ENCYCLOPEDIA OF THE UNITED STATES CONGRESS

ENCYCLOPEDIA OF THE UNITED STATES CONGRESS

Robert E. Dewhirst

John David Rausch, Jr., Associate Editor

Facts On File
An imprint of Infobase Publishing

Encyclopedia of the United States Congress

Facts On File, Inc.
An imprint of Infobase Publishing
132 West 31st Street
New York NY 10001

Library of Congress Cataloging-in-Publication Data

Dewhirst, Robert E.
Encyclopedia of the United States Congress / by Robert E. Dewhirst;
John David Rausch, Jr., associate editor.
p. cm.
Includes bibliographical references and index.
ISBN 0-8160-5058-9 (hc : alk. paper)
1. United States. Congress—Encyclopedias. I. Rausch, John David. II. Title.
JK1021.D48 2006
328.73003—dc22 2005028124

Facts On File books are available at special discounts when purchased in bulk
quantities for businesses, associations, institutions, or sales promotions. Please call our
Special Sales Department in New York at (212) 967-8800 or (800) 322-8755.

You can find Facts On File on the World Wide Web at http://www.factsonfile.com

Text design by Joan McEvoy
Cover design by Cathy Rincon
Illustrations by Dale Williams

Printed in the United States of America

VB Hermitage 10 9 8 7 6 5 4 3 2 1

This book is printed on acid-free paper.

Contents

List of Entries

List of Contributors

Ahuja, Sunil   Youngstown State University
Allen, Carmen R.   Eastern Illinois University
Aichinger, Karen   Natchitoches, Louisiana
Alam, Mohammed Badrul   Miyazaki International College, Japan

Baker, William D.   Arkansas School for Mathematics, Sciences, and the Arts
Baldino, Thomas J.   Wilkes University
Bass, Jeffrey D.   University of Connecticut
Behlar, Patricia A.   Pittsburgh State University
Bell, Lauren Cohen   Randolph-Macon College
Bell, Walter F.   Lamar University
Bobic, Mike   Emmanuel College
Bow, Shannon L.   University of Florida
Briley, Ron   Sandia Preparatory School
Brooker, Russell G.   Alverno College
Brownell, Roy E, II   United States Agency for International Development

Cammisa, Anne Marie   Suffolk University
Campbell, Colton C.   Florida International University
Clapper, Tomas   Oklahoma City, Oklahoma
Cobane, Craig T.   Culver-Stockton College
Connor, George E.   Missouri State University
Culver, William   State University of New York, Plattsburg
Curry, Brett   The Ohio State University

Dewhirst, Robert E.   Northwest Missouri State University
Ditslear, Corey   University of North Texas

English, Ross M.   University of Reading, United Kingdom

Farrier, Jasmine L.   University of Louisville
Fisher, Patrick   Seton Hall University
Frisch, Scott A.   California State University, Bakersfield

Gilmour, Terry   Midland College
Glassman, Matthew   Yale University
Glenn, Brian J.   Harvard University
Grose, Christian   Lawrence University
Galderisi, Peter F.   Utah State University
Goss, Robert P.   Brigham Young University

Harris, Douglas B.   Loyola College of Maryland
Hate, Vibhuti   Lawrence University
Hoff, Samuel B.   Delaware State University
Hoffman, Donna R.   University of Northern Iowa
Holst, Arthur   Governmental Affairs Manager, Philadelphia Water Department
Holman, Craig   Legislative representative

Jones, David R.   Baruch College, City University of New York

Kedrowski, Karen M.   Winthrop University
Kelly, Sean   California State University, Bakersfield
Kemper, Mark   Bridgewater State College
Kleeman, Kathy   Rutgers University
Kratz, Jessica   Washington, D.C.
Kraus, Jeffrey   Wagner College
Krutz, Glen S.   University of Oklahoma
Kubik, William   Hanover College

Langran, Robert W.   Villanova University
LeBeau, Justin   Undergraduate Research Center, University of Oklahoma
Lind, Nancy S.   Illinois State University
Lowrey, Phil   West Texas A&M University
Lyons, Michael   Utah State University

Maslin-Wicks, Kimberly   Hendrix College
McCurdy, Karen M.   Georgia Southern College

McGowan, Brian M.   Louisiana State University
Miller, Paul T.   Temple University
Miller, Gregory   Ohio State University
Mueller, Melinda A.   Eastern Illinois University

Norris, James Texas   A&M International University

Olivares, Jamie Ramon   Houston Community College
Opheim, Cynthia   Southwest Texas State University

Patten, Joseph   Monmouth University
Paulson, Darryl   University of South Florida
Pederson, William D.   Louisiana State University, Shreveport
Pollard, Vincent K.   University of Hawaii, Manoa

Rausch, John David, Jr.   West Texas A&M University
Rausch, Mary S.   West Texas A&M University
Ricks, Martin   University of Utah
Rocca, Michael S.   University of California, Davis
Romans, Maureen   Roberts Rhode Island College

Solowiej, Lisa A.   Binghamton University, State University of New York
Schraufnagel, Scot D.   University of Central Florida
Smith, Daniel E.   Northwest Missouri State University
Steiner, Michael   Northwest Missouri State University
Straus, Jacob   University of Florida
Sweet, Barry N.   Clarion University of Pennsylvania

Tien, Charles   Hunter College and the City University of New York Graduate Center
Turner, Charles California State University, Chico

Valero, Larry A.   University of Salford, United Kingdom
Van Der Slik, Jack R.   University of Illinois, Springfield
Vassilev, Rossen V.   Ohio State University

Waskey, Andrew J.   Dalton State College
Watkins, Peter   St. Joseph's College of Indiana
Williams, Jackson   AARP Public Policy Institute
Woods, Michael   Eastern Illinois University

Introduction

Congress is the major policy-making branch of the national government of the United States. It is also charged with major oversight and organizational responsibilities over the federal bureaucracy. The authors of the Constitution clearly preferred the legislative branch, making it the subject of Article I of their document. Likewise, visitors to Washington, D.C., will notice that the Capitol rotunda dominates the city's skyline and that the surrounding street network radiates from Capitol Hill, the highest point in the area. Congress is physically, symbolically, and literally the center of action in the nation's capital.

With 435 representatives and 100 senators, Congress always is a busy place. Its work and daily routine often appear contradictory, confusing, complex, and even messy to outsiders. Constituents, lobbyists, the news media, members of the federal bureaucracy, and tourists swarm Capitol Hill almost daily. Although Congress lacks the glamour of the presidency and the mystique of the Supreme Court, the legislative branch remains the place where the American people have tended to go when in need of help. For more than two centuries, Congress has proven to be the most eager, responsive, and resilient institution imaginable, always ready to adapt to changing needs placed upon it by the press of circumstances and the pleas of American society.

This encyclopedia of the United States Congress is organized alphabetically for ease of use. Most entries list bibliographic references, for those who wish to further explore their subjects. Entries bear the names of their authors: all entries not so designated were written by the volume's editor. It is hoped that this encyclopedia accurately reflects the dynamics, energy, and complexity of this thoroughly American of institutions. Although a reference work, this book is also meant to be a teaching tool wherein curious readers can learn about some unusual or interesting facts within the wealth of information available here.

Abscam

Abscam is the name given to a sting operation of the Federal Bureau of Investigation (FBI) that netted seven members of Congress, including one U.S. senator and six members of the House of Representatives in 1980. The term *Abscam* refers to Abdul Enterprises, Ltd., a fictitious company used by the FBI to lure public officials into accepting bribes. Seven members of Congress were convicted of accepting bribes from FBI agents posing as wealthy Arab businessmen.

The news that members of Congress were videotaped accepting bribes from FBI agents posing as Arab businessmen raised serious questions about both the integrity of the legislative process and FBI investigative tactics. U.S. representatives Richard Kelly, a Republican from Florida; Michael Myers, a Democrat from Pennsylvania; Raymond Lederer, a Democrat from Pennsylvania, and Frank Thompson, a Democrat from New Jersey, were all videotaped accepting money in exchange for supporting private immigration legislation on behalf of officials from the FBI front company. Representatives John Jenrette, a Democrat from South Carolina, and John Murphy, a Democrat from New York, were convicted of accepting money through middlemen.

Harrison A. Williams, a Democrat from New Jersey, the only U.S. senator convicted in the operation, was videotaped agreeing to use his influence to obtain government contracts for an imaginary titanium processing plant in exchange for a concealed financial stake in the fictitious company. The senior senator from New Jersey served as the chair of the Committee on Labor and Human Resources at the time. Williams was convicted of bribery and conspiracy in 1981 and served a three-year sentence for the crime. He resigned from the Senate after 23 years of service on March 11, 1982, in the face of overwhelming support for expulsion. He died proclaiming his innocence on November 17, 2001, at the age of 81.

All seven legislators were sentenced to be confined between 18 months and three years, and all served jail time.

However, Representative Kelly had his conviction overturned on an entrapment defense, despite videotape evidence showing him accepting $25,000 from FBI agents. Representatives Jenrette, Kelly, Murphy, and Thompson were all defeated in reelection bids, and Representative Lederer resigned from office. Representative Myers was expelled from the House of Representatives on October 2, 1980, marking the first time a member had been expelled since the Civil War and the last before James Traficant, a Democrat from Ohio, was expelled on July 24, 2002.

The FBI sting operation found its way to Congress's doorsteps via an unrelated investigation. The Abscam operation originated in 1978 in Long Island, New York, as a relatively routine investigation aimed at recovering stolen art and exposing fraud. The FBI recruited Melvin Weinberg, a recently arrested confidence man to assist in the operation. Weinberg posed as the chair of Abdul Enterprises. This FBI front company was created to attract thieves interested in selling stolen art or fraudulent security certificates. The FBI opened a bank account under the name of Abdul Enterprises and deposited $1 million into the account to establish credibility and to cover operating costs.

FBI agents posing as Arab businessmen quickly established a relationship with a professional forger, who eventually recommended that Abdul Enterprises open a gaming casino in Atlantic City, New Jersey. The agents were then assured that Camden, New Jersey, mayor Angelo Errichetti could arrange for a gaming license in exchange for a financial kickback. Errichetti was also a state senator and was generally regarded as the most powerful political figure in southern New Jersey. It was Mayor Errichetti's involvement in the investigation that ultimately steered the FBI to other public officials, including the seven members of Congress.

Mayor Errichetti eventually brought Representatives Myers and Lederer into the fold. Myers and Lederer were the first members of Congress to act on behalf of the FBI front company. They agreed to sponsor a private relief bill granting U.S. residency to Abdul Rahman and Yassir

Habib. Rahman and Habib were actually FBI agents posing as businessmen from Abdul Enterprises. Errichetti then recruited Representative Thompson, one of the most powerful Democratic figures in Washington. Thompson was videotaped accepting a briefcase holding $45,000 from an FBI agent posing as an Arab sheikh in exchange for sponsoring another private immigration bill. Thompson then recruited Representative Murphy. Thompson was arrested four months later while watching his alma mater play basketball on television in his Alexandria, Virginia, home. Other middlemen eventually recruited the others.

Plea bargaining was made difficult because most of the acts were captured on videotape and aired to a surprised nation on the nightly news. The defendants therefore employed three separate defense strategies including entrapment, due process, and play acting. Critics of the Abscam investigation raised questions about FBI investigative tactics, arguing that the legislators were entrapped into committing these crimes. Some of the defendants employed an entrapment defense, arguing that undercover agents are typically employed when there is either evidence of a crime or evidence that a crime is likely to be committed in the future. The crux of the defense was that the FBI lured them into committing crimes they would not have committed otherwise. However, entrapment law required the defendants to establish that the FBI did more than simply set a trap, but had actually induced them into committing the crime. Representative Kelly was successful in his entrapment defense because the videotape showed that he had initially rejected the bribe but was eventually persuaded to accept it by an FBI agent. The other defendants did not appear to need such persuasion and were thus found guilty.

A due process defense succeeded for a Philadelphia councilman who was also snared in the Abscam investigation. The judge in that case ruled that the government's investigative conduct was so outrageous that it rose to unconstitutional levels.

The play acting defense was used by Representative Kelly and Senator Williams. Kelly claimed that he accepted the money to use as evidence against the FBI agents trying to bribe him, while Williams claimed that he never made any specific promises to the agents and that he was simply pretending to be interested. The play acting defense was unsuccessful on both counts.

In the end the Abscam scandal remains one of the most embarrassing chapters in the history of the U.S. Congress. However, the clear message that public officials are expected to rise above the trappings of office still resonates today. On a positive note, it is also important to acknowledge that Senator Larry Pressler, a Republican from South Dakota, and many other public officials refused bribes offered by the FBI agents.

Further reading:
Green, Gary S. *Occupational Crime.* 2d ed. Chicago: Nelson-Hall, 1997; Maitland, Leslie. "At the Heart of the Abscam Debate," *New York Times Magazine,* 25 July 1982; Noonan, John T. *Bribes.* New York: Macmillan Publishing Co., 1984.

—Joseph Patton

adjournment

Adjournment terminates the proceedings of a congressional committee or a chamber of Congress. The motion to adjourn can be used to end a legislative day or an annual session of Congress. A motion, which ends a legislative day, is called Adjournment to a Day Certain; in these cases lawmakers set a date for the session to reconvene. The Adjournment to a Day Certain allows for time off during an annual session and is usually done for holiday observances, a summer respite, and other brief periods of time. These breaks in legislative activity that occur within an annual session are sometimes referred to as a recess. If the recess is to exceed three days (and often they do), the adjournment is done by concurrent resolution. This practice is necessitated by the constitutional provision found in Article 1, section 5, that stipulates that neither chamber of Congress may adjourn for more than three days (Sundays excepted) without the consent of the other.

When a motion to adjourn is done at the end of an annual legislative session, it is known as Adjournment *Sine Die* (adjournment without a day). This is also carried out by concurrent resolution. Although the *sine die* provision suggests that there is no particular day when Congress will reconvene, this is not actually the case. The Constitution has determined that Congress shall meet in annual session on January 3 unless the chambers decide to meet on a different day, which they often do. So the real difference between the two forms of adjournment is that the Adjournment to a Day Certain is an intersession break, and Adjournment *Sine Die* is an intra session adjournment or an adjournment to end a specific two-year Congress. It should be noted that, constitutionally, the president could require the Congress to adjourn on a specific date if the chambers are unable to agree on a day. However, this has never happened.

Further reading:
How Congress Works. 3d ed. Washington, D.C.: Congressional Quarterly Inc., 2000; Ru, Robert, Henry M. Robert III, William J. Evans, Daniel H. Honemann, and Thomas J. Balch. *Robert's Rules of Order.* 10th ed. Cambridge, Mass.: Perseus Publishing, 2000; Wetterau, Bruce. *Desk Reference on American Government.* 2d ed. Washington, D.C.: Congressional Quarterly Inc., 2000.

—Scot D. Schraufnagel

adjournment and recess (House of Representatives)

In the House of Representatives a motion to adjourn is highly privileged and, except for rare instances, is in order once a member has been recognized by the floor leader. One instance in which the motion to adjourn is not in order (or allowed) is when the chamber is meeting as the COMMITTEE OF THE WHOLE. The standard motion to adjourn does not require a quorum to be present, and the motion is not debatable. Of course, the motion to adjourn may be voted down by a majority of those present. Furthermore, a rules change in the 103rd Congress allowed the SPEAKER OF THE HOUSE to adjourn or suspend the business of the House of Representatives at any time, provided there is no question pending on the floor. The rules change also granted the floor leader the discretion at any time to recognize a motion from members that authorizes the Speaker to declare a recess.

The House, unlike the Senate, with few exceptions adjourns each calendar day. Once adjourned, the LEGISLATIVE DAY ends. The consequence of adjourning each calendar day (as opposed to a simple recess) is that legislative days and calendar days coincide with one another. This is not the case in the Senate. In the House of Representatives there is no ambiguity about what represents a day. Because the House adjourns each day, however, it must start the next day's session with all the normal proceedings that characterize the beginning of a legislative day in the House (such as approval of the JOURNAL, prayer, and the Pledge of Allegiance to the flag). There are times in the House when a unanimous consent agreement will dispense with some of the elements of the formal beginning of a legislative day.

See also ADJOURNMENT and ADJOURNMENT AND RECESS, SENATE.

Further reading:
Partner, Daniel. *The House of Representatives.* Broomall, Pa.: Chelsea House Publishers, 2000; Stewart, Charles. *Analyzing Congress.* New York: Norton, 2001.
—Scot D. Schraufnagel

adjournment and recess (Senate)

The Senate can end its daily proceedings by means of a motion to recess or a motion to adjourn. However, recesses are much more common. Strictly speaking, a recess is a "short intermission within a meeting which does not end the meeting or destroy its continuity as a single gathering." The significance of the Senate breaking each day via recess as opposed to adjournment is that it allows the Senate to dispense with the standard procedural events associated with the MORNING HOUR. The morning hour occurs at the beginning of each legislative day in the Senate and is filled

with procedural requirements such as correcting the journal from the previous day and considering resolutions. The morning hour normally lasts about two hours. When the Senate reconvenes after a recess it simply picks up where it left off on the previous calendar day. In short, by ending a day with a recess instead of an adjournment, the Senate is able to save time. Of course, this practice causes Senate LEGISLATIVE DAYS to be out of sync with the real-world calendar. However, it is commonly held that the convenience of being able to dispense with the morning hour easily offsets the problem of legislative days and calendar days being incongruent.

See also ADJOURNMENT and ADJOURNMENT AND RECESS, HOUSE.

Further reading:
Baker, Ross K. *House and Senate.* 3d ed. New York: Norton, 2000; Stewart, Charles. *Analyzing Congress.* New York: Norton, 2001.
—Scot D. Schraufnagel

advice and consent

Constitutional powers granted to the United States SENATE that requires that chamber to approve TREATIES and confirm presidential APPOINTMENTS have been termed advice and consent powers.

Article II, Section 2, of the Constitution provides the president the power, by and with the advice and consent of the Senate, to make treaties, provided two-thirds of the senators present concur. By and with the advice of the Senate, the president also has the power to appoint ambassadors, other public ministers and consuls, judges of the Supreme Court, and all other officers of the United States.

When the Senate acts on treaties and presidential appointments that come to it under Article II, it engages in executive business and follows a different procedure than it does when it engages in legislative business under Article I. The Senate maintains an executive calendar upon which treaties and nominations are placed when a committee reports them. The EXECUTIVE SESSION proceedings are recorded in a separate *Executive Journal.* Executive business is conducted in executive session. The Senate usually meets in legislative session each day. By MOTION or UNANIMOUS CONSENT, the Senate will resolve into executive session to deal with executive business. Senate Rule XXII governs the process of resolving into executive session.

Treaties are typically referred to the FOREIGN RELATIONS COMMITTEE. A treaty is a formal compact between the United States and one or more other nations. Senate Rule XXX governs the process of reviewing treaties. Most of the time the Senate considers treaties in open session, but there have been occasions when secret sessions were held to consider classified information. Treaties do not die at the end of a Congress if not approved by the Senate. In 1986 the Senate ratified the Genocide Treaty that had been submitted by President Harry Truman in 1947. If a president believes that he will not be able to get the Senate to approve a treaty, he may avoid the process by entering into an executive agreement. Such agreements do not require Senate approval.

During the 108th Congress, Senate Rule XXXI governed presidential nominations. The nominations are referred to the appropriate committee of jurisdiction. Some committees review a large number of nominations, while other committees consider very few. Nominations have to be approved by a majority vote of the Senate meeting in executive session. Rule XXXI stipulates that the presiding officer asks, Will the Senate advise and consent to this nomination? Nominations die at the end of a session. The Constitution permits the president to fill all vacancies that may happen during a Senate recess. These appointments are called recess appointments.

When a new president is elected, an official document, *U.S. Government Policy and Supporting Positions* (the "plum book"), lists positions that the president fills by appointment. Because of the large number of positions that need to be filled annually, a process has developed. About 99 percent of nominations are to minor positions. When a vacancy occurs, the White House identifies appropriate candidates. After a background check and a review of the intended nominee with senators in order to avoid problems with senatorial courtesy, the president announces a nominee. The nomination is sent to the Senate, where it is referred to a committee and public hearings are held. Prior to 1929 hearings were closed to the public. The committee then votes on the nomination and sends it to the Senate floor. Following debate the Senate votes on the nomination.

Most treaties and nominations to minor positions are approved with little controversy. Since 1789 only 21 treaties have been rejected by the full Senate. On March 9, 1825, the full Senate defeated a treaty with Colombia on the suppression of the African slave trade. This was the first treaty rejected by the Senate. The Senate rejected an annexation treaty with the Republic of Texas on June 8, 1844. On October 13, 1999, the Senate rejected the Comprehensive Nuclear Test Ban Treaty by a vote of 48 to 51.

One of the most famous treaties rejected by the Senate was the Treaty of Versailles, ending World War I and establishing the League of Nations. The Senate voted twice to reject the treaty, in 1919 and 1920. The treaty was defeated in part because a senator did not participate in the treaty negotiations. The question of whether senators should participate in treaty negotiations has never been answered definitively.

Nominees to major positions such as federal judges, members of regulatory bodies, and key executive and diplomatic personnel not covered by the merit systems, face the closest scrutiny. Historically, Supreme Court justice nominees have faced the most controversy, and such nominees have been rejected most often. Since 1789 27 Supreme Court appointees were either rejected or decided to withdraw under the threat of rejection. Some 20 of the failed appointments were in the 19th century. All Supreme Court justice appointees were confirmed in the period from 1930 through 1967. Since then, the Senate rejected two of President Richard Nixon's nominees to the Supreme Court in 1969. In 1987 the Senate rejected Judge ROBERT BORK, President Ronald Reagan's appointee.

Appointees to nonjudicial positions also have failed to be approved by the Senate. The first nominee to be rejected by the Senate was Benjamin Fishbourn of Georgia, nominated in 1789 by President George Washington to be a customs collector in Savannah. The Georgia senators exercised SENATORIAL COURTESY to block Fishbourn's appointment. In 1926 the Senate twice in six days rejected President Calvin Coolidge's nomination of Charles Warren to be attorney general. The Senate in 1989 rejected former Texas senator John Tower's nomination to be secretary of Defense in the George H.W. Bush administration, becoming the first cabinet nominee of a new president ever to be rejected.

The politics of the presidential appointment process was the subject of political fiction in the book *Advise and Consent*, written by Allen Drury, a Capitol Hill journalist, in 1959. The plot centers on the controversial nomination of liberal Robert Leffingwell to be secretary of State. Conservatives in the Senate mobilized to oppose him. The book was made into a Broadway play and a 1962 movie directed by Otto Preminger starring Henry Fonda as Robert Leffingwell.

Further reading:
Gerhardt, Michael J. *The Federal Appointments Process: A Constitutional and Historical Analysis.* Durham, N.C.: Duke University Press, 2000; McCarty, Nolan, and Rose Razaghian. "Advice and Consent: Senate Responses to Executive Branch Nominations, 1885–1996." *American Journal of Political Science* 43, no. 4 (1999): 112–143; United States Senate Committee on Foreign Relations. *Treaties and Other International Agreements: The Role of the United States Senate.* Senate Print 106-71. Washington, D.C.: Government Printing Office, 2001.

—John David Rausch, Jr.

agenda

Within the U.S. Congress an agenda is a list of legislative priorities. Before Congress can produce public policy outcomes, the issue or topic must reach the government agenda. The government agenda is a metaphorical list of issues that are important enough to warrant government attention. When something is said to be on the agenda, it means that politicians, bureaucrats, policy analysts, and interest groups who deal with the issue or problem are paying it serious attention.

Congress must work in an atmosphere that has at least four sources of agendas. Congressional leaders have agendas that they wish to see enacted, and they seek the assistance of their fellow partisans in both houses to push the issues through the legislative process. The president has an agenda of issues important to him that he works to enact. In the case of unified government, the majority leadership's agenda and the president's agenda usually include similar objectives. During periods of DIVIDED GOVERNMENT, the branches will come into conflict in trying to enact their agendas. Interest groups also have legislative agendas that they bring to the House of Representatives and the Senate. Finally, individual members of Congress have agendas on which they were elected or reelected. Members can add items to their agendas as they continue to serve in Congress.

Political scientists study the process through which items reach the agendas. The process is called agenda setting. Agenda setting is studied using a variety of methods. Scholars have tracked the agenda by counting the appearance of items in the *CONGRESSIONAL RECORD* and in major newspapers such as the *New York Times*. Other scholars have interviewed knowledgeable observers to determine what policy issues are important over a period of time. Some studies involve case analyses of the emergence of a particular issue across time within a given country or by comparing two or more countries.

One of the most publicized congressional agendas was the CONTRACT WITH AMERICA developed by House Republicans in 1994. During the 1994 congressional campaign, the House Republican leadership developed a coherent, specific, 10-point program they called the Contract With America. Most of the party's House candidates signed a pledge to follow the contract if elected. The party's effort was successful. By the time a self-imposed deadline of 100 days had passed, the House had approved nine of the 10 items. The only item that failed to pass the House was a constitutional amendment proposal to impose term limits on members of Congress. Senate Republicans were not bound by the contract, and many of the items failed to win Senate approval.

Further reading:
Kingdon, John. *Agendas, Alternatives, and Public Policies.* Boston: Little, Brown, 1984; Wolbrecht, Charles. "Female Legislators and the Women's Rights Agenda." In *Women Transforming Congress,* edited by Cindy Simon Rosenthal. Norman: University of Oklahoma Press, 2002.

—John David Rausch, Jr.

Aging, Senate Special Committee on

The Senate Special Committee on Aging was established in 1961 as a temporary committee. It was granted permanent status on February 1, 1977. As a SPECIAL COMMITTEE rather than a STANDING COMMITTEE, this panel does not have the authority to propose new laws, but it can study issues, oversee programs, and investigate reports of fraud and waste. The committee can also make recommendations to the full Senate for discussion of particular issues. Throughout its existence the Special Committee on Aging has served as a focal point in the Senate for discussion and debate on matters relating to older Americans. Often the committee has submitted its findings and recommendations for legislation to the Senate. In addition, the panel has published materials to assist persons interested in public policies related to the elderly.

The committee has had a reputation for being active, particularly in exploring health insurance coverage of older Americans prior to the enactment of Medicare in 1965. It collected much of the data used to enact the Medicare program. Since the passage of that legislation, the committee has continually reviewed Medicare's performance on an almost annual basis. The committee has also regularly reviewed pension coverage and employment opportunities for older Americans and has conducted oversight of the administration of major programs such as SOCIAL SECURITY and the Older Americans Act. Finally, it has crusaded against frauds targeting the elderly, from telephone scandals to electronic mail scandals. One of the committee's most influential reports dealt with unacceptable conditions found in nursing homes.

In addition, panel members worked to increase protections for seniors against age discrimination and evaluate the pay system used by Medicare. Specifically, Senator John Heinz, a Republican from Pennsylvania, reviewed Medicare's Prospective Payment System to verify that the system was forcing Medicare beneficiaries to be discharged "quicker and sicker." Other substantive areas of interest studied by the committee include pricing practices for prescription drugs and health care antifraud legislation. They also studied the impact and necessity of long-term care programs as well as abuses in the funeral industry. Over the years the committee has been at the center of the debate on issues of central concern to older Americans. In the 108th Congress Senator Larry Craig, a Republican from Idaho, was the chair of the committee. The most recent focus of committee members has been on examining predatory lending practices as well as responses to the threat of mad cow disease.

Further reading:
Goldreich, Samuel. "Status Quo for Panel on Aging." *Congressional Quarterly Weekly Report,* 9 November

2002, p. 2,928; United States Senate Special Committee on Aging. Available online. URL: http://aging.senate.gov/. Accessed January 16, 2006.

—Nancy S, Lind

Agriculture, House Committee on

Since 1820 agriculture has been a standing committee of the U.S. HOUSE OF REPRESENTATIVES. The Committee on Agriculture was established during the 16th Congress through a resolution introduced by Lewis Williams of North Carolina on May 3, 1820, with Thomas Forrest of Pennsylvania as its first chair. Forrest, a Federalist, served as chair for the duration of the Congress. Originally consisting of seven members, the committee's size of 51 was set in 2001.

In 1862 the committee approved legislation creating a Bureau of Agriculture within the executive branch of the federal government. The bureau was to be headed by a commissioner appointed by the president. The committee supported the establishment of a cabinet-level Department of Agriculture in 1889. During the recession following World War I, the committee chair, Gilbert Nelson Haugen of Iowa, joined with his counterpart in the Senate, Charles McNary of Oregon, to sponsor the McNary-Haugen Farm Bill. Beginning in 1924 the two introduced the bill that provided for the federal government to purchase surplus agricultural products for sale overseas. President Calvin Coolidge twice vetoed the bill (stating in his 1927 veto message that the bill went against an economic law as well established as any law of nature [Neal 1985: 101]). In 1928 Coolidge called the bill a system of wholesale commercial doles (Neal 1985: 105). The proposal was a forerunner of President Franklin Delano Roosevelt's NEW DEAL agricultural policies.

Originally, the committee's jurisdiction was subjects relating to agriculture. In 1880 House rules were amended to extend the committee's jurisdiction to forestry and reporting the appropriations for the Department of Agriculture. In 1920 jurisdiction over the Department of Agriculture's appropriations was returned to the House APPROPRIATIONS COMMITTEE. In 1933 the committee assumed jurisdiction for farm credit.

The current jurisdiction of the committee took effect in January 1947, when the House revised its rules as part of the LEGISLATIVE REORGANIZATION ACT OF 1946 and included the following areas of jurisdiction for the committee: adulteration of seeds, insect pests, and protection of birds and animals in forest reserves; agriculture generally; agricultural and industrial chemistry; agricultural colleges and experiment stations; agricultural economics and research; agricultural education extension services; agricultural production and marketing and stabilization of prices of agricultural products and commodities; animal industry and diseases of animals; commodity exchanges; crop insurance and soil conservation; dairy industry; entomology and plant quarantine; extension of farm credit and farm security; inspection of livestock, poultry, meat products, and seafood and seafood products; forestry in general and forest reserves other than those created from the public domain; human nutrition and home economics; plant industry, soils, and agricultural engineering; rural electrification; and rural development and water conservation.

During the 108th Congress, House Agriculture had five subcommittees: the Subcommittee on Conservation, Credit, Rural Development and Research; the Subcommittee on General Farm Commodities and Risk Management; the Subcommittee on Specialty Crops and Foreign Agriculture Programs; the Subcommittee on Department Operations, Oversight, Nutrition and Forestry; and the Subcommittee on Livestock and Agriculture. The committee's chair, Republican Bob Goodlatte of Virginia, assumed the chair at the beginning of the 108th Congress (January 3, 2003).

Among the important legislation that has been considered by the committee has been the Federal Meat Inspection Act of 1906, which authorized the Department of Agriculture to conduct meat inspections and condemn any meat deemed unfit for human consumption; the Soil Conservation and Domestic Allotment Act of 1935, which created a financial assistance program that aided farmers who engaged in soil conservation; the National School Lunch Act; the Poultry Products Inspection Act; the Food and Agriculture Act of 1962; the Food Stamp Act; the Child Nutrition Act of 1966; and the Federal Crop Insurance Reform and Department of Agriculture Reorganization Act of 1994, which repealed a number of the New Deal programs that provided financial assistance to farmers.

Further reading:
Neal, Steve. *McNary of Oregon: A Political Biography.* Portland, Ore.: Western Imprints, 1985; Opie, John. *The Law of the Land: 200 Years of American Farmland Policy.* Lincoln: University of Nebraska Press, 1994; United States House of Representatives Committee on Agriculture. *United States House of Representatives Committee on Agriculture 150th Anniversary,* House Document 91-350, 91st Congress, 2d session, 1970.

—Jeffrey Kraus

Agriculture, Nutrition, and Forestry, Senate Committee on

This standing committee in the U.S. Senate considers issues affecting American agriculture, forestry, and nutrition programs. The Senate created a standing Committee on Agriculture on December 9, 1825, the first new standing committee created after the establishment of the first

12 committees in 1816. The committee was created during a debate over dividing the Committee on Commerce and Manufactures. Senator William Findley of Pennsylvania argued that agriculture was one branch of the three great branches of domestic industry. Findley convinced his colleagues that agriculture was as important as commercial enterprises, especially in the new western states that had recently entered the Union. Findley was named the committee's first chair. The first piece of legislation considered by the new committee was a bill placing a duty on imports of alcoholic spirits, an issue important to Findley's Pennsylvania constituents.

During the first four decades of the committee's existence, the federal government had a limited role in agriculture. This was reflected in the small number of bills referred to the committee. In March 1857 the Senate adopted a resolution amending Senate rules to consolidate or abolish certain standing committees in order to increase efficiency. The Committee on Agriculture was abolished.

The committee was revived in 1863. The federal government's role in agriculture was growing as President Abraham Lincoln signed legislation creating the U.S. Department of Agriculture in 1862. Congress also had enacted the Homestead Act, making lands available in the new states and territories for the large number of immigrants coming to the United States. The Morrill Land Grant College Act of 1862 also provided impetus for the re-creation of the committee. Senators believed that there was now a need for a standing committee to consider legislation relating to agriculture.

The existence of the Committee on Agriculture was threatened in 1867 by the creation of a Committee on Appropriations. Jurisdiction over appropriations for agricultural programs slowly moved to the new committee, leaving some agriculture committee members fearing that their committee would be abolished. The committee tried to regain some of its jurisdiction in 1883, when it reported a resolution amending Senate rules to transfer jurisdiction over Department of Agriculture appropriations from the Committee on Appropriations back to the Committee on Agriculture. The full Senate did not take action on the resolution.

In 1884, after the Bureau of Forestry was added to the Department of Agriculture, the committee's name was changed to the Committee on Agriculture and Forestry. The power of all standing committees in the Senate was increased when the Senate approved a resolution amending the rules to require referral of certain general appropriations to authorizing committees. Department of Agriculture appropriations would be referred to the committee.

The committee's legislative role grew as the nation and the federal government grew. In 1906 the enactment of the Food and Drug Act gave the committee significant oversight of a new regulatory agency to ensure the safety of meat. Through the 1930s the committee was transformed as major farm programs were created to assist farmers hurt by the Great Depression. In 1946 the Committee on Agriculture and Forestry was granted formal jurisdiction over agricultural issues as defined by Senate rules approved after the LEGISLATIVE REORGANIZATION ACT was passed. This act provided the first written statements of committee jurisdictions in both chambers.

The committee's jurisdiction increased during the 1950s as Congress enacted legislation in the area of soil conservation. The Watershed Protection and Flood Prevention Act of 1954 authorized the Department of Agriculture through its Social Conservation Service to provide technical and financial assistance to local groups working to maintain watersheds and implement flood prevention. In 1955, recognizing the increased size of its jurisdiction, the committee created its first subcommittee, an action allowed under the Legislative Reorganization Act of 1946. Five subcommittees were created in that year: Soil Conservation and Forestry; Agricultural Credit and Rural Electrification; Agricultural Production, Marketing, and Stabilization of Prices; Agricultural and General Legislation; and Tobacco.

The federal government's involvement in school lunch and other nutrition programs widened the committee's jurisdiction. The Senate parliamentarian regularly referred food and nutrition bills to the Committee on Agriculture in spite of the lack of a jurisdictional direction because he believed that the committee had the best understanding of food production and distribution. In 1977 the committee's name was changed to the Committee on Agriculture, Forestry, and Nutrition to reflect the importance of these nutrition programs.

The Agriculture, Forestry, and Nutrition Committee was one of 16 standing committees in the 108th Congress (2003–04). It had 21 members (11 Republicans and 10 Democrats) primarily from southern, central, and western states. The chair was Mississippi senator Thad Cochran and the ranking Democrat was Iowa senator Tom Harkin. The committee had four subcommittees: Production and Price Competitiveness; Marketing, Inspection, and Product Promotion; Forestry, Conservation, and Rural Revitalization; and Research, Nutrition, and General Legislation. The subcommittees approximated the committee's jurisdiction.

Further reading:
Deering, Christopher J., and Steven S. Smith. *Committees in Congress.* 3d ed. Washington, D.C.: Congressional Quarterly Press, 1997; Fulton, Tom. *The United States Senate Committee on Agriculture, Nutrition, and Forestry 1825–1998: Members, Jurisdiction, and History.* Senate Document 105-24. Washington, D.C.: Government Printing Office, 1998.

—John David Rausch, Jr.

Albert, Carl Bert (1908–2000) *Speaker of the House of Representatives*

The "Little Giant from Little Dixie" became the 46th Speaker of the U.S. House of Representatives in January 1971. He served during a unique time in American history. Twice in the immediate line of succession to president of the United States, first after the resignation of Vice President Spiro Agnew and then President Richard Nixon, he was one of the few national leaders in the nation's capital who did not aspire to that high office.

The life and Speakership of Albert is a story of a talented, hard-working, self-effacing man who wanted to strengthen the institutions of democracy in the United States more than he wanted to wield personal political power. He was a transition figure, building a bridge between a past that no longer adequately functioned and a future that required a stronger centralized congressional leadership. Above all, he was an institutionalist. Albert loved the United States, its Constitution, Congress, and other democratic institutions as well as his home state of Oklahoma and district in "Little Dixie." His contributions to the reform of the U.S. House of Representatives, his transformation of the Speaker's position into a modern institution, and his ability to keep the Congress and the country united during times of great controversy and crisis were the result of hard, intelligent work behind the scenes instead of in front of the camera, microphone, or press. Carl Albert preferred private compromise over public confrontation.

The son of a coal miner and farmer, Earnest Albert, and his wife, Leona Albert, Carl Bert Albert was born on May 10, 1908, north of McAlester, in Pittsburg County, Oklahoma. It was as a young schoolboy that Carl Albert heard his local congressman, Charles D. Carter, speak and decided at that moment to make his career serving in the

President Gerald Ford addressing Congress as Speaker of the House Carl Albert (right) looks on, 1974 *(Library of Congress)*

U.S. Congress. He graduated from McAlester High School in 1927. The winner of a national oratory contest, Albert attended the University of Oklahoma, where he graduated Phi Beta Kappa in 1931 and was selected as a Rhodes Scholar in Oxford, England. He graduated in 1934 and was admitted to the bar in 1935. Returning from England, Albert worked for the Federal Housing Administration and later as an attorney practicing petroleum law. During World War II Albert served in the Pacific. He began as a private and ended the war a lieutenant colonel. He won a Bronze Star.

In 1946, when a vacancy occurred in his home Third Congressional District, the diminutive Albert campaigned in Little Dixie, a poverty-stricken region in southeastern Oklahoma and was elected by a margin of fewer than 400 votes. He was to serve for 12 more terms. While in the House of Representatives, Albert supported agriculture, public power, civil rights (later in his legislative career), hunting (until later in his career), and a strong national defense. Above all, he championed domestic programs that were designed to alleviate poverty in his home district.

Albert quickly became the protégé of Speaker SAMUEL RAYBURN, with whom he shared borders of their congressional districts. Rayburn recognized Albert's intelligence and above all his ability to count votes accurately. As a result, Albert was named his party's WHIP in 1955. At that time the power of the Speaker was the power to persuade. Albert was one of the party faithful who in 1961, under the leadership of Speaker Rayburn, stripped "Judge" Howard Smith of his iron grip on the U.S. House Rules Committee and strengthened the position of the Speaker.

When JOHN MCCORMACK moved up to the Speakership in 1962, Albert also moved up to the position of MAJORITY LEADER despite a challenge from Representative RICHARD BOLLING, a Democrat from Missouri. This was one of his few public victories. While Albert's political defeats were well reported, his triumphs were usually kept out of the public spotlight. For the next nine years Albert served as a broker between the established House leadership of Democrats and liberal Democratic reformers. Albert's head was with the reformers, but his heart was with the traditional leadership. It was Albert who in 1969 persuaded Speaker McCormack to revive the Democratic Caucus.

Albert's ascension to the Speakership in 1971 placed him in the middle of the debate over the Vietnam conflict. This was followed by a bitter election and the impeachment hearings of President Richard Nixon. During his tenure as Speaker, Albert presided over a House facing a nation torn over divisive social issues and severe economic challenges. A hawk on defense matters and international affairs, he was a bitter foe of the economic policies of both the Nixon and Gerald Ford administrations. During the

Nixon impeachment hearing, Speaker Albert stayed aloof, letting the process take its course without his personal involvement. As the highest elected Democratic official during both the Nixon and Ford administrations, Albert was thrown into the spotlight as Speaker for his party, a position he neither sought nor relished. Albert believed in national unity and resisted divisiveness in both the Congress and the country even at the cost of potential political power and popularity.

Albert's reform of the House of Representatives went almost unnoticed outside the institution. House business was handled fairly and efficiently in the face of war, bitter election campaigns, and impeachment hearings. Almost without fanfare he became chair of the DEMOCRATIC STEERING COMMITTEE and was able to nominate his party's membership of the HOUSE COMMITTEE ON RULES. He made wide use of ad hoc committees and task forces, laying the groundwork for the modern leadership. When Albert departed Congress the elected House leadership decided committee assignments and had some control over bills in the Rules Committee. The Democratic Caucus was a functioning body. Before his tenure none of this was true.

There was a wide perceptual gap between the Albert who was respected and admired by the members of his home congressional district and the national legislative leader who was routinely underestimated and unappreciated in the nation's capital. Albert had a strong local office handling constituent affairs in his home district but a weak public and media presence in the District of Columbia. Although later in his career he was probably more liberal than many of his constituents on matters of social and economic policy, they were proud of him as one of their own. Albert's public reputation both in Oklahoma and in the nation's capital was one of honesty, fairness, integrity, intelligence, hard work, and financial independence from interest groups.

Carl Albert did not seek reelection in 1976, retiring to McAlester, Oklahoma. He died February 4, 2000.

There are many institutional memorials to him in Oklahoma. Carl Albert State College in Poteau, Oklahoma, is probably the best known to those who live in his home state. However, it is the Carl Albert Congressional Research and Studies Center with its congressional archives and internship program at the University of Oklahoma in Norman, Oklahoma, that offers the greatest tribute to Albert's political career. This center has become a leading institution for research on the American Congress, dominating the scholastic world in this field of study.

Further reading:
Albert, Carl Bert, with Danney Goble. *Little Giant: The Life and Times of Speaker Carl Albert.* Norman: University of Oklahoma Press, 1990; Peabody, Robert L., and Nelson Polsby, eds. *New Perspectives on the House of Representatives.* 2d ed. Chicago: Rand McNally, 1969; Peters, Ronald M. Jr. *The American Speakership: The Office in Historical Perspective.* Baltimore: Johns Hopkins University Press, 1999; Peters, Ronald L. Jr., ed. *The Speaker: Leadership in the U.S. House of Representatives.* Washington, D.C.: Congressional Quarterly Press, 1995; DeCosta Wides, Louise. *Carl Albert, Democratic Representative from Oklahoma.* Washington, D.C.: Grossman (Ralph Nader Congress Project Citizens Look at Congress), 1972.

—Tom Clapper

Aldrich, Nelson W. (1841–1915) *Senator*

Nelson Aldrich was a prominent member of Congress for more than three decades. He was a Republican U.S. representative and U.S. senator from Rhode Island, Senate leader, and a coauthor of the Payne-Aldrich Tariff of 1909.

Born in Foster, Rhode Island, in 1841, Aldrich received an education in Connecticut and at the East Greenwich Academy in Rhode Island. At the age of 17 he became a clerk and bookkeeper for a grocery wholesaler in Providence, Rhode Island. During the Civil War he served with the Tenth Rhode Island Volunteers in Washington, D.C., returning to Providence after the war to become a partner in a grocery business.

A Republican since before the war, Aldrich entered political life in 1869 by winning election to the Providence City Council. He left the city council after winning a seat in the Rhode Island General Assembly in 1875, serving as speaker from 1876 to 1877. He was elected to the U.S. House of Representatives as a Republican in 1878 and reelected in 1880. In 1881 the Rhode Island legislature elected him to the U.S. Senate, succeeding the late general Ambrose Burnside. He was reelected to the Senate in 1886, 1892, 1898, and 1904.

In the Senate Aldrich worked to build the industrial capability of the United States. Opposing the federal regulation of business, Aldrich voted against the Interstate Commerce Act of 1887. Early in his career he was appointed to the SENATE COMMITTEE ON FINANCE, eventually rising to chair. He used his position to protect the interests of eastern manufacturers by using the protective tariff. Aldrich was involved in developing the "Mongrel Tariff" of 1883. He proposed the Republican alternative to the Mills Bill of 1888. He worked to shepherd the McKinley Tariff of 1890 through the Senate. When the Senate was under the control of the Democrats, Aldrich worked with the Democratic leadership to assure that tariff rates were not cut so sharply as to damage American manufacturing. He supported lower tariffs on imports that benefited eastern corporations. For example, he worked to lower or eliminate duties on raw sugar to benefit refiners in the East.

Some critics claimed that his support of industry stemmed from apparent close ties with the Standard Oil Company, an allegation Aldrich stridently denied. Despite the fact that his daughter Abby was married to John D. Rockefeller, Jr., Aldrich noted that he had met John D. Rockefeller, Sr., only three times.

When the Republicans controlled the Senate, he was a leader in that chamber. His seniority and position on the Finance Committee allowed Aldrich to extend his authority among the members of the Republican caucus. His ability to mobilize campaign contributions also allowed him to participate in making committee assignments. Aldrich's power stemmed largely from his political sense and strength of will, since, other than Finance Committee chairman, he held no official position in the Senate.

He was an opponent of free silver, working to enact the Gold Standard Act of 1900. He indicated that he would support bimetallism only if it was adopted around the world. Aldrich was not an isolationist, seeing the potential for profits in the markets of Latin America and East Asia. His support enabled the Senate to ratify the treaty providing for the acquisition of the Philippines and Puerto Rico after the Spanish-American War. He also worked for the passage of the Platt Amendment, allowing the United States to intervene in the internal affairs of Cuba.

In his role as a Senate Republican leader, Aldrich maintained a complex and often difficult relationship with progressive Republican president Theodore Roosevelt. Aldrich was not an ally of the progressives in the Republican Party. President Roosevelt recognized the senator's power and respected his ability to move legislation through that chamber. During the president's first term the men were on good terms. Aldrich supported Roosevelt's ventures in Panama, and Aldrich allowed Roosevelt to engage in some regulation of American business interests. The president deferred to Aldrich and his Senate allies on issues important to them, such as the tariff.

After 1904 Aldrich's relationship with the president became more complex. Part of the problem was that many of Aldrich's allies and friends in the Senate were retiring. The senator was not able to recognize the increasing power of progressivism in the Republican Party, and his positions were becoming much more isolated. He soon became identified with the special interests seen as controlling the Senate. In 1906 President Roosevelt sought to expand the authority of the Interstate Commerce Commission. Aldrich was able to limit the expansion by amending the Hepburn Act to provide for judicial review of commission decisions. The senator was able to block many of the items on the president's reform agenda for the rest of Roosevelt's term in office. The men's relationship was strained to the point that Aldrich refused to visit the White House for a number of years.

Despite a long career in the Senate, Aldrich is identified by name on few bills. One of these, the Aldrich-Vreeland Act of 1908, provided a method for banks to issue notes based on securities other than federal bonds. The legislation also created the National Monetary Commission that Aldrich chaired. The Payne-Aldrich Tariff of 1909 was one of the senator's last bills. Shortly after taking office President William Howard Taft asked Congress to enact tariff reform. A tariff bill written by House Ways and Means Committee chairman Sereno Payne, a Republican from New York, passed the House. Aldrich amended the bill in the Senate by raising the tariffs on most goods. One of the proposals the senator offered in working to secure passage of the tariff bill was a constitutional amendment authorizing a federal income tax. This maneuver was unusual because it had been a goal of the progressives. After a conference committee approved the changes, President Taft signed the bill enacting the first changes in tariff laws since 1897.

The bill was not a victory for Aldrich, as it caused a progressive Republican uprising against the more conservative Senate leadership, and the Rhode Island senator lost most of his power. Shortly after progressive members of the House of Representatives deposed Speaker Joseph Cannon, a Republican from Illinois, and removed him from the House Rules Committee, it was reported that many of the insurgents yelled "On to Aldrich." Progressive Republicans saw the senator as as much of an obstacle to progress as Cannon had been. This further isolated the aging senator, and he did not seek reelection in 1910.

The conflict between the conservative and progressive wings of the Republican Party eventually allowed the Democrats to regain control of Congress after the election of 1910. Many of the same progressives left the party in 1912, supporting former president Roosevelt on the Bull Moose ticket. Aldrich continued to work on currency reform as the chair of the National Monetary Commission. In 1911 the commission presented the "Aldrich Plan" proposing a National Reserve Association, something similar to a centralized bank. Regional banks, organized in districts, would be able to share reserves, allowing the money supply to grow and shrink as the national economy warranted. The American Bankers' Association endorsed the plan, but it failed in Congress in part because Aldrich was too closely aligned with special interests. In 1912 the Democratic Party won the presidency campaigning on a platform that included a rejection of the Aldrich Plan. Democrats in Congress were able to pass the Federal Reserve Act in 1913, a bill similar to Aldrich's idea of a central banking association. The former senator opposed the 1913 act because he questioned the abilities of a Federal Reserve Board comprised of political appointees. His proposal included a board of directors appointed by the member banks. Nelson Aldrich died of a stroke on April 16, 1915, in New York City.

Further reading:
Kolko, Gabriel. *The Triumph of Conservatism: A Reinterpretation of American History, 1900–1916.* New York: Free Press of Glencoe, 1963; Rothman, David J. *Politics and Power: The United States Senate 1869–1901.* Cambridge, Mass.: Harvard University Press, 1966; Stephenson, Nathaniel W. *Nelson W. Aldrich: A Leader in American Politics.* Port Washington, N.Y.: Kennikat Press, 1971.
—John David Rausch, Jr.

amending

The process of changing the content of legislation as it is considered in committee markup sessions or on the floor of the HOUSE OF REPRESENTATIVES or the SENATE is called amending. A bill may be amended at as many as seven different stages of the legislative process. The legislation may be amended in a House subcommittee, in that subcommittee's parent committee, and on the House floor. A bill also may be amended in a Senate subcommittee and in the Senate committee as well as on the Senate floor. Finally, the bill may be amended when the House and Senate try to reach final agreement on the bill's content, either in the conference committee or by an exchange of amendments between the two chambers.

Most bills are considered first by a subcommittee in the House or the Senate. After holding public hearings on the bill, the subcommittee decides whether to consider amendments to it at a markup session. After making additions and deletions to the bill, the subcommittee debates the final product before voting to report it to the full committee. In the full committee the bill may go through the same process of hearings and markup.

The process is essentially the same in the Senate. The subcommittees and committees in both houses generally follow chamber rules for amending from the floor. The smaller size of the Senate subcommittees and committees results in a less formal amending process and structure than the process in House subcommittees and committees.

Chamber rules specify that only the full House and the full Senate may amend pieces of legislation. Committees and subcommittees only make recommendations in the form of amendments. The full chamber must approve committee recommendations before they are incorporated into the bill. Committee amendments are the first items to be acted upon when the bill reaches the floor of the House or Senate. House members or senators may amend the committee amendments before the amendments are voted on, but members may not introduce amendments to the bill before committee amendments have been considered. An exception to this general rule occurs when an amendment in the nature of a substitute is offered. Members are able to amend the substitute before it is considered.

According to the rules of the House and Senate, amendments must be submitted in writing and read aloud before the chamber may consider them. A first-degree amendment is one that changes the text of a bill. An amendment to an amendment is a second-degree amendment. These amendments may add language to a bill, delete language from a bill, or delete and replace language in a bill. Once an amendment has been approved, that amendment may not be amended further.

The amending processes in the House and Senate have differences. Because of its larger size, the amending process in the House is more systematic and regulated. Members of the House offer amendments to each section of a bill in sequence. Senators are permitted to offer their amendments to any part of a bill in any order. Representatives are allowed only five minutes each to debate their amendment. Senators are allowed unlimited time to debate and may filibuster to defeat an amendment they do not like. House amendments must be germane to the bill, or relate to the topic addressed by the piece of legislation. Senate rules apply germaneness in only limited situations.

The House usually considers amendments to legislation after it resolves itself into the COMMITTEE OF THE WHOLE House on the State of the Union. As a committee, it is easier to offer and debate amendments. Bills come to the floor of the House under rules established by the HOUSE COMMITTEE ON RULES to guide the consideration of the bill. The rule typically contains limitations on the number and type of amendments that may be offered to a piece of legislation. A closed rule prohibits all floor amendments except committee amendments. An open rule allows any germane amendment to be offered on the floor. A modified rule permits amendments only to specified sections of the bill, or allows specific subjects or specific amendments. The House must adopt the rule before debate on the legislation may begin. Senators usually consider legislation, including amendments, under unanimous consent agreements.

If both houses pass different versions of the same bill, they must work on amending the bill to make the versions identical. After the House passes amendments to a bill already passed in the Senate, or after the Senate passes amendments to a bill passed by the House, the other chamber must approve the amendments. If the other chamber does not pass the amended bill, a conference committee is convened to negotiate the differences in the bills.

Further reading:
Davidson, Roger H., and Walter J. Oleszek. *Congress & Its Members.* Washington, D.C.: Congressional Quarterly Press, 2004; Johnson, Charles W. *Constitution, Jefferson's*

Manual, and Rules of the House of Representatives. House Document No. 107-284. Washington, D.C.: Government Printing Office, 2003; Riddick, Floyd M., and Alan S. Frumin. *Riddick's Senate Procedure: Precedents and Practices.* Senate Document No. 101-28. Washington, D.C.: Government Printing Office, 1992.

—John David Rausch, Jr.

Anthony Rule

Named after Senator Henry B. Anthony, a Republican from Rhode Island, who proposed the rule, it is a Senate legislative procedure designed to regularize the process of moving pieces of legislation off the Senate CALENDAR. Senator Anthony served from 1859 through 1894. He introduced the rule in 1872 to reduce a backlog of bills on the Senate calendar. Senate rules before 1869 specified that after the opening MORNING HOUR, the General Orders Calendar should be called. Measures entered on the calendar first were considered first, but any BILL could be considered out of turn by a majority vote. Vital business was entered on the separate and privileged Special Orders Calendar by a two-thirds majority vote. The General Orders Calendar did not differentiate between public and private bills and between those bills that were unimportant and those that were vital. After the Senate had spent much time debating the order in which bills would be considered, Anthony proposed a solution. The rule was codified into Rule VII of the Senate rules in 1884.

Anthony proposed a straightforward solution. From the close of Morning Hour, usually 12:30, until 1:30, bills could be taken from the General Orders Calendar with the restriction that each senator could speak on the measure for five minutes or less. If a single senator objected, the legislation was returned to the calendar for later consideration without limitation on debate. Anthony's objective was to have noncontroversial measures be quickly passed or defeated.

The Anthony Rule remains in effect in the Senate, but it is rarely invoked because of the development of the legislative authority of the MAJORITY LEADER. The Majority Leader decides which items on the calendar will be put before the Senate. The automatic call of the calendar is avoided by unanimous consent.

Further reading:

Haynes, George H. *The Senate of the United States: Its History and Practice.* 2 vols. New York: Russell & Russell, 1960; Rothman, David J. *Politics and Power: The United States Senate 1869–1901.* New York: Atheneum, 1969.

—John David Rausch, Jr.

appeal

When the presiding officer rules on a POINT OF ORDER that has been raised on the floor of either chamber, any representative or senator is allowed to appeal that ruling. The appeal is made when the representative or senator formally questions the call of the presiding officer. When this appeal is made, the full House or the full Senate makes the final decision by voting on whether to sustain the ruling of the presiding officer or to reverse the ruling of the presiding officer. In sum, appeal is a parliamentary procedure for challenging the decision of a presiding officer by asking the members to uphold or reject the decision.

—Nancy S. Lind

appointment power

Congress shares the responsibility for appointing officials in the U.S. government with the president and the executive branch. The appointment powers are described in Article II, Section II, of the U.S. Constitution, which declares that the president

> shall have power, by and with the Advice and Consent of the Senate to . . . appoint Ambassadors, other public Ministers and Consuls, Judges of the supreme court, and all other Officers of the United States, whose Appointments are not otherwise herein provided for, and which shall be established by Law: but the Congress may by Law vest the Appointment of such inferior Officers, as they think proper, in the President alone, in the Courts of Law, or in the Heads of Departments.

Article II, Section II, also gives the president the exclusive authority to fill vacancies in these governmental positions during the times that Congress is in recess and, therefore, unavailable to consent to the president's selections. Such appointments expire at the conclusion of the next session of the Congress unless the Senate formally approves the president's appointee during the session. To date, there has never been a serious attempt to amend the Constitution's appointment provisions.

The framers of the Constitution appear to have intended the shared appointment power as an internal check on the power of both the Congress and the president. Edited transcripts of the Constitutional Convention of 1787 demonstrate that the framers did not want to vest the appointment power wholly in the Congress, which some delegates believed would lead to difficulty in reaching agreements about suitable candidates. Nor did the framers want the president to be fully responsible for selecting judges, ambassadors, and other public officials because they feared that presidents would seek to use such an appointment power to accumulate power. Alexander

Hamilton appears to be the author of the language in Article II that resolved the delegates' dilemma by causing the appointment power to be shared.

Over time the shared appointment process has been refined, as Congress sought to identify both expedient and appropriate methods of selecting men and women to work at the highest levels of government. Today Congress and the president work together on some appointments; the "advice and consent" of the Senate is required for appointments to many federal courts, for appointments of all ambassadors, and for the appointments of cabinet secretaries (heads of executive branch departments), high-level bureaucrats in some executive branch agencies, and many quasi-independent regulatory agencies, such as the Federal Reserve Board, Federal Trade Commission, and Securities and Exchange Commission. In other cases, however, the president is given exclusive responsibility for appointing officials to positions.

The appointment power remains a shared responsibility of the Senate and the president but in recent decades has become a source of tension between Congress and the president, especially during periods in which members of opposing parties control the Senate and White House. For example, during the 1990s the Senate refused to act on many nominations submitted by the president, leaving vacancies in federal courthouses and in the executive branch. During this period senators frequently accused presidents of ignoring the "advice" requirement of the "advice and consent" provision in Article II of the Constitution and retaliated by withholding their "consent."

See also ADVICE AND CONSENT.

Further reading:
Mackenzie, G. Calvin. *The Politics of Presidential Appointments.* New York: The Free Press, 1981; Abraham, Henry J. *Justices, Presidents, and Senators: A Political History of Appointments to the Supreme Court.* New York: Oxford University Press, 1996.

—Lauren Bell

apportionment and redistricting

Legislative bodies, whether large or small, are created to represent a larger body of people. A small town may have a council of five members that decides local policies for the population of the place. Such a body may be elected at-large, that is, at election time all the voters may vote to fill all five positions. While such arrangements make sense in a small community for a small number of representatives, more elaborate provisions are required when the electorate is numerous and the number of representatives is large, as in the case of the U.S. Congress. The Congress comprises two chambers: the 100-member Senate and the 435-member House of Representatives. Apportionment is the process for assigning the seats, or positions of authority, in the representational institution to political entities, in this case the states.

The apportionment of seats in the U.S. Senate is determined by the historic compromise hammered out in Philadelphia when the founders wrote the American Constitution. The Virginia Plan called for a national legislative body of two chambers with representation in both according to population. A counterproposal from the small states, referred to as the New Jersey plan, sought a single legislative body in which each state would be equally represented. The resulting compromise created a Congress with two chambers. Every state is represented in both chambers. The Senate apportionment plan provides that each state has two senators. In the House of Representatives each state has representation according to population, but each state has at least one representative. That compromise has endured, and the Senate's membership has grown from 26, when there were 13 states, to 100 members representing 50 states.

Originally the Constitution provided that senators be elected by state legislatures. However, during the PROGRESSIVE ERA around the turn of the 20th century, public support grew for the direct election of senators. Congress passed the SEVENTEENTH AMENDMENT to make that change in 1912, and it was ratified by the states in 1913. Senators are elected at large with voters from the entire state electing each member. The six-year terms of the senators are staggered so that under ordinary circumstances the two Senate seats in a given state are not up for election at the same time. Moreover, with congressional elections occurring every two years, normally in each state every third election lacks a Senate contest. However, in the case of the death or resignation of a senator, the state (typically the governor thereof) may appoint a replacement to serve until the next election. If any unexpired term remains (two years or four years), then an election takes place to fill the position for the remainder of that term.

Seats in the House of Representatives are apportioned to the states according to population. From the beginning the Constitution required a CENSUS every 10 years, beginning in 1790. The first House seated 65 members, but its membership was expected to grow as the nation's population increased. After the 1910 census the chamber size was set by law to remain at 435 members. A brief exception was allowed for new states in 1959, when Hawaii and Alaska were accorded statehood. Each was granted one House seat until the reapportionment following the 1960 census. As the nation has grown in population, the average number of Americans for each representative has risen. For example, after the 2000 census reported a population of more than 282 million Americans, the average per representative became nearly 647,000 people.

STATE POPULATION AND THE DISTRIBUTION OF REPRESENTATIVES

State	Population	Representatives 2002 to 2010
Alabama	4,461,130	7
Alaska	628,933	1
Arizona	5,140,683	8 [+2]
Arkansas	2,679,733	4
California	33,930,798	53 [+1]
Colorado	4,311,882	7 [+1]
Connecticut	3,409,535	5 [−1]
Delaware	785,068	1
Florida	16,028,890	25 [+2]
Georgia	8,206,975	13 [+2]
Hawaii	1,216,642	2
Idaho	1,297,274	2
Illinois	12,439,042	19 [−1]
Indiana	6,090,782	9 [−1]
Iowa	2,931,923	5
Kansas	2,693,824	4
Kentucky	4,049,431	6
Louisiana	4,480,271	7
Maine	1,277,731	2
Maryland	5,307,886	8
Massachusetts	6,355,568	10
Michigan	9,955,829	15 [−1]
Minnesota	4,925,670	8
Mississippi	2,852,927	4 [−1]
Missouri	5,606,260	9
Montana	905,316	1
Nebraska	1,715,369	3
Nevada	2,002,032	3 [+1]
New Hampshire	1,238,415	2
New Jersey	8,424,354	13
New Mexico	1,823,821	3
New York	19,004,973	29 [−2]
North Carolina	8,067,673	13 [+1]
North Dakota	643,756	1
Ohio	11,374,540	18 [−1]
Oklahoma	3,458,819	5 [−1]
Oregon	3,428,543	5
Pennsylvania	12,300,670	19 [−2]
Rhode Island	1,049,662	2
South Carolina	4,025,061	6
South Dakota	756,874	1
Tennessee	5,700,037	9
Texas	20,903,994	32 [+2]
Utah	2,236,714	3
Vermont	609,890	1
Virginia	7,100,702	11
Washington	5,908,684	9
West Virginia	1,813,077	3
Wisconsin	5,371,210	8 [−1]
Wyoming	495,304	1
Total	281,424,177	435

Congressional districts are not equal in population across the country because seats are apportioned on a proportional basis to the 50 states and no congressional district extends across any state boundary. Six states have only one seat, the constitutional minimum: Alaska, Montana, North Dakota, South Dakota, Vermont, and Wyoming. Of those states, Wyoming has the smallest population: 494,000. California has the most seats, 53, and the most people, 33.9 million. Recent population trends feature population growth in the South and Southwest of the United States, with less growth in the North and Midwest. States that gained two seats after the 2000 census are Arizona, Georgia, and Texas, while California, Colorado, Florida, and Nebraska each gained one. New York and Pennsylvania each suffered the loss of two seats, while Connecticut, Illinois, Mississippi, Ohio, Oklahoma, and Wisconsin declined by one.

States have the task of drawing districts for the number of seats obtained by the apportionment process. Historically states enjoyed significant latitude in making their arrangements. In the first half of the 20th century, rapid urban growth was virtually ignored by the state legislatures, which were themselves districted with little regard for population equality. For example, in Illinois urban voters challenged the inequality of districts in federal court in the case of *Colegrove v. Green*. District lines had not been redrawn since 1901, and district populations varied from 112,000 to more than 914,000. Colegrove, a Northwestern University political scientist, argued that the Constitution required the U.S. House of Representatives to be equitably districted according to population (Article 1, Section 2) and that the existing arrangements violated due process and equal protection under the law, as required by the Fourteenth Amendment. In 1946, however, and by a vote of 4-3 in the U.S. Supreme Court, the majority held that this was a legislative matter and a "political thicket" to be avoided by the courts. The people's remedy would lie in the processes of legislation or constitutional change.

After the 1960 census social critics denounced the obviously growing inequality evident in both the U.S. House and especially in state legislatures. In the California Senate the largest district population was more than 422 times as large as in the smallest district. The ratio in the New Hampshire House was 1,443 to 1. In Florida about 12 percent of the population could elect a majority of the state senate, while a slightly different 12 percent could elect a majority of the state house. These inequities led to much speculation about the discriminatory policies that could result when small percentages of the people in a states could dominate the legislative process.

More legal challenges resulted, and the U.S. Supreme Court accepted one, *BAKER V. CARR*, for a decision in 1961. Baker, a voting citizen in Nashville, Tennessee, argued that population inequality deprived him of "due process of law" and "equal protection of the laws," as guaranteed by the

Fourteenth Amendment. Although Baker did not get the relief he hoped for, in 1962 the U.S. Supreme Court did decide that the federal courts could decide cases and provide relief in matters of state legislative districts. In short, such issues were now justiciable, no longer a forbidden political thicket as far as the courts were concerned.

Soon the courts were flooded with cases. In 1964 the U.S. Supreme Court rendered another important decision in WESBERRY V. SANDERS. It questioned the fairness of two Georgia congressional districts where one had three times the population of another. The court required that, "as nearly as is practicable, one man's vote in a congressional election is to be worth as much as another's." On the basis of these cases and more, the principle of "one voter, one vote" became the standard for U.S. House congressional districts, county boards, city councils, school boards, as well as both chambers of state legislatures. As the decades since the 1960s have passed, redistricting to maintain population equality in the face of population growth and mobility has taken place everywhere following each decennial census. While one voter, one vote provided a major criterion for equitable districts, major fairness issues remain. Redistricting implies changing an existing balance of political power. Adding congressional seats to a state contributes to its political power at the expense of states that lose seats. After the 1990 and 2000 censuses New York's congressional delegation declined by five members to number 29, while California gained eight to number 53. To squeeze five New York Congress members out of office and allow California voters to add eight representatives to their congressional delegation is a meaningful redistribution of power.

Within the states redistricting means shifting legislative district lines, creating more districts in places of population growth and enlarging the area of districts where population is stagnant. But when district lines are subject to change, there is opportunity for GERRYMANDERING, defined as manipulating district boundaries to the advantage of particular political interests.

Historically there have been two predominating particular interests in the battles over redistricting. Because redistricting by definition means change in existing lines, the people with stakes in the old lines, the legislators themselves, seek personal advantage. So redistricting has usually favored the reelection prospects of incumbents who desire to stay in office. Second, there is the prospect of party advantage. Typically the majority party seeks to concentrate the minority party voters into as few districts as possible while creating as many districts with consistently winnable majorities as possible.

After the 1982 amendments to the CIVIL RIGHTS ACT OF 1964, the courts enforced redistricting plans that concentrated people of racial and language minorities while maximizing the number of districts that would come under electoral control of these minorities. Such districts are referred to as "majority minority districts." In 1993, for example, there were 16 new African-American members, with 13 coming from predominantly black populated districts created after the 1990 census. The number of black members in the House increased from 17 prior to 1990 redistricting to 37 after the 2000 election. Hispanics in the House increased from five to 19 in the same period.

Redistricting after the 1990 census raised legal and political questions about how far redistricting efforts should go to concentrate minorities. In North Carolina, for example, a congressional district followed Interstate 85 between Charlotte and Durham, assembling small concentrations of black Americans along the way into a district that promptly elected a black congressman. While the shape of North Carolina's 12th district was extreme, the national effort produced 15 new districts predominated by African Americans and nine by Hispanics. However, Democrats noted a political consequence. Although all the new minority districts elected Democrats, the increasingly white districts around them, formerly held by Democrats, were taken over by the Republicans. The result was that Democrats suffered a net loss of seats. A court challenge to Georgia's districts threw out a plan drawn with race as the "predominant factor" (*Miller v. Johnson*), but the Supreme Court accepted a revision that allowed one minority majority district and two others with substantial majority populations (*Abrams v. Johnson*). After the 2000 census the states avoided making race "the predominant factor" as they redrew district lines, but greater clarity about this aspect of redistricting may not come from the justices of the U.S. Supreme Court until some changes occur in the Court's membership.

Redistricting occurs as a highly political issue that arises every 10 years in the state legislatures. It remains, as the Supreme Court said in 1946, "a political thicket," but one that courts have repeatedly entered in the last half century. The result is that citizens are entitled to equal representation in the U.S. House as well as in state and local representative bodies on the basis of population. It is up to legislatures to make the political choices, but the resulting maps must be equitable regarding population. Moreover, protected minorities must be accorded representation where possible and certainly not divided up to prevent the election of minority representatives. These are the principles of fairness that the U.S. Supreme Court has said are protected by the Constitution.

A significant political consequence of decennial redistricting is that the prospects for change do threaten incumbents and do raise the stakes for political parties to win majorities. The shakeup stimulates new candidates and alters prospects for winning reelection by incumbents. Typically the House of Representatives and state legislatures are enlivened after redistricting by a bumper crop of freshman representatives.

Further reading:
Greenblatt, Alan. "The Mapmaking Mess." *Governing*, (January 2001) p. 1; Giroux, Gregory L. "Remaps' Clear Trend: Incumbent Protection," *Congressional Quarterly Weekly Report*, 3 November 2001, pp. 2,627–2,632; *Abrams v. Johnson* 521 U.S. 74 (1997); *Baker v. Carr* 369 U.S. 186 (1962); *Colegrove v. Green* 328 U.S. 549 (1946); *Miller v. Johnson* 515 U.S. 900 (1995).

—Jack R. Van Der Slik

Appropriations, House Committee on

The House Committee on Appropriations is one of the most powerful committees in Congress. Its influence stems in large measure from the prominent role it plays with respect to exercising Congress's "power of the purse," generally thought to be the most important legislative prerogative. This committee, along with its Senate counterpart, has sole responsibility for drafting the legislation that allocates the federal government's discretionary spending. Discretionary spending is federal spending the provision of which must be made every year or two. This type of spending is distinct from direct or mandatory spending, which involves the automatic allocation of funds according to a formula and certain eligibility requirements. Direct spending, unlike discretionary spending, is a product of authorizing legislation and generally does not require annual or biennial legislative renewal. The Appropriations Committee's authority over discretionary funds includes the power to set ceilings on spending levels, mandate expenditure of funds, withhold federal monies altogether, specify the purpose of the expenditure, and condition funding on the satisfaction of certain criteria.

Due to its control over large amounts of federal expenditure, it is not surprising that this powerful committee has attracted and/or helped catapult to prominence some of Congress's most important members. Two former members have gone on to become president of the United States: James Garfield and Gerald Ford. Other members include men who went on to become Speaker of the House: Samuel J. Randall, JOSEPH CANNON, and Joseph Byrnes. The committee has also been home to scores of other notable figures such as Thaddeus Stevens, Clarence Cannon, George Mahon, John Rhodes, Jamie Whitten, Robert Michel, TOM DELAY, and NANCY PELOSI.

The House Committee on Appropriations was established in 1865. Prior to that the WAYS AND MEANS COMMITTEE was the House body that exercised control over how federal funds were spent. At the time the Ways and Means Committee was thought to be overburdened, and in response the House created the Appropriations Committee and the COMMITTEE ON BANKING AND CURRENCY (to be followed two years later by the SENATE APPROPRIATIONS COMMITTEE). Since 1865 the power of the Appropriations Committee has waxed and waned as the House has modified its rules and procedures, as Congress has restructured the budget process, and as political and budgetary pressures have fluctuated. Nevertheless, for most of its history the committee has been among the most influential institutions in Congress.

The 1970s witnessed a number of events that affected the committee. The internal congressional reforms of this period had a significant impact on the Appropriations Committee. These efforts ended much of the "star chamber" quality of its proceedings. Increasingly, HEARINGS and markups were opened to the public so the public could scrutinize member votes and statements in committee much more easily. In addition, these reforms undercut what had been the unshakeable law of seniority that had largely insulated committee members from internal House pressures. The manner in which committee members were selected, subcommittee chairmen appointed, and bills considered on the floor were all modified, making the committee more accountable to the parent chamber.

Enactment of the CONGRESSIONAL BUDGET AND IMPOUNDMENT CONTROL ACT OF 1974 also altered the manner in which appropriators performed their functions, but in a more ambivalent fashion. Prior to this legislation appropriators were essentially permitted to allocate monies piecemeal, largely according to their wishes. This legislation created budget committees in each house that were given an important role in formulating overall discretionary funding levels, thus reducing the authority of the appropriators accordingly. However, the bill also strengthened the committee's hand by authorizing the chair to set the annual spending ceilings for each subcommittee. Rules of procedure, budgetary pressures, and political realities have ensured that these ceilings are difficult to breach by floor amendment. Moreover, from its inception a number of appropriators have automatically sat on the BUDGET COMMITTEE, thus assuring that the interests of the Appropriations Committee are represented.

In the 1980s and 1990s political pressure mounted for greater fiscal austerity. This also had a major, if again ambivalent, effect on appropriators. This trend bolstered the powers of the House leadership and Budget Committee, both of which played an increasingly prominent role in overall budget formation. The combination of an aging population, the political popularity of mandatory spending programs, and the problem of persistent budget deficits also has had the effect of "crowding out" discretionary spending, which is the preserve of the appropriators. Four decades ago discretionary spending made up the preponderance of federal spending. Today it totals approximately one-third. That leaves two-thirds of annual federal spending largely in the hands of authorizing committees, thus, in theory, reducing the power of the appropriators. Of course, jurisdiction over such programs and the exercise of actual control over such expenditures are often two very different things. Direct spending programs, such as Social Security, are exceedingly popular and therefore politically difficult to alter. Thus, paradoxically, the appropriators' "loss" of power over a large share of the budget may actually render them more powerful. As discretionary spending becomes more compressed, the more precious a commodity it becomes, thus increasing the appropriators' influence. Even with the explosion of direct spending, the monies controlled by the Appropriations Committee still fund the lion's share of executive branch activities.

The chair of the Appropriations Committee by his position traditionally ranks among the most influential members of the House. While this position does not command the type of power wielded by Clarence Cannon or John Taber in the 1950s and 1960s, it still carries immense clout. First, the chair and ranking member (of the minority party) serve as ex officio members of each subcommittee. Second, the chair hires and fires committee and subcommittee staff members. Third, he or she controls the schedule for committee hearings and works with the House leadership to schedule floor time for bills. Fourth, and perhaps most important, the chair is responsible for setting the annual spending ceilings for each subcommittee.

The bulk of the committee's work is carried out at the subcommittee level. The committee is made up of 13 subcommittees, and the jurisdiction of these subcommittees touches upon virtually every aspect of government operations, ranging from the military to the postal service. These subcommittees enjoy a great deal of autonomy, wielding immense authority over matters within their jurisdiction. Actions taken by subcommittees are rarely overturned by the committee and often pass unamended on the House floor. The prominence enjoyed by the subcommittee chairs is such that they have been dubbed "cardinals," drawing comparisons to Vatican prelates. They put together the first draft of their subcommittee's bill and, given their staffing advantage, are well positioned to defend the "chair's mark" in subcommittee proceedings. Although House subcommittee chairs are not as well positioned to defend their mark at this stage of the process as are their Senate counterparts—Senate subcommittee chairs work with colleagues who spend much less time on subcommittee matters—that relative disadvantage is more than offset on the House floor, where appropriations bills stand a much better chance of passing without amendment than they do on the Senate side. In short, the appropriations cardinals often wield greater power than do chairs of authorizing committees.

Because of its power, the committee has long been among the most coveted committee assignments. The committee, with 65 members, has the third-largest membership of any committee in Congress (behind the HOUSE TRANSPORTATION AND INFRASTRUCTURE and House Ways and Means Committees). Those who get on the committee tend to stay there, remaining on the committee until they retire, die, are defeated, or are elevated to House leadership.

One of the key relationships that the committee maintains is with its Senate counterpart. Most observers have concluded that the House Committee on Appropriations is the more powerful of the two, and many persuasive arguments can be marshaled to support this claim.

First, it is almost certainly true that the House committee exercises greater power within its respective chamber than does the Senate committee. This is largely because House rules and procedures make it much more difficult for appropriations bills to be amended on the floor.

Second, by custom the House usually produces its version of an appropriations bill first. In this way the House sets the parameters for debate on appropriations law for that year. Traditionally, the Senate has filled more of an appellate role by offering agencies and groups an opportunity to revisit the House's decisions. In recent years, however, the Senate has played less of an appellate and more of a proactive role, a trend that has been reinforced by the budgetary timetables prescribed by the Congressional Budget and Impoundment Control Act. This has elevated the Senate body in many ways to a position of near equality with respect to its House counterpart, because the timetables enable Senators to become more active in the details of the budget earlier in the process.

Third, House appropriators generally sit on only one committee—Appropriations (there are some exceptions, most notably the handful of members who also serve on the Budget Committee). Senators, on the other hand, often serve on a number of other committees and consequently have less time to devote to their appropriations duties. Therefore, when dealing with the Senate, House member knowledge of the subject matter is often superior. The impact of the imposition of TERM LIMITATIONS on committee and subcommittee chairs by congressional Republicans, however, may have an effect on this equation, but it is difficult at present to draw any definitive conclusions on this issue.

Despite the institutional advantages enjoyed by House appropriators, their relative power over their Senate colleagues may be less than meets the eye. Empirical research indicates that the upper house more than holds its own in disagreements during conference committee deliberations. This is in part because "going second" offers some advantages. Since the House has "shown its cards" first, the Senate can adjust its position accordingly, thus gaining a more favorable position heading into conference. In addition, by waiting the Senate can better factor in changes in the policy and political environments. On an individual level, senators have more authority than do individual House members, since they often have overlapping committee jurisdictions owing to membership on related authorizing committees. Finally, the Senate committee is a smaller body, permitting (at least in theory) each member a proportionately greater say in the resulting legislation.

In recent years the committee has been bolstered by the legislative atrophy of the authorizing committees. Powerful institutional incentives favor the appropriators in their competition with their authorizing counterparts. For the government to operate, appropriations bills must be passed. Authorization bills, as a general matter, are not as vital to government operations.

Authorizing legislation, at least theoretically, is supposed to precede appropriations bills in the budget process and to set legislative policy for the agencies. In reality, authorizing committees have often failed to enact legislation before their appropriations cousins, frequently passing their bills (if they are passed at all) after the appropriations bill has already been enacted. An extreme case is the example of the House and Senate Appropriations Subcommittees on Foreign Operations vis-à-vis their authorizer colleagues. Whereas the subcommittees produce an appropriations bill every year, there has not been a comprehensive foreign assistance authorization bill passed in almost two decades. Such failure by the authorizing committees leaves appropriations bills as "the only legislative game in town." To get their policy preferences translated into law, agencies, interest groups, and even authorizers themselves often must ask the appropriators to insert substantive measures into spending bills. This is all the more likely to happen when the appropriations bills are combined into a large omnibus package. Appropriators, however, are mindful not to encroach unduly onto the authorizers' turf since that can open up a Pandora's Box. Authorizers collectively far outnumber appropriators, and they have the potential to narrow the jurisdiction of the appropriators, an occurrence that is not without precedent. Appropriator-authorizer tension is generally more acute in the House, where committees provide members with most of their opportunities for legislative influence.

The culture of the House Appropriations Committee separates it from other House committees. First, the committee generally operates on a bipartisan basis. Even though members may be from different ideological backgrounds, it is in their mutual interests to "get along" since, by preserving the culture of comity, members are more apt to get funded the programs they favor. In some ways this bipartisanship is born of necessity, since appropriations bills must pass every year to fund government operations. Excessive partisanship could have a crippling effect on the committee's effectiveness. At the same time, the bipartisan tradition of the committee helps insulate it from outside forces looking to alter a bill or make its passage more difficult.

Second, the committee is different from other committees in that it rarely unveils grand undertakings or initiatives. Unlike other committees, it infrequently holds high-profile hearings. Its job is inherently reactive and workmanlike: poring over budgetary submissions and the minutiae of agency operations.

Despite or perhaps because of its great authority, the Appropriations Committee has often come under heavy criticism. First, the news media and the public are frequently critical of what they view to be the committee members' constant efforts to support parochial spending projects, or "pork," for their home districts. This perceived tendency to place "pork" in appropriations bills and reports has long been derided as wasteful of taxpayer dollars, self-serving to the members, and disruptive to agency planning. Second, agencies are often critical of the appropriators' tendencies to "earmark" (that is, to specify the use of) funds for particular programs or projects. The executive branch resents these actions as intrusions into its administrative discretion. Third, authorizing committees are often critical because they believe that the Appropriations Committee infringes on their prerogatives by legislating in spending bills. Finally, appropriators have been criticized for working too much at the margins, focusing on incremental budget adjustments, trimming, and pruning but rarely uprooting programs and implementing needed structural change. None of these criticisms is without foundation, although certainly some of them reflect frustration and resentment by outsiders at the immense power wielded by this committee.

Further reading:
Fenno, Richard F. *The Power of the Purse: Appropriations Politics in Congress.* Boston: Little, Brown & Company, 1966; Munson, Richard. *The Cardinals of Capitol Hill: The Men and Women Who Control Government Spending,* New York: Grove Press, 1993; Taylor, Edward T. *A History of the Committee on Appropriations, House of Representatives.* Washington, D.C.: Government Printing Office, 1941; White, Joseph. "The Functions and Power of the House Appropriations Committee," Ph.D. dissertation, University of California, Berkeley, 1989.

—Roy E. Brownwell, II

Appropriations, Senate Committee on

Much like its House counterpart, the Senate Committee on Appropriations is one of the most powerful panels in Congress. Its influence stems in large measure from the prominent role it plays with respect to exercising Congress's power of the purse, generally thought to be the most important legislative prerogative.

This committee, along with the HOUSE APPROPRIATIONS COMMITTEE, has sole responsibility for drafting the legislation that allocates the federal government's discretionary spending. (Discretionary spending is federal spending the provision of which must be made every year or two. This type of spending is distinct from direct or mandatory spending, which involves the automatic allocation of funds according to a formula and certain eligibility requirements. Direct spending, unlike discretionary spending, is a product of authorizing legislation and generally does not require annual or biennial legislative renewal.) The Appropriations Committee's authority over discretionary funds includes the power to set ceilings on spending levels, mandate expenditure of funds, withhold federal monies altogether, specify the purpose of expenditures, and condition funding on the satisfaction of certain criteria. It has long been accepted that the Senate committee is less influential than its House counterpart, although recent evidence suggests that this gap has closed somewhat over the past several years.

The Senate Appropriations Committee has numbered among its members some of the nation's most distinguished public figures. They include two presidents, LYNDON JOHNSON and Harry Truman; three vice presidents, HUBERT HUMPHREY, Charles Curtis, and Henry Wilson; and a number of Senate Majority or Minority Leaders: Thomas Martin, Oscar Underwood, JOSEPH ROBINSON, W. H. White, Kenneth Wherry, Styles Bridges, William Knowland, ROBERT TAFT, Lyndon Johnson, EVERETT DIRKSEN, Mike Mansfield, and ROBERT C. BYRD. This, of course, does not include other Senate powers who served on the committee such as John Stennis, Warren Magnuson, Kenneth McKellar, William Allison, Carter Glass, RICHARD B. RUSSELL, CARL HAYDEN, and JAMES G. BLAINE.

The Senate established its Appropriations Committee in 1867, two years after the House created its committee. Prior to that the COMMITTEE ON FINANCE was the Senate body that exercised control over how federal funds were spent. Since its founding the power of the Appropriations Committee has varied, as the Senate has modified some of its rules and procedures, as Congress has restructured the budget process, and as political and budgetary pressures have fluctuated. Nevertheless, for most of its history the committee has been among the most influential committees in the Senate.

The 1970s witnessed a number of events that affected the committee. The internal congressional reforms of this period had no small impact on the Appropriations Committee. These efforts ended much of the "star chamber" quality of Appropriations proceedings. Increasingly, hearings and markups were opened to the public, whereby member votes and statements in committee could be scrutinized by the public much more easily.

Enactment of the CONGRESSIONAL BUDGET AND IMPOUNDMENT CONTROL ACT OF 1974 (CBICA) also altered the manner in which appropriators performed their functions, but in a more ambivalent fashion. Prior to this

legislation appropriators were essentially permitted to allocate monies piecemeal largely according to their wishes. This legislation created budget committees in each house that were given an important role in the formulation of overall discretionary funding levels, thus reducing the authority of the appropriators accordingly. However, the bill also strengthened the committee's hand by authorizing its chair to set the annual spending ceilings for each subcommittee. Rules of procedure, budgetary pressures, and political realities have ensured that these ceilings are difficult to breach by floor amendment. Moreover, a number of appropriators have traditionally sat on the SENATE BUDGET COMMITTEE, thus assuring that the interests of the Appropriations Committee are not ignored.

In the 1980s and 1990s political pressure mounted for greater fiscal austerity. This trend also had a major, if again ambivalent, impact on the appropriators. It bolstered the powers of the Senate leadership and budget committees, both of which played an increasingly prominent role in overall budget formation. The combination of an aging population, the political popularity of mandatory spending programs, and the problem of persistent budget deficits also has had the effect of "crowding out" discretionary spending, which is the preserve of the appropriators. Four decades ago discretionary spending made up the preponderance of federal spending. Today it totals approximately one-third. That leaves two-thirds of annual federal spending largely in the hands of authorizing committees, thus, in theory, reducing the power of the appropriators. Of course, jurisdiction over such programs and the exercise of actual control over such expenditures are often two very different things. Direct spending programs, such as Social Security, are exceedingly popular and therefore politically difficult to alter.

Thus, paradoxically, the appropriators' "loss" of power over a large share of the budget may actually render them more powerful. As discretionary spending becomes more compressed, the more precious a commodity it becomes, thus increasing the appropriators' influence. Even with the explosion of direct spending, the monies controlled by the Appropriations Committee still fund the lion's share of executive branch activities.

The Appropriations Committee chair by his or her very position traditionally ranks among the most influential members of the Senate. First, the chair and ranking member of the minority party on the committee serve as ex officio members of each subcommittee. Second, the chair hires and fires committee and subcommittee staff members (even if, in reality, subcommittee chairs exercise much authority over subcommittee staff). Third, he or she controls the schedule for committee hearings and weighs in with the Senate leadership with respect to scheduling floor time for bills. Fourth, and perhaps most importantly, the chair is responsible for setting the annual spending ceilings for each subcommittee.

Much like the House committee, the bulk of the Senate committee's work is carried out at the subcommittee level. The committee is made up of 13 subcommittees, and the jurisdictions of these subcommittees touch upon virtually every aspect of government operations, ranging from the military to the postal service. These subcommittees enjoy a great deal of autonomy, wielding immense authority over matters within their jurisdictions. A subcommittee chair puts together the first draft of the subcommittee's appropriations bill and, since he or she enjoys a staffing advantage over his or her colleagues, is well positioned to defend the "chair's mark," better positioned, in fact, than his or her House counterpart, who works with colleagues who spend much more time on subcommittee matters. That relative advantage is offset, however, on the Senate floor, where bills stand a much better chance of being amended than in the House.

Because of its power, the committee has long been among the most coveted committee assignments. The committee, with 29 members, has the largest membership of any Senate committee. Those who get on the committee tend to stay there, remaining on it until they retire, die, are defeated, or are elevated to Senate leadership.

One of the key relationships that the committee maintains is with its House counterpart. As noted above, most observers have concluded that the House Committee on Appropriations is the more powerful of the two, although this advantage is less marked in recent years.

First, it is almost certainly true that the House committee exercises greater power within its respective chamber than does the Senate committee. This is largely because Senate rules and procedures make it much easier for appropriations bills to be amended on the floor.

Second, by custom the House usually produces its version of an appropriations bill first. In this way the House sets the parameters for debate on appropriations law for that year. Traditionally, the Senate has filled more of an appellate role by offering agencies and interest groups an opportunity to revisit the House's decisions. In recent years, however, the Senate has played less of an appellate and more of a proactive role, a trend that has been reinforced by the budgetary timetables prescribed by the CBICA. This has elevated the Senate body in many ways to a position of near equality with respect to its House counterpart.

Third, House appropriators generally sit on only one committee—Appropriations (there are some exceptions, most notably the handful of members who also serve on the Budget Committee). Senators, on the other hand, often serve on a number of other committees and consequently have less time to devote to their appropriations duties. Therefore, when dealing with the Senate, House member

knowledge of the subject matter is often superior. (Whether that is true at the staff level is a different matter altogether). The impact of the imposition of term limits on committee and subcommittee chairs by congressional Republicans, however, may have an effect on this equation, but it is difficult at present to draw any definitive conclusions on this issue.

On the other hand, despite the institutional advantages enjoyed by House appropriators, their relative power over their Senate colleagues may be less than meets the eye. Empirical research indicates that the upper house more than holds its own in disagreements during conference committee deliberations. This is in part because "going second" offers the Senate committee some advantages. Since the House has "shown its cards" first, the Senate can adjust its position accordingly, thus gaining a more favorable position heading into conference. In addition, by going second the Senate can better factor in subsequent changes in the policy and political environments. Moreover, in many ways individual senators have more authority than do individual House members, since they often have overlapping committee jurisdictions owing to membership on related authorizing committees. Finally, the Senate committee is a smaller body, permitting (at least in theory) each member a proportionately greater say in the resulting legislation.

In recent years the committee has been bolstered by the legislative atrophy of the authorizing committees. Powerful institutional incentives favor the appropriators in their competition with their authorizing counterparts. For the government to operate, appropriations bills must be passed. Authorization bills, as a general matter, are not as vital to government operations.

Authorizing legislation, at least theoretically, is supposed to precede appropriations bills in the budget process and to set legislative policy for the agencies. In reality, authorizing committees have often failed to enact legislation before their appropriations cousins, frequently passing their bills (if they are passed at all) after the appropriations bill has already been enacted. An extreme case is the example of the House and Senate Appropriations Subcommittees on Foreign Operations vis-à-vis their authorizing colleagues. Whereas the subcommittees produce an appropriations bill every year, there has not been a comprehensive foreign assistance authorization bill passed in almost two decades. Such failure by the authorizing committees leaves appropriations bills as "the only legislative game in town." To get their policy preferences translated into law, agencies, interest groups, and even authorizers themselves must ask the appropriators to insert substantive measures into spending bills. This is all the more likely to happen when the appropriations bills are combined into a large omnibus package. Senate appropriators, however, are mindful not to encroach unduly onto the authorizers' turf for reasons of comity. Appropriator-authorizer tension is less pronounced in the Senate, however, since member influence in the upper chamber is less tied to committee assignments.

The culture of the Senate Appropriations Committee separates it from other committees, although the difference between appropriators and authorizers is comparatively less dramatic in the Senate than in the House, where partisanship is more the norm. First, the committee generally operates on a bipartisan basis. Even though members may be from different ideological backgrounds, it is in their mutual interests to "get along," since, by preserving the culture of comity, members are more apt to get funded the programs they favor. In some ways this bipartisanship is born out of necessity, since appropriations bills must pass every year to fund government operations. Excessive partisanship could have a crippling effect on the committee's effectiveness. At the same time the bipartisan tradition of the committee helps insulate it from outside forces looking to alter a bill or make its passage more difficult.

Second, the committee is different from other committees in that it rarely unveils grand undertakings or initiatives. Unlike other committees, the committee infrequently holds high-profile hearings. Its job is inherently reactive and workmanlike: poring over budgetary submissions and the minutiae of agency operations.

Despite or perhaps because of its great authority, the Appropriations Committee has often come under heavy criticism. First, the press and the public are frequently critical of what they view to be the committee members' constant efforts to support parochial spending projects, or "pork," for their states. This perceived tendency to place "pork" in appropriations bills and reports has long been derided as wasteful of taxpayer dollars, self-serving to the members, and disruptive to agency planning. Second, agencies are often critical of the appropriators' tendencies to "earmark" (that is, to specify the use of) funds for particular programs or projects. The executive branch resents these actions as intrusions into its administrative discretion. Third, authorizing committees are often critical because they believe that the Appropriations Committee infringes on their prerogatives by legislating in spending bills. Finally, appropriators have also been criticized for working too much at the margins, focusing on incremental budget adjustments, trimming, and pruning but rarely uprooting programs and implementing needed structural change. None of these criticisms is without foundation, although certainly some of them reflect frustration and resentment by outsiders at the power wielded by this committee.

Further reading:
Fenno, Richard F. *The Power of the Purse: Appropriations Politics in Congress*. Boston: Little, Brown & Company, 1966; Munson, Richard. *The Cardinals of Capitol Hill: The Men and Women Who Control Government Spending*. New York: Grove Press, 1993; Horn, Stephen. *Unused Power: The Work of the Senate Committee on Appropriations*. Washington, D.C.: Brookings Institution, 1970; *Committee on Appropriations, U.S. Senate, 135th Anniversary*. Washington, D.C.: Government Printing Office, 2002.

—Roy E. Brownwell, II

appropriations bills

There are many types of appropriations bills. Regular appropriations bills occur after the president submits his budget to Congress and the Congress completes action on the budget resolution and the budget reconciliation bills. There are 13 regular appropriations bills required by federal law, and the subcommittees of the HOUSE OF REPRESENTATIVES and SENATE APPROPRIATIONS COMMITTEES reflect these 13 areas substantively. Each appropriations subcommittee receives a spending cap from the appropriations committee. Subcommittees hold hearings to divide up spending among federal agencies under their jurisdictions. Each subcommittee then submits their bills one at a time to the larger body for consideration. Once these 13 bills are passed and the president signs them, work on the regular budget or the on-budget items is done.

The federal fiscal year runs from October 1 to September 30, and fiscal years are named for the year in which they end (e.g., FY05 runs from October 2004 to September 2005). Often, Congress runs behind in finishing work on the 13 appropriations bills required to keep the government functioning. When this happens, typically the Congress and president agree to stop-gap spending measures (called continuing appropriations or continuing resolutions or just CRs), which continue the previous year's spending levels into the new fiscal year, allowing the decision makers some additional time to complete the budget. Once the 13 appropriations bills are completed and the fiscal year budget is being implemented, budgets need some augmentation. Supplemental appropriations (called deficiency appropriations at times in the past) are passed to provide this. When natural disasters hit or other focusing events occur (such as the terrorist attacks of September 11, 2001), such supplementals are often termed emergency appropriations bills.

The appropriations bills described above are all part of the discretionary side of the federal budget, or the so-called on-budget items. Many federal areas (a majority in fact) are formula-based entitlement programs. These are not on the table during the regular appropriations process. These include mostly formula-based programs, such as Social Security, Medicare, Medicaid, veterans programs, and many welfare programs. These programs constitute a slight majority of the federal budget each year but are not on the table in the regular process described above. They are called permanent appropriations because they are authorized and appropriated typically at one point in time via distinct public law (revisions are possible and often necessary down the road, but they need not be tackled annually like the on-budget items). These are typically completed via the lawmaking process of the authorizing committees, while the appropriations process is driven by the money committees.

Further reading:
Mikesell, John. *Fiscal Administration.* (6th ed.) 2002 5th ed. Belmont, Calif.: Wadsworth, Oleszek, Walter. *Congressional Procedures and the Policy Process.* 6th ed. Washington, D.C.: Congressional Quarterly (5th ed.), 2004; Schick, Allen, and Felix Lostracco, *Federal Budgeting.* Washington, D.C.: Brookings Institution Press, 2004.

—Glen S. Krutz

Architect of the Capitol
The office of the Architect of the Capitol was established in 1793, when George Washington selected Dr. William Thornton's design for the new capitol building after a failed design competition resulted in disappointing results that did not fit the vision of Congress. Thornton was then designated the first official architect and had the assistance of three professional architects in supervising the construction of the north wing of the capitol. Stephen Hallet (1793–94), George Hadfield (1795–98), and James Hoban (1798–1800) all assisted Thornton in the construction of the north wing.

Beginning in 1803 with the second Architect of the Capitol, Benjamin Henry Latrobe, the president appointed the architect for an indefinite term with the advice and consent of the Senate. In 1989 Congress passed legislation that changed the length of term for the architect. Beginning with the current architect, Alan Hantman, the architect is

Architectural rendering of the U.S. Capitol done by Alexander Jackson Davis, c. 1830 *(Library of Congress)*

appointed by the president for a 10-year term, with the advice and consent of the Senate from a list of three candidates recommended by a congressional commission. Upon confirmation the architect becomes an official of the legislative branch and is eligible for reappointment after the term. Hantman, appointed in 1997 by President Bill Clinton, is the 10th Architect of the Capitol.

In accordance with a law passed August 15, 1876 (19 Stat. 147; 40 U.S.C. 162-163), the architect's duties include maintaining the mechanical and structural integrity of the capitol building, providing upkeep and improvement to the grounds of the capitol and organizing the presidential inauguration and other events that take place on the grounds of the capitol.

In addition to the architect's duties in maintaining the structure and grounds of the capitol, the office is also responsible for the capitol complex, which includes the Senate and House office buildings, the Library of Congress buildings, the Supreme Court building, and the U.S. Botanical Gardens. Today the Architect of the Capitol is responsible for the creation and design of the new Capitol Visitor's Center, which will help guide the more than 3 million people who visit the grounds annually, as well as the continued upkeep of the buildings, grounds, and power plant for the capitol complex.

See also CAPITOL BUILDING; CAPITOL HILL.

Further reading:
Allen, William C. *History of the United States Capitol: A Chronicle of Design, Construction and Politics.* Washington, D.C.: U.S. Government Printing Office, 2001; "Office of the Architect." Available online. URL: http://www.aoc.gov/AOC. Accessed January 16, 2006.

—Jacob R. Straus

Armed Services, Senate Committee on
The Senate Committee on Armed Services was created in 1946 with the passage of the Legislative Reorganization Act. This act merged the existing Senate Military Affairs Committee (1816–1946) and the Naval Affairs Committee (1816–1946), marking the first time responsibility for the nation's defense was placed in a single committee. The Senate Military Affairs Committee and the Naval Affairs Committee were created on December 10, 1816, as two of the original standing committees created by Congress.

Prior to 1816 the Senate met as a committee of the whole and organized smaller ad hoc committees to grapple with the major issues of the day. This inefficient nature of decision making, stemming from unfocused congressional committees, caused leaders to conclude that this system was not a viable form of government. During the Continental

Congress, for instance, more than 3,200 ad hoc committees were created between 1774 and 1788. These inefficiencies caused a deliberate nudge toward the Constitutional Convention.

The core of the U.S. Constitution rests on the assumption that the process of checks and balances will assist in guarding against a tyrannical system of government. The fear of an unconstrained executive, in fact, propelled the framers of the Constitution to institute safeguards against presidential abuses of power. In Federalist Paper 51, Madison argued that structuring a government to ensure a system of checks and balances was the surest way to prevent the concentration of power in one branch of government. This basic tenet has served as an integral component to the U.S. political process.

Article 1, Section 8, of the U.S. Constitution states that the powers of Congress include the responsibility of the nation and empowers Congress

> to provide for the common defense, raise and support armies and to provide and maintain a navy.

The jurisdiction of the Senate Armed Services Committee encapsulates these broad powers. The committee's jurisdiction also includes

> aeronautical and space activities peculiar to or primarily associated with the development of weapons systems or military operations.

The U.S. Senate is currently organized around 20 committees and 68 subcommittees. The majority party controls both the chair of each committee and the majority of members on each committee. The Senate Armed Services Committee also consists of six subcommittees, which include the subcommittees on Airland, Emerging Threats and Capabilities, Personnel, Readiness and Management Support, Sea Power, and Strategic Forces.

The size of the committee has varied dramatically over the years from the original 13 members in 1946 to the 24 members who currently serve. In 2003 the committee was chaired by Senator John Warner (R-VA). Republican Senators also serving on the committee include Senators McCain (R-AZ), Inhofe (R-OK), Roberts (R-KS), Allard (R-CO), Sessions (R-AL), Collins (R-ME), Ensign (R-NV), Talent (R-MO), Chambliss (R-GA), Graham (R-SC), Dole (R-NC), and Cornyn (R-TX). The Ranking Minority Member on the committee is past chair Senator Carl Levin (D-MI), who is joined by Democratic senators Kennedy (D-MA), Byrd (D-WV), Lieberman (D-CT), Reed (D-RI), Akaka (D-HI), Nelson (D-FL), Dayton (D-MN), Bayh (D-IN), Clinton (D-NY), and Pryor (D-AR).

The committee met for the first time on January 13, 1947, and included some of the most prominent members of the Senate, including Senators H. Styles Bridges (R-NH), J. Chandler Gurney (R-SD), Leverett Saltonstall (R-MA), Millard E. Tydings (D-MD), Richard B. Russell, Jr. (D-GA), and Harry F. Byrd (D-VA). The committee played a major role in establishing a transformed military policy geared to the perceived threats of the cold war. After the "two shocks" of 1949, which included the Communist takeover in China and the emergence of a Soviet atomic bomb, U.S. military policy shifted to a more hard-line anti-communist approach that relied heavily on maintaining military superiority over the Soviets. The North Korean invasion of South Korea in 1950 also marked the first time the communist movement, perceived to be monolithic, was willing to use force to expand its base.

The committee quickly established a "bipartisan, consensus decision making style" and was particularly active during the early years, spearheading the National Security Act of 1947, the Selective Service Act of 1948, the Air Force Composition Act of 1948, and the Armed Forces Reserve Act of 1952. The committee also gained national exposure when it investigated President Truman's decision to relinquish General Douglas MacArthur from his post as the commander of UN forces in Korea in 1951.

Senator Russell (D-GA) was most closely identified with the committee during the early years. He chaired the committee from 1955 to 1969 and quickly catapulted the committee into one of the most prestigious committees in the Senate. The prestige of the committee attracted some of the most prominent senators during these years, including Senators Lyndon Johnson (D-TX), John C. Stennis (D-MS), W. Stuart Symington (D-MO), and Henry M. Jackson (D-WA). Chairman Russell is largely credited with organizing the first stable subcommittee system. The Preparedness Investigating Subcommittee, in fact, was chaired by Senator Lyndon Johnson (D-TX) until he resigned from the Senate to run for the vice presidency. It was in this role that Senator Johnson grew concerned about a "missile gap" that he believed made the United States vulnerable to a Soviet attack.

The breakdown in the cold war consensus, however, began to emerge during the Vietnam conflict. Senator John C. Stennis (D-MS) chaired the committee from 1969 to 1981, steering the committee through the Vietnam era and beyond. The committee played a large role in the development of the Draft Extension Act (1971), which replaced the draft with an all volunteer military. The committee also held high-profile hearings on the Strategic Arms Limitation Talks (SALT) and the Anti-Ballistic Missile (ABM) treaties with the Soviets.

The modern era continued the tradition of strong committee leadership with Senator John Tower (R-TX) serving from 1981 to 1985, Senator Barry Goldwater (R-AZ) serving from 1985 to 1987, Senator Sam Nunn (D-GA) serving as chair from 1987 to 1995, and Senator Strom Thurmond (R-SC) serving from 1995 to 1998. Senator Tower (R-TX) was the key ally to President Reagan's unprecedented peacetime expansion of the military. Senator Goldwater (R-AZ) chaired the committee during the 99th Congress. He was the chief sponsor of the Goldwater-Nichols Act of 1986, which both centralized the authority of the Joint Chiefs and elevated the position to serve as chief military adviser to the president. This act is generally recognized as the most significant defense reorganization since the National Security Act of 1947.

Senator Nunn (D-GA) is internationally recognized as a leader on defense issues. He and Senator Richard Lugar (R-IN) were the chief sponsors of the Soviet Nuclear Threat Reduction Act of 1991, also known as the Nunn-Lugar bill. This legislation provided financial assistance to help former Soviet republics dismantle weapons remaining from the cold war arsenal. Ironically, the committee, with Senator Nunn at the helm, voted 11-9 against Senator Tower's nomination as secretary of Defense for alleged "womanizing and excessive drinking" in 1989. Senator Thurmond is largely credited for negotiating a missile defense program with President Clinton after President Clinton vetoed the initiative a year earlier.

Today, the three leading issues facing the committee are the national missile defense system, privatization, and the occupation of Iraq. Senator John W. Warner (R-VA) has returned to chair the committee, a position he held from 1999 to 2001. Republicans successfully spearheaded the authorization of $7.8 billion to develop a national missile defense system over Democratic opposition. The Pentagon has also proposed privatizing 200,000 civilian positions, a plan staunchly opposed by the federal employees union.

However, the greatest challenge stems from the military occupation of Iraq. The cost in both blood and treasure has led to animated hearings between the Bush administration and committee members. The cost of the occupation is estimated at $60 billion a year, and the need to restructure the military to meet the increased threat of terrorism has once again cast the committee into the national limelight.

Further reading:
Deering, Christopher J., and Steven S. Smith. *Committees in Congress*. 3d ed. Washington, D.C.: Congressional Quarterly, 1997; Deering, Christopher J. "Decision Making in the Armed Services Committee." In *Congress Resurgent: Foreign and Defense Policy on Capitol Hill*, edited by Randall Ripley and James M. Lindsay. Ann Arbor: University of Michigan, 1993; Fessenden, Helen. "Lawmakers Brace for Long, Expensive Haul in Iraq." *Congressional Quarterly Weekly Report* 61, July 12, 2003, pp. 1,633–1,634; U.S. National Archives and Records Administration. "The Senate Committee on Armed Services, 1947–1996." *Committee Resource Guide*, 2003; Towell, Pat. "Armed Services Faces a Few Key Battles." *Congressional Quarterly Weekly Report* 60, November 9, 2002, pp. 2,937–2,938.

—Joseph N. Patten

Armed Services Committee, House

This is the STANDING COMMITTEE in the HOUSE OF REPRESENTATIVES that has jurisdiction over most aspects of U.S. national defense. Included are the Department of Defense, ammunition depots, forts and arsenals, the size and compositions of the armed forces, pay, promotion, retirement, and selective service. Additionally, the committee prepares legislation related to scientific research and development in support of the military, strategic and critical materials necessary for the nation's defense (including the military application of nuclear energy), and the conservation, development, and use of naval petroleum and oil shale reserves. More recently, the House has given the Armed Service Committee special oversight responsibilities for international arms control and disarmament treaties. The committee's jurisdiction over intelligence matters was curtailed when the House created the permanent Select Committee on Intelligence in 1977. The Armed Services Committee is considered among the chamber's most influential committees, and assignments to it are highly sought after by House members.

The current Armed Services Committee is the result of nearly 200 years of congressional committee evolution. The earliest predecessors of the committee were special subcommittees created by the Continental Congress to supervise military matters. Members frequently accompanied General George Washington onto the field to observe and offer advice and counsel. On March 13, 1822, Congress created the House Committees on Military Affairs and Naval Affairs. Another early component of today's committee was the Committee on the Militia, which existed from 1835 until its responsibilities were taken over by the Military Affairs Committee in 1911. In 1885 the Naval Affairs and Military Affairs Committees wrestled control of budgetary jurisdiction away from the APPROPRIATIONS COMMITTEE. By 1920 the pendulum swung back, and budgetary power was returned to the Appropriations Committee. Finally, on January 2, 1947, as part of the LEGISLATIVE REORGANIZATION ACT OF 1946, the House Military Affairs Committee and the Naval Affairs Committee were combined into the Armed Services Committee. The combination of these two committees was paralleled the following year by an executive branch reorganization, which united the Departments of War and the Navy in a single Department of Defense, created the National Security Council, and transformed the Office of Strategic Services (OSS) into the Central Intelligence Agency (CIA).

The other great 20th-century development for the committee was the Russell Amendment of 1959, which required annual program authorization of appropriations related to the procurement of military equipment. Prior to the amendment, only about 2 percent of defense activity required annual authorization. As a result of the Russell Amendment and subsequent legislative initiatives, the committee must authorize all defense activities. Thus, the committee has ensured at least a cursory role for itself in every activity related to national defense. Every year the Armed Services Committee, in conjunction with its corresponding Senate committee, prepares two authorization bills setting the Defense Department (DOD) limits on spending related to weapon systems, personnel, and facilities. The committee does not wield sole authority over defense spending, since the House BUDGET and Appropriations committees play a significant role in the funding process. The Armed Services Committee does, however, largely determine how and where the DOD spends the money.

During the first half of the 20th century, members serving on either the Military Affairs or Naval Affairs Committees could serve on no other House committees. The latter half of the century has seen the Armed Services Committee designated a major committee, allowing members an additional minor committee assignment. The size of the committee has grown over the past century. In the early 1900s the combined membership of the Military Affairs and Naval Affairs Committees was 37. The 1946 reorganization led to a consolidated Armed Services Committee with 33 members. The committee grew to 37 by 1965. Since then the committee's growth has accelerated, reaching 54 in 1991 and 61 in 2002. The growth in membership has not greatly affected the number of subcommittees used by the committee. Except for the 90th and 91st Congresses (1967–71), when the establishment of a set of specific subcommittees ballooned the total to 15, the committee normally operates with approximately seven subcommittees.

The modern history of the post-1946 reorganization saw a coalition of conservative pro-defense Republicans and southern Democrats control the Armed Services Committee for nearly a quarter century. The Democrats who chaired the committee during this time were famous for their autocratic style. The first of these iron-fisted chairs was Carl Vinson. a Democrat from Georgia, who ran the committee from 1949 to 1965, except for the years from 1953 to 1955, when Dewey Short, a Republican from Missouri, was chair. Mendel Rivers, a Democrat from South Carolina, was next and chaired the committee until his death in 1970. Rivers was often accused of running the

committee as his own personal fiefdom, steering a tremendous amount of military patronage to his home state.

The end of the Vietnam War saw an influx of Democrats, who were increasingly liberal, being elected to Congress. This changed the character of the committee because younger, more liberal, representatives joined the committee who were less supportive of the defense establishment and vocal in their opposition to excess military spending. The Armed Services Committee was not the only thing altered due to the election of reform-minded Democrats. Another reform undertaken was altering the House seniority system for selecting committee chairs. The existing system, which selected committee chairs according to length of service, was changed to a method based on elections within the House Democratic Caucus. One of the prime targets of the reformers was F. Edward Hebert, a Democrat from Louisiana, who chaired the committee from 1971 to 1975, when the Democratic caucus replaced him with the then 70-year-old C. Melvin Price, a Democrat from Illinois.

Hebert was one of three House committee chairs demoted as a result of the House revolution led by the 1974 WATERGATE "babies." During his 10 years as chair, 1975 to 1985, Price was best known for his support of the Reagan administration's first-term military buildup. By the mid-1980s growing federal budget deficits created pressure on Congress to reduce defense spending. In this fiscal environment Les Aspin, a Democrat from Wisconsin, replaced the aging Price, who had failed to provide energy or effective leadership. The liberal Aspin was selected over five more senior members for two reasons. First, he was considered one of Congress's top military experts, and second, the increasingly liberal House Democratic Caucus was sympathetic to Aspin's reform-oriented agenda. Aspin's tenure as chair saw him challenge many of the traditional assumptions of the military establishment, and under his leadership the Armed Services Committee undertook several controversial policies including military base closings, cuts in military personnel, and delays or cancellation of a military procurement.

Aspin provided strong, effective leadership of the committee until 1992, when President Bill Clinton appointed him secretary of Defense. The move away from southern dominance continued as Ronald V. Dellums, a Democrat from California and one of the most liberal members of Congress, was elected chair in 1993. Dellums, a prominent member of the Congressional Black Caucus, was first elected to Congress due in large part to his strong vocal opposition to the Vietnam War. Although considered antimilitary, Dellums provided fair and effective leadership during the two years he was chair. His political finesse earned him respect from even some of the most conservative members of the House.

The Republican Revolution in 1994 not only ended nearly 40 years of Democratic control of Congress, it also returned the chair to a southerner, Floyd Spence, a Republican from South Carolina. Spence, an old-style pro-defense southerner in the mold of Vinson and Rivers, fought hard and clashed often with both the Clinton administration and Republican budget cutters for substantial increases in defense spending. His term as chair is considered successful, having increased military spending substantially, but his low-key style contrasted sharply with the flamboyance of the previous two chairs. Therefore, he never gained the high profile of previous Armed Services Committee chairs. Spence's death in 2001 brought Bob Stump, a Republican from Arizona, to the chair for what would be, due to serious health problems, a single two-year term (2001 to 2002). Stump's decision not to run for reelection opened the door for conservative pro-defense Duncan Hunter, a Republican from California, who became chair of the Armed Services Committee in 2002.

Further reading:

Blechman, Barry M. The *Politics of National Security: Congress and U.S. Defense Policy.* New York: Oxford University Press, 1990; Deering, Christopher J. "Decision Making in the Armed Services Committees." In *Congress Resurgent: Foreign and Defense Policy on Capitol Hill,* edited by Randall B. Ripley and James M. Lindsay. Ann Arbor: University of Michigan Press, 1993; Rundquist, Barry S., and Thomas M. Carsey. *Congress and Defense Spending: The Distributive Politics of Military Procurement.* Norman: University of Oklahoma Press, 2002.

—Craig T. Cobane

Army-McCarthy hearings   *See* MCCARTHY-ARMY HEARINGS.

authorization bills

An authorization bill is one that provides the legal authority for a government program or a government agency to exist and determines its policy. Bills proposing that a new government department be established, that an existing agency be changed, that a new government program to help people be created, or that an existing program be changed in some way are all examples of possible authorization bills. A policy-making authorization bill is often contrasted with an appropriations or spending bill that provides budget authority to a government program or an agency to expend monies or incur obligations that will result in expenditures. The important congressional power of the purse is enhanced by this two-step authorization-appropriation process that is derived from HOUSE OF REPRESENTATIVES and SENATE rules.

Bills are one congressional form of proposed legislation; others include various types of resolutions. When introduced in the House a bill takes the form of H.R. with a number following, such as H.R. 129, whereas in the Senate a new bill is given an S. designation, such as S. 87. The subject matter of the introduced bill determines whether it is an authorization bill, an appropriations bill, or some other kind, and it also determines to which committee it will be referred after introduction by a member. Title language for an authorization bill is followed by an enacting clause that reads, for example,

> be it enacted by the Senate and House of Representatives of the United States of America in Congress assembled that . . .

Both House and Senate rules contain jurisdiction assignments to STANDING COMMITTEES, Rule X in the House and Rule XVII in the Senate. Most congressional committees (exceptions are appropriations or budget committees) receive authorization bill referrals and have the ability to report policy-making authorization bills related to the programs and agencies for which they have jurisdiction.

General appropriations bills, allowing agencies and programs to spend money, originate in the House by tradition. The annual budget proposal from the president as well as testimony from government officials and others before the Appropriations Committees of the House and Senate serve as a basis for both Appropriations Committees drafting appropriations bills. In contrast to authorizing bill language, the title of an appropriations bill may read something like "An act making appropriations for the Department of Justice for the year ending September 30, 2004." House and Senate Appropriations Committees report to their full chambers bills that provide regular appropriations, supplemental appropriations, or continuing appropriations providing stop-gap funding for programs and agencies.

Because authorization bills and appropriations bills perform different functions in Congress, they are generally considered in sequence. First, the authorization bill is considered and then the appropriations bill for discretionary spending purposes. For example, discretionary authorization bills establish, continue, or modify agencies or programs and thus perform their first function of providing the necessary legal authority to federal programs and activities. But such authorization bills also perform a second purpose by authorizing subsequent appropriations for agencies and programs, frequently setting spending ceilings for those agencies and programs. Possible language in an authorization bill may include language with selected amounts for particular fiscal years, or the language may include authorization to appropriate such sums as may be necessary. Permanent, annual, or multiyear authorizations can be authorized; if either of the latter two is provided, then future reauthorization bills will be necessary so that the agency or program does not expire with the passage of time. Once the chamber has passed an authorization act that gives a government agency or program a legal basis for operation, provides appropriate policy guidance, and then authorizes future appropriations, the chamber then traditionally considers an appropriations act that provides budget authority to incur financial obligations that will result in immediate or future outlays of government funds so that the agency or program can spend money to operate and function as authorized. Discretionary spending is the label applied to this process because Congress is not required to provide appropriations for a program that it has authorized, and if it does fund the program, it does not have to do so in an appropriations act at the full levels that were contained in the authorization act.

The successful separation between authorization on the one hand and appropriations on the other is enforced in the House and Senate through the rules of those chambers. First, the rules prohibit appropriations for unauthorized agencies and programs. They also limit an appropriation for the agency or program so that it cannot exceed the authorized amount. Second, chamber rules forbid the inclusion of legislative language in appropriations bills. Third, in the House but not in the Senate, appropriations are prohibited in authorizing legislation. These rules are enforced through members raising POINTS OF ORDER questioning the action being taken or the action proposed to be taken as contrary to the chamber's rules, practices, and precedents. For the rules to be enforced members must actually raise such points of order; they are not self-enforcing. This two-step authorization and appropriations process maximizes the power of the purse possessed by Congress, but it also allows Congress the flexibility to follow its own rules. Rules may be waived by not raising points of order, by SUSPENSION OF THE RULES, by UNANIMOUS CONSENT, or in the House by SPECIAL RULE. If unauthorized appropriations are enacted into law through one of these processes circumventing the rules, in most instances the government agency may expend the entire authorized amount.

This two-step authorization-appropriations process permitting discretionary funding through the annual appropriations process is viewed as the traditional one, but not all agencies and programs use this process. Indeed, budget authority for some agencies and programs has been provided over many years in authorization bills, thereby bypassing this two-step process in favor of direct spending or backdoor spending. In fact, approximately two-thirds of federal spending now occurs outside the annual appropriations process. This does not mean that agencies and pro-grams are spending federal monies that have not been approved. Rather, it means that such expenditures have been authorized by Congress in a single-step process in the authorization bill.

When budget authority has been provided outside this annual appropriations process, it is done through uncontrollable spending known as borrowing authority, contract authority, entitlements, and loan guarantees. For example, loan guarantees such as Guaranteed Student Loans, Federal Housing Administration (FHA) loans, and others are not handled through the authorization-appropriations process. Instead, the government merely promises that the loan will be repaid to the lender if the borrower fails to do so, thereby creating a governmental obligation to pay on behalf of the defaulting party. Similarly, entitlement programs include such large programs as Social Security, Medicare and Medicaid, food stamps, veterans' benefits, and federal employee pensions. Here the federal government has pledged to pay these benefits to the individuals entitled to receive them if those persons meet the eligibility criteria. The individuals have legally enforceable rights to these benefits for which they have qualified. Instead of the traditional two-step authorization-appropriations process used by Congress that allows the exercise of congressional discretion in spending all, a portion, or none of the authorization bill amounts, specific types of budget authority such as contract authority, borrowing authority, entitlements, and loan guarantees have been placed within authorization bills. The placing of both legal authority and budget authority within authorization acts results in mandatory spending.

Further reading:
Beth, Richard S. *Bills and Resolutions: Examples of How Each Kind Is Used.* Washington, D.C.: Congressional Research Service, 27 January 1999; Heniff, Bill, Jr. *Overview of the Authorization-Appropriations Process.* Washington, D.C.: Congressional Research Service, 23 July 2003; Johnson, Charles W. III. *How Our Laws Are Made.* Washington, D.C.: U.S. House of Representatives, 2003; Streeter, Sandy. *The Congressional Appropriations Process: An Introduction.* Washington, D.C.: Congressional Research Service, 29 July 2003; U.S. House of Representatives. *Rules of the House of Representatives: 108th Congress.* Prepared by Jeff Trandahl, Clerk of the House, 7 January 2003; U.S. Senate, Senate Committee on Rules and Administration. *Authority and Rules of Senate Committees, 2003–2004: A Compilation of the Authority and Rules of Senate and Joint Committees, and Related Materials.* 108th Cong., 1st Session, Senate Document 108-6, 2003.

—Robert P. Goss

B

backdoor spending

Much time and effort are invested in the regular federal budget process, or what is often called the on-budget part of the process or the discretionary budget. The other part, or off-budget part of the national budget, consists of entitlement programs such as Social Security, which are formula-based. They are sometimes called permanent appropriations because once the formula for funding citizens is enacted into law, the government has basically required itself to provide the funding no matter what happens. If a citizen has a certain level of need and meets other basic criteria, the government provides benefits, regardless of what is decided in the annual budget process. That is, the citizen is by law entitled to those funds. This approach is used widely in American national government in such entitlement areas as Social Security, Medicaid and Medicare, veterans' benefits, and social welfare programs. That entitlement funding makes up more than half of all government funding makes decision making on the other part of the budget (the discretionary side) all the harder when resources are constrained.

Through backdoor spending, members of Congress place funding for programs that really ought to be in the discretionary, or on-budget, part of the process in the off-budget entitlement legislation. Strategic lawmakers have discovered that the entitlement areas are less scrutinized than the regular budget and that it is easier to obtain funding in that area than in the rigorous, regular process of so-called on-budget items. If budget items can be presented to sound similar to the entitlement program or area, backdoor spending can be pulled off, and the member or his or her coalition can achieve a desired policy outcome. However, the aggregation of the various instances of backdoor spending leads to fiscal irresponsibility. Non–formula-based items ought to be in the regular process, where they can be scrutinized along with everything else. The more backdoor spending grows, the higher the annual budget deficits, and the overall debt climbs.

Further reading:
Oleszek, Walter. *Congressional Procedures and the Policy Process*. 6th ed. 5th ed. Washington, D.C.: Congressional Quarterly Press, 2004; Allen Schick. *Federal Budgeting*. Washington, D.C.: Brookings Institution Press, 2004.

—Glen S. Krutz

Baker, Howard H. (1925–) *Senator*

Howard Baker, a Republican from Tennessee, served in the U.S. SENATE from 1967 until his retirement in 1984. During this time he established himself as one of the foremost Republican Party leaders and one of the finest Senate leaders in the 20th century. Baker accomplished this record in the midst of some of the most tumultuous times for the Republican Party in the United States and in spite of his own close ties to the man who caused those troubles, President Richard Nixon. Baker's rise in the Senate and his success while serving there is a story of a remarkable man who often put the interests of the nation ahead of the interests of his party and his own personal ambitions.

Howard Baker was born on November 15, 1925, in Huntsville, Tennessee, to Howard Henry and Dora Ladd Baker. Baker's mother died when he was eight, so he was raised by his grandmother, Lillie Ladd Mauser. His father eventually remarried, and the Bakers lived in Huntsville while Baker grew up. Baker attended the McCallie School, a military preparation academy in Chattanooga and upon graduation in 1943 enlisted in the U.S. Navy. Baker took officer's training courses and studied electrical engineering at the University of the South in Sewanee, Tennessee, and at Tulane University. He completed his naval service and entered the University of Tennessee law program in Knoxville, Tennessee, in 1946. He earned his degree in 1949 and joined his grandfather's law firm.

Baker assisted his father in a successful bid for the U.S. HOUSE OF REPRESENTATIVES in 1950. During the campaign he met Joy Dirksen, the daughter of Senator

EVERETT DIRKSEN of Illinois. Dirksen was a well-known Republican senator, a confidant of President LYNDON JOHNSON, and a key supporter of Johnson's civil rights and Vietnam agendas. He was a skilled legislator whose leadership often allowed Republicans access to the agenda despite often overwhelming Democratic control of the Senate.

Baker's first encounter with Joy Dirksen ended when he tossed her into a rosebush because she had tempted his sister to smoke a cigar. He soon regretted his actions and a few days later asked her if he could come over and apologize. Less than half an hour into this meeting, Baker had asked Dirksen to marry him. She agreed, and the two remained married until her death in 1993. Baker has since remarried to former senator Nancy Kassebaum.

Baker's first taste of politics occurred when his father attempted to unseat Representative John Jennings, a Republican from Tennessee. The campaign was a difficult one, with allegations and charges on both sides rankling the Republican Party. Baker Sr. won the nomination and the general election and held the seat through the next six elections. When Baker Sr. died in 1964, party leaders asked Baker to be his successor. He was not interested in completing a House term, however, and encouraged his stepmother, Irene Baker, to finish the term. Baker was not finished with politics. Later in 1964 Senator Estes Kefauver died, and the party again asked Baker to run to fill the senator's uncompleted term. Baker decided to take this opportunity, and although he lost the special election in a close race, he was now ready to launch what would become a remarkable political career.

Baker's race for the Senate in 1966 was remarkable. The Democratic Party nominated former state governor Frank Clement over the incumbent senator Ross Bass. Clement was a solid campaigner and popular. Few of Baker's supporters believed he had much of a chance. Baker, however, had polling data indicating that he could beat Clement and launched an aggressive campaign. He visited all 95 counties in Tennessee, courting minorities, farmers, and conservative Democratic voters. His campaign strategy was brilliant, and in the end he upset Clement and won with 56 percent of the vote to become the first Tennessee Republican elected to the Senate.

Baker's first term (1967–72) placed him in the midst of the greatest political conflicts of the 20th century: race relations, state revenue sources, and efforts to protect the environment. Baker's positions on many of these issues placed him at odds with most of his own party, yet he was able to build coalitions across party lines and bring legislation successfully through the Senate.

Race relation legislation in the late 1960s revolved around three key issues: voting representation, housing rights, and the Civil Rights Act of 1968. Baker faced enormous challenges as a Republican because for the most part he supported efforts to expand civil rights. Baker's initial skirmish with his own party came over two critical Supreme Court cases: *Baker v. Carr* (1962), which required states to apportion seats in lower houses by population, and *Reynolds v. Simms* (1965), which applied the *Baker* doctrine to state upper houses, or senates. While most Republicans opposed the Reynolds decision as intrusive into states' rights, Baker worked hard to create rules to implement these decisions. Baker persuaded fellow Republicans to support his efforts by arguing that the malapportionment that existed actually favored Democrats and that this was a matter of basic justice. Baker's success in persuading Republicans to support legislation defining the one person, one vote rule rested on his ability to marshal empirical evidence and his appeal to core Republican values.

Baker had a much more difficult time persuading fellow Republicans to support open housing laws, federal requirements that private home sellers had to offer their homes to any qualified buyer regardless of race. Baker believed that such regulation infringed on the rights of private homeowners, even though he had called for Tennessee to adopt some form of open housing. Because Baker had already spoken on the issue, the bill sponsor, Walter F. Mondale, a Democrat from Minnesota, approached him to support his federal open housing plan. While Baker could not support Mondale's blanket approach, he was able to persuade Dirksen to meet with Mondale to work out a compromise. Baker's persistence paid off, and by February 1968 the Senate passed a compromise bill requiring realtors to offer homes to all qualified buyers, but not requiring individual homeowners to do so.

Finally, Baker assisted in gaining passage of the 1968 Civil Rights Act, which guaranteed blacks the right to home ownership, barred red zoning, or efforts by realtors to steer black clients into specific areas, and reauthorized provisions in the Civil Rights Act of 1964. Baker opposed parts of the 1968 act, particularly in relation to gun control and gun registration.

Baker strongly supported Nixon's efforts to enhance the power of states to deal with critical social and economic problems. A centerpiece of Nixon's "new federalism" was a plan that would allow the federal government to share revenue with state governments. The plan passed but was not as successful as Nixon and Baker had hoped. However, it would inspire President Ronald Reagan in the 1980s to pursue block grants as a way to enhance state revenues.

Baker served on the Air and Water Pollution Subcommittee of the Energy and Environment Committee. Edwin Muskie, a Democrat from Maine and subcommittee chair, recognized Baker's engineering background and emerging leadership skills and enlisted his aid in drafting the CLEAN AIR ACT OF 1970. During the raucous markup sessions, Muskie would often turn to Baker to help resolve conflicts between senators pressured by environmentalists and those pressured by big business. Baker's knack for turning political issues into procedural ones allowed him to bring together different groups and find middle ground. While the Clean Air Act was under debate, Tennessee industrialists argued that their companies could not bear the costs of installing exhaust scrubbing equipment to meet the clean air standards. Baker studied the problem and realized that while the scrubbers were the best solution, the weight of the materials being removed provided an alternative solution. If factories would increase the height of their smoke stacks, they could come into general compliance, as the particles Congress wanted to control would not escape these higher stacks.

Throughout his freshman term in the Senate, Baker demonstrated three key abilities that would make him a powerful senator and Senate leader. First, when Baker approached a policy issue, he sought out empirical evidence, from which he built a position. Second, Baker had a knack for finding common principles or ideas that unified different senators. Appealing to that common theme often allowed him to propose a compromise both factions could support. Baker was also knowledgeable of Senate rules and procedures. He could bring a debate to a conclusion by turning an ideological controversy into a procedural or structural matter. Finally, Baker was fearless in approaching party leaders on either side of the aisle to create support, and he was also willing to ask other senators for help. This knack allowed him to build trust among a diverse group of policy makers and earned him the nickname the "Great Conciliator." These abilities would be sorely tested in 1973, when Nixon led the nation into the worst constitutional crisis in American history.

Baker easily won reelection in 1972, defeating Democratic governor Ray Blanton. However, Baker and fellow Republicans quickly found themselves embroiled in a bitter political battle over the future of Nixon. The WATERGATE SCANDAL broke late in 1972. Senate Democrats called for hearings to investigate charges that Nixon had been involved in the break-in at Democratic headquarters in the Watergate apartment and office complex. Republican leader Hugh Scott called on Baker to serve as the senior Republican on the Watergate committee.

Baker initially believed that the hearings were nothing more than a political show by Democrats stung by their loss in the 1972 presidential election. He had intended to bring the investigation to a quick and decisive conclusion, but as more evidence appeared and Nixon grew more intransigent about executive privilege, Baker began to suspect that the conflict was more than a Democratic political vendetta.

The Watergate hearings began on May 17, 1973. Baker took a lead in questioning witnesses and attempting to establish motives for the various participants. He believed

that the committee was chasing rabbits and decided in June to press the issue much harder than the committee had done before. During a tendentious session, Baker questioned John Dean about the president's knowledge of the break-in, asking his famous question: What did the president know, and when did he know it? Dean's answer contradicted several previous accounts, for he implied that Nixon was aware of events as early as September 1972. Nixon had stated publicly that he did not know anything about Watergate until March 1973. Dean's testimony suggested that the president had been involved in illegal activities. Baker urged Nixon to make a full disclosure of all the events of Watergate for the good of the party and the nation. Nixon refused.

Baker's integrity and grit during the hearings had impressed many Americans, and he is credited for mitigating much of the damage the Republicans could have faced from Watergate. By 1976 he was back in the limelight of the party. He was the keynote speaker at the Republican National Convention, and Gerald Ford almost chose him to be his running mate. However, this was not to be, and so Baker returned to the Senate. After the election of 1976, Baker once again ran for Republican MINORITY LEADER in the Senate, and this time he won, defeating Bob Griffin of Michigan.

Baker took the reigns of a dispirited and disorganized party. The election of 1976 had been brutal. Republicans held the fewest seats in the Senate (38) since 1900. Baker had to mobilize and reinvigorate his colleagues and his party. His ability to organize his office and contact each member went a long way toward restoring the morale of Senate Republicans. They would need this morale, because although President Jimmy Carter had won a narrow electoral victory, he entered office with an aggressive agenda. Carter wanted to expand environmental protections, reduce America's dependence on foreign oil, and recast American foreign policy from Nixon's realism to an emphasis on human rights. Carter also wanted to reduce the size of the military and open dialogue in the Middle East.

As Minority Leader Baker was expected not only to pursue the interests of the party, but also to protect the prestige and power of the Senate. Many times he would face conflicting duties, and in most cases he would choose the national interest over personal or partisan interests.

Baker was fortunate in that the MAJORITY LEADER was Democrat Robert Byrd of West Virginia. The patrician Byrd was different from the stoop-shouldered Tennessean in appearance and temperament. Byrd was often abrupt and demanding, while Baker was soft-spoken and collegial. Despite their differences, the two forged a working relationship that allowed the Senate to address key issues with far less rancor than one would expect given the composition of the Senate. During the 1977–80 period the Senate ratified the Panama Canal Treaty, pursued a number of Middle

East initiatives, revised the Clean Air and Water Acts, attempted to televise Senate proceedings, and faced the Iranian revolution and hostage crisis.

Perhaps the most important issue for Baker was the Panama Canal Treaty, which was to return control of the canal to Panama by 2000. Baker's influence ensured that the treaty would pass, but his support almost cost him reelection in 1978; many observers believe it cost him the presidency in 1980. In 1978 Carter also asked Congress to authorize the sale of AWACS airborne radar planes to Saudi Arabia. Israel bitterly opposed this sale, but Carter was adamant. Baker and Byrd eventually persuaded Carter to reconsider, but the issue would reemerge once the Iranian revolution began.

Baker was also instrumental in assisting Carter to gain passage of the Strategic Arms Limitation Treaty (SALT I). However, when Carter attempted to gain passage of an extension of SALT (the SALT II Treaty), Baker abandoned his presidential bid to oppose the treaties. Once the Soviets invaded Afghanistan, SALT II was essentially dead.

Baker entered 1979 considering a bid for the presidency. However, events of 1979 and 1980 overwhelmed his efforts, and he dropped out of the race early in 1980. He then committed his time and energy to a Republican majority in the Senate. In November 1980 his efforts succeeded, as voters sent 53 Republicans to the Senate. Many of these new senators had held no public office before, and many of them were extremely conservative, far more so than Baker and even Reagan. If Baker were to lead this majority party, he was going to face hard-won struggles.

Republicans began 1981 in control of the Senate for the first time since Eisenhower. Baker's slim majority of 53 Republicans to 47 Democrats meant that he would have to hold his party together to an extraordinary degree in order to gain passage of Reagan's domestic agenda. Although Reagan had won a substantial victory, he still faced an experienced corps of Democratic senators and an inexperienced team of Republicans. Baker's leadership would be critical.

Baker successfully held his party together during the 1981–82 period. Although Reagan's agenda was much smaller than Carter's, it was no less daunting. Reagan had run on a platform of deep tax cuts and increased military spending, and it was Baker's job to get these bills through the Senate. Nevertheless, much of Reagan's budget and tax programs did pass the Senate in 1981 and 1982.

Baker faced greater difficulties with Reagan's military programs. Reagan intended to revive Carter's plan to sell AWACs to Saudi Arabia, but initially only 12 senators supported the idea. Baker negotiated a deal sending F-16 fighters to Israel, and the deal passed. Baker continued to support Reagan's programs, often against his own wishes. "If I must take a separate position, I will try to let you know in advance," Baker once told Reagan, but for the most part, Baker worked closely with Reagan. Many observers credit Baker with Reagan's remarkable success in his first term.

However, Baker had served in the Senate since 1967 and had seen a number of tumults and changes in the institution. By 1983 Baker began to discuss retiring from the Senate, and in 1984 he announced his resignation. Baker turned over the majority post to Robert Dole of Kansas, a gifted politician but not nearly as capable as Baker in building consensus and working across the aisle.

Baker intended to retire and practice law, but in 1987 the Reagan administration asked him to return to public life as the administration's chief of staff. Reagan's presidency was threatened by a growing scandal, the Iran-contra affair. Reagan had attempted to negotiate a release of hostages in the Middle East, and in the course of the negotiations the deal became an arms-for-hostages deal. In order to raise money for the arms, administration officials began to sell arms to Nicaraguan rebels fighting against the government. When the deal was revealed in 1986, Reagan denied knowledge of the deal. While it was never clear how much Reagan knew of the deal, the scandal harmed Reagan's popular support. Baker returned to public life in order to assist Reagan. He was able to assure Congress and the American people that Reagan himself had had no direct knowledge of the Nicaraguan side of the deal, but Reagan did admit trading arms for hostages. Baker's successful efforts helped to restore Reagan's presidency and assure the election of Vice President George H. W. Bush in 1988.

Baker has since retired to his law practice in Huntsville, Tennessee. He still participates in politics occasionally and makes speeches. The University of Tennessee in Knoxville has established the Howard Baker Institute to preserve his papers and his legacy.

Baker stands as one of the great Senate leaders in American history. His success can be attributed to his willingness to put his country ahead of personal or partisan interests, his ability to convert contentious political issues into procedural questions, his ability to build coalitions across party and ideological lines, and his determination to make good policy. Baker once offered 13 rules for Senate success, but it is the last one that captures the man: Be civil, and encourage others to do likewise.

Further reading:
Annis, Lee. *Howard Baker: Conciliator in an Age of Crisis.* Lanham, Md.: Madison Books, 1995; Annis, Lee, and Bill Frist. *Tennessee Senators 1911–2001: Portraits of Leadership in a Century of Change.* New York: Madison Books, 2001; Baker, Howard H. *Howard H. Baker Center for Public Policy.* University of Tennessee. Available online. URL: http://bakercenter.utk.edu. Accessed January 16, 2006.

—Mike Bobic

Baker v. Carr 369 U.S. 186 (1962)

The Baker case marked the beginning of an important political transition in American politics generally and legislative politics in particular. While the U.S. Supreme Court's decision in the case left a great many problematic issues unsettled, it made courts, the federal courts in particular, the referees regarding the fairness of legislative districts across the United States.

Baker brought a complaint to the federal district court about the unequally populated legislative districts in his state, Tennessee. He contended that this inequality violated his rights as a citizen under the U.S. Constitution because the Fourteenth Amendment forbids states from denying to any person within their jurisdiction equal protection of the laws. The factual situation was that the 1960 census revealed that the disparity in population between the largest and smallest Tennessee legislative districts was six to one for the state senate and 23 to one in the state house. Baker claimed that disparities such as these denied him and others in disproportionately large urban legislative districts from the same protection of the laws that citizens in overrepresented districts had.

The debasement of their votes by virtue of the incorrect, obsolete, and unconstitutional apportionment that Baker claimed in Tennessee was not unique in the American states. The dominance of rural interests in state legislatures was typical, reflecting population shifts to urban areas during the first half of the century that intensified after World War II. However, the extremity of matters in Tennessee provided an apt test case. Tennessee's 1870 constitution required reapportionment of seats in both the house and the senate every 10 years following a census. However, none had taken place since 1901. Appeals for change to the malapportionment fell on deaf ears in a legislature controlled by members who benefited from existing arrangements.

The Tennessee supreme court refused challenges in state courts. The U.S. Supreme Court precedent in *Colegrove v. Green* gave both state and federal courts an answer to this kind of legal challenge. Justice Felix Frankfurter wrote the majority opinion in that case, saying that the Court refused relief because of the "peculiarly political nature" of the question that was, therefore, not appropriate "for judicial determination." The basis of Frankfurter's deference was the principle of separation of powers. Matters of apportionment were particular responsibilities of the elected branches of government, not the courts.

Baker was prevented from other possible solutions to the unfairness he was contesting. The Tennessee state constitution did not allow any initiative or referendum process by which the people could put the issue of equal representation in the legislature on the ballot for a statewide vote of its citizens.

Baker lost in the U.S. district court for the middle district of Tennessee on two grounds. First, the court said it lacked jurisdiction in this political matter, and, second, that the complaint provided no appropriate remedy. The decision did acknowledge that the Tennessee legislature was in violation of the Tennessee constitution. Baker appealed to the U.S. Supreme Court.

Some significant changes had occurred on the Supreme Court since a 4-to-3 majority decided the *Colegrove* case in 1946. Three of Frankfurter's supporters in that decision had been replaced on the Supreme Court, and Earl Warren, former governor of California, was the new chief justice. Also, the Justice Department filed a friend of the court (amicus) brief in support of Baker. The Supreme Court heard three hours of oral arguments, giving the appellants an unusually long time to plead their case, and subsequently it allowed a reargument several months later.

With eight justices taking part, the Court decided in favor of Baker with a 6-2 majority. The opinion of the Court was by Justice Brennan, speaking for himself, Warren, and Black. Justices Clark, Douglas, and Stuart, each writing a separate concurring opinion, joined them. Dissents came from Frankfurter and Harlan, both of whom wrote an opinion. All the opinions together required 163 pages in the U.S. Supreme Court Report.

The majority settled some key matters. It ruled first that this matter was properly before a federal court and that the district court possessed jurisdiction over the case. That meant that although the Supreme Court would not spell out specific relief, the issues of the case would go back to the district court. Second, it rejected the idea that reapportionment issues were "political" questions beyond the reach of the Court. Apportionment of the state legislatures would properly come before the Court for relief as a justifiable matter. Finally, individual citizens have standing to sue for relief. Their right to relief under the equal protection clause of the Fourteenth Amendment was not diminished by the fact that the discrimination imposed related to their political rights.

Baker v. Carr did not settle all the issues of redistricting, but it opened the door to a process of trial and error in the courts. It did not fully overrule *Colegrove*. It distinguished the challengeable inequalities in state legislative districts from what might be challenged later with regard to congressional representation. Citizens aggrieved by unequal representation now have standing to raise issues of representation as a matter of equal protection under the Fourteenth Amendment. This would unleash grievances in most of the states and immediately place great political pressure on the state legislatures around the country. They were now subject to court challenge, and they possessed the authority to redistrict themselves according to more equitable standards.

The *Baker* decision powerfully conveyed the view that the right to equality in representation could no longer be refused to citizens by state legislatures, because citizens could get that relief from the courts backed by the U.S. Constitution. Moreover, the Justice Department took action on this issue as a powerful advocate for the equality principle in representation. Within five years there was action in the courts and legislatures regarding legislative districts in every state except Oregon. That state had reapportioned its representation on a population basis in 1952. In retrospect, Chief Justice Warren characterized this case as "the most vital decision" rendered during his years of service on the U.S. Supreme Court.

Opposition to the Court was widespread in state legislatures and Congress. There were efforts in Congress to pass legislation to deny the federal courts jurisdiction over redistricting issues. Congress considered possible constitutional amendments. However, all such proposals were defeated in 1964, 1965, and 1966. In the meantime, additional cases moved through the courts, and more equitable redistricting plans were put into place. Illinois, for example, under provisions of its state constitution, conducted an at-large election for its 177-member house. Doing so, the electorate replaced many of its former incumbent legislators.

As new district plans took effect in the various states, there came to be new rosters of incumbents elected under more equitable district plans. In many states the disproportionate power of rural and small town interests gave way to representation for urban and suburban concerns. The political resistance to equality in representation lost momentum, and a revolutionary change was fully implemented in Congress and the states by the close of the 1960s.

A clear consequence of the reforms that followed the *Baker* case was the increase in the number of urban and suburban legislative districts and a corresponding decline of those allocated to small towns and rural areas. The interests of the hinterlands, such as agricultural, mining, and forest industries were soon deprived of legislative strength. The cities and suburbs elected more highly educated candidates to office, including women, African Americans, and Hispanics. In many of the states the coming of new members into the legislatures stimulated reforms and modernization. Policy issues such as transit and metropolitan highways, the professionalization of schools and universities, health care issues, regulation of business, and a variety of social welfare concerns became much more prominent in state policy making. A process of professionalization began that added to the capacities and competencies of state legislatures to address the needs of their people. Legislatures beefed up their infrastructures for technical, professional, and partisan support, and the scope of state government expanded. Efforts at modernization

and reform became commonplace. Committee systems were streamlined, and as members learned to hire and use the abilities of professional staff, legislative processes took on a new level of professionalization. The capacity of legislatures to engage in oversight of executive agencies was enlarged, invigorating checks and balances in state political processes. As the states widely addressed the matter of democratic equity, they renewed the legitimacy of the legislatures in particular and state governments generally, causing a rebalance of governmental power in the American federal system.

See also APPORTIONMENT AND REDISTRICTING; GERRYMANDERING, PARTISAN; GERRYMANDERING, RACIAL; *WESBERRY V. SANDERS.*

Further reading:
Baker v. Carr 369 U.S. 186 (1962); *Congress and the Nation.* Vol. 2. Washington, D.C.: Congressional Quarterly, 431–435, 1969; Mikula, M. L., and M. Mabunda, eds. *Great American Court Cases,* Thomas Gale, Vol. 3, 597–598, 1999; Neal, P. C. "*Baker v. Carr*: Politics in Search of Law." In *The Supreme Court Review,* edited by P. D. Kurland, Chicago: University of Chicago Press, 1962, pp. 252–327.

—Jack R. Van Der Slik

Baldwin, Raymond E. (1893–1986) *Senator*
Raymond E. Baldwin was the only individual in Connecticut's history to serve as governor, U.S. senator, and chief justice of the state's supreme court. Born in Rye, New York, on August 31, 1893, Baldwin moved with his family to Connecticut when he was three. He graduated from Wesleyan University in 1916 and enrolled at Yale Law School. He postponed his studies to join the navy in World War I, serving on a destroyer, where he rose to the rank of lieutenant. Baldwin earned his law degree in 1921 from Yale and practiced in New Haven and Bridgeport before becoming a prosecutor and then town judge in Stratford. He served three years in the state house of representatives, from 1931 to 1933, where he quickly rose to the position of majority leader.

Republicans were the majority party in Connecticut for close to half a century prior to the Great Depression, which led to a change of control in the state house and governorship in 1930. In 1938 Baldwin won the Republican primary and then defeated the popular four-term governor, Wilbur Mills, in the general election, largely thanks to the presence of a Socialist Party candidate who split the Democratic vote. Baldwin lost his seat two years later, only to regain it in 1942, being reelected again in 1944. His youth, relatively progressive outlook, and friendly demeanor resonated well with the state's voters, and Baldwin became highly respected across the political spectrum. As a wartime Republican governor, he resisted increased control over the state's economy from Washington and directed an increase in state authority instead. Under his administration the state became far more active in housing, lower court reform, civil rights enforcement, job training, and economic planning. He also created administrative venues for employers and unions to work out grievances without having to resort to labor unrest. Although he was a fiscally conservative Republican, Baldwin did much to promote the interests of minorities and workers in Connecticut.

After winning a special election to fill the remainder of the term of Senator Francis T. Maloney, who passed away while in office, Baldwin resigned as governor in 1946. He served in Washington until 1949, where he allegedly became quite disenchanted with politics, especially after coming into conflict with Joseph McCarthy. Baldwin was nominated by Connecticut's Democratic governor to the position of associate justice of the state supreme court of errors, becoming the chief justice in 1959. He noted that his 10 years on the bench was the happiest period in his life. He retired in 1963 and chaired the state's constitutional convention in 1965. Baldwin died on October 4, 1986.

Raymond E. Baldwin was the most respected politician of his era in Connecticut. Baldwin Medals for public service are now conferred annually by Wesleyan University, Quinnipiac University School of Law, and the Connecticut Department of Education, while a state inn of court was also renamed in his honor.

Further reading:
Johnson, Curtiss S. *Raymond E. Baldwin: Connecticut Statesman.* Chester, Conn.: Pequot Press, 1972.

—J. Glenn

Bankhead, William B. (1874–1940) *Representative, Speaker of the House*

William B. Bankhead was a prominent Democratic U.S. representative from Alabama and Speaker of the House from 1936 to 1940. He was born in Moscow, Alabama, on April 12, 1874, the son of U.S. senator John Hollis Bankhead, also a Democrat from Alabama, and his wife Tallulah. Bankhead's older brother John H. II was a U.S. senator from Alabama also. In 1892 William Bankhead graduated from the University of Alabama. He received a law degree from Georgetown University School of Law in Washington, D.C., in 1895. After working briefly as an actor in New York and as a lawyer in Huntsville, Alabama, he entered a legal practice in Jasper, Alabama, with his brother John.

Bankhead worked as a county prosecutor from 1910 to 1914. In 1914 he unsuccessfully sought a seat in the U.S. House of Representatives. The Alabama legislature, of which his brother John was a member, drew a new congressional district, from which William was elected in 1916. He was reelected from that district 11 times.

As a member of the majority Democrats, Bankhead was a supporter of President Woodrow Wilson's administration. His impact in Congress was limited when the Republicans regained power in Washington in the 1920s. He spent his time becoming an expert on the rules of the House and working on programs involving grants-in-aid to provide aid to the states for specific purposes, usually on a matching basis. Grants-in-aid had been an interest of his father while in the Senate. Bankhead's other legislative interests included agriculture, labor issues, and health.

Bankhead advanced his interest in vocational education as a member of the House Education Committee. In 1920 he supported a bill providing federal aid to rehabilitate workers crippled in industrial accidents. The bill was enacted over the objections of Bankhead's more conservative colleagues, who claimed that the bill violated the tenets of federalism outlined in the U.S. Constitution.

The congressman's position on states' rights and private enterprise was complicated. Like many of his southern colleagues, he endorsed the idea of the private sector operating Muscle Shoals on the Tennessee River to produce fertilizer. By the end of the 1920s, many southern congressmen changed their position to favor government operation of the area to produce hydroelectric power. These congressmen almost unanimously supported President Franklin Roosevelt's plan for the Tennessee Valley Authority (TVA) in 1933. The TVA helped many of Bankhead's constituents obtain electrical power.

Working with Senator WILLIAM BORAH, a Republican from Idaho, Bankhead sponsored a soil reclamation bill. He also defended the legislation that funded the Boulder Dam project along the Colorado River. Most House members from the South opposed this bill. Unlike most southern congressmen, he defended the rights of labor, for which he was rewarded by being endorsed by organized labor in his reelection campaigns. His support for labor stemmed from his experience as a coal mine operator in western Alabama in the early 1900s. The Bankhead operation provided a form of workers' compensation to the miners as well as allowing the mineworkers local to meet in one of the company's buildings. The Alabamian voted for the Norris-LaGuardia Anti-Injunction Bill, a proposal supported by the mineworkers union but opposed by most southern members of Congress.

He was a loyal Democrat, and in 1928 he supported the presidential campaign of New Yorker Alfred E. Smith, even though many of his southern colleagues bolted from the party. The Bankhead family was rewarded for this loyalty when William's brother John was elected to the U.S. Senate in 1930.

William Bankhead recognized early that the problems presented by the Great Depression required unorthodox solutions. Among his proposals was a plan for employment relief, controversial because it required direct payments to unemployed workers, an innovation at the time. Bankhead gave his complete support to the New Deal legislation advanced by the new president, Franklin Roosevelt, in 1933. One of the measures, cosponsored with Senator John H. Bankhead II, was the Bankhead Cotton Control Act of 1934. This legislation was designed to strengthen the voluntary crop reduction plan in the Agricultural Adjustment Act of 1933, another bill supported by Bankhead. The voluntary plan was not working for cotton farmers, so the Bankheads designed a plan to limit cotton-ginning quotas. If two-thirds of all cotton farmers agreed, a tax of 50 percent of the market price would be placed on all cotton ginned by a farmer over his allotment. The bill passed over the objections of senators who believed the law went too far in constricting the activity of farmers. Despite the popularity of the measure, the act was repealed after the Supreme Court ruled that the processing tax established by the Agricultural Adjustment Act was unconstitutional. Officials in the Roosevelt administration believed that the Court would rule similarly on the Cotton Control Act.

At the beginning of the New Deal in 1933, Bankhead was the ranking Democrat on the House Rules Committee. Later in 1933 the chair, Edward W. Pou, a Democrat from North Carolina, fell ill, and Bankhead became de facto chairman. After Pou's death in 1934, Bankhead was named chair of the Rules Committee. In this position he worked to advance the legislation proposed by the Roosevelt administration. In many cases the Rules Committee wrote closed rules on administration bills, allowing for little debate and no amendments. Bankhead won respect from both Democrats and Republicans despite ruling with an apparent iron hand. He argued that the nation needed solutions to the problems of the Great Depression, and he was going to ensure that the House enacted these solutions.

Speaker of the House Henry T. Rainey, a Democrat from Illinois, died during the summer recess in 1934, thereby setting off a scramble for the office. Bankhead was among the leading candidates in the race that included Majority Leader Joseph Byrnes, a Democrat from Tennessee; Sam Rayburn, a Democrat from Texas; John Rankin, a Democrat from Mississippi; and James Meade, a Democrat from New York. Fellow Democrats dissuaded Bankhead from continuing his candidacy by arguing that he was needed to advance the party's agenda. He withdrew from the race and announced that he was seeking the Majority Leader position. On January 1, 1935, Bankhead suffered a heart attack. The House Democrats caucused on January 2 in anticipation of the convening of the new Congress on January 3. Bankhead's supporters in the House did not tell other Democrats how seriously ill he was, telling everyone that he only had a bad cold. While some Democrats objected to electing a Majority Leader in absentia, Bankhead was elected on the second ballot. Not knowing the extent of his illness, most newspapers and magazines applauded the selection. He spent the entire session recovering from the heart attack, returning to the floor of the House on January 1, 1936.

Despite Bankhead's leadership, Roosevelt's New Deal agenda began to break down. The president was losing the support of southern congressmen. Bankhead had objections with a number of the proposals, but he continued to support the president, primarily out of party loyalty. Among the bills the Majority Leader shepherded through the House was the court-packing scheme, executive branch reorganization, and the Fair Labor Standards Act of 1938.

Bankhead served as Majority Leader for about six months before Speaker James Byrns died on June 2, 1936. Democratic leaders met on June 3 and decided to elevate the Majority Leader to Speaker. The House on June 4, 1936, elected Bankhead without debate or opposition. As Speaker he continued his support of the New Deal. Newspaper accounts recorded the new Speaker's ability to rally Democrats behind the president. Bankhead relied largely on personal contact and persuasion rather than coercion to bring his party colleagues into line. Most of his party leadership was behind the scenes.

President Roosevelt delayed announcing his intention to run for a third term in 1940. Alabama Democrats promoted Bankhead as a candidate for president. He agreed to be a candidate with the stipulation that he be allowed to run on a New Deal platform. When the party learned of Roosevelt's plans to seek a third term, the Speaker's supporters began a Bankhead for vice president campaign. Roosevelt selected Henry Wallace as his running mate, stating that Bankhead was too old and in fragile health to serve as vice president. Respecting his pledge to Alabama Democrats, Bankhead did not withdraw from the campaign and received 327 votes to Wallace's 627. As a consolation and to gain his support, President Roosevelt named Bankhead the keynote speaker for the Democratic National Convention scheduled for September 10, 1940, in Baltimore. A short time before he was scheduled to give his speech, he was found unconscious on the floor of his hotel room. He died at the Naval Hospital in Washington, D.C., on September 15, 1940.

Further reading:
Heacock, Walter J. "William B. Bankhead and the New Deal." *Journal of Southern History* 21, no. 3 (1955): 347–359; Johnson, Evans C. "John H. Bankhead 2d: Advocate of Cotton." *The Alabama Review* 41, no. 1 (1988): 30–58; Peters, Ronald M. *The American Speakership: The*

Office in Historical Perspective. Baltimore: Johns Hopkins University Press, 1990.

—David Rausch, Jr.

Banking, Housing, and Urban Affairs, Senate Committee on

The Senate Committee on Banking, Housing, and Urban Affairs is responsible for reporting on all matters related to banking and all financial institutions, controlling prices of commodities, rents, and services, and deposit insurance and export controls. It also reports on all matters related to the promotion of export and foreign trade, stabilization of the economy, defense production, federal monetary policy including the Federal Reserve System, financial aid given to industry and commerce, money, credit, construction of nursing homes, veterans' housing, public and private housing, urban development and mass transit, and the renegotiation of government contracts. The committee also reviews matters related to international economic policy in order to report on the ways they affect the United States's monetary and urban affairs.

By 2004 the committee consisted of 21 members, 11 majority Republicans and 10 Democrats. The Banking, Housing, and Urban Affairs Committee also includes five subcommittees that may be authorized only by the majority of the committee. They are the Subcommittee on Economic Policy, which is made up of three members from each political party, the Subcommittee on Financial Institutions, which is made up of nine majority and eight minority members, the Subcommittee on Housing and Transportation, which consists of seven members from each party, the Subcommittee on International Trade and Finance, which is made up of seven majority members and six minority members, and the Subcommittee on Securities and Investment, which is made up of nine majority members and eight minority members.

The committee meets regularly on the last Tuesday of every month that the Senate is in session unless they have already met prior to the last Tuesday of that month, in which case the committee chair has the authority to cancel the regular meeting. The committee and the subcommittees are governed by similar rules the committee unanimously adopted on January 30, 2003. The committee can conduct investigations and hold hearings, which have to be authorized by the Senate, full committee, or the chair and the ranking member of the minority party. Subcommittees need only authorization from the Senate or the full committee. Committee hearings cannot be scheduled outside the District of Columbia unless the chair and the ranking minority party members agree to it or by a majority vote. In the case of subcommittees, a hearing can be held outside the District of Columbia. During the committee's proceedings, it is possible that confidential material or testimony will be presented. In this case no such information shall be made public by any means without being authorized by both the chair of the committee and the ranking member or by a majority vote of the committee. The same rule goes for the subcommittees, except that the authorization is obtained from the chair of the subcommittee and its ranking member or by a majority vote.

The chair of the committee or subcommittee has the right to deny a witness the privilege of testifying before it unless he or she complies with the rule that states that he or she must file 75 copies of a statement with the committee or subcommittee 24 hours before appearing. The statement also has to include a brief summary of the testimony that will be presented, which must not be longer than three pages. The statements that have been properly filed with the committee or subcommittee have no limit regarding their length. The witness is allowed to include any documents that he or she feels are necessary to fully present his or her views, but only those documents selected by the chair of the committee or subcommittee will be placed in the transcript of the hearings. Witnesses' oral presentations are limited to 10 minutes but may be reduced or extended at the discretion of the chair. In the committee or subcommittees, witnesses can be questioned only by members of the committee or subcommittee or professional staff that are authorized by the chair or the ranking member of the committee or subcommittee. The members are allowed five minutes each to question a witness if five or more members are present and 10 minutes if less than five members are present. After all members have asked their questions, a second opportunity to ask further questions is given with a five minute limit, and so on, until there are no further questions.

Witnesses who have been subpoenaed by the committee or subcommittee have the right to representation by a counsel of their choosing, who will advise them on their legal rights during the testimony. No witness will receive reimbursement for time unless otherwise agreed to by the chair and ranking member of the committee.

The Banking, Housing, and Urban Affairs Committee also deals with coinage legislation. Because of this, it considers legislation such as a gold medal or commemorative coin, bill, or resolution that has been cosponsored by at least 67 senators. The confirmation hearings of presidential nominees are also held before this committee.

Further reading:
Ralph Nader Congress Project. *The Money Committees: A Study of the House Banking and Currency Committee and the Senate Banking, Housing and Urban Affairs Committee.* Grossman, 1975; United States Congress. *Senate Committee on Banking, Housing and Urban Affairs.* Available

online. URL: http://www.access.gpo.gov/congress/senate/senate05.html. Accessed April 15, 2003.

—Arthur Holst

Barenblatt v. United States 360 U.S. 109 (1959)

In 1954 Lloyd Barenblatt, a former graduate student and teaching fellow at the University of Michigan, was called before the House UN-AMERICAN ACTIVITIES COMMITTEE (HUAC) to answer questions concerning a perceived rise of Communist influences in education. Barenblatt refused to answer any questions related to his personal, political, or religious beliefs. Citing the First, Ninth, and Tenth Amendments to the U.S. Constitution, he challenged the power of the subcommittee to conduct such an investigation. He was fined and sentenced in the federal district court to six months in jail for contempt of Congress. On appeal to the Supreme Court, Barenblatt argued that the statute authorizing investigation into Communist activities was too vague to allow generalized investigation of teachers, that he was not informed of the pertinence of the questions to any investigation of communism, and that the questions infringed on his First Amendment rights. The Supreme Court, in a 5-4 decision, upheld his conviction. In the process the Court confirmed the constitutional grant of wide-ranging, but not limitless, powers of investigation by Congress.

Generally, due to separation of powers concerns, the Supreme Court has been reluctant to make rulings that affect the powers of another branch of the federal government under an informal rule known as the political question doctrine. However, on occasion the court had ruled based upon the broader impact of the case. BARENBLATT V. UNITED STATES (1959) satisfied this exception to the general rule. The Supreme Court attempted to avoid infringing on the powers of another branch as much as possible. Here the court acknowledged the power of Congress to conduct hearings and investigations so long as those hearings were part of a legislated purpose and clearly set forth in the statute, even if those hearings did not result in legislation to address the subject matter of the hearings.

The Court had noted previously in *Watkins v. United States* (1957) that Congress must apprize the defendant of the pertinence of the committee's questions to the subject matter of the inquiry. The *Watkins* case opened the door for challenges to HUAC's ability to conduct fishing expeditions in search of Communists in all aspects of American life. The Court in *Barenblatt* made clear that limited circumstances would allow a hearing witness to refuse to answer a congressional inquiry. By enunciating the requirements and limitations on questioning witnesses, the Court told Congress how to frame its investigations to avoid judicial problems. The Court also indicated that it did not matter that the purpose of the investigation was primarily to expose individuals tied to Communist organizations, so long as the overall legislative purpose of the investigation was valid.

At the same time the Court sent a message that HUAC would not have free reign to conduct investigations that might cross into the realm of either judicial or executive powers granted in the Constitution. Furthermore, the Court clarified that congressional hearings were not exempt from First Amendment considerations. In the case of teachers, the First Amendment would have protected Barenblatt from investigations into whether he was teaching about communism in his class unless there was evidence that he was promoting Communist principles of overthrowing the government. However, HUAC was free to investigate any membership in Communist organizations and those groups advocating the violent overthrow of government. Other constitutional provisions applied to congressional hearings, including that witnesses cannot be compelled to give evidence against themselves and that they cannot be subjected to unreasonable search and seizures.

The *Barenblatt* case put the final stamp of approval, though with a few cautionary limitations, on Congress's ability to investigate Communist activities. Congress could investigate so long as it did not infringe upon the powers of another branch of government or violate one of the core individual rights in the Constitution.

Further reading:
The 1992–93 Staff of the Legislative Research Bureau. "PROJECT: An Overview of Congressional Investigation of the Executive: Procedures, Devices, and Limitations of Congressional Investigative Power." *Syracuse Journal of Legislation and Politics; Barenblatt v. United States*, 360 U.S. 109 (1959); Goodman, Walter. *The Committee: The Extraordinary Career of the House Committee on Un-American Activities.* New York: Farrar, Straus & Giroux, 1968; *Watkins v. United States*, 354 U.S. 178, 1957.

—Corey Ditslear

bargaining

Many political scientists and other observers look at the U.S. Congress as a bazaar where favors are traded, deals are hatched, and compromises forged. There are several types of bargains that typically take place in legislatures.

First, there are split the difference compromises whereby members make policy concessions for the practical purpose of getting legislation passed even if they believe they are voting for a less than optimal bill. For example, if two groups of legislators disagree on the proper level of funding in an education bill—one side prefers a version of the bill that spends $6 billion, while the other side prefers spending $10 billion—they may decide to split the difference between their positions and agree to join forces on a piece of legislation that spends $8 billion on education.

A second typical legislative bargain is known as pork barreling. PORK BARREL legislation involves federal spending on projects in enough districts and states to build a majority coalition of members whose support of the bill is bought by spending in their district or state. Again, under pork barrel legislation members of Congress might vote for overall legislative packages that they do not believe are in the broader public interest for the sole reason of getting their particularistic projects in the bill.

LOGROLLING is a third type of bargain that seeks to use the individual interests of members to build majority coalitions. In a logroll members of Congress agree to vote for a particular bill in exchange for a promise of future support for their preferred legislation. In this type of "I'll vote for your bill if you'll vote for mine" bargaining, winning coalitions are built not by developing legislation that can win majority support on its merits but rather by explicitly bundling different pieces of legislation so that the supporters of the first bill will trade their majority-making support for the second bill in exchange for the additional support needed to put the first bill over the top.

A less explicit kind of logrolling known as mutual noninterference is a fourth type of bargain whereby members of Congress avoid interfering with the legislative and electoral goals of their colleagues in the expectation that those colleagues will return the favor. In regard to the congressional committee system, such mutual noninterference became the norm of committee deference whereby members of Congress would seek to avoid amending or voting against the legislation produced by other committees in the expectation that reciprocity would preclude other members from amending or voting against the legislation produced by *their* committees. If not overtly logrolling on a given piece of legislation, such a system of committee deference has largely the same effect in that legislation is often passed that may or may not have gained majority support on its legislative merits.

A final type of legislative bargaining is the giving of aside payments to members to get their support on a particular piece of legislation. For instance, party leaders might offer members a preferred committee seat, an honorary appointment to a board or council, and even things as mundane as better offices in exchange for their vote on a bill. Recognizing the importance of such bargains demonstrates the extent to which Congress might be viewed as a small community in and of itself where favors, status, and material exchange may affect legislative outcomes.

Given its complexity, Congress offers a number of arenas whereby this variety of legislative bargains might be struck. STANDING COMMITTEES, for example, in which most important legislation is written and amended in mark-up sessions, are prime arenas for bargaining. Once out of committee, bill managers often must also compromise in their efforts to win the requisite number of votes needed for floor passage. Whereas committees and the floor are important arenas of bargaining in the SENATE as they are in the HOUSE OF REPRESENTATIVES, there are some key differences. First, Senate committees are generally less important than committees in the House both because senators tend to be policy generalists compared to specialized House committee experts and because a good deal more legislating takes place on the Senate floor than it does on the House floor. Moreover, on the floor individual senators have extraordinary autonomy and influence over what issues get debated and what issues actually get voted on. Individual senators' abilities to filibuster and put holds on legislation with which they disagree make for powerful incentives for advocates for a particular piece of legislation to seek to compromise and strike bargains with any senator who might object to a particular legislative proposal. And the different composition, electoral considerations, and processes of the House and the Senate also complicate the bargaining that takes place between the two chambers at they try to reconcile differences in legislation in CONFERENCE COMMITTEES.

Finally, if it is to enact laws, Congress as an institution must bargain with the president in order to avoid a veto and obtain his signature. Presidents often make their legislative priorities and preferences known to members of Congress throughout the legislative process and sometimes intervene either personally or through White House staff members to attempt to bargain with individual members and otherwise persuade them to support the president's positions. Such overt and explicit bargains often involve presidents using their own political resources and reputations to win legislative battles in Congress. Still, in many cases such interbranch negotiations between Congress and the presidency are implicit bargains. That is, by anticipating what the president will and will not accept, that is, what might provoke a presidential veto, Congress often makes important legislative concessions to the president. Still, on some occasions the president must accept certain legislative provisions with which he disagrees if vetoing legislation is too politically costly or he anticipates that his veto would be overridden.

Although Congress has always been open to bargaining, it is nevertheless the case that bargaining was most pronounced in the mid-20th century's textbook Congress in which a bargaining culture of the House was facilitated by a number of institutional factors that were specific to the era. Weak party discipline, individualistic members, bipartisanship, and a strong committee system all facilitated and perhaps necessitated the rise of bargaining as a dominant means of building legislative coalitions for policy passage. As these factors have changed, the House and Senate's bargaining cultures and institutions have been transformed.

Since the 1950s senators have become more independent, more partisan, and more sensitive to public and press perceptions of their legislative activities. By the same token, reforms in the House in the 1970s that weakened committees and proliferated power throughout the House membership, increased party leadership powers, and opened up the House to more press and public scrutiny similarly complicated bargaining. If, in the textbook Congress, bargains were often conducted within committees or cross-jurisdictional bargains were struck by committee chairs, then the committee system and the strength of committee chairs was key to the bargaining atmosphere within Congress. And if bipartisan bargaining was facilitated in the textbook Congress by relatively weak party alignments and party leaders, an increase in partisanship in the second half of the 20th century made bipartisan bargains more difficult to achieve. Whereas the increased independence of senators and House members makes bargaining more complicated and difficult, the increased impact of party influence makes members and senators less likely to bargain across the aisle. And, finally, the increased public and press scrutiny in both the House and the Senate make the sometimes unsavory compromises less likely to occur, as senators and House members do not want to bargain for fear of being seen as having sold out the positions held by their committed supporters.

None of this is to imply that legislative bargaining is no more. To be sure, bargains still take place in the contemporary Congress, but the proliferation and diffusion of power in the legislative process, the increased partisan polarization of the contemporary era, and the increased gaze of press and public attention make legislative bargains more difficult to achieve.

Further reading:
Bessette, Joseph M. *The Mild Voice of Reason*. Chicago: University of Chicago Press, 1991; Cooper, Joseph, and David W. Brady, "Institutional Context and Leadership Style: The House from Cannon to Rayburn." *American Political Science Review* 75 (1981): 411–425, Oleszek, Walter J. *Congressional Procedures and the Policy Process*. 6th ed. Washington, D.C.: Congressional Quarterly Press, 2004; Schattschneider, E. E. *Politics, Pressure and the Tariff*. New York: Prentice Hall, 1935; Sinclair, Barbara. *The Transformation of the United States Senate*. Baltimore: Johns Hopkins University Press, 1989.

—Douglas B. Harris

Barkley, Alben William (1877–1956) *Representative, Senator, vice president*

The last vice president to be born in a log cabin, Alben William Barkley was the son of a poor Kentucky tenant farmer who raised tobacco. He was born Willie Alben, but he reversed the order as soon as he was old enough to do so. As he wrote in his autobiography, *That Reminds Me*, "Just imagine the tribulations I would have had, a robust active boy, going through a Kentucky childhood with the name of Willie, and later trying to get into politics."

In 1891 his family moved to a wheat farm in Hickman County, Kentucky. He attended public schools and graduated in 1897 from Marvin College, a Methodist institution in Clinton, Kentucky, having worked as a janitor and teacher to pay his tuition. He studied law at Emory College (now Emory University) in Oxford, Georgia, and at the University of Virginia in Charlottesville but did not graduate because he could not afford to continue his studies. He returned to Kentucky, where he clerked for two attorneys before being admitted to the Kentucky bar in 1901. He practiced law in Paducah from 1901 to 1905. In 1903 Barkley married his first wife, Dorothy Brewer, and they later had three children: David Murrell, Marion Frances, and Laura Louis.

In 1904 Barkley was elected the prosecuting attorney for McCracken County, a post he held for four years. He then was elected McCracken County circuit court judge, serving from 1909 to 1913.

Barkley, a Democrat, was elected to the 63rd Congress in 1912 to represent Kentucky's First District in the HOUSE OF REPRESENTATIVES. He would serve there from March 4, 1913, to March 3, 1927 (63rd through 69th Congress). In the House he supported President Woodrow Wilson's Progressive program, taking a lead role in the passage of Wilson's roads and farm credit bills and the Clayton Anti-Trust Act.

In 1923 Barkley returned to Kentucky to campaign for the Democratic nomination for governor. He lost the primary to William J. Fields, the only electoral defeat in Barkley's political career. The campaign gave him statewide exposure and a nickname, Iron Man, in recognition of his tireless campaigning. Barkley became known for the power of his voice, as he was able to make a speech without the benefit of a microphone.

In 1926 he was elected to the SENATE, defeating incumbent Republican Richard P. Ernst. He was reelected in 1932, 1938, and 1944. He remained in the Senate until January 19, 1949, when he resigned to become vice president of the United States. In the early 1930s he moved into the Democratic Party's leadership in the Senate, as the vice chair of the Democratic Conference and assistant to Majority Leader JOSEPH T. ROBINSON of Arkansas. In 1932 he was selected by Franklin Roosevelt to be the keynote speaker at the Democratic National Convention in Chicago, beginning an alliance with Roosevelt that would last more than a decade.

Following Senator Robinson's death in 1937, Barkley became MAJORITY LEADER, defeating Senator Pat Harrison of Mississippi by one vote. While publicly neutral, President Roosevelt privately assisted Barkley, and the Kentucky senator's victory was seen as a win for Roosevelt. Harrison had opposed Roosevelt's court packing plan. Donald Ritchie suggests that Barkley was seen by his colleagues in the Senate as the White House's voice rather than as a spokesman for his fellow Democratic senators. Barkley supported Roosevelt in the years prior to American entry into World War II, leading the effort to repeal the Neutrality Act and sponsoring, in January 1941, the Lend-Lease Act. Along with Vice President Henry Wallace, the SPEAKER OF THE HOUSE, SAM RAYBURN, and the HOUSE MAJORITY LEADER, JOHN MCCORMACK, Barkley was a member of The Big Four, who regularly met with Roosevelt to discuss the administration's legislative strategy.

During World War II the relationship between Barkley and Roosevelt cooled as the president was preoccupied with the war effort. In February 1944 Roosevelt vetoed a $2 billion revenue bill that Barkley had worked on with the SENATE FINANCE COMMITTEE and shepherded to passage through the Senate. Roosevelt believed that the tax increase was not sufficient and labeled the bill not for the needy but the greedy. After urging his colleagues to override the president's veto, Barkley resigned as Majority Leader to protest Roosevelt's action. Barkley was unanimously reelected Majority Leader by his Democratic colleagues, who recognized that Barkley was now their spokesman.

While his act of defiance enhanced his prestige in the Senate, his relationship with the president suffered. That summer Roosevelt chose Senator Harry Truman of Missouri as his running mate, rejecting Barkley. After his party lost control of the Senate in the 1946 elections, Barkley became the MINORITY LEADER for the 80th Congress (1947–49).

In 1948 Barkley was again the keynote speaker at the Democratic National Convention in Philadelphia. In his speech he used the phrase "give them hell," which is often associated with Truman. His partisan speech triggered an hour-long demonstration, and Barkley was nominated as Harry Truman's running mate against the Republican ticket of New York governor Thomas E. Dewey and California governor Earl Warren. While Truman conducted his legendary whistle stop campaign, Barkley made more than 250 speeches in 36 states in what became known as the prop stop campaign.

Barkley was sworn in as the 35th vice president at the age of 72. Acknowledging the obscurity of the office, he often joked about the woman with two sons, one who ran away and went to sea, the other who was elected vice president of the United States, neither one of whom was ever heard from again. This was not the case with Barkley. As vice president Truman had had little contact with President Roosevelt and had not been informed about the development of the atomic bomb (the Manhattan Project) until

becoming president after Roosevelt's death. Truman made Barkley a key member of his administration, appointed him to the National Security Council (NSC), and had him regularly attend cabinet meetings.

Barkley was the only vice president to marry while in office when he married the 38-year-old Jane Hadley. Barkley was extremely popular and was affectionately known as the "Veep," a nickname given him by his young grandson that stayed with him after he left office.

Barkley was the last vice president to preside over the Senate regularly and often attended meetings of the Senate Democratic Policy Committee. He also was the last vice president not to maintain an office in the White House, working in the vice president's room, located just outside the Senate chamber in the Capitol.

In 1950 Barkley campaigned for Democratic congressional candidates while President Truman concentrated on the Korean War. While the Democrats lost seats, the party maintained majorities in both houses. In 1952, after Truman announced he would not run for another term, Barkley sought the Democratic Party's presidential nomination but was opposed by leaders of organized labor because they believed that, at age 75, he was too old. Barkley withdrew from the race, retiring to his native Kentucky.

Retirement would not last long. In 1954 Barkley was again elected to the Senate, defeating incumbent Republican John Sherman Cooper and giving the Democrats a one-seat majority in the Senate. His Democratic colleagues offered to seat him at the front of the Senate chamber with other senior members. Barkley declined, taking his seat with the other freshman senators. In 1956 he was invited by the students of Washington and Lee University to give the keynote speech at their mock convention. In what turned out to be his last speech, he referred to his freshman status in the Senate: "I'm glad to sit in the back row," he said, "for I would rather be a servant in the House of the Lord than to sit in the seats of the mighty." As the students wildly applauded, Barkley collapsed and died of a massive heart attack.

Barkley is buried in Mount Kenton Cemetery, outside Paducah, Kentucky. In his honor the debating society at Emory University is known as the Barkley Forum.

Further reading:
Barkley, Alben W. *That Reminds Me.* Garden City, N.Y.: Doubleday, 1954; Barkley, Jane R. *I Married the Veep.* New York: Vanguard Press, 1958; Davis, Polly Ann. *Alben Barkley: Senate Majority Leader and Vice President.* New York: Garland, 1979; Hatfield, Mark O., with the Senate Historical Office. *Vice Presidents of the United States, 1789–1993.* Washington, D.C.: Government Printing Office, 1997; Libbey, James K. *Dear Alben: Mr. Barkley of Kentucky.* Lexington: University Press of Kentucky, 1979;

Ritchie, Donald A. "Alben W. Barkley: The President's Man." In Richard A. Baker and Roger H. Davidson, eds. *First among Equals: Outstanding Senate Leaders of the Twentieth Century.* Washington, D.C.: Congressional Quarterly Press, 1991.

—Jeffrey Kraus

bells, legislative

The SENATE and the HOUSE OF REPRESENTATIVES have a system of bells and lights used to alert members of a QUORUM CALL or vote on their chamber floor. Because much of the work of Congress is done away from the House or Senate chambers, a system of bells or buzzers and lights is used to alert members of certain activities taking place in their respective chamber's. Congress has been wired for a system of buzzers since 1912. The Rules of the House identify the combination of bells and lights ordered by the SPEAKER OF THE HOUSE.

A visitor to the Senate may hear one of several signals. A long continuous ring indicates that the Senate is convening, and one light remains on at all times when the Senate is in session. One ring indicates that a yea or nay vote is being taken. A quorum call is signified by two rings. Three rings indicate a call for absentees. An adjournment or recess is indicated by four rings. Five rings indicate that there are seven and half minutes remaining on a yea or nay vote. Six rings (with the six lights turned off on the sixth ring) indicate the end of morning business. A short recess during daily session is signified by six rings with the six lights remaining on during the recess.

The House employs a similar system of using bells and lights. One long continuous ring indicates that the House is convening. One ring signifies a demand for a teller vote. Teller votes were discontinued at the beginning of the 103rd Congress. Two rings indicate a vote by electronic device. Two rings followed by a pause followed by two rings indicate a manual roll-call vote. Two rings followed by a pause followed by five rings indicate the first vote in a series of votes postponed from earlier consideration. Three rings indicate a recorded quorum call either in the House or in the Committee of the Whole. Three rings followed by a pause followed by three rings indicate a manual recorded quorum call. Three rings followed by a pause followed by five rings indicate a quorum call in the Committee of the Whole, followed immediately by a five-minute recorded vote. Adjournment is signified by four rings. Five rings indicate a five-minute vote. Six rings indicate a recess of the House. Twelve rings is a civil defense warning. When the House is in session, the light on the far right, light seven, remains illuminated.

Traditionally, Capitol Hill restaurants have signaled a vote to congressional diners by ringing dinner bells or buzzers. More modern forms of electronic communication have replaced that system. Pagers or cellular telephones notify members of votes. Members' offices learn about occurrences in the chambers by watching closed-circuit television or by being notified via electronic mail on their computers.

Further reading:
Dove, Robert B. *Enactment of a Law.* Washington, D.C.: United States Senate, 1997; Johnson, Charles W. *Constitution, Jefferson's Manual, and Rules of the House of Representatives.* House Document No. 107-284. Washington, D.C.: Government Printing Office, 2003.

—John David Rausch, Jr.

Benton, Thomas Hart (1782–1858) *Senator, Representative*

Benton was born on March 14, 1782, at Hart's Mill near Hillsboro in Orange County, North Carolina, to Jesse and Ann Benton. He was one of eight children. Benton's father was a lawyer and prominent Piedmont landowner who died in 1791, when Benton was eight years old. His mother, orphaned at a young age, was raised in the home of Thomas Hart, who was, like Jesse Benton, a prominent landowner. In 1821 Thomas Hart Benton married Elizabeth McDowell. The Benton's had five children, two daughters and three sons. The youngest son, McDowell, died at the age of four in 1835. Their daughter Jessie Ann married John

Thomas Hart Benton *(Library of Congress)*

Charles Frémont, the western explorer and presidential candidate. Benton's early schooling was in a private academy in Hillsboro. In 1798 he attended Chapel Hill College (now the University of North Carolina). In addition to threatening another student, Archibald Lytle, with a pistol, Benton was charged with theft and was expelled from Chapel Hill in 1799.

Relocating to Tennessee in 1801, Benton began his political career when he was admitted to the Tennessee bar in 1806. Three years later, in 1809, Benton was elected to the state senate. In the Tennessee senate he served on committees that restructured the state court system, protected the property rights of early settlers, and sought to establish fair trials for blacks. During the War of 1812, Benton served as a volunteer captain, a lieutenant colonel in the regular army, and an aide-de-camp to General Andrew Jackson. During an 1813 brawl in Nashville involving his brother Jesse and family honor, Benton shot Andrew Jackson in the arm. By 1815 Benton had relocated to St. Louis, Missouri.

In 1817 Benton was appointed to the board of trustees for schools in St. Louis. At the same time, he began writing editorials in the *Western Emmigrant* newspaper. In 1818 the paper was renamed the *St. Louis Enquirer,* and Benton was appointed editor. He held his first elective office in his new state as a member of the St. Louis board of trustees. Benton's prominence in the state rose to such a level that he was elected one of Missouri's first senators when the territory achieved statehood. Benton was first elected to the Senate in 1821, the year Missouri was admitted to the Union. He was the first U.S. senator to serve 30 consecutive years. Despite losing his bid for reelection in 1850, Benton was subsequently elected to the House of Representatives for one term in 1852.

Although an early supporter of the presidential aspirations of Henry Clay, Benton ironically became one of Andrew Jackson's most effective supporters in the Senate. As an unmatched spokesman for the West, Benton entered the famous 1830 Senate debate between Daniel Webster and Robert Hayne. However, Benton's rise to national prominence was inextricably linked to the federal monetary policies that divided both party and region. In 1832 Benton opposed the rechartering of the Bank of the United States, which, nonetheless, passed in both the House and the Senate. Benton supported President Jackson's veto, and the Senate failed in its override attempt. With Benton's endorsement Jackson removed the national government's deposits from the Bank of the United States in 1833. Reacting to the removal, Clay shepherded a censure resolution against the president in 1834. Three years later Benton's personal response to this rebuke of President Jackson culminated in his successful effort to expunge the censure from the Senate JOURNAL.

Similar debates led Benton to hold the party line on the tariff and the gold standard in successive Democratic administrations. During the tumultuous debates of 1828, 1832, and 1836, he generally endorsed the administration position on tariffs. While opposed to high tariffs in principle, Benton nonetheless voted for high duties on items produced in the West, such as Missouri's lead. As a staunch supporter of hard currency, Benton earned the endearing nickname Old Bullion and the negative sobriquet Gold Humbug in 1834. By 1840 Old Bullion had won the day with the passage of the Independent Treasury Bill.

The issue of slavery permeated Benton's career and illustrates the countervailing pressures of party and region. Although he supported slavery in principle, he opposed its extension into new territories during debates over the annexation of Texas in 1844. In 1847, however, Benton opposed the Wilmot Proviso that would have prohibited slavery in California and any other territory acquired from Mexico. Amid the tangle of issues that became the Compromise of 1850, Benton again voted against the extension of slavery into new territories. By all accounts, this vote was perceived by the people of Missouri as antislavery, and he was defeated for reelection in the general assembly. He was subsequently elected to the House of Representatives. However, by voting against the Kansas-Nebraska Act and further extension of slavery in the West, Benton sealed his political fate and was defeated for reelection. The repercussions of these votes continued to be felt in Benton's defeat in the Missouri gubernatorial election of 1856. Benton died on April 10, 1858, in Washington, D.C.

Further reading:
Belz, Herman, ed. *The Webster-Hayne Debate on the Nature of the Union.* Indianapolis: Liberty Fund, Inc., 2000; Benton, Thomas Hart. *Thirty Years View: A History of the Working of the American Government for Thirty Years.* 2 vols. New York: D Appleton & Company, 1854; Chambers, William Nisbet. *Old Bullion Benton: Senator from the New West.* Boston: Little, Brown, 1956; Smith, Elbert B. *Magnificent Missourian.* Westport, Conn.: Greenwood Press, 1957.

—George Connor

Beveridge, Albert Jeremiah (1862–1927) *Senator*
Albert Beveridge was a Progressive Republican who represented Indiana in the SENATE from 1899 to 1911. He was a supporter of President Theodore Roosevelt and championed American expansionism into the Far East. An accomplished historian, Beveridge was the biographer of John Marshall and Abraham Lincoln.

Beveridge was born October 6, 1862, in Highland County, Ohio, to the farming family of Thomas Beveridge and Frances Parkinson. Experiencing economic difficulties, the family moved to Illinois, where as a young man Beveridge worked as a laborer. He enrolled in Asbury College (now DePauw University), earning a reputation for his oratory. Following graduation in 1885, he sought admission to the Indiana bar.

As a young attorney, Beveridge successfully practiced law in Indianapolis until a skillful lobbying effort with the Indiana Republican legislative caucus secured his election to the U.S. Senate in 1899. At age 37 Beveridge was one of the youngest members in the Senate, and his political ambitions often antagonized Charles W. Fairbanks, the senior Republican senator from Indiana, who battled Beveridge for patronage and control of the Indiana Republican Party.

In the Senate Beveridge gained attention for his support of the Spanish-American War and imperialistic designs by the United States. Beveridge believed that territorial expansion would guarantee markets and investment opportunities for American business interests, avoiding the type of financial crisis that led to the Panic of 1893. The senator supported annexation of the Philippines and sought to repeal the Teller Amendment, which asserted that the United States had no territorial designs on Cuba. To foster trade, Beveridge championed access to American markets for Cuban and Puerto Rican exports. He insisted, however, that the people of the conquered territories were not prepared for self-rule and needed the guiding hand of Anglo-Saxon civilization. An advocate of the China market as a destination for American industrial production, Beveridge visited the Far East in 1901. Perceiving Japan as a threat to American interests in the region, Beveridge, in his book *The Russian Advance* (1903), called for the United States to support the Russians as a countervailing force to Japanese expansionism.

In 1901 Beveridge was named chair of the Senate Committee on Territories. In this capacity he sponsored the 1906 legislation establishing Oklahoma as a state. However, he blocked statehood legislation for the New Mexico and Arizona Territories. Officially, he maintained that the population of the two territories was simply too sparse. In reality Beveridge expressed reservations regarding the large Hispanic and Native American populations of the region. Following the assassination of William McKinley, Beveridge aligned with the new president Roosevelt and the Progressive wing of the Republican Party. Roosevelt's support was crucial in attaining Beveridge's reelection after Republicans captured control of the Indiana legislature in 1904.

During his second Senate term Beveridge established a reputation for supporting Progressive legislation. He sponsored the Meat Inspection Act of 1906, which was passed in response to the sanitary concerns expressed by Upton Sinclair in *The Jungle* (1906). In addition, the Indiana senator advocated a national child labor bill to prohibit

the interstate transportation of products made by exploiting the labor of children. His growing reservations regarding the economic and political powers of big business encouraged Beveridge to call for an independent tariff commission to depoliticize tariff construction.

A turning point in Beveridge's political career came in 1909, when he joined insurgent Republicans in opposing the Payne-Aldrich Tariff. He also earned the wrath of President William Howard Taft and the Republican congressional leadership for championing Gifford Pinchot in his environmental and bureaucratic squabbles with Secretary of the Interior Richard A. Ballinger. Beveridge also joined insurgents in supporting postal savings bank legislation and railroad regulation with the Mann-Elkins Act of 1910. Although he maintained a solid Progressive voting record, Beveridge lost his Senate seat when Democrats regained control of the Indiana legislature in 1910.

A disillusioned Beveridge followed his hero Theodore Roosevelt out of the Republican Party in 1912, serving as temporary chair and keynote speaker at the Progressive Party's national convention. He also accepted the Progressive nomination for the governorship of Indiana, but Beveridge and Roosevelt both went down to defeat. Two years later Beveridge was the Progressive candidate for the Senate in Indiana, but he finished third in the race. By 1916 he returned to the Republican fold.

Beveridge was a vocal critic of President Woodrow Wilson and moved increasingly in a more conservative political direction. He opposed organized labor and such legislation as the Adamson Act of 1916, which established an eight-hour day for railroad workers. Beveridge encouraged Wilson to take a more interventionist policy with the Mexican revolution. In regard to the war in Europe, Beveridge found Wilson to favor Britain, while the former Indiana senator's German sympathies were displayed in his *What Is Back of the War* (1915). Beveridge criticized Wilsonian internationalism and the League of Nations for undermining American independence.

Meanwhile, Beveridge turned his attention to history and biography, completing his four-volume *The Life of John Marshall* in 1919. The biography, which celebrated Marshall as a nationalist, was well received by critics, scholars, and the general public.

Despite the accolades for his scholarship, politics remained in Beveridge's blood. In 1922 he defeated incumbent senator Harry New in the Republican primary. In the general election campaign Beveridge denounced labor unions, high personal and corporate income taxes, and involvement with the League of Nations. He was defeated by the Democratic nominee, Samuel M. Ralston.

After this final foray into the political field, Beveridge returned to scholarship, preparing a multivolume biography of Abraham Lincoln. Before he could complete the biography, Beveridge died in Indianapolis on April 27, 1927. Historian Washington Ford completed the two-volume *Abraham Lincoln, 1809–1858* (1928). In recognition of Beveridge's scholarship his friends established an endowment fund in his honor with the American Historical Association.

Further reading:
Beveridge Papers, Library of Congress, Washington D.C.; Bowers, Claude G. *Beveridge and the Progressive Era.* New York: The Literary Guild, 1932; Braeman, John. *Albert J. Beveridge: American Nationalist.* Chicago: University of Chicago Press, 1971.

—Ron Briley

bicameralism

The root element in this word is *camera,* Latin for chamber, so the word refers to two chambers. The word is almost exclusively applied in a political context and refers to a preference for structuring a legislature with two chambers, or houses. A legislature with a single chamber is unicameral.

While history records the development of councils in various countries, the American pattern followed the English model, where two chambers emerged in the 17th century. The House of Commons was to represent ordinary people, and the House of Lords spoke for the nobility. The first government of the United States under the Articles of Confederation had as its key institution a unicameral Continental Congress. By the time of the Convention of 1787, 11 of the states had bicameral legislatures, while two were unicameral.

When the founders sought to form the republic, the central institution was the Congress. It would be there that representatives elected by the people would legislate and oversee the government's exercise of constitutionally limited powers. However, the Constitution drafting process promptly came to an impasse over competing proposals from the large states and the small states. The Virginia Plan featured a bicameral legislature with members elected to the first house directly by the people of the states and the second filled by nominees named by the state legislatures and elected by the first chamber. A crucial point in the plan was that representation in both chambers would be proportional to either the taxes paid by the states to the national government or the number of free inhabitants.

An alternative proposal, the New Jersey plan, was conceived as a revision of government under the Articles and held steadfastly to a unicameral legislature in which the states were equally represented. The small states would not yield the equal representation they enjoyed in the Continental Congress, fearing that a national government dominated by the larger states would obtain commercial preeminence at the small states' expense. The key to further progress in the convention was acceptance of the Connecticut Compromise, which provided representation of the states by population in the House and representation of the states on an equal basis in the Senate.

Always understood as the people's house, the House of Representatives was to be a relatively large chamber. The term of office was short, only two years. The seriously considered alternative was a one-year term. Qualifications for offices were simple: an age of 25 years, a citizen for seven years, and an inhabitant of the state where one was elected. These representatives were to be elected by the people directly. While the electorate's qualifications were not defined, they were to be as generous in each state as the states were regarding the voters electing representatives to the larger chamber of the state legislature. There are almost no limits in the Constitution about introducing bills except that Article I, Section 7, requires "all bills for raising revenues shall originate in the House of Representatives; but the Senators may propose or concur with amendments as on other bills." Tax bills were to begin in the people's House. The Senate's function was to review, amend, and concur. Indeed, during the early history of the Senate its part in the legislative process was largely as a revisory body that responded to House initiatives on all matters.

There was a clearer consensus among the founders about the nature of the House than of the Senate. Some saw the Senate as a mild parallel to the English House of Lords. Despite an absence of hereditary aristocracy, they expected that appointments from the states would favor persons with great stakes in land and commerce. Many had reservations about the tyranny of the many over the few, particularly the less well off over the owners of great wealth. Thus, the Senate should be a check upon the House. James Madison observed in the convention that "The use of the Senate is to consist in its proceeding with more coolness, with more system, and with more wisdom, than the popular branch." Although during the convention he had opposed the equal representation of the states in the Senate, Madison accepted the arrangement as a necessary compromise. In Federalist 62 he said, "Another advantage accruing from this ingredient in the constitution of the Senate is the additional impediment it must prove against improper acts of legislation. No law or resolution can now be passed without the concurrence, first, of a majority of the people, and then of a majority of the states." Despite his continuing reservations he allowed that "this part of the Constitution may be more convenient in practice then it appears in contemplation."

In Federalist 64 John Jay argued the merit in the Senate's particular role in foreign relations. The president's power to make treaties was limited with the requirement that they be made "by and with the advice and consent of the Senate . . . provided two-thirds of the Senators present concur." Jay argued that the president and senators would be "those who best understand our national interests, whether considered in relation to the several states or to foreign nations, who are best able to promote those interests, and whose reputation for integrity inspires and merits confidence. With such men the power of making treaties may be safely lodged."

The Senate was constituted to be quite different from the House. The six-year terms are much longer than those of representatives. Because of staggered terms any given election could replace at most a third of the Senators, and the Senate has the nature of a continuing body. It has a major role in confirming the president's appointees to both the executive branch and courts. It tries cases of impeachment, but only if the people's House brings charges.

In the primary task of lawmaking the House and Senate are equal and separate. Except for revenue measures and, by tradition, appropriation bills always starting in the House, other matters may originate in either chamber and, importantly, must pass both chambers in like substance to become law. The legislative override of vetoes by the president requires two-thirds majorities in both houses. Each chamber makes its own rules and keeps its own records. Hearings and committee systems are separate. Joint sessions are rare and mainly ceremonial.

While neither house is superior to the other, the pattern of careers reveals only one-way movement. Representatives often seek to move "up" to the Senate, and quite a few succeed. Only in rare cases have former senators sought election to the House. The reward from winning a Senate seat is a lengthy term and the opportunity to legislate as one of a 100-member body rather than one of 435. Senators take part in major governmental appointments and treaty making. Moreover, the prospects for serious consideration as a presidential or vice presidential candidate are much greater for senators than for representatives.

Although the Senate was conceived to be a check upon the tyranny of the majority operating through the House, it is difficult to demonstrate the success of that intention. Certainly, the Senate overrepresents the small states even more today then it did in 1790, the time of the first CENSUS. According to the 2000 census, for example, the two senators from California represent 33.9 million constituents, while Wyoming's 494,000 residents likewise have two senators. It is not obvious what interests benefit most from such variation from the one person, one vote standard that applies to the House of Representatives, but the states with the larger populations are obviously underrepresented in the Senate. As a consequence, urban minorities, such as citizens differentiated by race or language, appear to be disadvantaged in the Senate by a system of equal state representation. However, major political cleavages in American history have not pitted large states against the small in a fashion that has undermined the continuing acceptability of equal state representation in the Senate. Certainly, compared to the founding era, the present-day Senate is much more directly related to the people in each state because in 1913 the SEVENTEENTH AMENDMENT took senatorial selection away from state legislatures and assigned it to the voters.

The likelihood of undoing the Connecticut Compromise to make a unicameral Congress or to undo the equal representation of the states in the Senate appears to be very small. The typical procedure of amending requires two-thirds of both houses to propose an amendment, with ratification by three-fourths of the states. The concluding clause of Article V requires "that no state, without its consent, shall be deprived of its equal suffrage in the Senate." The constitutional protections for the biased structure of the U.S. Senate are formidable, and the future for bicameralism appears to be secure.

See also APPORTIONMENT AND REDISTRICTING; GERRYMANDERING, PARTISAN; GERRYMANDERING, RACIAL.

Further reading:
Dahl, R. A. *A Preface to Democracy.* Chicago: University of Chicago Press, 1956; Baker, R. A. "The Senate of the United States: 'Supreme Executive Council of the Nation', 1787–1800." *Prologue* (Winter 1989): 299–313; Kurland, P. B., and R. Lerner, eds. *The Founders' Constitution.* Available online. URL: http://press-pubs.uchicago.edu/founders. Accessed December 17, 2002; Hamilton, A., J. Madison and J. Jay. *The Federalist Papers.* Introduction by C. Rossiter, ed. New York: New American Library, 1961.
—Jack R. Van Der Slik

bills

A bill is a draft of a law presented to the HOUSE and/or the SENATE for enactment. Most legislative proposals before Congress are in a bill form. Public bills change PUBLIC LAW. If enacted into law, bills are published in *Statutes at Large* and given a public law number, such as P.L. 234. PRIVATE BILLS address matters affecting individuals, such as an immigration case, and if enacted into law are not reported in *Statutes at Large*.

Bills are officially designated H.R. (number) in the House and S. (number) in the Senate. Usually, bills are assigned numbers according to the chronological order in which they are introduced. Occasionally, however, members will request the bill clerk to reserve a particular number for political and symbolic reasons. Although legislation is given a number, it may be know by several names. Each bill is required to have a formal title along with its officially designated number. The naming of legislation can be an issue. An attractive title can potentially garner a bill useful media attention. The timing of introducing a bill can also be important. Members need to determine whether a controversial bill should be introduced early or late in a legislative session. A bill likely to be filibustered in the Senate, for example, should be introduced early to allow plenty of time to overcome the FILIBUSTER.

In the House introducing a bill simply requires a representative to drop it into the hopper, a wooden box at the front of the chamber, when the House is in session. In the Senate senators hand their draft legislation to a clerk or gain recognition to orally introduce it from the floor. Only members of the House may introduce bills in the House, and only senators can introduce bills in the Senate. A consequence of this is that even the president needs to find a member of both the House and the Senate to introduce his legislation, though doing so is never a problem. There is no limit to the number of bills that members can introduce in a session; members may introduce as many measures as they wish.

A member who introduces a bill becomes its sponsor. In both houses the chief sponsor of a measure may seek a cosponsor to show wide support for the legislation. As important as the number of cosponsors there are, so is their leadership status and ideological stance. Members sometimes introduce bills on request, as a favor to the president or someone else. When this is done it is indicated next to the sponsors' names at the top of the first page of the legislation, signaling that the sponsor does not necessarily endorse the provisions of the bill. Legislation is also often introduced by a committee chair on behalf of his or her committee, usually after the committee has drafted and approved the details. In such a case the chair is the formal sponsor, but the bill is recognized as a committee bill.

After a bill is introduced it is referred by the House or Senate PARLIAMENTARIAN to the STANDING COMMITTEE (or possibly committees) of jurisdiction. Since committees differ in membership and perspective, which committee receives the bill can make a difference to the ultimate success of the bill. Most referrals are routine, but occasionally referrals can become controversial. Large, complex bills often generate competition among committees with jurisdictions relevant to the legislation. In 1975 the House changed its rules and allowed the referral of legislation to more than one committee. Since the rules change, multiple referrals have become increasingly common, especially on major legislation.

A bill must pass an overwhelming number of hurdles in order to eventually become law. Most bills die in committee. After the committee holds HEARINGS and approves the bill, it is then sent to the floor of the appropriate chamber of Congress. After debating the merits of the bill, if both the House and Senate pass the bill it is then sent to a CONFERENCE COMMITTEE, where a compromise is sought between any differences between the House and Senate versions of the bill. If both the House and Senate approve the compromise version of the bill, it is then sent to the president for his signature. If the president vetoes the bill, Congress has the power to override a presidential veto with a two-thirds vote in both the House and the Senate, but this is unlikely. Less than 4 percent of presidential vetoes have ever been overturned. As a result, in order for a bill to become law it must usually have the good will (or at least not hostility) of the White House.

Only a relatively small number of bills ever become law. In the 105th Congress, for example, of the 7,732 bills and joint resolutions introduced, only 394 (5 percent) became law. Yet, at the same time, bills that are introduced are much more complex than they used to be. The average number of pages per law has increased from two and a half in the 1950s to more than 18 pages by the dawn of the 21st century. The contemporary Congress may pass fewer laws than it used to, but the bills that do become law are considerably larger.

Further reading:
Oleszek, Walter J. *Congressional Procedures and the Policy Process.* Washington, D.C.: Congressional Quarterly Press, 2001; Sinclair, Barbara. *Unorthodox Lawmaking.* 2d ed. Washington, D.C.: Congressional Quarterly Press, 2000; Smith, Steven. *The American Congress.* 2d ed. Boston: Houghton Mifflin, 1999.

—Patrick Fisher

Bipartisan Campaign Reform Act of 2002

The Bipartisan Campaign Reform Act of 2002 (BCRA) was signed by the president and enacted on March 27, 2002, as P.L. 107-155. BCRA capped a seven-year effort by its congressional sponsors to change federal campaign law and marked the most significant amendment to the Federal Election Campaign Act (FECA) in more than a quarter century. The Senate version of the final bill, S. 27, principally sponsored by John McCain, Republican senator from Arizona, and Russell Feingold, Democratic senator from Wisconsin, initially passed the Senate on April 2, 2001, and was submitted to the House for consideration. The House version, H.R. 2356, principally sponsored by Christopher Shays, Republican representative from Connecticut, and Martin Meehan, Democratic representative from Massachusetts, passed the House on February 14, 2002. On March 20, 2002, the Senate approved the House version by a 60-40 vote in order to avoid a conference committee that would have been composed by many of the leading opponents of the bill. A series of technical amendments (H.Con.Res. 361) were approved by the House later that day and subsequently ratified by the Senate on March 22, sending the final bill to the president.

Among its myriad of components, there are two key pillars of the Bipartisan Campaign Reform Act that have fundamentally transformed campaign finance law. First, the act prohibits raising and spending "soft money" by federal officeholders and candidates and by the national parties and severely restricts the use of soft money by state and local parties in relation to federal election activities. Second, the act redefines what constitutes a campaign advertisement, subject to the disclosure requirements, contribution limits, and contribution source restrictions of federal law.

In federal elections soft money is defined as funds that are otherwise prohibited by law for use in campaign activity, that is, funds that come from individuals in excess of the contribution limits or funds that come from corporate or union treasuries. Due to an exemption in the 1979 amendments to the Federal Election Campaign Act, state and local parties were allowed to spend soft money on grassroots organizing and voter mobilization activities that impacted state as well as federal elections. Subsequent regulations by the Federal Elections Commission (FEC) expanded the soft money exemption, allowing the national parties also to raise and spend soft money for party building and voter mobilization activities. In 1988 the FEC even permitted the national parties to use soft money to pay for partisan television advertisements that benefited both state and federal candidates, so long as the soft money was used to pay for the nonfederal share of the costs.

The parties had initially been slow to take advantage of this new source of revenue—until the 1996 reelection campaign of President Bill Clinton. In that election the Democratic Party realized the soft money exemption allowed the national party to raise unlimited amounts of soft money and then transfer the funds to state parties. State Democratic parties, in turn, could spend the soft money on nonfederal election activity, including television and radio advertisements, which directly benefited the Clinton campaign.

Both parties promptly turned their attention to soft money. In the 2000 election cycle national and congressional party committees broke all previous records in soft money fund-raising. National Republican Party committees raised $249.9 million in soft money and spent $252.8 million in soft money, while national Democratic Party committees raised $245.2 million in soft money and spent $244.8 million (see Figure 1). More than half of this soft money was transferred to state parties and used to pay for television advertisements. Overall, 77 percent of party-sponsored television commercials relating to federal elections in the 2000 election were paid for by state parties. The national party committees and federal congressional committees combined purchased about 23 percent of the party airwaves that addressed federal elections. Not surprisingly, most of this state party spending activity took place in the

nation's most competitive states in the presidential election: Florida, Pennsylvania, California, Michigan, Washington, and Ohio.

BCRA sharply curtailed the role of soft money in federal elections. Most of the provisions of the new campaign finance law went into effect on November 6, 2002. Federal officeholders and candidates and the national parties are now prohibited from raising or spending soft money in most instances. As part of a congressional compromise, however, entities may contribute up to $10,000 in soft money (known as Levin funds) to each state and local party organization if permitted by state law; the money may be spent for voter mobilization activity in federal elections. Additionally, the Federal Election Commission has promulgated a series of regulations to loosen the soft money ban somewhat, much to the consternation of the congressional sponsors, who have filed a lawsuit in response (*Shays v. FEC*).

Although the Federal Election Campaign Act regulates expenditures in connection with federal elections, subsequent court rulings have narrowly defined what constitutes a "campaign advertisement" subject to the regulations. In a footnote to the 1976 landmark decision *Buckley v. Valeo,* the U.S. Supreme Court drew what is facetiously known as the "magic words" standard. According to this standard, a political communication is subject to regulation if it expressly advocates the election or defeat of a candidate by using such words as "vote for," "elect," or "vote against." If such words of express advocacy are not used in the political communication, it is then deemed an "issue

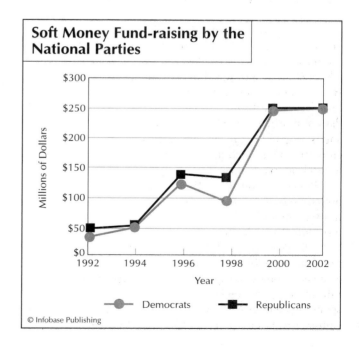

Soft Money Fund-raising by the National Parties

ad" rather than a campaign ad, beyond the scope of federal campaign regulations. The court recognized that all candidate advertisements, whether or not they use the magic words, are defined as campaign ads.

A series of academic studies in the 1996, 1998, and 2000 elections documented that very few political advertisements, even those sponsored by candidates, employ any of the magic words of express advocacy. In the 2000 elections, for example, 2 percent of television ads sponsored by political parties and independent groups used the magic words; only 10 percent of candidate ads used the magic words.

Yet, the bulk of political "issue ads" are nevertheless seen as promoting the election or defeat of specific candidates. For example, the following television ad aired in key states during the hotly contested Republican presidential primary race between George W. Bush, then governor of Texas, and Senator John McCain:

> Last year, John McCain voted against solar and renewable energy. That means more use of coal-burning plants that pollute our air. Ohio Republicans care about clean air. So does Governor Bush. He led one of the first states in America to clamp down on old coal-burning electric power plants. Bush's clean air laws will reduce air pollution more than a quarter million tons a year. That's like taking 5 million cars off the road. Governor Bush, leading, for each day dawns brighter.

Since the advertisement did not expressly advocate the election of George Bush or the defeat of John McCain, it was classified as an issue ad not subject to the disclosure requirements or contribution and source limitations of federal campaign laws.

The Bipartisan Campaign Reform Act provides a new definition of campaign ad versus issue ad. The law retains the magic words standard as well as the concept that any advertisement sponsored by a candidate is a campaign ad. But it also imposes a "bright-line standard" in which any broadcast advertisement that depicts a candidate within 30 days of a primary election or 60 days of a general election and is targeted to the voting constituency of that candidate constitutes an electioneering communication, subject to federal campaign laws.

Passage of the Bipartisan Campaign Reform Act did not come easily or quickly. The original version of BCRA, more commonly known as the McCain-Feingold bill, was introduced as S. 1219 in the 104th Congress on September 7, 1995. The original bill provided for more than restrictions on soft money. It also called for voluntary spending ceilings in congressional races, free broadcast time, reduced-rate mailing privileges to candidates who abided by the spending ceilings, and limits on self-financing of candidate campaigns. Each session of Congress thereafter, Senators McCain and Feingold introduced a modified version of their bipartisan campaign reform legislation.

The McCain-Feingold bill died short of a cloture vote in the Senate of the 104th Congress. In the following session the House succeeded in passing its companion bill, H.R. 2183, better known as the Shays-Meehan bill. Senate sponsors in the 105th Congress, however, failed three times to break a filibuster on the Senate version. In the 106th Congress, the House again passed the Shays-Meehan bill (H.R. 417), only to be thwarted by another filibuster in the Senate. Even a scaled-down Senate bill (S. 1593) in that same session providing only a ban on soft money was stopped by a filibuster.

Finally, in the 107th Congress the latest McCain-Feingold bill (S. 27) survived an onslaught of 38 potentially crippling amendments that were disposed of with 26 roll call votes. On April 2, 2001, the Senate approved the McCain-Feingold bill by a vote of 59-41. As passed, the bill contained 22 amendments offered on the floor; 16 additional amendments were rejected.

The momentum for campaign reform now moved into the House. The House Administration Committee initiated a series of hearings on campaign finance reform from March through May 2002. The committee favorably reported to the House a substantially weaker version of the Senate bill, known as the Ney-Wynn bill (H.R. 2360), and unfavorably reported the companion bill, H.R. 2356, sponsored by Representatives Shays and Meehan. On July 12 the House rejected by 203-228 a proposed rule to consider the campaign finance issue, leaving both bills suspended.

Beginning on July 19, 2001, a group of Blue Dog Democrats began circulation of a discharge petition ordering the House leadership to resume debate on the campaign finance bills. The petition needed 218 signatures to force a floor vote. On January 24, 2002, campaign finance reform proponents secured the last four signatures needed on the discharge petition. The House approved H.R. 2356 on February 7, 2002, on a 240-189 vote. The Senate approved an identical bill on March 22 in order to avoid a conference committee, which was signed into law by the president on March 27.

The tumultuous history of the Bipartisan Campaign Reform Act has not yet come to a close. Within a month of passage of the new campaign finance law, more than 80 plaintiffs—ranging from Senator Mitch McConnell (R-KY) to the AFL-CIO to the Republican Party—filed 11 different lawsuits challenging every provision of the act. The U.S. Department of Justice and the Federal Election Commission are the lead defendants in the suits, supported in their defense of BCRA by the principal congressional sponsors of the law, who intervened in the case. All the lawsuits have been consolidated into one case, *McConnell v. FEC*, in which the Supreme Court ruled in 2003 to uphold the act.

Further reading:

Cantor, Joseph. *Campaign Financing*. Congressional Research Service, Library of Congress, CRS Issue Brief, 2003; Cantor, Joseph, and L. Paige Whitaker. *Bipartisan Campaign Reform Act of 2002: Summary and Comparison with Previous Law*. Congressional Research Service, Library of Congress, CRS report, 2003; Corrado, Anthony, et al. *Inside the Campaign Finance Battle*. Washington, D.C.: Brookings Institution Press, 2003; Holman, Craig, and Luke McLoughlin. *Buying Time 2000: Television Advertising in the 2000 Federal Elections*. New York: Brennan Center for Justice, 2001; Magleby, David, ed. *Financing the 2000 Election*. Washington, D.C.: Brookings Institution Press, 2002.

—Craig Holman

Blaine, James G. (1830–1893) *Representative, Senator, Speaker of the House*

James G. Blaine was one of America's most prominent political figures in the years following the Civil War. A man of immense charisma, Blaine, known as the "Plumed Knight," served six years as SPEAKER OF THE HOUSE (1869–75), five years as U.S. senator (1876–81), was Republican nominee for president in 1884, and a two-time secretary of State.

Blaine was born to a prominent family near Pittsburgh in 1830. During his youth Blaine exhibited a keen mind and a strong interest in history and letters. He attended Washington College in Pennsylvania (now Washington and Jefferson College), where he displayed much promise. Upon graduation in 1847, Blaine moved to Kentucky to serve as a schoolteacher. In Kentucky Blaine experienced slavery firsthand. This exposure convinced Blaine of the iniquity of the "peculiar institution." After three years in Kentucky, Blaine returned to Pennsylvania for two years to teach at a school for the blind before making his way to Augusta, Maine, with his new bride, Harriet Stanwood.

In 1854 Blaine's fortunes took a dramatic turn when he purchased a stake in the *Kennebec Journal* and became coeditor. The Whig paper had a statewide readership and would provide Blaine with a platform on which to expound his political views. Blaine's timing could scarcely have been better. During this period the Kansas-Nebraska Act, which extended slavery into the hitherto "free" territories, prompted the creation of the Republican Party. Blaine's articles lambasted slavery, the Kansas-Nebraska Act, and President Franklin Pierce's efforts to annex Cuba. This helped elevate Blaine to prominence in the budding Republican party in Maine.

At age 26 he was chosen a delegate to the first national Republican convention. Blaine entered the Maine legislature soon thereafter. In 1859 he became the head of the Maine state party, a perch he would hold for more than two decades. In 1860 Blaine was elected to serve as Speaker of the lower state house. That same year he campaigned heartily for Abraham Lincoln and helped deliver Maine for the Republican nominee.

Once the Civil War broke out, Blaine became a strong supporter of Lincoln's war policies. Although he did not himself serve—Blaine paid for a proxy to serve for him—he was active in the state legislature in helping to supply the Union war effort. Blaine's popularity and ambition soon took him beyond the state house. He was elected to a seat in the U.S. House of Representatives in 1862.

Upon arriving in the House of Representatives, Blaine charted a moderate course. He continued his support for Lincoln's military efforts and allied himself with the Radical Republicans on issues related to the promotion of African-American rights. For instance, Blaine voted in favor of the Thirteenth Amendment, which abolished slavery, a measure that was initially defeated in the House. Blaine also advocated extending the franchise to freedmen. Blaine, however, parted company with the Radical Republicans on some of the more coercive Reconstruction measures. He also displayed his independence by crossing swords repeatedly with House leader and arch-Radical Thaddeus Stevens.

Like other Republicans, Blaine quickly grew disillusioned with Lincoln's successor, President Andrew Johnson. Blaine was particularly exasperated at Johnson's refusal to extend federal protection to pro-Union southerners. Blaine responded by voting to impeach Johnson. (In later years, he expressed regret at this action.)

By the time of Stevens's death in 1868, Blaine had emerged as one of the preeminent leaders of the House. When Schuyler Colfax vacated the Speaker's chair to assume the vice presidency, Blaine seized on the opportunity and easily outpaced his only competitor. At the age of 39 Blaine became Speaker of the House.

Blaine is generally considered the most powerful Speaker during the 50-year period following Henry Clay's departure from the Speakership in the early 1820s. Prior to the Civil War the Speaker's authority had largely atrophied. The issue of slavery had split the majority Democratic Party, rendering the House ungovernable at times. Furthermore, there was no coherent opposition party to mount an effective alternative to the Democrats.

Blaine's accession coincided with a number of trends favorable to a reinvigorated Speakership. During this period the Republican Party was emboldened by the successful war effort and was largely unified against President Johnson's Reconstruction policies. The party also suffered from few of the sectional divisions that plagued the Democratic Party, and it enjoyed a relatively coherent political ideology. During the period of Blaine's Speakership, the Democrats were in disarray and offered little in the way of serious political opposition.

Blaine took advantage of the political situation and astutely exercised his prerogatives as Speaker. He exercised great care with his committee appointments, garnering political capital from newly appointed members. Blaine used this power to support the growing American business sector, particularly the railroads. He also collaborated with the administration of President U.S. Grant on several foreign policy issues.

It was in his capacity as parliamentarian, however, that Blaine left his lasting imprint on the Speakership. Blaine used the Speaker's power of "recognition"—the power to formally permit members to speak and make motions on the floor—to particular advantage. Prior to Blaine's tenure Speakers often had only a generalized idea of what members were preparing to say or do on the House floor. Blaine demanded that members inform him ahead of time as to the exact reason they sought recognition. Those who tried to move forward with plans with which Blaine disagreed often found themselves unable to gain recognition until they modified their efforts more to Blaine's liking. In this way Blaine controlled the flow of legislative business. Blaine's recasting of the Speaker's right of recognition went a long way toward centralizing power to the office of the Speaker. It also helped to make floor activity less chaotic in a way that presaged the present-day responsibilities of the HOUSE COMMITTEE ON RULES. In sum, Blaine's parliamentary efforts paved the way for the apogee of the Speakership under Thomas B. Reed and Joe Cannon in the late 19th and early 20th centuries.

Blaine's Speakership was marred, however, by allegations of corruption, and the whiff of scandal would remain attached to him for the remainder of his public career. Blaine had amassed a considerable personal fortune during his career, thus making him a target for political opponents. While Speaker, Blaine was accused of personally benefiting from his ties with the railroad interests, which had granted him favorable treatment on several stock deals. In response to the allegations, Blaine appointed a select House committee to look into the matter. The committee never found evidence contradicting Blaine's version of events, and for a while it appeared Blaine might emerge unscathed. It was not to be. In 1876 the allegations resurfaced. This time Blaine dramatically took to the floor of the House to defend his actions. During his address he read excerpts from letters that had fallen at one point into the possession of a bookkeeper, James Mulligan. Blaine's selective reading of the "Mulligan Letters" saved him from political ruin, but the issue would never wholly disappear and may well have cost him the 1876 Republican presidential nomination. Most authorities today believe that his actions with respect to the railroad industry, if not illegal, certainly reflected poor ethical judgment on his part.

The elections of 1874 ushered in a Democratic majority in the House and ended Blaine's tenure as Speaker. As a member of the minority, Blaine struck a more partisan chord, most memorably with his incendiary speech against granting amnesty to former Confederate president Jefferson Davis.

Blaine was appointed to fill a Senate vacancy in 1876 and was selected by the Maine legislature the following year for a full term. Blaine served in the upper chamber until 1881. Blaine never achieved the level of distinction in the Senate that he had enjoyed in the House. His time in the Senate is perhaps best remembered for his demagogic efforts to halt Chinese immigration, a stance at odds with Blaine's forward-looking views on extending rights to African Americans. He also promoted efforts to expand American trade overseas, opposed the use of silver as a form of currency, and worked to revitalize the U.S. merchant marine.

As secretary of State the 1876 elections witnessed the first of several attempts Blaine made to win the presidency. That year Blaine could well have been elected but for concern about his relationship with railroad interests. The specter of impropriety that hung over Blaine's head provided Ohio governor Rutherford B. Hayes with sufficient opportunity to take the Republican nomination.

In the intervening four years Blaine represented the faction of the Republican Party known as the "Half Breeds," who favored some measure of civil service and governmental reform and who opposed President Grant's pursuit of a third term. This branch of the party was ardently opposed by the "Stalwarts," led by Senator Roscoe Conkling. Blaine's association with the "Half Breeds" and his sour personal relations with Conkling did not help his pursuit of the presidency in 1880. That year, despite Blaine's strong support within the party, the nomination ultimately went to Blaine's friend and fellow "Half Breed," James Garfield.

Garfield appointed Blaine secretary of State with the understanding that Blaine would serve as a "prime minister" of sorts. During his first secretaryship Blaine made strides toward establishing U.S. control over what would become the Panama Canal route. Blaine also went to great lengths to put together an inter-American conference and pushed for annexation of Hawaii. These efforts were interrupted by Garfield's assassination and Blaine's subsequent resignation from President Chester Arthur's cabinet.

The 1884 elections looked as if they might finally be the time for Blaine. The ethical questions surrounding his railroad stock transactions seemed to have largely subsided. Blaine had also bolstered his own standing by giving a moving eulogy to the slain President Garfield in 1882. Blaine received the Republican nomination and became locked in a close race with New York governor Grover Cleveland. Near the end of the race, at a political rally attended by Blaine, a Protestant minister, Samuel D. Burchard, denounced the Democrats as constituting the party of "Rum, Romanism and Rebellion." When it came time for Blaine to speak, he failed to repudiate the reverend's inflammatory comments. Blaine's opponents gleefully capitalized on his omission and used this against him during the final days of the campaign. This mistake cost him Catholic support in New York, a state he ultimately lost by only a few thousand votes. Blaine's defeat in New York cost him the presidency.

Even following the disappointing defeats of 1880 and 1884, Blaine remained politically popular and very much in the public eye. Following his departure from the Arthur administration, Blaine began to write the first volume of his memoirs, *Twenty Years of Congress*. The first volume appeared in 1884. Blaine would return to this project following his unsuccessful 1884 election effort and would also publish a book of his campaign speeches.

He returned to public life in 1888 in support of former Indiana senator Benjamin Harrison's quest for the presidency. After Harrison was elected he named Blaine secretary of State but without the special status he carried during the Garfield administration. During his second tenure as secretary he continued to pursue a vigorous foreign policy. This approach included continuing his earlier efforts at asserting American dominion over the yet-to-be-completed Panama Canal and urging the annexation of Hawaii. He also pushed to acquire Cuba and Puerto Rico. In 1889 he chaired the initial Pan-American Conference, a precursor to the modern-day Organization of American States. Blaine also consummated a number of reciprocal trade agreements with Latin American countries and colonies.

Despite his failing health, Blaine apparently still harbored presidential ambitions, and in summer 1892 he resigned from the cabinet, presumably to challenge Harrison for the Republican nomination. He was defeated easily by Harrison at the convention. Early the next year Blaine died at the age of 62.

Though his reputation is somewhat sullied by scandal, Blaine remains among the most noteworthy political figures of the Gilded Age. He is generally considered among the four or five most important Speakers of the 19th century, and he proved himself a capable secretary of State.

Further reading:
Crapol, Edward P. *James G. Blaine: Architect of Empire.* Wilmington, Del.: Scholarly Resources, 2000; Muzzey, David S. *James G. Blaine: A Political Idol of Other Days.* Port Washington, N.Y.: Kennikat Press, 1935; Peters, Ronald. *The American Speakership: The Office in Historical Perspective.* Baltimore: Johns Hopkins University Press, 1990; Stanwood, Edward. *James Gillespie Blaine.* Boston: Houghton Mifflin, 1905.

—Roy E. Brownnell, II

blocs and coalitions

Blocs and coalitions have been defined as groupings of legislators across party lines designed to further or block a particular legislative issue or group of issues. Blocs and coalitions form in almost every legislative body in the world. In multiparty parliamentary systems, such as those of Italy and France, party coalitions form in order to establish a government. No party has achieved a majority in parliament and must join with one or more smaller parties to create a governing coalition. In this sense a coalition is a combining of entire parties. Coalition governments are almost inevitable in multiparty systems but are nonexistent in stable, two-party systems such as the one in the United States. The odd number of seats in the HOUSE OF REPRESENTATIVES makes it almost impossible for either party to achieve a majority, barring a large number of members declaring themselves as independents. In the SENATE the potential for a tie is more real, but the Constitution grants the vice president of the United States, as the president of the Senate, the power to break ties. When the 107th Congress convened in January 2001, the Democrats and Republicans each held 50 seats in the chamber. For 17 days the Democrats enjoyed majority party status because Vice President Al Gore, a Democrat, broke tie votes, including those on organizing the chamber. After the incoming president and vice president were inaugurated, the Republican Party became the majority party, with Vice President Dick Cheney breaking tie votes.

A bloc is different from a coalition. While party members may join different blocs, entire parties create parliamentary coalitions. Since the U.S. Congress is a two-party system, and party coalitions are rare and unnecessary, bloc and coalition are used interchangeably when referring to the American national legislative body.

A related term is faction. A faction is any subgroup within a larger organization, such as the moderate faction of the Republican Party or the conservative faction of the Democratic Party. In a faction some party members feel a loyalty to a particular leader or have an interest in a particular issue not shared by other party members. Factions become particularly important during the organization of a new Congress when party leaders and chamber officers are being selected. Observers have noticed that blocs, coalitions, and factions are likely to appear when a new political party is being formed or the current political parties are being realigned. This is the reason that the study of coalitions is a central focus of political science.

Legislative coalitions predate the U.S. Constitution. There were coalitions in almost every colonial assembly.

Coalitions have existed in Congress since the early days of the republic. One of the first coalitions formed around the Compromise of 1790. In June 1790 Thomas Jefferson brought Federalist leader Alexander Hamilton and James Madison, leader of the Republicans, together at a dinner party to reach an agreement on two pieces of legislation: one to move the capital to the Potomac River and another to have the federal government assume the states' debts. After the agreement was reached, coalition members worked together to have the legislation passed by Congress. Passage of the bill moving the capital to the Potomac in exchange for the federal government's assumption of the states' debts became known as the Compromise of 1790.

The War of 1812 was the result of the efforts of the War Hawks, a bloc led by HENRY CLAY of Kentucky and John C. Calhoun of South Carolina, to convince a reluctant President James Madison to go to war with Great Britain. The factions that had emerged in Congress affected the presidential nomination process in 1816. The congressional caucus picked James Monroe of Virginia over William H. Crawford of Georgia to replace Madison as president. The influence of the congressional caucus was reduced after the election of 1824, when presidential support was divided among John Quincy Adams, Andrew Jackson, Henry Clay, and William Crawford. The House of Representatives eventually selected Adams even though Jackson had more popular votes. The resulting controversy led to the creation of the Democratic Party with the election of Jackson to the presidency in 1828.

The debate over slavery before the Civil War led to a number of congressional coalitions and factions. Both the Democratic and Whig Parties were divided over the slavery issue into northern and southern factions. These factions often decided the selection of the SPEAKER OF THE HOUSE as members crossed party lines to vote for the leader of their regional faction. The Civil War did not mark the end of factional politics in Congress. During Reconstruction efforts to reconcile the former Confederate states were blocked by Radical Republicans such as Pennsylvania representative Thaddeus Stevens.

During periods of one-party dominance in national politics, and especially in state politics, the majority party often divides into factions. In the latter part of the 1800s, the Republican Party divided into the Stalwart and Half-Breed factions. The Stalwarts emerged from the Radical Republicans and resisted reconciliation with the former Confederate states during the administrations of Presidents Ulysses Grant and Rutherford Hayes. The Stalwarts also opposed efforts to reform the civil service. Half-Breed Republicans, such as JAMES G. BLAINE of Maine and James Garfield and JOHN SHERMAN of Ohio, were more forward looking and reformist. They supported Garfield and his efforts to reform the civil service as president. In Congress the Stalwarts were often opposed by a coalition of Half-Breeds and Democrats.

At the turn of the century the Republican Party again was split by factional strife. Factions emerged over the tariff debate and the proper role of government in managing the economy. An eastern Republican bloc emerged under the leadership of NELSON W. ALDRICH of Rhode Island. These eastern Republicans, joined by Speaker of the House JOSEPH CANNON of Illinois, worked to block Progressive legislation favored by President Theodore Roosevelt, other liberal Republicans, and Democrats. Progressive Republicans included Senators Robert La Follette of Wisconsin, WILLIAM BORAH of Idaho, and ALBERT BEVERIDGE of Indiana.

In the early 20th century both parties were divided internally by region. Republican Progressives were divided into an eastern-oriented faction that followed Theodore Roosevelt's form of liberalism and a western faction led by La Follette, Albert Cummins of Iowa, and Coe Crawford of South Carolina. The Democratic Party was divided into an eastern, urban, industrial, anti-prohibitionist and immigrant wing led by Alfred Smith of New York and a rural, southern and western, prohibitionist, nativist, and Protestant wing led by William Jennings Bryan of Nebraska.

The FARM BLOC, an example of a cross-party coalition loosely organized around a set of issues, emerged in the 1920s. It was composed of the radical agrarian factions of both parties and worked to maintain farm price supports. Members of Congress from the eastern states regularly opposed the Farm Bloc. The Farm Bloc declined after President Franklin Roosevelt's New Deal and disappeared during the administration of President Dwight Eisenhower.

The New Deal of the late 1930s created a congressional bloc arrangement that lasted at least into the 1990s. The CONSERVATIVE COALITION, a bloc of Republicans and southern Democrats, emerged as opposition to the New Deal's domestic programs. Members of the coalition were concerned about the growing influence of organized labor, a swelling federal bureaucracy, expanded welfare programs, and increasing budget deficits. Opposing the Conservative Coalition was a liberal-labor bloc consisting largely of northern Democrats. Political observers are not certain if the Conservative Coalition survived until the end of the 20th century, as more southern House and Senate seats came to be held by Republicans.

Many small but cohesive coalitions based on ideology, region, policy areas, ethnicity, and gender emerged in Congress during the latter decades of the 20th century. Some of these groupings formed more tangible organizations recognized in chamber rules as caucuses. Examples of these groups included the DEMOCRATIC STUDY GROUP, the Sunbelt Caucus, the Mushroom Caucus, the Coal Caucus, the Western State Coalition, the Pro-Life Caucus, and the Congressional Black Caucus. Other less formally structured groups included the GYPSY MOTHS (moderate and liberal Republicans from the Northeast and Midwest), and the BLUE DOG DEMOCRATS (conservative Democrats, partially the successors of the "boll weevils").

Further reading:
Brady, David W., and Charles S. Bullock, III. "Party and Factional Organization in Legislatures." *Legislative Studies Quarterly* 8, no. 4 (1983): 599–654; Collie, Melissa P. "The Rise of Coalition Politics: Voting in the U.S. House, 1933–1980." *Legislative Studies Quarterly* 13, no. 3 (1988): 321–342; Hadley, John F. *Origins of American Political Parties, 1789–1803.* Lexington: University Press of Kentucky, 1986; Hinckley, Barbara. *Coalitions & Politics.* New York: Harcourt Brace Jovanovich, 1981; Manley, John F. "The Conservative Coalition." In *Congress Reconsidered,* edited by Lawrence C. Dodd and Bruce I. Oppenheimer, New York: Praeger, 1977; Nitschke, Lori. "Political Trends Come Together to Diminish Coalition's Clout." *Congressional Quarterly Weekly Report,* 3 January 1998, pp. 21–23; Shelley, Mack C., II. *The Permanent Majority: The Conservative Coalition in the United States Congress.* University: University of Alabama Press, 1983; Sinclair, Barbara. "Coping with Uncertainty: Building Coalitions in the House and the Senate." In *The New Congress,* edited by Thomas E. Mann and Norman J. Ornstein, Washington, D.C.: American Enterprise Institute for Public Policy Research, 1981.

—John David Rausch, Jr.

Blue Dog Democrats

The Blue Dog Democrats are a coalition of fiscal conservatives in the United States HOUSE OF REPRESENTATIVES who advocate, among other things, a balanced federal budget and paying down the nation's debt. Since the group's inception in 1995, their positions on many issues have bridged the gap between the more ideologically extreme positions held by leaders of the two major parties. In their brief history they have built a reputation as significant players in the policymaking process.

The group was formed in the 104th Congress in an attempt to give a voice to conservative and moderate Democrats in the wake of significant Republican electoral success in the 1994 congressional elections. The group's colorful name is a spin-off from an earlier euphemism for party loyalists. The earlier nomenclature referred to loyal southern Democrats as yellow dogs. In 1928 Senator Tom Heflin of Alabama broke with the party and supported Herbert Hoover, a Republican, for president over Al Smith, the Democratic Party nominee. In response to Heflin's disloyalty, party members from the South chastised him by stating that they would rather vote for a yel-

low dog than a Republican. The moniker YELLOW DOG DEMOCRAT has alternatively been used over the years in a positive light to distinguish party loyalty, and negatively to denote a person who is loyal to a fault, one who fails to consult his or her conscience when determining voting behavior.

Representative Pete Geren, a Democrat from Texas, allegedly coined the label *blue* when he claimed that moderate Democrats in the House had been "choked blue" (silenced) by liberals within the party. Geren's comment and the formation of the Blue Dog alliance are best understood in the context of the 1994 elections. In the wake of significant losses the Blue Dogs attempted to assert the role of moderate Democrats. Their plan was to right the Democratic Party ship and protect electoral opportunities for coalition members. Since 1995 the coalition has grown in significance, and the group has become more than an electoral strategy intended to stop the bleeding of Democratic Party losses in the early 1990s.

In the 104th Congress the Blue Dogs played a fundamental role in brokering a deal that produced welfare reform. Since then the group has been instrumental in blocking politically popular raids on the federal budget by both Democratic and Republican lawmakers. In the 107th Congress the group helped to orchestrate passage of campaign finance reform legislation. In the 2004 presidential campaign, Blue Dogs worked to inform the public about what they perceived to be the fiscally irresponsible tax policies of the George W. Bush administration. Their argument was that tax cuts had gone too far and resulted in deficit spending, an accumulation of debt, and increased interest payments on the debt. In the context of the 2004 election, which often focused on matters of national security, the Blue Dog Democrats tried to make the point that it is not possible to be free, strong, and broke.

Since 1995 more House members have allied themselves with the coalition. Among the new members, known as Blue Pups, were candidates who were singled out for support by Blue Dog coalition leaders. In the 108th House the group had 37 members, up from 29 in 1995. The table below lists the names and state affiliation of the Blue Dog Democrats in the 108th Congress. Although the group has southern roots, it should be noted that by 2004 members were from all regions of the country.

The southern roots of the coalition could be traced to a group known as the boll weevils, which existed from the 1950s to the 1980s. Many observers believe the support of this group of conservative southern Democrats was instrumental to the passage of wide-ranging policy changes during Ronald Reagan's administration. The "boll weevil" label, however, has been rejected by Blue Dog Democrats because the earlier term was often linked to the anti–Civil Rights positions of white southern Democrats.

BLUE DOG DEMOCRATS IN THE 108TH CONGRESS

Marion Berry (AR)	Stephanie Herseth (SD)	Mike Ross (AR)
Sanford Bishop (GA)	Baron Hill (IN)	Loretta Sanchez (CA)
Leonard Boswell (IA)	Tim Holden (PA)	Max Sandlin (TX)
Allan Boyd (FL)	Steve Israel (NY)	Adam Schiff (CA)
Dennis Cardoza (CA)	Chris John (LA)	David Scott (GA)
Brad Carson (OK)	William O. Lipinski (IL)	Charlie Stenholm (TX)
Ed Case (HI)	Ken Lucas (KY)	John Tanner (TN)
Ben Chandler (KY)	Jim Matheson (UT)	Ellen Tauscher (CA)
Jim Cooper (TN)	Mike McIntyre (NC)	Gene Taylor (MS)
Bud Cramer (AL)	Mike Michaud (ME)	Mike Thompson (CA)
Lincoln Davis (TN)	Dennis Moore (KS)	Jim Turner (TX)
Harold Ford, Jr. (TN)	Collin Peterson (MN)	
Jane Harman (CA)	Earl Pomeroy (ND)	

Source: http://bluedogdemocrats.com

The SENATE in 1999 also formed a group with a fiscally conservative agenda called the New Democratic Coalition. The group, who chose a more pedestrian name, had 20 members in 2004. Some Democratic Party leaders have criticized both the Senate group and the Blue Dog Democrats in the House for ignoring the well-being of lower-class Americans. They believe the groups' conservative economic positions ignore the needs of many poorer Americans in need of government services. Others have argued the move to the right by these Democrats has cost the party the support of key constituencies.

Further reading:
Carmines, Edward G., and Michael Berkman. "Ethos, Ideology, and Partisanship: Exploring the Paradox of Conservative Democrats." *Political Behavior* 16 (1994): 203–218; Harmel, Robert, and Keith E. Hamm. "Development of a Party Role in a No-Party Legislature." *Western Political Quarterly* 39 (1986): 79–92; Blue Dog Democrat Web site. Available online. URL: www.bluedogdemocrats.com. Accessed January 16, 2006.

—Scot D. Schraufnagel

blue ribbon commissions

The origins of the blue ribbon commission may be traced to a time when it was the practice of Congress to refer matters of particular importance to select committees. It was the short legislative session and the lack of technical skill that largely prompted the creation of the special committee or commission. By the 19th century blue ribbon commissions were usually composed of legislators of one or both houses of Congress (sometimes supplemented by nonmembers especially qualified for the delegated task) and were commonly employed in investigating some topic that was about to be the subject of legislative action. A notable example was the Armstrong Insurance Commission of New York that Congress created in 1905 to look into the life insurance business of that state. The commission's findings startled the nation with their revelations of neglect of duty on the part of the responsible insurance officials and prompted Congress to institute important reform legislation.

Blue ribbon commissions are formal groups established by statute. They have a varying number of members, with each commissioner sharing equally the responsibility for findings and recommendations. Most are "sunsetted," limited to a time frame to complete work, usually one to two years from the time of creation to the final report to Congress. In some cases, however, Congress may propose a blue ribbon commission to extend over several years. The Commission on a North American Economic Alliance, a precursor to the North American Free Trade Agreement, for example, was designed in 1979 to study the development and utilization of the resources of the United States, Mexico, and Canada, submitting annual reports to Congress until its termination in 1985.

Generally speaking, a commission's mandate includes a termination date often no more than three years after the date of creation or at a specified date upon submission of its recommendations or alternatives, which is anywhere from 30 to 90 days after its final report to Congress. Commissions come in various sizes and shapes, with membership ranging from nine to 20 commissioners, with 12 to 15 being the normal number of members. The final number of commissioners will generally accommodate equal appointments by the majority and minority in both the House and the Senate as well as by the president. Congress determines the mandate of a blue ribbon commission, then determines the extent of resources, time, money, and staff that it is willing to make available for the commission, and then provides for the selection of the commission members. A clear statement of scope in the enacting legislation guides commissioners and staff as to what they should accomplish.

Whether established by a freestanding bill or attached as an amendment, blue ribbon commissions are often authorized to use appropriated sums, such as for pay and travel expenses for commission members and staff to carry out their duties; Congress usually provides that upon the request of the director or chair. Commissions may also enlist the temporary or intermittent services of experts and consultants on a reimbursable basis, and any personnel of an executive department or agency on a reimbursable basis. The General Service Administration (GSA) frequently provides resources ranging from office space to advice on staff and the services of trained administrators who manage payrolls.

There are exceptions, however, as with the absence of congressional funding for the E-Commerce Commission. In 1998 Congress passed the Internet Tax Freedom Act (ITFA), which imposed a three-year moratorium on new Internet taxation. As part of the act, Congress established the Advisory Commission on Electronic Commerce to address issues related to Internet taxation. The blue ribbon commission conducted a thorough study of federal, state, local, and international taxation and tariff treatment of transactions using the Internet. This commission was unique in that Congress did not appropriate any funding but gave the commission gift authority. As a result, at its first meeting the commission approved a funding strategy that called for initial funding from the state of Virginia and the six corporate members of the commission. The initial funding provided by Virginia and the corporate members was eventually reimbursed as the commission closed its books.

Most blue ribbon commissions have a three-tier organizational structure, which consists of commission members who serve for the life of the commission, an executive director, who is usually chosen by the commission chair and confirmed by the commission, and research staff. Many also have a bipartisan membership. Specific provisions within the creating legislation often concern the number and joint appointment of members by the president, the Speaker of the House, the president pro tempore of the Senate, and/or the Majority and Minority Leaders of the House and Senate. According to one study, of the 562 total commissioners proposed to be appointed in legislation creating blue ribbon commissions between the 103rd (1993–94) and 105th (1997–98) Congresses, 27 percent were appointed by the president, 47 percent were congressionally appointed, and 26 percent were appointed by other sources, such as executive department and agency administrators, subnational governments, and the courts.

Because blue ribbon commissions vary widely in origin, authority, composition, and purpose, no standard method of submitting reports has emerged. Ordinarily, a commission has a policy formulation responsibility limited to a specific issue or to a group of related questions. But because these entities are largely advisory and rarely have power to implement their findings or recommendations, they are infrequently mandated with administrative authority, except for the powers conferred on them to assist them in collecting and gathering information. In many instances blue ribbon commissions hold hearings and request written submissions from interested persons and organizations, secure information from federal departments and agencies, conclude with the publication of a report, and close down.

Further reading:
Beard, Charles A. "Commissions in American Government." In Andrew C. McLaughlin and Albert Bushnell Hart, eds. *Cyclopedia of American Government*. Vol. 1. Gloucester: Peter Smith, 1963; Campbell, Colton C. *Discharging Congress: Government by Commission*. Westport, Conn.: Praeger Publishers, 2002; Wolanin, Thomas R. *Presidential Advisory Commissions: Truman to Nixon*. Madison: University of Wisconsin Press, 1975.

—Colton C. Campbell

blue-slip procedure

The blue-slip procedure, or the idea of senatorial courtesy, pertains to the advice and consent role played by the Senate in regard to filling seats on the lower federal court bench, which includes nominees to both district-level courts and also to the federal circuit court of appeals. The procedure begins when the counsel for the SENATE JUDICIARY COMMITTEE sends out blue-colored slips of paper to the two senators from the state in which the federal district court resides for appointees to the district court bench. However, since appellate court circuits cover several states, the blue slips usually go to all senators in the circuit involved, or sometimes just to those whose state claims the actual slot that the nominee would fill upon appointment.

If either of the blue slips is returned marked with an "objection" by either senator, regardless of party, the Judiciary Committee traditionally declines to schedule a hearing on the nomination. In addition, at certain times during the history of Congress, if even one of the senators withholds a blue slip, the head of the Judiciary Committee would decline to schedule a hearing on the nomination. Without hearings scheduled on a nomination, the nomination is successfully killed in the committee, since the Senate does not even have the opportunity to vote on it. Although the use of blue slips used to be anonymous, both parties have now agreed to disclose the names of senators using them. If all blue slips given to senators regarding a particular nomination are marked "no objection," then the committee counsel, with the consent of the chair of the Judiciary Committee, places notice in the *CONGRESSIONAL*

RECORD, which schedules a hearing on the nomination not more than seven days later.

Although Congress has used this procedure during the majority of its history, the procedure can change depending on the chair of the Judiciary Committee. Thus, the importance of blue slips and how easily they can be used to kill a nomination within committee varies with the changing chairs of the Judiciary Committee. For example, when Edward Kennedy became chair in 1979 he changed the procedure so that withholding a blue slip would not always kill the candidacy of a judicial nominee, but instead the nomination would be considered by all members of the Judiciary Committee to decide on a suitable course of action. Kennedy also made it so that even blue slips returned marked as objectionable would be discussed by the full committee, reserving their right to hold hearings on a nominee even in the face of an objectionable blue slip. This change obviously gave the Judiciary Committee more leeway to deal with obstructionist senators.

During the presidency of Bill Clinton, the chair of the Judiciary Committee, Orrin G. Hatch, a Republican from Utah, refused to schedule hearings unless both senators returned favorable blue slips. In fact, Clinton's nominations were commonly killed in committee because of blue slipping by Republican senators. However, the tide changed in 2001, when George W. Bush took office and Hatch made a proposal to drop the requirement of a favorable return of one blue slip, instead of two, in order to shorten the time from nomination until confirmation, thus making it easier for the Republican majority to push the new Republican president's nominees through the confirmation process. But when Democrats took narrow control of the Senate, Patrick J. Leahy, a Democrat from Vermont, became chair of the Judiciary Committee. Leahy reinstated the policy of the withholding of even one blue slip being enough to kill a nomination.

Further reading:
Binder, Sarah A., and Forrest Maltzman. "Senatorial Delay in Confirming Federal Judges, 1947–1998." *American Journal of Political Science,* 46 no. 1 (2002): 190–199; Davidson, Roger H., and Walter J. Oleszek. *Congress and Its Members.* 8th ed. Washington, D.C.: Congressional Quarterly Press, 2002; Goldman, Sheldon. *Picking Federal Judges: Lower Court Selection from Roosevelt through Reagan.* New Haven, Conn.: Yale University Press, 1997;

—Lisa A. Solowiej

Boehner, John A. (1949–) *representative, Majority Leader*

A native of southwestern Ohio, John Boehner served six years in the Ohio house of representatives before winning election to Congress in 1990. An eager member of the Republican "revolution" of 1994, he won a party leadership post in 1995 when he was selected chair of the Republican conference. However, Boehner soon was cast into political exile after he was identified as having participated in a failed Republican effort to oust Newt Gingrich from the Speakership. But with the subsequent demise of Gingrich, Boehner slowly worked his way back into the party's power circle. In 2001 he became chair of the House Education and Workforce Committee, a position he used to cultivate the support of lobbyists and campaign contributors. His crucial role in winning passage of President George W. Bush's "No Child Left Behind" bill underscored his growing legislative skills.

The son of a restaurant and tavern owner, Boehner became wealthy as the president of a plastics packaging business, Nucite Sales Inc. Upon his arrival in Washington he quickly developed a reputation as an excellent golfer, despite an unorthodox swing, and for hosting lavish corporate-financed parties in the American Legion Hall on Capitol Hill.

In January 2006, following the demise of Tom Delay, Boehner won a close Republican Caucus election to become House Majority Leader. He defeated Roy Blunt of Missouri on the second ballot, 122-109. On the first ballot Boehner attracted only 79 votes to 110 for Blunt, 40 for John Shadegg of Arizona, and two for Jim Ryun of Kansas. During the second ballot runoff contest Boehner received the bulk of support from the two eliminated candidates. Blunt, the party's whip under DeLay, was a protégé of and closely identified publicly with the controversial former Majority Leader. On the other hand, Boehner undoubtedly profited from an image as a party leader relatively untainted by the DeLay controversy.

Boehner, with numerous close ties to lobbyists himself, promised to support relatively modest lobbying reform efforts while continuing to work hard at raising funds to finance the party's reelection efforts the following fall.

Boland amendments

Boland amendments refer to a series of amendments sponsored by Representative Edward Patrick Boland, a Democrat from Massachusetts, intended to limit the type and scope of assistance that the U.S. government could provide to the contra rebels in Nicaragua. Boland served in the House from 1953 to 1989 and chaired the HOUSE INTELLIGENCE COMMITTEE.

The Central American country of Nicaragua was ruled for 43 years by members of the Somoza family. They were widely regarded as corrupt, authoritarian dictators. Following a bloody and costly civil war, President Anastasio Somoza Debayle, the youngest son of President Anastasio

Somoza García, who had ruled nearly continuously from 1937 to 1956, fled the country on July 17, 1979, as rebels, known as the Sandinistas, threatened to capture the capital. The Sandinistas reflected a range of opposition views within Nicaragua and instituted reforms that brought relief to a large segment of the population. In order to attract international assistance, the Sandinistas promised to create a liberal democracy, yet the Sandinista party organization gradually assumed the functions of government, seizing control of the television and radio stations and censoring newspapers. On September 19, 1980, the Sandinista government announced that it would not hold national elections until 1985.

Initially, the United States supported the new regime, with President Jimmy Carter providing $39 million in food assistance. But there was suspicion that the Sandinistas harbored a communist philosophy, and as intelligence determined that the new regime was establishing close relations with the Soviet Union and assisting Marxist rebels in nearby El Salvador, the administration of President Ronald Reagan withdrew American aid. Within Nicaragua opposition to the Sandinistas developed under a loose coalition known as the contras. The contras comprised three groups: former National Guardsmen and right-wing figures who had fought for Somoza and against the revolution; anti-Somocistas who had supported the revolution but felt betrayed by the Sandinista government; and Nicaraguans who had avoided direct involvement in the revolution but opposed the Sandinistas' increasingly antidemocratic regime. As the Sandinista administration became more openly Marxist, the Reagan administration moved to assist secretly those anti-Sandinista guerrillas operating from Honduras, known as the Nicaraguan Democratic Force, with funds and weapons.

While members of Congress heard rumors of secret American aid to the contras, Congress was officially informed of this assistance through its intelligence committees in December 1981. Immediately, bipartisan reservations were heard, and Boland wrote to CIA director William J. Casey to express his committee's concerns about the number of rebels funded and the ability of the Americans to direct their tactics. Efforts by Casey in early 1982 to convince the intelligence committees of the limited nature of American aid were undermined as reports from Central America strongly suggested that the contras numbered more than 10,000.

During House Intelligence Committee discussions in April 1982, liberal Democrats attempted but failed to cut off all aid to the contras. A compromise measure was adopted that prohibited covert American actions to overthrow the Sandinista regime or provoke a military exchange between Nicaragua and Honduras. It also stipulated that any aid be used only to cut off arms shipments from Nicaragua to the Marxist rebels in El Salvador. This same language was incorporated in the classified sections of the fiscal year (FY) 1983 intelligence authorization bill (PL 97-269), which finally cleared Congress in September 1983.

During public debate of the FY 1983 defense appropriation bill, Representative Tom Harkin, a Democrat from Iowa, led a small group of liberal Democrats in a futile attempt to attach an amendment that would have banned any military aid to the contras. When the effort failed, Boland offered an amendment prohibiting Americans from providing military aid to Nicaraguan rebels and from provoking a military exchange between Nicaragua and Honduras. Boland's amendment passed 411-0 and cleared the Congress as part of the FY 1983 continuing appropriations resolution (PL 97-377) on December 20. It was signed by the president on December 21, 1983. The conditions of the amendment expired on September 30, the end of the fiscal 1983 year.

With the secret aid to the contras now revealed, press coverage of the civil war in Nicaragua intensified. Extensive reporting in *Time,* the *New York Times,* and the *Washington Post* strongly suggested that the Central Intelligence Agency's assistance benefited former leaders of the Somoza regime (a faction not popular with many Democrats) and that the scope of the aid had moved beyond intercepting arms shipments to El Salvador.

In an address before the House in April, Boland said that "one with any sense, any legal sense, would have to come to the conclusion that the operation is illegal, that the purpose and mission of the operation was to overthrow the government in Nicaragua." Boland moved to insert a ban on further aid to the contras in a bill before the House Intelligence Committee on May 3, which also permitted $80 million to be spent openly to assist allies in Central America interested in interdicting weapons flowing to guerrillas. Clement J. Zablocki, a Democrat from Wisconsin and chair of the House Foreign Affairs Committee, steered a vote to support the language through his committee on June 7, but not without a struggle. Representative Gerry E. Studds, a liberal Democrat from Massachusetts, demanded stronger language banning aid, while Lee H. Hamilton, a moderate Democrat from Indiana, supported Boland. The House passed Boland's measure by a vote of 228–194 along nearly party lines on July 28, but when the SENATE INTELLIGENCE COMMITTEE failed to consider Boland's proposal, it died. Not to be thwarted, the House incorporated similar language into the FY 1984 intelligence authorization bill. The Republican-controlled Senate again rejected the ban, and instead, by voice vote, approved approximately $28 million in contra aid.

The logjam was broken when Boland negotiated a compromise during the conference committee meetings for the FY 1984 defense appropriations bill. His amendment read:

> During fiscal year 1984, not more than $24 million of the funds available to Central Intelligence Agency, the Department of Defense or any other agency or entity of the United States involved in intelligence activities may be obligated or expended for the purpose, or which would have the effect, of supporting, directly or indirectly, military or paramilitary operations in Nicaragua by any nation, group, organization, government or individual.

The same language was also included in the intelligence authorization bill. Both bills cleared the Congress on November 18 and were signed by the president a few weeks later.

Though the Reagan administration preferred an aid package of between $35 and $50 million, Republicans, such as Representative C. W. "Bill" Young from Florida, praised the compromise. For his part, Boland explained that the language was the best deal he could get under the circumstances. As with the first Boland amendment, the second amendment expired at the end of the fiscal year—September 30, 1984.

During spring 1984 news broke revealing that the CIA had assisted the contras in mining several Nicaraguan harbors. The timing could not have been worse for the Reagan administration, as it was asking Congress for $24 million in additional aid to the rebels. Most members of Congress were shocked, particularly leaders of the intelligence committees, Boland and Senator Barry Goldwater, a Republican from Arizona, who were furious that they had not been informed in advance of the mining. Despite this setback, Reagan pushed hard to have a supplemental appropriation for the contras approved, sending a letter to the Senate in which he wrote that the United States

> does not seek to destabilize or overthrow the government of Nicaragua; nor to impose or compel any particular form of government there.

The more conservative Senate complied and passed a $21 million package, but the House rejected the language in its supplemental bill, 241-177, on May 24.

The intensely partisan battle between the two chambers over the aid continued through the summer and into the fall, with the Senate including contra aid in various bills and the House deleting or rejecting the measures. Finally, under pressure to pass a continuing resolution to keep the government in operation, and with Reagan and his staff lobbying wayward Republicans and vulnerable Democrats in both chambers, a complicated deal was struck in conference committee on October 10. Boland's amendment was an important component of the agreement. It banned any U.S. government agency from spending money "for the purpose of or which would have the effect of supporting, directly or indirectly, military or paramilitary operations in Nicaragua by any nation, group, organization or individual."

Additional elements of the deal would cause the ban to end if, after February 28, 1985, the president sent a report to Congress that demonstrated that the Nicaraguan government was supporting guerrillas in El Salvador or other countries in the region, analyzed the military significance of that support, justified the amount and type of aid sought for the contras, and clearly explained the goals of U.S. foreign policy in Central America. Congress would have had to vote to approve the report using special, expedited procedures described in the agreement. Finally, a $14 million limit was placed on funding for military operations in Nicaragua, but this needed approval by joint resolution.

Over the next few years Boland continued to offer language similar to his previous amendments to a variety of bills in an effort to limit aid to the contras. In 1985 Boland worked to limit contra assistance to $27 million for "humanitarian" purposes and directed that funds be controlled by the State Department. President Reagan established the Nicaraguan Humanitarian Assistance Office (NHAO) within State to oversee the money, but as was later discovered during the IRAN-CONTRA INVESTIGATION, NHAO became part of the system of funneling military assistance to the contras. Subsequent attempts to limit the scope of the contra aid to nonmilitary functions were not as successful, but Boland managed to limit the amount of contra military assistance to $100 million.

The Boland amendments highlight the role that Congress may play in developing and implementing foreign policy. Presidents claim to have near-absolute authority over foreign policy, but the Constitution clearly gives Congress the power of the purse, which it can use to check presidents who do not seek the counsel of the legislature.

Further reading:
Report of the Congressional Committees Investigating the Iran-Contra Affair, With the Minority View. New York: Times Books, 1988; *Congressional Quarterly Almanacs, 1982, 1983, 1984, 1985.* Washington, D.C.: Congressional Quarterly Press; Fisher, Louis. "How Tightly Can Congress Draw the Purse Strings?" *The American Journal of International Law* 83 (1998): 758–771; Hicks, D. Bruce. "Presidential Foreign Policy Prerogative after the Iran-Contra Affair: A Review Essay." *Presidential Studies Quarterly* 26 (1996): 962–977.

—Thomas J. Baldino

Bolling, Richard Walker (1916–1991)

Representative, House Rules Committee Chair

Representative Richard Bolling, a Democrat from Missouri, served in the U.S. House from January 3, 1949, to January 3, 1983. He was elected from the Fifth District of Missouri, which included the heart of Kansas City, wealthy suburbs along with impoverished inner-city neighborhoods, the central city, as well as most of the industrial area, by the Missouri River.

Bolling is well noted for his leadership of reform efforts in the House, particularly those culminating in the reforms to the committee system in the early 1970s. He chaired the Select Committee on Committees in the 93rd Congress (1974–75), which proposed a reform plan that would reorganize committees, realign jurisdictions, reduce the number of committees, and restrict the absolute power of the baronial chairs. Not surprisingly, most of the procedural reforms proposed were defeated on the floor. The attempt to streamline the budgeting process, bringing fiscal responsibility to the separate appropriation and revenue decisions, did move forward with creation of the HOUSE BUDGET COMMITTEE. Representative Bolling became a protégé of Speaker SAM RAYBURN of Texas, receiving an assignment to the HOUSE RULES COMMITTEE in 1955. Bolling assumed the chairmanship of Rules for the 96th and 97th Congresses (1979–83). While he was known as a traditional economic Democrat by voting record, favoring a strong military and a strong labor movement, his liberal tendency was expressed in the desire for a responsive House, not necessarily for the social upheaval associated with his junior liberal colleagues elected in the 1960s and 1970s. Bolling favored procedural reforms that would block the hold of chairs born in the 19th century, who formed the leadership of the House during the 1950s and 1960s. He was a founder of the Americans for Democratic Action prior to being elected to Congress. Later in the House, he was among the founding members of the DEMOCRATIC STUDY GROUP in 1954, noted by the 1960s for its strategy sessions and ability to communicate important ideas in order to mobilize the Democratic liberal rank and file. Frustrated with the committee tactics blocking civil rights reform and other liberal policies from leaving Rules, Bolling, along with Frank Thompson of New Jersey, worked with Speaker Rayburn to expand the Rules Committee in 1961 from 12 to 15 members, thereby breaking the reactionary obstructionism of Chairman Howard V. Smith of Virginia.

Bolling was frustrated by the weakness in congressional leadership in the subsequent Speakership. This frustration led to his well-known congressional critique, *House Out of Order.* Representative Bolling remained committed to the institution, competing for leadership posts throughout his career even while publishing biting critiques. He was passed over for the WHIP position by Speaker JOHN MCCORMACK of Massachusetts and MAJORITY LEADER CARL ALBERT of Oklahoma when Hale Boggs of Louisiana was selected in 1962. During the second ballot for the Majority Leader post in 1976, he was narrowly defeated by JAMES WRIGHT of Texas, who went on to become Majority Leader and briefly Speaker before being forced to resign in 1989.

Born in New York City May 17, 1916, to his namesake, a prominent surgeon from Huntsville, Alabama, and a Vassar-educated mother, Florence Easton Bolling, Representative Bolling was educated at home, in private school, and at Phillips Exeter Academy. Upon his father's death when he was 15, he returned home to Hunstville, Alabama. He received a bachelor's (1937) and master's degree (1939) from University of the South, Sewanee, Tennessee. He taught at Sewanee Military Academy in 1938 and 1939 and at Florence State Teachers College in Alabama, working with the rural poor. Bolling attended graduate school at Vanderbilt University from 1939 to 1940 but interrupted his doctoral studies to enlist in the army as a private in April 1941. He served four year in Australia, New Guinea, and the Philippines and in Japan as assistant to the chief of staff to General MacArthur. He was awarded the Legion of Merit and Bronze Star. He was discharged a lieutenant colonel in July 1946. He took up residence in Kansas City after the war, joining his wife and accepting a position as director of student activities and veterans affairs at the University of Kansas City. Bolling was related to two members of Congress from Alabama, a great-great grandfather, John Williams Walker, and a great-great uncle, Percy Walker. Representative Bolling resided in Maryland until his death on April 21, 1991.

Further reading:
Bolling, Richard. *House Out of Order.* New York: Dutton, 1965; Bolling, Richard, *Power in the House: A History of the Leadership of the House of Representatives.* New York: Capricorn Books, 1974; Rieselbach, Leroy N. *Congressional Reform.* Washington, D.C.: Congressional Quarterly Press, 1986; *Oral History Interview Transcripts.* Truman Presidential Museum & Library. Available online. URL: www.trumanlibrary.org/oralhist/bolling.htm#oh2. Accessed January 16, 2006.

—Karen M. McCurdy

Borah, William E. (1865–1940) *Senator*

William Borah was a U.S. senator from Idaho, a western populist, and a leader of the Progressive wing of the Republican Party noted for his independent voting behavior in the Senate. Borah was born in Fairfield, Illinois, on June 29, 1865. An avid reader but indifferent student, he did not finish high school. Resisting his father's wishes that he join the ministry, Borah tried to sign up with a company of Shakespearean actors to play Mark Antony. His acting career was blocked by his father. In 1885 Borah moved to Kansas at the invitation of an older sister. He enrolled in the University of Kansas, but lack of financial resources and poor health forced him to drop out in 1887. He read the law in a local law office and later in 1887 was admitted to the bar in Kansas. After practicing law with his brother-in-law for three years, the young lawyer headed west. Although Borah's goal was Seattle, he stopped in Boise, Idaho, when his money ran out.

Borah enjoyed life in the rough frontier town of Boise. He quickly developed a reputation as a flamboyant criminal attorney. As a state prosecutor, he participated in a number of sensational criminal trials in the state. He also entered politics. In 1892 he was named chairman of the Republican State Central Committee. He served as secretary to Idaho governor William J. O'Connell and married the governor's daughter Mary in 1895.

William Edgar Borah, Idaho senator (left) and Hiram Warren Johnson, California senator *(Library of Congress)*

In 1896 he joined fellow "Silver Republicans" in leaving the party to support the Democratic presidential candidate William Jennings Bryan. Borah also campaigned unsuccessfully for a seat in the U.S. House of Representatives. He ran for the Senate in 1902 as a Republican. Despite being the most popular candidate, his candidacy was blocked by party regulars who remembered his defection in 1896.

Borah received national attention in 1906 as the prosecuting attorney in a murder trial involving the alleged attempt of William Haywood and other radical labor leaders to contract for the killing of the former governor of Idaho, Frank Steunenberg. Clarence Darrow represented the defendants. Borah's prosecution was unsuccessful, and before the end of the trial he was indicted for his participation in a number of fraudulent timber deals. He was acquitted. In 1907, with a majority of the Idaho legislature pledged to his candidacy, Borah was elected to the U.S. Senate.

In the Senate Borah considered himself a Progressive Republican but did not always vote with other Progressives. He voted against legislation that would curb the power of special interests, a key part of the Progressives' program, because he feared that it increased the power of the federal government. His proclivity to protest without taking action earned Borah a reputation for futility. He claimed some responsibility for the creation of the Department of Labor and the Seventeenth Amendment providing for the direct election of senators. Sensing a conspiracy, Borah opposed an American protectorate over Nicaragua because he believed it was a scheme of international bankers to reap significant profits.

The senator supported the Constitution while interpreting it to serve his purposes. He was a staunch supporter of civil liberties, especially during World War I and the Red Scare in the 1920s. He did not show as much enthusiasm for civil rights, allowing the states to establish laws regarding southern blacks' right to vote and women's suffrage. Borah, a lifelong teetotaler, also believed that the states were not allowed to interpret Prohibition.

A nationalist, he supported President Woodrow Wilson's interventions in Mexico in 1914 and 1916. He also voted in favor of war against Germany in 1917, stating that the war was good for national interests and not because of Wilson's crusade for world democracy. Borah was one of the 16 IRRECONCILABLES in the Senate who opposed U.S. membership in the League of Nations. Their inability to compromise with Wilson kept the country out of the new international organization.

Borah became chairman of the SENATE FOREIGN RELATIONS COMMITTEE in 1924. He was a leader in the Outlawry of War movement and helped enact the Kellogg-Briand Peace Pact in 1928. Despite his involvement in this movement, he was not an internationalist. He used the peace movement largely as a political device to keep the United States out of entangling alliances. Despite his inconsistent views on foreign policy, Washington observers recognized the senator's influence in foreign affairs when they said that "Secretary of State Frank B. Kellogg made foreign policy by ringing Borah's doorbell."

The senator was inconsistent in his foreign policy positions. The Washington Conference of 1921–22 resulted in part from a Senate resolution Borah introduced in 1920. By the time the conference completed its work, he was convinced that President Warren G. Harding and Secretary of State Charles Evans Hughes were trying to lead the United States into the League of Nations through the backdoor, and he voted against many of the conference's proposals.

After World War I Borah emerged as a leader in the Progressive movement. His ability to work with the press provided him a national following. Many of these followers became disillusioned with him because of his inability to develop a coherent program. In 1928 he endorsed the Republican presidential candidate Herbert Hoover. This endorsement upset many Borah supporters. The *Nation* called him "the sorriest figure in this campaign" and stated that he could "no longer be carried on the roster of independents and Progressives." Interestingly, Borah had attacked Hoover's work as Food Administrator after World War I. The senator subsequently was frequently critical of the Hoover administration's inability to solve the problems posed by the Great Depression.

Throughout his political career Borah was regularly mentioned as a candidate for national office. In 1924 President Calvin Coolidge summoned the Idahoan to the White House to offer him a place on the ticket as the Republican nominee for vice president. Borah declined the invitation. He played no role in the 1932 campaign and endorsed neither Hoover nor the Democratic nominee, Franklin D. Roosevelt. He spent the campaign making speeches that attracted national attention. In one speech Borah denounced as dishonest the American dollar based on gold, calling for a return to silver. He also proposed a 50 percent reduction in armaments worldwide. In 1936 he made a bid for the presidency, picking up delegates in a few western primaries. His candidacy had little support at the convention, however, and he withdrew from the race.

Borah lost influence after Roosevelt was elected president in 1932. As the Great Depression deepened, the senator came to realize that solutions to the economic situation would have to come from government intervention. He supported most New Deal proposals that provided work, direct relief, and aid to farmers. He opposed any proposal to benefit financial and industrial interests. As the New Deal began to succeed, Borah became a check on the activities of the Roosevelt administration. In 1937 he used his position on the Senate Judiciary Committee to help defeat Roosevelt's COURT PACK-

ING scheme. When Senator Hugo Black, a Democrat from Alabama, was nominated for a seat on the U.S. Supreme Court in 1937, Borah's office was flooded with telegrams stating that Black was a member of the Ku Klux Klan. Despite appearing to support Black by indicating that not one shred of evidence existed to prove Black's membership in the KKK, Borah voted against confirming the Alabama senator. In foreign policy Borah supported the administration's "Good Neighbor" policy toward Latin America. He also applauded American recognition of the Soviet Union.

With the outbreak of World War II in Europe in the 1930s, the senator argued for strict neutrality. He feared that Roosevelt was working the United States into an alliance with Great Britain and France. He was able to block Roosevelt's 1939 plan to amend the neutrality laws to permit the sale of arms. The amendments passed over Borah's objections after Germany invaded Poland.

Despite Borah's support of civil liberties, he became a lightning rod of controversy for his objection to an anti-lynching bill introduced by Senator Robert F. Wagner, a Democrat from New York. He argued that the measure was unconstitutional because it infringed upon states' rights. Borah supported the southern senators in their filibuster to defeat the bill. The Idahoan was a vocal opponent of any attempt to invoke cloture in the Senate. He believed that prolonged debate could kill a bad piece of legislation, saving taxpayers millions of dollars.

For all his years as a senator, he often appeared uncomfortable with the lavishness of his surroundings. Borah seldom dined out. He was not a careful dresser, a regular subject of complaint by Mrs. Borah. She objected to his wearing old, worn-out hats and unpressed baggy pants. "Why only today," he once said to his wife, "I was complimented by a Senator on being the best dressed man in the Senate." "Yes, and I know who that Senator was; it was Senator [Thomas] Gore," replied Mrs. Borah, referring to the Democratic senator from Oklahoma who was blind. Borah died on January 19, 1940, in Washington, D.C.

Further reading:
Ashby, LeRoy. *The Spearless Leader: Senator Borah and the Progressive Movement in the 1920's.* Urbana: University of Illinois Press, 1972; Maddox, Robert James. *William E. Borah and American Foreign Policy.* Baton Rouge: Louisiana State University Press, 1969; McKenna, Marian C. *Borah.* Ann Arbor: University of Michigan Press, 1961.
—John David Rausch, Jr.

Bork, Robert, Supreme Court nomination of
The unsuccessful nomination of Robert Bork to become a justice on the U.S. Supreme Court was marked by strong conflict over ideology and disagreements over the proper

role of the courts in American society. On June 26, 1987, Supreme Court Associate Justice Lewis Powell announced that he was retiring from the Court. The announcement was a surprise because many court observers believed that he should have retired earlier. At 78 years of age, Powell had been in and out of hospitals for several years. Upon receiving Powell's announcement, President Ronald Reagan asked the Department of Justice to compile a complete list of potential nominees to the Court. Reagan specifically asked that Judge Robert Bork be included on the list, since Bork had been a candidate for an earlier vacancy but had lost narrowly when Antonin Scalia was nominated.

White House Chief of Staff Howard Baker showed the list to Senate MAJORITY LEADER Robert Byrd, a Democrat from West Virginia, and JUDICIARY COMMITTEE Chairman Joseph Biden, a Democrat from Delaware. Biden reportedly told Baker that a Bork nomination might run into problems. Despite the potential for problems, the White House nominated Bork. Bork had served as solicitor general in the administration of President Richard Nixon. During the Watergate scandal in the Nixon administration, Bork had become famous as the person who fired Special Prosecutor Archibald Cox after the attorney general and deputy attorney resigned after refusing to fire Cox. The event became known as the "Saturday Night Massacre." After leaving the solicitor general's office in January 1977, Bork was at the American Enterprise Institute briefly before becoming a professor at Yale Law School. President Ronald Reagan nominated Bork to a seat on the U.S. Court of Appeals for the District of Columbia circuit in December 1981, and he was confirmed by the Senate in February 1982. On July 1, 1987, President Reagan nominated Bork to the Supreme Court.

Bork's nomination attracted the attention of liberal and conservative groups. Many liberal groups feared that he would tilt the Court in a more conservative direction. Women's groups thought Bork would vote to overturn *Roe v. Wade*, recriminalizing abortion. Civil rights groups believed he would overturn affirmative action programs for minorities. Civil libertarians were worried that Bork would read free speech guarantees too narrowly and that he would reduce the wall of separation between church and state. Conservative groups saw the nomination as the culmination of the Reagan revolution, reducing the power of the federal government and returning the nation to a more moral direction.

The Democratic Party was the majority party in the U.S. SENATE. Their initial strategy was to delay confirmation hearings to allow Bork's opponents time to build their case against him. Reagan called on Senate Democrats to schedule confirmation hearings as soon as possible. On July 7, 1987, Senate MINORITY LEADER Robert Dole, a Republican from Kansas, and Senator Strom Thurmond,

a Republican from South Carolina, the ranking Republican on the Judiciary Committee, took the Senate floor to urge Democrats to complete the confirmation process before the start of the Supreme Court session in October. The next day Biden announced that the Judiciary Committee would begin hearings on September 15 and that the hearings would take at least two weeks. Minority Leader Dole objected, but he was unable to convince Biden to move the hearings up. Biden also refused to specify the date that the nomination would be ready for a vote by the full Senate. Senator Dole went further in late July by suggesting that the president could appoint Bork to the Court through a recess appointment when the Senate was not in session.

Liberal groups were able to organize their opposition quickly and discussed their strategy even before President Reagan made Bork's nomination official. A week after the announcement three Democratic senators, Howard Metzenbaum of Ohio, Edward Kennedy of Massachusetts, and Biden, all members of the Judiciary Committee, met to discuss strategy. Senator Kennedy became the point man in the effort to mobilize public opinion against Judge Bork. The senators agreed to hold the hearings after the August recess in order to solidify the opposition's position. Kennedy's work resulted in the opposition being able to counter Bork's testimony during the confirmation hearings. Whenever Bork's testimony appeared to be different from positions he had previously taken on issues such as free speech and gender discrimination, position papers were brought out overnight by the American Civil Liberties Union (ACLU), the National Abortion Rights Action League (NARAL), and the Leadership Conference on Civil Rights. They described how "the new Bork" contradicted "the old Bork," thereby raising concerns about whether Bork's testimony could be trusted. The position papers were widely discussed in the mass media.

While the liberal groups opposing Bork's nomination used the time between Reagan's announcement and the confirmation hearings to build a strong case, the conservative groups supporting Bork seemed to lose momentum. In fact, several observers noted that it appeared as though Bork were left to defend himself. He spent hours talking individually with uncommitted members of the Senate Judiciary Committee. One of the senators Bork targeted was Senator Arlen Specter of Pennsylvania, a moderate Republican on the Judiciary Committee. The White House also played a limited role, upsetting some conservative activists who had hoped the president would use significant political capital to see that Judge Bork was seated on the Supreme Court. Reagan took his usual month-long vacation in August and was out of Washington during the time Bork supporters needed the president to contact uncommitted senators.

On September 15, 1987, Judge Bork appeared before the Senate Judiciary Committee for the first of five days of testimony. It was the longest confirmation hearing for any Supreme Court nominee since the committee began holding hearings in 1939. During his testimony Bork worked to portray himself as a moderate, easing some of his more controversial opinions. For example, in 1971 he had written that the constitutional protection of free speech applied only to political speech. During the hearing he argued that the First Amendment applied to news, opinion, and literature. The changes in Bork's opinions upset many of his supporters and angered his opponents. Uncommitted senators were left wondering who was the real Judge Bork.

At the beginning of the hearings before the 14 members of the Judiciary Committee, Senators Biden, Kennedy, Metzenbaum, and Paul Simon, a Democrat from Illinois, were opposed to Bork. Senators Thurmond and Orrin Hatch, a Republican from Utah, were the Judge's most ardent supporters. The uncommitted senators included Howell Heflin, a Democrat from Alabama, and Dennis DeConcini, a Democrat from Arizona, as well as the Republican Specter. After a second week of hearing testimony from witnesses from both sides of the nomination, Senators Heflin, DeConcini, and Specter joined the opponents' camp. On October 6 the Judiciary Committee voted 9-5 against confirming Bork. Most of Bork's supporters believed that he would withdraw from the process and were surprised that he continued the fight. On October 23 the full Senate voted 58-42 against his confirmation to the Supreme Court.

After Bork's nomination failed, President Reagan had to make two more nominations before the vacancy was filled. Conservative Judge Douglas Ginsburg withdrew from the confirmation process after nine days when he admitted having smoked marijuana in the 1970s. Judge Anthony Kennedy, Reagan's third choice, was confirmed by the Senate with little opposition.

William Safire's *Political Dictionary* added a new word, a verb, to bork, to describe what happened to Judge Bork: to attack viciously a candidate or appointee, especially by misrepresentations in the media. Judge Bork resigned from the federal court of appeals in February 1988.

Further reading:
Bork, Robert H. *The Tempting of America: The Political Seduction of the Law.* New York: The Free Press, 1990; Hodder-Williams, Richard. "The Strange Story of Judge Robert Bork and a Vacancy on the United States Supreme Court." *Political Studies* 36, no. 4 (1988): 613–637; Vieira, Norman, and Leonard Gross. *Supreme Court Appointments: Judge Bork and the Politicization of Senate Confirmations.* Carbondale: Southern Illinois University Press, 1998.

—John David Rausch, Jr.

Buckley v. Valeo, 424 U.S. 1 (1976)

In this controversial landmark decision, the Supreme Court ruled on the constitutionality of various provisions of the FEDERAL ELECTION CAMPAIGN ACT (FECA). Congress enacted FECA in an effort to curtail the corrupting influence of money, particularly in the form of large donors to individual campaigns, on federal elections. The most important components of FECA were:

- limits on contributions by individuals ($1,000) and political action committees ($5,000) to any one candidate during an election cycle, plus an annual limit of $25,000 for any individual contributor;
- limits on personal contributions by candidates (and their families);
- limits on spending in support of a particular candidate by independent individuals or groups ($1,000 per election);
- limits on overall spending by candidates in an election;
- record-keeping and public disclosure requirements for political action committees;
- establishment of a voluntary public funding system for general elections, in which taxpayers may choose to donate funds and candidates may receive federal funds if they agree to adhere to prescribed spending limits; and
- creation of the Federal Election Commission (FEC) to enforce FECA's provisions.

Senator James Buckley, former senator Eugene McCarthy, and other members and former members of Congress sued the HOUSE OF REPRESENTATIVES and SENATE (Valeo was the secretary of the latter) to bar enforcement of FECA, claiming, inter alia, that the contribution and spending limits violated the First Amendment's guarantee of freedom of speech. Congress countered that FECA was necessary to safeguard the integrity of federal elections against actual and perceived threats of corruption and, therefore, was sufficient to trump First Amendment claims. In addition, Valeo argued that expenditures of money are not equivalent to pure speech and do not warrant full First Amendment protection.

In a contentious per curiam opinion the Supreme Court upheld the voluntary public financing scheme with voluntary spending limits, reporting requirements, and limitations on campaign contributions but struck down the limitations on expenditures by campaigns, candidates, and independent individuals or groups and candidate contributions to their own campaigns. The Court agreed that political contributions and expenditures are entitled to First Amendment protection, recognizing that virtually all meaningful political communications in the modern setting involve the expenditure of money. Accordingly, mandatory limits on campaign spending were subjected to strict scrutiny and were struck down (although the voluntary limits established under the public financing scheme were acceptable). Limits on contributions by candidates (and their relatives) to their own campaigns were viewed as functionally no different from spending limits, and were similarly struck down.

The Court treated limits on contributions to candidates and campaigns somewhat differently. While still entitled to First Amendment protection—both speech and association—contributions were viewed as raising a substantial danger of quid pro quo arrangements between large donors and candidates. Particularly in light of the Court's rejection of limits on independent (uncoordinated) spending by individuals and groups in support of a candidate, the limits on contributions were deemed constitutional. Similarly, disclosure and reporting requirements were accepted as essential to the integrity of the electoral system and were not viewed as imposing significant burdens on freedom of speech or association.

Not surprisingly, reaction to *Buckley* and FECA has been mixed. First Amendment advocates have criticized the decision as imposing undue restrictions on political participation. Supporters of campaign finance reform have lamented the Court's rejection of spending limits, claiming that money increasingly determines outcomes, to the detriment of democracy. Others have noted that the act, limited by the Court's preservation of unlimited spending, perpetuates and augments the enormous advantages held by congressional incumbents, particularly House incumbents. Perhaps most troubling has been the "soft money" loophole. In *Buckley* and subsequent decisions the Court held that contributions to candidates or political parties, and spending by the parties, were not subject to FECA's limits or reporting requirements if not used to directly advocate the election or defeat of a candidate. The result was a proliferation of issue ads and attack ads that often plainly supported or opposed particular candidates but were not subject to limitations or disclosure requirements.

Following *Buckley*, the Court further restricted the scope of FECA in some respects. In *Federal Election Commission v. National Conservative Political Action Committee* (1985), the Court struck down limits on independent spending by political action committees, and in *Colorado Republican Federal Campaign Committee v. Federal Election Commission* (1996), the Court struck down limits on political party spending in Senate races. The Court did, however, uphold FECA's limits on party spending coordinated with a candidate's campaign (*Federal Election Commission v. Colorado Republican Federal Campaign Committee* [2001]) and reaffirmed the constitutionality of Congress's ban on direct corporate contributions to federal candidates, even by nonprofit corporations (*Federal Election Commission v. Beaumont* [2003]).

Buckley and its progeny regulated campaign fundraising and expenditures for nearly 30 years. In 2002 Congress overhauled FECA in the Bipartisan Campaign Finance Act (BCRA), commonly known as the McCain-Feingold law. Most notably, BCRA closed the soft money loophole, imposed restrictions on issue ads by corporations and unions using general organizational funds, established stringent disclosure requirements for political advertisements, established staggered contribution limits triggered by the level of spending from an opponent's personal funds (the so-called millionaire provision), and increased campaign contribution limits for individuals and organizations for the first time in nearly 30 years. In a fractured, complex decision reminiscent of *Buckley*, the Supreme Court upheld substantially all of BCRA in *McConnell v. Federal Election Commission*.

Further reading:
Federal Election Commission v. National Conservative Political Action Committee, 470 U.S. 480 (1985); *Colorado Republican Federal Campaign Committee v. Federal Election Commission*, 518 U.S. 515 (1996); *Federal Election Commission v. Colorado Republican Federal Campaign Committee*, 533 U.S. 431 (2001); *Federal Election Commission v. Beaumont*, 539 U.S. 146 (2003); *McConnell v. Federal Election Commission*, 540 U.S. 93 (2003); O'Brien, David M. *Supreme Court Watch 2004.* New York: Norton, 2004.

—Daniel E. Smith

Budget and Accounting Act of 1921

The U.S. Constitution establishes the basic rules for federal appropriations: The federal government spends money after Congress acts and the president agrees (except in the case when Congress overrides a president's veto). Congressional appropriation and presidential veto have been the foundation of federal budgeting since the country's first budget in 1789 and essentially were the only rules guiding the appropriations process until the enactment of the 1921 Budget and Accounting Act. In response to growing deficits from World War I and the public's desire for economy and efficiency in government, Congress passed the Budget and Accounting Act of 1921 to improve government efficiency and place more responsibility on presidents for the federal budget.

The movement at the turn of the 20th century for more economy and efficiency in government led President William Howard Taft to establish the President's Commission on Economy and Efficiency, which recommended a national budget system to replace the existing decentralized one. With objections from Congress, Taft ordered all department heads to send him a copy of the budget estimates they were sending to Congress. The budget estimates were used in filing the commission's second report to

Congress in 1913, which contained the first presidential budget request.

The appropriations process during the period before the 1921 Budget and Accounting Act is best described as "decentralized." At least eight committees were involved in annual appropriations in the HOUSE OF REPRESENTATIVES. From 1789 to 1794 Congress provided lump-sum appropriations in four areas: the civil list (federal government salaries and expenses, such as rent, stationary, printing, firewood, etc.), the Department of War, interest on the debt, and other listed expenditures. The first three APPROPRIATIONS BILLS passed by Congress were general in language (the first one in 1789 contained only 142 words). The House and SENATE decided spending levels after receiving requests from the individual departments through the Treasury Department. The secretary of the Treasury merely transmitted each department's book of estimates, and the president had no direct budgetary responsibilities in submitting estimates to Congress. This does not mean, however, that the president was uninvolved in the budget process.

The president, through the Treasury secretary, would often take liberties in using the funds appropriated by Congress. The Treasury secretary would often transfer appropriations from one area to another within departments, thus weakening Congress's power of the purse. Although the appropriations bills in the first three years of the government contained general language, the executive branch was not operating in a vacuum. The lump-sum appropriations were made with the understanding that money could be spent only on authorized projects and items and that the departments follow the estimates that were transmitted to Congress by the Treasury Department. This arrangement, of course, was not adhered to always, and Congress quickly became unhappy with this arrangement.

In 1791 Congress began including specific instructions for departments in their appropriations bills. Congress's main budgetary concern was controlling the specific expenditures made by the executive branch. Needless to say, the executive branch opposed the inclusion of specific instructions in appropriations bills. Alexander Hamilton, the first secretary of the Treasury, wrote that congressional micromanaging of the federal budget was preposterous. Hamilton argued for the need for executive discretion in spending. In response to Thomas Jefferson's call for increased congressional guidance in government spending, Hamilton said:

> Thus (to take a familiar example) in providing for the transportation of an army, oats and hay for the subsistence of horses are each susceptible of a definition and an estimate (from Congress), and a precise sum may be appropriated for each separately; yet in the operation in an army it will often happen that more than a sufficient quantity of the one article may be obtained, and not sufficient quantity of the other. If the appropriations be distinct and the officer who is making the provision be not at liberty to divert the fund from one of these objects to the other . . . , the horses of the army may in such a case starve and its movement be arrested in some situations the army itself may likewise be starved, by a failure of the means of transportation.

Conflict between the president and Congress over budgeting often has been over the control of spending within departments and not over the total spending levels for the departments, and this was especially true before 1921. This battle over controlling appropriated money within departments briefly subsided in 1798, when the Senate sided with the administration and forced passage of a military spending bill that did not include specific spending items. The practice of shifting money between accounts thus became an accepted custom, though it was considered illegal.

The 1921 Budget Act established the Bureau of the Budget (renamed the Office of Management and Budget (OMB) in 1970) and required presidents to review agency budget requests and then submit comprehensive and detailed budget proposals to Congress. Although the 1921 act was an attempt by Congress to control the executive, it actually gave presidents more control and power over the budget process. Congress tried consistently to control the executive by passing detailed appropriations bills. Part of the appeal to Congress of the 1921 act was that it was going to receive from presidents, through the very departments it was trying to micromanage, the detailed estimates it was trying to apply to the departments through the appropriations bills. Instead, the presidential budget has greatly helped presidents set a national agenda and determine spending levels for agencies. The creation of the budget proposal power allows presidents to set the parameters of discussion, because congressional action at each stage of the spending process is always compared to the president's proposal.

The budget proposal has also helped presidents because by going first presidents usually limit congressional action on politically sensitive issues. Congress often has been reluctant to tackle tough issues unilaterally. Congress has used the president's budget proposal as a document to give them cover. If a president cuts the budget or zeroes out a line-item, it allows Congress to take the same position, assuming they agree with it, and say they are simply reflecting the president's budget.

Further reading:
Fischer, Louis. *Constitutional Conflicts between Congress and the President.* 3d rev. ed. Lawrence: University Press of Kansas, pp. 186–215, 1991; Neustadt, Richard E. "Presidency

and Legislation: Planning the President's Program." In *The Presidency*, edited by Aaron Wildavsky, Boston: Little, Brown, 1969; Smithies, Arthur. *The Budgetary Process in the United States*. New York: McGraw-Hill, 1955; Willoughby, William F. *The National Budget System*. Baltimore: Johns Hopkins University Press, 1927.

—Charles Tien

Budget Committee, House and Senate

In part to recapture budgetary prominence lost to the president over the previous 50 years, Congress passed the 1974 Congressional Budget and Impoundment Control Act, which created a new annual budget process, new information resources through the Congressional Budget Office, reduced the president's rescission powers, and established the House and Senate Budget Committees to oversee these various reforms and create an annual fiscal framework to guide Congress's tax and spending decisions.

With the help of a large professional staff, the three basic duties given to the Budget Committees in the 1974 act were to report two concurrent resolutions on the budget each year (subsequently reduced to one), make several macroimpact reports of proposed and existing programs, and oversee the operations of the Congressional Budget Office. The Budget Committees were not designed to have any subcommittees to help in these tasks, but soon instituted a practice of ad hoc task forces to research various governmental programs and budgets. Unlike the division of the Appropriations Committee's work into subcommittees for each of the 13 annual spending bills, the Budget Committees' task forces are not strictly aligned with set fiscal or functional categories.

The most important of the two Budget Committees' tasks is creating, passing, and enforcing the annual congressional budget resolution, which is a broad tax and spend blueprint meant to guide the other fiscal policy committees' work, such as the Taxation and Appropriations Committees, during the rest of the session's budget-making process. After the president submits a budget in early February, the Budget Committees receive estimates from other congressional committees, then draft the budget resolution, and, ideally, adopt it in both chambers by April 15. This resolution is meant to set budget totals for the current year as well as for several years into the future, including total revenue, budget authority and outlays, and deficit or surplus levels. The resolution also specifies funding for the government's 20 functional spending categories for current and future fiscal years, which must adhere to the total numbers as well. The budget resolution may differ significantly from the president's request, but both should adhere to any budget laws in effect at the time regarding deficit and spending control.

According to budget expert Allen Schick, the House and Senate Budget Committees are both potentially powerful and weak. Although the budget resolution is presented to both chambers for a vote, it does not go to the president for signature, nor does it have the force of law. Sometimes the budget outcomes later adopted by the Tax and Appropriations Committees conform to the resolution, but other times they do not, even though congressional rules exist to help the budget committees enforce their work. At other times, however, the Budget Committees seem quite strong by developing a dramatic alternative to the president's plan and/or including reconciliation instructions in the budget resolution that direct the other committees to adhere to specific revenue and outlay numbers. But sometimes the resolution is ignored along the way or is completely irrelevant.

In 1998, for the first and only time in their history, the Budget Committees were unable to formulate a resolution due to House and Senate differences, even though both chambers were controlled by the Republican Party, but the rest of the budget process continued anyway. Oftentimes, though, the House and Senate Budget Committees must resolve their differences through a conference committee before the budget resolution is presented to both chambers. This is true not only on the few occasions in which the House and Senate are held by different parties, but also when one party dominates both chambers. As is the case in many aspects of congressional life, the senators of both parties are usually more centrist than their House counterparts.

Originally, the House Budget Committee (HBC) was given a strict formula for membership distribution: five members from Appropriations, five from Ways and Means, 11 from other standing committees, and one from each of the two parties' leaderships. According to Schick, this formula was developed because House liberals in the early 1970s feared the HBC would become an independent, fiscally conservative bully that would threaten the party's spending desires. In 1975 the HBC was enlarged from 23 to 25 members; the extra members were chosen from the other House standing committees. HBC members are now allowed to serve a maximum of six years out of every 10, whereas under the original act they could serve only two consecutive Congresses. Currently, the HBC has 33 members, with 24 Republicans and 19 Democrats.

In the House especially, the Budget Committee works closely with the majority party both in drafting the annual budget resolution and seeing it shepherded through the chamber. Party leaders are also necessary to smooth out differences between the Budget Committee and the others over taxation and spending. But there have been incidents of friction between the House Budget Committee and the majority party, such as that between Republican HBC chair John Kasich and the caucus in 1998.

Despite changes to the budget process in the 1980s and 1990s that somewhat diluted the original mission of the House and Senate Budget Committees, such as the Gramm-Rudman-Hollings deficit control laws in the mid-1980s and the 1990 Budget Enforcement Act and its 1993 and 1997 amendments, both Budget Committees still have important formal powers throughout the annual budget process.

However, on an informal basis, the Budget Committees' work may be heeded more or less depending on intra- and interchamber politics and policy clashes. A common source of tension between these various committees is that the tax-writing and entitlement policy committee of the House (called Ways and Means) has a different perspective from the Appropriations Committee, which sets outlays for the fiscal year, as well as the various authorization committees, which create and alter government programs. The House Budget Committee has the difficult and enduring duty of creating and enforcing a blueprint to keep all of these pressures under a larger short- and long-term budgeting plan.

Neither the Senate's Budget Committee's (SBC) number of members nor the selection process for choosing the members was included in the original 1974 act. There are no specific term limits for SBC members other than existing term limits for chairs passed by the Republican caucus in the mid-1990s. Currently there are 12 Republicans and 11 Democrats on the SBC.

Tensions have arisen from time to time between the Senate Budget Committee and the Appropriations Committee. In the 1990 budget process reform known as the Budget Enforcement Act, Senator Robert Byrd (D-WV) fought for a power shift to the Appropriations Committee, which he chaired at the time, at the expense of the SBC. Such conflicts have plagued the Budget Committees in both the House and the Senate because they were created as an additional layer to the budget-making process already fragmented with powers lodged in various authorization committees, as well as taxation and entitlements (Ways and Means in the House and Finance in the Senate), and Appropriations.

Further reading:
Schick, Allen. *Congress and Money: Budgeting, Spending, and Taxing.* Washington, D.C.: Urban Institute, 1980; Schick, Allen. *The Federal Budget: Politics, Policy, Process.* Rev. ed. Washington, D.C.: Brookings Institution Press, 1980; HBC. Available online. URL: http://www.house.gov/budget/. Accessed January 16, 2006.

—Jasmine L. Farrier

Budget Enforcement Act of 1990

The Budget Enforcement Act (BEA) of 1990 effectively ended the GRAMM-RUDMAN-HOLLINGS (GRH) sequestration budget process. Instead of cutting equal dollar amounts from defense and domestic discretionary spending when the overall deficit failed to meet the spending target, the BEA divided discretionary spending into three parts: defense, international, and domestic for three years. For fiscal years 1991, 1992, and 1993 there were separate spending limits (commonly called caps or ceilings) for each of the three categories. Sequestration would occur only in the category in which the limit was breached. In fiscal years 1994 and 1995 the three categories were combined back into one. The caps were extended into 1998 by President Bill Clinton's first budget in 1993. The BEA, however, essentially did away with sequestration by setting the spending caps at a sufficiently high level to accommodate expected spending and requiring the executive to adjust the deficit targets when necessary. Under the BEA, whatever the deficit is is what it is permitted to be.

The major issue in the 1990 budget fight was taxes as the country watched President George H. W. Bush break his campaign pledge and raise taxes when the savings-and-loan bailout and the blue smoke and mirror economic forecasts used to calculate past deficits finally caught up with administration budgets. The collapse of the savings-and-loan industry cost the federal government billions of dollars in payments to insured depositors in the deregulated industry. The total cost to taxpayers is estimated at more than $500 billion. To meet the GRH deficit targets and avoid sequestration, administrations had routinely relied on inflated estimates of economic growth and deflated estimates of unemployment to increase projected revenues and decrease projected outlays.

These problems caught up with budgeters in 1990. Adding to the problem that year was the attention the Social Security trust fund was receiving. Changes to Social Security in 1983 to handle the large number of future retirees resulted in trust fund surpluses of more than $50 billion. If not removed from budget calculations, the appearance was that Washington was robbing the trust fund to pay for other programs. The actual deficit for fiscal year 1991 was well over $200 billion after accounting for the savings-and-loan bailout and the Social Security trust fund. The fiscal year 1991 GRH deficit target was $74 billion (including the $10 billion cushion. Each year's target was given a $10 billion cushion so that as long as the deficit was within $10 billion of the target, no sequestration would be ordered).

The gap between target and reality was too large. For President George Bush to keep his campaign promise of not raising taxes, he would have had to slash more than $125 billion in discretionary spending and entitlement spending, a politically unacceptable amount. When White House staff and congressional leaders ended lengthy budget negotiations, the press focused on the story of the wealthiest Americans having to pay more income taxes, and more taxes on luxury items such as their boats and yachts. Receiving less attention was the fact that the GRH targets were effectively dead, and separate spending caps were placed on defense, international, and domestic spending for three years. Replacing the GRH targets were spending caps that placed a limit on how much could be appropriated for discretionary programs. The president, however, was required to adjust the spending caps when proposing the budget, which made the caps almost impossible to exceed.

The 1990 budget agreement was a five-year reconciliation agreement. It raised taxes and reduced entitlement spending by $246 billion for fiscal year 1991 through fiscal year 1995. More importantly, the BEA sought to control congressional action rather than focus on the deficit like GRH. The two main components of the BEA that tried to control congressional action were pay-as-you-go (PAYGO) requirements and caps on discretionary spending. PAYGO focused on entitlements and taxes and required that all changes in entitlement programs and taxes be revenue neutral. In other words, if Congress or the president proposed either an increase in entitlement spending or a tax cut, they also had to cut spending or raise taxes somewhere else so the proposal would not increase the deficit.

The caps on discretionary spending, on the other hand, placed a limit on how much could be appropriated for discretionary programs. The caps were harshest on defense spending. More than $180 billion in cuts were required over five years for an average of $36 billion per year. Domestic spending was actually given a slight increase of more than $20 billion for fiscal year 1991 through fiscal year 1993. The president, however, was required to adjust the spending caps when proposing the budget for changes in concepts, definitions, and inflation.

Further reading:
Schick, Allen. *The Federal Budget: Politics, Policy, Process.* Washington, D.C.: Brookings Institution Press, 1995; Shuman, Howard E. *Politics and the Budget: The Struggle between the President and the Congress.* 3d ed. Englewood Cliffs, N.J.: Prentice Hall, 1992.

—Charles Tien

Budget and Impoundment Control Act of 1974

Large deficits became a persistent major problem in the early to mid-1970s. Fiscal year 1969 was the last year that the federal government ran a budget surplus until the mid-1990s. When the Vietnam War, a recession, and President Lyndon Johnson's recently enacted Great Society programs started draining the federal treasury and when President Richard Nixon impounded appropriated funds, Congress responded by passing the Budget and Impoundment Control Act of 1974.

An impoundment occurs when the administration does not spend, for whatever reason, appropriated funds. There are, however, different types of impoundments. The two more pernicious types are "deferrals" and "rescissions." A deferral is when appropriated funds are temporarily withheld, while a rescission occurs when budget authority is actually cancelled. The Franklin Roosevelt, Truman, Eisenhower, Kennedy, and Johnson administrations all had impounded funds. Before the Nixon administration, impoundments were used to save taxpayer dollars, to follow Congress's directives, or to stop undesired projects.

Nixon's practice of impounding was a drastic departure from how previous administrations had impounded funds. In fact, they were well beyond the scope of impoundments from previous administrations. Nixon attempted to change national policy by refusing to spend money that Congress appropriated. Nixon's impoundments were in the form of rescissions. The Nixon administration impounded funds to cancel major programs such as the Rural Environmental Assistance Program, the Rural Electrification Administration, and parts of the CLEAN WATER ACT, among others.

Congress's response was the Impoundment Control Act of 1974, which was a separate section under the Budget and Impoundment Control Act of 1974. The impoundment provision attempted to limit the practice of executive impoundments of monies appropriated by Congress. The 1974 law required that deferral impoundments be subject to the approval of one house of Congress and that rescission impoundments be subject to the approval of both houses of Congress.

In addition, the 1974 law established Congress's reply to the president's budget, the comprehensive budget of its own called the congressional budget resolution. The congressional budget resolution is a concurrent resolution, which means it is passed by both the HOUSE OF REPRESENTATIVES and the SENATE in the same form but does not go to the president for signature. The congressional budget resolution does not have the force of law. The budget resolution provides a framework for the Appropriations Committees to work within and also sets goals for revenues and spending that direct the taxing and authorizing committees. The 1974 law also gave Congress more budget expertise by establishing the House and Senate BUDGET COMMITTEES and the CONGRESSIONAL BUDGET OFFICE (CBO).

Before the 1974 act Congress would consider each appropriations bill separate from the others. The total amount appropriated for the year was simply the sum of the various appropriations bills. The size of the deficit or surplus was calculated after revenues were counted against appropriations. There was no congressional blueprint for its annual budget decisions. The 1974 act forced Congress to consider how much to spend in total and how much to raise revenues at the beginning of the budget process rather than the end. The budget resolution constrained the Appropriations Committee by giving it a budget and could direct the other committees to raise or cut revenues and to increase or decrease entitlement spending.

The 1974 budget act requires Congress to pass a budget resolution by April 15, well before the start of the fiscal year, which the law changed to October 1 from July 1. This would give Congress almost six months to pass all its appropriations and reconciliations bills to meet the goals set out in the budget resolution.

Some supporters of the 1974 act believed that Congress would spend less if they considered aggregate spending levels before working on the individual appropriations bills. However, the 1974 budget process failed to constrain spending. The 1974 budget process resulted in higher levels of spending because members selected the overall level of spending in the budget on the House floor. Therefore, spending levels depended on the preferences of the members of the whole chamber, and the Budget and Appropriations Committee could not prevent spending levels from being set at levels below what the whole House desired. The Budget Committees have to accommodate the interests of the whole chamber when writing the budget resolution. With the floor demanding relatively high levels of spending through the Budget Committee, the House Appropriations Committee found it difficult to defend bills on the floor that did not meet or come close to meeting the levels set in the budget resolutions. "It's no secret that appropriators do not like the budget process, [they] would like to see the Budget Committee go away, [they] say it's not necessary. They don't like being told that you can't spend more than x amount of dollars, they would rather do it themselves" (House Budget Committee member, 1996).

One of Congress's goals in the 1974 act was to control the executive by passing new impoundment procedures, but establishing a parallel budget structure to the executive was also an attempt to gain leverage over the executive in spending outcomes. The CBO countered the Office of Management and Budget's (OMB) duty in producing economic estimates; the House and Senate Budget Committees countered OMB's function of forcing fiscal policy and policy preferences onto the micro budgetary decisions made by the other committees; the congressional budget resolution countered the president's budget as a comprehensive budget document.

Further reading:
Fisher, Louis. *Presidential Spending Power.* Princeton, N.J.: Princeton University Press 1975; Wildavsky, Aaron. *The New Politics of the Budgetary Process.* 2d ed. New York: HarperCollins, 1992.

—Charles Tien

budget process

The power of the purse is one of the central powers of Congress and was designed as such by the founding fathers. Due to the fear of "taxation without representation," there was an early recognition that financial issues would be primarily congressional concerns. Throughout the 19th century Congress considered itself to be the dominant branch of government, and it had relatively little contact with the White House on budgetary matters. As government grew in size and scope, however, Congress found itself forced to give up its powers over the purse gradually to the president. Even with an increasingly centralized budget process, however, Congress has had more and more difficulty limiting expenditures to revenues.

The restraints of time, the internal struggle for power within Congress, and conflict with the executive branch have changed the congressional budget process from a timely and predictable process to a struggle in which the smarts of the street are more important than an adherence to the traditional and ritualistic rules. Ideally, the budget timetable is the following:

October 1: Beginning of the new fiscal year. All action concerning the budget is to be completed.
February: The president submits a budget.
April 15: Congress is required to pass its budget resolution.
June 30: All 13 appropriations bills should have been passed by the House; this rarely happens.
September 30: Congress is supposed to have finished its budget work for the fiscal year that is supposed to start; it rarely does. The result is a series of continuing resolutions until the budget is finally passed.

Traditionally, the federal fiscal year began on July 1. In earlier eras when government was small and relatively uncomplicated Congress would have adjourned by summertime. Congress found this deadline more and more difficult to meet as budgeting became more complex, and finally in 1974 the fiscal year was shifted to October 1, giving Congress three additional months for its annual budget work. These three extra months, however, have often not been long enough, as Congress has on numerous occasions found itself unable to agree on a budget by October.

Following passage of the budget resolution in the spring, subcommittees of the Appropriations Committees consider specific appropriation bills, and the revenue committees consider their portion of the budget, with the Appropriation subcommittees supposedly staying within the budget resolution. The budget committees serve as watchdogs, making sure that legislation is not substantially at variance with the resolution, although the budget committees lack authority to override other committees.

The budget resolutions adopted by Congress each year constitute the heart of the budget process, expressing congressional decisions on fiscal policy by defining the balance between total spending and revenue. The breakdown of total spending by functional categories represents congressional priorities. Budget resolutions do not impose fixed limits on spending because the ceilings imposed can always be raised. Thus, in the absence of fixed limits, Congress can avoid the really unpleasant choices between spending programs. Congressional budget resolutions have no status in law, however, underscoring the fragility of the budget process. Resolutions are simply blueprints by which Congress sets goals for macro-level spending, taxing, and deficit decisions.

Regardless of the amounts set in the budget resolution, expenditures continue to be made according to legal requirements. The adoption of the RECONCILIATION procedure was supposed to fix this. The reconciliation process allows legislative proposals that normally would be separately considered to be incorporated into an omnibus bill, allowing both taxing and spending legislation to be taken up jointly. When created in the CONGRESSIONAL BUDGET AND IMPOUNDMENT CONTROL ACT OF 1974, reconciliation was designed to be a process in which the committees were instructed to adjust spending and revenue measures upward or downward to conform to the overall budget plan. The reconciliation process, however, comes too late in the legislative session for Congress to have an effective opportunity to change existing laws; by the time that reconciliation is supposed to be completed, the new fiscal year is ready to begin. As a result, reconciliation has been of limited effectiveness since it was added to the budget process.

Increasingly, Congress has been forced to rely on CONTINUING RESOLUTIONS due to its failure to pass its regular appropriations bills on time. Continuing resolutions are budget authority for specific ongoing activities in cases in which the regular fiscal year appropriations bill for such activities has not been enacted by the beginning of the fiscal year. At the end of the 97th Congress, for example, not one of the 13 appropriations bills had been signed by the president by the start of the new fiscal year, and only six were passed and signed when Congress adjourned in December. Continuing resolutions thus funded 78 percent of appropriated monies as Congress adjourned for Christmas. It can be said that the use of continuing resolutions has become symbolic of the failures of the budget process.

A whole range of committees deal with taxing and spending; there is no single focal point in the budget process. The major players in the committee organization relevant to the budget include the HOUSE and SENATE BUDGET COMMITTEES, the HOUSE and SENATE APPROPRIATIONS COMMITTEES, the HOUSE WAYS AND MEANS COMMITTEE, and the Senate FINANCE COMMITTEE and the authorization committees. The authorization committees set policy, the Appropriation Committees determine the levels and distribution of discretionary spending, and the taxation committees determine the volume of revenues and the distribution of the tax burden. All of these activities are supposed to be coordinated by the Budget Committees, so that Congress can meet its policy obligations and budget targets.

No appropriation can be made without authorization. Authorizations are the official expressions of the interests of Congress. The authorization requirement serves to highlight the fact that the primary responsibility of Congress is to provide services, not to make budgetary decisions. The authorization committees are organized according to governmental function. In the House a total of 18 committees share some authorization responsibility.

Appropriations Committee members traditionally see themselves in the role of watchdog of the budget process. The Appropriation Committees traditionally scrutinize presidential budgetary actions and compare them to authorization requests. If authorization requests are much different from the president's requests, Appropriations will often side toward the president's position. For most annual authorizations, however, the amount appropriated is more than 90 percent of the authorized level. Authorizations and appropriations, however, will usually diverge when the committees do not share the same attitudes toward a program.

The Ways and Means Committee in the House and the Finance Committee in the Senate create the legislation that generates the revenue for the federal government. In addition to being responsible for tax legislation, the committees are responsible for trade and many of the largest spending programs in the budget, including Social Security and Medicare. As a result, not only do the Ways and Means and Finance Committees have control of more than 100 percent of taxes, but they have control of more than half the federal government's spending as well. Since the tax-writing committees have almost complete control of the revenue side of the budget, control a good portion of the spending, and have jurisdiction over both the deficit and the national debt, some observers of Congress have argued that they have excessive control.

The balancing of congressional interests begins in the Budget Committees, which were created in 1974. Although they can take a hard line and try to block legislation that does not meet their rules, the Budget Committees try to accommodate the budget process to the diverse legislative interests of other committees, especially those of Appropriations and Ways and Means/Finance. The dilemma for the Budget Committees is to accommodate without giving up all meaningful enforcement. The Budget Committees, however, are largely unable to prevent other committees from doing what they want to do. Both Budget Committees can be said to be "adding-machine" committees that gather the demands of the spending committees and impose as much restraint on them as the current congressional mood allows. Neither Budget Committee has the authority to act as the sole interpreter of congressional preferences, greatly weakening their designated role as guardians of the budget process.

An important element in the budget process is the degree to which it is dominated by the executive or legislative branch. In the model of executive dominance, the chief executive is responsible for formulating the budget proposal, which reflects priorities and the policy agenda; the legislature acts essentially as a rubber-stamp body. In the legislative-dominated budget process, the committees write up their requests for spending with the assistance of legislators who want some particular expenditure. The U.S. budget process falls in between these two extremes. From the earliest days of American government, budget decisions have been treated as a struggle for power between the executive and legislative branches. Roots of the legislative budget go back to colonial times; there were extraordinary efforts of colonial legislators to control executives by limiting their expenditures. Anti-monarchy beliefs led to antiexecutive tendencies when it came to the power of budgeting and taxing. The experience of the United States, however, has tended to indicate that budgeting requires the central force of an executive.

The expansion of the role of government during the Progressive Era and World War I greatly strained the traditional congressional budget process. Before 1921, if agencies wanted money, they went directly to Congress—the president had little budgetary power. Congress, unable to cope with the new budgetary environment and realizing that more centralization was needed in the budget process, was forced to forfeit some of its power of the purse to the president. The 1921 Budget and Accounting Act required the president to send an annual budget plan to Congress, created the Bureau of the Budget (later Office of Management and Budget) to help the president in his new budgetary role, and formalized a new budget process that divided labor among the branches. The basic provisions of the 1921 act remained intact until the process finally broke down during the Nixon administration as the deficit skyrocketed. Congress reacted by overhauling the budget process with a 1974 act, in which Congress tried to exert more control over the budget process. The enormous deficits of the 1980s and the inability of Congress to come to agreement with President Bush in 1990 lead to the enactment of the Budget Enforcement Act of 1990, in which Congress abdicated budgetary power to the president.

That the president has the ability to command more public attention than Congress no doubt hinders congressional influence in the budget process. Yet, despite the increased budgetary power of the presidency, Congress still has an important role in protecting the public's interest. The major weapon of Congress is the constitutional delegation of the power of the purse—Congress must pass all budget decisions. The power of the purse is the heart of legislative authority and an essential check on the executive branch. Since the end of World War II, however, Congress has never changed the president's aggregate budget request by more than 3 percent. Thus, the executive branch is as dominant in the budget process as it has ever been.

Further reading:
Franklin, Daniel. *Making Ends Meet*. Washington, D.C.: Congressional Quarterly Press, 1993; Ippolito, Dennis. *Congressional Spending*. Ithaca, N.Y.: Cornell University Press, 1981; LeLoup, Lance. *The Fiscal Congress*. Westport, Conn.: Greenwood Press, 1980; Rubin, Irene. *The Politics of Public Budgeting*. Chatham, N.J.: Chatham House, 1990; Schick, Allen. *Congress and Money*. Washington, D.C.: American Enterprise Institute, 1980; Shuman, Howard. *Politics and the Budget*. Englewood Cliffs, N.J.: Prentice Hall, 1983; ———. *Politics and the Budget*. Englewood Cliffs, N.J.: Prentice Hall, 1992; Wildavsky, Aaron, and Naomi Caiden. *The New Politics of the Budgetary Process*. 3d ed. New York: Longman, 1997.
—Patrick Fisher

Budget Reconciliation Act

Put simply, the annual Budget Reconciliation Act, which is the third step in the congressional budget process, makes existing laws (authorizations) comply with the new budget as passed in the budget resolution. After requesting legislation from committees, the standing Budget Committees organize the material together, and the chambers pass it as an omnibus bill. If the authorizing committees complete their work (revising authorizations) and the sum total is not in line with the totals in the budget resolution, the budget committees have the authority (per the Congressional Budget and Impoundment Control Act of 1974) to make across-the-board cuts to bring them into line with the blueprint as passed in the budget resolution.

There is technically no reconciliation requirement. It is recommended in the 1974 act and had been used nearly every year until recent years after 9/11, when Congress has opted not to complete a budget resolution and hence reconciliation cannot occur because there is no baseline budget. In these recent years Congress moves straight to appropriations, and things are much more decentralized. In turn, spending tends to increase, and previous spending caps are ignored. The Budget Reconciliation Act forces Congress to follow its own blueprint for the macro budget and tends to lead to more responsible budgetary decision making and even deficit reductions.

Once the Budget Reconciliation Act is passed, Congress then proceeds to the 13 regular appropriations bills. Having done the resolution and reconciliation, the Appropriations Committees have a set of clear signals to work with in terms of completing work on appropriations.

Beginning with the 1981 reconciliation bill, the annual act became a massive measure that includes significant policy add-ons. In this regard it was an OMNIBUS BILL in its truest form because the reconciliation act contained a nucleus that had support such that add-ons received less scrutiny. Some of our nation's most daring policies, including deficit reduction and continuing health care coverage for employees after they leave a job, have been passed as part of the reconciliation act. In fact, the latter policy is often referred to by the name of the bill on which it was passed: COBRA, or Consolidated Omnibus Budget Reconciliation Act.

Further reading:
Krutz, Glen S. *Hitching a Ride: Omnibus Legislating in the U.S. Congress.* Columbus: Ohio State University Press, 2001; Mikesell, John. *Fiscal Administration.* Belmont, Calif.: Wedsworth. 5th ed. 2003; Oleszek, Walter. *Congressional Procedures and the Policy Process.* 5th ed. Washington, D.C.: Congressional Quarterly, 2004; Schick, Allen. *Federal Budgeting.* Washington, D.C.: Brookings Institution Press, 2004.

—Glen S. Krutz

budget terms

The federal budget process is perhaps the least understood aspect of congressional politics. Indeed, the lexicon of congressional budgeting is complex and full of jargon. In this entry several terms and definitions will be shared to help the reader better understand the budgeting process.

Beginning with a key distinction, it is important to know that budget figures are reported regularly in studies and by media outlets in two different currencies: budget authority and budget outlays. Typically, budget authority appears more erratic when plotted across time, while budget outlays (money actually being spent for programs and agencies during a fiscal year) track more smoothly longitudinally (some describe it as incremental). For example, the vast majority of budget authority for President Bill Clinton's AmeriCorps program was completed during one year, yet the budget outlays that resulted from that one year of authority were spent over several years.

The elected institutions of our national government, the Congress and president, together create budget authority through various policymaking channels. Hence, at the end of the appropriations process, the outcomes are in the form of budget authority, or permission to allocate funds, through the Office of Management and Budget to various agencies for budgetary and policy implementation. Budget outlays are the format that budget figures take when agencies are actually spending the money for various services, such as labor, materials, and (sometimes) investment. In brief, budget authority is produced by Congress and the president, while budget outlays are processed in the bureaucracy. The focus here will be with the area of budgeting that produces budget authority.

For federal dollars to be allocated as budget authority, two things must occur: authorization and appropriation. These things occur within Congress, with the president's approval (signature) required. Authorization gives areas of the budget and particular programs budgetary legal standing and typically frames budgetary areas in terms of upper and lower bounds. Appropriation involves actually doling out money by area and program. To eventually have budget authority (and by extension to have budget outlays during the fiscal year), areas of the budget must have both authorization and appropriation. It is possible to follow authorization and appropriation as dichotomous processes in the regular federal budget process, or what is often called the on-budget part of the process or the discretionary budget. The other parts, or off-budget part of the national budget, are entitlement programs that dichotomize well and accomplish authorization and appropriation simultaneously at one point in time.

Turning first to the regular, discretionary side of the budget process, five steps are followed to produce budget authority. First, the president submits his proposed budget to the Congress. Second, the HOUSE OF REPRESENTATIVES and SENATE produce a budget resolution, which originates in the BUDGET COMMITTEE of each chamber and is a blueprint for the budget. The budget resolution is at the macro level of budgeting and includes overall parameters and targets. Third, the authorizing committees complete their authorizations, and these authorizations are aggregated into the budget reconciliation bill by the Budget Committees. The term *reconciliation* is appropriate because the authorizations must be consistent with the overall plan passed by Congress in the budget resolution. If not, the law states that the budget committee may cut the authorizations to make them so. It is also important to note that the president must sign the reconciliation bill, but the budget resolution is required to be passed only by the

House and Senate. Once the resolution and RECONCILIA-TION are completed, the appropriations bills are introduced and completed. There are 13 regular appropriations bills required by federal law, and the subcommittees of the House and Senate Appropriations Committees reflect these 13 areas substantively. Once these 13 bills are passed and the president signs them, work on the regular budget, or the on-budget items, is done.

The federal fiscal year runs from October 1 to September 30, and fiscal years are named for the year in which they end (e.g., FY05 runs from October 2004 to September 2005). Often, Congress runs behind in finishing work on the 13 appropriations bills required to keep the government functioning. When this happens, typically Congress and president agree to stop-gap spending measures (called continuing appropriations, continuing resolutions, or just CRs), which continues the previous year's spending levels into the new fiscal year, allowing the decision makers some additional time to complete the budget. Once the 13 appropriations bills are completed and the fiscal year budget is being implemented, budgets need some augmentation. Supplemental appropriations (called deficiency appropriations at times in the past) are passed to provide this. When natural disasters hit or other focusing events occur (such as the terrorist attacks of September 11, 2001), such supplements are often termed emergency appropriations bills.

The other side of congressional budgeting pertains to the off-budget, or entitlement, areas of the budget. These include mostly formula-based programs, such as Social Security, Medicare and Medicaid, Veterans' programs, and many welfare programs. These programs constitute a slight majority of the federal budget each year but are not on the table in the regular process described above. They are called permanent appropriations because they are authorized and appropriated typically at one point in time via distinct public law (revisions are possible and often necessary down the road, but they need not be tackle annually like the on-budget items). These are typically completed via the lawmaking process of the authorizing committees, while the appropriations process is driven by the money committees.

A further blurring of which type of committee does what is seen through the BACKDOOR SPENDING and backdoor policy making. Through backdoor spending members of Congress place funding for programs that really ought to be in the discretionary, or on-budget, part of the process in the entitlement legislation. Backdoor spending empowers the authorizing committees at the expense of the Appropriations Committees. In contrast, backdoor policy making involves making policy (which typically takes place in the authorizing committees) via the budget process. This typically takes place in large omnibus packages, which contain a large budget nucleus together with many policy pro-

posals folded in (the budget reconciliation, for example, always has policy riders).

Further reading:
Krutz, Glen S. *Hitching a Ride: Omnibus Legislating in the U.S. Congress.* Columbus: Ohio State University Press, 2001; Mikesell, John. *Fiscal Administration.* 5th ed. Belmont, Calif.: Wadeworth, 2003; Oleszek, Walter. *Congressional Procedures and the Policy Process.* 5th ed. Washington, D.C.: Congressional Quarterly Press 2004; Schick, Allen. *Federal Budgeting.* Washington, D.C.: Brookings Institution Press, 2004.

—Glen S. Krutz

Byrd, Robert C. (1917–) *Senator*

Senator Robert C. Byrd took the senatorial oath on Tuesday, January 7, 2003, marking his 50th anniversary as a member of Congress. Byrd took office during the last few days of the administration of President Harry Truman and has served with 11 presidents. As of this writing, 11,707 men and women have served in Congress throughout the history of the United States, and Senator Byrd has served longer than all but two of them. Only Congressman Jamie Whitten, a Democrat from Mississippi, and Senator Strom Thurmond, a Republican from South Carolina, have served longer than Byrd.

He is a renowned defender of Congress's constitutional role in the American system of checks and balances and routinely challenges what he views as executive encroachments on these powers. He is openly critical of the modern Congress's tendency "to regard a chief executive in a role more elevated than the Framers intended." Accordingly, the *Almanac of American Politics* notes that Byrd may

Senator Robert Byrd, arms in the air at the conclusion of a civil rights filibuster in the Senate *(Library of Congress)*

come closer to the kind of senator the authors of the Constitution had in mind than any other.

Senator Byrd is also widely regarded as a Senate historian and the master of Senate rules and procedures. He gained this reputation by writing two books, *The Senate 1789–1989* and *The Senate of the Roman Republic,* and from his eloquent orations on the Senate floor. His floor speeches are typically filled with references to the classics, including Greek and Roman philosophers, Shakespeare, and America's founding fathers. He also has an uncanny ability to link the classics with modern policy issues, such as the line-item veto and tax policy.

Robert Carlyle Byrd was born Cornelius Calvin Sale, Jr., on November 20, 1917, in North Wilkesboro, North Carolina. His father sent him to live with his aunt and uncle in Stotesbury, West Virginia, after his mother died in the flu epidemic of 1918–19. He only learned of his real name at the age of 16. His foster father was a coal miner, roaming from town to town for employment. His meager beginnings sometimes resulted in suppers "with only lettuce and a little butter . . . and sugar on the table" and Christmases without presents. His only toy was a "little automobile he could pedal," which he kept until adulthood.

These impoverished beginnings shaped Senator Byrd's self-image. In a fiery exchange at a Senate Budget Committee hearing with former Treasury secretary Paul O'Neill, Senator Byrd declared,

> Well, Mr. Secretary, I lived in a house without electricity too. No running water, no telephone, a little wooden outhouse. I started out in life without any rungs in the bottom ladder, I can stand toe to toe with you.

Byrd overcame his meager beginnings with a thirst for knowledge. In fact, he was the valedictorian of Mark Twain High School in Stotesbury in 1934. However, Byrd spent only one semester at Marshall University in Huntington, West Virginia, unable to continue for financial reasons. Instead, Byrd spent the Depression years working in low-paying blue-collar jobs. He served as a gas station attendant and later worked in a grocery store. He eventually worked his way to a position as the head butcher before accepting welding positions in Maryland and Florida in the early 1940s. After World War II Byrd returned to West Virginia, where he opened a grocery store in Sophia.

Byrd taught a Bible class in Sophia, West Virginia. His discourses were so dynamic that a local radio station in nearby Beckley began broadcasting the lectures to a wider audience. In 1946 Byrd parlayed his fame into a political career. He was a charismatic campaigner who would entertain crowds with fiddle renditions of such bluegrass classics as "Cripple Creek" and "Rye Whiskey." He was elected to the West Virginia state house by a wide margin in 1946.

He was then elected by another wide margin to the state senate just two years later. Byrd took night classes at Morris Harvey College in Charleston and Marshall University in Huntington during this time.

Byrd ran for the U.S. House of Representatives in West Virginia's Sixth Congressional District in 1952. During the primary H. D. Ragland, one of Byrd's opponents, disclosed that Byrd had been an organizer for the Ku Klux Klan in 1942 and 1943. Byrd took the offensive and purchased radio and television advertisements attributing the membership to a mistake of youth. However, during the general election his Republican challenger produced a sympathetic letter Byrd had written to the imperial wizard of the Ku Klux Klan in 1946, three years after he allegedly left the organization. In the letter Byrd stated that "The Klan is needed today as never before and I am anxious to see its rebirth in West Virginia." While the letter cost him the support of the governor, Byrd went on to win with 57.4 percent of the vote and was reelected by greater margins in 1954 and 1956. During a television interview in 2001 Byrd said, "We all make mistakes; I made a mistake when I was a young man. It's always been an albatross around my neck, joining the Ku Klux Klan."

The race issue reemerged in the U.S. Senate when Byrd filibustered the Civil Rights Act of 1964 with a 14-hour speech, which is still one of the longest Senate speeches on record. Again, Byrd has expressed regret for this chapter of his career.

Byrd was elected to the U.S. Senate in 1958 at the age of 40. Taking advantage of the traditional unpopularity of sitting presidents during midterm elections, Byrd effectively ran against President Dwight Eisenhower's policies. Byrd became the first legislator in the history of Congress to earn a law degree while serving in Congress. He earned his law degree from American University in 1963 and had his diploma presented to him by President John F. Kennedy, who delivered the commencement speech.

Byrd quickly endeared himself to Majority Leader Lyndon Johnson, who rewarded Byrd's loyalty with a seat on the Senate Appropriations Committee during his first year. He rose to the level of assistant Majority Whip in 1965 and wrestled the whip position away from Senator Ted Kennedy, a Democrat from Massachusetts, in 1971, after Kennedy became distracted with the Chappaquiddick affair. He went on to become Senate Majority Leader after Mike Mansfield retired in 1976. He served as Majority Leader for six years (1977–80, 1987–88) and as the Senate Minority Leader from 1981 to 1986. Byrd did not enjoy serving as Majority Leader and resigned from the leadership position after the 1988 election. In 1989 he was unanimously elected President Pro Tempore of the Senate, placing him third in line of succession to the presidency. He has served in more leadership positions than any other senator in the history of the United States.

Byrd also became chair of the Appropriations Committee in 1989. While he is generally regarded as a loyal Democrat, he tends to place greater emphasis on the powers of the Senate and the economic welfare of West Virginia. In 1990 Byrd proudly stated that he wanted "to be West Virginia's billion dollar industry." He realized his dream 10 years later with the 2000 appropriations bill, which earmarked more than $1 billion of federal funds for West Virginia.

On the legislative front he has cast more than 16,000 roll-call votes, more than any other senator in the history of the United States. He also surprised some by casting the deciding vote against a proposed constitutional amendment banning flag desecration in 2000. He explained his vote by stating "the foolish and the dead alone never change their minds." He also played a leading role during the Clinton impeachment trial. While he personally believed Clinton's action rose to the level of impeachment, he voted against it because the public did not support removing Clinton from office. Byrd admonished the Senate for its unwillingness to debate the decision to invade Iraq in 2003.

We stand passively mute in the United States Senate, paralyzed by our own uncertainty, seemingly stunned by the sheer turmoil of events. Only on the editorial pages of our newspapers is there much substantive discussion of the prudence or imprudence of engaging in this particular war.

Byrd once stated that "people in West Virginia believe in four things: God Almighty; Sears and Roebuck; Carter's Little Liver Pills; and Robert C. Byrd."

The people of West Virginia demonstrated their belief once again by electing Byrd with 77.8 percent of the vote in the 2000 general election. For many observers Byrd came to personify the U.S. Senate.

Further reading:
Barone, Michael, Grant Ujifusa, and Douglas Matthews. *The Almanac of American Politics.* New York: E. P. Dutton, 2002; *Current Biography,* "Robert C. Byrd." New York: H. W. Wilson Co., 1978; *Politics In America.* Washington, D.C.: Congressional Quarterly Press, 2002.

—Joseph N. Patten

C

calendar

A congressional calendar is a list of those measures or other matters pending floor consideration. The House uses five calendars; the Senate uses two. Bills are numbered sequentially in the order in which they are placed on their respective calendar, but such numbers do not match subsequent consideration by the parent chamber. Rather, each house determines which measures and other matters to take up, when, and in what order.

In the Senate the calendar of business catalogs those bills, resolutions, and other items of legislative business eligible for floor consideration. This list contains all reported measures and any bills or joint resolutions not referred to committee and placed directly on the calendar. Once on the calendar, to be considered the matter must be called up for consideration either by unanimous consent or by a debatable motion to proceed to consideration. Measures not listed on the calendar either have been referred to a committee and are awaiting committee action or are held at the desk by unanimous consent.

The Senate's executive calendar identifies matters requiring the advice and consent of the upper chamber, namely, treaties and nominations. Like the calendar of business, numbers represent the order in which items are placed on the calendar but do not guarantee whether the Senate will consider them. Instead, the Senate must move to executive session, either by motion or by unanimous consent, to consider pending treaties and nominations. If a treaty or nomination is not on the calendar, it remains in the possession of the committee with jurisdiction, or it is held at the desk by unanimous consent, where it awaits referral to committee or direct floor consideration by unanimous consent.

The term calendar in the House of Representatives refers to several lists of measures and motions that are (or soon will become) eligible for floor consideration. The Union calendar (short for the Committee of the Whole House on the State of the Union, known as Committee of the Whole, where such measures are considered) lists bills and resolutions favorably reported by committees that deal with taxation, authorization, and appropriations. The House calendar lists other matters favorably reported by committees for further consideration by the House. If a measure is not on either one of these calendars, either it lies in limbo while awaiting action by one or more House committees to which it was referred or it is held at the Speaker's table in anticipation that the House may agree to consider it.

The House also uses three other calendars, primarily for special purposes. The private calendar lists those private bills and resolutions reported by committees that apply only to specified individuals, corporations, or institutions. These typically involve such things as claims against the federal government and immigration matters. Such measures are considered on the first and third Tuesdays of each month.

Created in 1995, the House's corrections calendar lists measures to repeal or correct various laws, rules, and regulations. The Speaker has the discretion to have any bill on the Union or House calendars placed also on the corrections calendar, although a bipartisan Corrections Day Advisory Group generally advises him or her on which measures should be placed on the calendar. Amendments are not permitted except for those recommended by the committee of jurisdiction or the chair's designee, and a three-fifths vote is required for passage. The House considers bills on this calendar on the second and fourth Tuesdays of each month under the one-hour rule of the House.

Finally, the discharge calendar enables members to bring to the House floor a bill or resolution that has been referred to a committee for at least 30 legislative days but that has not yet been reported. Such items may be made on the second or fourth Mondays of a month at least seven days after the petition is filed. A total of 218 members must sign the petition; they may add or remove their names until the petition has the requisite number of signatures and is then printed in the *Congressional Record*. The discharge process is ignored if the committee reports the bill before the actual motion to discharge is offered. The legislation may then be considered under another calendar.

Further reading:
Bach, Stanley, and Christopher M. Davis. *Calendars of the House of Representatives.* CRS Report 98-437 GOV. Washington, D.C.: Congressional Research Service, U.S. Library of Congress, 2003; Oleszek, Walter J. *Congressional Procedures and the Policy Process.* 5th ed. Washington, D.C.: Congressional Quarterly Press, 2000; Palmer, Betsy, and Stanley Bach. *The Senate's Calendar of Business.* CRS Report 98-429 GOV. Washington, D.C.: Congressional Research Service, U.S. Library of Congress, 2003.

—Colton C. Campbell

Calendar Wednesday

Since the adoption of Calendar Wednesdays in the House of Representatives in 1909, committees may be called on, in alphabetical order each Wednesday, to bring up any bill from the House or the Union CALENDAR, excluding privileged bills. Specifically, bills brought up during Calendar Wednesdays should not yet have a rule attached to them by the Rules Committee. The House is limited to a two-hour debate on each bill considered during Calendar Wednesdays. Furthermore, bills called up from the Union calendar are considered in the Committee of the Whole instead of in the House. The House does not observe Calendar Wednesday during the final two weeks of any session. Likewise, Calendar Wednesday may be dispensed with during any other time with a two-thirds vote of the House.

The creation of Calendar Wednesday was meant to give committees equal access to the floor, even in the face of opposition from the powerful Speaker of the House. In particular, during the era in which Calendar Wednesday was created, Speaker Joseph Cannon, a Republican from Illinois, was seen as an obstructionist Speaker. Before Calendar Wednesday was implemented, the Rules Committee and in turn the majority party, as well as the Speaker, strictly controlled the agenda. Therefore, Calendar Wednesday was seen as a way for members to be able to circumvent the regular orders of business, thus weakening the majority party's control of the floor. Essentially, Calendar Wednesday was a direct challenge to Cannon's control of the agenda that was meant to ensure that bills backed by either the Democratic minority and/or the Republican Progressives had a chance to be considered on the floor. Democrats, the minority party at the time, in general supported the adoption of Calendar Wednesday, while many Republicans feared the loss of power it would mean for the majority party.

Despite the original intentions of Calendar Wednesday, it has rarely been used in Congress, because the procedure is considered to be both impractical and unmanageable. In fact, although it still exists as a formal rule of the House, fewer than 15 bills have become law while using this procedure.

Further reading:
Binder, Sarah. *Minority Rights, Majority Rule: Partisanship and the Development of Congress.* New York: Cambridge University Press, 1977; Davidson, Roger H., and Walter J. Oleszek. *Congress and Its Members.* 8th ed. Washington, D.C.: Congressional Quarterly Press, 2002; Smith, Steven S. *The American Congress.* 2d ed. New York: Houghton Mifflin, 1999.

—Lisa A. Solowiej

campaign committees

Party committees in Congress that are charged with recruiting and supporting candidates for election to the HOUSE OF REPRESENTATIVES and SENATE are called campaign committees. Each of the two major political parties has a campaign committee in the House of Representatives and the Senate. In the House there is the Democratic Congressional Campaign Committee (DCCC) and the National Republican Congressional Committee (NRCC). The Democratic Senatorial Campaign Committee (DSCC) and the National Republican Senatorial Committee (NRSC) serve the Senate. Each campaign committee consists of members of Congress and professional staff. The members of Congress are selected by their party colleagues to serve on the committees, with each chair usually being selected by the party leadership in each chamber. The professional staff is hired based on political campaigning and communication expertise and organizational abilities.

The two House campaign committees were created after the Civil War during a period of political instability. The NRCC was organized in 1866 by radical Republicans opposed to President Andrew Johnson. The House Republicans wanted to distance themselves from the Republican National Committee that was under Johnson's nominal control. In response to the creation of the NRSC, House Democrats created the DCCC in 1868. The senatorial campaign committees were created in 1916, after the ratification of the SEVENTEENTH AMENDMENT turned the Senate into a popularly elected body.

The campaign committees did not become significant in congressional elections until campaign finance regulations were enacted in the early 1970s. Before the 1970s most congressional candidates were on their own when it came to their campaigns. A few candidates were able to receive campaign financing from party leaders, usually under the table. By the end of the 20th century, the committee staffs had grown and became more involved in candidate recruitment. Their ability to raise funds to contribute to candidates and to spend money on campaign consulting also increased their status.

Further reading:
Herrnson, Paul S. *Congressional Elections: Campaigning at Home and in Washington*. Washington, D.C.: Congressional Quarterly Press, 1995; Kolodny, Robin. *Pursuing Majorities: Congressional Campaign Committees in American Politics*. Norman: University of Oklahoma Press, 1998.
—John David Rausch, Jr.

Cannon, Joseph G. (1836–1926) *Representative, Speaker of the House*

The Speaker of the U.S. House of Representatives from 1903 to 1911, Joseph G. Cannon, a conservative Republican, dominated the body over which he presided through an array of formal powers concentrated in his office. His autocratic use of those powers and his inability to recognize the intensity of demands for democratic reform ultimately led to the weakening of the office of Speaker.

Joseph Gurney Cannon was born May 7, 1836, into a Quaker family in North Carolina. His father was a self-taught country doctor who, because of his hatred of slavery, moved the family west, and they settled in Parke County, Indiana. Young Joe Cannon lived in a log cabin and attended country schools. His childhood, however, abruptly ended at age 14, when his father drowned. Cannon then took jobs to help support the family. When he was 20, he began to read law in the office of an attorney in Terre Haute, Indiana, where he remained for a year. He attended Cincinnati Law School for six months, received his degree, and opened a law office in Shelbyville, Illinois, in 1858. Four years later he married. In 1876 the Cannons moved to Danville, Illinois. Danville, a small town that would always remain Cannon's home, became the geographic base of a political career containing both victories and defeats.

Cannon's political career did not have an auspicious beginning. He lost his first election when he ran for the position of district attorney of Coles County. The following year he did become a district attorney when he won an election in a district newly created by the state legislature. Because of the position he held, he did not volunteer for service in the Civil War.

Joe Cannon was elected to the U.S. House of Representatives in 1872. The House leadership granted his request for assignment to the Committee on Post Office and Post Roads. It was a position from which he could do things for his rural constituents. The first bill he introduced was an amendment to the postal code, and, among other things, it required publishers to pay the postage on magazines they mailed. Prior to passage of Cannon's bill, postage had been collected from the recipients. Cannon's first speech in the House was related to that bill and another that he had introduced. He was not a great orator, but he used large gestures and was always moving. From that point onward he became the subject of political cartoons. Those cartoons made Americans familiar with his lean, erect frame, narrow face, blonde hair, and beard. The beard was darker around the mouth, discolored by the many cigars he smoked.

Joe Cannon was an ambitious man. He aspired to become Speaker of the House, and he achieved that ambition. Cannon became Speaker through hard work, loyalty to the Republican Party in the House, and loyalty to the House as an institution. It was not until his third try at winning the Speakership that he was successful.

In his first unsuccessful attempt at the Speakership, the Republican caucus nominated Congressman Thomas B. Reed. Since the Republicans were the majority party, the speakership went to Reed, the Republican candidate. Cannon greatly admired Reed and loyally supported him, assisting in the preparation of Reed's rules of parliamentary procedure. Reed, for his part, appointed Cannon to the Rules Committee, which, along with the Speaker, ran the House of Representatives.

Cannon gained stature in the House when he stood up to the Senate, which had been accustomed to dominating the lower house in conference. He did not win the battle, but he won the respect of the House of Representatives, including members who were not his friends, although his friends were not in short supply. The battle with the Senate was over an appropriations bill that included a payment to the state of South Carolina. Senator Benjamin "Pitchfork Ben" Tillman insisted that the federal government owed his state $47,245.77 for actions taken by South Carolina in the War of 1812. Joe Cannon and the auditors in the Treasury Department acknowledged a debt of only 34 cents. The appropriations bill passed the two houses in different forms and, therefore, had to go to a conference committee. Cannon, chairman of the House Appropriations Committee, and the House conferees ultimately gave in and accepted a bill containing $47,000 for South Carolina because Tillman threatened to filibuster all other bills to come up in the Senate if his state did not get the money. The 57th Congress was due to adjourn on March 4, 1903, and it was imperative that all the appropriations bills be passed. Cannon reluctantly agreed with Senate conferees that a special session to pass the appropriations bills would cost the government more than the $47,000 included in the Senate bill. Cannon asked his colleagues to pass the bill even though it was the result of legislative blackmail. Some senators strongly objected to his use of

This cartoon by Clifford K. Berryman depicts the excessive use of power of Joseph G. Cannon before the revolt that stripped him of his Speakership. The majority of the House is portrayed as clones of Cannon. *(National Archives)*

the word *blackmail* but thereafter showed the House more respect. "Uncle Joe," as he was called, won the esteem of House members.

Later in 1903, on his third try, Uncle Joe Cannon was elected Speaker of the House. He supported business and tariffs and believed that the demands of labor were sheer nonsense. He had no sympathy for the reform movements of the late 19th and early 20th centuries. His lack of sympathy extended to reformers within his own party, including those who occupied the White House.

On a personal level Cannon was a kindly, likeable man, but kindness had nothing to do with the way he ran the House. He used the Reed rules but supplemented them with rules of his own. He would say which bills would pass and which would fail, and invariably they did. The Speaker controlled committee assignments. The Speaker named committee chairmen. House members could not speak on the floor without being recognized, and the Speaker could grant or withhold recognition. One of Cannon's innovations was a requirement that House members notify him in advance if they wanted to be recognized. The Speaker was chairman of the Rules Committee, which had jurisdiction over any resolutions introduced to change House rules. Any such resolutions would die in the Rules Committee because Cannon and his appointees would never permit them to go to the floor for a vote. Uncle Joe had become a tyrant.

In the congressional elections of 1908, Progressive House members launched a two-pronged attack against Speaker Cannon. One prong of the attack was to try to defeat him in his home district. William Jennings Bryan, the Democratic presidential candidate, went to the Danville area and spoke against Cannon's reelection. It was all to no avail. Cannon's constituents returned him to the House of Representatives. The second prong of the attack involved getting House candidates to commit themselves to vote for someone other than Cannon for Speaker if they won their elections. Again, the reformers failed. Cannon defeated the Democratic candidate for Speaker, Congressman Champ Clark of Missouri, by a vote of 204-166.

Speaker Cannon had no use for any Republicans who called themselves Progressives. He thought they ought to become Democrats. It was the Progressive Republicans who were deviating from Cannon's strongly held value of party loyalty. He was outraged when President William Howard Taft elevated Justice Edward Douglas White, a Democrat, to the position of Chief Justice of the Supreme Court.

Some Republicans feared that Cannon's iron rule could cost them control of the House in the 1910 elections. A group of Progressive Republicans began to meet to seek some way to put an end to Cannon's domination. The leader of the group was Congressman George W. Norris of Nebraska, who had entered the House in 1903, the same year that Uncle Joe Cannon had become Speaker. Norris and his group of insurgents had an opportunity to demonstrate their political muscle over a committee the House authorized in January 1910 to investigate the Department of the Interior and the Forest Service. Norris had been watching and observing. Whenever Cannon was not presiding, John Dalzell, a regular Republican from Pennsylvania, would preside. Norris observed that Dalzell was a man of strict habit who would leave the chair at exactly one o'clock to have lunch. At this point Walter Smith from Iowa, another regular Republican, would assume the chair. Norris considered Smith a fair man and a friend. Just as Dalzell was about to leave the chair for lunch, Norris asked Smith if he could have a few minutes on the floor. Smith replied that he would give Norris five minutes. After being recognized Norris moved that the members of the investigating committee be selected by the House membership rather than by the Speaker. Norris, 25 insurgent Republicans, and the Democrats voted in favor of the motion. It passed 149-146, and the Speaker was furious. He and several of his supporters had been absent during the proceedings. Norris and his group of insurgents were pleased but hardly satisfied, for they had a larger goal.

Norris drafted a resolution that would go beyond a special investigating committee. It would affect the House Rules Committee and the Speaker himself. Norris folded it, put it in his pocket, and hoped that he would have an opportunity to introduce it. The opportunity came in March 1910. When Cannon ruled that a bill dealing with a matter contained in the Constitution was privileged and could be taken out of order, he unwittingly gave Norris the break he needed. Norris announced that he wished to introduce a constitutionally privileged resolution dealing with House rules, since the Constitution allows each house of Congress to make its own rules. Norris sent the tattered resolution that he had been carrying in his pocket up to the clerk. His resolution required that members of the Rules Committee be selected from different geographic regions of the nation, that the members of the committee select the chair, and that the speaker be ineligible to serve on the Rules Committee.

Norris got most but not all of what he wanted. Without the Democrats, he would have gotten nothing. In order to retain the support of the Democrats, he had to compromise. The Democrats had hopes of winning control of the House in the November elections and did not like the idea of selecting Rules Committee members on a geographic basis. To hold the support of the Democrats, Norris amended his resolution to read that the members of the Rules Committee would be selected by the House. That would not restrict the majority party. The coalition of insurgent Republicans and Democrats held, the resolution passed, and Speaker Joseph Cannon's power was broken. Later in the session the House also adopted a discharge rule. The leadership of future Speakers would be based on bargaining rather than domination.

Cannon continued to serve as Speaker until the Democrats reorganized the House after winning a majority of the seats in the 1910 elections. Cannon held his seat in 1910 and moved to the office building that would come to bear his name. He lost his bid for reelection in 1912, sat out a term, was reelected in 1914, and continued to represent his district until he retired in 1923 at age 87. He lived another three years in Danville and died on November 12, 1926.

Further reading:
Bolles, Blair. *Tyrant from Illinois: Uncle Joe Cannon's Experiment with Personal Power.* New York: Norton, 1951; Busbey, L. White. *Uncle Joe Cannon: The Story of a Pioneer American.* New York: Henry Holt, 1927; Cooper, Joseph, and David W. Brady. "Institutional Context and Leadership Style: The House from Cannon to Rayburn." *American Political Science Review* 75 (June 1981): 411–425; Mooney, Booth. *Mr. Speaker: Four Men Who Shaped the United States House of Representatives.* Chicago: Follett Publishing, 1964; Norris, George W. *Fighting Liberal: The Autobiography of George W. Norris.* New York: Macmillan, 1945.

—Patricia A. Behlar

Capitol building

The symbol of the nation's government and of Congress, the Capitol building in Washington, D.C., has housed the U.S. HOUSE OF REPRESENTATIVES and the U.S. SENATE since 1793. A French engineer, Pierre Charles L'Enfant, planned the city to be named Washington, and selected what was then known as "Jenkins Hill" as the site for the nation's Capitol. The building, constructed 88 feet above the nearby Potomac River, was not complete when Congress first met there in 1800. The ARCHITECT OF THE CAPITOL was responsible for the design. Construction of the original building took 34 years and was directed by six presidents. The Capitol building initially housed not only the U.S. Congress but was also home to the LIBRARY OF CONGRESS, the Supreme Court, district courts, and a myriad of other offices.

The Capitol building was determined to be too small after its completion in 1826 and was subsequently enlarged. Given the continued crowding in the Capitol, the Library of Congress in 1897 moved eastward across the street to its own building, the Thomas Jefferson building. In addition, the House and Senate constructed separate House and Senate office buildings. Finally, members of the Supreme Court moved out in 1935 following completion of their new building, which was constructed just north of the Library of Congress. The neoclassical Capitol structure has long been noted for several prominent and historic architectural features, most prominently its dome. Constructed between 1855 and 1866, the 287-foot cast-iron dome, which dominates the Washington, D.C., skyline, replaced the smaller wooden dome completed in 1824. Construction of the dome continued throughout the Civil War. Standing atop the dome is a 19-foot, six-inch Statue of Freedom The dome consists primarily of more than 8.9 million pounds of ironwork. The entire project cost $1,047,291.

A large colorful rotunda dominates the center of the Capitol building's second floor. The rotunda connects the Senate wing of the building to the north with the House wing to the south. The rotunda, which is 96 feet in diameter and 180 feet tall, was constructed between 1818 and 1824. The sandstone walls of the rotunda extend 48 feet above the floor and feature numerous paintings, sculptures, busts, and other works of art depicting events in American history. The rotunda has been the scene of numerous ceremonial events and the lying in state of presidents and other prominent citizens.

North of the rotunda is the Old Senate Chamber, a semicircular, half-domed, two-story room in which the Senate met between 1810 and 1859. After the Senate began convening in its present room, the Old Senate Chamber was taken over by the Supreme Court, which used it from 1860 to 1935. The Supreme Court previously convened downstairs in the Old Supreme Court Chamber. The Supreme Court had been convening in its old chamber, a semicircular room with an umbrella-vaulted ceiling, from 1810 to 1860. In this room the Supreme Court announced such historic rulings as *Marbury v. Madison* (1803) and *McCulloch v. Maryland* (1819). Later the room served as a committee meeting room, law library, and storage room before being restored to its mid-19th-century beauty in 1975.

On the first floor and directly below the rotunda is the Capitol Crypt. The Crypt is a large circular area surrounded by 40 Doric brown stone columns that support sandstone arches that support the rotunda floor and the nine-ton iron dome above. Completed in 1827, the Crypt features a star in the center of its floor that represent the point from which the streets of the city were laid out and numbered.

Extending southward from the Crypt is the Hall of Columns, a 100-foot-long hall beneath the House of Representatives. The hall is lined with 28 fluted white marble columns, or which the hall is named. Constructed in the mid-19th century, the hall has housed part of the National Statuary Hall collection since 1976.

The main part of the National Statuary collection is housed one floor above in the Old Hall of the House, today commonly known as the National Statuary Hall. The two-story hall, located in a semicircular room just south of the Rotunda, was where the House of Representatives met for almost 50 years. Rebuilt between 1815 and 1819 following the British burning of the Capitol in 1814, the hall was constantly plagued by echoes as sound bounced off the smooth curved ceiling. Architects were never able to resolve this problem, necessitating moving the House to its present chamber in 1857. The history of the Old Hall of the House includes the inauguration of six early 19th-century presidents, the marquis de Lafayette becoming the first foreign citizen to address Congress, and the dramatic election of President John Quincy Adams in 1824. Today the chamber houses 38 statues and is the setting for numerous ceremonies, such as presidential luncheons and receptions for foreign dignitaries.

By the early 21st century activities in the Capitol building have been distributed among five levels. The ground floor is occupied by committee rooms and special spaces dedicated to congressional officers. The second floor houses the chambers of the House of Representatives and the U.S. Senate as well as congressional leadership offices. It is from the second floor that visitors can view the Capitol rotunda. The third floor provides public access to the galleries of the House and Senate, where visitors can view the proceedings when Congress is in session. Offices, committee rooms, and press chambers are also found on the third floor. The fourth floor and basement of the Capitol building house offices, workrooms, and other support areas.

Further reading:
"A Brief History of the U.S. Capitol Complex." Available online. URL: http://www.aoc.gov/cc/cc_history.htm. Accessed February 8, 2003; "The United States Capitol: An Overview of the Building and Its Function." Available online. URL: http://www.aoc.gov/cc/capitol/capitol_overview.htm. Accessed February 8, 2003.

—Nancy Lind

Capitol Hill

The neighborhood surrounding the Capitol building in Washington, D.C., is commonly known as Capitol Hill. Pierre L'Enfant, the engineer commissioned to lay out the plan of the new federal district in 1791, selected a hill at the eastern end of town to be the location for the Capitol building. He found the hill, known then as Jenkins Hill, to be a pedestal waiting for a monument. Even though the U.S. Supreme Court is located adjacent to the Capitol, the hill became synonymous with the legislative branch of government. When people say, "I am going up to the Hill," they are usually referring to business they have in the Capitol building.

Jenkins Hill was farmland owned by the Rozier-Young-Carroll family when L'Enfant designed the city. He placed the Capitol at the hub of the city, with the four sectors of Washington converging on the building. The proposed Capitol building was to face east, so land speculators bought land on the eastern part of the hill recognizing a good investment.

The first wing of the Capitol was completed in 1800. By that time a number of boardinghouses, private homes, and businesses had been built on Capitol Hill. Few of those buildings survived into the modern era. The older buildings one may find on Capitol Hill today were built during and after the administration of President Abraham Lincoln. Some of the older buildings were torn down to make room

The Capitol Dome viewed from the west *(Architect of the Capitol)*

for the physical growth of the federal government. The Library of Congress was built in 1889, and the Supreme Court, located directly across First Street from the Capitol, was completed in 1935. The House and Senate office buildings also are located on Capitol Hill. By the end of World War II, many of the row homes and businesses had fallen into a state of disrepair. After the war people began restoring the old buildings and refurbishing the area. The Capitol Hill neighborhood generally is considered to be the area between Massachusetts Avenue on the north, the foot of the Capitol on the west, E Street to the south, and Lincoln Park and 11th Street on the east.

Further reading:
Herron, Paul. *The Story of Capitol Hill.* New York: Coward-McCann, 1963; Overbeck, Ruth Ann. "Capitol Hill: The Capitol Is Just Up the Street." In Kathryn Schneider Smith, ed. *Washington at Home: An Illustrated History of*

Neighborhoods in the Nation's Capital. Northridge, Calif.:
Windsor Publications, 1988.

—John David Rausch, Jr.

careers, congressional

Many members of Congress currently expect to serve
lengthy periods of time in either the HOUSE OF REPRE-
SENTATIVES or the SENATE, and on a few occasions in both
chambers. Members of Congress in the early days of the
republic were likely to be experienced state or local officeholders who served a brief time in the national legislature.
After a two-year term many representatives decided not to
run for reelection. Many senators resigned before their first
term of office expired. Before the Civil War the average
member of Congress served roughly four years. At the start
of each new Congress, the majority of members in both
chambers were freshmen. There was no staff assistance or
offices; most members worked at their desks on the floor.
The federal government was small since states took care of
the largest portion of policy making. Most of the work could
be done in a few months each year.

After the Civil War tenure lengthened in the Senate
first, followed by the House. Members from southeastern
states were particularly able to serve long periods in
Congress. The development of committees allowed senators and representatives to begin to develop policy expertise. Strong party leaders emerged to appoint members to
committees and to enforce party voting. The size and
importance of the federal government also began to grow
with new policies on economic development, foreign
affairs, and business regulation. Turnover remained high
because local party organizations controlled nominations
and enforced a voluntary form of rotation in office.

At the turn of the 20th century, congressional careers
began to lengthen as the local party organizations began to
exert less control over nominations. The introduction of
direct primaries, in which voters could directly nominate
their choice of candidates, weakened party control. In 1913
the adoption of the SEVENTEENTH AMENDMENT providing
for the popular election of senators further diminished the
influence of local party organizations over candidate selection. Districts became safe for Republicans in northern
states and Democrats in southern states after the realigning
election in 1896. The only competition some members of
Congress faced was within their own party.

Internal changes in both chambers encouraged
careerism. The Senate adopted seniority as the method for
selecting committee chairs. The member of the majority
party who had the longest tenure on the committee became
the chair at the retirement of the previous chair. Seniority
was seen as an innovation that provided for an almost automatic selection process. In 1911, in the wake of deposing
their autocratic SPEAKER OF THE HOUSE, members of the
House also adopted seniority in selecting committee chairs.
The norm for selecting party leaders involved a ladder of
advancement after a long apprenticeship. The office of a
member of Congress grew with additional staff, increased
pay, and year-round sessions.

In the 1920s the mean length of service in both chambers was between eight and nine years. The number of
freshman members at the start of a specific Congress was
around 20 percent. Large freshmen classes in 1932, 1946,
and 1958 became the exception to the rule. Junior members
deferred to more senior members, knowing that when the
time came, they would have their chance at wielding power.

As the federal government grew in response to the
Great Depression, World War II, and the cold war, congressional workload also increased. Congress became a
complex and stable institution, and its members enjoyed
secure and predictable careers. By the 1960s a number of
new social issues emerged, and local and national party
organizations had declined to a low level of influence. A
new type of entrepreneurial, self-selected candidate
emerged to run for Congress. When elected these members sought additional power within their chambers in
order to enact a policy agenda to help their constituents.
The reelection rate reached 80 percent in the early 1960s.
By the 1980s the reelection rate had grown to more than 90
percent. Members of Congress engaged in permanent
campaigns, spending more time at home and building professional organizations in their congressional offices. New
subcommittees were created allowing more members
increased opportunity to be chairs. Individual legislators
became more autonomous, while the most senior chairs
lost control of their organizations.

Senior Democratic members chose to retire in the
1970s in reaction to their loss of personal power to the new
policy entrepreneurs in the legislature. Senior Republicans,
dismayed at never having the chance to be committee
chairs, also retired. By the 1980s this wave of retirements
had slowed, but congressional careers continued to be
demanding. There were constituents to serve and subcommittee and committee meetings to attend. In a letter to
constituents, Mo Udall, a Democrat representative from
Arizona, complained that with constituent service and
meetings, there was little time to do the true work of
Congress, legislation. In the 1990s many members complained that congressional careers were more demanding
and less rewarding than in the past. In 1992 several factors, including the House bank scandal and the ability to
convert campaign funds into personal use, combined to
encourage 66 representatives to retire.

The Republican Party's takeover of Congress in 1995
led to a number of retirements among senior Republicans.
Disregarding seniority, Speaker Newt Gingrich passed over

several senior members in appointing committee chairs. Three committees were eliminated, and the number of subcommittees also was reduced. The House Republican Conference limited chairs' terms to three years. While the importance of seniority was reduced, the Committee on Committees selected chairs from experienced members. Several of the newly elected Republicans vowed to serve only a few terms in Congress.

The term limitation movement emerged in the early 1990s as a reaction to the concern about legislative careerism. While the movement was most successful in enacting limits on the length of service of state legislators, the movement's leaders acknowledged that their goal was to enact limits on congressional service. Term limits on members of Congress were enacted in 23 states before the U.S. Supreme Court ruled in *U.S. Term Limits v. Thornton* that states could not add to the constitutional qualifications for congressional service.

Political science and American national government textbooks regularly note that congressional careers are much longer in the modern era than they were in earlier Congresses. The evidence of these lengthy careers is used to demonstrate that Congress has become institutionalized and professionalized, a positive trend in the eyes of most political scientists. The popular support for congressional term limits that continued at high levels despite the Supreme Court's ruling in *Thornton* indicated that many Americans do not think congressional careers are a positive feature of the legislative body.

Further reading:
Brady, David, Kara Buckley, and Douglas Rivers. "The Roots of Careerism in the U.S. House of Representatives." *Legislative Studies Quarterly* 24 (1999): 489–510; Coyne, James K., and John H. Fund. *Cleaning House: America's Campaign for Term Limits.* Washington, D.C.: Regnery Gateway, 1992; Hibbing, John R. *Congressional Careers: Contours of Life in the U.S. House of Representatives.* Chapel Hill: University of North Carolina Press, 1991; Hibbing, John R. "Legislative Careers: Why and How We Should Study Them." *Legislative Studies Quarterly* 24 (1999): 149–171; Polsby, Nelson W. "The Institutionalization of the U.S. House of Representatives." *American Political Science Review* 62 (1968) 144–168; Price, H. Douglas. "The Congressional Career: Then and Now." In *Congressional Behavior,* edited by Nelson Polsky, 14–27. New York: Random House, 1971; Rausch, John David. "Understanding the Term Limits Movement." In *The Test of Time: Coping with Legislative Term Limits,* edited by Rick Farmer, John Farmer, John David Rausch, and John C. Green, 225–236. Lanham, Md.: Lexington Books, 2003.

—John David Rausch, Jr.

Carlisle, John Griffin (1835–1910) *Speaker of the House of Representatives*

John G. Carlisle was born to a family of Irish-English Kentucky pioneers. The youngest son in a large family, Carlisle proved from a young age to be an eager student with an agile mind. After having earned a common grammar school education he moved to Covington, Kentucky, to study under John W. Stevenson, who later served as a senator and governor of Kentucky. An apparently extraordinary law student, he was soon practicing law, developing a reputation as a stump speaker in the Democratic Party, and by 1859 was serving in the state legislature. The secession of 1861 left the border state of Kentucky in turmoil, and Carlisle pled for compromise, though he was opposed to federal military action against the seceding states. Unfortunately for Carlisle, his constituents had stronger Union sentiments and refused to reelect him for a third term in 1861. Benefiting from a larger constituency in 1866, he began two terms as a state senator, attended the Democratic National Convention as a delegate, and was elected lieutenant governor of the state in 1871. Carlisle's experience in presiding over the state senate not only developed his skills as a legislator but also whetted his appetite for a role in national politics. He won election to the U.S. HOUSE OF REPRESENTATIVES in 1876 from the Sixth District of Kentucky.

As good a politician as he was a student, Carlisle developed a solid reputation among Democratic congressmen and at the start of his second term garnered a choice appointment to the WAYS AND MEANS COMMITTEE. Given that the money question dominated political debate at the time, this committee was a prized position for Carlisle, who had developed a keen interest in monetary and fiscal policy. Representing western interests demanded that he oppose the Specie Resumption Act of 1875, believing that the federal payment of gold for depreciated greenbacks established by the law would be damaging to western farmers, who would be hurt by deflation. Carlisle, however, was at heart a monetary conservative who opposed paper currency and advocated only limited coinage of silver to accompany gold.

With the resurgence of the South in national politics, Democrats gained control of both houses of Congress in 1878 and spent much of the Rutherford B. Hayes administration restoring home rule in the South. With Hayes's withdrawal of federal troops from the South and Democrats presiding over Congress, much of the civil rights work of Reconstruction collapsed. Carlisle wholeheartedly supported the repeal of Reconstruction reforms by promoting extensive use of riders to appropriations bills that repealed civil rights reforms. Given that Hayes opposed these rapid reversals and was especially bothered by the rider technique, Congress spent considerable time debating the issue in multiple attempts to override PRESIDENTIAL VETOES. In these debates Carlisle built his stature among Democrats as a tough opponent to Republican policy.

The issue that most defined Carlisle's congressional tenure was the tariff. As free trade and protectionist factions battled over tariff rates in a rapidly growing economy, the Democratic Party struggled with sectional fissures in it ranks over the issue. Keeping in line with the historic opposition of southerners to protectionism, Carlisle became one of the most visible opponents to the tariff. With strong support from free trade southern and western representatives, Carlisle managed to win election in 1883 as SPEAKER OF THE HOUSE over Pennsylvanian Samuel Randall, the leader of the protectionist faction.

Though really not a supporter of pure free trade, Carlisle argued in the House for a considerable reduction in tariffs in order to stimulate exports and decrease prices. While his position was driven in part by concern over the tremendous profits and concentration of wealth enjoyed by northern industrialists, he was also concerned by the potential damage to the economy caused by surpluses in federal revenue. He asserted that after having calmly stood by and allowed monopolies to grow fat, one should not be asked to make them bloated. Enormous surplus revenues were illogical and oppressive. He also lobbied to halt the granting of subsidies to corporations in a variety of industries, including sugar production and shipping. To Carlisle, the inconsistency of discouraging trade through tariffs and encouraging trade through subsidies to shippers smacked of corruption. Carlisle also attacked from the Speaker's chair what he believed to be excessive expenditure by Congress. While he garnered respect for his management of the House, he often promoted his causes by refusing to recognize his opponents on the floor, a technique that only enhanced his esteem within his party.

Briefly touted as a candidate for the Democratic presidential nomination in 1884, Carlisle threw solid support behind the party's candidate, Grover Cleveland, who went on to win the election. Cleveland shared Carlisle's distaste for tariffs, and both men focused much attention on the issue. In 1888 the House passed the Mills Bill, which would have lowered tariff rates considerably had protectionist Democrats in the Senate not allied themselves with Republicans to defeat the bill. Democrats faced a much larger setback when Republican Benjamin Harrison won the presidency over Cleveland that fall, and Republicans achieved a majority in both houses of Congress. The tariff debate reached a fevered pitch, with Carlisle as MINORITY LEADER, when Republicans successfully raised import duties to a record peacetime rate with the McKinley Tariff.

In 1890 he left his minority leadership in the House to take an appointment by the Kentucky legislature to finish the term of Senator James Beck (allowing him to vote against the McKinley Tariff twice). Carlisle used his SENATE seat to preach against the tariff and high government spending. The 1890 congressional elections showed that many Americans must have come to agree, as Democrats reversed their losses from two years earlier. With optimism running high among Democrats for the 1892 presidential election, Carlisle's name was again floated for nomination, but the party again went with Cleveland with success. Given the like-mindedness of the two men on monetary and fiscal policy, Cleveland appointed Carlisle secretary of the Treasury in 1893. It was an inopportune time to take the helm of the Treasury, since within weeks the country succumbed to a serious financial panic. The years that followed were difficult and contentious and proved the undoing of Carlisle's political career.

As panic set in to the market in spring 1893, speculators began to hoard gold, causing federal reserves to drop below the level deemed necessary to maintain the monetary system. Carlisle responded by demanding an end to silver coinage and tight adherence to a hard-money gold standard. As the situation worsened, a special session of Congress convened to debate the repeal of the Sherman Silver Purchase Act, which had allowed holders of silver certificates to redeem them for Treasury gold. While Carlisle's influence in the Senate won the fight for repeal, the Democratic Party found itself more profoundly split than ever. Worse, the repeal failed to stabilize the Treasury and halt the downward spiral. Congress responded to the deepening depression by turning to more protectionism through the Wilson-Gorman Tariff. Carlisle again voiced strong opposition to the tariff based on the same arguments he had given during the more prosperous 1880s. But Democrats had pushed hard for protectionism as a means for protecting wages and buttressing the failing economy.

In 1894 the president and his Treasury secretary reluctantly attempted to buttress gold reserves through the sale of federal bonds. The bonds sold, but most speculators paid for them with gold they were acquiring through the redemption of paper at the Treasury. Special issues of bonds to wealthy financiers such as J. P. Morgan also failed to recover the Treasury and brought charges of corruption against Carlisle. The secretary also pleaded with Congress to slash spending, and further charges of malfeasance came from his home district when he lobbied against the construction of another bridge across the Ohio River between Cincinnati and Covington. When word surfaced that Carlisle had served as an attorney for the existing private Suspension Bridge Company in Covington, the local townspeople labeled him a traitor.

By 1896 the economy began to recover, and a final bond issue stabilized the gold reserves. But considerable collateral political damage had accompanied the economic trauma of a half decade. The Democratic Party was divided on fundamental policy issues, with a majority of the party embracing the soft-money inflation promoted by Populists.

While most were still opposed to paper currency, the party built a platform on the coinage of silver. In 1896 the Democrats chose William Jennings Bryan as their candidate for the presidency, just as the Populist Party had also nominated Bryan as the national standard-bearer for loose monetary policy. Carlisle opposed Bryan's nomination and threw his support behind the minority conservative faction of the Democratic Party that had formed the National Democratic Party (the Gold Democrats).

As the Democrats absorbed the Populists and the Republicans began formulating a conservative progressivism, Carlisle found himself without a place in national politics and was shunted aside. Reelection from his home district in Kentucky was unlikely since he had alienated most of his old constituents, who hungered for currency and federally funded bridges. He returned to his hometown of Covington in 1896 to speak on the advantages of the gold standard and fiscal responsibility. Dodging vegetables, eggs, cigars, and a few bricks, he fled the stage and never looked back.

When Cleveland and his cabinet left Washington in 1897, John Griffin Carlisle eschewed his home in Kentucky for a law practice in New York. He was last visible on the national scene amid turn-of-the-century turmoil over foreign policy as an opponent of expansionism and vice president of the Anti-Imperialist League. He died in 1910 having lived at the center of the critical questions of his day and seen the time for his convictions pass. His final return to Covington, to be buried in the Linden Grove Cemetery, brought softened attitudes and eventually a school bearing his name.

Further reading:
Barnes, James. *John G. Carlisle, Financial Statesman.* 1931. Reprint, Gloucester, Mass.: P. Smith Co., 1967; Cherny, Robert W. *American Politics in the Gilded Age.* New York: Harlan Davidson, 1997; Logan, Rayford Whittingham. *The Betrayal of the Negro: From Rutherford B. Hayes to Woodrow Wilson.* New York: Da Capo Press, 1997; Sherman, John, Trumbul White, and John G. Carlisle. *Silver and Gold on Both Sides of the Shield: The Doctrines of Free Silver, Mono-Metalism, and Bi-Metalism.* Los Angeles: University Press of the Pacific, 2001; Weisman, Steven. *The Great Tax Wars: Lincoln to Wilson: The Fierce Battles Over Money and Power That Transformed the Nation.* New York: Simon & Schuster, 2002.

—Michael Steiner

Carswell, G. Harold, nominee to the U.S. Supreme Court

Immediately after the defeat of President Richard Nixon's first nominee to the Supreme Court, Clement F. Haynsworth of South Carolina on November 21, 1969, Nixon ordered his political adviser Harry Dent to "find a good federal judge farther down South and further to the right." Dent came up with G. Harrold Carswell of Florida, a member of the Fifth Circuit Court of Appeal to fill the seat vacated by the resignation of Justice Abe Fortas. Carswell was appointed by President Eisenhower to the U.S. District Court for Northern Florida in 1958. In 1969 President Nixon elevated Carswell to the Fifth Circuit and six months later nominated him to the Supreme Court.

The immediate reaction to the Carswell nomination was positive. Most observers felt that the Senate was not willing to engage in another battle over a Supreme Court nominee following the rejection of Haynsworth. The only initial opposition to emerge came from the NAACP and its Washington lobbyist Clarence Mitchell. The NAACP and other civil rights attorney's who had argued before Carswell found him to be insensitive to blacks and civil rights attorneys in his court. A few days after the nomination, a reporter uncovered a statement made by Carswell when running for political office in Georgia in 1948. Carswell, in a campaign speech, stated "I believe that segregation of the races is proper and the only practical and correct way of life in our states." Carswell immediately denounced his own remarks as "obnoxious and abhorrent to my personal philosophy." Defenders rallied to support Carswell, saying that the statements were 20 years old and no longer reflected his political views.

Opponents to the Carswell nomination used a strategy of delay in trying to defeat the nomination. They were concerned that a quick vote would result in Carswell's confirmation, but given sufficient time they would be able to mount a strong case against confirmation. The strategy proved to be successful. With every passing day, new information came in that raised concerns about whether Carswell was qualified to sit on the nation's highest court.

Legal scholars began to question Carswell's qualifications for the Court. The dean of the Yale Law School, Louis Pollack, testified that Carswell presented the weakest credentials of any Supreme Court nominee in the 20th century. In spite of the growing attack from the legal community on Carswell's credentials, the Senate Judiciary Committee voted 13-4 to favorably report the nomination to the Senate floor. The only hope of opponents was to delay the nomination and hope that additional damaging information would come forth. They got the time they needed when the Senate became bogged down in a debate over amendments to the 1970 Voting Rights Act.

With the delays in the confirmation process, additional information came out that showed that Carswell had assisted in the 1956 conversion of a publicly owned golf course in Tallahassee to a private one in order to prevent its integration. A document was uncovered that indicated that

Carswell sold property in 1966 that contained a restrictive covenant barring sale to African Americans. Although Carswell defended his actions in both cases, it raised concerns that Carswell had not abandoned the racial positions he had previously enunciated in his 1948 speech.

In response to the rapidly emerging criticism that Carswell did not possess the intellect to serve on the nation's highest court, several senators rose to defend Carswell and mediocrity. The most famous and damaging defense of Carswell came from Republican senator Roman Hruska of Nebraska, who took to the floor of the Senate to defend the selection of a mediocre Supreme Court nominee. Even if Carswell were mediocre, argued Hruska, "there are a lot of mediocre judges and people and lawyers. They are entitled to a little representation, aren't they, and a little chance? We can't have all Brandeises and Frankfurters and Cardozas and stuff like that there." Hruska hardly helped Carswell with his ringing defense of mediocrity.

On April 8, 1970, the Senate, rejected the Carswell nomination in a 51-45 vote. With the rejection of Carswell, President Nixon became the first president since Grover Cleveland to have two successive Supreme Court nominees rejected. Nixon attributed the defeat of both Haynsworth and Carswell to an "anti-South" bias of the Senate. "As long as the Senate is constituted the way it is today," said Nixon, "I will not nominate another southerner and let him be subjected to the kind of malicious character assassination accorded both judges Haynsworth and Carswell." Senate critics of the president said there were plenty of "strict constructionists" from the South who could win Senate confirmation, just not these two.

Unlike Haynsworth, who stayed on the federal bench and served with distinction for two decades, Carswell retired from the federal courts two weeks after his rejection. He returned to his native Florida and entered the Republican Senate primary against Representative William Cramer, who was one of the developers of the modern Republican Party in Florida. Republican governor Claude Kirk urged Carswell to enter the race, much to the consternation of the Republican establishment. Carswell lost to the better-known Cramer, but the disputed primary would weaken Cramer and allow long-shot Democrat Lawton Chiles the opportunity to win the election and delay the Republicans in taking political control of the state. Carswell disappeared from the political scene after being arrested for soliciting sex from a male police officer at a Tallahassee mall.

Further reading:
Dent, Harry S. *The Prodigal South Returns to Power.* New York: Wiley & Sons, 1978; Harriss, Richard. *Decision.* New York: Ballatine Books, 1970; Kotlowski, Dean. *Nixon's Civil Rights.* Cambridge, Mass.: Harvard University Press, 2001.
—Darryl Paulson

Case Act of 1972

The Case Act is the law requiring that the executive branch transmit the text of all international agreements not submitted to the SENATE as treaties within 60 days after the agreements take effect. It also is known as the Case-Zablocki Act.

In August 1970 the administration of President Richard Nixon entered into an executive agreement with Spain extending an earlier agreement governing American use of military bases in Spain. A number of senators were concerned that the agreement was not negotiated as a treaty, requiring Senate ratification. On December 11, 1970, the Senate passed Senate Resolution 469, expressing the sense of the Senate that nothing in the executive agreement should be considered to be a national commitment by the United States toward Spain.

The Nixon administration concluded executive agreements with Portugal and Bahrain in December 1971, providing for continued stationing of American military personnel at a base in the Azores and continued use of facilities in Bahrain. The Senate FOREIGN RELATIONS COMMITTEE responded by introducing Senate Resolution 214, stating that any agreement with Portugal should be submitted to the Senate as a treaty. In January 1972 Senator Clifford Case, a Republican from New Jersey, introduced an amendment to the resolution calling for the agreement with Bahrain to be submitted as a treaty. The resolution was approved.

Neither resolution had the force of law. In December 1970 Senator Case introduced legislation that became the Case-Zablocki Act. His action was in response to secret security agreements previous presidential administrations had made with foreign governments committing the United States without the knowledge of Congress. The bill introduced by Senator Case had been proposed in 1954, 1955, and 1957. The earlier bills had been passed by the Senate but died in the HOUSE OF REPRESENTATIVES. Case's bill called for the submission of all executive agreements to the Senate within 60 days after the agreements took effect. After it was reintroduced in February 1971, the bill successfully made it through the legislative process to become Public Law 92-403. Companion bills had been introduced in the House in April 1972 by Representatives Clement Zablocki, a Democrat from Wisconsin, and Charles Whalen, a Republican from Ohio.

Under the Case-Zablocki Act, all executive agreements must be sent to Congress within 60 days after they take effect. Agreements that have been classified because of their effect on national security also must be submitted to Congress. The receipt of the executive agreements is noted in the *CONGRESSIONAL RECORD,* and unclassified agreements are listed in committee publications. Members of Congress may review the agreements in the offices of the Foreign Relations Committees in each chamber.

Further reading:

Crabb, Cecil V., and Pat M. Holt. *Invitation to Struggle: Congress, the President, and Foreign Policy.* 4th ed. Washington, D.C.: Congressional Quarterly Press, 1992; Johnson, Loch. *The Making of International Agreements: Congress Confronts the Executive.* New York: New York University Press, 1984; United States Senate. Committee on Foreign Relations. *Treaties and Other International Agreements: The Role of the United States Senate.* Senate Print 106-71. Washington, D.C.: Government Printing Office, 2001.

—John David Rausch, Jr.

casework

Casework refers to efforts by a member of Congress to solve a constituent's problem with an entity of the government. Those problems take many forms. The classic example is helping a widow get a lost pension check from the Social Security Administration. Americans call upon their representatives and senators for a great range of particular services: help to get a passport, assistance to a student needing information for a term paper on some aspect of government activity, help to a veteran to receive a medal for a war experience in an earlier era, support for a grant application from a local government or university, support for a particular business seeking relief from a governmental regulation, nominations for young people to obtain appointments to military academies, appointments to congressional internships, and summer jobs. Constituents ask for help with immigration problems, military regulations, taxation issues, and the like. They seek benefits such as government loans, jobs, grants, and patents. Visiting CAPITOL HILL with their children during vacation, constituents may want a picture with a congressperson, passes to one of the congressional GALLERIES, or a visit to a congressperson's office.

From time immemorial one of the rights of the citizen has been to write one's congressperson a letter about a grievance with some agency of government. The basic idea is that the representative can and should stand up for the concerns of an individual constituent, no matter how humble the constituent or how insignificant the request. Thus, representatives often function as special pleaders on behalf of constituent interests. Biographies of representatives often report the unusual requests they dealt with and the lengths to which they and their staff went to satisfy their constituents' needs. Such requests come in all forms of communication: letters, telephone calls, E-MAILS, and faxes. Congressional offices receive hundreds, even thousands, of communications each week.

If the demand side of the relationship is obvious, the supply side has particular dynamics as well. Many congressmembers feature in their communications to citizens' invitations and encouragements to get help from them. Indeed, a major function of both paid and volunteer STAFF in congressional offices is to act upon citizen requests. Members of Congress give priority to their public service function. When the House did a study of its own operations in 1977, 79 percent of the members expressed as one view of their job that they perform as a constituency servant. Many congressional offices resemble small businesses. They treat their constituents like customers, and the customers' needs are serviced with efficiency and good grace. According to David Mayhew, "Each office has skilled professionals who can play the bureaucracy like an organ— pushing the right pedals to produce the desired effects."

Congressional offices take pride in performing effective casework. Caseworkers take up constituents' problems, typically focusing requests on liaisons in the various executive agencies that administer the government service that is subject to question. Paperwork, phone calls, and e-mail often bring a solution in a matter of days or weeks. In difficult cases most members of Congress become personally involved in finding a solution for the constituent. The constituent typically receives a letter from the congressmember taking credit for the solution or putting the best face on the outcome that was achieved.

Members of Congress acknowledge that good constituent service is good politics. In an influential political analysis, Mayhew identified reelection as the primary goal of incumbent members of Congress, and to pursue the goal they engage in credit claiming, advertising, and position taking. By vigorously pursuing casework, congresspeople can ingratiate themselves with constituents, thereby trying to activate them as loyal voters. In contrast with position taking on the issues, which can alienate voters whose views on issues differ from those of the representatives, casework help is rarely controversial and usually welcomed and applauded by the beneficiaries. Mayhew and others made the argument that this major aspect of representation helped to explain why representatives, after winning a close initial election, often experience a "sophomore surge" and increase their margin of victory in the next election. A larger argument indicated that casework accompanied by credit claiming helped incumbents repeatedly win reelection with safe margins of victory. As a consequence of these safe margins and the growing phenomenon of incumbent reelection, the number of marginal districts, where congressional election contests were close, was "vanishing."

Although political scientists have struggled with methodological difficulties in trying to sort out explanations for the electoral success of incumbents, they observed clear evidence that Congress itself increased its staff resources to do constituent service. They increased the allocation of staff to district offices and locally based services, increased the volume of direct mail to constituents, and increased the time and exposure that incumbents devoted to their districts to engage in credit claiming activities.

In the 1980s and 1990s the matter of staff size and staff salaries became increasingly costly and controversial. Personal staffs of House members number about 18. Senators have larger staffs, and their staff payrolls vary according to the size of their state constituency. In recent years the sizes of committee staffs actually declined, indicating the priority that members give to constituency service over programmatic expertise.

Critics of casework argue that repetitious casework requests, even the proverbial Social Security check for the widow, should spur Congress to solve the bureaucratic problems underlying such specific problems with comprehensive policy changes. Congress should improve upon its piecemeal efforts at getting one check to one constituent accompanied by a letter that claims credit for a victory over the bureaucracy. Instead it should reform government procedures and streamline government services with effective legislation and achieve appropriate and efficient administration by means of systematic congressional oversight. Some critics suggest that casework requests should be referred to an ombudsman, as in the United Kingdom, where a civil servant has the task of impartially investigating citizen complaints against a public authority or institution in order to bring about a fair settlement or solution to a problem. This would, it is argued, appropriately meet citizens' needs without encouraging scandalous political favors for friends of congresspeople under the cover of the word *casework.*

Moreover, the critics say, members of Congress should put the resources of their time and staff entirely into solving the policy problems related to legislation. Representatives and senators ought not expend their energy on retail politics and the particular needs of individual constituents when complex matters of economic development, environmental problems, taxation, national defense, and foreign relations deserve every bit of effort and intelligence that they can bring to bear.

Despite these objections, the function of representation carries the strong implication that the representative will make wide-ranging efforts to act in the interests of constituents. Their concerns regarding government ought to be tended to, and each representative's stakes in keeping such a constituent happy incline the representative to persist in providing that kind of service by means of casework.

Further reading:
Mason, D. M. "Let Congress Be Congress." *Policy Review* Fall (1992): 31–37; Mayhew, D. R. *Congress: The Electoral Connection.* New Haven, Conn.: Yale University Press, 1974; Mezey, M. L. "Legislatures: Individual Purpose and Institutional Performance." In *Political Science: The State of the Discipline,* edited by A. Finifter, Washington, D.C.: American Political Science Association, 1993; Sarra, G., and D. Moon. "Casework, Issue Positions, and Voting in Congressional Elections: A District Analysis." *Journal of Politics* (1994): 200–214; *Congressional Quarterly's Guide to Congress.* 2d ed. Washington, D.C.: Congressional Quarterly, 1976.

—Jack R. Van Der Slik

caucus, party

The party caucus is the collection of members of either major political party (Democratic or Republican) elected to either the HOUSE OF REPRESENTATIVES or the SENATE. The Democrats in either chamber refer to this group as the Democratic Caucus; the Republicans' name is the Republican Conference.

In the House the majority party caucus is responsible for selecting the SPEAKER OF THE HOUSE, MAJORITY LEADER, Majority Whips, and Deputy Whips. The minority party caucus selects the MINORITY LEADER (who also is the minority party's candidate for Speaker), Minority Whip, and Deputy Whips. Each caucus also appoints members to a Steering Committee, which works with the party leader to appoint members to House committees and to select the committee chair or ranking member. The House Democratic caucus elects all committee chairs or ranking members and all chairs or ranking members of the 13 APPROPRIATIONS COMMITTEE subcommittees, a practice instituted in the 1970s. Both the House Democratic Caucus and the Republican Conference have chairs that run the meetings of the caucus and a secretary, another important leadership position.

In the Senate the party caucuses are responsible for choosing the minority and majority party leaders and majority and minority whips, as appropriate. The Steering Committee, a committee of the Democratic Caucus, coordinates Senate Democrats' committee assignments. Senate Republicans' assignments are coordinated by the Committee on Committees. All committee assignments, including those selected as chair and ranking member, are approved by the full party caucus and are subject to Senate rules regarding committee assignments. The looser structure of the Senate, coupled with rather expansive leadership opportunities, means that practically every member of either party caucus may hold a formal party leadership position if he or she wishes.

Aside from their organizational function, the party caucuses also meet regularly to formulate legislative strategy. For the majority party this includes choosing which legislative alternatives to support, moving items through the committees, and plotting floor strategy. For the minority party, whose ability to move legislation is limited, caucus meetings focus on legislative and public relations strategies as a means to block objectionable legislation and/or embarrass the majority party. Party caucus leaders may work with members of the opposing party to craft compromise legislation. However, as both chambers have become more partisan in the 1990s and 2000s, such bargaining is becoming less frequent.

Party caucuses, especially in the much larger House, are not monolithic. Over time various informal groups, comprised of members of a particular ideological bent, have organized to influence the decisions of the larger party caucus. For instance, in the 1970s and 1980s conservative Democrats, primarily from the South, formed the Conservative Democratic Forum, also known as the "Boll Weevils." On several issues, most notably the Reagan tax package of 1981, they joined forces with the Republican conference when they could not move the Democratic caucus. The Boll Weevils were replaced by the "Mainstream Democratic Forum" in the late 1980s and early 1990s. This group later evolved into the BLUE DOG DEMOCRATS, a group of moderate and conservative Democrats from all over the country.

On the other end of the political spectrum, the DEMOCRATIC STUDY GROUP (DSG) began in the 1970s as a collection of the most liberal Democrats who wanted an organization to study and interpret legislation independent of the leadership, whom they perceived as controlled by those sympathetic to the Boll Weevils. The DSG eventually organized as a LEGISLATIVE SERVICE ORGANIZATION and became a well-respected clearinghouse for information on upcoming legislative proposals. Similarly, the Congressional Progressive Caucus unites some of the most liberal members of the House and Senate and provides a platform for their policy alternatives. Anchoring the center is the New Democrat Coalition, formed in 1997, which claims to support core Democratic values but says it is "pro-growth and development."

The Republicans have their groups as well. The Conservative Opportunity Society (COS) was formed in the early 1980s by former Speaker NEWT GINGRICH. COS members used the new medium of C-SPAN to spread their message and to attack the Democratic majority. Also in the 1980s, a group of moderate and liberal Republicans, primarily from the Northeast and Midwest, formed the Gypsy Moths as a means to ensure the conference leadership considered their positions on issues. Some, such as the House Wednesday Group, another moderate Republican organization, boasted Senate counterparts. The Republican Study Committee, which boasts some 85 members in the 108th Congress, promotes a conservative economic and social agenda.

The development of these informal groups, many registered as congressional member organizations, troubles the formal party leadership. Many leaders saw them as a threat and as potentially divisive to the party caucus as a whole. However, over time these informal groups have become an important way for different factions of the parties to gain legitimacy and articulate their common interests and for members to gain important leadership skills.

Further reading:
The Blue Dog Coalition. Available online. URL: http://www.house.gov/baronhill/bluedogs/. Accessed January 16, 2006 Congressional Progressive Caucus. Available online. URL: http://bernie.house.gov/pc/. Accessed January 16, 2006; Copeland, Gary W. and Moen Matthew C. *The Contemporary Congress: A Bicameral Approach.* Belmont, Calif.: West/Wadsworth, 1999; Hammond, Susan Webb. *Congressional Caucuses in National Policy Making.* Baltimore: Johns Hopkins University Press, 1998; House Democratic Caucus. Available online. URL: http://www.dems.gov/. Accessed January 16, 2006 House Republican Conference. Available online. URL: http://gop.gov/; Accessed January 16, 2006 New Democrat Coalition. Available online. URL: http://www.house.gov/adamsmith/news/ndc_press.html. Accessed January 16, 2006 Republican Study Committee. Available online. URL: http://johnshadegg.house.gov/rsc/. Accessed Senate Democratic Caucus. Available online. URL: http://democrats.senate.gov/. Accessed January 16, 2006 Senate Republican Conference. Available online. URL: http://republican.senate.gov/. Accessed January 16, 2006.

—Karen M. Kedrowski

caucuses, or congressional member organizations
Caucuses, or congressional member organizations (CMOs), are informal groups of members of Congress who share some common interest. The first such groups developed in the earliest Congresses, when members from a particular region or political party roomed together in boarding houses. These members not only plotted legislative strategy after hours in the boarding house, they often voted together on the floor of the House.

Today caucuses serve three primary functions, depending upon the group's mission and level of cohesion. The first is educational. The caucus provides information on legislation, policy evaluations and other developments to its members. Caucuses may plan policy briefings or develop briefing papers. The second is agenda setting. Caucus members may work together to bring their issue(s) onto the legislative agenda. Common strategies include sponsoring and cosponsoring legislation, endorsing particular legislation when several competing bills have been introduced, circulating "Dear Colleague" letters, meeting as a caucus with party leadership, and/or working with committee chairs to include provisions favored by the caucus into the committee draft of legislation. The final function is to deliver a block of votes on the floor in support of or to block legislation on the floor. Only the most cohesive and homogeneous caucuses can perform this function consistently and effectively.

While caucuses exist in both the HOUSE OF REPRESENTATIVES and the SENATE, they are more popular in the House. Senate rules of open debate and permitting nongermane amendments, coupled with the greater number of committee assignments, allows senators to pursue multiple interests simultaneously. The House of Representatives, on the other hand, limits committee assignments, emphasizes specialization and seniority, and strictly limits opportunities for floor debate. All of these rules prohibit a representative from becoming active in several unrelated policy areas. Caucus memberships, however, provide just such an outlet. They also provide leadership opportunities for junior members and opportunities to serve constituent interests and to work in a bipartisan or bicameral organization. At one time congressional leaders saw caucuses as an outlet for junior members primarily. However, today many senior members of Congress and those in formal leadership positions join caucuses.

The COMMITTEE ON HOUSE ADMINISTRATION oversees congressional member organizations (CMOs, the official name for caucuses); it reports that 207 caucuses are registered in the 108th Congress. The types of caucuses vary widely. However many CMOs can be broken down into the following categories: regional, demographic, partisan, and special interest.

Examples of regional caucuses include the Appalachian Caucus, the California Congressional Delegation, the Chesapeake Bay Watershed Task Force, the Congressional Coastal Caucus, the Congressional Friends of the Florida Keys Caucus, the Congressional Northern Border Caucus, the I-69 Caucus, the Interstate 49 Caucus, the Upper Mississippi River Basin Task Force, and the Northeast-Midwest Coalition.

Demographic caucuses are those that describe the members themselves and those that focus around a particular demographic group of constituents. Examples of the first include the Congressional Black Caucus, the Congressional Caucus for Women's Issues (which also permits male members to join), the Congressional Hispanic Caucus, and the Congressional Hispanic Conference. Examples of the latter include the caucuses that focus on refugees, Iraqi women, children, commuters, persons with disabilities, fathers, and ethnic and racial groups such as Asian Pacific Americans, Israelis, Sri Lankans, Turks, and Native Americans.

Partisan caucuses include the Blue Dog Coalition, the Republican Israel Caucus, the New Democrat Coalition, the Progressive Coalition, and the Republican Study Committee.

Interest caucuses constitute the largest group. They include caucuses on a wide variety of issues. Health and health care is one such popular cause, with particular caucuses focusing on rural health, diabetes, addiction, brain injuries, fetal alcohol syndrome, community health centers, digestive diseases, hearing, heart disease and stroke, kidney diseases, and mental health. Another popular set of issues deals with foreign affairs and trade. Examples of these caucuses include those focusing on arms control, national security, human rights, free trade, and military (army, coast guard, and electronic warfare) and caucuses that focus on relations with a particular country or region (such as the Caribbean, Brazil, Denmark, Korea, Bulgaria, and Morocco, among others). Several caucuses focus on economic development. They include industries such as travel and tourism, hunting, entertainment, skiing and snowboarding, furniture, steel, and agriculture. Finally, several groups focus on a particular issue, such as abortion (Bipartisan Pro-Life Caucus), environment, firearms, and taxation, among others.

How effective are the caucuses, especially in terms of their most important function—delivering a block of votes? The answer varies. Among the most closely studied caucuses is the Congressional Black Caucus (CBC). It was highly cohesive for much of its history, comprised almost entirely of African-American Democrats who represented urban districts outside the South. It was a highly cohesive group and held some sway within the Democratic Caucus especially. The CBC also annually submits its own budget alternative as a means to shape congressional debate about spending priorities. The CBC became much larger after 1990 redistricting with its emphasis on creating majority-minority districts. Many of the new members were centrist African-American Democrats representing rural southern districts. While the CBC's cohesiveness declined and its influence waned when the Democratic Party became the minority party in 1995, scholars also argue that the CBC's new generations of members are highly effective legislative strategists.

The same level of cohesion has never been realized by the Congressional Hispanic Caucus, in part because the Hispanic Caucus is smaller and more diverse ideologically and ethnically. However, the bipartisan nature of the Hispanic Caucus makes it able to influence policy in both the Republican Conference and the Democratic Caucus.

The Congressional Caucus for Women's Issues (CCWI) is a bipartisan organization of women in the House of Representatives. Since the CCWI operates on a consensus basis, it found that it could not adopt the comprehensive feminist agenda that many of its leaders wanted. Especially divisive were issues surrounding abortion, reproductive choice, and fetal stem cell research. Therefore, in the 1990s especially, as the size of its membership increased, the CCWI focused on women's health issues. The CCWI was particularly influential in creating the Office of Women's Health at the NIH, forcing the NIH to enforce its own regulations regarding the inclusion of women in clinical trials and increasing funds for breast cancer research.

Other caucuses have not undergone the same level of scrutiny as these three caucuses. However, in her analysis of congressional roll-call voting behavior, Susan Webb Hammond found that caucus membership was related to floor votes for approximately half of the caucuses she examined. It was significant in some caucuses of all types that she reviewed. In short, caucuses matter.

Further reading:
Canon, David T. *Race, Redistricting and Representation.* Chicago: University of Chicago Press, 1999; Gertzog, Irwin N. *Congressional Women: Their Recruitment, Integration and Behavior.* 2d ed. Westport, Conn.: Praeger, 1995; Hammond, Susan Webb. *Congressional Caucuses in National Policy Making.* Baltimore: Johns Hopkins University Press, 1998; Kedrowski, Karen M., and Marilyn Stine Sarow. "Gendering Cancer Policy: Media Advocacy and Congressional Policy Attention." In Cindy Simon Rosenthal, ed. *Women Transforming Congress.* Norman: University of Oklahoma Press, pp. 240–259, 2003; Singh, Robert. *The Congressional Black Caucus: Racial Politics in the U.S. Congress.* Thousand Oaks, Calif.: Sage Publications, 1998; Swain, Carol. *Black Faces, Black Interests.* Cambridge, Mass.: Harvard University Press, 1993; Vigil, Maurilio E. *Hispanics in Congress.* Lanham, Md.: University Press of America, 1996.

—Karen M. Kedrowski

census

The nation's census is a constitutional mandate that all residents of the United States be counted in order to properly apportion the seats in the HOUSE OF REPRESENTATIVES. Article I, Section 2, Clause 3, of the U.S. Constitution provides for the House of Representatives to be apportioned among the states according to an actual enumeration of the population that is to be made every 10 years in such manner as Congress shall direct. In addition to counting residents, the modern census provides much of the demographic information used by Congress to make domestic policy. The form, contents, and length of the census questionnaires is debated and negotiated within the executive and legislative branches.

In 1790 the nation's first census was conducted by 650 federal marshals going house-to-house unannounced. The marshals recorded the names of the heads of households and counted the other residents. The census cost $45,000 and took 18 months to complete, counting 3.9 million people. Federal marshals and their assistants conducted the census until 1880. The census of 1810 included the first questions on U.S. manufacturing capabilities. At this time the United States needed to export agricultural products and import manufacturing goods. In 1840 Congress asked the Census Bureau to collect information on social matters such as idiocy and mental illness. More questions on commerce and industry were added, lengthening the form to 80 questions.

By 1850 significant reforms had been made in the process of collecting census data. The federal government asked the scientific community, funded by the financial community, to discuss what kinds of questions should be asked, how the information should be collected, and how it should be reported. The census of 1850 was the first time that detailed information about all members of a household was collected.

The Census Bureau introduced mechanical tabulators in 1890. The census would never again be hand-tabulated. The 1930 census included questions about unemployment, migration, and income in order to help the federal government formulate policies to address the Great Depression. In 1940 the Census Bureau applied modern sampling techniques and created the first long form that was sent to only a subset of the population. The rest of the population was counted using a shorter form of more basic questions. The census of 1950 was tabulated for the first time using an electronic digital computer that worked 1,000 to 1 million times faster than previous equipment.

The 1960 census was the last one in which enumerators visited every U.S. household. In 1970 60 percent of American households were asked to complete their census forms themselves and mail them back to the Census Bureau for processing. Households were contacted by enumerators only if they failed to return their form or if there were errors on the form. The remaining 40 percent of households were visited by enumerators. The 1980 census expanded the mailing to almost 90 percent of households, and in 1990 almost all households received the census form by mail.

One of the challenges with the census is the problem of undercount. Since the Census Bureau sends a questionnaire to every household to complete and return, there is the problem of being unable to reach some households. The portion of the population not reached by the Census Bureau is the census undercount.

The Census Bureau has been measuring the census undercount since 1940, and the undercount rate has been the subject of public debate since the 1970s. After the 1980 census the bureau faced 54 lawsuits, many by civil rights groups, charging it with improper and unconstitutional methods of counting. Some identifiable groups, including certain minorities, children, and renters, have historically

This cartoon by Clifford K. Berryman depicts Uncle Sam and Congress regarding the results of the 14th census, which will affect the House of Representatives. *(National Archives)*

been undercounted. Historically, the Census Bureau tried to increase the number of persons from whom it obtained information through various means including advertising and setting up a toll-free number to help people fill out the form.

In 1991 Congress passed the Decennial Census Improvement Act instructing the secretary of Commerce to contract with the National Academy of Sciences to study the means by which the government could achieve the most accurate population count possible. The academy

concluded that the undercount could not be reduced without the use of statistical sampling and recommended that statistical sampling be used in the 2000 census. The Census Bureau developed plans to include sampling in the 2000 enumeration, drawing two separate legal challenges claiming that the use of sampling to apportion representatives among the states violates the census clause of the Constitution. The Supreme Court agreed, ruling in *Department of Commerce, et al. v. United States House of Representatives, et al.* (525 U.S. 316 [1999]).

Further reading:
Anderson, Margo J., and Stephen E. Fienberg. *Who Counts? The Politics of Census-Taking in Contemporary America.* New York: Russell Sage Foundation, 1999; Samuelson, Robert J. "Politics and the Census." *Newsweek,* 8 February 1999, p. 48; Samuel, Terence. "A Liberal in Winter." *U.S. News & World Report,* 11 March 2002, pp. 29–30.
—John David Rausch, Jr.

chaplains

Both chambers of Congress employ full-time chaplains to serve as ministers and pastoral counselors to members and their aides. The SPEAKER OF THE HOUSE OF REPRESENTATIVES has traditionally selected the chamber's chaplain at the beginning of each new Congress for a two-year term. The selection process had become more decentralized in the waning years of the 20th century, but the Speaker still played a dominant role.

The SENATE chaplain has been selected by Senate leaders, has not had a set term, and did not need to be reappointed at the beginning of each new Congress. Chaplains have been considered officers in their respective chambers. Language in the Constitution allowed Congress to choose officers to justify those positions. One of the chaplain's primary duties has been to open each legislative session with a formal prayer.

In 2000 the position of chaplain stirred some controversy in the House when the committee in charge of winnowing the list of candidates ranked a Roman Catholic priest, Timothy J. O'Brien, as their first choice. Republican leaders were criticized for failing to follow the bipartisan committee recommendation. The controversy was settled after a second round of interviews resulted in the selection of a different Catholic, Daniel P. Coughlin. The previous 58 chaplains in the House had all been Protestants. The Senate had a Catholic chaplain for one year, in 1832. The current Senate chaplain, Barry C. Black, a Seventh-Day Adventist, became the first African American to serve in the capacity of chaplain in either chamber.

Historic documents suggest that the original motivation for the position of chaplain was to provide lawmakers with pastoral care and guidance when they were away from home in the same way a chaplain provides services to military troops. Today, besides tendering the daily morning prayer, the chaplain offers invocations at a number of official events in the nation's capital. Chaplains also conduct wedding ceremonies for members of Congress and their staffs and assist members in their contacts with religious groups.

Further reading:
Amer, Mildred. *House and Senate Chaplains.* Washington, D.C.: Congressional Research Service, Library of Congress, 2003; Stokes, Anson Phelps, and Leo Pfeffer. *Church and State in the United States.* Vol. 1. New York: Harper & Row, 1964; Tong, Lorraine H. *Senate Administrative Officers and Officials.* Washington, D.C.: Congressional Research Service, Library of Congress, 2003.
—Scot D. Schraufnagel

checks and balances

The initial organization of American national government was provided in the Articles of Confederation. Its primary institution was the Continental Congress. This original governing form was intentionally weak and poorly coordinated because the colonial experience had taught Americans to resist the tyranny of governmental rule. However, the deficiencies of a weak and spastic governing system became quickly apparent, so leading politicians of the day gathered in Philadelphia to formulate a new constitutional arrangement.

Despite disappointment in the performance of government under the Articles of Confederation, there remained great concern about centralizing too much power in the national government. James Madison articulated the point in Federalist 47, saying: "the accumulation of all powers, legislative, executive, and judiciary, in the same hands, whether of one, a few, or many, and whether hereditary, self-appointed, or elective, may justly be pronounced the very definition of tyranny." The elemental solution that the founders conceived was to distribute power into a variety of institutional forms and structures so that the centralization of power under some future tyrant would be unlikely, if not impossible. We capture the essence of this distribution of governmental power in the phrase *checks and balances.*

Clearly the PRESIDENTIAL VETO is a check upon the legislative majorities that have the power to tax, spend, and legislate. Congress has a variety of powers to check the president and the courts. Presidential appointees to the executive agencies and the courts require Senate CONFIRMATION. Judicial interpretations of law can be reshaped by subsequent legislation. Although the Constitution does not explicitly equip the courts with powers of review over acts of the president and Congress, the Supreme Court successfully attributed to itself the power of judicial review—to enforce the Constitution by invalidating actions or legislation that are contrary to it. This was the opinion and precedent that came from Chief Justice John Marshall in *MARBURY V. MADISON* in 1803.

The primary institutional expression of checks and balances is in the separation of the three kinds of power that Madison took note of in the quotation above. But the checks and balances extend beyond the attributes of American government immediately annexed to separation of powers.

State and local governments legitimately exercise a great range of governing activities apart from the national government's authority. In terms of constitutional authority, for example, states have whatever powers their people invest in them in their state constitutions. The U.S. Constitution asserts only the powers that the states delegated to the national government. The scope and range of U.S. constitutional power is not infinitely elastic. For example, the police power over most of what Americans know to be criminal behavior is exercised under state authority. Most American law enforcement officers are local: sheriff's officers and municipal police. Thus, there is a strong check upon the Federal Bureau of Investigation, a limited organization of federal police, in the fact that only state governments have police power in the United States and they administer that power through the many police organizations at the state and local levels of government.

Madison perceived the prospect that if different people were endowed with particular but separate powers, they would check one another from overreaching the legitimate use of the powers vested in their offices. In Federalist 51 he suggested that "the great security against a gradual concentration of power in the same department consists in giving to those who administer each department the constitutional means and personal motives to resist encroachments. . . . Ambition must be made to counteract ambition. . . . In framing a government which is to be administered by men over men, the great difficulty lies in this: you must first enable the government to control the governed; and in the next place oblige it to control itself."

There are abundant checks and balances within the separate branches of government. The most conspicuous is that in the legislative branch. A House and Senate, whose members come from distinctly different constituencies with different terms of election, must act by majorities in both institutions to jointly pass laws and budgets. Either can block the other, and often they do just exactly that.

Courts oversee courts. Trial courts try cases. Appellate courts consider appeals from trial participants, but the appellate courts do not retry cases. Appellate courts deal in constitutional and statutory interpretation and errors in trial procedures. In this three-layered system most cases are settled before or at trial. Only a few receive scrutiny that upholds or overturns what happens at trial, but the opinions rendered by appellate courts become precedents to guide trial courts in subsequent cases.

Sometimes well-intentioned citizens find that checks and balances in the governing system frustrate their desire for fast action in problem solving. However, the protections that checks and balances provide against tyranny have preserved American democracy and are worth the inconvenience that they cause.

See also FEDERALIST PAPERS.

Further reading:
Hamilton, A., J. Madison, and J. Jay. *The Federalist Papers.* New York: New American Library, 1961; Singer, R. G. "Police Power." In *The Guide to American Law.* St. Paul, Minn.: West Publishing Company, 1984; *Marbury v. Madison,* 1 Cranch 137 (1803).

—Jack R. Van Der Slik

Chinagate

The infamous Watergate case is well documented, and subsequent government debacles have been made famous by the simple addition of *gate.* Irangate, Filegate, and Donorgate are but a few examples. Chinagate (which is considered to be a part of Donorgate) is no exception. This potentially explosive situation between the United States and the People's Republic of China was filled with espionage, finger pointing, paper trails going back as far as the mid-1980s, and a cover-up that may have extended to the top of the American political hierarchy. Did the Chinese government influence the 1996 presidential elections with unorthodox efforts and illegal campaign donations? Did the Chinese nuclear program make exceptional gains with the help of secrets extracted from Los Alamos? Did these tumultuous events take place under the supervision of high-ranking American government officials? All of these issues lay at the heart of Chinagate. There are conflicting reports and opinions as to the players, their involvement, and the severity of actions taken in the theft of top-secret U.S. information by the Chinese government.

The basic issue of Chinagate was how much influence within the U.S. government did China have, and what military secrets were obtained under dubious conditions? Even the Carter administration admitted that plans for the W-70 warhead, a top-secret neutron bomb, had been stolen during their watch. The concern during Chinagate was to what extent the American officials knew about the leak of secrets to China, and what they did or did not do to curb this breach of security. This had a direct impact on a variety of American foreign policy decisions. For example, with Most Favored Nation status at stake, the Chinese government seemed to regain admittance to this sacred list despite their well-documented abuses of human and civil rights. The fact that this was occurring at the same time that the Democratic Party was amassing huge sums of campaign money, even from Asians who were not American citizens, seems a bit too coincidental.

It is also clear that not all parties involved agreed upon the severity of these acts. The CIA and the Department of Energy both agreed that nuclear secrets had been relayed to the Chinese. The CIA tended to view the leak as more severe, while the Department of Energy claimed the material was not of top-secret nature and was intended to be shared with other nations in a more open policy toward nuclear technology.

Meanwhile, Asian reports tended to view the entire incident as minor. One report went as far to say "it would be a tragedy of potentially historic proportions if a petty, partisan squabble on the banks of the Potomac River were to undermine what is increasingly recognized as the most important bilateral relationship of the 21st century—that between China and the United States. Certainly in Asia, stable Sino-American ties are seen as a linchpin of the region's peace and prosperity." Many Chinese officials stated that they were merely mirroring efforts by Taiwanese officials starting in early 1995 by wooing and attempting to influence U.S. government policymakers. The inherent problem was did these efforts by Chinese officials cross the line and breach U.S. security and campaign finance laws? Unfortunately, the majority of documents related to this case are not available to the general public. Some have called Chinagate the greatest leak of American intelligence to a foreign power in history. Unfortunately, only time will reveal the severity of the acts committed by those on both sides of the Pacific.

Further reading:
Risen, James, and Jeff Gerth: "China Stole Nuclear Secrets from Los Alamos, U.S. Officials Say, *New York Times*, 6 March 1999. Available online. URL: www.nytimes.com/library/world/asia/030699china=nuke.html. Accessed May 9, 2006.

—Nancy S. Lind

circular letters

Circular letters were widely used in the 18th century. They served as an essential tool to the politicians in publicizing their views and stances on public issues, legislative activity, and affairs of state. They were mostly sent by members of the HOUSE OF REPRESENTATIVES from western and southern states. At the time senators were not popularly elected, as was the case of representatives. They therefore were not as interested in sending circular letters to their constituents. An example of a circular letter was a letter from the Massachusetts legislature to other colonial assemblies. In this circular Massachusetts urged the colonists to resist taxation without representation by the British Parliament.

The content of circular letters varied, from copies of official reports and simple listings of legislation that had passed to more elaborate explanations and comments on national affairs. They were formulated in a certain way to make the sender look good since one of their focuses was the next election. The recipients of circular letters were mostly individuals and at times also included postmasters. They covered the cost of printing, while the government covered the cost of mailing the letters through the FRANK-ING PRIVILEGE, which allows congressmembers and other public officials to send mail at no charge for their office purposes. The senders of circular letters were interested in spreading the word and encouraged the recipients to do so in print.

This practice continues to this day but mostly in a different manner. With the development and advancement of the Internet, many politicians post their circular letters on their Web sites for everyone to see. This advancement in technology has also made it possible for not only politicians but also for large national and international companies and organizations to post their own circular letters on the Internet.

Further reading:
Cunningham, Noble E., Jr., ed. *Circular Letters of Congressmen to Their Constituents, 1789–1829.* 3 vols. Chapel Hill: University of North Carolina, 1977; U.S. Congress. Senate. "Franking." *Precedents Relating to the Privileges of the Senate of the United States.* Comp. by George P. Furber. Washington, D.C.: Government Printing Office, 1893.

—Arthur Holst

City of Boerne v. Flores 521 U.S. 507 (1997)

In *City of Boerne v. Flores* the U.S. Supreme Court, in a 6-3 decision, held that the Religious Freedom Restoration Act of 1993 was unconstitutional. The Fourteenth and First Amendments to the U.S. Constitution and the document's separation of powers doctrine were analyzed. This case is significant because the Court set limits on Congress's powers. The archbishop of San Antonio sought to enlarge St. Peter Catholic Church in the city of Boerne, Texas. The parish had been growing rapidly, and the 70-year-old mission style church was no longer large enough. Local officials denied a building permit to enlarge the church because of a historic preservation ordinance. The archbishop sued under a federal statute, the Religious Freedom Restoration Act (RFRA), claiming the denial of the building permit interfered with the free exercise of religion. RFRA had been passed in response to the Court's holding in *Employment Division v. Smith* (1990).

In the *Smith* decision, the Court employed a narrower interpretation of the Free Exercise Clause in the First Amendment when balancing religious freedom against governmental interests. In pre-*Smith* cases the Court had carved out exemptions from generally applicable state laws when they incidentally infringed upon religious freedom. The law would be sustained only if the government could demonstrate a compelling interest. In *Smith* two Native Americans were fired from their jobs as drug rehabilitation counselors because they used peyote during a religious ceremony. They then applied for unemployment compensation but were denied benefits because they were fired for misconduct. The Court held that Oregon's drug laws were generally applicable. Therefore, the denial of unemployment benefits was constitutional. The state no longer had to demonstrate a compelling governmental interest. In prior cases involving an incidental burden on religious freedom and the denial of unemployment benefits, maintaining the financial integrity of unemployment compensation funds was not considered compelling. The elimination of the compelling interest requirement meant that more laws would withstand a Free Exercise Clause challenge.

Capitol Hill's reaction to the *Smith* decision was swift and negative. Congress responded by passing RFRA, which not only required the prior showing of a compelling interest but also imposed a least-restrictive means requirement. The government would have to show that the law served a compelling interest and that no less-restrictive means were available to achieve that interest. If the government failed to do this, the incidental burden on religious freedom would be in violation of RFRA. Congress claimed it had the power to pass RFRA in accord with Section 5 of the Fourteenth Amendment. Section 5 granted Congress the power to enforce the due process and equal protection provisions of the Fourteenth Amendment with appropriate legislation. Congress passed RFRA to reestablish greater protection for religious freedom. In other words, Congress was legislating a fortified version of the prior, or pre-*Smith*, standard of judicial review for alleged freedom of religion violations.

The Supreme Court had to decide in *Boerne* if Congress had exceeded the scope of its Fourteenth Amendment enforcement power by attempting to change the meaning of the Free Exercise Clause of the First Amendment. Was RFRA an attempt to remedy or prevent constitutional violations, or was it an attempt to change the substantive meaning of a constitutional provision? The majority opinion, written by Justice Anthony Kennedy, concluded that the statute exceeded Congress's grant of power under Section 5 of the Fourteenth Amendment. Citing *Marbury v. Madison*, Kennedy made clear that it is the role of the judiciary to determine the constitutionality of laws. Congress passed RFRA seeking to reinterpret the meaning of the Free Exercise Clause. Kennedy made a distinction between legislation passed to enforce the Free Exercise Clause and that which sought to alter its meaning. He acknowledged that the line of demarcation could not always be easily discerned but asserted that RFRA clearly went over it.

The dissent, led by Justice Sandra Day O'Connor, basically agreed with the majority's interpretation of Congress's Section 5 enforcement power. However, the dissenters disagreed with the standard set in the *Smith* case. If the *Smith* interpretation of the Free Exercise Clause were overturned, RFRA would be less objectionable. With the exception of the least restrictive means requirement, the legislation would merely reflect the Court's interpretation of the Free Exercise Clause.

Boerne is important because it set limits on congressional power. It also demonstrated that the Supreme Court would vigorously defend its role within the separation of powers framework. The decision restated that it is the Court's role to determine what the Constitution means. Consequently, a law, passed with near unanimous support in Congress and signed into law by President Bill Clinton, was struck down as unconstitutional.

Further reading:
City of Boerne v. Flores, 521 U.S. 507 (1997); *Employment Division, Department of Human Resources of Oregon v. Smith*, 494 U.S. 872 (1900); Hall, Kermit L., ed. *The Oxford Guide to United States Supreme Court Decisions.* New York: Oxford University Press, 1999; O'Brien, David M. *Constitutional Law and Politics: Struggles for Power and Governmental Accountability.* 5th ed. New York: Norton, 2003; Yarbrough, Tinsley E. *The Rehnquist Court and the Constitution.* New York: Oxford University Press, 2000.
—Barry N. Sweet

Civil Rights Act of 1964

Congress passed a Civil Rights Act in 1875, and it would take more than three-quarters of a century for Congress to pass another civil rights bill. In 1957 and 1960 the Eisenhower administration introduced modest civil rights legislation that was passed by Congress. These two laws were so weak that civil rights advocates pushed the new administration of President John F. Kennedy to introduce a stronger and more sweeping provision. It was not until two and a half years later that Kennedy finally sent his bill to Congress. Racial demonstrations in the South in 1963, especially the Birmingham, Alabama, demonstrations where police arrested 700 schoolchildren and turned fire hoses and police dogs on protesters finally pushed Kennedy to reassess his position.

On June 11, 1963, the same day that Governor George Wallace stood in the doorway at the University of Alabama in his symbolic attempt to defy the federal court ordered desegregation of the school, Kennedy went on national television to announce his sweeping civil rights proposal. Kennedy argued that the time was right for moral reasons. It was also necessary, said the president, to move the problem "from the streets to the courts," to prevent the leadership of both whites and blacks from falling into the hands of extremists, and it was necessary because the United States was losing support from the newly emerging third world nations that were critical of the racial discrimination occurring in the United States.

The civil rights legislation was sweeping in its scope. Its provisions prohibited racial discrimination in voting, public accommodations and public facilities, education, and employment. The two most important provisions of the act were Title II and Title VII, which provided judicial remedies for racial discrimination in public accommodations and employment. Also, like previous civil rights legislation, southerners in Congress led the opposition to passage and tried to weaken the bill at every opportunity.

The Kennedy bill was considered first by the House Judiciary Committee, which has jurisdiction over civil rights legislation. The Judiciary Committee quickly reported the bill, and after a temporary delay in the Rules Committee, the bill was sent to the floor and approved by a margin of 290-130. As in the past, civil rights supporters knew that the real test would come in the Senate, where the filibuster had made it virtually impossible to pass civil rights legislation.

By jurisdiction, civil rights legislation must be sent to the Senate Judiciary Committee. The problem with this was that the chair of the committee was Senator James Eastland, a Democrat of Mississippi, and Senator Eastland was one of the leading segregationists in Congress. He was not about to let his committee report a civil rights bill. To bypass this stumbling block, about 90 percent of the bill was sent to the Judiciary Committee, but one provision was sent to the Senate Commerce Committee. The provision dealing with ending discrimination in public accommodations was sent to the Commerce Committee because Congress's authority to regulate interstate commerce was based on the Commerce Clause of the Constitution. The Commerce Committee, chaired by Senator Warren Magnuson, a Democrat of Washington, quickly approved the public accommodations provision and sent it to the Senate floor. As soon as that provision reached the floor, the rest of the civil rights bill was added on as an amendment.

Southerners were incensed that the Senate leadership had bypassed the Judiciary Committee, but they knew the real battle would be on the Senate floor, where the southern senators could use the filibuster to defeat the legislation. While Congress was debating the passage of the civil rights bill, President Kennedy would be assassinated, and his vice president, Lyndon Johnson, assumed the presidency. This caused great concern in the civil rights community, because as a southern senator, Lyndon Johnson had consistently voted against civil rights legislation. Nevertheless, five days after the assassination, President Johnson addressed a joint session of Congress and urged them to pass the civil rights bill as a tribute to Kennedy. The time for talk was past, said

Johnson, and now Congress needed to act in order to end racial discrimination in the United States.

Civil rights opponents began a two-stage filibuster in the Senate. The first filibuster was an attempt to prevent the Senate from even taking up consideration of the House bill. After 16 days the first filibuster ended when the Senate voted 67-17 to begin consideration of the House legislation. In the second stage of the filibuster, southerners filibustered the bill itself and did everything possible to try to weaken or kill the bill. The second filibuster lasted 74 days and ended when 71 senators, or four more than were needed at the time, voted to invoke cloture and stop the filibuster. This was monumental. For the first time in the history of the Senate, senators had agreed to end a filibuster on the subject of civil rights.

Ultimately, the Senate voted on final passage of the 1964 Civil Rights Act, and it passed by a margin of 73-27. Democrats voted 46 to 21 for the bill, and Republicans supported passage by a vote of 27-6. Of the 21 Democrats who voted against passage, 18 were from the South, and the other three were from border-South states. Of the six Republicans who voted in opposition to the act, the most prominent was Barry Goldwater of Arizona. Goldwater would become the Republican presidential candidate in 1964, and his selection would affect partisan change in the South over the next several decades. Goldwater carried five southern states from the "solid Democratic South" in 1964, but they were states that Republicans had not won in 75 years: Alabama, Georgia, Mississippi, Louisiana, and South Carolina. States that had begun voting Republican for Eisenhower and Nixon in 1952, 1956, and 1960 supported Johnson in 1964. In other words, political loyalties were turned upside down, and this would have a major long-term impact in the South.

As previously mentioned, Titles II and VII are considered the most significant aspects of the 1964 Civil Rights Act. Title II banned discrimination in public accommodations such as hotels, restaurants, and places of amusement. Legal challenges were quickly launched against its provisions. On December 14, 1964, the Supreme Court upheld the public accommodations provisions in two unanimous decisions, *Heart of Atlanta Motel v. United States* and *Katzenbach v. McClung.* In these companion cases the Court ruled that even though the hotel and restaurant were local operations, food, supplies, and customers impacted interstate commerce. If minorities could not eat at restaurants or stay at hotels, this would have an adverse impact on interstate commerce, "no matter how small the pinch."

Title VII banned discrimination in hiring, paying, promoting, and firing workers. It also established the Equal Employment Opportunity Commission (EEOC). It was EEOC rulings on "affirmative action" that established policies that continue to divide the American electorate today.

In *Griggs v. Duke Power* a unanimous Supreme Court struck down the use of tests and other employment practices that are not job related but would have an adverse impact on minority hiring. Where union "seniority systems" collide with affirmative action, the courts have sided with the unions and against affirmative action.

It is impossible to overestimate the impact the 1964 Civil Rights Act had on changing the politics, economics, and culture of the South, in particular, and the nation as a whole. The provisions of the 1964 act were originally focused on African Americans in the South, but the provisions would later be applied to other minority groups, the aged, handicapped, women, and gays and lesbians. Whereas the nation had reached consensus about the need for laws to protect against racial discrimination, that consensus broke down as more and more groups fell under the protection of civil rights laws. "White backlash" and "reverse discrimination" emerged as political issues as more and more Americans felt the 1964 Civil Rights Act was being stretched to the breaking point.

Further reading:
Berman, Daniel M. *A Bill Becomes a Law: Congress Enacts Civil Rights Legislation.* New York: Macmillan, 1964; Lawson, Steven. *Black Ballots: Voting Rights in the South, 1944–1969.* New York: Columbia University Press, 1976; Loevy, Robert D., ed. *The Civil Rights Act of 1964: The Passage of the Law That Ended Racial Segregation.* Albany, N.Y.: SUNY Press, 1997; Whalen, Barbara, and Charles Whalen. *The Longest Day: A Legislative History of the 1964 Civil Rights Act.* Washington, D.C.: Seven Locks Press, 1985.

—Darryl Paulson

Clark, James Beauchamp Champ (1850–1921)
Representative, Speaker of the House

Clark was born on March 7, 1850, near Lawrenceburg in Anderson County, Kentucky. He was one of three children born to John and Althea Clark. His father was a carriage and buggy maker and an itinerant dentist; his mother died when he was three years old. In 1881 Clark married Genevieve Davis Bennett. They had four children, of whom Bennett Champ and Genevieve survived beyond infancy. Bennett Champ Clark served in the U.S. Senate from Missouri between 1932 and 1944.

Clark attended common schools in Kentucky. After being expelled from Transylvania University (later Kentucky University) for shooting at a fellow student, he graduated from Bethany College in West Virginia with highest honors in 1873. He was named president of Marshall College in 1873 at the age of 23. Clark graduated from Cincinnati Law School in 1875. He began his law practice in Wichita,

Kansas, but quickly relocated to Pike County, Missouri, in 1876. Clark briefly taught school in Renick and was a newspaper editor-owner in Louisiana, Missouri, before becoming the city attorney for Bowling Green and Louisiana, and a deputy prosecuting attorney and prosecuting attorney for Pike County. He served one term in the Missouri house of representatives between 1889 and 1891. In the general assembly Clark introduced the Australian ballot, wrote the state's antitrust law, and was one of the leaders of an effort to reorganize the state university system.

Clark was first elected to the House in the 53rd Congress in1893. Although he lost his bid for reelection to the 54th Congress, he was subsequently elected to the 55th Congress and served through the 66th Congress, when he lost his bid for reelection in 1921. Clark served on both the Ways and Means and Foreign Relations Committees. He was appointed to fill the unexpired term of Democratic Minority Leader John Sharp Williams during the 60th Congress and served as Minority Leader during the 61st and 66th Congresses. He was elected SPEAKER OF THE HOUSE during the 62nd Congress in 1911 and served as Speaker through the 65th Congress, until Republican Frederick Gillett assumed the Speakership in 1919. Clark was defeated for reelection when a split within the Missouri Democratic Party over President Wilson's proposed League of Nations and statewide dissatisfaction with farm prices led to a Republican sweep of Missouri politics. The Republicans, led by Governor Arthur Hyde, won all open executive offices, both houses of the general assembly, and 14 of Missouri's 16 seats in the U.S. House of Representatives.

While Clark had delivered lectures and had given speeches throughout Missouri, he first rose to national prominence with his July 4, 1893, speech before Tammany Hall challenging the accepted conceptions of the West. As a freshman Clark attracted the attention of his peers during a special session of Congress with an address in favor of free silver. Unafraid of the contentious issues of the day, Clark also spoke against the protectionist Republican tariffs even though his own Democratic Party was divided on the subject. As a member of Congress Clark joined each of his fellow Missouri representatives in support of the declaration of war against Spain in 1898. As a practical matter, both Kansas City and St. Louis had economic ties to Cuba. Clark, with some skepticism, also endorsed the concept of Manifest Destiny with respect to American possession of Puerto Rico, Guam, and the Philippines. Near the end of his career, Clark rose to speak against conscription and press censorship and in favor of women's suffrage.

For all of his other legislative accomplishments, Clark is probably best known for his role in one of the most significant restructuring efforts in the history of the House of Representatives. Clark, along with George Norris and

Oscar Underwood, was instrumental in the bipartisan 1910 revolt against then Speaker of the House JOSEPH CANNON. The Speaker had amassed enormous personal and institutional authority through his power of appointment of both committee chairs and members and his chairmanship of the House Rules Committee. While Cannon's power was curtailed and the Speaker was removed from the Rules Committee, it was not until 1911, when the Democrats had gained a majority and Clark had become Speaker, that the Speaker's power over committee assignments was constrained. The revolt against Cannon led to the decline of the Speaker's formal powers and the rise of the party caucus. As a result, Clark's own powers as Speaker were surpassed by the power of Oscar Underwood, the Democratic Party's Majority Leader.

Outside the House, Clark was influential in national Democratic Party politics. In 1904 Clark chaired the Democratic National Convention, held in St. Louis, which nominated Alton Brooks Parker of New York for president and Henry Gassaway Davis of West Virginia for vice president. Clark's most significant political role was his campaign for the Democratic presidential nomination in 1912. With a victory in the Illinois primary and the support of publisher William Randolph Hearst, Clark went into the Democratic National Convention in Baltimore well positioned to win his party's nomination. However, the party's nomination required a two-thirds majority, which Clark could not garner. He entered the convention with a majority of delegates and actually led the delegate count through 30 ballots until three-time Democratic nominee William Jennings Bryan gave his support to the party's eventual nominee, Woodrow Wilson. Although Clark and Bryan formally reconciled their differences, Clark's autobiography betrays a degree of ironic bitterness, given his early support of Bryan and the free silver movement. Clark died on March 2, 1921, in Washington, D.C.

Further reading:
Clark, Champ. *My Quarter Century of American Politics.* 2 vols. New York: Harper & Row, 1920; Hechler, Kenneth W. *Insurgency: Personalities and Politics of the Taft Era.* New York: Columbia University Press, 1940; Webb, W. L. *Champ Clark.* New York: Neale Publishing Group, 1912; Hollister, Wilfred R. *Five Famous Missourians.* Kansas City, Mo.: Hudson Kimberly, 1900.

—George Connor

Clay, Henry (1777–1852) *Representative, Speaker of the House, Senator*
Known by the titles "The Great Compromiser" and the "Great Pacificator" in honor of his legislative accomplishments, Clay served in state and national politics for a half

century. He helped to define and strengthen the role of SPEAKER OF THE HOUSE and is regarded as one of the most influential members of the U.S. SENATE in American history. He was a leader of two major political parties that opposed the Democrats and supported nationalist policies.

Henry Clay was born in Hanover County, Virginia, on April 12, 1777. His father died when Henry was just four years old. Though he had little public schooling, Clay's stepfather helped him secure a position with the Virginia Court of Chancery in 1792. After studying law with Chancellor George Wyche, Clay also gained legal experience in the office of Virginia attorney general Robert Brooke. Clay was licensed to practice law in 1797 and moved to Kentucky the same year. His legal and oratorical skills led to his election to the Kentucky state legislature (1803–06) and a stint as a professor of law at Transylvania University (1805–07).

Clay's tenure in the U.S. Congress began in November 1806, when he was asked to fill the unexpired term of John Adair in the U.S. Senate. He served there for about six months before returning to the Kentucky state legislature. In 1810 he was again selected to serve in the U.S. Senate, this time to fill the term of Buckner Thruston. Later that year he was elected to the U.S. HOUSE OF REPRESENTATIVES. On the first day of the new session in 1811, he was selected SPEAKER OF THE HOUSE, a position he held over the next decade except for a brief hiatus to assist in the peace negotiations ending the War of 1812. Clay left the House in 1821 to practice law and recoup financial losses but returned in 1823 and resumed his post as Speaker. He stepped down in 1824 to run for U.S. president. Although he lost in a four-way race, he was tapped by the eventual winner, John Quincy Adams, as secretary of State (1825–29).

In November 1831 the Kentucky legislature elected Clay a U.S. senator. A month later he was nominated by the National Republicans to run for president against incumbent Democrat Andrew Jackson. Clay lost the 1832 presidential election but retained his seat in the Senate. He served there until 1842, when he resigned amid political disagreements with the Democrats. As the nominee of the Whig Party, he ran unsuccessfully for president in 1844. In February 1848 the Kentucky legislature again chose him to represent the state in the Senate, where he remained until his death on June 29, 1852.

Clay's list of legislative accomplishments set him apart from his contemporaries. He was the longest-serving Speaker of the House in the 19th century. In the House he engineered passage of a series of bills that he dubbed the American System, including chartering of the Second Bank of the United States, protective tariff measures, public works projects, and transportation improvements. He was the author of the Missouri Compromise of 1820–21 and the Compromise of 1850, both of which successfully balanced the interest of slave and nonslave states. Additionally, he quelled the threat of South Carolina's secession with the Compromise Tariff of 1833.

Though he favored war with Great Britain in 1812, Henry Clay subsequently pursued policies of peace and freedom for the rest of his career. Though a slaveholder, he advocated gradual emancipation and freed his slaves upon his death. He was well known in Latin America for his friendly relations. For instance, during his service as secretary of State in the John Quincy Adams administration, he gained congressional approval of U.S. participation in the Pan American Congress. When he ran for president in 1844, Clay rejected annexation of Texas, fearing that it would provoke war with Mexico. When that war did occur, he opposed it. Clay also sought to have land returned to the Five Civilized Tribes of Indians.

Besides his congressional career, Clay was a three-time presidential candidate, running for the office in three different decades. Although he placed third in the four-way 1824 race, Clay's support of John Quincy Adams assured the House selection of Adams after no one received a majority of electoral votes in the election. In the 1832 election Clay lost to Andrew Jackson by a 56.5 to 43.5 percent popular vote margin. Clay came closest to being elected president in 1844, when James Polk defeated him by a 49.6 to 48.1 percent popular vote tally. Although Clay was considered by Whig leaders in 1848, Zachary Taylor received the party's presidential nomination that year. Despite his pursuit of the nation's highest office, Clay refused to compromise his principles for votes, stating that he would rather be right than be president.

Henry Clay had a deserved reputation as an outstanding orator. This skill, acquired from observing such luminaries as Patrick Henry and from devoted practice, served him well as both a politician and a lawyer. He argued many cases before the U.S. Supreme Court, including *Ogden v. Saunders* (1927), which defined the constitutional limits of state bankruptcy laws. Clay gained enormous wealth from his law practice, in part due to his popularity and bold style of arguing cases.

Though viewed by some as lacking ideas and criticized by others for his ambition, Clay's impact on national politics during the first half of the 19th century was significant. He is often classified with Daniel Webster and John Calhoun as constituting the triumvirate of American statesmen of the period. After their passing the country spiraled downward toward eventual civil war. Clay's career coincided with the development of political parties in the United States. The successor to the parties he led, the National Republicans and the Whigs, was the Republican Party, which trumpeted many of the issues Clay advocated during his lifetime. Clay was eulogized after his death by Abraham Lincoln, who would become the first Republican elected to the presidency.

Henry Clay *(Library of Congress)*

Further reading:
Colton, Calvin. *The Life and Times of Henry Clay.* Whitefish, Mont.: Kessinger Publishing, 2004; Eaton, Clement. *Henry Clay and the Art of American Politics.* Boston: Little Brown, 1957; Kelly, Regina. *Henry Clay: Statesman and Patriot.* Boston: Houghton Mifflin, 1960; Remini, Robert. *Henry Clay: Statesman for the Union.* New York: Norton, 1993; Schurz, Carl. *Henry Clay.* New York: Chelsea House Publishing, 1980.

—Samuel B. Hoff

Clean Air Acts

Problems associated with air pollution have affected metropolitan areas of the United States since the 19th century. While major cities such as Chicago and Cincinnati had instituted their own legislation to tackle the problem as early as 1881, it was not until after World War II that Congress made a serious attempt to legislate on the issue. Before this pollution and other environmental problems were areas that were considered to be the preserve of state rather than federal government.

By the 1950s the problem of air pollution was gaining public attention, with serious smog reported in cities such as Los Angeles, leading to fears for public health. Members of Congress claimed their rights to intervene on the grounds that as polluted air did not respect state boundaries, the issue could legitimately be considered one of interstate commerce. Beneath such arguments also lurked the fact that state governments were often reluctant to place restrictions on industry, fearful that regulations would prompt business to relocate to neighboring states with less stringent standards.

The Air Pollution Act of 1955 (and subsequent amendments in 1960 and 1962) laid the groundwork for the regulations that exist today. The act itself did little to reverse the emission of pollutants. Instead, choosing to appropriate funds for research into the issue, it recognized the problem for the first time and established the right of Congress to legislate in the area. The scope of the legislation was increased with the passage of the Clean Air Act of 1963 (amended in 1965, 1966, 1967, and 1969) to include areas such as motor exhaust emissions. The legislation was still based on providing money for research and encouraging states to establish emission standards and reduce the impact on the environment of coal and oil sources.

Under the legislative leadership of Senator Ed Muskie, a Democrat from Maine, the Clean Air Act of 1970 broke new ground by establishing national emission standards, strictly regulating new sources of pollution and emissions from motor vehicles. It also allowed citizens to take legal action against any organization (including government) ignoring the new standards. While the states retained primary responsibility for enforcing the reduction of pollution, the act was a strong piece of legislation that yielded results. Its main weakness was in the ambitious nature of its targets, especially concerning motor vehicle emissions, which industry lobbyists insisted were unreachable in the mandated time frame.

Partly as recognition of this and partly to avoid the act becoming irrelevant once its stated target years passed without full compliance, the deadlines were extended in 1977. The compromise drew criticism from both sides: Industry sources claimed that the new targets were still too tight, and environmentalists complained that the amendments simply allowed industry longer to continue to pollute the environment. The amendments did more than just extend deadlines, and for the first time the problem of ozone depletion was incorporated into the law.

It was 13 years before Congress revisited the Clean Air Act in any major way. The Clean Air Act of 1990 rewrote the law to set a new timetable for abatement efforts, raised the automobile emission standards, and encouraged the use of low-sulfur fuels. It also mandated the standard of technology required to reduce the level of toxins released into the atmosphere. While the problems of air pollution still exist and compliance with the Clean Air Act has not been complete, the law still forms the backbone of the federal government's efforts to require states to ensure cleaner air.

Further reading:
Findley, T. W., and D. A. Farber. *Environmental Law in a Nutshell.* 3d ed. St. Paul, Minn.: West Publishing, 1992; Holland, K. M., F. L. Morton, and B. Galligan, eds. *Federalism and the Environment: Environmental Policymaking in Australia, Canada and the United States.* Westport, Conn.: Greenwood Press, 1966; Lester, J. P., ed. *Environmental Politics and Policy: Theories and Evidence.* Durham, N.C.: Duke University Press, 1989.

—Ross M. English

Clean Water Acts

Congress first legislated to control the effects of water pollution as early as 1889, when the Rivers and Harbors Act attempted to deal with the problems shipping faced from waste blocking navigable waters. While further legislation was passed in 1912 and 1924, state governments remained the governing bodies with primary responsibility for the issue.

The first recognition of water pollution as a national problem occurred in 1948, when the Water Pollution Act (guided through Congress by Senators ALBEN BARKLEY, a Democrat from Kentucky, and ROBERT TAFT, a Republican from Ohio) began the first active federal intervention in the nation's water quality. The law encouraged research into the problem and authorized loans to municipalities for the construction of sewage treatment facilities. Amendments to the legislation were passed in 1956 and 1961. Under the leadership of Senator Ed Muskie, a Democrat from Maine, the Water Quality Act of 1965 went further and enlarged the scope of federal involvement to mandate states to ensure the quality of interstate waters.

By the early 1970s it had become clear to reformers that fewer than half of states had taken appropriate action, and the current regulations were proving inadequate in terms of enforcement. The quality of America's waters still varied greatly from state to state, and a change in approach was needed. The resulting legislation, under Muskie's leadership, was the Federal Water Pollution Control Act of 1972, which became more commonly known as the Clean Water Act.

The Clean Water Act declared as its objective "to restore and maintain the chemical, physical, and biological integrity of the Nation's waters" and set a goal that "the discharge of pollutants into navigable waters be eliminated by 1985." The major departure from previous approaches (borrowing from similar initiatives concerning air pollution) was that the law moved away from focusing on the "ambient" quality of particular bodies of water and instead allowed the Environmental Protection Agency (EPA) to mandate the type of technology to be installed into industrial plants and to establish a permit program that would specify the type and amount of pollution that was allowed to be discharged from any one source. The municipal sewage construction grants program was also extended further. The Clean Water Act passed Congress with overwhelming support, which was confirmed when President Richard Nixon's veto of the legislation was subsequently overturned.

Major amendments to the Clean Water Act were passed in 1977 and 1987 (the latter over the veto of President Ronald Reagan). The amendments were necessary not only to extend deadlines that the EPA was struggling to meet but to increase the scope of the legislation in an attempt to counter causes of pollution other than simple point sources of industrial discharges. The 1977 amendments began to tackle the disappearance of wetlands. This issue would prove to be politically difficult because many wetlands are found on private land, especially farms, and any attempt by Congress to regulate their use starts to involve questions of property rights. The Water Quality Act of 1987 further strengthened the act by addressing the issues of toxic chemicals, acid rain, and pollution from non-point sources such as agricultural runoff, sewer overflows, and runoff from urban areas. It also saw Congress step back from its commitment to continue subsidizing the construction of municipal sewage treatment plants and instead institute a revolving loan fund.

The Clean Water Act has undoubtedly been a successful piece of legislation and has done much to improve the state of America's waters. However, it is still far from its original goal of eliminating the discharge of pollutants. As the scope of the legislation has increased, so have the political and practical problems in framing a solutions. This is perhaps one of the reasons that Congress has not successfully overhauled the act since 1987, instead choosing to deal with many of the issues in distinct pieces of legislation.

Further reading:
Congressional Research Service. *A Legislative History of the Water Quality Act of 1987.* 4 vols. Washington, D.C.: Government Printing Office, 1988; Findley, T. W., and D. A. Farber. *Environmental Law in a Nutshell.* 3d ed. St. Paul, Minn.: West Publishing, 1992; Lieber, H. *Federalism and Clean Waters,* Lexington, Mass.: D.C. Heath, 1975.
— Ross M. English

Clerk of the House
The Clerk of the House is one of the officers that Article I, Section 2, of the Constitution grants the House authority to choose. The clerk is not chosen from the membership of the House because his or her duties are administrative in nature. At the beginning of every new Congress, both PARTY CAUCUSES submit candidates for clerk, SERGEANT AT ARMS, CHAPLAIN, and chief administrative officer. The majority party's candidates prevail because this is a party-line vote.

Rule II of the House of Representatives establishes the duties of the clerk. Among the clerk's major duties are to maintain the roll of members, maintain the constitutionally required journal of the proceedings of the chamber, and notify members of reports that are required from other government officials pursuant to current law. All formal documents issued by the House must go through the clerk's office. The clerk oversees the engrossment of bills and the enrollment of bills before they are sent to the president and is the officer who delivers enrolled bills to the president if they originated in the House. The clerk sends the messages of the House, and when the House is not in session, it is the clerk who receives messages from the Senate and the president. The clerk's office maintains a library of all documents sent by the House and is responsible for the administration of a member's office if they die, resign, or are expelled during a Congress. The House Oversight Committee oversees the clerk's office.

Further reading:
U.S. House of Representatives. *Office of the Clerk.* Available online. URL: http://clerk.house.gov. Accessed January 16, 2006 U.S. House of Representatives. Rule II. Available online. URL: http://clerk.house.gov/index.html. Accessed January 16, 2006.
— Donna R. Hoffman

cloakrooms
When the U.S. Congress originally convened, House and Senate members did not have their own offices. As a result, centralized cloakrooms were organized according to congressional chamber and party affiliation as a place for representatives and senators to store their coats and other personal belongings when they were on the floor. When the House of Representatives gave personal offices to its members in 1908 and the Senate gave personal offices to its members in 1909, the cloakrooms were turned into private lounges. Each cloakroom, of which there are four (Democratic House, Democratic Senate, Republican House, and Republican Senate), is located in the U.S. CAPITOL BUILDING, and their doors lead directly into the House and Senate chambers. They are long enclosed rooms at the back of each chamber. Many members of Congress use the cloakrooms to enter and exit the floor of their chamber.

Inside each cloakroom are numbered phone booths, and the cloakroom staff indicate to each member of

Congress which phone booth he or she may use to make or receive calls. The party Whip offices leave schedules in the cloakrooms indicating the floor schedule for debate of bills and copies of letters from the leadership of their respective party and chamber. Interest groups also leave information on their positions on bills being debated in chamber.

Access to the cloakrooms is restricted. Leadership staffs have come-and-go privileges, as do all the pages. No other staff members may enter the chambers without being summoned by a legislator. Each cloakroom has its own staff that answers the phones and takes and delivers messages to legislators on the floor. Journalists also regularly call the cloakroom for up-to-date information on legislative debates. Cloakroom staff have even established a hot-line, updated throughout the day to provide current information on the status of bills. Rather than sitting on the floor of their respective chambers, many legislators use the cloakroom as a "getaway" where they can hide from staff for privacy, wait in between votes, have political conversations with each other, or just relax.

Further reading:
C-span.org. "Public Affairs on the Web." Available online. URL: http://www.c-span.org/questions/weekly2.asp. Accessed February 6, 2003.

—Nancy S. Lind

cloture

Cloture is a parliamentary petition to end debate in the U.S. SENATE. The small size of the Senate has encouraged collegiality and a reluctance to limit the abilities of senators to participate in free debate and deliberation. Senate Rule XXII provides senators with a means to end a FILIBUSTER on any matter the Senate is considering. A total of 16 senators must initiate a cloture petition by presenting a motion to end the debate. The Senate does not vote on the cloture motion until the second day after the motion is made. It usually requires the votes of at least three-fifths (60) of all senators to invoke cloture. Two-thirds of the senators present and voting are required to support a motion to invoke cloture on a proposal to amend the Senate's standing rules. If cloture is invoked, a maximum of 30 additional hours is allotted for considering the pending matter. The 30-hour period includes all time consumed by roll-call votes, QUORUM CALLS, and other actions, as well as time for debate. During the 30 hours each senator may speak for no more than one hour.

The cloture rule was adopted in 1917. Prior to this the Senate relied on UNANIMOUS CONSENT AGREEMENTS to end debate, usually impossible during a filibuster. The only other factor the Senate could use to end debate was a hope that the speaker or speakers would give up because of exhaustion. Walter Oleszek said the Senate was prompted to act on a formal way to limit debate by a filibuster that killed a bill that would have allowed U.S. merchant ships to be armed against the threat posed by attacks by German submarines immediately before the United States entered World War I. President Woodrow Wilson criticized the filibuster and called the Senate into special session. The Senate adopted the cloture rule in 1917.

Cloture was rarely invoked for the next 20 years. From 1937 until the early 1960s, cloture was invoked most often when southern Democratic senators engaged in filibusters of civil rights bills. Cloture was rejected in every instance. Efforts to reduce the cloture requirements were defeated in 1957, 1963, 1965, and 1967. These efforts were led by liberal senators who wanted to reduce the cloture vote requirement to three-fifths or to a simple majority of senators. In 1975 the Senate voted to change the cloture rule. The pressing Senate workload was exaggerating the effect of a filibuster and frustrating senators who wanted to enact public policy to solve the country's problems. The cloture vote requirement was changed from two-thirds of those present and voting to three-fifths of all the senators.

In the 108th Congress MAJORITY LEADER WILLIAM FRIST, a Republican from Tennessee, sought changes in the rules governing debate to discourage Democrats from filibustering President George W. Bush's judicial nominations. Frist was unsuccessful.

Further reading:
Beth, Richard S., and Stanley Bach. *Filibusters and Cloture in the Senate.* Washington, D.C.: Library of Congress, Congressional Research Service, 2003; Binder, Sarah A., and Steven S. Smith. *Politics or Principle? Filibustering in the United States Senate.* Washington, D.C.: Brookings Institution Press, 1997; Oleszek, Walter J. *Congressional Procedures and the Policy Process.* 6th ed. Washington, D.C.: Congressional Quarterly Press, 2004.

—John David Rausch, Jr.

clubs

Congress is not only a place to work. For its members Congress also provides important social outlets for members after hours. Predictably, important legislative negotiations may occur at these social events. Thus, having access to these organizations becomes an important means for members to influence policy. Former representative and WAYS AND MEANS COMMITTEE chair Dan Rostenkowski, a Democrat from Illinois, reportedly dined at a Washington steak house regularly. Sharing a meal with him was a unique opportunity to bend his ear about important issues regarding the tax code.

In addition, some members of Congress have organized into clubs that meet periodically. Their meetings mix business and pleasure. Among the oldest and most prestigious were SOS and the Chowder and Marching Society. Formed by Republican House members in 1953 and 1949, respectively, both were influential in shaping policy and formulating legislative strategy. Members of the Chowder and Marching Society were well represented in the senior ranks of prestigious committees. Meetings of such clubs apparently included food, alcoholic beverages, smoking, relaxing, conversations of questionable taste, and, of course, legislative bargaining and logrolling.

Another example of such a contemporary club is the Wednesday Group, a group of moderate House Republicans that meets regularly. Since 1942 a group of House members has met on Thursday mornings while Congress is in session for a prayer breakfast.

Another venue for combining business and pleasure is the House gymnasium, where pick-up games of basketball regularly occur. While not a "club" in a formal sense, the gym is regularly frequented by members who develop friendships that are a basis of legislative bargaining later. They once also enjoyed the camaraderie that developed from the exclusively all-male environment (the gymnasium excluded women for many years) and the locker room banter.

Congressional clubs came into some criticism because they historically excluded female members of Congress. Club members privately asserted that the men would be uncomfortable in the company of women, colleagues or not, because of the damper they would put on men's behavior and because of the gossip such meetings might generate. Some, however, at least perceived that the women's effectiveness in the institution might be compromised by their exclusion from such clubs. Even the venerable groups SOS and Chowder and Marching Society eventually admitted women. The gymnasium today is co-ed. However, women still have difficulty penetrating the cliques who meet for a pick-up game of basketball or paddleball.

Further reading:
Gertzog, Irwin N. *Congressional Women: Their Recruitment, Integration and Behavior.* 2d ed. Westport, Conn.: Praeger, 1995.

—Karen M. Kedrowski

coattail effect
Conventional wisdom has maintained that in years when there is a presidential election, the party that wins the White House will also make gains in that year's congressional elections. Victorious members of Congress are said to be pulled into office on "the president's coattails."

In the modern era there is considerable evidence for the existence of the coattail effect. Between 1944 and 1984 the party of the winning presidential candidate also saw its position improved in the House of Representatives in all but one instance (the 1956 election). With fewer seats up for election, the situation has not been so marked in the Senate, but it is notable that only twice during that 40-year period did the victorious presidential candidate's party see its representation in the Senate diminish (1972 and 1984). Determining the exact nature of the connection between the presidential and congressional elections can be problematic. However, it is clear that in many competitive races the popularity of a party's national candidate provided a boost for the local campaign. Many of these gains proved short lived, with the opposition party bouncing back in the mid-term elections, when holding the White House can act as more of a hindrance than a help.

Since 1988, however, the effect of presidential coattails on congressional elections has begun to be questioned. In the four presidential elections since then only once has the victorious party been rewarded a net gain in the House (1996) or the Senate (1992).

Three factors can be suggested for the demise of the coattail phenomenon. First, fewer congressional races are truly competitive. The rate at which incumbents are successfully reelected frequently exceeds 90 percent. Aside from the traditional advantages of office and the developments in technology and direct mailing techniques that have helped incumbents in their reelection bids, the rising cost of campaigning has seen running for office increasingly become a rich person's preserve. Additionally, in the 2000 election 15 percent of the seats in the House of Representatives were won with no major party opponent. Additionally, more than 70 percent of winning candidates faced a major opponent but swept to victory with more than 55 percent of the vote. Hence, the fewer seats that can be counted as genuinely competitive, the less opportunity there is for any party to make large gains in either the House or the Senate.

Second, the connection between presidential and congressional campaigns has been diminished by the growth in "split-ticket" voting. Not only are more of the electorate rejecting the traditional party labels to consider themselves independent, but voters are also increasingly willing to vote for different parties for different posts, even if the elections take place on the same day. The importance of the issues, the campaigns, and the candidates themselves appear to have become far more important than the party label, which inevitably reduces the effect of a Republican or a Democratic victory in the race for the White House on the success of their congressional counterparts.

Finally, in the 1992, 1996, and 2000 presidential elections, the winning candidate failed to gain 50 percent of the popular vote. In 1992 and 1996 the presence of H. Ross Perot as a significant third-party candidate restricted President Bill Clinton to 43 percent and 49 percent of the popular vote, respectively. In 2000 George W. Bush won 48 percent, losing the popular vote, but emerged victorious in the Electoral College via the Supreme Court. With presidents winning the White House with a minority of the ballots cast, it is hardly surprising that their parties' congressional candidates do not experience a coattail effect. Whether the peculiar circumstances that have surrounded the last three presidential elections have exaggerated the extent to which the coattail effect has shrunk will be seen only over time.

Further reading:
Campbell, J. E. *The Presidential Pulse of Congressional Elections.* Lexington: University Press of Kentucky, 1997; Cook, R. "The Election of 2000: Part Retro, Part New Age." *Public Perspective* (November/December, 2001); Jacobson, G. C. *The Politics of Congressional Elections.* New York: Longman, 2001; Moos, M. C. *Politics, Presidents and Coattails.* New York: Greenwood Press, 1969.

—Ross M. English

Colfax, Schuyler (1823–1885) *Representative, Speaker of the House, Vice President*

The grandson of General William Colfax of George Washington's Life Guard, Schuyler Colfax was born in New York City in 1823. His career took him from ambitious young Whig journalist to congressman, to SPEAKER OF THE HOUSE, to vice president, and to discredit and relative obscurity. Known throughout his political career as an affable and diplomatic man (nicknamed "The Smiler"), Colfax deftly negotiated the volatile decades of the 1850s and 1860s from the ground floor of Republicanism through the party's contentious intramural battles between conservatives and radicals. While he cultivated strong supporters along the way, including a close ally, Salmon Chase, he also generated suspicions that his cool smile masked selfish ambition.

Born to a notable but financially diminished family, Colfax attended public school to age 10, after which he worked as a store clerk following the death of his father. In 1826 his mother married George Mathews, who moved the family to Indiana, where Schuyler pursued an eager self-education through reading newspapers. In 1841 Mathews was elected county auditor as a Whig in South Bend and appointed young Colfax his deputy. Colfax had taken up political writing, earning a post reporting on the state legislature for the *Indiana State Journal*. By age 19 he was tapped by Whigs to edit the *South Bend Free Press*. As a thoroughly devoted Whig, dedicated fully to the platform of the party and especially temperance, Colfax purchased a share of the *Free Press* in 1845 and renamed the Whig organ the *St. Joseph Valley Register.*

Colfax's headlong drive into politics led him to the Whig convention of 1848 and Indiana's constitutional convention of 1849, where he established himself as an opponent to antiblack provisions. Indiana Whigs convinced him, probably with little arm twisting, to run for Congress in 1851. Losing to a Democratic incumbent by a narrow margin, he made a second run in 1854 amid the collapse of the Whigs and the birth of the Republican Party. The congressman found himself in 1855 a cautious supporter of Know-Nothingism, amenable to the movement's nativist position but more concerned about pushing its antislavery plank. By the next election Colfax announced his candidacy as a Republican and won his seat back in the sectional fracas over Kansas that enveloped Congress. He gained a reputation as a fiery opponent to slavery in the territories and used his diplomatic skills (and the substantial patronage he had available as chair of the Post Office Committee) to help forge the loose confederation of abolitionists, free-soilers, and Republicans of various stripes into the unified party of 1860.

With southern secession and the evacuation of southern Democrats from Congress, Colfax used a moderate stance on the many issues that tugged the new party in contentious directions to establish himself as a House leader, capable of holding the party together through the war. Opposition to the war in the North by late 1862 diminished Republican hegemony in congressional races, and Colfax was forced to fend off tough opposition from David Turpie in his district. A narrow victory in a tough race, however, at a time when a number of key Republicans had lost their seats further enhanced Colfax's reputation in the Republican Party. When Congress convened in December 1863, the Republican majority chose "Smilin' Schuyler" as their Speaker of the House.

Colfax thrived as Speaker. He was popular and by the accounts of his contemporaries in Congress managed the House enthusiastically, even pushing the boundaries of decorum and several times establishing procedural precedents. More cynical observers fretted that Colfax was too radical and too ambitious, including President Abraham Lincoln, who had opposed him from the start. Nonetheless, Colfax was at the center of Civil War policy, in frequent meetings with Lincoln and present at the White House for the signing of the Emancipation Proclamation. While Colfax avoided open confrontation with Lincoln, he quietly supported the bid of his close friend Salmon Chase for the presidential nomination in 1864. Lincoln and Colfax biographers alike agree that Lincoln referred to him as a little intriguer. While the chronology of Colfax's specific ambitions is unclear, it seems likely that from the Speaker's chair he envisioned a path to the Oval Office. Trained as a journalist, he enjoyed more support from the press than most Speakers and manipulated the press with all the clever media tools that would become essential to politicians over the next century and a half.

As Speaker, however, his real influence over wartime policy and legislation is uncertain. He spoke as a Republican moderate but was tolerant of policy ideas emanating from leading radicals such as Thaddeus Stevens, who emerged as the most significant Republican power in the House. The pairing of approaches, however, was to the benefit of Republicans politically. While radicals seemed unconcerned with the electoral dangers of open partisanship in pressing for greater rights for blacks, Colfax used the press effectively to instead substitute a resonance of Republican patriotism.

Having declined an invitation by the president to join his ill-fated evening at Ford's Theater in April 1865, Colfax began the postwar Reconstruction with a western tour. While the trip was ostensibly a survey of western mining potential, the fanfare that accompanied him and the more than 70 speeches made by the Speaker must have served as an interesting trial run for his ambitions. Returning to Washington in November, he attempted to lead a middle course on Reconstruction that would compromise the interests of radicals and conservatives and bridge presidential and congressional policy. To do so he announced that he supported Andrew Johnson's efforts to move quickly on Reconstruction, in advance of legislation, with the understanding that the restoration of southern states would include civil equality for freedmen (though without mentioning suffrage). Popular support for the position and Republican optimism fragmented, however, as Johnson rapidly undermined Reconstruction through generous terms for southern governments and complete disregard for freedmen's rights. The chasm that opened between Republicans in Congress and the president led to Johnson's impeachment under his violation of the Tenure of Office Act. While the executive's obstinacy had made compromise between branches impossible, Colfax continued to show managerial skill by holding together several Republican factions to support conviction of the president. Critical defections in the Senate, however, saved Johnson from removal. But congressional Republicans had taken the helm of Reconstruction, and Colfax continued to gain respect as the glue of compromise and solidarity in the party.

The election of 1868, with Ulysses Grant the popular choice for the Republican nomination, provided Colfax with the opportunity to advance his path to the White House through the vice presidency. While there was little contest for the Republican presidential nomination, the second spot on the ticket required multiple ballots at the convention in Chicago. Colfax challenged from behind Senators Ben Wade of Ohio and Henry Wilson. President Pro Tempore of the Senate, Wade was the early leader at the convention, but with each subsequent ballot support for Colfax grew. What seems to have tipped the scales in his favor was the unimpeachable integrity and virtue he would bring to the ticket. Colfax had long worked the temperance and Sunday school circuit as a popular promoter of sobriety and Christian virtue and would balance the rougher, hard-drinking reputation of Grant. With temperance groups a significant factor in the election, the choice for vice president was a popular one in the party, and his adversaries for the post conceded with strong praise, aided perhaps by the fact that Colfax was at the time betrothed to Wade's niece, Ellen.

Neither the first nor the last to discover the vice presidency to be a calm that permanently took the wind out of his sails, Colfax's choice of path proved a poor one for his ambitions. Unfortunately, too, the virtue and marriage that cemented his place on the ticket served to undermine his ambitions as well. Recommitted to a life of fastidious virtue by election speeches and a new wife and baby, the vice president distanced himself from the numerous valuable friends he had made in the Washington press corps. He also failed to develop a close partnership with Grant. As a variety of scandals began to emerge around the president's administration, this distance from Grant appeared at first to be a great advantage.

Colfax took the opportunity to attempt a risky ploy to make a bid for the 1872 nomination. In 1870 he announced his intent to resign from public life at the end of his term. The plan was apparently to further distance himself from Grant and signal to Republicans that he desired the presidential nomination in 1872. The plan failed miserably. The press took his announcement and his personal distance seriously and ignored him, while Republicans prepared to nominate Henry Wilson on a ticket with Grant. By the time he retracted his claim to retirement in the fall of 1862 an even bigger problem surfaced, known as the CREDIT MOBILIER SCANDAL that would prove his undoing.

Never a man of wealth and reluctant to risk insulting friends, colleagues, and supporters, Colfax had regularly accepted gifts of all sorts during his tenure in Washington. In 1868 he had accepted from Oakes Ames, a friend and colleague in the Senate, stock in the finance company called Credit Mobilier that was underwriting the Union Pacific Railroad's transcontinental line. Ames had been recruited by the company to distribute stock to congressmen to encourage them to bless the company with generous federal subsidies. Like others embroiled in the scandal that followed, Colfax claimed to have paid a fair market price for the stock, hoping that this would make legitimate the inflated dividends that resulted from their votes in Congress. A House investigation in 1873 revealed that a cash-poor Colfax had not paid for the stock up front, presumably hoping the dividends would pay later. When confronted with a $1,200 dividend check that had found its way into his bank account, the vice president concocted a far-fetched lie that left the virtuous half of the Grant ticket in shame. Had his term not expired in just a few weeks, Smilin' Schuyler would probably have been impeached. With the press no longer an ally, the disgraced vice president bore much of the blame in the public mind a year later when the financial failure of the railroads precipitated a depression. The good fortune of many of his former colleagues was that Colfax's infamy lightened the pressure considerably on many other guilty men whose political careers survived the scandal.

Schuyler Colfax left public life in disgrace but managed to make a good living afterward as a public lecturer. Even if scorned as a crook and a hypocrite, the hearty appetite of Americans for stories of the martyred Abraham Lincoln provided the man who had spent many intimate hours with Lincoln during the war with a ready trade in speaker's fees. Colfax died of a heart attack in 1885 on a train platform in Mankato, Minnesota, eulogized in the press not for his skill as Speaker of the House and engineer of the Republican Party, but rather for the genial manner and winsome smile that masked a flawed character. With little more to recommend him, historians have largely set him aside. The last substantial biography of the man who chaired the House of Representatives through the Civil War was published in 1952.

Further reading:
Anbinder, Tyler. *Nativism and Slavery: The Northern Know Nothings and the Politics of the 1850's.* New York: Oxford 1992; Benedict, Michael Les. *A Compromise of Principle: Congressional Republicans and Reconstruction 1863–1869.* New York: Norton 1974; Bogue, Allan G. *The Congressman's Civil War.* New York: Cambridge 1989; Martin, Edward Winslow. *The Life and Public Service of Schuyler Colfax.* New York: United States Pub. 1868; Smith, Willard Harvey. *The Life and Times of Hon. Schuyler Colfax.* Indianapolis: Indiana Historical Bureau, 1952: Summers, Mark Wahlgren. *The Era of Good Stealings.* New York: Oxford 1993.
—Michael Steiner

comity

Comity is the obligation that members of Congress have to adhere to a system of behavioral norms in how they treat fellow members. Comity has at certain times in history been central to the individual behavior of members.

These norms are usually described as including courtesy, gentility, and reciprocity. Thus, comity is more than members simply being nice to one another. Reciprocity is the foundation of comity because when legislators are civil and polite to another legislator, there is a certain expectation under a regime of comity that others will behave in the same civil manner. That is, a regime of comity does not exist if one individual is polite while the other individual involved in the interaction is rude. Historically, congressional comity refers to both individual standards of behavior for members as well as a mutual respect of the two chambers for each other. It is also important to note that a norm of comity does not imply cooperation between individuals or between chambers but does indeed facilitate the type of cooperation necessary for public policy making.

Levels of comity within Congress change over time. Despite conventional ideas that contemporary members are increasingly uncivil toward one another, the behavior of modern members seems somewhat tame compared to their behavior prior to the Civil War. It is hard to imagine that in certain eras brawls and duels within Congress were somewhat commonplace, particularly in the antebellum era. After what was considered a low point for comity in Congress, comity was reestablished as the norm in the late 19th century. However, during both the 1890s and the 1920s, levels of incivility once again increased, although these breaks in comity were less aggressive than those that took place during the antebellum era. The last era in which comity was the norm in Congress was from the 1950s until the late 1960s. A renewed incivility began to take over Congress beginning in the 1970s.

Eric Uslaner argues that the norm of comity in Congress trails the cycle of partisan realignments. Thus, the antebellum era, the late 19th century, and the 1920s all showed drastic increases of incivility, which all coincided with the arrival of the weakest party systems Congress has ever seen. After each realignment occurs, there is typically a period of increased partisanship as well as a more majoritarian government. This shift is typically followed by more restrained behavior, which is signaled by the return to comity, both between and within political parties.

However, unlike previous declines in comity, the new incivility that began in the 1970s does not seem to coincide with a new partisan realignment. Thus, while the decrease of civility seemed to occur in line with its typical cyclical pattern, there was no corresponding realignment. Uslaner argues that the current decline of comity reflects not partisan realignments but larger changes within societal values. Other explanations for the increasing incivility found in contemporary Congresses include factors such as the congressional reforms of the 1970s, the increasing occurrence of divided government, individual membership changes in Congress, the surfacing of a liberal majority in the 1960s, and an increasingly important media.

Further reading:
Uslaner, Eric M. *The Decline of Comity in Congress.* Ann Arbor: University of Michigan Press, 1993.
—Lisa A. Solowiej

commerce power

The Constitution's grant of power to Congress "to regulate Commerce with foreign Nations, and among the several States, and with the Indian Tribes," in Article I, Section 8, of the Constitution, is the source of most federal regulatory authority and federal criminal law. The vast range of federal regulation of the workplace (e.g., minimum wage, 40-hour work week, collective bargaining, occupational safety), apportionment of the broadcast spectrum, environmental protection laws, antitrust laws, and consumer protection agencies (e.g., Federal Trade Commission, Food and Drug Administration, National Highway Traffic Safety Administration) are all based on the commerce power. Congressional enactments under the Commerce Clause can preempt states' laws, such as rules governing lawsuits for personal injuries. Most federal criminal laws, such as those making kidnapping and bank robbery federal offenses, are based on the power to regulate interstate commerce.

In granting Congress authority over interstate commerce, the Constitution implicitly denied that authority to individual states. The commerce power is not only affirmative, in that it grants Congress latitude to legislate, but it is also exclusive, making it the foundation of the system of free trade among the states.

Ultimately, the boundaries of Congress's commerce power are delineated by the U.S. Supreme Court. A century ago the Court gave strict interpretation to the word *commerce*, distinguishing between "distribution" of goods, which it said involved a "direct" effect on commerce, and "production" of goods, which it said had merely "indirect" interstate effects. The Court permitted Congress to regulate only "direct" activities, which curtailed government regulation of business substantially. For instance, in *Schechter Poultry Corp. v. United States*, the Court held that Congress could not regulate the wages and hours of employees of poultry processors, finding that once live chickens had been delivered to a slaughterhouse for local distribution, the "flow in interstate commerce had ceased." The Court said that such distinctions were "fundamental" and "essential" to the constitutional system, for without them "there would be virtually no limit to the federal power."

By 1937, with *National Labor Relations Board v. Jones & Laughlin Steel Corp.*, the distinctions broke down. The Court held that the impact of an activity on interstate commerce, rather than its source, determined whether Congress had jurisdiction. The Court went so far, in *Wickard v. Filburn*, as to hold that even crops grown for household consumption could be regulated, since they reduced demand for food purchased in the market. These decisions ushered in an era of expanded federal power to regulate business as well as to desegregate public accommodations.

For more than half a century the Supreme Court declined all entreaties to invalidate laws passed pursuant to the Commerce Clause, but this streak ended in 1995 with *United States v. Lopez,* in which the Court struck down the Gun-Free School Zones Act. The Court noted that even its "modern-era precedents which have expanded congressional power under the commerce clause confirm that this power is subject to outer limits," and cited language from *Jones & Laughlin Steel* warning that the scope of the power "must be considered in the light of our dual system of government and may not be extended so as to . . . obliterate the distinction between what is national and what is local and create a completely centralized government."

In *Lopez* and in *United States v. Morrison*, the Court created a new dichotomy. Congress could regulate "economic" activity but could not regulate "non-economic, violent criminal conduct." The Court rejected arguments that a criminal carrying a gun or committing a rape could have a substantial effect on commerce, saying that if Congress could regulate

> any activity that it found was related to the economic productivity of individual citizens [such as] family law . . . it is difficult to perceive any limitation on federal power, even in areas such as criminal law enforcement or education where States historically have been sovereign.

Some observers view the *Lopez* and *Morrison* decisions as a reprise of early 20th-century decisions by conservative justices substituting their ideological views for Congress's. A more benign view would suggest that different branches of government will have different views of the appropriate division of power between state and national governments. Political scientist Paul Peterson has posited two theories to explain the exercise of congressional power in a federal system. Under a "functional" theory the logic behind maintaining separate levels of government would dictate what legislation is passed by Congress. Activities that require regulation on a uniform national basis, or problems that spill over from one state to another, are the best candidates for exercise of the commerce power pursuant to this theory.

Under a "legislative" theory, on the other hand, "policies are shaped by the political needs" of members of Congress. Members may feel demands to address issues such as sexual assaults or gun violence in schoolyards quite apart from whether such activities affect interstate commerce. The courts are more insulated from political demands and may form a different judgment of whether a congressional enactment squares with an idealized allocation of functions.

Further reading:
Schechter Poultry Corp. v. United States, 295 U.S. 495; *National Labor Relations Board v. Jones & Laughlin Steel*

Corp., 301 U.S. 1; *Wickard v. Filburn*, 317 U.S. 111; *United States v. Lopez*, 514 U.S. 549; *United States v. Morrison*, 529 U.S. 598; Peterson, P. *The Price of Federalism.*

—Jackson Williams

Commerce, Science, and Transportation, Senate Committee on

The Committee on Commerce, Science, and Transportation has the broadest jurisdiction of any standing committee in the U.S. SENATE. A number of committees have held the jurisdiction given to the Committee on Commerce, Science, and Transportation. In fact, many separate committees simultaneously shared the jurisdiction held by the committee in the 108th Congress (2003–04). The Committee on Commerce, Science, and Transportation can trace its history to one of the first substantive standing committees created by the Senate in 1816, the Committee on Commerce and Manufactures. Prior to 1816 the Senate relied on temporary (select) committees to provide in-depth consideration of a particular bill or issue. A resolution adopted by the Senate during the second session of the 14th Congress created 11 standing committees, including the Committee on Commerce and Manufactures.

The committee focused primarily on compiling statistical reports and conducting investigations requested by the full Senate on matters such as harbor improvements, foreign trade, canal construction, and the regulation of shipping. By the mid-1820s the committee began to debate the question of tariffs. The tariff issue badly split the committee's membership. Recognizing that the committee was divided on its two major subjects, the Senate voted in 1825 to divide the committee into two separate committees: the Committee on Commerce and the Committee on Manufactures.

The railroad industry grew in the decades following the Civil War. In 1872 President Ulysses Grant called on the Senate to investigate some of the railroads' more questionable practices. The Senate responded by creating a select committee that investigated and proposed several reforms. No action was taken on the reforms. In 1885 Illinois senator Shelby Cullom introduced a resolution to create a temporary committee to consider ways to regulate the railroads. The resolution was approved, and the Select Committee on Transportation by Railroad between the Several States was created.

A select committee to investigate interstate commerce also was created in early 1885. By December 1885 the permanent Committee on Interstate Commerce replaced the select committee. The Interstate Commerce Act of 1887 was one of the most important bills reported out of the new committee.

At the end of the 19th century, the Senate became concerned about the state of the maritime industry in the United States. In 1899 the Senate created the Committee on Interoceanic Canals. One of the bills reported out by the committee was the Spooner Act of 1902, the bill that authorized the construction of the Panama Canal.

In 1921 the Senate reorganized its committee structure. Many senators believed that the number of committees had become unwieldy and voted to reduce the number from 73 to 33. The Committee on Commerce, the Committee on Manufactures, the Committee on Interstate Commerce, and the Committee on Interoceanic Canals all survived the reorganization in 1921.

The Senate reorganized itself again in the mid-1940s as a result of the LEGISLATIVE REORGANIZATION ACT OF 1946. The act was intended to improve the efficiency of Congress. It reduced the number of Senate standing committees from 33 to 15. The Committee on Commerce, the Committee on Manufactures, the Committee on Interstate Commerce, and the Committee on Interoceanic Canals were voted out of existence. Most of their jurisdiction was given to the new Committee on Interstate and Foreign Commerce.

In the 1950s the promise of space travel and the need for policy to guide the development of a space program led to the creation of the Committee on Aeronautical and Space Sciences in the Senate. The Commerce Committee reemerged again in 1961, when the name of the Committee on Interstate and Foreign Commerce was shortened. Most people had been calling it the Commerce Committee.

In 1976 the Senate created the Select Committee to Study the Senate Committee System. Among the select committee's recommendations was to change the name of the Committee on Commerce to the Committee on Commerce, Science, and Transportation. The Committee on Aeronautical and Space Sciences was eliminated in 1977 and its jurisdiction turned over to the new Commerce Committee. With the committee's name change, it was given jurisdiction over the regulation of consumer products and services and charged with developing the country's science, engineering, and technology policy. It also was given the responsibility for nonmilitary aeronautical and space science policy as well as communication policy.

The Commerce, Science, and Transportation Committee was one of 16 standing committees in the Senate in the 108th Congress. With 23 members (12 Republicans and 11 Democrats), it was one of the larger committees. Reflecting its varied jurisdiction, the committee had seven subcommittees: Aviation; Communication; Competition, Foreign Commerce, and Infrastructure; Consumer Affairs and Product Safety; Oceans, Fisheries, and Coast Guard; Science, Technology, and Space; and Surface Transportation and Merchant Marine.

Further reading:

Cohn, Peter. "Major Reauthorizations for Commerce." *Congressional Quarterly Weekly Report,* 62 (2002): 2,917; Hall, Richard L. "Participation, Abdication, and Representation in Congressional Committees." In Lawrence Dodd and Bruce I. Oppenheimer, eds. *Congress Reconsidered.* Washington, D.C.: Congressional Quarterly Press, 1993; Sharma, Amol. "Overlapping Interests, Jurisdictions Complicate Efforts to Reauthorize Satellite Television Law." *Congressional Quarterly Weekly Report,* 62 (2004): 1,809.
—John David Rausch, Jr.

committee assignments (House and Senate)

Party committees in each chamber are responsible for assigning members to committees. Democratic and Republican party leaders at the beginning of each Congress negotiate the size of each committee. The number of seats on each committee allocated to each party (committee ratio) is roughly determined by the percentage of seats in the chamber held by each party (party ratio), although the majority party in the House typically maintains an extraordinary majority on the most powerful committees (Appropriations, Rules, and Ways and Means) to ensure control over important aspects of the legislative agenda. Committee ratios in the Senate tend to reflect closely the party ratio in the chamber due to the rules of that body.

At the beginning of each new Congress newly elected and returning members of the House and Senate are asked by their respective party leaders to submit their requests for committee assignments. Incumbent members are entitled to retain their existing assignments except under extraordinary circumstances; they need only submit a request if they are seeking a change in their committee assignments. Any member requesting to serve on a committee is required to submit a written rank-ordered list of committees on which he or she would like to serve. It is the responsibility of the party committee to determine the number of open seats their party has on a committee and select those members who will fill the empty seats. In many cases the number of requests for a seat on a particular committee—especially the most sought after committees, Appropriations, Rules, and Ways and Means in the House, and Appropriations and Finance in the Senate—outstrips the number of available seats. Members of Congress seeking a preferred committee will often engage in campaigns, similar to the campaigns that they waged to get elected, within the House or Senate aimed at influencing the votes of party committee members.

Political scientists have tried to understand the factors that influence the success of a member pursuing a committee assignment (request success) in the House. Typically request success is considered to be a function of seniority, geographic balance, and partisan loyalty. The relative importance of these factors varies between the parties and over time. In the pre-1970s Democratic Party, when the Ways and Means Committee was responsible for committee assignments, seniority and geographic balance were the most important considerations. However, once the committee assignment process was taken over by the Democratic Steering and Policy Committee, geography and partisan loyalty became dominant factors in determining the success of member applications.

Due to the structure of the Republican committee selection process prior to the 104th Congress, committee assignments were largely determined by large-state Republicans making geography (but not necessarily balance) important in the selection process, followed by seniority. In the 104th Congress the Republican leadership, specifically the Speaker, took a much larger role in the selection process, emphasizing party loyalty and geographic balance over seniority.

In the Senate Charles Bullock has demonstrated that seniority is a powerful factor influencing who receives a committee assignment in the Democratic Party. During the tenure of LYNDON JOHNSON as Democratic leader, committee assignments were at least partially decoupled from seniority. The "Johnson Rule" held that newly elected Democrats were entitled to at least one "good" committee assignment, which generally required setting aside the seniority rule. It also provided Johnson a means of rewarding or punishing the personal loyalty of senators. In the Senate, Republican Committee assignments are determined by seniority; the most senior member requesting a committee assignment receives the committee seat. More recently the Republican Senate leader was given the power to make one committee assignment to each incoming Republican member in an attempt to make assignments at least partially dependent on party loyalty.

In addition to examining request success, political scientists have invested a great deal of effort attempting to explain why individual members of Congress seek to serve on particular committees and studying the policy consequences of those individual choices. The dominant interpretation is referred to as the distributive theory of congressional assignments. Distributive theory is based on a set of four assertions: 1) Members of Congress request membership on committees that will best serve their constituency and, in turn, their interest in reelection; 2) the congressional party committees seek to accommodate member requests above all else, placing them on the committees that they request; 3) committees, as a result, are composed of members with extreme preferences on policy issues under the committee's jurisdiction; and 4) public policy is skewed in favor of the extreme positions of committee members, often resulting in an oversupply of benefits (spending) for the districts of committee members through LOGROLLING by committees.

The classic examples of how distributive theory works are the House and Senate Agriculture Committees. First, requests for membership on an Agriculture Committee will come to the party committee from members who represent rural districts or states. Second, the party committee will accommodate the request by assigning the member to the Committee. Third, as a result of this self-selection process, the Agriculture Committee will be composed of members representing similar constituencies—farmers and those employed in farm-related industries—who are seeking to be responsive to their constituencies by providing exces-sively high levels of benefits to their constituents. Finally, the Agriculture Committee will gain support for its poli-cies by cooperating with other committees. For instance, the Agriculture Committee will get support for its policies from members of the Armed Services Committee and will return the favor by supporting the Armed Services Com-mittee in its quest for benefits. In short, distributive theory suggests, the quest of individual members of Congress for committee assignments that will help them to get reelected will result in overspending in all categories of federal gov-ernment spending.

This cartoon by Clifford K. Berryman depicts Senator Robert Taft and Senator Arthur Vandenberg as the "ring-masters" in charge of committee assignments in the U.S. Senate. *(National Archives)*

Despite the intuitive appeal of the distributive theory, recent research suggests that distributive theory may not explain why members pursue preferred committee assignments, nor the policy consequences of committee assignments. Drawing on committee requests from Democratic and Republican members of the House over most of the post–World War II era, Frisch and Kelly are critical of the four postulates of the theory.

First, they demonstrate that members of Congress mention reelection less than half the time as a motivation for pursuing a preferred committee, more often citing policy concerns and a desire to exercise institutional influence. Furthermore, they were able to find only modest evidence supporting the assertion that constituency characteristics are related to committee requests. In fact, the strongest evidence is for the Agriculture and Armed Services Committees, mentioned above as classic examples, but they found little relationship otherwise. Second, they cast doubt on the idea that party committees simply accommodate member requests for committee assignments. According to their analysis, about half of requesting Democrats and about a third of requesting Republicans received a preferred committee assignment. Third, consistent with the findings of others, Frisch and Kelly show that most committees (with the notable exceptions of Agriculture and Armed Services) are not made up of members with similar policy interests. Finally, their data analysis suggests that members who serve on a particular committee, such as Agriculture, do not usually deliver higher levels of benefits to their districts than do members who do not serve on that committee.

See also DEMOCRATIC STEERING COMMITTEE, HOUSE; REPUBLICAN STEERING COMMITTEE, HOUSE.

Further reading:
Deering, Christopher J., and Steven S. Smith. *Congressional Committees.* Washington, D.C.: Congressional Quarterly Press, 1997; Frisch, Scott A., and Sean Q. Kelly. *Committee Politics.* Norman: University of Oklahoma Press, forthcoming; Krehbiel, Keith. *Information and Legislative Organization.* Ann Arbor: University of Michigan Press, 1991; Shepsle, Kenneth A. *The Giant Jigsaw Puzzle.* Chicago: University of Chicago Press, 1978.

—Scott A. Frisch and Sean Q. Kelly

Committee of the Whole

The Committee of the Whole, technically "the Committee of the Whole House on the State of the Union," is a legislative device used to expedite the consideration of bills on the floor of the House of Representatives. After a bill has been considered in and reported out of committee, it is sent to the House Rules Committee, where it receives a special rule (usually referred to simply as a "rule"), which schedules the bill for floor debate and sets the parameters for that debate. The rule then is sent to the floor along with the bill. Before the bill can be considered, there is a vote on the rule. If the rule passes, the bill is taken up immediately for consideration, which occurs in the Committee of the Whole. The Committee of the Whole is technically a committee whose membership includes every member of the House. In reality, the Committee of the Whole is simply the House of Representatives operating under a different name.

The House, a rather unwieldy body with 435 members, has strict rules and procedures about how business may be conducted on the floor. If bills were to be considered under those rules, the process would be quite time consuming and make it almost impossible for legislation to pass. The Committee of the Whole is designed to move legislation through more quickly by by-passing the rules. Once the special rule (itself a method of by-passing the rules) has been voted on, the House immediately resolves itself into the Committee of the Whole. As a signal that this has happened, the ceremonial mace, which is usually kept upright on the dais next to the Speaker, is lowered. (One can tell, when watching C-SPAN, whether a bill is being considered by the position of the mace.)

The Committee of the Whole is used to debate and amend legislation. The bill is "read" (usually by section title), and Representatives make amendments to each section as allowed by the rule. Once the legislation has been amended and is ready for a vote on final passage, the Committee of the Whole rises and reports the measure back to the House. Since the Committee of the Whole is a committee, it does not have the authority to vote on final passage. The mace is again placed in an upright position, the Speaker announces that a vote on the previous question has been ordered, and debate on the bill is complete.

The Committee of the Whole concept is derived from British parliamentary history. During the Stuart monarchy Parliament developed its own Committee of the Whole as a mechanism to get around its rules. The committee met without its speaker (who would report proceedings to the king) and was therefore able to discuss tax bills in secret. The Committee of the Whole in the U.S. House of Representatives is not a secret body, but it is also a method to operate under streamlined rules. In the Committee of the Whole a quorum (the number of members that must be present in order for a body to do business) is 100 instead of the usual 218 (half of the Members plus one). Obviously, it is easier to round up 100 representatives than 218.

In the House, where members specialize in one or two issue areas (as opposed to the smaller Senate, where senators are forced to be generalists), representatives are not necessarily interested in being present for debate on each and every bill that is considered. Given the large number of issues any Congress must face, a representative has a limited amount of time on any given day to perform his or her own committee work, constituency services, and other administrative duties. He or she is often glad to follow leadership or trusted colleagues on legislation outside his or her expertise. With a quorum of 100, the Committee of the Whole allows those who worked on a particular piece of legislation to have it considered on the floor while still allowing those who might not have an overarching interest in the issue to attend to other business. When the vote on final passage comes, however, the quorum is again 218.

Debate is also curtailed under the Committee of the Whole. General debate on a bill is usually limited to one hour (although for complex bills significantly more time may be allotted), with each party taking about half of the debate time. Instead of the usual one-hour rule, debate on amendments is limited to five minutes on each side, streamlining the process for what may be a great number of amendments. The five-minute rule makes it possible for legislation to be considered and debated in a timely fashion. In practice, representatives routinely speak for more than the five minutes allowed, often requesting unanimous consent to speak longer or to yield some or all of their time to other representatives. The number and content of amendments are also limited by the rule associated with the bill.

The Speaker of the House does not preside in the Committee of the Whole. He or she steps down, and while he or she may remain in the House and debate, he or she appoints a presiding officer from the majority party to guide the debate. Usually, he or she is not someone from the committees that worked on the legislation. The Speaker does not usually vote in the Committee of the Whole, unless in the case of a tie. The Speaker resumes his or her position when debate on the bill is completed, and the House returns to its usual rules.

Further reading:
Davidson, Roger H., and Walter J. Oleszek. *Congress and Its Members.* 7th ed. Washington, D.C.: Congressional Quarterly Press, 2000; Froman, Lewis, Jr. *The Congressional Process.* Boston: Little, Brown, 1967; Oleszek, Walter J. *Congressional Procedures and the Policy Process.* 5th ed. Washington, D.C.: Congressional Quarterly Press, 2001.

—Anne Marie Cammisa

committees: joint

Permanent committees made up of equal numbers of members of the HOUSE OF REPRESENTATIVES and the SENATE are called joint committees. Modern joint committees are permanent panels that do not have legislative

authority but exist to conduct studies or perform housekeeping tasks. The chair of joint committees usually alternates between the House and Senate in alternating Congresses. A CONFERENCE COMMITTEE is a temporary joint committee formed to negotiate the differences between competing House and Senate bills. Conference committees draft compromises between the positions of the two chambers. These compromises are then submitted to the full House and Senate for approval.

Joint committees are rarely given legislative authority, in part because the chairs of permanent STANDING COMMITTEES are unwilling to give up some of their jurisdiction to the joint panels. The last joint committee with legislative authority was the Joint Committee on Atomic Energy, which disbanded in 1977.

Joint committees provide an important service to Congress. There were four joint committees in the 108th Congress. Two of the joint committees performed shared administrative housekeeping functions. The JOINT COMMITTEE ON THE LIBRARY oversaw the Library of Congress, and the JOINT COMMITTEE ON PRINTING oversaw the Government Printing Office. The JOINT ECONOMIC COMMITTEE and the Joint Taxation Committee provide Congress with additional staff specialists on economic and tax matters.

In earlier years both houses of Congress used joint committees more extensively than they do today for purposes of legislative and administrative coordination. During Congress's first century of operation, both chambers had a system of joint rules in addition to their individual chamber rules. This system of joint rules was abandoned as unworkable in 1889.

Throughout history Congress has relied on different joint committees. A Joint Committee on the Disposition of Useless Papers existed from 1889 until the Joint Committee on Disposition of Executive Papers replaced it in 1935. This joint committee was disbanded in 1970. Frustrated with the course of the Civil War in 1861, Congress established the Joint Committee on the Conduct of the War. It was disbanded in 1865. Since 1901 all presidential inaugural ceremonies at the U.S. Capitol have been organized by the Joint Congressional Committee on Inaugural Ceremonies.

Further reading:
Carr, Thomas P. *Committee Types and Roles.* Washington, D.C.: Library of Congress, Congressional Research Service, 2003; Deering, Christopher J., and Steven S. Smith. *Committees in Congress.* 3d ed. Washington, D.C.: Congressional Quarterly Press, 1997.

—John David Rausch, Jr.

committees: jurisdiction

Jurisdiction refers to authority a committee has to deal with particular subject matter and is defined by House and Senate rules. Because of the large workload of Congress and the vast array of issues with which it is concerned, each house subdivides itself into committees and subcommittees, which are the places where most of the work of Congress is done. As Woodrow Wilson wrote,

> Congress in session is Congress on display. Congress in committee is Congress at work.

There are several types of committees in Congress. Select committees are ad hoc committees formed to deal with a single issue. They generally disband at the end of the two-year session of Congress and do not usually have authority to consider major legislation. Joint committees are committees comprised of both senators and representatives. Like select committees, they usually examine a single issue for the purposes of investigation, oversight, and review. Joint committees (with the exception of conference committees, a special subset of joint committee created to reconcile differences between House and Senate bills) also do not have legislative authority. The legislative function has historically been placed in the third, most common type of committee, a permanent standing committee. These committees work out details of legislation, and each has legislative authority over a discrete (in practice, sometimes not so discrete) subject area, for example, agriculture, appropriations, the environment, small business, or veterans affairs. In turn, the committees are divided into subcommittees, each of which concerns itself with a particular subset of the subject matter.

Once a bill is introduced in the Senate or the House, it is referred to committee. Officially, the SPEAKER OF THE HOUSE and the presiding officer in the Senate refer a bill to the appropriate committee. In practice, however, it is usually the parliamentarians of each chamber who do the referrals. BILLS are referred to committee based on jurisdiction, which sometimes can be difficult to ascertain. Jurisdiction in the House is defined by House Rule X, which, as amended, sets out the guidelines for committees' subject matter. Some referrals are automatic: The WAYS AND MEANS COMMITTEE in the House of Representatives has jurisdiction over all tax bills (and it is constitutionally mandated that all bills raising taxes originate in the House of Representatives), as does the FINANCE COMMITTEE in the Senate. The Appropriations Committees in both the House and Senate have automatic jurisdiction over each of the 13 appropriations (spending) bills that Congress must consider each year. The jurisdiction of each of the committees' 13 subcommittees neatly corresponds to the subject matter of the 13 bills.

Other bills, however, may be properly referred to one or more committees, since jurisdiction often overlaps. For example, a bankruptcy bill falls under the jurisdiction of both the House FINANCIAL SERVICES COMMITTEE, since it deals with banking and financial

---

A SAMPLE OF COMMITTEE JURISDICTION

House Committee on Education and the Workforce, 108th Congress

Child labor
Gallaudet University and Howard University and Hospital
Convict labor and the entry of goods made by convicts into interstate commerce
Food programs for children in schools
Labor standards and statistics
Education or labor generally
Mediation and arbitration of labor disputes
Regulation or prevention of importation of foreign laborers under contract
Workers' compensation
Vocational rehabilitation
Wages and hours of labor
Welfare of miners
Work incentive programs

House Committees in the 108th Congress

Agriculture
Appropriations
Armed Services
Budget
Education and the Workforce
Energy and Commerce
Financial Services
Government Reform
House Administration
International Relations
Judiciary
Resources
Rules
Science
Small Business
Standards of Official Conduct
Transportation and Infrastructure
Veterans' Affairs
Ways and Means

Senate Committees in the 108th Congress

Agriculture, Nutrition, and Forestry
Appropriations
Armed Services
Banking, Housing, and Urban Affairs
Budget
Commerce, Science, and Transportation
Energy and Natural Resources
Environment and Public Works
Finance
Foreign Relations
Governmental Affairs
Health, Education, Labor, and Pensions
Indian Affairs
Judiciary
Rules and Administration
Small Business
Veterans' Affairs

matters, and the JUDICIARY COMMITTEE, since it also involves legal issues. What is to be done when committee jurisdictions overlap, as they often do? Sometimes a political decision is made, and the bill is referred to the committee that is most likely to report it out favorably (or not, depending on the preferences of the majority leadership). Sometimes a decision is made out of courtesy, and the bill is referred to the committee of the person who sponsored it. Other times the bill is referred to each of the committees that have jurisdiction over it. This is known as multiple referral and may be joint (sent to two committees at once), split (each section sent to the committee with jurisdiction over it), or sequential (sent to one committee and then another). Multiple referrals, once common in the House, have become more streamlined under the Republican majority. And they are much less common in the Senate, where senators are given broad leeway to make amendments to legislation during floor consideration.

Reforms in the 104th Congress created several changes that affected committee jurisdiction in the House. New rules put multiple referrals in the Speaker's control, eliminated joint referrals, and required that any multiple referrals specify a committee that will have "primary jurisdiction" over the legislation. The Republican majority in the House abolished four existing committees (District of Columbia, Merchant Marine and Fisheries, Post Office, and Civil Service), redistributing the matters under their jurisdiction to other committees, some of which were given new names more in keeping with Republican interests and concerns. Committee and subcommittee staff sizes were also drastically reduced. In addition, committees were limited to no more than five subcommittees, and ad hoc task forces were routinely used to draft and consider legislation. The 104th Congress also consolidated leadership in Speaker NEWT GINGRICH (R-GA), centralizing control over committees in the Speaker rather than committee chairs. Subsequently, chairs have regained some of their powers over committees. These reforms were not the first attempt at reorganizing the committee structure. The LEGISLATIVE REORGANIZATION ACT OF 1946 and reforms in 1970, 1974, and 1980 also significantly restructured committees, making changes in jurisdiction and referrals.

Further reading:
Deering, Christopher, and Steven S. Smith. *Committees in Congress.* 3d ed. Washington, D.C.: Congressional Quarterly Press, 1997; Fenno, Richard. *Congressmen in Committee.* Berkeley, Calif.: Institute for Governmental Studies, 1995; Oleszek, Walter J. *Congressional Procedures and the Policy Process.* Washington, D.C.: Congressional Quarterly Press, 2001.

—Anne Marie Cammisa

committees: leadership

SENATE and HOUSE OF REPRESENTATIVE committees and SUBCOMMITTEES are led by chairs and rankings members. In both chambers the majority and minority parties each designate formal leaders for each committee and subcommittee. The majority party appoints the chairs of all committees and subcommittees, and the minority party appoints a ranking minority member for every committee and subcommittee. Historically, the seniority system specified that the member with the longest continuous service on the committee or subcommittee serve as chair, but seniority broke down somewhat in the last decades of the 20th century. There are limitations on the number and type of chairs a member may hold.

The Senate developed a system of STANDING COMMITTEES by 1816, and the House developed its system a few years later. As standing committees matured, members became specialized in the issues over which the committee had jurisdiction. Committees became more resistant to control by party and chamber leaders. After the revolt against a SPEAKER OF THE HOUSE, JOSEPH CANNON, a Republican from Illinois, in 1910, committee chairs became the center of power in the House of Representatives. The chairs were so powerful that Speaker JOHN MCCORMACK, a Democrat from Massachusetts, advised freshmen members of the House, "Whenever you pass a committee chairman in the House, you bow from the waist. I do."

The seniority system served to increase the power of chairs. Since they were automatically appointed based on their length of service, chairs did not need to have loyalty to their party's leaders in the chamber or even to the president of the United States. By the late 1960s and 1970s a large number of newly elected members began questioning the seniority system as conservative and outdated. They wanted to change the system for appointing chairs, and working with more senior members of the House, the younger members pushed through rules changes that diffused power.

In the post-reform Congress House and Senate committee chairs and ranking minority members must be elected by their party colleagues. In this way party leaders are able to ensure the party loyalty of committee chairs. Republican Party rules for the 108th Congress stated, "The Chairman on each committee has an obligation to ensure that each measure on which the Republican Conference has taken a position is managed in accordance with such position on the Floor of the House of Representatives."

On most full committees the chair is the most powerful member. The chair determines the committee's agenda, presides during meetings, and controls most of the funding allocated by the chamber to the committee. Chamber rules allow others a share in controlling the committee's business. For example, a majority of members of a committee may call a committee meeting. To distribute committee power, chamber and party CAUCUS rules limit the number of full and subcommittee chairs or ranking minority positions a member may hold. Only the Republicans have committee leadership TERM LIMITS. No House Republican may serve as chair (or ranking minority member) of a committee or subcommittee for more than three consecutive terms, effective with the 104th Congress, and no Senate Republican may serve more than six years as chair or six years as ranking minority member of any standing committee, effective with the 105th Congress. Members may request waivers to avoid the term limits.

Further reading:
Deering, Christopher J., and Steven S. Smith. *Committees in Congress.* 3d ed. Washington, D.C.: Congressional Quarterly Press, 1997; Schneider, Judy. *The Committee System in the U.S. Congress.* Washington, D.C.: Library of Congress, Congressional Research Service, 2003.
—John David Rausch, Jr.

committees: reports

Because so much of the work done by Congress occurs within its STANDING COMMITTEES, committees prepare reports for either the full HOUSE OF REPRESENTATIVES or the entire SENATE to consider. Often such committee documents accompany legislation voted out of committee, but reports may also include findings on matters that have been under investigation by a committee. The sheer volume of BILLS and RESOLUTIONS introduced into the Congress has required each chamber to establish an organized way of considering proposed legislation using a division of labor among its members, and assigning responsibility for particular committees to assess the worth of the many ideas and concepts represented by the introduced legislation or matters to be investigated. As "little legislatures," committees may change or rewrite the bills and resolutions referred to them, they may develop their own legislative recommendations, and they may engage in investigations of problems and oversight of government agencies.

Written reports frequently accompany proposed legislation suggested by a committee, including the reasons and background information for their recommendations, thus aiding the two chambers in handling a growing workload. Committee reports are classified as those from the House or Senate, numbered consecutively in the order in which they are filed preceded by the session of Congress (i.e., House Report 108–393), and governed by the rules of their respective chambers under Article I, Section 5, of the Constitution. For example, House Rule XIII: Calendars and Committee Reports requires that reports of House committees be delivered to the CLERK OF THE HOUSE for printing and reference to the proper calendar, affirms the duty of each committee chair to promptly report measures or matters approved by the committee and take steps to bring the matter or measure to a vote, and also sets seven calendar days as the time within which the report of the committee must be filed, signed by a majority of the members of the committee.

Correspondingly, Senate rules apply to the reports issued by Senate committees. For instance, the vote of any committee to report a measure or matter requires the concurrence of a majority of the members of a committee who are present, and committee reports must include a tabulation of the votes cast by each member of the committee in favor of and in opposition to such measure or matter. Further, when proposed legislation has been referred to more than one Senate committee jointly, only one report may accompany any proposed legislation that is jointly reported by the committees. Senate and House rules regarding committee reports are similar, but not identical. It is the usual practice for Senate committees to have a written report, although it is not required, but in the House a written report accompanying a reported bill is necessary.

Because the Senate has unique responsibilities under Article II, Section 2, to approve treaties negotiated by the executive branch as well as provide advice and consent for presidential nomination of ambassadors, judges, and executive branch officers, another category of congressional reports involves Senate Executive Reports. These include those from the Senate FOREIGN RELATIONS COMMITTEE dealing with treaties submitted to the Senate for ratification, and when the committee reports a need for changes, the full Senate may amend the treaty. Others deal with individual nominations of all federal judges, with cabinet and independent agency and military service appointments, with those in the Foreign Service and uniformed civilian services, and with U.S. attorneys and marshals.

The volume of written records of Congress and its committees has increased substantially since the First Congress in 1789. After permanent standing committees were created, preserving records and materials that represented the work of such committees became more important. During the 1800s individual petitions, claims demanding government compensation for injuries such as occurred during the Civil War, and memorials from individuals, organizations, and states, including recording the correspondence and evidence supporting such requests, represented major activities of committees. Added to such citizen sources during the 1900s were the studies and reports of many federal agencies. Public hearings were used to gather information, and the results of those hearings were sometimes published in written committee reports.

Committee reports are of growing significance not only to Congress but to interest groups, executive branch agencies, and the courts. They serve as a critical part of a bill's legislative history. Agencies charged with implementing a law, courts attempting to interpret statutes that become subjects of future disputes, and individuals and interest groups seeking to take advantage of the provisions of a law or to avoid its penalties may all seek guidance through committee reports. When written in conformance with their respective House and Senate governing rules as well as associated laws that Congress has enacted, they sustain such usage. To illustrate, House committee reports generally must contain CONGRESSIONAL BUDGET OFFICE or committee fiscal statements of costs associated with the reported legislation, as well as an executive branch agency's estimated cost, so that House members and others can understand the nature and magnitude of the bill's proposed budget impact in the present and succeeding five fiscal years.

A clear explanation of how existing law is changed by the proposed legislation being reported, often termed the "Ramseyer rule," named after the former House member who proposed this concept, is also necessary. So is inclusion of the committee's oversight findings and recommendations, as well as statements of general performance goals and objectives for which funding is authorized. And these documents must include a statement of unfunded federal mandates that may be imposed by the legislation on state and local governments. The reports must also include the supplemental, minority, or additional views of committee members that have been submitted prior to filing the report and committee evaluations of the regulatory impact of the recommended legislation, including the economic impact of such regulation on individuals, consumers, and businesses affected, the paperwork that will result from any regulations to be developed in accordance with the bill, and a determination of the impact upon personal privacy of the individuals affected.

Further reading:
Lucas, M. Phillip. "Legislative Records and Publications." In *Encyclopedia of the American Legislative System,* edited by Joel H. Silbey, New York: Charles Scribner's Sons, 1994; Schneider, Judy. *House Committee Reports: Required Contents.* Washington, D.C.: Congressional Research Service, 1999; U.S. House of Representatives. *Constitution, Jefferson's Manual, and Rules of the House of Representatives, 108th Congress.* Compiled by Charles W. Johnson, Parliamentarian, 107th Cong., 2d sess., 2001. H. Doc. 107-284; U.S. House of Representatives. *House Practice: A Guide to the Rules, Precedents, and Procedures of the House.* Compiled by William Holmes Brown and Charles W. Johnson, 108th Cong., 1st Sess., 2003; U.S. Senate, Senate Committee on Rules and Administration. *Authority and Rules of Senate Committees, 2003–2004: A Compilation of the Authority and Rules of Senate and Joint Committees, and Related Materials.* 108th Cong., 1st sess., 2003, Senate document 108-6.

—Robert P. Goss

committees: select or special

Panels without legislative authority established in the SENATE or HOUSE OF REPRESENTATIVES to study emerging issues and problems are termed select or special committees. Select committees usually are established by a resolution passed by the committee's parent chamber. They typically are charged with conducting investigations and studies, but they may consider pieces of legislation. Select committees may be permanent or temporary, but historically most select committees have been temporary. Traditionally, select committee members were elected by the Senate or the House, and special committee members were appointed by the leadership. In the modern Congress the two types of committees tend to be so similar in structures and functions that distinguishing between the two is difficult. On occasion select or special committees have been transformed into STANDING COMMITTEES.

Select committees are created for several reasons. They may be established in response to the concerns of individual members. Special committees may serve as points of access for interest groups. Select committees assist the standing committees by examining issues and concerns that the standing committees do not have time for.

The House and Senate have created select and special committees in response to a number of different situations. In 1987 the House established the House Select Committee to Investigate Covert Arms Transactions with Iran (the Iran-Contra Committee). In 1984 the Senate created the Senate Select Committee to Study the Senate Committee System. The Senate created the Select Committee on Presidential Campaign Activities, chaired by Senator Sam Ervin, a Democrat from North Carolina, to investigate illegal and improper activities alleged to have occurred during the 1972 presidential campaign and election. The committee, also known as the Senate Watergate Committee or the Ervin Committee, concluded its investigation in June 1974 and was disbanded.

Senator Harry Truman, a Democrat from Missouri, attracted national attention as the chair of the Senate Special Committee to Investigate the National Defense Program in 1941. The House Special Committee on Un-American Activities Authorized to Investigate Nazi Propaganda and Certain Other Propaganda Activities was established in 1934 and issued its report in 1935. It was the forerunner of the House Un-American Activities Committee.

During the consideration of the LEGISLATIVE REORGANIZATION ACT OF 1946, a proposal was introduced to prohibit the establishment of select committees. The original version of the bill approved by the Senate included a section that stated: "No bill or resolution, and no amendment to any bill or resolution, to establish a special or select committee, including a joint committee, shall be received or considered in either the Senate or the House of Representatives." The House refused to enact this prohibition and returned the bill to the Senate without it. The House prevailed.

Most select and special committees exist for one or two Congresses before being disbanded. Few have continued over several Congresses. In the 103rd Congress select and special committees were criticized as wasteful, and the House eliminated all four of its select committees.

In the 108th Congress senators served on the Select Committee on Ethics, the Select Committee on Intelligence, and the SPECIAL COMMITTEE ON AGING. Representatives served on the Permanent Select Committee on Intelligence and the Select Committee on Homeland Security. The latter select committee was established at the start of the 108th Congress to provide oversight of the new Department of Homeland Security. It was made a standing committee at the start of the 109th Congress.

Further reading:
Davidson, Roger H., and Walter J. Oleszek. *Congress & Its Members.* 9th ed. Washington, D.C.: Congressional Quarterly Press, 2004; Deering, Christopher J., and Steven S. Smith. *Committees in Congress.* 3d ed. Washington, D.C.: Congressional Quarterly Press, 1997.

—John David Rausch, Jr.

committees: standing

Permanent committees are subject to specific jurisdictional subdivisions of the U.S. House of Representatives and Senate, from which legislation is reported to the floor and oversight of the executive branch agencies is conducted. Standing committees are a microcosm of their chambers, alternately characterized as the little legislatures or the workrooms of Congress.

The modern congressional committee system came into being in the 80th Congress (1947–49), a result of the LEGISLATIVE REORGANIZATION ACT OF 1946. This reform reduced the number of committees by more than half in each chamber, from 35 to 15 in the Senate and from 48 to 19 in the House. The outcomes of the reform were ephemeral and needed to be repeated at regular intervals. The reforms of the 1970s and 1990s had similar components in restricting the number of committees and the number of assignments allowed to members. Membership

on committees is typically determined at the beginning of a congressional term, with membership on the standing committees of the Senate and House carrying over from one Congress to the next, allowing members to accrue seniority on the committee.

Until 1975 the route to committee leadership was to become the most senior member of the majority party serving on a particular committee or the second-most-senior member in the event that a lucky individual rose to the top of seniority on two different committees at the same moment and could hold only one chair. The committee chair carried immense power over agenda setting until the reforms of the early 1970s. It was not uncommon during this baronial period for a committee chair to refuse to schedule a meeting of the committee and thereby block the committee majority or even the floor majority from voting.

This course of events led quickly to unrest among the junior members of several committees. Representative RICHARD BOLLING, a Democrat from Missouri, described the situation for the general public in his book *House Out of Order,* published in 1965. Procedural reform in Congress passed through several joint committees and several select House committees and Senate commissions between 1965 and 1980. Rationalization of the committee system and realignment of jurisdiction was supported in the Senate, resulting again in a reduction in the number of committees in 1977. Reform in the House was more drawn out, with those standing to lose influence and power better able to block comprehensive action. Instead, the reforms were more incremental and involved altering both House and party CAUCUS rules.

The end result of committee reform was similar in both chambers, a reduction in the power of the chairs, an increase in staff, the recording of committee actions required, a weakening of seniority, and limitations on the number of committees representatives and senators could serve on simultaneously. A rise in the role and power of subcommittees resulted from the 1970s round of reforms and continued unabated until 1995, when the Republican Party congressional candidates adopted their Contract with America reforms at the beginning of the 104th Congress. Three committees were abolished (Merchant Marine and Fisheries, District of Columbia, and Post Office and Civil Service), and limits were set at three terms for committee chairs, although their power in relation to the subcommittee chairs was increased through control of staff hiring. The seniority norm had been the major factor involved in choosing committee leaders until the reforms of the 1970s, although seniority was routinely followed in determining committee chairs until the reforms of 1995.

Congressional committees are responsible for reporting legislation to the floor, holding hearings in advance of committee mark-ups, providing oversight to the executive branch agencies charged with implementation, and making budgetary appropriations. Oversight can be a regular annual exchange of information with very little attention or controversy, or a product of a crisis or scandal that generates a tremendous amount of visibility for the hearing process. Congressional committee hearings serve a variety of purposes for the committee as well as individual members, from fact finding to constituency education, and sometimes as pure media events.

The size of committees, the number of subcommittees, and the political party ratio is set at the beginning of each Congress in the Senate and House rules. The desirability of particular committees varies slightly over time, with committees growing in size to reflect important policy agendas and strong demand from members for seats, and conversely committees shrinking in size because of a decline in demand. Size can also fluctuate up or down as the desire of the chamber party leadership for influencing the policy consensus varies. Committees can even be eliminated, as happened in 1947 and 1995. Committees are designated by the Senate and House as exclusive, major, and minor, which limits the number of assignments that a member may hold.

See also COMMITTEE ASSIGNMENTS; COMMITTEES: JOINT; COMMITTEES: JURISDICTION; COMMITTEES: LEADERSHIP; COMMITTEES: REPORTS; REORGANIZATION OF CONGRESS.

Further reading:
Deering, Christopher J., and Steven S. Smith. *Committees in Congress.* 3d ed. Washington, D.C.: Congressional Quarterly Press, 1997; Rieselbach, Leroy N. *Congressional Reform.* Washington, D.C.: Congressional Quarterly Press, 1986.

—Karen M. McCurdy

Common Cause

Common Cause is a public interest lobbying organization with a mission to promote governmental reforms that increase accountability, improve efficiency and effectiveness, and enhance the ethical conduct of elected and appointed officials. Much of its lobbying effort is directed at Congress, and its state chapters target individual state legislatures. Common Cause is a nonpartisan organization that accepts no financial support from government, foundations, labor unions, or corporations.

Founded by John W. Gardner, Common Cause initially followed in the tradition of the Progressives of the early 20th century in targeting what have been called "structure and process" issues, though the organization quickly broadened its cache of causes to include substantive issues such as opposition to the Vietnam War. In the summer of 1970, Gardner, who had served as president of the Carnegie Foundation and secretary of Health, Education and Welfare from 1965 to 1968, was directing the Urban Coalition. The most successful component of the coalition was its lobbying unit, the Urban Coalition Action Council (UCAC), but with changes in the tax laws in 1969, the coalition could no longer finance UCAC. Gardner decided to spin off UCAC as an independent entity, but to do so it needed a dependable source of funding. A mass mailing and newspaper ad campaign drew a response from 100,000 mostly white, upper-middle-class people for a "people's lobby"— Common Cause. Membership has since fluctuated from a high of more than 300,000 to its current number of more than 200,000.

Gardner's vision for the new organization was for it to immerse itself in politics to attain its objectives. Using a small, professional, full-time staff of lobbyists supplemented by volunteers, the organization does little original research but instead relies on the research of other groups to support its positions and press its agenda on Congress. Gardner also believed that the group's membership should assist in identifying the organization's priorities. A national governing board of members is elected by the mass membership to three-year terms. The board meets three times each year in Washington, where it discusses and produces its issue agenda and monitors the organization's operation. In 2000 Common Cause voted to create the Common Cause Educational Fund (CCEF) as a 501 (c) (3), tax-exempt, public education and research affiliate, since membership dues and contributions to Common Cause itself are not tax deductible. In its first years CCEF focused on campaign finance and electoral reform and corporate accountability.

Campaign finance reform was one of the first significant issues championed by Common Cause. Despite some serious resistance within Congress that melted in the heat following the WATERGATE SCANDAL, Common Cause, working with the League of Women Voters and Ralph Nader's Public Citizen, lobbied in support of the Federal Election Campaign Acts of 1971. The laws established contribution limits to presidential and congressional candidates and public funding of presidential elections. The leadership of Common Cause realized that much more needed to be accomplished in this area and during the next two decades pushed for additional major changes to close loopholes (e.g., soft money) that were discovered in the earlier laws, only to be repeatedly foiled. At last, a major success occurred with the passage of the McCain-Feingold Act in 2002.

Regulation of interest group spending, disclosure of their contributions, and limits on some of their tactics held a high place on Common Cause's agenda from 1971 as well. The organization shares responsibility for passage of laws that restrict the cost of meals provided to lawmakers and their staffs as well as trips paid for by interest groups.

Efforts by Republican leaders in 2003 to scale back these limits drew the ire of the organization.

Internal congressional rules have also been a favorite target of Common Cause. It lobbied for "sunshine" laws for years and was rewarded in 1976 with the passage of the Government in Sunshine Act that applied to most federal agencies but not cabinet departments. Congress eventually followed with a SUNSHINE RULE that opened nearly all its committee meetings. In the mid-1970s Common Cause backed a number of major House reforms that reduced the power of committee chairs and the role of seniority in selecting the chairs. It successfully worked to end honoraria for legislators but coupled that with support for higher salaries for members. It also fought a long but unsuccessful battle in federal court to end the FRANKING PRIVILEGE. The adverse decision was rendered in 1983, *Common Cause v. William E. Bolger.*

Demanding ethical behavior by government officeholders has caused the organization to feel the wrath of some major figures on Capitol Hill. It lobbied intensively for passage of the Ethics in Government Act of 1978 and called for investigations into the questionable practices of each of the following: Representative Robert Sikes, a Democrat from Florida, in 1976; Speaker Jim Wright, a Democrat from Texas, in 1988; Majority Whip Tony Coelho, a Democrat from California, in 1989; the so-called KEATING FIVE in 1990 (Senators Alan Cranston, a Democrat from California; Dennis DeConcini, a Democrat from Arizona; John Glenn, a Democrat from Ohio; John McCain, a Republican from Arizona; and Donald W. Riegle, Jr., a Democrat from Michigan); Representative Dan Rostenkoski, a Democrat from Illinois, in 1994; Senator Robert Packwood, a Republican from Oregon, and Speaker Newt Gingrich, a Republican from Georgia, in 1998, among others. In most cases the chamber of the member in question conducted investigations that led to the punishment or resignation of the member. In a few cases the investigations also resulted in changes in laws or chamber rules or practices that contributed to the member's ethical lapse.

Common Cause has not restricted itself to structure and process issues. From the beginning the organization decided to address questions such as the Vietnam War. Common Cause was an active opponent of the war in the early 1970s, supporting measures to end the conflict, such as the McGovern-Hatfield, Cooper-Church, and Mansfield Amendments. The organization has also lobbied against production of the B-1 bomber, the MX missile, and the funding, research, and deployment of the Strategic Defense Initiative, popularly known as Star Wars. Common Cause also took stands in support of the consumer. For instance, it worked for the deregulation of the trucking and airline industries but opposed the major overhaul of the Glass-Steagall Act in 1999 (the Finan-

cial Services Reform Act), the personal bankruptcy reforms in 2000, and the FCC's rule changes on media ownership in 2003. Common Cause continues as a visible and vocal presence in Washington pressing for legislation to improve the quality of government.

Further reading:
McFarland, Andrew S. *Common Cause: Lobbying in the Public Interest.* Chatham, N.J.: Chatham House Publishers, 1984; Rothenberg, Lawrence S. "Agenda-Setting at Common Cause." In *Interest Group Politics*, 3d ed., edited by Cigler, Allan J. and Burdett A. Loomis, Washington, D.C.: Congressional Quarterly Press, 1991; Rothenberg, Lawrence. "Organizational Maintenance and the Retention of Decision in Groups." *American Political Science Review* 82 (1988): 1,129–1,152.

—Thomas J. Baldino

concurrent powers

Concurrent powers are those powers that, in the American federal system, do not belong exclusively to either the national government or the states. They are powers that may be exercised by both levels of government. Such an abstract definition, however, provides no statement of what it is that the national government and the states may do at the same time. The U.S. Constitution does not clarify the matter; it makes no explicit mention of concurrent powers.

In spite of the lack of any constitutional language concerning concurrent powers, Alexander Hamilton recognized a concurrent power of taxation in the FEDERALIST PAPERS, the series of essays in which he, James Madison, and John Jay attempted to convince the people of New York to ratify the Constitution. Hamilton said that state governments would retain all rights of sovereignty except those that the Constitution placed exclusively in the national government or prohibited to the states. He noted that the Constitution did not by its language make the grant of taxing authority to the national government exclusive. He further noted that the Constitution prohibited the states, without the consent of Congress, to lay imposts or duties on imports or exports. This, according to Hamilton, implied that the states' authority to tax extended to all other situations that were outside the language of the prohibition. In taxation, however, as in other areas, the states would be subject to the Supremacy Clause.

Political conflict over the Bank of the United States and the Supreme Court case of *MCCULLOCH V. MARYLAND*, which it engendered, made Hamilton's abstract discussion somewhat clearer. The state of Maryland had attempted to drive the Bank of the United States outside the state's borders. Maryland was opposed to the bank, contended Congress had no authority to create it, and used state taxing power to place on the bank a destructively heavy tax burden. The Supreme Court, in an opinion by Chief Justice John Marshall, upheld Congress's authority to create the bank and acknowledged that the states legitimately have the power to tax. Marshall denied, however, that even a legitimate state power, the concurrent power of taxation, could be used to destroy a validly created instrument of the U.S. government. He pointed to the Supremacy Clause of Article VI of the Constitution, according to which the Constitution, all laws pursuant to the Constitution, such as the law creating the Bank of the United States, and treaties made under the authority of the United States are the supreme law of the land. When state actions, even those that might otherwise be valid, conflict with valid actions of the national government, the Supremacy Clause requires that the state yield.

A few years later the Supreme Court interpreted the Commerce Clause for the first time in *GIBBONS V. OGDEN.* Ogden, operating steamboats in New York waters under license from the holders of a monopoly granted by the state of New York, defended the legitimacy of his license on grounds that in granting the monopoly, the state of New York had exercised a concurrent power, the power to regulate commerce within its borders. Ogden contended that this power was comparable to the power to tax, which was recognized as a concurrent power. The Supreme Court, however, rejected this analogy. Chief Justice Marshall noted that when a state taxes, it does so to accomplish state purposes, in which congressional power does not extend. Marshall, however, did not say that the regulation of commerce was not a concurrent power.

Whether there was a concurrent power to regulate commerce was left unanswered. The Supreme Court did not have to answer that question because Gibbons, who had been operating his steamboat in New York waters under a federal coasting license, appealed to the Supreme Court after his vessel was seized for violating New York's monopoly grant. Relying on the Supremacy Clause, the Supreme Court decided for Gibbons, noting that Congress had power under the Commerce Clause to regulate navigation, but the monopoly of New York conflicted with the exercise of that power. The state had to yield. It was not until 1852, in *Cooley v. Board of Wardens of the Port of Philadelphia,* that the Court recognized that the states could regulate commerce within their borders when Congress had not acted and the thing being regulated required diversity in its regulation.

In some areas of policy, the states are foreclosed from regulating once Congress has taken action, even if the states might have occupied that policy area in the absence of congressional action. Hamilton had recognized the existence of such situations but provided no examples. By the 20th century this occupying of a particular area by Congress and the concomitant exclusion of the states came to be known as fed-

eral preemption. When Congress preempts a field of activity, it sometimes says so in the language of a statute. Other times, however, federal courts find a congressional intent to preempt a field, even though it was not stated by Congress. For example, the Supreme Court, in *Pennsylvania v. Nelson,* interpreted several federal statutes as together implying that Congress intended to take over the protection of the United States against sedition even though Congress had not actually said so. The Supreme Court, therefore, reversed a conviction under a Pennsylvania law that prohibited sedition against the United States. Defenders of state authority to act concurrently with Congress generally find preemption by judicial interpretation more objectionable than preemption by express congressional language. From Hamilton's day to the 21st century, "concurrent powers" has remained a concept laden with vagueness.

Further reading:
U.S. House of Representatives, Subcommittee on National Economic Growth, Natural Resources, and Regulatory Affairs of the Committee on Governmental Reform. *Hearing on the Federalism Act of 1999.* 106th Cong., 1st Sess., 1999; Wright, Benjamin Fletcher, ed. *The Federalist.* Cambridge, Mass.: Harvard University Press, 1961; Zimmerman, Joseph F. *Federal Preemption: The Silent Revolution.* Ames: Iowa State University Press, 1991.

—Patricia Behlar

conference committees

In order for a bill to become law, it must pass both the HOUSE OF REPRESENTATIVES and the SENATE in identical form. Given the complexities of the legislative process (BILLS must be considered, amended, and reported from committees and subcommittees in both bodies; floor consideration in each house is likely to include amendments and modifications), it is unlikely that even bills introduced in identical form in the House and Senate will remain identical after passage. And many times several versions of the same or a similar bill will be introduced and considered in each house. For minor, noncontroversial legislation, a bill passed in one chamber will be sent to the other, where it may be voted on as is, or amended, in which case the amended version is sent back to the original chamber, and the back and forth continues until the two chambers agree on identical wording. The vast majority of legislation is passed in this manner.

For major, more controversial legislation, an extra step is often necessary for a bill to become law. Such bills are too unwieldy and potentially contentious to go through the back and forth process of amendment by each chamber. Usually in these cases the House and Senate have each passed a similar bill with significant differences. A conference committee is appointed to reconcile the two bills. The conference committee includes both senators and representatives. The membership of the conference committee is usually (though not always) roughly proportional to the party makeup of each house. House and Senate leadership from each party appoint the members of the committee, usually drawing from the standing committees that had original jurisdiction over the bill. The leadership makes their appointments based on the recommendation of the chairs of the committees in each house that considered the bill. Thus, conference committee members (called conferees) will be those senators and representatives who worked on the original bill in each house.

While conference committees used to be relatively small (less than a dozen or so lawmakers), the complexity of legislation since the 1980s means that they can be quite large, sometimes even in the hundreds of legislators (in such a case, the conference committee will be divided into subcommittees). In addition, with the rise of multiple referrals, that is, bills being referred to more than one committee, and mega bills covering a great deal of legislative territory, conference committees sometimes have complicated arrangements. For example, separate conferees might be appointed to work out differences on separate parts of the bill.

A conference committee is a temporary, ad hoc committee appointed solely for the purpose of reconciling differences on one piece of legislation. When those differences are ironed out (or the committee decides they cannot be), the conference committee disbands. Unlike a permanent, standing committee, which has jurisdiction over a general legislative area (such as health or veterans' affairs), a conference committee is concerned only with one piece of legislation.

The conferees meet to discuss the particulars of the legislation, and their goal is to resolve differences between the two bills (one reported from each chamber). Conference committees are theoretically limited in their discussions: They are not to go beyond the scope of the original bills (for example, by proposing larger or smaller dollar amounts than what is contained in the House and Senate bills), and they can make amendments only to those parts of the bills in which there is disagreement. In practice, however, conference committees sometimes substantially revise legislation beyond the areas of disagreement and may even rewrite the entire bill or add unrelated amendments to it.

As at all stages of the legislative process, there is a possibility that the bill will die in conference. That is, the members of the committee might not be able to come to agreement and report a bill back to their respective houses. Conference committees have at least two sources of potential conflict: based on party and based on institution. As one would imagine, Democrats and Republicans are likely to disagree on policy issues. In addition, senators and representatives may be partial to the bill passed by their own chamber. Either because of institutional loyalty, or because they know what their own chamber will or will not accept, members of one house often see themselves defending their chamber from encroachments by the other. In fact, leadership in each chamber will also give committee members specific instructions as to how much or how little change they should make to the bill. Often, tensions between the two houses are played out in conference committees. In recent years frustrations between House and Senate Republicans have made for difficult conference committee debates.

Instructions to the conference committee may come from the party leadership or may involve a more formal vote, as happened in 2003, when major Medicare legislation went to conference. House Democrats proposed an instruction to House conferees to accept Senate provisions on competition and prescription drug coverage. Not surprisingly, the proposal was voted down on the floor by the Republican-ruled House.

The president may play an indirect role in the conference committee proceedings. By indicating that he may veto a bill that contains particular provisions, the president signals to the conference committee where battle lines are drawn. The committee may or may not take the veto threat into consideration, and the president may or may not follow through on it.

If Democrats and Republicans, senators and representatives do come to agreement and a majority signs off on it, then they will report the bill out of conference committee. This new version of the bill, called the "conference report," goes to both the House and the Senate. In each chamber the bill is scheduled for a vote on final passage (or not; the leadership may decide to sit on the bill, effectively killing it). The vote on the conference report is a simple up or down vote. No amendments to the report are allowed in either chamber. Unless and until the report is passed as is by both chambers, it will not become law. If, as rarely happens, the conference report is rejected by one or both houses, a new conference committee may be appointed, or the bill will be considered dead and legislators must start from scratch, introducing new legislation. Once the conference report has been passed by both the House and the Senate, it still has at least one more hurdle: It must be signed by the president. If signed, the bill is now law. If vetoed, the two chambers have a chance to override that veto by a two-thirds vote in both the House and the Senate.

Although the conference committee, like much of the legislative process, may seem an annoyance designed to block legislation, it is actually a useful tool. The conference committee, as a small group of experts on a particular piece of legislation, is able to hammer out differences and make compromises without a lot of interference. (Theoretically, at least. conference committee negotiators may be lobbied by interest groups, the president, and other members of Congress not on the committee.) Because it includes members from each house, the conference committee forces senators and representatives to work out differences between the chambers. And members of each house may be more willing to vote for legislation knowing it has been vetted by interested legislators from each chamber. On the other hand, the conference committee is an extra-constitutional tool that wields a great deal of power, to the point that it is sometimes referred to as "the third house" (implying that conference committees are in some way coequal to the House of Representatives and the Senate). Since the 1970s conference committees have been subject to "sunshine laws," meaning that they must be open to the public. Unless the full House votes to have closed conference committee meetings, the proceedings must be public. C-SPAN sometimes provides live television coverage of conference negotiations. In practice, conferees in recent years sometimes circumvent the openness rules, hammering out differences in smaller groups before the compromise is presented to the committee. The fact remains that conference committees are one more place where a variety of political voices may wrangle, and that is not by accident. The system was set up to ensure minority voices would be considered and not to facilitate speedy passage of legislation.

Further reading:
Longley, Lawrence D., and Walter J. Oleszek. *Bicameral Politics: Conference Committees in Congress.* New Haven, Conn.: Yale University Press, 1989; Steiner, Gilbert. *The Congressional Conference Committee, Seventieth to Eightieth Congresses.* Urbana: University of Illinois Press, 1951; Van Beek, Steven D. *Post-Passage Politics: Bicameral Resolution in Congress.* Pittsburgh: University of Pittsburgh Press, 1996; Volger, David. *The Third House: Conference Committees in the U.S. Congress,* Evanston, Ill.: Northwestern University Press, 1971.

—Anne Marie Cammisa

confirmation

Confirmation is the final hurdle for a presidential nominee. If a nomination is confirmed by the U.S. SENATE, the nominee will be sworn in and will assume the office to which he or she was nominated by the president of the United States.

The Senate confirmation process is the mechanism by which the Senate grants its "consent" to a presidential nomination, in accordance with Article II, Section 2, of the Constitution, which requires the Senate's consent to be given to presidential nominees for significant positions in the federal government, such as ambassadorships, cabinet secretary positions, and federal judgeships.

When a president makes the decision to nominate an individual to a position requiring the Senate's approval, he sends that individual's name to the Senate, where it will be read on the Senate floor and assigned by the Senate parliamentarian a number on the Senate's executive calendar (the calendar devoted exclusively to nominations and treaties submitted by the president and requiring Senate approval). The nomination will then be referred to the appropriate standing committee. Referral is made based on the committees' jurisdiction. For example, the SENATE JUDICIARY COMMITTEE processes all nominations for the federal courts, while the SENATE FOREIGN RELATIONS COMMITTEE processes all nominations to serve as a U.S. ambassador to another country.

Once in the committee, the committee investigators will conduct their own background check on the nominee. Once the investigators have cleared the nominee, the committee chair will schedule a hearing on the nomination. In most cases it is entirely at the discretion of the chair whether to hold a hearing. If no hearing is held, the nomination will not be confirmed. Following the hearing the members of the committee will meet in executive session in order to discuss and vote on pending nominations. An affirmative vote of a majority of committee members is required in order to send the nomination to the full Senate for its consideration. In most cases a tie vote kills the nomination, although in some cases (such as nominations to the Supreme Court), the committee will allow the nomination to proceed to the Senate floor on a tie but will refuse to endorse the nominee. The referral of the nomination back to the floor or the defeat of a nomination during a vote in executive session concludes the committee's role in the process.

After being voted out of committee, the nomination will be scheduled by the SENATE MAJORITY LEADER for debate and for a vote by the full Senate. In order to be confirmed, a majority of senators voting must cast an affirmative vote. Once a nomination has been endorsed by the full Senate, the president is notified and the nominee is sworn in.

The Constitution, although it requires the Senate's approval of nominations for important positions, says nothing about the mechanism the Senate should employ for granting its consent. The process outlined above is the modern version of the process, but it is different from the one used early in the country's history, when there were no committees in Congress. Throughout the late 18th century and early 19th century the process appears to have consisted of the president selecting nominees and transmitting their names, by letter, to the Senate for approval. Once the names arrived at the Senate, evidence suggests that the names were simply read from the floor during the EXECUTIVE SESSION, and senators expressed their opinions about the nominees. The vast majority of nominees were confirmed, usually within a matter of hours and almost always within a day or two of receiving the name.

Confirmation, even during the late 18th century, was never assured, however. The Senate, as a condition for confirmation, requires that in cases in which a nominee has been selected to serve within a particular state, the senators from that state grant their approval to the nomination before the full Senate will confirm. The process of deferring to home-state senators is known as senatorial courtesy, and even George Washington had to contend with the requirement.

The confirmation process within the Senate has evolved dramatically over time. Changes to the process have been driven by several factors, including an increased number of positions requiring Senate confirmation, the decentralization of power from the full chamber to the committee structure (the modern Senate committee structure is largely a function of the LEGISLATIVE REORGANIZATION ACT OF 1946, as well as additional acts of Congress, which streamlined the number of committees within the chamber, set jurisdictions, and gave autonomy to committees as they carried out their responsibilities), and changes in the political environment surrounding the Senate and the confirmation process.

According to political scientist Paul Light, writing in *Thickening Government*, the number of top-level positions in the executive branch grew from 196 in 1960 to 786 in 1993. The number of federal judgeships requiring confirmation likewise has increased; from the 1980s to the 1990s nearly 100 additional federal judgeships were created, an increase in the size of the federal judiciary of nearly 13 percent. Moreover, whereas the number of nominees submitted to the Senate for confirmation was generally less than 15,000 per Congress (including military promotions in rank) through the 1930s, by the 1990s the Senate was regularly called upon to act on more than 70,000 nominations in a given Congress.

More positions, of course, mean that a greater proportion of senators' time must be devoted to the consideration of executive nominations. They also mean that even if the proportion of controversial nominees has remained the same over time (generally less than 5 percent of the total), there are a greater number of nominations to which the Senate gives careful scrutiny. The volume of nominees combined with the increased scrutiny applied to those nominees that are deemed controversial has dramatically slowed the pace of the confirmation process. The number of days between nomination and confirmation for judicial nominees has increased in the last 30 years. While there has been more fluidity in the pace of confirmations for nomi-

nees to the cabinet, beginning with the 103rd Congress the trend for both judicial and cabinet nominees has been sharply upward, denoting marked increases in the number of days a nominee waits for confirmation from the day his or her nomination is received by the Senate.

At the same time that the number of nominations requiring Senate confirmation was increasing, changes within the Senate altered the nature of the process as well. For example, through the middle of the 20th century internal Senate norms of comity, respect for seniority, and the sanctity of committee processes were adhered to by members of the Senate. With regard to the Senate confirmation process, what this meant was that presidents typically had only to persuade a few powerful committee chairs to support their nominees, and the rank-and-file junior senators would acquiesce.

As Mark Silverstein makes clear in his 1994 book *Judicious Choices: The New Politics of Supreme Court Confirmations*, prior to the Senate's consideration of Abe Fortas in 1968 to be chief justice of the U.S. Supreme Court, presidents could assume the compliance of the full Senate when the leadership had reached an agreement with the president. But Fortas's rejection was forced by junior senators, most of whom were Republicans and therefore opposed to the president's nominee in part on partisan and ideological grounds. The defection of junior senators on such a high-profile matter as the confirmation of a Supreme Court chief justice was shocking to many in the institution, which until that point had valued adherence to the norms of deference and seniority as a mandatory condition of service.

In addition to the breakdown of adherence to internal norms, the shifting nature of committee power in the chamber also contributed to the changed nature of the institution. Indeed, the vast majority of the power to control the fate of nominations rests not in the hands of the majority and minority leaders in the Senate, but instead in the hands of the powerful committee chairs who control the committees with jurisdiction over presidential nominations. For example, it is the chairs of committees who decide whether to schedule hearings on particular nominations, and when the committee chair is opposed to a nominee, he or she can choose not to bring the nominee in for a hearing. Without a hearing the nomination is effectively dead. This was the case in 1998, when Senator Jesse Helms refused to schedule a Senate Foreign Relations Committee hearing to consider former Massachusetts governor William Weld's nomination to be the ambassador to Mexico. Helms was ultimately forced (through arcane parliamentary procedures) to hold a hearing, but the power granted to him as chair of the committee meant he controlled the hearing, as well. When the hearing opened, Helms announced that the hearing would last roughly 30

Secretary of State nominee Alexander Haig before the Senate Foreign Relations Committee, 1981 *(National Archives)*

exchange for campaign support or even funding for the next campaign.

In short, the confirmation process today has grown into a fully mature system, with highly routinized committee and floor procedures that are similar to those that developed in the Senate more broadly as part of its institutionalization. But along with these developments, the contemporary confirmation process is frequently slow. Recently, advocates of reform both from within Congress and from the outside have been successful at demonstrating the need for reform within process in order to keep seats at the cabinet table and seats on the federal bench filled and engaged with the nation's business.

See also APPOINTMENT POWER.

Further reading:
Bell, Lauren Cohen. *Warring Factions: Interest Groups, Money, and the New Politics of Senate Confirmation.* Columbus: Ohio State University Press, 2002; Carter, Stephen. *The Confirmation Mess.* New York: Basic Books, 1994; Mackenzie, G. Calvin. "Starting Over: The Presidential Appointment Process in 1997." New York: The Twentieth Century Fund, 1998.

—Lauren Bell

minutes; he then proceeded to make a lengthy statement that consumed most of the time. About 30 minutes after the hearing began, Helms dropped the gavel to signal its conclusion—without taking a word of testimony or allowing a single question from the nominee.

The external political environment of the Senate is also different today from it was even at mid-century. The dramatic expansion of interest groups and the rise of electronic media—especially 24-hour news channels and the Internet—have increased the incentives for individual senators to oppose nominees and work to prevent their confirmation. This is because the public typically knows little about any of the men and women nominated to fill high-ranking positions in government, and therefore individual senators can use the occasion of a blocked nomination to promote themselves as the protectors of the executive branch or of the courts. In addition, recent studies have demonstrated that interest groups now use the confirmation process to effect policy change, since high-level federal bureaucrats and high-ranking federal judges may have a greater short-term influence on public policy in some instances than the legislators that have traditionally been targeted by the interest groups. As Lauren Cohen Bell points out in her book *Warring Factions: Interest Groups, Money, and the New Politics of Senate Confirmation,* interest groups frequently encourage senators to oppose nominees in

Congressional Budget and Impoundment Control Act of 1974

The Congressional Budget and Impoundment Control Act of 1974 attempted to restructure the role Congress played in the federal budgetary process by seeking to control spending and to counteract the growth of presidential power in budgeting. In 1972 Congress established a Joint Study Committee on Budget Control. The committee, composed of members from the HOUSE OF REPRESENTATIVES and SENATE appropriations and tax-writing committees as well as two at-large members from each chamber, held seven days of hearings and gathered testimony from 37 witnesses during March 1973. The recommendations presented in the committee's report included finding a way to improve the ability of Congress to examine the budget from an overall point of view, together with a congressional system of deciding priorities.

The HOUSE RULES COMMITTEE, the SENATE GOVERNMENTAL AFFAIRS COMMITTEE, and the SENATE RULES AND ADMINISTRATION COMMITTEE reviewed the committee's recommendations and added refinements to the proposals. Since in early 1973 the House Rules Committee and the SENATE JUDICIARY COMMITTEE had conducted 13 days of hearings on the president's ability to impound appropriations, legislation to limit presidential impoundment activity was merged with the effort to strengthen congressional budgetary controls.

Writing the recommendations of the joint study committee into law, Congress passed the Congressional Budget and Impoundment Control Act in 1974. The legislation was widely supported in both houses, passing the House by 401-6 and the Senate by 75-0. President Richard Nixon, under intense public scrutiny for his role in the WATERGATE break-in, signed the bill in July 1974. Understanding that it had to play a role in controlling federal spending and trimming budget deficits, the legislative body also was responding to President Nixon's attempts to cut federal spending at his own discretion.

The new law gave Congress additional power in the making of the budget. It provided for additional committees and staff. The House and Senate Budget Committees were created to coordinate congressional consideration of the federal budget. The CONGRESSIONAL BUDGET OFFICE (CBO) was established as a counterweight to the power of the Office of Management and Budget (OMB) in the executive branch. The CBO was to provide nonpartisan analysis relating to the budget and the national economy. It developed an alternate budget forecast for Congress, which previously had to rely solely on numbers from the OMB.

The act also specified a timetable for congressional action on the budget and established a method for coordinating the various portions of the budget. The concurrent budget resolution forces congressional action at specified times but does not require the president's signature. The resolution was required to be drafted by the Budget Committees by April 15 of each year and passed by Congress no later than May 15. The resolution allowed Congress to act on the budget as a whole, and it provided a budget blueprint for the authorizing and appropriations committees in both houses. The concurrent budget resolution was an innovation that allowed Congress to continue using its traditional processes of authorization and appropriation with some form of control. By September 15 Congress was required to pass a second budget resolution setting binding spending totals. The actions of the appropriations committees had to be reconciled with the second resolution's numbers. The start of the new federal FISCAL YEAR was moved from July 1 to October 1 in order to provide Congress with more time to enact a budget.

Both chambers developed procedures for handling the budget resolutions. In the House the budget resolution is considered under a rule issued by the Rules Committee. While alternative budget proposals are allowed to be debated, the leadership-supported resolution usually wins on a party-line vote. During the 108th Congress the House used a rule first originated by Representative Dick Gephardt, a Democrat from Missouri, in 1979 and deleted from the rules in the 107th Congress. After successful adoption of the budget resolution the House would automatically be "deemed" to have passed a bill to increase the debt ceiling.

In the Senate floor action is governed largely by the requirements of the act as well as by UNANIMOUS CONSENT AGREEMENTs negotiated by the leadership. Concurrent budget resolutions are privileged. They have a 50-hour statutory debate limitation. Amendments may be offered and voted on after the 50 hours have expired, but without debate. Amendments offered to the resolutions are required to be germane, but this regulation may be waived if 60 senators agree.

The president's ability to impound money appropriated by Congress was limited under the act. Impoundments were divided into two categories. RESCISSIONs, permanent cancellations of budget authority, required congressional approval before the rescission was made. Temporarily deferring spending was allowed unless specifically rejected by Congress. Decisions regarding both types of impoundments became the jurisdiction of the appropriations committees in the House and the Senate.

Further reading:
Gilmour, John B. *Reconcilable Differences? Congress, the Budget Process, and the Deficit.* Berkeley: University of California Press, 1990; Schick, Allen, and Felix LoStracco. *The Federal Budget: Politics, Policy, Process.* Rev. ed. Washington, D.C.: Brookings Institution Press, 2000; Wander, W. Thomas, F. Ted Hebert, and Gary W. Copeland, eds. *Congressional Budgeting: Politics, Process, and Power.* Baltimore: Johns Hopkins University Press, 1984.

—John David Rausch, Jr.

Congressional Budget Office

The BUDGET AND ACCOUNTING ACT OF 1921 created a Bureau of the Budget in the executive office of the president. The Bureau of the Budget evolved into the Office of Management and Budget (OMB), the president's central budget office and hegemony of budgetary power in Washington ever since. OMB regulates budget preparation and execution in the executive branch agencies, makes revenue estimates, and prepares the president's budget to be proposed to Congress, to name just a few of its major duties. Congress agreed to give the president a staff in 1921 such that the president would be the official initiator in the budget process and the official proposer of a unified national budget. Congress would then respond to the budget, especially at the microlevel of detail.

It was this recognition by Congress in the mid-20th century that the existing process and institutional apparatus greatly favored and empowered the president that led to a call for reform on CAPITOL HILL. Members of Congress wanted to be on more equal footing with the president on the broad contours of the budget, in addition to maintaining their traditional role on the particulars of appropriations.

Put more bluntly, their attitude was "if the president gets a budget office, then we should get one, too." Among many other things that improved congressional budgeting and made Congress look at the budget at the macrolevel (like the budget resolution), the creation of the Congressional Budget Office (or CBO as it is typically called) was accomplished as part of the BUDGET AND IMPOUNDMENT CONTROL ACT OF 1974. This act was passed over a veto by President Richard Nixon, who thought the act's provisions would have a detrimental effect on the power of the presidency. Given that the act curbed his flexibility in impounding funds and created a rival budget office to his OMB, he was at least partially right.

The Congressional Budget Office, like OMB, furnishes information on all stages and elements of the federal budget. CBO studies the economy and entertains revenue estimates on a frequent basis. It has a reputation for being nonpartisan and for making conservative revenue estimates, especially in entitlement areas. OMB, in contrast, tends to make more rose-colored projections and is a more jealous advocate of the president than the more balanced CBO is of the Congress. Like OMB, CBO prepares a congressional budget or alternative to the president's proposal during each regular budget process. In addition, when the president's budget is sent to Capitol Hill shortly after the State of the Union Address, it is first analyzed by CBO in concert with the House and Senate Budget Committees. CBO, the budget committees, and the new 1974 budget process (to include a budget resolution and reconciliation) served to strengthen Congress's hand at the macrolevel of the budget.

One of the more interesting hobbies undertaken by Washington insiders is to follow the differences in revenue estimates provided by CBO and OMB. For example, in the budget process of 2002, which yielded the fiscal year 2003 (FY03) federal budget, the differences in short-term and long-term forecasts were striking. The following table shows the differences in total budget surplus or deficit for two time periods:

Time Period	CBO Estimate	OMB Estimate
FY03–FY07	$929 billion deficit	$392 billion deficit
FY03–FY13	$1 trillion surplus	$2.3 trillion surplus

These considerable differences, driven by different assumptions about the health of the economy now and in the future, affect revenues and debt service costs in particular. OMB has a track record of being more optimistic than CBO in its estimates.

Further reading:
Mikesell, John. *Fiscal Administration*. 5th ed. Belmont, Calif.: Wadsworth 2003; Oleszek, Walter. *Congressional Procedures and the Policy Process*. Washington, D.C.: Congressional Quarterly Press. 5th ed., 2004; Schick, Allen. *Federal Budgeting*. Washington, D.C.: Brookings Institution Press, 2004.

—Glen S. Krutz

Congressional Directory

Constituents often have concerns about issues of public policy or their own personal situations whereby they need to contact a legislative official. Citizens often contact their legislators to provide their opinions on key issues under debate, to give legislators a chance to demonstrate their support or opposition to an issue, or to gather information to investigate or expose a problem. This means that constituents need to find their legislators.

The *Congressional Directory* is an official publication of the U.S. Congress that makes this information accessible to the public. The *Congressional Directory* provides a short biography of each member of the House of Representatives and the Senate as well as presenting a listing of each member's committee membership, terms of service, and direct contact information. The publication also lists officials of the courts, military establishments, and federal departments and agencies and governors and foreign diplomats.

A new *Congressional Directory* is written for each Congress, prepared by the Joint Committee on Printing and printed by the Government Printing Office. The document is available in print at numerous public and university libraries and is accessible on the Internet at the following link: http://www.access.gpo.gov/congress/cong 016.html.

Further reading:
Government Information Archives. Available online. URL: http://library.usak.ca.lists/govinfo/1999/0087.html. Accessed February 6, 2003.

—Nancy S. Lind

congressional elections: financing

There are five primary sources of funding for congressional campaigns: the candidates themselves, individual contributions, POLITICAL ACTION COMMITTEES, party committees, and interest groups. Individual contributions account for about two-thirds of SENATE campaign funds and more than half of funds for HOUSE OF REPRESENTATIVES campaigns.

The cost of funding congressional elections sets new records each election year. The average cost for a Senate campaign is about $4 million, while the average cost for a House of Representatives campaign is slightly less than $1 million. The record for a candidate-financed campaign is held by Jon Corzine, a Wall Street investment banker who in 2000 became a Democratic senator from New Jersey after spending $63 million, almost all from his own funds, to finance his campaign.

Incumbent candidates, regardless of their region, seniority, party affiliation, or ideology, regularly have more money to spend than their challengers. For the average incumbent fund-raising is an activity that continues throughout his or her term of office. Incumbent advantages include close interest group relationships established through committee assignments and the likelihood of winning reelection campaign. Donors are more eager to give to a likely winning candidate, plus they want to give to a candidate whose legislating and oversight activities are most likely to affect the donor directly. Incumbents also have helped assure their reelections by compiling enormous campaign war chests and publicizing their holdings to discourage ambitious potential challengers. On the other hand, an incumbent failing to accumulate a large war chest will probably attract an eager and well-financed challenger. In addition, incumbents enjoy free (for them) publicity provided at government expense by carrying out their duties while in office. Incumbents also have a FRANKING PRIVILEGE and limited printing subsidies to help them keep constituents informed about their activities in office.

One of the most common questions asked is if donors are buying legislator votes. Legislators in both chambers and both major parties tend to defend their accepting donations by saying that donors do not buy votes, but that they do buy access. Members of Congress frequently promise to listen to, but never to be bound by, the pleas of campaign donors. Moreover, members of Congress often assert that typically votes they cast involve their choosing between viewpoints, whereas they receive contributions from donors on each side of the issue. Therefore, when casting most votes legislators are simultaneously deciding in favor of and against the wishes of campaign donors. Other critics, however, maintain that most members of Congress receive far more funds from business and producer interests than they do from consumers or the average citizen.

Numerous efforts have been made to establish and then alter the rules governing federal campaign disclosure of donations. Congress passed laws in 1972, 1974, 1976, and 1979, plus the seminal BIPARTISAN CAMPAIGN REFORM ACT OF 2002. In addition, court cases such as *Buckley v. Valeo* in 1976 also set the rules governing campaign finance.

Campaign funding is policed by the bipartisan Federal Election Commission (FEC), a group nominated by the president and confirmed by the Senate. Duties of the FEC include collecting and disseminating records of individual campaign donors and expenditures. The FEC also adopts regulations and issues advisory opinions governing campaign finance practices. It also can investigate allegations of violations and prosecute offenders.

Each major political party in each chamber of Congress has established a campaign committee to collect and distribute campaign funds: the Democratic Senatorial Campaign Committee (DSCC), the Democratic Congressional Campaign Committee (DCCC), the National Republican Senatorial Committee (NRSC), and the National Republican Congressional Committee (NRCC).

—Mark Kemper

congressional elections: incumbency

How strong is the electoral check that voters exercise over Congress? Cynics argue that members of Congress enjoy an almost insurmountable advantage over incumbents in elections. Candidates having won a congressional seat and running for reelection have seen their share of the vote increase significantly in recent years, and incumbents now lose fewer congressional races than they have at any time in American history. Few races with an incumbent, especially in the House, are even close. Incumbents have been able to increase their ability to make themselves better known at the same time that challengers have become increasingly invisible during campaigns.

As a result, there has been a dramatic increase in the percentage of congressional voters who defect from their party identification to vote for an incumbent from the other party. One's party identification is the single best predictor of how one will vote for Congress, and party identification is a far more important determinate of congressional than of presidential voting. Partisanship, however, has become less important in voters' decisions on how to vote as incumbency has risen as an electoral force. When party and incumbency are in conflict, the latter appears to be the more powerful electoral force.

The result is that though it is undoubtedly extremely difficult to get elected to Congress, it is relatively easy to get reelected. Ironically, the founding fathers feared that Congress might become an unstable and unprofessional body with great turnover. Technically, after all, it is possible today that 435 new members could be elected every two years to the HOUSE OF REPRESENTATIVES. Now one of the biggest complaints about the House is that incumbents are too entrenched and there is not enough turnover. The movement for congressional term limits over the past two decades is one result of this lack of turnover.

Why are congressional incumbents so successful when seeking reelection? Some potential explanations explaining incumbent success include:

1. ***Name Recognition.*** The most important advantage incumbents have is name recognition—incumbents are almost always better known than challengers. House challengers in particular often tend to be invisible. There is a rising tendency for voters to vote for candidates they know, and voters are much more likely to be aware of the incumbent than the challenger.

2. ***The Rise of Independents.*** Since the 1960s there has been a decrease in the percentage of voters who identify themselves as Democrats or Republicans and an increase in the number of voters who consider themselves independents. At the same time, those who still identify with one of the major political parties seem to be using it less and less as a vote-making guide. There has become an increasing unwillingness of voters to use party identification as a voting cue as voters become increasingly willing to use incumbency as a voting cue. Fewer people vote automatically against a party, thereby helping incumbents. The use of incumbency as a voting cue has resulted in decreasing the number of competitive seats.

3. ***Home Style.*** The concept of "home style" refers to the relationship between a member of Congress and his or her constituents. Public ratings of Congress as an institution have gone down, even though the number of incumbents defeated for reelection has also declined. This finding is consistent with the popular belief (borne out by public opinion polls) that people hate Congress but like their own congressional representatives. Members of Congress are able to cultivate popularity because they are consistently engaged in activities directed toward appeasing their constituents. Members of Congress try to portray an image that will be a vote winner in their district, and they are usually successful in this endeavor.

The nation's legislators are constantly concerned with their constituencies' impressions of them. As a result, the nation's representatives engage in "home style" when presenting themselves to their constituents—activities intended to make representatives look good in the eyes of constituents, including appearing to be like a typical constituent (in terms of clothing, language, important issues, etc.).

4. ***Casework and Perks.*** Members of Congress enjoy the electoral advantage of being able to help constituents in nonpolitical manners through CASEWORK done by congressional STAFF. Legislators also can use the FRANKING privilege, free postage for material sent to constituents. Though officially material sent to constituents is not directly related to campaigning, the ability to send literature highlighting one's legislative record and governing philosophy for free is not a benefit that challengers to incumbents have. Similarly, members of Congress have become more electorally secure in part because they have become adept at cutting through bureaucratic red tape and serving as ombudsmen for their constituents.

5. ***Pork Barreling.*** PORK BARRELing is the practice of legislators trying to bring government projects or appropriations to their districts in hopes of helping themselves politically. The ability to bring federal money for projects within one's district is a way to make a member of Congress look good in a way that transcends politics.

6. ***Redistricting.*** Redistricting may help incumbents electorally because incumbents have the incentive to make their districts safer when districts are reapportioned among the states and lines are redrawn every 10 years. There is no doubt that this happens in some cases, such as in California after the 2002 House reapportionment, but in other instances incumbents are made worse off. Sometimes incumbents even lose their district altogether. Overall, the impact of redistricting on incumbency safety is probably benign.

7. ***Legislative Pragmatism.*** There exists a high degree of agreement between the popular opinion of a district and its representative in Congress. The advantage incumbents enjoy could be simply a result of pragmatic politics whereby a legislator tries to gauge popular opinion in his or her district. A representative's floor behavior is strongly influenced by the preferences of his or her constituency. Ironically, members may overrate their visibility; constituents tend to have a low degree of knowledge of their representatives' stances.

8. ***Campaign Finance.*** The role of money in congressional elections clearly has emerged as a significant factor favoring incumbents. In an era in which congressional campaigns have gotten outrageously expensive, incumbents hold a significant fund-raising edge. Many, if not most, challengers are not able to raise enough resources to be competitive. It takes about $500,000 to seriously challenge an incumbent in most House districts, and in areas with expensive media markets the price tag can go over $1 million. Few challengers can raise this much money, so the gap between incumbent and challenger spending has grown dramatically. Incumbents have far greater potential to raise vast sums of money when it is needed, in part because POLITICAL ACTION COMMITTEE (PAC) donations, which make up 40 percent of campaign financing in the House, are heavily tilted toward incumbents. Challengers need to raise more money to become more competitive, but money tends to flow to incumbents based on the perception that the incumbent is more likely to win, creating a cycle whereby challengers need money to be competitive but are unable to raise enough money because of the perception that they are probable losers.

The amount spent by a challenger is far more important in accounting for voters' decisions than is the amount spent by an incumbent. The more challengers spend, the more votes they receive, and the more likely they are to win. The more incumbents spend, on the other hand, the lower their vote, and the greater their chances of losing because incumbents are likely to spend more when facing a difficult reelection. Since voters are demonstrably reluctant to vote for candidates they know nothing about, challengers have a great deal to gain by making themselves better known to the electorate. The level of campaign activity for challengers thus has a strong influence on how well they do at the polls. The probability of initially favoring the challenger increases from .15 to .44 as total spending rises from nothing to $900,000. The probability of switching to the challenger goes up and of switching to the incumbent goes down, the more the challenger spends. Greater spending by challengers attracts voters from supporters of both parties much more even-handedly than spending by incumbents.

9. Weak Challengers. You cannot beat someone with nobody. Most challengers for congressional seats are amateurs with no previous elective experience. Incumbents have an enormous advantage over challengers because they are more visible and experienced. Incumbents are thus generally able to win by large margins only due to the weakness of their challengers. For incumbents running for reelection, the quality of his or her challenger is the most important factor in determining the likelihood of political success.

Though Senate incumbents possess considerable advantages when running for reelection, it is important to note that the electoral advantage for senators is considerably less than it is for members of the House. Senators face extra obstacles that make incumbency less powerful than it is for House members. Winning reelection is more difficult for senators because they represent larger and more diverse constituencies; winning reelection in the state of California, with more than 35 million people, for example, is much more difficult than winning reelection in a typically (relatively) homogeneous House district with about 650,000 constituents. Voters also tend to be better informed in Senate elections because senators tend to get more media coverage. Senators are also more likely to face experienced and well-financed challengers. Finally, the longer term of senators (six years as opposed to two years) may make it easier for senators to fall out of touch with voters.

Undoubtedly, incumbents enjoy significant advantages over challengers. This does not mean, however, that members of Congress enjoy insurmountable advantages in their attempts for reelection. In fact, congressional seats may not be as safe as they may seem—58 percent of those in the House have had a close race for reelection at least once in their careers. Just because an incumbent wins a reelection attempt by a large margin does not mean that the potential is not there for a serious challenge in the future. Incumbents also may not be as invincible as they are made out to be because incumbency reelection rates are inflated by the

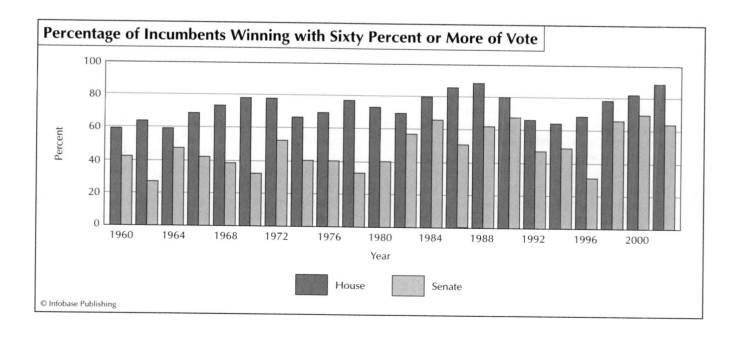

Percentage of Incumbents Winning with Sixty Percent or More of Vote

© Infobase Publishing

fact that many incumbents who face difficult reelection prospects, especially after a scandal, choose not to run for reelection.

Further reading:
Fenno, Richard. *Home Style.* Boston: Little, Brown, 1978; Jacobson, Gary. *The Politics of Congressional Elections.* 9th ed. New York: Longman, 2000; Mayhew, David. *Congress: The Electoral Connection.* New Haven, Conn.: Yale University Press, 1976.

—Patrick Fisher

congressional elections: media

As political party structures weakened in the latter half of the 20th century, the media became the principal means by which voters received information about political candidates during campaign season. Campaigns for seats in the U.S. HOUSE OF REPRESENTATIVES and the U.S. SENATE are no exception. Candidates compete for voters' attention using both news coverage and paid advertisements.

Candidates compete for news coverage so they can reach voters. Securing news coverage is desirable because it is far less expensive than paid advertising. There are no production costs and no need to purchase ad time or space. The "costs" of generating news coverage are primarily staff time and efforts to plan campaign events, schedule interviews, and send out media releases. Second, news coverage and editorial endorsements have legitimacy that paid advertising simply does not carry. However, candidates cannot control the message voters receive from news coverage. Reporters may choose to focus on issues that candidates might rather avoid, such as controversial votes or scandals, and place little emphasis on the issues that form the central themes of the campaign.

News coverage is not evenly distributed. Incumbents are able to generate news related to their official activities: sponsoring or passing legislation, constituency service, and making local appearances. Incumbents also tend to benefit from "horserace" coverage of their campaigns, which is likely to highlight incumbents' higher levels of name recognition and/or leads in candidate preference polls.

By contrast, the typical challenger can count on only four news stories: announcement, primary victory, candidate profile, and the final defeat. One strategy a challenger often uses to generate publicity and reach voters is to challenge the incumbent to a debate. The negotiations provide fodder for news stories, and the incumbent receives negative publicity should he or she refuse to debate. As a result, most incumbents accept challengers' invitations to debate. The debates not only generate additional news coverage, but they provide the challengers an opportunity to be seen on an equal footing with the incumbents.

News coverage of female and racial minority candidates has additional variations. Reporters are likely to focus on the "unusualness" of their candidacies, especially when they face a male or a white person. They are also likely to highlight issues traditionally considered important to these groups, such as affirmative action, crime and safety, education, and health. Recent studies have found that women candidates are likely to benefit when campaigns focus on "women's" issues but suffer at the polls when campaigns focus on "men's" issues, such as defense and foreign policy.

Senate races, because they cover an entire state, are more likely to receive news coverage and to see that coverage appear in a variety of outlets. However, local coverage of House races varies widely. Candidates running in districts embedded within large metropolitan areas are not likely to receive much news coverage because of the large number of House districts within the media market. Similarly, candidates campaigning in sprawling districts that span several media markets may find that news coverage is uneven across the district and difficult to generate.

As a result, candidates, whenever possible, turn to paid advertisements in mass media of all sorts. The most powerful is television. Virtually every household has at least one television, and TV is most voters' primary source of information about politics. Consequently, approximately 90 percent of all Senate campaigns and 70 percent of House campaigns use paid television advertising. The major benefit of paid television ads is the opportunity to reach thousands of potential voters with a completely unfiltered message. Well-crafted visual and audio messages can establish a candidate's credibility and allows the candidate to focus on the primary themes of the campaign.

Television's major drawback is its cost. Candidates pay the same rate for commercial time as do other advertisers. This amount varies by the size of the media market and the popularity of the show during which the ad appears. Larger markets and popular programming ensure exposure to the most potential voters. Thus, to ensure that their ads appear during desirable times, candidates must pay top dollar.

Another problem arises because of the lack of congruence between media market boundaries and state and congressional district lines. Television ads will be seen by a large number of viewers who live outside the candidate's district. The message and the money spent to put it there are wasted on those viewers.

In response to these problems, House and Senate candidates are increasingly making use of less expensive, targeted mass media. Two of the most popular are cable television and radio. Both are less expensive than network television, and both allow candidates to tailor their ads to highly targeted audiences, such as African Americans or Spanish speakers. Radio has the added benefit of low production costs and does not require a telegenic candidate.

Candidates also like to purchase newspaper advertisements, even though newspaper readership is declining, because they are quite inexpensive in comparison to television.

The most recent campaign communication tool is the Internet. House and Senate campaigns set up Web sites and use the Internet in more and more sophisticated ways. Relatively inexpensive to set up and maintain, candidate Web sites are no longer "virtual yard signs." They provide opportunities to Webcast television ads and candidate speeches, target messages to particular voters through buttons (e.g., "labor issues") or different languages, recruit volunteers, motivate supporters, and solicit donations.

Internet sites with similar URLs (Web addresses) can be used to parody or criticize the candidate's official site, especially if the candidate did not secure all versions of his or her URL, such as "janesmithforcongress.com" and "janesmithforcongress.org." Such uses, if properly registered with the Federal Election Commission, are perfectly legal. They can, however, be a source of headaches for candidates and confusion to voters.

Further reading:
Herrnson, Paul S. *Congressional Elections: Campaigning at Home and in Washington.* 2d ed. Washington, D.C.: Congressional Quarterly Press, 1998; Kahn, Kim Fridkin. *The Political Consequences of Being a Woman: How Stereotypes Influence the Conduct and Consequences of Political Campaigns.* New York: Columbia University Press, 1996; Terkildson, Nayda, and David F. Damore. "The Dynamics of Racialized Media Coverage in Congressional Elections." *Journal of Politics,* vol. 61, no. 3 (1999), pp. 680–700; Thurber, James A., and Colton C. Campbell, eds. *Congress and the Internet.* Upper Saddle River, N.J.: Prentice Hall, 2003.

—Karen Kedrowski

congressional elections: midterm

Midterm elections are regularly scheduled elections held in the years when a presidential election is not held (e.g., 1998, 2002). Unlike presidential election years, congressional races (especially those for the SENATE) may be the highest-profile races on the ballot during midterm elections. As THOMAS O'NEILL famously declared, "All politics is local." This truism is particularly apt when it comes to midterm elections, though local political circumstances are often interpreted through a national lens. Midterm elections are extremely useful to political observers and scholars, as they can garner information on voting and electoral patterns in Congress unfettered by effects that may be related to presidential elections.

Midterm elections are also noteworthy because during these elections power in Congress can shift dramati-

cally. Testimony to this claim is that the president's party has lost seats in the House in almost every midterm election from 1934 to the early 21st century. In both 1998 and 2002, though, this historic trend was not borne out because the parties of both President Bill Clinton and President George W. Bush picked up seats (Clinton in 1998 and Bush in 2002). Generally, though, when voters are dissatisfied with the performance of the administration, midterm elections provide an indirect opportunity to express this dissatisfaction by punishing the president's House and Senate partisans. Although evidence is mixed on the extent to which voters engage in this sort of punishment behavior (relative to voting primarily because of local concerns), the results of midterm elections are often interpreted as votes of confidence or lack thereof for the existing partisan order. Thus, midterm elections are significant by shaping perceptions of presidential power in relation to the power of Congress.

A number of factors distinguish midterm elections from congressional elections held during presidential years. For instance, the makeup of the electorate during a midterm election and an election during a presidential year are likely to differ dramatically. According to the theory of surge and decline, midterm elections receive significantly less attention compared to presidential elections, and thus voters in midterm elections are considerably different from their counterparts in presidential election years. A direct result is a noticeable variation in turnout, as midterm elections draw a much lower percentage of the electorate than in elections in presidential years (both in the aggregate nationally and in individual states or House districts). According to Gary Jacobson, turnout drops by approximately 13 percent in midterm elections. This drop in turnout during midterm elections is often explained by a lack of motivating factors to attract voters to the polls in the absence of a presidential contest. Typically, voters are less informed about congressional elections than presidential elections as well.

In addition to lower turnout, the partisan makeup of the electorate in midterm elections differs from elections held in presidential years. During midterm elections a larger portion of the electorate is likely to have strong partisan ties (though recent research suggests this proposition is debatable). Voters with weak partisan ties or true independents are more likely to vote in presidential years than in midterm years. Therefore, congressional candidates' campaign strategies are likely to differ in midterm and presidential year elections. In midterm elections candidates are more concerned with mobilizing their base of partisan supporters.

In addition, some midterm elections have been described as corrections to electoral outcomes from two years prior (or six years prior in the case of Senate elections).

In presidential election years there are typically some candidates thought to be elected to Congress on presidential coattails. Analyses of congressional elections suggest that some members of Congress are elected to their first terms on the coattails of a popular presidential candidate of their own party. In some marginal districts in particular, voters may cast a ballot for their preferred presidential candidate and also vote for the congressional candidate of the same party. Consequently, incumbents of the president's party initially elected by a small margin in the preceding presidential election year are more likely to lose in a midterm election than are other congressional incumbents. This explanation also accounts in part for the loss of congressional seats by the president's party during midterm elections. This pattern was evident in the 1986 midterm elections, when many first-term Republican senators, initially elected with Ronald Reagan in 1980, were defeated.

Finally, while congressional midterm elections tend to focus on district- or state-specific concerns in individual races, national political conditions and issues can have an influence as well. According to the referendum theory of midterm elections, the midterm congressional vote is strongly related to the state of the economy and the public performance rating of the current administration. Beyond the discussion of presidential coattails and the difference in partisanship among the electorate, voters in midterm elections will hold the party of the administration responsible for the state of the economy during congressional midterms. Thus, the better the economic conditions and the higher the president's approval ratings, the better the president's party does in midterm congressional elections.

Two recent congressional midterm elections, both during the Clinton administration, were particularly historic: the 1994 and 1998 midterms. In 1994 the Republicans achieved a majority in the House of Representatives for the first time since 1952. In 1998, following a controversial impeachment, the president's party beat the odds and gained seats in Congress during a midterm election.

In 1994 the Republican Party gained a majority in the House of Representatives by picking up 52 seats. Democratic House giants such as former Speaker Thomas Foley of Washington, Dan Rostenkowski of Illinois, and Jack Brooks of Texas were handily defeated by Republican insurgents with little political experience. According to Jacobson, one of the main reasons for the Republicans' success in 1994 was that they were able to blame national problems on a unified Democratic government. Voters in 1994 were in a particularly strong anti-Washington mood, and Republican congressional candidates deftly turned this voter animosity against the majority party Democrats. Also, when 12 years of divided government ended with the 1992 election, voters anticipated subsequent policy changes. Bill Clinton, perhaps pulled leftward by the Democratic

Congress, did make new policies but did not deliver in ways many who had supported him in 1992 had hoped.

In 1994, led by Newt Gingrich, the Republicans successfully nationalized the midterm congressional election. In many districts Republican candidates exploited the national discontent within the context of the local political circumstances of their districts and states. While the 1994 midterm election was a surprise given decades of Democratic dominance in Congress, in many ways it demonstrated the empirical regularities common to midterm elections (e.g., midterms as referendum elections, surge and decline, and a decline in the share of congressional seats held by legislators from the president's party).

The 1998 midterm election was not only surprising but bucked historic trends. For the first time since 1934, the president's party gained seats in the House during a midterm election. While the Republicans still maintained control of the House, the Democratic pickup of five seats was unexpected because the Lewinsky scandal had erupted and the president had been accused of perjury and obstruction of justice. By the end of 1998, Clinton would become the second president to be impeached by the House.

Contrary to the historical anomaly, Jacobson holds that the 1998 Democratic pickup of House seats should not be surprising at all: The voters cast their ballots as a reflection of their opinions regarding the existing Clinton administration and were expressing approval for the political status quo. In spite of Clinton's personal peccadilloes, in 1998 Americans gave him high ratings, and the economy was booming. Thus, the 1998 midterm elections can be interpreted as an endorsement of the referendum theory of midterm congressional elections. Alan Abramowitz, though, presents an amendment to the referendum theory in the context of the 1998 elections. According to Abramowitz, salient issues that parties in the House take conflicting stands on can significantly influence the outcome of a midterm election. Thus, in 1998 the aggregate election results may have had as much to do with the highly salient issue of impeachment as with the president's popularity or the state of the economy.

Further reading:
Abramowitz, Alan. "It's Monica Stupid: The Impeachment Controversy and the 1998 Midterm Election." *Legislative Studies Quarterly* 26 (2001): 211–226; Campbell, Angus. "Surge and Decline: A Study of Electoral Change." *Public Opinion Quarterly* 24 (1960): 397–418; Campbell, James E. *The Presidential Pulse of Congressional Elections.* Lexington: University of Kentucky Press, 1993; Jacobson, Gary C. *The Politics of Congressional Elections.* 5th ed. New York: Addison Wesley Longman, 2001; Tufte, Edward R. "Determinants of the Outcomes of Midterm Congressional Elections." *American Political Science Review* 69 (1975):

812–826; Tufte, Edward R. *Political Control of the Economy.* Princeton, N.J.: Princeton University Press, 1978.

—Vibhuti Ashe Hate and Christian R. Grose

congressional elections: open seats

Open seats exist in districts, states, or other electoral units in which no incumbent officeholder runs for reelection. Seats become open when an incumbent retires, dies in office, seeks higher office, or loses renomination in a primary. Although traditionally used to refer to races for the U.S. HOUSE OF REPRESENTATIVES, the term can also be applied to nonincumbent elections for U.S. SENATE, governor, state legislator, and the like.

Congressional incumbents almost always win reelection, particularly in the U.S. House, and their margins of general election victory are substantial. Since 1980 the number of House incumbents who sought and won reelection dropped below 90 percent only once (1992) and surpassed 98 percent in 1998, 2000, and 2002. The number of incumbents who won comfortably, gaining at least 60 percent of the two-party vote, ranged between 63 and 88 percent in that same period. Much of this was due to the partisan makeup of each member's district, with incumbents usually sharing the partisan affiliation of a majority of their constituents. Incumbents, however, also benefit from generally positive name recognition, fostered by the constituency service and PORK BARREL benefits that they provide and that they can advertise by way of their FRANKING privilege. Given such odds, quality challengers from the opposition party are hard to come by, thus increasing the odds that an incumbent will be easily reelected.

Without the benefits of incumbency coming into play, however, open seats are considered more competitive than when an incumbent runs for reelection. Consequently, parties target open seats to maintain or alter the balance of legislative power, and usually a set of higher-quality candidates strategically decides to enter those races. Parties, candidates, and campaign contributors apply disproportionate resources to winning. In 2002, for example, incumbent House members raised an average of $935,420 to spend on their reelection bids. Their general election challengers spent an average of only $276,332.2 Candidates vying for open seats, however, spent an average of $985,738 and more than $1.25 million if they won. Even in districts that are fairly noncompetitive between parties, an open seat usually attracts more and higher-quality candidates within the predominant party's primary election.

Because states, unlike many house districts, are fairly competitive, and because the U.S. Senate offers higher visibility and prestige than the U.S. House, incumbent senators tend to attract higher-quality challengers (reelection rates in the Senate have ranged from 55 to 97 percent since

1980). Even in the Senate, however, open seats tend to produce better-financed campaigns. The average 2002 figures for Senate incumbents, challengers, and open seat candidates were approximately $5.63 million, $1.93 million, and $5.59 million, respectively.

Membership turnover in Congress comes mainly by way of open seats. From 1980 to 2002 the number of House freshmen who won open seats exceeded the number who defeated incumbents in the general election by better than two to one, even though open seat races never exceeded 20 percent of all House elections. Freshman senators winning open seats exceeded those beating incumbents by roughly 70 percent. The importance of open seat elections in altering the balance of power between parties is also striking. Since 1980 roughly 40 percent of House and Senate seats that changed party have come from open seats, far surpassing the percentage of election contests those seats represented. Open seats provided disproportionate opportunities for the Republicans as they took over control of both congressional chambers in 1994. A total of 22 of the 57 districts that changed from Democratic to Republican control in that year came from open seats, even though only 52 total open seats were contested, with only 32 of that number being previously held by a Democrat. The effects of open seats were even more pronounced in the Senate, as Republicans picked up six of their eight gains in states where an incumbent chose not to seek reelection.

Open seats for the U.S. House, although usually proportionally few in number, are more likely in elections that follow reapportionment and redistricting. The reapportionment of seats from one set of states to another automatically creates new and thus open seats in states that gain districts through reapportionment. A total of 12 such open seats were created in 2002. Additionally, boundary changes that follow redistricting often add new voters to an existing member's district, voters for whom the incumbent's name recognition and service advantages are not so relevant. This change of district boundaries that must occur in most states, regardless of whether a state gains, loses, or maintains the same number of districts, thus tends to increase the number of incumbents who choose to retire. This was particularly true in 1992, when redistricting coupled with the congressional banking scandal contributed to the retirement of 65 incumbent members of the U.S. House. Also, 1992 was the last year that retiring members could take any campaign funds left over from previous elections with them, thus providing an extra incentive to vacate a seat.

Open seat elections have become more prevalent in state legislatures due to the increasing number of states, mainly in the West, that have instituted TERM LIMITS. The 16 states that maintained term limits collectively produced more than 300 forced retirements in 2002 alone (with only 11 of those states holding elections affected by term limits that year). These "term limited" open seats constituted anywhere from 7 to 71 percent of all election contests in their respective states. Self-imposed term limits can also produce open seats in the U.S. Congress. Mandated term limits in the House and Senate, however, were declared unconstitutional by the U.S. Supreme Court in 1995 (*U.S. TERM LIMITS V. THORNTON*), thus limiting the opportunity for massive, forced vacancies in those chambers. In all likelihood, term limited state legislators become prime candidates for competing in congressional elections, particularly those in which an incumbent need not be challenged, that is, in open seats.

Further reading:
Gaddie, Robert K., and Charles S. Bullock, III. *Elections to Open Seats in the U.S. House: Where the Action Is."* Lanham, Md.: Rowman & Littlefield, 2000; Despoato, Scott W., and John R. Petrocik. "The Variable Incumbency Advantage: New Voters, Redistricting, and the Personal Vote." *American Journal of Political Science* 47, 1 (2003): 18–33; Jacobson, Gary C. "Terror, Terrain and Turnout: Explaining the 2002 Midterm Elections." *Political Science Quarterly* 118 (2003): 1–22; Jacobson, Gary C., and Samuel Kernell. *Strategy and Choice in Congressional Elections.* New Haven, Conn.: Yale University Press, 1983; Stanley, Harold W., and Richard G. Niemi. *Vital Statistics on American Politics, 2001–2002.* Washington, D.C.: Congressional Quarterly Press, 2002.

—Peter F. Galderisi

congressional elections: pivotal nineteenth-century contests

As the American experiment with republican government matured in the 19th century, pivotal congressional elections occurred in 1800, 1828, 1854, and 1894. These elections were pivotal because they signified a party in Congress making great gains in their representation, and subsequent years were defined by that party's power. Disconnecting presidential and congressional elections in this period is often difficult; most historical accounts focus mainly on presidential contests. In addition, only the House of Representatives was directly elected in the 19th century, and unified government was the rule, not the exception it became in the 20th century. As with the pivotal elections of 1800 and 1828, they coincided with important presidential contests. However, the congressional elections of 1854 and 1894 were ones that foreshadowed a party's fortune in the next presidential election. Those presidential elections received the most attention and, as with both 1860 and 1896, are termed critical. The identified congressional elections are significant, however, because they mark new partisan relationships in the Congress.

The election of 1800 was pivotal because it marked a peaceful transfer of political power from one party to another, the first such transfer in American history. It also established a new ruling party, the Jeffersonian Republicans or Democratic-Republicans. In the few years before the 1800 election, partisanship between the Federalists and the Jeffersonians had grown. In 1800 the Jeffersonian Republicans wrested control of both Congress and the presidency from the previously dominant Federalists. The Federalists never again attained majority status in either chamber of Congress and never again held the presidency; 1816 was the last election in which they ran a candidate for president.

In the presidential election, Jefferson and his running mate, Aaron Burr, each received 73 electoral votes to incumbent John Adams's 65. This being prior to the adoption of the Twelfth Amendment in 1804 providing for separate presidential and vice presidential ballots, the election was thrown into the House of Representatives, where on the 36th ballot Jefferson was selected president.

In Congress Jefferson's party after the 1800 election controlled 67 percent of the House and 53 percent of the Senate. From the 1800 elections until 1824, the Democratic-Republicans controlled both Congress and the presidency. In the Seventh Congress the dominance of the Democratic-Republicans marked a retreat from the more elitist policies of the Federalists, who favored a vigorous national government to the more participatory, state-centered view of politics held by the Jeffersonians. In addition, the 1800 election marked the success of both the Democratic-Republican appeals to the electorate, which Federalists were loath to do, and their organizational skills at state and local levels. The Democratic-Republican Party was decentralized, mirroring its political philosophy. In addition, large reservoirs of antiparty feeling in the United States still existed. Over the next several elections, however, the Democratic-Republicans were able to build on their popularity. By the Ninth Congress (1805–07), they held 79 percent of the seats in both the House of Representatives and the Senate.

In the 1820s party identities were re-forming. The Federalists had ceased to be competitive at the national level in the 1810s, and the Democratic-Republicans were succumbing to factionalism within the party by the 1820s. The 1824 presidential election was a four-way race between various personalities within the Democratic-Republican party. While Andrew Jackson won the popular vote and received more electoral votes than any other candidate (but not a majority), the House of Representatives chose John Quincy Adams to be president in what Jacksonians labeled a corrupt bargain between Adams and Henry Clay. Jackson successfully avenged his 1824 loss in the 1828 presidential election, a rematch with Adams. In 1828 the mass-based political party came to fruition in the form of Jacksonian Democrats. Jacksonians commanded majorities in both chambers in the 21st Congress (1829–31), holding 67 percent of the seats in the House of Representatives and 52 percent of the seats in the Senate. However, it should be noted that the Jackson era was one marked by executive leadership over the legislative branch. By 1832 Jackson and his followers called themselves Democrats. The Whig Party coalesced as the opposition to Democrats during this period, and by the mid-1830s two-party competition was fierce and close between the Whigs and Democrats.

In 1854 Congress passed the Kansas-Nebraska Act that left the question of slavery in the territories to popular sovereignty, contrary to the Missouri Compromise of 1820. Anti-Nebraska forces quickly coalesced into the Republican Party, which came to dominate both the executive and the legislative branches by the election of 1860. All of the electoral success in Congress of the new Republican Party after 1854 cannot be attributed solely to its stance on slavery, however. Some nativist sentiments were also incorporated into the Republican Party's stances after the 1854 election, which enabled it to attract members of the nativist American Party (Know-Nothings). It was, however, the 1854 congressional election that was crucial in marking pivotal congressional elections.

In the 33rd Congress (1853–55) there was not a single Republican. After the 1854 election a plurality of House members were of the new Republican Party. The Senate, much slower to change due to indirect election and lengthier terms, remained in the hands of the Democrats until 1860. Republican numbers in the House atrophied in the 1856 election; they lost more than a dozen seats, but they made gains in the Senate. Republicans, however, rebounded in the 1858 election, increasing their numbers in both House and Senate, while remaining the minority. In the election of 1860, Republicans captured majorities in both the House and the Senate. The Republican Party was thus able to achieve majority status in Congress in 1860 as well as capture the presidency, an election that would precipitate the Civil War. The dominance of the Republican Party during the Civil War and afterward during Reconstruction shaped the structure and nature of American politics for more than a century.

The election of 1894 was pivotal because Republicans made great gains in Congress. The Panic of 1893 doomed the majority Democrats in the 1894 midterm elections. In the subsequent 54th Congress (1895–97) the House was 69 percent Republican; in the Senate Republicans held a plurality of seats and constituted 49 percent of that chamber.

Divisions on the economy played a key role in the elections of 1894 and 1896. The issue of the monetary standard's composition pitted rural interests against industrial

ones, as did the other key issue of tariffs. In 1894 the issue of the monetary standard was still partially a cross-cutting one within the Democratic and Republican Parties. There were some silver Republicans and some gold Democrats. However, the popularity of the Populist Party in some regions came at the expense of Democratic candidates. In addition, punishment for the depression was dealt to the ruling party, the Democrats. Republicans were able to take majority party status away from the Democrats in Congress. Only after the 1894 election did the two parties take polar stances on economic issues, with Republicans favoring the gold standard and industrial interests and Democrats favoring bimetallism and other Populist issues, leading to the realignment of 1896. Republicans dominated Congress well into the 20th century and become a party based in the industrial Northeast and the Midwest, favoring industrial interests. The Democrats appealed to the South, West, and agricultural interests.

Further reading:
Brady, David W. *Critical Elections and Congressional Policy Making.* Stanford, Calif.: Stanford University Press, 1988; Cunningham, Nobel E., Jr. *The Jeffersonian Republicans in Power.* Chapel Hill: University of North Carolina Press, 1963; Goodman, Paul, ed. *The Federalists vs. the Jeffersonian Republicans.* New York: Holt, Rinehart, & Winston, 1967; Silbey, Joel H., ed. *Political Ideology and Voting Behavior in the Age of Jackson.* Englewood Cliffs, N.J.: Prentice Hall, 1973; Sundquist, James L. *Dynamics of the Party System.* Washington, D.C.: Brookings Institution Press, 1983; U.S. House of Representatives, Office of the Clerk. Party Divisions. Available online. URL: http://clerk.house.gov/histHigh/Congressional_History/partyDiv.php Accessed 30 June 2003; U.S. Senate. *Party Division in the Senate, 1789–Present.* Available online. URL: http://www.senate.gov/pagelayout/history/one_item_and_teasers/partydiv.htm Accessed 30 June 2003.
—Donna R. Hoffman

congressional elections: primaries

Primary elections are the most common method for political parties to select their nominee for a SENATE or HOUSE OF REPRESENTATIVES seat. Direct primaries feature two or more candidates competing to be their party's standard bearer in the subsequent general election in November. Direct primary elections became popular in the early years of the 20th century as one of the reforms advocated by the Progressive movement. They sought primaries as a key tool to eliminate boss-dominated local and state political parties. The goal was to have candidates determined by a vote of party constituents rather than bosses making closed deals in smoke-filled rooms.

Congressional primaries in which an incumbent is seeking reelection normally are not competitive elections. Only about 30 percent of incumbent representatives and 40 percent of incumbent senators typically even face a token primary challenger. Moreover, an incumbent member of Congress rarely is ever defeated in a primary election. Incumbents widely perceived as vulnerable normally will watch a competitive primary in the rival party. On the other hand, competitive primary elections most often occur to fill an open House or Senate seat. States or House districts dominated by one political party will probably have competitive contests in that party's primary and little or no activity in the minority party's primary. Thus, primaries in one-party-dominant areas tend to determine the winner of the subsequent general election.

States vary in their laws governing citizen qualification to vote in primary elections. Closed primaries that require voters to declare their party affiliations before voting in primary elections are held in 26 states. On the other hand, 20 states have open primaries, in which citizens can vote in either party's primary just by requesting that party's ballot at the polling place. Three states (Washington, Alaska, and California) had a controversial blanket primary system whereby each voter was given a ballot listing all candidates from each party. Persons ware allowed to vote for only one person (regardless of party) for each office. However, in 2000 the Supreme Court eliminated this system, ruling that it violated citizens' First Amendment right of freedom of association.

Finally, Louisiana has the most distinctive system. That state has a nonpartisan primary on the national election day in November in which all candidates are listed on the same ballot. Any candidate who receives a majority of popular votes on election day wins the office outright. However, if no candidate receives a majority of the votes, then a second, or runoff, election is held later between the top two vote-getters regardless of their party affiliation in the November election.

State and national party leaders have been known to try to attempt to influence the outcome of their parties' primaries for selected offices. Most states allow party organizations to endorse favored candidates running in primary elections. National party leaders have been known to either recruit or endorse favored congressional candidates. National leaders also at times have tried to avoid a possibly divisive primary in a state by discouraging a candidate from running. Such candidates can be threatened with retaliation or promised a position elsewhere if they opt not to run for office.

Interest groups also have increasingly taken on a role in primary elections. Sometimes they endorse a candidate or back one of their followers seeking a party's nomination to the House or Senate. Interest groups have been known to determine the outcome of a primary election by mobilizing a large number of voters to go to the polls.

Voter turnout for primaries tends to be significantly lower than for general elections the following November. Hence, a well-organized block of voters, such as citizens affiliated with one or a group of allied interest groups, can sway a primary election. They might even nominate a candidate possessing little appeal among regular voters in that party. Such interest group–backed candidates often have ideologies unrepresentative of the constituents as a whole and thereby suffer a major defeat in the general election.

Further reading:
Herrnson, Paul S. *Congressional Elections: Campaigning at Home and in Washington.* 4th ed. Washington, D.C.: Congressional Quarterly Press, 2004; Jacobson, Gary. *The Politics of Congressional Elections.* 6th ed. New York: Longman, 2004.

—Robert E. Dewhirst

congressional elections: special elections

Special elections are held in either the SENATE or the HOUSE OF REPRESENTATIVES to fill seats vacated normally by a member's death or resignation. However, each chamber has distinctive ways for filling its vacancies.

Each state is directed to establish a system for nominating House candidates and conducting special elections. States require special elections to fill vacancies that occur during the first year of the two-year House term. On the other hand, for vacancies that occur during the second year of the term some states simply allow the seat to remain vacant, while other states hold a special election as soon as possible or wait until the next scheduled election and hold two elections, one to complete the current term and another to fill the seat for the next term.

Although special elections can be employed to fill Senate vacancies, most states authorize their governors to appoint a temporary successor to hold the seat until a special election can be held in conjunction with the next general election. Because senators serve six-year terms, a special election might place a senator in office for two or four years until the original term has expired. Senators appointed during the last two years of a term normally serve until the end of that term.

Special elections traditionally have been characterized by low voter turnout on election day and for attracting ambitious candidates with the ability to work quickly, assemble a campaign organization, and attract sufficient funds virtually overnight. Normally, there is little lead time to prepare for a special election campaign to fill vacancies that typically occur suddenly. With no incumbent in the contest, special elections can become particularly competitive and, if there is a narrow balance of power on Capitol Hill, attract considerable national publicity and financial support.

Further reading:
Herrnson Paul S. *Congressional Elections: Campaigning at Home and in Washington.* 4th ed. Washington, D.C.: Congressional Quarterly Press, 2004; Sigelman, Lee. "Special Elections to the U.S. House: Some Descriptive Generalizations." *Legislative Studies Quarterly* (1981).

congressional intelligence oversight

Congress was an aggressive investigative body of U.S. intelligence activities upon the creation of the Central Intelligence Agency (CIA) in 1947, a situation reminiscent of the intelligence investigations of the mid-1970s. The highly critical Pearl Harbor Report by a joint congressional committee provided instrumental recommendations for the creation of a centralized intelligence bureaucracy.

The earliest years of the CIA's relations with Congress were actually strained by the anticommunist fervor that swept through the country in the late 1940s and early 1950s. Senator JOSEPH MCCARTHY of Wisconsin suspected and accused the CIA of harboring communists. Allen Dulles, President Dwight Eisenhower's director of central intelligence (DCI), worked vigorously to overcome these accusations and develop a close political relationship between the CIA and Congress by creating an atmosphere of trust around his office. His administrative style was to appear voluntarily before a group of federal legislators, usually after working hours, smoke a bit of his pipe, and tell a few good old-fashioned spy stories. He became a master of congressional manipulation. The politically astute Dulles cultivated bipartisan, yet conservative, support for the CIA with senior southern Democrats and northeastern Republicans.

Senator Leverett Saltonstall of Massachusetts, a former member of the ARMED SERVICES and APPROPRIATIONS COMMITTEES, once described how the practice of oversight worked during the Dulles years: Dominated by the committee chairs, members would ask few questions that dealt with internal agency matters or with specific operations. The most sensitive discussions were reserved for one-on-one sessions between Dulles and individual committee chairs. Nothing was put in writing, and no known records were kept about these meetings. Representative Gerald Ford of Michigan once expressed complete surprise that a CIA appropriations briefing delivered by DCI Dulles did not even mention the word *dollar.*

Not all federal legislators were content with the cozy relationship between Congress and the CIA. In 1955 Senator Mike Mansfield of Montana, drawing upon the recommendations of the congressionally mandated Hoover Commission, made the first attempt to formally establish a committee to oversee the CIA. In 1956 the Mansfield resolution, although it gained the support of 35 cosponsors, met fierce opposition from entrenched senators, who jealously guarded their personal influence with the CIA. Dulles easily persuaded 12 cosponsors to withdraw their support for the Mansfield resolution after expressing his concern for the possibility of committee staffers leaking intelligence methods and sources. When the Mansfield resolution came to a vote on April 11, 1956, it was easily defeated 59-27.

Nevertheless, Senator Mansfield's defeated resolution led to a compromise agreement of sorts. In 1956 Senator RICHARD RUSSELL of Georgia formed a CIA subcommittee of the SENATE ARMED SERVICES COMMITTEE, and the following year the SENATE APPROPRIATIONS COMMITTEE followed suit. These CIA subcommittees were informal bodies that usually met in joint meetings between the Armed Services and Appropriations Committees. In the HOUSE OF REPRESENTATIVES intelligence oversight was somewhat more organized as Congressman Carl Vinson of Washington established a CIA subcommittee for the HOUSE ARMED SERVICES COMMITTEE. Congressman Clarence Cannon of Missouri and the chair of the HOUSE APPROPRIATIONS COMMITTEE monitored the CIA with an informal special group of five members who advised their full committee directly on intelligence issues.

This failure of the Mansfield resolution was followed in 1961 by another doomed resolution to create an intelligence oversight body; its sponsor was Senator Eugene McCarthy of Minnesota. This was followed by yet another failed oversight resolution in 1966 by Senator J. William Fulbright of Arkansas, the chair of the SENATE FOREIGN RELATIONS COMMITTEE.

The war in Vietnam, the nuclear arms race, and increasing international tensions throughout the 1960s forced the CIA to gradually become more accessible to a concerned Congress and the American public. DCI Richard Helms responded to growing demands for greater CIA openness by increasing the number of CIA briefings to congressional committees. In 1967 17 committees were offered detailed briefings by agency officials. Still, many of these briefings were made before the House and Senate intelligence subcommittees, but an ever-growing number of presentations were made to the full House and Senate Armed Services Committees as well as the Foreign Relations Committee in the Senate, the FOREIGN AFFAIRS COMMITTEE in the House, and the Joint Committee on Atomic Energy. These briefings remained largely informal, but the floodgates had been opened for a more formal oversight system to be adopted by Congress in following years. Top CIA officials such as the DCI and the deputy director of Central Intelligence soon averaged 30 to 35 briefings before Congress annually.

By the mid-1970s the political climate in Congress was changing even more significantly in response to scandals in the White House and the Pentagon and controversial press revelations regarding the U.S. intelligence community. There were credible reports of foreign assassination plots and domestic surveillance of civil rights leaders and the antiwar movement. The first congressional reaction to these public disclosures was the 1974 passage of the Hughes-Ryan Amendment to the Foreign Assistance Act of 1961.

The Hughes-Ryan Amendment, which followed in the wake of U.S. covert action in Chile, prohibited the use of appropriated funds for operations in foreign countries, other than activities intended solely for obtaining necessary intelligence, unless and until the president found that each such operation was important to the national security of the United States. The president was also required by the Hughes-Ryan Amendment to report in a timely fashion a description and scope of such operations to the appropriate committees of Congress. The appropriate committees then included a total of six: Armed Services, Foreign Relations/Affairs, and Appropriations of both the Senate and House. This was later modified under the Intelligence Oversight Act of 1980 to include just the two permanent committees on intelligence.

The Hughes-Ryan Amendment was widely assumed to be the demise of plausible deniability in covert operations, which had been established during the Truman administration with the approval of NSC 10/2. This principle gave the U.S. government a means to disavow any authorization or knowledge of a covert operation. From then on every president would be forced to place his signature and political reputation on the line when it came to the CIA's covert activities. However, the Hughes-Ryan Amendment also tied the hands of Congress as well. No longer would members of Congress be able to complain to the press and the American public that they were left in the dark when it came to unfavorable secret activities.

Following the adoption of the Hughes-Ryan Amendment on January 27, 1975, the Senate appointed a select committee under the leadership of Senator Frank Church of Idaho to investigate a host of alleged illegal activities committed by American intelligence agencies. The Church Committee, formally known as the Senate Select Committee to Study Government Operations with Respect to Intelligence Activities, conducted an exhaustive 15-month investigation. The Church Committee also carried out 21 days of hearings, released six final reports, and made 183 formal recommendations to improve the effectiveness and legality of American intelligence operations. The Church Committee was one of the most thorough investigations in the history of Congress, and its recommendations set the stage for a formal oversight committee of intelligence in the Senate.

The House also created a select investigative committee during the mid-1970s to examine the U.S. intelligence community. On February 19, 1975, Congressman Lucien Nedzi of Michigan was selected to be the chair of the HOUSE SELECT INTELLIGENCE COMMITTEE. However, the troubled and partisan Nedzi Committee failed to get its investigation started. The initial difficulties centered on the selection of the committee's staff director. The committee Democrats then revolted when they learned that Chair Nedzi, also a fellow Democrat, failed to respond to alleged intelligence abuses while serving as the chief overseer of the House Armed Services subcommittee for intelligence. The Nedzi Committee's leadership was essentially undermined, making any investigations into the U.S. intelligence community impossible.

The House moved quickly to create a second select intelligence committee, this time under the leadership of Congressman Otis Pike of New York. The Pike Committee included 13 members and had a mandate to conduct investigations and make recommendations for the U.S. intelligence community. The Pike Committee was plagued from the same internal political strife that racked the Nedzi Committee but managed to conduct 28 days of public hearings. The Pike Committee's zealous investigations also led to open conflict with the executive branch, particularly the White House.

On January 29, 1976, the full House repudiated the Pike Committee's tactics and voted 246-124 to suppress the committee's final report. Soon after, a draft copy of the committee's final report was leaked to CBS news correspondent Daniel Schorr. The Pike Committee report was then passed by Schorr to the *Village Voice*, a liberal weekly published in New York City. The public disclosure of the Pike Committee's final report, after the full House had voted to suppress it, prompted an official investigation into the matter. All 13 members of the committee and 32 members of the staff were forced to testify under oath about the leak of the report. The investigators had become the investigated, and the reputation of the Pike Committee was irreparably tarnished.

Despite all the sensational revelations regarding the U.S. intelligence community, the lasting legacy of the Church and Pike Committees was their separate recommendations for a formal and permanent oversight committee system on intelligence. Both committees made it clear in no uncertain terms that existing legal and policy constraints on U.S. intelligence activities were inadequate and that proper supervision and accountability within the executive branch and Congress were sorely lacking.

Senate plans to establish a formal oversight committee on intelligence followed closely the example set by the Church Committee. On May 19, 1976, after extensive committee review and 10 days of floor debate, the Senate voted 72-22 in favor of Senate Resolution 400, 94th Congress, which created a Senate Select Committee on Intelligence (SSCI). Although the term *select* usually refers to committees appointed by the MAJORITY and MINORITY LEADERS that serve only a limited period of time, the SSCI has continued to operate uninterrupted with the bipartisan support of the Senate.

Meanwhile, the House was working on the passage of its own resolution for intelligence oversight. The House worked hard to disassociate itself from the controversial Nedzi and Pike Committees. House Resolution 658 eventually passed by a vote of 227-171 on July 14, 1977. The House resolution differed from its Senate counterpart in that it established a House Permanent Select Committee on Intelligence (HPSCI), a body considered truly permanent under the rules of the House. Both of these select committees took the position that they were the appropriate committees for notification of covert operations under the Hughes-Ryan Amendment and, like other congressional standing committees, they had the authority to recommend legislation.

The U.S. intelligence community, and particularly the CIA, is now the subject of two political masters, the executive branch and Congress. Since the mid-1970s Congress has become a voracious consumer of intelligence. In 1988 alone the CIA's Office of Congressional Affairs reported that more than 1,000 substantive intelligence briefings had been provided to individual members of Congress, committees, and staff. This upward trend continued throughout the 1990s, despite the end of the cold war and the collapse of the Soviet Union. In 1993 1,512 meetings took place between members of Congress and the CIA's legislative staff, along with 154 small group meetings between the legislators and the DCI, 26 congressional hearings with the DCI as a witness, 128 hearings with other CIA witnesses, 317 contacts with legislators, and 887 meetings and contacts with legislative staff, while the CIA provided 4,976 classified and 4,668 unclassified documents to Congress.

The passage of the 1991 Intelligence Authorization Act in response to the Iran-contra scandal served to solidify the oversight position of Congress with respect to the U.S. intelligence community. The 1991 act repealed provisions of the Hughes-Ryan Amendment but required that presidential findings on covert action be made in writing and reported directly to Congress. Retroactive findings were prohibited. Once the exclusive domain of the presidency, the U.S. intelligence community now sits roughly equidistant between the executive and legislative branches of the federal government.

Further reading:
Conner, William E. *Intelligence Oversight: The Controversy behind the FY 1991 Intelligence Authorization Act.* McLean, Va.: Association of Former Intelligence Officers, 1993; Johnson, Loch K. *A Season of Inquiry: Congress and Intelligence.* Chicago: Dorsey Press, 1988; Knott, Stephen F. *Secret and Sanctioned: Covert Operations and the American Presidency.* Oxford: Oxford University Press, 1996; Olmsted, Kathryn S. *Challenging the Secret Government: The Post-Watergate Investigations of the CIA and FBI.* Chapel Hill: University of North Carolina Press, 1996; Smist, Frank J. *Congress Overseas the United States Intelligence Community 1947–1994.* 2d ed. Knoxville: University of Tennessee Press, 1994; Snider, L. Britt. *Sharing Secrets with Lawmakers: Congress as a User of Intelligence.* Washington, D.C.: Center for the Study of Intelligence, 1997.

—Larry A. Valero

Congressional Quarterly

Popularly known as "CQ," Congressional Quarterly is a privately owned publisher that reports on the U.S. Congress, the federal government, and national politics. It also publishes a variety of directories and reference works. The flagship publication of the organization is the *CQ Weekly Report,* a news magazine on Congress and its activities. This magazine tracks legislation from its proposal at the subcommittee level through final conferences involving congressional leadership.

Congressional Quarterly was founded in 1945 by Henrietta and Nelson Poynter, who wanted a privately owned publication to cover Congress in a nonpartisan manner. The *Weekly Report,* one of its earliest publications, distilled large amounts of legislation into a more easily understood form and in political and governmental context.

One of the most valuable services Congressional Quarterly provides researchers and the public is how it presents roll-call votes in the HOUSE OF REPRESENTATIVES and SENATE. The House roll-call reports list House members alphabetically by state, then identify each member by district and party affiliation. The roll-call votes by the Senate are also listed alphabetically by state, with the majority party members listed first. This innovative way of presenting roll-call vote information allows researchers to conduct roll-call analysis more easily and also gives insight into congressional behavior and attitudes at any given time.

Congressional Quarterly's roll-call tallies have also contributed to the study of political science by creating measurements that have become standards in the field of congressional studies. One was simply a measure of attendance at roll calls. CQ also began interviewing members of Congress who were absent from a particular vote on how they would have voted if they had been present on the floor. Another measure was a party voting index that measured party cohesiveness in Congress as well as the degree of differentiation between the two parties. A third measure, presidential support scores, showed legislative support for presidential initiatives. The last commonly used measure, the conservative coalition index, measured ideological voting by weighing the combined vote of Republicans and southern Democrats against those of nonsouthern Democrats in Congress. These voting measures have been used in almost every recent study of the U.S. Congress.

Congressional Quarterly evolved into a reference book publisher when it began to compile its own reports in its journal *Congress and the Nation,* published every four years to coincide with four-year presidential terms. Other current publications include *CQ Researcher, Guide to U.S. Elections, America Votes, Presidential Elections,* and *U.S. Primary Elections,* just to name a few. Congressional Quarterly also publishes a large number of books on an array of different subjects. *CQ Today* (formerly the *CQ Daily Monitor*) is a legislative daily that provides a morning news report on Congress and scheduled hearings and mark ups of congressional committees. The *CQ Researcher* focuses each weekly issue on a single topic of current interest.

Congressional Quarterly also provides comprehensive and timely legislative tracking information on its Web site. Content available at www.CQ.com includes coverage of bill action, votes, schedules, and member profiles. There are also direct links to relevant texts of bills, committee reports, testimony, and transcripts of hearings.

Further reading:
Austin, Jan, ed. *CQ . . . Almanac Plus, 2003.* Washington, D.C.: Congressional Quarterly Press, 2004; Cohn, Mary, ed. *Congressional Quarterly's Guide to Congress.* 4th ed. Washington, D.C.: Congressional Quarterly Press, 1991.
—Mary S. Rausch

Congressional Record

The published account of the proceedings, debates, and floor votes of the U.S. Congress is called the *Congressional Record.* The *Record* is published daily when one or both chambers of Congress are in session and is available the day after Congress meets. A bound, permanent edition is issued after each two-year Congress. The *Congressional Record* began in 1873 and is still published by the Government Printing Office. The federal courts and many federal agencies use the *Congressional Record* to help interpret legislative intent, and scholars often use it to track a bill's legislative history.

The *Congressional Record* is not an exact record of proceedings, and it includes much more than legislative matters. Roll-call votes, the texts of bills, amendments, con-

ference reports, and floor debates are all reported in the publication. It also contains articles reprinted from magazines and newspapers, speeches on a vast array of topics, communications from the president and executive branch memorials, petitions, and other information on legislation. Committee activities are not usually reported in the body of the *Record* other than the mentioning of reports made to the HOUSE OF REPRESENTATIVES and SENATE or notices of meetings.

The House and Senate journals are actually the official records of the House and Senate proceedings. The journals, which are similar to minutes of a meeting, discuss only in passing the procedural actions and votes that occur on any given day and do not contain the transcripts of debates on legislation or any other extra material. The *Congressional Record* is a more complete source of legislative activity and debate.

Each daily edition of the *Congressional Record* is divided into four numbered sections: the Daily Digest, the Proceedings of the House, the Proceedings of the Senate, and the EXTENSION OF REMARKS. The Proceedings of the House and Senate alternate in appearing first in each daily printing whenever schedules permit.

Members of both the House and the Senate are allowed to edit the transcript of their remarks before being published in either the daily or permanent *Record.* House members may be granted permission to revise and extend their remarks by unanimous consent. Senators may be given permission to have any unfinished remarks inserted in the *Record* at the point where they stopped speaking.

The Extension of Remarks section follows the House and Senate proceedings and is used by House members to include additional legislative comments not delivered on the floor of the House. It also includes the text of speeches given outside Congress, letters from and tributes to constituents, and newspaper and magazine articles.

The Daily Digest pages appear at the back of each issue. These pages summarize the day's floor and committee activities and act as a table of contents for that issue. The section summarizes legislative action that took place in each chamber by giving brief descriptions of the bills and amendments considered. It also lists committee meetings held, usually including the names of any witnesses who may have testified.

While there is no electronic version of the permanent edition of the *Congressional Record,* full-text electronic versions of the daily edition of the *Record* have been available since the mid-1980s from various commercial vendors such as Congressional Quarterly, WestLaw, and LexisNexis, as well as from Thomas from the Library of Congress. In 1994 the Government Printing Office also made the daily *Record* available via the Internet through its GPO Access online service. There is also a cumulative annual *Congres-*

sional Record index to the daily editions available through GPO Access.

Further reading:
McKinney, Richard J. "An Overview of the Congressional Record and its Predecessor Publications." *Law Library Lights* 46, 2 (2002): 16–22; Amer, Mildred. *The Congressional Record: Content, History, and Issues.* Washington, D.C.: Congressional Research Service, Library of Congress, CRS Report 93-60, 1993.

—Mary S. Rausch

Congressional Research Service

The Congressional Research Service (CRS) is a Division of the LIBRARY OF CONGRESS that produces policy research for the U.S. Congress. The Congressional Research Service was established in 1914 as the Legislative Reference Bureau (LRB). Funding for the service had been included in the fiscal year 1915 appropriations bill by Senator Robert LaFollette, a Republican from Wisconsin. LaFollette had been governor of Wisconsin when the state government established a specialized library unit to assist the legislature in policy research. Seven bills to establish a legislative reference bureau had been introduced in Congress in 1911, encouraging Herbert Putnam, the Librarian of Congress, to investigate the costs and benefits of creating a reference bureau. He studied all the bureaus that existed in the states as well as consulted parliamentary libraries in Europe. At the conclusion of his research, Putnam sent a 20,000-page report to Congress documenting what was required to establish a Legislative Reference Bureau for Congress. The House of Representatives held hearings on a bill introduced by Representative John Nelson, a Republican from Wisconsin, to duplicate the Wisconsin Legislative Reference Bureau on a grander scale. The bill lacked significant support in part because the proposal called for a reference bureau to draft legislation. A number of House members believed that this function was best left to members of Congress.

In 1913 six additional bills were introduced in Congress. The Senate held hearings on Senator LaFollette's bill. This bill eventually became the amendment to the appropriations bill that was enacted for fiscal year 1915. According to the amendment, the Librarian of Congress was to "employ competent persons to prepare such indexes, digests, and compilations of law as may be required for Congress and other official use."

The Legislative Reference Bureau was made a separate division of the Library of Congress and officially renamed the Legislative Reference Service (LRS) in 1946. Under the Legislative Reorganization Act of 1970, the LRS was renamed the Congressional Research Service and given a clearer mission, to "provide Congress with comprehensive and reliable research, information, and analysis that is timely, objective, nonpartisan, and confidential."

In fiscal year 1999 the CRS began a realignment of its research divisions. At the completion of the realignment, employees were organized into six interdisciplinary research divisions: American Law; Domestic Social Policy; Foreign Affairs, Defense, and Trade; Government and Finance; Information Research; and Resources. The divisions were further divided into subject specialist sections. This reorganization was intended to improve the ability of the CRS to respond to the need for information during the legislative process while also reducing costs. In fiscal year 2002 the CRS was appropriated $81 million and had 694 employees.

By the late 1990s the research agency was the focus of controversy because it did not release its products directly to the public. Members of the public who needed access to the reports had to submit a request to their representative or senators. Some documents also were made available on House members' Web sites as part of a pilot project. Legislation was introduced in the 105th and 106th Congresses to provide easy public access to CRS reports. The agency's response to the legislation was that the CRS was not designed to provide a public information function. It also argued that interest groups and lobbyists would flood the agency with comments and complaints, causing the CRS to lose its nonpartisan stature and slowing down the research process. In 2003 Senator John McCain, a Republican from Arizona, along with Senators Patrick Leahy, a Democrat from Vermont, and Tom Harkin, a Democrat from Iowa, introduced a resolution to help open the CRS to the public. The bill, S. Res. 54, was supported by a large number of groups, including the American Library Association, the National Taxpayers Union, and the Consumer Federation of America.

Further reading:
Faler, Brian. "Access to Congress's Advisors." *Washington Post,* 17 February 2003, p. A29; Goodrum, Charles A. *The Library of Congress.* New York: Praeger Publishers, 1974; Library of Congress, *The Annual Report of the Librarian of Congress for the Fiscal Year Ending September 30, 2000.* Washington, D.C.: Government Printing Office, 2001.

—John David Rausch, Jr.

Conkling, Roscoe (1829–1888) *Representative, Senator*

Roscoe Conkling was born in Albany, New York, on October 30, 1829. His family moved to Auburn, New York, in 1839. Conkling was admitted to the New York bar in 1850 and established a practice in Utica. He served as district attorney for Oneida County and mayor of Utica from 1858 to 1859. In 1855 Conkling married Julia Seymour, sister of two-term Democratic governor of New York Horatio Seymour. Roscoe Conkling was first elected to the House of Representatives in 1858, and after serving two terms, he lost his bid for reelection in 1862. He returned to the House to serve a single term from 1865 to 1866 before being elected to the U.S. Senate in 1867. He held the seat until his resignation in 1881.

As the head of the stalwart faction of New York's dominant Republican Party, Senator Conkling is usually noted for his devotion to party politics, oratorical skills, fiery temper, and propensity to hold a grudge. Conkling biographer Andrew Jordan asserts that Conkling did not have much impact on Reconstruction because, in his words, "[t]here was too much ideology in Reconstruction; Roscoe Conkling was never much for ideology."

It is certainly fair to say that Conkling devoted more of his time to issues of patronage than to issues of public policy, and he concerned himself with relatively few substantive policy questions over the course of his career. There is a certain ideological consistency to the positions that he took and the policies that he advocated.

Though Conkling's politics remained firmly grounded in the prevailing view of the time of a limited role for government, particularly a limited role for the federal government, he consistently advocated, for example, extension of and protection for the political rights of former slaves. Though he had been a member of the House only two years, Conkling's progressive but not radical position on the abolition of slavery caught President Lincoln's attention, and Lincoln requested that Conkling be the one to introduce his compensation for emancipation bill in March 1862. The bill encouraged southern states to voluntarily emancipate slaves by offering federal compensation to states that chose to free slaves. The bill passed the House on March 11, 1862. Moreover, as a member of the Joint Committee on Reconstruction and the subcommittee on Virginia, North, and South Carolina, Conkling played an active role in the drafting and debating of the Civil War amendments. He was particularly interested in the Fourteenth Amendment and offered his own draft of the section on representation. Conkling's version of the amendment contained five provisions. The most controversial was also the one that most interested Roscoe Conkling. Conkling suggested tying representation in national politics to rights of suffrage within a state, which would increase a state's representation in both the House of Representatives and the Electoral College to the degree that the state extended the right of suffrage within the state to former slaves, different ethnic groups, women, and persons under the age of 21. In describing his proposed amendment, Conkling argued:

It contains but one condition and that rests upon a principle already imbedded in the Constitution, and as old as free government itself. That principle I affirmed in the beginning, namely, that representation does not belong to those who have not political existence, but to those who have. The object of the amendment is to enforce this truth. It therefore provides that whenever any State finds within its borders a race of beings unfit for political existence, that race shall not be represented in the Federal Government. Every state will be left free to extend or withhold the elective franchise on such terms as it pleases, and this without losing anything in representation if the terms are impartial to all. Qualifications of voters may be required of any kind. . . . But whenever in any State, and so long as a race can be found which is so low, so bad, so ignorant, so stupid, that it is deemed necessary to exclude men from the right to vote merely because they belong to that race shall likewise be excluded from the sum of Federal power to which that State is entitled.

Conkling's position harkened back to the pre-Revolutionary slogan "no taxation without representation." Any segment of the population that was subject to taxation was entitled to suffrage.

At the same time, he had a narrow view of the federal government's authority over state policy. Four years later, Conkling opposed an amendment offered by Congressman Morton that would have allowed Congress to return a state to territory status if it withdrew the right of suffrage from former slaves after being readmitted to the union. Conkling felt that the federal government did not have that authority to dictate to a state legislature.

Why, sir, can it be that lawyers or laymen can differ in opinion upon the doctrine that after we have restored Virginia, after we have crowned her again with that sovereignty, that statehood, that relationship, call it what you may, which she has lost, we can dictate to her the action of her Legislature and can expel her representatives unless she attends to our behests? And I ask can lawyers doubt that an argument which will prove that conclusion will show that Maine or Missouri can be made to lie down upon the bed which we prescribe, and be stretched if they are too short, or shortened if they overmatch in length?

While Conkling never advocated extending the role of the federal government in order to guarantee political rights of African Americans, he advocated human and political rights for African Americans, women, and other ethnic groups within the confines of the existing federal system. His ideological commitment to civil rights was recognized by the *Cleveland Gazette* following Conkling's death.

'He was among the foremost advocates of the Civil Rights Bills.' This fact in itself is sufficient to impress upon us the fact that another *race friend* has passed away. So shallow, selfish and mercenary is the political world, that few are its active and foremost members on whom we can depend as *bona fide race friends* . . . it must be a genuine inborn and high-bred sense of 'all men being created equal,' that would lead a man of such sterling qualities and disposition to champion the cause of a despised race. . . . We must feel that it was the highest, purest and bravest sense of RIGHT which lead this man's mighty voice and influence to our aid and feeling thus we can mourn his demise as that of a *true friend,* made not by machinations of men and politics, but of God.

The other issue about which Conkling felt strongly throughout his political career was the economy. A fiscal conservative, Conkling opposed all efforts to deviate from the gold standard and the issuance of paper currency. During the Civil War the Union attempted to finance the war by issuing paper currency. Moreover, an increase in paper currency was used in an attempt to alleviate recessionary conditions in the aftermath of the war. Conkling violently objected to such efforts, claiming they were not based on sound economics. It was most likely Conkling's advice that President Grant heeded in 1874, when he vetoed the "Ferry bill," which would have expanded the supply of paper money. Later in his career Conkling also opposed the efforts to coin silver.

Senator Conkling also played an important role in the controversial election of 1876, perhaps somewhat surprisingly given his status as a staunch Republican. And a staunch Republican he was, but also a stalwart Republican. Rutherford B. Hayes came from the reform segment of the party and made civil service reform an issue in the election, driving a wedge between the stalwart and reformist factions of the Republican Party. Conkling did not campaign for Hayes, ostensibly due to illness. As the election controversy unfolded, Conkling kept his views private. While he certainly opposed a Democratic administration, he had mixed feelings about a Republican administration led by Hayes, particularly since Hayes had pledged to make civil service reform a priority, and probably felt that Tilden had rightfully won the election. Moreover, Conkling was concerned by reports that Hayes supporters intended to have him inaugurated by force if necessary.

Conkling found himself in the unfamiliar position, relatively speaking, of political neutrality, and he was appointed to the special joint committee on the election. In that capacity and probably with the encouragement of President Grant, Conkling drafted a bill providing for an electoral commission to determine the outcome of the election, consisting of five senators, five representatives, and

Senator Roscoe Conkling *(Library of Congress)*

five members of the Supreme Court. Opposition to the commission was considerable on both sides of the aisle. On January 23 and 24 Senator Conkling took the floor to defend his proposal in what biographer Andrew Jordan describes as his finest moment. Conkling defended his proposal in one of the most important speeches of his career, and it was quickly adopted by both chambers. Though his name was suggested as a possible member of the commission, it drew considerable criticism from within his own party, and Conkling made it publicly known that he had no intention of serving on the commission, most likely in order to improve the bill's prospects.

One of the most controversial and strangest aspects of Senator Conkling's career was the way it ended. During the contentious Republican convention of 1880, in which 36 ballots were required to select a candidate, Conkling nominated Ulysses S. Grant to be the Republican candidate, for the third time. Moreover, Conkling attempted to rally all his supporters to ensure Grant's nomination. He was sorely disappointed when the nomination went instead to James Garfield and Chester Arthur consented to be the vice presidential candidate despite Conkling's advice to the contrary. Despite his intense disappointment in the party ticket, Conkling reluctantly agreed to actively campaign on behalf of the Republican ticket in exchange for Garfield's support in New York's political appointments.

After the election the rivalry between Garfield and Conkling intensified when Garfield nominated one of Conkling's most bitter enemies, William Robertson, to fill one of the most sought-after posts in New York, Custom House Collector. Conkling attempted to defeat the nomination in the Senate, and when the Senate approved the nomination despite his objections, he and the junior senator from New York, T. C. Platt, resigned. Platt and Conkling returned to New York and actively sought reappointment by the New York legislature. After extensive debate and 56 ballots, the legislature selected Elbridge Lapham to succeed Roscoe Conkling as senator from New York. Roscoe Conkling returned to the practice of law and died in 1888.

Further reading:
Chidsey, Donald Barr. *The Gentleman from New York: A Life of Roscoe Conkling.* New Haven, Conn.: Yale University Press, 1935; Conkling, Alfred R. *The Life and Letters of Roscoe Conkling: Orator, Statesman, Advocate.* New York: Charles L. Webster & Company, 1889; Jordan, David. *Roscoe Conkling of New York: Voice in the Senate.* Ithaca, N.Y.: Cornell University Press, 1971.

—Kim Maslin-Wicks

conservative coalition

The conservative coalition was a voting bloc of Republicans and conservative southern Democrats that frequently formed in both committee and on the floor in both the HOUSE OF REPRESENTATIVES and SENATE. The coalition has largely faded into history, forming rarely and on relatively insignificant legislation by the late 1990s. For much of the period from the late NEW DEAL through the Reagan era, the coalition determined the fate of major civil rights, economic, and labor legislation.

The standard measure of a conservative coalition voting bloc developed by *Congressional Quarterly* is a case in either the House or the Senate when a majority of Republicans and a majority of southern Democrats combined in opposition to a majority of northern Democrats. The *Congressional Quarterly* definition of the South includes the 11 states of the former Confederacy (Alabama, Arkansas, Florida, Georgia, Louisiana, Mississippi, North Carolina,

South Carolina, Tennessee, Texas, and Virginia) plus Kentucky and Oklahoma.

The fortunes of the conservative coalition reflected the strength of divisions in the Democratic Party. The origins of the coalition are found in the opposition to President Franklin Roosevelt's proposal in 1937 to expand the size of the Supreme Court in order to facilitate friendlier rulings on his New Deal proposals. Divisions in the Democratic Party tended to be sectional in character, with southern members being more conservative on many economic and social issues, especially those involving race. This conservatism made for ready coalitions with Republicans, although many Republicans held more progressive positions on civil rights issues than southern Democrats.

The conservative coalition's fate became increasingly intertwined with the electoral fortunes of Republicans in the South. The coalition's death knell came in 1965 with the adoption of the VOTING RIGHTS ACT. The effect of the act was to radically change the constituency of both parties in the once Democratic solid South. An influx of African-American voters into the Democratic Party meant that candidates seeking nomination as Democrats had to move substantially to the left to win renomination. This helped force the erosion of the old southern Democratic coalition of working-class and affluent whites. With the end of segregation and the enfranchisement of African Americans, conservative southern voters started abandoning the region's traditional party for the Republicans. The election of Ronald Reagan to the presidency briefly arrested the steady decline in the number of votes on which the coalition formed. Reagan ran well in the South, and many southern Democrats, or Boll Weevils, supported his budget, tax, and defense proposals in 1981.

The conservative coalition continued to fade by the late 1980s as intraparty unity among Democrats increased, although it successfully formed in 1993 to pass the North American Free Trade Agreement. The coalition continued to enjoy residual success on social issues such as school prayer, sex education, and gay rights through 1994. After Republicans took control of Congress in 1995, the coalition's relevance ended for the foreseeable future as Republicans no longer need the votes of southern Democrats to pass their bills.

The formal rules of the House and Senate greatly facilitated the ability of the conservative coalition to shape policy outcomes. Southern Democrats controlled a disproportionate number of committee chairs in both chambers. Reliance on seniority as the mechanism for assigning committee chairs coupled with the lack of effective party opposition in the South and the incumbent-friendly nature of candidate-centered elections in the region meant that southern Democrats were overrepresented among the senior members of both Democratic caucuses. Given that chairs enjoyed a wide variety of powers, including that to set the agenda of their committees, most liberal bills on major issues either languished in committee or faced substantial revision in order to pass.

The HOUSE, COMMITTEE ON RULES came to exemplify the institutional power of the conservative coalition. Chaired by Howard W. Smith, a Democrat from Virginia, from 1955 to 1967 but long dominated by the Smith-led conservative coalition, Rules became the graveyard of liberal legislation. The committee could force changes in bills in return for granting favorable rules for floor debate or any rule at all. Smith frequently refused to grant a hearing for bills opposed by the coalition. The most controversial act of the committee during this period was to deny the House a rule in 1960 to allow the House to go to conference with the Senate on a major bill that would dramatically increase federal aid to education. Flouting the House and Senate, Smith brought the wrath of liberal and moderate Democrats down on himself and the conservative coalition dominating the committee. Following a major gain in seats in the North during the 1958 election, the region and ideological centers of gravity in the Democratic caucus shifted dramatically, weakening Smith's procedural majority that allowed the committee to act as an obstruction to congressional majorities.

In 1961 these Democrats, President John F. Kennedy, and Democratic Speaker SAMUEL RAYBURN of Texas successfully defeated the bipartisan coalition that had tacitly supported Smith. In that year a change to the House's rules representing leadership accountability to the majority and to the majority party took the first step to curb the power of the conservative coalition on the Rules Committee by increasing the size of the committee from 12 to 15 members. The additional members were more trustworthy Democrats who helped defeat Smith and the conservatives dominating the committee.

Subsequent reforms in the House likewise reduced the influence of the conservative coalition. The most important were changes in the Democratic rules regarding the selection of committee chairs when the Democrats held the majority. Previously determined by seniority and challengeable only by an awkward mechanism in the Democratic caucus, beginning in 1975 Democrats could call for a secret ballot in the caucus on the selection of individual chairs. In the first year of use three conservative chairs were dethroned and replaced by much more mainstream Democrats. The lesson was learned quickly and well: Conservative Democratic chairs increasingly looked to represent the center of their caucus, and their floor voting patterns quickly became indistinguishable from mainstream Democrats. The institutional basis of the conservative coalition in the House was eroding.

In the prereform Senate a combination of rules and norms biased outcomes in the direction of the conservative coalition. Respect for seniority in making committee assignments meant that senior members tended to dominate the more significant committees while junior members were overrepresented on minor committees. Given that southern Democrats enjoyed on average greater seniority than their northern colleagues, the conservative coalition tended to dominate the writing of major legislation.

Senate norms likewise frustrated liberals and bolstered coalition influence. The norm of legislative work held that senators should devote the bulk of their time to committee work and the floor at the expense of personal publicity. The effect was to dampen attempts to seek publicity for personal gain or the advancement of liberal issues. Similarly, the norm of specialization held that senators should focus on their committees' jurisdictions and on issues directly pertaining to their constituents. The result was to dampen the influence of junior liberal Democrats on significant legislation. Courtesy required that political conflicts not become personal, while reciprocity meant that senators were to keep bargains and obligingly help colleagues whenever possible. These norms diffused ideological conflict. The apprenticeship norm held that junior senators were to restrain themselves from full participation in the work of the Senate while learning how the institution operated, thus limiting challenges to the stasis of the institution. Lastly, institutional loyalty meant that members were expected to extol the virtues of the Senate and uphold its claims to being the world's greatest deliberative body, even if the institution frustrated any attempt to markedly change national policy.

What underlaid these norms was the power of the Senate's conservative coalition to filibuster liberal legislation. Were a liberal senator to challenge any of these norms and attempt to submit a liberal bill in a major policy area such as labor rights, the bill would die in a coalition-dominated committee. If that same member attempted to offer his or her measure as an amendment to another bill, the amendment would meet with a FILIBUSTER. Repeated attempts to upset the policy equilibrium of the chamber would be met with a potential cutoff of attributable benefits to the member's state, damaging the member's reelection chances.

Successful challenge to the conservative coalition's power in the Senate came in the same form as that in the House, an influx of new members who found the institution's folkways stifling. The first formal rules change came with the rise of LYNDON JOHNSON of Texas to the post of Democratic MAJORITY LEADER in 1955. He quickly instituted the Johnson rule, which guaranteed every Democrat irrespective of seniority an assignment to a major committee. Combined with an influx of liberals beginning with the 1958 election, norms that favored limited participation by liberals and enhanced the prerogatives of conservatives fell by the wayside. The conservative coalition became increasingly less likely to form as electoral shifts produced either increasingly less conservative southern Democrats or southern Republicans uninterested in forming coalitions with Democrats. Lastly, changes in the Senate's rules dropping the votes needed to invoke cloture from two-thirds of senators present and voting to three-fifths of the Senate (60 votes) made it more difficult for southern Democrats to successfully filibuster civil rights bills.

While conservative coalition voting blocs may continue to form in Congress on occasional bills, their significance to the passage of legislation on the floor depends on the cohesiveness of the parties and which party is the majority. Should the Republicans maintain a majority in a chamber and remain highly cohesive, they will not need southern Democratic votes to pass bills.

Further reading:
Binder, Sarah A., and Steven S. Smith. *Politics or Principle: Filibustering in the United States Senate.* Washington, D.C.: Brookings Institution Press, 1997; *Congressional Quarterly Almanac.* Washington, D.C.: Congressional Quarterly Press; Dierenfield, Bruce J. *Keeper of the House: Congressman Howard W. Smith of Virginia.* Charlottesville: University of Virginia Press, 1987; Rohde, David W. *Parties and Leaders in the House.* Chicago: University of Chicago Press, 1991; Rohde, David, Norman J. Ornstein, and Robert L. Peabody. "Political Change and Legislative Norms in the U.S. Senate, 1957–1974." In *Studies in Congress,* edited by Glenn R. Parker, Washington, D.C.: Congressional Quarterly Press 1985.

—William Kubik

contempt of Congress

Contempt of Congress is the power of Congress to jail persons who refuse to cooperate in its investigations or who threaten the legislative process. The process of being held in contempt of Congress begins when a congressional committee reports a resolution specifying the reasons for the contempt charge. The House or Senate must adopt the resolution. After the relevant chamber approves a resolution recommended by one of its committees, the matter is referred to a U.S. attorney. The U.S. attorney may take the case to a grand jury to consider indicting the individual. The punishment for contempt of Congress is no more than one year in prison and/or $1,000 in fines.

The Supreme Court has upheld the power of Congress to hold people in contempt. In *Anderson v. Dunn,* the Court recognized the inherent contempt power of Congress. The power included the ability of the House and the Senate to punish contempt by jailing an individual. The Court limited this power when it specified that imprisonment could not extend beyond the adjournment of Congress. This limitation on the contempt power was removed when in 1857 Congress enacted a statute (2 U.S. Code 192) outlining the current procedure. The statute limits contempt citations to matters relating to legislative purposes and that fall within the jurisdiction of the affected committee. Contempt citations primarily have been issued for reasons of refusing to testify or failing to provide Congress with requested documents or answers. Citations also can be issued for bribing or libeling a member of Congress.

During the cold war and congressional investigations of communism, the House UN-AMERICAN ACTIVITIES COMMITTEE (HUAC) regularly issued contempt citations. In September 1947 the HUAC interviewed 41 people who were working in Hollywood. These witnesses provided the names of several people who they accused of holding left-wing views, but 10 of the accused, known as the "Hollywood Ten," refused to answer any questions. They claimed that the Fifth Amendment of the U.S. Constitution gave them the right to refuse to cooperate. The HUAC disagreed and found the 10 in contempt. The Hollywood Ten lost on appeal to the courts and each was sentenced to six to 12 months in prison.

During the cold war the Supreme Court changed its position on the ability of Congress to force witnesses to testify. In *Watkins v. United States* the Court stated that a witness could be held in contempt only for not answering questions that were relevant to the investigation. The Court moved away from that position in *BARENBLATT V. UNITED STATES,* stating that Congress had a significant interest in learning about Barenblatt's activities and could compel the witness to provide information.

The House Energy and Commerce Committee voted in 1982 to hold Secretary of the Interior James Watt in contempt for refusing to turn over subpoenaed documents. Environmental Protection Agency administrator Anne Gorsuch Burford was held in contempt by the House for refusing to provide documents on the Superfund project. Burford was not prosecuted after the administration of President Ronald Reagan agreed to allow access to the requested documents.

In 1998 the House Government Reform and Oversight Committee voted along party lines to cite U.S. attorney general Janet Reno for contempt of Congress for refusing to release internal memos relating to the investigation of 1996 campaign financing abuses by the Clinton reelection campaign. The House adjourned before acting on the issue.

Further reading:
Beck, Carl. *Contempt of Congress: A Study of the Prosecutions Initiated by the Committee on Un-American Activities, 1945–1957.* New Orleans: Hauser Printing, 1959; House Committee on the Judiciary, *Clarifying the Investi-*

gatory Power of the United States Congress. Washington, D.C.: Government Printing Office, 1988.

—John David Rausch, Jr.

continuing resolutions

A continuing resolution (CR), also known as a stopgap spending bill, provides temporary money for federal agencies whose annual APPROPRIATIONS BILLS have not been passed by Congress and signed by the president by the start of each new fiscal year on October 1. CRs are a common occurrence because it is highly unusual for Congress and the president to pass all 13 appropriations bills by the start of the new fiscal year. At least one CR has been enacted every year since 1954 except for 1988, when the final appropriations bill passed one minute before the start of the new fiscal year. A CR can be as brief as 24 hours, or it can set the spending levels for agencies for the rest of the fiscal year by replacing the appropriations bill. This occurred often during the 1980s and in fiscal year 1996, when Congress funded selective programs for the remainder of the fiscal year.

Continuing resolutions are negotiated and bargained over. Sometimes the funding levels of agencies in the CR are determined by a simple formula of temporarily funding them at the lowest of the House-passed appropriations bill, or the Senate-passed bill, or the previous year's spending level. Washington insiders refer to this formula as the Michel Rule, after former Minority Leader Bob Michel, a Republican from Illinois, who offered the formula as a way to fund CRs during the 1990 budget battle. The fiscal year 1996 budget battle suggests that the Michel Rule would be abandoned when there were large differences between the president and Congress over program spending levels. The first fiscal year 1996 continuing resolution (H.J. Res 108, PL 104-31) abandoned the Michel Rule when it funded agencies at no less than 90 percent of the previous year's level even if both the House and Senate voted to zero the agency out. The continuing resolution President Bill Clinton vetoed (H.J. Res 115) called for some agencies to function at no less than 60 percent of the previous year's level. The fourth continuing resolution of the fiscal year (H.J. Res 122, PL 104-56) funded agencies at 75 percent of the previous year's level if Congress zeroed them out. Other agencies in the bill were funded according to the Michel Rule. The remaining 10 continuing resolutions for fiscal year 1996 followed the same agreement of 75 percent for zeroed out programs and funding levels determined by the Michel Rule for the remaining programs.

Since 1980, failure to pass a CR or an appropriations bill has led to a government shutdown. In 1980 President Jimmy Carter's administration, in reevaluating a law passed in 1870, the Anti-deficiency Act, ruled that agencies without appropriations had to close operations. The 1870 law said that "[I]t shall not be lawful for any department of the government to expend in any one fiscal year any sum in excess of appropriations made by Congress for that fiscal year, or to involve the government in any contract for the future payment of money in excess of appropriations." The Carter administration's ruling of the 1870 Anti-deficiency Act required agencies without appropriations to shut down immediately.

The first agency to ever shut down from a lapse in appropriations was the Federal Trade Commission (FTC). The FTC shut down for one day in 1980 because Congress refused to pass a full-year appropriation for the agency until it had authorizing legislation. President Ronald Reagan's administration used the shutdown guidelines the following year when Reagan vetoed a continuing resolution that resulted in a three-day broader government shutdown. The government has shut down (partially) a total of at least 11 times since 1980; the fiscal year 1996 budget battle included two lengthy government shutdowns. To avoid or end a government shutdown, the president and Congress must pass either the regular appropriations bill or a continuing resolution.

Further reading:
Fenno, Richard F. Jr. *The Power of the Purse: Appropriations Politics in Congress.* Boston: Little, Brown, 1966; Schick, Allen. *The Federal Budget: Politics, Policy, Process.* Washington, D.C.: Brookings Institution Press, 1995.

—Charles Tien

Contract with America

The Contract with America was a 10-point legislative agenda on which Republican candidates ran for the House of Representatives in 1994. It was highly unusual, in that political parties in the United States (unlike in parliamentary systems) do not have a platform on which congressional candidates run. Instead, elections focus on individual candidates, who take their own stands on various issues. The 1994 election was different, however. Perhaps because Republicans had been the minority party in the House for 40 years (Republicans briefly controlled the Senate during the Reagan years), or perhaps because partisan animosity toward Democratic president Bill Clinton was so strong, Republicans decided on a new strategy. Led by Representative Newt Gingrich (R-GA), they developed a platform and pledged to vote on it in the first 100 days of the 104th Congress. In a surprising and overwhelming upset, Republicans took the majority in both houses of Congress (as well as in state governorships). The Contract with America served as a "mandate," or marching orders, for the newly elected majority. Although most Americans were not familiar with the contract when they cast their votes in the congressional elections that year, they voted for Republicans in large numbers. Republicans in the House, already energized by their historic victory, were able to focus that energy on a specific legislative plan, one that clearly distinguished them from Democrats in Congress (and the White House, for that matter). And the newly elected Speaker Gingrich was intent on pushing the contract as quickly as possible.

The contract came about as a result of a political retreat in early 1994 for Republican congressional candidates. Gingrich and Representative Dick Armey (R-TX), who became House Speaker and Majority Leader, respectively, pushed for a platform on which candidates could run. The platform, developed from legislative proposals that had died in previous Democratic Congresses, was geared toward policies that polled well with the public. It included eight procedural reforms and 10 legislative items. On September 27, 1994, 367 Republican candidates signed the contract on the steps of the U.S. Capitol, pledging to bring it to a vote immediately if they won the majority in November.

The preface of the contract contained proposed changes in the way Congress would do business (procedural reforms). These were partly a reaction against Democratic control, under which Republicans had chafed for decades. Among other things, the procedural reforms would require that Congress become subject to the same workplace and nondiscrimination laws as any other workplace; that there would be fewer committees, with their staffs cut by one-third, meetings open to the public, and chairs term-limited; and that a three-fifths majority (rather than a simple majority) would be required to enact tax increases.

The remainder of the contract was devoted to 10 legislative issues (or 10 "planks" of the platform): 1) the Fiscal Responsibility Act (proposing a line-item veto and a balanced-budget amendment), 2) the Taking Back Our Streets Act (crime-prevention legislation), 3) the Personal Responsibility Act (welfare reform), 4) the Family Reinforcement Act (tax breaks for families, among other things) 5) the American Dream Restoration Act (repealing the "marriage penalty" in taxes and creating a child tax credit), 6) the National Security Act (strengthening defense), 7) the Senior Fairness Act (expanding Social Security benefits), 8) the Job Creation and Wage Enhancement Act (policies to assist small businesses and elimination of "unfunded mandates"), 9) the Common Sense Legal Reforms Act (intended to reduce litigation), and 10) the Citizen Legislatures Act (limiting congressional terms).

Although the contract received much media attention as it wended its way through the 104th Congress, its lasting effects were somewhat limited. The procedural reforms, as promised, were enacted on the first day of the new Congress (causing the House to be in session until 2 A.M.), and, also as promised, every single one of the 10 planks was voted on in the first 100 days. The Republican Party, in a remarkable show of party unity in the United States, voted overwhelmingly for the contract items (indeed, in 73 of the first 139 roll call votes, the Republican Party was unanimous). But if one examined closely the Republicans promise in the contract, one discovered that it was not a matter of passing legislation, but merely of bringing it to a vote. Of course, a favorable vote in the House was all but guaranteed, given the unity among the new Republican majority. Even so, enough House Republicans defected on an anti–ballistic missile bill, part of the National Security Act, to kill that particular provision. It is important to remember that in order to become law, a bill must be passed in identical form by both houses of Congress and be signed by the president. No matter how much unity he commanded in the House, Speaker Gingrich could not control the Senate or, obviously, the president. The Senate, which considers itself a more deliberative body, was in no rush to push through the House contract legislation. In fact, although the contract was signed by every Republican running for a House seat, it was not signed by any senators, who felt no compunction to act on it within 100 days or even within the 104th Congress, for that matter.

The House of Representatives acted a bit like a parliamentary system when it pushed through its legislative platform, but it was stymied by the American system of checks and balances. At the end of the 104th Congress, only three items had been signed into law: welfare reform, the line-item veto, and the elimination of "unfunded mandates" (federal requirements for state and business actions for which they are not compensated). President Clinton used his veto only once on contract legislation, on a welfare reform bill which was later retooled and eventually signed by him. And the line-item veto was ultimately declared unconstitutional by the Supreme Court, which said it gave the president too much legislative power, a violation of the separation of powers.

The Contract with America was a significant event in the life of the United States Congress. Its procedural reforms have changed greatly the way Congress does business, and it served as a unifying, even nationalizing, force for the Republican Party. Its real importance, however, may be found in the limits of its success. The framers of the Constitution intended that Congress *not* be subject to quick change. The system of checks and balances that they set up, giving power to the minority, allowing one chamber of Congress to be a brake on the other, and giving both the president and Supreme Court some power over legislative action ensured that the contract, or any other massive legislative changes, would be slowed, stymied, and ultimately limited.

Further reading:
Davidson, Roger H., and Walter J. Oleszek, eds. *The 104th Congress: A Congressional Quarterly Reader*. Washington,

D.C.: Congressional Quarterly Press, 1995; Gillespie, Ed, and Bob Schellhas. *Contract with America: The Bold Plan by Rep. Newt Gingrich, Rep. Dick Armey and the House Republicans to Change the Nation.* New York: Times Books, 1994; Gimpel, James J. *Fulfilling the Contract: The First 100 Days.* Boston: Allyn & Bacon, 1996; Manuel, Paul C., and Anne Marie Cammisa. *Checks and Balances: How a Parliamentary System Could Change American Politics.* Boulder, Colo.: Westview Press, 1999.

—Anne Marie Cammissa

Cook v. Gralike et al. 531 U.S. 510 (2001)

In *U.S. TERM LIMITS V. THORNTON* the U.S. Supreme Court dealt a critical blow to the term limits movement by ruling that states could not impose term limits on members of Congress. In response to this ruling Missouri amended article VIII of its constitution in 1996 to promote the establishment of congressional term limits at the federal level. Article VIII directs all members of the state's delegation to the U.S. Congress to "use all of [their] delegated powers to pass the Congressional Term Limits Amendment advocated by the State. Should a Senator or Representative fail to take one of eight acts outlined in Article VIII, then DISREGARDED VOTER INSTRUCTION ON TERM LIMITS shall be posted next to his/her name on the next electoral ballot. Similarly, any candidate for Congress from Missouri refusing to sign a term limit pledge shall have the statement DECLINED TO PLEDGE TO SUPPORT TERM LIMITS next to his/her name on the ballot." Article VIII was dubbed the Scarlet Letter provision by the state's own general counsel and several members of the judiciary.

Ruling in favor of Gralike, a candidate for the U.S. House, the district judge, a unanimous 6th Circuit panel, and a unanimous Supreme Court rejected Missouri's attempted end-run around the *Thornton* decision. The Court ruled that eligibility to hold national legislative office was established in the Qualifications Clause, Article I, 4, cl.1, of the Constitution and cannot be altered by the states. In addition, mandating a term limit pledge violates the First Amendment rights of candidates and legislatures by requiring them to take a particular substantive position or suffer electoral disadvantage.

—Daniel Smith

Court-packing fight

President Franklin D. Roosevelt (FDR) wanted to demonstrate that the American political system was responsive to the Great Depression during an otherwise totalitarian era in world history. The NEW DEAL was his ad hoc and experimental public policy agenda launched during his first presidential term. Riding the crest of his 1936 landslide reelection, he quickly set in motion legislation to expand and strengthen the executive branch of government while developing a plan that would prevent the Supreme Court from declaring further acts of the New Deal unconstitutional. It was quickly dubbed FDR's Court-packing plan.

FDR's first attorney general, Homer S. Cummings, secretly drafted the plan after the president agreed that it would take too long to enact a constitutional amendment to limit the Court's power or to give Congress additional power. Cummings cloaked the proposal's real purpose by broadening the legislation to allow for 44 new judges on the lower federal benches and up to six additional Supreme Court justices. It covered everyone with 10 years of service who did not retire within six months after reaching the age of 70, and six of the sitting nine justices were already older than 70. Besides the president, the attorney general, and two of his top assistants, only Solicitor General Stanley F. Reed and Robert H. Jackson, Reed's subsequent replacement, knew of the plan.

Court enlargement schemes had precedents dating from the Lincoln and Grant administrations. Ironically, the previous attempt to assure a younger judiciary had been made in 1913 by James C. McReynolds, then Woodrow Wilson's attorney general, who was now one of the four most conservative and elderly activists on the Court, the so-called Four Horsemen, a designation suggesting the legendary Four Horsemen of the Apocalypse. The conservative bloc voted consistently against New Deal economic and social legislation.

FDR announced the proposal to a stunned Congress on February 5, 1937. Immediately, Republicans and then newspaper editors and the organized bar came out against the plan. Nonetheless, it attracted considerable support among Democrats. Hatton W. Sumners, a Democrat from Texas and chair of the HOUSE JUDICIARY COMMITTEE, favored the retirement of senior justices, and Henry F. Ashurst, a Democrat from Arkansas and chair of the SENATE JUDICIARY COMMITTEE, initially favored the proposal. It was supported by several future justices in Congress and the administration, for example, Fred Vinson, Solicitor General Stanley F. Reed, and his successor, Robert H. Jackson, who was later an attorney general and who helped prepare the president's March 9 fireside chat justifying the proposal. Ultimately, FDR was counting on the popular leadership of Senate Majority Leader Joseph T. Robinson, a Democrat from Arkansas, to carry the Senate fight. It was made clear that Robinson would be the president's first nominee to the reconstituted Court.

Beyond this institutional support, Democrats were divided on the issue. The bipartisan opposition was led by Burton K. Wheeler, a Democrat from Montana, who had first attracted national attention that forced the resignation of Harry M. Daughterty, Warren Harding's attorney general. Wheeler had been the first national figure to endorse FDR, but the Court-packing plan led to their permanent break. Wheeler became the model of the senatorial hero in Frank Capra's classic 1939 movie *Mr. Smith Goes to Washington.*

The ultimate fate of the bill was doomed after four nearly simultaneous strikes against it. First, in late March 1937, under the leadership of Charles Evans Hughes, the Supreme Court suddenly began to reverse itself on New Deal measures. Second, on May 18 conservative activist Justice Willis Van DeVanter, one of the Four Horsemen, announced his retirement. That same day the Senate Judiciary Committee released its negative report on the bill. Finally, Robinson suffered a fatal heart attack on July 14 only eight hours after the formal Senate debate began. Just as suddenly, a group of freshman Democratic senators announced opposition, while others no longer felt bound to their previous pledges to Robinson. On July 22 Senator Mavel Logan, a Democrat from Kentucky, moved that the bill be recommitted to the Judiciary Committee. As a face-saving measure, on August 26 FDR signed the Judiciary Procedures Reform Act, which reformed lower court procedures without mentioning judicial enlargement.

It was a costly and unnecessary first political blunder for an activist administration. The president would have been better off withdrawing the bill after the Court modified its stance. The controversy postponed for more than two years FDR's plan to strengthen and reorganize the executive branch, and it also weakened the New Deal coalition by contributing to the rise of the CONSERVATIVE COALITION of southern Democrats and Republicans. Ironically, the president, who was unable to name a single justice to the Court during his first term, would eventually name more justices than any president since George Washington, and he did so in a way that did pack the Court.

Further reading:
Jackson, Robert H. *That Man. An Insider's Portrait of Franklin D. Roosevelt.* New York: Oxford University Press, 2003; Leuchtenburg, William E. *The Supreme Court Reborn: The Constitutional Revolution in the Age of Roosevelt.* New York: Oxford University Press, 1995; McKenna, Marian C. *Franklin D. Roosevelt and the Great Constitutional War. The Court-Packing Crisis of 1937.* Bronx, N.Y.: Fordham University Press, 2002; Shaw, Stephen K., William D. Pederson, and Frank J. Williams, eds. *Franklin D. Roosevelt and the Transformation of the Supreme Court.* Armonk, N.Y.: M. E. Sharpe, 2003.
—William D. Pederson

courts and Congress
Understanding the relationship between the federal courts and Congress begins with an appreciation of the constitu-

tional framework established for creating and operating the two branches. Article III of the U.S. Constitution established the Supreme Court but granted Congress the power to create any inferior courts it deemed necessary to administer justice. All courts created under this authority to handle the general trial and appellate matters in the federal system are called Article III, or constitutional courts, to distinguish them from courts established to address a specific congressional power under Article I of the Constitution. These specific jurisdiction Article I, or legislative courts, were established by Congress to carry out specific powers under Article I, Section 8, of the Constitution. The primary legislative courts currently include the tax court, court of veteran appeals, court of federal claims, and court of military appeals, whose jurisdictions are not wholly legal in nature but include some more legislative tasks. For instance, the tax court handles complaints against Internal Revenue Service decisions.

Not only has Congress been given the power to create the lower federal courts, it also has the ability to control the appellate jurisdictions of the courts. Thus, Congress can change the types of cases that the federal courts are allowed to review. Congress and the courts interact in a number of other ways mandated by the Constitution. In the realm of impeachment there are two types of interactions. First, judges may retain their seats on good behavior, thereby making impeachment the only recourse for Congress to remove a federal judge from office. A recent example of a federal judge who was impeached and removed from the bench is that of Walter L. Nixon, Jr., a district court judge from Mississippi (*Nixon v. United States,* 506 U.S. 224, 1993). In the case of impeachment of the president, the chief justice of the Supreme Court presides over the trial in the Senate, as was the case when William Rehnquist presided over the IMPEACHMENT OF PRESIDENT BILL CLINTON in 1999. The final constitutionally established relationship between Congress and the courts dictates that the Senate must confirm all nominations to the federal bench.

In accord with its constitutional mandate, early Congresses quickly established an extensive federal judicial system in support of the Supreme Court and clarified the jurisdiction of the federal courts. The Judiciary Act of 1789 established the lower federal district and appellate courts and granted them specific powers to hear cases, but not the full range of powers listed in Article II of the Constitution. The structure of the original system remains largely unchanged as courts were added to meet the needs of a growing nation. The Judiciary Act of 1789 also created six seats on the Supreme Court because the Constitution did not establish the number of justices. Over the years the number of justices fluctuated between five and 11 until 1869, when the current number of nine justices was approved. No changes have been made since that time.

However, occasionally a president or members of Congress have made largely political threats to change the size of the Supreme Court. The most notable such effort was the COURT-PACKING plan proposed by Franklin D. Roosevelt in the late 1930s.

The Constitution does not establish the right of either the Court or Congress to interpret the Constitution or statutes. That power was claimed by the Supreme Court in the case of *MARBURY V. MADISON* (1803). Chief Justice John Marshall, writing for the Court, asserted that the power of judicial review of constitutional provisions and statutes rested with the Court. This decision created a balance of power between the Court and Congress that remains largely unchanged today. The creation of judicial review has not always allowed for smooth relations between the Court and Congress. However, rarely has Congress completely disregarded a constitutional ruling by the Supreme Court.

The two separate interpretive functions of the Court have given rise to different reactions from Congress. The statutory interpretation role of the Court means that Congress has the ability to clarify the Court's decisions or even correct them when an error is perceived. As the lawmaking body, Congress may either amend a statute or even completely rewrite it. The Court must then rule on the new, presumably clearer, language in the statute. There has been much debate among legal scholars concerning what factors should be considered when interpreting a statute. Some, including Chief Justice William Rehnquist, have advocated the use of any information that might better inform a justice's decisions, including the legislative history and committee reports of the statute. The idea has been to understand the expressed intent of the enacting legislature. Arguing against the use of legislative history have been Justices Antonin Scalia and Clarence Thomas. They have asserted that since the legislature did not enact the legislative history or committee reports as part of the law, those sources cannot be consulted. They would look to the plain meaning of the statute as the guide to interpretation. Neither of these approaches has assured that the Court's interpretation would be accepted by Congress. Congress has been known to incorporate harsh reprimands of judicial decisions when they were forced to revisit a statute to correct what they thought to be errant interpretations of the Court. The Court, on the other hand, has tended to view this process as necessary for ensuring stable and clear laws. In fact, there is some evidence that when Congress has failed to act or has been less than clear in its pronouncements, the Court would issue statements in opinions refusing to correct grossly unfair statutes and tell Congress that it needed to fix the problems.

On the other side have been the constitutional interpretations of statutes. When the Supreme Court has ruled that a statute contained language violating some provision of the Constitution, Congress has been left with little recourse to correct the error. In many instances efforts to alter the language of a statute to avoid the constitutional issues have been insufficient. For example, after the Supreme Court ruled in 1989 that burning the American flag was constitutionally protected speech (*Texas v. Johnson*), Congress attempted to rewrite the statute to bypass the constitutional issue. The Supreme Court struck down the new statute as unconstitutional as well (*United States v. Eichman*, 1992), leaving Congress with only one recourse—to amend the Constitution. Thus far, continued efforts to do so have failed. On rare occasion such efforts have succeeded, as was the case with the federal income tax struck down by the Court in *POLLOCK V. FARMER'S LOAN AND TRUST COMPANY* in 1895, with the Constitution amended 18 years later in 1913 with the adoption of the Sixteenth Amendment.

In a slightly different situation in which Congress did not need the courts for prosecution of statutory violations, Congress could choose to ignore the rulings of the Supreme Court, even when those rulings were made on constitutional grounds. This has rarely happened because doing so raises the separation of powers problem to a constitutional crisis. However, in at least one recent instance Congress has chosen to ignore a constitutional pronouncement of the Supreme Court. In the case of *INS v. Chadha* the Supreme Court ruled that legislative vetoes of executive decisions were an unconstitutional violation of the separation of powers doctrine. However, since then Congress has continued to include legislative veto provisions in grants of power to the executive branch. Although such provisions are unconstitutional, members of both the executive branch and Congress, normally for political reasons, have ignored the Court ruling.

This ever-present potential tension between the courts and Congress implies much conflict, but the norm largely has been one of cooperative effort. The Court has deferred to the position of the U.S. Solicitor General so much that the government's position wins much more often than any other litigant before the Court. This is important because the Solicitor General represents the government's position defending statutes and the position of Congress unless there is a conflict between Congress and the president on an issue, something that happens infrequently. The political question doctrine mentioned above also suggests that the Supreme Court will tend not to interfere with Congress's use of constitutionally mandated powers, although it is not reluctant to determine which powers are constitutionally mandated.

In substantive terms this has led to the Court determining that the House of Representatives may not refuse to seat a duly elected representative (*POWELL V. MCCORMACK*, 1969), but that the states cannot impose term limits on senators and representatives (*U.S. TERM LIMITS V. THORNTON*). The Supreme Court has time and again found that the SPEECH OR DEBATE CLAUSE (Article I, Section 6) insulates members of Congress from civil or criminal liability for statements made as part of their legislative duties, but not necessarily when similar statements are made in press conferences or news releases (*HUTCHINSON V. PROXMIRE*). The investigatory powers of Congress are wide reaching but not without limits as to scope, as the Court in *BARENBLATT V. UNITED STATES* proclaimed. While the Commerce Clause powers of Congress have been restricted and expanded many times since the 1920s, the Supreme Court has rarely restricted the legislative powers of Congress in most other areas.

In the end the two branches need each other's assistance for the smooth operation of the federal government. Without the power of judicial review in the federal courts, Congress would be required to be more specific in its statutory enactments to avoid ambiguous or incomplete language, which the federal courts currently address. When Congress has failed to act, it would otherwise have to revisit many statutory issues that are satisfactorily resolved through the courts. The courts, on the other hand, rely on Congress to shape statutes in such a way as to guide interpretation and to define the scope of their jurisdiction. While conflicts between the courts and Congress have most often been remembered, it is the congruence of their positions that more commonly has been the norm.

Further reading:
Barenblatt v. United States, 360 U.S. 109 (1959); Biskupic, Joan, and Elder Witt. *The Supreme Court and the Powers of the American Government*. Washington, D.C.: Congressional Quarterly Press, 1997; *Eichman v. United States*, 496 U.S. 310 (1992); *Hutchinson v. Proxmire*, 443 U.S. 111 (1979); *INS v. Chadha*, 462 U.S. 919 (1983); Katzmann, Robert A. *Courts and Congress*. Washington, D.C.: Brookings Institution Press, 1997; *Marbury v. Madison*, 5 U.S. 137 (1803); Murphy, Walter F. *Congress and the Court*. Chicago: University of Chicago Press, 1962; *Pollock v. Farmer's Loan and Trust Co.*, 157 U.S. 429 (1895); *Powell v. McCormack*, 395 U.S. 486 (1969); *Texas v. Johnson*, 491 U.S. 397 (1989); *U.S. Term Limits, Inc. v. Thornton*, 514 U.S. 779 (1995).

—Corey A. Ditslear

Credit Mobilier scandal

Among the many scandals that plagued American government during the Gilded Age, perhaps none was as egregious as the Credit Mobilier affair of 1863 to 1872. The construction of the transcontinental rail system, approved through the Pacific Railway Act of 1862, created a dangerous marriage between federally funded projects unprecedented in scope and private contractors who were awarded generous subsidies to complete the jobs. To build the first line the Central Pacific and Union Pacific Railroads were contracted to construct a transcontinental route from railheads on the Missouri River to California, with the federal government providing the land, generous loans, and subsidies to complete the line. Investors in these firms were already experienced in the art of blending private capital investment with government contracts and subsidies through often complex corporate structures that allowed the creation of substantial private profit from public money. What made the Credit Mobilier affair unique were its scale and the degree to which it involved corruption in the halls of Congress.

Credit Mobilier began as a federally chartered railroad bond agent called the Pennsylvania Fiscal Agency. Vice president of the Union Pacific Railroad Thomas Durant gained control of the company in 1863 and, along with a number of important investors, including Representative Oakes Ames from Massachusetts, engineered its transformation into a subsidiary of the Union Pacific Railroad that would manage financing and construction of the transcontinental line. The Union Pacific, whose principal shareholders were also the principal shareholders in the subsidiary, in effect contracted the construction of the line to themselves with payments to Credit Mobilier of approximately $60,000 per mile of construction. Within the first year of construction, it became apparent that the payments were terribly inflated when Peter Dey, the Union Pacific chief engineer, resigned in disgust over the financing. Ames, however, had softened concern in Washington by enticing at least 16 fellow members of Congress to buy stock in Credit Mobilier at prices well below the firm's rapidly growing market value. These included the SPEAKER OF THE HOUSE, SCHUYLER COLFAX, who subsequently won election to the vice presidency on the Grant ticket in 1868. Ames was so anxious to wed the operation to the private fortunes of his colleagues that he offered loans to several to buy the stock.

By the time the nation celebrated the driving of the final spike in the transcontinental line in 1869, investors in Credit Mobilier and the Union Pacific had amassed fortunes in federal subsidies, having charged by contemporary and modern estimates about double the actual cost of construction. The graft became public knowledge in 1872, when investor H. S. McComb filed affidavits in Pennsylvania court and the *New York Sun* published a story based on letters written by McComb that revealed the fraud. Facing public outrage, the HOUSE OF REPRESENTATIVES convened a committee to investigate the charges. Chaired by J. W. Wilson of Indiana, the committee determined that Credit Mobilier had overcharged the Union Pacific Railroad, and hence American taxpayers, by $23 million.

The repercussions were, for those directly involved, relatively limited. Ames was merely censured by the House, though he died a short time later a humiliated man. While some members of Congress talked of impeaching Vice President Colfax, fellow Republicans in charge determined that he could not be sanctioned as vice president for offenses committed while Speaker of the House. The affair ruined for certain, however, Colfax's already failing ambitions for the presidency. While a number of other members of Congress had participated in the scheme, only one other representative, Democrat James Brooks, was censured for his actions. The Credit Mobilier scandal later became the principal example of the corruption that surrounded the Grant administration and Reconstruction politics, inspiring movements for reform in the three decades that followed.

Further reading:
Les Benedict, Michael. *A Compromise of Principle: Congressional Republicans and Reconstruction 1863–1869.* New York: Norton, 1974; Foner, Eric. *Reconstruction: America's Unfinished Revolution.* New York: Harper & Row, 1988; Hoopes, Roy. "It Was Bad Last Time Too: The Credit Mobilier Scandal of 1872." *American Heritage* pp. 42, 58–60, February/March 1991; Summers, Mark Wahlgren. *The Era of Good Stealings.* New York: Oxford University Press, 1993.

—Michael Steiner

Crockett v. Reagan 720F 2d 1355, 1356

(DC, Cir 1983)
This case was brought by George Crockett, Jr., acting in his capacity as a member of the U.S. House of Representatives, against President Ronald Reagan. Representative Crockett, a Democrat from Michigan suing on behalf of the House of Representatives, charged that President Reagan willingly sent U.S. military officials and troops into El Salvador. Crockett charged that in making the decision to send military personnel into El Salvador, President Reagan failed to report to Congress in relation to these matters. Crockett sued based on the contention that President Reagan's failure to report to Congress was a violation of both the WAR POWERS RESOLUTION and the War Powers Clause noted in the Constitution.

Crockett, on behalf of the House, was seeking an immediate injunction as a remedy to this situation. This injunction would direct the United States to withdraw immediately all U.S. armed forces, weapons, military equipment, and aid from El Salvador. The injunction would also prohibit any further aid of any nature. The case origi-

nated in the U.S. District Court for the District of Columbia. The court ruled in favor of President Reagan. The U.S. Court of Appeals for the District of Columbia later heard the case and affirmed the decision of the district court. Circuit Judge Robert Bork wrote the opinion of the appellate court. Judge Bork argued that Crockett lacked the proper standing necessary to sue in this matter. The component of standing that was lacking from Crockett's argument was that of injury-in-fact. Bork wrote that in order to make a legitimate claim for diminishing congressional influence on behalf of a member of Congress, which would constitute the necessary component of injury-in-fact, that member of Congress must prove that there has been a virtual nullification of his or her vote.

In this case the appellate court did not see any indication that the plaintiff had lost any part of his right to vote, and therefore had not suffered any cognizable injury that would give him the necessary components of standing that would allow him to sue. Additionally, Bork altered case law by establishing that separation of powers considerations are properly addressed as part of the standing requirement. Previously, the district court had maintained that separation of powers would have no bearing on the analysis of standing and instead devised and implemented a "doctrine of equitable discretion" to address concerns of separation of powers. Bork attested that the two court panels, which operated under this doctrine of equitable discretion, were attempting to change the law without submitting the issue to the full court. Therefore, Bork felt in no way obligated to follow this lead and to return to the original practice of including separation of powers into the standing requirement.

Crockett appealed to the U.S. Supreme Court, where it was denied certiorari, and the decision of the court of appeals stood. The underlying result that can be derived from this case is that the judicial system is refusing to answer questions of a political nature. This case is only one of a series of cases that resonates these sentiments of the judiciary's hands-off approach to politics.

Further reading:
Crockett v. Reagan, 720 F. 2d 1355, 1356 (DC Cir. 1983).

—Nancy S. Lind

C-SPAN

C-SPAN is the acronym for Cable-Satellite Public Affairs Network and was the brainchild of Brian Lamb. In the course of his career in politics and the media, Lamb became concerned that the dominance of the three major networks gave the public only part of the information they needed to be informed citizens. He felt that the growth of cable television in the 1970s provided a unique opportunity to furnish the American public programming about public affairs that would not be filtered by traditional media outlets. Because of his efforts, the cable industry started C-SPAN, a nonprofit corporation. It is not funded by the government or by commercial advertising, but by subscription fees from the cable services that carry it.

C-SPAN began broadcasting gavel-to-gavel coverage of the House of Representatives in 1979 and of the Senate in 1986. Today C-SPAN offers three networks. C-SPAN offers full coverage of the House of Representatives. C-SPAN2 features coverage of the Senate, and C-SPAN3 focuses on more general public affairs and historical programming. In addition, there are C-SPAN Radio and C-SPAN.org, where all the networks can be accessed, viewed, and heard over the Internet. Besides offering live coverage of the floor proceedings of the House and Senate, C-SPAN offers government briefings, committee hearings, policy conferences, call-in programs, *Booknotes,* and other original programming such as *American Presidents* and *America & the Courts.* According to the C-SPAN Web site, its coverage of floor debates from the House of Representatives today makes up only 13 percent of its total programming.

The C-SPAN Web site boasts that more homes now receive C-SPAN (85,000,000) than MTV and that its viewers voted at a rate of 90 percent in the 2000 election. C-SPAN's effect has been large. First, it has provided a source of unfiltered information on public affairs for politically active citizens. C-SPAN has shed light on processes that were largely inaccessible to most of the American public. It has even spawned the phenomenon of C-SPAN "junkies," viewers who routinely watch the coverage of the American political system in action and take note of what elected officials are doing. Second, members of Congress recognize the importance of the television cameras in their chambers. Members and their offices monitor floor debate through C-SPAN and keep track of events as they are happening without having physically to be in the chamber. It has allowed politically savvy members of Congress, such as Newt Gingrich in the 1980s and early 1990s, to build public followings that would have taken them much longer to establish if they had had to rely solely on traditional media or the seniority dominated structure of Congress. Today, members of Congress routinely take to the floor with visual props designed for the C-SPAN audience.

Finally, C-SPAN has changed the nature of journalism in the United States. It provides an alternative outlet for both the news and journalists. C-SPAN creates a permanent record of the happenings of Congress that other media outlets can turn to should they feel a story warrants mainstream attention. Journalists also have a forum that allows them to experiment with news formats. Larry King was able to expand his exposure to a national audience when C-SPAN began broadcasting his radio talk show. C-SPAN has also alleviated some mediating effects of journalists. Viewers are provided access to a direct look at events.

Further reading:
C-SPAN.org. Available online: URL: http://www.cspan.org. Accessed 15 April 2000; Frantzich, Stephen. "Don't Get Mad, Get Evenhanded." In *Citizen Democracy.* Lanham, Md.: Rowman & Littlefield, 1999; Frantzich, Stephen, and John Sullivan. *The C-SPAN Revolution.* Norman: University of Oklahoma Press, 1996.
—Donna R. Hoffman

customs and mores of Congress

In 1984 Speaker Tip O'Neill learned that the Speaker could be called to account for improper speech. Georgia representative Newt Gingrich provoked Speaker O'Neill by disparaging the patriotism of Democratic members of the House. O'Neill left his seat on dais, an action rarely taken by a Speaker, to move to the podium in the well to take Gingrich to task. After gaining recognition, O'Neill angrily stated that the Republican's statement was "the lowest thing I have ever seen in my thirty-two years in Congress." A Republican House member rose and demanded that O'Neill's words be taken down or stricken from the record. The House Parliamentarian ruled against O'Neill, finding that the Speaker had violated the prohibition against personal insult. For the first time since 1789, a Speaker of the House was chastised for his language.

Some observers have noted an increase in incivility in the Congress, especially in the House. While there has been an increase in the number of times words are "taken down," incidents of physical assault are rare. There was one reported case of physical assault in 1985. New York representative Thomas J. Downey allegedly accosted California representative Robert Dornan by grabbing Dornan's shoulder and spinning him around to demand whether Dornan had referred to him as a "draft-dodging wimp" in a floor speech. Dornan reacted to Downey's attack by grabbing the New Yorker by the necktie and hoisting him off the floor. Neither member was punished.

The casual observer of Congress might be surprised to learn that several famous aspects of the legislature are customs and not part of the rules of either the House or the Senate. The seniority system, on which committee assignments are made and that helps determine who becomes a committee chair, is based solely on custom. The custom is much stronger in the House than in the Senate, as a number of senior House Republicans learned in 1995, when they were passed over for chairs after the Republicans became the majority party. The dress code noticed by a C-SPAN viewer also is a custom not denoted by the rules. Male representatives and senators wear coats and ties when they are in their chambers. Colorado representative and senator Ben Nighthorse Campbell regularly challenged the custom by wearing his bolo tie on the floor.

At the turn of the 21st century, observers outside Congress and members themselves became concerned about the decreasing level of civility in the House. The Annenberg Public Policy Center of the University of Pennsylvania began monitoring the quality of discourse in the House starting with the 104th Congress (1995–96). In the fall of 1996, the House held the first of several biennial "civility retreats," traveling to Hershey, Pennsylvania, to build better relationships among the representatives. Despite the efforts to improve civility, by the 108th Congress (2003–04) many members observed that incivility and rudeness continued to be a problem.

Further reading:
Asher, Herbert B. "The Learning of Legislative Norms." *American Political Science Review* 67, 2 (1973): 499–513; Grove, Lloyd. "Politics of Politeness." *Washington Post,* 25 September, p. B1; Jamieson, Kathleen Hall, and Erika Falk. "Continuity and Change in Civility in the House." In Jon R. Bond and Richard Fleisher, eds. *Polarized Politics: Congress and the President in a Partisan Era.* Washington, D.C.: Congressional Quarterly Press, 2000; Matthews, Donald R. *U.S. Senators and Their World.* Chapel Hill: University of North Carolina Press, 1960; Wallison, Ethan. 'Curses! A Brief Senate History,' *Roll Call,* p. 1, 28 June 2004.

—John David Rausch, Jr.

D

Daschle, Thomas (1947–) *Representative, Senator, Senate Majority Leader, Senate Minority Leader*

Senator Tom Daschle is a Democrat from South Dakota who served in the House of Representatives and later the Senate, where he gained prominence as a leader of the minority and majority delegations. Daschle was born on December 9, 1947, in Aberdeen, South Dakota. The son of a bookkeeper at a store for automobile parts, Daschle received his B.A. in 1969 from South Dakota State University and served in the U.S. Air Force from 1969 to 1972. Upon ending his stint in the air force, he soon embarked on his legislative career.

Daschle arrived on Capitol Hill in 1973 as a legislative assistant to Senator James G. Abourezk, a Democrat from South Dakota. In 1976 Daschle relocated to his home state to serve as field director for Abourezk. However, Daschle soon began to prepare for his own elective career. He took the opportunity of an open seat in 1978 in eastern South Dakota being vacated by Larry Pressler, who was running for the Senate, to launch his first bid for the U.S. House of Representatives. He beat former representative Frank Denholm in the Democratic primary and then won a hard-fought battle in the general election against the Republican nominee and former Vietnam prisoner of war Leo Thorsness by a mere 139 votes on a recount.

Daschle served in the House for four terms from 1978 to 1986. Upon arriving in the House, Daschle soon began to develop a political network. He befriended then representative Morris K. Udall (D-AZ), who became his political mentor and began to plant the seeds of legislative leadership in Daschle. Udall encouraged him to represent his region in the Democratic whip organization. In 1983 Daschle was elected to the Democratic Steering and Policy Committee in the House.

Daschle faced a tough reelection fight in 1982. Due to loss of population in South Dakota, after the 1980 census the state was reduced to one House seat. In this merger, Daschle, who represented the eastern "Corn Belt" half of the state, faced off against Republican Clint Roberts, the other congressman, who represented the western ranching part of the state. The 1982 contest was therefore a face off between the two major parties, the state's two regions, and the state's two major economic concerns. In the end Daschle emerged as the winner, defeating Roberts by 52 to 48 percent.

As the lone representative from his state in the House, Daschle already had positive name recognition throughout the state. In 1986 he decided to run for the Senate against incumbent Republican senator James Abdnor. He charged that after nearly three decades in Washington, Abdnor had become ineffective. After a nasty campaign of accusations and counteraccusations, Daschle beat Abdnor by a narrow margin of 52 to 48 percent, despite then President Ronald Reagan's support for the Republican incumbent. Daschle won his next two reelections to the Senate handily, beating Charlene Haar by 65 to 33 percent in 1992 and Ron Schmidt by 62 to 36 percent in 1998. He was poised to win reelection in 2004 despite the fact that his state had become increasingly Republican over the years.

As could be expected, Daschle was a vigorous defender of the concerns of his state and thus acquired a reputation as a "prairie populist." He worked relentlessly on issues dealing with agriculture, American Indian affairs, veterans' affairs, and health care, among others. He served on the agriculture committees in both houses of Congress and constantly resisted cuts in farm subsidies and other forms of federal support for farmers. Among his other public policy interests were the development and use of ethanol and benefits to veterans exposed to Agent Orange and to their children.

Every August Daschle visited all 66 counties in South Dakota in an effort to stay in touch with his constituents. He was known to drive himself around in casual clothes and engage in informal chats with voters about their concerns. He prided himself about close and personal contact with the folks back home and was amply rewarded by these connections at the polls.

Daschle's casual and low-key demeanor carried over to Washington. In the Senate, a chamber full of superstars, Daschle was mild mannered and unassuming. He often went unrecognized by the regular people, who looked for such political giants as Byrd and Kennedy but not for Daschle. Upon arriving in the Senate, Daschle soon began to develop a political base, just as he had done upon entering the House. He became a protégé of Senator George Mitchell (D-ME), who began his service as the Democratic leader of the Senate in January 1989. The new leader named Daschle the cochair of the Senate Democratic Policy Committee, effectively making him the number 2 member in the Senate.

It is not an understatement to say that Daschle has been underestimated throughout his political career. This signature carried over when he sought the Senate Democratic leadership. When Mitchell announced in March 1994 that he would retire, Daschle soon began his bid for the leadership slot. He was considered an underdog from the beginning, as he was thought to be too junior, a lightweight without much legislative experience and not tough enough to deal with the Republicans. When his first opponent, Senator Jim Sasser (D-TN), lost reelection in November 1994, Senator Christopher Dodd (D-CT) quickly stepped in for the race, supported by some senior members. However, in an extremely tight race Daschle secured the vote of then Senator Carol Moseley-Braun (D-IL), to whom he gave his Senate Finance Committee slot. Daschle won by a vote of 24-23. To be sure, Daschle was supported by many junior but also some senior senators, who wanted a fresh face for the party leadership.

Daschle faced some early hurdles as the party leader. His first test came when a constitutional amendment to balance the budget was up for debate and vote. He had previously endorsed the proposal, but Senator Robert C. Byrd (D-WV), a former Democratic leader of the body, had vehemently opposed it and led the fight against it. Daschle offered a measure to exclude using Social Security funds to balance the books, and when that proposal failed he voted against the amendment, which failed by one vote. The Social Security issue provided cover not only for him but also for five other Democrats who switched their positions as well. Also early in his leadership, Daschle came under scrutiny about whether he had improperly used his influence with federal officials to prevent them from grounding unsafe airplanes on behalf of a constituent. The Senate Ethics Committee investigated the matter and dismissed all charges of impropriety. He also had to contend with the fact that Dodd, his former opponent for the leadership race, rose to new prominence in January 1995 as the new leader of the Democratic National Committee (DNC), giving Dodd virtually equal visibility and standing in national politics.

However, Daschle soon established himself as the Democratic leader. He developed a reputation as a tough negotiator. Despite his image as an affable and modest person, he was not someone to be rolled over. He worked extremely hard, focuses on building consensus, could be a fierce partisan, and was about as tough as any. These qualities served him well in his dealings with the Republican leaders. Despite being a tenacious partisan, Daschle established comfortable working relationships with each of the Republican leaders. He worked closely with Senators Robert Dole (R-KS) and Trent Lott (R-MS), as he did with Senator William Frist (R-TN). The Senate's norms and procedures mandate that the leaders of the two parties work together if the Senate's business is to get done.

Within his own caucus Daschle sought unity and loyalty. The emphasis on individualism in the Senate's rules and procedures makes it impossible for any leader to demand faithfulness and threaten reprisals. He encouraged dialogue and understood disagreement but asked his Democratic colleagues to regularly consult with him and not to go public if they disagreed with the party's stands. He thus produced a fairly unified caucus. Daschle also had a much more amicable relationship with the media than have any of his Republican counterparts. He met with reporters routinely to discuss the party's agenda and the Senate's schedule. Moreover, Daschle was not shy about employing the Senate's procedures to his party's advantage, particularly when the Democrats were in the minority. He often used them to demand accommodation from the Republicans or to threaten gridlock. Even when he knew that Democratic bills and amendments would lose, he frequently demanded a vote so as to showcase Democratic priorities to the public.

In that sense, Daschle won a major victory when the 2000 election produced an equally divided Senate. He brokered a power-sharing agreement with Lott, who had been the Majority Leader until then, that called for equal membership on all the committees and equal staff and office resources. This agreement infuriated some Republicans, but Daschle took a hard line and kept his caucus united regarding equality. When Democrats lost their majority status after the 2002 election (having gained it after Senator James Jeffords of Vermont became an independent in June 2001, producing a Senate of 50 Democrats, 49 Republicans, and 1 independent), Daschle insisted on proportional representation on committees and proportional resources. That was unheard of, as the minority always got less than the majority. However, Daschle secured almost everything he sought, again at the resentment of some Republicans.

Daschle maintained a close relationship with President Bill Clinton but also asserted some degree of independence from the White House. He staunchly backed Clinton's proposals, ranging from health care to spending priorities to

American involvement in Bosnia and Kosovo to permanent normal trade relations with China. He strongly defended the president during his trial procedures in the Senate following impeachment in the House. He accused Republicans of treating Clinton unfairly and kept his caucus united such that not a single Democrat voted for the conviction. On the other hand, Daschle consistently opposed most of President George W. Bush's initiatives, ranging from tax cuts to judicial nominations to the American-led war in Iraq. Daschle has maintained a generally liberal voting record throughout his congressional career.

Daschle pondered a presidential run for the 2004 election. He would have been a formidable candidate, but he bowed out since the campaign would have often taken him away from Capitol Hill and South Dakota. Instead, he opted to run for reelection to his Senate seat. In a surprise outcome, Daschle lost his bid for reelection in 2004. He lost a close and bitter contest to John Thune, a Republican recruited and supported by President Bush and the White House. Daschle became the first party leader to lose reelection since 1952, when Republican Barry Goldwater of Arizona defeated Majority Leader Ernest W. McFarland, a Democrat from Arizona. While Daschle may not be placed in the annals of history among the giants of the Senate's leadership, such as Lyndon Johnson and Mike Mansfield, he proved to be an effective, capable, and strong leader of his party.

Further reading:
Daschle, Tom, with Michael D'Orso. *Like No Other Time: The 107th Congress and the Two Years That Changed America Forever.* New York: Crown Publishers, 2003.
—Sunil Ahuja

debate and oratory

Debate in Congress takes place both on and off the floors of the House of Representatives and Senate. Off-floor debate most commonly occurs during committee proceedings, where legislation is discussed and fine tuned. In turn, there are two types of floor debate: legislative and nonlegislative. Legislative debate consists of periods in which members of Congress address current or pending legislation, such as during general debate in the House and Senate (thus, debate during committee proceedings can also be considered legislative). Nonlegislative debate, on the other hand, consists of forums in which members may address any topic they wish, be it policy or nonpolicy in nature. Examples of these forums are ONE-MINUTE SPEECHES and SPECIAL ORDER ADDRESSES in the House and the MORNING HOUR during Senate proceedings.

The focus here is on legislative floor debate in the House and Senate. Floor debate—and general debate in particular—is arguably the most recognizable form of debate in Congress and thus the focus of this discussion. These debates can be examined in three parts: first, the purpose of debate and oratory in general; second, general debate in the House and Senate specifically; and third, the political significance of debate in Congress.

As Walter Oleszek notes, floor debate in Congress consists mostly of set speeches rather than typical give-and-take debate. He writes that because committees and subcommittees shape the fundamental character of most legislation, only a limited number of representatives participate in debate, and those who do usually are members of the committee that drafted the legislation. However, he also acknowledges the value of debate: "A . . . general debate has an intrinsic value that is recognized by most House members and experts on the legislative process."

Oleszek discusses its symbolic and practical purposes. First, it assures both legislators and the public that the House makes its decisions in a democratic fashion, with due respect for majority and minority opinion. A House Republican remarked that Congress is the only branch of government that can argue publicly. Indeed, tourists who visit Washington and feel they should see Congress usually attend a debate session of the House or Senate. Thus, floor debate has significant symbolic meaning.

Oleszek lists some of its more important practical purposes in today's Congress:

> General debate forces members to come to grips with the issues at hand; difficult and controversial sections of a bill are explained; constituents and interest groups are alerted to a measure's purpose through press coverage of the debate; member sentiment can be assessed by the floor leaders; a public record, or legislative history, for administrative agencies and the courts is built, indicating the intentions of proponents and opponents alike; legislators may take positions for reelection purposes; and, occasionally, fence-sitters may be influenced.

Thus, general debate can be used to send signals to constituents, other branches or agencies, lobbyists or campaign donors, and even other members of Congress. Members must send signals to constituents that they are effective and responsible legislators in order to get reelected. Participating in debate, especially for policies important to a district, can help representatives send those signals. Further, legislators use general debate to take positions on important issues that their constituents care about. Indeed, the viability of general debate as a position-taking activity only increased after C-SPAN began televising congressional proceedings in 1979.

In addition, junior members can use activities such as debate to send signals to leaders that they are active and engaged legislators. Leaders might in turn reward them with promotions or desirable committee assignments. Moreover, debate can also be used to send informational signals. As one noted political scientist argues, Congress is organized to encourage efficient transmittal of information. Members, especially committee leaders, use general debate to explain complicated policy to other members of Congress.

Although debate in Congress takes place in a variety of settings—during committee proceedings and nonlegislative forums, for instance—arguably the most recognizable forum is general debate. In the House general debate is the first order of business after the Speaker declares the House resolved into the COMMITTEE OF THE WHOLE. General debate on a particular bill occurs after the bill has been reported out of a STANDING COMMITTEE and sent to the floor of the House. One hour of debate is usually allowed for each bill, equally divided between the minority and majority parties and managed by members from the committee of jurisdiction (each party has a FLOOR MANAGER). For more complex legislation as many as 10 hours of debate may be scheduled. Due to significant time constraints in the House, members on average rarely speak for more than two minutes at a time.

It is the floor managers' responsibility to direct the course of debate on each bill. The manager on the majority side is usually the chair of the committee that reported the legislation to the floor. The senior minority member of the reporting committee is usually the manager for the minority side. The floor managers' roles are important to policy outcomes; effective management increases the chances for smooth passage. Their principal tasks are as follows: inform colleagues of the contents of the bill, explain the controversial issues in the bill; explain why the committee did what it did, and provide lawmakers with reasons to vote for the legislation.

In some respects general debate in the Senate is similar to debate in the House. For instance, debate on a bill occurs after it has been reported out of the standing committee of jurisdiction and is coordinated by floor managers representing the majority and minority parties. There are some significant differences between the Senate and House debate proceedings, however. One important difference is that unlike general debate in the House, the Senate follows a principle of unlimited debate. Once a lawmaker is recognized by the presiding officer, that senator may hold the floor for as long as he or she chooses. Only when senators yield the floor may others be recognized to speak.[1] This opens the door to FILIBUSTER, a time-delaying tactic used by a minority to prevent a vote on a bill or amendment. Although there are a variety of types of filibusters, the most recognizable tactic takes the form of an endless speech. This tactic is not possible in the House because general debate is governed by rules that restrict the amount of time members may address the chamber.

Whether general debate has any effect on electoral outcomes is not clear. As David Mayhew notes, the effect of position taking, in general, on electoral behavior is difficult to measure. Still, the electoral consequences of general debate are most likely small due to its limited audience. But Mayhew also explains, however, that there can be no doubt that congressmembers believe positions make a difference. So despite the inability to find systematic political consequences of position taking such as general debate, it is important to note that members of Congress behave *as if* these activities make a difference.

While general debate is an important position-taking and entrepreneurial activity, it is most likely *not* important to the final vote. As one House Republican noted, general debate is akin to professional wrestling; The outcome is predetermined. Oleszek writes, however, that once in a while debate, especially by party leaders just before a key vote, can change opinion. He recounts a 1983 speech by Speaker THOMAS O'NEILL on U.S. involvement in Lebanon. One House Democrat told him that it was one of the few times on the House floor when a speech changed a lot of votes.

Relative to other congressional actions, such as voting and sponsoring legislation, the effect of debate and oratory in Congress on policy and election outcomes is probably tenuous at best. However, debate has important symbolic and practical purposes, and for those reasons congressional debate and oratory will always be politically significant.

Further reading:
Fenno, Richard F. *Home Style: House Members in Their Districts.* New York: HarperCollins, 1978; Krehbiel, Keith. *Information and Legislative Organization.* Ann Arbor: University of Michigan Press, 1991; Oleszek, Walter J. *Congressional Procedures and the Policy Process.* Washington, D.C.: Congressional Quarterly Press, 2001.

—Michael S. Rocca

debt limit

Debt limits are statutory restriction on the amount of federal public debt that may be issued and outstanding at any given time. The public debt limit is the maximum amount of money the government is allowed to borrow without receiving additional authority from Congress. Prior to 1917 Congress approved each issuance of debt and determined its interest rate and term. The Second Liberty Bond Act of

---

[1] There are four restrictions to unlimited debate, however: unanimous consent agreements may limit debate; invoking cloture, which stops debate by a 3/5 vote; a motion to table; or debate-limiting features actually built into bills.

1917 was the basis for the current debt limit law. This act allowed the Department of the Treasury to borrow as much money as necessary to finance federal government activities up to an amount set by Congress. The law was needed during World War I because it was difficult to predict how much money would be needed to finance the war. The limit continued after the war and was raised periodically as the public debt increased.

In 1941 Congress combined the separate limits on different types of federal debt, bills, notes, and bonds into a single limit. Congress began to use temporary limits in the 1950s. These limits were enacted with expiration dates and were combined with the permanent limit to produce the total debt limit. The purpose of the temporary limits was to work on reducing the public debt. In 1983 the permanent and temporary debt limits were combined into a single permanent limit. Between January 1980 and September 1997 the debt limit was extended by Congress 37 times.

The initial debt limit in 1917 was $11.5 billion, and the actual federal debt was $3 billion. By 1947 the debt limit had been raised to $275 billion, where it remained through most of the 1950s. Actual federal debt during that period ranged from $255.8 billion to $323.1 billion. The limit was $752 billion in 1977, and it had risen to $2.8 trillion by 1987. In 1992 the limit was set at $4.145 trillion. The debt limit was $5.95 trillion in 2001. In one of its last acts before adjourning the 108th Congress in November 2004, Congress voted to extend the limit to $8.18 trillion, an increase of $800 billion over the previous limit. If Congress had adjourned before increasing the debt limit in 2004, the Treasury Department warned that it would no longer have any maneuvering room to avoid passing the limit. When the federal debt reaches the limit, the government is no longer able to borrow additional funds, pay interest on existing financial notes and bonds, or repay lenders with matured securities. The increase was expected to cover Treasury borrowing for about a year.

Both chambers have different methods for handling proposals to raise the debt limit. During the 108th Congress the HOUSE OF REPRESENTATIVES used a rule first originated by Representative Dick Gephardt, a Democrat from Missouri, in 1979 and deleted from the rules in the 107th Congress. After successful adoption of the budget resolution, the House would automatically be "deemed" to have passed a bill to increase the debt ceiling. The SENATE treats the debt limit legislation as any other resolution it receives from the House. It can accept, reject, or modify the increase in the debt limit. When the Senate accepts the House's increase, the bill is sent to the president for signature. If the Senate rejects or modifies the increase, the resolution is either returned to the House or sent to a CONFERENCE COMMITTEE for negotiation.

The debt limit may be changed by attaching it to or including it in some other piece of legislation as an amendment. The 108th Congress passed the bill as a stand-alone resolution, but not before the Republican leadership had considered strategies for avoiding a direct vote, including attaching the provision to the omnibus appropriations bill. Constituents had little say in the November 2004 debt limit increase, as the vote occurred after election day.

Further reading:
Crittenden, Michael R. "Debt Limit Increase Clears; Democrats Use Deadline Vote to Attack GOP Fiscal Policy." *CQ Weekly Report*, 20 November 2004, p. 2,692; United States Government Accountability Office. *Federal Debt: Answers to Frequently Asked Questions, An Update.* GAO-04-485SP. Washington, D.C.: Government Accountability Office, 2004; Winters, Philip D. *The Debt Limit.* IB93054. Washington, D.C.: Library of Congress, Congressional Research Service, 2001.

—John David Rausch, Jr.

DeLay, Tom (Thomas Dale DeLay) (1947–)
Representative, Majority Leader

Known as "the hammer" by friend and foe alike, Tom DeLay is widely identified as being among the most partisan and combative members of the HOUSE OF REPRESENTATIVES. A native of Laredo, Texas, DeLay spent much of his childhood in Venezuela, where his father was employed as an oil-drilling contractor. He attended Baylor University in Waco, Texas, before graduating from the University of Houston in 1970. DeLay and his wife, Christine, had one child and moved to Sugarland, Texas, a Houston suburb. Before entering Congress DeLay was a member of the Texas House of Representatives and owned Albo Pest Control in Sugarland.

Throughout his political career DeLay has been known as a staunch conservative on both social and economic issues. He first won election to the House in 1984 to represent Texas's 22nd District, which encompassed southwest Houston and the nearby suburbs spanning Fort Bend and Brazoria Counties. He rapidly ascended the Republicans' House hierarchy. In his freshman term Delay won a seat on the Republican Committee on Committees, which he followed the next term with a seat on the coveted HOUSE APPROPRIATIONS COMMITTEE. In December 1992 DeLay defeated incumbent Bill Gradison to become Republican Conference secretary. Two years later he won a majority of votes on the first ballot, defeating two rivals to become the Republicans' House whip, the third-ranking position in the chamber behind the SPEAKER OF THE HOUSE AND THE MAJORITY LEADER. He thus became his party's chief vote-counter in the House.

Throughout his CAPITOL HILL career DeLay has been known for controversy, political fund-raising skills, and efforts to deregulate business to help Republican allies in the private sector. He frequently has fought to eliminate or reduce federal regulation of businesses concerning the environment and workers. One of his more controversial efforts was a failed attempt in 1997 to oust NEWT GINGRICH as Speaker. During a Republican Conference meeting following the coup attempt, DeLay admitted his role in the plot. His admission reportedly helped solidify his support among Republicans over his other rival, Majority Leader Dick Armey. Following Gingrich's resignation in November 1998, DeLay rejected notions of becoming the new Speaker, reportedly saying that he was too much a national polarizing figure. Instead, he supported the candidacies of first Robert Livingston and then Dennis Hastert, DeLay's chief deputy whip. Armey subsequently retired from the House, thereby paving the way for DeLay to become Majority Leader.

DeLay stepped up his aggressive efforts on behalf of Republicans in general and those on Capitol Hill in particular. He quickly established a thorough and effective whip operation to count votes and hold together party coalitions in the House. DeLay also put together a powerful fund-raising machine, operating a personal political action committee and the Republican Majorities Issues Campaign, a Section 527 group. Regularly one of the largest Republican fund-raisers on the national scene, DeLay repeatedly has fought off efforts at campaign finance reform.

Another continuing partisan effort has been DeLay's campaign to replace Democratic lobbyists within the A to K Street corridor of Washington, D.C., with Republicans. DeLay's aggressive approach to this task, coupled with his equally aggressive fund-raising techniques, earned him the nickname, "the Hammer." He worked closely with business lobbyists to craft legislation designed to meet their public policy needs. Such efforts attracted vehement criticism from environmental and worker interest groups and even a lawsuit from the Democratic Party.

In 1997 DeLay had a famous altercation with a Democrat, David Obey of Wisconsin, on the House floor. During an intense and vehement argument DeLay reportedly shoved Obey, and the two had to be separated by nearby staff members. DeLay's battles with Democrats subsequently included a lawsuit, which was later dismissed, and numerous ethics complaints, which led to his receiving several letters of reprimand from the House Ethics Committee.

Nonetheless, his aggressive partisanship remained unabated. In 1998 DeLay quickly assumed a leading role in pushing the House to vote out articles of impeachment against President Bill Clinton, despite mounting evidence that the effort would fail a Senate vote and increasingly run contrary to public opinion. Two years later, with the outcome of the presidential election in the balance, DeLay campaigned aggressively both publicly and within the House against Democratic efforts both in the court system and in Florida.

The intensity of DeLay's partisanship crested in 2003. After capturing both houses of the Texas legislature the previous fall, the new Republican majority approved DeLay's plan to redistrict the state's congressional districts to assure the addition of at least five party members to the state's House delegation. Democrats, both in Texas and in the nation's capital, bitterly fought the maneuver, which had helped Republicans maintain a slim majority in the House. By the end of 2005, the controversy had reach the United States Supreme Court.

However, ominously for DeLay, the Texas redistricting struggle cost him his Majority Leader position. Many of his fund-raising efforts on behalf of Republican Texas legislative candidates led to his indictment in 2005 on campaign finance conspiracy and money-laundering charges. While the conspiracy charges were later dismissed, the pending trial on money-laundering charges made Republicans on Capitol Hill nervous about its possible impact on their reelection chances in 2006.

DeLay's legal and political fortunes were further threatened by a major federal investigation of one of his closest political allies, Jack Abramoff—a powerful Washington lobbyist whose staff was filled with former DeLay aides. In September 2005 DeLay temporarily relinquished the Majority Leader post and turned over the position on an interim basis to the party's House whip, Roy Blunt of Missouri. DeLay's political position with fellow House Republicans became untenable after Abramoff subsequently reached a plea agreement with federal prosecutors.

Delay's House career ended early the following year. First, his hope of regaining the Majority Leader position concluded in January 2006 when he announced he would not seek to return to the post. The Republican House caucus subsequently replaced him with JOHN BOEHNER of Ohio, who defeated Blunt in a close contest. The following months found De Lay fighting for his political life in an expensive and bitter reelection campaign, first to defeat a primary challenger and then to take on a likely strong Democratic challenger the following November. Finally, on April 4, 2006, DeLay announced he would abandon his campaign for a 12th term and retire from the House within the next two months. Retirement would allow him to devote all of his time and money to fight legal battles stemming from his political activities in Texas and Washington, D.C.

Further reading:
Dubose, Lou, and Jan Reid. *The Hammer: Tom DeLay, God, Money, and the Rise of the Republican Congress.* New York: Public Affairs Press, 2004.

—Darryl Paulson

delegate

A delegate is a representative elected to the U.S. House of Representatives from a land or territory other than an American state. Delegates enjoy all the rights and privileges of representatives, such as holding committee assignments, entering into debate, offering motions (except to reconsider), and voting in committees, but delegates are not permitted to vote in the Committee of the Whole House or the full House. Most delegates serve two-year terms, but the Resident Commissioner from Puerto Rico is elected to a four-year term. Currently, the Territory of American Samoa, the District of Columbia, the Territory of Guam, the Commonwealth of Puerto Rico, and the U.S. Virgin Islands send delegates to the House.

The tradition of delegates may be traced to the Northwest Ordinance of 1787. The ordinance provided that once the population of a new territory reached 5,000 free adult males, the people could elect their own territorial government and have the territorial legislature elect a delegate to represent their interests in the House. William Henry Harrison was one of the first delegates elected from the Ohio Territory and helped secure the passage of the Land Act of 1800.

As the United States obtained other territories—from the Louisiana Purchase of 1803, the treaty with Spain in 1819 for Florida, the lands ceded from Mexico after the war of 1848, the purchase of Alaska from Russia in 1867, and the annexation of Hawaii in 1898—the nascent states had the option of electing delegates. Alaska and Hawaii were the last two territories sending delegates to become states, Alaska in 1958 and Hawaii in 1959. The peoples of other countries or lands acquired through conquest or other means, such as Cuba, the Philippines, Puerto Rico, Guam, and Samoa, were not automatically extended constitutional rights and privileges or the right to send delegates. (This matter was clarified somewhat in the Supreme Court's decision in the Insular Cases of 1901.) Of the territories now considered "insular areas" under the authority of the Department of the Interior (American Samoa, the Commonwealth of the Northern Mariana Islands, the Federated States of Micronesia, Guam, the Marshall Islands, Palau, and the U.S. Virgin Islands), only American Samoa, Guam, and the U.S. Virgin Islands are permitted delegates.

The District of Columbia presents a different scenario. As the seat of the capital, the territory is not a state. Thus, technically under the Constitution its people, while American citizens, could not vote in presidential or congressional elections. (Voting in presidential elections was granted with the Twenty-third Amendment in 1961.) Responsibility for governing the district was placed in committees of Congress. In the early part of the 19th century, District of Columbia residents were extended the privilege of electing a delegate, but this was withdrawn prior to the Civil War. In 1871 Congress established a territorial government for the district, but this was removed in 1875.

It was not until 1970 that the question of representation for the district was successfully resurrected. Democrats sought statehood for the district, but Republicans were suspicious because the voters of the district were mostly Democrats. President Richard Nixon agreed to support a constitutional amendment granting statehood, but until such time as a constitutional amendment was adopted, he signed a law passed on September 9, 1970, that gave the people of the district the privilege of electing a delegate to the House. On March 23, 1971, Walter E. Fauntroy, a Democrat, was elected and served continuously until 1991, when he resigned to run for mayor of the district. He was replaced by Eleanor Holmes Norton, a Democrat, who has held the position ever since.

All delegates were extended voting privileges only in standing committees in the early 1970s, and the SPEAKER OF THE HOUSE may appoint delegates to special, select, or ad hoc committees and conference committees. On January 5, 1993, the Democratically controlled House adopted a rule change that gave the five delegates in the chamber (from American Samoa, the District of Columbia, Guam, Puerto Rico, and the Virgin Islands) the right to vote on the House floor while the House was convened as the Committee of the Whole. The rule had a significant caveat, however: If the outcome of a vote taken in the Committee of the Whole was affected by votes cast by the delegates, an immediate members-only revote must be taken, essentially negating the influence of the delegates' votes. Originally proposed by Delegate Norton, the measure passed along a strictly party line vote. Republicans were livid because all five delegates would likely vote with the Democrats, and the Republicans had gained 10 seats in the 1992 election.

The Republicans took the matter to federal district court, where arguments were heard by Judge Harold H. Greene on February 9, and he ruled on March 8 that the rule change was "meaningless." Republicans claimed a partial victory with the decision because the judge agreed to at least hear the case. Lawyers for the Democrats argued that the court should declare this a political question and not accept the case. Republicans ultimately appealed the verdict. In the interim Republicans strategically demanded separate votes on nearly all amendments passed by the Committee of the Whole, as delegates could not cast votes on these. Democrats labeled these votes as dilatory tactics. On January 25, 1994, the Court of Appeals for the District of Columbia Circuit let stand the decision of Judge Greene.

The Republicans ultimately succeeded in their efforts to restrict the delegates' voting privilege when they regained control of the House following the 1994 elections.

In a party line vote a rule change banned delegates from voting on the House floor in any configuration but continued their privilege of voting in committees.

Further reading:
McLaughlin, Andrew C., ed. *Cyclopedia of American Government.* New York: Peter Smith, 1914.

—Thomas J. Baldino

Democratic Steering Committee, House

Prior to 1974 the Democratic members of the HOUSE COMMITTEE ON WAYS AND MEANS were responsible for making Democratic committee assignments in the House of Representatives. Under the control of its powerful chair, Wilbur Mills of Arkansas, the secretive Ways and Means Committee assignment process became a source of suspicion for many rank-and-file Democrats. The caucus reforms that preceded the 94th Congress stipulated that the Democratic Steering and Policy Committee (DSPC) assume responsibility for committee assignments. Consistent with the general spirit of other congressional reforms of the time, members sought to democratize the committee selection process by creating a representative system that would reflect the interests of the Democratic caucus. More junior members of the Democratic Caucus, many of whom sought access to seats on more influential committees, probably believed that creating a more representative process would enhance their chances of obtaining a sought-after committee assignment.

Also consistent with other caucus reforms of the time, Democrats gave an expanded role to the party leadership in constituting the DSPC. The purpose of giving additional power to the party leadership was to create a direct linkage in the minds of Democratic members between committee assignments and loyalty to the Democratic Party. Using the committee assignment process, reformers reasoned, the party leadership could reward partisan loyalty and thereby advance the Democratic legislative agenda in the House. The DSPC as originally constituted was composed of three sets of members. First, the Democratic leadership: the Speaker, who served as the chair of the DSPC, Democratic Leader, Democratic Whip, and Caucus Chair. Second, eight members were appointed to the committee by the Speaker. Finally, the Democratic Caucus through "zone" elections chose 12 regional members. This provided the party leadership with half the votes in the DSPC; since 1974 the party leadership has assumed a greater role in the process, now composing more than half of the DSPC membership.

Prior to convening the DSPC for purposes of making committee assignments for the next Congress, the 12 regional members are chosen by members of their regional caucus. Regional zones are determined based on two criteria. First, states were included in a zone to emphasize geographic compactness, that is, grouping together states with common interests. Second, the number of states in a zone is determined so that the number of Democratic members within each zone is roughly equal. Caucus rules limit zone representatives to two consecutive terms on the DSPC. It is the responsibility of the zone representatives to promote the committee requestors from their zone in committee deliberations and fight for geographic balance.

Despite the heavy influence of the leadership in the committee selection process, the leadership does not dictate committee assignments. In the case of many committees peripheral to the leadership's legislative agenda, the leadership has little interest in dictating committee assignments. When the leadership takes an interest in influencing committee assignments, they are often successful, but not always. A former member of the DSPC elaborated in an interview with the authors. When asked if the leadership would seek to impose a slate of committee assignments on the DSPC, the member responded:

> Oh absolutely. But it might not be done publicly. And when I say publicly, I mean within the meeting, it would be done prior to that time. They'd say these are some people that we are interested in. And it wouldn't be hard to figure out who the leadership supported because you'd see the leadership people all lining up behind those people. Sometimes [they would win] . . . and sometimes people on Steering would have a very different view or different agenda and the leadership did not win.

A second role of the DSPC, often overshadowed by its responsibility for making committee assignments, is to formulate and promote a Democratic legislative agenda in the House. Beginning with Speaker Tip O'Neill of Massachusetts in the 95th Congress, Democratic leaders used the DSPC as a means for consensus building and to signal to Democratic members of the House matters of "party policy" in an attempt to increase support for measures that were considered important by the party leadership. Voting with the DSPC position was often considered important for future consideration for committee assignments. As former Speaker James Wright of Texas explained in an interview with the authors:

> Maybe eight times in a year, the Speaker and the leadership will ask Steering and Policy to pass a resolution calling on the members to vote for this bill or for this amendment or against that amendment . . . party regularity votes. These are counters. In those days we would try to enforce the idea that if you expect to get on a committee, if you expect consideration of that nature from the

leadership, and you are free to vote any way your conscious dictates, we would never ask you to vote against the wishes of your constituency. But when the Steering and Policy Committee called on somebody to vote on something that is party policy. That's party policy. . . .

It is difficult to know with certainty whether the goal of increasing party loyalty was achieved through changes in the committee assignment process. In the years since the 94th Congress party loyalty has increased significantly among House Democrats. However, it is also the case that party loyalty among Republicans increased over the same period despite only minor changes in their committee assignment process.

A recent major alteration in the DSPC occurred when the Democrats lost the majority in 1994. Minority Leader Richard Gephardt (MO) initiated a change that broke the Steering and Policy Committee into two parts—a Steering Committee to assign members to standing committees and to select ranking members (or chairs if the Democrats were in the majority) and a policy committee to help formulate and publicize party policy. The creation of separate committees had the benefit of including more Democrats in responsible party leadership positions. In the wake of the tremendous losses in the number and quality of committee assignments suffered by Democratic members, Gephardt sought to create additional positions of importance for many of his members.

See also CAUCUS, PARTY.

Further reading:

Deering, Christopher J., and Steven S. Smith. *Congressional Committees*. Washington, D.C.: Congressional Quarterly Press, 1997; Frisch, Scott A., and Sean Q. Kelly. *Committee Politics*. Norman: University of Oklahoma Press, forthcoming; Shepsle, Kenneth A. *The Giant Jigsaw Puzzle*. Chicago: University of Chicago Press, 1978.
—Scott A. Frisch and Sean Q. Kelly

Democratic Study Group

The Democratic Study Group (DSG) is a group composed of moderate and liberal members of Congress, mostly Democrats drawn predominantly from the House, that offers a forum for its members to discuss and develop policies outside the formal congressional party organizations. It became the first LEGISLATIVE SERVICE ORGANIZATION (LSO) officially certified by the HOUSE ADMINISTRATION COMMITTEE (now titled House Oversight). While its structure, membership, and visibility may have changed over the years, the DSG continues to supply its highly valued research reports to members and works to support liberal legislation and good government reforms.

The DSG evolved from meetings led by liberal representative Eugene McCarthy, a Democrat from Wisconsin, in the mid-1950s with like-minded colleagues (known as McCarthy's Mavericks or McCarthy's Marauders) who were frustrated in their efforts to pass progressive social programs by the votes of the conservative coalition. Rather than continue to operate as a loose coalition, McCarthy sought to formalize the group and in 1959 created the DSG with Representative Lee Metcalf, a Democrat from Montana, as its chair. With a membership of approximately 100, drawn mostly from the Northeast and Midwest and funded by dues of $100 per member plus whatever individual members wished to contribute from their congressional staff funds, the group hired a professional staff, established an informal whip network, and produced research reports, bill analyses, and statements on upcoming legislative issues.

With a Democratic president in the White House, the DSG became a dependable ally for President John Kennedy in his quest to pass his New Frontier programs. Senior conservative Democrats, however, held many committee chairs and blocked his initiatives, key among them Howard W. ("Judge") Smith, a Democrat from Virginia and chair of the HOUSE RULES COMMITTEE. In a bold attempt to weaken Smith's control, DSG members proposed increasing the size of the Rules Committee from 12 to 15, with the three new seats going to more junior liberal Democrats. Despite strong objections from Smith, the rule change passed, marking an early major victory for the DSG. In 1965 the DSG supported another mechanism to undermine the Rules Committee chair: a rule that would allow a bill buried in Rules to be discharged without a rule after 21 days with the approval of the SPEAKER OF THE HOUSE if the standing committee chair that handled the bill requested its release. This motion passed as well. When Johnson moved into the Oval Office and with the Vietnam War intensifying, the DSG's agenda included support for the president's Great Society programs and opposition to the war in Vietnam.

In 1968 the DSG hired a new staff director, Richard Conlon, and under his leadership the group's focus moved from advocating substantive legislation to structural reforms, particularly in the House, though it continued to do bill analyses and reports and encouraged its members to support liberal legislation. According to Conlon, DSG leaders understood that fundamental changes in House rules would create a chamber that was more open and responsive to the increasingly liberal electorate. To this end, the DSG actively supported the LEGISLATIVE REORGANIZATION ACT OF 1970, an important first step in modernizing Congress.

In succeeding years the DSG successfully lobbied for rule changes to record teller votes, open committee and subcommittee deliberations to the public, and weaken the grip of the seniority system on the process of gaining committee chairs. In several instances the DSG had bipartisan support from "Rumsfeld's Raiders," a group of Republicans led by Donald Rumsfeld, a Republican from Illinois.

With the election of 1974, an unusually large entering class of liberal Democrats, who came to be known as "the Watergate Babies," entered the House eager to change how Congress did business. DSG chair Phillip Burton, a Democrat from California, tapped into their energy and impatience. One of the most liberal Democrats in the House, Burton chafed for years under the conservative leadership of his party and with the addition of these new members, mounted a serious assault on the seniority system that allowed the conservatives to retain power. Among its victories, the DSG could number adoption of rules for a SUB-COMMITTEE bill of rights, caucus voting to approve committee chairs, and the enlargement of the Ways and Means Committee from 25 to 37. Unfortunately, despite it best efforts, the DSG could not help win adoption of the Bolling Committee's proposal for a major overhaul of the standing committee system in the House.

The accomplishments of the DSG brought the formation of many other LSOs, with the number of officially certified groups reaching 27 by the early 1980s and the number of informal caucuses to more than 100. With Republicans recapturing the presidency in 1980, increasing their numbers in the House, and gaining control of the Senate, the DSG exerted more time and effort supplying its members with reports and bill analyses in an attempt to hold a liberal voting bloc together in the face of a popular president's legislative agenda.

Following the 1992 election concerns about unresponsive and out-of-touch committee chairs resurfaced. Representative Robert Wise, a Democrat from West Virginia and chair of the DSG, voiced unhappiness with the lack of focus of the party's agenda, a consequence of committee chairs pursuing their individual goals. The DSG called for caucus rule changes that would have a party work group on policy establish legislative priorities, with membership coming from the rank and file as well as leadership. Moreover, the group sought to have the caucus vote to approve subcommittee chairs (rather than leave the decision to a subcommittee's members alone) and full committee chairs without any reference to seniority. The caucus created a Committee on Organization, Study and Review chaired by Louise M. Slaughter, a Democrat from New York, to mediate the dispute, which eventually brought a split of the DEMOCRATIC STEERING COMMITTEE into two separate entities. The DSG failed, however, to achieve its principal objective: caucus control over committee and subcommittee chairs.

The 1994 elections brought Republican control to the House and with it entirely new rules regarding LSOs. During the campaign then MINORITY LEADER NEWT GIN-GRICH, a Republican from Georgia, promised to abolish LSOs because he saw them as wasting taxpayer money. On January 4, 1995, a package of rule changes stripped all LSOs and informal caucuses of their funding and their offices in congressional buildings. The DSG, along with the Congressional Black Caucus and Congressional Caucus for Women's Issues, managed to reorganize and survive. (As part of its reorganization, the DSG sold its publishing unit to Congressional Quarterly Press.) Though it is somewhat less visible, the DSG remains active, producing its reports and keeping its members informed of important developments affecting liberal legislation.

A new Democratic Study Group emerged in 2003 in the Senate, taking its name from the organization discussed above. With Senator Richard Durbin, a Democrat from Illinois, as its informal leader, the group of approximately 20 liberal members has had some success in convincing congressional leaders to be more publicly critical of President George W. Bush's economic and social policies.

Further reading:
Ferber, Mark F. "The Formation of the Democratic Study Group." In *Congressional Behavior*, edited by Nelson Polsby, New York: Random House, 1971; Hammond, Susan Webb. *Congressional Caucus in National Policy Making*. Baltimore: Johns Hopkins University Press, 1998; Kofmehl, Kenneth. "The Institutionalization of a Voting Bloc." *Western Political Quarterly* 17 (1964): 256–272; Steven, Arthur, Arthur Miller, and Thomas Mann. "Mobilization of Liberal Strength in the House 1955–1970: The Democratic Study Group." *The American Political Science Review* 66 (1974): 667–681.

—Thomas J. Baldino

Department of Commerce v. United States House of Representatives 525 U.S. 316 (1999)

This U.S. Supreme Court case was a result of two legal challenges questioning the use of sampling techniques used by the U.S. Department of Commerce in conducting the 2000 CENSUS. Specifically at issue was whether the Department of Commerce could use sampling techniques to apportion congressional seats among the states.

Article I, Section 2, of the U.S. Constitution states that "Representatives . . . shall be apportioned among the several States . . . according to their respective numbers." It further requires that "the actual Enumeration shall be made within three Years after the first meeting of Congress of the United States, and within every subsequent Term of ten years, in such Manner as they shall by Law direct." The Constitution's census clause authorized Congress to direct an "actual enumeration" of the American public every 10 years to provide a basis for apportioning congressional representation. Given this authority, Congress enacted the Census Act that directed the secretary of Commerce to conduct the decennial census. Using this information, the secretary was required to inform the president of the population of each state. The president, in turn, was to transmit to Congress a statement showing the population of each state and detailing the number of representatives each state would be entitled to.

In understanding the significance of this case, it is important to review the historical background of the U.S. census conducted by the Department of Commerce. The current Census Act was adopted by Congress in 1954, and it specified that a census enumerator must personally visit every household to collect data for the census. The law was amended in 1957 to allow the Department of Commerce to use sampling procedures for all purposes of the census with the exception of determining the population for APPORTIONMENT of legislative districts. Then, in 1976, the Census Act was amended to allow the secretary of Commerce increased discretion in conducting the census. Specifically, it seemed to allow the use of sampling in some circumstances.

In preparing for the 2000 census, the Department of Commerce indicated that it intended to use two forms of statistical sampling to help account for a serious problem of "undercounting" in the decennial census. The undercounting problem was such that certain groups of individuals, particularly minorities, children, and renters, were not counted in the census. As a response to this plan, two sets of plaintiffs filed separate suits challenging the legality and constitutionality of the plan. The original cases, which were combined in this lawsuit, were *Clinton v. Gavin and U.S. House of Representatives v. U.S. Department of Commerce.* The lower court in both cases found that the Census Act prohibits sampling for purposes of congressional apportionment. The U.S. Supreme Court ruled 5-4 that the Census Act amendments bar the use of sampling methods to compile the state population totals used to apportion the 435 seats in Congress among the 50 states. Neither the lower courts nor the Supreme Court ruled on the constitutionality issues in this case.

Further reading:
Department of Commerce v. United States House of Representatives, 525 U.S. 316, 1999; "Legal Challenges to Sampling in the 2000 Census." *Census 2000 Fact Sheet.* Available online. URL: http://www.census2000.org/facts/legal.html. Accessed 23 January 2003.

—Nancy S. Lind

Department of Homeland Security Act
After September 11, 2001, the United States recognized that historic steps were necessary to defend the country and to protect citizens against further terrorist attacks. President George W. Bush signed new legislation on November 26, 2002, by which Congress created a cabinet-level department, the Department of Homeland Security, to address those threats. This new department analyzes threats to citizens, guards borders and airports, protects critical infrastructure, and coordinates responses to future emergencies. The reform was enacted with the support of strong bipartisan majorities in the House and the Senate.

The Department of Homeland Security constitutes a significant reorganization of the federal government in that the nation now has a single department whose primary mission is to secure the homeland. The mission of the department is to prevent terrorist attacks within the borders of the United States as well as reduce America's vulnerability to terrorist activities. Further, the department was designed to minimize the damage from any attacks that might occur.

The primary mission of the department includes the following:

- prevent terrorist attacks within the borders of the United States
- reduce the vulnerability to terrorist activities
- minimize damage and assist in the recovery efforts if terrorist attacks do occur
- carry out all functions transferred to the department
- ensure that the functions of agencies within the department that are not directly related to securing the homeland are not diluted except by acts of Congress
- ensure that the overall economic security of the United States is not diminished by activities to protect the homeland
- monitor connections between illegal drug trafficking and terrorism and sever such connections whenever possible

To accomplish those goals, the department was organized into four primary divisions: Border and Transportation Security; Emergency Preparedness and Response; Chemical, Biological, Radiological, and Nuclear Countermeasures; and Information Analysis and Infrastructure Protection. Further, the department was assigned to minimize the overlap among federal government agencies. This was to be accomplished by transferring all functions related to homeland security to the new department. Thus, for example, the department assumed responsibility for the U.S. Coast Guard, the U.S. Customs Service, the Immigration and Naturalization Service, the Animal and Plant Health Inspection Service, and the Transportation Security Administration. It was hoped that this would streamline government activities. In addition, the responsibilities of the U.S. Secret Service were transferred to the department to protect the president and other top government leaders.

The Department of Homeland Security was created specifically to allow the United States to identify clear lines of authority and responsibility in the decision-making processes of government bureaucrats. It was established to provide a unified effort against terrorism. President Bush's signature of this legislation signified the country's intention of taking terrorist threats seriously and developing plans to prevent or minimize the disruption from any future attacks.

Further reading:
Bush, George W. "Message to the Congress of the United States," June 2002. Available online. URL: http://www.whitehouse.gov/news/releases/2002/06/20020618-5.html. Accessed 22 January 2003; "How to Protect the Nation: Proposed Department of Homeland Security: Pro and Con—Should the House Pass the Homeland Security Act?" *Congressional Digest* 81 (October 2002): 225–256; "President Bush Signs Homeland Security Act: Remarks by the President at the Signing of H.R. 5005 of the Homeland Security Act of 2002." Available online. URL: http://www.whitehouse.gov/news/releases/2002/11/20021125-6.html. Accessed January 21, 2003.

—Nancy S. Lind

dilatory motion

When a legislative body meets it is important for that body to have some control over the proceedings that occur on the floor. A dilatory motion is an action taken to kill time and prevent the legislature from taking action on a bill or amendment before a legislative chamber or a legislative committee. The U.S. House of Representatives has outlawed the use of dilatory motions. The determination of whether a motion is dilatory is entirely at the discretion of the Speaker of the House or the chair of the Committee of the Whole. The rationale behind the dilatory motion is that every deliberative assembly has the inherent right to protect itself from being imposed upon by members using parliamentary procedures to prevent it from enacting legislation. An example of a dilatory motion is when members of Congress consistently ask for quorum calls to slow down the order of business. The U.S. Senate does not ban dilatory rules except when they are operating under procedures of cloture. When the Senate is operating under the cloture rule, it may limit consideration of a pending bill to 30 additional hours, but only by a vote of three-fifths of the Senate membership.

Further reading:
"Deschler's Precedents." Available online. URL: http://www.access.gpo.gov/congress/house/precedents/chap23.html. Accessed 9 February 2003; "Dilatory Motion or Tactic."

Available online. URL: http://www.thecapitol.net/glossary/def.htm. Accessed February 9, 2003.

—Nancy S. Lind

direct election of Senators   *See* SEVENTEENTH AMENDMENT.

Dirksen, Everett (1896–1969) *Representative, Senator, Senate Minority Leader*

Everett McKinley Dirksen was a Republican senator (1951–69) and representative from Illinois (1933–49) and is considered among the most prominent lawmakers of the post–World War II era, in addition to one of the most colorful. Dirksen served as Senate MINORITY LEADER from 1959 until his death in 1969. He is perhaps best remembered today for the crucial role he played in securing passage of the landmark CIVIL RIGHTS ACT OF 1964, VOTING RIGHTS ACT OF 1965, and Civil Rights Act of 1968.

Dirksen was born to modest means in Pekin, Illinois, in 1896. As a boy Dirksen was an avid reader and displayed what Dirksen himself would call "an irrepressible urge for

Everett Dirksen *(Library of Congress)*

expression." The latter trait would manifest itself in Dirksen's lifelong love of public speaking. As a young man Dirksen attended the University of Minnesota. However, he cut his education short to serve in World War I. Following his return from Europe, Dirksen became involved in local politics through the American Legion, and in 1927 he was elected to the Pekin city council. Later that same year he married Louella Carver, a union that would produce one daughter, Danice Joy, who would later marry senator and Senate Republican leader Howard Baker.

Dirksen ran for Congress in 1930 but was narrowly defeated in the Republican primary. Undeterred, he ran again in 1932 and this time was elected, one of the few new Republicans to win in an otherwise thoroughly Democratic year. Upon arrival in the House, Dirksen quickly established himself as a diligent and capable member of the legislature. He supported a number of New Deal measures but maintained a strong isolationist streak, a stance he would later repudiate just months prior to the Japanese attack on Pearl Harbor. This would not be Dirksen's last volte-face. By the end of the war, Dirksen had become a proponent of the establishment of the United Nations and later a supporter of the Marshall Plan.

By the early 1940s Dirksen had achieved a measure of national prominence. In 1943 he mounted a campaign for the presidency, although his effort came to little. In 1946 *Pageant* magazine polled House members, and Dirksen (along with Sam Rayburn) was ranked as the second-most-able representative. His effectiveness was reflected by his work in securing passage of the historic Legislative Reorganization Act of 1946, which provided much-needed staff support for Congress while it streamlined the committee structure.

Then, in late 1947 Dirksen began to experience difficulty with his vision, a condition that threatened him with blindness. Dirksen believed that the end of his political career was at hand, and the following year he announced his retirement from public life.

Following the remarkable recovery of his vision, Dirksen decided to return to the political arena. In 1950 he challenged Democrat Scott Lucas, the MAJORITY LEADER, for his Senate seat. Dirksen prevailed over Lucas in a hard fought race, but Dirksen was sharply criticized throughout for reversing himself on a number of issues.

Dirksen's first several years in the Senate were marked by fierce partisanship and a lurch to the right. He was sharply critical of President Harry Truman's approach to the Korean War, and his fierce anticommunist sentiments led him to become a friend and ally of Joe McCarthy. Even after McCarthy became politically isolated, Dirksen refused to abandon him, voting against his censure.

At the 1952 Republican National Convention, Dirksen's oratory was on full display when he spoke in support of Robert A. Taft. After Dirksen thundered against two-time presidential nominee Thomas Dewey, mayhem erupted on the floor of the convention hall. Despite Dirksen's best efforts, General Dwight Eisenhower received the Republican nomination, and for the first few years of the Eisenhower presidency Dirksen found himself out of step with the administration. Dirksen's conservatism during this period did not extend to civil rights, however, as he continued to take a forward-looking approach to the issue.

As the 1950s progressed, Dirksen began slowly gravitating toward the popular president. Following Dirksen's reelection in 1956, he emerged as one of Eisenhower's closest Senate allies and as one of the leaders of the Republican caucus. The following year Dirksen was elected MINORITY WHIP. After Republican leader William Knowland left the Senate in 1959, Dirksen became Minority Leader.

Upon his elevation to the office of Minority Leader, Dirksen was quick to consolidate power, in many ways doing what Democratic leader Lyndon Johnson had done a few years earlier on the other side of the aisle. Dirksen ingratiated himself to younger members by distributing committee assignments more equitably. He also assiduously courted his party colleagues, albeit in a less heavy-handed fashion than Johnson. During this time Dirksen and Johnson developed a close working relationship, in large part due to Dirksen's rare ability to assail his political opponents without engendering personal bitterness in the process.

In 1960 John F. Kennedy was elected president, and Dirksen's political fortunes improved still further. With a Democrat in the White House, Dirksen, along with House Minority Leader Charles Halleck, became the national spokesmen for the Republican Party. The two developed what would come to be known (at first derisively) as "the Eve and Charlie Show," a weekly press conference at which both leaders would hold forth on the political issues of the day. This gathering not only reflected Dirksen's enjoyment of the spotlight but also a concerted effort on his part to cultivate the Washington press corps. Dirksen's outreach to the media reflected his prescient understanding of the need for the opposition party in Congress to use the media to get its message out to the public.

Kennedy courted Dirksen with some success. Dirksen played a key role in bringing bipartisan support to a number of Kennedy foreign policy initiatives, such as the Peace Corps, the nuclear test ban treaty, and Kennedy's response to the Cuban missile crisis. Following Kennedy's assassination and Johnson's accession to the presidency, Dirksen's influence grew still further.

In addition to his good relations with the press and his status as a national Republican cospokesman, there were several other factors that contributed to Dirksen's exceptional influence in the 1960s. First, Dirksen enjoyed a number of important personal relationships, the most important of which was with Johnson. For Johnson, Dirksen provided political cover on his right flank and secured important Republican votes on many of his more contentious initiatives. For Dirksen, Johnson provided significant amounts of patronage, prestige from the status he conferred upon Dirksen as a presidential confidante, and a voice in decision making at the highest levels. Dirksen's friendship with Senate Majority Leader Mike Mansfield was also central to his success despite the marked differences between the two men. While Dirksen was every bit the showman and clearly reveled in the limelight, Mansfield was quiet and reserved, happily permitting Dirksen to take center stage on matters such as civil rights.

Second, Dirksen benefited from the structural makeup of the Senate at the time. Senate Democrats easily outnumbered Senate Republicans during the 1960s, but these majorities were less meaningful than they might appear at first blush. A significant number of Senate Democrats were well-placed conservative southerners who shared little of the prevailing Democratic ideology. Contentious measures such as civil rights legislation could not pass the Senate without Republican assistance. In addition to the split within the Democratic ranks, Dirksen benefited from a leadership void that emerged in the early 1960s as a number of prominent members either left the Senate (Johnson), died (Styles Bridges, Robert Kerr), or watched their political support dwindle (Richard Russell). The Senate ethos of the time also benefited Dirksen in that it discouraged legislative individualism, making it easier for a party leader to guide his caucus.

Finally, Dirksen had a number of unique personal attributes that contributed to his success. His magniloquent oratory, disheveled appearance, frequent anecdotes, and colorful conversational style all enhanced his media-savvy approach to the job of Minority Leader. At the same time, these traits also hid a keen mind, a diligent work ethic, and a shrewd political touch. Dirksen prided himself on his mastery not only of the internal politics of the Senate chamber but also of legislative detail. He was both a "show horse" and a "work horse."

By the early 1960s African Americans in the South were staging widespread nonviolent protests to eliminate the system of de jure segregation and subjugation that pervaded the region. In response President Kennedy introduced legislation prohibiting racial discrimination in public establishments. The bill, however, languished in Congress. Standing in the path of this legislation was the southern bloc led by Russell. At the time, in order to end a filibuster in the Senate and permit a bill to come to the floor, a two-thirds vote of all Senators was required (the requirement is three-fifths today). Because of the southern conservatives, Democrats could not shut off debate on their own. Therefore, Republican votes were crucial. Dirksen artfully

maneuvered his way to the center of the debate, refashioned the bill more to his liking, and produced 27 Republican votes (out of 33) for cloture. The vote was the first time in history that cloture had been successfully invoked on a civil rights bill, and it permitted the legislation to be enacted into law.

Despite the 1964 bill, African Americans still faced major obstacles such as restrictions on their right to vote. In 1965 Dirksen again produced important Republican votes for cloture that paved the way for enactment of the Voting Rights Act. This bill was another landmark piece of legislation, providing greatly improved access to the ballot box for African Americans.

Dirksen also proved himself a formidable obstructionist. He was a key player in blocking repeal of a section of the Taft-Hartley Act that permitted states to enact right-to-work legislation. Dirksen was less successful, however, in initiating legislation. Despite his strong commitment to causes such as reinstituting prayer in public schools, Dirksen could not escape the fact that his power was largely reactive: He could position himself so that Democrats had to come to him to negotiate in order to secure a two-thirds vote, but when he sought to affirmatively push his own initiatives, the political support was simply not there.

By the mid 1960s Dirksen began to come under increasing pressure from his Senate Republican colleagues. They were frustrated at Dirksen's close relationship with Johnson, particularly when it manifested itself in Dirksen's vocal support for Johnson's Vietnam policy. Johnson's own party was highly critical of the war, and Dirksen's defense of Johnson made Republican criticism that much more difficult. (In private Dirksen urged Johnson to take stronger measures against North Vietnam, but Dirksen would not publicly air such views until late in the Johnson administration.)

In many ways Dirksen's last hurrah occurred in 1968, when he helped secure cloture for civil rights legislation that allowed better access to housing for African Americans. Passage of the bill, however, could not mask Dirksen's poor showing in rounding up Republican votes, revealing his diminished standing within his caucus.

Dirksen's status would receive a severe blow with the election of Richard Nixon as president in 1968. Whereas with the two previous Democratic presidents Dirksen had enjoyed warm personal relations and had served as national Republican cospokesman, under Nixon Dirksen enjoyed neither advantage. To make matters worse, Dirksen's health also began to fail.

In August 1969 Dirksen died of complications following a difficult surgery. He passed away at the height of his reputation, if not his powers. Like his hero, Abraham Lincoln, Dirksen's body lay in state at the U.S. Capitol (only the fourth senator at that time to have been so honored). President Nixon eulogized him in glowing terms, comparing him favorably to the majority of U.S. presidents. In 1972 the new Senate office building was renamed in his honor.

Everett Dirksen is open to criticism on a number of fronts. His indiscriminate anticommunism during the McCarthy era was unfortunate, and his reflexive support for Johnson's policy in Vietnam in many ways was an abdication of the Minority Leader's role as leader of the loyal opposition. Dirksen can also be criticized for his tendency to flip flop on a number of policy matters. That said, there can be no disputing Dirksen's stature as one of the most prominent Minority Leaders in history. Dirksen's role in the enactment of monumental civil rights legislation of the 1960s can scarcely be overstated; this in and of itself would assure him a significant place in history. When coupled with his pivotal role in both the Senate and the House on scores of other legislative measures ranging from the nuclear test ban treaty to the Legislative Reorganization Act, the full measure of his impressive legacy is brought into view.

Further reading:
Hulsey, Byron. *Everett Dirksen and His Presidents: How a Senate Giant Shaped American Politics.* Lawrence: University Press of Kansas, 2000; Loomis, Burdett. "Everett McKinley Dirksen: The Consummate Minority Leader." In *First Among Equals: Outstanding Senate Leaders of the Twentieth Century,* edited by Roger H. Davidson and Richard A. Baker. Washington, D.C.: Congressional Quarterly Books, 1991; Macneil, Neil. *Dirksen: Portrait of a Public Man.* New York: World Publishing, 1970; Schapsmeier, Edward L. *Dirksen of Illinois: Senatorial Statesman.* Urbana: University of Illinois Press, 1985; Whelan, Charles, and Barbara Whelan. *The Longest Debate: A Legislative History of the 1964 Civil Rights Act.* Washington, D.C.: Seven Locks Press, 1985.

—Roy E. Brownell, II

discharge of committees

Rule XV, Clause 2, of the House of Representatives permits a majority of members the means by which to discharge a committee of a bill and bring the unreported measure to the floor for consideration 30 days after the measure has been referred to committee (normally equal to days the House is in session). In the House the discharge process begins when any member files a discharge petition with the clerk. The petition is then made available for other members to sign, and they may add or remove their names until the discharge petition acquires the requisite 218 signatures (a majority of the chamber), at which time the list is then frozen. Once the necessary signatures are obtained and the committee does not report the measure, the discharge motion is then made by any member who signed the petition. This motion is made either on the second or last Monday of a month that falls at least seven days after the petition is filed or during the last six days of a congressional session. However, if the committee not reporting the measure does report before the discharge motion is offered, the measure is considered under other procedures.

Often, to preserve its role as gatekeeper (when a discharge petition does receive the needed number of signatures) the Rules Committee will intervene and report its own special rule in order to vitiate the discharge and recover the legislative agenda. Such action transpires during the required layover period before a discharge motion can be brought to the floor.

The House has maintained a discharge rule since 1910, although the current method was not adopted until 1931. In 1935 the number of signatures required on the petition was changed, increasing the total from 145 to 218. In 1991 the House permitted debate on and amendment of a special rule reaching the floor through discharge. Two years later, when the Republicans captured the House, the discharge rule was amended to make public the names of members signing discharge petitions by publishing them once a week in the *Congressional Record.* And in 1997 the House prohibited any special rule that would effectively permit nongermane amendments or that would provide for the consideration of more than one measure.

Leadership generally discourages members from using the discharge procedure. According to one study, between 1967 and 2002 only 12 discharge petitions obtained enough signatures to discharge committees, with the House voting for only six of the petitions and considering the other six measures under other procedures.

Senate rules do not provide an equivalent to relieve a standing committee from further consideration of matters referred to it. By practice and precedent unanimous consent will discharge committees. In practice senators have alternative ways of bringing measures to the floor. They may offer the text of an unreported measure as a nongermane amendment to some other measure or introduce an identical measure and have it placed directly on the calendar. Also, by unanimous consent a measure may be multiply referred with a provision that one or more Senate committees are to be automatically discharged if they do not report by a specified time.

See also DISCHARGE RULES.

Further reading:
Beth, Richard S. *The Discharge Rule in the House: Principal Features and Uses.* CRS Report 97-552 GOV. Washington, D.C.: Congressional Research Service, Library of Congress, 2003; Beth, Richard S. *The Discharge Rule in the House: Recent Use in Historical Context.* CRS Report 97-856 GOV. Washington, D.C.: Congressional Research Service, Library of Congress, 2003; Riddick, Floyd M., and Alan S. Frumin. *Riddick's Senate Procedure: Precedents and Practices.* Washington, D.C.: Government Printing Office, 1992.

—Colton C. Campbell

discharge rules

Discharge rules in both the SENATE and the HOUSE OF REPRESENTATIVES are intended to check the discretion of standing committees. When a committee refuses to consider a legislative initiative put before it, discharge rules allow chamber members a mechanism to force floor consideration. These rules are rarely used, however, in part because the norm of committee discretion is so highly valued in Congress.

Because the Senate allows for nongermane amendments to be attached to pending legislation, the discharge rule is rarely used in the upper chamber. Members interested in moving legislation out of committee can simply attach the entire bill to a different piece of legislation to force floor consideration. Committee discharge is also unlikely because motions to discharge must be made and the debate completed during MORNING HOUR. Because the Senate is more inclined to recess from one day to the next, instead of adjourning, morning hours are rare. Moreover, it is unlikely that debate on a discharge motion could be completed in this limited amount of time. Lastly, the motion to discharge in the Senate is open to debate, thus establishing opportunities for FILIBUSTER. Even if a discharge petition in the Senate made it to the Senate calendar, it is improbable that a unanimous consent agreement could be brokered to allow for consideration on the floor.

In the House of Representatives a discharge petition is more likely. However, it is still a relatively rare occurrence. The opportunity to petition for committee discharge was established by House rules in 1910. The rule was adopted in response to the centralizing and authoritative maneuvers of a SPEAKER OF THE HOUSE, JOSEPH CANNON, a Republican from Illinois. The basic procedures for committee discharge in the House today were adopted in 1931. However, there was a significant change made to the rules in 1993. Now, the names of members signing a discharge petition are made public. This recent change creates the possibility that a discharge petition can be used as a political tactic to put legislators on the record as either supporting or opposing particular legislation.

The table below provides a list of the number of discharge requests that were filed with the CLERK OF THE HOUSE in each Congress since 1931. A much smaller number of petitions garnered sufficient signatures or actually forced legislation out of a committee. Discharge attempts were most common in the period 1933 to 1950, when Democrats often had control of both chambers of Congress and the presidency. A coalition of Republicans and southern Democrats were often behind these discharge efforts in the House.

The discharge rule (Rule XV, clause 2) in the House of Representatives spells out the procedures for forcing floor consideration of legislation caught in a committee. A member wishing to discharge legislation files a request with the Clerk of the House, who draws up the petition. At least 30 days must have passed from the date that a committee received the legislation before a discharge request will be considered by the Clerk's office. Most often, representatives wait much longer than 30 days and attempt other strategies to prompt committee consideration. The discharge petition

| DISCHARGE PETITIONS FILED IN THE HOUSE OF REPRESENTATIVES (1931–2004) ||
Congress (Years)	Total Petitions Filed
72nd (1931–1932)	12
73rd (1933–1934)	31
74th (1935–1936)	33
75th (1937–1938)	43
76th (1939–1940)	37
77th (1941–1942)	15
78th (1943–1944)	21
79th (1945–1946)	35
80th (1947–1948)	20
81st (1949–1950)	34
82nd (1951–1952)	14
83rd (1953–1954)	10
84th (1955–1956)	6
85th (1957–1958)	7
86th (1959–1960)	7
87th (1961–1962)	6
88th (1963–1964)	5
89th (1965–1966)	6
90th (1967–1968)	4
91st (1969–1970)	12
92nd (1971–1972)	15
93rd (1973–1974)	10
94th (1975–1976)	15
95th (1977–1978)	11
96th (1979–1980)	14
97th (1981–1982)	24
98th (1983–1984)	13
99th (1985–1986)	10
100th (1987–1988)	5
101st (1989–1990)	8
102nd (1991–1992)	8
103rd (1993–1994)	26
104th (1995–1996)	15
105th (1997–1998)	8
106th (1999–2000)	11
107th (2001–2002)	12
108th (2003–2004)	16

Source: Beth, Richard S. *The Discharge Rule in the House: Recent Use in Historical Context.* Washington, D.C.: Congressional Research Service, 2001.

is usually considered a last recourse for members trying to bring legislation to a vote.

The petition must be signed by a majority of all representatives, currently 218 members.[2] If the requisite number of signatures is obtained, the list is frozen; the names of the people who signed the petition are printed in the CONGRESSIONAL RECORD, and the motion to discharge is placed on the discharge calendar. Private bills and House resolutions attempting to establish investigating committees are not subject to discharge motions. Delegates from the territories and Washington, D.C., are not permitted to sign a discharge petition.

The discharge calendar is called the second and fourth Mondays of each month while Congress is in session. The motion to discharge may be offered on either of these days, provided that day's session is at least seven legislative days after the motion was first entered on the calendar. The motion, once recognized, is debated for 20 minutes on the floor, with the time split evenly between opponents and supporters of the motion. If after the debate a majority of members present support the motion, the committee is discharged and the floor can consider the legislation.

Further reading:
Beth, Richard S. *The Discharge Rule in the House: Recent Use in Historical Context.* Washington, D.C.: Congressional Research Service, Library of Congress, 2003; Durden, Barry C. "The Discharge Rule and Majoritarian Politics in the U.S. House of Representatives." Presented at the annual meeting of the American Political Science Association, Philadelphia, 2003; Smith, Steven S. *The American Congress.* 2d ed. New York: Houghton Mifflin, 1999.
—Scot D. Schraufnagel

discipline of members
The Constitution grants each house of Congress the power to form its own rules and to enforce those rules. The only punishment expressly stated in the Constitution, however, is expulsion, which requires a two-thirds majority vote of the respective body. A member can also be impeached by the HOUSE OF REPRESENTATIVES and removed by the SENATE under Congress's IMPEACHMENT POWERS. Only one senator has been impeached, but the Senate chose to expel him instead of finding him guilty of the specified charges.

Only 19 members of Congress have been expelled since the body formed, and 17 of those were expelled for disloyalty during the Civil War. In order to enforce the rules, each house has developed a system to discipline its members through punishments short of expulsion. The

procedures for each house are fairly similar and range from an informal call to order by the chair to a formal censure.

The most dramatic form of discipline available short of expulsion is censure. More than 30 members of Congress have been formally censured by their colleagues for a variety of offenses. Censuring a member of either house is easier than expulsion because it requires only a majority vote. Perhaps the most famous case of censure occurred in the Senate. In 1954 Senator JOSEPH R. MCCARTHY, a Republican from Wisconsin, was censured for insulting senators and a variety of other charges stemming from his committee hearings on communist infiltration of the federal government. The actual language of the resolution against McCarthy used the word *condemned* instead of *censure,* but historians have reached a consensus that McCarthy's condemnation had the same force and effect as a censure.

While the procedures used to reach a vote on censure are similar between the houses, there are a few important differences. In the Senate a senator being investigated is given the right to speak on his or her behalf. The House decides whether a member can speak on his or her behalf on a case-by-case basis, and often the House has chosen not to let the member speak. The most striking difference between the houses, however, is the method by which the members are presented with a censure. In the Senate the censure resolution is read aloud in the chamber to the senator in question, but the senator is allowed the usual dignity reserved for a member of that body. On the other hand, the House treats a member being censured as if he or she were a criminal, which was the case in at least some cases. The SPEAKER OF THE HOUSE summons the member to stand before the chamber as the resolution is read aloud. The House's procedures are more reminiscent of a criminal sentencing than anything ordinarily found in the chamber.

A less severe form of punishment, developed by the House STANDARDS OF OFFICIAL CONDUCT COMMITTEE in 1976, is the reprimand. The only major difference between a reprimand and a censure in the House is that a member of the House is not publicly admonished by the Speaker in the chamber. The Senate has only reprimanded one member, Senator Alan Cranston, a Democrat from California, and he was treated in the same manner as if he were being censured. The only difference was that the Ethics Committee issued the reprimand, and the full body never voted on the resolution.

In recent decades other forms of minor punishments have been developed by each chamber's ethics committees. The early 1990s saw the introduction of the formal rebuke by the Senate Ethics Committee. Like the reprimand, the committee acts on behalf on the entire body. Even more recently the committees have begun issuing public or private letters of reproval when the transgressions are appro-

---

[2] The requirement that a majority of all members (218) must sign the petition was established in 1935.

priately minor. The most recent case of a committee issuing a letter of reproval was the case of Senator Robert G. Torricelli, a Democrat from New Jersey. Even though there was no formal action taken against him by the full Senate, he was forced to withdraw from his reelection campaign.

An even less severe form of punishment can be handed out by the party caucus instead of either the full house or the appropriate ethics committee. If a majority of the member's party agrees, he or she can be stripped of any chairs or other leadership positions the member holds. The most recent case of this was for Senator Trent Lott, a Republican from Mississippi, who lost his position as MAJORITY LEADER through pressure from his party.

In 1975 the House established a rule that was subsequently added to the House Code of Official Conduct stating that any representative charged with a crime that carries a penalty of imprisonment for two years or more loses the right to participate in House votes or committee hearings. The member regains the ability to participate in House activities if the charges are reversed on appeal or the member is reelected.

Further reading:
Congressional Quarterly. *Congressional Quarterly's Guide to Congress.* 3d ed. Washington, D.C.: Congressional Quarterly Press, 1982; U.S. Congress, House Committee on Standards and Official Conduct. *Ethics Manual for Members, Officers, and Employees of the U.S. House of Representatives.* 102d Cong., 2d sess. Washington, D.C.: Government Printing Office, 1992; U.S. Congress, Senate Select Committee on Ethics. *Senate Ethics Manual.* 108th Cong., 1st sess. Washington, D.C.: Government Printing Office, 2003.

—Brian M. McGowan

District of Columbia

The District of Columbia is the official seat of the federal government, or capital, of the United States. It lies on the Potomac River between Maryland and Virginia and is home to approximately 570,000 Americans, including the president of the United States. Most members of Congress maintain a residence either inside the district or in nearby surrounding towns.

Within the District of Columbia lie many of the most important federal government buildings, such as the Capitol, the White House, and the Supreme Court. The downtown area also is home to many famous national monuments and archives including the Lincoln, Washington, and Jefferson Memorials, the Smithsonian national museum system, the National Archives, and the Vietnam Memorial.

The city is named for George Washington and Christopher Columbus. Originally, *Washington* referred to just the city and *District of Columbia* to the two surrounding 10-

mile-square tracts of land ceded to the federal government by Virginia and Maryland for its creation, but the city now occupies the whole of the district. In 1845 Virginia was given back its tract of land, although many important government buildings, such as the Pentagon, are on the Virginia side of the Potomac.

Washington, D.C., was the United States' first planned city. The creation of the District of Columbia was mandated by the Constitution, which called for a permanent national seat of government to be built for use by the new government. After some haggling in Congress over the location, the Potomac was chosen. Architect Pierre L'Enfant was given the job of planning the city. Work began in 1791, and President John Adams moved from Philadelphia to Washington in June 1800. The December session of Congress took place in Washington the same year.

The District of Columbia has been the capital of the United States since 1800 and has served as the location for virtually every major battle in Congress during the past 200 years. The district itself has been at the center of several political battles. Early opponents of slavery attempted to ban the practice in Washington, despite the district being firmly lodged between two slave states. In more recent times the voting rights of Americans who live in Washington have become controversial. The Twenty-third Amendment gave Washington electoral votes in presidential elections, but citizens who live inside the district still do not have representatives in either the House of Representatives or the Senate.

See also CAPITOL BUILDING.

Further reading:
Arnebeck, Bob. *Through a Fiery Trail: Building Washington, 1790–1800.* New York: Madison Books, 1991; Wurman, Richard Saul. *Access Washington, DC.* 7th ed. New York: AccessPress, 2002.

—Matthew Glassman

districts

Members of Congress are elected by and represent people from particular geographic areas, or territorial jurisdictions, called districts. While the term *district* is also widely used for elected officials at all levels of government in the United States for state legislators, county commissioners, city council members, and local school board members, for example, the unique application of the term to Congress stems from the U.S. Constitution.

The geographic area is easily identified for a U.S. senator because the specific defined territory is the entirety of a single state. Article I, Section 3, Clause 1, of the Constitution requires that the SENATE be composed of two senators from each state, and thus residents of each state have two individuals representing them since ratification of the Seventeenth Amendment in 1913 requiring direct election through a statewide vote of the people; previous to this amendment senators were chosen by the state legislature. Because a district for a senator is identical to a state's geographic area, the custom has been not to use the term district but to identify and introduce senators by using the state's name, as in Senator WILLIAM FRIST of Tennessee, for example.

The use of the term *congressional district* applies to the HOUSE OF REPRESENTATIVES. The concept of the geographic area or congressional district for a member of the House is more complicated because Article I, Section 2, Clause 3, requires that the number of representatives be apportioned among the states on the basis of their population. While the Constitution does not specify the exact size of the House membership, its current 435-member size was established in Public Law 62-5 and took effect in 1913. Until that time the House allowed itself to expand to accommodate both new states and the country's population growth. Every state, regardless of population, has at least one representative.

Currently, seven states with relatively small populations (Alaska, Delaware, Montana, North Dakota, South Dakota, Vermont, and Wyoming) have only one representative. Accordingly, districts for each of these seven members are equivalent to their own state's geographic area, just as for senators from these same states. These seven House members are described as members-at-large, meaning they have been elected by the voters statewide rather than those within a numbered congressional district.

However, most states have been apportioned more than one seat in the House because their relative percent-

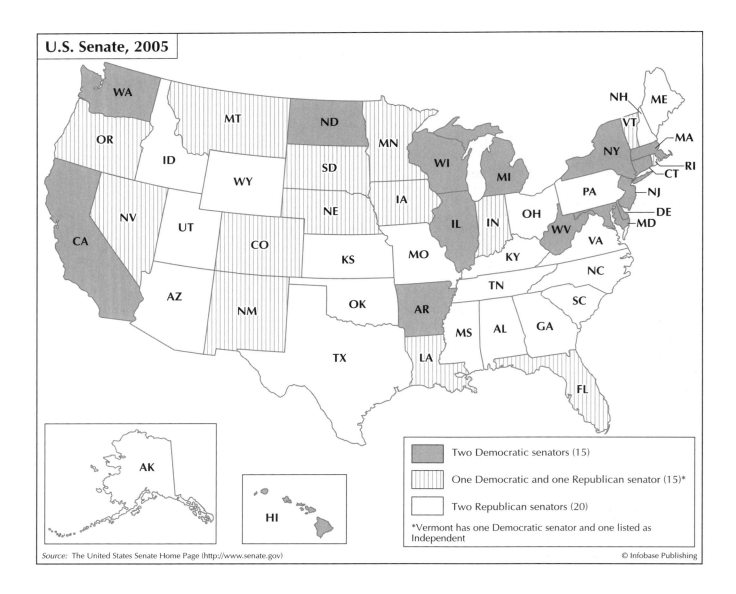

U.S. Senate, 2005

Two Democratic senators (15)

One Democratic and one Republican senator (15)*

Two Republican senators (20)

*Vermont has one Democratic senator and one listed as Independent

Source: The United States Senate Home Page (http://www.senate.gov)

© Infobase Publishing

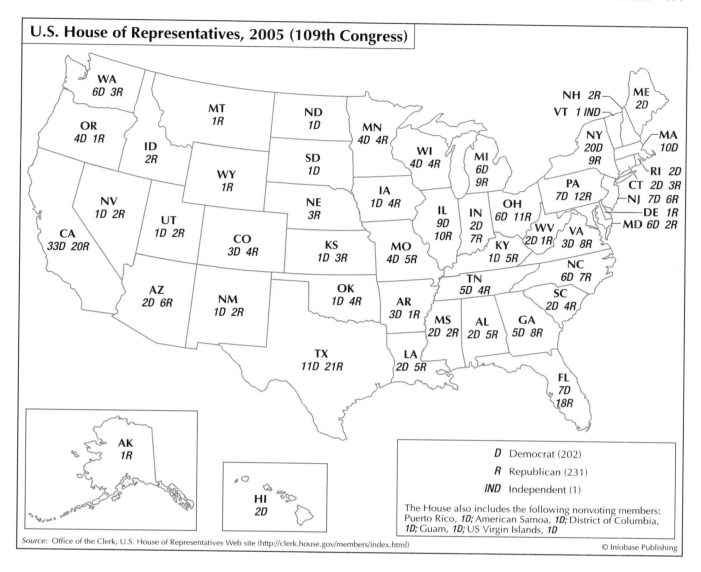

U.S. House of Representatives, 2005 (109th Congress)

WA 6D 3R
OR 4D 1R
MT 1R
ID 2R
WY 1R
NV 1D 2R
CA 33D 20R
UT 1D 2R
CO 3D 4R
AZ 2D 6R
NM 1D 2R
ND 1D
SD 1D
NE 3R
KS 1D 3R
OK 1D 4R
TX 11D 21R
MN 4D 4R
IA 1D 4R
MO 4D 5R
AR 3D 1R
LA 2D 5R
WI 4D 4R
IL 9D 10R
MS 2D 2R
MI 6D 9R
IN 2D 7R
KY 1D 5R
TN 5D 4R
AL 2D 5R
OH 6D 11R
WV 2D 1R
VA 3D 8R
NC 6D 7R
SC 2D 4R
GA 5D 8R
FL 7D 18R
NH 2R
VT 1 IND
NY 20D 9R
PA 7D 12R
ME 2D
MA 10D
RI 2D
CT 2D 3R
NJ 7D 6R
DE 1R
MD 6D 2R

AK 1R

HI 2D

D Democrat (202)
R Republican (231)
IND Independent (1)

The House also includes the following nonvoting members:
Puerto Rico, *1D;* American Samoa, *1D;* District of Columbia,
1D; Guam, *1D;* US Virgin Islands, *1D*

Source: Office of the Clerk, U.S. House of Representatives Web site (http://clerk.house.gov/members/index.html)

© Infobase Publishing

age of the nation's total population justifies it. California, the most populous state from the 2000 census, has been apportioned 53 of the 435 seats using congressionally established procedures because its state population constitutes approximately 12 percent of the national population. There are 53 California congressional districts for these 53 House members. The next largest state, Texas, has 32 congressional districts; New York has 29, Florida 25, and so forth. For each state having more than one member in the House, congressional districts are numbered consecutively. In California there exists a 1st District through a 53rd District. Just as a senator may be introduced as the Senator from California, for example, a member of the House may be introduced as the representative from California's 53rd District. Each numbered congressional district following the 2000 census has a population of about 650,000.

The U.S. Supreme Court ruled in *Department of Commerce v. U.S. House of Representatives* that an actual enumeration and not a sampling or estimate of population is required by Article I, Section 2, Clause 3, of the Constitution. A population census is conducted every 10 years by the U.S. Census Bureau in the Department of Commerce. Results of this decennial census can mean gains or losses in the number of representatives in a state from one decade to the next. Following the 2000 census Arizona, Florida, Georgia, and Texas gained two seats, and California, Colorado, Nevada, and North Carolina gained one. Correspondingly, New York and Pennsylvania lost two seats each, and Connecticut, Illinois, Indiana, Michigan, Mississippi, Oklahoma, and Wisconsin lost one seat.

It is not Congress, however, that creates and numbers the congressional districts from which House members serve. Article I, Section 4, of the U.S. Constitution grants to state legislatures the right to prescribe congressional districts, subject to constraints established by Congress and the Supreme Court. In most states the exact legal geographic territory constituting a congressional district is determined by the state legislature, but some states have established special redistricting commissions or identified by state law other means to fulfill these obligations, usually after a decennial census has been completed. In cases in which state legislatures, often because of partisan disputes, have been unable to produce redistricting plans to send to governors for signature (or possible gubernatorial veto, after which the legislation is returned to the legislature for possible veto override requiring super-majority votes in each chamber of the state legislature), the task of congressional redistricting has sometimes fallen to the courts. Recent court decisions have recognized that states may undertake redistricting more than once in a decade unless state or federal law prohibits it.

Incumbent members who intend to stand for reelection to Congress take a keen interest in the work of state legislatures or other bodies undertaking a congressional redistricting process. Many House members may even be involved in the process of suggesting or responding to plans to make changes in their district boundaries, often through colleagues and friends from their own political party who are serving in the state legislature or the governor's office.

By its very nature the congressional redistricting process is a highly political one, and the partisan stakes are high because even small shifts in the number of voters identified with political parties in a district can often change election outcomes. Candidates for Congress can be either advantaged or disadvantaged in the congressional redistricting process depending upon whether their political party controls either or both of the chambers in the state legislature or has a governor from their party serving to sign or veto the bill when it reaches the state chief executive's desk. Even in cases in which the party of the House member does control the state legislative branch, there may be difficulty in making district boundary decisions that would please an incumbent or a possible challenger due to many competing considerations.

The congressional redistricting process undertaken by a state legislature, whether because the census has determined that the number of representatives should be increased or decreased, or simply because populations within the state have shifted, is a complicated one. In *Department of Commerce v. U.S. House of Representatives* (525 U.S. 316, 1999) the Supreme Court narrowly ruled as unconstitutional the Census Bureau's planned use of statistical samplings in the 2000 Census. However, the Census Bureau ignored the ruling and used the statistical technique, termed "hot-deck imputation," which enabled offi-

cials to estimate the number of uncounted citizens in a state. The Bureau's use of this technique ignited a second lawsuit, *Utah v. Evans* (536 U.S. 452 2002), when Utah officials charged that the "hot-deck imputation" system awarded a fourth House seat allocated for their state to North Carolina instead. The 5-4 Utah decision upheld the statistical technique that had been approved by Congress.

In undertaking congressional redistricting, a state legislature or other body may try to keep whole counties or cities or towns in a single congressional district if possible. These units have traditionally served as the building blocks in the redistricting process. There have also been attempts to have each congressional district be compact and contiguous or connected. Indeed, as early as the Apportionment Act of 1842 Congress sought to require that districts be contiguous, and the Apportionment Act of 1901 required compactness. While no federal legislation since 1929 has required compactness and contiguity for congressional districts, they are still viewed as desirable characteristics for districts. But these may run headlong into other critical demands and requirements as well, specifically those set by court rulings.

As late as the 1960s many congressional districts were malapportioned, having severely unequal populations. Often growing urban populations were systematically underrepresented. The U.S. Supreme Court in *Karchev v. Daggett,* 462 U.S. 725 (1983), sought adherence to strict standards of numerical equality among congressional districts, and New Jersey's effort that produced a range of 0.70 percent in size differences among its districts was struck down because the evidence indicated the state legislature could have reduced the range to 0.45 percent. An earlier case before the Supreme Court, WESBERRY V. SANDERS, 376 U.S. 1 (1964), required that as nearly as practicable one person's vote in a congressional election be worth as much as another's. This one-person, one-vote principle, based on the Equal Protection Clause of the Fourteenth Amendment, has become an overriding standard during state redistricting.

A second significant standard during redistricting has involved compliance with the VOTING RIGHTS ACT OF 1965 and amendments in 1982 that outlawed the effect of dilution of the political influence of minorities. In *Thornburg v. Gingles* (1986) the Supreme Court found that a state legislature should redistrict in such a way as to effectuate an increase in African-American and other minority representation in Congress, and the makeup of Congress after the 1990 census resulted in such increases.

In a later case, *SHAW V. RENO* (1993), the Supreme Court considered a complaint from North Carolina residents who objected to the creation of a new congressional district that stretched approximately 160 miles along Interstate 85 and for much of its length was no wider than the I-85 corridor. It was alleged that this proposed district concentrated a majority of black voters arbitrarily without regard to considerations such as compactness, contiguousness, geographical boundaries, or political subdivisions. A closely divided Court found that appearances do matter and that an apportionment plan that included in one district individuals who belonged to the same race but who were otherwise separated by geographical and political boundaries and who may have had little in common with one another but the color of their skin bears an uncomfortable resemblance to political apartheid and thus remanded the case to the lower federal court to determine whether the plan incorporated any common interest other than race. Ultimately, the North Carolina legislature redrew the district boundaries somewhat from the original proposed district.

Drawing congressional district boundaries requires a careful balancing of racial and ethnic but not necessarily partisan fairness, contiguity of district shape and demographics, and respect for existing political subdivisions and communities of interest while adhering to the one-person, one-vote standard. While peculiarly shaped districts have often been created to provide one political party a majority in as many districts as possible, commonly known as PARTISAN GERRYMANDERING, the above-described affirmative RACIAL GERRYMANDERING and even incumbent protection gerrymandering has been made more feasible through the use of census tract data and the use of computer technology to produce particular results for the required single-member congressional districts called for in the 1967 Public Law 90-196.

House of Representatives single-member districts, those requiring that only one individual in an election contest will be a winner and thus be the sole representative of the particular geographic area, are not specified in the Constitution. Indeed, a majority of the original 13 states in the first congressional election used multimember districts. In the first handful of apportionments no particular direction to the states was given by Congress, and consequently the states elected representatives in several ways, including electing their entire House delegation statewide, having congressional districts elect more than one representative, and combinations of single-member district elections for some congressional districts and multimember district elections for other congressional districts.

It was not until the Apportionment Act of 1842 that single districts were first required by Congress, and even then a few states (Georgia, Mississippi, Missouri, and New Hampshire) elected their representatives at large, and the House of Representatives after debate still seated them. By 1967 Congress finally enacted legislation that followed up its earlier passage of the Voting Rights Act of 1965, prohibiting both at-large and other multimember elections for congressional districts in states apportioned more than one

House seat. Only the states of Hawaii and New Mexico were directly affected by that legislation. The concept and tradition of single-member congressional districts is now required by law.

See also APPORTIONMENT AND REDISTRICTING.

Further reading:
Hacker, Andrew. *Congressional Districting: The Issue of Equal Representation.* Washington, D.C.: Brookings Institution Press, 1963; Martis, Kenneth C. *The Historical Atlas of United States Congressional Districts, 1789–1983.* New York: Free Press, 1982; National Conference of State Legislatures Redistricting Task Force. *Redistricting Law 2000.* Denver, Colo.: NCSL, 1999; Office of the Clerk, U.S. House of Representatives. Available online. URL: http://clerk.house.gov/index.html. Accessed January 16, 2006.

—Robert P. Goss

divided government

The term *divided government* has dominated discussions of American national politics inside Washington and in the academic world for several decades now. The concept of divided government (and its opposite, unified government) has to do with control of the elected branches of American national government by the two major political parties, the Democrats and the Republicans. Unified government occurs when control of Congress and the presidency is exercised by the same political party. When both parties control some aspect (the presidency, the HOUSE OF REPRESENTATIVES, or the SENATE), then divided government occurs.

Though having unified government in the administration of President George W. Bush, divided government has been the trend in recent decades. For example, between 1981 and 2000 there was constant divided government except for 1993–94 (Democratic president Bill Clinton governed with a Democratic House and Senate). During the presidency of Ronald Reagan, a Republican, the Democrats held the House all eight years and for three Congresses the Senate, also. During the Clinton presidency six years featured Republican control of Congress.

Since the traditional thinking on political parties is that they unify what the founders (namely James Madison) sought to splinter apart in an institutional sense, many elites in American society (some in academia such as Samuel Huntington, many in the media such as Mark Shields) have regarded the rise of divided government as a bad thing. Here is how this thinking goes: We could get more done in our gauntlet of American government if the same party controlled everything. The commonsensical idea is that it is hard enough to govern without the parties trying to block each other's initiatives, which happens, it is reasoned, when divided government occurs. When one party has the presidency and the other at least one house of Congress, those individuals who control the institutional levers of power in one institution will have vastly different policy preferences than the leaders of the other institution, especially in the recent era of polarized parties in Washington.

This conventional wisdom became widely spouted in the media (it still is) and at academic conference panels to a point that assumptions about the negative effects of divided government became a deeply rooted assumption, almost an ideology of sorts. If we only had unified government, things would get done, many would say. Divided government was an ideology, that is, until David Mayhew came along and got academics, at least, to reexamine their thinking about party control. Mayhew made the basic observation that many major policy innovations enacted in the latter half of the 20th century occurred during times of divided government. For example, most of President Clinton's major policies were enacted when the opposition party (the Republicans) controlled Congress.

Perhaps, Mayhew reasoned, we should test empirically to determine whether divided government truly halts innovation, as everyone assumes it does. The title of his book on the subject, *Divided We Govern*, says it all. Mayhew found roughly equal levels of landmark enactments in periods of divided government and unified government.

In his impressive study, Mayhew examined acts that passed into law, comparing the propensity of innovation (landmark acts culled through two fairly systematic sweeps of various sources) in times of divided government as compared to unified government. But, scholars would say, if there is to be an effect of divided government, it should be in blocking things from passing in the first place. Hence, George Edwards and associates argued, we should look at what did not pass (legislative failures) for the effects of party control on lawmaking. They used various CONGRESSIONAL QUARTERLY sources to enumerate all significant legislative failures from 1949 to 1994. When they used Mayhew's measures as a numerator and their failures count plus Mayhew's count as a denominator, they found a significant negative effect for divided government. Legislative productivity, in other words, went down as a percentage of significant bills considered during times of divided government. More things passed, controlling for what was attempted, in unified government.

Regarding the legislative effects of divided party control, scholars now engage in debates about the effects, rather than assuming there is a base effect. In fact, a whole path of inquiry in congressional studies (the information, or median voter, model) assumes that political parties have no substantial effect on legislative organization and outcomes beyond their preferences. Still, many legislative scholars argue that parties matter greatly in legislatures and that party control, likewise, is an important determinant of legislative outcomes, qualitatively if not quantitatively. Outside of academic circles, the conventional wisdom about divided government never really went away. One of the often quoted sound-bites on the talk show circuit is that divided government makes it impossible to get anything done. In the final analysis, perhaps Mayhew had it at least partially right in noting that things still get done in divided government.

Further reading:
Edwards, George C., Andrew Barrett, and Jeffrey Peake. "The Legislative Impact of Divided Government." *American Journal of Political Science* 41, no. 2 (1997): 545–564, 1997; Krehbiel, Keith. *Information and Legislative Organization.* Ann Arbor: University of Michigan Press, 1991; Mayhew, David R. *Divided We Govern.* New Haven, Conn.: Yale University Press, 1991; Rohde, David W. *Parties and Leaders in the Post-reform House.* Chicago: University of Chicago Press, 1991.

—Glen S. Krutz

Dole, Robert J. (1923–   ) *Representative, Senator*
Bob Dole, a Republican from Kansas, is one of the largest political figures of 20th-century American politics. He was born on July 22, 1923, in Russell, Kansas. The son of a working-class family, Dole suffered through the depths of the Great Depression early in his life. He attended the University of Kansas from 1941 to 1943 and the University of Arizona from 1948 to 1949. He received undergraduate and law degrees from Washburn University in Topeka, Kansas, in 1952. From 1943 to 1948 he served in the army, where in April 1945 in Italy he suffered a serious injury that paralyzed his right hand. He spent the next four years in hospitals recovering from the injury.

Dole was elected to the Kansas state house in 1951 and served for two years. He served as the Russell County prosecutor from 1953 to 1961. He was then elected to the U.S. House of Representatives in 1960, where he remained for the next eight years. In the Republican primary in 1960, Dole beat Keith G. Sebelius for an open House seat by a mere 982 votes but went on to defeat his Democratic opponent in the general election in a solidly Republican district. As a result of redistricting, the state's two western seats were united in 1962, and Dole easily defeated J. Floyd Breeding, the Democratic incumbent. Dole had a tougher time in 1964, a year that favored the Democrats nationwide, but he still won against Bill Bork, his Democratic opponent.

In 1968 Dole decided to run for the U.S. Senate when incumbent Republican senator Frank Carlson chose to step down. Dole won the Republican nomination against former governor William H. Avery and went on to easily defeat William I. Robinson, the Democratic nominee and a Wichita lawyer, in the fall. Dole had a tougher contest in his first reelection to the Senate in 1974, a bad year nationally for the Republicans due to the Watergate scandal. His Democratic opponent, William Roy, a four-year House member, perhaps played the Watergate card a bit too much, and Dole won in the end. After that he coasted through reelections in 1980, 1986, and 1992.

As a legislator Dole first and foremost sought to protect the interests of his home state. As a member of the Senate Agriculture Committee, he routinely supported farm programs and food stamps, even by breaking ranks with the Republican conservatives who opposed these programs. As an old-fashioned midwestern Republican, he believed in balanced budgets and advocated higher taxes to avoid deficits. He ardently supported many civil rights laws, especially the rights of the handicapped, an issue near and dear to his heart because of his personal injury. On the other hand, he opposed abortion and advocated a strong military and an assertive American foreign policy. In the 1980s he helped win passage of assistance to the Nicaraguan contras, and in 1991 he helped steer the resolution authorizing the Persian Gulf War. As such, in his policy stands Dole possessed both moderate and conservative streaks. He maintained a generally conservative voting record throughout his congressional career.

Dole came to national prominence upon entering the Senate. As a freshman member of the minority party when he arrived, Dole had little influence either in the committees or on the floor. He thus spent most of his time on the floor defending the policies of President Richard Nixon. A loyalty to his party's presidents became a hallmark of Dole's congressional career. In response in 1971 Nixon appointed him chair of the Republican National Committee (RNC), a position he held until 1973. Dole's star continued to rise in Republican politics, as President Gerald Ford chose him to be his vice presidential running mate in 1976. However, the Republicans lost the election. Dole then launched his own unsuccessful bid for the presidency in 1980.

Upon the election of President Ronald Reagan in 1980, the Republicans gained majority seats in the Senate and hence control of congressional committees. Dole became chair of the coveted SENATE FINANCE COMMITTEE in 1981, and his senatorial career began to skyrocket. In his capacity as chair of the finance committee, he again displayed his characteristic of advancing his president's agenda when he guided Reagan's tax cut package of 1981. After the 1984 election, when then Senate majority leader Howard H. Baker, Jr., a Republican from Tennessee, retired, the Republicans selected Dole as their leader. Dole had now "arrived" in Washington politics. He got the pres-

Robert J. Dole *(Library of Congress)*

idential itch again in 1988 but after scoring some early victories in the nomination process, lost the nod to George H. W. Bush. After the election Dole faithfully "carried the water" for Bush on CAPITOL HILL.

As a leader Dole displayed two somewhat contradictory traits: partisanship and pragmatism. He practiced traditional conservatism and hardball politics, yet he was ready to compromise and cut deals. He relentlessly stood by his party's agenda yet quickly yielded to the other side when he thought it was necessary. Dole employed the pragmatic approach because he understood, more than most, that in order to get anything done in the fragmented American political system, he must work with those on the other side of the aisle. Throughout his career he was known as someone who could go behind closed doors with his adversaries and quickly come out with a deal.

Dole never shied away from using his power to keep his troops in line, sometimes through force, sometimes persuasion, and sometimes tongue-lashing. Due to his aggressive use of the Senate's rules and procedures and his friendly relations with many Republicans and Democrats, he demonstrated that the Senate of 100 "prima donnas" could, in fact, be led. He peppered his legislative style with a biting sense of humor and a quick wit. His leadership style was in sharp contrast to the cordial Baker, his immediate predecessor as the Republican leader of the Senate.

Personally, Dole has always believed in the puritanical work ethic. Hard work and perseverance characterized his childhood in Kansas as he struggled through the Depression years, his World War II years as he battled through his injury, and his political years as he fought his opponents in elections and on the Senate floor for his issues and ideas. As a thinker, Dole believes in an America where anyone can succeed at anything provided one is willing to put in what it takes.

In the 1990s Dole became a larger-than-life political figure. The election of Bill Clinton as president in 1992 brought renewed prominence to Dole. Although the House and Senate were still in Democratic hands, Dole was the Republican leader of the Senate, making him the leading Republican in the nation and the party's standard-bearer. He rejected Clinton's economic stimulus program in 1993 and opposed his budget and tax packages. He showed some interest in Clinton's health care reform initiatives but refused to compromise, favoring modest rather than grand changes. He criticized the president on Whitewater issues as well as on his Bosnia policy.

The election of 1994 gave Dole even greater standing in American politics. The Republicans won the House for the first time in 40 years and regained control of the Senate. Given the rules and procedures of the Senate that make it extremely easy to block initiatives and given the heady reforms being proposed in the House by the conservative reformers, this meant that Dole would, in fact, control the Republican agenda. Early in his career Dole had had an icy relationship with Newt Gingrich (R-GA), the new Speaker of the House, but in 1994 Dole endorsed many of the reforms embodied in the CONTRACT WITH AMERICA being railroaded in the House by Gingrich and his lieutenants. Many reforms passed the House but fizzled in the Senate due to lack of support in that chamber.

The younger conservatives, however, not just in the House but in his own caucus in the Senate as well, caused headaches for Dole. The Republicans elected in the 1980s and 1990s, particularly those from the South, showed little regard for negotiating, compromising, bargaining, or getting along with the other side. They also showed little patience for the Senate's deliberative procedures and traditions. This approach to politics contrasted sharply with Dole's pragmatism. In the 101st Congress he thought about stepping down as the Republican leader, and in the 102nd Congress considered leaving the Senate altogether. But the 103rd and 104th Congresses brought renewed vigor and purpose to Dole, especially as the Republicans regained control of Congress in the 104th Congress, as noted above.

The newfound energy and his majority leadership status made Dole the focal point of American politics in the mid-1990s, and he was riding high in the polls. He thus decided to challenge Clinton for the White House in 1996, especially as Clinton appeared weak after the Democrats lost control of both houses of Congress to the Republicans in 1994. However, Dole soon realized that the demands of his job as the Majority Leader made it impossible for him to keep that position and pursue his presidential dream. In a stunning speech on the Senate floor in July 1996, he announced his resignation as the Majority Leader and that he would not return to the Senate if he lost his presidential bid.

However, the third time would not be a charm for Dole's presidential aspirations. He secured the Republican nomination this time, as opposed to his previous two efforts, in 1980 and 1988, and indeed was leading in the early polls against Clinton. But as the campaign entered the fall of 1996 the older Dole fell behind and lost the presidency to the younger Clinton.

That ended a distinguished career in 20th-century American politics. Dole served 35 years in Congress, 28 of those in the Senate. He served as the Senate Majority Leader for four years (from 1984 to 1986 and again from 1994 to 1996) and as the Senate minority leader for eight years (from 1986 to 1994), making him the Senate Republican leader for a longer time than anyone else in history. Throughout his career Dole was not a political theorist but rather a deal-maker. He was a master politician who stood up for his party but who also understood the necessity of getting along with the other side.

In his postcongressional life Dole remains an influential figure in Republican politics. Away from the restraints of electoral shackles, he has even reacquired his humor, making commercials for Viagra and Pepsi.

Further reading:
Cramer, Richard Ben. *Bob Dole.* New York: Vintage, 1995; Hilton, Stanley. *Senator Bob Dole: An Unauthorized Biography.* New York: St. Martin's, 1995; Wertime, Marcia. *Bob Dole: Politician.* Philadelphia: Chelsea House, 1997.

—Sunil Ahuja

Doorkeeper of the House

The elected officer of the HOUSE OF REPRESENTATIVES whose duties include enforcement of the privileges of the House is called the Doorkeeper. On April 2, 1789, the First Congress established the office of the Doorkeeper of the House of Representatives by passing a resolution: "That a door-keeper and an assistant door-keeper be appointed for service of this House." The first Doorkeeper was Gifford Dalley, and his assistant was Thomas

Claxton. Claxton was elected Doorkeeper in 1795 and held the post until 1821. The most famous Doorkeeper was William M. "Fish Bait" Miller of Pascagoula, Mississippi. Miller served as Doorkeeper from 1949 to 1953 and again from 1955 until the House Democratic caucus rejected his bid for reelection in 1974. Miller chronicled his experiences in his book *Fish Bait: The Memoirs of the Congressional Doorkeeper*. The entire House elects the Doorkeeper after nominations from the majority and minority parties.

Much of the public recognition of the Doorkeeper came from the ceremonial role of announcing the president of the United States and other visiting dignitaries to the House chamber. The Doorkeeper and his staff were also assigned administrative duties including overseeing the House pages, the doormen, the document room, the cloakrooms, and the House photographer. The Doorkeeper also manages the galleries and work areas set aside for daily newspapers. The office of the Doorkeeper was abolished at the beginning of the 104th Congress in 1995. The duties of the Doorkeeper were combined with those of the House SERGEANT AT ARMS.

Further reading:
Johnson, Charles W. *Constitution, Jefferson's Manual, and Rules of the House of Representatives*, House Document No. 107-284. Washington, D.C.: Government Printing Office, 2003; Miller, William M., and Frances Spatz Leighton. *Fish Bait: The Memoirs of the Congressional Doorkeeper*. Englewood Cliffs, N.J.: Prentice Hall, 1977.
—John David Rausch, Jr.

drafting

The point of origin for a PUBLIC LAW begins with the drafting of a BILL. Drafting is the process of writing the preliminary version of a bill and is the first stage of the LEGISLATIVE PROCESS. Drafting legislation is an art, not a science. A well-drafted bill results from thorough knowledge of the subject and careful attention to detail.

The drafting of legislation has many different origins. Some bills are drafted due to the LOBBYING of interest groups or individuals. Some come from the White House or federal government agencies, some are the result of media coverage, and some represent a member's own personal policy priorities. Legislation may be drafted by anyone, including a congressional staff member, the executive branch, a committee, and lobbyists. Members of the House can seek aid drafting a bill through the Office of the Legislative Counsel (HOLC), the legislative drafting service of the House. The HOLC is among the main drafters of House legislation. Although the members are not required to use the HOLC, most legislation in the

House is worked on by attorneys in the HOLC. The HOLC is impartial as to issues of legislative policy and does not advocate the adoption or rejection of any proposal or policy.

After draft legislation is introduced in the form of a bill, the House Speaker or the Senate's presiding officer refers it to the appropriate STANDING COMMITTEES. The manner in which legislation is drafted can favorably influence the referral decision. Bill sponsors often consider how to draft legislation in such a fashion that it will be referred to a committee likely to act favorably instead of one whose members might be considered to be less sympathetic. In the drafting process policy advocates keep the committee of jurisdiction and especially its leaders (chair and ranking minority member) in mind. Both the form and the content of a bill are drafted with the desire to clear the committee hurdle, and strategic choices are made accordingly. One approach is to word the measure ambiguously so that it can legitimately fall within the jurisdiction of more than one committee. Another strategy is to introduce legislation that amends statutes over which the committees have jurisdiction.

Drafting a bill has many tactical implications. From the vantage point of individual legislators, drafting legislation can allow them to claim credit for addressing an issue that is important to their constituents or perhaps enable them to become a central player on a legislative issue, even if the bill fails to win approval. What is included in a bill draft, the form in which the provisions are cast, and the detail in which policy proposals are spelled out all contribute to the ways in which Congress treats the proposal.

In order to design proposals that will ultimately win legislative approval, a number of issues must be addressed. One difficulty is the question of the content of legislation. The amount of money or authority to seek is inevitably a thorny issue. To ask for too much is to risk being defeated and not getting anything. On the other hand, to demand too little may put achieving one's desired policy purposes at risk. There is also the problem of the manner in which to allocate the power of the funds sought. Another set of issues that confronts bill writers pertains to the form in which to cast the proposal. An important decision for bill drafters is whether to have a multipart OMNIBUS BILL or a series of narrower measures. With an omnibus bill, linking several desirable policies is likely to attract considerable attention and may arouse sufficient interest to win passage. An omnibus measure also may facilitate LOGROLLING, making it easier to gain support from more legislators. On the other hand, a narrowly focused freestanding bill may make it easier for the bill to avoid controversy. Also, the task of drafting is more straightforward for a limited-purpose bill. Finally, a bill drafter must determine the specificity of the various statutory provisions proposed because the amount of detail included when drafting a bill can affect congressional treatment. An absence of specificity may keep a coalition intact by not giving legislators enough of a reason to vote against the proposal, but too little detail may appear deceptive.

Further reading:
Oleszek, Walter J. *Congressional Procedures and the Policy Process.* Washington, D.C.: Congressional Quarterly Press, 2000; Sinclair, Barbara. *Unorthodox Lawmaking.* 2d ed. Washington, D.C.: Congressional Quarterly Press, 2001.

—Patrick Fisher

E

Economic Committee, Joint

Congress's Joint Economic Committee (JEC) was established by the Employment Act of 1946, which also created the President's Council of Economic Advisers (CEA). The Employment Act was designed "to promote maximum employment, production, and purchasing power," as is stated in the law, so to these ends both the council and JEC were meant to examine the nation's economy and report to their respective branches regarding the real or projected consequences of the government's past and future tax and spending decisions. The CEA helps the president prepare his annual economic report, which is required by the 1946 act and is presented to Congress each year. The JEC then makes its own study of the president's report and submits its findings to Congress. According to budget expert Howard Shuman, while the JEC has no power to propose legislation and is therefore less formally involved in the annual budget than Congress's other fiscal policy committees (Ways and Means in the House, Finance in the Senate, and Appropriations, Budget, and Authorizations Committees in both), its hearings and reports are important components of public information on government economic data, policy alternatives, and legislative oversight of the executive branch's economic activities.

The JEC examines a wide variety of economic issues related to the U.S. and world economies, some related to national and international economic events and others to the annual budget cycle. For example, in the first half of 2003 the JEC held hearings and issued reports on a variety of newsworthy topics, from rebuilding Iraq's economy to regulating prescription drug costs in Medicare reform. On a more regular basis the chair of the Federal Reserve Board of Governors testifies in front of the committee, as does the president's chief national economic adviser. And the JEC, along with the Joint Taxation Committee, report to Congress's other budget committees at the beginning of the annual budget cycle on their analyses of the president's budget proposal and other issues, such as long-term projections of outlay and authority estimates.

Although the JEC was created by a law that delegated extensive powers from Congress to the president to monitor and control the economy, early in its history the JEC enjoyed moments of being in the spotlight and influencing the nation's economic policy. According to Shuman, in 1954 JEC chair Paul H. Douglas helped the Federal Reserve and Treasury Department reach an agreement to allow fluctuating interest rate policy to match the nation's economic cycles. In 1960 the JEC made an important study of employment, prices, and growth that greatly impacted economic policies through 1965. Many of the committee's staff, witnesses, and advisers later went on to be part of the CEA, and President John F. Kennedy himself was a member of the JEC as a senator. Shuman argues that the economic policies enacted in the early 1960s based on the JEC study of 1960 greatly contributed to the nation's economic growth early in that decade.

Like all other congressional committees, the JEC is chaired by one person of the majority party in that member's chamber. The chair is usually the most senior member and alternates between senators and House members each Congress.

Further reading:
Joint Economic Committee. Available online. URL: http://jec.senate.gov/. Accessed January 16, 2006; Shuman, Howard. *Politics and the Budget: The Struggle between the President and the Congress.* Englewood Cliffs, N.J.: Prentice Hall, 1992.

—Jasmine L. Farrier

Education and the Workforce, Committee on

This committee was originally created in 1867 in the aftermath of the Civil War and the growth of American industry and was called the Committee on Education and Labor. In 1883 the original committee was divided into two standing committees: Committee on Education and

Committee on Labor. In 1947 the functions were again combined under the LEGISLATIVE REORGANIZATION ACT. In 1995 it was renamed the Committee on Economic and Educational Opportunities. The current Committee on Education and the Workforce was established in 1997. While Congress has been concerned about education and labor issues for many years, a separate committee was not established for nearly 100 years after the First Congress. Many in Congress and in the rest of the country maintained that education was primarily a responsibility of the states.

The current committee is composed of 49 members of the House of Representatives, with the members chosen to serve on the committee by their respective party caucuses. In 2004 there were 27 Republicans and 22 Democrats on the committee. The committee traditionally has been composed of highly partisan members generally bringing a strong ideological perspective to the proceedings.

One of the major programs the House Education and the Workforce Committee has dealt with has been implementation of the No Child Left Behind Act. This legislation was designed to bring oversight to the schools and to ensure that improvement occurs in America's schools. A provision of this act was that all 50 U.S. states and the District of Columbia and Puerto Rico were required to submit accountability plans to the U.S. Department of Education by January 31, 2003. These plans were to summarize each state's efforts to provide annual testing of public school students in reading and mathematics in grades 3 to 8, provide report cards to parents on school achievement levels, and ensure that new options are available for those in underachieving schools. The legislation also provided resources for states to help reduce qualified teacher shortages. In addition, every local school district was to be given new freedom and decision-making authority to use much of its federal funds for local initiatives.

Another major program of the House Education and the Workforce Committee has focused on holding American higher education institutions accountable for their results. The committee launched hearings on this issue in May 2003, and many were interested in evaluating the horror stories brought to them by constituents: college graduates entering the workforce needing to take remedial courses upon employment, teacher colleges graduating teachers who were not prepared to teach, and American companies unable to find college graduates with the necessary skills. Many committee members were concerned with establishing assessment and accountability programs to deal with these issues.

Rule X of the Rules of the House of Representatives specifies the legislative jurisdiction of the committee and identifies areas under its jurisdiction, including child labor, labor standards, mediation and arbitration of labor disputes, worker compensation, wages and labor hours, and work incentive programs. The goal of the recent House Education and the Workforce Committee included efforts to empower students and teachers to provide students with the best education possible and to give American workers access to the skills necessary to compete successfully in the workforce.

Further reading:
"Committee Leaders Launch Effort to Ensure Accountability and Quality in U.S. Higher Education." *News from the Committee on Education and the Workforce,* May 13, 2003; "History of the Committee on Education and the Workforce." Available online. URL: http://edforce.house. gov/committee/history.htm. Accessed February 28, 2004; "Implementing the No Child Left Behind Act: A Progress Report." Available online. URL: http://wwws.house.gov. Accessed February 28, 2004.

—Nancy S. Lind

E-Government Act of 2002

The E-Government Act of 2002, signed by President George W. Bush in November 2002, is a sweeping change to the way in which government conducts its business with the public. Sponsored by Senator Joseph Lieberman, a Democratic senator from Connecticut, the law is intended to force federal agencies to make wider use of the Internet to provide information and services to citizens.

A key aim of the legislation is to improve the federal Internet portal, FirstGov, to make it more "user friendly" so that citizens can find information and services they seek from the federal government more quickly and efficiently. A goal of the legislation is to provide citizens with secure online information and services. Further, the E-Government Act also strengthens protections on privacy to prevent government agencies from releasing inappropriate personally identifiable information that is maintained by federal agencies. In effect, the law lays out the rules of engagement for agencies providing information and services online.

This law affects nearly every federal government agency in their provision of information to the public. It defines e-government and its basic parameters, from identifying Web sites to providing electronic archives that give the public easier access to government information. The law also created a new government position, a permanent position in the Office of Management and Budget (OMB) appointed by the president with Senate confirmation, to develop and oversee all policies related to e-government. This individual serves as the key administrator in a new Office of Electronic Government within the Office of Management and Budget.

The legislation makes the administrator responsible for the implementation of the following functions:

- advising the OMB director on the resources necessary to operate the information technology system
- helping to establish information resource management policies and requirements for all federal agencies
- sponsoring dialogue with leaders on electronic government in the executive branch agencies and legislative and judicial branches as well as with other levels of government
- administering the Office of Electronic Government

This is only a sampling of the responsibilities created by the E-Government Act of 2002. The 21st century has brought an increasing use of computers and technology by average citizens, and hence this law is an attempt to bring government in an accessible form directly to the people. The law is intended to achieve more efficient performance by government agencies and increase citizen participation in government. The law also promotes interagency collaboration in providing electronic government services by integrating related functions and reducing the duplication of agencies placing their databases online. In addition, the law provides enhanced access to government records without compromising personal privacy, national security, or medical information. Moreover, the law makes the federal government overall more transparent and accountable for its actions.

See also INTERNET AND CONGRESS.

Further reading:
"E-Government Act of 2002." Public Law 107-347, December 17, 2002; Hasson, Judi. "E-Government Act Promotes Web Standards, Procurement Reform, Security Policies." *Federal Computer Week,* 2 December 2002; Matthews, William. "E-Gov Act on Its Way to President." *Federal Computer Week,* 18 November 2002.

—Nancy S. Lind

Electoral College

This is the constitutional system created by the founding fathers for the election of the president and vice president of the United States of America. It is also the colloquial term used to describe a group of electors nominated by state political parties, and popularly elected, who vote for those two offices. The term *electoral college* is not found in the Constitution. Article II of the Constitution refers to *electors,* a term also used by Alexander Hamilton in Federalist 68. In the early 1800s the term *electoral college* came into general use but did not appear in federal statutes until 1845.

Members of the Constitutional Convention examined a variety of methods for selecting a president. The deliberations in many respects mirrored debates on other issues

related to the new Constitution. The election process was intended to maintain the principles of separation of powers and checks and balances, while balancing the interests of three important sets of competing constituencies: small states versus large states, the individual states versus the newly proposed national government, and those who desired increased popular representation versus those skeptical of mass democracy and popular passions.

Three proposals dominated discussions on the election process. The first had Congress selecting the president, the second gave the power of choosing the president to state legislatures, and the third called for the president to be elected by direct popular vote. The first proposal was deemed unacceptable because it would upset the separation of powers between the executive and legislative branches. In order to increase chances of reelection, the president might be influenced to appease Congress by signing proposed legislation. The second proposal was problematic because it could upset the balance of power between states and the national government. The founders believed the authority of the national government could be compromised in exchange for support from state legislatures. The third proposal was rejected out of distrust of mass democracy and popular passions. Technological and geographical impediments to communication between the 13 states meant voters would not know enough about candidates from outside their states to make informed voting decisions. This would lead to people voting only for "favored sons" from their own state. The compromise, which drew from each proposal, was the basis for the system we use today.

The original system was intended to function in a country without political parties or national campaigns. Each state was allotted a number of electors equal to its congressional delegation (i.e., its two U.S. Senators plus the number of its U.S. House of Representatives members), which is based on the state's population. The electors, popularly elected on election day, meet in their state capitals on the first Monday after the second Wednesday in December and cast two votes for president. The candidate with the most electoral votes (and a majority) becomes president. If there is a tie, the House votes, with each state having one vote. If no one receives a majority, again the House decides, choosing from one of the top five electoral vote recipients. The person with the second-highest total becomes vice president, and the Senate is authorized to make a selection in case of a tie. To avoid the potential problem of "favored sons," the electors could not vote for two people from the same state. This is the reason Dick Cheney, then residing in Houston, Texas, changed his legal residence back to Wyoming (where he was a former congressman) prior to being selected by then governor of Texas, George W. Bush, as a vice presidential running mate for the 2000 election.

The Electoral College was designed to deal with a variety of competing interests and produce a viable presidential candidate; it was never intended to be a perfect system. In other words, there have been some interesting anomalies. In the 1800 election Thomas Jefferson and Aaron Burr (both nominees of the Democratic-Republican Party) each received 73 electoral votes. Although Jefferson had been designated the party's presidential candidate, it was not until the 36th ballot and much political bargaining in the House that Jefferson was selected. Because the Electoral College was intended to prevent this type of unseemly "politicking," the Twelfth Amendment was ratified. Two important changes included electors being required to cast one vote for president and a separate vote for vice president, and in case of a tie the House would consider only the top three vote recipients.

The only other election to end up in the House was in 1824, when four strong candidates emerged: John Quincy Adams, Andrew Jackson, Henry Clay, and William H. Crawford. When the electoral votes were counted, no candidate had received the requisite 131 votes. Jackson, who had the most popular votes, led with 99 electoral votes (compared to Adams's 84, Crawford's 41, and Clay's 37). Reforms of the Twelfth Amendment meant only the first three candidates' names were passed on to the House. As a result of some political intrigue, Clay committed his supporters in the House to Adams, who became president and then made Clay his secretary of State. Jackson's successful 1828 campaign relied heavily on the contention that "political deals" in the House thwarted the will of the people in 1824.

Candidates who received fewer popular votes, but the majority of the electoral votes, won several other elections as well. In 1876 nearly unanimous support from small states gave Rutherford B. Hayes a one-vote margin in the Electoral College despite losing the popular vote to Samuel J. Tilden by more than 264,000 votes. The election involved an Electoral College dispute, which was ultimately resolved by an ad hoc Electoral Commission created by Congress and consisting of five members of the Senate, House, and Supreme Court. Benjamin Harrison in 1888 lost the popular vote by 95,713 votes to Grover Cleveland but won in the Electoral College by 65 votes. In this instance the Electoral College worked as it was intended by preventing a candidate from winning based on support from one region of the country. Six southern states gave Cleveland more than 425,000 more votes, but he lost the rest of the country by more than 300,000 votes. Finally, in the 2000 election Al Gore received 48.23 percent of the vote to George W. Bush's 47.87 percent (a difference of approximately 500,000 votes) but lost the electoral vote 271-266 (one of Gore's electors abstained from voting).

Today the Electoral College includes 538 electors, 435 members of the House, 100 members of the Senate, and,

by virtue of the Twenty-third Amendment (1961), three electors from the District of Columbia. The Constitution gives each state the authority to choose its own method of selecting electors. Generally, there is a slate of electors for each party (Republican, Democratic, Libertarian, etc.) involved in the election. On the Tuesday after the first Monday in November, voters go to the polls and select the electors who are pledged to the candidate of their choice. If the Republican nominee receives the most votes, then that state's slate of Republican electors is selected and the candidate (presumably) receives all of the state's electoral votes. This is known as the "winner take all" system. Maine since 1969 and Nebraska since 1988 are the exceptions; they allocate their electors by a system in which the candidate receiving a plurality of the votes in the state's congressional districts (two in Maine and three in Nebraska) gets that district's Electoral College vote. The state's other two electoral votes, which correspond to the state's Senate seat, are allocated by a statewide plurality vote.

The Constitution gives little guidance on who may be an elector, although it does state that members of Congress and federal employees are prohibited. Electors "pledge" themselves to the party's nominee. However, the issue of potential "faithless electors" (electors pledged to one candidate but who vote for another) has led 27 states to enact state laws binding electors to their pledges. From 1900 to the 2000 election there have been only eight cases of faithless electors. The two most recent included a 1988 elector from West Virginia who voted for Lloyd Bentsen for president and Michael Dukakis for vice president instead of the other way around and the 2000 election, in which an elector from the District of Columbia abstained from voting for Al Gore in protest of the district's lack of full representation in Congress (mentioned earlier). Overall, well over 99 percent of electors have voted as pledged, and no elector has ever been prosecuted for failing to vote as pledged.

Since its inception there has always been controversy surrounding the Electoral College. Today people complain it is an 18th-century anachronism that gives too much power to small states, depresses voter turnout, and fails to represent the popular will. As a result, there have been a myriad of proposals for abolishing the Electoral College. The U.S. Senate in the 1970s supported President Jimmy Carter's proposed amendment abolishing the Electoral College, but the proposal failed to garner the two-thirds majority necessary to pass.

The Electoral College has performed its function for more than 200 years by ensuring that the president of the United States has both sufficient popular support to govern and that the support is sufficiently distributed throughout the country to enable effective governing. Additionally, while the Electoral College was designed to solve one set of problems, it has served to solve an entirely different set of problems, a tribute to the genius of the founding fathers and to the durability of the American federal system.

Further reading:
Berns, Walter, ed. *After the People Vote: Steps in Choosing the President*. Washington, D.C.: American Enterprise Institute, 1983; Longley, Lawrence D., and Neal R. Pierce. *The Electoral College Primer 2000*. New Haven, Conn.: Yale University Press, 1999.

—Craig T. Cobane

e-mail and Congress

E-mail—written messages transmitted electronically over the Worldwide Web—is the most recent communications innovation to come to Congress. The e-mail era began in 1993, when Senator Charles (Chuck) Robb (D-VA) established and publicized his e-mail address. By the end of 1994, most members of Congress established e-mail addresses as part of a larger telecommunications revolution underway in the institution.

Prior to 1998 the typical House office received several dozen e-mail messages a week; the typical Senate office received several hundred. However, during the HOUSE OF REPRESENTATIVES' impeachment proceedings of President Bill Clinton in 1998, congressional offices were deluged with e-mail messages. For a few years congressional offices unsuccessfully coped with the volume of e-mail, which increased by 1 million messages a month.

The sheer volume of e-mail posed practical difficulties for congressional staff and threatened to undermine Congress's representational function. Sorting through thousands of e-mail messages to determine subject matter and whether the author was a constituent was time consuming and difficult. As a result many offices were reluctant to deal with e-mail. Some responded to e-mail with letters sent through the U.S. Postal Service. Offices routinely ignored any that could not be directly traced to constituents. Others ignored e-mails altogether. Some observers worried that such practices might further undermine public opinion of Congress.

Various technological innovations have slowed the increase in volume of e-mail and helped offices cope with the influx. Mail management programs help sort and direct mail. Most offices have eliminated traditional e-mail addresses in favor of Web-based forms, which include zip code filters that restrict messages to those living in the members' district or state. Other members use their Web sites to provide information on voting records, members' positions on high-profiles issues of the day, and other "frequently asked questions." Today more offices have developed the capacity to respond to e-mail with e-mail and have begun to encourage this type of correspondence from constituents. Several congressional offices realized the potential advantages of e-mail in the wake of the anthrax contamination event in 2001, which delayed postal service for weeks or months.

Staff members have also discovered that by cutting and pasting language from e-mails into memos to members helps them communicate the nature of their constituent communications with more nuance than a simple "yes or no" can do. However, e-mail poses another challenge to representation: how to interpret the depth of the opinion expressed in the messages. Member offices have long understood that letters that were individually composed and mailed from someone's home or office expressed a depth of opinion that outweighed a preprinted postcard generated by an interest group. Yet e-mails can be written quickly and sent with a click of a button. Thus, it is more difficult to ascertain the degree of thought that went into each message.

In addition, e-mail poses questions about the deliberative function of Congress. Deliberation by definition is slow and thoughtful. It benefits from some distance from the passions of public opinion. As a result, some commentators worry that members of Congress will become even more concerned with public opinion or that the "permanent campaign" will become even further entrenched.

Further reading:
Congressional Management Foundation. *E-mail Overload in Congress: Managing a Communications Crisis*. Washington, D.C.: Congressional Management Foundation. Available online. URL: http://www.congressonlineproject.org. Accessed January 16, 2006; Congressional Management Foundation. *E-mail Overload in Congress—Update*. Washington, D.C.: Congressional Management Foundation. Available online. URL: http://www.congressonlineproject.org. Accessed January 16, 2006; Thurber, James A., and Colton C. Campbell, eds., *Congress and the Internet*. Upper Saddle River, N.J.: Prentice Hall, 2003.

—Karen M. Kedrowski

emergency powers

In some countries the executive is authorized by the national constitution to make policy in time of emergency without participation by the legislature. Such is not the case in the United States; the Constitution confers no emergency powers on the president. As Supreme Court justice Robert Jackson explained in his concurring opinion in *Youngstown Sheet & Tube Co. v. Sawyer* in 1952, the framers of the Constitution well understood that governments sometimes face emergency situations, yet that did not induce them to authorize the president, acting alone, to make policy. Justice Jackson believed that if American presidents had been given emergency powers, they would have succumbed to the temptation to create emergencies in order to justify the exercise of those powers, and he attributed that belief to the framers of the Constitution as well.

Presidents have nevertheless exercised emergency powers in a variety of situations, and Congress, also recognizing emergencies, has enacted legislation delegating broad power to the president or validating its exercise after the fact. The economic emergency of the Great Depression led President Franklin D. Roosevelt to turn to the use of emergency powers in his efforts to combat it. In his inaugural address President Roosevelt stated that he hoped that the nation's problems could be met within the normal balance of legislative and executive authority, but he also recognized that it might not be possible. The next day, March 9, 1933, he called Congress into special session, and the members adopted a law approving actions already taken by the president or that he would take thereafter. His previous actions included the declaration of a bank holiday to stave off the withdrawal of funds by panicked account holders to the point that the banks were drained of funds and had to close their doors. The action, a kind of "time out," allowed the sense of panic to weaken, as evidenced by the fact that people began to deposit money again, even more than they withdrew. The president issued numerous other executive orders ranging far beyond banking to make policy changes with greater speed than Congress could act.

War, even more than economic crises, has led to the exercise of emergency powers by the president and Congress. During the Civil War President Abraham Lincoln took a variety of emergency actions, including the seizure of railroad and telegraph lines. Congress later validated the president's actions. Later wars led to the seizure of railroads, communication facilities, and facilities producing needed materials. Courts have considered war an emergency sufficient to justify legislative and executive actions that in other circumstances would have been considered a violation of constitutionally protected civil liberties. In *Schenck v. United States* (1919) the Supreme Court affirmed a conviction under the Espionage Act of 1917. The offense was the circulation of leaflets in opposition to the military draft, which urged men subjected to the draft peacefully to resist. The Court said that there were things that would be constitutionally protected in peacetime that Congress may prevent when men are fighting. In upholding the Emergency Price Control Act of 1942, the Supreme Court went so far as to state in *Yakus v. United States* (1944), although it was not the issue before the Court, that Congress could in time of war take numerous actions, even permitting the personal liberty of citizens to be restrained on a temporary basis without violating the constitutional guarantee of due process of law. When Japanese Americans were removed from the West Coast and sent to relocation centers, the Supreme Court found no constitutional violation in 1944. The process began with an executive order that was later validated by the congressional enactment of sanctions on violations of the exclusion policy.

In 1950, during the era of the cold war, Congress recognized that in the event of a nuclear attack by the Soviet Union, which had exploded a nuclear device the previous year, there might be need for emergency powers on the home front. Congress passed the Federal Civil Defense Act. Among the emergency powers given to the Civil Defense administrator was the power to take private property for public purposes without going through any judicial proceedings. The legislation provided some limited protection of property in that government could not take title to the property unless Congress specifically authorized it. Congress initially placed the powers created by the Federal Civil Defense Act in the hands of the Civil Defense administrator, but they were later given to the president or an official subject to his direction.

When Congress granted emergency powers to the president or other executive officials, it often placed no time limit on the authorization. This omission was not always intentional. Congress would sometimes become caught up in the sense of emergency for which it was legislating and exercise less care than it normally would. On other occasions Congress recognized that it could not foresee how long the emergency would last. But as it attempted to rein in the "imperial presidency" in the 1970s, one thing it did was eliminate open-ended grants of emergency powers. The Senate Special Committee on the Termination of the National Emergency found 470 grants of emergency power from the presidencies of Harry Truman through Richard Nixon. In the Emergencies Act of 1974, Congress terminated in 1976 all emergencies previously declared. Future emergencies declared by the president would have only a two-year life span.

Further reading:
Cooper, Phillip J. *By Order of the President: The Use and Abuse of Executive Direct Action.* Lawrence: University Press of Kansas, 2002; Franklin, Daniel P. *Extraordinary Measures: The Exercise of Prerogative Powers in the United States.* Pittsburgh: University of Pittsburgh Press, 1991; McCarey, John, and Matthew Soberg Shugart, eds. *Executive Decree Authority.* Cambridge: Cambridge University Press, 1998; Rankin, Robert S., and Winfried R. Dallmayr. *Freedom and Emergency Powers in the Cold War.* New York: Appleton-Century Crofts, 1964.

—Patricia A. Behlar

enacting clause

An enacting clause gives the legal force of law to proposed legislation. The enacting clause is mandated by 61 Statute At Large, Section 101, which requires the following statement immediately following the bill number: "Be it enacted by the Senate and House of Representatives of the United States of America in Congress assembled." If there is a motion in either the House or the Senate to strike the enacting clause, the proposed legislation is killed. This technique of striking the enacting clause is usually used to extend the period of debate.

—Nancy S. Lind

Energy and Commerce, Committee on

The Committee on Energy and Commerce is a standing committee in the U.S. HOUSE OF REPRESENTATIVES with jurisdiction over a wide range of matters including energy policy, commerce, safety, and health. The committee is considered one of the most important committees in the House of Representatives. As the third standing committee created by the House, it is one of the oldest. The Committee on Commerce and Manufactures was established in 1795 to help the House manage its constitutional authority to "regulate Commerce with foreign Nations, and among the several states." In 1819 the committee's name was changed to the Committee on Commerce after a new Committee on Manufactures was created. This division of responsibilities was necessary due to the growing scope and complexity of American commercial activity. The jurisdiction of the Committee on Commerce included

commerce, Life-Saving Service, and light-houses, other than appropriations for Life-Saving Service and light-houses.

President Franklin D. Roosevelt, flanked by members of the cabinet seated in the first row, shown during his report to Congress, 1945 *(Library of Congress)*

Other committee responsibilities were regulation of both interstate and foreign commerce, customs collection, ports of entry, regulations and appropriations of navigable waters and their works, establishment of public health and the prevention of infectious disease, and regulation of the purity of food. In 1883 the Committee on Commerce lost its jurisdiction over appropriations for the improvement of rivers and harbors to the new Committee on Rivers and Harbors.

The committee's name changed in 1892 to the Committee on Interstate and Foreign Commerce, but there was little change in its jurisdiction. Apparently, a losing candidate for Speaker of the House was appointed chair and he felt that his committee should have a more dignified sounding name. Later that decade the committee experienced several jurisdictional changes. In 1895 jurisdiction over customs districts, ports of entry and delivery, the transportation of dutiable goods, and officers and employees of the customs service was given to the Committee on Ways and Means. In addition, much of the jurisdiction over matters relating to water transportation slowly shifted to the Merchant Marine and Fisheries Committee. A House rule approved in 1935 dropped matters relating to the Life-Saving Service and lighthouses from the jurisdiction of the Committee on Interstate and Foreign Commerce, but the committee acquired jurisdiction over radio-related matters from the Merchant Marine and Fisheries Committee.

The jurisdiction of the Committee on Foreign and Interstate Commerce was further changed by the LEGISLATIVE REORGANIZATION ACT OF 1946. House rules written to incorporate the law's provisions defined the jurisdiction of the committee as interstate and foreign commerce generally; regulation of interstate and foreign transportation, except transportation by water not subject to the jurisdiction of the Interstate Commerce Commission; regulation of interstate and foreign communications; civil aeronautics; weather bureau; interstate oil compacts; petroleum and natural gas, except on the public lands; securities and exchanges; regulation of interstate transmission of power, except the installation of connections between government water power projects; railroad labor and railroad retirement and unemployment, except revenue measures relating thereto; public health and quarantine; inland waterways; the Bureau of Standards, the standardization of weights and measures, and the metric system. According to a committee print published in 1974, the committee's jurisdiction overlapped with those of more than half of the other House committees.

In 1981 the committee's name was changed to the Committee on Energy and Commerce. This change reflected the increased role of Congress in guiding national energy policy, an important element of commerce. When the Republican Party reorganized the committee system after becoming the majority party in 1995, the committee was renamed the Committee on Commerce. In addition, about 20 percent of its jurisdiction was transferred to other committees. The committee lost responsibility over reform of the Glass-Steagall securities law, railroads, food inspection, the Trans-Alaska Pipeline, and energy research and development.

House rules adopted at the beginning of the 107th Congress in 2001 transferred jurisdiction over securities and exchanges and insurance from the Committee on Commerce to the newly renamed Committee on Financial Services. The Committee on Commerce also was renamed the Committee on Energy and Commerce. Because of overlap, the two committees executed a memorandum of understanding clarifying jurisdictions. The Committee on Energy and Commerce retained jurisdiction over bills dealing broadly with electronic commerce, including electronic communications networks. The Committee on Financial Services kept its jurisdiction over bills amending securities laws to address the specific type of electronic securities transaction currently governed by special Securities and Exchange Commission regulations.

The Committee on Energy and Commerce was one of 19 standing committees in the 108th Congress. With 57 members (31 Republicans and 26 Democrats), it was one of the largest committees. The committee's six subcommittees reflect its broad jurisdiction: the Subcommittee on Commerce, Trade, and Consumer Protection; the Subcommittee on Energy and Air Quality; the Subcommittee on Environment and Hazardous Materials; the Subcommittee on Health; the Subcommittee on Telecommunications and the Internet; and the Subcommittee on Oversight and Investigations.

Further reading:
Sheffner, Benjamin. "25 Panels Are Axed." *Roll Call*, 5 December 1994; U.S. House of Representatives. Committee on Interstate and Foreign Commerce. *Historical Data Regarding the Creation and Jurisdiction of the Committee on Interstate and Foreign Commerce.* House Document 234. Washington, D.C.: Government Printing Office, 1957; U.S. House of Representatives, Committee on Energy and Commerce. *Report on the Activity of the Committee on Energy and Commerce.* Washington, D.C.: Government Printing Office, 2005.

—John David Rausch, Jr.

Energy and Natural Resources, Senate Committee on

The Senate Committee on Energy and Natural Resources is responsible for oversight of the public lands and all energy and natural resource matters of importance to the

U.S. government. Frequently this mission has placed the committee at the center of some of the most dramatic economic development and demographic decisions facing the nation in any particular decade. In the 19th century the committee was involved in facilitating westward expansion by encouraging population migration to the interior. This was initially done by public land sales and grants and the development of the railroads. Major pieces of legislation ultimately reflected the national consensus on public subsidy of land ownership in the Homestead Act of 1862, the Mining Law of 1872, and their successors. The committee jurisdiction expanded as the complexity of managing the national lands grew. Concern for conservation in the late 19th and early 20th centuries led to the first national park in 1872, the first national forest in 1891, and the first national wildlife refuge in 1902. The executive agencies created to professionally manage the public lands and national resources followed soon after: the Department of the Interior in 1849, the Division of Forestry in 1898 that eventually led to the creation of the Forest Service (1905), and the National Park Service in 1916. These, too, expanded the responsibilities and workload of the committee. Alternate energy sources such as nuclear, solar, and hydroelectric were added to the committee's responsibility for traditional energy sources such as petroleum, natural gas, and coal in 1977.

The current configuration of the Energy and Natural Resources Committee came into being at the Senate reorganization of 1977. It was a direct successor to the Interior and Insular Affairs Committee (1948–77), which was simply a renaming of the Public Lands Committee that had been consolidated in the 1946 Legislative Reorganization Act. The Public Lands Committee was created in 1816 as one of the Senate's original standing committees and in 1946 was one of five committees that were part of the consolidation (Indian Affairs, Territorial and Insular Affairs, Mines and Mining, and Irrigation and Reclamation). The 1977 Committee System Reorganization Amendments ended the Energy and Natural Resources Committee responsibility for Indian affairs by creating a temporary select committee (now Indian Affairs). In 1946 the committee gained responsibility for all aspects of public lands development and the accompanying controversy as the nation debated economic development and natural preservation philosophies in public lands policy through the late 20th century.

Since 1946 the Senate committee has been in the control of western state senators, particularly those from states that have large amounts of federal lands within their borders, rich concentrations of natural resources that have traditionally been exploited for economic development, and slow-growing populations that valued consistent public policy for their region. The extractive and production industries have strong roots in the region and exert influence in both state and national politics. The public debate on environmental protection begun in the 1960s found its way onto the committee agenda curiously without the animosity that resulted in other venues. Energy and Natural Resources was responsible for shaping and reporting the National Environmental Policy Act (1969) to the Senate floor. The energy crisis of the 1970s intensified the interchamber rivalry between the House and Senate; the Senate committee was controlled by members from energy producing states, while the House Energy and Commerce Committee was controlled by members from energy consuming states. This cleavage between eastern consumer states and western producer states is more likely on the committee than the traditional political party breakdown seen in most other policy areas. The committee has been noted for its bipartisan spirit and consensus decision making. In part this can be explained by the regional focus of the membership and the policy concerns they manage. It may also have something to do with the outlook and style of one of the most influential chairs of the committee, Senator Henry M. (Scoop) Jackson of Washington, who chaired the panel from 1963 to 1981.

Committee jurisdiction for the 108th Congress found in Senate Rule 25 includes coal production, distribution, and utilization; energy policy; energy regulation and conservation; energy-related aspects of deepwater ports; energy research and development; extraction of minerals from oceans and outer continental shelf lands; hydroelectric power, irrigation, and reclamation; mining education and research; mining, mineral lands, mining claims, and mineral conservation; national parks, recreation areas, wilderness areas, wild and scenic rivers, historical sites, military parks and battlefields, and, on the public domain,

Chairman	State and Political Party	Years
Hugh A. Butler	Nebraska, Republican	1947–1949, 1953–1954
Joseph C. O'Mahoney	Wyoming, Democrat	1951–1953
Eugene D. Millikin	Colorado, Republican	1954–1955
James E. Murray	Montana, Democrat	1955–1961
Clinton P. Anderson	New Mexico, Democrat	1961–1963
Henry M. Jackson	Washington, Democrat	1963–1981
James A. McClure	Idaho, Republican	1981–1987
J. Bennett Johnston	Louisiana, Democrat	1987–1995
Frank Murkowski	Alaska, Republican	1995–2001
Jeff Bingaman	New Mexico, Democrat	2001–2003
Pete V. Dominici	New Mexico, Republican	2003–

preservation of prehistoric ruins and objects of interest; naval petroleum reserves in Alaska; nonmilitary development of nuclear energy; oil and gas production and distribution; public lands and forests, including farming and grazing thereon, and mineral extraction therefrom; solar energy systems; and territorial possessions of the United States, including trusteeships.

Further reading:
Fenno, Richard J., Jr. *Congressmen in Committees.* Boston: Little, Brown, 1973; U.S. Senate. *Committee on Energy and Natural Resources. History of the Committee on Energy and Natural Resources.* 100th Cong., 2d sess., 1989. S. Doc 100-46; Magida, Arthur J. "The House and Senate Interior and Insular Affairs Committees." In *The Ralph Nader Congress Project: The Environment Committees.* New York: Grossman, 1975; Rieselbach, Leroy N. *Congressional Reform.* Washington, D.C.: Congressional Quarterly Press, 1986.

—Karen M. McCurdy

engrossed bill

An engrossed bill is, in political terms, a bill that has the ability and necessity to be amended by the HOUSE OF REPRESENTATIVES and by the SENATE. In legal terms, the preparation of a copy of a legislative bill in the format in which it has passed the House can be a detailed and politicized process. The Democrats and the Republicans strive to inculcate their political agendas into the bill.

Due to the large number and complexity of proposed amendments to some bills adopted by the House, an engrossed bill becomes a politically important battle involving heated debates over amendments. Frequently, these amendments are offered during a spirited debate with little or no prior formal preparation. Since the advent of the American political party system in the 19th century, political parties have sought to extend power and control in the process of developing a bill. One of those changes was allowing amendments to be introduced to change bills from their purest and rawest form. The amendment may be introduced for the simple purpose of inserting new and less politicized language, substituting dissimilar words from those introduced in the original bill, or, if necessary, deleting portions of the bill that may be politically volatile. Indeed, throughout the course and process of an engrossed bill, the measures can undergo a significant amount of change. Usually, the resulting bill is vastly different from the original bill.

It is not unusual to have more than 100 amendments adopted by the standing committee, including any changes proposed by the committee at the time the bill is originally accounted and those offered from the House floor during the consideration and debating of the bill in the chamber. In certain instances amendments offered from the floor are written in traditional longhand for the purpose of clarity and political expediency. These changes and amendments ensure that the language of the bill can, at any point in the future, be changed for the sake of political expediency.

Moreover, each amendment must be inserted in precisely the proper place in the bill, with the spelling and punctuation exactly as the House adopted the bill. It is extremely important that the Senate receive a copy of the bill in the precise form in which it has passed the House. In order for the Senate to accurately debate the correct and important issues, the bill must be distributed to the Senate in its purest form. In order to ensure this process, an enrolling clerk is contracted to prepare such a functioning copy. In the House of Representatives the enrolling clerk serves and works under the CLERK OF THE HOUSE.

In the Senate the enrolling clerk, or the person charged with ensuring the accuracy and clarity of the language of the bill, serves under the Secretary of the Senate. The enrolling clerks receive the entire set of papers relating to the bill, including the official clerk's copy of the bill as reported by the House standing committee as well as each amendment adopted by the House pertaining to the bill. From this material the enrolling clerk prepares the engrossed copy of the bill as passed, containing all the amendments agreed to by the House. At this point the clerk declares the bill an engrossed bill, and the measure ceases to be defined as a bill and is subsequently termed "An Act," signifying that it is the act of a unified body of the whole Congress, although it is still popularly (and incorrectly) referred to as a bill. The process of passage then escalates to deliberation in the Senate as the act, or bill, is set to become official. The clerk then performs the task of sending the engrossed bill to the Senate for deliberation. The engrossed bill is printed on blue paper and is signed by the Clerk of the House.

Essentially, an engrossed bill is an amended bill that is at times a grossly raw bill, with changes and amendments without a clear set of ideological assumptions. Every bill must reflect the ideological partisanship of both parties. An engrossed bill signifies that partisanship, as both parties seek to place their political interests into the bill before it reaches the Senate. In its finality an engrossed bill is the initial phase of a bill development, and it shows the process for gaining accuracy in the language of a bill.

Further reading:
de Grazia, Alfred, ed. *Congress, the First Branch of Government.* Garden City, N.Y.: Anchor Books, 1967; Keefe, William J. *The American Legislative Process: Congress and the States.* Englewood Cliffs, N.J.: Prentice Hall, 1981;

Reid, T. R. *Congressional Odyssey: The Saga of a Senate Bill.* San Francisco: W. H. Freeman, 1980.

—Jamie Ramón Olivares

enrolled bill

When a bill has been agreed to in identical form by both the HOUSE OF REPRESENTATIVES and the SENATE through either no amendment or changes by the Senate, by House concurrence with Senate amendments, by Senate agreement with any House amendments, or by a formal agreement in both houses to the conference report, a copy of the bill is then enrolled for presentation to the president of the United States. The preparation of an enrolled bill is a painstaking and important task. The enrolled bill must reflect the precise nuances and effects of all amendments, either through deletion, substitution, or addition, that were concurrently agreed to by both houses of Congress. The enrolling CLERK OF THE HOUSE, with respect to bills originating in the House, receives the original engrossed bill, the engrossed Senate amendments, an affixed conference report, several messages from the Senate, and any written notation of final action to be taken by the House for the simple purpose of preparing an enrolled copy. The enrolling clerk then must meticulously prepare the final form of the bill as it was agreed to by both Houses for formal presentation to the president. On numerous bills as many as 500 amendments have been adopted, each of which must be set out in the enrollment exactly as agreed to, and all punctuation and language must agree, in text and tone, with any action taken.

The enrolled bill is printed on parchment paper and certified by the Clerk of the House stating that the bill originated in the House of Representatives. A bill originating in the Senate is examined and certified by the Secretary of the Senate. In turn, the House bill is then examined for accuracy by the clerk. When satisfied with the accuracy of the bill, he or she attaches a slip stating that he or she observed the bill truly enrolled. He or she dispatches the bill to the Speaker of the House for a final examination and signature. All bills, regardless of the body in which they originated, are signed first by the SPEAKER OF THE HOUSE and then by the vice president of the United States, who constitutionally functions as the President of the Senate. The President Pro Tempore of the Senate also has the power to sign enrolled bills. The Speaker of the House may even sign enrolled bills whether or not the House is in session. Oddly, the President of the Senate may sign bills only while the Senate is actually sitting, but advance permission is normally granted to sign during a recess or after adjournment. If the Speaker or the President of the Senate is unable to sign the bill, it may be signed by an authorized member of the respective House. After both signatures are affixed, a House bill is returned to the clerk for presentation to the president for

action under the Constitution. A Senate bill is presented to the president by the Secretary of the Senate.

Both houses must pass a CONCURRENT RESOLUTION to recall an incorrectly enrolled bill already sent to the president or to make changes in the text of an enrolled bill still in the possession of the Congress. Essentially, an enrolled bill is the penultimate stage in the life of a bill. The process involves attaining the permission and approval of both houses. Indeed, it is the process of attaining that approval that contributes to the dynamic process. In its final form an enrolled bill is ready for a vote in the Senate. The process can assume political tones, but on the whole the enrolled bill is an important stage in the passage of a bill.

Further reading:
U.S. Congress. *Calendars of the US House of Representatives and History of Legislation Library of Congress.* Washington, D.C., 1789–1958; U.S. Department of Commerce. *Historical Statistics on the United States: Colonial Times to 1957.* Washington, D.C.: Bureau of the Census, 1967.

—Jamie Ramón Olivares

entitlements

Entitlements are government spending programs for which Congress has set eligibility criteria, such as age, income, location, or occupation. If a recipient meets the criteria, she or he is "entitled" to the money. Federal entitlement programs range from the largest, such as Social Security and Medicare, to the comparatively small, such as an indemnity program for dairy farmers whose milk is contaminated by chemicals. While most entitlements go to people, some also go to other units of government. The Title XX Social Services block grant, for instance, goes to states based on population. What makes entitlements different from the other major form of congressional spending is that they are mandatory; money must be provided until the program is changed by Congress. By contrast, discretionary spending is good for only one year, and Congress has to renew it annually through the appropriations process.

Since entitlements are mandatory, they are broadly considered to be "uncontrollable" to some. Classifying entitlement spending as uncontrollable is somewhat misleading, however; while Congress cannot control levels of eligibility in the population, it can control benefit levels under the law (cost of living adjustments, for example). Nevertheless, it would be accurate to say that politically entitlements are relatively uncontrollable. Entitlements are available for a vote, but only if Congress decides to arrange one. Congress can change or repeal any law it passes, and lawmakers can revisit entitlements at any time to reduce or eliminate them. However, Congress rarely chooses to eliminate existing entitlement programs.

There are good policy reasons for entitlement spending. Entitlements can be an efficient way for the government to provide services, and it seems logical that the government may want to avoid the political difficulty of not being able to maintain its promises regardless of the financial condition of the government, which is, after all, highly reliant on the state of the economy. A criticism of entitlements, however, has been that to a large degree they go to fund what has been called "middle-class welfare." That is, entitlement benefits have been dispensed largely on the basis of criteria other than income (such as age). Programs that require proof of low income to receive benefits are a small part of entitlements.

Less than a third of the budget during the administration of President John Kennedy, entitlements now make up more than half of the federal budget. During the 1960s and 1970s the creation of programs such as Medicare, Medicaid, and food stamps combined with expanded Social Security benefits to provide an enormous boost to entitlement spending. All told, from 1966 to 1976 entitlements more than doubled in relation to the size of the economy. Today entitlements are growing more than twice as fast as the gross domestic product, and the federal government annually spends more than $1 trillion on entitlement programs (see Table).

Conservatives fear that the result of the growth in entitlements will be higher taxes and deficits; liberals fear that entitlements will squeeze out other programs and, if they keep growing, use up future revenue increases. Yet both conservatives and liberals in Congress have been unwilling to confront the growth in entitlements. Critics argue that the difficulty in reducing or eliminating entitlements is exactly what the architects of entitlements had intended and exactly what contemporary Congresses ought to be doing. Entitlement programs dole out funds automatically so that basic benefits are not subject to the year-to-year inconsistencies of the appropriations process. Furthermore, entitlements are growing as they were supposed to, especially during periods of a bad economy. The so-called automatic stabilizers such as unemployment insurance and food stamps are designed to pick up the slack during bad economic periods.

Entitlement programs, however, do not always have the effect their creators intended. Times change, but often established entitlements are unable to change as new circumstances dictate. A problem with entitlements is that it is much easier to start an entitlement for an apparently needy group than it is to terminate an entitlement after it no longer makes sense. Most subsidy programs, for example, began for the same reason as did programs to benefit individuals—that is, they were a response to hardship cases. In their early days aid was targeted on the basis of an immediate need or a significant national purpose. Over the years many of these programs, especially in agriculture, lost their focus as conditions changed. Instead of being phased out, many were expanded for political purposes.

Some of the largest and most expensive programs in the federal budget are entitlements, such as Social Security and Medicare, which are politically the most difficult programs to alter. Social Security, in fact, is called by politicians "the third rail of American politics"—touch it and die. Social Security is the largest single spending program in the federal budget, costing $429 billion in 2001 and accounting for 23 cents of every dollar the federal government spends. Medicare, the federal health insurance for the elderly and disabled, and Medicaid, the joint federal-state health program for the poor, are currently by far the fastest growing entitlements and together are almost as expensive as Social Security. To critics of entitlements, the costs of Social Security, Medicare, and Medicaid are rising so fast that they risk crowding out the rest of domestic spending.

Further reading:
Pascall, Glenn. *The Trillion Dollar Budget.* Seattle: University of Washington Press, 1985; Wildavsky, Aaron, and Namoi Caiden. *The New Politics of the Budgetary Process.* 3d ed. New York: Longman, 1997.

—Patrick Fisher

THE TOP ENTITLEMENTS

Rank Program	Expenditures (billions of $)	% of GDP
1. Social Security	429.4	4.2
2. Medicare	237.9	2.3
3. Medicaid	129.4	1.3
4. Other Retirement/Disability	92.7	0.9
5. Unemployment	27.9	0.3
6. Farm Price Supports	22.4	0.2
7. Total Means Tested	248.7	2.5
8. Total Non–Means Tested	846.5	8.3

Source: Congressional Budget Office. Figures are for the 2001 fiscal year.

enumerated powers

The powers offered to the U.S. Congress via the citizens are established in the nation's Constitution under Article I, Section 8. This clause is often denoted as the enumerated powers clause, as the authorities granted to Congress are rolled out one by one in numerical fashion, specifically laying out the duties granted to Congress.

Within this article one finds the foundation for every functional activity of Congress in effect to date. These functions include but are not limited to the powers to lay and collect taxes; to borrow money on the credit of the United States; to regulate commerce; to establish a uniform rule of naturalization; to establish a uniform law on bankruptcies; to coin money and regulate the value thereof; to fix the standard of weights and measures; to establish post offices and post roads; to promote the progress of science and useful arts; to constitute tribunals inferior to the Supreme Court; to define and punish piracies and felonies committed on the high seas; to declare war; to raise and support armies; to provide and maintain a navy; to make rules for the government and regulation of the land and naval forces; to provide for calling forth the militia to execute the laws of the union; to provide for organizing, arming, and disciplining the militia; to exercise authority over all places purchased by the consent of the legislature of the state in which the same shall be for the erection of forts, magazines, arsenals, dockyards, and other needful buildings; and to make all laws which shall be necessary and proper for carrying into execution the powers vested by the Constitution in the government of the United States, or in any department or officer thereof.

The difficulty that has been associated with the enumerated powers clause over the years has been the extent to which each itemized power has been interpreted. Many people believe that the authors of the Constitution were aware of the public's fear that the independence and authority of the states would become diluted with the establishment of a centralized national government. The public frame of reference for this fear was the growth of power experienced by the Parliament in Britain. Having been initially intended to function as a check on the power of the monarchy, the Parliament's sphere of influence gravitated into one of virtually unlimited power.

Those who believe this theory assert that the framers were intentionally limiting the realm of congressional power by itemizing the powers delegated to Congress. There are significant historical data to back up these claims. Within the Constitution itself, these sentiments have been thought to be expressed through the Tenth Amendment, which declares the following:

> The powers not delegated to the United States by the Constitution are reserved to the states respectively, or to the people.

Additionally, observers have looked to historical documents created by the framers to obtain a stronger understanding of their intentions. James Madison, in Federalist 45, specifically addresses to the people of the state of New York the dichotomy created between state and federal power. The title of this essay gives a perfect portal into some citizen concerns of the time. It reads "Alleged Danger from the Powers of the Union to the State Governments Considered." The summation of Madison's argument can be epitomized by his closing remarks:

> If the new Constitution be examined with accuracy and candor, it will be found that the change which it proposes consists much less in the addition of NEW POWERS to the Union, than in the invigoration of its ORIGINAL POWERS.

Madison also addressed the concern over the loss of state power in Federalist 39 by offering that the Constitution

> leaves to the several States a residuary and inviolable sovereignty over all other objects.

Constitutional analysts who believe the enumerated powers clause to have been created as limiting in nature argue that contemporary legislatures have gone far beyond their scope of authority with expansive interpretations of the clause. The framers of the Constitution implemented checks on the legislative branch to avoid an unbalanced government and dominant legislative branch. These checks included direct election of senators by the state legislatures (overturned by the SEVENTEENTH AMENDMENT), the PRESIDENTIAL VETO, and use of the Supreme Court to decide where the boundaries of power between the state and federal jurisdictions lie. However, critics argue that these checks on the legislative branch are ineffective because they are "external checks."

External checks are perceived as ineffective checks on Congress, as they rely on a purely unconstitutional act being exerted from Congress in order for them to be spurred into action. Interpreting the Constitution is still a matter of working within the parameters set forth by the framers of the Constitution and therefore does not trigger the flashing red light that would cause a response from the checks systematically put into place. These critics suggest that some form of internal check on Congress is needed to achieve the framers' original intentions for the legislative branch.

Whether the framers intended for the powers enumerated in Article I, Section 8, be limiting or not will probably never receive a definitive answer, as the debate over this issue has been waged for decades. What we do know is that the ambiguity that leads to problems within the Constitution can also lead to solutions.

See also CHECKS AND BALANCES; COURTS AND CONGRESS.

Further reading:
Baldacchino, Joseph. "Committees on Enumerated Powers: How Congress Can Revive the Constitution." *Center*

for Constitutional Studies Available online. URL: http://www.nhinet.org/revive.htm. Accessed January 30, 2006; Madison, James. "Alleged Danger from the Powers of the Union to the State Governments Considered." *The Federalist No. 45: Independent Journal,* 1788; Available online. URL: http://www.federalistjournal.com/fedpapers/fed_45.htm. Accessed 30 January 2006; Madison, James. "Conformity of the Plan to Republican Principles." *The Federalist No. 39: Independent Journal,* 1788. Available online. URL: http://www.federalistjournal.com/fedpapers/fed_39.htm. Accessed January 30, 2006.

—Nancy S. Lind

Environment and Public Works, Senate Committee on

The Senate Committee on Environment and Public Works began life as the Committee on Public Buildings and Grounds. Established in 1837, its original remit was to oversee the growing number of federal buildings in Washington, D.C.. Renamed the Committee on Public Works in 1947, it eventually received its existing title in the reorganization of 1977.

Throughout the 20th century the committee's jurisdiction grew from its original remit to include consideration of issues such as America's interstate highway system, flood control, and matters of navigation. The largest change, however, occurred in 1963, when the committee was given responsibility for pollution control, rural economic development, and natural disasters relief programs. The 1960s saw the issue of environmental protection rise in prominence on the national agenda. Such policy had previously been considered an area that was primarily the responsibility of state governments. However, with public concern growing over the issue, Congress looked to reform the federal law. In contrast to the HOUSE OF REPRESENTATIVES, where environmental issues were divided among a number of committees under the leadership of, among others, Chair Jennings Randolph (D-WV), Ranking Minority Member John Sherman Cooper (R-KY), and Air and Water Subcommittee Chair Edmund Muskie (D-ME), the Senate panel soon developed a reputation as the body's primary source for environmental policy. This reputation was established further with the passage of the groundbreaking CLEAN AIR ACT of 1970 and federal Water Pollution Control Act of 1972. Over the next decades environmental matters began to dominate the committee's agenda. The reorganization of 1977 brought such issues as endangered species, fish and wildlife refuges and programs, and nonmilitary nuclear power under its jurisdiction. Indeed, by 1992 five of its six subcommittees dealt with matters pertaining to environmental protection. The number of subcommittees has since been reduced to four, with three of them covering issues relating to the environment.

The committee gained a reputation for maintaining a bipartisan approach to environmental policy and as such managed to score some notable legislative successes. Major clean water legislation was passed in 1972 and 1987 over the vetoes of Presidents Nixon and Reagan, respectively. The committee could not repeat these successes in 1990 and suffered a blow to its authority when the Senate rejected its amendments to the Clean Air Act in favor of a compromise negotiated between the White House and SENATE MAJORITY LEADER George Mitchell (D-ME).

Conflict between the committee and the White House has not been restricted to environmental matters. Because of its public works remit, the committee has often been associated with senators seeking to acquire PORK BARREL. Former chair Jennings Randolph was frequently accused by opponents of using his position on the committee to benefit the economy of his home state. On public works legislation the deliberations of the committee have been described by William Riker as

> bi-partisan and consensual, characterized by norms of reciprocity and universalism.

Unsurprisingly, the dual responsibilities for environmental protection and public works legislation brought the committee into conflict with the Reagan administration as the White House sought to cut spending and relax regulations on industry. Such conflict occurred despite the fact that moderate Republican senator Robert Stafford (R-VT) chaired the committee.

Under Stafford the full committee began to dominate the formulation of environmental policy. Legislation concerning the Superfund and the Clean Air Act was not referred to subcommittees at all during this period, although amendments to the Clean Water Act were. This was partly a matter of Stafford's leadership style but also reflected the technical nature of environmental policy that can lead to a few legislators dominating deliberations.

During the 107th Congress Stafford's successor as senator from Vermont, Senator James Jeffords (I-VT), chaired the committee. Jeffords was awarded the position by the new Democratic majority leadership following his change of political affiliation from Republican to independent. His leadership of the committee majority was short-lived, however, and with control of the Senate switching back to the Republicans in 2003, Senator James Inhofe (R-OK) took over as the full committee chair.

Further reading:
U.S. Congress, Senate, Committee on Environment and Public Works. *History of the Committee on Environment*

and Public Works. Washington, D.C.: Government Printing Office, 1988.

—Ross M. English

Equal Rights Amendment

The Equal Rights Amendment (ERA) was formally proposed as the 27th amendment to the U.S. Constitution by Congress in 1972. The amendment's language, originally adopted in 1943 by the renowned women's rights activist Alice Paul, read simply:

> Equality of rights under the law shall not be denied or abridged by the United States or by any state on account of sex.

Upon its proposal the amendment was submitted to the states. When the requisite 38 states failed to ratify the amendment in 1982 after an extension of the deadline, the ERA became the first proposed amendment in post–Civil War history to expire after congressional passage.

The ERA was first introduced in 1923 by Alice Paul; the amendment was reintroduced in every session of Congress until it passed in 1972. In the early 1940s both the Democrats and the Republicans endorsed the amendment in their party platforms. However, opposition quickly developed from various sources, among them some women's groups. There was a tendency for business and professional women, many of whom were Republican at the time, to support the amendment, while working-class women, generally Democrats, opposed it.

The most persistent opposition to the ERA from its introduction in 1923 until a year after Congress formally proposed it in 1972 was from organized labor. The latter saw the amendment as a threat to protective labor legislation for women that it had worked so hard to pass. Working women were afraid that the amendment would strip them of protections such as the eight-or nine-hour work day. The inclusion of sex (almost by accident) into the 1964 Civil Rights Act undercut protective legislation that was often discriminatory. Thus, the AFL-CIO endorsed the ERA for the first time in 1973.

In 1970 several events brought the ERA to the forefront of Congress's attention. The prohibition against sexual discrimination that was included in the CIVIL RIGHTS ACT OF 1964 precipitated a barrage of complaints, well over one-third of the complaints received by the Equal Employment Opportunity Commission in its first year of operation. That summer two members of Congress, Edith Green and Martha Griffiths, launched a campaign to bring the ERA resolution to the House floor. The amendment had been bottled up in Chair Emanuel Cellar's Judiciary Committee for 22 years without a hearing.

Representative Green, who chaired the Judiciary's Subcommittee on Education, launched hearings on what was ostensibly discrimination against women in education. In reality, the hearings brought out complaints from women in many other areas. The hearings served as an important context for the amendment's eventual passage by the House.

While de facto hearings took place in Green's subcommittee, Representative Griffith filed a petition to discharge the HOUSE JUDICIARY COMMITTEE of further responsibility for the ERA resolution. This was a bold move indeed. Before 1974 it was difficult to challenge the power of committee chairs. Up until this time only 24 bills had ever received the 218 signatures required for discharge from a congressional committee. But the political climate was right, and eventually the discharge resolution was approved. The House voted 352-15 in favor of the ERA. In March 1972 the Senate passed the amendment 84-8, 22 votes more than the necessary two-thirds. However, the amendment also included an unusual provision that it be ratified within seven years.

Proponents of the ERA argued that a constitutional amendment would strengthen existing laws prohibiting certain inequities, laws that were often ignored or enforced indifferently. The amendment would provide a higher constitutional standard, a standard that would have symbolic as well as practical value for the issue of gender equality. The amendment would benefit men by reducing economic discrimination against women and enhancing family income; it would benefit homemakers by recognizing unpaid work as a contribution to the household. To opponents, who claimed that the Fourteenth Amendment's guarantees of equal protection were sufficient, advocates countered that those provisions were originally meant to protect African Americans against racial discrimination and would not be applied as stringently to gender. Finally, proponents argued that the United States remained one of a handful of democratic nations that did not provide constitutional protection of equal rights for women.

Opponents to the ERA began to emerge quickly. Arguments against it ranged from deep-seated philosophical issues to silly objections such as the fear that the amendment would force the use of unisex restrooms. One of the most vocal and powerful opposition movements was organized by an Illinois homemaker, Phyllis Schlafly, whose group "Stop ERA" led the attack. This organization's and other opponents' most serious objection was that the amendment's emphasis on feminist individualism would threaten the traditional structure of the family. Their practical arguments included such concerns as forced military service, challenges to laws requiring husbands to support the family, and an end to women's favored position in child custody matters.

Once proposed, the amendment needed three-fourths of the states to approve. Although 35 states ratified the ERA by 1977, the opponents' case quickly gained momentum. When the time elapsed in 1982, the amendment was still three states short of the necessary 38. The states that failed to approve the ERA were Alabama, Arizona, Arkansas, Florida, Georgia, Illinois, Louisiana, Mississippi, Missouri, Nevada, North and South Carolina, Oklahoma, Utah, and Virginia.

In March 2001 Representative Carolyn Maloney, a Democrat from New York, and Senator Edward M. Kennedy, a Democrat from Massachusetts, introduced the ERA once again to both houses of Congress. The bill had 162 original sponsors in both houses but only a handful of support from Republicans in the House. Supporters claimed that wage and pension gaps as well as conservative assaults on abortion and affirmative action made constitutional protections necessary, but opponents to the ERA quickly mobilized. It appears that after 80 years the political battle over the ERA is not over.

—Cynthia Opheim

Ex parte McCardle, 74 U.S. 506 (1869)

Article III, Section 2, of the U.S. Constitution authorizes Congress to make exceptions and regulations with respect to the Supreme Court's appellate jurisdiction. Strictly speaking, this means Congress may, by legislation, bar the Court from hearing certain cases or classes of cases, should it so decide. This power, commonly referred to as "court-stripping," has been invoked on numerous occasions, but it has been exercised only once in American history: in the case of *Ex parte McCardle*.

McCardle, a Mississippi newspaper editor, was taken into custody and held for trial before a military tribunal for allegedly publishing libelous articles regarding the occupation of the postwar South during Reconstruction. McCardle filed a writ of habeas corpus in federal circuit court alleging unlawful restraint by military force. Upon denial of the writ, he sought appeal to the Supreme Court pursuant to the Judiciary Act of 1789, as amended in 1867 to specifically authorize such appeals. The Court heard oral arguments in the case in early March 1868. Fearing that an adverse decision by the Court in McCardle's case would undermine Reconstruction legislation, Congress hurriedly amended the Judiciary Act to repeal the Court's jurisdiction over habeas corpus denials; the act was signed by the president on March 27, 1868, before the Court had rendered a decision on the merits.

The Court was faced with a dilemma: challenge Congress's exercise of the court-stripping power and face a constitutional crisis or accept a significant curb on its authority. The Court chose the latter and dismissed McCardle's appeal for lack of jurisdiction. While the justices certainly understood that Congress had legislated expressly to block McCardle's case, the Court's opinion stated that "we are not at liberty to inquire into the motives of the legislature. We can only examine into its power under the Constitution."

Shortly thereafter the Court appeared to distance itself from the McCardle decision in *U.S. v. Klein*, 80 U.S. 128 (1872). In that case the Court rejected congressional removal of jurisdiction, which would "prescribe rules of decision to the Judicial Department . . . in cases pending before it." Citing Klein, Justice Douglas questioned the vitality of McCardle in a 1962 dissenting opinion, but the Court has never overruled McCardle. Court-stripping thus remains a potentially powerful curb on judicial power. While it has not been used since, it has been invoked increasingly in recent years, most recently regarding potential challenges to the Defense of Marriage Act.

Further reading:
U.S. v. Klein, 80 U.S. 128 (1872); *Glidden Co. v. Zdanok*, 370 U.S. 530, 605 (1962) (Black, J., dissenting); Gunther, Gerald, and Kathleen M. Sullivan. *Constitutional Law.* 14th ed. New York: Foundation Press, 2001.

—Daniel E. Smith

executive agreements

Executive agreements are agreements made by the president of the United States or other executive official with executive officials of other nations. They differ from treaties in that the legislative branch has no role in the process. According to Article II, Section 2, of the Constitution, a treaty must be ratified by the Senate by a two-thirds majority of the senators present. This means that a minority of the Senate—a third of those present plus one additional senator—can effectively veto a treaty that the president has submitted. The president faces no such obstacles in relation to executive agreements. However, insofar as executive agreements are used rather than treaties with the required Senate participation, the foreign policy process loses public involvement. Senate debate on a treaty would receive media coverage, but executive agreements do not receive such attention and, in fact, are sometimes made in secret.

Although they are not mentioned in the Constitution, presidents have entered into executive agreements since George Washington's day. Presidents used them for fairly routine matters in the early years of the nation. Therefore, they were not controversial. However, during the presidency of Franklin D. Roosevelt and to an even greater extent in the post–World War II years, the number of executive agreements that presidents concluded rose significantly and dealt with matters far from routine.

Franklin D. Roosevelt exercised the constitutional authority granted to the president to receive ambassadors to extend diplomatic recognition to the Soviet Union. In 1933, as a part of the process of establishing diplomatic relations, the two nations entered into an executive agreement for the purpose of resolving financial claims that American nationals had against the Soviet Union. According to the agreement, the Soviet Union, in what was known as the Litvinov Assignment, turned over to the United States the right to all amounts owed to it by Americans. The United States was to use these assets to satisfy claims American nationals had against the Soviet Union. The executors of the estate of New York banker August Belmont challenged the validity of the agreement when funds in Belmont's bank, over which the Soviet Union had previously claimed ownership, were to be turned over to the United States to satisfy American claims. In *United States v. Belmont* (1937) the Supreme Court upheld the validity of the executive agreement, noting that not all international compacts are treaties that require Senate ratification. In further litigation related to the Litvinov Assignment, in *United States v. Pink* (1942), the Court called the executive agreement a modest implied power of the president and, like treaties, the supreme law of the land.

The conflict between the United States and Iran following the seizure of the American embassy in Tehran on November 4, 1979, and the taking of American embassy personnel as hostages, provided the basis for another executive agreement related to frozen assets. On January 19, 1981, the United States and Iran, as they attempted to bring closure to the conflict, entered into an executive agreement in which each country agreed to halt all litigation in its country by its own nationals against the other party to the agreement. Instead of civil trials within the two countries, they would establish an Iran-United States Claims Tribunal to provide binding arbitration. The Supreme Court upheld the executive agreement against challenge in *Dames & Moore v. Regan* (1981). In upholding the agreement the Court noted that Congress had not enacted any legislation authorizing this executive agreement. However, in other legislation over the years, Congress had accepted the authority of the president to enter into agreements regarding the settlement of international claims of American nationals. Whether the executive agreement would have been valid had there been congressional opposition rather than acceptance was left unanswered.

Not all executive agreements have dealt with international financial claims. In the post–World War II period there were important military treaties but even more executive agreements concerning such matters as military base rights in foreign countries as well as agreements to protect the security of other countries by going to their aid if attacked by communist forces. During the cold war there were secret executive agreements regarding intelligence gathering and covert activity, some of them not even with nations but with resistance groups within nations that had communist governments. Congress came to know of such agreements much later, only after they were in effect, and sometimes only because of leaks in the executive branch.

In the 1970s Congress began to assert itself against the "imperial presidency." Congress passed the Case-Zablocki Act in 1972 requiring the secretary of State to send to Congress the text of all executive agreements. If national security might be jeopardized by making such information public, the statute permitted the text to be sent to the relevant congressional committees only. The act, with its 1978 amendment, was only moderately successful. Congress, however, showed that it would not unquestioningly accept absolute presidential power, even in foreign affairs.

Further reading:
Glennon, Michael J. *Constitutional Diplomacy.* Princeton, N.J.: Princeton University Press, 1990; Johnson, Loch K. *America as a World Power: Foreign Policy in a Constitutional Framework.* 2d ed. New York: McGraw-Hill, 1995; Johnson, Loch K. *The Making of International Agreements: Congress Confronts the Executive.* New York: New York University Press, 1984; Lipson, Charles. "Why Are Some International Agreements Informal?" *International Organization* 45 (Autumn 1991): 495–538.

—Patricia A. Behlar

executive branch and Congress

The baron de Montesquieu, a French political philosopher of the 18th century, is credited with expounding what were to become key distinctions in the governmental principles of the U.S. Constitution. To legislate is to formulate the public laws. To execute is to carry out the laws and administer them. The judicial power is the interpretation of the laws and their application to actual disputes and cases. These are the three main things that the government can and should do. According to Montesquieu these three functions should be allocated to the three branches of government: the legislature, the executive, and the judiciary.

The American founders agreed with Montesquieu that the various functions should be assigned to distinct institutions of government that would function substantially, but not entirely, independently from one another. Of the three branches Federalist 78 told Americans, "—The judiciary is beyond comparison the weakest of the three departments of power; that it can never attack with success either of the other two; and that all possible care is requisite to enable it to defend itself against their attacks." The preeminent branches were expected to be and have always been the executive branch and Congress.

Clearly, it was Madison's view that "the legislative department" was the branch with the most extensive powers, including, he noted in Federalist 48, "access to the pockets of the people." But the founders prepared solutions to the problem. "The remedy for this inconveniency is to divide the legislature into different branches; and to render them, by different modes of election and different principles of action, as little connected with each other as the nature of their common functions and their common dependence on the society will admit." Madison counted on the House and Senate to be competing bodies, distinctly constituted, that would check and balance each other, thereby restraining the dangerous power of the preeminent legislative branch.

Even divided, Madison feared that the legislative branch would encroach on the separate responsibilities of the other branches. Therefore, "the weakness of the executive may require . . . that it be fortified." That fortifying power was to put the veto authority into the hands of the president, not an "absolute negative" but a qualified one that the legislature could override with two-thirds majorities in both houses.

Congress lacks any centralized leadership. The Senate's nominal leader is the vice president, who presides (when he cares to) and breaks tied votes. In practice, however, the Senate's leadership has devolved upon its majority party leader, not really a spokesperson for the Senate as a whole. The Speaker of the House is more prominent and powerful, but those in the office have always functioned as creatures of the House, a challenging and sometimes unruly large body of persons with equal votes. While some speakers have visibly played a public role (most recently Speaker Newt Gingrich, 1995–99), most have primarily managed the legislative process without actually dominating the policy agenda of the House, much less that of Congress as a whole. The result is that the broad and complex policy agenda in Congress belongs to whichever senators and representatives manage to use the rules of procedure along with their talents and personal leadership abilities to articulate policy ideas, win votes, and gain approval from their colleagues. The openness of the House and Senate to alternative policy leaders among their membership means that Congress is unable to speak to the American public with a single voice. Congress is home to a multitude of voices, mostly uncoordinated and often expressing competing views, that advocate to both the public and their colleagues for and against a variety of policy proposals.

Congress as an institution remains the most powerful branch. With its legislation it formalizes all the laws and the budget for the business of government. But it works by the action of majorities in two separate chambers that have no central management to coordinate them. Because majorities usually work their will slowly, Congress is a reactive body, often playing catch-up to problems imposed on the policy agenda by external events. To illustrate, the attacks against the United States on September 11, 2001, prompted the most sweeping restructuring of the federal bureaucracy since World War II. It took a year and a half to enact a new Department of Homeland Security, putting together elements from 22 different federal agencies. This legislation establishes a new framework, but the task of enacting all the details of this structure is far from complete. That huge task absorbed the energy of members throughout Congress and at the same time simply forcing many other policy issues off the legislative policy agenda.

While the powers of the executive branch are not nearly as sweeping as those entrusted to Congress, Article II of the Constitution immediately addresses the leadership issue. Section 1 opens by saying, "The executive power shall be vested in a President of the United States of America." The president as chief executive holds the reins for the entire executive establishment. While it would be inaccurate to say that the chief executive is the controlling leader of the national political system, there is no other authority who can regularly impose upon him or her. The president controls political instruments including the bureaucracy, political appointees, staff, and the military. He or she proposes the budget, conducts foreign relations, oversees the spending, and manipulates the veto. The SPEAKER OF THE HOUSE, the SENATE MAJORITY LEADER, political party officials, the chief justice of the Supreme Court, interest group speakers, and media commentators may rival the president's influence in particular circumstances, but on the broad range of issues with which the government deals, the president most often prevails. Hamilton in Federalist 70 had an explanation for the practical effectiveness of the president.

> Energy in the executive is a leading character in the definition of the government. It is the president who can take initiative, with other countries through the Secretary of State and the ambassadors, in domestic matters by means of the departments and civil servants.

While presidents have varied in the form and manner of their deference to Congress, from Washington to the present presidents have sent messages to Congress, putting their policy requests on the legislative agenda. From the beginning the Constitution authorized that,

> He shall from time to time give to the Congress information of the state of the Union, and recommend to their consideration such measures as he shall judge necessary and expedient.

Certainly since Franklin D. Roosevelt took the initiative to revitalize a Depression-ridden economy in the 1930s, the people have expected the president to propose remedies for national problems of the day with that energy Hamilton remarked about.

A president has about 2.4 million civilian employees subject to his or her direction. However, in terms of leadership tasks, only a small part of that number is significant. About 1,200 direct the agencies of the administration, and, although subject to Senate confirmation and duty-bound to appear before congressional committees to account for their performance, they are appointed and serve at the pleasure of the president. Such appointees are recruited from careers and experience directly related to the industries or segments of society most affected by the agency to which they are appointed. Many of the ideas for policy come from them and the career employees they direct. The presidency also has formalized agencies to advise the president about broad areas of policy concern. These include the National Security Council, the Office of Policy Development, the Office of Management and Budget, and the Council of Economic Advisers.

The inner core of presidential advisers is the White House staff. While many of these people bring their own varieties of experience, they are not expected to represent specific interests in the policy process. Their notable qualities are their anonymity and their loyalty to the president they serve. Presidents vary in their personal style for exercising and overseeing staff. President William Clinton's style was more spontaneous, less formal and disciplined than that of his successor, George W. Bush. White House staff possess no legal authority to "do" anything. They serve on the president's behalf and at his pleasure. The paperwork they generate is subject to the Presidential Records Act. They are not answerable to Congress about what they do on the president's behalf (except in the case of criminal investigations, as in Watergate). Through this staff the president keeps continuously informed about what politically relevant events are happening domestically and abroad. Staff supply both information and evaluation. They make decisions in the president's name and prod others on his behalf. A significant portion of staff effort goes to stimulating and coordinating departments and agencies. Another portion is devoted to congressional relations. The president's staff equips him with greater control over information than any other political rival has. This vast information base is a major resource for presidential leadership.

The presidency affords the incumbent preeminent visibility. In a media-conscious world the president can use his or her authority and information to make things happen and, in effect, make news. In contrast especially to Congress, the president speaks with a single voice. Therefore, he or she is well positioned to advocate innovations and changes to public policy. Some innovations he or she can effectuate by orders. Others require legislative action. The president's assets make him or her the preeminent policy promoter in the political system.

Despite the president's powers, budgets expire every year. New programs require legislative authority. Appointments necessitate Senate confirmations. Treaties take effect only with Senate approval. Budget plans must be backed with appropriations that begin in the House. Despite the separation of powers the executive branch depends for its sustenance on Congress. If Congress needs the executive's energy, the president cannot sustain the executive function without congressional support.

There is a rhythm to the continuing interactions and rivalry of the executive branch with Congress. That rhythm is set by congressional elections every two years, presidential elections every four years, and the two-term limit upon incumbent presidents. The president and his or her appointees in the executive branch turn over relatively quickly. Despite short elected terms, many in Congress have through their success with reelection seen several presidents of both political parties come and go. Such an accumulation of political experience lends continuity to the nation's political rhythm, sustaining both the forces for change and stability that balance the often stressful give-and-take between Congress and the executive branch.

See also CHECKS AND BALANCES; DIVIDED GOVERNMENT.

Further reading:
The Constitution of the United States; Hamilton, A., J. Madison and J. Jay. *The Federalist Papers.* C. Rossiter, ed. New York: New American Library, 1961; *The United States Government Manual 2002–03.* Washington, D.C.: Government Printing Office, 2003; Patterson, B. H. *The White House Staff: Inside the West Wing and Beyond.* Washington, D.C.: Brookings Institution Press, 2000; Greenberg, E. S. and B. I. Page. *The Struggle for Democracy.* 5th ed. New York: Longman, 2002; Vile, M. J. C. *Constitutionalism and the Separation of Powers.* Indianapolis: Liberty Fund, 1998.

—Jack R. Van Der Slik

executive session
Closed or secret floor or committee meetings in the HOUSE OF REPRESENTATIVES and SENATE when the bodies considers treaties, nominations, and business sent from the executive branch are called executive sessions. An executive session of a congressional committee or the full Senate or House of Representatives is a meeting that is closed to the press and the public. Witnesses frequently appear before committees in executive session because

they are discussing topics of a sensitive nature, usually national security. Most committee meetings in Congress are open to the public as required by SUNSHINE RULES. The Senate also may meet in closed sessions when deliberating an impeachment proceeding. Executive session may refer to a meeting of the Senate called to discuss functions related to the executive branch, such as the confirmation of presidential nominations and the ratification of treaties.

Congress derives its ability to hold secret sessions from Article I, Section 5, of the Constitution. The section states:

> Each House shall keep a journal of its proceedings, and from time to time publish the same, excepting such parts as may in their judgment require secrecy.

All normal rules of debate apply during secret sessions in both the House and Senate, except for impeachment deliberations in the Senate.

In the House secret sessions are governed by Rule XVII, Clause 9, which specifies what business may be conducted in secret. A motion to resolve into a secret session may be made only by the House meeting as the House of Representatives, not by the Committee of the Whole House. Rule X, Clause 11 (D–F), specifies that the House Select Committee on Intelligence may move that a secret session be held to determine whether classified information held by the committee may be released to the public.

Senate Rules XX and XXIV have been interpreted by the Senate to require that deliberations during impeachment trials be held in secret. Senate Rules XXI, XXIX, and XXXI govern secret sessions for legislative and executive business. The Senate can close its doors once a motion has been made and seconded. The vote on whether to close the meeting to the public is made behind closed doors. Under Senate Rules consideration of treaties is to be conducted in secret unless a majority of senators votes to lift the "injunction of secrecy." Most treaties have been deliberated in open session. Presidential nominations are to be considered in open session unless the Senate votes to close the session.

Further reading:
Amer, Mildred. *Secret Sessions of Congress: A Brief Historical Overview.* RS20145. Washington, D.C.: Library of Congress, Congressional Research Service, 2004; Johnson, Charles W. *Constitution, Jefferson's Manual, and Rules of the House of Representatives.* House Document No. 107-284. Washington, D.C.: Government Printing Office, 2003; U.S. Senate, *Senate Manual, Senate Document 107-1.* Washington, D.C.: Government Printing Office, 2002.
—John David Rausch, Jr.

expedited consideration

Expedited consideration allows the U.S. HOUSE OF REPRESENTATIVES and SENATE to adopt special procedures that allow Congress to greatly hasten action on committee or floor decisions. Expedited consideration allows Congress to in effect bypass its own rules and regulations. The traditional legislative procedures of the House and Senate are intentionally time-consuming, so that bills do not get enacted without sufficient scrutiny, but these procedures also provide no guarantee that the resolutions presented will be debated quickly in committee or on the floor. In some instances, however, members of Congress decide that certain measures are so critical that they should be given preferential, or "fast track," treatment by Congress. These special procedures protect the resolutions from being blocked or delayed by procedural obstacles. Expedited consideration has most commonly been granted to budget resolutions and reconciliation bills, measures related to the use of U.S. armed forces in accord with the WAR POWERS RESOLUTION OF 1973, and measures to implement international trade agreements consistent with the Trade Act of 1974.

The CONGRESSIONAL RESEARCH SERVICE has specified that expedited consideration has included many, though not necessarily all, of the following elements:

- a detailed definition of the types of bills and resolutions to which expedited consideration applies
- mandatory introduction of such a measure, often promptly after the House and Senate receive a message that the president is required to submit
- a requirement for the committee that is assigned the bill to report it to the floor within a certain number of days
- a provision for automatic discharge of a bill if the committee fails to report the measure within the timeframe provided
- privileged access for the bill to be heard on the House and Senate floor for consideration
- limitations on the length of debate for the resolution
- prohibitions against legislators proposing floor amendments to the measure
- procedures for immediate floor action in either house when a companion bill passes in the other chamber

In sum, expedited consideration allows Congress to shorten the time required for a bill to become a law. In some cases it is important to note that expedited consideration may prompt fast committee action in one house but not in the other. The use of expedited consideration is designed to bring immediate action on a resolution rather than delaying the measure to the extent that it might not reach the president for possible signature and enactment into law.

See also CLOTURE; DILATORY MOTION; FILIBUSTER; RULES AND PROCEDURES, HOUSE; RULES AND PROCEDURES, SENATE.

Further reading:
Bach, Stanley. "Expedited or 'Fast-Track' Legislative Procedures." Congressional Research Services Report for Congress RS20234, 1999; Bach, Stanley. " 'Fast Track' or Expedited Procedures: Their Purposes, Elements and Implications." Congressional Research Services Report 98-888, 1998.

—Nancy S. Lind

extension of remarks

The extension of remarks is a method by which members may insert statements, charts, graphs, newspaper articles, letters from constituents, and many other materials not spoken or presented on the floor into the CONGRESSIONAL RECORD. Though it is not the official record of Congress's work (each house publishes a JOURNAL that serves this purpose), the *Congressional Record* is an important source of information for scholars and judges who seek to understand the motives or reasons for congressional decisions, sometimes referred to as congressional intent. Over time the rules to add more material have been made more stringent because of the increased expense of printing the *Congressional Record* (by one estimate the cost per page is approximately $260.00) and mounting criticism by those who claim members use the *Record* for political purposes. Members may request reprints of pages from the *Record* to mail to constituents via the FRANKING privilege, extolling their accomplishments or justifying positions they have taken, among other things. Such tactics increase the advantages enjoyed by incumbents in their reelection bids.

Extension of remarks is different from revision of remarks, though both are often requested simultaneously on the floor if the member asks for "unanimous consent to revise and extend my remarks at this point in the Record." Since the earliest Congresses, members have sought and been granted permission by the chamber's presiding officer to edit statements made on the floor prior to publication. In the House material added through the request for extension appears in a separate section of the *Congressional Record* titled "Extension of Remarks," while revised comments appear in the main text of the *Record* in a different font. In the Senate extended material and revised statements are printed in the proceedings of the *Record*, but they are demarcated by black dots. These practice of differentiating revisions and extensions via font styles began in 1978.

House procedures for requesting an extension of remarks are rather specific. A member may physically appear on the House floor and request an extension, or the member may obtain a form for this purpose from the member's leadership table, complete it, and personally sign it before submitting it. For those who choose to file a form, each party has a member on duty at the end of the day whose responsibility is to request permission to extend remarks for all the members of the party filing that day. The deadline for submitting requests is 5:00 P.M. or 15 minutes after the House adjourns. Extended materials may not exceed two pages. Members may, however, request an exception in person at the start or end of each day by personally standing and asking for recognition by the presiding officer, and say "I ask unanimous consent to extend my remarks in the *Record* and to include therein extraneous material notwithstanding the fact that it exceeds two pages and is estimated by the GPO (Government Printing Office) to cost $—." Members must have investigated the true cost of the additional pages by seeking an estimate from the GPO.

—Thomas J. Baldino

F

Farm Bloc

The Farm Bloc was a small group of senators and representatives who sought to influence legislation and government policy on agriculture. It originated in the severe post–World War I depression that particularly affected American farmers. The collapse of world prices for grain and cotton that began in 1919 resulted in a wave of farm failures in the Midwest, far West, and South. When it became apparent that the incoming Republican administration of Warren G. Harding had no positive program, a group of U.S. senators from agricultural states decided to take action. At the behest of W. S. Kenyon, a Republican senator from Iowa, a bipartisan group of 12 senators met in the Washington offices of the American Farm Bureau Federation on May 9, 1921, to formulate their own program.

The Senate group subsequently doubled to 24, with 12 additional participants (six from each party). Led initially by Kenyon and later by Arthur Capper (Republican from Kansas), the bloc included many influential senators. Particularly active were George W. Norris (R-NE), Charles McNary (R-OR), Frank Kellogg (R-MN), Claude Swanson (D-VA), and Robert M. La Follette, Jr., (R-WI). Congressman Lester Dicksinson, also an Iowa Republican, organized a similar but less formal Farm Bloc of nearly 100 members in the HOUSE OF REPRESENTATIVES.

Despite warnings in the eastern press about manifestations of agricultural radicalism, the Farm Bloc did not press for radical reforms and actually did little to alleviate the difficulties confronting American farmers in the early 1920s. Bloc members confined their activities to issues on which they agreed. Their main agenda was legislation to stabilize prices for commodities (particularly corn, pork products, tobacco, and cotton), the regulation of processors, and the expansion of farm credit. The Farm Bloc enjoyed considerable power in the 67th Congress (1921–23) and took credit for the enactment of several bills of interest to farmers, including the Future Trading Act, the Packers and Stockyards Act, the Capper-Volstead Cooperative Marketing Act, and the expansion of the activities of the Intermediate Credits Act.

The Farm Bloc was unwilling, and to some extent unable, however, to go beyond these measures. It lacked ideological cohesiveness, and attachments varied with each issue depending on sectional considerations and political outlook. Members could not agree on larger measures needed to stabilize farm exports and farm income. As a result, numerous sectional and ideological differences led to the breakdown of the Farm Bloc in the next Congress. Prodded by the Farm Bureau Federation and its director, George N. Peek, midwestern and southern elements in the bloc worked to reconstitute the bloc later in the 1920s. The struggle to pass the McNary-Haugen Bill in 1927 and 1928 did lead to partial reunification in sufficient strength to push the measure through both houses of Congress, but it did not survive President Calvin Coolidge's veto. Facing hostility from Presidents Coolidge and Hoover, both of whom opposed direct government intervention to stabilize commodity prices, the Farm Bloc as a cohesive political force in Congress disappeared for the remainder of the 1920s and the early 1930s.

In the friendlier atmosphere of Franklin D. Roosevelt's NEW DEAL, with its support for farm interests and its emphasis on price stabilization and production controls, the bloc thrived. Led by a bipartisan groups of midwestern Progressive senators, such as George Norris and Burton K. Wheeler (D-MN), and southern New Deal Democrats such as John H. Bankhead (D-AL), JOSEPH ROBINSON (D-AR), and J. W. Elmer Thomas (D-OK), the bloc was instrumental in passing of the Agricultural Adjustment Acts of 1933 and 1938 and bills addressing the stabilization of specific commodities, such as the Bankhead Cotton Control Act and the Kerr-Smith Tobacco Act (both enacted in 1934).

Reciprocity, particularly between the midwestern and southern elements in the bloc, enabled its members to maintain unity. Its strength was enhanced by strategic committee assignments, the seniority of many of its midwestern Republican and southern Democratic leaders, and ties to farm lobbies (particularly the American Farm Bureau Federation) and the federal government's agricultural bureaucracy. Its priority during both the New Deal and World War II was the securing of price supports for corn, cotton, tobacco, and meat products and market stabilization. Its influence continued to be strong into the post–World War II years, and it had a strong voice in the continuing controversies surrounding congressional legislation and government policy toward the agricultural surpluses that marked agricultural politics in the late 1940s and the 1950s.

Despite its political successes, however, the Farm Bloc did not address many fundamental structural problems of American agriculture, such as the decline of the family farm, the displacement of many small and tenant farmers, and the impact of new technology. Its strength in recent years has been undermined by the declining number of farms and the agricultural population. The rise of consumer and environmental issues has weakened support for farm subsidies among labor and the suburban middle classes. The use of the term *Farm Bloc* has virtually disappeared from the American political dialogue. Nevertheless, the bloc remains one of the best examples of how interest groups can influence congressional legislation and public policy and how a small but well-connected and cohesive political body can exercise political power out of proportion to its size.

Further reading:
Browne, William P. *Private Interests, Public Policy, and American Agriculture.* Lawrence: University Press of Kansas, 1988; Campbell, Christina McFadyen. *The Farm Bureau and the New Deal: A Study in the Making of National Farm Policy,* 1933–1940. Urbana: University of Illinois Press, 1962; Fite, Gilbert C. *George N. Peek and the Fight for Farm Parity.* Norman: University of Oklahoma Press, 1954.

—Walter F. Bell

Federal Election Campaign Act of 1971

The first of a series of bills seeking to reform financing of federal elections was the Federal Election Campaign Act of 1971. The law, which actually was passed in January of the following year, sought to mandate disclosure of and establish selected limits to contributions made to federal election campaigns.

This law was amended by measures passed in 1974, 1976, and 1979 and the BIPARTISAN CAMPAIGN REFORM ACT OF 2002. Such restrictions on campaign funding were challenged through lawsuits. In 1976 the Supreme Court ruled in the *BUCKLEY V. VALEO* decision that there could be no limit to how much of their own money individual candidates could spend on their campaigns.

See also CONGRESSIONAL ELECTIONS: FINANCING.

—Mark Kemper

Federalist Papers

The Federalist Papers were a series of essays prepared for New York newspapers in 1787 and 1788 arguing for the ratification of a new Constitution to replace the Articles of Confederation. The authors were Alexander Hamilton, James Madison, and John Jay. Both Hamilton and Madison were convention delegates. The signers of the proposed Constitution completed their work in Philadelphia on September 17, 1787. Using the pen name "Publius," the three authors contributed 85 essays that began to appear in New York newspapers in late October 1787. These essays were published steadily until April of the next year and after a 10-week break appeared from mid-June to mid-August. The essays were collected into two volumes, making the entire corpus of arguments available to other advocates as well as editors of newspapers throughout the 13 states.

Hamilton was a leading Federalist in New York and actively campaigned for ratification of the proposed Constitution. Thus, Hamilton became the prime mover in the project, and he wrote most (51) of the essays. He recruited the two additional authors. The youngest of the three, Hamilton had been an active pamphleteer in promoting the American Revolution. He was a young officer under the command of George Washington during the war and had worked diligently to get the Constitutional Convention under way. He was a member of the New York delegation to the convention of 1787 but was apparently neutralized there by Robert Yates and John Lansing, prominent anti-Federalists also in the New York delegation. To gain ratification of the proposed Constitution at the state convention in his home state, Hamilton persuaded New York newspapers to publish the series of essays he would develop on behalf of the Constitution.

John Jay was the oldest and, at the time, the most distinguished of the three essayists. He was a major draftsman of the New York constitution adopted in 1777. He had been a significant spokesman for America in the postwar peace negotiations when the nation's independence was internationally acknowledged in 1783. Under the Articles of Confederation Jay was America's secretary for Foreign Affairs and, thus, unavailable to serve as a convention delegate. When he was not in government service he was active as a lawyer in New York. Although well suited to the task of writing such essays, he contributed only five, presumably because of sickness suffered in late 1787. Later, of course, Jay became the first chief justice of the Supreme Court by appointment from George Washington.

James Madison was the third of the essayists. He was from Virginia and an early supporter of the revolutionary cause. He served on Virginia's council of state under the first elected governors there, Patrick Henry and Thomas Jefferson. He took part in developing Virginia's bill of rights, adopted in 1776. He developed a reputation as a tireless legislator in the Continental Congress, where he became a friend of Hamilton. During the Constitutional Convention Madison diligently supported the ideas of the Virginia Plan and was a major force for advocating a strong central government. Madison's notes on that convention are the most detailed record of what happened because there was no official journal for the body. Madison was anxious to advocate the Constitution that he did so much to produce, so he became a willing ally in the Publius series. Contemporary historians typically credit Madison as being the "father of the Constitution." After ratification was achieved Madison became a crucial figure in the development of the Constitution's first ten amendments, popularly referred to as the Bill of Rights. Later, of course, Madison was secretary of State for another of his close political allies, Thomas Jefferson, and succeeded Jefferson to the presidency in 1809.

The Federalist Papers appeared in rapid succession. After the convention, opposition to the Constitution quickly became apparent. Several of its prominent members, including Alpheus Mason, Edmund Randolph, and Elbridge Gerry, refused to sign the proposed Constitution. John Lansing and Robert Yates, anti-Federalists from New York, left the convention early to begin urging rejection of the proposed Constitution at the New York state convention. Opponents of the Constitution would argue that the power of the states was threatened by the Constitution more than it had ever been by England's King George and its Parliament. Therefore, the Federalists set about making their case quickly as well. The first essay appeared on October 27, 1787, and in it Hamilton promised a series of papers that would explain all aspects of the proposed Constitution. He was quick to note that

> the vigor of government is essential to the security of liberty and that regarding this Constitution,
>
> I am clearly of opinion it is your interest to adopt it. . . . I frankly acknowledge to you my convictions, and I will freely lay before you the reasons on which they are founded.

The three authors took up a stunningly broad list of subjects. They warned about a hostile world and the need for unity and strength by the United States. They warned about the weaknesses and wickedness of human nature and the fearsomeness of violence among the states. In Federalist 10 Madison famously analyzed the nature and effect of factions. He argued that the multiplicity of factions (interests) and the largeness of the republic over which power would be dispersed would keep factions in check. Hamilton argued that a strong political union would facilitate economic growth and widespread prosperity. The three authors provided much criticism of the deficiencies of government under the Articles of Confederation as well as in other confederations of world history. Hamilton defended the strengths of national taxation. Madison made elaborate arguments in favor of the separation of powers in representative government. In Federalist 51 Madison says,

> You must first enable the government to control the governed; and in the next place, oblige it to control itself.

His solution was a large republic, separated power, checks and balances, and a competing variety of political interests and factions. He asserted the strengths of a bicameral Congress. Jay argued on behalf of the Senate's role in forging international treaties. Hamilton discussed the qualities of the presidency and in an often quoted line noted that,

> energy in the executive is a leading character in the definition of good government

Hamilton is also famous for saying,

> whenever a particular statute contravenes the Constitution, it will be the duty of the judicial tribunals to adhere to the latter and disregard the former

In 1803 Hamilton's reasoning became an established precedent of the Supreme Court in the case of *Marbury v. Madison*. Hamilton completed his review of the proposed Constitution saying why a Bill of Rights was unneeded, but he acknowledged that the means for amendment were available in the Constitution.

The Federalist case prevailed in all the states but Rhode Island and North Carolina, so the Constitution gained ratification in 1788. There is no clear evidence that the Federalist Papers were decisive to the state contests. However, in the home states of the authors, New York and Virginia, the issues were highly contested, and the outcomes were close. In the New York convention the proposition carried by only three votes, and approval came after threats from New York City that people might detach themselves from the state in order to form a new one. In both states the Federalist case prevailed, and the state conventions approved the Constitution.

Collected together, the Federalist Papers have remained a kind of catechism that explains the intentions of the founders. They continue to be the subject of analysis and debate. It is commonly argued that Hamilton projects a more nationalistic tone and emphasizes power, while Madison is more concerned about controlling governmental power and mischievous majorities that might exploit it.

The continuing significance of the Federalist Papers is evidenced by more than scholarly attention. The official expositor of the U.S. Constitution is the Supreme Court. Its historic decisions are accompanied by its opinion, often added to with both concurring and dissenting opinions. Recent scholarship reports that these opinions have increasingly cited the Federalist Papers and that the rate of such citations was never higher than in the 1990s. As of 1996 the five most frequently cited papers have been noted in at least 25 Supreme Court decisions. The most frequently cited, 33 times, is Federalist 42, in which Madison discusses the powers of the new government in the conduct of foreign affairs, regulating commerce, and providing for harmonious relations among the states. Hamilton's Federalist 78 has been cited in 30 Supreme Court decisions. In it he describes the independence of the federal judiciary and argues for the courts' role in judicial review. Doubtless it is the best-known Federalist essay among lawyers and law students along with the third-ranking essay, 81, also by Hamilton. It has been cited in 27 decisions, and it, too, deals with the judiciary, particularly relations among the levels of federal courts as well as with the state courts. Madison's Federalist 51, dealing with checks and balances, ranks fourth and has been cited in 26 cases. Nearly all these citations were after 1960, the modern era when such issues became subjects of increasing court litigation. In fifth place is Hamilton's Federalist 32, which discusses taxation and the respective powers of the national government and the states. Cited in 25 cases, the great majority of these cases were settled more than a quarter of a century ago.

Argumentation about the Constitution and its applications remains a lively matter in American democracy. For example, during the height of controversy regarding the impeachment of President Bill Clinton, advocates on both sides and analysts in the media of the day supported their positions with quotations from the venerable Federalist Papers. The intelligence and insights recorded there by the authors of the papers still have weight and meaning in contemporary controversies of American politics.

Further reading:
Hamilton, A., J. Madison, and J. Jay. *The Federalist Papers.* C. Rossiter, ed. New York: American Library of World Literature, 1961; Elkins, S., and E. McKitrick. *The Age of Federalism.* New York: Oxford University Press, 1963; Lupu, I. C. "The Most Cited Federalist Papers." *Constitutional Commentary* (Winter 1998): 403; Walker, D. B. *The Rebirth of Federalism: Slouching toward Washington.* Chatham, N.J.: Chatham House, 1995.

—Jack R. Van Der Slik

filibuster

The filibuster is the procedural device used primarily in the U.S. SENATE to delay consideration of a BILL or to prevent its enactment. Widely believed to be derived from the Dutch word *vrijbuiter*, which signifies a "pirate," the filibuster today is perceived to permit a senator to speak on a piece of legislation until his or her "knee hits the floor"—in other words, until he or she is simply physically unable to continue to deride the measure under consideration.

Although the filibuster is not expressly provided for in the Standing Rules of the Senate, it exists de facto as a result of the Senate Rules' grant of the privilege of speaking for as long as a member of the Senate wishes to hold the floor. Rule XIX, Section A(1), specifies: "No Senator shall interrupt another Senator in debate without his consent." This short phrase provides the basis for the filibuster, which, according to Sarah Binder and Steven Smith, writing in *Politics or Principle? Filibustering in the United States Senate,* "has been responsible for killing or delaying enactment of a considerable body of legislation otherwise headed for enactment into law. The filibuster also has political consequences for legislative outcomes and procedures."

In order to understand the filibuster, it is necessary to understand the institutional history of the Senate. Created by the framers of the Constitution to be the "upper house," the Senate was originally designed to consist of elder statesmen whose seniority and depth of experience would be ensured by the process of selecting senators by their respective state legislatures. The Senate was also designed by the framers to mitigate what the framers feared would be the more impulsive nature of the popularly elected HOUSE OF REPRESENTATIVES.

Because of the small number of senators (26 in the first several Congresses), each senator was selected by the legislators of his respective state and was considered to be formally equal to every other senator. Nonetheless, the first Senate adopted a rule that allowed a majority of members to close debate. However, in 1806 the Senate revised its rules and dropped the debate-ending provision from its standing rules. As the movement for "states' rights" gained momentum, and because of the linkage between senators and their states (because of the selection of senators by their respective state legislatures), the early Senates of the 19th century did not wish to permit the senators from several states to dominate the views of senators from a smaller number of states or even a single state. As Robert Caro points out in his history of Lyndon Johnson's Senate career, the only way to bring about the end of a filibuster under the 1806 version of the Standing Rules on the matter was to obtain the unanimous consent of all senators that the filibuster be brought to a close, an impossibility given that one of the required votes would have to be obtained from the person conducting the filibuster.

In 1917 the Senate again made a change to its Standing Rules. This time, the Senate enacted Rule XXII, the so-called cloture rule. Under Rule XXII, if 16 senators petitioned to end debate and two-thirds of the members of the Senate agreed, debate would be ended on the measure after allowing each member of the Senate up to one additional hour of debate. In 1975 the Senate amended the cloture rule to reduce the number of senators needed to enact cloture from two-thirds to three-fifths, or 60 senators. Today, the votes of three-fifths of the membership of the Senate remain necessary in order to end a filibuster.

When a member of the Senate makes the decision to filibuster, he or she will typically seek to identify other like-minded senators who will agree to participate. Although filibusters through the mid-20th century were most often undertaken by individual senators (the record is held by the late senator Strom Thurmond who individually—but ultimately unsuccessfully—led a 24-hour filibuster on a mid-century civil rights bill), the contemporary filibuster rarely resembles the filibuster made famous by Jimmy Stewart's character in the film *Mr. Smith Goes to Washington*. Today, successful filibusters usually require the

This Clifford K. Berryman cartoon refers to the unusual efforts by Charles G. Dawes, when he was vice president under Calvin Coolidge, to limit the Senate filibuster. *(Library of Congress)*

participation of a small group of senators. This is not only because of the less stringent cloture rule, but also because filibustering senators discovered that they could yield the floor to other like-minded individuals who would continue the filibuster. Thus, the contemporary filibuster is typically a group effort.

Once a member or members of the Senate have made the decision to filibuster, the filibusterer(s) often alert the leadership. This is not only a matter of courtesy; since most legislation is brought up for floor debate under unanimous consent agreements, the leadership may decide not to bring up an issue for debate simply because the threat of a filibuster demonstrates that unanimous consent will be impossible to achieve. If the legislation does make its way to the Senate floor, the filibusterer(s) will seek recognition from the presiding officer of the Senate. Once a filibusterer has been granted the privilege of the floor, he or she will begin the filibuster. It continues until one of four events occurs: the filibusterer(s) voluntarily relinquish the floor (usually because they have been granted some important concession), the speaker inadvertently yields the floor to someone who is hostile to the filibuster, the opponents of the filibuster are successful in invoking cloture, or the majority leader "pulls the bill down," that is, takes the bill off the floor, effectively killing it.

Different senators use filibusters for different reasons. While some senators have substantive concerns about pending legislation, others use the filibuster to signal their displeasure with the chamber's leaders, to appease an interest group or key constituency group, or simply to stall for additional time to negotiate for compromises with other members of the Senate. According to CONGRESSIONAL RESEARCH SERVICE researcher Stanley Bach, filibustering is used "not only to prevent action, but also to extract substantive policy concessions from the majority, whether it is partisan or bipartisan." Although there are varied reasons for senators to use the filibuster, recent studies have identified some patterns with regard to the ways in which individual senators make the decision to filibuster.

First, because the filibuster is often the only option available to those senators who find themselves in the minority on an item of pending business, senators who are on the ideological fringes of their respective parties use it frequently. This is so because decisions about calling up items of pending business for debate in the Senate are usually made in tandem by the Senate MAJORITY LEADER and MINORITY LEADER through UNANIMOUS CONSENT AGREEMENTS. Since unanimous consent agreements typically require both sides to make concessions and the concessions that each leader is likely to accept are generally those that are not too ideologically extreme, senators with interests in the pending legislation whose ideological per-

spectives and proposed changes are too far from center are unlikely to have their interests represented effectively during the negotiations. Binder and Smith also suggest that the increasingly partisan and ideological nature of debate in the Senate has given senators increasing incentives to filibuster legislation.

Second, L. Marvin Overby and Lauren Cohen Bell reveal that senators who have made the decision to retire from the Senate also appear to filibuster slightly more frequently than those whose careers will continue in the institution. Their analysis indicates that it is likely that retiring senators are less likely to fear retribution from their colleagues and thus are more willing to engage in filibustering on legislation that they oppose.

Despite the considerable attention the filibuster has received in both the scholarly and popular presses, filibusters are rare. Less than 1 percent of all legislation pending on the Senate floor during any given Congress is filibustered; the percentage is reduced to a fraction of 1 percent when all measures introduced in the Senate are considered. Nonetheless, the use of the filibuster has increased over the last several decades. As Barbara Sinclair has noted, between 1951 and 1960 there was an average of one filibuster per two-year Congress; that number increased to 4.6 filibusters per two-year Congress between 1961 and 1970. However, since the mid-1990s there has been an average of nearly 30 filibusters per two-year Congress. There is no sign that the increasing number of filibusters is abating, although the relative rate of filibustering has not changed much over time due to the increasing volume of legislation proposed in the contemporary Congress.

Nevertheless, the increasing number of filibusters has led to frustration from both the leadership and the rank-and-file members of the Senate. It has also led to calls for reform not only from members of the chamber but from political pundits and the media as well. Proposals range from eliminating the possibility of filibustering at all on nonlegislative business, such as judicial and executive branch nominations, to another reduction in the number of senators whose consent is required in order to invoke cloture. In 2005 majority Senate Republicans proposed eliminating the filibuster when considering nominees to the courts only.

Further reading:
Beth, Richard S. "Filibusters in the Senate, 1789–1993." Memorandum. Washington, D.C.: Congressional Research Service, 1994; Binder, Sarah, and Steven Smith. *Politics or Principle: Filibustering in the United States Senate.* Washington, D.C.: Brookings Institution Press, 1997.

—Lauren Bell

Finance, Senate Committee on

Finance is the standing committee of the U.S. SENATE that considers issues involving the financing of the American government as well as Social Security and trade and tariff legislation. The Senate Committee on Finance was one of the original standing committees created by the Senate in December 1816. The committee has its origins in the early Senate practice of appointing select committees to review issues and then disband at the end of a Congress. In December 1815 the Senate established the Select Committee on Finance and a Uniform National Currency to consider parts of a message delivered by President James Madison. The select committee was unusual in that when its responsibilities were completed, it was not disbanded. It continued to meet through the entire first session of the 14th Congress. It considered the Tariff of 1816 and the creation of the Second Bank of the United States. The select committee became a standing committee at the beginning of the second session of the 14th Congress in December 1816.

The committee's original jurisdiction included matters relating to the collection of revenue through customs duties and taxes, regulation of customs collection and ports of entry, banking, currency, and the national debt. The Finance Committee also considered appropriations bills. In 1869 jurisdiction over appropriations bills was transferred to the new Committee on Appropriations. Jurisdiction over bank and currency matters was transferred to the new Committee on Banking and Currency in 1913.

The Finance Committee has jurisdiction over income and excise taxes, Social Security and its related programs, the funding of welfare, unemployment insurance, and trade and tariff bills. During World War I issues related to veterans' benefits became part of the committee's jurisdiction. Between the wars the committee became responsible for matters concerning vocational rehabilitation and medical treatment for veterans. After World War II the Finance Committee considered the Servicemen's Readjustment Act of 1944, the GI Bill of Rights. When the Committee on Pensions was abolished by the LEGISLATIVE REORGANIZATION ACT OF 1946, the Finance Committee considered matters dealing with veterans' compensation, while the Committee on Labor and Public Welfare handled bills relating to the vocational rehabilitation, education, medical care, and civilian readjustment of veterans. The LEGISLATIVE REORGANIZATION ACT OF 1970 transferred jurisdiction over all issues relating to veterans to the newly established Committee on Veterans' Affairs in 1971.

The Finance Committee was one of 16 standing committees in the Senate in the 108th Congress. With 21 members (11 Republicans and 10 Democrats), it was one of the larger committees. The committee had five subcommittees: the Subcommittee on Health Care, the Subcommittee on International Trade, the Subcommittee on Long-Term Growth and Debt Reduction, the Subcommittee on Social Security and Family Policy, and the Subcommittee on Taxation and Internal Revenue Service Oversight. In the 108th Congress the Finance Committee had jurisdiction over the debt of the United States, customs and ports of entry and delivery, deposit of public moneys, general revenue sharing, health programs under the Social Security Act, reciprocal trade agreements, and revenue matters generally.

Because of its jurisdiction over tax, trade, Social Security, and Medicare issues, the Senate Finance Committee is one of the most powerful and most desirable committees in the Senate. As such it has been identified as a "Super A" committee. Senators may serve on only one of the four "Super A" committees, including Appropriations, Armed Services, and Foreign Relations, as well as Finance.

The Senate Finance Committee works closely with the Joint Committee on Taxation. Several members of the Finance Committee also serve on the Joint Committee on Taxation.

Further reading:
United States Senate. *Committee on Finance, History of the Committee on Finance.* Senate Document 97-5. Washington, D.C.: Government Printing Office, 1981; United States Senate. *Committee on Finance, Report on the Activities of the Committee on Finance of the United States Senate during the 106th Congress.* Report 107-8. Washington, D.C.: Government Printing Office, 2001.

—John David Rausch, Jr.

financial disclosure

Members of Congress and certain congressional staffers are required to file annual reports detailing their personal financial affairs. These reports also must provide information about the personal finances of the member's or employee's spouse and dependent children. The financial disclosure requirements for members of Congress and other high-ranking officials in the federal government were originally enacted into law in the Ethics in Government Act of 1978. Disclosure is important because the financial interests of members of Congress and employees may present conflicts of interest with official duties. Members and employees are not required to sell their assets upon assuming their positions. They also do not have to excuse themselves from voting on issues that generally affect their personal financial interests. Reporting provides a means of monitoring for potential conflicts.

Financial disclosure reports must be filed by May 15 of each year by all members of Congress and by congressional staffers who are paid more than 120 percent of the base salary for a GS-15 (General Schedule, grade 15) government employee. If there are no employees on a member's staff with a salary at that level, then the member must designate at least one staffer to file a disclosure report. House and Senate candidates also are required to file within 30 days of becoming a candidate, or on or before May 15, whichever is later, but in any event at least 30 days before an election. Financial disclosure rules use the Federal Election Commission's definition of "candidate" to determine who must file.

Members and employees of the House of Representatives file their reports with the Clerk of the House. Senators and Senate employees file with the Secretary of the Senate. The ethics committees in each house, the House Committee on Standards of Official Conduct and the Senate Select Committee on Ethics, receive copies of the reports. The public also has access to the reports and may review and copy files after identifying themselves and agreeing not to use the data in the reports for commercial, credit, or fundraising purposes. Files are maintained for six years.

The disclosure report forms record information about the sources and types of outside earned and unearned income received by the filer in amounts in excess of $200; gifts received with a value of more than $100; gifts of travel, food, or lodging accepted, or reimbursements for such expenses, along with an itinerary of such travel if more than $250; interests in income-producing assets and investments of more than $1,000; liabilities owed exceeding $10,000; the description and date of transactions in real estate or stocks, bonds, or other financial instruments that exceed $1,000 in value; positions held in businesses and organizations, including whether any compensation exceeding $5,000 has been received from any one source during the preceding two years; and any agreements or arrangements for future employment, leaves of absence, or continuing compensation from any source other than the federal government. Information must also be provided about the income, gifts, reimbursement, assets, liabilities, and financial transactions of the member's or employee's spouse and dependent children. The reports do not list exact dollar amounts. Rather, a range of values is reported for each asset or item.

Members and employees are allowed to established blind trusts if approved by the House or Senate ethics committee. Only the income from the blind trust needs to be reported and not the specific items held by the trust. Blind trusts shield officials from knowing what assets they own, protecting them from potential conflicts of interest.

The House and Senate have required some financial disclosure by rule since 1968 and public reporting by statute since 1978. The impetus for this level of financial disclosure was the revelation of financial wrongdoing by Senate staff aide Bobby Baker in the 1960s. The Senate Rules Committee investigated the Baker case and recommended that the Senate create a committee on standards of official conduct and adopt limited, confidential financial disclosure for senators. The Ethics in Government Act of 1978 required annual financial disclosure by all senior federal employees, including senators and some Senate employees. The Ethics Reform Act of 1989 revised and condensed the different requirements that had covered the different branches into one code covering the entire federal government.

Further reading:
Bunch, Sonny. "The Roll Call 50 Richest." *Roll Call*, 13 September 2004. Washington, D.C.: Congressional Quarterly Press. *Congressional Ethics: History, Facts, and Controversy.* Washington, D.C.: Congressional Quarterly Press, 1992.

—John David Rausch, Jr.

Financial Services, House Committee on

Since January 3, 2001, a standing committee of the U.S. HOUSE OF REPRESENTATIVES, the Committee on Financial Services oversees the entire financial services industry, including banking, housing, insurance, and securities. The committee also has jurisdiction over the Federal Reserve, the Department of the Treasury, the Office of the Comptroller of the Currency, and the Securities and Exchanges Commission (SEC).

Standing committees with jurisdiction over banking date back to 1865. Prior to that time there were three select committees concerned with banking that were established for short periods by the House. A Select Committee on the Conduct and Management of the Bank of the United States was established on November 30, 1818, and was terminated on January 16, 1819. A Select Committee on the Petition of the Bank of the United States was established on December 13, 1820, and was terminated on March 7, 1822. A third select committee, the Select Committee on United States Bank Affairs, functioned from March 14, 1832, until June 25, 1834.

The Committee on Banking and Currency was established in the House on March 3, 1865, to reduce the workload of the WAYS AND MEANS COMMITTEE. The committee's jurisdiction included the chartering and oversight of national banks; the issuance of national bank loans; the issuance, taxation, and redemption of national bank notes; and the authorization of bond issues. It was also responsible for legislation on the deposit of public funds, strengthening of the public credit, and the issuance of silver certificates as currency. Oversight of the Freedman's Savings and Trust Company (which was established by an act of Congress in March 1865 but collapsed as a result of the Panic of 1873 in 1874) was also part of its jurisdiction. In the wake of the panic, the committee conducted investigations into the failures of a number of banks.

In 1912 the committee's chair, Arsene P. Pujo, a Democrat from Louisiana, led an investigation into the money trust. The hearings of the committee featured the interrogation of financier J. P. Morgan by the committee's counsel, Samuel Untermeyer. The committee found evidence that a few financial leaders controlled the nation's money and credit. The revelations led to the passage in 1913 of the Federal Reserve Act creating the Federal Reserve System.

In 1921 part of the jurisdiction of the House Committee on Coinage, Weights, and Measures relating to stabilization of the currency was transferred to the Banking and Currency Committee. In 1946, under the Legislative Reorganization Act, the coinage responsibilities of the Coinage, Weights, and Measures Committee were transferred to the Banking and Currency Committee. The committee's jurisdiction now included the following subjects: banking and currency; control of the price of commodities, rents, and services; deposit insurance; the Federal Reserve System; financial aid to commerce and industry; gold and silver; public and private housing; and the valuation and revaluation of the dollar.

On January 3, 1975, the name of the committee was changed to the Committee on Banking, Currency and Housing. Two years later the name was again changed to the Committee on Banking, Finance and Urban Affairs.

At the beginning of the 105th Congress on January 4, 1995, when the Republicans took control of the House of Representatives for the first time in two generations, the committee was renamed the Committee on Banking and Financial Services. The committee took on its present name at the beginning of the 107th Congress. The committee conducted a number of hearings on accounting irregularities in 2002, investigating WorldCom, Global Crossing, and Enron.

By 2004 there were 70 members of the committee (37 Republicans, 32 Democrats, and an independent who sits with the Democrats), making it the second-largest committee in the House of Representatives. The panel has five subcommittees: the Subcommittee on Capital Markets, Insurance, and Government Sponsored Employees; the Subcommittee on Domestic and International Monetary Policy, Trade and Technology; Subcommittee on Financial Institutions and Consumer Credit; the Subcommittee on Housing and Community Opportunity; and the Subcommittee on Oversight and Investigations.

Rule X, clause 1 (g), of the Rules of the House of Representatives grants the Committee on Financial Services jurisdiction over the following: banks and banking, including deposit insurance and federal monetary policy; economic stabilization, defense production, renegotiation, and control of price commodities, rents, and services; financial aid to commerce and industry (other than transportation); insurance generally; international finance; international financial and monetary organizations; money and credit, including currency and the issuance of notes and redemption thereof; gold and silver, including the coinage thereof; valuation and revaluation of the dollar; public and private housing; securities and exchanges; and urban development.

In the wake of the Enron scandal, the committee passed the Sarbanes-Oxley Act of 2002, named for Senator Paul Sarbanes of Maryland and committee chair Michael Oxley. The law established a Public Company Accounting Oversight Board (PCAOB) to restore investor confidence in the accounting industry.

Further reading:
United States House of Representatives, Committee on Financial Services. *Rules for the Committee on Financial Services, 108th Congress, First Session.* Washington, D.C.: Government Printing Office, 2003.

—Jeffrey Kraus

fiscal year

The 12-month period used by the U.S. federal government for budgeting and appropriations is termed a fiscal year. Federal departments, agencies, and most programs are funded one fiscal year at a time. The funding levels for these departments are determined in appropriations bills. The fiscal year for the federal government starts annually on October 1. The starting date of the fiscal year was changed in 1976 from July 1 to October 1 to give Congress three more months to pass all APPROPRIATIONS BILLS. However, even with three more months to work, Congress has seldom managed to pass all of the appropriations bills by the start of the fiscal year. In 1988 the final appropriations bill passed one minute before the start of the new fiscal year. When Congress and the president cannot agree on spending levels for departments or programs in an appropriations bill by the start of the fiscal year, they rely on continuing appropriations to avoid a government shutdown.

—Charles Tien

floor leader, Senate

A floor leader is a political party leader, chief strategist, and spokesperson in the Senate. Beyond designating the vice president of the United States as the President of the Senate, the U.S. Constitution is largely silent on the issue of leadership in the chamber. The authors of the Constitution believed that the Senate would not need leadership because it would be a collegial institution comprised of senior statesmen reviewing the legislative output of the HOUSE OF REPRESENTATIVES. The framers also did not consider the potential influence of political parties as instruments to organize the work of the Senate.

From 1789 until the early 20th century, floor leadership was conducted largely by committee chairs and various influential senators. Political scientist Woodrow Wilson observed in 1885 that no senator was the acknowledged leader of the chamber. As the strength of the parties increased in the early 1900s, their caucuses began to select individuals to guide the parties' policy agenda through the Senate.

The Democrats were the first party to officially name a senator as leader. Acting on the request of President Woodrow Wilson, the Democrats elected Indiana senator JOHN WORTH KERN as party chair and floor leader in 1913. Wilson, who had been elected in 1912 as the result of a split in the Republican Party, wanted someone to help direct his policy agenda through the Senate and enforce party unity in voting. Senator Kern had served in the Senate only two years before being elected leader. Wilson also sought the assistance of influential committee chairs and other allies in the Senate. By the 1920s both parties routinely elected floor leaders. The leaders adopted the titles MAJORITY LEADER or MINORITY LEADER, depending on which party was the majority in the Senate. Nowadays, the Minority Leader usually prefers to be called the Democratic leader or Republican leader, as the case may be. In 1927 the Democratic leader began the custom of occupying a front-row, center-aisle desk. The Republican leader did the same starting in 1937.

Floor leaders are elected to a two-year term by a majority vote of their respective party conferences. In the rare instance that there are more than two candidates for the position, the senator receiving the lowest number of votes on the first ballot is removed from the race. Balloting continues until one senator receives a majority. Incumbent party leaders are often elected with unanimous votes because they have obtained commitments from a majority of party members before the vote. This strategy discourages other senators from entering the race.

The Majority Leader, working with the Minority Leader and committee chairs, is the Senate's legislative agenda setter and scheduler. The Majority Leader usually works closely with the Minority Leader so that, as Kansas senator ROBERT DOLE explained, "we never surprise each other on the floor."

Senator Dole was in a unique position to comment on the relationship between the Majority Leader and the Minority Leader. He served as the Majority Leader in the 99th Congress (1985–87) and as the Minority Leader from 1987 until 1996, when he resigned from the Senate to campaign as the Republican presidential nominee.

In the absence of formal rules, the leader must rely on UNANIMOUS CONSENT AGREEMENTs to efficiently conduct the Senate's business. Unanimous consent agreements set limits on time, amendments, and motions. The leader often must negotiate with individual senators to assure that one senator will not hold up Senate business. Despite his or her apparent stature, the Senate Majority Leader is far less powerful than the SPEAKER OF THE HOUSE and can muster less party discipline than the House of Representatives leadership.

Floor leaders do have control over setting the Senate's schedule. In order to get cooperation from a potentially uncooperative senator, the leader may threaten to cancel a scheduled recess or keep the Senate in session late into the night to achieve legislative goals. Leaders also exercise influence using their power over committee assignments, legislative scheduling, and Senate administrative operations. Part of the floor leaders' legislative power flows from the first recognition rule and precedent and custom. Senate Rule XIX indicates that when a senator desires to speak, he or she shall rise and address the presiding officer. The presiding officer recognizes the senator who first addresses him or her. When a senator has the floor, no other senator may interrupt him or her seeking to be recognized. By precedent the Majority and Minority Leaders are recognized first if either leader or another senator seeks recognition at the same time. By custom only the Majority Leader (or his or her designee) makes motions or requests affecting the Senate's schedule.

Since the Senate operates formally on the basis of consensus, floor leaders, especially the Majority Leader, have to be adept at maintaining open communications with other senators. A Majority Leader from the party that controls the White House faces challenges as the leader of the Senate and the president's chief legislator. Such a leader might be asked to advocate the interests of his or her party, the full Senate, or the president.

A number of statutory responsibilities have been given to the floor leaders over the years. In 1978 Public Law 95-521 created the Joint Leadership Group in the Senate. The Joint Leadership Group consists of the Majority and Minority Leaders, the President Pro Tempore, the chair and ranking minority member of the SENATE JUDICIARY COMMITTEE, and the chair and ranking minority member of the Senate committee with jurisdiction over the Senate's contingent fund. The Joint Leadership Group makes appointments to offices, boards, and commissions through recommendations to the President Pro Tempore.

Democratic floor leaders chair their party conference and the committee that sets the party's legislative agenda. The Democratic leader also chairs the committee that appoints Democrats to Senate committees. Republican leaders typically do not chair these types of committees. Because floor leaders have additional responsibilities, they also receive a higher salary than other senators. They also are allotted additional funds for staff and office expenses. The floor leaders occupy office suites adjacent to the Senate floor.

While each floor leader has made a contribution to the development of the office, Texas senator LYNDON JOHNSON has been credited with employing all of the powers inherent in the office of Majority Leader. Johnson, a Democrat, was Minority Leader in the 83rd Congress (1953–55) and Majority Leader from 1955 until he resigned in 1961 to become vice president of the United States. When the Democratic Caucus elected Johnson Minority Leader, he had been a senator for four years. He was noted for his ability to get his colleagues to do what he wanted, especially after being subjected to some arm-twisting and the "Johnson treatment." Other senators who have served as floor leader include Kentucky senator Alben Barkley, California senator William Knowland, Illinois senator Everett Dirksen, Montana senator Mike Mansfield, Senator Hugh Scott of Pennsylvania, Senator Howard Baker of Tennessee, West Virginia senator Robert Byrd, and Maine senator George Mitchell.

Few of Senator Johnson's successors have been as able as he to wield the power and influence of the Senate. With the rise of partisanship and an increase in egalitarianism in the Senate, floor leaders have had difficulty managing their colleagues. Since the turn of the 21st century the office of floor leader has experienced some turbulence. The 107th Congress convened on January 3, 2001, with a membership equally divided between the Democrats and the Republicans. Because Democratic vice president Al Gore was able to break tie votes, the Democrats were able to organize the chamber, and South Dakota senator THOMAS DASCHLE became Majority Leader. Daschle had been Minority (Democratic) Leader since 1995. On January 20, 2001, Republican Dick Cheney was sworn in as vice president of the United States. His vote allowed Mississippi senator TRENT LOTT to regain his position as Majority Leader. Lott and Daschle reached an agreement in which both parties would share power. All committees had equal numbers of members from both parties. The leaders would schedule measures of importance to each party.

In May 2001 Vermont senator Jim Jeffords changed his party affiliation from Republican to independent, caucusing with the Democrats for organizational purposes. The parties changed power in the middle of a session, an unprecedented event. Daschle became Majority Leader, and Lott returned to Minority (Republican) Leader.

Senator Lott was unanimously reelected floor leader by the Republican conference on November 13, 2002. Since the Republican Party controlled a majority of the seats in the Senate, Lott would regain his position as Majority Leader. At the retiring South Carolina senator Strom Thurmond's 100th birthday celebration, incoming Major-

ity Leader Lott made racially charged comments, praising Thurmond for his 1948 campaign for the presidency on the segregationist "Dixiecrat" platform. After many Republicans called for his removal, the resulting controversy led Senator Lott to resign as floor leader. The Republican conference then elected Tennessee senator WILLIAM FRIST floor leader. Frist became the first floor leader elected by telephone conference call.

Daschle's term as leader of the Senate Democrats ended with his narrow electoral defeat in 2004. He was replaced by Senator Harry Reid of Nevada.

Further reading:
Baker, Richard A., and Roger H. Davidson, eds. *First among Equals: Outstanding Senate Leaders of the Twentieth Century.* Washington, D.C.: Congressional Quarterly, 1991; Davidson, Roger H., and Walter J. Oleszek. *Congress & Its Members.* 9th ed. Washington, D.C.: Congressional Quarterly Press, 2004; Lott, Trent, Mike Mansfield, Howard H. Baker, and Robert C. Byrd. *Leading the United States Senate.* Senate Publication 105-63. Washington, D.C.: U.S. Senate, 1998; Riddick, Floyd Millard. *Majority and Minority Leaders of the Senate: History and Development of the Offices of the Floor Leaders.* Senate Document 100-29. Washington, D.C.: Government Printing Office, 1988.
—John David Rausch, Jr.

floor manager

A floor manager is a legislator (usually the chair and ranking minority member of the committee or subcommittee that reported a bill) who works to guide a bill through debate and amendment to a final vote in his or her chamber. During the process of impeaching a federal official, HOUSE OF REPRESENTATIVES members serve as prosecution floor managers in a trial held in the SENATE.

After a committee has reported a bill it returns to the floor for debate, possible amendment, and final vote. The chair and ranking minority member of the committee or subcommittee that reported the bill act as its managers on the floor. The majority floor manager must defend the committee's version of the bill. The minority floor manager works to alter the bill prior to passage or to defeat the bill. Floor managers explain their party's position on the bill, and they control the time allotted for debating the bill. The floor managers also defend the bill against amendments or offer amendments to the legislation to change the bill to reflect the party's agenda.

Managers usually serve as their chamber's representative on CONFERENCE COMMITTEES to work out the differences between House and Senate versions of a bill. In this role the managers are known as conferees. The conferees are responsible for making sure that their chamber's version of the legislation stays intact while also working toward the goal of reaching an agreement with the other chamber. Conferees are appointed by their chamber's presiding officer upon the recommendation of the chair or ranking minority member of the original committee of jurisdiction.

House members who serve as managers during impeachment proceedings are elected by House resolution. They serve as the prosecutors during the Senate trial and present the articles of impeachment against the accused official.

Further reading:
Beth, Richard S. *Senate Floor Managers: Functions and Duties.* Washington, D.C.: Library of Congress, Congressional Research Service, 1987; Brown, Wm. Holmes, and Charles W. Johnson. *House Practice: A Guide to the Rules, Precedents, and Procedures of the House.* Washington, D.C.: Government Printing Office, 2003.

—John David Rausch, Jr.

Foley, Thomas S. (1929–) *Representative, Speaker of the House*

Thomas Stephan "Tom" Foley was born in Spokane, Washington, on March 6, 1929, the only son of Ralph E. Foley and Helen Marie Higgins. Ralph Foley was a Spokane County prosecutor and a superior court judge. Thomas Foley attended Gonzaga High School in Spokane, where he became a champion debater. During summers he worked at the local Kaiser Aluminum plant. In 1947 Foley enrolled at Gonzaga University in Spokane. During his junior year the dean warned him to improve his grade point average or leave the university. He left and transferred to the University of Washington in Seattle. He received a degree in 1951. Foley then entered the law school at the University of Washington, but he left the school after the first day of class and registered at the university's Graduate School of Far Eastern and Russian Studies. Two years later he returned to the law school and earned his degree in 1957.

Returning to Spokane, Foley practiced law in partnership with his cousin Hank Higgins. In 1958 he became the deputy prosecutor of Spokane County. He was appointed assistant state attorney general in 1960. In 1961 he was hired by Senator Henry M. Jackson, a Democrat from Washington state, to work as a special counsel on the Senate Interior and Insular Affairs Committee. In 1964, encouraged by Jackson, Foley decided to challenge the incumbent representative in the Fifth Congressional District around Spokane, Republican Walt Horan. He filed for the race only minutes before the filing deadline. After impressing the voters with his knowledge of agricultural issues and with the fund-raising assistance of Senator Jackson and Senator Warren Magnuson, a Democrat from Washington state, Foley was elected. The strong Democratic landslide on President LYNDON JOHNSON's coattails helped him.

Foley was one of 71 Democrats elected to the U.S. House in 1964. Recognizing that his victory was due in part to President Johnson's coattails, Foley supported all of the programs that constituted the administration's Great Society. He was appointed to the AGRICULTURE COMMITTEE, where he could serve his constituents. He also was appointed to the Interior Committee. Foley was reelected in 1966 with 57 percent of the vote in a strongly Republican district. As a member of the Agriculture Committee, he helped draft the Meat Inspection Act of 1967. In 1968 he voted against an anticrime bill that was enacted by the House in response to the assassinations of Martin Luther King, Jr., and Senator Robert F. Kennedy and the rioting in primarily black inner cities. Foley was one of only a few members to vote against the bill. His opposition was due to a provision granting wiretapping authority to all levels of government.

Foley married Heather Strachan on December 19, 1968. She was a lawyer he had met when both worked on Senator Jackson's staff. Mrs. Foley joined her husband's staff as an unpaid adviser.

In 1972 Foley received 81 percent of the vote in his reelection. Over the next four elections his margin of victory declined, as his Republican opponents were able to portray him as ultraliberal and out of touch with his conservative district. He almost lost in 1978 and in 1980. While Foley built a generally liberal voting record, he stopped short of joining the extreme left wing of the Democratic Party. Although he was a Roman Catholic in a district with a large Catholic population, Foley sided with the pro-choice side in the abortion controversy. He also supported the Equal Rights Amendment and opposed capital punishment, prayer in public schools, and military aid to the Nicaraguan rebels fighting the Marxist government. Foley voted to cancel funding for MX missile production and supported a nuclear freeze. Following the wishes of a majority of his constituents, Foley regularly opposed any attempts at gun control.

Foley reached the first step in the leadership ladder in 1974, when he was elected chair of the DEMOCRATIC STUDY GROUP, an organization of moderate and liberal House Democrats. He led the fight to open committee hearings to the public and to weaken the power of committee chairs. The 75 new Democratic members of the House who were elected in 1974 assisted him. One of the first targets was the chair of the House Agriculture Committee, W. R. Poage, a Democrat from Texas. Despite being the second-ranking Democrat on the committee, Foley did not participate in removing Poage. In fact, he nominated the chair in the Democratic Caucus. After he was defeated for chair, Poage returned the favor and nominated Foley for the position. After Foley was elected, he named Poage vice chair of the committee.

In 1976 Foley defeated Representative Shirley Chisholm, a Democrat from New York, to become chair of the Democratic Caucus. He was not active in the position. Despite almost losing his seat in the Republican victory of 1980, Foley benefited from the positions opened because others lost their seats. John Brademas of Indiana, the Democratic WHIP, and Al Ullman of Oregon, chair of the HOUSE WAYS AND MEANS COMMITTEE, were both defeated in their campaigns for reelection. The SPEAKER OF THE HOUSE OF REPRESENTATIVES, THOMAS O'NEILL of Massachusetts, offered Representative Dan Rostenkowski of Illinois the choice of becoming whip or chairing Ways and Means. Rostenkowski chose Ways and Means. O'Neill then appointed Foley Majority Whip.

As whip, Foley worked to get his Democratic colleagues to support the party agenda. Instead of using threats of punishment, the new whip persuaded using fairness and integrity. In August 1982 Foley delivered the Democrats' televised response to President Ronald Reagan's call for public support of a compromise tax increase to reduce the budget deficit. He urged fellow Democrats to support the president's initiatives.

In the 1980s he became one of the Democratic Party's leaders on foreign policy and budget matters. He worked to save the Gramm-Rudman-Hollings deficit reduction act in 1985. The Republican-controlled Senate passed the law, and House Democrats were prepared to reject that version. Foley proposed an alternative bill that divided funding cuts equally between domestic programs, except for Social Security, and defense.

Speaker Tip O'Neill retired at the end of the 1986 session. MAJORITY LEADER JAMES WRIGHT, a Democrat from Texas, was elected Speaker. Foley moved up to become Majority Leader, while Representative Tony Coelho, a Democrat from California, became whip. As Majority Leader, Foley served on the Permanent Select Committee to Investigate Covert Arms Transactions with Iran. He became a respected member on Capitol Hill. He was among these Democratic presidential nominee Michael Dukakis considered for his running mate. Not wanting national office, Foley withdrew his name before Dukakis made a decision.

On May 31, 1989, Speaker Wright resigned from Congress after the House Ethics Committee found that he had violated House Rules in 69 instances. Foley was elected Speaker in a straight party-line vote. On the same day that Foley was elected, the Republican National Committee issued a memo entitled "Tom Foley: Out of the Liberal Closet." The memo compared Foley's voting record with that of Representative Barney Frank, a Democrat from Massachusetts, one of the House's most liberal members and an acknowledged homosexual. Leading Republicans were forced to apologize for the memo, and Foley was forced to announce publicly that he was not gay. He spent the remainder of the 101st Congress trying to repair the damage to the institution caused by Wright's ethical violations.

During the 102nd Congress (1991–92) Speaker Foley had to work to defuse the scandal involving members' overdrafts at the House bank. His usual calm, measured approach to solving problems was seen by some colleagues as indecision. A large number of the members implicated in the scandal were defeated in the 1992 election, and Foley's leadership seemed threatened. He reacted by advocating a number of reforms of House procedures. The House bank was closed. An independent administrator was hired to oversee House operations. Foley was reelected Speaker for the 103rd Congress (1993–94). He worked to keep his colleagues' attention focused on the Democratic agenda being pushed by the new Democratic president, Bill Clinton of Arkansas. He was able to get most of the new president's proposals through the House, including Clinton's budget, an economic stimulus package, and the North American Free Trade Agreement (NAFTA).

Representative Foley faced a strong challenge from Republican George Nethercutt in his 1994 campaign for reelection. Throughout his congressional career Foley had enjoyed the support of the National Rifle Association (NRA) because of his opposition to gun control. In 1994 he said that he favored a ban on some assault-style weapons after six people were killed by a gunman using an assault rifle at Fairchild Air Force Base in Washington. This position cost Foley the endorsement of the NRA. He also was one of the most vocal opponents of congressional term limitations. He filed a lawsuit challenging the term limits enacted in 1992 by the voters of Washington. Nethercutt used Foley's participation in the lawsuit as an indicator that the Speaker was out of touch with his constituents and all the voters in the state of Washington. In November Foley lost to Nethercutt, part of a Republican midterm election landslide that cost the Democrats control of both houses of Congress. Foley became the first Speaker defeated by his constituents since 1862.

Foley joined the Washington, D.C., law firm of Akin Gump Strauss Hauer & Feld after leaving the House in 1995. In 1996 President Clinton appointed him chair of the President's Foreign Intelligence Advisory Board. From November 1997 until January 2001, Foley served as ambassador to Japan. Returning to the United States, he rejoined Akin Gump. Working with former Speaker NEWT GINGRICH, a Republican from Georgia, in 2002 Foley released a proposal on how to keep Congress running if a large number of members died in a catastrophic attack on Washington, D.C.

Further reading:
Biggs, Jeffrey R., and Thomas S. Foley. *Honor in the House: Speaker Tom Foley.* Pullman: Washington State University Press, 1999; Egan, Timothy. "Foley, Defending Congress to the Last, Concedes Election Defeat by Newcomer." *New York Times,* 10 November 1994, p. B1; Oreskes, Michael. "Foley's Law," *New York Times Magazine,* 11 November 1990, p. 64.

—John David Rausch, Jr.

Foreign Relations, Senate Committee on

The Senate Committee on Foreign Relations was created on December 10, 1816, as one of the original 11 standing committees created by Congress. Prior to 1816 the Senate met as a Committee of the Whole and organized smaller ad hoc committees to grapple with the major issues of the day. From 1789 to 1797, for instance, the Senate formed 19 committees to review treaties. This practice originally developed in the Continental Congress, where more than 3,200 ad hoc committees were created between 1774 and 1788. However, the sheer number of presidential nominations and the increased activity generated from the War of 1812 motivated a more structured process.

The Constitution of the United States grants special foreign policy powers to the Senate, including the sole power to ratify treaties with a two-thirds vote and the power to confirm foreign appointments with a majority vote. In addition, the Constitution explicitly authorizes Congress the power to declare war. The Senate Foreign Relations Committee spearheads these discussions. The committee's jurisdiction also includes foreign economic, military, technical, and humanitarian assistance. It is also granted oversight powers in these areas.

The size of the committee has varied dramatically over the years, from the original five members in 1816 to 23 members in 1946. Committee size is established by party leaders with the approval of the Senate as a whole.

In 2003 the committee was chaired by Senator Richard Lugar (R-IN). Other Republican senators serving on the committee included Senators Hagel (R-NE), Chafee (R-RI), Allen (R-VA), Brownback (R-KS), Enzi (R-WY), Voinovich (R-OH), Alexander (R-TN), Coleman (R-MN), and Sununu (R-NH). The Ranking Minority Member was past chair, Senator Joe Biden (D-DE). He was joined by Senators Sarbanes (D-MD), Dodd (D-CT), Kerry (D-MA), Feingold (D-WI), Boxer (D-CA), Nelson (D-FL), Rockefeller (D-WV), and Corzine (D-NJ).

Today the Senate is organized around 20 committees and 68 subcommittees. The majority party controls both the chair of each committee and the majority of members on each committee. The Senate Foreign Relations Committee also consists of seven subcommittees, including African Affairs, East Asian and Pacific Affairs, European Affairs, International Economic Policy, Export and Trade Promotion, Near Eastern and South Asian Affairs, and Western Hemisphere, Peace Corps, and Narcotics Affairs.

The committee quickly gained a reputation as a launching pad for national leadership. Presidents Andrew Jackson, James Buchanon, Andrew Johnson, Benjamin Harrison, Warren Harding, and John F. Kennedy all served as members prior to ascending to the presidency. In addition, 19 members have gone on to serve as secretary of State, including 16 of the 18 secretaries of State serving between 1816 and 1877.

It has also historically played an integral role in the formation of American foreign policy and is generally recognized as one of the most prestigious and powerful committees in the Senate. From Chair Henry Cabot Lodge's (R-MA) leadership in opposing U.S. entry into the League of Nations in 1919, to Chair Arthur H. Vandenberg's (R-MI) decisive role in establishing bipartisan support for the Truman Doctrine in 1947 and the Marshall Plan in 1948, to Chair J. William Fulbright's (D-AR) leadership in opposing U.S. involvement in Vietnam, to Chair Jesse Helms's (R-NC) role in defeating the Comprehensive Test Ban Treaty in 1999, the committee has played a pivotal role.

The president and Congress have struggled for control over foreign policy throughout history. While Washington, Adams, and Jefferson were all relatively sympathetic to Madison's notion of a congressional centered foreign policy, subsequent presidents have challenged this arrangement. Madison's belief that foreign affairs should be the responsibility of Congress was manifested in the Constitution's provision that Congress be granted the powers to declare war. Perhaps the first major challenge to congressional dominance over foreign policy occurred during James Polk's term in 1846. Polk, recognizing that the Senate committee, not to mention Mexico, stood in the way of America actualizing its manifest destiny, provoked a skirmish with Mexican soldiers along the Rio Grande border. This event demonstrated that although Congress had the authority to declare war, presidents could easily manipulate events so that Congress had little alternative but to declare one. Subsequent to World War I the pendulum began to swing back to a congressional centered foreign policy. Chair Henry Cabot Lodge's opposition to President Woodrow Wilson's attempted creation of collective security, the League of Nations, highlighted a new and stronger wave of isolationism in the committee. Lodge successfully opposed U.S. entry into the League of Nations because he believed the institution threatened American sovereignty and would bind the United States to destabilizing international commitments.

Foreign policy was dominated by an isolationist Congress during the interwar period. Perhaps the crowning moment came with the passage of the Neutrality Act in 1935. Members of the committee reasoned that since U.S. entries in past wars were precipitated by the deaths of Americans on the high seas (e.g., *The Maine* in 1908, *Lusitania* in 1915) the United States could stay out of harms way by prohibiting the president from transferring arms to any belligerent nation.

The second half of the 20th century witnessed executive encroachment on the powers of Congress. The general perception of congressional ineptitude, fostered largely by an isolationist Congress that failed to check Hitler, led to the ascendancy of executive power on matters of foreign affairs. Presidents were essentially given carte blanche in foreign affairs during the cold war. Following World War II Harry Truman worked feverishly to ensure the United States did not return to its policies of isolationism. The Truman Doctrine and the Marshall Plan both reflected a U.S. commitment to remain in Europe, and the U.S.-designed international structure (e.g., the United Nations and International Monetary Fund) represented a pledge to manage the international system. The committee's chair, Arthur H. Vandenberg (R-MI), however, played a key role in helping Truman craft the Truman Doctrine speech and played a vital role in securing Republican support for his policies.

U.S. foreign policy was shrouded in secrecy throughout the 1950s and mid-1960s. Eisenhower's willingness to use covert operations in Iran and Latin America in the 1950s was generally perceived to be an efficient way to conduct foreign policy. Covert operations were, after all, relatively inexpensive, and they enabled the president to implement policy without the knowledge of Congress. Despite President John F. Kennedy's role in the Bay of Pigs fiasco in Cuba and his relative inexperience in foreign affairs, Congress was again extraordinarily deferential in foreign affairs. The Berlin predicament and the Cuban missile crisis enabled Kennedy to project his authority on the international scene with little congressional interference.

However, a breakdown in the cold war consensus began to emerge during the Vietnam War. The committee's chair, Senator J. William Fulbright (D-AR), led nationally televised hearings, which played a large role in galvanizing public opinion against the war. These hearings also came to symbolize a transition in presidential-congressional relations on foreign policy. Committee member senator Jacob Javits (R-NY) sponsored the War Powers Resolution in 1973. This resolution was passed over President Richard Nixon's emphatic veto. The resolution calls on the president to consult with Congress before committing troops to combat areas and requires the president to withdraw troops within 90 days unless Congress explicitly approves the commitment. To date, the resolution has never been invoked.

The foreign policy landscape has changed dramatically over the last 30 years. The Vietnam War and Watergate have called into question the wisdom of an "unchecked" executive branch, and the end of the cold war has removed the threat that justified executive dominance in the first place. The first major test of the "New World Order" occurred in the Persian Gulf War in the early 1990s. While President Bush cultivated a spirit of cooperation in the United Nations, he faced major opposition in the Democratically controlled Congress, which only narrowly approved expelling Iraq from Kuwait.

The committee also played a large role in shaping the debate over America's role in the world in the 1990s. Jesse Helms (R-NC) rose to the chair after Republicans took control of the Senate in 1994. He earned the nickname "Senator No" for his unilateralist approach to foreign policy and for his willingness to oppose popular policies. For instance, he cast the only vote in the Senate against a resolution supporting Britain in the war with Argentina over the Falkland Islands. A leading critic of the United Nations, Helms ironically became the first sitting legislator to address the United Nations Security Council on American sovereignty and the need for reform in the United Nations. Ultimately, the United States agreed to authorize payment of its debt in exchange for a UN agreement to reform. Senator Helms also led the charge against the passage of the Comprehensive Test Ban Treaty in 1999.

President George W. Bush came to power after winning one of the closest presidential elections in U.S. history. The Senate was evenly split at 50-50, reflecting the intense competition between the two parties. The political drama intensified when Senator Jeffords (I-VT) withdrew from the Republican ranks. While Jeffords became a declared independent, his defection effectively gave Democrats a one-vote majority in the Senate. Then, a dramatic change in world events occurred when members of the al-Qaeda organization hijacked American passenger planes on September 11, 2001, and crashed them into the heart of the American financial district, bringing down both the World Trade Center and old ways of thinking about American foreign policy.

The Senate was largely supportive of Bush's foreign policy immediately following the attack but soon demonstrated it was not going to grant Bush carte blanche in foreign affairs. For example, when Senator Inhofe (R-OK) drafted an amendment giving the president the power to unilaterally waive sanctions against countries who might be willing to join the antiterrorism coalition, committee members senator Biden (D-DE) and senator Helms fervently opposed it, causing President Bush to back away from the proposal.

However, James Lindsay, a congressional scholar from the Brookings Institution, believes the committee lost some of its prestige during the 1990s. Senator Robert C. Byrd

Secretary of State Dean Rusk testifying about the Vietnam War before the Senate Foreign Relations Committee, 1968 *(Library of Congress)*

(D-WV) echoed these concerns when he recently admonished the Senate for its unwillingness to debate the decision to invade Iraq, saying "We stand passively mute in the United States Senate, paralyzed by our own uncertainty, seemingly stunned by the sheer turmoil of events. Only on the editorial pages of our newspapers is there much substantive discussion on the prudence or imprudence of engaging in this particular war."

The committee might gain some of its prestige back because international events now dominate the policy agenda. The committee is currently grappling with the issues of rebuilding Iraq and Afghanistan, the Israeli-Palestinian conflict, the proliferation of weapons of mass destruction, the nuclear showdown with North Korea, and the need for skillful diplomacy with western Europe, China, Japan, and Russia, areas that will invariably be impacted by America's new activism abroad.

Further reading:
Deering, Christopher J., and Steven S. Smith. *Committees in Congress.* 3d ed. Washington, D.C.: Congressional Quarterly Press, 1997; DiClerico, Robert E. *The American President.* Englewood Cliffs, N.J.: Prentice Hall, 1995; Gaddis, John Lewis. *Strategies of Containment: Past and Future.* Stanford, Calif.: Hoover Institution, 2001; Nye, Joseph S. *Understanding International Conflicts: An Introduction to Theory and History.* New York: HarperCollins 1993; U.S. Senate. *Committee on Foreign Relations: Millennium Edition 1816–2000.* Washington, D.C.: Government Printing Office, 2000.

—Joseph N. Patten

foreign travel

Members of Congress often use public funds to travel to foreign nations. The Capitol Hill term denoting such travel is CODEL (short for congressional delegation). Critics have attacked this practice, claiming that while traveling, representatives and senators waste taxpayers' money by traveling lavishly, eating in expensive restaurants, and staying in luxurious hotels. The word *junket* also is used to describe foreign trips taken by members of Congress. The word carries an implication that such travel is unwarranted and wasteful. Members of Congress justify the trips as an important part of Congress's oversight function.

Senate records indicate that some members were reimbursed for foreign travel as far back as 1830, and some records show that senators ventured abroad even before that. In 1943 Senator RICHARD B. RUSSELL, a Democrat from Georgia, led a five-member delegation to England and North Africa to inspect the equipment being used to fight in World War II. Senate Majority Leader Mike Mansfield, a Democrat from Montana, led a delegation that traveled to Vietnam in 1965 to view how Senate appropriations were being spent in the conduct of the war in Southeast Asia.

Some junkets are paid for by foreign governments or lobbying organizations. This practice has been vigorously criticized for leaving the perception, whether true or false, that foreign governments and lobbying organizations could improperly purchase influence with members of Congress. Former secretary of State Dean Rusk stated in 1985, "Give a member of Congress a junket and a mimeograph machine, and they think they are secretary of State."

According to the gift and travel booklet published by the HOUSE COMMITTEE ON STANDARDS OF OFFICIAL CONDUCT, the Constitution prohibits U.S. government officials from accepting any gift from a foreign government without the consent of Congress. Congress has consented to the acceptance of certain gifts from foreign governments under limits specified in the Foreign Gifts and Decorations Act (FGDA) of 1966 and its amendments and the Mutual Educational Cultural Exchange Act (MECEA) of 1961. To travel under the terms of the FGDA, any travel paid for by a foreign government must take place entirely outside the United States, must be consistent with the interests of the United States, and must be permitted under the regulations issued by the Committee on Standards of Official Conduct. The representative may not accept expenses for travel from the United States to the foreign country. Any such travel must be disclosed within 30 days of returning to the United States. A member of the House may accept travel expenses from a foreign government in order to participate in an approved MECEA program. The representative may not accept expenses for a spouse or family member traveling with the member. The travel expenses must be paid by the foreign government and not by a private source of funding. Senators must follow similar guidelines presented in Rule XXXIX.

Examples of questionable travel practices abound. The Taiwanese National Security Bureau used a slush fund to purchase influence with members of Congress and their staffers from both political parties from 1988 through 2000. The Saudi government has long been suspected of using its oil wealth to curry favor with the U.S. government by providing funding to bring members of Congress to the kingdom. The American Israel Political Affairs Committee (AIPAC) is widely known to use free foreign travel to Israel to influence the perception members of Congress have about the Israeli-Palestinian conflict.

While the majority of congressional trips have been to Europe, the American military response to the terror attacks of September 11, 2001, and the 2003 war in Iraq led to numerous congressional delegations traveling to potentially dangerous areas of the world. Representatives and senators argued that they needed to have a first-hand perspective of the fighting in Afghanistan and Iraq in order to justify the military actions to their constituents. American officials in those countries feared for the safety of the members of Congress because such important visitors would be the terrorists' targets. Officials also were concerned about having to provide security for the visitors. A number of CODELs were cancelled because of security concerns, but some legislators conducted independent trips to the war zones.

Members of Congress have been killed while traveling to foreign countries on official business. Representative Leo Ryan, Democrat of California, is believed to be the first member killed when he was gunned down by a member of a cult in Guyana in 1978. He was in the South American country investigating the People's Temple cult at the request of some of his constituents. In 1983 Representative Larry McDonald, a Democrat from Georgia, was traveling to South Korea to attend a conference commemorating the 30th anniversary of the U.S.-South Korea mutual defense treaty when over the Sea of Japan a Soviet fighter shot down the Korean airliner in which he was a passenger.

Further reading:
Allen, Jonathan. "A History of Congressional Travel, From Bimini to Baghdad." *CQ Weekly*, 1 May 2004, p. 1,008; Keller, Amy. "Overseas Travel Increases Sharply." *Roll Call*, 19 March 1998.

—Phil Lowrey and John David Rausch, Jr.

franking privilege

The franking privilege originated in the American Continental Congress in 1775 and was first codified into law in 1789. It allowed members of Congress and other federal officials to send mail free of charge by placing their signatures on the upper-right-hand corner of the envelopes in place of stamps. The practice was designed to encourage the exchange of information across the republic and to foster the relationship between representatives and constituents. Senators and representatives took full advantage of the privilege, and the amount of mail sent using the frank increased after the Civil War as members of Congress began to use rubber stamps to reproduce their signatures. Inevitably, stories of the system being abused became widespread, with the accusation that members were sending all kinds of personal mail and electioneering material using federal funds. One probably apocryphal story from the early 19th century told of a senator who signed his horse's bridal to send the animal back home.

In 1873, with the postal service showing a large deficit, the frank was abolished. However, exceptions to the ban were gradually introduced, and in 1891 full franking privileges were restored to members of Congress. Since that time the practice has continued to stimulate controversy. The law governing the use of the frank forbids members from using the privilege for personal business, for the purpose of electioneering, or for any mail that,

> specifically solicits political support for the sender or any other person or any political party, or a vote or financial assistance for any candidate for any public office.

A problem arises in that the distinction between a mailing that keeps constituents informed of their representative's activities in Congress and one that "solicits political support" can be a fine one indeed. It can be argued that the ability of senators and representatives to contact their voters at the government's expense gives incumbents a huge electoral advantage over their opponents, who must spend much of their campaign finances to achieve similar contact. Indeed, studies have shown that the members who use the franking privilege most are those who face the closest electoral battles.

Attempts have been made to tighten the regulations governing the use of the frank. In 1989 the HOUSE OF REPRESENTATIVES limited the number of districtwide mailings that could be sent, and it banned explicit partisan references and prescribed how many times a reference to the member could occur on each page. Mass mailings within 60 days of a primary or general election were also outlawed, although members have continued to send smaller, more specifically targeted mail in the run up to election day. In 1992 the House attempted to ban use of the frank for mail sent to recipients outside of members' districts. However, following a court ruling, a limited amount of such mail is currently allowed to be sent.

Further reading:
Simpson G. R. "Surprise! Top Frankers Also Have the Stiffest Challenges." *Roll Call*, 22 October 1992, pp. 1, 15; U.S. Congress. *House Commission on Congressional Mailing Standards, Regulations on the Use of the Congressional Frank by Members of the House of Representatives.* Washington, D.C.: Government Printing Office, 1996.

—Ross M. English

freshmen

Freshmen are members of a legislature serving in their first terms. Freshmen are an intriguing group of politicians. They come to Washington with a vast array of experience and at different stages of life. Once they arrive they must adapt to life on CAPITOL HILL. The networks they create and the problems they encounter shape their perceptions and help them become accustomed to the hectic life members of Congress lead. These early experiences help determine whether careers are failures or successes.

Once elected, freshmen are in a unique situation. They are not fully aware of the history and practices of the institution yet are expected to contribute to its everyday operation. This provides a challenge for many freshmen, as they arrive with limited political knowledge and must work hard to understand their institutional roles. If new members do not learn from their early experiences they will most likely fail, just as if they learn from mistakes they may be successful.

Freshmen, regardless of their prior experiences, are challenged by the practices and traditions of Congress. David Price recalls the confusion he experienced when he was first elected to Congress. In an effort to make the transition process easier, both the Democrats and the Republicans hold orientation sessions for freshmen in Washington, D.C., and at Harvard University.

> . . . the adjustments confronting any new member are profound: from campaigning to organizing legislative and constituent services offices, from the expectations and demands of one job or profession to those of another, from hometown family life to the bifurcated existence of an airborne commuter.

The orientation process is designed to ease the transition and help freshmen sort out their anxieties about balancing representation with what is best for the country.

Once freshmen overcome their initial fears, they must make the adjustment from campaigning to governing. This transition can be difficult, as the emphasis in Congress is on creating policy. Many freshmen find that writing and advocating policy outcomes are different from debating and discussing policy during the campaign. In order to make sense of the numerous issues and demands on their time, many freshmen work to create niches for themselves. This can be accomplished through appropriate committee assignments with the help of congressional staff members.

Once freshmen are established as members of Congress, they gain an advantage over possible challengers in future elections. Incumbents, members of Congress who are at minimum finishing their first term in office, tend to win elections at extremely high rates. When a current member of Congress runs for reelection, he or she often does so from a "safe seat." These safe seats are districts in which the incumbent candidate received at least 55 percent of the vote in the previous election. Those members who run in safe seats have reduced competition and may become members of the congressional leadership more quickly as a result of their electoral dominance.

More important, however, is the changing proportion of safe House seats over time. Before 1966 about three-fifths of the seats were safe, but after the mid-1960s approximately three-fourths of the seats fell into that category.

While Albert Cover and David Mayhew's study was conducted looking at elections in the 1960s and 1970s, the trend they identified still exists today. More recent studies illustrate that incumbents continue to win elections at high levels, with as high as 98 percent of incumbents winning in the 2002 midterm election.

Even with the advantages that freshmen gain during their first terms, not all freshmen share the same fate. Some freshmen are able to turn close initial elections into safe seats, while others continue to experience tough reelection competition. These differences can be attributed to a number of factors, including the personality of the member, the district, and their ties to their party leadership. Freshmen, to be successful, must create their own image and place within Congress. Without these, they will not have a chance to become sophomores.

Further reading:
Brady, David W., Brandice Canes-Wrone, and John F. Cogan. "Differences in Legislative Voting Behavior between Winning and Losing House Incumbents." In David W. Brady, John F. Cogan, and Morris P. Fiorina, eds. *Continuity and Change in House Elections.* Stanford, Calif.: Stanford University Press, 2000; Canon, David T. *Actors, Athletes, and Astronauts: Political Amateurs in the United States Congress.* Chicago: University of Chicago Press, 1990; Cover, Albert D., and David R. Mayhew. "Congressional Dynamics and the Decline of Competitive Congressional Elections." In Lawrence C. Dodd, and Bruce I. Oppenheimer, eds. *Congress Reconsidered.* Washington, D.C.: Congressional Quarterly Press, 1981; Killian, Linda. *The Freshmen: What Happened to the Republican Revolution?* Boulder, Colo.: Westview Press, 1998; Price, David E. *The Congressional Experience: A View from the Hill.* Boulder, Colo.: Westview Press, 1992.

—Jacob R. Straus

Frist, William H. (1952–   ) *Senator, Senate Majority Leader*
A heart and lung transplant surgeon from Tennessee, Bill Frist was elected Republican Senate Majority Leader to replace Trent Lott shortly before the start of the 2004 session of Congress. William Harrison "Bill" Frist was born in Nashville, Tennessee, on February 22, 1952. He was the son of Thomas F. Frist, Sr., a physician and the founder of the Hospital Corp. of America, and Dorothy Frist. He attended public and private schools in Nashville. He graduated from Montgomery Bell Academy. Frist attended the Woodrow Wilson School of Public Policy and International Affairs at Princeton University, where he specialized in health care policy. During the summer of 1972, he worked as an intern in the Washington, D.C., office of Representative Joe L. Evins, a Democrat from Tennessee. Frist received a bachelor's degree from Princeton in 1974.

In 1978 he earned an M.D. with honors from Harvard University. Frist spent the next seven years as a surgical trainee at Massachusetts General Hospital in Boston, Southampton General Hospital in England, and the Stanford University Medical Center in California. He married Karyn Jean McLaughlin in 1981; they had three sons.

After gaining board certification in general surgery, Frist joined the faculty of the Vanderbilt University Medical Center in Nashville, Tennessee, in 1985. In 1986 he founded the Vanderbilt University Multi-Organ Transplant Center. He served as the director of the center's Heart and Lung Transplantation Program. He was an assistant professor of cardiac and thoracic surgery at the Vanderbilt University School of Medicine from 1985 until he took a leave of absence in 1994 after being elected to the U.S. Senate. Frist also served as a surgeon on the staff of the Nashville Veterans Administration Hospital from 1986 until 1993. As a surgeon he performed more than 200 heart and lung transplant procedures.

A busy surgeon, Frist did not register to vote until he was 34. In 1992 Tennessee governor Ned McWherter, a Democrat, appointed Frist to chair a task force on Medicaid reform in the state. The task force's proposals became the basis for TennCare, the state's innovative health plan for low-income residents. Frist also led a statewide campaign to link organ donation with drivers' licenses. To publicize the need for organ donation, he wrote his first book, *Transplant*, a first-person account of his work as a transplant surgeon and the work of the Vanderbilt Transplant Center.

In 1994 Frist challenged three-term Democratic senator Jim Sasser. After defeating five opponents in the Republican primary, Frist faced Senator Sasser. He ran on a platform endorsing welfare reform, voluntary school prayer, and spending and tax cuts. He also advocated congressional term limitations, promising to serve only two terms in the Senate. Frist defeated the incumbent with 56 percent of the vote. He was the only challenger to defeat a full-term incumbent senator in 1994. Frist became the first physician elected to the Senate since 1928.

During his first year in the Senate, the new senator introduced several pieces of health-related legislation, including bills on medical savings accounts, patient confidentiality, and a reform of the Food and Drug Administration. In 1995 President Bill Clinton nominated Nashville physician Henry Foster to serve as surgeon general. This nomination was Senator Frist's first political test, and it put him at odds with his more conservative Republican colleagues in the Senate. Foster, the chair obstetrics and gynecology at Meharry Medical School in Nashville, reportedly was pro-choice on abortion and had been associated with a controversial birth control study by the Tuskegee Institute. Frist focused on Foster's work as a physician and worked with Democrats and moderate Republicans to end a filibuster blocking Foster's confirmation. Although Foster eventually was denied confirmation, Frist's actions brought him public attention and the respect of senators from both parties.

A believer in the principle of a citizen legislature, Senator Frist introduced the Citizen Congress Act in November 1995. This piece of legislation would have abolished many of the perquisites and privileges enjoyed by members of Congress, including the franking privilege. It would have reduced the congressional pension program, terminated automatic congressional pay increases, eliminated the special parking lots available to members of Congress, diplomats, and Supreme Court justices at Washington airports, and prohibited the use of military aircraft for congressional delegations traveling on business. Representatives Wayne Allard, a Republican from Colorado, and Representative Mark Sanford, a Republican from South Carolina, introduced a companion bill in the House of Representatives.

Senate Majority Leader Bob Dole, a Republican from Kansas, appointed the Tennessee senator to head the Senate Republican Medicare Working Group, a task force to examine policies to strengthen Medicare. From 1998 to 1999 he served on the National Bipartisan Commission on the Future of Medicare. Frist has served on the Senate Commerce, Science, and Transportation Committee and its subcommittees on Aviation, Communications, Manufacturing and Competitiveness, Surface Transportation and Merchant Marine, and Science, Technology, and Space. He also served on the Foreign Relations Committee and its subcommittees on International Operations and Terrorism, International Economic Policy, Export, and Trade Protection, and African Affairs; the Health, Education, Labor, and Pensions Committee; the Budget Committee; and the Small Business Committee. In 1997 Frist founded the Senate Science and Technology Caucus.

In 1999 Frist joined with Senator John Breaux, a Democrat from Louisiana, to introduce the Medicare Preservation and Improvement Act of 1999 (Breaux-Frist I). This bill would have subsidized prescription drug costs based on a patient's income. It also would have paid most, but not all, of the premiums for senior citizens to join private sector health plans. The senators introduced a modi-

fied version of their bill, called Breaux-Frist II, or the Medicare Prescription Drug and Modernization Act, in 2000. The new legislation would have created an independent Medicare agency to oversee all of the private sector health plans competing for senior citizen members. It also would have included prescription drug coverage in Medicare. Neither piece of legislation was enacted into law.

Frist was named Deputy Republican Whip in 1999. In 2000 he was the Senate liaison to Texas governor George W. Bush's presidential campaign. After Bush's election Frist served as an adviser to the transition team. The senator was reelected to his second term in the Senate, defeating Democrat Jeff Clark by the largest margin ever in a statewide election in Tennessee. In 2001 his Senate Republican colleagues elected Frist chair of the National Republican Senatorial Committee, the committee that raises money and works to elect Republicans to the Senate. The Republicans regained control of the Senate as a result of the 2002 elections.

Working with Senators Jim Jeffords, then a Republican from Vermont, and Breaux, Frist introduced the Bipartisan Patients' Bill of Rights of 2001. The bill would have allowed injured patients to sue managed care organizations in federal court only and to collect damage awards for lost earnings, medical expenses, and related costs. Nonmonetary damages, such as pain and suffering, would have been limited to $500,000, and punitive damages would have been prohibited. The bill was attacked by both Democratic and Republican senators, health insurance companies, and the American Medical Association (AMA). Senators John Edwards, a Democrat from North Carolina, and Edward Kennedy, a Democrat from Massachusetts, introduced an alternative bill favored by many Democrats.

Frist worked with Democrats. He cosponsored a bill with Senator Kennedy that authorized grant programs for research on children's health. He also sponsored legislation to create a Center for Research on Minority Health at the National Institutes of Health.

On December 5, 2002, Senate Republican leader Trent Lott toasted Senator Strom Thurmond, a Republican from South Carolina, on the occasion of Senator Thurmond's 100th birthday. Lott stated at the televised event that "the nation wouldn't have had all these problems" had Thurmond, the segregationist Dixiecrat candidate, been elected president in 1948. Lott apologized, but the questionable comments angered the Bush administration. It pressured Lott to step down as Republican leader. Senator Don Nickles, a Republican from Oklahoma, and Senator Rick Santorum, a Republican from Pennsylvania, expressed an interest in running for the position. The Bush administration quietly discouraged both men and encouraged Frist to seek the position. With the support of the Bush administration and after seeking the advice of former Republican leaders Senators Howard Baker of Tennessee and Bob Dole, Frist agreed to run for the post. He was elected by a unanimous vote.

As Senate Majority Leader, Frist worked to push the Bush administration program through the Senate. He was frustrated at the Democrats' ability to filibuster the president's nominees for federal court positions. He drew criticism for attempting to limit the use of the filibuster. He also was criticized for breaking Senate tradition by personally campaigning for Senate Democratic leader Tom Daschle of South Dakota's Republican opponent in the 2004 election.

Although a senator, Frist kept his doctor's bag at hand. In 1995 he resuscitated the Reverend Graeme Sieber, who had suffered a heart attack on the fifth floor of the Dirksen Senate Office Building. The senator also helped save the lives of several tourists and the life of Russell E. Weston, Jr., who was accused of fatally shooting two Capitol police officers before being shot himself, in 1998. In January 2003, shortly after being elected Senate Majority Leader, Frist was traveling on a Florida highway when he came upon an accident. He helped clear the windpipe of a woman and resuscitated two of the other injured, remaining on the scene until paramedics had the situation under control. He also regularly traveled to Africa to work with children infected with the AIDS virus.

The senator also brought his medical training to bear on the issue of bioterrorism. Shortly after the anthrax attacks on several senators' offices in 2001, Frist wrote *When Every Moment Counts: What You Need to Know about Bioterrorism from the Senate's Only Doctor.* After the 2004 presidential election and the Republican Party's success in increasing the number of Republicans in the Senate, Frist was mentioned as a potential candidate for the Republican presidential nomination in 2008.

Further reading:
Frist, William H., with J. Lee Annis. *Tennessee Senators, 1911–2001: Portraits of Leadership in a Century of Change.* Lanham, Md.: Madison Books, 1999; Martin, Charles. *Healing America: The Life of Senate Majority Leader William H. Frist, M.D.* Nashville: W Publishing Group, 2004; Simon, Richard, and Mary Curtius. "Majority Leader Faces Balancing Act in the Senate." *Los Angeles Times,* 10 November 2004, p. 1; Waller, Douglas, and Matthew Cooper. "Bush's Cool Operator." *Time,* 1 December 2003, p. 42.

—John David Rausch, Jr.

G

gag rule

A gag rule is a formal restriction of political speech. In the U.S. Congress the term refers to a rule limiting congressional debate on a particular issue. Although both houses of Congress have enacted gag rules, the HOUSE OF REPRESENTATIVES has done so more frequently than the SENATE.

The most notorious use of a gag rule occurred in the years 1836–44, when the House of Representatives limited debate on issues related to slavery. In the early 1830s abolitionists and other social reformers intensified their antislavery campaigns. These reformers sent hundreds of thousands of petitions to Congress, most asking that slavery and the slave trade in the District of Columbia be ended or that American slavery be abolished outright. Congress had received antislavery petitions since its first session in 1789, but never in such overwhelming numbers. Many of these petitions were placed before the House by members of Congress representing northern states, most notably by John Quincy Adams, a Whig from Massachusetts.

Most members of the House, however, wished to avoid debating the issue of slavery. Some believed that Congress lacked the constitutional authority to interfere with slavery in the states or to pass legislation restricting slavery in the District of Columbia. Others feared that addressing slavery would be disruptive to the harmony and tranquility of the union. In order to evade abolitionist pressure, the House passed a resolution to table all memorials, petitions, and papers on slavery. Tabling the petitions, in effect, disposed of them without debate. This resolution, passed on May 26, 1836, became known as the "gag rule" and soon became a standing rule of the House.

Over the next few years the gag rule itself became a major issue. Many citizens, including nonabolitionists, were angered because they felt the rule was antidemocratic. Critics also claimed the rule was unconstitutional, arguing that it violated the First Amendment clause prohibiting Congress from making any law that restricts the right of citizens to petition their government for the redress of grievances. As a result, petitions against the gag rule flooded Congress, joining the continuing stream of antislavery petitions.

The House enacted a gag rule in each of the next four Congresses over the constant objections of Adams. Adams continually dodged the gag rule by reading antislavery petitions and delivering long monologues on slavery on the floor of the House. On December 3, 1844, Adams's resistance prevailed, and the House passed a resolution rescinding the gag rule. Although the resolution officially repealed the gag rule, the House continued to table many slavery-related petitions, including those that opposed the admission of Texas as a state and those that argued for repeal of the fugitive slave law.

During this era there were attempts to institute a gag rule in the Senate. In late February and early March 1836, John C. Calhoun, a Nullifier from South Carolina, made a motion to refuse all petitions related to slavery. The Senate rejected Calhoun's motion but did agree to a motion from James Buchanan, a Jacksonian from Pennsylvania, to receive the petitions and then to immediately reject the petitioner's plea.

Today, the term *gag rule* is used to describe any attempt to limit debate on the floor. For example, closed rules are generally thought of as gag rules. A closed rule prohibits the full House from making amendments to a bill. Once general debate on the bill ends, the House must immediately vote on final passage. Closed rules are normally reserved for tax bills or other legislation that is highly technical, although this is not always the case. Closed rules were used during the legendary "first 100 days" of Franklin Roosevelt's presidency. Many proposals, such as those that would become the Emergency Banking Act, the Agricultural Adjustment Act, the Tennessee Valley Authority, and the National Industrial Recovery Act, were brought to the House floor under closed rules in order to expedite the approval process.

See also RULES, HOUSE COMMITTEE ON; RULES AND ADMINISTRATION, SENATE COMMITTEE ON; RULES AND

PROCEDURES, HOUSE; RULES AND PROCEDURES, SENATE; RULES FOR HOUSE AND SENATE DEBATE.

Further reading:
Fehrenbacher, Don E. *The Slaveholding Republic: An Account of the United States Government's Relations to Slavery.* New York: Oxford University Press, 2001; Miller, William Lee. *Arguing about Slavery: The Great Battle in the United States Congress.* New York: Knopf, 1996.

—Jessie Kratz

galleries

Situated above the floors of the HOUSE OF REPRESENTATIVES and SENATE are the public and media galleries. The majority of the viewing area is open to any member of the public in possession of a relevant gallery pass. For U.S. citizens, passes for either galley are available free of charge from the offices of their representatives or senators. International visitors can obtain passes from the screening area. The regulations that govern the public's behavior when in the galleries differ slightly between House and Senate, but the general rule is that visitors must remain seated, silent, and in no way disrupt the proceedings of the floor. The media galleries in the House and Senate are divided between the daily print press, television and radio, and periodical journalists. Only those with official accreditation are allowed to use these galleries.

While most visitors to the galleries behave impeccably, they have on occasions been the scenes of demonstrations. The most extreme incident took place during a debate in the chamber of the House on March 1, 1954. As a quorum count was taking place of the 243 members present at that time, two men and a woman sitting in the public gallery jumped to their feet, shouting "Free Puerto Rico," pulled out Luger automatic pistols, and opened fire on the members below. Five representatives were hit; all survived, but the injuries left Kenneth Roberts (D-AL) in a wheelchair for the next two years. Today all visitors must pass through a metal detector before entering the viewing gallery.

—Ross M. English

Garner, John Nance (1868–1967) *Representative, Speaker of the House, Vice President*

John Nance "Cactus Jack" Garner was born in Blossom Prairie, Red River County, Texas, on November 22, 1868, the son of John Nance Garner III and Sarah Guest, farmers. After attending school at Bogata and Blossom Prairie and saving money from doing farm chores and playing semiprofessional baseball, Garner traveled to Nashville, Tennessee, to attend Vanderbilt University. He stayed only one semester. Sources indicate that he was hindered by inadequate preparation and a respiratory illness. He returned to Texas, read the law, and was admitted to the bar in 1890. He set up a law practice in Clarksville, Texas, at the age of 21. He also made an unsuccessful bid for city attorney. Garner contracted tuberculosis and in 1893 moved to the drier climate in Uvalde, Texas, a small town west of San Antonio.

Garner joined the law firm of Clark and Fuller in Uvalde and was appointed to fill a vacancy as county judge. When he ran for a full term in 1893, his opponent was Mariette Rheiner. He was successful in this campaign, defeating Miss Rheiner, who he married on November 25, 1895. Garner served as county judge from 1893 to 1896. In 1896 the Garners' son was born.

Garner was elected to the Texas house of representatives in 1898. In the Texas house he gained a reputation as a man who studied issues and supported progressive measures to regulate insurance companies and the railroads. He worked to broker compromises that led to regulation without stifling business. Garner was reelected to the legislature in 1900.

After the 1900 census Texas gained a new congressional district. During the 1901 legislative session Garner was appointed chair of a special redistricting committee. As chair he drew the new 15th Congressional District that included the town of Uvalde. In 1902 he was elected to the U.S. HOUSE OF REPRESENTATIVES as a Democrat from the new district.

Garner spent the first few years of his congressional career silently observing the folkways of the House, developing friendships, and building a record of party loyalty. His party loyalty earned him several coveted committee appointments. He also was respected by the congressional leaders of both parties, President Theodore Roosevelt, and President William Howard Taft. In 1911 Garner was appointed Democratic Whip, and he gained a place on the WAYS AND MEANS COMMITTEE in 1913. While gaining respect for his legislative work, he also was adept at securing government benefits for his constituents. Despite differences with President Woodrow Wilson, a Democrat, Garner did agree with the president's proposals for independence for the Philippines, a graduated income tax, and the Federal Reserve System. Garner also worked to create improved credit and marketing programs for farmers. He became a close ally of the president when the United States entered World War I in 1917. When other influential Democrats spoke against the war, Garner supported the war and gained Wilson's respect. He became a spokesman for the administration in Congress, especially on issues relating to taxes and trade.

After the 1918 elections the Republicans gained a majority in the House of Representatives, and a Republican was elected president in 1920. After these two events Gar-

John Nance Garner *(Library of Congress)*

ner contemplated retirement and a return to Uvalde and his law practice. He decided to stay in Congress to show his opposition to the Ku Klux Klan.

By the 1920s Garner's seniority had made him the ranking Democrat on the Ways and Means Committee. He also was the chair of the Democrats' Committee on Committees. As the ranking Democrat on the tax-writing committee, he regularly attacked Secretary of the Treasury Andrew Mellon's economic programs, gaining the Texan a national reputation as a populist. Garner normally differed with the Republican president and Republicans in Congress on tariff and tax measures, offering constructive opposition to their proposals. Since he also opposed free trade, he likewise was likely to disagree with some of his fellow Democrats. Despite his position, Garner rarely introduced legislation or spoke from the floor. Most of his work was conducted behind the scenes. In fact, Representative Garner introduced only four pieces of legislation during his entire career in the House.

In 1929 Garner became Democratic floor leader. The Democratic Party endured dramatic losses in the election of 1928 and was suffering from low morale. Since the leader of the minority party has few formal powers, Garner used what

informal powers he could to build relationships with the majority Republicans. He built a close rapport with Speaker of the House NICHOLAS LONGWORTH of Ohio. The two men created the Bureau of Education, an informal gathering of representatives that was to become more famous later as the Board of Education under Speaker SAMUEL RAYBURN. The bureau provided a place for politicians to relax and get to know one another over a drink, despite the Prohibition imposed by the Eighteenth Amendment.

Between the 1930 congressional elections and the opening of the 72nd Congress on December 7, 1931, 14 members-elect, including Speaker Longworth, died. After special elections had been held, the Democrats became the majority party, with a 219 to 214 advantage. As party leader Garner was elected Speaker and became the national leader of the Democrats. Garner did not have a close relationship with the new Minority Leader Bertrand Small of New York. The parties had become polarized over proposals to solve the problems presented by the Great Depression. Garner also had to ensure that his Democratic colleagues were on the floor to protect the slim majority. Garner's party discipline led to many complaints from his colleagues. Representative Sam Rayburn called Speaker Garner "a terrible, table-thumping Democrat."

A fiscal conservative, Speaker Garner was willing to have government interfere with the economy if it would help end the Great Depression. He worked to build a bipartisan consensus in support of President Herbert Hoover's economic proposals, including the Reconstruction Finance Corporation and the Glass-Steagall banking bills. He was even willing to accept a national sales tax designed to increase government revenue. In 1932 Garner suffered a defeat when Democrats and Progressive Republicans united to kill the sales tax proposal.

A Garner for President movement emerged in January 1932 fueled by an editorial campaign in William Randolph Hearst's newspaper. In addition to Hearst, Garner's supporters included many conservative southern and western politicians and those who believed that he was the only candidate who could block New Yorker Franklin Roosevelt. Garner was not interested in becoming president, but he was concerned that the Democrats nominate a candidate with long enough coattails to keep the Democrats in the majority in Congress after the 1932 elections. He believed that Roosevelt was the candidate most likely to mobilize voters to choose the Democrats. At the Democratic National Convention in Chicago, Garner placed third on the first ballot behind Roosevelt and former candidate Al Smith. By the third ballot his vote total increase slightly, and Roosevelt's advisers noticed that they needed Garner's delegates to reach the two-thirds vote necessary for nomination. After meeting with Garner's campaign manager, the two groups reached an agreement in which Garner's delegates would vote for Roosevelt in return for the vice presidential nomination. Garner was elected vice president on the same day he was reelected to the House of Representatives in 1932.

As vice president Garner was the President of the SENATE. He was fair as presiding officer and allowed new senators opportunities to preside over the chamber in order to learn parliamentary procedure more quickly. He was able to work closely with fellow Texans and House Democratic leader Sam Rayburn. A conservative, Garner differed with Roosevelt on a number of issues, but he supported most New Deal policies out of party loyalty. He was regularly consulted by the president, especially on issues relating to dealing with Congress. Garner remained on the Democratic ticket in 1936 and was reelected.

By 1937 his differences with Roosevelt became sharper. Garner objected to the president's plan to add justices to the Supreme Court. He moved further away from Roosevelt when the president attempted to block the reelection of conservative Democrats in Congress. The vice president became more vocal in his opposition to Roosevelt's quest for a third term. Garner conducted a short-lived campaign for the presidency in 1940 before he withdrew after Texas Democrats would not come out against Roosevelt's quest for a third term. At the Democratic National Convention in Chicago in 1940, Roosevelt was renominated on the first ballot with 946 votes. Garner had 61 votes. He was removed from the ticket. Not only did Garner not campaign for Roosevelt in the 1940 election, he did not vote in the election.

After the inauguration in 1941, Garner retired to Uvalde after 38 years of government service. He spent his retirement in relative seclusion, rethinking his 1932 decision to accept the vice presidential nomination. In a 1957 interview, Garner lamented, "If I hadn't been nominated for Vice President, I might still be Speaker today." He died in Uvalde on November 7, 1967.

Further reading:
Fisher, O. C. *Cactus Jack*. Waco, Texas: Texian Press, 1982; Hatfield, Mark O., with the Senate Historical Office. *Vice Presidents of the United States, 1789–1993*. Washington, D.C.: Government Printing Office, 1977; Peters, Ronald M. *The American Speakership: The Office in Historical Perspective*. Baltimore: Johns Hopkins University Press, 1990; Timmons, Bascom. *Garner of Texas: A Personal History*. New York: Harper, 1948.

—John David Rausch, Jr.

Gephardt, Richard A. (1941–) *Representative, House Majority Leader, House Minority Leader*

Richard Gephardt was born in St. Louis on January 31, 1941. He was one of two sons born to Louis and Loreen Gephardt. His father was a milk truck driver, and his mother was a legal secretary. Gephardt graduated from Northwestern University in 1962 and received a law degree from the University of Michigan Law School in 1965. He served in the Air National Guard from 1965 to 1971. Between 1965 and 1971 Gephardt was a partner in the law firm of Thompson & Mitchell. In 1966 Gephardt married Jane Byrnes. They have three children: Matt, Chrissy, and Katie.

Gephardt began his political career with his election to the St. Louis board of Aldermen, where he served from 1971 until 1976. He was elected to the U.S. House of Representatives from Missouri's Third Congressional District in 1976. Gephardt served as chair of the Democratic Caucus from 1984 until 1988. Also in 1984 Gephardt was elected chair of the moderate Democratic Leadership Council (DLC). He became the Democratic MAJORITY LEADER in 1989. He became his party's MINORITY LEADER when the Republicans took control of the House in 1995 under Speaker Newt Gingrich, a Republican from Georgia. Gephardt relinquished his power as Minority Leader after significant Democratic losses in the 2002 midterm congressional elections.

While his most prominent legislative activities have focused on fiscal policy such as his "flat" and "fair" tax proposals, both in terms of substantive policy and party politics, Gephardt's congressional career has been defined by his close association with Democratic party leaders. With the help of his mentor, RICHARD BOLLING, a Democrat from Missouri, Gephardt was appointed to both the WAYS AND MEANS and HOUSE BUDGET COMMITTEES as a freshman. Within the Democratic PARTY CAUCUS his steady rise has been attributed to the patronage of Gillis Long, a Democrat from Louisiana. While Gephardt's career has benefited by these associations, his eventual rise to the position of Majority Leader came as the result of political scandal. The Speakership of JAMES WRIGHT, a Democrat from Texas, ended after an ethics investigation into a publishing contract. Similarly, MAJORITY WHIP Tony Coelho, a Democrat from California, resigned after an ethic's investigation into junk bond disclosures. The net result of these investigations and resignations was the elevation of THOMAS FOLEY, a Democrat from Washington, to the Speakership and Gephardt to Majority Leader.

For a congressman so enmeshed in his party's leadership structure, Gephardt's prominent opposition to the North American Free Trade Agreement (NAFTA) may seem surprising. In opposing NAFTA he opposed both the Democratic Speaker of the House and the Democratic president of the United States, Bill Clinton. Gephardt's opposition provides an important reminder that congressional party leaders have constituents. As was evident in his floor speech on November 16, 1993, Gephardt's position on NAFTA was simply a reflection of the position endorsed by his core unionized supporters.

Congressman Gephardt has twice sought the Democratic presidential nomination. He first declared his candidacy in 1987, and, although he won the early Iowa caucuses, his campaign never gained national momentum. Similarly, while garnering the endorsement of a significant number of major labor unions (including the AFL-CIO), his 2003 presidential campaign in a crowded Democratic field essentially ended with his second-place finish in Iowa. Not long afterward Gephardt announced his retirement from the House.

Further reading:
Brown, Lynne P., and Robert Peabody. "Patterns of Succession in House Democratic Leadership: Foley, Gephardt, and Gray." In *New Perspectives on the House of Representatives*. 4th ed. Baltimore: Johns Hopkins University Press, 1992; Gephardt, Richard A., and Michael Wessel. *An Even Better Place: America in the 21st Century.* New York: Public Affairs, 1999; Martinez, Gebe. "Gephardt's Uneven History Left Behind for 2004 Run." *Congressional Quarterly Weekly Report* 61 (31 May 2003): 1,314–1,324.
—George E. Connor

germaneness

Germaneness is a rule specifying that amendments must relate to the subject of the legislation to be amended. The germaneness rule was adopted by the HOUSE OF REPRESENTATIVES in 1789 and amended in 1822. During the 108th Congress the rule was found in Clause 7 of House Rule XVI. The rule is based on the principle that the House should consider only one subject matter at a time. Germaneness applies to an amendment and its relationship to a bill or another amendment. It does not apply to the relationship between two provisions of the bill itself. The amendment's proponent is required to prove that the amendment is related, or germane, to the underlying proposal. The chair rules on questions of germaneness. The entire amendment is ruled out of order if even a portion of the amendment is nongermane.

Germaneness is not the same as relevancy. An amendment may be related to a proposition in a bill, but it may still be ruled nongermane. The effect of the germaneness rule is to enable the majority party to specify the legislative agenda. If the majority party refuses to bring a representative's proposal to a vote, germaneness blocks the representative from simply offering the proposal as an amendment to an unrelated bill.

To assist the chair in determining whether an amendment is germane, a number of tests have been developed. A SPEAKER OF THE HOUSE, John Carlisle (D-KY), established a brief test for germaneness: "After a bill has been reported to the House, no different subject can be introduced into it by amendment whether as a substitute or otherwise. When, therefore, it is objected that a proposed amendment is not in order because it is not germane, the meaning of the objection is merely that it [the proposed amendment] is a motion or proposition on a subject different from that under consideration." The test established in this statement has been refined. An amendment must relate to the subject matter under consideration. The fundamental purpose of the amendment must relate to the fundamental purpose of the bill. The purpose of the bill is judged from its text, not from debate statements. An amendment should be within the subject matter of the committee of jurisdiction of a bill. This test does not apply when the jurisdiction of a bill overlaps several committees. In general, an amendment must be germane to the pending piece of legislation, not to the underlying law to be changed. The determination of whether a bill that amends existing law opens the entire law to amendment follows the principles that a general proposition can be amended by specific propositions (or subsets) of the same class.

The SENATE does not require germaneness except in special situations, such as cloture and budget resolutions. Senate tradition permits senators to offer amendments on any subject even if unrelated to the bill's topic. This may result in "Christmas tree" bills emerging out of the Senate.

In 1996 Representative John Conyers (D-MI) offered an amendment to add crimes of fraud and deception to a bill on crimes of violence against children and the elderly. The amendment was ruled out of order because it was not germane to the issue of crimes of violence. Conyers offered another amendment. The additional amendment dealt with environmental crimes and was ruled out of order for not being germane. A third amendment was offered by Conyers to include environmental crimes as a subset of crimes of violence under the appropriate section of the U.S. criminal code. A point of order challenging the germaneness of this amendment was overruled, as the chair stated.

> This amendment offered by the gentleman from Michigan ensures that the definition of a crime of violence under section 16 of Title 18 may include a crime involving the environment as a subset of a crime of violence for the purposes of the pending bill. As such, the amendment does not disturb the coherence among the provisions of the bill. It is confined to the subject of violent crimes against vulnerable persons and punishments therefore.

The *Congressional Record* records that after some debate about the relevance of the underlying bill, Representative Conyers's final amendment was agreed to.

Further reading:
Johnson, Charles W. *Constitution, Jefferson's Manual, and Rules of the House of Representatives.* House Document No. 107-284. Washington, D.C.: Government Printing Office, 2003; Oleszek, Walter J. *Congressional Procedures and the Policy Process.* 6th ed. Washington, D.C.: Congressional Quarterly Press, 2004.

—John David Rausch, Jr.

gerrymandering, partisan

Gerrymandering is the practice of drawing congressional (or other legislative) district boundaries in a way that promotes the election prospects of politicians rather than an ideal of fair and effective representation. The term originated in 1812, when Massachusetts governor Elbridge Gerry devised a salamander-shaped congressional district that carved Jeffersonian-leaning towns away from Federalist-leaning coastal towns.

Gerrymandering may be undertaken for two purposes: to protect individual, incumbent members of Congress or to increase one party's seats in a state's congressional delegation. In the former instance, members of different political parties may collude in the drawing of boundaries to prevent incumbents from facing each other in a single election district or to prevent an incumbent from facing a serious challenge. In the latter instance, the party controlling a state legislature seeks to gain congressional seats at the expense of the other party. In either case, the goal is to decrease the competitiveness of future elections by creating "safe" districts.

Pursuant to a unique state law in Iowa, that state's congressional districts are laid out by the nonpartisan Legislative Service Bureau using compactness, county boundaries,

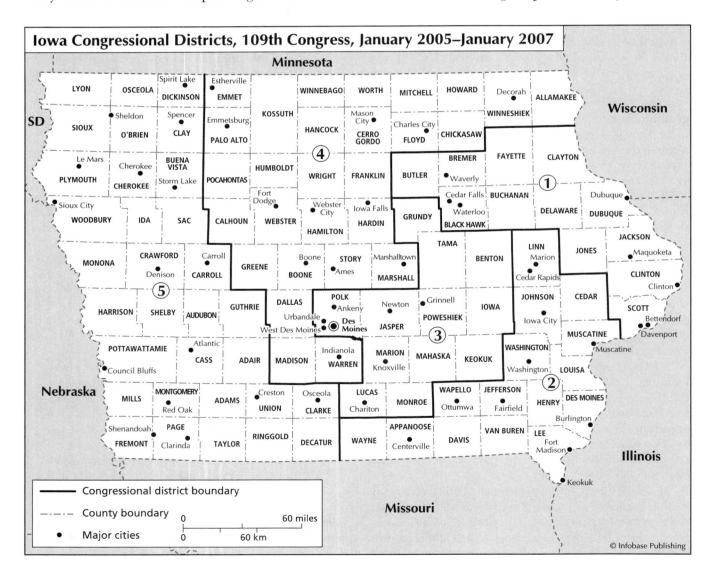

Iowa Congressional Districts, 109th Congress, January 2005–January 2007

Illinois Congressional Districts, 109th Congress, January 2005–January 2007

Wisconsin

Lake Michigan

Michigan

Iowa

Indiana

Missouri

Kentucky

JO DAVIESS
STEPHENSON
WINNE-BAGO
Rockford
McHENRY
LAKE
Waukegan
⑧
⑨
⑩
Skokie
⑤
④
Chicago
⑦
④
③
②
①
BOONE
CARROLL
OGLE
⑯
DeKALB
Elgin
KANE
De Kalb
⑥
DuPAGE
COOK
Dixon
Sterling
LEE
⑭
KENDALL
⑬
WHITESIDE
Joliet
WILL
Moline
Rock Island
ROCK ISLAND
BUREAU
LA SALLE
MERCER
HENRY
Kewanee
PUT-NAM
Streator
GRUNDY
⑪
KANKAKEE
Kankakee
STARK
MARSHALL
Galesburg
Monmouth
WARREN
KNOX
PEORIA
WOODFORD
LIVINGSTON
IROQUOIS
HENDERSON
⑰
Peoria
McLEAN
FORD
McDON-OUGH
Canton
Pekin
Normal
Bloomington
⑮
HANCOCK
Macomb
FULTON
TAZEWELL
Rantoul
VERMILION
SCHUYLER
MASON
⑱
DE WITT
CHAMPAIGN
Champaign
Urbana
Danville
ADAMS
BROWN
CASS
Beardstown
MENARD
LOGAN
Lincoln
MACON
PIATT
DOUGLAS
EDGAR
Quincy
Springfield
Decatur
MORGAN
SANGAMON
MOULTRIE
COLES
CLARK
Pittsfield
SCOTT
CHRISTIAN
Pana
CUMBER-LAND
PIKE
GREENE
MACOUPIN
MONTGOMERY
SHELBY
JASPER
CRAWFORD
CALHOUN
JERSEY
FAYETTE
Vandalia
EFFINGHAM
Effingham
Olney
LAWRENCE
Alton
MADISON
BOND
CLAY
RICHLAND
East St Louis
CLINTON
MARION
⑲
Centralia
WAYNE
EDWARDS
WABASH
Belleville
ST CLAIR
WASHINGTON
Mount Vernon
Carmi
MONROE
JEFFERSON
HAMIL-TON
WHITE
RANDOLPH
⑫
PERRY
FRANKLIN
SALINE
GALLATIN
JACKSON
Carbondale
WILLIAMSON
UNION
JOHN-SON
POPE
HARDIN
ALEXANDER
PULASKI
MASSAC
Cairo

— Congressional district boundary
—·—·— County boundary
• Major cities

0 ____ 60 miles
0 ____ 60 km

© Infobase Publishing

and population equality as the only criteria. The random grouping of counties gives no intentional advantage to any party or officeholder. Under the 2001 map Republicans hold 4 of the state's 5 seats and probably would do no better under a partisan map. But Democrats, if they exercised an opportunity to draw a partisan map, could probably add a second seat by grouping pro-Democratic counties in eastern Iowa into one district.

The map of Iowa districts contrasts markedly with the Illinois district map drawn by the Illinois general assembly in 2001. The Illinois map is an example of a collusive gerrymander in which Democratic and Republican members collaborated to preserve their districts. Unlike the Iowa map, the Illinois map divides many counties and cities among two or more congressional districts. The homes of previous and potential election challengers were placed in different districts from the incumbents they threatened.

The 1981 Indiana congressional district map is considered a classic partisan gerrymander accomplished through packing and fracturing of geographically cohesive blocs of voters. The Republican legislature and governor fractured Democratic voting strength by dividing Monroe County between the Eighth and Ninth Districts, making the Eighth District more Republican. Some of the Monroe County Democrats were "packed" into the Ninth District, already a Democratic stronghold, where their votes would be redundant. Democratic voters were also packed into the 10th District, where two Democratic incumbents were forced to run against each other in a primary election.

There are few limitations on gerrymandering of congressional districts. While many state constitutions require that state legislative districts be "compact," there is no such requirement for congressional districts. The U.S. Supreme Court held in *Gaffney v. Cummings* that a collusive gerrymander did not violate the Constitution if it was fair in allocating seats between the parties and ruled in *Davis v. Bandemer* that partisan gerrymandering is acceptable unless it would "consistently degrade a voter's or a group of voters' influence on the political process as a whole." Justice O'Connor went so far as to say, in *Bush v. Vera*, that

> we have recognized incumbency protection, at least in the limited form of avoiding contests between incumbents, as a legitimate state goal.

Congressional districts must have substantially equal populations, but this requirement has probably fostered gerrymandering more than it has curtailed it, since it has led to the abandonment of compactness and other neutral redistricting principles.

While the Supreme Court has tolerated gerrymandering, many commentators, including judges, have criticized it. By diminishing the competitiveness of elections, gerry-mandering discourages challengers and in theory reduces members' responsiveness. Noncompact districts may divide a single media market among two or three members of Congress, driving up the price of scarce commercial air time and reducing the amount of news coverage devoted to each race. Gerrymandering can divide "communities of interest"—geographic concentrations of voters with similar concerns, such as blue-collar workers, Armenian Americans, and citizens of a resource-poor municipality—making it harder for them to demand attention to their common concerns.

Modern gerrymandering is aided by the use of sophisticated computer programs that combine census data with election returns on a precinct-by-precinct basis. Members of Congress dip into their war chests to retain consultants for redistricting. For example, 30 Democratic members from California paid $20,000 apiece to one consultant in 2001.

A recent gerrymandering development has been the effort of House Majority Leader Tom DeLay, in 2003, to reopen the redistricting of Texas congressional districts that was completed in 2001. In the past custom has dictated that congressional districts be redrawn only following each decennial census. DeLay's attempt at and success in spurring the Texas legislature to redraw congressional boundaries following Republican gains in the 2002 state legislative elections may set a precedent for future mid-decade gerrymanders.

See also GERRYMANDERING, RACIAL.

Further reading:
Chicago Tribune. "Political Opponents Cast Out by Remap," p. 1, 27 June 2001; *Orange County Register.* "All Bow to Redistrict Architect." 26 August 2001; *Congressional Quarterly. Politics in America.* Washington, D.C.: Congressional Quarterly Press, 1984; *Gaffney v. Cummings,* 412 U.S. 735; *Davis v. Bandemer,* 478 U.S. 109; *Bush v. Vera,* 517 U.S. 952.

—Jackson Williams

gerrymandering, racial

Gerrymandering is the drawing of election district lines for partisan advantage. Racial gerrymandering has generally been viewed as the drawing of election district lines for the advantage of whites and to the disadvantage of African Americans and Latinos, although critics of racial gerrymandering contend it is now being used to draw district lines to the advantage of minority group members. While the courts have been reluctant to involve themselves in questions of partisan gerrymandering, they have been active in the area of racial gerrymandering.

Until the 1960s the federal courts refused to get involved in any gerrymandering issues under the belief that these were "political" questions that should be left to the discretion of legislative bodies. This began to change in the 1960 U.S. Supreme Court case of *Gomillion v. Lightfoot.* Black voters in Tuskegee, Alabama, charged that the Alabama legislature passed a law that changed the city boundaries of Tuskegee in order to exclude all but a few black voters from the city. Tuskegee went from a traditional city with boundaries on the south, north, east, and west to a 28-sided figure in order to eliminate blacks from the city. Blacks, who constituted almost 80 percent of Tuskegee's residents, suddenly became less than 1 percent of the residents. Throughout the South white administrations were using racial gerrymandering to combat the growing clout of the emerging black voter.

The federal district court dismissed the complaint and the Fifth Circuit Court of Appeals affirmed the lower court decision. A unanimous Supreme Court would reverse the decision and strike down Tuskegee's racial gerrymander. Justice Felix Frankfurter, a leading critic of courts involving themselves in gerrymandering issues, justified the Court's intervention in this case on the basis of the Fifteenth Amendment and its protection against denying the right to vote. As Frankfurter wrote in his majority opinion, "When a legislature thus singles out a readily isolated segment of a racial minority for special discriminatory treatment, it violates the Fifteenth Amendment."

The courts continued to shy away from the issue of racial gerrymandering until after the passage of the 1965 Voting Rights Act and its later amendments. In 1982 Congress amended the Voting Rights Act to prevent the passage of laws that might have the effect of reducing minority voting strength. States were prevented from diluting or "cracking" votes and were encouraged to "pack" districts in order to encourage the election of minority candidates. In a 1986 decision, *Thornburg v. Gingles,* the Supreme Court established a test to determine whether a minority group's representation had been compromised. The three-pronged test asked whether the minority group was large enough and compact enough to elect a representative in a district. Second, was the minority politically cohesive? Finally, was there evidence of racially polarized voting by the majority against the minority?

The 1982 amendments to the Voting Rights Act, along with the Thornburg decision, led the Justice Department in the George H. W. Bush administration to push for the creation of as many majority-minority districts as possible. Republicans suddenly became the defenders of minority districts, and Democrats became the leading opponents. Democrats charged that packing minorities into congressional districts would lead to the election of more minorities, but it would also lead to the election of fewer Democrats who traditionally had supported minority interests and issues. This prediction was borne out to some

degree based on the 1992 congressional elections, the first reapportionment elections after the Voting Rights changes and the Thornburg decision. A total of 15 new African-American majority-minority districts were created, for a total of 32 in the nation, and the number of blacks in Congress jumped from 26 to 39, roughly proportional to the percentage of blacks in the general population. There was also a significant increase in the number of Latino members of Congress. The 1990s also found Republicans winning control of Congress and many state legislative bodies, especially in the South.

Supreme Court decisions in the 1990s began to challenge the notion of majority-minority districts. In *Shaw v. Reno,* the Supreme Court, in a 5-4 decision, found two North Carolina districts so strangely shaped that they could not "be understood as anything other than an effort to segregate voters . . . on the basis of race." Two years later, in *Miller v. Johnson,* another 5-4 Court rejected two Georgia congressional districts because race was the predominant factor in their creation.

In the 2000 round of reapportionment, Democrats were able to persuade African Americans and Latinos to reduce the number of minority voters in congressional districts. Most minority members have retained their seats with the advantage of incumbency, and Democrats were able to pick up some seats in both Congress and the state legislatures.

The 5-4 decisions on racial gerrymandering indicate how closely divided the Supreme Court has been on the subject. Does "affirmative action gerrymandering," as it has been called, violate the constitutional guarantees of "equal protection"? Why do Republicans oppose affirmative action in other areas, but not in gerrymandering? Finally, why do Democrats, who have long been the supporters of minorities, oppose them on the issue of majority-minority districts?

See also GERRYMANDERING, PARTISAN.

Further reading:
Bositis, David, ed. *Redistricting and Minority Representation.* Washington, D.C.: Joint Center for Political Studies, 1998; Butler, David, and Bruce Cain. *Congressional Redistricting.* New York: Macmillan, 1992; Lublin, David. *The Paradox of Representation: Racial Gerrymandering and Minority Representation in Congress.* Princeton, N.J.: Princeton University Press, 1997.

—Darryl Paulson

Gibbons v. Ogden 22 U.S. (9 Wheat) (1824)

In *Gibbons v. Ogden* Chief Justice John Marshall laid the foundation for broad congressional commerce clause power. Marshall wrote the majority opinion with a concurrence by Justice William Johnson. This case reflects Marshall's desire to enhance the power of the national government. The case involved a dispute between rival steamboat operators. Aaron Ogden had a monopoly license granted by the state of New York to operate steamboats in its waters. Thomas Gibbons had a federal coasting license issued in accord with the Coastal Licensing Act of 1793. Both men ran boats between New York and New Jersey. Ogden sought to stop Gibbons by filing suit in a New York state court. The court ruled for Ogden, and its decision was sustained by a New York appellate court. Gibbons hired Daniel Webster and appealed the case to the U.S. Supreme Court.

Gibbons's argument basically was that either the federal license preempted the state license or the state was simply precluded from issuing a license because Congress was granted the power under the Commerce Clause. In other words, the state and national governments had concurrent power to license steamboats, but that the federal license took precedence if both sovereigns acted. In the alternative, Congress had exclusive authority to legislate in this area, and the state legislation was a violation of the Commerce Clause, even if Congress did not act.

The Court also had to determine what exactly constituted commerce and interstate commerce. Marshall, wanting to expand the national government's powers, cautioned against a strict constructionist interpretation of the enumerated powers. Therefore, he advocated a broad definition of commerce. He rejected Ogden's argument that the definition of commerce was limited to trafficking in commodities. Marshall stated that commerce included navigation and transportation of people; it involves all commercial intercourse. This broad definition was important because steamboats were becoming a popular method of travel. Marshall further expanded the reach of the Commerce Clause by stating that control of foreign commerce does not stop or start at the national border. If the foreign trip begins or ends at an inland port, Congress may exercise its Commerce Clause powers within that state. Marshall went on to say that this commerce power equally applied to commerce among the several states. As a result, Congress can even exercise its authority over foreign and interstate commerce taking place within state borders.

Marshall did acknowledge a concurrent state power to regulate purely intrastate commerce. Therefore, he did not decide the case on the exclusivity of congressional power over commerce. Instead, Marshall based his opinion on the existence of at least partially concurrent powers, but with federal preemption when Congress chose to regulate what could be considered interstate commerce. Since Congress had acted, the New York law could not stand. Interestingly, Justice Johnson, in his concurrence, took the more extreme view. He stated that even if the federal licensing act were repealed, the New York statute would violate the Constitution. The issue of when states could

not act in the absence of congressional regulation would have to be decided at a later date. Furthermore, the Gibbons case did not address the issue of when Congress could use its Commerce Clause power to regulate noncommercial activity. These two issues were not thoroughly addressed until the latter half of the 19th century.

Around the end of the 19th and the beginning of the 20th century, the Court struck down a considerable portion of state and federal efforts to regulate economic activity. The Court was accused of adhering to the principles of laissez-faire. Starting in 1937 the Court declared most federal legislation constitutional as long as Congress claimed it was acting in accord with its commerce powers. Important legislation such as the CIVIL RIGHTS ACT OF 1964 was based on the national government's commerce power. Arguably, Marshall's expansive reading of the commerce clause has provided the basis for far-reaching congressional power. More recently, however, the Court has been narrowing its reading of the clause. It has not allowed Congress to regulate guns at schools (*United States v. Lopez*) or provide civil remedies for violence against women (*United States v. Morrison*). Nonetheless, the Commerce Clause and Marshall's interpretation of it in *Gibbons v. Ogden* remains one of Congress's most important enumerated powers.

See also UNITED STATES V. LOPEZ.

Further reading:
Epstein, L., and T. Walker. *Constitutional Law for a Changing America: Institutional Powers and Constraints.* 4th ed. Washington, D.C.: Congressional Quarterly Press, 2001; *Gibbons v. Ogden*, 22 U.S. (9 Wheat.) 1 (1824); Hall, Kermit L., ed. *The Oxford Companion to the Supreme Court of the United States.* New York: Oxford University Press, 1992; *United States v. Lopez*, 514 U.S. 549 (1995); *United States v. Morrison*, 529 U.S. 598 (2000).
—Barry N. Sweet

Gillett, Frederick H. (1851–1935) *Representative, Senator, Speaker of the House*

Frederick Huntington Gillett was a Republican politician who served in the U.S. HOUSE OF REPRESENTATIVES from 1893 to 1925 and in the U.S. SENATE from 1925 to 1931, when he retired from politics. The pinnacle of his career was his election as SPEAKER OF THE HOUSE for three Congresses, the 66th, 67th, and 68th.

Representative Gillett was born in Westfield, Massachusetts, on October 16, 1851, the son of Edward and Lucy Fowler Gillett. His father was a successful lawyer who was well known for his polished speaking style. The elder Gillett took a keen interest in his son's education and helped the future Speaker hone his own oratorical talents. Representative Gillett attended the Westfield public schools and then spent a year studying in Germany. In 1870 he entered Amherst College, where he studied political science and constitutional law, displayed his leadership potential as the captain of the baseball team and president of his junior and senior classes, and won prizes for rhetoric and writing. After graduating from Amherst in 1874, he attended Harvard University's law department. Upon completion of his legal studies in 1877, he passed the Massachusetts bar and set up a law practice in Springfield, Massachusetts. From 1879 to 1882 he served as the Massachusetts assistant attorney general and from 1890 to 1891 was a member of the Massachusetts house of representatives.

In 1893 Representative Gillett won the first of his 16 elections to the U.S. House of Representatives. In his first speech on the House floor, he vigorously defended the voting rights of African Americans from a Democratic initiative to suspend federal supervision of southern elections. At the end of his speech, senior Republicans congratulated him on an outstanding debut, an event that Representative Gillett considered one of the highlights of his career.

In the next Congress the Republicans were returned to the majority, and THOMAS REED of Maine became Speaker. Representative Gillett demonstrated his knack for making friends by establishing an easy rapport with the new Speaker. When Representative Gillett proposed making the residency requirement for divorce one year in the territories, Speaker Reed asked the congressman, a bachelor at the time, if his interest in this issue was purely anticipatory.

During the Republican ascendancy in the House from 1893 to 1911, Representative Gillett received several desirable committee assignments including, Appropriations, Foreign Affairs, Judiciary, and Military Affairs. From 1900 to 1911 he chaired the Reform in the Civil Service Committee, in which he staunchly protected the Pendleton Act from encroachments by some of his fellow Republicans. His greatest interest, however, was in the budgetary process. From his vantage point on the APPROPRIATIONS COMMITTEE from 1902 to 1918, he advocated setting up a bureau of the budget in the executive branch, so that a unified budget could be prepared for presentation to Congress as opposed to having every executive agency compile a separate budget. In addition, he favored having only the Appropriations Committee handle spending in the House rather than using a multicommittee approach. Both of these reforms were enacted during his tenure as Speaker, when he was especially influential in persuading Congress to pass the BUDGET AND ACCOUNTING ACT OF 1921.

During World War I as the ranking Republican member on Appropriations, he worked closely with the Democratic chair, Representative John Fitzgerald of New York, to pass the money needed for the war, although he ruefully noted that as a New Englander he really preferred econ-

omy in government. While supportive of the war, he consistently opposed legislation to expand President Woodrow Wilson's powers to deal with the emergency. For example, in 1918 he was one of only two House Republicans to vote against a bill that would diminish the Senate's power to confirm executive branch officials and permit the president to reorganize executive departments without congressional approval. In this period he also had his first taste of party leadership. When Minority Leader James Mann of Illinois became ill in 1917, Representative Gillett filled in for him. Although he tried as a leader to keep criticism of the war to a minimum, he admitted that there were times when his silence required much self-restraint.

In 1919, with the Republicans again in the majority, there was strong interest in the Speakership. The new Speaker would be the first Republican to hold the office since the powerful and autocratic JOSEPH CANNON had been stripped of his power in the famous 1910 revolt. Initially, expectations were high that Minority Leader Mann would win. Mann had skillfully led the House Republicans during their eight years in the minority, but the Minority Leader had several liabilities. He was an ally of Speaker Cannon—in fact, the former Speaker was his campaign manager. Consequently, there was fear that Mann would bring back Cannonism, a development that could hurt the Republicans in the upcoming 1920 elections. Other Republicans thought Mann's acceptance of free steaks from a meat packing company could also tarnish the party's image. Furthermore, Mann had antagonized a number of Republicans with his refusal to push any bill that might embarrass President Wilson while he was abroad at the peace conference. In contrast, Gillett pledged that if he were elected there would be no return to Cannonism, particularly the Speaker's exclusive prerogative to appoint committee chairs. Moreover, Gillett declared himself to be "100 percent American" as a way of indicating that he would press ahead with the Republican agenda regardless of President Wilson's wishes. Representative Gillett was also the most senior Republican in the House in terms of continuous service. However, perhaps his biggest advantages were his amiability and reputation for fair play that assured members that he would be a reasonable presiding officer but not an overly assertive party leader. In the caucus, with the assistance of Nicholas Longworth of Ohio and his followers, Gillett easily defeated Mann 138-69. Philip Campbell of Kansas, who thought Mann's ties to the beef industry and Gillett's opposition to women's suffrage and Prohibition disqualified them both, received 13 votes, with the rest scattered.

Even in defeat Mann displayed his exceptional ability to wheel and deal by gaining control of the newly formed Committee on Committees, which not only made committee assignments but also nominated the majority leader,

WHIP, and five-member Steering Committee. The Committee on Committees selected Mann as the new Majority Leader, but he declined the offer. Although Frank Mondell of Wyoming served as floor leader under Speaker Gillett, Mann continued to play a powerful role behind the scenes in the House until his death in 1922 and undercut Speaker Gillett's ability to lead the House.

In his first year as presiding officer, Speaker Gillett got into a couple of procedural tussles with the Democrats. In July 1919 he ruled that a Democrat could not introduce a resolution welcoming General John Pershing back to the United States because that was a right of the majority party, and he would have to confer with the Steering Committee before permitting it. In the next month he outraged Minority Leader Champ Clark of Missouri when he refused to let William Igoe of Missouri introduce a resolution criticizing the high price of shoes. Whether Speaker Gillett was again deferring to the Republican Steering Committee or protecting an important Massachusetts industry from an unwanted investigation is unclear.

In 1921 Speaker Gillett easily won reelection and in 1923 appeared to be headed to another easy victory when the Republican Caucus renominated him over token opposition. In a stunning miscalculation, the caucus did not make the vote for Speaker binding, thus paving the way for a revolt on the House floor. In 1922 the Republican majority had been reduced from 303 to 225 members. Of these 225 Republicans, there were 15 Progressives and a large FARM BLOC, which had been organized in the preceding Congress to publicize the serious economic plight of midwestern farmers. Although most Farm Bloc Republicans did not share the Progressives' critique of mainstream conservatism, there was concern that Speaker Gillett was too tied to eastern business and industrial interests to be responsive to agricultural problems. With the Democrats holding 205 seats, the insurgents in the Republican Party had the power to delay or even prevent Speaker Gillett's reelection altogether simply by withholding their votes when the full House elected the Speaker. For two days and eight ballots, 22 insurgents, mostly Wisconsin Progressives and a handful of the most alienated Farm Bloc members, steadily refused to vote for Speaker Gillett. When Majority Leader Longworth could not round up the votes needed to put the Speaker back into office, he reluctantly agreed to negotiate with the insurgents. In the end, the insurgents voted for Speaker Gillett in return for placing John Nelson of Wisconsin on the Rules Committee and reducing the number of signatures required on a discharge petition from 218 to 150.

In 1924 Speaker Gillett announced that he would run for the Senate, even though he had told the House he would rather be Speaker of the House than hold any other position in the world. Fellow politicians believed President Calvin Coolidge urged him to take on the Senate race. During the campaign Speaker Gillett switched his position on Prohibition. In 1918 he had voted against the Prohibition amendment, but in 1924, to win "dry" votes in Massachusetts, he became a supporter. In the general election he defeated incumbent senator David Walsh by 18,585 votes, which was a fairly narrow margin considering that President Coolidge carried Massachusetts by more than 420,000 votes. Except for his 1910 victory of fewer than 500 votes when Cannonism was the issue, it was Speaker Gillett's closest election.

In the Senate he was a tireless advocate of American participation in the World Court. Given his reservations about the League of Nations, Senator Gillett's support for the World Court was somewhat surprising, but in the past he had shown considerable respect for international law. In 1914, for instance, during the Mexican unrest, he had reminded the Wilson administration that blockading ports was an act of war under international law. As a member of the FOREIGN RELATIONS COMMITTEE, Senator Gillett prodded the Senate to reopen debate on the World Court and helped rally public opinion through speeches and newspaper articles.

After one term Senator Gillett decided to retire. In his last years he wrote a biography of George Frisbie Hoar, a former senator from Massachusetts. Speaker Gillett had a professional as well as a personal interest in the topic. In 1915, at the age of 64, he had married Christine Rice Hoar, widow of Congressman Rockwood Hoar and daughter-in-law of Senator Hoar. On July 31, 1935, Speaker Gillett died from leukemia and was buried in Westfield, Massachusetts.

As Speaker, Gillett had little real power. Scholars have called him a figurehead, a transitional figure, and a moderator, but all agree that while he brought dignity to the office, he had limited control over day-to-day politics in the House. During his tenure power in the House became diffused. The Majority Leader, the Steering Committee, and key committee chairs all played important roles, unlike during the Cannon years. In fact, although the Steering Committee met daily, Gillett had to be invited to these sessions because he did not have a formal seat on the committee and appeared to have little influence over the Steering Committee's decisions.

Yet there is more to Speaker Gillett's years of service in Congress than his weakness as Speaker suggests. He was an effective legislator who concentrated on his committee assignments, worked well with colleagues, and was respected for his thoughtful preparation. He did not give many speeches, but when he did speak, his remarks were brief, carefully crafted, and well delivered. His approach to constituents was to leave his district alone. He seldom visited, preferring to keep in touch by exercising the franking privilege to the fullest. He believed that as a member of

Congress his first priority was to the national interest, not to his district's welfare. Upon observing the difficulty Gillett had in lobbying for his district, cabinet member Elihu Root commented that the necessities of politics were at war with the instincts of a gentleman.

Further reading:
Davidson, Roger H., Susan Webb Hammond, and Raymond W. Smock, eds. *Masters of the House: Congressional Leadership over Two Centuries.* Boulder, Colo.: Westview Press, 1998; Frederick H. Gillett. *George Frisbie Hoar.* Boston: Houghton Mifflin, 1934; Gillett, Frederick H. *The United States and the World Court.* New York: American Foundation, 1930; Russell, Henry B. "Frederick H. Gillett: American Statesman." *Amherst Graduates' Quarterly* 21 (November 1931): 3–17; Peters, Ronald M., Jr. *The American Speakership: The Office in Historical Perspective.* 2d ed. Baltimore: Johns Hopkins University Press, 1997.
—Maureen Roberts Romans

Gingrich, Newt (1943–) *Representative, Speaker of the House*

Newton Leroy "Newt" Gingrich was born in Harrisburg, Pennsylvania, the son of Kathleen McPherson. At three he was adopted by Robert Gingrich, his mother's second husband. The elder Gingrich was an army officer, so Newt attended schools at various military bases in Kansas, France, and West Germany. He graduated from high school in Columbus, Georgia. He followed his high school math teacher to Emory University in Atlanta, where she had been given a teaching job. Gingrich married Jacqueline Battley in 1962; they later divorced.

Gingrich graduated from Emory in 1965. He then enrolled in Tulane University in New Orleans, where he received a master's degree in 1968 and a Ph.D. in modern European history in 1971. As a graduate student he campaigned for Governor Nelson Rockefeller of New York for president in 1968 because the New Yorker supported civil rights. Before completing his doctoral dissertation, Gingrich joined the faculty of West Georgia College in Carrollton, Georgia. Popular in the classroom, by 1974 he had become restless teaching. In 1974 he challenged Representative John Flynt, a Democrat from Georgia, for the state's Sixth Congressional District seat, almost defeating the incumbent. Gingrich challenged Flynt again in 1976, narrowly losing because of President Jimmy Carter's coattails in Georgia.

Flynt retired in 1978. Gingrich ran again on a platform of lower taxes and opposition to the Panama Canal Treaty. He defeated Democratic state senator Virginia Shepherd. As a freshman Republican in a HOUSE OF REPRESENTATIVES securely controlled by Democrats, Gingrich was unwilling to serve as a quiet backbencher. Leading a small group of young Republicans, he criticized his party's leadership for failing to adequately challenge the Democratic majority. He worked to develop a Republican challenge to the Democrats' budget proposals, emphasizing the need to cut spending and reduce taxes.

Believing that both political parties failed to have workable visions, Gingrich began work to develop a new direction for the Republican Party. In February 1983 he began meeting with other young conservative representatives, a group that Gingrich called the Conservative Opportunity Society. The group used parliamentary tactics to force votes on controversial issues such as school prayer and trade with communist countries. Gingrich's group took advantage of the new Cable-Satellite Public Affairs Network (C-SPAN) and the live televising of House proceedings. In 1980 the group began a series of "special order speeches," publicizing their conservative agenda.

On May 8, 1984, Gingrich and Representative Robert Walker, a Republican from Pennsylvania, read from a report by the Republican Study Committee that criticized foreign policy statements made by about 50 Democrats over the past 15 years. The cameras focused on Gingrich, who paused at intervals to allow Democrats to respond. C-SPAN viewers could not see that Gingrich was speaking to a largely empty House chamber. Two days later, during floor debate, the SPEAKER OF THE HOUSE, THOMAS O'NEILL, a Democrat from Massachusetts, left his seat on the dais, an action rarely taken by a Speaker, to move to the podium in the well to berate Gingrich. After gaining recognition, O'Neill angrily stated that the Republican's statement was "the lowest thing I have ever seen in my thirty-two years in Congress." A Republican House member rose and demanded that O'Neill's words "be taken down," or stricken, from the record. The House PARLIAMENTARIAN ruled against O'Neill, finding that the Speaker had violated the prohibition against personal insult. Gingrich was ecstatic over the publicity the event gained for his cause.

A strong supporter of President Ronald Reagan's fiscal policies, Gingrich regularly criticized fellow Republicans who he felt were blocking the president's agenda. He once called Senator ROBERT DOLE, a Republican from Kansas and chair of the SENATE FINANCE COMMITTEE, "the tax collector for the welfare state." Gingrich criticized Office of Management and Budget director David Stockman, calling him "the greatest obstacle to a successful revolution from the liberal welfare state to an opportunity society." Gingrich outlined his political philosophy in the book *Window of Opportunity: A Blueprint for the Future* that he published in 1984. In writing the book he collaborated with his second wife, Marianne, and David Drake, a science fiction writer.

In 1984 Gingrich and his supporters were able to get the Republican National Convention to adopt a platform more conservative than the one proposed by the Reagan reelection campaign. The platform included a commitment not to increase taxes, a proposal to end abortion, and the inclusion of the phrase "conservative opportunity society." In Congress Gingrich continued to support the Reagan administration's military spending and its aid to the contra rebels fighting against the Marxist-led Sandinista government in Nicaragua. He joined Democrats in supporting the creation of a federal holiday in honor of Martin Luther King, Jr. Gingrich was easily reelected in 1984 and 1986.

Gingrich decided to challenge Speaker JAMES WRIGHT, a Democrat from Texas, in 1987. For months Gingrich had called for an ethics investigation into some of Wright's financial dealings, including a contract for Wright's book *Reflections of a Public Man*. The book was not sold in a normal way. Instead, Wright developed a system that allowed him to collect large royalties on bulk sales to his supporters. Since House ethics rules allowed royalties as acceptable outside income, Wright was able to get

House Speaker Newt Gingrich holding a copy of the Republicans' "Contract with America," 1995 *(Corbis)*

around House rules. In May 1988 Gingrich was able to persuade many of his fellow Republicans, with the exception of House MINORITY LEADER Robert Michel, a Republican from Illinois, to join him in formally requesting an investigation by the House COMMITTEE ON STANDARDS OF OFFICIAL CONDUCT. After the probe found evidence that Wright violated House rules, the Speaker resigned in May 1989.

In March 1989 President George H. W. Bush nominated House Minority WHIP Dick Cheney, a Republican from Wyoming, to be the secretary of Defense. Gingrich began collecting pledges of support for a bid to be whip. Minority Leader Michel was able to persuade Representative Edward Madigan, a moderate Republican from Illinois, to run against Gingrich. The younger Republicans in the House, who shared his desire to have the Republican Party gain control of the chamber, supported the Georgian. Gingrich was narrowly elected by a vote of 87 to 85.

Gingrich became the subject of an Ethics Committee investigation in April 1989. Representative Bill Alexander, a Democrat from Arkansas, charged that the Minority Whip had violated House rules on outside income by benefiting from two partnerships created to finance and promote two books, including *Window of Opportunity*. A second ethics probe was launched in July 1989 when it was reported that Gingrich had taken two staff members off the payroll in order for them to work on his reelection campaign and then rehired them after the election with large increases in salary. Neither investigation resulted in action by the House.

In 1990 Gingrich almost lost his seat when his opponent attacked him for supporting a congressional pay raise and opposing a government bailout of Eastern Airlines. He was almost a victim of redistricting in 1992, when the Georgia legislature put him in a new district farther out from Atlanta with Representative Richard Ray, a Democrat from Georgia. Gingrich moved to the more Republican Sixth District, but he had to face an opponent in the primary election.

As a member of leadership, he continued to look for ways to move up to Republican House leader. He had inherited the political action committee GOPAC from Delaware Governor Pete duPont. He used the money raised by GOPAC to elect Republicans to the House when the party's fund-raising was limited. In October 1993 Minority Leader Michel announced his retirement from Congress. Gingrich began a campaign for leader. Initially he was challenged by Representative Gerald Solomon, a Republican from New York, but Solomon realized that Gingrich had more vote pledges and withdrew after five days. Gingrich effectively became the Republican's leader. Although working with the Democratic president Bill Clinton to enact the North American

Free Trade Agreement, he opposed Clinton's health care plan. He also started work on the Contract with America, a series of 10 proposals Gingrich promised that Congress would vote on if Republicans were elected to the majority. In November 1994 the Republican Party gained control of both houses of Congress. His colleagues nominated Gingrich for Speaker, and he was elected in January 1995.

Most of the power Gingrich exercised as Speaker stemmed from the support he gained from the 73 Republican freshmen elected in 1994. He ignored the seniority system and appointed his allies to chair key STANDING COMMITTEES in the House. Nine of the 10 items on the contract passed the House; term limits failed to garner the required two-thirds support. Not long after becoming Speaker, Gingrich found himself presiding over a large political misstep, a government shutdown that infuriated the public and all but guaranteed a second term for President Clinton and a nine-seat gain in the House for Democrats in the 1996 election.

Late in 1996 the Speaker was investigated by federal law enforcement officials who claimed he had violated federal tax laws. He was reprimanded by the Ethics Committee and required to pay a $300,000 fine. Rank-and-file Republicans began to call for internal changes to weaken the power of the Speaker. Gingrich also was the target of an unsuccessful attempt to remove him from the Speaker's office. The impeachment of President Clinton seemed to reenergize Gingrich, and the Republicans regained their focus. In 1998 the Republican Party lost seats in the House. Even though he was reelected, Gingrich resigned as Speaker in December 1998 and did not take his seat for the 106th Congress.

After retiring from Congress, he founded The Gingrich Group, a communications and management consultant firm in Atlanta. He also served as a senior fellow at the American Enterprise Institute and worked as a political analyst for the Fox News Channel. Working with former Speaker Tom Foley, a Democrat from Washington state, Gingrich in 2002 released a proposal on how to keep Congress running if a large number of members died in a catastrophic attack on Washington, D.C.

Further reading:
Gingrich, Newt, with Marianne Gingrich and David Drake. *Window of Opportunity: A Blueprint for the Future.* New York: Tor, 1984; Gingrich, Newt. *Lessons Learned the Hard Way: A Personal Report.* New York: HarperCollins, 1998; Miller, Matthew. "The Newt in Winter." *Fortune,* 6 September 2004, pp. 68–69; Steely, Mel. *The Gentleman from Georgia: The Biography of New Gingrich.* Macon, Ga.: Mercer University Press, 2000.

—John David Rausch, Jr.

Government Accountability Office (GAO)

Created in 1921, the General Accounting Office quickly became popularly known simply as the GAO. In 2004 it was renamed the Government Accountability Office while retaining its popular abbreviated title.

The Constitution gives Congress the power of the purse, that is, the power to raise and spend money in the public's interest, but until 1921 the legislature's ability to oversee the executive branch's use of funds was haphazard at best. Moreover, neither the executive nor the legislative branches prepared a unified budget that listed all department and program funding needs and revenues to pay for them. Soaring budget deficits following World War I finally triggered congressional action with the passage of the BUDGET AND ACCOUNTING ACT OF 1921. The act created the Bureau of the Budget (BOB), housed it in the Treasury Department, and gave it authority to "assemble, correlate, revise, reduce, or increase the estimates of the several departments or establishments." Essentially, the president now had authority to create and propose a single budget for all parts of the executive branch. But in the same act Congress established for itself the GAO to ensure its ability to oversee the budget and all expenditures made pursuant to it.

The first comptroller general, John Raymond McCurl, a Republican, laid the foundation for the agency's independence as a watchdog of the public's money. His rigorousness in pursuing questionable expenditures, including many early New Deal programs, caused some people, most notably FDR, to call for the elimination of the GAO. But the agency survived and during its first 20 years spent much of its energy checking if vouchers, the forms used by government officials to record information on their spending, had been properly filed.

World War II increased government spending exponentially, which taxed the GAO and the government's accounting system like nothing before. In 1949 Comptroller General Lindsay C. Warren took several steps to address the weaknesses uncovered during the war. He proposed the "comprehensive audit," a full study of a unit's financial operation done on site and with an eye on its authorizing legislation, an unprecedented approach for the time. He also agreed to have the GAO, Treasury, and BOB coordinate their efforts to modernize and improve the government's financial management system by entering into the Joint Accounting Improvement Program. With the passage of the Budget and Accounting Procedures Act of 1950, Congress formally recognized the executive branch's responsibility for reporting and accounting methods and that the GAO had authority to determine which reporting and accounting methods must be used. The law also formalized the GAO's power to undertake comprehensive audits.

The GAO established the first of its 11 regional field offices and an office in Paris in 1952. Great Society social programs, particularly the War on Poverty, brought calls from lawmakers to have the GAO conduct evaluations to determine whether the programs were actually meeting their objectives. The success of the GAO's early foray into program evaluation prompted Congress to include language in the LEGISLATIVE REORGANIZATION ACT OF 1970 that formally extended the agency's authority to undertake these studies and gave it more staff to accommodate the extra work.

In 1985 Congress passed the GRAMM-RUDMAN-HOLLINGS Debt Reduction Act as a response to the spiraling national debt. To achieve a balanced budget, the act mandated that Congress and the president meet annual budget deficit targets over a six-year period. Should Congress and the president fail to make the cuts necessary to meet the targets, based on data from independent analyses done by the CBO and OMB (the former BOB), the comptroller general had the authority to issue a sequestration order that automatically reduced spending. The Supreme Court declared the act unconstitutional in *Bowsher* (the comptroller general at the time) *v. Synar* (a Democrat from Ohio who brought the suit). The Court ruled that because the comptroller general was a part of the legislative branch, his actions to reduce spending, an executive function, violated the separation of powers principle.

Since the 1990s the GAO has organized itself to reflect its emphasis on issue areas. There are 13 research, audit, and evaluation teams (the newest, national preparedness, is a "virtual" team) focused on policy areas such as health care and information technology. With more than 3.200 employees with specialties in a variety of fields, the GAO remains a critical arm of Congress, assisting it in its oversight responsibility.

Further reading:
Brown, Richard E. *The General Accounting Office: Untapped Source of Congressional Power.* Knoxville: University of Tennessee Press 1970; Havens, Harry S. *The Evolution of the General Accounting Office: From Voucher Audits to Program Evaluations.* Washington, D.C.: General Accounting Office 1990; Mosher, Frederick C. *The General Accounting Office: The Quest for Accountability in American Government.* Boulder, Colo.: Westview Press, 1979; Pois, Joseph. *Watchdog on the Potomac: A Study of the Comptroller General of the United States.* Washington, D.C.: University Press of America, 1979; Trask, Roger R. *Defender of the Public Interest: The General Accounting Office, 1921–1966.* Washington, D.C.: General Accounting Office, 1996.

—Thomas J. Baldino

Governmental Affairs, Senate Committee on

Governmental Affairs is a standing committee in the SENATE with jurisdiction to oversee the operations of the federal government and to find government inefficiency, waste, and official corruption. The Senate's Governmental Affairs Committee has its historic roots in the Committee on Retrenchment, a standing committee created by the Senate in 1842 to examine the expenditures of the government and determine if government spending could be reduced without harming the public service. The Retrenchment Committee was abolished in 1857. In 1866 Congress created the Joint Select Committee on Retrenchment. The Joint Select Committee expired at the end of the 41st Congress in 1871. A majority of senators wanted to continue their investigations and voted to create the Committee on Investigations and Retrenchment on December 14, 1871. The major target of the investigations conducted by this committee was the graft and corruption in the New York City customs house. The committee expired at the end of the 42nd Congress in March 1873.

The Committee on Civil Service and Retrenchment replaced the Committee on Investigations and Retrenchment. Created in 1873, the Committee on Civil Service and Retrenchment remained a standing committee until 1921. From the 1880s until the early 20th century, the Senate tried a number of different committees to control federal government expenditures as well as administrative and organizational oversight committees. The Committee on Expenditures of Public Money was created in 1884 and abolished in 1889, with little evidence that it had any significant legislative impact. The committee was replaced by the Committee on the Organization, Conduct, and Expenditures of the Executive Departments, which continued in various forms until the 1920s.

The current Committee on Governmental Affairs has a direct lineage to the Committee on Expenditures in the Executive Departments created by the Senate in 1920. The first piece of legislation received and considered by the new committee was the BUDGET AND ACCOUNTING ACT OF 1921. This legislation created the Bureau of the Budget, the General Accounting Office, and the first centralized system for budgeting and auditing in the federal government. Despite this auspicious beginning, the Committee on Expenditures in the Executive Departments produced little legislation for the next 25 years.

The committee's stature improved with the passage of the LEGISLATIVE REORGANIZATION ACT OF 1946. The act officially recognized congressional responsibility for administrative oversight and provided the committee with more staff to conduct this oversight. While other committees were abolished or consolidated, the Senate retained the Committee on Expenditures in the Executive Departments and gave it official jurisdiction over budget and accounting measures other than appropriations. Under the Legislative Reorganization Act the committee became a major Senate committee. It was involved in writing the Executive Reorganization Act of 1949, the development of the Federal Property and Administrative Services Act of 1949, and the passage of the Budgeting and Accounting Procedures Act of 1950.

To investigate government operations the committee made use of its Subcommittee on Investigations, one with its own independent heritage. The Subcommittee on Investigations grew from the Senate Special Committee Investigating the National Defense Program chaired by Missouri senator Harry S. Truman during World War II. From 1953 through 1954 the subcommittee was chaired by Wisconsin senator JOSEPH MCCARTHY. McCarthy staged a series of highly publicized anticommunist investigations, including an inquiry into communism within the U.S. Army. The Army-McCarthy Hearings, as the investigation became known, were televised. The subcommittee made a detailed investigation of the Italian mafia in the 1960s. In the 1970s the subcommittee investigated energy shortages. Later in the century the subcommittee examined off-shore banking practices, money laundering, child pornography, and the federal government's drug control policy.

In 1952 the committee's name was changed to the Committee on Government Operations to more accurately represent its jurisdiction. The committee's name was changed again in 1979 to the Committee on Governmental Affairs.

The Committee on Governmental Affairs was one of 16 standing committees in the Senate during the 108th Congress. With 17 members (9 Republicans and 8 Democrats), it was one of the Senate's smaller committees. It had three subcommittees. One of the subcommittees, the Permanent Subcommittee on Investigations, probably has wider public recognition than the full committee. The other two subcommittees are the Subcommittee on Financial Management, the Budget, and International Security and the Subcommittee on Oversight of Government Management, the Federal Workforce, and the District of Columbia.

Despite the small number of members, the Committee on Governmental Affairs has a broad jurisdiction. It has jurisdiction over legislation and issues related to the Archives of the United States, budgeting and accounting measures other than appropriations, the census and collection of other statistics, congressional organization, the federal civil service, intergovernmental relations, the municipal affairs of the District of Columbia, organization and management of U.S. nuclear policy, organization and reorganization of the executive branch of the government, and the U.S. Postal Service.

Further reading:
Endersby, James W., and Karen M. McCurdy. "Committee Assignments in the U.S. Senate." *Legislative Studies Quarterly* 21, no. 2 (1996): 219–233; U.S. Senate: Committee on Government Operations. *Committee on Government Operations, United States Senate: 50th Anniversary History, 1921–1971.* Senate Document 31. Washington, D.C.: Government Printing Office, 1971; U.S. Senate. *Committee on Governmental Affairs, Executive Sessions of the Senate Permanent Subcommittee on Investigations of the Committee on Government Operations: Index to Hearings.* Senate Print 107-84. Washington, D.C.: Government Printing Office, 2003.

—John David Rausch, Jr.

Government Printing Office

The Government Printing Office (GPO) is the public printer for the federal government. Established by statute in 1860, the GPO provides public printing for the federal government through its own facilities and by procuring commercial services. The GPO captures, stores, authenticates, produces, and disseminates information from Congress and other federal agencies for the public to access directly and through the Federal Depository Library Program.

The Public Printer, who serves as the GPO's chief executive officer, is nominated by the president and confirmed by the SENATE. The GPO operates under the authority of the public printing and documents chapters of Title 44 of the United States Code. The congressional Joint Committee on Printing oversees the GPO.

The GPO was initially created to take care of the printing needs of Congress and today prints and disseminates information for the entire federal community. Approximately 130 federal departments and agencies, along with Congress and the White House, depend on the GPO's services. Congressional publications, federal regulations and reports, census and tax forms, and U.S. passports are among the documents produced by or through the GPO. In the early days of its existence, the GPO's mission was accomplished with conventional printing presses. Today the GPO provides government information in a wide range of formats, including print, microfiche, CD-ROM, DVD-ROM, and the Internet via GPO Access.

Unlike most federal agencies, the GPO operates much like a business, since it is reimbursed for services rendered to its customers. The GPO also receives two appropriations from Congress: one to pay for the cost of congressional printing and the other to fund the cataloging, indexing, distribution, and online access to government documents through the Federal Depository Library Program (FDLP) as required by law.

Approximately three-quarters of the GPO's printing revenues are from agencies for work procured by GPO from the private printing industry. The GPO has a long-established partnership with America's printing industry to provide for the government's printing needs. In 2003 the GPO competitively bought products and services from nearly 2,300 private firms in all 50 states. It is one of the government's most successful procurement programs, assuring cost-effective use of taxpayers' printing dollars.

In the age of the Worldwide Web, the public demands immediate access to official government information. To meet this demand, GPO Access, at http://www.gpoaccess.gov, makes online information products available to the public. GPO Access is a leading online source of free, official government information. Its publicly available resources, which cover all branches of the federal government, include the CONGRESSIONAL RECORD, the United States Code, Government Accountability Office Reports, congressional bills and reports, PUBLIC LAWS, the Federal Register, and many more. There are more than 250,000 titles available on the GPO servers. GPO Access also hosts 20 federal Web sites, including the Web site for the Supreme Court. Most electronic documents appear on the day they are published, exactly as they appear in print, and are the official published version. The GPO maintains permanent public access to all government information residing on GPO Access.

Further reading:
U.S. Government Printing Office. *GPO/2001: Vision for a New Millennium.* Washington, D.C.: Government Printing Office, 1992; U.S. Government Printing Office. *Public Printer's Annual Report, Fiscal Year 2003.* Washington, D.C.: Government Printing Office, 2004; U.S. Government Printing Office. *Biennial Report to Congress on the Status of GPO Access.* Washington, D.C.: Government Printing Office, 2001.

—Mary S. Rausch

Government Reform, House Committee on

A standing committee of the HOUSE OF REPRESENTATIVES since January 1995, the Committee on Government Reform possesses broad investigative and oversight powers over the operations of the federal bureaucracy. The committee's origins date back to 1814, when a Committee on Public Expenditures was established in the House. The committee subsequently was terminated in 1880. In addition, six separate Committees for Expenditures were established in 1816 to oversee the Navy Department, the Post Office Department, the Treasury Department, the State Department, the War Department, and Public Buildings. In later years Committees on Expenditure would be established to watch over the Interior Department (1860), the Justice Department (1874), the Agriculture Department (1889), and the Commerce and Labor Departments (1905; in 1913 the jurisdiction of this committee would be divided between Committees on Expenditure to review each department). In 1927 the Committee on Expenditures in

the Executive Departments was created by consolidating the separate standing committees.

As the principal investigative arm of the House, the committee conducted investigations and held hearings on various activities of the federal government. Much of the committee's work (as well as the work of its successors) was through subcommittees. One of the more notable investigations was conducted in 1947 by the Subcommittee on Paroles, which was trying to determine why four of organized crime figure Al Capone's friends received early paroles.

On July 3, 1952, the committee was renamed the Committee on Government Operations. This change reflected the committee's mandate to study government operations to improve economy and efficiency. Toward this end the committee oversaw the implementation of the recommendations of the second of the two Commissions on Organization of the U.S. Executive Branch (which functioned between 1953 and 1955 and was popularly known as the Hoover Commission after its chair, former president Herbert Hoover). During 1954 the Subcommittee on Anti-Racketeering investigated racketeering in Cleveland, Baltimore, and Washington, D.C.

The committee became the House Government Reform and Oversight Committee in 1995 following the Republican takeover of the House after four decades of Democratic control. This name change reflected the new majority party's belief that the federal government needed to be reformed. The committee also assumed the jurisdictions of the Committee on the Post Office and the Civil Service and the Committee on the District of Columbia, both of which were abolished. In 1999 the committee took on its present name when it dropped Oversight in order to avoid confusion with the House Oversight Committee. The newly renamed committee conducted a number of hearings into the activities of the administration of President Bill Clinton. These included hearings into the firing of White House Travel Office employees, the handling of Federal Bureau of Investigation files on prominent Republicans by the administration, and, following the president's reelection in 1996, the financing of the Clinton campaign. In the 107th Congress (2001–03) the committee investigated Clinton's last-minute pardons. Since the September 11, 2001, terrorist attacks the committee has conducted a number of hearings related to the federal government's ability to wage the war on terrorism.

In the 108th Congress the committee was organized into eight subcommittees: Census; Civil Service and Agency Organization; Criminal Justice, Drug Policy and Human Resources; District of Columbia; Energy Policy, Natural Resources and Regulatory Affairs; Government Efficiency, Financial Management and Intergovernmental Relations; National Security, Veterans' Affairs, and International Relations; and Technology and Procurement Policy.

The committee's jurisdiction includes budget and accounting measures other than appropriations; the overall economy and efficiency of government operations and activities, including federal procurement; reorganizations in the executive branch of the government; intergovernmental relationships between the United States and the states and municipalities and general revenue sharing; and the National Archives.

Significant legislation considered by the committee and its predecessors include the Privacy Act of 1974. A number of pieces of legislation that were part of the Republican party's 1994 CONTRACT WITH AMERICA became law during the 104th Congress after originating in the committee. These included the Unfunded Mandates Reform Act of 1995, a bill to stop Congress from passing unfunded mandates; the Line Item Veto Act, which granted the president the authority to strike individual items from tax and spending bills (in 1998 the act was ruled unconstitutional by the Supreme Court in *Clinton v. the City of New York*); and the Paperwork Reduction Act of 1995, a bill reducing the paperwork burden that the federal government imposes on state and local governments, individuals, and businesses. In 2002 the committee approved the creation of the Department of Homeland Security, the largest reorganization of the federal government since the Great Depression.

Further reading:
U.S. Congress. House. Committee on Government. *Activities of the House Committee on Government Reform.* Washington, D.C.: Government Printing Office, 2001–2003. U.S. Congress. House. Committee on Government Reform and Oversight. *Activities of the House Committee on Government Reform and Oversight.* Washington, D.C.: Government Printing Office, 1997–1999. U.S. Congress. House. Committee on Rules. *Investigative Authorities: Hearings before the Committee on Rules, House of Representatives, 105th Congress, first session on H. Res. 167, to provide special investigative authorities for the Committee on Government Reform and Oversight, June 18, 1997.* Washington, D.C.: Government Printing Office, 1998.

—Jeffrey Kraus

Gramm-Rudman-Hollings Bills (1985 and 1987)

The 1985 Gramm-Rudman-Hollings Act (GRH I) was a response to the unheard of (at the time) $200 billion deficits of the early to mid-1980s ($207.8 billion in 1983). GRH I attempted to reduce the budget deficit to zero gradually over six consecutive years by $36-billion reductions each year. Deficit reduction was to start in fiscal year (FY) 1986 with a $171.9-billion target and end in FY 1991 with a balanced budget. GRH I attempted to give teeth to the spending limits in the congressional budget resolution. GRH I was an amendment offered by Senators Phil Gramm, a Republican from Texas; Warren Rudman, a Republican from New Hampshire; and Ernest Hollings, a Democrat from South Carolina. It passed without any hearings or debate by any congressional STANDING COMMITTEE.

After failing to meet the deficit targets for the first two years, Congress passed the 1987 Emergency Deficit Control Reaffirmation Act (GRH II). The new GRH law pushed back the targets, delayed the zero year to FY 1993, and corrected for a U.S. Supreme Court ruling that deemed part of GRH I unconstitutional. The Supreme Court ruled that by requiring an agent of Congress (the Government Accounting Office) to advise the president on what and how much to sequester, GRH I placed Congress in the middle of executing the law, which is a constitutional responsibility of the executive.

The GRH targets were deficit targets. GRH set no limits on spending. Congress and the president could spend as much as they wanted under GRH as long as they passed reconciliation bills that raised taxes and/or cut entitlement spending to meet the deficit target. The targets had $10-billion cushions (except for the last year), so that as long as Congress came within $10 billion of the target, automatic spending cuts would be avoided.

Under GRH members of Congress were faced with two alternatives when voting on their initial budget resolution that was required to meet the GRH deficit target. They could either vote to reduce spending (order their chamber's APPROPRIATIONS COMMITTEE to spend less), or they could spend more than that amount by including reconciliation instructions in the budget resolution. Reconciliation orders required virtually every major congressional committee but Appropriations to make changes in tax or mandatory spending legislation (that is, "entitlements" such as Medicare,

DEFICIT TARGETS UNDER GRH I AND GRH II (IN BILLIONS OF DOLLARS)		
Fiscal Year	**1985 GRH I targets**	**1987 GRH II targets (not including the $10 billion cushion)**
1986	171.9	
1987	144	
1988	108	144
1989	72	136
1990	36	100
1991	0	64
1992	28	
1993	0	

Medicaid, farm subsidies, etc.) to raise revenues or cut spending enough to meet the GRH deficit targets.

Regardless of the alternative chosen, if Congress failed to meet the deficit target by even one dollar for whatever reason, sequestration would meet the target for them. The sequestration process under GRH II involved an Office of Management and Budget (OMB) budget deficit estimate taken on August 15 for the upcoming fiscal year that started on October 1. On August 25 the president would order a sequester if the deficit targets were not met, which would take effect on October 1. Congress would have the opportunity to act between August 25 and October 10 to make any further reductions in the deficit. Then on October 15 a final sequester report would be issued and take effect. If sequestration was required under GRH II, OMB would issue equal across-the-board cuts to defense and nondefense spending to meet the GRH target if the president and Congress failed to do so through any mix of spending cuts and tax increases.

Sequestration was the core concept of GRH. Members of Congress originally described sequestration as the sword of Damocles, Draconian, and a planned train wreck. Proponents of the law believed that sequestration would be so distasteful to members of Congress that it would force members to act on their own to lower the deficit. This meant that members would either reduce spending by passing appropriations bills that met the targets, or, if they wanted to spend more they would also have to pass a reconciliation bill that raised revenues or reduced entitlement spending by an amount needed to reach the deficit target. Failure to pass a reconciliation bill would trigger the sequestration process, which cuts equal dollar amounts from spending for defense and nondefense discretionary programs to meet the target. The sequestration process exempted debt interest and entitlements such as Social Security, Medicaid, and Aid to Families with Dependent Children, and cut by limited amounts entitlements such as Medicare and Guaranteed Student Loans. In fact, only 27 percent of the budget was entirely sequesterable.

Only once during GRH's existence was a full-year sequestration carried out, and that was in the first year of the law (FY 1986). The FY 1988 sequestration was rescinded, and the FY 1990 sequester was in effect for five months.

The federal deficit reached a low of $149 billion in 1987 before rocketing up to more than $220 billion three years later when the GRH target was $100 billion. Anomalies like the savings-and-loan debacle in the late 1980s exacerbated the deficit and put the GRH targets beyond reach. The 1990 Budget Enforcement Act (BEA) effectively ended the GRH sequestration process.

Further reading:
Shuman, Howard E. *Politics and the Budget: The Struggle between the President and the Congress.* 3d ed. Upper Saddle River, N.J.: Prentice Hall, 1992; Wildavsky, Aaron, and Naomi Caiden. *The New Politics of the Budgetary Process.* 4th ed. New York: Longman, 2001.

—Charles Tien

grandfathering

The practice of applying a specific exemption from meeting new standards to a group that has previously existing circumstances is termed grandfathering. The term originated with the grandfather clause found in some southern state constitutions after the Civil War and Reconstruction. The grandfather clause was an attempt to permit poor whites to register to vote while keeping blacks disenfranchised. The provisions specified that those who had enjoyed the right to vote prior to 1866 or 1867, or their decedents, were exempt from the voting requirements. In recent times the term has been applied to provisions in laws that contain a specific exemption from regulation. It also has been applied to certain exceptions and exemptions to limitations appearing in the rules of the House and Senate.

Grandfathering has played a role in committee assignments. Members of Congress receive committee assignments according to a complex series of party procedures and chamber rules. The number of committee assignments per member is limited. Because not all committees are appealing to all members, some seats on less attractive committees are difficult to fill. Party caucuses have assigned members to these seats that already have committee assignments. This type of assignment was called a "grandfather." In 2003 junior Democrats protested this apparent lack of fairness in Democratic committee assignments in the HOUSE OF REPRESENTATIVES. Members with less seniority were concerned that they were missing out on better committee assignments because they were not allowed to hold another committee slot. Democratic rules generally prohibit members serving on exclusive committees, such as WAYS AND MEANS, APPROPRIATIONS, and ENERGY AND COMMERCE, from serving on other standing committees.

Members of Congress have found other ways to benefit from grandfather provisions. In 1979 Congress amended the FEDERAL ELECTION CAMPAIGN ACT OF 1971. One of the SENATE amendments was a provision prohibiting all past and present members of Congress from using campaign funds for personal purposes, a prohibition already in Senate rules. Without a similar rule, House members were able to keep anything left in their campaign accounts if they were retiring and if they paid income taxes on it. A grandfather provision was inserted subjecting all current members of the House and Senate to their respective chamber's rules. Members sworn in after January 8, 1980, would be subject to the new amendments prohibiting personal use.

This grandfather clause was phased out as part of a 1989 House pay raise bill. The clause terminated in January 1993 at the beginning of the 103rd Congress. Members who had been in the House before 1980 had to either retire in 1992 or stay in Congress and forfeit the chance to use their campaign funds for personal use.

Grandfathering also is used to describe provisions written into law that exempt people with specific existing conditions from the regulations or benefits created by the law. For example, a Senate bill on Internet taxes debated in 1998 included a grandfather clause. The clause would have allowed at least a dozen states that collected taxes on Internet access to continue collecting the taxes after the law was enacted. To prohibit these states from collecting taxes on Internet service would have created an unfunded mandate, something that the majority Republicans did not want to do.

Further reading:
Billings, Erin P. "Rules Fight Coming," *Roll Call* (10 February 2003). Available online. URL: http://www.rollcall.com/issues/48_57/news/474-1.html. Accessed February 8, 2006. Groseclose, Timothy, and Keith Krehbiel. "Golden Parachutes, Rubber Checks, and Strategy Retirements from the 102d House." *American Journal of Political Science* 38, no. 1 (1994): 15–99; Gruenwald, Juliana. "Senate Bill to Place Moratorium on New Internet Taxes." *CQ Weekly Report*, 10 October 1998, p. 2,744.

—John David Rausch, Jr.

grants-in-aid

Federal grants-in-aid are funds that the federal government pays to state and local governments to finance state and local programs or payments to individuals. In fiscal year 2001 the federal government made $339 billion in grant awards to state and local governments from 668 separate programs, which amounted to 19.1 percent of all federal spending. The major grant programs are classified as either formula or project grants. The *Catalogue of Federal Domestic Assistance*, the government document that compiles information on all federal grant programs, defines formula grants as "Allocations of money to States or their subdivisions in accordance with distribution formulas prescribed by law or administrative regulation, for activities of a continuing nature not confined to a specific project." Project grants are defined as

> The funding, for fixed or known periods, of specific projects. Project grants can include fellowships, scholarships, research grants, training grants, traineeships, experimental and demonstration grants, technical assistance grants, survey grants, and construction grants.

Although most programs are project grants, the largest are distributed through formula grants.

The evolution of the grant system has lacked planning and coordination. In 1862 Congress enacted the Morrill Act to help states establish and fund land-grant colleges. Grants in the form of financial assistance were limited in scope prior to the Great Depression. In 1902 there were only five grant programs in operation; total federal spending on these five programs was only $3 million. In 1929 only about 3 percent of the federal budget was distributed in the form of grants. However, during the administration of Franklin Delano Roosevelt, numerous social programs were established that fundamentally altered the role of the federal government. By 1939 39 percent of all federal expenditures were made through grant spending. New Deal grant-in-aid programs included awards to the states for direct relief to citizens, aid to the unemployed, and grant programs to address health, maternity, and the physically disabled.

A second major increase in the grant system occurred between 1964 and 1971, when the number of federal grants increased from 51 to 530. Unlike previous grants, which had been mainly formula grants, many of the new assistance programs enacted as part of Lyndon Johnson's War on Poverty were project grants. This was the period known as "creative federalism," and requirements that those seeking funding submit project proposals were meant to ensure that grants would reward innovative solutions to public problems.

Over the years Congress at times has acted to make the grant system more rational through program consolidation. For example, the Omnibus Budget Reconciliation Act of 1981 consolidated a number of social service programs into nine block grants that allowed for greater state and local autonomy and flexibility in using funds to meet federal policy goals. Congress consolidated a number of welfare-related programs into the Temporary Assistance for Needy Families block grant in 1996. In spite of these efforts at improving the grant system, each period of consolidation has been followed by a proliferation of new federal programs.

> In 2003 testimony, Paul L. Posner of the General Accounting Office claimed the federal grant system continues to be highly fragmented, potentially resulting in a high degree of duplication and overlap among federal programs.

There are 50 different grant programs for the homeless that are administered by eight different federal agencies. In addition, a small number of programs account for the vast majority of grant spending. While the 20 largest grant programs account for 78 percent of total grant spending, there are 169 small grant programs that receive less than $5 million annually.

Political scientists often view grants as opportunities for members of Congress who are interested in reelection to serve their constituents and subsequently claim credit for the successful receipt of grant money. David Mayhew claimed:

> In fact the categorical grant is for modern Democratic Congresses what rivers and harbors and the tariff were for pre–New Deal Republican Congresses. It supplies goods in small manipulable packets.

Members of Congress certainly devote resources to assisting constituents in pursuing grant funding. Many scholars have found that members of Congress are most influential in stimulating demand for grants by informing constituents of the availability of funding and by assisting in the preparation of grant applications. Evidence that members of Congress influence the success or failure of project grant applications is very limited. In addition, some scholars have argued that there is a tendency for Congress to universalize grant programs, thereby ensuring continued authorization by providing benefits to virtually all congressional districts. Research by Stein and Bickers contradicts this claim; they found that three-quarters of all domestic grant programs provide spending in less than a third of all House districts.

Most members do devote staff resources to assisting constituents in navigating the complex grant environment. According to a report published by the Congressional Research Service:

- The congressional office is seen by constituents as a potential source of assistance in:
- Providing facts about financial and nonfinancial assistance available through federal programs;
- Clarifying the intricacies of proposal development, application, and follow-up procedures;
- Writing letters of support from the member to the granting agency;
- Resolving problems that occur when an application is unsuccessful in obtaining funds;
- Suggesting other sources for grant assistance in both the private and the public sectors.

Although members may not be able to influence the success or failure of a grant application, there is some evidence that they may influence the timing of awards. In addition, they are often informed of a grant award by the federal agency prior to the recipient and therefore are allowed to be the bearer of good news. According to the same CRS report,

Although there is some variation, the usual announcement procedure in cases of allocated federal funds is for the agency making the award to notify the Senate office first (a Senator of the president's party may be first notified), then the House office and finally the recipient. This allows members of Congress an opportunity to notify recipients of grants.

The complex and substantial grant-in-aid system certainly provides significant opportunities for members to assist constituents. The degree to which this translates into votes, however, has never been empirically demonstrated.

Further reading:
The Catalog of Federal Domestic Assistance, U.S. General Services Administration. Available online. URL: http://www.cfda.gov. Accessed January 16, 2006; Gerli, Merete F. *CRS Report for Congress: Grants Work in a Congressional Office.* Washington, D.C.: Congressional Research Service, The Library of Congress, 2002; Mayhew, David R. *Congress: The Electoral Connection.* New Haven, Conn.: Yale University Press, 1974; Posner, Paul L. *Federal Assistance: Grant System Continues to Be Highly Fragmented.* Washington, D.C.: General Accounting Office [GAO-03-718T], 2003; Stein, Robert M., and Kenneth N. Bickers. *Perpetuating the Pork Barrel: Policy Subsystems and American Democracy.* Cambridge: Cambridge University Press, 1995.
—Scott A. Frisch and Sean Q. Kelly

Gravel v. U.S., 408 U.S. 606 (1972)

In *Gravel v. U.S.* the Supreme Court set forth what remains today the definitive interpretation of the Speech and Debate Clause, found in Article I, Section 6, of the U.S. Constitution. The provision immunizes members of Congress from civil or criminal liability for any speech or debate in either House, but does not define the scope of immunity beyond actual statements made in session. The Court established general guidelines in Kilbourn v. Thomson (1881). Activities generally done in a session of the House by one of its members in relation to the business before it are protected but prior to Gravel had not been reexamined in light of media growth and a corresponding expansion of members' political and communicative as opposed to purely legislative activities in the modern era. Nor had it addressed to what extent members' staffs were protected by the privilege.

After the Supreme Court ruled in *New York Times Co. v. U.S.,* 403 U.S. 713 (1971), that the government could not bar publication of the Pentagon Papers, Senator Gravel read excerpts from the papers before his subcommittee and entered their entire contents into the public record. He also arranged to have the papers published commercially by the Beacon Press. Leonard Rodberg, an aide to the senator, was subpoenaed by the federal grand jury investigating the theft and release of the Pentagon Papers. The senator and Rodberg sought to quash the subpoena in its entirety.

In a 5-4 decision the Court made explicit that the clause protected members of Congress and their aides insofar as the conduct of the latter would be a protected legislative act if performed by the member. But the Court otherwise rejected Senator Gravel's broad reading of the Speech and Debate Clause. It limited protection to legislative activities that are an integral part of the deliberative and communicative processes by which members participate in committee and House proceedings regarding legislation or other constitutionally authorized duties of Congress. Senator Gravel's activities in connection with the subcommittee meeting were therefore protected. However, his discussions and arrangements with the Beacon Press and his aide's participation in those discussions were deemed to be mere informing activities that were in no way essential to the deliberations of the SENATE. Thus, the subpoena was valid regarding such information. Justices William Brennan and William Douglas filed dissents asserting that the informing function, and communicating with the public in general, are essential legislative tasks that ought to be protected by the Speech and Debate Clause. The ruling in Gravel was extended and clarified in HUTCHINSON V. PROXMIRE, 443 U.S. 111 (1979), which excluded press conferences, newsletters to constituents, and other political activities from Speech and Debate Clause immunity.

Further reading:
Kilbourn v. Thompson, 103 U.S. 168 (1881); Hutchinson v. Proxmire, 443 U.S. 111 (1979); Dickson, Del, ed. *The Supreme Court in Conference (1940–1985)*. Oxford: Oxford University Press, 2001.

—Mark Kemper

Gypsy Moths

The Gypsy Moths were members of an informal group of moderate Republicans from northeastern and midwestern states organized to protect federal programs vital to their districts from budget-cutters in the administration of President Ronald Reagan. In early 1981 a small group of moderate Republican House members, mainly from urban areas in the Northeast and Midwest, began meeting to discuss issues of common interest. These House members held an organizational meeting in June. They did not have a staff, dues, or officers. A steering committee was appointed in September 1981, when the group began to attract more publicity. By October 1981 the group had more than 20 members, although the informality of the group made an accurate count impossible. An article in the *Washington Post* identified the following Republican representatives as active Gypsy Moths: Lawrence Coughlin of Pennsylvania, Robert W. Davis of Michigan, Lawrence J. DeNardis of Connecticut, Jim Dunn of Michigan, Millicent Fenwick of New Jersey, Hamilton Fish, Jr., of New York, Benjamin Gilman of New York, Bill Green of New York, Margaret M. Heckler of Massachusetts, Harold C. Hollenbeck of New Jersey, Frank Horton of New York, James M. Jeffords of Vermont, Stewart B. McKinney of Connecticut, Marc L. Marks of Pennsylvania, Carl D. Pursell of Michigan, Ralph S. Regula of Ohio, Marge Roukema of New Jersey, Claudine Schneider of Rhode Island, Olympia Snowe of Maine, Thomas J. Tauke of Iowa, and Lyle Williams of Ohio.

The name *Gypsy Moth* was coined by Representative DeNardis, one of the members of the group's steering committee and a founder of the group. According to DeNardis, the name was meant to be similar to the Boll Weevils, conservative southern Democrats who supported the Reagan administration budget cuts. The gypsy moth was as much a pest to vegetation in New England and the Great Lakes states as the boll weevil was to cotton-growing states in the South. DeNardis also identified a political connotation of the name:

> The Gypsy moth goes through a unique metamorphosis from worm to fly and I told House Minority Leader Robert Michel (a Republican from Illinois) that we preferred not to remain as worms but to fly with the leadership—if we could get some help from the administration on the transition.

To assure the Gypsy Moths that their voices were heard in the Republican Conference, Michel appointed Edward Madigan of Illinois to serve as an "ambassador" to the group.

The Gypsy Moths based their opposition to the Reagan administration on regional concerns. There was no ideological test for membership. They held to the norm that a member of the House should vote for his or her district first. This orientation made their presence more tolerable to the House Republican leadership and the Reagan administration. In the first eight months of 1981, the Moths voted for the Reagan tax cuts while bargaining behind the scenes to protect those programs vital to their constituents. This bargaining appeared to be successful when the administration announced in August that it was restoring $4 billion to programs on mass transit, low-income fuel assistance, and food stamps. The Reagan administration stated that any additional cuts would come from the defense budget. When second rounds of cuts were announced in September threatening the programs they thought they had saved, the Gypsy Moths went public with their opposition. They voted against the Labor, Health and Human Services appropriation in October 1981. The group also proposed reducing defense expenditures by $9 billion. They failed in their effort to rework the budget to their specifications, but they were able to get the Republican leadership to support a tax increase and save Medicaid, the guaranteed student loan program, and mass transit subsidies.

Most of the Gypsy Moths were junior House Republicans with little chance to attain leadership positions. They complained that conservatives in the Republican Conference blocked their membership on key House committees. No Gypsy Moth served on the Rules or Ways and Means Committees. Representative Regula was a member of the Appropriations and Budget Committees and was identified as being a member of the Gypsy Moths. He did not consider himself an official member of the group, however, stating that he attended Gypsy Moth meetings to keep the group informed on the budget process. Only one, Hamilton Fish, served on the HOUSE JUDICIARY COMMITTEE. The Moths claimed that ideological purity kept them out of the seats of power.

Several Gypsy Moths were defeated for reelection in 1982, including Representatives DeNardis, Dunn, Heckler, and Hollenbeck. They were defeated in part because of a bad economy and redistricting. Millicent Fenwick of New Jersey left the House after an unsuccessful U.S. Senate campaign. Marc Marks of Pennsylvania retired. The Gypsy Moths' power in the House was weakened by the resurgent Democrats, who gained 26 seats, increasing that party's majority and decreasing the importance of swing votes. A number of Gypsy Moths continued in the House, but the group was never as effective as it had been during 1981.

Further reading:
Arieff, Irwin B. " 'Gypsy Moths' Poised to Fly against Reagan's New Cuts; Charge Pledges Were Broken." *Congressional Quarterly Weekly Report,* 10 October 1981, pp. 1,950–1,952; Broder, David S. " 'The Gypsy Moths,' *Washington Post,* 27 July 1981, p. A1; Rae, Nicol C. *The Decline and Fall of the Liberal Republicans from 1952 to the Present.* New York: Oxford University Press, 1989.

—John David Rausch, Jr.

Hammer v. Dagenhart, 247 U.S. 251 (1918)

The *Hammer* decision marked the high-water mark of Supreme Court opposition to Congress's constitutional authority to regulate interstate commerce. For more than 20 years, until overruled in UNITED STATES V. DARBY LUMBER CO. (1941), *Hammer* imposed a remarkably narrow and formalistic interpretation of commerce that blocked Congress's efforts to legislate for what the Court deemed illegitimate purposes.

At issue in *Hammer* was the Federal Child Labor Act of 1916, which prohibited interstate shipment of goods produced in factories by children under 14, or by children less than 16 working excessive hours. In striking down the law, the Court's 5-4 majority followed UNITED STATES V. E. C. KNIGHT CO., 156 U.S. 1 (1895) in holding that manufacturing (production) is distinct from distribution (commerce), and Congress may regulate only the latter. The Court distinguished prior cases allowing Congress to regulate interstate shipment of prostitutes, lottery tickets, and impure food because those goods were considered harmful per se, whereas the goods produced by child labor were themselves harmless. The Court thus articulated a direct-indirect doctrine, under which Congress was not to use the commerce power to achieve indirectly that which it lacked power to achieve directly.

In dissent Justice Oliver Wendell Holmes derided the majority's application of the commerce clause as overly formalistic and driven by improper reliance on conservative economic theory. If an act is within the powers specifically conferred upon Congress, he wrote, it is not made any less constitutional because of the indirect effects that it may have.

The Court repudiated the production-distribution distinction in NATIONAL LABOR RELATIONS BOARD V. JONES & MCLAUGHLIN STEEL CORP. (1937), signaling an end to its resistance to NEW DEAL legislation. Congress responded by passing the Fair Labor Standards Act of 1938, which mirrored the legislation struck down in *Hammer.* The Court unanimously upheld the act in *Darby,* overruling *Hammer* in some of the most emphatic language in Supreme Court history. In the words of Justice Harlan Stone,

> The distinction on which the decision [in *Hammer*] was rested . . . was novel when made and unsupported by any provision of the Constitution. . . . was a departure from the principles which have prevailed in the interpretation of the commerce clause both before and since the decision.

The production-distribution rule was thus placed on the scrap heap of history. Notwithstanding its repudiation in *Darby,* however, the direct-indirect doctrine continued to elicit discussion in dissents for the next 50 years and has enjoyed a partial revival in the Rehnquist Court's restrictions on congressional use of the commerce clause since 1995.

Further reading:
United States v. E. C. Knight Co., 156 U.S. 1 (1895); *U.S. v. Darby Lumber Co.,* 312 U.S. 100 (1941); *NLRB v. Jones & McLaughlin Steel Corp.* (1937).

—Daniel E. Smith

Hastert, J. Dennis (1942–) *Representative, Speaker of the House*

J. Dennis Hastert, a Republican from the 14th District in central Illinois just west of Chicago, currently serves as SPEAKER OF THE HOUSE of the U.S. House of Representatives. In 1994 he was named Chief Deputy Whip by Majority Whip THOMAS DELAY and became Speaker of the House upon the resignation of NEWT GINGRICH in 1999.

Prior to his service in Congress, Hastert served three terms in the Illinois house of representatives. While in Illinois, Hastert promoted legislation regarding economic development, property tax reduction, excellence in education, and child abuse prevention. He also supported the passage of a reformed public utilities act to enhance the residents of Illinois's access to utilities.

Hastert's policy agenda has changed little since his service in the Illinois house. In his acceptance speech on January 6, 1999, Speaker Hastert outlined his agenda to lower taxes, improve education, strengthen Social Security and Medicare, and improve national defense. In this speech he advocated limited and efficient government as well as a spirit of bipartisanship. He asserted,

> In the turbulent days behind us, debate on merit often gave way to personal attacks. . . . Solutions to problems cannot be found in a pool of bitterness . . . but in an environment in which we trust one another's word.

His first act in this bipartisan spirit was to hand the gavel to Minority Leader RICHARD GEPHARDT, allowing him the opportunity to briefly preside over the day's proceedings.

According to colleagues, Hastert's commitment to bipartisanship has been a positive influence in the House. His dedication to making the House a cohesive, functioning legislative process has earned the respect of House Republicans and Democrats alike. His efforts have helped the House pass important legislation addressing economic problems and foreign threats, times when agreement could not be more crucial. Additional legislation included measures to decentralize education, to reduce taxes, and to improve antiterrorism measures. Other Republicans say Hastert has been a calming influence and knows how to diffuse pressure points within the party, both attributes that are highly important to the cohesiveness of a political party in the legislature.

Although not currently serving on any House committees, Hastert previously served on committees that produced important legislation. He was chair of the House Government Reform and Oversight Subcommittee on National Security and International Affairs and also a member of the House Commerce Committee, where he exerted influence in policy areas including energy policy, telecommunications deregulation, and drug control legislation.

Hastert served as cochair of the House Working Group on Health Care Quality, which produced the Patient Protection Act of 1998. The Patient Protection Act, passed by the House in July 1998 but defeated in the Senate, sought to make health care more widely available and less restricted to all Americans. He also has chaired a steering committee on health and the Resource Group on Health and coauthored the Health Care Reform Bill that was signed into law by President Bill Clinton in 1996. That law allows insured workers to keep their insurance should they leave their jobs; it also limits insurance companies' tenden-

cies to refuse coverage to citizens with what they call a "preexisting condition." Since becoming Speaker Hastert's influence over health care legislation has continued. He is dedicated to the passage of a comprehensive Patient's Bill of Rights, which, among other things, would severely limit the influence of health maintenance organizations (HMOs) in the patient-doctor relationship and allow the relationship to be preserved in spite of the possible costs of care, which HMO's have tried to keep as low as possible. Hastert served as chair of the House Government Reform and Oversight Subcommittee on National Security, International Affairs, and Criminal Justice.

Hastert has also been active on legislation concerning gun control. He supported mandates for trigger locks, the enforcement of stricter restrictions on sales made at gun shows, and the banning of the importation of ammunition clips. Concerning senior citizens, Hastert has battled Senator John McCain, a Republican from Arizona, concerning the Social Security Earnings Limit, which had taxed Social Security–receiving seniors' income over the established amount of 50 percent. Hastert also advocated tax reduction. He cosponsored and supported bills aimed to permanently repeal the inheritance tax, to provide marriage tax reduction, to increase the child credit, to phase out estate and gift taxes, and to reduce federal income taxes.

Further reading:
Duncan, Phil. "Career Paths: How They Got Where They Are." *Campaigns and Elections* 20 (1999); Killian, Linda. "The Reluctant Speaker." *The American Spectator* 32 (1999); VandeHei, Jim. "Housemaster." *The New Republic* 221 (1999).

—Nancy S. Lind

Hastings, Alcee Lamar (1936–) *Representative*
Although not widely known, Alcee Hastings (D-FL) is a unique member of the U.S. House of Representatives. An African American who was a foot soldier in the Civil Rights movement during the 1960s, Florida's first black federal judge and the sixth federal judge in history to be convicted by the U.S. Senate on impeachment charges, he was elected to the U.S. House in 1992.

The 1990 census confirmed that Florida was entitled to four additional seats in the House of Representatives for the 1992 elections. U.S. Supreme Court precedents necessitated a state districting plan that would enhance office opportunities for Florida's blacks and Hispanics. The new district lines created three black majority districts, two of which were new. If the 23rd District lacked compactness, stretching about 100 miles, from the black enclave west of Miami Beach north to Fort Pierce and west to the sugarcane farms abutting Lake Okeechobee, it had one dominating characteristic: 50 percent of its residents were black. In 1992 Hastings saw his opportunity. He came in second in the Democratic primary, won a runoff primary, and defeated the Republican candidate in the general election.

What is unique about Alcee Hastings is the portion of his career before election to Congress. For 13 years he had a "y'all come" general practice law office. Appointed circuit judge by Governor Rubin Askew, he served two years until President Jimmy Carter appointed him Florida's first black federal judge in 1978. In 1981 he tried a case of two brothers charged with racketeering. After the accused were found guilty, Judge Hastings had legal control of $1.5 million in assets. The FBI came to believe that Hastings and the racketeers' attorney entered into a bribery scheme. The attorney was promptly convicted in federal court. Hastings was indicted and tried but successfully refuted the government's circumstantial case against him. A jury found Hastings not guilty on all counts.

Although legally innocent, Hastings's judicial colleagues used a 1980 judicial discipline law (PL 96-458) to investigate him, concluding that Hastings lied and fabricated evidence for his acquittal. The report went to the U.S. Judicial Conference and by its vote was referred to the U.S. House, saying, "consideration of impeachment may be warranted."

During unsuccessful appeals of procedural issues, Hastings was quoted, "If I were white, I wouldn't be facing impeachment." The Congressional Black Caucus maneuvered to put Hastings's case before a subcommittee with an African-American chair. John Conyers (D-MI), a founder of the Congressional Black Caucus, led the subcommittee investigation. However, after failing to uncover exculpatory material on Hastings's behalf, Conyers became his accuser. With Conyers's active support, the House passed a resolution to impeach by a vote of 413-3.

Despite legal challenges by Hastings, the Senate appointed 12 senators to hear the case from the House. The House case described Hastings as a corrupt judge who wrongfully obtained a courtroom acquittal with fabricated evidence. Hastings's witnesses portrayed him as an outspoken but innocent black judge who became the FBI's target.

On October 28, 1989, Hastings became the sixth judge convicted on impeachment charges by the Senate. Convicted on eight counts and acquitted on three, the Senate declined to vote on six others. The first count alleged conspiracy to obtain a bribe. It was agreed to 69-26. The vote exceeded the two-thirds requirement. Seven more counts passed with between 67 and 70 votes. Interestingly, the two senators who cochaired the Senate's ad hoc committee voted not guilty.

Bereft of his federal judgeship but a free man, Hastings sued in federal court to overturn his Senate conviction

U.S. Representative Alcee L. Hastings speaking in protest of the Florida electoral vote during the counting of the electoral votes in the U.S. House of Representatives *(Corbis)*

and returned to his law practice. When the opportunity came in 1992 to run for the House, Hastings took it. He carried his campaign to the people of south Florida, particularly the African-American half of the electorate. His reputation among them was as the embattled black federal judge who as a civil rights attorney had fought for the concerns of ordinary minority people. He forcefully proclaimed his innocence and suffering as a victim of FBI harassment. In the primary runoff election Hastings's white opponent attacked his integrity as an impeached federal judge. With exquisite timing two weeks before the election, a federal judge announced a decision to overturn the Senate's conviction on impeachment. The judge said Hastings was entitled to a trial by the full Senate, not a committee thereof. Proclaiming himself an "unimpeached federal judge," Hastings said he would rather be in Congress. He won the runoff 58 to 42 percent and went on to win the election, running a bit behind President Bill Clinton at the head of the ticket. On January 5, 1993, Alcee Hastings was seated in the U.S. House.

Hastings has since won reelection five times, winning after redistricting in 2002 with 78 percent of the vote. Anticlimactically, after his election to the House, the U.S. Supreme Court overruled the district court regarding the Senate's impeachment procedures. However, since then he has served in the House, and in 2001 his Democratic colleagues entrusted him with a seat on the House Rules Committee. Still not a household name in American politics, Alcee Hastings has demonstrated the tenacity and diligence necessary to win back public trust and succeed among his colleagues, some of whom voted for his impeachment a dozen years before.

Further readings:
Baron, A. I. "The Curious Case of Alcee Hastings." *Nova Law Review* 19 (1995); Haskins, James. "Hastings, Alcee Lamar." In *Distinguished African-American Political and Governmental Leaders.* Phoenix, Ariz.: Oryx Press.
—Jack R. Van Der Slik

Hayden, Carl Trumbull (1877–1972) *Representative, Senator*

Known as the Silent Senator for his reluctance to make speeches on the floor of Congress, Carl Hayden served the state of Arizona in the HOUSE OF REPRESENTATIVES and SENATE from 1912 to 1969, a longer combined service than any other representative in American history. During his extensive tenure in Congress, Hayden served as President Pro Tempore of the Senate and chair of the APPROPRIATIONS COMMITTEE while establishing a reputation as one of the leading architects of federal reclamation policy.

Hayden was born October 2, 1877, in Hayden's Ferry (now Tempe), Arizona, to Charles Trumbull Hayden, a mill owner, and Sallie Davis. The young man grew up in a small town founded by his father. After graduating from Tempe Normal School in 1896, Hayden entered Stanford University. He failed to complete his degree at Stanford because his assistance was needed with the business interests of his ailing father.

Hayden's political career began in 1902, when he was elected to the Tempe town council. Two years later he was appointed a delegate to the Democratic National Convention in St. Louis. In 1907 he was selected as sheriff of Maricopa County, a post he held five years. A year later he married schoolteacher Nan Downing.

In 1912 Arizona achieved statehood, and Hayden ran for the House of Representatives, becoming the state's first representative. In the House Hayden served on numerous committees important to the interests of his western state, including Indian Affairs, Irrigation and Arid Lands, Public Lands, and Water Power. Although his chief focus was on reclamation and water rights, the young legislator introduced a joint resolution in 1913 calling for a women's suffrage amendment (in honor of his mother, who was a suffragette), and in 1913 he sponsored the Grand Canyon National Park Act. Hayden also gained a progressive reputation for defending the rights of organized labor. He denounced the 1917 forced deportation of more than 1,000 striking copper miners from Bisbee, Arizona, into the New Mexico desert.

After serving seven terms in the House, Hayden was elected to the Senate. During his tenure in the upper chamber from 1927 to 1968, Hayden served on the Appropriations, Mines and Mining, Territories and Insular Affairs, Printing, Post Office and Post Roads, and Rules and Administration Committees. He gained the attention of the Senate when he joined with the state's senior senator, Henry Ashurst, to filibuster the Swing-Johnson Bill. The proposed legislation called for the construction of a hydroelectric dam on the Colorado River and a canal to deliver water to California's Imperial Valley. Arizona's junior senator asserted that the bill would endanger Arizona's development by limiting the state's access to Colorado River water. The Arizona senators halted their filibuster when their colleagues agreed to place a limitation of 4.4 million acre feet on California's Colorado River allotment.

During the NEW DEAL Hayden also demonstrated an interest in transportation issues, joining with Congressman Wilburn Cartwright of Oklahoma to sponsor the 1934 Hayden-Cartwright Act, or Federal Highway Act of 1934. This piece of legislation established that allocation of federal highway funds would be on the basis of area rather than population. The Hayden-Cartwright Act also provided the framework for the more extensive Federal Highway Act of 1956, which was also sponsored by Hayden.

In the post–World War II era Hayden returned his focus to the western issues of water and reclamation, with his championing of the Central Arizona Project, an extensive aqueduct system to bring Colorado River water to the arid regions of central and southern Arizona. Hayden criticized California legislators for blocking the project, asserting that development in Arizona deserved the same degree of support as that accorded California. The Central Arizona Project was simply a matter of fairness to the Arizona senator. Nevertheless, the legislation was stalled until 1968, when as chair of the Senate Appropriations Committee, Hayden was able to shepherd the Central Arizona Project through the Congress. This bill was the capstone of Hayden's legislative career, which also included such reclamation projects as construction of the Coolidge Dam on the Gila River and the San Carlos irrigation project, in addition to authorizing local water-use associations to take over the care, maintenance, and operation of federal reclamation projects.

During his tenure in Washington, the senator usually supported the policies of Democratic presidents Franklin D. Roosevelt, Harry Truman, John Kennedy, and LYNDON JOHNSON. Nevertheless, on race relations and civil rights he identified with the southern conservative wing of the Democratic Party, voting in 1948 to uphold the poll tax and failing to support efforts at curtailing southern FILIBUSTERS. Despite his conservative record on civil rights, Hayden was convinced by President Johnson to vote in favor of the 1964 CIVIL RIGHTS ACT and 1965 VOTING RIGHTS ACT.

After serving more than 50 years in Congress, the President Pro Tempore of the Senate retired in 1968. Hayden returned to Arizona, where he engaged in historical projects focusing on the state's pioneer families. On January 25, 1972, Hayden died in Mesa, Arizona, at age 94.

Further reading:
August, Jack. *Vision in the Desert: Carl Hayden and Hydropolitics in the American Southwest.* Fort Worth: Texas Christian University Press, 1999; *Carl Hayden Papers.* Hayden Library, Arizona State University, Tempe; Rice, Ross Richard. *Carl Hayden: Builder of the American West.* Lanham, Md.: University Press of America, 1994.

—Ron Briley

Haynsworth, Clement F., nomination to the U.S. Supreme Court

As vice president under Dwight Eisenhower from 1953 to 1961, Richard Nixon was a proponent of strong civil rights legislation. In fact, in the 1960 presidential election many leading civil rights activists openly supported Nixon over John F. Kennedy, who frequently voted with southern senators against stronger civil rights bills. In the 1968 election Nixon substantially changed his views on civil rights and vigorously pursued a "southern strategy" in winning a three-way presidential contest against Democrat Hubert Humphrey and American Party candidate George Wallace. While campaigning in the South, Nixon told audiences that he opposed the recently passed 1968 Civil Rights Act and that he would appoint a "strict constructionist" to the U.S. Supreme Court.

Nixon had the opportunity to appoint a "strict constructionist" when former justice Abe Fortas resigned because of conflict of interest charges while serving on the bench. Nixon nominated Clement F. Haynsworth, chief judge of the Fourth Circuit Court of Appeals in Richmond, Virginia, to replace Fortas. Philip Kurland, a leading constitutional scholar at the University of Chicago, called Haynsworth "a Southerner but not too Southern. He's not going to be unacceptable to anybody." But he was. Immediately after the nomination opposition voices began to emerge. Objections were raised by those who saw the

Haynsworth nomination as a Nixon "payoff" to the South and to Senator Strom Thurmond in particular. Senator Thurmond had played a key role in persuading white southerners not to defect to George Wallace in the 1968 election. Thurmond had argued that a vote for Wallace was really a vote for Humphrey. If enough southerners voted for Wallace and prevented Nixon from winning a majority of the electoral vote, the Democratic-controlled House would clearly choose the liberal Humphrey over Richard Nixon. Critics found it more than coincidental that both Haynsworth and Thurmond were South Carolinians.

Democrats controlled the Senate and the Judiciary Committee that had the responsibility for reviewing all federal court nominees. Two issues emerged during the committee debate that would influence the final decision relating to confirmation. First, Haynsworth was accused of participating in court decisions in which he had a conflict of interest. In one case Haynsworth was accused of owning a one-seventh interest in a firm that supplied vending machines to a textile mill. Haynsworth contended that the vending machine company would not profit no matter what decision the court reached in the case. In addition, Haynsworth's profit from the company at this mill was $390, hardly sufficient to sway his decision one way or the other. Critics contended that since Justice Fortas had just stepped down because of a conflict of interest charge, the Senate had to be particularly scrupulous in reviewing this issue with respect to Fortas's replacement. The "appearance of impropriety" would inflict great damage on the Haynsworth nomination.

Haynsworth's supporters argued that the conflict of interest charge was bogus and produced numerous legal scholars who found no conflict to exist. In reality, his supporters argued, the conflict of interest charge was merely a cover for opposing Haynsworth on ideological grounds. Haynsworth, according to his backers, was being opposed because he was a southerner and because he was a "strict constructionist."

The second issue raised against Haynsworth, primarily by the NAACP and AFL-CIO, was that Haynsworth's race relations decisions were often overturned by the Supreme Court. All eight black members of Congress sent a letter to President Nixon condemning the appointment of "a man whose views have been so often at odds with a Supreme Court which achieved distinction through its attack on the malaise of racial discrimination in this country."

Although the SENATE JUDICIARY COMMITTEE voted 10-7 to favorably report Haynsworth as someone who was "extraordinarily well qualified" to serve on the Supreme Court and although the American Bar Association had given Haynsworth a "high" recommendation to serve on the Court, the full Senate rejected the nomination on November 21, 1969, by a 55-45 vote. Particularly harmful to Haynsworth was the last minute defection of a number of key Republican senators, including Edward Brooke, the only black member of the Senate, and Senate Minority Leader Robert Griffin of Michigan. A total of 26 Republicans and 19 Democrats supported Haynsworth, while 17 Republicans and 38 Democrats opposed his confirmation.

After his defeat Judge Haynsworth returned to his position on the Fourth Circuit Court of Appeals, where he would serve until his death in 1989. Even the *Washington Post*, clearly not Richard Nixon's favorite newspaper, supported the Haynsworth nomination in 1969 and wrote that his defeat "resulted more from ideological and plainly political considerations than from ethical ones."
Overcoming what was clearly one of the most painful episodes in his life, Judge Haynsworth spent two more decades serving the federal judiciary with distinction.

Further reading:
Dent, Harry S. *The Prodigal South Returns to Power.* New York: John Wiley & Sons, 1978; Harris, Richard. *Decision.* New York: Ballantine Books, 1970; Kotlowski, Dean J. *Nixon's Civil Rights.* Cambridge, Mass.: Harvard University Press, 2001.

—Darryl Paulson

Health, Education, Labor, and Pensions, Senate Committee on

The standing committee in the U.S. SENATE with a wide-ranging jurisdiction over matters relating to health, education, and human resources is the Health, Education, Labor, and Pensions Committee. The Senate Committee on Health, Education, Labor, and Pensions had its origins in the Committee on Education established by the Senate in 1869. Senator Justin Morrill (R-VT), as a member of the HOUSE OF REPRESENTATIVES, had sponsored the bill creating land-grant colleges, introduced the resolution creating the Committee on Education. Slightly more than a year after its creation, the committee name was changed to the Committee on Education and Labor in 1870. This change was in recognition of the increasing number of petitions the Senate was receiving after the passage of the first eight-hour workday law in 1868.

During the rest of the 19th century and the early part of the 20th century, the committee focused largely on legislation concerning the working conditions of federal employees and federal aid to education. The committee produced little legislation except for the Smith-Hughes Act of 1917 funding vocational rehabilitation programs. Most legislation related to labor was referred to other committees as late as the 1930s. In 1935 the committee attracted attention when it considered the National Labor Relations Act, followed by the Walsh-Healey Public Contracts Act of

1936 and the Fair Labor Standards Act of 1938. Almost all labor legislation was referred to the committee by the 1940s, including the Taft-Hartley Act of 1947.

During World War II the committee investigated the problems caused by a lack of physical fitness among military draftees. It also considered nurse training legislation. In 1944 jurisdiction over the Public Health Service was moved from the Commerce Committee to the Committee on Education and Labor. The Education and Labor Committee considered the Hospital Survey and Construction Act of 1946, which modernized the American hospital system.

A provision of the LEGISLATIVE REORGANIZATION ACT OF 1947 changed the name of the committee to the Committee on Labor and Public Welfare. The act also expanded the committee's jurisdiction to include legislation affecting the rehabilitation, health, and education of veterans. In 1949 the committee's jurisdiction was expanded again to include mine safety legislation. Four members of the Labor and Public Welfare Committee served on the Select Committee to Investigate Improper Activities in the Labor and Management Field in the late 1950s.

In the 1960s the committee was the primary committee handling the package of legislation that became known as President Lyndon Johnson's War on Poverty. It considered the Economic Opportunity Act of 1964 as well as other major pieces of legislation in the health, education, and manpower areas. The LEGISLATIVE REORGANIZATION ACT OF 1970 transferred most of the committee's jurisdiction over veterans' affairs to the new Committee on Veterans' Affairs.

The committee's name changed again in 1977, becoming the Committee on Human Resources, although its jurisdiction remained unchanged. By 1979 the name was changed to the Committee on Labor and Human Resources. In 1999 Senator James Jeffords (R-VT) announced that the committee's name would be the Committee on Health, Education, Labor, and Pensions, with the abbreviation HELP. The senator indicated that the name change, without a change in jurisdiction, would highlight the "committee's role in dealing with those quality-of-life issues that people face."

The Health, Education, Labor, and Pensions Committee was one of 16 standing committees in the Senate during the 108th Congress. With 21 members (11 Republicans and 10 Democrats), it was a moderate-sized committee. It had four subcommittees: the Subcommittee on Aging; the Subcommittee on Children and Families; the Subcommittee on Employment, Safety, and Training; and the Subcommittee on Substance Abuse and Mental Health Services.

Further reading:
Fenno, Richard F. *The Making of a Senator: Dan Quayle.* Washington, D.C.: Congressional Quarterly Press, 1989;

U.S. Senate. *Committee on Labor and Human Resources, History of the Committee on Labor and Human Resources, United States Senate, 1869–1979.* Senate Document 96-71. Washington, D.C.: Government Printing Office, 1981; *United States Senate Committee on Labor and Human Resources Report on Legislative Activities of the Committee on Labor and Human Resources.* Senate Report 105-5. Washington, D.C.: Government Printing Office, 1997.

—John David Rausch, Jr.

hearings

Hearings are the method by which congressional committees collect and analyze information in the early stages of the legislative process. Committees and subcommittees in the HOUSE OF REPRESENTATIVES and in the SENATE hold hearings to collect and analyze information to be used by the committee or subcommittee. The decision to hold hearings is made by committee or subcommittee chairs. The chair determines the schedule for any hearing. Committee hearings serve an important purpose as a way for members to learn about a policy problem or issue. Witnesses from the executive branch, other members of Congress, interest group representatives, academic experts, and regular citizens appear before a committee to provide their insights into the merits or problems of a particular piece of legislation.

Committee hearings can be held in one of five different formats: traditional, panel, joint, field, and high-tech. In the traditional hearing witnesses usually read or summarize their prepared statements while a few committee members listen. When the formal testimony is completed, each committee member is allowed to ask the witness questions. House rules allow at least five minutes per committee member to question witnesses. Senate rules permit each committee to establish its rules governing committee procedures. In a panel hearing two or more witnesses of similar or different opinions sit at a table in front of committee members. Committees use this format to either dramatize a problem or speed the hearing process. Joint hearings are sessions scheduled with other committees or even committees from the other chamber. Field hearings are held at sites away from CAPITOL HILL. Congressional committees and subcommittees increasingly use high-tech and interactive hearings during which witnesses can testify before committees using videoconferencing technology.

There are four basic types of congressional committee hearings: legislative, oversight, investigative, and confirmation. Legislative hearings are the most common type and the ones with which most C-SPAN viewers are familiar. Committees gather information about the subject matter of one or more pieces of legislation in preparation for a markup session and the eventual reporting of the bill to the full chamber. A bill does not have to be introduced and referred to a committee for the panel to hold a legislative hearing. A hearing can be held for the purposes of drafting a piece of legislation that will eventually be introduced.

Oversight hearings are one part of the process of reviewing, monitoring, and supervising the implementation of public policy. Hearings may be held because a committee is committed to reviewing ongoing programs and agencies. The committee also may hold a hearing because it believes that a program is being poorly administered. Hearings are held when a program is about to expire and needs to be reauthorized.

Investigative hearings examine allegations of wrongdoing by public officials acting in their official capacities, or private citizens whose activities may suggest the need for legislation. Investigative hearings tend to be more controversial and confrontational. Both chambers have rules that govern this type of hearing because witnesses are more likely to appear under a subpoena and are sworn to tell the truth. A major investigation sometimes requires the passage of a House or Senate resolution. This resolution will specify the procedures for holding hearings. Some investigative hearings are noted for the drama they brought to the halls of Congress. These investigations include the Teapot Dome inquiry in 1923, the Senate Watergate hearings of 1973 and 1974, the IRAN-CONTRA SCANDAL INVESTIGATION in 1987, the 2000 Firestone and Ford hearings into whether vehicle crashes were caused by defective tires, and the 2003 joint hearings into the disintegration of the space shuttle *Columbia* as it was returning to Earth.

Confirmation hearings are held by Senate committees to consider the president's nominations to executive and judicial positions. Article II of the Constitution provides the president with the power to nominate certain government officials with the "advise and consent" of the Senate. While Senate Rule XXXI establishes the procedures for handling presidential nominations, it does not indicate how confirmation hearings are to be held. Senate committees are not required to hold confirmation hearings. Most nominations, such as for military promotions, go directly to the Senate floor for approval. Hearings are commonly held for cabinet nominations and for appointments to the federal judiciary. Among the most controversial hearings held in the Senate, and those that attract the most public attention, are JUDICIARY COMMITTEE hearings to confirm nominees for seats on the U.S. Supreme Court.

Further reading:
Aberbach, Joel D. *Keeping a Watchful Eye: The Politics of Congressional Oversight.* Washington, D.C.: Brookings Institution Press, 1990; Mackenzie, G. Calvin, *The Politics of Presidential Appointments.* New York: Free Press, 1981; Oleszek, Walter J. *Congressional Procedures and the Policy*

Process. 6th ed. Washington, D.C.: Congressional Quarterly Press, 2004.

—John David Rausch, Jr.

Heart of Atlanta Motel, Inc. v. U.S., **379 U.S. 241** (1964) **and** *Katzenbach v. McClung,* **379 U.S. 294** (1964)

In these cases the U.S. Supreme Court sustained the landmark CIVIL RIGHTS ACT OF 1964, thereby affirming the power of Congress to ban discrimination by private as well as public actors and further expanding the scope of the Commerce Clause as a source of Congress's regulatory authority. The Civil Rights Act, also referred to as the Public Accommodations Act, was passed over the vehement opposition of southern Democrats in the Senate only after being subject to an 82-day filibuster. Once the act finally cleared the Senate and was signed by President Lyndon Johnson, it was immediately challenged as an unconstitutional exercise of national power. The plaintiffs, a large motel in Atlanta and a family-owned neighborhood restaurant in Birmingham, had powerful precedent on their side: In 1875 Congress had passed a somewhat analogous public accommodation statute, which the Court had struck down in the Civil Rights Cases (1883) for exceeding Congress's power under the Fourteenth Amendment. The Court reasoned that the Equal Protection Clause was explicitly limited to state action, and, therefore, Congress could not reach private acts of discrimination. This time, however, Congress avoided the fate of the 1875 act by relying upon the Commerce Clause rather than Section 5 of the Fourteenth Amendment. The record before Congress documented a relationship between racial discrimination and economic hardship, most notably difficulties faced by African-American travelers in finding food and lodging, which discouraged travel and other economic activities by a large segment of an increasingly mobile population.

The Heart of Atlanta Motel's arguments were easily rejected by the Court, largely on the factual record that demonstrated that the hotel solicited, indeed catered to, interstate travelers. In addition, Justice Tom Clark's opinion for a unanimous Court noted the statute carefully targeted for regulation enterprises having a direct and substantial relation to the interstate flow of goods and people; this language, of course, closely tracked the Court's approach in its post-1937 Commerce Clause decisions. In *McClung,* three justices expressed minor reservations about whether Ollie's Barbecue sufficiently affected interstate commerce, but the Court ultimately ruled unanimously that obtaining its produce from interstate sources was sufficient to invoke congressional authority. The Court's acceptance of the act under the Commerce Clause was critical to Congress's ability to bring its power to bear on the divisive issue of racial discrimination. Despite several judicial decisions prior to the act,

segregation remained firmly entrenched in the laws and private practices of the South until this act signaled the full-scale opposition of the national government. The decision also broadened the Court's acceptance of Congress's power to regulate commerce. In conference several justices expressed a preference that the act be deemed appropriate legislation under the Fourteenth Amendment, but they viewed the Commerce Clause as the path of least resistance. Prior to these cases the Court had permitted regulations of commercial activities with only a remote impact on interstate commerce, but the regulations targeted economic activity, even if the ultimate objective was to right a moral wrong. For example, in *U.S. V. DARBY LUMBER CO.* (1941) the Court upheld a ban on interstate trade in goods manufactured by employees receiving less than a minimum wage; although the object of the law was to enforce a minimum wage, the law itself banned a commercial activity. Here, the law regulated arguably noncommercial behavior—discrimination. The Court had no problem taking this further step as long as Congress was able to show a rational basis for finding that racial discrimination had an effect on commerce and that the means for eliminating the discrimination were reasonable.

The expansive reading of the Commerce Clause espoused by the Court in *Heart of Atlanta* and *McClung,* premised upon deference to Congress's fact-finding duties and abilities, was unchallenged until 1995, when in *Lopez v. U.S.* the Rehnquist Court signaled that it would no longer uphold regulations whose connection to commerce appeared too attenuated, nor would it defer to Congress in determining whether a sufficient nexus exists.

Further reading:
The Civil Rights Cases, 109 U.S. 3 (1883); *U.S. v. Darby Lumber Co.,* 312 U.S. 100 (1941); *United States v. Lopez,* 514 U.S. 549 (1995); Dickson, Del, ed. *The Supreme Court In Conference (1940–1985).* Oxford: Oxford University Press, 2001; Lucas A. Powe, Jr. *The Warren Court and American Politics.* Cambridge, Mass.: Harvard University Press, 2000.

—Daniel Smith

holds

Holds are formal requests made by individual members of the SENATE to the Senate MAJORITY LEADER to delay action on pending legislative business. Not found in any Senate rule book, the Senate hold is nonetheless a significant parliamentary tool used by senators to direct the flow of legislation through the upper house of the national legislature. In an institution in which the majority can rule only when the minority agrees, the hold is the ultimate weapon to prevent tyranny of the majority. All it takes is one senator to place a hold on a piece of pending business and to refuse to release it, and the item that was pending is dead.

Originally conceived of as a method by which senators who needed more time to read a piece of legislation or consult with constituents could be granted more time, today holds are more frequently used as a method to delay consideration of a piece of legislation about which a member of the Senate has concerns. In some cases holds are used to kill a piece of legislation outright.

Because holds do not appear in the Senate's formal rules, it is difficult to know when they began. Moreover, because of their originally benign purpose of allowing senators extra time to prepare for debate, few congressional scholars thought them worthy of attention until the 1960s, when it became clear that some senators had begun to use them to extract concessions from political opponents. More recently the Senate's practice of allowing holds to be placed on legislation in secret has come under attack, since in recent years it has been revealed that hold requests are frequently made by members of the Senate staff and that sometimes the senators for whom they work do not know that it is their office that is delaying consideration of pending business.

In practice a senator who wishes to have more time to consider a piece of pending business or who wishes to place a hold on a bill or nomination for another reason will simply contact the Majority Leader and inform him or her of the desire to place a hold on the item. The Majority Leader will generally ask for an ending date for the hold, although in many cases the end date is left open because the senator placing the hold really is not certain when he or she will be ready to proceed to consideration of the legislation or nomination. Majority Leaders have discretion with regard to whether to honor the hold request, but most such requests are honored out of respect for the Senate's longstanding norms of courtesy toward and respect for each individual member of the body. Majority Leaders may have other, more practical reasons to honor holds as well; it is possible that a senator who truly does not wish to debate a piece of legislation would use other delaying tactics, such as the filibuster, to forestall consideration of the pending business if the hold were not honored.

In addition to pointing out their increased frequency, Senate staffers also note that holds can be used for different purposes. For example, some senators may legitimately want more time to consider a piece of legislation, although that scenario has grown rare. In other cases holds are used to express disagreement with a proposed public policy that would result from passage of a piece of pending legislation. Still other holds are personal; senators who wish to extract a concession from a colleague will hold up his or her legislation or a nominee for his or her home state until an agreement can be reached. In extreme cases senators will use holds to attempt to kill a piece of legislation or block a pending nomination outright; they care little about securing concessions, only about defeating the proposal at hand. In these cases, because holds are secret, there is little that the proponent(s) of the pending proposal can do to salvage it.

Over the past decade several proposals have been advanced to reform the hold procedure. Indeed, between 1998 and 2000 provisions to eliminate secret holds were twice approved by the Senate as riders to other legislation, but the provisions were removed by the House-Senate conference committees that considered the larger proposals. During the first session of the 107th Congress in 2001, Majority Leader TRENT LOTT and Minority Leader THOMAS DASCHLE encouraged senators to share their concerns about pending business with the authors of the legislation and with the committee of jurisdiction. However, there was no formal policy proposed nor a formal action taken by the Senate to change the way holds are administered.

Proposals for change are made in nearly every Congress. Most commonly these proposals include some kind of "sunshine" clause, which would end the secret nature of the Senate hold. The logic behind these proposals is the idea that if senators had to disclose the holds they placed on pending business, they would be more judicious and more sparing in their placing of holds. In April 2002 Senators Charles Grassley (R-IA) and Ron Wyden (D-OR) proposed S. Res. 244, a proposal to eliminate secret holds. The resolution stated:

> A Senator who provides notice to party leadership of his or her intention to object to proceeding to a motion or matter shall disclose the notice of objection (or hold) in the Congressional Record in a section reserved for such notices not later than 2 session days after the date of the notice.

However, the Senate adjourned in October 2002 without taking action on S. Res. 244. Until such time as holds become public or are eliminated altogether, in any given Congress many items of pending business will perish because a single senator or a handful of senators places holds on them.

Further reading:
"Statement of Senator Grassley Concerning S. Res. 244." *Congressional Record,* 2002; Washington, D.C.: Government Printing Office; Oleszek, Walter. "Proposals to Reform Holds in the Senate." *CRS Report for Congress,* Washington, D.C.: Congressional Research Service, 31 December 2002.

—Lauren Bell

House Administration, Committee on

A standing committee of the U.S. HOUSE OF REPRESENTATIVES since 1947, the Committee on House Administration publishes important books: the *Members Congressional*

Handbook, which contains the regulations for the member's representational allowance; the *Committee's Congressional Handbook,* which governs all expenditures of committee funds; the *Employee Handbook,* which sets forth the rules of conduct for employees of the House of Representatives; and the *New Member Pictorial Directory,* which presents photographs of newly elected members of the House of Representatives.

The committee was created by the LEGISLATIVE REORGANIZATION ACT OF 1946, which merged the Committees on Enrolled Bills (originally established as a joint committee in July 1789, the joint committee was dissolved in 1876 and replaced by separate committees in each house of Congress); Elections (created in 1789); On Election of the President, Vice President, and Representatives in Congress (created in 1893); Accounts (created in 1803); Printing (created in 1846); Disposition of Executive Papers (created in 1889); and Memorials (created in 1929). In addition, some functions of the Joint Committee on the Library of Congress (created in 1806) were assigned to the Committee on House Administration.

In 1975 the committee's jurisdiction was expanded to include oversight of parking facilities and campaign contributions to House candidates. In 1995 jurisdiction was added to include oversight of the Commission on Congressional Mailing Standards (known as the Franking Commission). The commission is responsible for reviewing all congressional mass mailings to ensure their compliance with mailing standards.

Under the Congressional Accountability Act of 1995, the committee was given oversight responsibilities for Congress's compliance with federal employment and labor laws. The statute was part of the House Republicans' 1994 CONTRACT WITH AMERICA, a series of proposals that the party's House conference and candidates promised would be brought to the floor in the first 100 days of a Republican-controlled House of Representatives. In recent years some members of Congress have attempted to shield themselves from lawsuits brought under this act by asserting that a clause in Article I of the Constitution protects them from being questioned about speech or debate in either House and in any other place. As of this writing (2004), no case on this matter has reached the U.S. Supreme Court.

In 2003, under its jurisdiction over services provided to the House of Representatives, the committee ordered that the cafeterias in the House buildings change the names of certain menu items. The name changes were intended to rebuke France for that nation's opposition to the American invasion of Iraq. French fries were to be known as freedom fries, while French toast would henceforth be known as freedom toast.

The committee has nine members and operates with no subcommittees. During the 108th Congress (2003–04) the committee ratio was six Republicans to three Democrats.

The committee's jurisdiction includes oversight over the LIBRARY OF CONGRESS, the Smithsonian Institution, the Franking Commission, the CONGRESSIONAL RECORD, the Inspector General, the CLERK OF THE HOUSE of Representatives, the SERGEANT AT ARMS, and the Chief Administrative Officer. The committee also has jurisdiction over House staffing, office space assignments, services to the House of Representatives (including the House restaurant, parking facilities, the House office buildings, and the House wing of the Capitol), and federal elections. Five members of the committee also serve as members of the JOINT COMMITTEE ON PRINTING, which oversees the functions of the GOVERNMENT PRINTING OFFICE and the printing procedures of the federal government.

The committee's most important legislative work has been on the conduct of federal elections. In 1993 the committee approved the National Voter Registration Act, popularly known as the Motor Voter Act. The act was intended to increase the number of eligible citizens who register to vote in elections for federal office by allowing them to register to vote when applying for a driver's license.

Following the contested presidential election of 2000, the committee supported the passage of the Help America Vote Act. The law provided funds to the states to introduce new elections technology, created an Elections Assistance Commission to assist states with the administration of elections, and mandated that states verify the identity of new voters in order to ensure the integrity of the electoral process.

The committee supported the BIPARTISAN CAMPAIGN REFORM ACT OF 2002. Popularly known as McCain-Feingold (after its two principal Senate sponsors, John McCain of Arizona and Russ Feingold of Wisconsin), the House version was sponsored by Christopher Shays of Connecticut and Marty Meehan of Massachusetts. The statute prohibited foreign contributions and soft money, unlimited political contributions made by corporations and labor union political action committees (PACs) to political party organizations. It also placed limits on independent expenditures campaign spending by third parties that are not coordinated with campaign committees. The constitutionalities of more significant provisions of the statute were subsequently upheld by the Supreme Court in 2003.

Further reading:
Nelson, Suzanne. "Johnson Takes Senators' Tack in Suit." *Roll Call* 49, no. 145 (28 June 2004): 1; U.S. Congress. House. Committee on House Administration. *Report on the Activities of the Committee on House Administration of the House of Representatives.* Washington, D.C.: Government Printing Office, published on a biennial basis.

—Jeffrey Kraus

House bank and post office scandals

The house bank and post office scandals were actually two separate but embarrassing incidents that significantly contributed to the Republican Party's capture of Congress in the 1994 elections. News of the bank scandal broke in fall 1991, while the post office incident became public in spring 1992. Two other equally shameful activities also came to light during this period: members not paying their tabs at the House restaurant and legislators having their D.C. parking tickets "fixed" by the SERGEANT AT ARMS. Though these particular events concerned the House, the Senate endured its own trials at the time, such as the KEATING FIVE episode and the accusations of sexual misconduct by Senator Robert Packwood, a Republican from Oregon. Many citizens came to believe that members abused their generous perquisites, and public approval of Congress plummeted to 22 percent as recorded in a July 1992 CBS News/NY Times poll. Republicans capitalized on these developments. Following a strategy devised by Minority Leader NEWT GINGRICH, a Republican from Georgia, the Republicans sought to nationalize the 1994 election and campaigned under the slogan "the CONTRACT WITH AMERICA," promising to clean up an institution that had become corrupt after nearly 40 years of Democratic rule. With success at the polls, Gingrich quickly instituted rule changes to end the practices that brought disfavor upon Congress.

The House bank was not a traditional, commercial institution. Rather, it was an office located off the House floor that allowed only members to open non–interest bearing checking accounts while also cashing checks for members, staff, and journalists working on CAPITOL HILL. Since the 19th century members could cash personal checks even if there were insufficient funds in their accounts. They could do so essentially without penalty. Though records indicate that congressmen abused this privilege as early as 1831, it was not flagged as a serious problem until 1988, when the General Accounting Office (GAO) issued a report strongly recommending that the House adopt rules to prevent check floating. Jack Russ, then Sergeant at Arms and the official responsible for overseeing the bank, proposed but never implemented check cashing guidelines. An audit in 1990 discovered more instances of check floating, and again the GAO called for reform. Finally, on September 18, 1991, the GAO released an audit that uncovered more than 8,000 instances of overdrawn checking accounts in a one-year period. When the story ran in the national media, the public was outraged. A bipartisan effort by Speaker THOMAS FOLEY, a Democrat from Washington, and MINORITY LEADER ROBERT MICHEL, a Republican from Illinois, to address the problem and deflect further criticism had little effect, because their plan did not disclose the identity of check floaters. Conservative freshman Republi-

cans John A. Boehner from Ohio, Scott L. Klug from Wisconsin, and Rick Santorum from Pennsylvania took to the floor demanding that the abusers be named. Under pressure that fall, leadership supported H Res. 236 that closed the bank and permitted the COMMITTEE ON STANDARDS OF OFFICIAL CONDUCT to conduct its own investigation into the matter. After some controversy within the ethics committee that necessitated Louis Stokes, a Democrat from Ohio, be replaced as chair by Matthew F. McHugh, a Democrat from New York, the committee discovered more than 12,000 overdrafts dating to 1972 but agreed to reveal only those 355 current and former members it deemed the most egregious offenders, a list that included influential lawmakers from both parties.

What began in 1991 as an investigation by the U.S. attorney's office into allegations of drug sales and embezzlement by staff at the House post office expanded to include several charges but especially that members exchanged stamps purchased with office funds for cash that they then used for personal expenses. Controversy surrounded the House post office in 1976 and again in the mid-1980s, when misuse of stamps and funds allotted for stamp purchases prompted the leadership to discontinue the legislators' ability to "cash out" office accounts for personal use and severely restricted use of stamps. It was believed that the FRANKING privilege made stamps practically unnecessary.

In May the House was made aware of the federal inquiry when the records of Joseph Kolter, a Democrat from Pennsylvania, Austin J. Murphy, a Democrat from Pennsylvania, and Dan Rostenkowski, a Democrat from Illinois and chair of the WAYS AND MEANS COMMITTEE, were subpoenaed by a grand jury. As several post office employees and supervisors pleaded guilty and cooperated with prosecutors, Republicans called for full disclosure of the charges against the three and an independent examination of the post office by the House. After much resistance Democrats agreed to permit an investigation by the House Administration Committee in February 1992. The committee's findings, released in July, revealed partisan differences. Both sides agreed on the following: 1) the office was mismanaged, with particular criticism aimed at its director, Robert V. Rota; 2) "that the patronage system caused a substantial portion of the dysfunction" leading to shoddy performance and staff catering to the needs of their political benefactors; 3) cashing out stamps was not a significant problem; and 4) the post office had illegally cashed personal checks for members. In their report Democrats played down the scandal and targeted managers as the main culprits, while Republicans blamed the Democrats for the problems, noted several "ghost employees," and highlighted the use of postal staff to assist in campaign work, a clear violation of the rules. On July 22 the matter was sent to the Committee on Standards of Official Conduct for a full and impartial review.

Closing the bank and making the post office a part of the U.S. Postal Service were among a number of structural reforms undertaken by Democrats in the aftermath of the scandals. Responsibility for the management of internal House operations was centralized in a new position, director of Non-Legislative and Financial Services, in 1992. Democrats moved to reorganize the House administration at the same time, but the Republicans instituted additional changes after the 1994 elections.

The scandals left their greatest impact on the political landscape of Capitol Hill. A number of representatives of long tenure and influence, such as Speaker Foley, were defeated, while some rising stars, such as Vin Weber, a Republican from Minnesota, resigned rather than face reelection. Rostenkowski, defeated in his 1994 primary, was convicted and served time in federal prison. And, of course, Gingrich became Speaker of the House and instituted a major restructuring and significant reforms of House administrative rules.

Further reading:
Beard, Edmuynd, and Stephen Horn. *Congressional Ethics: The View from the House.* Washington, D.C.: Brookings Institution Press, 1975; Congressional Quarterly. *Congressional Ethics: History, Facts, and Controversy.* Washington, D.C.: Congressional Quarterly Press, 1992; Dobel, J. Patrick. *Public Integrity.* Baltimore: Johns Hopkins University Press, 1999; Thompson, Dennis F. *Ethics in Congress: From Individual to Institutional Corruption.* Washington, D.C.: Brookings Institution Press, 1995.

—Thomas J. Baldino

House of Representatives
The House of Representatives, often called simply the House, is the larger of the two chambers of the U.S. Congress, the legislative branch of the federal government. Like its counterpart, the SENATE, it was established by the Constitutional Convention of 1787. The constitutional framers had deadlocked over the problem of representation in Congress. Delegates from states with large populations argued that representation should be determined by population, but those from states with smaller populations favored equal representation for every state. In the end a compromise was reached, according to which representation in the House was based on population, while each state was accorded two senators regardless of population.

The first Congress that met in 1789 originally had 59 members in the House of Representatives, which grew to 65 members by the end of that Congress. Membership of the House reached 435 in 1912, a number made permanent by law in 1929, even though the House expanded itself temporarily to 437 members after the admission of Alaska and Hawaii as states in 1959. The allocation of House seats is based on the population of each state and is apportioned and redistricted every 10 years following the decennial population census. Several of the least populated states have only one member (Alaska, Delaware, Montana, North Dakota, South Dakota, Vermont, and Wyoming), because the Constitution entitles all states to have at least one representative in the House regardless of the size of the state's population.

Members of the House (usually called representatives or congressmen and congresswomen) are elected every two years by plurality vote from single-member districts of approximately equal population created for this particular purpose. Today each member of the House represents approximately 600,000 people. The constitutional provisions regarding eligibility for membership in the House of Representatives require a minimum age of 25, U.S. citizenship for at least seven years, and residence in the state from which the representative is elected. The founding fathers intended the House to be the chamber that represents the popular will, as its members are directly elected by the people, rather than indirectly, as was originally practiced in the Senate. Standing so frequently for reelection was believed to draw representatives much closer to their constituencies and make them more sensitive to any changes in popular mood and preferences.

The two chambers are considered constitutionally equal. The House of Representatives shares with the Senate equal responsibility for lawmaking. Both chambers must concur in and adopt identical legislation in order for it to be enacted into law. Whenever an item of legislation is approved in varying forms by the Senate and the House, language differences must be negotiated and reconciled by a conference committee that includes members of both chambers. The president must then sign congressional legislation for it to become law, but a presidential veto of legislation can be overridden by a two-thirds vote in each of the two chambers.

The Constitution vests certain exclusive powers in the House of Representatives, among the most important of which is the right to originate revenue bills, a right that over the years has extended to spending bills as well. The House is thus charged with the constitutional duty of raising revenue for the U.S. government, mainly through the collection of taxes, duties, fees, and tariffs. But by custom it also originates all bills appropriating money. That is, it distributes federal revenue through legislative appropriations. The other important constitutional responsibility conferred upon the House is the right to initiate impeachment proceedings against the president (a prerogative it has used only twice in

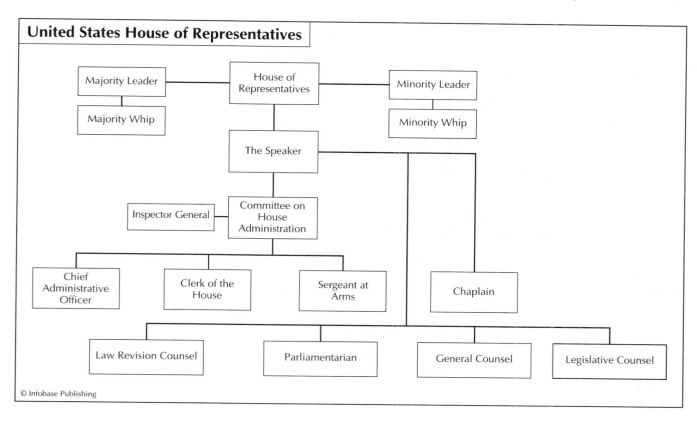

United States House of Representatives

Majority Leader — House of Representatives — Minority Leader

Majority Whip — Minority Whip

The Speaker

Inspector General — Committee on House Administration

Chief Administrative Officer — Clerk of the House — Sergeant at Arms — Chaplain

Law Revision Counsel — Parliamentarian — General Counsel — Legislative Counsel

© Infobase Publishing

its history) and other high government officials for what the Constitution describes as high crimes and misdemeanors.

The Constitution makes the Speaker the presiding officer of the House. The Speaker has always been a member of the House, even though there is actually no constitutional requirement for him or her to be a representative. The SPEAKER OF THE HOUSE presides over floor sessions and gives representatives permission to debate. The Speaker also appoints the House members of the four JOINT COMMITTEES, which consist of members of both chambers of Congress. He or she decides upon the legislative agenda in close consultation with the MAJORITY LEADER and the MINORITY LEADER, STANDING COMMITTEE chairs, and occasionally other senior members of the House. Given the numerous legislative and other duties, the Speaker is often absent from the House and has to turn over procedural responsibilities to the Speaker Pro Tempore, a representative from the majority party appointed by the Speaker to be a designated stand-in.

The Speaker is officially elected by the full House but actually has already been chosen at the meeting of the majority party (either the Democratic Caucus or the Republican Conference) that takes place in January after every congressional election. Following tradition, both parties nominate their candidate for Speaker, and then the entire membership votes for their choice on the opening day of a new Congress (the House goes out of existence every two years at the close of the old Congress). But the House election simply confirms the majority party's choice because representatives always vote for their party's candidates for leadership positions. The members of the majority party also select the Majority Leader of the House at their meeting. The candidate for Speaker chosen by the minority party becomes the Minority Leader. Each party also elects an assistant leader called a WHIP. The Majority and Minority Whips work to maintain party discipline, which includes persuading representatives of their party to support party policies. However, party discipline is not particularly strict in a chamber whose members run for reelection every two years and who tend therefore to look for support in their electoral DISTRICTS rather than from their party leadership.

Committees do most of the actual work of the House of Representatives. Almost all bills are first referred to a committee, and the House usually acts on a bill only after the committee has approved it for floor action. The committee system also plays an important role in the control exercised by Congress over the executive branch of government. Departmental secretaries, heads of government agencies, and other senior executive officials are often summoned before the House committees to explain or defend current policy. For this reason and in order to avoid other conflicts of interest, the Constitution (Article I, section 6) prohibits members of Congress from holding office in the executive branch of the federal government.

Representatives from each party can serve on four types of House committees: (1) standing (permanent), (2) SELECT OR SPECIAL, (3) CONFERENCE, and (4) joint. Each committee is controlled by the majority party. Standing committees are the most important and are organized around major policy areas, each having a supportive staff, a budget, and several SUBCOMMITTEES. They hold hearings on issues of public interest, propose legislation that has not been formally introduced as a bill or resolution, and may also conduct investigations.

The House has 19 standing committees, each of which deals with a particular field of legislation: AGRICULTURE (51 members); APPROPRIATIONS (65 members); ARMED SERVICES (60 members); BUDGET (43 members); EDUCATION AND THE WORKFORCE (49 members); ENERGY AND COMMERCE (57 members); FINANCIAL SERVICES (70 members); GOVERNMENT REFORM (44 members); HOUSE ADMINISTRATION (9 members); INTERNATIONAL RELATIONS (49 members); JUDICIARY (37 members); RESOURCES (52 members); RULES (13 members); SCIENCE (47 members); SMALL BUSINESS (36 members); STANDARDS OF OFFICIAL CONDUCT (10 members); TRANSPORTATION AND INFRASTRUCTURE (75 members); VETERANS' AFFAIRS (31 members); and WAYS AND MEANS (41 members). With each standing committee divided into several subcommittees, the House normally has more than 100 subcommittees. The heads of committees and subcommittees are senior members of the majority party who are elected by a secret ballot at either the Democratic Caucus or the Republican Conference. The proportion of Republicans and Democrats on the standing committees generally tends to reflect that of each party's membership in the House. The Democratic Caucus and the Republican Conference choose the committee assignments, which are then confirmed by the entire House. But it is the Speaker who nominates the majority party's members of the important Rules Committee, which decides whether a bill will reach the entire House for consideration.

Select committees of the House, also called special committees, are usually temporary bodies formed for investigations or other special purposes, such as the Permanent Select Committee on Intelligence (20 members) and the Select Committee on Homeland Security (49 members). Conference and joint committees have members from both the House and the Senate. Conference committees resolve differences between competing versions of bills that have passed in both chambers. Joint committees handle matters of concern to both chambers of Congress: the JOINT ECO-NOMIC COMMITTEE; the JOINT COMMITTEE ON THE LIBRARY OF CONGRESS; the JOINT COMMITTEE ON PRINTING, and the Joint Committee on Taxation.

Further reading:
Currie, James T. *The United States House of Representatives.* Malabar, Fla.: R. E. Krieger, 1988; Deering, Christopher J., and Steven S. Smith. *Committees in Congress.* Washington, D.C.: Congressional Quarterly Press, 1997; Ripley, Randall B., and Grace A. Franklin. *Congress, the Bureaucracy and Public Policy.* Belmont, Calif.: Wadsworth, 1991; Sinclair, Barbara. *Legislators, Leaders, and Lawmaking: The U.S. House of Representatives in the Postreform Era.* Baltimore: Johns Hopkins University Press, 1995; Smith, Steven S. *The American Congress.* Boston: Houghton Mifflin, 1999.

—Rossen V. Vassilev

House rules and Manual

The handbook governing the rules and operations of the HOUSE OF REPRESENTATIVES is called the House Manual. Officially *The Constitution, Jefferson's Manual, and the Rules of the House of Representatives of the United States,* this publication serves as the fundamental source for parliamentary procedure used in the House of Representatives. The manual includes the Constitution of the United States, applicable provisions of Jefferson's manual, Rules of the House, provisions of law and resolutions having the force of Rules of the House, and pertinent decisions of the SPEAKER OF THE HOUSE and other presiding officers of the House and COMMITTEE OF THE WHOLE interpreting the rules and other procedural authority used in the chamber. The interpretations include citations to CONGRESSIONAL RECORD pages or the volumes of House Precedents in which the interpretations are listed in full. The manual is authorized by House resolution at the end of one Congress for printing at the beginning of the next Congress.

The preface is the first section of the House Manual. It provides information on the substantive rules changes made by the House resolution adopting the rules of the previous Congress. The next section, the table of contents, identifies rules and the page on which they appear. A table follows the table of contents. This table displays rules changes in rules numbers in order to make it easier to find rules changes after the House recodified its rules in 1999. A one-page description of the General Order of Business and the Special Order of Business follows.

The U.S. Constitution and the 27 amendments are printed in their entirety in the manual. The documents are accompanied by annotations providing the reader with additional information about how the provisions of the Constitution and the amendments have been interpreted over time.

The next section of the manual is JEFFERSON'S MANUAL. Thomas Jefferson served as vice president of the United States and President of the Senate from 1797 until 1801, when he was elected president of the United States. He wrote a manual of rules for his use during his tenure presiding over the Senate. In 1837 the House adopted a rule providing that Jefferson's Manual should govern the House in all cases in which it is applicable and in which it is not inconsistent with the standing rules and orders of the House and joint rules of the Senate and House. The portions of Jefferson's Rules that refer to Senate procedures are omitted from the House Manual.

The remainder of the volume contains the 28 Rules of the House with notes and annotations explaining precedents and interpretations. At the end of the rules, the provisions of the LEGISLATIVE REORGANIZATION ACT OF 1946 and the LEGISLATIVE REORGANIZATION ACT OF 1970 that apply to both houses are reprinted. JOINT AND SELECT COMMITTEES are listed and identified with a note that four House select committees were abolished in the 103rd Congress and a Select Committee on Homeland Security was established in the 107th Congress. House and congressional offices including the CONGRESSIONAL RESEARCH SERVICE, the CONGRESSIONAL BUDGET OFFICE, and the office of the parliamentarian, among others, are listed. The manual concludes with information on the early organizational meetings of the House held in December of an election year, congressional budget legislation, congressional disapproval provisions, and a detailed index.

Further reading:
United States House of Representatives, Constitution, Jefferson's Manual, and Rules of the House of Representatives of the United States, 108th Congress. Compiled by Charles W. Johnson. House Document 107-284. Washington, D.C.: Government Printing Office, 2003.
—John David Rausch, Jr.

House Un-American Activities Committee *See* UN-AMERICAN ACTIVITIES COMMITTEE, HOUSE.

Humphrey, Hubert (1911–1978) *Senator, Vice President*
Hubert Horatio Humphrey, Jr., longtime senator from Minnesota, is generally regarded as one of the most well known and effective legislators in the history of the American Congress. A firebrand Democratic liberal, Humphrey displayed a deep commitment to assisting those less fortunate. His record of legislative achievement is both extensive and impressive. In many ways he defined the political era in which he served.

Born on May 27, 1911, in Wallace, South Dakota, Humphrey experienced first-hand the Great Depression, which would have a great influence on his political views. After being educated in the public schools of South Dakota, he earned a pharmacy degree from the Capitol College of Pharmacy in Denver, Colorado, in 1933. For several years he made his living in his family-owned pharmacy. However, his interest in politics led him to eventually pursue a degree in political science at the University of Minnesota. Graduating in 1939, he then earned a masters degree in political science from Louisiana State University a year later.

Humphrey's early jobs were academic. He held teaching posts at Louisiana State University, the University of Minnesota, and Macalester College. The onset of World War II gave Humphrey his first government experience. He was appointed state director of war production training and reemployment and state chief of the war service program in Minnesota in 1942. In 1943 he was named assistant director of the War Manpower Commission. Humphrey lost his first bid for elective office when he ran for mayor of Minneapolis in 1943, but he won election to that office in 1945 and was reelected in 1947. With the backing of the Farmer-Labor Party, he won a seat in the U.S. SENATE in 1948, becoming the first Democrat to represent Minnesota since 1901 and the first Democrat popularly elected to the Senate from that state.

Vice President Hubert Humphrey (right) chatting with Dr. Martin Luther King, Jr., 1965 *(Library of Congress)*

Once in the Senate Humphrey combined a strong anticommunist position in foreign policy with ardent liberalism, identified by some as prairie populism. It was in the latter area that he made the greatest impact. Humphrey initiated legislation addressing a host of issues, including health insurance, school aid, and labor policy, among others. His support of the Democratic Party's 1948 civil rights plank was a prelude to his leadership on the issue, which would manifest itself in later legislation. But in the tradition-laden, go-along-to-get-along Senate, Humphrey's bold position on civil rights made him a target of conservative critics for more than a decade.

Although reelected to the Senate in 1954, Humphrey's reform agenda was largely stalled by the Republican presidential administration of Dwight Eisenhower. Yet his legislative proposals for a Peace Corps, Medicare, a Youth Conservation Corps later named the Job Corps, and the Food for Peace Program came to fruition in the 1960s.

After the election of Democrat John Kennedy to the White House in 1960 and his own reelection to the Senate that year, Humphrey was elevated to Majority Whip, a position he held until 1965. During this period Humphrey worked hard for passage of a civil rights law. Though two previous acts dealing with civil rights had been enacted, one in 1957 and one in 1960, neither had the influence or comprehensiveness to guarantee progress on equal rights for minorities. The CIVIL RIGHTS ACT OF 1964 stands as one of the major legislative accomplishments of the 20th century, and Humphrey deserves primary credit for its passage.

From the mid-1950s Humphrey was committed to the principle of nuclear disarmament. He gained much credence as a spokesman on that matter following a 1958 meeting with Soviet leader Nikita Khrushchev. After the Cuban missile crisis of 1962, Humphrey pushed for a treaty between the United States and the Soviet Union. The result of his effort was the 1963 Limited Test Ban Treaty.

Tapped as LYNDON JOHNSON's vice presidential candidate in 1964, Humphrey left the Senate for the executive branch after Johnson's landslide victory that year. He was again elected to the U.S. Senate in 1970. After his reelection in 1976 he was slowed by cancer, but he worked on a final piece of landmark legislation, the Humphrey-Hawkins Bill, which set national economic goals dealing with employment. Following his death on January 13, 1978, the bill was enacted by Congress.

For much of Humphrey's political career he chased the elusive dream of the presidency. In 1956, when Democratic nominee Adlai Stevenson allowed the party's national convention to select the vice presidential nominee, he lost out to Senator Estes Kefauver for that post. In 1960 Humphrey made his first of three bids for the presidency. He faced Senator John Kennedy, who was better looking and better financed. Kennedy defeated Humphrey in crucial primaries in Wisconsin and West Virginia amid accusations that Humphrey had avoided the draft in World War II. Of course, Kennedy went on to win the nomination and the general election for president.

When Johnson announced his refusal to seek another term as president in early 1968, Humphrey, then vice president, again sought the Democratic nomination for president. But his party was wracked by the divisive split over Vietnam War policy. Humphrey became the Democratic nominee. In the general election campaign he was challenged not only by Republican nominee Richard Nixon but by George Wallace's American Independent Party. In one of the closest elections in American history, Nixon bested Humphrey by just a half million votes out of more than 70 million votes cast. Finally, Humphrey unsuccessfully sought the Democratic nomination for president in 1972, losing to Senator George McGovern.

Humphrey's political career has been the subject of some negative commentary. For instance, he was accused of siding with the red-baiters of the McCarthy era in the early 1950s. Second, his support of deficit spending was lambasted by conservatives. Third, some scholars believe that he depended too much on Johnson for his direction and chose not to separate himself from Johnson's policies as his vice president. Finally, Humphrey was criticized for the manner by which his emotion often influenced his public discourse. Yet these points are counteracted by Humphrey's extraordinary legislative career. Upon his death in 1978, Humphrey was given the rare tribute of lying in state in the rotunda of the U.S. Capitol. In 1980 he was posthumously awarded the Presidential Medal of Freedom by President Jimmy Carter. His positive outlook and commitment to public service earned him the well-deserved nickname the "Happy Warrior."

Further reading:
Cohen, Dan. *Undefeated: The Life of Hubert H. Humphrey.* Minneapolis, Minn.: Lerner Public Group, 1978; Engelmayer, Sheldon, and Robert Wagman. *Hubert Humphrey: The Man and His Dream.* New York: Methuen, 1978; Hatfield, Mark, with Senate Historical Office. *Vice Presidents of the United States: Hubert Humphrey, 1965–1969.* Washington, D.C.: Government Printing Office, 1997; Hernon, Joseph Martin. *Profiled in Character: Hubris and Heroism in the U.S. Senate, 1789–1990.* Armonk, N.Y.: M. E. Sharpe, 1997; Solberg, Carl. *Hubert Humphrey.* New York: Borealis Books, 2003.

—Samuel B. Hoff

Hutchinson v. Proxmire, 443 U.S. 111 (1979)

Article I, Section 6, of the U.S. Constitution insulates members of Congress from civil or criminal liability for any speech or debate in either House. But what activities are included within the scope of speech or debate? This question, initially explained in *KILBOURN V. THOMPSON* (1881), was narrowed in light of expanded communicative activities by members of Congress in *GRAVEL V. U.S.* (1972) and was again clarified in the amusing case of *Hutchinson v. Proxmire.*

In 1975 Senator William Proxmire of Wisconsin created a monthly "Golden Fleece Award," a mock award media stunt designed to highlight wasteful government spending. The senator announced each award in a humorous speech on the SENATE floor followed by press releases and newsletters mailed to his constituents publicizing the award. The second Golden Fleece was given to federal agencies, including NASA, the National Science Foundation, and the U.S. Navy, for funding the research of Dr. Ronald Hutchinson, a research behavioral scientist studying animal aggression. In announcing the award Senator Proxmire belittled Dr. Hutchinson's search for an objective measure of stress and aggression in animals with statements such as "Dr. Hutchinson's studies should make the taxpayers as well as his monkeys grind their teeth. In fact, the good doctor has . . . made a monkey out of the American taxpayer."

Dr. Hutchinson sued Senator Proxmire for defamation, claiming that his professional reputation had been damaged and that he had lost actual and potential earnings as a result. The senator countered that his actions were protected by the Speech and Debate Clause of the Constitution.

In resolving the case, the Court followed its decision in *Gravel* by distinguishing between legislative and political activities. Thus, statements made on the Senate floor and read into the *CONGRESSIONAL RECORD* were deemed immune from civil action. However, the senator's press releases, newsletters, and telephone calls made in connection with the Golden Fleece Award were unprotected by the Speech and Debate Clause and therefore fair game for Hutchinson's libel action. The latter activities were neither essential to the deliberations of the Senate nor actually part of the legislative process. The Court stated that providing information to constituents and the general public regarding matters of public concern is certainly important, but mere expressions of an individual member's views outside the legislative forum are simply not entitled to immunity. The vote was 8-1, with Justice William Brennan dissenting. In his view legislators' public criticism of wasteful government expenditures should be deemed legislative acts.

Hutchinson's libel suit was ultimately settled for $10,000, and the Senate was obligated to cover Senator Proxmire's legal expenses, which amounted to nearly $125,000. Due to the public controversy over this amount (and perhaps not wanting to appear in the same light as his Golden Fleece recipients), the senator repaid much of this expense from his book royalties.

Further reading:
Dickson, Del, ed. *The Supreme Court in Conference (1940–1985).* Oxford: Oxford University Press, 2001; *Kilbourn v. Thompson,* 103 U.S. 168 (1881); *Gravel v. U.S.,* 408 U.S. 606 (1972).

I

Immigration and Naturalization Service v. Chadha 462 U.S. 919 (1983)

Immigration and Naturalization Service v. Chadha is a landmark case dealing with the separation of powers. The case is best known for declaring the LEGISLATIVE VETO unconstitutional. In a 7-2 decision the U.S. Supreme Court struck down a provision in the Immigration and Nationality Act that permitted either house of Congress to veto a deportation suspension granted by the attorney general. The legislative veto was not a new development. It first appeared during the administration of President Herbert Hoover. Congress had authorized the president to reorganize the executive branch but wanted to retain some control over the eventual outcome. As the administrative state grew in subsequent decades, the legislative veto became an increasingly popular mechanism that provided Congress with a check on the rule-making power it was delegating to the executive branch. In fact, by the time of the *Chadha* decision nearly 200 statutes contained legislative veto provisions.

The *Chadha* case finds its origins in the struggle of a foreign student to stay in the United States. Jadish Rai Chadha was born in Kenya in 1944. He was of East Indian descent. His parents were from South Africa and India. After independence from Great Britain in 1963, the Kenyan government made everyone born in Kenya who did not have Kenyan parents apply for citizenship. While trying to obtain citizenship in 1966, Chadha secured a British passport and a student visa to study in the United States. After completing his schooling Chadha began to look for work, but his visa was about to expire. He was discouraged by the British government from looking for employment in Britain and told to try to stay in the United States. Attempting to return to Kenya was also an unattractive option. By the time Chadha asked the Immigration and Naturalization Service (INS) about staying in the United States, his student visa had expired. A hearing was scheduled, and he had to show cause as to why he should not be deported. The INS court decided that Chadha would face extreme hard-

ship if deported to his place of birth or Great Britain. Consequently, his deportation was suspended.

Congress was informed of the suspension as required by law. The House of Representatives then passed a resolution nullifying the suspension of Chadha's deportation. Chadha then challenged the constitutionality of the legislative veto. The INS court refused to rule on the issue, resulting in a deportation order. Chadha appealed to the Board of Immigration Appeals, which sustained the INS court's decision. Chadha then appealed to the Ninth Circuit Court of Appeals. Since both the INS and Chadha agreed that the legislative veto was unconstitutional, the Ninth Circuit invited both the House and the Senate to submit "friends of the court" briefs. The Ninth Circuit ruled that the legislative veto was unconstitutional because it violated the principle of the separation of powers.

The case then moved on to the Supreme Court. When deciding separation of powers cases the justices tend to use one of two approaches. The first approach is more functional in perspective. It recognizes the need for checks and balances and the fact that the branches exercise interdependent powers. This approach is more flexible and allows more creative power-sharing arrangements. The second approach is formalistic and strict constructionist in nature, requiring closer adherence to the actual text of the Constitution. Both of these approaches are seen in the *Chadha* case.

The majority opinion written by Chief Justice Warren Burger used the formalistic approach. Burger argued that the legislative veto violated two requirements of the Constitution. First, Article I, Section 7, requires that bills be passed by the House of Representatives and the Senate. This is the bicameral requirement. Second, all bills must then be presented to the president before they can become law. This is the presentment requirement. Burger went on to argue that the House in effect legislated unilaterally. It altered the legal rights of Chadha when it invalidated his deportation suspension. Any law altering Chadha's rights should have been passed by both houses and then presented to the president for signature. Congress had delegated to the executive branch the discretion to determine who could stay in the United States. It could not alter the exercise of that discretion through the use of a legislative veto.

Justice Byron White's dissent took the functional approach to analyzing separation of powers claims. White argued that the legislative veto adhered to the spirit of the Constitution, if not the letter. The attorney general had the discretion to suspend the deportation of an otherwise deportable alien. This suspension did not grant the alien permanent residence status. A permanent change in the alien's status required the agreement of both houses and the executive branch. If both houses passed a private bill and the president signed it, the status of the alien could be changed. The legislative veto in effect reversed the order. The executive branch moved first and then waited for Congress to act. If neither house acted, their silence indicated agreement with the executive's action and the alien's status was changed. If either house disagreed, it could pass a resolution of disapproval, the alien's status would not change, and the suspension would be lifted. White argued that these two methods of changing an alien's status are functionally equivalent. In both cases an alien's status could not be changed without the agreement of the House, the Senate, and the executive branch.

White also made a well-reasoned argument for the necessity of the legislative veto in a modern administrative state. Congress frequently passes legislation with broad language and instructs executive and independent agencies to fill in the details. The legislative veto allowed Congress to retain some control over this delegated power. White stated that Congress was left with a "Hobson's Choice" without the legislative veto. Congress has to either completely abdicate its rule-making power to the executive branch and independent agencies or attempt the impossible by writing laws capable of dealing with every possible exigency.

The decision did not prove to be as catastrophic for Congress as some may have predicted. The executive branch and Congress have used informal methods that retain some of the benefits of the legislative veto. More recently Congress has passed the Congressional Review Act of 1996. This act requires agencies to submit regulations for congressional review. Congress has 60 days to review the proposed regulations. If Congress passes a joint resolution within 60 days and the president signs it, the regulations do not go into effect. The president can veto the resolution that can then be overridden by a two-thirds vote in both houses. Therefore, agencies can promulgate regulations that a majority in Congress do not support. The Congressional Review Act was first successfully used in 2001 to repeal ergonomic rules adopted by the Occupational Safety and Health Administration.

See also COURTS AND CONGRESS.

Further reading:
Barron, Jerome A., and C. T. Dienes. *Constitutional Law: In a Nutshell.* St. Paul, Minn.: West Group, 1999; Foster, James C., and Susan M. Leeson. *Constitutional Law: Federal Governmental Powers and Federalism.* Upper Saddle River, N.J.: Prentice Hall, 1998; Hall, Kermit L., ed. *The Oxford Companion to the Supreme Court of the United States.* New York: Oxford University Press, 1992; *Immigration and Naturalization Service v. Chadha,* 462 U.S. 919 (1983); Mason, Alpheus T., and Donald G. Stephenson, Jr. *American Constitutional Law: Introductory Essays and Selected Cases.* Upper Saddle River, N.J.: Prentice Hall, 2002.

—Barry N. Sweet

immunity, congressional

Constitutional protection from lawsuits and criminal charges that may result from the performance of legislative duties has been termed congressional immunity. Congressional immunity is provided by the Speech and Debate Clause in the U.S. Constitution. The framers of the Constitution wanted to guarantee the independence of the legislative branch, and they believed that congressional immunity would achieve this goal. Congress was to be free from executive and judicial scrutiny inappropriate under the separation of powers. The Speech and Debate Clause states that members of the HOUSE OF REPRESENTATIVES and SENATE

> shall in all Cases, except Treason, Felony and Breach of Peace, be privileged from Arrest during their Attendance at the Session of their respective Houses, and in going to and returning from the same; and for any Speech or Debate in either House, they shall not be questioned in any other Place.

Despite the definitive statement in the Constitution, there have been questions about limitations on congressional immunity. Members of Congress appear to have immunity from being arrested while in the capital or conducting congressional work. The courts have decided that the immunity only applies to arrests in civil, not criminal, matters. Members of Congress remain subject to criminal and civil charges for actions taken outside of Congress. Behavior within Congress is monitored by the other members of Congress, who may discipline colleagues for unethical behavior.

Court rulings on the subject of congressional immunity have not been definitive. There is a fine line between legislative and nonlegislative actions. A member of Congress can be protected from legal action concerning a floor speech but not immune from charges related to circulating a printed copy of the same speech. Judicial decisions have often been inconsistent.

The federal courts have established limits on congressional immunity. In HUTCHINSON V. PROXMIRE the Supreme Court ruled that immunity covered only Wisconsin senator William Proxmire's comments on the floor of the Senate, not a press release or newsletter. In August 2004 a federal district judge ruled that the Constitution does not automatically provide members of Congress immunity from employment discrimination suits brought by senior legislative aides.

Members of Congress have rejected a claim of congressional immunity, even when it was offered them by legal authorities. In May 1999 West Virginia senator ROBERT BYRD was driving to West Virginia on a Friday afternoon when he hit the rear bumper of a van that had stopped in traffic. He initially was charged with failing to keep proper control of his car and given a ticket by a police officer on the scene. Later police commanders and the local district attorney decided that the ticket was void because of congressional immunity established by the Constitution. Several days after the incident Senator Byrd called the police and asked that the ticket be reinstated. He was not actually on Senate business when the accident occurred. He pleaded "no contest" in Fairfax County, Virginia, traffic court and was assessed $30 in court costs.

Further reading:
Jackman, Tom. "Sen. Byrd Has His Day in Traffic Court." *Washington Post*, 20 July 1999, p. B1; Nelson, Suzanne. "Judge Rejects 'Speech or Debate' *CAA Defense.*" *Roll Call* (31 August 2004). Available online by subscription. URL: http://www.rollcall.com/issues/50_20/news/6573-1.html. Accessed 8 February 2006.

—John David Rausch, Jr.

impeachment of President Andrew Johnson

In 1868 in the wake of the conclusion of the upheaval of the Civil War, Congress for the first time in history impeached a president of the United States. The HOUSE OF REPRESENTATIVES voted out 11 articles of impeachment against President Andrew Johnson. The articles were immediately forwarded to the SENATE for a subsequent trial and final votes on each charge.

The impeachment effort culminated a lengthy and intense power struggle between radical Republicans in Congress and the president over the nature of Reconstruction of the defeated southern states following the end of the Civil War. Radical Republicans wanted to punish southern states for seceding from the Union, while first President Abraham

Lincoln and then President Johnson wanted reconciliation and healing of differences between the two sides. The congressional Republican campaign against the president intervening in their efforts to punish southern states began the year before the end of the war. They vocally rejected President Lincoln's liberal plan to readmit states when at least 10 percent of their electorate took loyalty oaths to the Union.

A key event in this power struggle between branches occurred in 1867, when Congress passed the Tenure in Office Act. This law prohibited the president from removing from office all civil officials, including members of the president's own cabinet. A confrontation between the Radical Republicans and the president was assured when later that year Johnson fired his secretary of War, Edward Stanton. Congress immediately responded by beginning impeachment proceedings in the House.

On February 24, 1868, the House voted to impeach the president. The next month members began voting out a series of articles of impeachment. Representatives subsequently wrote 11 articles of impeachment against the president, with nine charges focusing on the president's dismissal of Stanton, an article consisting of a confusing collection of statements taken from speeches Johnson had

George T. Brown, Sergeant at Arms of the House of Representatives, serving the impeachment summons to President Andrew Johnson in the White House; illustration in *Harper's Weekly,* March 28, 1868 *(Library of Congress)*

delivered in 1866, and a final charge chastising him for resisting Congress.

The subsequent trial and vote in the Senate was as tense as it was dramatic. Eight Republican representatives were selected to argue for conviction, while five members, three Republicans and two Democrats, were named defense counsel. Haggling over procedures delayed the start of the trial five weeks. The trial itself also moved slowly, continuing to the end of May, when the Senate voted first on the vague 11th article. The Senate acquitted the president when the vote fell one short of the two-thirds majority the Constitution requires for conviction. All Senate Democrats voted for acquittal. They were joined by seven Republicans who braved intense political pressure and threats to end their political careers.

Following a lengthy recess so that Republicans could attend their national convention, the Senate resumed deliberations. Then, in separate votes senators subsequently defeated two additional articles of impeachment on votes identical to their previous tally on the 11th article. Not long afterward anti-Johnson forces abandoned their efforts to remove the president.

Subsequent analyses have tended to identify at least three factors that helped save the embattled president. Some senators were reluctant to replace the president with his successor, the Senate President Pro-Tem and a Radical Republican, Benjamin Wade. In addition, Johnson quietly agreed to cooperate with willing congressional Republicans on making and implementing future Reconstruction efforts. Finally, the Republican presidential nominee, U.S. Grant, was both a war hero and a moderate whose nomination acceptance speech preached a return to peace.

See also IMPEACHMENT OF PRESIDENT BILL CLINTON; IMPEACHMENT OF PRESIDENT RICHARD NIXON.

Further reading:
DeWitt, David M. *The Impeachment and Trial of Andrew Johnson.* New York: Russell & Russell, 1967; LesBenedict, Michael. *The Impeachment and Trial of Andrew Johnson.* New York: Norton, 1973.

—Robert E. Dewhirst

impeachment of President Bill Clinton

The lengthy investigation and subsequent impeachment proceedings against President Bill Clinton finally ended with his acquittal on February 12, 1999. The SENATE failed to produce a majority of votes for either of two articles of impeachment, far short of the two-thirds majority the Constitution requires for conviction.

Kenneth Starr, an independent counsel appointed to investigate numerous allegations against the president, on September 9, 1998, presented a report of his findings to the

HOUSE OF REPRESENTATIVES. The report contained numerous details about the president's sexual encounters with a White House intern. While less sensational but much more ominous, Starr's report suggested that the president could have committed two impeachable offenses, perjury and obstruction of justice. On October 8 the House voted to begin an impeachment inquiry into the allegations made in the Starr report.

The HOUSE JUDICIARY COMMITTEE began holding hearings the following month. The public sessions featured extensive partisan bickering and numerous exchanges of allegations. The committee produced a written list of 81 questions for the president to answer under oath. In December the committee held another group of hearings and concluded their deliberations by submitting four articles of impeachment to the full House. Two of the articles focused on perjury allegations, another article alleged obstruction of justice, and the final article charged the president with abusing his power.

Throughout much of this time, extensive debate, both on Capitol Hill and throughout the news media, surrounded proposals to censure rather than impeach the president. House Republican leaders firmly rejected efforts even for a floor vote on censure, opting instead to proceed with the impeachment process.

On December 19, 1998, the full House approved two of the four articles of impeachment presented by the Judiciary Committee. The House, without the support of the Democratic minority, approved a charge of presidential perjury before a grand jury and obstruction of justice. The House rejected the other two proposed articles, a second perjury charge and abuse of power.

The Senate began its trial the following January 14. The House prosecution team took three days to present its case against the president. This was followed by three days of arguments from the president's defense team. The effort to censure the president interrupted impeachment deliberations. On February 12 the Senate passed a censure motion, 56-43, but short of the two-thirds majority needed to suspend Senate impeachment trials.

Later that day the Senate also failed to produce the 67 votes needed to convict the president on either article of impeachment. The article alleging perjury failed on a 45-55 vote, and the obstruction of justice article failed on a 50-50 vote. All 45 Senate Democrats voted "not guilty" on each article. A total of 10 Republicans voted "not guilty" on the first article, and five voted "not guilty" on the second article.

The lengthy and unsuccessful effort to oust the president reflected the deep partisan divisions rampant throughout American politics in general and on Capitol Hill in particular. Republicans were adamant about removing the president, while Democrats were equally forceful in wanting to retain him in office. Meanwhile, public opinion clearly sided with the Democrats; President Clinton's public approval ratings climbed steadily throughout the impeachment effort. However, his presidency would be forever tainted by the embarrassing personal revelations that fueled the impeachment effort.

Further reading:
Baker, Peter. *The Breach: Inside the Impeachment and Trial of William Jefferson Clinton.* New York: Scribner, 2000; Posner, Richard. *An Affair of State: The Investigation, Impeachment and Trial of President Clinton.* Cambridge, Mass.: Harvard University Press, 1999; Rozell, Mark, and Clyde Wilcox. *The Clinton Scandal and the Future of American Government.* Washington, D.C.: Georgetown University Press, 2000.

impeachment of President Richard Nixon

On August 9, 1974, Richard Nixon resigned from the presidency in response to his widely anticipated removal from office through the congressional impeachment process. Although he was never found guilty or even impeached, Nixon became the only president in American history to be forced to leave office before the end of his term.

In late July 1974 the HOUSE JUDICIARY COMMITTEE voted out five articles of impeachment against President Nixon in response to numerous charges stemming from the WATERGATE SCANDAL. The Judiciary Committee, working nonstop from January 1974, gathered evidence into the summer months, when it held often dramatic televised hearings. Its work included listening to numerous hours of taped conversations the president had with his aides and others plus closely interviewing nine witnesses. On July 24 committee members began six days of debating proposed impeachment articles.

Within a few weeks the committee had voted three articles of impeachment out to the full HOUSE OF REPRESENTATIVES. During the votes the impeachment articles gathered a limited but crucial amount of bipartisan support among committee members. A majority of committee Democrats approved all charges, while a majority of panel Republicans opposed each proposal. However, throughout this time a group of seven representatives, four Republicans and three southern Democrats, proved to be a key bloc in the proceedings. By remaining cohesive this group held the balance of power on committee impeachment votes. Hence, during committee debates bloc members succeeded in having the committee drop some proposed articles and either helped write or wrote themselves articles to present to the committee.

The five articles of impeachment the Judiciary Committee debated for nearly a week and considered reporting for a vote of the full chamber were as follows: Article one charged the president with obstruction of justice by personally orchestrating efforts to hinder the investigation of the Watergate scandal. For example, the committee charged Nixon with bribing witnesses, suborning perjury, and pressuring the Federal Bureau of Investigation to drop its investigation. The House Judiciary Committee approved this article by a 27-11 vote.

Article two focused on allegations that the president illegally sought to stifle opponents of America's presence in the Vietnam War. The article included charges that Nixon directed the Internal Revenue Service to audit tax returns of his political opponents and have subordinates establish a plumbers unit to spy on critics. The House Judiciary Committee approved this article by a 28-10 vote.

Article three charged the president with contempt of Congress for not complying with all of the subpoenas submitted to him by the House Judiciary Committee. The article particularly focused on the incomplete and misleading written transcripts of audio tapes of conversations he had held with subordinates. He refused to turn over to Congress the tapes themselves until he was compelled to do so by a Supreme Court ruling. The House Judiciary Committee approved this article by a 21-17 vote.

Article four concerned Nixon's handling of the Vietnam War. It accused the president of misuse of his commander in chief powers by directing and then covering up the 1969 bombing and 1970 invasion of a legally neutral nation, Cambodia. This was the only article to address the Vietnam War issues that had divided the nation for so long. It also was the first of two articles to be rejected by the committee, on a 12-26 vote in which nine Democrats joined the entire panel's Republicans in voting against the proposal.

Article five dealt with allegations that the president sought financial gain by evading paying income taxes and having the government illegally finance improvements to his homes in Florida and California. The House Judiciary Committee defeated this article on a 12-26 vote as each member voted identical to his position on the previous article.

Nixon's fate essentially was sealed on August 5, when he reluctantly obeyed a July 24 unanimous Supreme Court ruling to turn over to the special prosecutor tapes of conversations he had had with his staff. The tapes revealed that the president indeed had nurtured and helped plan the cover-up of the Watergate burglary.

Nixon resigned the presidency on August 9, 1974, before the House of Representatives could begin deliberating the three articles. His resignation followed a steady erosion of his support among both fellow Republicans in the House and Senate and in public opinion, when fewer than 30 percent of citizens polled reportedly favored his remaining in office. While a growing majority of Democrats called for Nixon's removal, Republicans also were increasingly abandoning the president. Some Republicans reportedly were appalled by mounting evidence of his behavior, while others viewed his remaining in office as a growing liability to their future electoral fortunes.

In sum, although the Senate was never given the opportunity to hear the case of the impeachment of President Richard Nixon, the constitutional process of impeachment essentially was the legal mechanism that ultimately compelled his resignation from office. Finally, on September 8, 1974, after his staff consistently denied that he was considering taking such action, President Gerald R. Ford pardoned Richard Nixon of any possible criminal charges against him stemming from the Watergate crisis.

Further reading:
Bernstein, Carl, and Bob Woodward. *All the President's Men.* New York: Simon & Schuster, 1974; Kutler, Stanley I. *Watergate: The Fall of Richard Nixon.* St. James, N.Y.: Brandywine Press, 1996; White, Theodore H. *Breach of Faith: The Fall of Richard Nixon,* New York: Atheneum; *United States v. Nixon,* 418 U.S. 683 (1974).

—Robert E. Dewhirst

impeachment powers and process

The founding fathers originally considered the issue of impeachment, defined as a proceeding in which accusations are brought by a legislative body against government officials, during the Constitutional Convention. In Federalist 65 Alexander Hamilton described impeachment as a process designed "as a method of national inquest into the conduct of public men." The response was to make impeachment a difficult process as well as a process developed to guard against the intrusion of Congress into the political activities of the judicial and executive branches. Impeachment was to be used only for legal reasons and never for political reasons.

In the United States the power to impeach resides in the House of Representatives, and the power to try an impeachment is with the Senate. The Constitution sets the general principles that control the procedural aspects of impeachment. Article I, Section 2, provides that the House of Representatives

"shall have the sole Power of Impeachment."

Article I, Section 3, states that

The Senate shall have the sole Power to try all Impeachments. When the President of the United States is tried, the Chief Justice shall preside; and no Person shall be convicted without Concurrence of two-thirds of the Members present.

It further states that judgment in the case of impeachment shall not extend further than removal from office and disqualification to hold future office. Article II, section 2, specifies that "The President . . . shall have Power to grant Reprieves and Pardons for offenses against the United States, except in cases of Impeachment." Both the House and Senate have adopted procedures to implement these constitutional principles.

Impeachment proceedings must initially commence in the House, and several procedures are available for bringing the initial charges. A member of Congress may bring charges by presenting a list of offenses while under oath or may deposit a resolution of impeachment in the hopper. Persons outside Congress may initiate actions whereby the judicial branch recommends that the House may wish to commence proceedings against a federal judge or when an independent counsel advises the House that it has evidence of impeachable offenses. Likewise, the president may send a message to the House initiating impeachment proceedings.

The most common type of impeachable offense occurs when charges are brought against someone within the category of impeachable officers under Article II, Section 4, of the U.S. Constitution. This includes the president, vice president, and all civil officers of the United States. The charges are generally referred to the HOUSE JUDICIARY COMMITTEE, though they can be referred to other committees as well. The Judiciary Committee normally refers such charges to one of its subcommittees to conduct an investigation.

The focus of the investigation is to determine if the person involved has engaged in an impeachable offense, defined as treason, bribery, or other high crimes and misdemeanors. If the committee decides there are grounds for impeachment by majority vote, a resolution citing specific acts of misconduct is reported to the full House.

The resolution is then debated on the floor of the House of Representatives. At the conclusion of the debate, the House may either vote on the articles of impeachment as a whole or vote on each charge separately. The full House may vote to impeach even if the Judiciary Committee does not recommend impeachment. A vote to impeach requires a majority vote. If the House votes to impeach, House managers who serve as prosecutors are chosen to report the matter to the Senate.

The House managers then appear before the Senate and report the charges voted on by the House. Impeachment proceedings in the Senate then commence. The Senate issues a writ of summons asking the government official under consideration to appear before the Senate to answer the charges. The respondent may appear in person or be represented by legal counsel. If the respondent does not appear, the assumption is made that the respondent is entering a "not guilty" plea. In addition, the respondent may argue that he or she is not a civil official subject to impeachment or that the charges do not fit the constitutional charges necessary for impeachment.

Once the respondent has presented his or her case or failed to appear, the Senate sets a trial date. It further issues subpoenas to compel witnesses to testify. If the president is being impeached, the chief justice of the Supreme Court presides. If other officials are being impeached, the Senate serves as both judge and jury.

During the trial the Senate operates as a court and collects evidence and testimony. If the full Senate chooses not to do this, the task can be assigned to a special committee that will then report its findings to the full Senate. The Senate may always take further testimony before the full Senate.

The House managers and counsel for the person being impeached present the opening arguments to the Senate outlining the charges and responses to the charges. Witnesses may be examined and cross-examined. House managers then get to make final closing arguments.

The Senate as a whole then meets in closed session to deliberate on the charges. Senators then move to an open session in which their votes to impeach or not are publicly recorded from the floor of the chamber. Conviction requires a two-thirds vote of all senators present. If conviction results the respondent is notified of his or her removal from office. If any single charge is voted as an impeachable offense, the remainder of the charges do not need to be considered, as the result remains the same for one conviction or many: removal from office. Lastly, the Senate may elect to vote on whether the charges are so severe as to disqualify the respondent from holding any future office. This decision requires a simple majority vote.

Further reading:
Berger, Raoul. *Impeachment: The Constitutional Problems.* Cambridge, Mass.: Harvard University Press, 1973; Brandt, Irving. *Impeachment: Trials and Errors.* New York: Knopf, 1972; Halstead, T. J. "An Overview of the Impeachment Process." *CRS Report* (October 6, 1998). Available online. URL: http://usembassy.state.gov/colombia.wwwsimpe. shtml. Accessed February 7, 2003.

—Nancy S. Lind

implied powers

Chief Justice John Marshall, in commenting on a decision by his Court, acknowledged,

> Undoubtedly, there is an imperfection in human language, which often exposes the same sentence to different constructions.

This applies as well to the continuing discussion and court cases surrounding the language of Article I, Section 8, that sets forth specific congressional powers. Clause 18 of this section,

> makes all Laws which shall be necessary and proper for carrying into Execution the foregoing Powers, and all other Powers vested by this Constitution in the Government of the United States, or any Department or Officer thereof.

This statement has often been at the center of debate of the question of the rise of authority in the administrative state. The Constitution established a system of government that divides power among the three branches. This was intended to establish checks and balance on the power base of each. But the administrative agencies of today often combine powers the Constitution separates. More importantly, agencies are not subjected to the checks that are imposed upon the three established branches. With this background some have maintained that the administrative state is unconstitutional. But as recently as 30 years ago, how could society see the rise of technology with new innovations that occur frequently? So who can fault the framers of the Constitution with not being able to foretell the enormous growth of the new nation they were creating?

In fact, supporters of the Constitution in the ratification debates of 1787–89 minimized the scope of the necessary and proper power. They maintained that the prohibitions of Article I, Section 9, which barred congressional passage of designated legislation, did not imply the authority to enact measures not specially mentioned. James Madison maintained that had the people believed the necessary and proper clause would enlarge the federal power beyond that specifically stated, the Constitution might never have been ratified.

Throughout the FEDERALIST PAPERS both Alexander Hamilton and Madison addressed the issue of the scope of national power. They were emphatic in their defense of the necessary and proper clause, explaining that the language was needed to eliminate a complete digest of laws on every subject to which the Constitution relates. Unlike legal documents such as contracts, constitutions are unique; they are specially drafted documents that allow interpreters substantial discretion. This is unavoidable, seeing as to the longevity of the document, the growth of the nation, and the absence of the original authors.

One of the first questions arising in regard to the necessary and proper clause was the congressional passage of the Bank Bill in 1791. In brief, after much discussion and a seeming reversal of sentiment by Hamilton in regard to the power of Congress, the bill was approved. The bank was established and time passed. In 1818, as the charter was being terminated, again the question arose as to the authority of Congress to create this particular action.

In *McCulloch v. Maryland*, March 7, 1819, Chief Justice John Marshall answered in the affirmative. Marshall maintained that Congress has the power to incorporate a bank, setting precedence for passing legislation legitimately furthering specified powers. Naturally, this set off a firestorm of protests from those supporting the rights of the states and for limiting the authority of the national government. However, the first challenge to the necessary and proper clause was passed.

James Wilson, a principal architect of the Constitution's scheme of representation, believed that sovereign people must transfer substantial power to representatives for government to be efficient. He recognized the possibility of inadequacies in this system but believed that the Constitution and the people themselves would monitor activities of the representatives. He believed that for government to be both efficient and effective, power must be delegated to representatives. Additionally, as issues became more complex and intertwined with other issues, the general population would have difficulty casting an informed vote.

But as time has progressed this has in turn applied to the body of legislators and their ability to address the many issues of the day. So the rise of the administrative bureaucracy has taken over some of the duties of the legislative body. This swell in the federal bureaucracy is a creation of Congress. The ebb and flow of this development has taken place over time and in the context of change within Congress and the nation itself. As Congress evolved into a more professional institution, the need for more administrative tasks developed.

During the Depression and NEW DEAL era, regulation of these agencies came to the forefront. The LEGISLATIVE REORGANIZATION ACT OF 1946 outlined the area of congressional responsibility for oversight of the administration. Another wave of reform took place after the WATERGATE SCANDAL in the early 1970s. While these reforms were done to install another checks and balances system in the government, it was also taking place during a time of struggle for power within Congress. Committees were becoming more powerful, and members sought to be part of the committees that could offer the most to their congressional constituencies.

At the same time the Supreme Court has not invalidated the existence of these many agencies and their actions. The size of the federal bureaucracy was approximately 3,000 officials at the turn of the 19th century. It now numbers in the millions. All three branches have acquiesced to this growth and change in structure over time.

Further reading:
Dodd, Lawrence C., and Richard L. Schott. *Congress and the Administrative State.* New York: Wiley, 1979; Hamilton,

Marci A. "Power, Responsibility, and Republican Democracy." *Michigan Law Review* K1313 (May 1995): 1,539–1,558; McCutchen, Peter B. "Mistakes, Precedent, and the Rise of the Administrative State: Toward a Constitutional Theory of the Second Best." *Cornell Law Review* K3.07 (November 1994): 1–42; Siegan, Bernard H. *The Supreme Court's Constitution.* New Brunswick, N.J.: Transaction Books, 1987.

—Nancy S. Lind

impoundment of funds

Impoundment is defined as the failure to use appropriated money in the legally prescribed timeframe. It is done within the budget implementation process by executive branch officials with the approval of the president through his Office of Management and Budget. Impoundments are different from rescissions, which involve not ever spending the money, because impoundments are eventually spent; they are simply deferred. Still, if a fiscal year's budget has a section of a functional budget that is deferred for several months and not all the money appropriated is spent by the end of the fiscal year, the impoundment essentially becomes a RESCISSION. Hence, the two types of nonappropriation are related.

Congress would obviously prefer that the president and the executive branch spend the money exactly as outlined in law. After all, appropriations bills are enacted via congressional passage and presidential signature. That is, they reflect a contract or deal of sorts. However, a couple of things warrant some flexibility for presidents in their implementation of the national budget. First, it is impossible to predict what will happen when budgets are implemented; things change, such as citizens' needs and other issues that arise. Second, Congress does not typically pass laws (or budgets) with the amount of detail necessary for bureaucrats to know precisely what to do during budgetary implementation. There are always gray areas, and hence some executive branch flexibility is generally thought permissible by congressional leaders, though they certainly keep a watchful eye on the executive as budgets are implemented.

The flexibility typically afforded to presidents by Congress was seriously reconsidered and then codified in the early 1970s, when President Richard Nixon made aggressive use of both impoundments and rescissions. Nixon was using the budget-changing techniques to steer budgetary implementation outcomes closer to his policy preferences and away from congressional intent as contained in the laws and budgets as passed (and signed by the president!). This strategy made Congress angry, and both parties sought to assert their institutional prerogative on behalf of the legislative branch. Legislation was passed to overhaul the congressional budget process and to clarify what presidents can and cannot do as they implement budgets during the fiscal year. Nixon opposed the latter portion of the bill and vetoed the package. Congress passed the budget reform bill over his veto in a near unanimous vote, meaning that many of Nixon's own partisans opposed their president. This case shows how party cleavages sometimes are replaced by other power cleavages, in this case of the institutional variety.

The name of the reform was the CONGRESSIONAL BUDGET AND IMPOUNDMENT CONTROL ACT OF 1974, and it set rules for how to spend appropriated money. It clarified the two classifications of deferral and rescission. The president must submit a request to Congress for either, and Congress has 45 days to act on the request. If no action is taken, the money must be spent as directed in the appropriations package previously approved by Congress and signed by the president (e.g., per the public law).

Further reading:
Mikesell, John. *Fiscal Administration.* 5th ed. Belmont, Calif.: Wedsworth, 2003; Oleszek, Walter. *Congressional Procedures and the Policy Process.* 5th ed. Washington, D.C.: Congressional Quarterly Press, 2004; Schick, Allen. *Federal Budgeting.* Washington, D.C.: Brookings Institution Press, 2004.

—Glen S. Krutz

Indian Affairs, Senate Committee on

As presently constituted, the Senate Committee on Indian Affairs is a permanent select committee with jurisdiction over a variety of issues that affect American Indians, ranging from land management to health care to loan programs. While the designation *select* is meant to indicate that the committee's primary responsibilities are oversight and study of problems through congressional hearings for a limited time, and to distinguish it from standing committees, the fact that the committee was made permanent in 1984 and has the authority to report legislation to the Senate suggests that for all practical purposes it behaves as a standing committee. One important exception is that service on this committee does not count against the total number of committees on which a senator may serve or the leadership positions a senator may hold. This exception guarantees that senators interested in American Indian issues will not have to sacrifice service on another standing committee to take part in this one.

The Committee on Indian Affairs has the authority to consider and report all legislation pertaining to American Indians, conduct studies and investigations of problems affecting American Indians, and hold hearings on issues of concern to American Indians. In the 108th Congress (2003–05), the committee consisted of 15 members and

was chaired by Republican senator Ben Nighthorse Campbell of Colorado, a member of the Northern Cheyenne tribe and the first American Indian to chair the committee. All 15 of these senators represented western states, many of which contain Indian reservation land or a significant American Indian population.

Though an Indian Affairs committee has not been a continuous feature of the Senate, it does have a long history. From 1820 until 1946 there was an Indian Affairs Committee in the Senate. The Legislative Reform Act of 1946 eliminated this committee and placed jurisdiction over American Indian concerns first in the Senate Committee on Public Lands (80th Congress, first session) and then in the Senate Committee on Interior and Insular Affairs (80th Congress, second session through the 94th Congress). During this era Indian legislation was handled at the subcommittee level. Since senators serving on the Interior Committee often had little specific interest in Indian Affairs, the concerns of American Indians were sometimes neglected. This situation led to a period known as the "Termination Era," in which the general approach to Indian policy was to attempt to sever formal relations between Indian tribes and the federal government. Termination policy created tensions and a sense of injustice in American Indian communities, resulting in an American Indian civil rights movement beginning in the late 1960s and continuing into the next decade.

A series of notable protests in the early 1970s resulted in the reestablishment of an Indian Affairs Committee in the Senate. The most dramatic of these was the American Indian Movement's 1973 occupation of Wounded Knee—a location on the Pine Ridge reservation in South Dakota where hundreds of Indians were massacred by the U.S. Cavalry in the late 19th century. This event led to a 10-week standoff with the FBI that left several American Indian activists wounded and two dead. Both the gravity and location of this event led South Dakota Democratic senator James Abourezk to propose an American Indian Policy Review Commission. Among other findings, the commission concluded that a full committee on Indian affairs was needed. Thus, on February 4, 1977, a Select Committee on Indian Affairs was established in the Senate. Though created as a short-term solution, the committee's existence was extended several times and eventually made permanent on June 4, 1984.

Since its reestablishment this committee has been responsible for several important pieces of legislation affecting American Indians. The Indian Child Welfare Act of 1978 ensured tribal court jurisdiction over the custody and adoption of American Indian children. The 1988 Indian Gaming Regulation Act formalized a mechanism for tribes to negotiate with states to establish casinos on reservation land. In 1990 the committee secured passage of the Native American Graves Protection and Repatriation Act, a law that requires the return of many Indian remains and artifacts to the Indian nations that claim them.

Further reading:
Gross, Emma R. *Contemporary Federal Policy toward American Indians.* New York: Greenwood Press, 1989; Meyer, John M., ed. *American Indians and U.S. Politics: A Companion Reader.* Westport, Conn.: Praeger, 2002; Turner, Charles C. "American Indian Policy in Committee: Structure, Party, Ideology, and Salience." *Politics and Policy* 29 (2001); U.S. Senate Committee on Indian Affairs. "History of the Committee on Indian Affairs." Available online. URL: http://indian.senate.gov/cominfo.htm. Accessed Jaury 16, 2006.

—Charles C. Turner

intelligence oversight   *See* CONGRESSIONAL INTELLIGENCE OVERSIGHT.

International Relations, House Committee on

The primary STANDING COMMITTEE in the HOUSE OF REPRESENTATIVES that exercises broad jurisdiction over many aspects of American relations with other countries is the chamber's International Relations Committee. Included in these areas are American diplomatic relations, foreign aid programs, international conferences and organizations, and international economic and overseas trade policy.

Although the committee's jurisdiction is broad and has significant responsibilities, it traditionally has little impact on the direction of American foreign policy (with a few notable exceptions). The reason is enshrined in the Constitution, which provides the SENATE far more powers related to foreign policy than the House. Consequently, the SENATE FOREIGN RELATIONS COMMITTEE, with its exclusive power over international treaties and nominations, is far more influential than the House International Relations Committee. The International Relations Committee traditionally has used the constitutional authority conferred to the House, "the power of the purse," to influence the direction of the nation's foreign affairs. In the modern era the executive branch's increased authority related to foreign affairs and the expansion of authority by other House committees with interests in foreign policy (e.g., ARMED SERVICES COMMITTEE and the SELECT COMMITTEE ON INTELLIGENCE, etc.) have exacerbated the already substantial constitutional limits on the International Relations Committee. The International Relations Committee, while still considered one of the chamber's less prestigious committees, has gradually grown in importance as the role of the nation in global affairs increased.

The House International Relations Committee traces its lineage to preindependence America. On November 29, 1775, the Continental Congress created the Committee of Correspondence, later known as the Committee of Secret Correspondence, with Benjamin Franklin as its chair. These committees were the first institutions created to represent the soon-to-be United States in the area of foreign affairs. The Constitution of 1789, which organized Congress, conferred powers to each legislative body but left internal organization up to the individual chambers. The House originally created ad hoc committees to oversee foreign relations. In 1807, as a result of predatory actions by both the French and the British against American commercial shipping, the House created a special committee known as the Aggression Committee. Its findings led President James Madison to send a war message to Congress, thus initiating the War of 1812. A decade later the Committee on Foreign Relations was officially designated a standing committee of the House of Representatives. The committee's name did not vary for more than 150 years until it was changed in 1975 to the International Relations Committee. In 1979 the original name was restored until 1994, when the newly elected Republican majority, as part of its reorganization of the House, changed the name back to the International Relations Committee.

At the time of the CONGRESSIONAL REORGANIZATION ACT OF 1946, membership on the committee was limited to 25, a number that had not changed since 1933. The 1946 reorganization, the cold war, and a concomitant larger American presence in global affairs led to a steady increase in the size, scope, and power of the committee. During the 101st Congress (1989–90), membership grew to 44, and by the 108th Congress (2003–04) the committee had 49 members. The growth in overall size of the committee has not seen an expansion in the number of subcommittees. Committee rules restrict the number of standing subcommittees to six. Instead of creating a proliferation of new subcommittees, chairs of the International Relations Committee changed the names of existing subcommittees to reflect the evolution of foreign relations. For example, in January 2003 Chair Henry J. Hyde, a Republican from Illinois, abolished the Subcommittee on International Operations and Human Rights in order to create a new subcommittee intended to reflect the exigencies of a post–September 11 world called the Subcommittee on International Terrorism, Nonproliferation and Human Rights.

The lower prominence of the committee in the early cold war years could be seen in the quick succession of chairs. Between 1947 and 1959 the committee was presided over by six different chairs, none of whom stayed more than one term in the position. Most left the committee's obscurity for committees of greater legislative and political stature. In 1959 Thomas E. Morgan, a Democrat from Pennsylvania, took over the committee, becoming the longest-serving chair in the committee's long history. He retired from Congress and his position as chair in 1977. Morgan's tenure is remembered for President Richard Nixon's use of the committee's larger and more hawkish membership as a political counterweight to the Senate's smaller and more dovish Foreign Relations Committee during heated congressional debates regarding the Vietnam War. The next chair was Clement J. Zablocki, a Democrat from Wisconsin, who ran the committee from 1977 to 1983.

Dante B. Fascell, a Democrat from Florida, replaced Zablocki and provided a decade of strong leadership with a marked increased in the committee's influence and prestige (1983–93). Fascell is remembered for his leadership on two important issues. First, the committee's work on H.R. 1460, the Anti-Apartheid Act of 1985, which, many argue, altered the course of history in South Africa. Second, he organized a group of key Democratic House committee chairs to back House Joint Resolution 77 giving President George H. W. Bush congressional authorization for military action leading to the 1991 Persian Gulf War.

Lee H. Hamilton, a Democrat from Indiana and a well-respected foreign affairs expert, was chair during the 103rd Congress (1993–94) until the Republican revolution of 1994 took control of Congress away from the Democrats for the first time since 1955. The first Republican chair of the committee in nearly five decades was Benjamin A. Gilman, a soft-spoken moderate and one of the last remaining moderate "Rockefeller Republicans," who, although not raising the profile of the committee as had some of his predecessors, facilitated the merging of two independent foreign affairs agencies into the State Department and provided the secretary of State greater authority over the U.S. Agency for International Development. Gilman's six-year term as chair, a limit imposed as part of the Republican's 1994 reorganization of the House, ended in 2001. He was replaced by the well-respected and capable but much more conservative Henry J. Hyde, a Republican from Illinois.

Further reading:

Hinckley, Barbara. *Less Than Meets the Eye: Foreign Policy Making and the Myth of the Assertive Congress.* Chicago: University of Chicago Press, 1994; McCormick, James M. "Decision Making in the Foreign Affairs and Foreign Relations Committees." In Ripley, Randall B., and James M. Lindsey, eds. *Congress Resurgent: Foreign and Defense Policy on Capitol Hill.* Ann Arbor: University of Michigan Press, 1993.

—Craig T. Cobane

Internet and Congress

The most recent telecommunications revolution that has come to Congress is the Internet. The earliest efforts to bring Congress to the Worldwide Web began in the 103rd Congress (1993–94) under Representative Charlie Rose (D-NC), former chair of the House Administration Committee. The House Administration Committee administered the House Information System, an interactive computer system that connected House offices and a provided a now-antiquated gopher system. The gopher included party leadership and committee membership lists and selected House documents. Also in 1994 Senator Edward Kennedy (D-MA) built the first congressional Web site.

In the 104th Congress (1995–96) Republican Speaker Newt Gingrich began to create the online Congress. On January 5, 1995, Speaker Gingrich revealed the THOMAS Web site (http://thomas.loc.gov/). Named for Thomas Jefferson, THOMAS is managed by the Library of Congress. THOMAS includes numerous searchable databases, including the full text of legislation and public laws, legislation scheduled for floor debate, roll-call votes for both the House and the Senate, daily session calendars, full text of the *Congressional Record,* and various historical documents. In addition, THOMAS includes links to committee Web sites. The Library of Congress reports that THOMAS is visited hundreds of millions of times per year, and information is transferred to domain names all over the world.

Each chamber of Congress now has an institutional Web site that provides information specific to the chamber and its operations (http://www.house.gov and http://www.senate.gov). Each site is searchable and provides quick links to individual members' Web sites. They also provide information also available on THOMAS, such as information on the legislative process and current legislation. In addition, each committee has a Web site controlled by the majority party. House committee Web sites also include buttons that link to a site controlled by the minority party. Altogether, there are more than 600 official congressional Web sites controlled and maintained by various congressional offices. In addition, the House of Representatives and the Senate each have intranet sites that allow staff and members to access documents from the Library of Congress, Congressional Research Service, and General Accounting Office in addition to the resources available to the public through THOMAS.

The Congressional Management Foundation (CMF), a nonpartisan nonprofit corporation that provides technical assistance on management matters to congressional offices, has studied and evaluated congressional Web sites for the past three years. Its goal is to help offices design better, more useful Web sites. CMF studies found that Internet users want different information from congressional Web sites than from commercial Web sites. They want useful information about the member, the legislative process, and current issues; they also want easily navigable sites. Users do not want self-promotion or flashy commercial graphics. Based on these preferences, the CMF "graded" congressional Web sites in 2002 and found most of them sorely lacking. More than 90 percent received "grades" of "C" or lower; Republican Web sites earned slightly higher overall grades. By 2003, however, the CMF found that congressional Web sites had improved markedly. More than half earned grades of "A" or "B" by the CMF criteria.

The Internet has affected congressional operations in a myriad of ways. On the one hand, accessing information and conducting research for members and constituents is much easier and faster for congressional staff members. The Internet has also impacted legislative work; Congress is now confronted with many policy issues relating to the Internet. For example, Congress is considering whether and how to tax items sold via the Internet and is attempting to safeguard children from exposure to inappropriate Web sites or to sexual predators on the Internet. Since the Internet is not specifically included in the jurisdiction of any particular committee of either chamber, many committees are now grappling with Internet issues and regulations. As a result, a number of institutional rivalries have resurfaced.

Finally, the soul of the Internet is speed. One can easily download reams of information instantaneously. However, the soul of Congress is deliberation, which, if done well, is slow and cautious. Several commentators worry that the emphasis on instant information and speedy action will further jeopardize Congress's deliberative role by adding even more pressure to move quickly and to respond to public pressure.

Further reading:
Congressional Management Foundation. *Congress Online 2003: Turning the Corner on the Information Age.* Available online. URL: http://www.congressonlineproject.org/webstudy2003.html. Accessed January 17, 2006. Owen, Diana, Richard Davis, and Vincent James Strickler. "Congress and the Internet." *Harvard International Journal of Press/Politics* 4 (1999): 10–30; Thurber, James A., and Colton C. Campbell, eds. *Congress and the Internet.* Upper Saddle River, N.J.: Prentice Hall, 2003.

—Karen M. Kedrowski

investigations

Congressional investigations involve exercising congressional oversight of the executive branch through detailed examination of agency and program operations. Congress has always acted on the assumption that it has the power to conduct investigations. The framers of the Constitution realized that the legislative body had to be able to inspect the conduct of the offices of the executive branch. They also believed that both chambers had to be able to investigate their own actions and punish those members who failed to conduct themselves appropriately. The Constitution provides no express powers for Congress to conduct investigations, however.

Congress has conducted investigations of executive branch operations since the first Congress. In 1790 Robert Morris requested that the House investigate his conduct as superintendent of Finance during the Continental Congress. A three-member select committee was assigned to conduct the investigation. The Senate asked President George Washington to appoint three commissioners to investigate Morris's conduct and report back to Congress. The House committee reported on February 16, 1791. The House inquiry decided that it was necessary for Congress to acquire information in order to "do justice" to the country and its public officers.

In 1792 the House conducted an investigation of Major General Arthur St. Clair's expedition against Native Americans in the Ohio Territory. The investigation was an attempt to determine why St. Clair's force suffered such heavy losses in the action. President Washington allowed papers relating to the expedition to be furnished to the investigating committee. The committee also heard from witnesses and received a written statement from General St. Clair. While the committee cleared the general of any blame for the military disaster, it failed to publish its report because it reflected badly on the secretary of the Treasury and the secretary of War.

The topics of investigations conducted by the House of Representatives and the Senate are varied. Congress has conducted investigations on immigration, strike-breaking in the railroad industry, western land speculation, the New York Stock Exchange, the surprise attack on Pearl Harbor, communists working in the federal government, the Internal Revenue Service, the Watergate scandal in the Nixon administration, and the covert sale of weapons to Iran and the diversion of the profits to assist the Nicaraguan contra forces fighting the Sandinistas. During 1997 and 1998 various congressional committees launched investigations of alleged illegal and improper campaign fund-raising activities during the 1996 presidential election campaign. In February 2002 the Senate Select Committee on Intelligence and the House Permanent Select Committee on Intelligence agreed to conduct a joint inquiry into the activities of the U.S. intelligence community in connection with the terrorist attacks perpetrated against the United States on September 11, 2001.

Congress uses investigations for five reasons. Investigations have proven useful in gathering information to be used in drafting legislation. Investigations have been an important tool in the oversight of agencies within the executive branch. Investigations are a highly visible means by which members of Congress can inform and educate the public about important issues. Investigations have been used by both chambers to police themselves through the ethics committees or to improve internal procedures. Investigations can be used as "safety valves" allowing potentially divisive issues to be decided in the hearing rooms of Washington rather than in the streets of the country.

Congressional investigations are normally conducted by committees. In some cases special or select committees must be established to deal with investigations of special problems. For example, the Senate Select Committee on Improper Activities in the Labor or Management Field in 1959 investigated connections between organized crime and the labor unions. In 1973 the Senate Select Committee on Presidential Campaign Activities (the Senate Watergate Committee) examined the Nixon administration's attempted bugging of the Democratic Party's national headquarters and the resulting cover-up. The Legislative Reorganization Act of 1970 provided each standing committee with the power to conduct oversight activities of executive branch agencies, including investigations.

The Supreme Court has indicated that Congress has broad powers of investigation, but the powers are not without limits. In *Watkins v. United States* (1957) the Court ruled that Congress may not force testimony unless it is pursuing a legitimate legislative goal. The goal must be found within the scope of its enumerated powers. In the same opinion the Court also defined the proper outlines of a congressional investigation, stating that Congress can collect whatever information it needs to conduct oversight, expose corruption, and judge the validity of an election and whether to expel a member of Congress.

Congressional investigations also are limited by the Bill of Rights, the first 10 amendments to the U.S. Constitution. The Supreme Court has ruled that under the Bill of Rights witnesses are required to receive timely notice of their date of appearance before a committee and to know why Congress wants the information they may be able to provide. Witnesses also have the right to have their testimony recorded correctly in writing as well to have counsel present during a hearing. Witnesses cannot demand that a closed hearing be opened to the public. In *Quinn v. United States* (1955) the Court ruled that witnesses at congressional hearings may exercise their Fifth Amendment privilege against self-incrimination. Witnesses may use it to protect themselves, but not other people or organizations. Witnesses cannot refuse to answer questions if Congress has provided them with immunity from prosecution.

The first use of "use immunity" by a congressional committee was during the 1973 investigation by the Senate Select Committee on Presidential Campaign Activities, or the Watergate Committee. Use immunity prohibits prosecutors from using a witness's testimony against himself or herself, allowing the witness to testify freely to an investigating committee without fear of self-incrimination. A witness could still be convicted in court, but only using evidence collected from other sources. The committee granted use immunity to John Dean, President Richard Nixon's former White House counsel and the key witness to the Watergate cover-up.

In the 1970s private citizens and government officials tried to use the courts to block requests that they appear before congressional investigating committees. In *Eastland v. United States Servicemen's Fund* (1975) the Supreme Court ruled that a congressional committee had the right to issue a subpoena to the United States Servicemen's Fund and that the Court could not interfere in a proper legislative investigation.

One challenge faced by investigating committees is the president's use of executive privilege to keep information from Congress. In 1973 President Nixon tried to withhold from Congress and the courts a set of audiotapes recorded in the White House. The Supreme Court rejected Nixon's claim of executive privilege in *United States v. Nixon* (1974). In 1981 and 1982 President Ronald Reagan claimed executive privilege in House investigations involving Secretary of the Interior James Watt and Environmental Protection Agency Administrator Anne Gorsuch. The House was able to overcome the claim of executive privilege and get the witnesses to testify before the committees. In its investigations of the Clinton administration, the House almost had to invoke its power of CONTEMPT OF CONGRESS on two occasions. During the 1995 investigation of the 1993 firings of seven White House Travel Office employees, White House counsel Jack Quinn initially refused to release information about the firings. After the House Committee on Government Reform and Oversight voted to hold Quinn in contempt, the records were sent to the committee. In 1998 the House Government Reform and Oversight Committee voted along party lines to cite U.S. attorney general Janet Reno for contempt of Congress for refusing to release internal memos relating to the investigation of 1996 campaign finance abuses by the Clinton reelection campaign. The House adjourned before acting on the issue.

Further reading:
House Committee on the Judiciary. *Clarifying the Investigatory Power of the United States Congress.* Washington, D.C.: Government Printing Office, 1988; Nather, David. "Congress as Watchdog: Asleep on the Job?" pp. 1,190–1,195. *CQ Weekly Report,* 22 May 2004; U.S. Senate Select Committee on Intelligence and U.S. House Permanent Select Committee on Intelligence. *Joint Inquiry into Intelligence Community Activities Before and After the Ter-*

rorist Attacks of September 11, 2001. Senate Report 107-351, House Report 107-792. Washington, D.C.: Government Printing Office, 2002.

—John David Rausch, Jr.

Investigations, Senate Permanent Subcommittee on

The Senate Permanent Subcommittee on Investigations is a subcommittee of the Senate GOVERNMENTAL AFFAIRS COMMITTEE with jurisdiction to investigate the efficiency and economy of operations of all branches of the government as well as the compliance of corporations, companies, and individuals with the rules, regulations, and laws governing the various governmental agencies and their relationships with the public. Although panel members term the subcommittee permanent, there is no statutory authority for doing so.

Although a subcommittee of the Senate Governmental Affairs Committee, the Senate Permanent Subcommittee on Investigations has its own independent heritage. The Subcommittee on Investigations grew from the Senate Special Committee Investigating the National Defense Program (the Truman Committee) chaired by Senator Harry S. Truman, A Democrat from Missouri, during World War II. At its creation in 1948, the subcommittee was part of the Committee on Expenditures in the Executive Department.

Until 1957 the subcommittee's jurisdiction focused on waste, inefficiency, and illegality in government operations. The subcommittee was granted additional jurisdiction in the late 1950s and early 1960s. In 1957, using information gathered by the subcommittee, the Senate created the Select Committee on Improper Activities in the Labor or Management Field. Senator John McClellan, a Democrat from Arkansas, who also was chair of the Investigations Subcommittee, chaired the select committee. The select committee shared office space and personnel with the subcommittee. The select committee was allowed to expire in early 1960, and its jurisdiction and files were transferred to the Permanent Subcommittee on Investigations.

In 1961 the subcommittee received authority to investigate matters relating to syndicates, or organized crime. After riots and other civil disturbances in 1967, the subcommittee was directed to investigate the riots and to recommend policy actions to be taken to address the issues raised by the riots. In January 1973 the subcommittee was merged with the National Security Subcommittee. The merger gave the Permanent Subcommittee on Investigations the power to examine the adequacy of national security staffing and procedures, relations with international organizations, and technology transfer issues. The subcommittee's jurisdiction was broadened again in 1974, when in reaction to the Arab oil crisis and energy shortages the sub-committee received authority to investigate government operations involving the control and management of energy resources and supplies.

The first chair of the Subcommittee on Investigations was Senator Homer Ferguson, a Republican from Michigan. Working with his chief counsel, William P. Rogers, Ferguson continued investigating fraud and waste in U.S. government operations, the job inherited from the Truman Committee. Ferguson was succeeded by Senator Clyde Hoey, a Democrat from North Carolina. Under Hoey the subcommittee investigated the "five-percenters," Washington lobbyists who charged their clients 5 percent of the profits from any federal contracts they obtained on the clients' behalf.

In 1953 Republicans regained the majority in the Senate, and Senator Joseph McCarthy, a Republican from Wisconsin, became the chair of the subcommittee. Under McCarthy the subcommittee began a series of anticommunist investigations, including the famous Army-McCarthy hearings. Near the end of the investigation into communist activities in the U.S. Army, the parent committee examined McCarthy's attacks on the army. Because of this investigation into his methods, McCarthy stepped down as chair, and Senator Karl Mundt, a Republican from South Dakota, became the subcommittee's acting chair. The Senate censured McCarthy in 1954. The subcommittee adopted new rules protecting the rights of witnesses in 1955.

Senator McClellan became the chair of the Subcommittee on Investigations in 1955. He appointed Robert F. Kennedy the subcommittee's chief counsel. The members of the subcommittee were joined by members of the Senate Labor and Public Welfare Committee to form a special committee to investigate labor racketeering. The special committee focused much of it attention on the Teamsters Union. Union leaders Dave Beck and Jimmy Hoffa were called to testify. After the special committee had completed its work, the Subcommittee on Investigations continued an examination of organized crime. In 1962 the subcommittee held hearings during which Joseph Valachi described the activities of La Cosa Nostra, or the Mafia. Attorney General Robert F. Kennedy used the information gathered by these hearings to prosecute several prominent Mafia leaders. The hearings also resulted in the passage of the Racketeer Influenced and Corrupt Organizations (RICO) provision of the Crime Control Act of 1970.

The subcommittee continued to examine waste and inefficiency in the federal government. From 1962 until 1970 the Subcommittee on Investigations probed the effects of politics on the awarding of government contracts for the Department of Defense's TFX (tactical fighter, experimental) program. The subcommittee also investigated charges of corruption in U.S. servicemen's clubs in Vietnam and other countries.

Senator Henry ("Scoop") Jackson, a Democrat from Washington state, became chair of the subcommittee in 1973. Senator Charles Percy, a Republican from Illinois, became the ranking minority member. Under Jackson the subcommittee investigated the reasons behind the energy shortages of the mid-1970s. From 1979 until the Republicans regained the majority in the Senate in 1981, Senator Sam Nunn, a Democrat from Georgia, chaired the subcommittee. Nunn was replaced by Senator William Roth, a Republican from Delaware, who served from 1981 until 1986. The Democrats became the majority party in 1987, and Nunn became the subcommittee chair again. Roth was the chair from 1995 until 1996. The subcommittee investigated commodity investment fraud, off-shore banking schemes, money laundering, child pornography, federal drug policy, abuses in federal student aid programs, airline safety, and health care fraud.

In 1997 Senator Susan Collins, a Republican from Maine, became the first woman to chair the Subcommittee on Investigations. In June 2001 the Democrats gained control of the Senate, and Senator Carl Levin, a Democrat from Michigan, became chair. Senator Norm Coleman, a Republican from Minnesota, assumed the chair at the beginning of the 108th Congress in 2003. During the 108th Congress the Permanent Subcommittee on Investigations examined safety issues related to Internet drug sales, problems in the consumer credit counseling industry, and issues related to file-sharing and intellectual property on the Internet. In 2003 the subcommittee released papers and documents from executive sessions held during the McCarthy period in 1953 and 1954.

Further reading:
United States Senate Committee on Government Operations. Committee on Government Operations. *United States Senate: 50th Anniversary History, 1921–1971.* Senate Document 31. Washington, D.C.: Government Printing Office, 1971; United States Senate. Committee on Governmental Affairs. *Executive Sessions of the Senate Permanent Subcommittee on Investigations of the Committee on Government Operations: Index to Hearings.* Senate Print 107-84. Washington, D.C.: Government Printing Office, 2003.
—John David Rausch, Jr.

Iran-contra scandal investigation

In 1986 two secret federal government operations were publicly exposed that potentially implicated officials in the administration of President Ronald Reagan with participating in illegal activities and possibly disregarding congressional powers. The Iran-contra scandal concerned two secret Reagan administration policies coordinated by the National Security Council (NSC). The first was an Iranian

President Ronald Reagan (center) and Senator Edmund Muskie (right) listening as Senator John Tower (left) reports on his commission's investigation into the Iran-contra initiative *(Reagan Library)*

operation involved in efforts in 1985–86 to obtain the release of Americans held hostage through the sale of U.S. weapons to Iran despite a congressional embargo on such sales. The second secret program was a contra operation that involved efforts in 1984–86 to provide governmental support to military and paramilitary activities in Nicaragua despite congressional prohibition of this support. The Iran and contra operations were merged when funds generated from the sale of weapons to Iran were diverted to support the contra military efforts in Nicaragua. A "diversion memo" was written by Oliver North, a Marine lieutenant colonel assigned to the NSC staff, that detailed a scheme to skim millions of dollars from the U.S. arms sales to Iran to finance the contra rebels in violation of a congressional ban known as the Boland Amendment.

In 1984 Congress passed Boland Amendment II to further strengthen congressional opposition to U.S. support for the contras. This amendment prohibited the use of any funds "available to the Central Intelligence Agency . . . or any other agency or entity of the United States involved in intelligence activities" on behalf of the contras during fiscal year 1985. By the time this amendment was passed, the Reagan administration was embedded in efforts to sustain the contra rebels in Nicaragua.

President Reagan had been a vigorous opponent of the Sandinista regime that had seized power in Nicaragua in 1979. As a presidential candidate Reagan advocated cutting all aid to the Nicaraguan government. Once in office Reagan stepped up American activities against the Sandinistas and embraced their opponents, known as the Nicaraguan Democratic Resistance, or contras.

Congressional investigations into the matter as well as an independent counsel investigation provided a record of the military and political operations, both overt and covert, that served as the foundation for a significant American scandal. The Report of the Congressional Committee Investigating the Iran-Contra Affair noted that the president is required to conduct foreign policy "in consultation with Congress" but in this instance showed disrespect for Congress and prevented Congress from exercising its oversight role by withholding information from Congress. Despite the large amount of information from a variety of sources, by early January 1987 most central Iran-contra operatives had refused to testify, invoking their Fifth Amendment privilege against self-incrimination. This group included John Poindexter, a retired admiral and National Security Advisor to the president; North; North's secretary Fawn Hall; retired air force major general Richard V. Secord; and his business partner Albert Hakim. Others would follow this course as the investigation reached them.

As a result of these operations, Attorney General Edwin Meese III sought the appointment of an independent counsel to assist in the investigation of these activities. Lawrence Walsh was appointed independent counsel. It was clear there would be few, if any, friendly witnesses available to his investigation. The individuals most directly involved in the Iran and contra operations, North, Poindexter, Secord, and Hakim, by early 1987 had all refused to testify, invoking their Fifth Amendment protection against self-incrimination. The independent counsel viewed his mandate as a charge to determine who had committed crimes and how high up the true responsibility for those crimes went. Liaison with Congress and the White House was of highest importance during the early phases of the investigation.

Weekly meetings were held with representatives of the Select Iran/Contra Committees before central figures gave their immunized testimony. Cabinet officers and presidential advisers generally professed little knowledge of the Iran and contra activities. In investigative terms, much of the information on the Iran arms sale initiative in 1986 was laid out in official documents. The independent counsel's most pressing concern from the outset was that the House and Senate Select Committees would grant immunity to targets of the criminal investigation, compelling them to testify before Congress while guaranteeing that nothing they said could be used against them in a criminal proceeding. The law was clear that Congress controlled the political decision of whether immunity grants were justified by the importance of the hearings even though they could destroy a criminal prosecution.

During the course of the investigations, 14 persons were charged with criminal violations, including operational crimes in which money was illegally diverted to contra activities and cover-up crimes in which false statements were made to congressional committees investigating the events. All of the individuals were convicted except for one CIA official whose case was dismissed on national security grounds and several officials who received pardons from President George H. W. Bush. The cost of the investigation was more than $47 million. The investigations clearly demonstrated that high-ranking Reagan administration officials violated laws in the Iran-contra matter.

The office of independent counsel obtained further evidence that members of Reagan's cabinet as well as White House chief of staff, Donald Regan, withheld information that would have helped Congress obtain a much clearer view of the Iran-contra scandal. There was never any credible evidence presented that President Reagan himself violated any criminal statute. There was, however, evidence that the Reagan administration engaged in efforts to evade congressional oversight.

Overall, many issues emerged during the Iran-contra scandal investigations. The underlying facts are that President Reagan and some of his cabinet members committed themselves to two operations contrary to congressional policy and contrary to national policy. Despite the extraordinary difficulties imposed by the destruction and withholding of records and the congressional grants of immunity to some of the key actors, the independent counsel, at times working with congressional investigators, was able to bring criminal charges against some key government officers.

Further reading:
Arnson, Cynthia. *Crossroads: Congress, the President and Central America, 1976–1993.* University Park: Pennsylvania State University Press, 1993; Crothers, A. Lane, and Nancy S. Lind. *Presidents from Reagan through Clinton, 1981–2000.* Westport, Conn.: Greenwood Press, 2003; Draper, Theodore. *A Very Thin Line: The Iran-Contra Affairs.* New York: Hill & Wang, 1991; Kornbluh, Peter. "The Iran-Contra Scandal: A Postmortem." *World Policy Journal,* 5 (1988).

—Nancy S. Lind

iron triangles

Also known as "subgovernments" or "cozy triangles," iron triangles consist of congressional subcommittees, government agencies, and interest groups. Each side of the triangle makes its own contributions to the policymaking process in a particular issue area. Congressional subcommittees create legislation and oversee agency activities, government agencies fashion regulations and implement the laws, and interest groups represent those individuals or institutions most affected by the laws. So, for example, an iron triangle around early childhood education might involve the House and Senate subcommittees dealing with primary education, the Department of Education, and teachers associations, such as the NEA (National Education Association). Similarly, subcommittees of the Veterans' Affairs committees in the House and Senate, the Department of Veterans' Affairs, and veterans associations such as the VFW (Veterans of Foreign Wars) make up an iron triangle for veterans' issues. Agencies that have a discrete constituency, such as the Department of Veterans Affair and the Department of Agriculture, are known as "clientele agencies" and are more likely to be part of an iron triangle.

The term *subgovernment* is used to illustrate the fact that these policy groupings operate at a level that may be below the radar screen of the public (or even other parts of the government) and points to the somewhat secretive, or at least hidden, nature of their activities. The *cozy* in cozy triangles refers to the fact that the actors have a familiar relationship and are comfortable with one another. It also connotes a lack of accountability, with governmental agencies and congressional committees feeling beholden to those they are supposed to be governing. Finally, "iron" triangles are strong and unbreakable, implying imperviousness to outside influence and an unbending notion of how things should be done. The three sides of an iron triangle leave no room for other competing groups to get inside.

The complexity of issues with which Congress must contend is the underlying cause of iron triangles. Throughout most of the 20th century the U.S. government expanded its scope of operations. As a result, new governmental agencies were set up, and congressional committees and subcommittees were formed. These committees not only create the legislation that gives agencies their mandates, but they also oversee the activities of the agencies. The proliferation of committees and the concomitant decentralization of leadership in Congress led to an increasing need for subcommittees to rely on interest groups for information and in some cases to become advocates for the very groups that the subcommittees are supposed to be regulating. Fragmentation is a result, with a larger and larger number of groups entering the process, each dealing with a narrow band of issues. It logically follows that there will be a lack of coherence in overall policy making. Iron triangles are government at a micro-level: they look at the small picture of how a policy will affect a particular group of people, rather than the large picture of how policies fit into the overall goals of government. Iron triangles make policies one issue at a time, removed from other issues and concerns.

Iron triangles may be seen as a good thing, in that those people most affected by a particular set of laws are interacting with those people who make and implement the laws. Iron triangles allow various interest groups to bring their expertise to subcommittees in Congress. They also help members of Congress by providing information. Thus, as Congress considers legislation in a particular area, the executive agencies in that area can have input on the feasibility of specific provisions, and interest groups representing various constituencies can also explain in what ways the laws may benefit or harm them. Iron triangles are also a natural by-product of constitutional freedoms of association and petition, the very freedoms that promote the use of interest groups in the United States. On the negative side, the term *iron* refers to the fact that these subgroups are firm and closed. Input from other opposing interest groups and citizens themselves is limited. The democratic process is supposed to be open and fluid, rather than closed and rigid, as iron triangles imply. The term *captured* is also used to describe the government players in an iron triangle, who feel themselves beholden to a particular interest group (perhaps more so if that interest group has made sizeable campaign donations). An agency set up to regulate a particular industry, for example, may find itself sympathetic to the industry's plight, perhaps at the expense of the public good. While an iron triangle may streamline the policy-making process, there is something at least a bit unseemly about those being regulated having some control over the regulations. Some consider it akin to having the inmates running an asylum. The resultant fragmentation of policy making means that broad, overarching concerns are not often taken into consideration and that one iron triangle may be creating policies at odds with another. Iron triangles also preserve the status quo at the expense of innovation and encourage incrementalism (making changes a little bit at a time) rather than rational, comprehensive change.

The term *iron triangle* never appears in the Constitution, and it is not a concept that was consciously put into place. Rather, the term is an attempt to describe reality, but there are those who believe the term is not even an accurate description of reality, or at least not in all cases. Political scientist Hugh Heclo in his article "Issue Networks and the Executive Establishment" states that the term *iron triangle* is "not so much wrong as it is disastrously incomplete." Instead, Heclo argues that policies are made through a series of issue networks (also called "sloppy large hexagons"), which are much more fluid than iron triangles. Interest groups "flow in and out of" various issue networks, attempting to influence a broad range of policies wherever they can. For example, the National Organization of Women (NOW), concerns itself with legislation about welfare, child care, reproduction, affirmative action, and more and contends with different networks of interest groups for each issue. Children's advocates, welfare rights advocates, religious groups, and civil rights groups flow in and out of these issue networks depending on their interest in the issue involved. And each issue not only includes coalitions of interest groups in favor of a particular policy, but also coalitions that oppose it. These coalitions themselves change, with some interest groups lining up against each other on one issue (NOW and the Catholic Church on either side of the abortion debate for example) and aligning together on another (NOW and the Catholic Church on the expansion of benefits to welfare recipients). Rather than an iron triangle, Heclo contends, there is a seamless web of interest groups that interact with Congress and the executive branch.

This seamless web is made up of temporary, ad hoc coalitions formed around a particular policy problem and disbanded when that problem is resolved or becomes obsolete. Issue networks, fluid and open rather than rigid and closed, are themselves problematic. Partisan zealots may advocate for narrowly defined policy changes, the process may be unstable or unpredictable, and competing interests may serve only to complicate policy debates.

On the other hand, the concept of issue networks is compatible with democratic theory, which holds that the governmental process should be open to various interests and individuals. As such, issue networks describe what is called interest group pluralism. In a large, complex society such as the United States, citizens have little direct impact on decision making, particularly at the national level. Instead, interest groups representing the wide array of citizen interests compete with one another in the marketplace of ideas and policy making and influence federal decision makers in creating policies. The end result, or so the argument goes, is that compromises are made that reflect the overall will of the people. Like the "invisible hand" of the economic marketplace, interest group pluralism controls the ups and downs of the political marketplace.

Which describes reality, iron triangles or issue networks? Probably both. Both terms describe what is known as a "policy subsystem," another phrase to describe a group of actors who work together on a policy issue. On some issues, particularly those involving clientele agencies, some form of iron triangle probably does predominate. In those cases, there is often not a competing interest group to work in opposition. On the majority of issues, however, issue networks are probably a more apt description of reality. Although Congress has made some strides in curtailing subcommittees, and Republicans have attempted to roll back the functions of federal government, there is still quite a wide variety of issues before policy makers. It looks as if both iron triangles and issue networks are here to stay.

Further reading:
Kingdon, John W. *Agendas, Alternatives, and Public Policies.* New York: HarperCollins, 1984; Heclo, Hugh. "Issue Networks and the Executive Establishment." In Anthony King, ed. *The New Political System.* Washington, D.C.: American Enterprise Institute for Public Policy Research,

1978; Stillman, Richard. *The American Bureaucracy: The Core of Modern Government.* 2d ed. Chicago: Nelson Hall, 1996.

—Anne Marie Cammisa

Irreconcilables, the

Following his return from the Versailles Peace Conference in 1919, President Woodrow Wilson's Versailles Treaty ran into difficulty almost immediately upon its submission on July 10, 1919, to the SENATE for ratification. The Republicans had regained control of Congress in the elections of 1918 by a 49 to 47 margin after six years of Democratic control. Republican leaders were resentful over what they felt had been Wilson's politicization of World War I during the midterm campaign. Wilson's failure to invite any Republicans to accompany him to Europe as part of the American peace delegation had further antagonized key party senators, who were now eager for an opportunity to exploit some of the more controversial elements of the treaty.

Leading the Senate opposition to the treaty was Massachusetts senator HENRY CABOT LODGE, the chair of the SENATE FOREIGN RELATIONS COMMITTEE and a staunch opponent of Wilson's, eager to hand his rival an embarrassing political defeat. Although 80 of the 96 members of the Senate had expressed some degree of support for the treaty, resistance coalesced around Article X, the provision establishing the newly formed League of Nations as a collective security arrangement, in which member states would be obligated to come to the defense militarily of any member state threatened by hostile action from others states. Despite their internationalism and support for American imperialism, Lodge and his Republican allies were concerned that Article X threatened American sovereignty by usurping Congress's constitutional authority to declare war and that American soldiers might be forced into conflicts in which there were no clear American strategic or political interests. Lodge asked his colleagues "Are you willing . . . to put your soldiers and sailors at the disposition of other nations?"

Nevertheless, the concerns of Lodge and his 34 fellow Reservationists might be addressed through the adoption of certain amendments to the treaty. Others, however, including California senator HIRAM JOHNSON, Idaho senator WILLIAM BORAH, and Wisconsin senator Robert LaFollette, were unyielding and adamantly opposed to the treaty, earning them the sobriquet Irreconcilables. After several weeks of stalling tactics in the form of committee hearings, expert testimony, and debate in the summer of 1919, a Republican Senate delegation to the White House failed to convince President Wilson to compromise on any of their treaty concerns. Instead, Wilson decided to embark on a national tour to sway public opinion in favor of the treaty. In late September, however, Wilson became ill and was forced to return to Washington, where he suffered a massive stroke on October 2.

The Irreconcilables, 12 Republicans and three Democrats, were led by the committed isolationist Borah, who, despite the fact that he had never left U.S. soil, was widely regarded by his colleagues as an expert on international politics. Borah and his allies were fearful that U.S. participation in the League of Nations would inevitably lead to the country becoming entangled in the sordid political disputes and alliances of the European powers. Borah famously declared, "[I]f the Savior of men would revisit the earth and declare for a League of Nations . . . I would be opposed to it."

Following Wilson's stroke and extended convalescence, Senate Democrats found themselves without effective leadership from the White House. Concerned that the addition of amendments to the treaty might require that it be renegotiated, Lodge instead elected to report the treaty to the Senate floor with 14 reservations. The White House let it be known that, while some minor reservations might be acceptable, Wilson was unwilling to budge on Article X. On the anniversary of the armistice that had ended the war in Europe, Lodge's treaty bill was defeated in the Senate by a vote of 39-55, with Senate Democrats allying with Irreconcilables to defeat the bill; it was the first time the Senate had ever rejected a peace treaty. A subsequent vote on Wilson's original treaty, without the reservations, was voted down by a margin of 34-53, this time with the Reservationists and Irreconcilables uniting to defeat the bill.

In the face of public outrage at Lodge's tactics and what was seen as Republican obstructionism, the Senate took up the treaty once again in February 1920, this time with 15 reservations. Following weeks of contentious debate, the treaty was defeated once again on March 19 by a 49-35 vote, seven votes short of the two-thirds margin necessary for ratification. Despite Wilson's opposition to this version of the treaty, several Democrats joined with the Reservationists in the failed attempt to approve the treaty. In May, having failed to approve the peace treaty, Congress instead voted to formally end the war, although Wilson vetoed the measure.

The idealism and optimism that had surrounded U.S. entry into World War I and the subsequent Versailles Peace Conference had devolved into partisan rancor and personal vendettas. Wilson's intransigence and political missteps, perhaps intensified by his stroke in the waning months of his administration, almost certainly doomed the Versailles Treaty, although Lodge's personal bitterness toward Wilson and insistence on denying the Democrats a political victory certainly played a role. Although Wilson attempted to make the elections of 1920 a referendum on the treaty, the Republican Party's strong showing in House and Senate elections and Warren G. Harding's election as president effectively sealed its fate. In 1921 a joint resolution passed by the House and Senate formally ended the war as far as the United States was concerned, and the nation retreated once again into relative isolationism.

Further reading:
Stone, Ralph A. *The Irreconcilables: The Fight against the League of Nations.* Lexington: University Press of Kentucky, 1970; Knock, Thomas J. *To End All Wars.* Princeton, N.J.: Princeton University Press, 1995; Margulies, Herbert F. *Mild Reservationists and the League of Nations Controversy in the Senate.* Columbia: University of Missouri Press, 1989.

—William D. Baker

J

Jefferson's Manual

Thomas Jefferson, third president of the United States (1801–09), is appropriately remembered as a Renaissance man who studied music, science, geography, and philosophy while in office serving at the highest levels of government. He maintained a wide correspondence with other leaders of his time. Prior to the presidency he held local and state offices (including the governorship of Virginia) and was a member of the Continental Congress, ambassador to France, secretary of State to George Washington, and vice president under John Adams. He was the principal draftsman of the Declaration of Independence.

Being of a meticulous and orderly mind, Jefferson took seriously the major responsibilities that came to him during his tenure as vice president, namely, to preside over the Senate as its president. The Senate had a simple compilation of rules when he assumed his position in 1797. His predecessor, John Adams, had been criticized about the inconsistencies of his decisions as the Senate's first presiding officer as well as for joining in on the Senate's debates.

Jefferson searched for documentary sources about legislative procedures in the United States, but he depended most on the parliamentary practices of England, in particular precedents of proceedings in the House of Commons and debates in the House of Commons. He wrote his manual during his four years as vice president and committed himself to completing it during the last year of his term, intending it as his legacy to the Senate.

The manual is organized into 53 sections. It records the rules and practices of the Senate in italics. They are backed and supported by or distinguished from parallel considerations then observed in England's Parliament. He felt duty-bound to preside according to "a known system of rules" so as to preserve objectivity and fairness in the Senate's proceedings and debates. The rules, he intended, would serve as a check on the majority and as a protection for the minority.

Published as a manual of parliamentary practice for the Senate, it was printed by Samuel Harrison Smith in 1801. The Senate continues to reference the Senate's rules according to Jefferson's compilation. In 1834 the House of Representatives, a rowdy institution in those days, adopted a rule providing that Jefferson's Manual "shall govern the House in all cases to which they are applicable, and in which they are not inconsistent with the standing rules and orders of the House."

The manual remains a part of the published rules of the U.S. House. Jefferson's Manual became a sourcebook to various state legislatures and later to developing democracies around the world.

Further reading:
Malone, D. *Jefferson and the Ordeal of Liberty.* Boston: Little, Brown, 1962; *Jefferson's Manual.* See the *House Rules Manual.* House document 104-272. Accessible online. URL: http://www.gpo.gov.

—Jack R. Van Der Slik

Jeffords, James (1934–) *Representative, Senator*

Senator James Merrill Jeffords, an independent from Vermont, was born on May 11, 1934, to the former chief justice of the Vermont supreme court Olin and Marion Jeffords. The Jeffords family had been living in Vermont since 1794. Jeffords received his undergraduate education at Yale University and a J.D. from Harvard Law School. Jeffords also served in the navy and retired as a naval reserve captain in 1990.

Jeffords's political career began as a Republican in the Vermont state senate. He won his first statewide campaign in 1969, when he became Vermont's attorney general. In 1975 Jeffords was elected to the U.S. House of Representatives. During his time in the House Jeffords served as the ranking Republican on the House Education and Labor Committee and served on the HOUSE AGRICULTURE

COMMITTEE. In 1988 Jeffords was elected to the U.S. Senate, where he has served as chair of the Health, Education, Labor and Pensions Committee and also as the cochair of the Northeast-Midwest Senate Coalition.

On May 24, 2001, a development that had started in the 1960s came to fruition. At a news conference at the Radisson Hotel in Burlington, Vermont, Jeffords announced he was leaving the Republican Party to become an independent, thus shifting the balance of power in the Senate and cementing the liberal tendencies developing in New England over the previous 40 years. Jeffords had many personal reasons for switching parties, but none was larger than the pressure he was feeling as a representative of the people of Vermont.

While his decision had broad consequences for governing on the national level, it was a by-product of representation in Vermont and the changing nature of the state's electorate. Jeffords no longer felt that being a Republican was the best way to represent the people of Vermont.

> Increasingly, I find myself in disagreement with my party. I understand that many people are more conservative than I am, and they form the Republican party. Given the changing nature of the national party, it has become a struggle for our leaders to deal with me, and for me to deal with them.

Republican politics in Vermont has a long history of fiscal conservatism infused with moderate positions on social issues. Jeffords's record in Congress has often reflected this ideology. When he first arrived in 1975 as a member of the House of Representatives, he lived in a camper because of $40,000 in campaign debt. Yet while he may have been fiscally conservative, Jeffords continuously supported the National Endowment for the Arts and was one of the five

Republicans who voted against convicting Clinton after his impeachment trial in 1999.

By 1999 James Jeffords was becoming increasingly uncomfortable with the current trends within the Republican Party even though his family were longstanding members. At that time Jeffords went on record with his concerns over the Republicans' role in the impeachment of President Bill Clinton. By 2001 the issues were different, but his uneasiness with the party remained.

Jeffords's problems continued with the policy programs advocated by the George W. Bush White House. As a Republican, Jeffords felt that he should support his party, which had recently regained control over the White House and both Houses of Congress for the first time in more than 40 years. However, he disagreed with the scope and measure of Bush's tax cuts and had promised his constituents a plan different from the president's proposal. Jeffords campaigned on a plan that called for $2.7 trillion to be set aside for Social Security and Medicare and another $1.8 trillion that should be split three ways. The first third should be set aside for both the expected and the unexpected, the second third should be spent on national priorities such as fully funding special education and providing drug benefits under Medicare, and the final third should be given back to the taxpayers in the form of tax cuts. His stance ran counter to the president's plan, but he believed his idea made the most sense for the people of Vermont and the nation.

The event that finally convinced Jeffords that action was inevitable was the failure of the Republicans to include full funding for special education programs in the 2002 budget. Jeffords had been advocating full funding to be included within the budget, but the Republican leadership would not agree to support this issue. Considering the government had promised to fully fund special education in 1975 and had yet to do so, Jeffords felt increasingly marginalized by the party's leadership. When the budget passed without this measure in place, Jeffords realized not only that he no longer fit into the Republican ideological mold but also that the current leadership disregarded his seniority and policy expertise. The only solution was a dramatic partisan shift to realign Vermont back toward its progressive principles.

Jeffords's decision caught the White House by surprise and shifted the balance of power in the Senate to the Democrats. Jeffords's switch was dramatic because of the unprecedented party-sharing agreement created in an evenly divided Senate. However, while Jeffords's switch was significant for senatorial control, he was not the first senator within American history to change party affiliation.

Jeffords's decision to leave the Republican Party reflected the nature of politics in Vermont and the com-

JEFFORDS' JOB PERFORMANCE

	Excellent	Good	Fair	Poor	Undecided
Sept. 1992	44%	25%	13%	9%	
June 1994	14%	58%	23%	3%	2%
Sept. 1994	9%	45%	32%	10%	4%
Sept. 1996	5%	47%	27%	14%	3%
Dec. 1997	12%	44%	29%	14%	1%
Aug. 1998	18%	44%	28%	4%	6%
May 2001	39%	31%	17%	11%	1%

Mason-Dixon Polling and Research Inc. of Washington, D.C., conducted this poll on the evening of May 24, 2001. A total of 552 registered Vermont voters were interviewed statewide by telephone. The margin of error is plus or minus 4.3 percentage points.

mitment he felt to his constituents. While some believe that the White House lost his loyalty with its conservative stances, in reality other factors were pushing Jeffords away from the Republican Party and into step with the more progressive and independent ideas that already existed in Vermont. In fact, Jeffords may have become more popular in Vermont as a result of his independence. Table 1 shows the results of the *Burlington Free Press* poll that was taken the night of his announcement.

Jeffords's approval rating increased from 62 percent rating him as excellent or good in 1998 to 70 percent in 2001. While this difference is not huge, the striking numbers are his approval over time (especially in the excellent category). Jeffords received a tremendous increase in the excellent category after his announcement and enjoyed more support than at any other time in his career.

Jeffords did not come to his decision lightly. It took years of frustration with the Republican leadership over issues important to the people of Vermont for him to make his ultimate decision to leave the party of his family. Jeffords did not easily abandon Vermont's Republican Party, but he wanted to move away from the conservative viewpoints of the national leadership.

Further reading:
Alter, Jonathan. "The Odyssey of 'Jeezum Jim.'" *Newsweek*, 4 June 2001 p. 20,; "Burlington Free Press/ WPTZ Poll on Jeffords." *Burlington Free Press*, 24 May 2001 p. A1; Christensen, Mike. "Anguished Transformation from Maverick to Outcast." *CQ Weekly Report*, 26 May 2001; Fineman, Howard. "What Bush Needs to Learn." *Newsweek*, 4 June, 2001; Jeffords, James M. *My Declaration of Independence.* New York: Simon & Schuster, 2001; Killian, Linda. *The Freshmen: What Happened to the Republican Revolution?* Boulder, Colo.: Westview Press, 1998; Rudin, Ken. "The Seismic Result of Jeffords's Decision." *Washington Post*, 25 May 2001.
—Jacob R. Straus and Shannon L. Bow

Johnson, Hiram Warren (1866–1945) *Senator*
Known by his contemporaries as the "political evangelist," Hiram Johnson spent nearly 35 years in public service, first as governor of California, then as a five-term senator from that state. During that span, bracketed by both world wars, Johnson developed a national reputation as one of the country's best orators, a dedicated Progressive, and a fiery opponent of internationalism.

Johnson was born in 1866 in Sacramento, California, to Grove Johnson, whose own political career was as dubious as Hiram's would be esteemed. Pure tenacity and skill from the stump allowed the elder Johnson to serve in the

California assembly, the California senate, and the U.S. HOUSE OF REPRESENTATIVES despite repeated charges of ballot fraud (including one bizarre scheme involving disappearing ink). Hiram Johnson cut his political teeth as an assistant in his father's law firm and campaign staff. Grove's scandalous connections to the Southern Pacific Railroad led to a split between father and son, and Hiram set out on his own.

Having overcome a childhood speech impediment, Johnson dedicated his education to wide-ranging knowledge and oratorical skill and proved successful as a trial lawyer with a penchant for sharp argument and dramatic delivery. His success earned him a post as a prosecutor for the district attorney in San Francisco. It was there that Johnson began his lifelong crusade against the corruption targeted by muckrakers and Progressives through the next 20 years. His successful prosecution in 1908 of Mayor Eugene Schmitz and crime boss Abraham Reuf for graft propelled Johnson into a statewide campaign against corruption and particularly the Southern Pacific Railroad. Members of the Lincoln-Roosevelt League, a reform movement within the Republican Party, tapped Johnson as a candidate for governor in 1910. Overcoming his father's connections to the railroad, he took the vanguard of Progressivism in California to a slate of Progressive Republican victories in state elections. Over the next year the state legislature passed a host of reforms proposed and supported by Johnson, including more than 20 reform amendments to the state constitution. These changes included the initiative, the referendum, the recall, a statewide advisory vote on U.S. senator elections, ballot reform, civil service reform, conservation laws, and control of shipping rates.

These successes gained California Progressives, and particularly Hiram Johnson, national acclaim. When President William Howard Taft toured California in 1911 hoping to secure Republican support for his reelection, Progressives within the party were disappointed to find the candidate critical of radicals in the Lincoln-Roosevelt League. The reformers endorsed Theodore Roosevelt for the Republican nomination in 1912 and chose Johnson to deliver his seconding speech at the convention in Chicago. In the midst of a contentious and chaotic convention, Taft managed a solid defense of his reelection bid, and the Progressives were forced to retreat to a rump convention that would launch a third-party campaign. Hoping to lure liberal Democrats into the Progressive camp, the new party asked William Jennings Bryan to run as Roosevelt's vice president. When Bryan declined they turned to Hiram Johnson, whose speeches at the convention had been sensational. While the 1912 Progressive campaign did not return Roosevelt to the presidency, it did mount the nation's most successful third-party bid and provided a platform from which Hiram Johnson built a national reputation as an impassioned speaker for the rights of the common man.

Californians returned Johnson to the governor's seat, but his second term was less fulfilling and changed the direction of his concerns. Having secured enactment of numerous reforms, Johnson turned his attention to the question of immigration to California. With cultural exceptionalism running high among white Americans, Johnson joined the tide of anti-immigrant sentiment in California. While the popular wish was to exclude Japanese immigration (Congress had already excluded the Chinese), the state legislative goal became a ban on alien ownership of land. Arguing the cause of American nationalism, Johnson paired his Progressivism with a devotion to an antiforeign stance and unilateralism, the two becoming the twin pillars of his career in national politics.

Having found the limits of his usefulness in state politics, Hiram Johnson made a successful run in 1916 for the U.S. SENATE. Perhaps more than any other politician of his time, Johnson mastered the technique of whistle stop campaigning and stump speaking. His eloquent attacks on big business combinations, special interests, and corruption were popular, and the frugality of his strategy allowed him to refuse big contributions. Having long shed the stigma of his father's crooked politicking, Johnson was praised even by his opponents for unquestionable integrity. Biographers agree as well that his convictions were true and never intended merely to solicit popular favor. His first vote as a senator in support of American entry into World War I served as an ironic introduction to national policy making. Convinced by Wilson that the war was a righteous defense of human rights and American interests, Johnson quickly recoiled at the centralization of power that came with war mobilization. His opposition to the Espionage Act as an unnecessary violation of the First Amendment garnered substantial and sympathetic coverage from the press.

Even more frightful to the senator and many of his colleagues was the Treaty of Versailles and proposed League of Nations. By 1919 Johnson had become a dedicated foe of Wilson's interventionist foreign policy (including the ill-fated intrusion into Russia). In a remarkable political drama Wilson mounted a stump campaign across the country attempting to make a direct appeal to support the treaty. Johnson literally followed him in a cross-country debate, though the two men never directly confronted each other. While Wilson defended his Fourteen Points, the heart of the Treaty of Versailles, generally by casting his opponents as ignorant isolationists, Johnson crafted a detailed assault on the provisions of the treaty itself. While opponents referred to Johnson

as an isolationist, he argued that his position was better described as unilateralism, a policy by which the United States would engage in conflict overseas based only on the dictates of individual circumstances and direct American interests. Treaties, he argued, exposed Americans to the avarice of untrustworthy foreign leaders. After a month of touring the president's health failed, as did his plea to sign the treaty. The tour had produced for Johnson not only a political victory, but also established the organizational contacts and confidence for a run at the Republican nomination for president in 1920.

From the start the campaign was problematic for Johnson. His Progressive history and continued dedication to liberal reforms bothered conservative Republicans, while his vehement anti-League stance offended moderates in the party. A shortage of funds and weak organization hobbled the campaign as well. Despite these problems, his showing was impressive, particularly his primary victory in California over Herbert Hoover, but the national convention proved to be a gauntlet of conservative party leaders through which the fiery Progressive made little headway.

The Senate race of 1922 provided an opportunity for political redemption. His commitment to both reform and antiforeign unilateralism put Johnson in a political bind since his old base of California Progressives were largely internationalists. Mustering all his skill in persuasive speech, he bravely highlighted his unswerving position on the League of Nations as proof of his integrity. He also had cosponsored a bill in the Senate proposing the Boulder Dam project that would bring a controlled water supply and electricity to Southern California. Another stump campaign worked, and California sent Johnson back to the Senate. Bolstered by reelection, he longed for another bid for the presidency but was convinced that Warren Harding would have no difficulty getting the nomination. For the time being he dedicated himself to opposing the internationalists and their new bid to bring the United States into the World Court. Harding's death in August 1923, however, opened the door for another shot at the nomination. The 1924 run proved even more difficult than 1920. The conservative majority in the party was growing and committed to incumbent president Calvin Coolidge. Diehard Progressives offered their support to popular Progressive and internationalist Robert LaFollette. Johnson contented himself, thereafter, to give up on the presidency and focus on his work in Congress. But having openly challenged two popular presidents and a majority of the congressmen in his party posed a significant obstacle to influence in the Senate. To overcome this position, Johnson relied heavily on the rhetorical skills that had served him well all along.

Dedicating himself to the proposition that opposing internationalism was faithful to Progressive Democracy, he used the floor of the Senate to battle against the World Court, the cancellation of foreign debt, and arms treaties that would reduce the size of America's defensive force. His speeches regularly drew audiences and press in the Senate disproportionate to support for his cause. The only international treaty he supported during the late 1920s was the Kellogg-Briand Pact (Treaty for the Renunciation of War), which declared war an illegitimate means of settling international disputes. Not wanting to vote against a peace pact, he voted in favor of the treaty, fully confident that it was a useless and nonbinding agreement. Johnson viewed international relations with pure pessimism. Sensing anti-American sentiment in governments around the world, he coupled his opposition to treaties with a demand for increased defense spending, particularly for naval power.

During the late 1920s Johnson continued to pursue domestic reform. He sponsored federal programs to aid American Indians, disabled veterans, the unemployed, and farmers. Amid the conservatism of Republican politics in the late 1920s, most of these bills met quiet deaths in committee. Having failed to turn reforms into law, Johnson remained true to his beliefs and continued to enjoy esteem among his colleagues for his integrity and rhetorical skill and favor among his constituents in California. The collapse of the economy in 1929, however, would breathe new life into his power in the Senate.

Given his disdain for the Harding, Coolidge, and Hoover administrations, Johnson crossed party lines in 1932 and supported Franklin Roosevelt for the presidency. In return, Roosevelt offered him the position of secretary of the Interior. Johnson declined. He preferred to remain in the Senate, where he enthusiastically supported Roosevelt's New Deal reforms. The two made good political allies on domestic issues but clashed on matters of foreign policy. Johnson fretted that the power of the presidency used for good on domestic issues would prove dangerous in foreign policy. He proposed legislation banning federal government loans to nations already in default on securities sold to American citizens. The Johnson Act passed in the spring of 1934, though Roosevelt was terribly reluctant to begin limiting executive power in foreign affairs.

The anti-internationalism favored by Johnson was gaining popularity as affairs in Asia and Europe began to threaten war on the global horizon. Congress followed in 1935 and 1937 with a series of neutrality acts designed to keep America out of these conflicts. Roosevelt countered with a move to bring the United States into the World Court, with confidence that he could garner the two-thirds vote necessary in the Senate. Having long relied on his talent from the podium, Johnson delivered what he believed to be the most important speeches of his career in opposition to the World Court. With growing support from the public and encouraged by famous anti-internationalists such as W. R. Hearst, Father Coughlin (the radio priest), and national hero Charles Lindbergh, court ratification lost by a narrow margin. Amid Progressive New Deal reforms and growing opposition to internationalism, life in politics was good for Johnson in 1935. Unfortunately, the years that followed would provide new and more difficult challenges.

In June 1936 Johnson suffered a stroke that left him incapacitated for months and impaired to some degree for years. Unable to walk for several weeks, the more enduring damage affected Johnson's precious gift of speech. Perhaps frustrated by his circumstances and increasingly worried by the president's pressure for greater international involvement, Johnson became convinced that Roosevelt was a grave danger. Even in domestic policies that should have appealed to Johnson, the senator saw a scheme to centralize power in the presidency for the purpose of foreign policy. As German and Japanese aggression drew two continents into war, Johnson battled his physical limitations to hold the nation fast to its isolation from war. To continue the fight at age 74, he won his fifth term in the Senate in 1940.

Following the collapse of France under German aggression, Roosevelt pleaded with Congress in 1941 to bolster Great Britain through a lend-lease plan that would arm them on generous credit terms. Johnson viewed the proposal as equivalent to a treaty and a declaration of war. He mustered his voice to take his campaign against the bill to the public through radio broadcasts. While the comfort of isolation appealed to millions of American listeners, Congress disagreed and handed Johnson a major defeat by creating a lend-lease program. Through the rest of 1941 Johnson continued to protest from the corner that America was sacrificing its liberty to war. The Japanese attack on Pearl Harbor in December ended his fight.

As America entered World War II, Hiram Johnson's body began to fail. In spring 1943 he suffered a second stroke that left him paralyzed for the rest of the year. Though he kept his seat in the Senate, he was no longer a fully active member. With his fiery rhetoric quieted by failing health, Johnson managed one last parry in summer 1945 by casting the only ballot in the Senate FOREIGN RELATIONS COMMITTEE in opposition to the United Nations charter.

On August 6, 1945, the United States dropped an atomic bomb on Hiroshima, Japan, asserting with fearsome power America's dominant role in world affairs and laying to rest any remaining notions of isolation. On that same day the nation lost the senator who sincerely believed that America could preserve the well-being and liberty of its people regardless of rank or station by remaining aloof from the problems of the world.

Further reading:
Lower, Richard Coke. *A Bloc of One: The Political Career of Hiram W. Johnson.* Stanford, Calif.: Stanford University Press, 1993; Mowry, George Edwin. *The California Progressives.* Berkeley and Los Angeles: University of California Press, 1951; Olin, Spencer C., Jr. *California's Prodigal Sons: Hiram Johnson and the Progressives, 1911–1917.* Berkeley and Los Angeles: University of California Press, 1968; Weatherson, Michael A., and Hal W. Bochin. *Hiram Johnson: A Bio-Bibliography.* Westport, Conn.: Greenwood Press, 1988; Weatherson, Michael A., and Hal W. Bochin. *Hiram Johnson: Political Revivalist.* Lanham, Md.: University Press of America, 1995.

—Michael Steiner

Johnson, Lyndon Baines (1908–1973)
Representative, Senator, Senate Majority Leader, President of the United States

Lyndon Baines Johnson (LBJ) was the 36th president of the United States, serving from 1963 until 1969. Previously, he had served in the House of Representatives (1937–49) and the Senate (1949–60).

Johnson, a Democrat, was a larger-than-life character, in some ways a quintessential American success story and proof that any American can aspire to the presidency. He was born into poverty in rural Texas and devoted his early adult life to education, having worked his way through teachers college. He was moved by the plight of the impoverished Mexicans who he taught in schools in Texas and felt empathy for those in poverty for the rest of his life. But his personality was far from that of a meek and mild altruist. He was ambitious, driven, and extremely politically savvy. His father had served in the Texas state legislature, and LBJ was able to use his father's connections to start his own political career. Through his father he knew Representative Sam Rayburn (D-TX) and started his congressional career as Rayburn's secretary. Johnson eventually ran for the House himself as a New Deal Democrat, dedicated to President Franklin D. Roosevelt's policies of government programs to help the poor and those dispossessed by the Great Depression. He also served in the navy during World War II, earning a Silver Star in the process, and was a member of the Naval Affairs Committee in the House.

As a representative Johnson learned the ropes and quickly moved ahead. He was always a master at "working the system." Johnson also never forgot where he came from and never missed a chance to send pork barrel to benefit his home state of Texas. He had a keen mind for legislative details and, even more importantly, an innate understanding of human motivations. He knew how to use connections to gain power and had an uncanny ability to get people to do what he wanted. These skills served him well in the position that it seemed he had been born to occupy, that of Senate Majority Leader, which he became in 1955. After six terms in the House, LBJ won a Senate seat in 1948, very narrowly defeating his primary opponent and gaining the nickname "landslide Lyndon." As was characteristic of him, Johnson's great personal victory (he had run for a Senate seat in 1941 and lost) came with a taint: accusations of strong arm tactics and fraud.

Johnson became Minority Leader of the Senate in 1953 and Majority Leader when the Democrats took the majority two years later. He was able to work with a Republican president (Eisenhower) and used a vast array of tools to move legislation: bargaining, persuasion, and the doling out of favors, to name a few. Persuasion was perhaps his strong suit. When Johnson backed a senator into a corner (as he often did—literally), he used his physical presence (Johnson was a large, tall man) and larger-than-life personality to convince that senator to go along with what Johnson asked, whatever it was. He was so well known for these tactics, nicknamed the "Johnson Treatment," that they became legendary, and senators were known to run for cover when the Johnson Treatment was coming on. LBJ achieved great success as Majority Leader, and one of his proudest accomplishments was the passage of civil rights legislation in 1957—the first since Reconstruction. This was especially admirable given that southern Democrats historically had been associated with Jim Crow and racial segregation.

In 1960 candidate John Fitzgerald Kennedy tapped Johnson as his running mate, a surprising move done mostly to gain the vote of southern Democrats who were likely to feel alienated by a Harvard-educated, East Coast, Irish Catholic. Johnson's selection as running mate probably did contribute to Kennedy's win, which was by a narrow majority. Johnson was less well suited to the office of vice president than he had been to that of Majority Leader of the Senate. He often felt out of place among the Kennedys and their friends, who he felt treated him as something of a country bumpkin. Even so, he was a loyal and active vice president.

When Kennedy was assassinated in 1963, gunned down in Dallas, Texas, by Lee Harvey Oswald, Johnson became president. He was sworn in on Air Force One with Jackie Kennedy by his side, still in her blood-stained suit. He wanted to move quickly and decisively to bring some sense of order to a country that was reeling from an unexpected blow. His was a very difficult job. Although he certainly had aspirations to the presidency, no one would want to get it under such circumstances. Johnson devoted himself to Kennedy's legislative agenda, pushing for passage of civil rights legislation and tax reduction legislation, among others. His years of practice shepherding legislation in the Senate served him well. Johnson was also devoted to military preparedness and space exploration, (It is not by chance that the National Air and Space Administration, NASA, is headquartered in Houston, Texas, and not Cambridge, Massachusetts, its original home.) In 1964 Johnson ran for the presidency on his own, with Hubert Humphrey (D-MN) as his running mate. In a stunning personal and political victory, Johnson won 60 percent of the popular vote. This was extremely important to Johnson, who, despite his tenacity and drive, could also be thin-skinned and sensitive about deserving his position.

Unfortunately, Johnson's first full term in office served as his political undoing despite impressive legislative gains. On the positive side, LBJ was able to pass a broad variety of legislation under his "Great Society" program, also known as the War on Poverty. Drawing from his own early personal experiences and association with the New Deal, Johnson pledged to eliminate poverty from American society. It was shameful, he felt, that in the midst of the land of plenty there should be pockets of great poverty. He guided passage of legislation in a variety of areas, from medical care for the elderly (Medicare) to early childhood education (Head Start). He shepherded passage of the Voting Rights Act and legislation creating jobs for youths. He expanded food stamps and welfare. Unbeknownst to him, these programs would serve as the last Democratic hurrah of the 20th century and would be overshadowed by his biggest fiasco, the war in Vietnam. As conservatives became more vocal and active regarding domestic social programs in the 1970s, 1980s, and 1990s, they criticized Johnson's Great Society, which they claimed exacerbated rather than eradicated poverty. While liberals still hotly defend the success of the Great Society, it nonetheless was not the unmitigated success story that Johnson would have liked as his legacy.

But by far the largest stain on LBJ's presidency was his handling of the war in Vietnam. Having served in World War II and having been a member of the Naval Affairs Committee in the House and Armed Services Committee in the Senate, Johnson was committed, as New Deal Democrats generally were, to containing the spread of communism. The latest threat of communism came not from the Soviet Union, the traditional adversary, but from China, which was encouraging guerrilla insurrections in Asian countries. (There was some suspicion that the Soviet Union may also have been providing military assistance.) Communist North Vietnam, aided by China, supported Vietcong troops who were attempting to take over the government in South Vietnam, a democratic country with the backing of the United States.

Johnson sent troops to aid the South Vietnamese government, hoping that the insurrection could be put down relatively quickly. As it became clearer that the Vietcong were winning the fight, Johnson felt he had no choice but to send in more and more American troops, who continued to fight what seemed to be a losing battle. Hostilities erupted on the home front as well. Many Americans, especially young Americans, were disillusioned with Johnson and with war. They did not see the war as a containment of communism but rather an example of American imperialism. Others, particularly older Americans, many of whom had fought in World War II, supported sending troops to Vietnam and criticized the president for not providing enough force. Johnson felt caught between a rock and a hard place, and became increasingly unpopular.

Vice President Lyndon B. Johnson standing on rostrum of the Senate, 1961 *(Library of Congress)*

Protests erupted and students picketed night and day in front of the White House, chanting, "Hey, hey, LBJ, how many kids have you killed today?"

At the same time, his preoccupation with the war in Southeast Asia drew his attention away from his expansive Great Society programs, which were losing funding anyway in the battle between "guns and butter," which guns were clearly winning.

An increasingly beaten and bitter man, LBJ finally announced in March 1968 that he would not run for president as he had intended, and that he would halt bombing in North Vietnam. His vice president, Hubert Humphrey, got the Democratic nomination but was defeated by Republican Richard Nixon. The country was divided over the war, over governmental spending, and over how representative American democracy truly was. A "generation gap" had been created. Johnson, a man destined for greatness, left the presidency in great despair.

Johnson retired to his ranch in 1969, and died three years later of a sudden heart attack. A portrait of human achievement and of human failure, Johnson was, ultimately, just that: human.

Further reading:
Caro, Robert A. *Master of the Senate.* New York: Knopf, 2002; Johnson, Lyndon B. *The Vantage Point: Perspectives of the Presidency, 1963–1969.* New York: Holt, 1971; Kearns, Doris. *Lyndon Johnson and the American Dream.* New York: Harper, 1976; Schandler, Herbert. *The Unmaking of the President: Lyndon Johnson and Vietnam.* Princeton, N.J.: Princeton University Press, 1977; White, Theodore H. *The Making of the President, 1964.* New York: Atheneum, 1964.

—Anne Marie Cammisa

Joint Committee on Reconstruction

In the aftermath of the Civil War the issue of the political status of former Confederate states was paramount. Three different perspectives on this question emerged that at their core differed in their understanding of secession and the proposed policies for dealing with rebellious states. Radical Republicans, such as Thaddeus Stevens of Pennsylvania, took the position that former Confederate states had seceded from the Union and, after the Union's victory, amounted to conquered territory. Given this interpretation, the Union was well within its prerogative to impose conditions or reparations on a conquered state. Radical Republicans took the position that the federal government could and should impose stringent conditions on the southern states prior to readmitting them to the Union, such as requiring southern states to enfranchise former slaves.

The more moderate wing of the Republican Party, including Roscoe Conkling (NY) and William Fessenden (ME), argued that the southern states could not secede but that it was possible for states to lapse from the republican form of government guaranteed by Article IV of the Constitution. In those cases states reverted to territory status, and it was appropriate for the federal government to take some steps to determine when they could be readmitted to the Union as full-fledged states. The Democrats, including President Andrew Johnson, agreed that it was not possible for states to secede from the Union and felt that the federal government did not have the authority to impose policy upon any state. Voting rights and qualifications had typically been left to the states to determine. Democrats found no justification for fundamentally overhauling the balance of power between the federal and state governments, which is precisely what would happen, they argued, if the federal government imposed voting rights on the states. Many Democrats demanded the immediate reinstatement of southern representation in national institutions.

It was in this political climate that Congress appointed the Joint Committee on Reconstruction, also known as the Committee of Fifteen, which consisted of six senators (William Fessenden [ME], James Grimes [IO], Ira Harris [NY], J. M. Howard [MI], George Williams [OR] and Reverdy Johnson [MD]) and nine Representatives (Thaddeus Stevens [PA], Elihu Washburn [IL], Justin Morrill [VT], John Bingham [OH], Roscoe Conkling [NY], George Boutwell [MA], Henry Blow [MS], Andrew Rogers [NJ], and Henry Grider [KY]).

The committee served from December 1865 to June 1866, when they submitted their final report. It was chaired by the moderate William Pitt Fessenden of Maine. It consisted of four subcommittees, which were responsible for gathering information about different states. They held hearings and interviewed a total of 144 witnesses, including eight African Americans, 57 southerners, and 77 northerners living in the South in an effort to gather information about the treatment of former slaves, the attitude of Confederate leaders toward the federal government, and the need for federal troops in the South.

Critics charged that the committee was captured by the radical Republicans and the witnesses had been selected in order to justify radical Reconstruction. The committee concluded that federal intervention was necessary in order to guarantee the protection of former slaves and proposed the controversial Fourteenth Amendment in order to protect the social, economic, and political rights of former slaves. The committee argued that the amendment was a compromise between the radical and moderate wings of the Republican Party since it would lead to universal male suffrage, without imposing it on the states and thereby avoided intervening in state affairs. The committee concluded that political power should be possessed in all the states exactly in proportion as the right of suffrage should be granted, without distinction of color or race. This it was thought would leave the whole question with the people of each state, holding out to all the advantage of increased political power as an inducement to allow all to participate in its exercise. Such a provision would be in its nature gentle and persuasive, and would lead, it was hoped, to an equal participation of all without distinction, in all the rights and privileges of citizenship, thus affording a full and adequate protection to all classes of citizens, since all would have, through the ballot box, the power of self-protection.

Further reading:
Donald, David H. *The Politics of Reconstruction, 1863–1867.* Baton Rouge: Louisiana State University Press, 1965; James, Joseph B. *The Framing of the Fourteenth Amendment.* Urbana: University of Illinois Press, 1956; Kendrick, Benjamin Burks. *The Journal of the Joint Committee of Fifteen on Reconstruction, 39th Congress, 1865–1867.* New York: Columbia University Press, 1914.

—Kimberly Maslin-Wicks

joint session

Joint sessions are combined meetings of the SENATE and the HOUSE OF REPRESENTATIVES held after the adoption of a concurrent resolution by both chambers. A joint session differs from a joint meeting. A joint meeting of both chambers occurs when each body adopts a unanimous consent agreement to recess to meet with the other body. Joint sessions are held to hear an address from the president of the United States, while joint meetings are held to hear an address from a foreign dignitary or American visitors other than the president. Joint sessions also are held to count the electoral votes after a presidential election.

The SPEAKER OF THE HOUSE of Representatives presides over joint sessions and joint meetings. The Constitution requires that the president of the Senate, the vice president of the United States, preside over a joint session called to count the electoral votes.

While the Congress met in New York City from 1789 to 1790, joint sessions and joint meetings were held in the Senate Chamber in Federal Hall. In Philadelphia joint gatherings were held in the Senate Chamber from 1790 until 1793 and in the Hall of the House of Representatives from 1794 until 1799. In 1800 Congress moved to the Capitol in Washington, and the Senate Chamber served as the location of joint meetings and sessions until 1805. Since 1809 joint gatherings have been held in the House chamber.

Presidential messages on the state of the union were originally called the Annual Message, but since 1947 they have been called the State of the Union Address. From 1800 until 1913 the messages were read by clerks to the individual bodies. Since 1913 the president has delivered the address to a joint session of Congress.

Inaugurations also are considered formal joint gatherings. Congress has hosted inaugurations since the first in 1789. Inaugurations are joint sessions when both houses of Congress are in session, with the ceremony becoming part of the business of the day.

There were six joint gatherings held during the 108th Congress (2003–04). President George W. Bush gave his State of the Union address on January 28, 2003, before a joint session of Congress. Great Britain's prime minister Tony Blair addressed a joint meeting on July 17, 2003. President Bush delivered another State of the Union address on January 20, 2004. José Maria Aznar, president of Spain, spoke before a joint meeting on February 4, 2004. Afghanistan's president Hamid Karzai addressed a joint meeting of Congress on June 15, 2004. The interim prime minister of Iraq addressed a joint meeting on September 23, 2004.

Further reading:
United States Congress, Joint Committee on Printing. *Congressional Directory.* Washington, D.C.: Government Printing Office, 2003.

—John David Rausch, Jr.

journalists

Approximately 6,000 credentialed news reporters cover the U.S. Congress, or approximately 11 reporters for every member of the House and the Senate. This group is extremely diverse by every measure. They work for a wide range of media: wire services, newspapers, magazines, newsletters, television and radio, online publications, and news conglomerates. They include freelance writers and photographers and foreign correspondents. Some specialize in particular issues, such as defense or higher education. Others focus on a particular state or region. Still others are generalists, simply there to cover "Congress" or "Washington." Some work out of Congress daily in space allocated in the galleries. Others may come to Congress only occasionally. Their one common characteristic is that they are full-time journalists. Only full-time news reporters can be credentialed through the congressional media galleries.

Among the credentialed congressional reporters are the employees of Cable-Satellite Public Affairs Network (C-SPAN). Congressional reporters see C-SPAN as a different medium. Its emphasis on simply presenting floor debate and hearings is a departure from the usual types of reporting, which include editing, placing debate in a larger context, and interpretation. Instead, C-SPAN provides what one reporter calls "raw data," which is a valuable source for the other congressional reporters.

While the congressional beat may not be the most prestigious in Washington, it is a desirable one. Most congressional correspondents appear to enjoy their jobs. One reason is that the complex organization, full of a variety of strong personalities, is interesting. Another reason is that there is a plethora of stories from which to choose when Congress is in session. A third reason is that Congress provides a variety of sources and perspectives when writing a story. Members, staff, affiliated organizations such as the General Accounting Office, and congressional testimony and floor statements are all available as possible sources. If one person is not willing to comment, another will be.

Many observers characterize the relationship between members of Congress and reporters, especially local reporters, as symbiotic. Members need the local media to communicate with their constituents and to enhance their chances of reelection. Reporters, on the other hand, need news stories. Members of Congress can provide numerous stories in their own right or provide a means to localize a national story by commenting on the issues of the day. It is not unusual to see local news stories that reproduce a large part or all of a member's press release. Thus, members may be in the enviable position of writing their own news stories. Of course, many reporters are more independent, and some are downright hostile to the members they cover. Nonetheless, generally speaking, the relationship between members and the media is one of mutual dependence. One former member of Congress summed up the relationship by saying, "Yes, [I like the press] if they write a favorable story. No, if they don't."

The mutual dependence between national reporters and the members of Congress is less obvious. National coverage yields less immediate benefit to rank-and-file members, and national reporters can tap many sources for their stories. However, most members are excited to receive national coverage and will make time for it even if most of their efforts are geared to securing local coverage.

What do reporters think of Congress? The answer is, "It depends." Reporters who specialize in covering Congress usually have a fairly high opinion of Congress. They give Congress especially high marks for its ability to raise issues and its responsiveness to constituents. Other reporters, especially editors and radio talk show hosts, are more hostile to the institution. Editors, who determine story placement and headlines, have a lower opinion of Congress than do their correspondents who are likely to write the stories. This perception gap may explain, in part, the increasingly negative tone of congressional news coverage. Radio talk show hosts, however, are the group of journalists who hold the lowest collective opinion of Congress. They generally rate Congress's effectiveness as "poor" and see it as a party to PACs and special interests.

See also CONGRESSIONAL ELECTIONS: MEDIA; C-SPAN; MEDIA GALLERIES.

Further reading:
Center for Responsive Politics. *"Dateline: Capitol Hill: Congress, the Public and the News Agenda."* Washington, D.C.: Center for Responsive Politics, 1990; Frey, Lou, Jr., and Michael T. Hayes. *Inside the House: Former Members of Congress Reveal How Congress Really Works.* Lanham, Md.: University Press of America, 2001; Hess, Stephen. *Live from Capitol Hill: Studies of Congress and the Media.* Washington, D.C.: Brookings Institution Press, 1991; Mann, Thomas E., and Norman J. Ornstein, eds. *Congress, the Press and the Public.* Washington, D.C.: American Enterprise Institute and Brookings Institution Press, 1994.
—Karen M. Kedrowski

journals
The journal is a record of the proceedings of each legislative day in the HOUSE OF REPRESENTATIVES and the SENATE. It is the official record of the proceedings of the U.S. Congress, and certified copies of the journals may be used in judicial proceedings.

Article I, section 5, of the U.S. Constitution requires the House of Representatives to keep a journal and to publish it except in cases in which secrecy is necessary. From its inaugural session the Senate has kept a journal of its proceedings in accordance with Article I, Section 5, of the Constitution, which provides that "Each House shall keep a journal of its proceedings, and from time to time publish the same, excepting such parts as may in their judgment require secrecy; and the yeas and nays of the members of either House, on any question, shall, at the desire of one-fifth of those present, be entered on the journal."

Journals should be seen as the minutes of floor action. They note the matters considered by the House of Representatives and the Senate and the votes and other actions taken. In addition, the Senate has maintained a separate record of its executive proceedings as they relate to the Senate confirmation process of presidential appointees and the Senate ratification of treaties. This journal is referred to as the Senate Executive Journal.

Further reading:
"House Journal." Available online. URL: http://memory. loc.gov/ammem/amlaw/lwhj.html. Accessed February 8, 2003; "Senate Executive Journal." Available online. URL: http://memory.loc.gov/ammem/amlaw/lwej.html. Accessed

8 February 2003; "Senate Journal." Available online. URL: http://memory.loc.gov/ammem/amlaw/lwsj.html. Accessed 8 February 2003.

—Nancy S. Lind

Judiciary Committee, House

The House Judiciary Committee is perhaps best known recently for its passage of articles of impeachment against two 20th-century presidents, Richard Nixon and Bill Clinton. Yet, as the Ralph Nader Congress Project noted in 1975, the routine, daily work of the Judiciary Committees has a far more profound effect on the nature and quality of American life than even the impeachment of a president. At that time Nader's team noted that the ordinary fare of the Judiciary Committees included such issues as abortion, civil rights, wiretapping by law enforcement agencies, drug laws, gun control laws, and the war on crime. More than a quarter century later, little had changed: The House Judiciary Committee still debates the most explosive issues in American politics.

The Committee on the Judiciary was established by the HOUSE OF REPRESENTATIVES on June 3, 1813, to consider legislation relating to judicial proceedings. Since then, the scope of the committee's official jurisdiction has expanded to encompass a mixed bag of legal issues. Its areas of responsibility fall into nine categories (quotations below are from House Rule X): 1) The judiciary and judicial proceedings, and 2) patents, the Patent and Trademark Office, copyrights, and trademarks, which are considered by the Subcommittee on Courts, the Internet, and Intellectual Property. 3) Commercial law, including bankruptcy and protection of trade and commerce against unlawful restraints and monopolies, and 4) administrative practice and procedure, which are considered by the Subcommittee on Commercial and Administrative Law. 5) Civil rights, and 6) constitutional amendments, which are considered by the Subcommittee on the Constitution. 7) Immigration and naturalization, and 8) claims against the United States, which usually means petitions by individuals for relief from hardships, are considered by the Subcommittee on Immigration, Border Security, and Claims. 9) Federal criminal law, including drug enforcement, sentencing, prisons, terrorism, and internal security, is considered by the Subcommittee on Crime, Terrorism, and Homeland Security. The ninth category can be characterized as government housekeeping matters, including presidential succession, state and territorial boundary lines, interstate compacts, apportionment of representatives and meetings of Congress; attendance of members, delegates, and the resident commissioner; and their acceptance of incompatible offices.

Typically between 40 and 70 measures processed by the committee become public laws every two years, most of which involve the more mundane subjects of its jurisdiction. Each term the committee also processes between five and 20 private laws that pay claims, grant benefits, or waive immigration restrictions for individual persons.

The work of the House Judiciary Committee differs considerably from that of its Senate counterpart. The SENATE JUDICIARY COMMITTEE has a unique role in confirming judicial nominations, which occupies a considerable amount of its time. The House Judiciary Committee's unique role, initiating impeachments of federal officials, is only seldom exercised. As such, the House committee has pursued a broader, more active agenda. For instance, from the 104th through 107th Congresses (1995–2002), the House Judiciary Committee issued reports on about 106 measures each term. The Senate Judiciary Committee issued reports on an average of only 15 measures per term during the same period. Often the House Judiciary Committee approved bills that had no counterpart in the Senate, and the full House would pass Judiciary-approved bills that were never to be taken up by the Senate Judiciary Committee.

House Judiciary is known for its propensity to deal with hot-button issues, and it has often tackled them with relish even when the committee's work is unlikely to result in a law being passed. For example, in February 1995 the committee held two days of hearings on the issue of whether the losing side in a civil lawsuit should pay the winning side's attorneys' fees. Following the hearings, the Committee advanced a bill, the Attorney Accountability Act, to the House floor, where committee members spent seven hours over two days managing debate on the bill. The bill ultimately passed the House but never had a serious chance of becoming law. The Senate Judiciary Committee held a cursory hearing on a bill containing a similar provision but did not mark up either bill.

Perhaps it is because of its controversial nature that, while gaining much public attention, the committee's work has not always translated into a proportionately large number of laws enacted. During the 99th Congress (1985–86), House Judiciary had a hand in nine of 90 laws passed that were classified as major legislation by the CONGRESSIONAL RESEARCH SERVICE. But during the 102nd Congress (1991–92), House Judiciary was involved in only two of 112 major enactments. One of them, the Civil Rights Act of 1991, had been passed in similar form the year before but vetoed by President George H. W. Bush. The committee devoted much effort during the 102nd Congress to an omnibus crime bill that failed to become law but was revived and ultimately passed the following term.

House Judiciary is said to be one of the most partisan and ideologically skewed committees in Congress. Without a doubt, it played the central role in the contentious debate of the conservative CONTRACT WITH AMERICA measures following Republican victories in the 1994 congressional elections. Four of 10 Contract with America elements, civil justice, criminal justice, and balanced budget and term limit amendments to the Constitution, were under Judiciary Committee jurisdiction. In the end the House voted on 18 contract measures, nine of which had originated in the House Judiciary Committee.

Further reading:
Schuck, Peter H. *The Judiciary Committees: A Study of the House and Senate Judiciary Committees.* New York: Grossman Publishers, 1975; Deering, Christopher J., and Steven S. Smith. *Committees in Congress.* 3d ed. Washington, D.C.: Congressional Quarterly Press, 1997.

—Jackson Williams

Judiciary Committee, Senate

Judiciary is the standing committee in the U.S. Senate that considers constitutional issues, the structure of the judiciary, and the confirmation of the president's nominees to serve on federal courts. The Senate Committee on the Judiciary was one of the original standing committees of the Senate and was established in 1816. The committee's original jurisdiction included matters relating to the courts, federal law enforcement, and judicial administration. By 1820 the committee had expanded its jurisdiction to include controversies over bankruptcy policy, the boundaries of the states, admission of new states to the Union, and contested Senate elections. After the Joint Committee on Reconstruction was abolished in 1867, the committee became responsible for legislation relating to bringing the former Confederate states back into the Union. In 1871 the Judiciary Committee lost its jurisdiction over contested Senate elections to the Committee on Privileges and Elections.

The LEGISLATIVE REORGANIZATION ACT OF 1946 returned some jurisdiction the committee had lost during the early 20th century. Legislation controlling the apportionment of the House of Representatives had been considered by the Judiciary Committee in 1821, but it lost its jurisdiction over apportionment to the Committee on Commerce, which had it until 1946. In 1837 jurisdiction over issues related to patents, trademarks, and copyrights was transferred to the Committee on Patents. Jurisdiction over matters relating to immigration was transferred to the Committee on Immigration in 1889. The Committee on the Judiciary regained jurisdiction over these matters in 1946.

The Judiciary Committee had jurisdiction over proposals relating to women's suffrage from the late 1860s until 1882, when the Senate established a Select Committee on Woman Suffrage. The select committee was abolished in 1921 when the Nineteenth Amendment giving women the right to vote in federal elections was ratified.

The early Judiciary Committee also considered claims made by private citizens against the U.S. government. This jurisdiction was transferred to the Committee on Claims and the Committee on Revolutionary Claims. The Legislative Reorganization Act of 1946 returned jurisdiction over claims to the Judiciary Committee.

The Committee on the Judiciary was one of 16 standing committees in the 108th Congress. With 19 members (10 Republicans and 9 Democrats), it was a moderately sized committee. It had six subcommittees: the Subcommittee on Administrative Oversight and the Courts; the Subcommittee on Antitrust, Competition Policy and Consumer Rights; the Subcommittee on the Constitution, Civil Rights and Property Rights; the Subcommittee on Crime, Corrections and Victims' Rights; the Subcommittee on Immigration, Border Security and Citizenship; and the Subcommittee on Terrorism, Technology and Homeland Security.

While the Judiciary Committee focuses largely on constitutional amendments, the federal judiciary, immigration, antitrust laws, and civil liberties, it is its role in confirming the president's judicial nominees that often attracts public attention. The committee is not as powerful as other committees in the Senate, but it attracts activists from both ends of the political spectrum who work to enact their political philosophies. One way that committee members have to do this is by confirming or not confirming federal judges who may share the same political philosophy. The Judiciary Committee's role is largely to recommend to the full Senate whether to confirm nominees to judicial positions. The full Senate rejects about one out of every five nominees. The Bork confirmation of 1987 and the Thomas confirmation in 1991 were two famous sets of hearings held by the Judiciary Committee.

Because of its polarized membership, the committee rarely produces major legislation that is enacted by Congress and signed into law by the president. Measures that do become law tend to be in the areas of criminal law and in juvenile justice and administrative law.

Further reading:
Samuel, Terence, and Kenneth T. Walsh. "Clubhouse Catfight," *U.S. News & World Report,* 22 November 2004, p. 28; Schuck, Peter H. *The Judiciary Committee: A Study of the House and Senate Judiciary Committees.* New York: Grossman Publishers, 1975; U.S. Senate, Committee on the Judiciary. *History of the Committee on the Judiciary, United States Senate.* Senate Document 97-18. Washington, D.C.: Government Printing Office, 1982.

—John David Rausch, Jr.

jurisdiction

Jurisdiction is a congressional committee's area of legislative or oversight responsibility. Committee jurisdiction is complex and has been determined by a number of factors. David King has identified two ways committees receive jurisdiction. The first way is statutory jurisdiction. Statutory jurisdiction is defined in the rules of the HOUSE OF REPRESENTATIVES and the SENATE that are approved by a majority vote of each body. Except in a few instances in the history of Congress, the rules of each chamber change very slightly from one Congress to the next.

The second type of jurisdiction is common law jurisdiction. When jurisdictionally ambiguous bills are introduced, they have to be referred to a STANDING COMMITTEE or multiple committees within 24 hours. The House and Senate PARLIAMENTARIANS, unelected employees in each chamber, refer bills and make decisions about which committee has jurisdiction. The referrals establish binding precedents for all future bills on the same subjects.

In addition to the sources of jurisdiction, there are two different types of jurisdiction. Legislative jurisdiction is the authority to consider and report bills to the full chamber. Oversight jurisdiction is the authority to review or investigate, usually a specific government function. Oversight jurisdiction usually is assigned by the resolution creating a committee, but it can be obtained when a committee accepts responsibility for reviewing broad topical areas.

The most important statements about standing, or permanent, committee jurisdictions are House Rule X and Senate Rule XXV. These rules identify the subject matter of legislative and oversight jurisdiction of each committee. The rules list the jurisdictions in broad topical terms rather than specific programmatic references, in most cases.

SELECT and SPECIAL COMMITTEE jurisdiction is included in the resolution creating the panel. Select committees usually do not have jurisdiction to write legislation and do not have bills referred to them. The jurisdiction of special and select committees usually refers to investigative responsibility.

One can usually determine the jurisdiction of a particular standing committee by referring to the committee's name. In some cases, however, it is difficult to precisely determine the committee's jurisdiction solely from its name. In part, this is because jurisdictional boundaries are not completely clear. In other cases jurisdictional divisions appear arbitrary. Subcommittee jurisdictions also serve to make the broad topical areas more specific. The jurisdiction of a particular subcommittee is identified in the rules adopted by the full committee. Most subcommittees in the House and Senate have formally defined jurisdictions.

House Rule X and Senate Rule XXV are broad because they are the products of an era when the role of the federal government was not as extensive. The rules consist of precedents from the 19th and early 20th centuries as codified by the LEGISLATIVE REORGANIZATION ACT OF 1946. The act reduced the number of standing committees from 33 to 15 in the Senate and from 48 to 19 in the House, and for the first time committee jurisdictions were presented in writing in chamber rules. In 1974 committee reform reached the agenda when the Bolling Committee reported its proposals on committee realignment. Most of the proposals were defeated in the House Democratic Caucus. A modified set of proposals was adopted changing the statutory jurisdictions of a number of committees, including transportation, health, and banking. Congress tried to enact jurisdictional reform in 1980 to bring energy issues under one committee, but it failed to remove the authority over energy issues from the House Commerce Committee.

When the Republicans gained control of Congress in the 104th Congress (1995–96), they modified committee jurisdiction by abolishing three House committees. The jurisdictions of the Committee on the District of Columbia and the Committee on the Post Office and Civil Service were given to the COMMITTEE ON GOVERNMENT REFORM. The jurisdiction of the Committee on Merchant Marine and Fisheries was divided among the COMMITTEE ON RESOURCES, the COMMITTEE ON TRANSPORTATION AND INFRASTRUCTURE, the Committee on National Security, and the COMMITTEE ON SCIENCE.

Because statutory changes in jurisdiction are slight and major changes are infrequent, most jurisdictional change is through common law. Once a measure has been referred to a committee, all future bills like it are also referred to that committee. When determining to which committee a bill should be referred, the presiding officer, in consultation with the chamber's parliamentarian, may take into account the committee assignment and issue expertise of the bill's sponsor. The timing of introduction also affects referral. Each chamber has different rules governing the referral of the same bill to multiple committees.

Because the modern Congress deals with a number of broad topics, committee jurisdictions often overlap. In order to deal with overlapping jurisdiction, committees often formulate a memorandum of understanding to informally specify jurisdiction. At the start of the 107th Congress (2001–02), the House adopted rules that renamed the Banking Committee the Financial Services Committee and transferred jurisdiction over securities and exchanges and insurance from the Commerce Committee to the Financial Services Committee. The Commerce Committee also was renamed the ENERGY AND COMMERCE COMMITTEE. The two committees executed a memorandum of understanding clarifying several jurisdictional issues. The Committee on Energy and Commerce retained jurisdiction over bills dealing broadly with electronic commerce, including electronic communications networks. The Committee on Financial Services kept its jurisdiction over bills amending securities laws to address the specific type of electronic securities transaction currently governed by special SEC regulations as Alternative Trading Systems.

Further reading:
Deering, Christopher J., and Steven S. Smith. *Committees in Congress.* 3d ed. Washington, D.C.: Congressional Quarterly Press, 1997; King, David C. *Turf Wars: How Congressional Committees Claim Jurisdiction.* Chicago: University of Chicago Press, 1997; Pershing, Ben, and Ethan Wallison. "Hastert Mediates Flap Over New Panel's Jurisdiction." *Roll Call,* 15 January 2001.

—John David Rausch, Jr.

K

"Keating Five" scandal

What became popularly known as the Keating Five scandal was linked to the collapse of the savings-and-loan industry (S&Ls for short) in the late 1980s, which cost U.S. taxpayers close to $1.4 trillion. The Keating Five were Senator Alan Cranston of California, Senator Dennis DeConcini of Arizona, Senator John Glenn of Ohio, Senator Donald Riegle of Michigan, and Senator John McCain of Arizona. S&L high rollers such as the notorious Arizona developer Charles Keating, Jr., had taken advantage of relaxed government regulation to make risky investments in the highly speculative market of commercial real estate as well as in high-interest consumer loans, both of which involved substantial risk to their thrifts (as the S&Ls are also known). Many of them also plundered the savings of their depositors, freely dipping into other people's money with the knowledge that the federal deposit insurance (up to $100,000 per savings account) would protect them from ever having to pay back what they stole. Like Keating and Texas S&L banker Don Dixon, most of them were wheeler-dealer real estate operators who saw their newly acquired thrifts as a source of unlimited funds (that is, the deposits guaranteed by the Federal Savings & Loan Insurance Corporation) to be used for their own enrichment and as favors for their friends and relatives. Not only did Dixon employ his own wife, sister-in-law, step-daughter, and other relatives in his S&L bank, he also bilked the bank out of millions of dollars to buy houses, expensive art and furniture, planes, yachts, and "dream trips" abroad, as well as to pay for his extravagant living expenses.

As the failing thrifts headed for financial ruin, Keating, Dixon, and other S&L executives turned for support to key congressmembers to help them cover up the ailing state of the poorly managed S&L industry. For example, Dixon turned to House Majority Whip Tony Coelho, who had been using Dixon's 112-foot yacht *High Spirits* for Democratic fund-raising and other parties on the Potomac River. Coelho in turn contacted Majority Leader Jim Wright, who was about to become the next Speaker of the House. On Christmas Day in 1986, Wright telephoned Edwin J. Gray, the chair of the Federal Home Loan Bank Board (FHLBB) and the chief S&L regulator, to plead on Dixon's behalf. However, he was too late, for federal regulators had just put Dixon out of business.

But no one linked to the S&L debacle—not even Dixon—was as powerful or well-connected as Keating, the flamboyant homebuilder antiporn crusader with a shady past. With help from "junk bond king" Michael Milken from the Beverly Hills office of Drexel Burnham Lambert, Keating had bought a California-based thrift, the Lincoln Savings and Loan Association. Like Dixon and other new thrift operators, Keating took advantage of the Reagan-era deregulation to pump up Lincoln Savings using brokered deposits and junk bonds to move out of the traditional homebuyers market and into the "red-hot" nonresidential real estate (like his chain of Phoenician resort hotels, which later became the biggest bust in the history of the U.S. hotel industry). Like Dixon, he used his thrift to get himself and his family rich using the depositors' money. Keating, for example, hired his 26-year-old son, Charles Keating III, as a senior bank manager, a spectacular rise for a former busboy and country club waiter. Using a tax-sharing plan allowed by the Internal Revenue Service, he siphoned $94.8 million out of Lincoln Savings.

The Lincoln Savings and Loan Association finally collapsed in April 1989, becoming the single largest thrift bankruptcy in U.S. history. When the government seized the failed bank, it was estimated that a bailout would cost several billion dollars, and Keating, as the chair of Lincoln's parent company, the Phoenix-based American Continental Corporation, was personally blamed for this costly failure. In November 1990 the House Banking Committee began televised hearings on the Lincoln collapse. Keating testified before the committee that this was the fault of overzealous regulators, who had pursued a personal vendetta against him and his businesses. But Edwin Gray, the ex-chair of the

Federal Home Loan Bank board, testified that the board, which regulated the thrift industry, became aware of the growing S&L problems in the mid-1980s and tried to reimpose stricter government controls to prevent a further deterioration of the worsening situation and a potential financial disaster. However, the Reagan administration, which was ideologically committed to a policy of deregulation, refused to go along and turned down all requests for personnel and budget funds required to monitor the sinking thrift institutions. Nor was Congress, especially its House and Senate Banking Committees, willing to consider the passage of new legislation to ensure the reregulation and future viability of the S&L industry.

Gray also testified that he had been approached by a number of influential senators to discontinue the federal investigation of the Lincoln Savings and Loan Association. Later, after the inevitable collapse of Lincoln and many other freewheeling S&Ls, it was revealed that these senators had received substantial amounts of money, both directly and indirectly, from Keating and his associates, totaling more than $1.3 million. A number of official investigations began as to whether these senators had acted improperly and whether Keating had been able to buy influence through his campaign contributions. One of these investigations was conducted by the Senate Ethics Committee, which focused on the controversial actions of the five senators implicated: Cranston, DeConcini, Glenn, Riegle, and McCain. These men were dubbed the Keating Five.

Together, the five senators had accepted more than $300,000 in direct campaign contributions from Keating. Robert Bennett, the special counsel to the Senate Ethics Committee, recommended that Senators Glenn and McCain be dropped from the investigation because they were not substantially involved. But after months of hearings had revealed that all five senators had acted improperly by intervening on Keating's behalf, the committee rejected his recommendation (years later Bennett would represent President Bill Clinton in the Paula Jones case). In their testimony each of the Keating Five maintained that they were not involved in any wrongdoing and were just following normal campaign funding practices.

But the five senators had a lot of explaining to do. As the preliminary investigation of the Senate Ethics Committee revealed, the first to be approached by Keating was Senator DeConcini, one of his most loyal friends in Congress. Not only had DeConcini received tens of thousands of dollars in campaign contributions from the Arizona developer, but at one point he had pushed Keating for U.S. ambassador to the Bahamas, where the Keatings owned a luxurious vacation home. In April 1987 DeConcini set up two meetings in his congressional office between the Keating Five and various thrift regulators.

Gray, the chair of the Federal Home Loan Bank Board and Keating's nemesis, was present at the first meeting, held on April 2. The second meeting was on April 19 and was attended by several federal and California auditors, who were investigating Keating for cooking the books and for violating the "direct investment" rules that prohibited S&Ls from taking substantial ownership of established companies.

The five senators' unambiguous message to the thrift regulators was to drop their case against Lincoln Savings and to get off Keating's back. As Senator Glenn told them bluntly,

> . . . you should charge them or get off their backs. If things are bad there, get to them. Their view is that they took a failing business and put it back on its feet. It's now viable and profitable. They took it off the endangered species list. Why has the exam dragged on and on and on?

In the end the investigation, which described Lincoln Savings as spiraling out of control, was scrapped in May 1988. Its report, recommending that the ailing thrift should be seized by the government, was ignored by the highly politicized Federal Home Loan Bank Board. After Senator Cranston had publicly chastised him for leaning too hard on the thrift industry and Senator DeConcini had demanded his resignation, Gray was replaced as chair of the board by Senator Jake Garn's administrative assistant, Danny M. Wall, who was much friendlier to Keating. Despite this temporary reprieve, however, Lincoln Savings continued to lose ground. As a new federal audit dragged on through 1988 and 1989, Keating finally declared bankruptcy, taking down the five senators with him.

The report of the Senate Ethics Committee concluded that Senators Cranston, DeConcini, and Riegle had improperly interfered with the regulators' enforcement responsibilities at the behest of Keating. In August 1991 the Senate Ethics Committee recommended that the full Senate censure Senator Cranston for "improper and repugnant" conduct (such as asking Keating for half a million dollars as his price for leaning on thrift regulators who were closing in around Lincoln Savings). The other four senators were formally reprimanded for exercising "poor judgment," a relatively mild rebuke given their questionable conduct. Senator Cranston had already decided not to seek reelection, citing medical problems. Senators Glenn and McCain were the only ones among the Keating Five to seek and obtain reelection (Glenn has since retired from the Senate). Senator McCain, the only Republican in the group, had not only taken about $112,000 in campaign contributions from Keating but had also accepted free flights aboard Keating's corporate jet and expense-free family vacations at Keating's Bahamas retreat. However, his dubious involvement in the

S&L scandal and the negative publicity it generated transformed him into a tireless advocate of campaign finance reform.

Shortly after his Lincoln Savings and Loan Association failed (with a record $3.4 billion in excess liabilities), Keating was asked if he thought that his campaign contributions to the five senators had led to the adoption of "favorable" federal banking regulations. He replied with a grin, "I want to say in the most forceful way I can: I certainly hope so." In January 1993 a federal jury convicted Keating of 73 counts of wire and bankruptcy fraud in the collapse of his homebuilding company, American Continental Corporation, and its S&L subsidiary, Lincoln Savings. He was sentenced to 12 years and 7 months imprisonment but served just 50 months in a white-collar prison before his conviction was overturned on a technicality. In 1999, at age 75, Keating pleaded guilty to four counts of fraud for looting American Continental before declaring bankruptcy in 1989. He was sentenced to time served.

As Daniel K. Inouye, the long-serving senator from Hawaii, told the Senate Ethics Committee in 1990, the Keating Five hearings were not just an investigation of the actions of a few colleagues but a trial of the entire U.S. Congress and the way it does business. As a result of the Keating Five scandal, a number of Senate and House bills on campaign finance reform were introduced, calling for campaign spending limits and a ban on unearned honoraria. Major campaign finance reform legislation, sponsored by Senators McCain, Russ Feingold (a Wisconsin Democrat), and Thad Cochran (a Mississippi Republican), was passed by Congress and signed into law by President George W. Bush on April 27, 2002. But the main provision of this legislation, the ban on so-called soft money (the unlimited contributions to political parties from corporations, labor unions, and individuals), has since been challenged in the courts.

Further reading:
Adams, James R. *The Big Fix: Inside the S&L Scandal. How an Unholy Alliance of Politics and Money Destroyed America's Banking System.* New York: John Wiley & Sons, 1990; Binstein, Michael, and Charles Bowden. *Trust Me: Charles Keating and the Missing Billions.* New York: Random House, 1993; Calavita, Kitty, Henry N. Pontell, and Robert H. Tillman. *Big Money Game: Fraud and Politics in the Savings and Loan Crisis.* Berkeley: University of California Press, 1997; Day, Kathleen. *S&L Hell: The People and the Politics behind the $1 Trillion Savings and Loan Scandal.* New York: Norton, 1993; Long, Robert Emmet, ed. *Banking Scandals: The S&Ls and BCCI.* New York: H. W. Wilson, 1993.

—Rossen V. Vassilev

Kefauver, Estes (1903–1963) *Representative, Senator*
Carey Estes Kefauver was a Democratic Party representative and senator who represented the state of Tennessee from 1939 to 1963. Kefauver gained national attention as chair of the Senate Crime Investigating Committee in 1950–51. He unsuccessfully sought the Democratic presidential nomination in 1952 and 1956, although he was selected as Adlai Stevenson's vice presidential running mate in 1956.

Kefauver was born July 26, 1903, in Madisonville, Tennessee, to Robert Cooke Kefauver, a hardware merchant, and Phredonia Bradford Esters. He entered the University of Tennessee in 1922, where he edited the campus newspaper and served as president of the student body. Following his graduation in 1924 with a bachelor of arts degree, Kefauver spent a year teaching mathematics and coaching high school football in Hot Springs, Arkansas. He then entered Yale University, earning a law degree in 1927.

The young attorney returned to Tennessee, where he pursued a lucrative corporate law practice in Chattanooga. In 1938 Kefauver sought election to the Tennessee senate, but the reform-minded lawyer was defeated by the local Democratic machine. He was then appointed a state finance and taxation commissioner by Governor Prentice

Senator Estes Kefauver *(Library of Congress)*

Cooper. When Representative Sam McReynolds of Tennessee's Third District, which included Chattanooga, died in 1939, Kefauver won a special election to fill the seat.

In the HOUSE OF REPRESENTATIVES Kefauver generally supported the policies of President Franklin Roosevelt, earning a reputation as a southern liberal sympathetic to organized labor. He was also an advocate of congressional reform and an opponent of monopoly, chairing a small business subcommittee critical of corporate concentration. Kefauver also emerged as a champion of public power, defending the Tennessee Valley Authority against the efforts of Tennessee senator K. D. McKellor to exercise political control over the agency.

Kefauver was elected to the SENATE in 1948, winning a three-way Democratic primary in which the Tennessee liberal defeated incumbent senator Tom Steward and Judge John Mitchell, who was backed by the political machine of Memphis mayor Edward Hull Crump. An infuriated Crump referred to Kefauver as a pet coon diverting its master's attention while stealing from his pockets. In response Kefauver donned a coonskin cap as a campaign symbol that the senator employed for the remainder of his political career.

In the Senate Kefauver maintained his reputation as a southern liberal, supporting organized labor, civil liberties, and the foreign policies of the Truman administration. Although he acknowledged that he was personally uncomfortable with integration, he was considered a moderate on racial issues and generally backed the civil rights initiatives of President Truman.

The Tennessee senator gained national fame in 1950–51 when he chaired the Senate Crime Investigation Committee. Seizing upon popular fears of a crimewave, Kefauver determined that the hearings would focus on allegations of nationwide gambling syndicates controlled by Italian-American gangsters. The senator also authorized that the hearings be publicized through the new medium of television. The committee conducted hearings in 14 major cities, receiving considerable media attention. Although little legislation resulted from the hearings, Kefauver emerged as one of the most admired men in the United States.

Kefauver used the crime hearings to launch a presidential campaign in which he challenged President Truman for the Democratic nomination. The Democratic Party disapproved of his candidacy, viewing the Tennessean as overly ambitious and blaming his crime commission for placing many Democratic mayors in an unfavorable light. Kefauver used a personal door-to-door campaign greeting voters in his folksy style, which was effective in the small state of New Hampshire. Kefauver upset Truman in the March 1952 New Hampshire primary, and two weeks later Truman dropped out of the race. The Tennessee senator continued to fare well in the Democratic primaries, losing only in Florida and Washington, D.C.

Kefauver entered the 1952 Chicago Democratic National Convention with considerable popular support, but he was opposed by party professionals, who engineered the nomination of Illinois governor Adlai Stevenson.

Following Dwight Eisenhower's victory over Stevenson in the general election, Kefauver was a frequent critic of the new Republican administration. He opposed the controversial Dixon-Yates contract, which called for private power companies to replace the Tennessee Valley Authority as an energy provider. As a civil libertarian, he cast the sole dissenting Senate vote against the 1954 Communist Control Act, which outlawed the Communist Party. Accused of being soft on communism and a liberal out of touch with his southern constituents, Kefauver, nevertheless, easily defeated his conservative Democratic challenger, Pat Sutton, in the 1954 Tennessee senatorial primary.

With his home base secured, Kefauver again sought the Democratic presidential nomination against his old rival, Stevenson. After early victories in the New Hampshire and Minnesota primaries, Kefauver was defeated by Stevenson in a string of primaries, including the pivotal state of California. Kefauver withdrew from the race and endorsed his former rival. When Stevenson allowed the 1956 Democratic National Convention to select his running mate, however, Kefauver's name resurfaced. He was selected for the second spot on the Democratic ticket over Massachusetts senator John Kennedy. Despite Kefauver's fierce populist campaigning, the popular Eisenhower won a landslide victory.

The 1956 national defeat curtailed Kefauver's national ambitions, and the legislator focused on his Senate duties. In 1957 he ascended to the chair of the Antitrust and Monopoly Subcommittee, conducting a series of hearings into administered prices in the steel, automobile, bread, drug, and electrical equipment industries. Kefauver asserted that administered prices encouraged inflation, endangering small businesses and consumers. Although he voted in favor of the 1957 Civil Rights Act, his support of jury trials for those accused of interfering with voting rights was perceived as weakening the legislation.

Kefauver was elected to a third Senate term in 1960. He worked with the Kennedy administration to gain passage of the Kefauver-Harris Drug Control Act of 1962, which strengthened federal safeguards on prescription drugs. Kefauver also led the Senate effort to approve the Twenty-fourth Amendment to abolish the poll tax. On August 10, 1963, Kefauver collapsed on the Senate floor and died from a heart aneurysm.

Further reading:
Estes Kefauver Papers. University of Tennessee, Knoxville; Kefauver, Estes. *Crime in America.* Garden City, N.Y.: Doubleday, 1951; Kefauver, Estes. *In a Few Hands:*

Monopoly Power in America. New York: Pantheon, 1955; Fontenay, Charles L. *Estes Kefauver: A Biography.* Knoxville: University of Tennessee Press, 1980; Gorman, Joseph Bruce. *Kefauver: A Political Biography.* New York: Oxford University Press, 1971.

—Ron Briley

Kennedy, Edward (1932–) *Senator, Majority Whip*
Edward Moore ("Ted") Kennedy was born in Brookline, Massachusetts, on February 22, 1932. He was the fourth son and youngest child of Joseph P. and Rose Fitzgerald Kennedy. He attended several different private schools before entering Milton Academy in 1946. He graduated from Milton in 1950 and enrolled at Harvard University. He was expelled from Harvard at the end of his freshman year for cheating on a Spanish final examination. Kennedy enlisted in the army and was assigned to SHAPE (Supreme Headquarters Allied Powers, Europe) headquarters in Paris. At the end of his two-year enlistment, he returned to Harvard and graduated in 1956. He enrolled in the University of Virginia law school. He received his law degree in 1958 and was admitted to the Massachusetts bar in the same year. In 1958 Kennedy married Virginia Joan Bennett; they had three children and were divorced in 1981.

He managed his brother John's SENATE reelection campaign while still a law student. In 1960, when John F. Kennedy was seeking the presidency, Ted served as western states coordinator for the Democratic nomination. John Kennedy's election as president left his Senate seat vacant. An arrangement with the governor of Massachusetts allowed a temporary "seat warmer" to be appointed until Ted reached the constitutional age to serve in the Senate. In the meantime, he served as assistant district attorney in Suffolk County, Massachusetts.

In 1962 Kennedy faced a tough primary campaign against the nephew of SPEAKER OF THE HOUSE of Representatives JOHN MCCORMACK, a Democrat from Massachusetts. After winning the nomination Kennedy easily defeated Republican George Lodge in the general election. In 1964, a year after President Kennedy's assassination, Senator Kennedy was elected to a full six-year term, winning 74 percent of the vote despite being unable to campaign because of a critical back injury suffered in a plane crash.

Ted's brother Robert also was elected to the Senate from New York. Through most of the 1960s, Ted remained in his older brother's shadow. In 1965 he successfully worked a significant piece of legislation through the process, leading the campaign for passage of the Immigration and Nationality Act ending the national origins quota system. By 1967 he was becoming an outspoken opponent of the Vietnam War. He focused on proposals for draft reform and was critical of the American inability to help Vietnamese refugees. In early 1968 Kennedy visited Vietnam, a trip that made him even more critical in his statements on the war.

In June 1968 Robert Kennedy, Ted's only living brother, was assassinated in a California hotel. Ted became more strident in denouncing the Vietnam War. Elements within the Democratic Party tried to draft him for the 1968 Democratic presidential nomination, but he resisted.

Kennedy was elected Senate Majority WHIP in January 1969. In June he was driving away from a party when he drove his car off a narrow bridge on Chappaquiddick Island in Massachusetts. The accident resulted in the drowning death of his companion, Mary Jo Kopechne, a staffer for Senators George Smathers, a Democrat from Florida, and Robert Kennedy. Kennedy did not report the accident for more than nine hours, resulting in being charged with leaving the scene of an accident. In a televised speech a week after the accident, he asked his constituents to advise him as to whether he should remain in office. His constituents believed he should stay in office. The local court suspended Kennedy's sentence.

Despite the public attention of the Chappaquiddick incident, Kennedy continued to focus on his work in the Senate. He opposed President Richard Nixon's antiballistic missile deployment proposal and supported several proposals to end the war in Vietnam. He also led a campaign to allow 18 year olds to vote in federal elections. Kennedy was easily reelected in 1970, but he lost his Majority Whip position to Senator Robert Byrd, a Democrat from West Virginia, in a close vote in 1971. His attacks on President Richard Nixon's policies led many to believe that Kennedy was going to run for president in 1972. He denied having any presidential ambitions. He did not attend the Democratic National Convention and even refused Democratic nominee George McGovern's offer of the vice presidential nomination.

Kennedy became a leading spokesperson on the issues of handgun control and compulsory national health insurance in the early 1970s. He introduced the Kennedy-Griffiths Health Security Act and wrote a book, *In Critical Condition: The Crisis in American Health Care,* to expose the health care crisis in the United States. He served as chair of the Senate Health Subcommittee, where he heard testimony about the high cost of health care from patients who were dismissed early from hospitals because of their inability to pay the bills. He also favored proposals for amnesty for Vietnam-era draft evaders and the right of women to receive federal assistance to have abortions. Recognizing how controversial his positions were, he once commented that he would love to run against his own record.

In late 1974 he announced that he would not seek the Democratic presidential nomination in 1976, despite leading in public opinion polls. He was reelected to the Senate in 1976 with 70 percent of the vote. In 1977 he was appointed chair of the Senate JUDICIARY COMMITTEE. He worked to deregulate airlines and to enact no-fault insurance legislation. He also supported President Jimmy Carter's foreign policies, including normalization of relations with the People's Republican of China and the Panama Canal Treaty.

In November 1979 Kennedy declared his candidacy for the Democratic presidential nomination, even though President Carter was seeking reelection. His campaign was marred by a series of early mistakes, including a televised interview that mentioned the Chappaquiddick incident. He also suffered from the temporary public support Carter received at the beginning of the Iranian hostage crisis. Kennedy lost to Carter in several early caucuses and primaries but remained in the campaign until the convention.

Republicans gained control of the Senate in 1981, and Kennedy lost his position as Judiciary Committee chair. He focused his energies on social programs and labor issues. In 1982 he was reelected with 60 percent of the vote. By this time he had risen to seventh in Democratic seniority in the Senate. He used his position to criticize many of President Ronald Reagan's domestic and foreign policies. During the 1987 hearings on the confirmation of Supreme Court nominee ROBERT BORK, Kennedy took the lead in organizing the liberals' campaign against Bork's confirmation.

In 1982 Kennedy announced that he would not seek the presidency in the future. After deciding against running for president in 1988, he said, "I know this decision means that I may never be president. But the pursuit of the presidency is not my life. Public service is." He was reelected easily in 1988.

His standing in public opinion was challenged again in the early 1990s. On Easter weekend in 1990, a woman accused Kennedy's nephew William Kennedy Smith of raping her at the Kennedy family's estate in Palm Beach, Florida. The senator's actions were challenged in part because it was his suggestion that he and his nephew go to the bar where Smith later met the accuser. Smith was acquitted of all charges in 1991, but not before Kennedy's reputation was injured. A senior member of the Senate Judiciary Committee, the senator had to remain largely out of the scene during the confirmation hearings for Supreme Court nominee CLARENCE THOMAS. In 1992 Kennedy married attorney Victoria Reggie.

Kennedy supported the presidential campaign of Arkansas governor Bill Clinton in 1992. After Clinton's election the senator worked to move the new president's proposals through Congress. Kennedy worked to pass direct student loans, AmeriCorps, and the School-to-Work Opportunity Act. He also sponsored the Family and Medical Leave Act that had been vetoed by President George H.

W. Bush and was the first piece of legislation signed by President Clinton. He was frustrated by his inability to move the Clinton health care plan through Congress.

In 1994 Kennedy's Republican opponent was businessman Mitt Romney, the son of a Michigan governor and presidential candidate in the 1960s. The campaign was the second-most expensive in 1994, with Kennedy spending $11.5 million and Romney spending $7.6 million. By September Romney had a slight lead in public opinion polls. Desperate, the Kennedy campaign began to question Romney's Mormon faith and ran a series of negative television ads questioning Romney's business practices. Kennedy won 58 percent to 41 percent. The Republican Party gained control of the Senate, however.

As a member of the minority party, Kennedy became a leading liberal voice on issues dealing with health care, education, children, and raising the minimum wage. He was reelected easily in 2000, receiving 72 percent of the vote. In 2001 Senator Jim Jeffords, an independent from Vermont, left the Republican Party, thereby giving the Democrats control of the Senate. Kennedy became the chair of the HEALTH, EDUCATION, LABOR, AND PENSIONS COMMITTEE. He became the ranking member on the committee after the Republicans regained majority status after the 2002 elections. He also continued his service on the Judiciary, Armed Services, and Joint Economic Committees.

Further reading:
Clymer, Adam. *Edward M. Kennedy: A Biography.* New York: Morrow, 1999; McGinnis, Joe. *The Last Brother.* New York: Simon & Schuster, 1993; Samuel, Terence. "A Liberal in Winter." *U.S. News & World Report.* 11 March 2002, pp. 29–30.

—John David Rausch, Jr.

Kern, John Worth (1849–1917) *Senator, Senate Majority Leader*

A progressive Democratic U.S. senator from Indiana, John Worth Kern in 1913 became the Senate's first MAJORITY LEADER.

Kern was born on December 20, 1849, in Alto, Indiana. In his youth the Kern family moved to Iowa but returned to Alto after the death of his mother when John was 14. He attended the local schools and the normal college at Kokomo, Indiana. After graduation he became a schoolteacher in Alto and later in a nearby town. He gained renown as a debater, engaging numerous debates on local issues with other residents of his community. Kern entered law school at the University of Michigan in 1867 and received his law degree in 1869. He then moved to Kokomo to begin his legal practice. His debating skills brought him many satisfied clients and a reputation as an effective trial lawyer. He remained in Kokomo for the next 15 years.

Kern family members were Democrats, and he soon became a local party leader. He was elected secretary of the Democratic county central committee in 1870. The committee nominated him for a seat in the Indiana legislature only a few months later and before he turned 21 years of age. Because Kokomo was Republican territory, Kern was unsuccessful in this first campaign. In 1871 he became Kokomo city attorney, serving in this position until 1884. That year he was nominated for reporter of the Indiana supreme court and was elected. He served four years in that position. Kern was renominated for the position in 1888, but every Democrat seeking a statewide office was defeated. At the expiration of his term in 1889, he remained in Indianapolis and established a residence and a legal practice.

In 1892 he was elected to the Indiana senate; he was reelected in 1894. During his first term Kern was a member of the majority. The Democrats lost control of the senate in 1894, so he was in the minority. Kern's legislative agenda included support for labor unions, the child labor issue, and internal legislative affairs. He was a member of the senate rules committee. In 1896 he met William Jennings Bryan, the Democratic nominee for president. Despite Kern's opposition to free silver, the men became friends. He left the senate in 1897, returning to his legal practice and remaining active in Democratic politics.

Kern won the Democratic nomination for governor in 1900 and was nominated again in 1904, but he lost both contests to the Republican candidate. He did attract some national attention when he ran ahead of the Democratic presidential candidates in both contests. In 1904 he brought the Indiana delegation to the support of New York judge Alton Parker at the Democratic National Convention in St. Louis, seconding the judge's nomination at the convention. He returned to his legal practice after the 1904 campaign. In 1906 ill health led him to spend several months in a sanitarium in Asheville, North Carolina. He returned to Indianapolis in March 1907.

In 1908 Kern entered presidential politics. Bryan was the Democratic nominee, and the party needed to find a vice presidential candidate to share the ticket. Most of the party leadership looked for a Democrat in the eastern states, but Bryan looked in the Midwest. Thomas Taggart of Indiana, chair of the Democratic National Convention, pushed Kern for the position. Bryan agreed, and the convention chose the Indianan. Observers noted that the ticket included a man who was twice defeated for the presidency and one who was defeated twice for governor. The Democrats lost the election to Republican William Howard Taft.

Despite the presidential defeat, the Democratic Party enjoyed a good year in Indiana in 1908. Thomas R. Marshall was elected governor, and the Democrats gained a majority in the Indiana house of representatives. The party had a slim minority in the senate. Because of this situation, the Democrats would elect the next U.S. senator. Most political observers assumed that Kern would become the next senator. He was disappointed when in 1909 the Democrats nominated former house member and gubernatorial candidate Benjamin Shiveley on a secret ballot. Newspaper editorials condemned the vote buying that provided Shiveley with the margin of victory. Again, Kern returned to his legal practice full-time, assuming that his political career was over at the age of 60. In 1910 Indiana's other Senate seat became vacant, and the Democrats sent him to Washington.

Kern entered the U.S. Senate during a time of significant change in America. Despite his lack of seniority, Kern took a leading role in the Senate as a member of the progressive Democrats dedicated to shaking up the conservative leadership of the party. In 1910 10 new Democrats were elected to the Senate, most of them progressives. When President Taft called a special session in April 1911, these new senators became involved in a struggle over the chair of the Democratic Caucus. Conservative senator Thomas S. Martin of Virginia was the leading candidate with the support of the southern Democrats. Bryan traveled to Washington to actively campaign against Martin. The nominal leader of the national Democrats worked to encourage progressive Democrats to run for the chair. Kern nominated fellow Indiana senator Shiveley, but on April 7, 1911, Martin defeated Shiveley on a 21-16 roll-call vote in the caucus. This was the first roll-call vote in 16 years; previous chairs had been elected by the unanimous consent of the caucus.

After Shively's defeat Oklahoma senator Robert Owen offered a resolution to reform the steering committee. Instead of allowing the caucus chair to appoint and chair the steering committee, Owen's proposal would have required that Democrats be divided into three groups according to seniority with three senators from each group appointed to the committee. Owen withdrew his resolution after Martin promised that all Democratic senators would be treated fairly. Shiveley was named vice chair of the caucus, and Kern and another progressive were appointed to the steering committee. Kern also was appointed to the Committee on Privileges and Elections and the FINANCE COMMITTEE.

Kern was an active supporter of campaign finance reform. In fact, the first bill he introduced was "an act providing for the publicity of contributions made for the purpose of influencing elections at which Representatives in Congress are elected." The Bryan-Kern ticket in 1908 had disclosed before the election the names of all contributors who donated $100 or more to the campaign. Kern's bill died in the Privileges and Elections Committee, but a similar measure passed by the House also passed the Senate and was signed into law by President Taft.

During his first two years in office, the senator rarely took the floor. His primary legislative issues included pension reform for Civil War veterans, the rights of laborers, and federal election reform. He favored tariff reform as a member of the Finance Committee. As a member of the Privileges and Elections Committee, he decided the fate of Senator William Lorimer, a Republican from Illinois. The Illinois legislature had elected the Republican boss of Chicago to the U.S. Senate in 1909. Kern played a prominent role in the investigation that led to Lorimer's election being invalidated.

The Democrats took the White House and gained a majority in the Senate in 1912. The Democrats had selected a ticket of New Jersey governor Woodrow Wilson and Indiana governor Thomas Marshall. Wilson shared many of the reformist ideas held by the progressive Democratic senators such as Kern. While the Indiana senator campaigned briefly for the ticket, he was occupied with business through most of the campaign season. The Senate did not adjourn until August 26, 1912. Kern then became involved in the McNamara case in Indianapolis. Labor union president James McNamara was accused of dynamiting a newspaper plant in Los Angeles. Kern served as one of the lead defense attorneys in the case that went on before and after election day. The Indianan also was suffering from lung ailments that limited his campaign activities.

In January 1913 the majority Democrats met to select a caucus chairman. Progressive Democrats again offered a plan to weaken the role of seniority in assigning leadership positions. With 11 new Democrats elected to the Senate in 1912, they joined with 20 other junior Democrats to form a significant faction within the party caucus. Senator Hoke Smith of Georgia offered a reorganization plan to weaken the power of senior Democrats in the Senate. Kern learned of this plan while back in Indianapolis working on the McNamara case. One of the leaders of the reorganization effort wired Kern and asked if he would agree to be considered for party leader. Kern agreed. President-elect Wilson, concerned that the progressives' efforts might lead to intraparty conflict, did not openly encourage the junior senators. When Kern returned to Washington in mid-January 1913, he went to work assuring more senior Democrats that they would have a role in a Senate under Kern's leadership. The Indianan was elected party leader unanimously on March 5, 1913.

Kern ascended to the Majority Leadership during a period of change in executive-legislative relationships. Congress had dominated policy making during the decades following the Civil War. During the Wilson administration the center of policy making shifted to the White House, and Majority Leader Kern became an important voice for Wilson in the Senate. Using the collective power of the Senate Democratic Caucus, Kern was able to shepherd most of Wilson's agenda through the chamber. Some senators criticized Kern for his scheduling plan. The Senate met daily usually all day and into the evening. Under Kern the Senate adopted rules changes, including UNANIMOUS CONSENT AGREEMENTS, allowing a second agreement to revoke the first with one day's notice. Another innovation was the creation of a WHIP position to assist the Majority Leader. Because of the grueling schedule, the Democrats were plagued with absenteeism. Senator J. Hamilton Lewis of Illinois was elected the Senate's first whip in 1913. Lewis's primary task was to ensure a quorum so the Senate could conduct its—and President Wilson's—business.

Most progressives like Kern favored the direct election of senators. In his 1916 reelection bid Kern became victim to the new constitutional amendment when Indiana voters failed to reelect him by a narrow margin. The Majority Leader was again suffering from a lung ailment and began campaigning late. The Republican Party was well organized in Indiana, and few national Democrats came to the state to speak on behalf of Senator Kern. Prominent Democrats recommended that Kern be nominated to some high federal position, and President Wilson agreed. Unfortunately, the former Majority Leader died on August 17, 1917, before Wilson could find a position for Kern.

Further reading:
Bowers, Claude G. *The Life of John Worth Kern.* Indianapolis: Hollendeck Press, 1918; Oleszek, Walter J. "John Worth Kern: Portrait of a Floor Leader." In Richard A. Baker and Roger H. Davidson, eds. *First among Equals: Outstanding Senate Leaders of the Twentieth Century.* Washington, D.C.: Congressional Quarterly Press, 1991.

—John David Rausch, Jr.

Kerr, Robert S. (1896–1963) *Senator*

Politics as well as nature abhor a vacuum. When LYNDON B. JOHNSON moved up from U.S. Senate Majority Leader to vice president in 1961, the vacuum created by his departure was filled by Robert S. Kerr, a Democrat from Oklahoma who earned the sobriquet "The Uncrowned King of the Senate." During the two-year period from Johnson's elevation to vice president until Kerr's death on January 1, 1963, the Democratic senator from Oklahoma was unquestionably the most influential and powerful member of the Senate. President John Kennedy made a famous visit to Oklahoma in order to pay his respects to the man who was "Wagon Master of the New Frontier."

Kerr was born in the Chickasaw Indian Territory near what is now Ada, Oklahoma, on September 11, 1896. Graduating from East Central Norman School in Ada in 1911, he enrolled in Oklahoma Baptist University and also attended East Central State College. Kerr studied law at the University of Oklahoma, was admitted to the Oklahoma bar in 1922, and began a law practice. However, it was his interest in the oil business that eventually made him a wealthy man as cofounder and chair of the board of Kerr-McGee Industries.

Kerr served as a second lieutenant with the First Field Artillery from 1917 to 1919 during World War I. He continued to serve in the military in the Oklahoma National Guard, where he was promoted to captain and then major. Kerr also rose to the top of the American Legion in Oklahoma, making it one of the cornerstones of his political career.

The Democratic Party, however, was Kerr's primary base of power. He was an active party loyalist starting in 1919 until his death in 1963. He served as national committeeman from Oklahoma in 1940. Kerr was elected governor of Oklahoma in 1942, and was the state's first native-born governor. As a result of his oratorical power he was selected as the keynote speaker at the 1944 Democratic National Convention.

Considered a possible running mate for Harry Truman in 1948, such was his popularity that Kerr was the first Oklahoma governor to be elected to the U.S. Senate that same year. Unsuccessful in his quest for the Democratic nomination for president in 1952, Kerr put his considerable talents to work amassing untold influence and power in Congress. He was reelected to the U.S. Senate in 1954 and 1960.

While in the Senate Kerr served on the Appropriations Committee, Finance Committee, Public Works, Aeronautics and Space Sciences Committee, and Select Committee on National Water Resources. Virtually unknown outside Congress and his home state of Oklahoma, Kerr wielded enormous political power behind the scenes. A feared debater, Kerr was more concerned with how to get things done than on parliamentary niceties. Thanks to his strong, outgoing personality, Kerr developed a reputation as a wheeler-dealer who looked after his personal interests, Oklahoma's interests, and national interests as if the three were identical. To him they probably were.

Kerr died unexpectedly on January 1, 1963. An early supporter of conserving natural resources, among his legacies are the McClellan-Kerr Arkansas River Navigation Project and America's manned space program.

Further reading:
Baker, Bobby, with Larry L. King. *Wheeling and Dealing: Confessions of a Capitol Hill Operator.* New York: Norton, 1978; Morgan, Anne Hodges. *Robert S. Kerr: The Senate Years.* Norman: University of Oklahoma Press, 1977; Stephenson, Malvina. *King of the Senate: The Early Life of Robert S. Kerr and Other Insights with His Wit and Humor.* Tulsa, Okla.: Cock-A-Hoop Publishing, 1995.

—Tom Clapper

Kilbourn v. Thompson, 103 U.S. 168 (1881)

This case established limits on congressional investigatory power under Article I of the Constitution. It also served to define the scope of immunity for members of Congress under the Speech and Debate Clause, Article I, Section 6, of the U.S. Constitution, until the Court narrowed and clarified the scope of immunity in GRAVEL V. U.S. and HUTCHINSON V. PROXMIRE.

Hallett Kilbourn was subpoenaed by a committee of the HOUSE OF REPRESENTATIVES investigating a real estate transaction in the District of Columbia (in which the U.S. government was a creditor). After refusing to answer certain questions he was jailed for contempt of Congress. Kilbourn brought a false imprisonment charge against the House SERGEANT AT ARMS and the members of the House committee. The circuit court ruled against Kilbourn, but the Supreme Court reversed and dismissed the charges. The investigation was deemed to be judicial, with a punitive rather than prescriptive purpose.

The Court did not rule that Congress lacked power to punish witnesses for contempt, but it announced strict limitations on the investigatory power. To be constitutional, congressional investigations must be limited to matters about which Congress is authorized to legislate, and the congressional resolution(s) authorizing an investigation must specify an intent to legislate on the subject being investigated. Further, investigations may not intrude into subjects reserved for the executive or judicial branches.

The Court, however, rejected Kilbourn's claim of false imprisonment with respect to the House members who spoke at his hearing. Notwithstanding the House exceeding its authority, its members were nonetheless protected by the Speech and Debate Clause. Members' immunity under the clause, said the Court, extends to things generally done in a session of the House by one of its members in relation to the business before it.

While Kilbourn continues to govern Congress's power to investigate and compel witnesses to testify, the Court has accepted a broader interpretation of legislative purpose, particularly allowing greater leeway in investigating the executive branch and acquiescing during the red scare of the 1940s and 1950s. In *Mcgrain v. Daugherty* (1927) the Court allowed the SENATE to subpoena private citizens in its investigation of the Teapot Dome scandal; the Court reasoned that investigations may address both pending legislation and subjects of potential legislation. In *Watkins v. U.S.* (1957) the Court cautioned against abuse of the investigatory power for the sake of mere exposure and ensured that witnesses called to testify are afforded due process rights. It accepted the broad powers of Congress to convene committees such as the House Un-American Activities Committee, provided the committee charter set reasonable parameters. Regarding speech and debate immunity, 90 years later in *Gravel* the Court modified the *Kilbourn* precedent to include congressional aides performing functions that would be protected if performed by a member and limit protected activities to those integral to the deliberative and communicative processes of the House of Representatives or Senate, specifically excluding activities such as disseminating information to the public.

Further reading:
McGrain v. Daugherty, 273 U.S. 135 (1927); *Watkins v. U.S.,* 354 U.S. 178 (1957); *Gravel v. U.S.,* 408 U.S. 606 (1972); *Hutchinson v. Proxmire,* 443 U.S. 111 (1979).
—Daniel E. Smith

killer amendments

A killer amendment is an amendment that, if adopted, is expected to cause a bill to fail. In its purest form, the killer amendment comes into play by strategy—offered by opponents of a bill to slice off some of the support necessary for the bill's passage by adding an obnoxious provision. The term is also applied to amendments offered by a supporter of a bill who sincerely desires both passage of the bill and inclusion of a provision obnoxious to other supporters of the bill. In either scenario, the amendment creates a dilemma for a subgroup of a bill's supporters and threatens the bill's passage.

The strategic killer amendment comes in two main types: the strengthening amendment and "new issue" amendment. The strengthening amendment threatens the bill by making it so extreme that moderate supporters will be alienated. For instance, during consideration of the Bipartisan Campaign Finance Reform Act (BCRA) in 2002, opponents offered an amendment to put the reforms into effect during the upcoming election. Many of the bill's most ardent proponents would have preferred immediate implementation but had to vote against the amendment to preserve the bill's viability. The strengthening amendment can have an additional benefit to opponents of a popular bill, allowing them to claim that they would have favored the bill if only it were tougher!

The new issue amendment adds another dimension to a debate. A new-issue killer amendment offered to the campaign finance reform bill, dubbed "paycheck protection," would have prevented withholding from workers' pay the portion of union dues used for political donations. This provision, which ordinarily would have enjoyed support from Republicans, was anathema to Democrats who supported campaign finance reform. It placed the Republicans whose support was necessary to pass the bill in the awkward position of rejecting one of two measures they supported.

The use of killer amendments is circumscribed in the House by the requirement that amendments be germane to a bill's subject matter and by the HOUSE RULES' COMMITTEE's control over what amendments may be offered on the floor. But when a chamber's leadership opposes a bill that enjoys support of a majority, a different killer amendment strategy comes into play. If either chamber's leadership opposes a bill, as was the case with campaign finance reform, an identical bill needs to pass both chambers without resort to a CONFERENCE COMMITTEE. This is because leaders appoint conferees and can consign a bill to limbo by refusing to appoint conferees or by appointing conferees hostile to the bill. Under these circumstances any amendment that alters the bill passed by the other house can become a killer. During House consideration of BCRA in 2002, the Rules Committee permitted 20 amendments to be offered over a 15-hour period. BCRA sponsors were forced to hold together their coalition on each and every vote to ensure a final bill acceptable to the Senate.

A study of 76 amendments labeled "killers" during the 103rd and 104th Congresses found that no bills had, in fact, been defeated due to a killer amendment strategy. More problematic is the "sincere" killer amendment, put forth by a member of Congress favoring a bill but who also feels strongly that the bill should not pass without addressing a pet issue. When the amendment addressing that issue commands majority support but alienates a bloc of the bill's supporters, the amendment has the effect of killing the bill.

During the 107th Congress Senator Charles Schumer, a Democrat from New York, added an amendment to the bankruptcy reform bill to prevent bankruptcy judges from discharging fines levied on abortion protesters for blocking access to clinics. Anti-abortion Republicans who otherwise would have supported the bill refused to vote for it, and the bill died. Another famous example of a sincere killer amendment was Representative Adam Clayton Powell's (a Democrat from New York) amendment to the 1956 School Construction Aid bill denying federal funds to schools that practiced racial segregation. Northern Democrats felt compelled to support the amendment even though its inclusion in the bill alienated southern Democrats, whose support was necessary for passage. The Powell amendment eventually became law in 1964.

Further reading:
Wilkerson, John D. " 'Killer' Amendments in Congress." *American Political Science Review* 93, 3 (September 1999): 535–552; Lancaster, John. "Sorting out the 'Poison Pills.' " *Washington Post,* 13 February 2002; Editorial. "Why the Code Won't Change in 2003." *Consumer Bankruptcy News,* 26 December 2002.
—Jackson Williams

L

"lame duck"

When presidents or members of Congress will not be returning to office, they become known as "lame ducks." The term applies to persons occupying their offices between the election and the inauguration of their successors. All these outgoing officeholders continue to exercise the full authority of their positions, but their influence is considered "lamed" by the fact that they will soon be relinquishing the reins of power.

From the start the lame duck period was a problem, most famously illustrated in the *MARBURY V. MADISON* case, in which lame-duck appointments by President John Adams set the stage for a landmark Supreme Court decision with his series of late night, last-minute appointments. Experience has shown that allowing a lame-duck session to be extensive often bring about undesirable legislative conditions. The result is a hurried situation whereby members of Congress can pass legislation without regard to its consequences, since they will not have to face the electorate again. Such sessions can take an unpredictable shape, with defeated lawmakers taking one last stab at winning legislative items for their favorite constituencies or interest groups. Representative David Obey, a Democrat from Wisconsin said,

> Nobody will have to answer for their actions. It's garbage time. An unleashed Congress is a dangerous thing. About anything is possible, including self-immolation.

Departing members have less at stake than members who will be facing voters again, and that can be reflected in modest changes in the way they vote or whether they vote at all. Congressional lame ducks are no longer accountable to their constituents but still can vote if lame-duck sessions are held. Lame-duck sessions historically were used to approve congressional pay raises and to improve the benefits and perks of retiring members. They also have provided an opportunity to pass unpopular legislation not mentioned during the campaign, since blame can then be placed on the nonreturning members. The TWENTIETH AMENDMENT was adopted to address this set of problems.

Further reading:
"Senate Plans Lame-Duck Session." *Arizona Daily Wildcat,* 2 November 2000; U.S. Constitution, Twentieth Amendment, 1933.

—Nancy S. Lind

"lame duck" amendment   *See* TWENTIETH AMENDMENT.

leadership, House of Representatives

The most important leaders who play a central role in the operations of the HOUSE OF REPRESENTATIVES are the SPEAKER OF THE HOUSE, the MAJORITY and MINORITY LEADERS and their deputies, and the Majority and Minority WHIPs. Most representatives in the House are members of either the Democratic Party or the Republican Party. At any given time it is the political party in the majority that is responsible for organizing and presiding over the business of the House. The majority party in the House chooses the Speaker, the Majority Leader, and the Majority Whip. It has a majority on each committee and controls the appointment of the committee chairs and most committee staff members. The Speaker and the other leaders are more influential than the rest of the House members, and they also enjoy certain additional privileges, including larger offices and staffs as well as chauffeured limousines.

The Constitution makes the Speaker the presiding officer of the House. He or she is third in line of constitutional authority and succession after the president and the vice president. Legally, the Speaker does not have to be but by custom has always been a member of the House. The

Speaker of the House is the leader of the majority party who attains leadership only after many uninterrupted terms of service. The Speaker presides over floor sessions and gives representatives permission to debate. He or she decides on the legislative agenda in consultation with the Majority Leader and the Minority Leader, committee chairs, and sometimes other senior members of the House. The Speaker also appoints most House members of the four JOINT COMMITTEES, which consist of members of both chambers of Congress. As presiding officer the Speaker is also the principal arbiter of the procedural rules and is assisted in this by the House PARLIAMENTARIAN. Only a vote by the majority of House members can overrule the Speaker's interpretations or applications of the RULES AND PROCEDURES.

Historically, the Speaker used to be more powerful and less responsive to the preferences of other members of the House. The Speaker set the agenda for floor debate to suit his or her own purposes and also appointed House committees, sometimes even ignoring seniority in designating the chairs. But at the beginning of the 20th century the members of the House rebelled, removing the Speaker from the RULES COMMITTEE and stripping the power to appoint committees and determine the legislative agenda. Since then the Speaker has relied more on informal influence among House members than on the formal authority of office.

Given the numerous legislative and other political duties, the Speaker is often absent from the House and has to turn over procedural responsibilities to the Speaker Pro Tempore, a senior representative from the majority party appointed by the Speaker to be a designated substitute. The Speaker is officially elected by the full House but actually has already been chosen at the caucus of the majority party (either the Democratic Caucus or the Republican Conference), which takes place in January after every congressional election. Following tradition, both parties nominate their candidate for Speaker, and then the entire membership votes for their choice on the opening day of a new Congress. But the House election simply confirms the majority party's choice because representatives always vote for their party's candidates for leadership positions. The members of the majority party also select the Majority Leader of the House at their caucus. The candidate for Speaker chosen by the minority party becomes the Minority Leader.

Each party also elects an assistant floor leader called a whip. Acting at the discretion of their respective floor leaders, the Majority Whip and the Minority Whip are charged with tracking forthcoming votes on important legislation in the House and with maintaining party discipline, which most often means trying to persuade party members to support their party's position. Party discipline is not particularly strict in the House, whose members run for reelection every two years and tend to look for support in their electoral districts rather than from the party leadership. In the absence of the party floor leader, the party whip often serves as acting floor leader. The majority leadership of the House is firmly in control of calling up legislation and deciding on the terms of its debate and amendments.

The heads of STANDING COMMITTEES and their SUBCOMMITTEES are a further dominating element of House leadership. These are senior members of the majority party, who are elected by a secret ballot at the party caucus at the beginning of each new Congress. After the Democratic Caucus and the Republican Conference have selected their choices, their committee assignments are confirmed by the entire House. But it is the Speaker who nominates the majority party's members of the important Rules Committee, which decides whether a bill will appear before the entire House for consideration.

Beginning in the 1920s the House followed the rule of its SENIORITY SYSTEM for determining members' rank on standing committees and in selecting committee chairs. The member of the majority party with the longest continuous record of service on each House committee automatically became its chair. But in an effort to democratize the selection process, the seniority system was reformed in the early 1970s. Now all members of the majority party can participate by secret ballot in selecting committee chairs, and each member may be elected to a committee chair regardless of seniority rank.

Further reading:
Currie, James T. *The United States House of Representatives.* Malabar, Fla.: R. E. Krieger, 1988; Deering, Christopher J., and Steven S. Smith. *Committees in Congress.* Washington, D.C.: Congressional Quarterly Press, 1997; Sinclair, Barbara. *Legislators, Leaders, and Lawmaking: The U.S. House of Representatives in the Postreform Era.* Baltimore: Johns Hopkins University Press, 1995; Smith, Steven S. *The American Congress.* Boston: Houghton Mifflin, 1999.

—Rossen V. Vassilev

leadership, Senate

Under the Constitution the vice president of the United States is the formal presiding officer, or president of the Senate, even though he or she spends little time in the Senate. Constitutionally, the vice president can vote only when the votes of senators are evenly divided on a controversial measure. Because the vice president is present only at ceremonial occasions and at meetings of special importance or to cast a tie-breaking vote, in his or her absence the most senior senator of the majority party (the party with the larger membership in the Senate) acts as the President Pro Tempore. Each is addressed as "Mr. President" when presiding over Senate proceedings.

Given his or her seniority the President Pro Tempore is also often absent, usually due to other duties as a chair of Senate STANDING COMMITTEES and/or their SUBCOMMITTEES. (While most House members serve on only one committee, all senators serve on two or three committees and a large number of subcommittees.) The business of presiding over the Senate is then assumed by junior senators, usually from the majority party, who guide debate in most sessions. These different temporary presidents rotate during floor sessions, each spending about an hour in the chair.

Even though political parties are not mentioned in either the Constitution or the procedural rules of the Senate and the House, the majority party takes the responsibility for managing official leadership positions in each chamber. The party conferences (known also as party caucuses), which are private meetings open to all members of the party, are held before each new session of Congress begins. These separate party meetings elect party floor leaders for a two-year term. The offices of Senate MAJORITY LEADER and MINORITY LEADER, which are not mentioned in the Constitution, developed gradually over the past century. The Senate designated its first Democratic floor leader only in 1920 and its first Republican floor leader in 1925. Having been elected by a majority vote of all the senators of their own party, the Majority and Minority Leaders act as the elected spokespersons in the Senate for their respective political parties and seek to maintain unified party action and discipline.

The authority to call up a measure to the floor is reserved by tradition for the Senate Majority Leader, who schedules the daily legislative agenda in consultations with the Senate Minority Leader. The majority leader, or another designated senior senator from the majority party, is present on the floor every day when the Senate is in session to make sure that the agenda is carried out to the party's satisfaction. Similarly, the minority leader, or another senior senator from the minority party, always remains on the floor to protect the interests of the minority.

The party conferences also elect the party WHIPS, the assistant floor leaders who act at the discretion of the Majority and Minority Leaders. The Majority and Minority Whips are charged with tracking forthcoming votes on important legislation in the Senate and with trying to persuade party members to support their party's position. In the absence of the party floor leader, the party whip often serves as acting floor leader. The work of the Senate is usually organized by the Majority Leader and the Majority Whip.

The Senate leadership also includes the conference chairs that are the chairs of the Democratic Caucus and the Republican Conference. The party conferences (or party caucuses) elect floor leaders, make committee assignments, and set legislative agendas. The Democratic floor leader serves as chair of the party caucus, while the Republican Party elects a chair for the party conference separate from the post of floor leader. The chairs of the party policy committees are also included in the Senate leadership. Established by the Senate in 1947, the Democratic and Republican Policy Committees help schedule bills for floor consideration and plan the legislative strategy of their parties. Both party policy committees now elect their chairs separately from the party floor leaders. Democrats and Republicans in the Senate also appoint campaign committees to raise contributions for Senate elections. Chaired by senior senators, these committees distribute money to incumbent senators and promising candidates. The senatorial CAMPAIGN COMMITTEE chairs are also considered part of the Senate leadership.

True to their customary decentralized style of leadership, Senate leaders have traditionally relied more on informal influence than on formal authority. They must maintain continued support as leaders because they are subject to periodic reelection by fellow senators from their own political party. In daily practice much of the legislative business of the Senate is conducted on the basis of unanimous consent agreements negotiated between the floor leaders of the two parties and aiming to achieve procedural and policy consensus. Floor leaders work together to expedite legislative consideration by placing voluntary restrictions on debate and amendment while trying to accommodate the scheduling and policy needs of the individual senators. However, most of the work in the Senate is performed by standing committees in which senators from both the majority and the minority parties are represented but are chaired by senior members of the majority party. The majority member whose continuous service on the committee is the longest is usually the chair.

Further reading:
Evans, C. Lawrence. *Leadership in Committee: A Comparative Analysis of Leadership in the U.S. Senate.* Ann Arbor: University of Michigan Press, 2001; Hickok, Eugene W., Jr. *The Senate: Advice and Consent and the Judicial Process.* Washington, D.C.: National Legal Center for the Public Interest, 1992; Lee, Francis E., and Bruce I. Oppenheimer, eds. *Sizing Up the Senate: The Unequal Consequences of Equal Representation.* Chicago: University of Chicago Press, 1999; Oppenheimer, Bruce I., ed. *U.S. Senate Exceptionalism.* Columbus: Ohio State University Press, 2002; Ripley, Randall B. *The Congress: Process and Policy.* New York: Norton, 1988.

—Rossen V. Vassilev

Legal Counsel, Office of Senate

The Office of Senate Legal Counsel was created through Title VII of the Ethics in Government Act of 1978 (95 Pub. Law 521; 92 Stat. 1824). The Office of the Senate Legal Counsel consists of the Senate Legal Counsel, a Deputy Senate Legal Counsel, and as many Assistant Senate Legal Counsels and other personnel as needed to perform the duties of the office. The Senate Legal Counsel and the Deputy Senate Legal Counsel are appointed by the President Pro Tempore of the Senate based on the recommendations of the Senate Majority and Minority Leaders. The Office of the Senate Legal Counsel acts under the direction of the Senate Joint Leadership Group.

Prior to 1978 the Solicitor General was in charge of representing the interests of the government, both the executive and the legislative branches. Whenever a conflict between the two branches' interests arose, Congress was advised to retain its own special counsel. With increasing disputes between the executive branch and Congress in the wake of the Watergate scandal and the high cost of retaining special counsel, the Senate deemed it necessary to protect its own interests in Supreme Court proceedings rather than rely primarily on the Solicitor General. The office was created to represent the Senate before the Supreme Court when the interests of the executive branch as represented by the Solicitor General and the interests of the Senate conflict. This occurs for two primary reasons. First, a statute may in effect limit the powers of the president. Second, the attorney general may feel that a statute is so clearly unconstitutional that the executive branch will not support it. When either of these situations arise the attorney general is required to notify the Office of the Senate Legal Counsel so that the office may proceed if they so choose. Under most circumstances, when the interests of the Senate and the executive branch are consistent, the Solicitor General represents the government's interest. However, whenever a conflict arises the Office of the Senate Legal Counsel takes over, and the Solicitor General is relieved of any responsibility for presenting the Senate's interests.

In addition to its role as the attorney for the Senate before the Supreme Court in matters when a conflict between the executive branch and the Senate exists, the Office of the Senate Legal Counsel is responsible for defending any member or employee of the Senate in any lawsuit whether in state or federal court when that person was acting in that person's official capacity, enforcing subpoenas issued by the Senate, filing amicus curiae (a friend of the court) briefs in the federal appellate courts, advising the Senate or its members on legal matters pertaining to their official capacities, obtaining grants of immunity from the U.S. district courts when the Senate has agreed to immunity for a witness, and defending the constitutional powers of the Senate.

The original intent was to form an Office of Congressional Legal Counsel to serve the interests of both the Senate and the House of Representatives, but the House was unable to agree on the conditions. As a result, the Office of the Senate Legal Counsel was the only one enacted. While the House has never joined the office or created its own, it has used its internal rule-making powers to grant similar responsibility to the Speaker's legal counsel.

Further reading:
Days, Drew S., III. "Lecture: In Search of the Solicitor General's Clients: A Drama with Many Characters." *Kentucky Law Journal*, 83 (1994): 485; Salokar, Rebecca Mae. *The Solicitor General: The Politics of Law.* Philadelphia: Temple University Press, 1992.

—Corey A. Ditslear

Legislative Counsel Office

The Legislative Counsel Office of the HOUSE OF REPRESENTATIVES and the OFFICE OF THE LEGAL COUNSEL OF THE SENATE were established on October 26, 1970, by the LEGISLATIVE REORGANIZATION ACT OF 1970 and amended by the Legislative Branch Appropriation Act of 1972. They were created to aid the House, the Senate, their committees, and members in drafting legislation. This office evolved from the Legislative Drafting Service, which was established by the Revenue Act of 1918 and enacted on February 24, 1919. The Legislative Drafting Service was created mainly due to the efforts of Middleton Beaman and Thomas I. Parkinson in presenting and convincing Congress of the benefits that the professional drafting service could offer. The Office of the Legislative Counsel advises and assists members of Congress in order to advise and assist in the achievement of a clear, faithful, and coherent expression of legislative policies (Title V of the Legislative Reorganization Act of 1970).

Presiding officers appoint the legislative counsels for their respective chambers. The legislative counsels in turn appoint their own staff with the approval of the presiding officer of the chamber in which they are located. The criterion for appointment is that the appointees should be able to carry out the work. Both offices have no political affiliation, and it is common for the same attorney to work with opposing sides on legislative policy issues. The attorneys are concerned only with making certain that the legislation they are drafting reflects the policy of the member or committee for whom it is being drafted. In order to do this, they have to consult with the members and their assistants and committees, attend sessions of both chambers, attend committee markups, and so on to clearly understand the problems. All communications with the office are kept confidential.

Further reading:
Lee, Frederic P. "The Office of the Legislative Counsel." *Columbia Law Review* 29, no. 4 (April 29, 1929): 381–403; Jones, Harry W. "Bill-Drafting Services in Congress and the State Legislatures." *Harvard Law Review* 65, no. 3 (January 1952): 441–481.

—Arthur Holst

legislative day

The time period that extends from one adjournment until the next adjournment in either the House or the Senate is the legislative day. Although a legislative day is similar in definition in both chambers, in reality it means different things from chamber to chamber. Since the House normally adjourns at the end of each day, legislative days and calendar days within the House usually coincide. However, legislative days in the Senate can take weeks or even months to complete. Instead of officially adjourning from day to day, the Senate instead chooses to recess at the end of each day, which is merely taking pause in legislation but not officially ending the proceedings for the day.

The Senate engages in this practice to avoid interrupting unfinished business with an adjournment. This is based on the Senate rule regarding the MORNING HOUR. Morning business, which includes introducing bills, filing committee reports, and receiving messages from the president and the House of Representatives, has to be done at the beginning of each session that the Senate meets directly after an ADJOURNMENT. Additionally, during the morning hour senators, as long as it is agreed to with UNANIMOUS CONSENT AGREEMENTS, can make short speeches and can also move to consider any bill that has already been placed on the calendar. However, the bill cannot be debated and cannot be FILIBUSTERed. Morning business can be extensive and time consuming, often taking well over two hours to complete.

Essentially, the legislative day is a parliamentary invention that ensures as few interruptions in the day-to-day work of the Senate as possible. When legislative days are extended to avoid the morning hour, the work of the morning hour is normally done, when necessary, with unanimous consent agreements.

See also ADJOURNMENT AND RECESS, HOUSE; ADJOURNMENT AND RECESS, SENATE.

Further reading:
Oleszek, Walter J. *Congressional Procedures and the Policy Process.* 5th ed. Washington, D.C.: Congressional Quarterly Press, 2001; Stewart, Charles III. *Analyzing Congress.* New York: Norton, 2001.

—Lisa A. Solowiej

legislative process

The steps through which a bill must travel before becoming a law have been termed the legislative process. The U.S. Constitution in Article I, Section 1, created the legislative branch of the federal government and assigned it the primary duty of making laws. While all legislative powers are vested in a Congress of the United States, the Constitution is largely silent about the exact process by which the legislative branch will exercise its legislative powers. Other than a few specific requirements for legislation, such as requiring all bills raising revenue to originate in the HOUSE OF REPRESENTATIVES, the Constitution, in Article I, Section 5, allows each chamber to determine the rules of its proceedings.

The legislative process usually is described as a flowchart, with each piece of legislation moving quickly through the process. In reality, the process is much more complex. Some bills move through the process quickly. Others are delayed while compromises are reached. Some legislation becomes part of other legislation, while some bills languish in committee, left to die a silent death at the end of a Congress. Far more bills are blocked by the process than are allowed to become law. During the 107th Congress (2001–02), only about 4 percent of the measures introduced became law.

All legislation traditionally begins as an idea. While only members of the House of Representatives and the SENATE may introduce bills in their respective chambers, anyone may provide an idea for a piece of legislation. The president, federal departments and agencies, state government officials, interest groups, and congressional staff may provide suggestions for legislation. Constituents, as individuals or in groups, may petition Congress, as is their right under the First Amendment to the Constitution. Members of Congress have been known to introduce a proposal knowing that it had no chance to succeed. The members wanted to go on record as supporting the idea represented by the proposal. No matter where the idea came from, a member may consult with the legislative counsel of the House or the Senate to frame the ideas in suitable legislative language and form before introduction.

The member introducing a piece of legislation is known as the bill's sponsor. Other members may choose to associate with the proposal and are called cosponsors. Identifying a large number of cosponsors suggests to other members of the chamber that the idea has wide support. In the House bills are introduced by dropping them into the hopper, a large wooden box located on the dais of the SPEAKER OF THE HOUSE. In the Senate bills are handed to a clerk. The bills are printed and distributed to all members of the chamber. Copies of bills also are made available to the public.

Legislative proposals take one of four forms: BILL, JOINT RESOLUTION, CONCURRENT RESOLUTION, or SIMPLE

RESOLUTION. While *bill* often is applied to all pieces of legislation introduced in Congress, a bill can be different from the other forms. A bill is identified in the House as H.R. xxxx (for example, H.R. 1002) and in the Senate as S. xxxx (for example, S. 1002). There is no difference between a bill and a joint resolution. During the 107th Congress (2001–02), 8,948 bills and 178 joint resolutions were introduced in both houses. Of the total number introduced, 5,767 bills and 125 joint resolutions originated in the House of Representatives. Several traditions apply to bills and joint resolutions. Proposals to amend the Constitution are drafted as joint resolutions. Some appropriations bills also are identified as joint resolutions. Bills and most joint resolutions must pass both chambers and be signed by the president before they become law. Joint resolutions proposing constitutional amendments must comply with the amending process.

Concurrent resolutions are used to take an action on behalf of Congress as a whole or to express congressional opinion on a matter. The Supreme Court has ruled that concurrent resolutions are not legislative. A concurrent resolution originating in the House of Representatives is designated "H. Con. Res." followed by its individual number, while a Senate concurrent resolution is designated "S. Con. Res." together with its number. On approval by both houses, they are signed by the CLERK OF THE HOUSE and the SECRETARY OF THE SENATE and transmitted to the Archivist of the United States for publication in a special part of the Statutes at Large volume covering that session of Congress.

A simple resolution involves a matter concerning the rules, the operation, or the opinion of either chamber alone. A resolution affecting the House of Representatives is designated "H. Res." followed by its number, while a Senate resolution is designated "S. Res." together with its number. Simple resolutions are considered only by the body in which they were introduced. Upon adoption simple resolutions are attested to by the Clerk of the House of Representatives or the Secretary of the Senate and are published in the *CONGRESSIONAL RECORD*.

After introduction most measures are referred to a legislative STANDING COMMITTEE or committees. Each chamber's rules govern the process through which referral is made. The Speaker of the House makes the referral decision based on advice from the parliamentarian. In the Senate the presiding officer refers legislation based on recommendations from that chamber's parliamentarian. Some measures are referred to a number of committees because they include subject matter within the jurisdiction of more than one committee. The committee phase is the most important part of the legislative process. Because much of the legislation that fails to become law does not clear the committee process, the decision on which committee to refer a bill to is crucial. Members of Congress have become creative in drafting legislation in order to avoid referral to a particular committee.

The committee may keep the bill for action by the full committee or it may send it to one of its subcommittees. This practice is governed by individual committee rules. The committee or subcommittee may schedule the bill for public HEARINGS. The hearings may develop information from experts about the value of the measure under consideration or to determine whether the legislation is even necessary. The individual committee develops the rules governing a hearing.

After hearings are completed, the subcommittee usually will consider the bill in a session known as the "markup" session. The views of both sides are studied in detail, and at the conclusion of deliberation a vote is taken to determine the action of the subcommittee. It may decide to report the bill favorably to the full committee, with or without amendment, unfavorably, or without recommendation. The subcommittee may also suggest that the committee "table" it, or postpone action indefinitely. Each member of the subcommittee, regardless of party affiliation, has one vote. Proxy voting is no longer permitted in House committees or subcommittees.

After hearing the report of the subcommittee, the full committee may also mark up the bill. These sessions end with a vote on whether to report the revised version of the legislation to the House or Senate floor with a recommendation for passage by the chamber. The measure must be reported out of committee by a vote taken when a quorum of the committee is present.

Measures are accompanied by committee reports when they are sent to the chamber's floor for further consideration. Committee reports are required in the House but are optional in the Senate. A report must include the committee's oversight findings and recommendations; a statement required by the CONGRESSIONAL BUDGET AND IMPOUNDMENT CONTROL ACT OF 1974 if the measure is a bill or joint resolution providing new budget authority (other than continuing appropriations) or an increase or decrease in revenues or tax expenditures; a cost estimate and comparison prepared by the director of the CONGRESSIONAL BUDGET OFFICE whenever the director has submitted that estimate and comparison to the committee prior to the filing of the report; and a statement of general performance goals and objectives, including outcome-related goals and objectives for which the measure authorizes funding. The committee report is an essential part of the bill's legislative history. If a committee fails to take action on a bill, both chambers have rules providing for a bill to be discharged from committee and sent to the floor without a report.

Legislation reported from a House committee is placed on one of five CALENDARS: the Union Calendar, the

House Calendar, the Private Calendar, the Corrections Calendar, and the Calendar of Motions to Discharge Committees. When a public bill is favorably reported by all committees to which it was referred, it is assigned a calendar number on either the Union Calendar or the House Calendar, the two principal calendars of business. In the Senate all bills are placed on the Calendar of General Orders. Placement on a calendar does not guarantee floor consideration. The majority leadership in both chambers sets the floor agenda.

The House considers most legislation under SUSPENSION OF THE RULES, a procedure in which the regular rules of order are waived. Under suspension of the rules measures may be debated for no more than 40 minutes and may not be amended from the floor.

Most controversial measures considered by the House are called up under a special rule drafted by the HOUSE RULES COMMITTEE. A special rule replaces the regular rules of order and becomes the guide for considering the bill. The special rule must be approved by the House before it can take effect. Special rules generally do four things for a piece of legislation. The first provision makes it in order to call up the bill for consideration. The second provision sets a time limit and allocates the time between the majority and minority parties. The third provision establishes the amending procedures and can include rules allowing no amendments, a few amendments, or specific amendments. The final provision may prohibit points of order. Special rules tend to be controversial.

The consideration of a bill on the Senate floor is much simpler. Most measures are brought up by a simple request to turn to a bill's immediate consideration. Without objection, the bill is considered, debated, and amended without any restrictions. The Senate also can consider a bill using a UNANIMOUS CONSENT AGREEMENT that may include time limitations on debate, restrict the number of amendments, and provide for a vote for final passage. Unlimited debate in the Senate means that a FILIBUSTER is possible. Filibusters can be ended by a CLOTURE vote of 60 or more senators.

Most of the debating and amending activity in the House is conducted after the House resolves itself into the COMMITTEE OF THE WHOLE on the State of the Union. In the Committee of the Whole, business is still conducted in the House chamber but under different procedures. These procedures make it easier to expedite the consideration of a bill. The five-minute rule operates in the Committee of the Whole, meaning that the proponents and opponents of any amendment may speak for five minutes. After general debate on the bill, the Committee of the Whole considers amendments. When the amendments are considered and disposed of, the Committee of the Whole arises and transforms itself back into the House of Representatives. The amended bill is then reported to the House for its consideration.

The House votes on final passage using one of four voting methods. The bill may pass by unanimous consent. If one member objects the presiding officer puts the question to a voice vote. After the voice vote any member may demand a standing vote, in which members stand to have their votes counted. The final method of voting is the recorded vote. If a recorded vote is ordered members vote by electronic device. The recorded vote is published in the *CONGRESSIONAL RECORD*. The Senate uses the same four voting methods, but the recorded vote is conducted by roll call. The Senate does not have an electronic device to record the votes, so the clerk calls each senator by name, and tellers record each senator's vote.

The House and Senate must enact identical versions of a bill before the legislation is sent to the president for signature or veto. There are two methods for reconciling differences between the two chambers. The first method is called amendments between the two houses. In this method the text of a bill is passed from the House and Senate until one chamber agrees with the amendments added by the other. The second method is to use a CONFERENCE COMMITTEE. A conference committee is a temporary committee comprised of House members and senators who meet to negotiate the differences between the two versions of a bill. After reaching an agreement the conference committee issues a report that must be agreed to by a majority of both chambers.

After a bill has been approved in identical form by both the House and the Senate, it is sent to the enrolling clerk, who prepares it for presentation to the president. The president is given 10 days to review the legislation, during which he or she has four options. The president can sign the legislation into law. Second, he or she can permit the bill to become law without signature, which occurs after 10 days pass if Congress remains in session. The president's third option is to hold the bill for 10 days in a pocket veto, which occurs after Congress has adjourned. Finally, the president can veto a bill and return it to the chamber that originated it with a veto message outlining his or her objections to the measure. Two-thirds of the chamber may vote to override the president's veto and send it to the other chamber. If two-thirds of the second chamber votes to override, the bill becomes law over the president's objections. Among more recent presidents, Congress overrode nine of President Ronald Reagan's vetoes, one of President George H. W. Bush's, and two of President Bill Clinton's.

Further reading:
Dewhirst, Robert E. *Rites of Passage: Congress Makes Laws.* Upper Saddle River, N.J.: Prentice Hall, 1997; Elving, Ronald D. *Conflict and Compromise: How Congress Makes the Law.* New York: Simon & Schuster, 1995; Johnson, Charles W. *How Our Laws Are Made.* House Document

108-93. Washington, D.C.: Government Printing Office, 2003; Sinclair, Barbara. *Unorthodox Lawmaking: New Legislative Processes in the U.S. Congress.* Washington, D.C.: Congressional Quarterly Press, 1997.

—John David Rausch, Jr.

Legislative Reorganization Act of 1946

Considered by many scholars to mark the beginning of the modern Congress, the Legislative Reorganization Act of 1946 (PL 79-60) was the first major structural and procedural overhaul of the entire institution since the Civil War. While several of its innovations failed to bring improvement, the act laid a foundation for future reform movements that were more successful.

Congress needed to modernize following World War II in order to compete effectively for influence with an executive branch whose capacity had expanded in response to the war as well as to meet the growing demands of an increasingly diverse and complex nation. Criticism of Congress's antiquated approach to lawmaking came from many quarters. For example, the American Political Science

This Berryman cartoon refers to the Legislative Reorganization Act of 1946. *(National Archives)*

Association issued a study of the institution in 1945 that found fault with its structure and methods, and Representative EVERETT DIRKSEN's (R-IL) talk "What Is Wrong With Congress?" was widely quoted. Public displeasure rose to such a level that Congress was forced to act. Both chambers voted in 1945 to form the Joint Committee on the Organization of Congress (JCOC) composed of six members from each house with equal numbers of Republicans and Democrats. The cochairs were Representative A. S. Mike Monroney (D-OK) and Senator Robert M. LaFollette, Jr. (R-WI). The committee met publicly for four months, from March to June, to take testimony and issued its final report on March 4, 1946. While the scope of the proposal was impressive, notably absent from it was any mention of curtailing the power of the Rules Committee in the House, easing the cloture mechanism in the Senate, or reducing the role of seniority in the designation of committee chairs in both houses. Subsequent floor debate over several months resulted in amendments and the removal of a number of dramatic JCOC recommendations, despite their popularity with many lawmakers. Among the rejected proposals were: Provide home rule to the District of Columbia, thereby relieving Congress of the burden of managing the District; create a centralized Civil Service type system to test and hire congressional staff for all offices and committees; and establish policy committees for both parties in each chamber to serve as advisory bodies to the leadership. The bill was eventually enacted on August 4, 1946.

In an effort to streamline its structure, the act drastically slashed the number of standing committees in both houses by eliminating committees that dealt with obsolete subjects or that were inactive and by combining committees that had overlapping jurisdictions. The House went from 48 standing committees to 19, while the Senate shrank to 15 from 33. This reduction was no mean feat, because entrenched committee chairs resisted all attempts to remove or limit their turf.

Beyond scaling back the number of committees, the act also attempted to make committee chairs more responsive and accountable to their fellow members. All standing committees except the Appropriations Committees were required to establish schedules and hold regular meetings. In the past chairs could hold legislation they opposed hostage by not meeting. Moreover, chairs were directed to move bills within their committees to a final vote as expeditiously as possible and then to push the bills approved by committee to the floor. But in order to thwart a capricious chair, no bill could be forwarded to the floor without a vote of the majority of committee members present. Chairs were also mandated to maintain all records of their committee's work including votes taken and to hold open public meetings, except for mark-ups and voting, unless a majority of the committee voted to close its doors because

discussion turned to matters of national security or issues deemed sensitive.

To improve legislative support, the act provided that four professional and six clerical staff be added to each standing committee, except for the Appropriations Committees, which had no limitation on number of staff. In addition, the Library of Congress's staff was reorganized, with the Legislative Reference Service (now known as the Congressional Research Service) becoming a distinct unit dedicated to conducting research for members.

The act sought to use members' time more efficiently by severely restricting the use of private bills. Private bills had become vehicles for members to have their constituents receive federal pensions and tort settlements or have their military records corrected. These seemingly trivial matters took large amounts of time. In addition, some members used private bills to have roads and bridges constructed in their districts. The act banned members from employing private bills for such things. For senators the act made it more difficult to include nongermane amendments in conference committees and restricted conferees from including unrelated amendments that the Senate had not previously debated. It also fixed a date for adjournment of July 31, except in times of national emergency or if either house voted to extend the session.

The failure of congressional salaries to keep pace with inflation was a source of discontent among lawmakers, and the act addressed this issue by raising salaries to $12,500 from $10,000; the salaries of the vice president and Speaker were set at $20,000. The members' retirement benefits were improved by having Congress covered by the Civil Service Retirement Act. Members may retire at 62 if they have served a minimum of six years in office.

Concerned over its inability to rein in excessive spending by the executive, Congress included a provision in the act that created a Joint Budget Committee composed of members of the Ways and Means, Finance, and Appropriations Committees from each house. The new committee then would produce a unified, comprehensive budget for the entire federal government estimating all revenues and expenditures. The committee would also issue a report and a concurrent resolution that, if passed, established the budget for the fiscal year and that limited the total appropriations available for all federal departments. The act also required that Congress increase the federal debt if it sought to spend more than the revenues anticipated for the fiscal year.

Title III of the act, the Federal Regulation of Lobbying Act, was the first attempt by Congress to oversee the activities of special interest groups. Lobbyists were required to register and file reports of their spending with the Clerk of the House. Failure to comply was not punished, however.

With the passage of time, experience demonstrated that parts of the act were unworkable or insufficient. In

1949 Congress did away with the Joint Budget Committee because it was too cumbersome and failed to limit growth in spending. While there were fewer standing committees, the number of subcommittees exploded in subsequent years, placing greater demands on members' time as well as causing more jurisdictional confusion and disputes. Everyone quietly ignored the toothless lobbying provision, while the number and autonomy of staff increased. But perhaps of most importance, the act did nothing to halt Congress's declining power vis-à-vis the executive.

Further reading:
Diamond, Robert A. *Origins and Development of Congress.* Washington, D.C.: Congressional Quarterly Press, 1976; Josephy, Alvin M., Jr. *On the Hill: A History of the American Congress from 1789 to the Present.* New York: Touchstone Books, 1979.

—Thomas J. Baldino

Legislative Reorganization Act of 1970

The Legislative Reorganization Act of 1970 was another milestone in the evolution of the modern Congress that began with the Legislative Reorganization Act of 1946. Remembered as much for its shortcomings as its accomplishments, the act set the stage for a decade's worth of more successful reform efforts. Interestingly, many of the provisions contained in this act paralleled those included in the 1946 law principally because their goals were similar: to make Congress more open to public scrutiny and its structure more responsive to the will of the majority.

The origins of the act may be traced to a group of liberal members of varying seniority from both houses unofficially led by Senator Joseph S. Clark (D-PA) that emerged in the mid-1960s. Frustrated with the difficulty in moving progressive social legislation through the Congress because of rules that gave southern conservative committee chairs powers to kill bills in committee and floor rules that gave tactical advantages to the Conservative Coalition (Republicans and conservative southern Democrats), disgruntled liberals saw structural change as essential if they were ever to achieve power appropriate to their numbers. They demanded that a study committee be formed, and in 1965 the Democratic leadership relented. The Joint Committee on the Reorganization of Congress (JOCO) was established with Senator A. S. Mike Monroney (D-OK) and Representative Ray J. Madden (D-IN) as cochairs. The JCOC s met for nearly all of 1966, taking testimony and preparing detailed recommendations, before issuing its report. A bill containing many of the JCOC's recommendations was taken up in both houses in 1967, though a number of its controversial proposals were removed, mainly those that concerned limiting the power of the Rules Committee and

the seniority system, banning all proxy voting in committees, and having the *CONGRESSIONAL RECORD* become a more accurate account of what transpires in each chamber. The Senate debated, amended, and passed its version of the bill early in the 90th Congress, but it died at the end of the session, buried in the Rules Committee. Few held out much hope that there would be any future action on the bill, so it was a great surprise when the Rules Committee established a special subcommittee in April 1969, chaired by B. F. Sisk (D-CA), which reported out a bill on terms it could accept in June 1970. Additional public proddings by liberals such as Representative Thomas M. Rees (D-CA) were needed before House leaders scheduled floor debate on the bill in mid-September, this after three prior dates to debate the bill were laid aside. The House passed the bill on September 17. The Senate had debated and passed its version of the bill earlier in the session, but revisited it, modified it to conform to the House version, and passed it on October 6. It became law as PL 91-510 on October 8, 1970, and took effect on January 3, 1971.

Title I, the longest and most detailed part of the act, deals with the committee system and has separate but parallel sections for each house. Nearly every rule change in this section attempted, either directly or indirectly, to constrain the extensive powers of committee chairs. For instance, the ranking majority member on a committee may convene the committee in the absence of the chair, something that was informally available in the House but not at all in the Senate. All House committee meetings must be open to the public unless a majority of the committee votes to close them. In the Senate meetings must also be open except for mark ups, votes, or if the majority votes to close the proceedings for any reason. Moreover, open hearings may be broadcast over radio and television if a majority of the committee votes to approve it. (In the Senate broadcast would be determined by rules adopted by each committee.) Public notice must be given at least one week in advance of a hearing except for extenuating circumstances. A majority of the minority party has the opportunity to call witnesses on at least one day of hearings. Every member's roll-call vote in committee must be recorded and included in the committee's report on a bill, and the report be made available to the public. If a majority of a committee requests it in writing, the report must be filed within seven days, though this was not extended to the Rules Committee. Limits were placed on proxy voting, but the number of exceptions allowed chairs to continue to manipulate proxy votes. Any committee member may file a minority, supplemental, or additional report if the member expresses the intention of doing so within three days. These other reports must accompany the main report. (This did not apply to the Rules Committee.) With few exceptions (e.g., declaration of war), committee reports must be available at least three days prior to floor consideration of a bill by either house.

One of the most significant reforms was the recorded teller vote. In the past only the total was documented for a teller vote, allowing members' positions on important bills or motions, especially at that time those dealing with the Vietnam War, to remain unknown to their constituents. With the reform, members' votes were either electronically or manually counted and reported, a major blow for lawmaker accountability.

Title II involved procedural changes in the fiscal area. Among other things, the act required that a common system for processing financial and budgetary data be adopted and charged the Office of Management and Budget (OMB) and Treasury Department with responsibility for developing it. Information produced by the new system must be made available to Congress upon request. The president must submit five-year projections of the costs of each new or expanded program as part of the annual budget, and updates for these projections must be submitted at midyear. Once a budget is received, the House Appropriations Committee must hold open hearings within 30 days and accept testimony from the Treasury secretary, director of OMB, and the chair of the Council of Economic Advisors. It extended the authority of the General Accounting Office to conduct program evaluations at the request of members, agencies, or on its own initiative.

The demand for more and better information was addressed in Title III by increasing the number of standing committee staff from four to six, with two to be chosen by the minority party. Neither the Appropriations Committees nor the House ethics committee was included in this change. Standing committees could hire professional consultants and send current staff for specialized training. The Legislative Reference Service was renamed the Congressional Research Service and given additional resources and an expanded portfolio of responsibilities to support the legislative needs of members.

Titles IV and V reorganized, eliminated, and created committees in both houses, though none of the major standing or joint committees were affected. The Office of Legislative Counsel was created for the House.

While these reforms brought progress in some areas, notably increasing the number and professional quality of the staff and the recorded teller vote, committee chairs continued to wield immense powers. Chairs determined the number and jurisdiction of subcommittees, their chairs and membership, and what bills would be referred to them. A chair also could exercise a "vest pocket veto" by not bringing a bill to the full committee for a vote. The next wave of reform just a few years away would bring greater and more lasting change, particularly for chairs. And the institution's struggle with the president for equal stature in the constitu-

tional system would take a dramatic turn with the near-impeachment of a president and the passage of the War Powers and the Budget and Impoundment Control Acts.

Further reading:
Clark, Joseph S. *Congress: The Sapless Branch.* Westport, Conn.: Greenwood Press, 1964; Clark, Joseph S. *Congressional Reform: Problems and Prospects.* New York: Thomas Y. Cromwell, 1965; Diamond, Robert A. *Origins and Development of Congress.* Washington, D.C.: Congressional Quarterly Press, 1976; Davidson, Roger H., and Walter J. Oleszek. *Congress against Itself.* Bloomington: Indiana University Press, 1977; Rieselbach, Leroy N. *Congressional Reform.* Washington, D.C.: Congressional Quarterly Press, 1986.

—Thomas J. Baldino

Legislative Service Organizations ("LSOs")

Legislative Service Organizations (LSOs) were a special subset of congressional caucuses that existed from 1979 to 1995. Established to further the policy and political interests of representatives and senators, LSOs were distinguished from other caucuses by virtue of their formal designation as LSOs by the House Administration (now Oversight) Committee. For a caucus to apply for and receive certification, a group of members needed to write by-laws and elect officers. Once certified, an LSO was permitted access to office space, if available, in a House or Senate office building and to hire staff and purchase office supplies with funds coming from official congressional budgets. Members could pay their LSO dues or make contributions directly from their office accounts.

Some LSOs drew members exclusively from one chamber, while others were bicameral. All LSOs, however, attempted to influence public policy. LSOs were formed around commodities (e.g., automobiles, steel, textiles), geographic areas (rural, Sunbelt, Northeast, Midwest), age, racial, and gender issues (children, the elderly, Blacks, Hispanics, women), abstract policy issues (foreign policy, the environment, human rights), and partisan political goals (liberal Democratic to Populist to conservative Republican). LSOs delivered information to their members in the form of reports and bill analyses, publicized their issue positions within Congress and to the nation as a whole, and presented a unified voice that lobbied the LSOs' positions before congressional committees, party caucuses, and the White House.

The first caucus to become an LSO was the Democratic Study Group (DSG). Organized in 1959 by liberal Democrats in the House, the DSG was officially recognized by the House Administration Committee as a caucus soon thereafter and granted office space in a House building.

Caucus numbers grew slowly and then took off in the early 1970s. The proliferation of caucuses brought concerns from some lawmakers who alleged improprieties in their funding and operation.

The House Committee on Administrative Review, created in 1976 and chaired by David Obey (D-WS), considered the place of caucuses in the structure of the House as part of its larger study of House workload. The Obey Commission, as it was called, made several recommendations on caucuses, among them that caucuses with long tenure receive formal certification by the House, which, in turn, would confer privileges (office space, dedicated House funding) but also require that caucuses file regular financial statements and accept the same restrictions on the use of staff and official House funds that members have. None of the recommendations concerning caucuses were adopted at that time, but they became the basis for the rules adopted by the House using proposals from the Administration Committee in 1979.

House Administration was given authority to recognize caucuses as LSOs, the first time the designation was formally adopted. Once recognized, the LSO received a House account from which it could draw funds to pay staff and purchase supplies. The LSO also could have office space in a congressional building, if space was available. But the LSO was required to file income and expenditure reports twice each year. Those caucuses not designated LSOs were unable to draw expenses or have members pay caucus dues from members' office accounts.

In 1981 the Better Government Association conducted an investigation of all caucus funding, and its findings raised serious questions. An Ad Hoc Subcommittee on LSOs was formed within House Administration to study the use of public monies. On the basis of the subcommittee's report, the House required LSOs to file quarterly expenditure and income statements and restricted LSOs from accepting contributions from outside interest groups.

As LSOs continued to promote their agendas, successfully in many instances, more members questioned the source and use of funds as well as whether LSOs were becoming vehicles for special interest groups to circumvent congressional rules that limited interest groups' ability to lobby and donate money to lawmakers and parties. More task forces on LSOs were formed in 1986, 1988, and 1990, and each one called for more regulation of and reports from LSOs. Those LSOs that had research or publishing "institutes" associated with them were forced to sever those relationships. LSOs were forbidden to solicit or accept contributions from organizations outside Congress; no outside funds could be used to support the operation of LSOs.

Despite the added regulations, LSOs underwent investigations in 1992 and 1993. Representative Charlie Rose (D-NC), chair of House Administration, called for a major GAO audit of LSOs in 1993 in an effort to quell the anger of Republicans who continued to challenge the integrity of LSO behavior. In 1994 Representative Pat Roberts (R-KS), the ranking minority member on House Administration, sought to abolish all LSOs, but his motion failed in committee. The election of 1994, however, brought Republican control of both houses, and on January 4, 1995, H Res 6, section 222, was approved, dissolving LSOs. A total of 96 LSO staff positions were eliminated, 16 offices became available, and $4 million that had been used to fund LSO activities was returned to the office accounts of members.

In place of LSOs, Congress created the Congressional Membership Organization (CMO), defined as

> an informal organization of members who share official resources to jointly carry out activities. The CMO has no separate corporate or legal identity apart from the members who comprise it, is not an employing authority and no staff may be appointed by or in the name of the CMO nor can it have separate office space.

CMOs may not use the FRANKING PRIVILEGE or purchase office supplies with public monies. The Committee on House Oversight (formerly Administration) was given responsibility to monitor the transition from LSO to CMO.

Of the 28 LSOs that existed in 1995, 25 continued to operate either as CMOs or as informal groups. Among the more well-know LSOs that survived are the Congressional Caucus on Women's Issues, the Congressional Black Caucus, and the Coalition, a group of conservative Democrats. The DSG merged with the House Democratic Caucus but was led by members other than formal party leaders. CMOs and other informal groups remain active players in the legislative process, though in somewhat different garb.

Further reading:
Hammond, Susan Webb. *Congressional Caucus in National Policy Making.* Baltimore: Johns Hopkins University Press, 1998; Hammond, Susan Webb. "Congressional Caucuses in the 104th Congress." In Lawrence C. Dodd and Bruce I. Oppenheimer, eds. *Congress Reconsidered.* 6th ed. Washington, D.C.: Congressional Quarterly Press, 1997; Loomis, Burdett A. "Congressional Caucuses and the Politics of Representation." In Lawrence C. Dodd and Bruce I. Oppenheimer, eds. *Congress Reconsidered.* 2d ed. Washington, D.C.: Congressional Quarterly Press, 1981; Thompson, Joan Hulse. "The Congressional Caucus for Women's Issues." In Sarah Slavin, ed. *Women's Issues Interest Groups.* Denver: Greenwood Press, 1993; Vega, Arturo. "Congressional Informal Groups as Representative Responsiveness." *American Review of Politics,* 14 (Autumn 1993): 355–373.

—Thomas J. Baldino

legislative veto

The legislative veto is a tool by which Congress attempts to exert its oversight authority over the executive branch. The U.S. Constitution created a system with separation of powers, wherein Congress has the legislative power (to make laws), the president has the executive power (to execute or carry out laws), and the Supreme Court (in conjunction with lower courts) has the judicial power (to interpret laws). The system of checks and balances also gives each branch a little power over the other two. Thus, the president must sign congressional legislation before it becomes law, while Congress has the power to override a presidential veto and to approve presidential appointees. The president appoints Supreme Court justices, who must be approved by the Senate. The Supreme Court can rule on the constitutionality of presidential actions or congressional laws. These checks of power by one branch over another are intended to ensure that no one branch of government can become too powerful.

The legislative veto allows one house of Congress (or sometimes one committee in Congress) to overrule executive action related to a specific law. The veto is written into the law: Congress allows the executive branch to take action subject to Congress's later approval. In its legislative function, Congress passes laws authorizing the executive branch to carry out a particular policy. Generally, congressional statutes are so broadly written that the executive branch needs to promulgate regulations that fill in the specifics of how a particular policy will be carried out. A legislative veto written into the law specifies that those regulations or other specified agency actions must be sent to Congress, which then has the authority to approve or disapprove of them.

At various times in U.S. history, the executive branch (the presidency and the administrative agencies of government) and the Congress have each asserted their power over the other. In the 1970s in particular, the Democratic Congress attempted to rein in what it saw as the "Imperial Presidency" of Richard M. Nixon. The legislative veto was one weapon in its arsenal, and Congress used it frequently both to thwart the Nixon administration and as a method of overseeing the vast amount of regulatory legislation Congress itself was passing.

Use of the legislative veto continued into the 1980s, and its constitutionality was eventually considered by the U.S. Supreme Court. The case was *IMMIGRATION AND NATURALIZATION SERVICES (INS) v. CHADHA* (1983). Chadha was a Kenyan-born East Indian with a British passport. He had come to the United States on a nonimmigrant student visa, and he stayed beyond the expiration of his visa. The INS began deportation proceedings against him but after a hearing decided to suspend the deportation and grant him permanent resident status. The attorney general ordered the suspension and under the Immigration and Nationality Act sent the suspension order to Congress for its approval. The chair of the House Judiciary Committee on Immigration, Naturalization and International law introduced a resolution to invalidate the order, thus requiring Chadha (along with five others) to be deported. The resolution was passed by the House. The action of Congress was in keeping with the Immigration and Nationality Act, which provided that either house could invalidate or suspend deportation rulings. This provision was a legislative veto: Congress had written into the law its own authority over executive deportation decisions. Congress had the power to overrule executive branch decisions in this regard.

Chadha appealed the decision, and the case went to the Supreme Court, which decided in Chadha's favor. The Court ruled that the specific provision in the Immigration and Nationality Act in particular and the legislative veto in general were unconstitutional. According to the Court, the legislative veto violated the principle of bicameralism (laws are to be made by both houses of Congress; the legislative veto allows the decision of only one body to invalidate an executive action). It also violated the separation of powers by having Congress too intimately involved in executive decision making, and it violated the presentment clause—all laws must be presented to the president for signature.

The initial reaction of Congress to the ruling was to repeal legislative vetoes and turn instead to other methods of oversight. Gradually, however, the legislative veto crept back into legislation, and it is, in fact, still widely used today. The legislative veto is in some ways a benefit to the executive branch. Congress is more likely to give increased authority to executive agencies if it knows that it has the right to oversee how that authority is used. In addition, the executive branch in some cases appreciates the guidance that a legislative veto might give. For these reasons, and because Congress has wide powers over executive agencies, the executive branch is acquiescent in the use of legislative vetoes.

Further reading:
Fisher, Louis. "The Legislative Veto Invalidation: It Survives." *Law and Contemporary Problems* (Autumn 1993): 273–292; *Immigration and Naturalization Service v. Chadha* (1983) 462 U.S. 919.

—Anne Marie Cammisa

libraries of the House and Senate

Members of the HOUSE OF REPRESENTATIVES and SENATE are served by library collections made for each chamber of government. The libraries of both the House of Representatives and the Senate had their beginnings in the Second Congress in 1791. Both the House and Senate passed resolutions that directed their respective officers to procure and deposit in his office the laws of the several states for the use of members. These actions are considered to be the foundation of the present-day libraries of the two legislative bodies, which serve mainly as legislative libraries.

Under this directive the secretary of the Senate developed collections of state and federal materials. As the collections grew throughout the 1800s the Senate library needed more space and improved management. In 1871 the Senate designated a suite of third-floor Capitol rooms for the U.S. Senate Library and appointed George S. Wagner the first Senate librarian. The Capitol suites and an additional fourth-floor area, added in 1900, served as the Senate library until February 1999. At that time the library opened a new facility in the Russell Senate Office Building. The move has allowed the library to offer improved patron services, plan for the latest technology, and house its expanding collection.

Since 1871 the library's mission has expanded from collecting materials to providing the Senate with legislative, legal, and general reference in an accurate, quick, and nonpartisan manner. The Senate library's resources are reserved for the use of members of the Senate, Senate staffs, Senate and House committees, and members of the press. The library's main collection is made of Senate and House materials dating from 1789, including bills, hearings, reports, and debates. The library has a large book collection, newspaper and magazine subscriptions, maps and atlases, and access to a variety of online resources.

The library of the House of Representatives is the older of the two legislative libraries. The CLERK of the House of Representatives has maintained a legislative and legal reference library since the Second Congress in 1792. In 1995 the House library, along with the House Historical Services, the House Document Room, the Office of Legislative Information, and the Office of Records were combined to form the Legislative Resource Center (LRC), which is under the direct supervision of the Clerk of the House of Representatives. The Legislative Resource Center assists with the retrieval of legislative information and records of the House for congressional offices and the public. The LRC provides centralized access to all published documents that have originated in the House and its committees, to the historical records of the House, and to public disclosure documents. It has a small staff to assist researchers and maintains a study area for library patrons.

Both the Senate library and the House Legislative Resource Center act as the official internal libraries of record for their respective houses. They are independent of the Library of Congress but often work closely with the Library of Congress's CONGRESSIONAL RESEARCH SERVICE on policy issues.

Further reading:
Burger, Timothy J. "House Historian's Office to Be Folded into New Legislative Resources Center Under Carle Plan." *Roll Call*, 11 May 1995. Available online by subscription. URL: www.rollcall.com. Accessed February 7, 2006. Library of Congress. *Journals of the Continental Congress.* Vol. 1, United States. Congress. Senate. Library, 2003. United States Senate Library. S. Pub. 108-7.
—Mary S. Rausch

Library, Joint Committee on the

The Joint Committee on the Library is one of four JOINT COMMITTEES in the 108th Congress (2003–05). The panel is a permanent committee that continues to exist from one Congress to the next, but does not have any legislative authority.

An equal number of legislators from the HOUSE OF REPRESENTATIVES and SENATE serve as members of the joint committee. In the 108th Congress five senators and five representatives served on the committee. The chair of the committee rotates between House and Senate members. Senator Ted Stevens of Alaska chaired the committee during the 108th Congress. The committee chair during the 109th Congress (2005–07) will be a member of the House of Representatives. The vice chair of the committee is a member of the legislative house not holding the chair during that particular Congress.

Congress organized temporary library committees as far back as 1800. In fact, the first joint committee ever established by Congress was the Joint Committee on the Library, established in 1802. The permanent joint committee was established on December 7, 1843, and was given authority to manage the Library of Congress.

More recently, the joint committee remains an administrative unit that handles routine internal matters. Much of the work of the Librarian of Congress and the Architect of the Capitol falls under the direction of the committee. The committee's jurisdiction in the 108th Congress included management of the Library of Congress and CONGRESSIONAL RESEARCH SERVICE, development and maintenance of the United States Botanic Garden, receipt of gifts for the benefit of the Library of Congress, and matters concerned with receiving and placing statues and other works of art in the U.S. Capitol.

Further reading:
United States House of Representatives. Joint Committee on the Library. *Organizational Meeting of the Joint*

Committee on the Library. Washington, D.C.: Government Printing Office, 2003; United States Senate. Joint Committee on the Library. Hearing before the Joint Committee on the Library of Congress. Senate Hearing 108-431, 2004.

—Mary S. Rausch

Library of Congress

The Library of Congress was established in Washington, D.C., on April 24, 1800, when President John Adams approved legislation that set aside $5,000 in order to purchase "such books as may be necessary for the use of Congress." Today, while still fulfilling its original remit of supporting the legislative activities of Congress, it has grown to become the largest library in the world. Open to the public, the Library of Congress now holds more than 18 million books and 54 million manuscripts as well as numerous maps, recordings, and photographs.

The foundation and development of the Library of Congress are inexplicably linked with the ideas and enthusiasm of Thomas Jefferson. During his presidency Jefferson took a keen interest in the library, and when an attack by British forces in 1814 led to the destruction of its holdings, Jefferson offered to sell his private collection of more than 6,000 volumes to restock the library. It was the purchase of Jefferson's collection, which contained works covering a diversity of disciplines in a variety of languages, that began to enlarge the scope of the Library of Congress from its original role as a legislative aid to the center of learning that it is today. The transformation to become the nation's library owes much to the work of Ainsworth Rand Spofford, Librarian of Congress from 1865 to 1897, who managed to establish a balance between the demands of Congress and the nation.

In 1897 the library moved from the Capitol to its own building, which in 1980 was renamed for Thomas Jefferson. A second building (now named after President John Adams) was opened in 1939 and a third (the James Madison Memorial Building) was added in 1981 as the library continued its expansion. The buildings and extraordinary collections are today maintained by more than 4,000 staff and are visited by nearly 1 million researchers and visitors each year from all over the world.

Further reading:

Cole, J. Y. *Jefferson's Legacy: A Brief History of the Library of Congress*. Washington, D.C.: Library of Congress, 1993; Johnston, W. D. *History of the Library of Congress: Volume I, 1800–1864*. Washington, D.C.: Government Printing Office, 1904; Wyeth, S. D. *History of the Library of Congress*. Washington, D.C.: Gibson Brothers, 1868.

—Ross M. English

Livingston, Robert L. ("Bob") (1943–)

Representative

Robert L. Livingston, a Republican, represented the First Congressional District of Louisiana in the U.S. House of Representatives from 1977 to 1999. Victory in a special election brought Livingston to Congress after the incumbent had been forced to resign. In time, Livingston, often described as a courtly southerner with a hot temper, rose to chair the HOUSE APPROPRIATIONS COMMITTEE and almost became SPEAKER OF THE HOUSE. A scandal, however, of a different sort than that of his predecessor led to his own resignation. Just as he had entered the House via a special election, so would his successor.

Livingston was born April 30, 1943, into a family that had left its mark on American history. One Livingston had signed the Declaration of Independence and another had administered George Washington's oath of office. It was after the Louisiana Purchase that some of the Livingstons went south to Louisiana. Bob Livingston, however, derived little benefit from his ancestry. His father deserted the family, and it was Mrs. Livingston who supported her son and her daughter by working as a secretary at Avondale Industries, a shipyard. Bob, too, went to work at Avondale when he was only 14 years old. After high school he joined the navy. Following his discharge from the navy, he returned to Avondale to put himself through college. He earned bachelor of arts and law degrees from Tulane University, then spent the better part of his early career as a prosecutor.

Louisiana electoral shenanigans, in which Livingston played no part, set the stage for his election to the House of Representatives. Following the 1976 Democratic primary in the First Congressional District, the second-place finisher accused the winner of vote fraud but was unsuccessful in state court. The winner of the Democratic primary was elected and took his seat in Congress. The candidate who claimed to be the victim of vote fraud was later vindicated by a House investigation. The forced resignation of the congressman from the First Congressional District made necessary a special election, which Livingston won on August 27, 1977. Livingston was honest, and his constituents approved of his conservatism. His constituency consisted of a white, fairly affluent section of New Orleans, some nearby suburbs, and some parishes (equivalent to counties) in the southeastern part of the state. Livingston's conservative constituents returned him to Congress again and again by large margins.

It was not honesty and conservatism alone that produced Livingston's large majorities. He worked hard at protecting the interests of his constituents. The military was a major employer in his district. Congressman F. Edward Hebert, a Democrat who had represented the district for many years and had chaired the HOUSE ARMED SERVICES COMMITTEE, brought many of the military jobs to the area.

Livingston protected those jobs when they were threatened by budget cuts. When the navy awarded a contract to replace old assault ships with new LPD-17 vessels in 1997, the contract went to Avondale Industries, where Livingston had once worked, rather that Ingalls Shipbuilding on the Mississippi Gulf Coast. The navy later appeased irate senator TRENT LOTT of Mississippi (then Senate Majority Leader) by giving Ingalls a contract for four destroyers. The army, too, awarded an important contract to a company in Livingston's district. Livingston helped Textron Marine and Land Systems win a contract to build a new field howitzer, which was expected to bring 225 new jobs into the area. Such things tend to get a congressperson reelected.

Livingston's rise to power in the House was gradual. As a young congressman he served as Republican regional WHIP for Texas, Louisiana, and Mississippi. He served on the powerful Appropriations Committee and its Defense Subcommittee. He was also appointed to the Intelligence Committee. But he did not walk an unbroken line of political successes. When he ran for the office of governor of Louisiana in 1987, he failed to make it into the runoff. When he was feuding with another Louisiana Republican, Richard Baker of Baton Rouge, he endorsed Baker's Republican opponent in 1992. Baker nevertheless won reelection, and the two Republicans eventually reconciled.

It was after the 1994 congressional elections, when the Republicans won control of both houses of Congress, that Livingston became a powerful figure in the House. NEWT GINGRICH of Georgia had become Speaker of the House and moved Livingston ahead of four Republicans with more seniority to be chair of the Appropriations Committee. The committee's ranking Republican was under indictment though later exonerated, and Gingrich feared that the other three would not be sufficiently supportive of the conservative "revolution" and the budget cutting it would entail. Gingrich believed that Livingston was more committed to reform than the others. John Kasich, an Ohio Republican and chair of the House Budget Committee, feared, however, that Livingston and the Appropriations Committee would try to protect some programs from cuts. Kasich wanted to be able to determine what would be cut, but Livingston was unwilling to be dominated by Kasich. It was not their first clash. In 1993 he had opposed a bill cosponsored by Kasich that would have decreased congressional pensions. Congressman Timothy Penney, a Democrat from Minnesota, reported that he could hear Livingston shouting obscenities at Kasich all the way across the House chamber. In this later clash between Livingston and Kasich, Gingrich entered the fray and left specific cuts in the hands of the Appropriations Committee and the WAYS AND MEANS COMMITTEE, which had jurisdiction over entitlements. But Gingrich made it clear that if these committees did not get the job done, he would ask

Kasich to designate specific spending cuts. That did not become necessary.

Livingston did not have things all his own way, but he remained loyal to the man who gave him his chair. He objected to the practice of inserting policy RIDERS on appropriations bills. He thought they should focus on fiscal matters. On this issue Livingston was rebuked by Speaker Gingrich. But when Gingrich was reprimanded by the House of Representatives for using tax-exempt funds for political purposes and submitting inaccurate statements to the House Ethics Committee, Livingston supported him. The House voted to fine Gingrich $300,000. Livingston and only 27 other House members voted against the fine. He thought it was excessive because Gingrich had derived no personal gain from his actions, and there had been no proof that he had deceived the Ethics Committee intentionally.

After budgetary clashes between congressional Republicans and President Bill Clinton resulted in government shut-downs in 1995–96, with the public blaming the Republicans more than the Democratic president, Clinton was reelected. In the 1998 congressional elections the Republicans saw their House majority diminished. Soon after the results were in, Newt Gingrich announced that he would not stand for Speaker and would leave Congress at the end of the year. House Republicans designated Bob Livingston as their candidate for Speaker in the next Congress. But before the year was out, impeachment proceedings against President Clinton were underway in the House growing out of his affair with White House intern Monica Lewinsky and his lies while under oath. Larry Flynt, publisher of *Hustler* magazine, accused members of Congress of hypocrisy, since several of them were guilty of marital infidelity. He threatened to expose them. Livingston was one such congressman. He addressed the House on December 19, 1998. He said that he would vote to impeach the president but that under the circumstances he would not stand for Speaker and would retire from the House about six months into the 106th Congress, when he would ask the governor of Louisiana to call a special election to choose his successor. He called upon President Clinton to resign as well. The president did not do so.

Livingston departed from Congress but not from politics. He went on to establish his own successful lobbying firm. His client list included Louisiana companies, national companies, and foreign governments.

Further reading:
Barone, Michael, and Grant Ujifusa. *The Almanac of American Politics*. Washington, D.C.: National Journal, 1986; Drew, Elizabeth. *Showdown: The Struggle between the Gingrich Congress and the Clinton White House*. New York: Simon & Schuster, 1996; Penney, Timothy J., and Major Garrett. *Common Cents: A Retiring Six Term Congressman Reveals How Congress Really Works and What We Must Do*

to Fix It. Boston: Little, Brown, 1995; Stone, Peter H. "Starting Over." *National Journal,* 26 February 2000 pp. 604–610; Taylor, Andrew. "Is Livingston the Manager the House Needs?" *Congressional Quarterly Weekly Report,* 14 November 1998.

—Patricia A. Behlar

lobbying

Lobbying involves communicating with members of Congress and other government officials in order to try to influence governmental decisions. It is undertaken by individual constituents, but it is also done by groups, businesses, associations of individuals and companies, and many other entities on behalf of members, employees, shareholders, customers, citizens, and other individuals or interests affected by decisions that members of Congress have made or are considering making.

Lobbying has come to have a pejorative connotation, yet it is based on the guarantees of First Amendment speech and association rights and particularly the right of Americans to petition the government for redress of grievances. This constitutional basis for lobbying anticipates the active involvement and participation of citizens and interest groups in the governmental decision-making process. Recent years have shown an enormous increase in petitions and requests for Congress to act on many issues, and thus reflected vigorous lobbying.

The term *lobbying* originated from England in the 17th century, referring to the habit of citizens and organized interest representatives waiting in the lobby or anteroom of Parliament's House of Commons so they could see and speak with their members in that house. Similarly, people in Washington, D.C., wait in lobbies, offices, meeting rooms, or even hallways of the U.S. Capitol or House and Senate office buildings to see members of Congress. Unlike earlier times, when constituents and interest groups were limited to either meeting members in person or writing letters or telegrams to them, now lobbying also includes the use of individual and group telephone calls, satellite and Web-based conference meetings, faxes, e-mails, and a host of new technologies. This change in communications technology has helped to differentiate two kinds of lobbying, inside lobbying and outside lobbying.

Inside, or direct contact, lobbying is often done by professional lobbyists inside the capital or government offices and involves meetings with members of Congress and their staffs, testifying at committee or subcommittee hearings, negotiating with governmental policy makers and other interest groups, and offering information and analysis to legislators and their staff members. On the other hand, outside, indirect, or grassroots lobbying takes place outside the capital, aided by TV, radio, and Internet near-instantaneous

transmission of congressional actions and opportunities and can involve many more people than professional lobbyists in efforts to change public opinion and thus affect congressional actions. Grassroots activities undertaken by associations or interest group members, employees of businesses, and constituents include visits to legislators in their districts, broad-based letter writing and e-mail campaigns, news conferences, visits to editorial board writers to take a group's concerns to the wider public, and generally building broad-based coalitions with others who may care similarly about issues. Whereas inside lobbying historically relied upon the ability of a few individuals to successfully articulate and persuade members of Congress of the importance and need for certain causes and concerns on behalf of members or clients, outside lobbying has now become an increasingly important strategy because it allows strong group interests to involve greater numbers of participants in persuading and influencing members of Congress to act in accordance with constituent desires.

Professional lobbyists are paid for their lobbying activities to influence government actions and policies. For example, in-house lobbyists are full-time employees who lobby on behalf of their employer whether that employer is a business or another organization such as a labor union, trade association composed of several business interests, professional society, or individual membership association. Functions undertaken by in-house lobbyists include monitoring the activities of Congress in a specific field of interest to the employer, helping to set the policy objectives to be pursued by the employer in this field, submitting suggested changes that could be incorporated into legislation that Congress might introduce in the form of bills or amendments, testifying at committee hearings, representing the employer with government officials and agencies, and involving the employer and others in grassroots lobbying efforts. Examples of employers using in-house lobbyists to represent them include, for business interests, entities such as the National Federation of Independent Business, U.S. Chamber of Commerce, National Association of Manufacturers, American Hospital Association, American Farm Bureau Federation, and National Association of Home Builders. Labor union examples include the AFL-CIO, National Education Association, and the International Brotherhood of Teamsters. Professional societies include the Association of Trial Lawyers of America and the American Medical Association, while individual membership associations include the AARP, the National Rifle Association of America, and the American Israel Public Affairs Committee.

These organizations consistently rank among the most powerful and influential lobbying groups in the nation. In contrast to in-house lobbyists, outside lobbyists are members of a lobbying firm, partnership, or a sole proprietorship who represent outside clients. While they are also professional lobbyists, they are not employees of their clients. Instead, they contract with their clients to perform the same types of lobbying activities as those performed by in-house lobbyists. Outside lobbyists often have multiple clients that they represent simultaneously.

Professional lobbyists usually use labels other than *lobbyist* to describe their activities and functions, including legislative counsel and government relations or public affairs consultant. Excellent lobbyists are compensated well in the form of salaries and benefits. Their important knowledge and ability to provide information and effective advocacy has resulted in their becoming known as the third house.

Many successful lobbyists are former members of Congress or legislative staffers or have had prior government service in the executive branch, such as in the cabinet or White House. Previous connections and familiarity with members of Congress and officials within the executive branch give these experienced people an advantage in representing an employer or client through their ability to open doors and talk to former colleagues and acquaintances. Skills needed by lobbyists include, in addition to experience and access to decision makers, knowledge of the relevant issues and processes of government. Good people skills, the capacity to make good political judgments, persistence, and a willingness to work hard are also important. In general, good lobbyists must be available day and night to pursue the causes that engage them. And they find both exhilaration and exhaustion in those causes.

Among the most famous of lobbyists was the legendary Samuel Ward, who described himself as "King of the Lobby" as he wined and dined members of Congress, often in an extravagant manner, during the years following the Civil War. The term *lobbyist* may conjure images of well-dressed and well-healed men such as Sam Ward advocating on behalf of wealthy clients, but it is also applicable to many Americans urging Congress to act on behalf of causes near and dear to them. Examples include the suffrage movement that secured passage of the Eighteenth and Nineteenth Amendments (Prohibition and the right to vote) in the early 1900s, as well as recent efforts by college students to secure federal financial aid programs.

Included in the First Amendment rights of speech, association, and petition that serve as the basis for people to lobby Congress is freedom of the press for print media such as newspapers, magazines, and books as well as broadcast media such as TV and radio. Various media have often portrayed lobbying as sinister and against the public interest, with special interests seeking to improperly influence the votes of members of Congress. Journalists and broadcasters have viewed themselves as watchdogs over Congress, including activities involving lobbyists, yet the media companies for whom they work have also sought to influence legislative votes, including powerful organizations such as the National Association of Broadcasters. Nevertheless, the perception that lobbyists can and do use the purchase of meals, entertainment, and gifts to curry favor with members of Congress and their staffs as a part of lobbying, and perhaps more importantly their contributions of money to reelection races for members of the House and Senate who may then feel some dependency upon them, are real problems. These activities raise the possibility of impropriety and corruption through lobbying, adversely affecting the confidence of citizens in their government and the work of their elected officials.

A first congressional effort to require registration of lobbyists and the disclosure of lobbying activities directed toward Congress was the Federal Regulation of Lobbying Act of 1946, which the Supreme Court upheld in 1954. Because not all lobbyists were required to register and report their employers or clients, and since the financial reports filed did not properly reflect lobbying expenditures, that act was strengthened by the Lobbying Disclosure Act of 1995. Lobbying has also been affected by the Foreign Agents Registration Act and House and Senate rules members have imposed on themselves. In addition, lobbyists and attorneys have developed and applied their own ethical self-regulation rules.

The Lobbying Disclosure Act of 1995 has specific thresholds for registration and relatively broad definitions for lobbyist and lobbying. Organizations with in-house lobbyists must register if their expenses for a six-month period exceed $22,500; lobbying firms (for outside lobbyists) must register if their expenses exceed $5,500 for the same filing period. Under this statute a lobbyist is one who spends at least 20 percent of his or her time for the employer or client on lobbying activities during the six-month period, and lobbying activities are broadly defined to include contacts with a member of Congress, congressional staffs, and senior executive branch officials, but also include background activities and similar efforts in support of such lobbying contacts. Lobbyists register with the CLERK OF THE HOUSE and the SECRETARY OF THE SENATE on forms that identify the lobbyist, the employer or client, any other entities beyond the client that contribute more than $10,000 for lobbying activities and have a major role in overseeing or controlling them, any foreign entity that owns 20 percent or more of the client or controls or is affiliated with the client, and the topics the lobbyist anticipates lobbying or has lobbied for the employer or client. Lobbyists are required in both oral and written communications to governmental officials to identify their clients, state whether they are registered, and disclose any interests of foreign affiliates. Registration reports are public records and are available online. Foreign agents register with the attorney general.

Other laws and rules that have particular applicability to lobbying include provisions that place additional restraints on lobbying to help eliminate or reduce undue or wrongful influence. Federal contractors, grantees, loan recipients, and agency employees are prohibited from using federal monies to lobby Congress. Charitable organizations are limited in the lobbying they are able to undertake if they wish to keep their eligibility to receive income tax–deductible contributions from individual and business donors. There are specific post employment and revolving door conflict of interest restrictions on some people in the federal government that may work to restrict their lobbying of Congress for a period of time after they leave office.

Congressional ethics rules include provisions that generally prohibit members and congressional staff from receiving or soliciting gifts from private parties, including but not limited to lobbyists. But there are exceptions to the gifts (including the gift of a meal) worth less than $50 and gifts from family members and friends. Gifts or payments in the form of honoraria formerly made available to members giving a speech to a group, writing an article, or making a personal appearance at a meeting are now explicitly prohibited for members and congressional staff. Generally, outside earned income or compensation is also impermissible for these same individuals. There are continuing restrictions on campaign contributions, including ones on members of Congress converting them for personal use. Offering any campaign contribution in exchange for a particular vote is illegal as bribery. Furthermore, congressional members have to make gift and travel filings as well as financial disclosure reports.

Lobbying limitations and restrictions described above represent attempts to eliminate corruption and undue or wrongful influence and reduce the appearance of impropriety in a manner that still permits people to use precious First Amendment freedoms to properly access and petition Congress, while also allowing Congress to adequately perform its functions to listen, receive information, deliberate, consider or reconsider, legislate, serve, and otherwise act to be a government of the people, by the people, and for the people. Reasonable regulation of lobbying that emphasizes disclosure represents a careful balance of competing freedoms and may undergo further rebalancing in the future.

Further reading:
Birnbaum, Jeffrey H. The *Lobbyists: How Influence Peddlers Get Their Way in Washington.* New York: Random House, 1992; Maskell, Jack. *Lobbying Congress: An Overview of Legal Provisions and Congressional Ethics Rules.* Washington, D.C.: Congressional Research Service Report to Congress, 2001; U.S. House of Representatives. *Constitution, Jefferson's Manual, and Rules of the House of Representatives, 108th Congress.* Compiled by Charles W. Johnson, Parliamentarian. 107th Cong., 2d sess., 2001. H.

Doc. 107-284; Wolpe, Bruce, and Bertram J. Levine. *Lobbying Congress: How the System Works.* 2d ed. Washington, D.C.: Congressional Quarterly Press, 1996.
—Robert P. Goss

localism

The localism tradition is the tendency of members of Congress to support policies that favor their state congressional DISTRICTS. In a representative democracy such as the United States, one would expect a representative to be significantly influenced by his or her constituency. Since members of Congress would like to be reelected, constituency pressures impose meaningful constraints on congressional decision making.

The nature of congressional REPRESENTATION, in which the nation's legislators are elected from individual districts representing distinct constituencies in a system of relatively weak political party cohesion, encourages parochial behavior by members of Congress. That is, the priority of a member of Congress is his or her individual district. As a result, what is good for an individual member of Congress is not necessarily good for the institution as a whole. What is good for an individual congressional district, furthermore, is not necessarily good for the nation as a whole. The legislative process in Congress reflects these congressional facts of life. The localism tradition tends to serve the political interests of individual members well, but not necessarily the interests of the institution as a whole.

The classic form of localism is PORK BARREL, whereby federal appropriations yield benefits (such as patronage positions, increased employment, or public spending) to a congressional district. Members of Congress are supportive of pork barrel projects because they are a mechanism that makes them look good in a nonpartisan way. Therefore, pork barrel funds are sought by members of Congress as a means of helping themselves electorally. Thus, one result of Congress's localism tradition may be to encourage excessive spending through the process of pork barreling. A popular criticism of the congressional budget process is that in their desire to please their constituents, members of Congress try to get special projects or funds for their districts to the detriment of the budget as a whole. That is, localism may cause members to look too much at how budget proposals affect their own districts and not enough at whether the budget is in the best interests of the nation. Whereas accountability toward the nation may require spending cuts or revenue increases to balance the budget, accountability toward one's constituency may require making sure that one's constituency is getting its fair share of whatever spending is done, as the localism tradition demands. An ironic result of this is the spectacle of members of Congress calling for budget cuts while simultaneously lobbying for federal funds for projects in their own districts.

The potential problems of localism for Congress can be seen by comparing the institution to the presidency. The president, unlike Congress, is elected by the entire nation and is expected to represent the entire nation. Though the president is undoubtedly more supportive of particular interests and groups than others, he or she is also the symbolic leader of the entire nation, whose success is judged by the condition of the nation as a whole. The problems the president faces are considerably different from those of Congress. Congress is a diverse group of 535 members (100 senators and 435 representatives) who represent different constituencies that have different interests and needs. Consequently, it should be expected that members of Congress will have numerous views on public policy. Parochial interests make it difficult for Congress to produce public policy with the nation's collective good in mind.

The degree to which a constituency affects the actions of a member of Congress has extremely important policy implications. If a legislator is responsive to the wants of his or her constituents, it suggests that constituents have the potential of playing an important, if indirect, role in the creation of the nation's public policy. At the same time, if the people are letting their demands be known, it becomes important to analyze what these demands are.

In the localism tradition of American legislative politics, the legislator has the responsibility of representing his or her constituency and promoting its interests. Strong popular opinion in a district strongly correlates to a member's vote. On many issues, however, it is not clear what the preferences of the constituents are. For most of the population below elites, there is only modest consistency among political beliefs and opinions. As a result, members of Congress must rely on factors other than constituency preferences to make their voting decisions.

As borne out by public opinion polls, people tend to dislike Congress as an institution while liking their own congressional representatives. These seemingly contradictory attitudes are a direct result of the localism tradition of the American legislative process. As the term denotes, voters expect legislators to "represent" them, supposedly by defending the interests of their home district, but at the same time voters expect Congress to solve the social and economic ills facing the nation as a whole. These two expectations do not necessarily go hand-in-hand. In fact, often they are in direct conflict.

Further reading:
Edelman, Murray. *Politics as Symbolic Action.* Chicago: Markham Publishing, 1971; Fenno, Richard F. *Home Style: House Members in Their Districts.* Boston: Little, Brown, 1978; Fiorina, Morris. *Divided Government.* 2d ed. Boston: Allyn & Bacon, 1996; Kingdon, John. *Congressmen's Voting Decisions.* 3d ed. Ann Arbor: University of Michigan Press, 1989; Page, Benjamin I., Robert Y. Shapiro, Paul W. Gronke, and Robert W. Rosenberg. "Constituency, Party, and Representation in Congress." *Public Opinion Quarterly* 48 (1984): 741–756.

—Patrick Fisher

Lodge, Henry Cabot (1850–1924) *Representative, Senator*

Henry Cabot Lodge served the state of Massachusetts in the HOUSE OF REPRESENTATIVES and SENATE from 1887 to 1924. As the Republican chair of the SENATE FOREIGN RELATIONS COMMITTEE, Lodge led the opposition to President Woodrow Wilson and American entrance into the League of Nations following World War I.

Lodge was born May 12, 1850, in Boston, Massachusetts, to John Ellerton Lodge, an affluent merchant and ship owner, and Anna Cabot. Reflecting his old-stock Bostonian roots and social class, Lodge attended Harvard College. Following graduation in 1871, Lodge enrolled in Harvard Law School and studied history under the direction of Henry Adams. After securing a law degree in 1874, Lodge earned a Ph.D. in history two years later, publishing his dissertation on Anglo-Saxon land law. In 1877 Lodge began teaching history at Harvard, establishing a solid scholarly reputation with volumes on George Cabot (1878), Alexander Hamilton (1882), Daniel Webster (1883), and George Washington (1889).

Influenced by his mentor, Henry Adams, Lodge entered politics as a reformer dedicated to addressing the corruption of the Grant presidency. He was elected as a Republican member of the Massachusetts general court in 1878. As a delegate to the 1884 Republican National Convention, Lodge was critical of the party presidential nominee, James G. Blaine, who Lodge characterized as corrupt. Nevertheless, Lodge was a party loyalist and supported the Blaine candidacy.

Lodge's allegiance was rewarded in 1884 with a Republican nomination for a Massachusetts congressional seat. However, the scholar-turned-politician was defeated. Two years later Lodge's quest for a position in the House of Representatives proved successful. In the House Lodge established a reputation for hard work and serving his constituents. He supported the traditional Republican Party position of fostering industry with a high protective tariff. However, Lodge was usually perceived as a somewhat moderate Republican. He allowed for currency inflation by favoring bimetallism, and he argued for expanded civil service reform. Concerned about the disenfranchisement of black voters in the South, Lodge sponsored the Federal Elections or Force Bill of 1890, calling for federal supervision of elections in the region. A southern FILIBUSTER in the Senate, however, blocked passage of the legislation.

In 1893 Lodge sought to represent Massachusetts in the Senate, replacing the retiring Henry L. Dawes. In the Senate Lodge elected to focus on foreign affairs and was assigned to the Senate Foreign Relations Committee. He was an avid expansionist who was influenced by the ideas of Captain Alfred Thayer Mahan regarding the importance of sea power in promoting national prominence. Lodge was also a champion of the Monroe Doctrine, supporting President Grover Cleveland's rebuke of the British in an 1895 boundary dispute with Venezuela.

Lodge emerged as an imperialist as he embraced the Spanish-American War and annexation of Hawaii, Puerto Rico, and the Philippines. He regretted that the Teller Resolution prohibited annexation of Cuba. Lodge favored expansion into Asia as a means to tap the potentially lucrative China market, supporting the "open door" policy and opposing any restrictions on American trade and investment opportunities in China. Lodge also backed President Theodore Roosevelt's aggressive acquisition of the Panama Canal.

Lodge and his fellow Harvard historian Theodore Roosevelt were good friends, and Lodge usually backed the Progressive reform agenda of the president. He favored moderate reform as a means to limit more radical legislation such as government ownership of public utilities. In addition, Lodge, reflecting his aristocratic class origins, was critical of economic plundering by some "robber barons." Nevertheless, he entertained doubts about such democratic reforms as direct election of senators and the initiative, referendum, and recall.

When William Howard Taft won the presidency in 1908, Lodge attempted to steer a middle course between Republican insurgents and the president. He hoped that Roosevelt would return to public life and regain control of the party. When Roosevelt failed to wrest the presidential nomination from Taft, Lodge refused to follow his friend into the Progressive Party. In 1912 Lodge maintained his party loyalty and voted for Taft.

The Republican split in 1912 paved the way for the election of Democratic president Woodrow Wilson, who earned little respect from Lodge. The Massachusetts senator opposed Wilson's foreign policy, faulting the president for not taking a stronger stand against the chaos of the Mexican Revolution. Although he was opposed to intervention in the European conflict that broke out in 1914, Lodge perceived Germany as the aggressor and Wilson as timid in his response to such provocations as the sinking of the *Lusitania* by a German submarine. The Massachusetts senator welcomed American entrance into the war in 1917, but he was critical of the president's failure to pursue a policy of unconditional surrender for the Central Powers.

Senator Henry Cabot Lodge *(Library of Congress)*

Nevertheless, Lodge approved of many points negotiated by Wilson at the Paris Peace Conference in 1919, but he had serious doubts regarding the proposed League of Nations. In particular, Lodge was concerned with Article Ten of the covenant, which required all league members to defend any other member who might become the target of aggression. Lodge believed this provision undermined American sovereignty. As chair of the Senate Foreign Relations Committee, Lodge moved deliberately to hold hearings and build opposition to the league. The Senate opposition led by Lodge proposed 14 reservations to the league, most focusing upon Article Ten and insisting that only Congress, and not the League of Nations, could commit American troops to hostilities. Suffering from the effects of a massive stroke, Wilson refused to negotiate with Lodge and the reservationists of the Senate. The failure to reach a compromise resulted in Senate rejection of the Versailles Treaty in votes taken in November 1919 and March 1920.

The controversy over the league and postwar disillusionment resulted in sweeping Republican congressional victories and the election of Warren G. Harding in 1920. Lodge, on the other hand, struggled when he sought reelection to a seventh Senate term in 1922. He was reelected by a slim margin of 7,000 votes, and the Massachusetts Republican Party was increasingly under the control of Vice President Calvin Coolidge. However, President Harding did appoint Lodge a delegate to the Washington Disarmament Conference of 1922, and he ushered the ensuing agreement through the Senate. The loyal Republican senator died on November 9, 1924, following a prostate operation.

Further reading:
Garraty, John. *Henry Cabot Lodge.* New York: Knopf, 1953; *Henry Cabot Lodge Papers.* Massachusetts Historical Society, Boston; Henry Cabot Lodge. *Early Memories.* New York: Charles Scribner's Sons, 1913; Lodge, Henry Cabot. *The Senate and the League of Nations.* New York: Charles Scribner's Sons, 1925; William, Widnor C. *Henry Cabot Lodge and the Search for an American Foreign Policy.* Berkeley: University of California Press, 1980.
—Ron Briley

logrolling
Logrolling is an agreement between two or more members of Congress who have little in common except the need for each other's support on legislation. To ensure passage of a BILL favorable to his or her constituency, a legislator will offer to vote for a bill favored by another legislator; in return, the second legislator is expected to vote for legislation supported by the first. As put succinctly, by Congressman B. F. Butler in 1870, "If you will vote for my interest . . . I will vote for yours. That is how these tariffs are log-rolled through."

The term is derived from an 18th-century American frontier practice. Families would work together to cut and trim trees into logs; they rolled the logs to the location needed by one of the families. In return, the family that benefited would help those who provided assistance at another time. In the same manner, to get support for their preferred legislation congressmembers will pledge their future support on another member's legislation. This process of political mutual aid has been around since the earliest days of the republic. Today hundreds of logrolling deals are made each year, and while there are no official books to keep a record, it would be a poor party leader whose WHIPs did not know who owed what to whom.

Logrolling may be applied by members working on a single OMNIBUS BILL or on separate unrelated bills working their way through the legislative process. In the first context a member who lacks a majority to support his or her piece of legislation searches out members in a similar situation. They create a bloc, or coalition, to support the omnibus bill. The overall result is the passage of a legislative measure containing programs for each member of the logrolling coalition. A frequently cited example of this type of logrolling occurred in 1964, when northern Democrats traded support for southern Democrats' legislation providing price supports for cotton and wheat in order to get the latter's support for the Food Stamp program.

The second type of logrolling involves two or more completely unrelated pieces of legislation. This type of vote trading coalition implicitly involves a quid pro quo agreement and thus tends to be unstable and short-lived. Reciprocity of this kind is designed to facilitate the need for legislators to be seen as "delivering the goods" back to their districts. This process of providing for the home district is closely tied to PORK BARREL politics. Critics of Congress have argued that the tendency to create logrolling coalitions has created an environment that focuses on narrow special interest legislation to the detriment of more general national interest legislation.

More recently, legislative and committee leaders are employing a modified form of logrolling to promote the leaders' policy preferences. Leaders use their positions to tack targeted district benefits onto legislation, using them as currency to purchase the votes of additional legislators for the leaders' policy preferences, much as political action committees (PACs) make campaign contributions hoping to sway members' votes. This type of logrolling strategy is successful when the distributive benefits the leaders offer are more important to the recipient than the policy matters on which they oppose the leaders. Additionally, in this manner entrepreneurial leaders can gather support through the process of logrolling for legislation with a broader national focus.

Logrolling, with its attendant political pork for the home DISTRICT, has invariably led to increased spending. Many argue that the institutional culture of logrolling during the 1960s and 1970s played a role in the federal budget deficits of the 1980s. During this time of high federal debts, members of Congress used the logic of logrolling to distribute the effects of spending cuts across an array of districts. In other words, logrolling was a way to share burdens rather than win rewards.

The problems caused by excessive logrolling have led Congress to find creative ways to circumvent the tendency to create coalitions. One example is the Defense Base Closure and Realignment Act passed in 1988. For several decades prior to the law, Congress had been unable to close military bases because of the tendency to logroll in order to protect parochial district interests (i.e., "you protect my base, I will protect your base"). The act established a bipartisan commission to make recommendations to Congress and the secretary of Defense related to closures and realignment of bases. This innovative approach has been successful in circumventing the traditional logrolling strategy and led to the closing of more than 100 bases.

The tendency to logroll is greatest when the leadership and discipline of a party is weak. This provides opportunities for members to "cross the aisle" and support bipartisan legislation that members believe or have been promised will provide benefits for their constituents. Regardless of the political environment, logrolling is an inevitable component of the American legislative process because, in the words of former SPEAKER OF THE HOUSE, SAMUEL T. RAYBURN, "If you want to get along, go along."

Further reading:
Davidson, Roger H., and Walter J. Oleszek. *Congress and Its Members.* 9th ed. Washington, D.C.: Congressional Quarterly Press, 2004; Evens, Diana. "Policy and Pork: The Use of Pork Barrel Projects to Build Policy Coalitions in the House of Representatives." *American Journal of Political Science* 38 (1994): 894–918; Ferejohn, John. "Logrolling in an Institutional Context: A Case Study of Food Stamp Legislation." In Gerald C. Wright, Jr., Leroy N. Rieselbach, and Lawrence C. Dodd, eds. *Congress and Policy Change.* New York: Agathon Press, 1986.

—Craig T. Cobane

Longworth, Nicholas III (1869–1931)
Representative, Majority Leader, Speaker of the House of Representatives

Nicholas Longworth III was the only son of a Cincinnati-based federal judge, Nicholas, Jr., and Susan Walker. They also had two daughters, Clara and Annie Rives. His uncle was Bellamy Storer, who represented Ohio's First Congressional District from 1891 to 1895. His grandfather, also named Nicholas, is regarded as the father of the American wine industry. Nicholas Longworth later became well known as the husband of President Theodore Roosevelt's daughter, Alice Lee.

Longworth attended the Franklin School in Cincinnati, then considered one of the best boys' schools in the city, and graduated from Harvard University in 1891, where he was a member of the Porcellian Club, Harvard's most exclusive club, whose past members included future U.S. senator Charles Sumner, the poet James Russell Lowell, a future Supreme Court justice, Oliver Wendell Holmes, and future president (and Longworth's father-in-law) Theodore Roosevelt.

He spent one year at the Harvard Law School and graduated from the Cincinnati Law School with an LL.B. degree in 1894. He was admitted to the Ohio bar in 1894 and began practicing law in Cincinnati. In 1897 Longworth became involved in Republican Party politics in Cincinnati, joining the Young Men's Blaine Club, part of Republican boss George B. Cox's Hamilton County (Cincinnati) political machine. Cox, along with Cleveland's Marcus A. Mark

Hanna, dominated Ohio politics in the late 19th and early 20th centuries. Longworth's sister wrote that: "many of our old friends were unstinted in their criticism; the name of Longworth, said they, should never be connected with that of George B. Cox, qualified as a vicious Boss."

In 1898 Longworth became a member of the Cincinnati board of education. Later that year he was elected to the Ohio state house of representatives, where he served one term (1899–1901). He then was elected to the state senate, where he also served one term (1901–03). In the legislature he supported the development of roads, canals, and waterways. In 1900 he became a member of the Ohio state Republican committee, a post he would hold until his death.

Elected to the 58th Congress from Ohio's First Congressional District in 1902, Longworth developed a reputation as one of Washington's most eligible bachelors. He was also a violinist (he had received musical training as a young boy) and lover of fine wine who was often seen in the company of attractive women. He also developed a friendship with President Roosevelt, who took a liking to the young congressman because of what they had in common: their alma mater, membership in the Porcellian Club, and their aristocratic backgrounds.

Longworth was assigned to the Foreign Affairs Committee, where he proposed that the government own its embassies and legations in foreign countries. Through his efforts funds were appropriated for the construction or purchase of buildings to house American diplomats. In 1907 Longworth became a member of the WAYS AND MEANS COMMITTEE, serving on that panel until he was defeated in 1912. He would serve again on Ways and Means from 1914 to 1923.

In 1905 Longworth and the president's daughter were part of a party that traveled with Secretary of War William Howard Taft to the Philippines. After visiting the Philippines they sailed to China, where they were entertained by the dowager empress in her palace in Beijing. Upon their return they became engaged to be married. In 1906 Longworth married Alice Roosevelt, who was 15 years his junior, in a White House wedding. The wedding was described by his sister, Clara Longworth Chambrun (1933):

> Bride and groom appeared with their accustomed natural and cordial vivacity against a background which bristled with "officialdom." The entire Supreme Court, the Senate and the House were invited, en masse, as well as the higher officials of the large Diplomatic Corps, and my impression was that none of these eleven hundred persons failed to appear.

However, despite marriage, Longworth is alleged to have continued his playboy ways. In Washington it was common knowledge that his was a marriage in name only.

When Alice gave birth to a daughter, Paulina, there was speculation that the child was not Congressman Longworth's. However, Longworth adored this child, taking her to his office and having members of the House sing happy birthday to her.

In 1912 Longworth was defeated for reelection by 97 votes by Democrat Stanley Bowdle. Longworth, rather than supporting his father-in-law, Progressive Party candidate Theodore Roosevelt, remained loyal to the Republican Party and supported President William Howard Taft's reelection. To retaliate, the Progressive Party nominated a candidate in Ohio's First District, siphoning enough votes from Longworth to ensure the Democrat's election.

In 1914 he was again elected to the House of Representatives, defeating Bowdle by 7,000 votes. Returning to Congress, he developed a reputation, in the words of Representative JOHN NANCE GARNER, a Democrat from Texas, as;

> a constructive legislator of immense learning, specialized on all subjects connected with external and internal revenue, appropriations and parliamentary procedure, whose qualities were those of a self-made and conscientious statesman and had nothing to do with political or family connections

Despite the large German population in his district, he was a supporter of American preparedness and entry into World War I. In a 1916 speech on the House floor, Longworth said, "I am in favor of every measure looking toward adequate national preparedness that is before Congress."

In 1923 Longworth was elected the MAJORITY LEADER in the House of Representatives. Two years later he was elected SPEAKER OF THE HOUSE, a position he held until his death. Congressman Fiorello LaGuardia of New York said that Longworth had the same domineering strength and control that JOSEPH CANNON exercised, although he exercised it without creating friction and protest. He left quite a record in the legislative history of the country.

Longworth and Democratic MINORITY LEADER John Nance Garner developed a close personal relationship. In describing their relationship, Garner said, "I was the heathen and Nick was the aristocrat."

The two cohosted a daily bipartisan group known as the Bureau of Education in the basement of the Capitol. The informal gatherings allowed members to get to know each other over a drink (notwithstanding Prohibition, which Longworth had opposed) and engage in off-the-record communications and negotiations. According to Garner, in these conferences were often discussed the policies of the Congress in a patriotic spirit, and many propositions were solved. A good many of them are on the statute books today.

In 1930 Longworth was challenged by a group of insurgent Republicans from the Northwest who wanted the rules of the House liberalized or they would abstain in the vote for Speaker, permitting a Democrat to win. The insurgents relented, and Longworth was reelected Speaker.

On the last day of the 71st Congress, Longworth prophetically addressed the House for the last time. Acknowledging that the closeness of the 1930 elections (218 Republicans, 216 Democrats, and one independent) made it a possibility that a Democrat could be Speaker by the time the Congress convened that December, Longworth said:

> I do not mean to insinuate that I regard it is a probability, but I must admit it is a possibility. With whatever Providence may decree I am absolutely satisfied. I ought to be, for all but three Speakers of the House in history will have had a longer term of consecutive service than I have had. I have esteemed every member here during my six years of service without one single exception.

Longworth died on April 9, 1931, of lobar pneumonia while visiting the winter home of James F. Curtis in Aiken, South Carolina. His funeral was attended by President Herbert Hoover, Vice President Charles Curtis, and members of Congress from both parties. He was one of 14 members of the House of Representatives who died between the November 1930 election and the opening of the 72nd Congress in December 1931. The results of the special elections held to fill these seats shifted control of the House of Representatives from the Republicans to the Democrats, a precursor to the Democratic sweep of 1932.

Longworth is buried in the Spring Grove Cemetery in Cincinnati, Ohio. The Longworth House Office Building, completed in 1933, was named in his honor in 1962 to recognize that he had been Speaker of the House of Representatives when the building's construction was authorized in 1929.

Further reading:
Chambrun, Clara Longworth, comtesse de. *The Making of Nicholas Longworth; Annals of an American Family.* New York: R. Long & R. R. Smith, 1933; Hatfield, Mark O., with the Senate Historical Office. *Vice Presidents of the United States 1789–1993.* Washington, D.C.: Government Printing Office, 1997; Longworth, Alice Roosevelt. *Crowded Hours.* New York: Scribners, 1933, and *Special to the New York Times, Won Way to Position By Years of Hard Work, New York Times,* 10 April 1931.

—Jeffrey Kraus

Lott, Trent (1941–   ) *Representative, House Republican Whip, Senator, Senate Majority Leader*

Trent Lott was born in Grenada, Mississippi, on October 9, 1941, the only child of Chester Lott, a shipyard worker, and Iona Watson Lott. He grew up in Pascagoula, attending school in that Gulf Coast town. As a student at the University of Mississippi, he was elected head cheerleader after an unsuccessful race for student body president. He received a bachelor of science in public administration in 1963. He earned a law degree from the University of Mississippi in 1967 and joined the law firm of Bryan & Gordon. In 1968 he traveled to Washington, D.C., to work in the office of Representative William Colmer, a Republican from Mississippi.

In 1972 Colmer decided not to run for reelection. Lott declared his candidacy for the seat as a Republican. He defeated the chair of the state senate banking committee, gaining 55 percent of the vote.

Lott entered the HOUSE OF REPRESENTATIVES as a freshman Republican in January 1973 as Congress began debating President Richard Nixon's role in the 1972 break-in at the Democratic National Headquarters in the WATERGATE office complex, in Washington, D.C. Lott was a member of the HOUSE JUDICIARY COMMITTEE that in 1974 began holding hearings on whether the president should be impeached. He was one of 10 Republicans who initially rejected the five articles of impeachment under consideration. Lott's support of Nixon increased his popularity back in his district. Nearly 87 percent of the district's voters had voted for Nixon in 1972. Despite his district's strong popular support of the president, after Nixon released transcripts of his conversations calling for a halt in the investigation of the Watergate break-in, Lott joined the other nine Republican representatives and voted for the first article of impeachment, obstruction of justice.

Lott was reelected in 1974. In 1975 he was appointed to the HOUSE RULES COMMITTEE, a position he held until he left the House in 1989. As a member of the minority party, he worked to frustrate Democratic legislative initiatives. He also worked to strengthen his relationship with his constituents. He was reelected to the House seven times, each by gaining more than 60 percent of the vote.

In 1980 Lott served as the chair of the Republican National Convention's platform committee, a position he also held in 1984. He also served as California governor Ronald Reagan's campaign manager in Mississippi. During the party's December 1980 congressional organizational meetings, Representative Lott was elected Minority WHIP by a vote of 96 to 90 over Representative Bud Shuster, a Republican from Pennsylvania. Lott became the first Deep South Republican to be elected House Minority Whip. Working with newly elected Republican MAJORITY LEADER Bob Michel of Illinois, Lott developed a member-to-member buddy system to try to persuade Democratic members of the House to support President Reagan's proposals.

Lott defied the president when he felt it was necessary. In 1985 he worked to block consideration of a tax overhaul bill favored by Reagan because Lott felt the bill did not meet Reagan's goals. He voted to override the president's veto of a highway spending bill in 1987 because the bill would have brought a highway demonstration project to his district.

By 1987 Lott had become frustrated with being in the minority in the Democratic-controlled House. In 1988 Senator John Stennis, a Democrat from Mississippi, announced that he was retiring. Lott declared his candidacy for the Senate. He defeated Representative Wayne Dowdy, a Democrat from Mississippi, with 54 percent of the vote. As a senator he worked with Republican president George H. W. Bush on most pieces of legislation. Lott opposed the 1990 budget summit agreement put together by the administration and congressional leaders because he would not support any increase in taxes. He called on Democrats to support the president during the vote to allow an American military response to the Iraqi invasion of Kuwait in 1990. He warned Democrats that opposing the president could be considered giving aid and comfort to the enemy.

In 1989 Senate MINORITY LEADER ROBERT DOLE, a Republican from Kansas, appointed Lott to the Senate Ethics Committee. Lott was appointed to the BUDGET COMMITTEE in 1991. In 1992 he was elected secretary of the Senate Republican Conference, defeating Senators Christopher Bond of Missouri and Frank Murkowski of Alaska. Dole placed Lott in charge of a party task force charged with reviewing President Bill Clinton's cabinet appointments in 1993. Lott was reelected to the Senate in 1994, the year the Republican Party became the majority in both houses of Congress. Although earlier he had not strenuously opposed Clinton's nominees, he was able to gather enough votes in 1995 to block the nomination as Surgeon General of Henry Foster.

Lott was elected Senate Majority Whip in December 1994, defeating Senator Alan Simpson, a Republican from Wyoming, by one vote. He was elected with the support of younger conservatives in the Senate; the more senior Republican senators backed Simpson. Lott worked with Majority Leader Dole but also worked to enact his own agenda. He negotiated a proposal that allowed long-distance companies to enter local phone markets, a bill signed into law by President Clinton in 1996.

As whip, Lott restructured his organization to be more effective. He recruited his colleagues to track fellow senators. In addition to six regional whips who reported to Senate leadership, Lott appointed a whip of the day who would be on the Senate floor at all times. His organizational abilities allowed him to be elected MAJORITY LEADER in 1996, when Senator Dole resigned to focus on his presidential campaign. Lott was elected with 44 votes. Eight senators voted for Senator Thad Cochran, also from Mississippi, and one abstained. Lott was able to maintain his position after the 1996 elections.

As Majority Leader in 1996, Lott was able to get a vote on welfare reform, a compromise health care bill, and the Safe Drinking Water Act. He also established a working relationship with Senate Minority Leader THOMAS DASCHLE, a Democrat from South Dakota. When the SPEAKER OF THE HOUSE, NEWT GINGRICH, a Republican from Georgia, was threatened with ethics charges, Lott became the most visible national Republican leader. In 1997 he angered Democrats by not working harder to enact a campaign finance reform bill and when he proposed investigating the results of the U.S. Senate race in Louisiana. Lott angered conservatives by working with the Clinton administration and against the Senate FOREIGN RELATIONS COMMITTEE chair, Jesse Helms, a Republican from North Carolina, to secure ratification of the Chemical Weapons Treaty. He encountered more controversy in 1998 when he stated that homosexuality was an illness similar to alcoholism.

Lott's leadership skills were tested during the impeachment of President Clinton in 1998. After the House approved articles of impeachment, Lott supported a proposal to allow four days of argument in the impeachment trial to be followed by a vote on whether the charges justified impeachment. If the vote fell short of the two-thirds required, the trial in the Senate would be adjourned. House Republican managers of the articles of impeachment expressed their disgust with Lott's actions and found support among conservative Republican senators. After reaching an agreement that the trial would be held without the calling of witnesses, the Senate did not vote for Clinton's removal from office.

Lott was reelected easily in 2000. Because the parties each held 50 seats in the Senate, he served as Minority Leader for 20 days in 2001 until President George W. Bush was inaugurated and Vice President Dick Cheney broke the tie in organizing the Senate. In June 2001 Senator JAMES JEFFORDS, an independent from Vermont, left the Republican Party, giving the Democrats control of the Senate. Lott and Minority Leader Daschle switched offices. In December 2002 Lott was preparing to reassume his role as Majority Leader in the 108th Congress, but he was forced to resign after causing controversy with comments made at an event honoring Senator STROM THURMOND, a Republican from South Carolina, the prosegregation Dixiecrat candidate for president in 1948. Lott told Thurmond that Mississippians were proud to have voted for him at the time, adding that if the rest of the country had followed their lead, America would not have had so many problems over the years. Lott apologized, but he had lost the support of his Republican colleagues and the Bush administration. The Republicans elected Senator WILLIAM FRIST, a Republican from Tennessee, to replace Lott as Majority Leader.

Lott was discouraged from retiring from the Senate because Mississippi's Democratic governor probably would have appointed a Democrat to the vacancy. This would have threatened Republican control of the Senate. Lott became chair of the SENATE COMMITTEE on RULES AND ADMINISTRATION. He also continued service on Finance, Commerce, and Intelligence Committees.

Further reading:
Connelly, William F., and John J. Pitney. *Congress' Permanent Minority? Republicans in the U.S. House.* Lanham, Md.: Littlefield Adams Quality Paperbacks, 1994; Lott, Trent. *Herding Cats: A Life in Politics.* New York: HarperCollins, 2005; Lott, Trent. *Master of the Game: Tales from a Republican Revolutionary.* New York: Regan Books 2005; Stolberg, Sheryl Gay. "For Lott, Uneasy Role as One of 100 in Senate." *New York Times,* 1 March 2003, p. A1.

—John David Rausch, Jr.

M

mace, House

The mace of the HOUSE OF REPRESENTATIVES is the symbol of the SERGEANT AT ARMS of the House. The House, during the 1st Congress in 1789, established the mace as the symbol of the Sergeant at Arms with one of the first resolutions passed by the young Congress. The House has used three different maces since its first session. The first mace was destroyed when the British burned the Capitol in 1814. Between 1814 and 1841 the mace was wooden. However, the current mace, made of ebony and silver, was commissioned to be similar to the one destroyed in 1814. New York silversmith William Adams crafted the current mace in 1841.

The 10-pound mace is a 46-inch column made up of 13 tiny ebony rods, which represent the 13 original states. The mace is bound together by 4 crossing sterling silver bands that are adorned with floral borders. The shaft is topped by a 4.5-inch silver globe that is engraved with the seven continents, the names of the oceans, the lines of longitude, and the major lines of latitude. Furthermore, the globe is bordered with a silver rim, on which is perched a silver eagle with a 15-inch wingspan.

Typically, each day when the House convenes the Sergeant at Arms or his or her assistant places the mace on a green marble pedestal, which is located to the Speaker's right. However, it is taken down from the table and moved to a lower pedestal when the Speaker hands the gavel to the chair of the Committee of the Whole. Thus, visitors to the House and the members coming onto the floor can tell from a lowered mace when the House is operating as the Committee of the Whole instead of as the House of Representatives. In addition, the mace appears at each presidential inauguration carried by either the Sergeant at Arms or an assistant. The Sergeant at Arms or an assistant leads the procession of the members as they arrive at the inauguration ceremony and then proceeds to stand behind the members, still holding the mace, for the remainder of the ceremony.

The original use for the mace was to restore order in the case of unruly members. When members became disorderly, the Speaker would order the Sergeant at Arms to take the mace from the pedestal and present it before the unruly member(s), thereby restoring order. Although in current times this procedure is rarely, if ever, used, the mace remains an important symbol of the House.

Further reading:
Office of the Clerk. U.S. House of Representatives, 2003; Oleszek, Walter J. *Congressional Procedures and the Policy Process.* 4th ed. Washington, D.C.: Congressional Quarterly Press, 1996.

—Lisa A. Solowiej

Majority Leader, House

The floor leader of the majority party in the HOUSE OF REPRESENTATIVES and the second ranking official in the chamber is the Majority Leader. Formally created in 1899, the House Majority Leader position is the majority party's deputy leader, behind the SPEAKER OF THE HOUSE. The Majority Leader was personally selected by the Speaker until the Democratic Party gained control of the House in 1910. Usually, the Speaker selected a trusted lieutenant or a political rival when necessary to promote party unity.

In 1910 a rebellion against the Speaker bolstered the power of the Majority Leader and led to the position being elected by the members of the party caucus. The first Majority Leader thus elected by the party caucus was Representative Oscar Underwood of Alabama. Underwood proved to have more power than the Speaker, JAMES BEAUCHAMP CHAMP CLARK of Missouri, because Underwood had the support of the party caucus. The Majority Leader chaired the party caucus. He also chaired the House WAYS AND MEANS COMMITTEE. Democrats on the Ways and Means Committee also acted as the party's Committee on Committees that was responsible for making committee assignments.

After Underwood left the House for the Senate, the power of the Majority Leader was diminished relative to the power of the Speaker. By the early 1920s both parties relieved their leaders of committee assignments. This remains the custom even though the leader will chair select or special committees and task forces on occasion. The primary duties of the Majority Leader are to be the principal floor defender, negotiator, and spokesperson for the party. The leader helps plan the party's legislative agenda and works to promote the purposes and programs of the majority party.

One goal of the Majority Leader has been to keep the party in the majority so that he or she will become Speaker. Almost all Speakers of the 20th century served as Majority Leader before being elevated to Speaker.

Sereno Payne, Republican of New York, was Majority Leader from 1899 until the Democrats regained the majority in 1911. Representative Underwood was the first leader elected by the Democratic Caucus. Claude Kitchin, Democrat of North Carolina, served as Majority Leader from 1915 to 1919. Frank Mondell, Republican of Wyoming, was the Majority Leader from 1919 until he was replaced by NICHOLAS LONGWORTH, Republican of Ohio, in 1923.

When Longworth became Speaker in 1925, the Republicans elected John Tilson of Connecticut. Tilson served until the Democrats gained the majority in the House in 1931. The Majority Leader in the 72nd Congress (1931–33) was Henry Rainey, Democrat of Illinois. He was replaced by Joseph Byrnes, Democrat of Tennessee, in the 73rd Congress (1933–35). William Bankhead, Democrat of Alabama, served as Majority Leader in the 74th Congress (1935–37) before being elected Speaker in 1936. SAMUEL RAYBURN, Democrat of Texas, was elected Majority Leader in 1936 and served in that position until being elected Speaker of the House in 1940.

Representative JOHN MCCORMACK, Democrat of Massachusetts, was elected Majority Leader in 1940. He served in that position until being elected Speaker in 1962, except for the 80th Congress (1947–49) and the 83rd Congress (1953–55), when the Republicans were the majority party in the House. Charles Halleck, Republican of Indiana, was the Majority Leader during the 80th and 83rd Congresses.

In 1962 CARL ALBERT, Democrat from Oklahoma, was elected Majority Leader, serving until 1971, when he was elected Speaker. Hale Boggs, Democrat of Louisiana, served as Majority Leader from 1971 until he went missing in an Alaskan airplane crash in 1973. THOMAS "TIP" O'NEILL, Democrat of Massachusetts, was elected to replace Boggs, serving as Majority Leader until becoming Speaker in 1977. James Wright, Democrat of Texas, served

as Majority Leader from 1977 until he was elected Speaker in 1987. Thomas Foley, Democrat of Washington, was elected Majority Leader in 1987 and became Speaker in 1989 after Wright resigned from Congress. In 1989 RICHARD GEPHARDT, Democrat of Missouri, was elected Majority Leader and served until the Republicans became the majority party in Congress in the 104th Congress (1995–96).

Richard Armey, Republican of Texas, was elected Majority Leader in 1995, the first Republican to hold the position in 40 years. Because of his involvement in a 1997 attempt to unseat Speaker NEWT GINGRICH, Armey was not a candidate for Speaker. In fact, he defeated two well-qualified challengers to retain his post at Majority Leader. Armey retired at the end of the 107th Congress in 2002. He was replaced by TOM DELAY, Republican of Texas.

Further reading:
Connelly, William F., Jr., and John J. Pitney. "The House GOP's Civil War: A Political Science Perspective." *PS: Political Science and Politics* 30 (1997): 699–703; Davidson, Roger H., Susan Webb Hammond, and Raymond Smock. *Masters of the House: Congressional Leadership over Two Centuries.* Boulder, Colo.: Westview Press, 1998; Sinclair, Barbara. *Majority Leadership in the U.S. House.* Baltimore: Johns Hopkins University Press, 1983.

—John David Rausch, Jr.

Majority Leader, Senate

The Majority Leader is the head of the majority party in the SENATE as well as the de facto leader of the Senate. (Though the vice president is the constitutional President of the Senate, the vice president seldom presides over Senate sessions.) The Majority Leader is chosen by secret ballot of majority party members in the Senate. A Majority Leader tends to be chosen to the post because he or she has earned respect as a trustworthy spokesperson for that party.

The role of Majority Leader is not mentioned in the Constitution and is a relatively recent creation that dates from the early 1900s. Historically, the Senate has always had some sort of leader, but in the 18th and 19th centuries no single senator was given the responsibility to exercise the central management of the legislative process as is today's Majority Leader. By the beginning of the 20th century, however, party leaders emerged as an identifiable force in managing the Senate's proceedings.

Senate Majority Leaders have two primary roles, party spokesperson and party strategist. The main function of the Majority Leader is to guide the party as it tries to create a record on which to stand at subsequent elections and from the majority party's perspective, maintain a majority of Senate seats. Agenda setting is the prime prerogative of the

Majority Leader, and agenda setting involves determining the party strategy in the Senate.

The Majority Leader possesses most of the same powers as the SPEAKER OF THE HOUSE. The Majority Leader can offer rewards for compliance through committee assignments, can assist senators with their constituents by providing support for constituency-oriented projects such as parks, highways, and universities within their respective states, and can provide campaign assistance at election time.

One of the most important formal powers of the Majority Leader is the scheduling of bills on the floor, and this is central to his or her ability to devise a legislative strategy for the majority party. The Majority Leader wants the Senate to focus on the majority party's agenda; the minority party, by contrast, wants to be able to advance its priorities by offering nongermane amendments to whatever bill lends itself to that objective. If the Senate has come to an impasse on an issue because of various stalling tactics, the Majority Leader can threaten to make members work long days, through the weekend, and even through planned recesses until the matter is resolved. The influence over the scheduling of Senate business is much more important today than it used to be due to the fact that for political reasons senators travel back to their home states much more than before. Thus, an important role of modern-day Majority Leaders is to accommodate the needs of individual lawmakers. This can be done, among other means, by attempting to arrange roll-call votes around the travel plans of senators. Predictable scheduling enhances the ability of senators to achieve their personal goals and thus may generate goodwill for Majority Leaders.

The influence of Majority Leaders tends to be informal, and the most powerful tool in the Majority Leader's arsenal is the "power of persuasion." LYNDON B. JOHNSON, a Democrat from Texas, was a master of this and is widely considered to be the most powerful Senate Majority Leader ever. In fact, Johnson's awesome display of face-to-face persuasion had a name: the Johnson treatment. Johnson revolutionized the position of Majority Leader. Before him the position was relatively anemic. After Johnson became Majority Leader in 1955, however, the post was transformed into one of considerable influence and preeminence.

Despite the Majority Leader's considerable powers, there are definitely considerable limits to a Majority Leader's power. In particular, the individualistic nature of the Senate and partisanship can work to undermine a Majority Leader's efforts. The existence of an extensive arsenal of persuasive weapons should not obscure that Majority Leaders have no way to ensure that bargains with members will work. Successful Majority Leaders will be able to promote the party orientation at the expense of competing foci of loyalty.

The importance of the Majority Leader as a primary spokesperson for the majority party can be seen in the resignation of TRENT LOTT, a Republican from Mississippi, as Majority Leader. On November 13, 2002, Lott was unanimously reelected by his Republican colleagues to be Majority Leader of the 108th Senate after the Republicans regained majority control in the 2002 elections. Three weeks after he was reelected, however, Lott made comments praising retiring senator STROM THURMOND's 1948 run for the presidency on a segregationist Dixiecrat ticket at a celebration for Thurmond's 100th birthday. Lott's remarks were denounced by many Republicans, including President George W. Bush, and in the political inferno that developed Lott was eventually forced to step down. Bill Frist, a Republican from Tennessee, was selected to replace him as the Republican Party leader in the Senate. The controversy surrounding Lott's comments demonstrates just how important a symbol the position of Majority Leader has become for the majority party. Lott lost the position as Majority Leader in large part because many in the Republican Party felt that he no longer could be an adequate spokesperson for the party after the controversy and could potentially cost the party electoral support. Nowadays, the Majority Leader is expected not only to be a leader of the majority party in the Senate but also, to some degree, to be a personification of the majority party.

Further reading:
Davidson, Roger, and Walter J. Oleszek. *Congress and Its Members.* 9th ed. Washington, D.C.: Congressional Quarterly Press, 2004; Rieselbach, Leroy N. *Congressional Politics: The Evolving Legislative System.* 2d ed. Boulder, Colo.: Westview Press, 1995; Sinclair, Barbara. *The Transformation of the U.S. Senate.* Baltimore: Johns Hopkins University Press, 1989.

—Patrick Fisher

Manhattan Project
The Manhattan Project was the code name for the top-secret effort to develop a nuclear weapon in America during World War II. The project was officially begun in 1942 with the creation of the Manhattan Engineer District, headed by Brigadier General Lesley Groves (who had overseen the building of the Pentagon). Robert Oppenheimer directed the centerpiece of the project in Los Alamos, New Mexico, building a nuclear reactor and creating an atomic bomb. Scientists from around the country were recruited for the effort. Enrico Fermi built a prototype reactor underground in Chicago, and secret facilities employing thousands of workers were set up in Los Alamos, Hanford, Washington, and Oak Ridge, Tennessee. The effort was speedy and highly secretive, with the goal of producing a bomb before Germany or Japan could.

Initially, Congress was not even informed of the massive military project, which was spending millions of dollars. When Congress did become involved, it began raising questions about the project and its expenditures. The directors knew that the project was controversial and set about to quickly and successfully accomplish their task in order to mitigate opposition. The first explosion of an atomic bomb occurred as a test at Alamogordo, New Mexico, in July 1945. In August of that year, bombs were dropped on Hiroshima and Nagasaki, devastating the cities, killing hundreds of thousands of people, and ending World War II.

The Manhattan Project was successful in its mission and can be seen as a testimony to American ingenuity, determination, and scientific research. That success came at a high cost, however. The project left in its wake moral questions about the staggering loss of life caused by the bomb and a debate about the use—and threat of use—of weapons of mass destruction. Once having developed nuclear weapons, the United States entered into an "arms race" with the Soviet Union. The threat of nuclear warfare was central to the cold war, which occupied the U.S. government for decades to come.

Further reading:
Norris, Robert S. *Racing for the Bomb: General Leslie R. Groves, the Manhattan Project's Indispensable Man.* South Royalton, Vt.: Steerforth Press, 2002; Rhodes, Richard. *The Making of the Atomic Bomb.* New York: Simon & Schuster, 1987.

—Anne Marie Cammisa

Marbury v. Madison 1 Cranch (5 U.S.) 137 (1803)
This Supreme Court case, decided in 1803, established the doctrine of judicial review, that the Court has the power to declare acts of Congress unconstitutional. The case played out against a backdrop of party competition. Although George Washington, the first president of the United States, warned against parties, a two-party system quickly emerged. The Federalists won the election of 1796, when John Adams was elected president. Because the Constitution mandated that the vice president be the person who came in second in the election, Adams's vice president was his political rival, Thomas Jefferson, who had run against him as a Jeffersonian Democratic-Republican. In the election of 1800, Thomas Jefferson defeated John Adams (only after the election was decided in the House of Representatives; Jefferson and his vice presidential running mate had tied in electoral college votes, and the Constitution sends a tied election to the House).

Under the Constitution the election was held in November, but the new government would not be inaugurated until March. (This was changed with the Twentieth Amendment, adopted in 1933.) Although Adams's Federalist Party had lost both the presidency and the majority in Congress, they had six months to pass a flurry of legislation to thwart the Jeffersonian Democratic-Republicans, who the Federalists distrusted immensely. Adams himself made a series of midnight appointments to the judiciary, trying to pack the courts with Federalists. One of those appointees was William Marbury, who was to be justice of the peace for the District of Columbia. President Adams's secretary of State, John Marshall, signed the commissions, but he failed to deliver several, including the one to Marbury.

The midnight appointments were not the only way the Federalists attempted to keep control over the judiciary. They also passed the Judiciary Act of 1801 (referred to as the Midnight Judges Act), which set up an additional layer of appellate courts. Theoretically, this system would reduce the Supreme Court justices' workload. Practically, it gave the Federalists a number of new judicial positions to fill with supporters of their party.

When the Democratic-Republicans took over Congress and the presidency in March of 1801, they were justifiably upset with Federalists attempts at controlling the judiciary. So they repealed the Midnight Judges Act, effectively "firing" the new circuit judges appointed by the Federalists. And in the Judiciary Act of 1802, the Jeffersonian-Republicans did away with the Court's 1802 term. The repeal of the Midnight Judges Act combined with the new Judiciary Act served as a threat to the Federalist judges on the courts. The Democratic-Republicans were asserting their authority and implying that they could get rid of other Federalists justices if they saw fit.

In the meantime, when President Jefferson's secretary of State, James Madison, found the signed commissions that Marshall had neglected to deliver, Jefferson ordered him not to deliver them, refusing to help his opponents by placing more Federalists on the judiciary. Marbury sued Madison for failure to deliver the document, requesting a writ of mandamus (in other words, asking that the document be delivered, giving him the appointment that was rightfully his). Under the Judiciary Act of 1789, the case went directly to the Supreme Court. That put the chief justice, John Marshall, in a no-win situation. In the first place, as Adams's secretary of State, he was the very person who had failed to deliver the documents (and, as newly appointed chief justice, another example of Federalist court packing). Under today's jurisprudence, Marshall would have recused himself from the case. In 1803 Marshall felt no conflict of interest. He did, however, face a political dilemma. If Marshall decided for Marbury, saying that the commission should be delivered, he knew that Madison would simply refuse to deliver it, and Marshall himself would probably face impeachment. If Marshall decided for Madison, he would be deciding in favor of his party's political enemies and would also appear to be acting out of fear. Either way, Marshall—and the Supreme Court—would look weak. And either way, the Federalists would be repudiated. Marshall also knew that a weakened Supreme Court would be a large threat to the future of the fledgling nation. In fact, the very partisan political bickering that was occurring over the judiciary was itself a threat to the future of American democracy.

Marshall came up with a brilliant plan. Writing for a unanimous court, he first said that Marbury was right, that Madison was required to deliver the commission signed by the previous secretary of State (that is, Marshall himself). The commission was, in fact, legal, as the Federalists asserted. But, Marshall said, that point was moot, because the law under which the case came to the Supreme Court was unconstitutional. The Judiciary Act of 1789 (which set up the original court system and was passed prior to the partisan wrangling of the Federalists and Jeffersonian-Democrats) gave the Supreme Court the power to issue writs of mandamus as part of its original jurisdiction. (In other words, such writs would go to the Supreme Court directly, rather than through the usual appeals process.) Since the Constitution spelled out in Article III precisely what cases constitute original jurisdiction ("all cases affecting ambassadors, other public ministers and consuls and those in which a state shall be a party"), and since writs of mandamus were not among those cases, Marshall reasoned that that section of the Judiciary Act of 1789 was unconstitutional, and the case was not properly before the Supreme Court. In so doing, he declared himself and his political party in the right while avoiding an ugly and protracted partisan fight with the Democratic-Republicans. (He also avoided facing potential impeachment.) In addition, Marshall established the primacy of the Supreme Court by clearly articulating the doctrine of judicial review: The Supreme Court has the power of deciding what laws are constitutional. "It is emphatically the province and duty of the judicial department to say what the law is." Marshall took a case that had the potential to severely weaken the Supreme Court and through ingenious legal reasoning used it to broaden and solidify the Court's power instead.

Further reading:
Clinton, Robert Lowry. *Marbury v. Madison and Judicial Review.* Lawrence: University Press of Kansas, 1989; Nelson, William E. *Marbury v. Madison: The Origins and Legacy of Judicial Review.* Lawrence: University Press of Kansas 2000; Levinson, Sanford, and Jack M. Balkin. "What Are the Facts of *Marbury v. Madison?" Constitutional Commentary* 6. (2003): 255.

—Anne Marie Cammisa

marking up bills

Marking up legislation is the term given to committee consideration of a bill. Ordinarily, a bill will be reported out by a STANDING COMMITTEE before it is brought to the House or Senate floor.

A mark-up session (sometimes referred to as an EXECUTIVE SESSION) begins with the committee chair calling up a bill for consideration. This will not always be the bill as originally introduced but may be an "amendment in the nature of a substitute" or "chair's mark" that reflects alterations, refinements, or agreements made prior to the session. The measure is then open for amendment.

Members are recognized in order of seniority, alternating by party, to offer amendments. In the House each member may speak for five minutes for or against an amendment; in Senate committees, keeping with that body's tradition, there are no time limits on debate.

Controversial provisions may be deleted from the original bill prior to the mark up if it appears that support for them is lacking. On the other hand, the mark up may be an opportunity to provide "death with dignity" for such provisions. For instance, it was apparent early on that there was inadequate Republican support for a school voucher program to pass as part of President George W. Bush's education reform bill in 2001. Nevertheless, the provision was deleted by the HOUSE EDUCATION AND THE WORKFORCE COMMITTEE in a mark-up session, allowing conservatives to champion the program in a public forum.

Legislative activity at a mark-up session varies depending on how controversial the measure is. Some bills are quickly approved by voice vote, but bills involving contentious issues generally provoke marathon mark ups. When a mark up is in this contentious mode, the minority party will offer a series of "message amendments" that prolong the mark-up process. Such amendments may be designed to carve out particular constituencies from the bill's reach, allowing the minority party to argue that the majority is subjecting a group (e.g., women) or cause (e.g., the environment) to unfair treatment. Other amendments may be intended to suggest hypocrisy or overreaching by the bill's sponsors. Frequently, an amendment will be offered to change a word or phrase in the bill in a way that renders the bill's provisions impotent; often, the proponent of that amendment will candidly admit the amendment's mischievous purpose is "to gut the bill."

Marathon mark-up sessions are tedious and appear absurd to casual observers, yet they serve two purposes. The minority party inflicts inconvenience on the majority party when it moves a controversial bill and in so doing reduces the overall amount of legislation that the majority party can include in its program. By offering and voting for doomed message amendments, members also can demonstrate their commitment to causes important to party constituencies and campaign contributors.

Mark-up sessions are an opportunity for members to attach pet provisions to a bill. This activity is especially likely to occur at mark ups of bills expected to pass with bipartisan support and is particularly important in the House, where opportunities to offer amendments on the floor are limited. Sometimes such amendments are withdrawn when the committee chair publicly promises the proponent that the pet idea will be fully considered at a later mark up. Sometimes amendments agreed to at a mark up can overload a bill with costly or controversial provisions and must be deleted at a later stage of the legislative process.

A bill that advances from a mark up is "ordered reported." The committee staff will draft a written report containing the text of the bill reflecting any amendments agreed to in committee, the votes on amendments offered at mark up, and the rationale for approving the bill. A bill altered at mark up may be reported as a "clean" or "original" bill with a new bill number.

Further reading:
Hall, Richard, and Frank Wayman. "Buying Time: Moneyed Interests and the Mobilization of Bias in Congressional Committees." *American Political Science Review* 84 (1990): 797.

—Jackson Williams

mavericks

Both chambers of Congress, but particularly the SENATE, have a lengthy history of a few members exhibiting independent political behavior and trying to attain goals unique to themselves. As early as the 1840s members such as Representative John Quincy Adams, a Whig from Massachusetts, became known for their "maverick" behavior. Named after unbranded stray animals on the American frontier, maverick legislators on Capitol Hill were known for frequently and conspicuously not abiding by their party's line.

Members' maverick behavior has been thought to stem from many origins. The member, such as Senator Huey Long, a Democrat from Louisiana, might simply seek the spotlight on himself and/or have a disdain for the norms of the Senate. Others, such as Senator Joseph McCarthy, a Republican from Wisconsin, might have a combative personality coupled with a strong ideological conviction. Likewise, later in the 1950s several liberal legislators developed maverick reputations because they sought public floor debate and amendment efforts to bypass standing committees, which were dominated by conservative chairs kept in place by seniority. On the other hand, Senator William Proxmire, a Democrat from Wisconsin, attracted national attention and regular reelection by publicizing what he believed to be wasteful and at times comic spending by government agencies. His annual "golden fleece award" always attracted nationwide news coverage. In later decades senators such as Wayne Morse of Oregon and JAMES JEFFORDS of Vermont broke with the Republican Party and declared an independent status.

Many mavericks regularly won reelection to continue their independent political behavior because they shared the distinctive policy goals of their constituents but ran counter to prevailing nationwide views. Hence, the mavericks continued waging their lonely policy battles on Capitol Hill. Regardless of their era, political party, or chamber membership, maverick members of Congress clearly have rejected the common Capitol Hill notion of "to get along you have to go along."

Further reading:
Huitt, Ralph K. "The Outsider in the Senate: An Alternative Role." In Ralph K. Huitt and Robert L. Peabody, eds. *Congress: Two Decades of Analysis.* New York: Harper & Row, 1969; Sinclair, Barbara. *The Transformation of the U.S. Senate.* Baltimore: Johns Hopkins University Press, 1989.

—Martin Ricks

McCarthy, Joseph R. (1908–1957) *Senator*

Joseph ("Joe") Raymond McCarthy, Republican senator from Wisconsin (1947–57), achieved national prominence, power, and notoriety in the early 1950s with his sensational but unproven charges of communist penetration in high government circles. He attacked alleged communist subversion within the administrations of presidents Harry S. Truman and Dwight D. Eisenhower, but failed to identify a single communist agent in the government. After the U.S. Senate officially censured him in 1954 for his vicious personal attacks on people he claimed to be subversive, his influence quickly faded until he died in 1957.

Senator McCarthy was born in Grand Chute, Wisconsin, on November 14, 1908, to a family of devout Roman Catholic farmers. He dropped out of school at the age of 14 to work as a chicken farmer but in 1928 returned to finish his high school studies. He graduated with a law degree from the Jesuit University at Marquette in 1935 and worked as a Wisconsin attorney, but his private law practice was lackluster. Joe McCarthy was originally a New Deal Democrat, but after failing to win the Democratic Party's nomination for district attorney, he switched parties and became the GOP candidate in an election for circuit court judge. He won after a dirty electoral campaign in which he reportedly smeared and slandered his opponent, accusing him of senility and financial improprieties. McCarthy served three years (1940–42) on the circuit court before resigning to enlist in the U.S. Marine Corps during World War II. In 1944, on leave from military service in the South Pacific, he ran unsuccessfully for the Republican senatorial nomination in Wisconsin.

Two years later he won the GOP nomination for the Senate in a stunning upset primary victory over Wisconsin senator Robert M. LaFollette, Jr. During the primary McCarthy attacked LaFollette for not enlisting during the war, even though the latter was too old to join the armed forces, and falsely accused him of war profiteering. He easily won the November 1946 ballot to capture LaFollette's Senate seat. But later "Tail-Gunner Joe," as McCarthy referred to himself on the campaign trail, faced charges that he had embellished his wartime record by claiming to have flown 32 combat missions when, in fact, he had held a desk job and had flown only in a few training exercises.

Senator McCarty was initially a quiet and undistinguished legislator who got into trouble when he came under investigation for tax evasion and for taking bribes from the Pepsi-Cola Company. On February 9, 1950, he launched a highly publicized campaign to expose alleged communists in the federal government. His explosive charge that there were 205 "card-carrying Communists" in the State Department known to Secretary of State Dean G. Acheson created a nationwide furor that catapulted him overnight from total political obscurity into the news headlines across the country. But when he subsequently testified before the Senate Committee on Foreign Relations, he was unable to produce the name of a single communist in any government office. Nevertheless, the junior senator from Wisconsin gained popular support for his campaign of vitriolic and fraudulent accusations by exploiting the nation's fears and frustrations over the Soviet acquisition of the atomic bomb, the "loss of China" to Mao Zedong's Communists, and the stalemated and inconclusive Korean War. He had the support of many of his Republican colleagues, who believed that the reds-in-the-government issue was vital to their victory in the 1950 midterm elections.

On February 20, 1950, Senator McCarthy delivered a five-hour speech on the Senate floor in which he charged that the Truman administration was riddled with communist subversives. He claimed to have a list of 57 spies forming a Soviet espionage ring within the State Department but refused to reveal their names or the source of his information. Because of his bluffing and his demagogic attacks on Secretary of State Acheson and other high-ranking government officials, Democratic senators accused him of smear tactics, insinuation, and indiscriminate character assassination. In response, Senator McCarthy charged that all Democrats, including President Truman, were dangerous liberals who were wittingly or unwittingly part of this communist conspiracy. This reckless accusation was used against those of his Democratic critics who were up for reelection, a number of whom lost in 1950 and 1952, making other Democrats fearful and reluctant to incur the Wisconsin senator's anger. Collaborating secretly with FBI director J. Edgar Hoover and other archconservatives, he helped instigate a militant anticommunist crusade, which contributed to the "Red Scare" hysteria of the early 1950s. To his many supporters the fanatically anticommunist senator McCarthy appeared as a true patriot and dedicated champion of the American way of life. To his detractors, however, he was an amoral, prevaricating, and headline-grabbing bully whose redbaiting tactics of lies, slander, and smear were undermining the nation's First Amendment traditions of civil liberties and individual rights.

Senator McCarthy claimed that high-level treason and internal subversion were behind all the failings of American foreign policy, with Secretary of State Acheson and his immediate predecessor, U.S. Army general George C. Marshall, being his favorite and most prominent individual targets. Acheson courageously defended his department, including Alger Hiss, the former State Department officer and New Dealer accused of spying for the Soviet Union in the 1930s, and refused to fire any of his subordinates named in the congressional hearings on subversion. However, President Truman avoided facing down the junior senator from Wisconsin, as did subsequently President Eisenhower.

Senator McCarthy was reelected in 1952 and obtained the chair of the Senate Government Committee on Operations and of its Permanent Subcommittee on Investigations. For the next two years he was constantly in the public eye, investigating various government departments and grilling in public numerous witnesses about their suspected communist ties. Assisted by Roy Cohn, his hand-picked chief counsel of the Permanent Subcommittee on Investigations, Senator McCarthy threatened the witnesses with prosecution for contempt and also made it clear to them that the only way of demonstrating that they had abandoned their erstwhile left-wing views was by naming other communists in high places. From his new post he leveled treason charges not just against liberal Democrats but also against members of the new Eisenhower administration. Moving deftly from one groundless accusation to another, Senator McCarthy intimidated his critics and brushed aside demands for concrete evidence. Sometimes he even claimed that there was no official evidence to prove that his victims were not indeed "Communists." As part of his anticommunist drive he also launched a campaign to purge public libraries of books he claimed to be "un-American." As a result, more than 30,000 books of the U.S. Information Libraries alone were removed from library shelves.

Encouraged by other Republicans angry over their fifth consecutive defeat in a presidential election, the Wisconsin senator accused the Franklin D. Roosevelt and the

Truman administrations of "twenty years of treason." Shrewd at public relations and media manipulation, he garnered a large and loyal GOP following. But among his supporters were even Democratic stalwarts such as Ambassador Joseph P. Kennedy Sr., one of whose sons, future New York senator Robert Kennedy, served as assistant counsel to the Senate Permanent Subcommittee on Investigations chaired by McCarthy. Although Senator McCarthy failed to make a credible case against anyone, his wild and baseless accusations drove many out of their jobs and brought popular condemnation to others. The persecution of innocent people on the unsubstantiated charge of being secret members of the communist underground and the imposed ideological conformity that this wide-ranging witch-hunt brought to American public life became known as McCarthyism. McCarthyism was used mainly against New Dealers in and out of government, who were accused of protecting known communists and being "soft on communism," if not of outright espionage and treason.

Senator McCarthy's inflammatory and vituperative attacks came to include President Eisenhower and other top Republican leaders. In October 1953 he began investigating communist infiltration into the military, trying in particular to discredit Robert T. Stevens, the secretary of the army, which reportedly infuriated the White House. But his influence began to wane in 1954 as a result of the sensational, nationally televised 36-day Permanent Subcommittee on Investigations hearing on his charges of communist conspiracy involving civilian officials and military officers of the U.S. Army. His failure to substantiate his claims of communist penetration of the military and the extensive television exposure of his brutal and dishonest interrogative methods discredited him and helped to turn the tide of public opinion against McCarthyism in America. Matters were made even worse for McCarthy by the army's accusations that, among many other misdeeds, he and Roy Cohn had abused congressional privilege by trying to prevent G. David Schine, Cohn's chief consultant and best friend, from being drafted in November 1953. When that failed they tied to pressure the military into giving Private Schine preferential treatment, such as special assignments or an officer's commission. The Wisconsin senator also became the target of hostile media coverage and damaging rumors about his drunkenness, dishonesty, bigotry, secret presidential ambitions, and suspected homosexuality, as well as an alleged homosexual affair between Cohn and Schine.

Although widely seen as cynical and out of control, Senator McCarthy was still a powerful figure until the Republicans lost control of the Senate in the midterm elections of November 1954. He was replaced as chair of the Senate Government Committee on Operations and of its Permanent Subcommittee on Investigations. He lost his power base at a time when many of his colleagues were eager to condemn him for his irresponsible personal attacks against a large number of senators over the years, a serious violation of Senate etiquette. In a rare move on December 2, 1954, the Senate officially censured the increasingly erratic and alcoholic Wisconsin legislator on a vote of 67-22 for conduct "contrary to Senate traditions." Senator McCarthy was largely ignored by his colleagues and by the media thereafter, but his fall from public grace did not take place before the wave of red hysteria, which he had helped instigate, destroyed numerous reputations, careers, and lives.

Senator McCarthy, who against the advice of his doctors had been drinking heavily for many years, was diagnosed with having cirrhosis of the liver and died in the Bethesda Naval Hospital in Maryland on May 2, 1957. But McCarthyism seems to live on as exemplified by the efforts of conservative scholars (such as author Arthur Herman) to exonerate him and his blatant assaults on constitutional rights and freedoms, as well as by renewed attacks on liberals as "anti-American" and "treacherous" in neo-McCarthyite books such as Ann Coulter's *Treason*.

See also UN-AMERICAN ACTIVITIES COMMITTEE, HOUSE.

Further reading:
Feuerlicht, Roberta S. *Joe McCarthy and McCarthyism.* New York: McGraw-Hill, 1972; Griffith, Robert. *The Politics of Fear: Joseph R. McCarthy and the Senate.* Lexington: University Press of Kentucky, 1970; Herman, Arthur. *Joseph McCarthy: Reexamining the Life and Legacy of America's Most Hated Senator.* New York: Free Press, 2000; Oshinsky, David M. *A Conspiracy So Immense: The World of Joe McCarthy.* New York: Free Press, 1983; Reeves, Thomas C. *The Life and Times of Joe McCarthy.* New York: Stein & Day, 1982.

—Rossen V. Vassilev

McCarthy-army hearings

The legendary McCarthy-army hearings, held from April 22 through June 16, 1954, came as a result of Republican senator Joseph R. McCarthy's wide-ranging and highly publicized campaign against what he claimed was internal subversion by communist agents lurking in all walks of American life, but especially inside the federal government. His shrill and vicious denunciations of the Democratic administration of President Harry S. Truman had helped Republican candidate Dwight D. Eisenhower win the 1952 presidential election, finally turning the Democrats out, who McCarthy had accused of "twenty years of treason." But the Wisconsin senator, who privately feared losing his senatorial job and thus his place in American politics, was temperamentally unable to suspend his immensely popular anticommunist crusade. By 1953 his inflammatory and vituperative attacks came to include President Eisenhower and other top Republican leaders, who McCarthy accused of hiding communists or being "soft on communism." His attention turned from the Department of State under the Democrats to the U.S. Army under the Republicans, which now became the main focus of his witch hunt for subversives.

But Senator McCarthy's enormous influence began to crumble in 1954 as a result of the sensational, nationally televised 36-day special hearing before his own Permanent Subcommittee on Investigations. The hearing was held to investigate the charge that the senator and two members of his staff had abused congressional privilege by trying to coerce the U.S. Army into giving special treatment to Private G. David Schine, a wealthy college dropout and former "chief consultant" to Roy M. Cohn, the notorious chief counsel of the Senate Permanent Subcommittee on Investigations, chaired by McCarthy. The Democratic minority of the Permanent Subcommittee on Investigations, which had been boycotting its sessions since the summer of 1953 because of its chair's outrageous tactics, returned to investigate these accusations as well as McCarthy's counter-charges that the military was using blackmail and intimidation to derail his investigation of a communist conspiracy involving civilian officials and military officers of the army. Senator McCarthy's failure to substantiate his claims of communist penetration of the military and the extensive television coverage of his boorish behavior and bullying interrogative methods discredited him and helped to turn the tide of public opinion against McCarthyism in America.

It was in October 1953 that the junior senator from Wisconsin first began investigating purported communist infiltration of the military, trying in particular to discredit Robert T. Stevens, the secretary of the army. Stevens had angered Senator McCarthy first by recently drafting Schine into the army and then by refusing to release him from military service. McCarthy and Cohn accused the army of having conscripted Schine—according to them, an indispensable "expert" on internal subversion despite his apparent youth (he was in his early 20s)—and holding him "hostage" in order to prevent their embarrassing exposure of "traitorous" communists in the military ranks. However, information released during the hearings indicated that Senator McCarthy was simply using his investigative powers to support the personal vendetta against the army pursued by Cohn, who had openly promised to end the investigation if his close friend Schine was given an officer's commission or was transferred to the CIA.

Senator McCarthy launched his first public challenge to the ideological integrity of the army by attacking Major Irving Peress, an army dentist stationed at Camp Kilmer,

Senator Joseph McCarthy chatting with his attorney, Roy Cohn, during Senate subcommittee hearings on the McCarthy-Army dispute *(Library of Congress)*

who at the time of his conscription had refused to answer some of the questions on the Loyalty Oath questionnaire inquiring about his affiliation with "subversive" groups. Even though Dr. Peress had been inducted into the army under the McCarthy-sponsored Doctors and Dentists Draft Act and was now being voluntarily discharged due to an illness in his immediate family, the senator demanded that the army dentist be court-martialed. Subpoenaed to appear before McCarthy's Permanent Subcommittee on Investigations, Peress had declined to testify, citing the Fifth Amendment. He was cleared by the army's loyalty board, composed of high-ranking military officers and well-respected civilians, but this only led to the board becoming a target for Senator McCarthy, who demanded to interrogate its anonymous members. He also demanded to know the names of those army officials responsible for the promotion of Peress to the rank of major and his subsequent honorable discharge. The army, backed in this matter by the White House, rejected his demands.

As a result, Brigadier General Ralph W. Zwicker, the Camp Kilmer commander and a highly decorated war hero, was brutally interrogated and humiliated by McCarthy when he appeared before the Permanent Subcommittee on Investigations but obviously followed orders from above not to disclose the information demanded by the Wisconsin senator. Furious with the brigadier general's failure to cooperate, McCarthy called him a "Fifth Amendment general . . . unfit to wear the uniform," accused him of not having even "the brains of a five-year-old," and suggested that

Zwicker should be relieved of duty for having shielded "traitors and communists." When transcripts from the closed hearings were leaked and revealed in the mass media, this exposure of McCarthy's belligerent rhetoric and odious demeanor tarnished his reputation in the eyes of the American public and even many of his media supporters.

But Senator McCarthy's "Waterloo" proved to be the open and televised 188-hour Permanent Subcommittee on Investigations hearings on his conspiracy charges against the military and especially his memorable confrontation with Boston attorney Joseph N. Welch, special counsel for the army. With remarkable skill, bravado, and calm patience, Welch goaded the volatile Wisconsin senator into displaying his utter arrogance, pettiness, and vindictiveness before an audience of some 20-million television viewers. Not only did McCarthy respond to Welch's questions with evasive answers and rude attacks, but under cross-examination he even refused to be bound by his own oath "to tell the truth, the whole truth, and nothing but the truth."

Just before the hearings Senator McCarthy had privately agreed not to attack Fred Fisher, a young lawyer in Welch's Boston law firm of Hale & Dorr, who had withdrawn from working on the army's case because he had once belonged to a leftist organization known as the Lawyers' Guild. In return, Welch had promised not to raise questions about Cohn's avoidance of military service as well as his rumored homosexual affair with Schine. But infuriated by Welch's probing questions and sarcastic remarks during the hearings, on June 9, 1954, a noticeably inebriated and ill-mannered Senator McCarthy reneged on his promise, prompting this memorable rebuke by his inimitable nemesis: "Until this moment, Senator, I think I never really gauged your cruelty or your recklessness. . . . Little did I dream you could be so reckless and so cruel as to do an injury to that lad. . . . If it were in my power to forgive you for your reckless cruelty, I would do so . . . but your forgiveness will have to come from someone other than me. . . . Let us not assassinate this lad further, Senator. You have done enough. Have you no sense of decency, Sir, at long last? Have you left no sense of decency?" When at that dramatic moment the hushed audience in the room erupted into stormy applause, a bewildered and visibly shaken Senator McCarthy turned to Cohn and asked, "What happened?"

Partly as a result of his bizarre antics and his ignominious defeat at the hearings, the Wisconsin senator became the target of hostile media attention and damaging rumors about his drunkenness, dishonesty, bigotry, secret presidential ambitions, and suspected homosexuality. Although widely seen as amoral and out of control, Senator McCarthy was still a powerful figure until the Republicans lost control of the Senate in the midterm elections of November 1954. He was replaced as chair of the Senate Government Committee on Operations and of its Permanent Subcommittee on Investigations. He lost his power base at a time when many of his colleagues were eager to condemn him for his irresponsible personal attacks against a large number of senators over the years, a serious breach of Senate etiquette. As a result of his attacks on the army, McCarthy had also lost the support of many Republicans. On December 2, 1954, a Senate resolution, introduced by Republican senator Ralph E. Flanders, officially censured the increasingly disgraced and alcoholic Wisconsin legislator on a vote of 67-22 for conduct "contrary to Senate traditions." On the recommendation of the Senate Select Committee chaired by Republican senator Arthur V. Watkins (also known as the Watkins Committee), the Senate resolved that McCarthy had "acted contrary to senatorial ethics and tended to bring the Senate to dishonor . . . and to impair its dignity; and such conduct is hereby condemned."

Many Americans hoped that McCarthyism would disappear along with McCarthy, who died from cirrhosis of the liver on May 2, 1957. But the senator is now lionized once again as a true patriot and loyal defender of the American way of life by conservative scholars such as Arthur Herman and right-wing authors such as Ann Coulter. Yet the famous army-McCarthy hearings still remind us of the grave dangers to constitutional freedoms and democratic principles and even to decency in public life inherent in McCarthy's shameless exploitation of patriotism and his selfish manipulation of the American public for ulterior political purposes.

See also McCarthy, Joseph R.

Further reading:
De Antonio, Emile, and Daniel Talbot. *Point of Order! A Documentary of the Army-McCarthy Hearings.* New York: Norton, 1964; Feuerlicht, Roberta S. *Joe McCarthy and McCarthyism.* New York: McGraw-Hill, 1972; Griffith, Robert. *The Politics of Fear: Joseph R. McCarthy and the Senate.* Lexington: University Press of Kentucky, 1970; Oshinsky, David M. *A Conspiracy So Immense: The World of Joe McCarthy.* New York: Free Press, 1983; Reeves, Thomas C. *The Life and Times of Joe McCarthy.* New York: Stein & Day, 1982.

—Rossen V. Vassilev

McConnell v. Federal Election Commission, 540 U.S. 93 (2003)

In *Buckley v. Valeo* (1976) the U.S. Supreme Court ruled on the constitutionality of various provisions of the Federal Election Campaign Act (FECA), which Congress enacted to curtail corruption and the appearance of corruption in federal elections. The Supreme Court upheld FECA's voluntary public financing scheme, reporting requirements, and limitations on campaign contributions but struck down on First Amendment grounds its limitations on expenditures by campaigns, candidates, and independent individuals or groups.

In the decades following *Buckley* the regulatory scheme established by Congress received mixed reviews. Those initially skeptical of FECA applauded the Federal Election Commission's (FEC) emphasis on disclosure and reporting rather than additional limits on campaign spending and applauded the Court's further objections to spending limits. Proponents of campaign finance reform, however, became increasingly troubled by the Supreme Court's continued hostility to limits on expenditures, gaps in enforcement by the FEC, loopholes in FECA that allowed for unlimited contributions by wealthy donors, and a corresponding dramatic increase in contributions and spending in federal elections. Most troubling were the soft money loophole and lack of restrictions on independent third-party issue and attack advertisements. In *Buckley* and subsequent decisions the Court held that contributions to political parties and spending of those funds by the parties were not subject to FECA's limitations or reporting requirements if not used to directly advocate the election or defeat of a candidate. The result was the proliferation of issue ads and attack ads that omitted the "magic words" "vote for" or "vote against" but were, for all intents and purposes, indistinguishable from regulated campaign spending.

Beginning in the early 1990s a handful of members of Congress began advocating further campaign finance reform to address the shortcomings of FECA. These efforts were largely unsuccessful due in large measure to the reality that the existing system maintained the advantages held by congressional incumbents. Finally, after the public took notice of the dramatic increase in soft money in the 1996 and 2000 elections (nearly $500 million in soft money was spent in the 2000 presidential race, more than half of which was donated by only 800 individuals and groups) Senators John McCain and Russell Feingold obtained support for their legislation. In 2002 Congress passed the BIPARTISAN CAMPAIGN FINANCE ACT (BCRA), commonly known as the McCain-Feingold law, which significantly overhauled FECA. The BCRA closed the soft money loophole created by *Buckley,* imposed restrictions on issue ads falling under a broader definition of electioneering communications by corporations and unions using general organizational funds, established stringent disclosure and broadcaster record-keeping requirements for political advertisements, and increased campaign contribution limits for individuals and organizations, which had not been increased or adjusted for inflation since FECA was adopted in 1971.

Immediately after President George W. Bush signed the BCRA into law, Senator Mitch McConnell (R-KY) and multiple interest groups from across the political spectrum challenged the legislation in federal district court. A three-judge panel issued a frighteningly detailed 1,700-page decision upholding many of the law's provisions but striking down the soft money ban. Multiple appeals of the decision were filed (no doubt partly in hopes of deciphering the district court's treatise on campaign finance); the Supreme Court consolidated the appeals and took the case on an expedited basis in the fall of 2002.

In a decision reminiscent of *Buckley* in its fractured nature and complexity, the Court upheld each of the BCRA's key provisions (although it did strike down the BCRA's ban on contributions by individuals under 18 years of age). Justices John Paul Stevens and Sandra Day O'Connor issued the Court's opinion, supported by a 5-4 margin, upholding the ban on soft money and independent electioneering issue ads. Justice William Breyer penned the Court's 5-4 opinion upholding publicly available record-keeping requirements for broadcasters airing political programming. Chief Justice William Rehnquist wrote a third opinion, supported unanimously by the Court, holding that the millionaire provision was nonjustifiable as presented to the Court. Multiple dissents were filed, most notably Justice Antonin Scalia's assertion that the Court had eroded its "money is speech" doctrine set forth in *Buckley.*

The Court's holding that the BCRA is constitutional dramatically affects the campaign finance landscape rules. *Buckley* allowed limitations on contributions, but there and in several subsequent decisions the Court sided decisively with First Amendment advocates in striking down limits on expenditures. In *McConnell,* however, the Court deferred to Congress's findings that the integrity of the election system was in crisis and that significant restrictions on both contributions and expenditures were essential. Further campaign finance reform appears likely to garner similar support by a majority of the Court.

As for the practical effects of the ruling, in the short term little appears to have changed. The 2004 election cycle proceeded without soft money spending by the national parties and without corporate or union spending on issue ads. Hard money, subject to FEC reporting requirements, increased dramatically, as did the numbers of small contributors to candidates. However, issue and attack ads did not decrease, they simply found new sources: independent nonprofit political organizations unaffiliated with corporations, unions, or political parties. These 527 corporations, named after the section of the BCRA recognizing such entities, raised and spent more funds than the BCRA eliminated. As a result, total spending during the 2004 election cycle skyrocketed to $2 billion.

Further reading:
Buckley v. Valeo, 424 U.S. 1 (1976); O'Brien, David M. *Supreme Court Watch 2004.* New York: Norton, 2004.

—Daniel E. Smith

McCormack, John W. (1891–1980) *Representative, Speaker of the House*

One of 12 children and born on December 21, 1891, to Joseph H. McCormack, a bricklayer, and Mary Ellen (Brien), John W. McCormack was reared in South Boston's Andrew Square neighborhood. His family was so poor that they were often evicted when they could not pay their rent. Nine of the McCormack children died as infants or in their youths. He graduated from the John Andrew Grammar School shortly before his father passed away. At the age of 13 he left school and became the family breadwinner, working as a hod carrier (a laborer who carried material to masons and bricklayers). He also had a paper route. He then went to work as an office boy making $4 a week in a law firm. He would study law books when not running errands and was admitted to the Massachusetts bar in 1913. In 1920 he married Harriet Joyce. They would be married 51 years until her death in 1971.

McCormack entered politics as a delegate to the Massachusetts state constitutional convention in 1917–18. Years later, McCormack detailed his career choice, explaining:

> politics was a natural to me. I always knew that I'd go into it some day. Where I was brought up the people were poor. Probably no district in America is more political than mine.

While this position gave him an automatic exemption from military service, he enlisted in the U.S. Army in 1917 following American entry into World War I. McCormack did not serve overseas and when the war ended he was discharged from the military as a sergeant major, the highest rank a noncommissioned officer could attain.

McCormack served in the Massachusetts house of representatives (1920–22) and the Massachusetts senate (1923–26). He was the Democratic floor leader in the state senate in 1925 and 1926.

McCormack was defeated in his first run for Congress in 1926, losing to James A. Gallivan in the Democratic primary in Massachusetts's 12th Congressional District. He won a special election from the same district to the HOUSE OF REPRESENTATIVES in 1928 to fill a vacancy in the 70th Congress (1927–29) caused by Representative Gallivan's death. He took his seat on November 6, 1928. At the same time he was elected to a seat in the 71st Congress (1929–31). He was reelected every two years until his retirement on January 3, 1971. Until 1963 McCormack represented the 12th District. From that point until he retired, he represented the 9th District. McCormack was also a delegate to the 1932, 1940, 1944, 1948, and 1960 Democratic National Conventions.

When he entered the House McCormack became the protégé of two Texas Democrats: JOHN NANCE GARNER, who was then Minority Leader and would later serve as SPEAKER OF THE HOUSE (1931–33) and as vice president of the United States during President Franklin D. Roosevelt's first two terms (1933–41), and SAMUEL RAYBURN, who would later precede McCormack as Speaker (1940–47, 1949–53, 1955–62).

An early indication of McCormack's relationship to Garner and Rayburn was his appointment to the HOUSE WAYS AND MEANS COMMITTEE in 1931. Assignment to this powerful committee generally was limited to members with much more seniority than McCormack, who had not completed two full terms in the House. So important was this assignment that McCormack turned down offers from both the Democratic and the Republican parties to run for mayor of Boston and for the U.S. SENATE. McCormack would spend more than three decades as an important figure in the Democratic House leadership.

A fervent anticommunist, McCormack was a member of the House UN-AMERICAN ACTIVITIES COMMITTEE after it was empanelled in 1937 and introduced a number of anticommunist measures during the 1930s. He supported the reinstatement of the military draft in the years prior to World War II and supported President Harry S. Truman's cold war policies in the late 1940s and early 1950s. In the 1960s he defended President LYNDON BAINES JOHNSON's Vietnam War policies.

During his more than four decades in Congress he supported a number of domestic policy initiatives. He supported civil rights legislation, Franklin Roosevelt's NEW DEAL programs, the SOCIAL SECURITY ACT of 1936, the National Labor Relations (Wagner) Act, the Housing Acts of 1937, 1949, 1965, and 1969, federal aid to education, and lowering the voting age from 21 to 18.

In the House he was chair of the Committee on Territories (1928–29) and the Select Committee on Astronautics and Space Exploration (1957–59). In 1958 he introduced the legislation creating the National Aeronautics and Space Administration (NASA).

McCormack developed a reputation as a fierce partisan. He was the House MAJORITY LEADER (1939–47, 1949–53, 1955–62) and MINORITY WHIP (1947–49, 1953–55) and became Speaker of the House of Representatives on January 10, 1962, following Speaker Sam Rayburn's death. McCormack was the first Roman Catholic elected to the post.

While Speakers historically had refrained from participating in House debates, McCormack left the podium to enter debate more often than his predecessors. When he became Speaker there was considerable speculation about how well he and President John F. Kennedy would get along. The president's brother, Edward Moore Kennedy, was opposing McCormack's nephew, Massachusetts attorney general Edward McCormack, for the Democratic nomination for the Senate. (Kennedy would defeat McCormack for the nomination.) Notwithstanding the Senate contest, McCormack loyally supported the president's legislative agenda. The only issue on which the two men openly differed was the issue of federal financial assistance to parochial schools. McCormack, who had close ties to the Roman Catholic Church, supported federal aid, while the president was opposed.

Following Kennedy's assassination on November 22, 1963, McCormack was a heartbeat away from the presidency until HUBERT HUMPHREY was sworn in as vice president on January 20, 1965. (Under the Presidential Succession Act of 1947, 61 Stat. 380; 3 U.S.C. 19, the Speaker of the House of Representatives becomes president if both the presidency and vice presidency are vacant.) McCormack rejected around-the-clock Secret Service protection because he wanted to retain his privacy.

As Speaker he helped guide through the House the avalanche of domestic legislation that made the mid-1960s one of the most productive eras in congressional history. Major legislation enacted under McCormack's leadership included the CIVIL RIGHTS ACT of 1964, the Economic Opportunity Act of 1964, the VOTING RIGHTS ACT of 1965, Medicare, the Elementary and Secondary Education Act, and the Civil Rights Act of 1968.

He was regarded by his allies as a master of the House's rules, which allowed him to influence committee assignments, shape legislation, and control debate. His critics regarded him as the symbol of all that was wrong with Congress: its intricate procedures, its rigid seniority system that placed power in the hands of a small number of members (mostly conservative southern Democrats in McCormack's time), and its clubby nature.

In 1969 McCormack was able to repel efforts to remove him as Speaker. It was rumored at the time that McCormick had survived as Speaker by committing to a number of wavering Democratic members that he would give up the Speaker's post at the conclusion of his term in January 1971.

Later in 1969 two of McCormack's closest associates, chief aide Martin Sweig and lobbyist Nathan Voloshen, were indicted for perjury and bribery. It was alleged they had traded on their relationship with McCormack by engaging in influence peddling. While there were allegations that McCormack had personally been involved in Voloshen and Sweig's influence peddling, they were never substantiated. However, McCormack's standing as Speaker was tarnished by the indictments. At Sweig's trial McCormack testified that he was not aware that his close friends were using his office for the benefit of their clients. McCormack would testify, "I'm not an inquiring fellow." After initially announcing he would run for reelection in 1970, McCormack later announced that he would retire from Congress at the conclusion of his term on January 3, 1971. He was succeeded as Speaker by CARL B. ALBERT, a Democrat from Oklahoma.

Following his retirement from the House, McCormack spent most of his time at the bedside of his wife in Washington, D.C.'s, Providence Hospital. She died in December 1971. He then returned to Boston, where he sold the home in Dorchester that he and his wife had occupied whenever Congress was not in session. In September 1980 he contracted pneumonia and was hospitalized. He subsequently died in his sleep on November 22, 1980, and was buried in Saint Joseph Cemetery, West Roxbury, Massachusetts.

Further reading:
Gordon, Lester I. "John McCormack and the Roosevelt Era," Ph.D. diss., Boston University, 1976; Nelson, Garrison. "Irish Identity Politics: The Reinvention of Speaker John W. McCormack of Boston." *New England Journal of Public Policy* 15 (Fall/Winter 1999/2000); Weisman, Steven R. "McCormack, Ex-Speaker, Is Dead." *New York Times,* November 1980 p. A1, 23 .

—Jeffrey Kraus

McCulloch v. Maryland 17 U.S. 316 (1819)

McCulloch v. Maryland is a landmark case that greatly expanded the power of the national government. It is a classic example of Chief Justice John Marshall interpreting the Constitution broadly in order to enhance national power. The Necessary and Proper Clause, the Supremacy Clause, and the Tenth Amendment were analyzed. The case found its origins in a dispute between the national government and the state of Maryland. The dispute was part of a larger and longer-running debate over the constitutionality of a national bank. Congress had chartered the Second Bank of the United States in 1816 in the wake of the economic collapse following the War of 1812. Even though the bank was deemed necessary by a majority of Congress due to the economic conditions, the Second Bank continued to face considerable opposition. At least six states, including Maryland, passed legislation taxing the bank's branches. Other states were not quite able to pass taxing legislation. Two states simply prohibited banks not chartered by their legislatures to operate within their borders. Maryland's attempt to tax the Second Bank brought the debate to the U.S. Supreme Court.

McCulloch was the cashier of the Baltimore branch of the bank. The cashier was not merely a teller, but actually operated as the branch manager. In 1818 an agent of Maryland visited the Baltimore branch and demanded payment. McCulloch refused to pay the tax. Maryland then sued McCulloch in state court and, of course, won. Maryland also won on appeal to the state appellate court. McCulloch then appealed to the U.S. Supreme Court. Marshall wrote the unanimous opinion that reversed the Maryland appellate court. Marshall's opinion was well structured and forceful. He stated that first it must be determined whether Congress had the power to create a bank. And if it did not, then the Court needed to determine if Maryland could tax the bank. In order to answer the first question, Marshall revisited the debate on the source of the national government's power. Was the national government empowered by the states or the people, he asked? He quickly dismissed the argument that the states empowered the national government, because then it would be subordinate to the states. He repeatedly emphasized that it was the people, at the state ratifying conventions, who approved the Constitution. Marshall then moved on to a discussion of the enumerated powers. He acknowledged that the national government was limited in its powers but that it was supreme when permitted to act. He further acknowledged that there was no enumerated power to create a bank. However, neither was there a prohibition. Marshall pointed out that the Tenth Amendment, unlike the Articles of Confederation, did not reserve to the states the powers not expressly delegated to the national government. The restrictive language of the articles had crippled the national government. Consequently, the Constitution was written in general terms so that its meaning could adapt to the times.

If the national government was not limited to express powers, it must also have implied powers. Marshall found the implied powers in the Necessary and Proper Clause. He reasoned that the placement of the clause indicated that it was meant to enhance, not limit, the national government's power. The Necessary and Proper Clause is listed among Congress's powers in Section 8 of Article I, not in Section 9, where the limitations on Congress's powers are found. Therefore, the clause should be read broadly, hence granting Congress the additional implied power to create the bank, he said.

Marshall then moved on to the issue of whether Maryland could tax the bank. In this section of his opinion, Marshall made reference to the Supremacy Clause found in Article VI of the Constitution. This provision states that the Constitution and all laws made in pursuance thereof is the supreme law of the land. When a national law and a state law contradict, the state law must yield. In effect, the Maryland tax on the bank contradicted national law. Marshall asserted that the power to tax involved the power to destroy also. If Maryland were allowed to tax the bank, it could be taxed out of existence. What might Maryland tax next, the post office, the courts, and the mint? The states conceivably could tax the entire national government out of existence. Such a possibility would fly in the face of the Supremacy Clause. Therefore, the states cannot tax an instrument of the national government.

McCulloch v. Maryland is one of Marshall's most significant opinions. It is extremely well written and reflects his predilection toward national power. He read the Tenth Amendment, the Necessary and Proper Clause, and the Supremacy Clause in ways that expanded the reach of the national government and restricted the powers of the states. Congress subsequently has frequently relied on Marshall's broad interpretation of the Constitution when legislating.

Further reading:
Gunther, Gerald. *Constitutional Law*. Westbury, N.Y.: Foundation Press, Inc., 1991; Hall, Kermit L., ed. *The Oxford Companion to the Supreme Court of the United States*. New York: Oxford University Press, 1992; *McCulloch v. Maryland,* 17 U.S. (4 Wheat.) 316 (1819).
—Barry N. Sweet

McNary, Charles Linza (1874–1944) *Senator, Senate Majority Leader*

Charles L. McNary was many things in his life: a lawyer, farmer, law professor, state court judge, U.S. senator, Senate Republican leader, and unsuccessful candidate for president and vice president of the United States. McNary was born on a farm near Salem, Oregon, the ninth of 10 children born to Hugh Linza McNary and Mary Calggett McNary. His mother died shortly before his fourth birthday, and his father moved the family into Salem, where he operated a variety store. However, Hugh McNary's health was failing and he died in 1883, when Charles was nine years old. He was then reared by older brothers and sisters. One of his youthful acquaintances was a future president of the United States, Herbert Hoover, who moved to Salem in 1888 and worked in the office of his uncle's business.

McNary attended the public schools in Salem and the Capital Business College in Salem and took college preparatory courses at Willamette University in Salem. In 1896 McNary, following Hoover's example, entered the Leland Stanford Junior University in Palo Alto, California. He stayed for a year before returning home, at his family's behest, to complete his studies at Willamette University in 1898. He studied law in his brother's law firm and was admitted to the Oregon bar in 1898. He began practicing law in Salem, Oregon, as a partner in his brother's firm and also taught property law at Willamette. In 1902 McNary married Jessie Breyman, the daughter of a Salem merchant. She was killed in an automobile accident near Salem in 1918. In 1923 he married Cornelia Morton, a former member of his staff who had become the Massachusetts director of the League of Women Voters, and they adopted a child, Charlotte, in 1935.

McNary managed his brother's successful campaign for district attorney in 1904 and became the deputy district attorney of Oregon's Third Judicial District, serving from 1904 to 1911. He became dean of the law department at Willamette University, serving from 1908 to 1913. During his tenure as dean, he revised the curriculum, moved the department's classes from off-campus sites to the Willamette campus, and increased the enrollment.

McNary also operated the family farm. In 1909 McNary established the first commercial filbert tree orchard in the nation. He also developed the imperial prune. In the same year, in order to promote local agriculture, he organized the Salem Fruit Union. He served as the organization's president for the rest of his life. He also became president of the Salem Board of Trade, lobbying for reduced railroad freight rates.

In 1913 the Oregon state legislature increased the size of the state supreme court from five to seven members. Although he was a Republican, McNary was appointed to one of the newly created seats as an associate justice of the Oregon state supreme court by Governor Oswald West, a Democrat. In his short time on the court, McNary wrote a number of important decisions, including decisions to uphold Oregon's workers' compensation law and a state wages and hours law. The following year he lost the statewide Republican primary for the post. In a disputed outcome that took more than three months to resolve, McNary lost the nomination for election to a full term on the court by one vote.

After leaving the supreme court he returned to the practice of law and became chair of the Oregon state Republican Party in 1916. As leader, McNary unified the party's regular and Progressive wings and delivered the state for Charles Evans Hughes, the Republican presidential nominee. It was the only western state that Hughes carried as President Woodrow Wilson was reelected.

On May 29, 1917, McNary entered the U.S. SENATE when he was appointed by Governor James Withycombe to a vacancy caused by the death of Senator Harry Lane, a Democrat. Lane had been one of six senators voting against U.S. entry into World War I. Lane was denounced by President Wilson and became the target of a recall effort. He suffered a nervous breakdown and died.

In taking the seat, McNary declared

I am a progressive. Neither am I a hide-bound partisan. I shall support President Wilson in all his progressive legislation. I shall stand behind him in all matters relating to our war in Germany

McNary was appointed to the Commerce, Public Land, Railroads, Public Health, and Indian Affairs Committees.

In 1918 McNary ran for a full six-year term, defeating former governor West with 54.2 percent of the vote. While McNary had been elected to a six-year term, Frederick W. Mulkey was elected to serve out the remainder of Lane's term. McNary vacated his seat on November 5, 1918, in favor of Mulkey. McNary then resigned, allowing Governor Withycombe to appoint McNary to the vacancy, giving him seniority over the other newly elected members. McNary was reelected to the Senate in 1924, 1930, 1936, and 1942. His most difficult race took place in 1936, when President Franklin Roosevelt won 64 percent of the vote in Oregon. McNary defeated his Democratic challenger, Mayor Willis Mahoney of Klamath Falls, 49.7 to 48.3 percent. The 1936 election left McNary with a conference of 16 Republicans to oppose 76 Democrats. McNary served as chair of the Committee on Irrigation and Reclamation of Arid Lands (1919–27), chair of the Select Committee on Reforestation (1923–24), chair of the Committee on Agriculture and Forestry (1925–33), and chair of the Republican Conference and SENATE MINORITY LEADER (1933–44).

Early in his Senate career he was one of the few Republican senators to support the Versailles Treaty and U.S. participation in the League of Nations. An internationalist, he was the leader of a small group of Republican senators known as the mild reservationists, who favored ratification of the treaty, including the League of Nations Covenant, with some minor reservations. President Wilson's unwillingness to accept any reservations to the treaty doomed it to failure.

Notwithstanding their differences over the League of Nations, McNary and Senate MAJORITY LEADER HENRY CABOT LODGE of Massachusetts developed a close relationship. McNary became a member of Lodge's inner circle, served as the Majority Leader's liaison to other western Republican senators, and was given a slot on the powerful Committee on Committees, which was responsible for making committee assignments.

When the Depression at the end of the 1920s devastated the nation's farms, McNary emerged as a spokesman for rural America, joining with a group of Progressive senators to form a FARM BLOC. The group was led by William Kenyon of Iowa and included George Norris of Nebraska, Robert LaFollette of Wisconsin, Arthur Kapper of Kansas, and fellow Oregonian Robert Stanfield. He sponsored a number of farm aid measures, notably the McNary-Haugen Farm Bill. Beginning in 1924 McNary would introduce the bill (along with Iowa congressman Gilbert N. Haugen), which provided for the federal government to purchase surplus agricultural products for sale overseas. President Calvin Coolidge twice vetoed the bill (1927 and 1928), stating in his 1927 VETO message that the bill went against "an economic law as well established as any law of nature." In 1928, Coolidge called McNary-Haugen "a system of wholesale commercial doles." McNary's proposal was a forerunner of Franklin Roosevelt's NEW DEAL.

McNary was a conservationist and a major proponent of hydroelectric power. As chair of the Senate Select Committee on Reforestation (established by a Senate resolution that he had sponsored), he was the Senate sponsor of the Clarke (named for a New York congressman, John D. Clarke)-McNary Act of 1924. The act authorized technical and financial assistance to the states for forest fire control, provided for acquisition of land for national forests, and encouraged federal-state cooperation with the lumber industry in reforestation. Four years later McNary and Representative John R. McSweeney of Ohio authorized an expanded Forest Service research program. He was the principal sponsor of the Bonneville Dam (opened in 1938), the first of eight such dams that the U.S. Army Corps of Engineers would construct on the Columbia River in the Pacific Northwest.

As Minority Leader he supported much of Franklin Roosevelt's New Deal, including the Emergency Banking Relief Act, Agricultural Adjustment Act (based on the McNary-Haugen legislation of the 1920s), the National Recovery Act, which he described as "the most important proposal that has ever been presented to this or any other Congress," and the SOCIAL SECURITY ACT. He opposed the Reciprocal Trade Agreements Act, the Federal Emergency Relief Act, and Roosevelt's court-packing plan. During this period McNary resisted the pressure of conservative Republicans who believed that the party should oppose the New Deal. McNary believed that the depth of the crisis required Republicans to work with Roosevelt to restore the nation's economic health.

During the 1930s McNary was an isolationist, insisting that there would not be a major war. However, as Hitler's armies conquered Europe, McNary changed his position. He voted in favor of the nation's first peacetime military draft and for the Lend-Lease Act (1941), which gave the president the authority to sell, transfer, exchange, or lend equipment to any country to help it defend itself against the Axis powers (Germany, Italy, and Japan). One of the first American politicians to express outrage over Nazi Germany's persecution of the Jews, he became the cochair (with Senator Robert Wagner of New York) of a national organization dedicated to the creation of a Jewish homeland in Palestine.

In 1940, after unsuccessfully seeking his party's presidential nomination, he was drafted by the Republican National Convention to become Wendell Wilkie's running mate. They were defeated in the general election by the Democratic ticket of Franklin D. Roosevelt (seeking his third term) and Henry Wallace (who replaced Vice President John Nance Garner on the ticket).

In the Senate McNary was the precursor of what Richard Fenno would later describe as the politico, acting as an instructed delegate on issues important to his constituents while using his own judgment on matters in which his constituents lacked interest. In 1940 he said

> I've always cast my lot with the voting groups of my state and my section, and I've found if they consider me the guardian of their interests, they'll allow me considerable independence on questions that don't affect them.

In November 1943 McNary was found to have a brain tumor. He died on February 25, 1944, and was buried in the Pioneer Cemetery in Salem, Oregon. His body was later reinterred at the Belcrest Memorial Park in Salem.

Further reading:
DeWitt, Howard A. "Charles L. McNary and the 1918 Congressional Election." *Oregon Historical Quarterly* 68 (June 1967); Hoffmann, George C. "Political Arithmetic: Charles L. McNary and the 1914 Primary Election." *Oregon Historical Quarterly* 66 (December 1965); Johnson, Roger T. "Charles L. McNary and the Republican Party during Prosperity and Depression." Ph.D. diss., University of Wisconsin, 1967; Neal, Steve. *McNary of Oregon: A Political Biography.* Portland, Ore.: Western Imprints, 1985.

—Jeffrey Kraus

media galleries

Reporters have covered Congress since the First Congress was convened. In the early Congresses the Senate met in closed session; no observers were allowed to witness the deliberations. The House of Representatives met in open session. However, reporters had to compete with the members' spouses and other visitors for spaces in the public seats. Reporters' workspaces were off the Capitol grounds, usually on "Newspaper Row," named for the large number of newspaper offices located on 14th Street between the Willard and Ebbitt Hotels, which were clustered within walking distance of the local telegraph office.

The Capitol building was renovated and expanded in the 1860s, at which time both the House and the Senate constructed new chambers. The new chambers included larger public balconies with reserved spaces for news reporters. At the same time, each chamber constructed separate press galleries, or workspaces, for the congressional correspondents. These ornately decorated spaces are a few steps away from the chambers so that reporters can duck into the chambers to witness votes or floor debates at a moments' notice. They were equipped with the latest technological innovation, a telegraph, which enabled reporters to file stories from the Capitol building itself.

Today there are four Senate media galleries: one each for press (i.e., newspapers), periodicals (i.e., magazines and newsletters), radio and television, and photographers. The House of Representatives has three media galleries: one each for press, periodicals, and radio and television. Each gallery employs a small number of people who facilitate meetings between congressional offices and correspondents. All galleries are within a few steps of either the House or the Senate chamber, although the galleries also control other locations, such as designated spaces on the grounds for outdoor news conferences. Today's galleries are equipped with telephones and televisions, which are often tuned to C-SPAN so that reporters can monitor floor activities. The galleries are not open to the public. Only credentialed members of the press, members of Congress, and congressional staff are allowed access.

Since 1879 the Standing Committee of Congressional Correspondents, an elected body comprised of members of the congressional news corps, has governed all the House media galleries. It began to govern the Senate galleries in 1884. The committee was established in response to a growing number of congressional reporters who augmented their meager salaries with lobbying activities and positions within executive agencies or Congress. One of the first rules promulgated by the committee was to define a reporter as someone who receives his or her primary income from news reporting and ban all lobbyists and executive branch employees from becoming credentialed correspondents.

Today the committee issues all congressional press credentials, hires gallery staff, provides some workspace for credentialed reporters, and establishes the rules and regulations reporters must abide by when covering Congress. The rules are highly complex. For example, they specify the amount of lighting that may be brought to committee hearing rooms; delineate the designated "stake out" areas, where reporters can wait for members to emerge from closed-door meetings; and include a list of rooms where television lighting and flash photography are not permitted. Interestingly, the only television cameras allowed on either the House or the Senate floor are the cameras used to broadcast floor proceedings on C-SPAN, which are controlled by the House and Senate leadership.

See also C-SPAN; JOURNALISTS; CAPITOL HILL; CAPITOL BUILDING.

Further readings:
Hess, Stephen. *Live from Capitol Hill: Studies of Congress and the Media.* Washington, D.C.: Brookings Institution Press, 1991; Ritchie, Donald A. *Press Gallery: Congress and the Washington Correspondents.* Cambridge, Mass.: Harvard University Press, 1991; U.S. House of Representatives. "Media Galleries." Available online. URL: http://www.house.gov/house/mediagallery.html. Accessed 18 January 2006. U.S. Senate. "United States Senate Media Galleries." Available online. URL: http://www.senate.gov/galleries/. Accessed 18 January 2006.
—Karen M. Kedrowski

membership: African-American women

African-American women come from an activist tradition. From the outset they were involved in organization and institution building, volunteerism, and protest in order to secure basic rights for themselves and their families. Their actions typically fell into one of two general dimensions: creating spheres of influence within existing structures wherein they were able to indirectly resist and undermine oppression, and affecting change by transforming existing structures. Prior to the 1960s most African-American women who struggled for civil rights acted independently, as in the case of Ida B. Wells-Barnett, or orchestrated like-minded women into organizations such as black women's clubs. And especially in the case of the club movement, many African-American women, infused with moral tenacity and an inclusive vision of what America could become, felt driven to undertake public service for positive change.

Before the Fifteenth Amendment was ratified in 1870, few African-American men could vote, none held congressional office, and no women, black or white, were allowed to vote. Between 1870 and 1901 only 22 African-American men from eight southern states served in Congress, and it was not until 1928 that, with the support of Ida B. Wells-Barnett, Oscar De Priest, a Republican from Illinois, became the first African American elected to Congress in the 20th century.

Furthermore, it was not until 1917 that the first woman, Jeannette Rankin, a Republican from Montana, was elected to the House. It was nearly a full century after the first African-American men were elected to Congress before the first African-American woman, Shirley Chisholm, a Democrat from New York, was elected to the House of Representatives in 1968.

The turning point that best facilitated African-American women gaining elected office was the Voting Rights Act of 1965. This act, designed mainly to address the South's 95 years of failure in implementing the Fifteenth Amendment guaranteeing all adult American citizens the right to vote, gave the U.S. attorney general and the Justice Department discretionary power to appoint federal officials as voting examiners who would make sure that African Americans could register to vote without interference.

In fact, African-American women legislators from the South whose terms in office began prior to 1985 reveal that the greatest obstacles to gaining office were structural, for example, using poll taxes and literacy tests to bar black voter registration and practicing minority vote dilution through the use of gerrymandering predominately black districts out of effective operation. As a result, only four African-American women were elected to Congress.

Between 1965 and 1975 the Voting Rights Act paved the way for many women to gain necessary and valuable experience at local and state levels before making the move to the House of Representatives. For example, of the 14 African-American women to have served in the House between 1968 and 1995, only three had never held elective office at the local or state level before holding national office.

Although running for and serving in the U.S. Congress poses challenges for all those who take it up, African-American women face unique circumstances in their bids for elected office. While funding, effective campaigning, and balancing political and family life are issues for all prospective candidates, African-American women must also wrestle with two factors that many people fail to realize still maintain significant sway in America—racism and sexism. One example of the racism that African-American women have faced is that they have had to prove their qualifications in a manner substantially more rigorous than their white counterparts. For example, even though of the 20 African-American women who served in the House between 1968 and 2000, 16 held political office previously, 17 earned college degrees, and 15 earned advanced degrees, many Americans cling to such negative stereotypes of African-American women as welfare dependents, uneducated dropouts, and unsophisticated ghetto mothers rather than face the reality that these women are well educated, articulate, intelligent, and qualified for office.

Even Shirley Chisholm, the nation's first African-American congresswoman, noted that voters of all kinds believed things about African-American candidates that they would not have readily believed about European-American candidates. She indicated that African-American leaders have less leeway and must conform to higher standards, or they will be brought down by their adversaries.

In addition, African-American women running for office often have had to contend with issues surrounding gender that have not typically been problems for men. One such issue surrounds the family. For instance, if a female candidate has children, voters are likely to consider whether she will be able to devote the necessary time to raising "her" children and completing the work required of public office, while no such consideration is given to a father's role in raising children. Such unfair assumptions are further exacerbated if the woman is a single mother, as were seven of the 14 African-American women who were serving in Congress in 2000.

African-American women's participation in congressional politics is a natural outgrowth of their history of activism combined with greater opportunities for inclusion within the American political system. Although they must contend with both the racism and the sexism inherent in American politics, the African-American women who have gained congressional office have proven to be well educated, politically adroit, and generally progressive while helping to shape this nation's domestic and foreign policies.

Further reading:
Chisholm, Shirley. *Unbought and Unbossed.* Boston, Mass.: Houghton Mifflin, 1970; Darling, Marsha. "African-American Women in State Elective Office in the South." In *Women and Elective Office: Past, Present, and Future,* edited by S. Thomas and C. Wilcox. New York Oxford University Press, 1998; Davidson, Chandler, ed. *Minority Vote Dilution.* Washington, D.C.: Howard University Press, 1984; Gill, La Verne. *African American Women in Congress: Forming and Transforming History.* New Brunswick, N.J.: Rutgers University Press, 1997; Hill Collins, Patricia. *Black Feminist Thought: Knowledge, Consciousness, and the Politics of*

Congresswoman Shirley Chisholm *(Library of Congress)*

Empowerment. New York: Routledge, 1991; Project Vote Smart. Available online. URL: http://www.vote-smart. org/vote- smart/votes.phtml?ID?COH45325&votid'2676. Accessed January 2006; Rogers, Mary Beth. *Barbara Jordan: American Hero.* New York: Bantam Books, 1998; Witt, L., K. Paget, and G. Matthews. *Running as a Woman: Gender and Power in American Politics.* New York: Free Press, 1994.

—Paul T. Miller

membership: African Americans

After the Civil War, the Thirteenth, Fourteenth, and Fifteenth Amendments to the U.S. Constitution were ratified. These amendments ended slavery, provided citizenship rights to blacks, and furnished the right to vote for African-American males over age 21; they combined with federal legislation such as the Civil Rights Act of 1866 to facilitate initial black representation in Congress.

The first African American selected to Congress was Hiram Revels, who was chosen by the Mississippi legislature in January 1870 to fill an unexpired Senate term created when the state seceded. From 1870 through 2004, 115 black Americans have been elected to Congress, including 110 in the House and five in the Senate. The majority of black members of Congress have been men (92) and Democrats (88). The longest-serving African-American congressman is John Conyers, first elected in 1965 and reelected to a 21st term in 2004. A total of 15 black members of the HOUSE OF REPRESENTATIVES and one black member of the SENATE have chaired committees. The most African Americans elected as freshmen was 17 in the 1992 election. A total of 40 African Americans served in each two-year Congress from 1993 through 1998; this was the most blacks in the national legislature at any point in American history. The state electing the largest number of African Americans to Congress is Illinois (16), followed by California (10), South Carolina (9), New York (8), and Georgia and North Carolina (7).

Trends in black representation in Congress reveal four distinct periods: 1870–1901, 1929–66, 1967–92, and 1993 to the present. The first period of African-American service in Congress began with Reconstruction and ended at the beginning of the 20th century. A total of 22 blacks were elected during this period, including 20 to the House of Representatives and two to the Senate. All members who served over the three decades from 1870 to 1900 were Republicans, and most came from the former slave states of the South, which possessed high black populations. Two black representatives from South Carolina, Joseph Rainey and Robert Smalls, each served a decade over this span. The initial period of black representation in Congress ended due to a racist climate that featured intimidation of black voters and Jim Crow laws.

In the second period of African-American representation in Congress, which covered the period 1929 through 1966, a total of seven blacks served in the House of Representatives. Although the first member of Congress elected in this period was a Republican, the other six were Democrats. This period corresponded with the NEW DEAL era and was a high point of American liberalism. In fact, black voters converted en masse to the Democratic Party in the early 1930s and have strongly supported that party ever since. One trait of black members who served during this span was their longevity; the shortest tenure was six years.

The third period of black representation in Congress began with the 90th Congress in 1967. This period was distinguished by several factors. First, Republican Edward Brooke was elected by Massachusetts voters to the U.S. Senate in the 1966 election, becoming the first African American to serve in that body in more than 80 years. Second, there was an exponential increase in the number of black members overall in Congress, with a total of 46 serving over the entire period. Many of these persons, including Andrew Young and John Lewis, among others, were active in the Civil Rights movement that had begun in earnest a decade earlier. Third, Shirley Chisholm, Democrat of New York, became the first black woman elected to Congress.

The most recent period of black representation in Congress began with the 103rd Congress in 1993 and continues to the present. It has witnessed the election of the fourth and fifth black members of the U.S. Senate. Carol Moseley-Braun, Democrat of Illinois, in 1992 became the first black woman and first black Democrat to be elected to the Senate. Though she was defeated for reelection in 1998 after one term, another Illinois Democrat, Barack Obama, was elected to the upper chamber in 2004. Further, the number of black representatives has been augmented due to legislation that strengthened the Voting Rights Act. An all-time high of 42 black members served in the 109th Congress, including four freshmen.

Many African-American members of Congress have gone on to serve in noteworthy positions within society. For instance, Barbara Jordan of Texas became a professor of public affairs; William Gray of Pennsylvania led the United Negro College Fund; Kweisi Mfume of Maryland was president of the National Association for the Advancement of Colored People; Andrew Young of Georgia took a post as U.N. ambassador; Harold Washington of Illinois served as mayor of Chicago. Other black representatives such as Ronald Dellums of California and Charles Rangel of New York, elected together in 1970, continue their distinguished service after more than three decades in Congress.

Further reading:

Amer, Mildred. *Black Members of the United States Congress: 1870–2004.* Washington, D.C.: Congressional Research Service, 2004; Christopher, Maurine. *America's Black Congressmen.* New York: Thomas Y. Crowell, 1971; Ornstein, Norman, Thomas Mann, and Michael Malbin. *Vital Statistics on Congress, 2001–2002.* Washington, D.C.: AEI Press, 2002; Swain, Carol. *Black Faces, Black Interests: The Representation of African Americans in Congress.* Cambridge, Mass.: Harvard University Press, 1993.

—Samuel B. Hoff

membership: Asian Americans

By the time of the 108th Congress the national legislature had five Asian-Pacific-American members in the HOUSE OF REPRESENTATIVES and two in the SENATE (including a nonvoting delegate from American Samoa). These seven members are part a small group of 20 Asian-Pacific-Americans who have been elected to the U.S. Congress as members or delegates. The most Asian-Pacific-American members to serve at one time was nine in the 103rd, 104th, and 107th Congresses. In addition to these 20 Asian Pacific Americans, 13 resident commissioners were elected from the Philippine Islands from 1907 to 1946.

The first elected Asian-Pacific member of Congress was Dalip Singh Saund, a Democrat from California, who served from 1957 to 1963. The first Asian-Pacific senator was Hiram Leong Fong, a Republican from Hawaii. Fong was elected as one of Hawaii's first two senators in 1959. Fong served from 1959 to 1977. Fong was also the first Chinese American elected to Congress. Fong has been one of only five Asian Pacific Americans to serve in the Senate. The others are Daniel K. Inouye, a Democrat from Hawaii, 1963–present; Samuel I. Hayakawa, a Republican from California, 1977–83; Spark M. Matsunaga, a Democrat from Hawaii, 1977–90; and Daniel K. Akaka, a Democrat from Hawaii, 1990–present.

Asian-Pacific-American members of Congress have been elected from American Samoa, California, Guam, Hawaii, Oregon, and Virginia (Robert Scott [D-VA] is an African American with Filipino heritage). A look at districts with more than 10 percent Asian Americans provides some insight into Asian representation in Congress. During the 1980s and 1990s Hawaii's First Congressional District had the highest number of Asians, with 67 percent, and was briefly represented by Patricia Saiki, an Asian Republican woman, from 1987 to 1990. Every Asian member of Congress during the 1980s and 1990s was elected at some point in their careers from one of these districts with more than 10 percent Asians. Asian Pacific Americans, however, are also capable of getting elected from districts with relatively few Asians. A pair of Democrats from California, Robert Matsui and Norman Mineta, were elected from districts with 6.5 percent and 6 percent Asians, respectively, from 1983 to 1992, and more recently David Wu of Oregon was elected in 1998 from a district that is only around 3 percent Asian American.

In 1994 the Congressional Asian Pacific Caucus was formed by then representative Norman Mineta to advocate for the needs of Asian Pacific Americans. The caucus has an executive committee that grants membership based on either being an Asian-Pacific member of Congress, representing an Asian-Pacific-American majority district, or exhibiting consistent and extraordinary dedication to the goals of the caucus.

Asian-Pacific-American members of Congress listed alphabetically: Akaka, Daniel Kahkini (D-HI), 1977–90, House, 1990–present, Senate. Blaz; Ben Garrido (R-Guam delegate), 1985–93 House; Faleomavaega, Eni F. H. (D-American Samoa delegate), 1989–present, House; Fong, Hiram Leong (R-HI), 1959–77 Senate; Hayakawa, Samuel Ichiye (R-CA), 1977–83, Senate; Honda, Michael M. (D-CA), 2001–present, House; Inouye, Daniel Ken (D-HI), 1963–present, Senate; Kalanianaole, Jonah Kuhio (R-HI delegate), 1903–22, House; Kim, Jay C. (R-CA), 1993–99, House; Matsui, Robert Takeo (D-CA). 1979–present, House; Matsunaga, Spark M. (D-HI), 1963–77, House, 1977–90, Senate; Mineta, Norman Yoshio (D-CA), 1975–95, House; Mink, Patsy Takemoto (D-HI), 1965–77, 1990–2002, House; Saiki, Patricia Fukuda (R-HI), 1987–91, House; Saund, Dalip Singh (D-CA), 1957–63, House; Scott, Robert C. (D-VA), 1993–present, House; Sunia, Fofo Iosefa Fiti (D-American Samoa delegate), 1981–88, House;Underwood, Robert Anacletus (D-Guam delegate), 1993–2002,House; Won Pat, Antonio Borja (D-Guam delegate), 1973–85, House; Wu, David (D-OR), 1999–present, House.

Further reading:

Tong, Lorraine H. *Asian Pacific Americans in the United States Congress.* Washington, D.C.: Congressional Research Service, 2003.

—Charles Tien

membership: Hispanic Americans

In the 108th Congress of 2003–04, Hispanics constituted approximately 13 percent of the national population but made up only slightly more than 5 percent of the HOUSE OF REPRESENTATIVES (23 of 435) and 0 percent of the SENATE. The number of Hispanics serving in Congress had risen sharply in the past 20 years. There were only six Hispanic members serving in the 97th Congress (1981–82) compared to the 23 serving in the 108th Congress.

One factor contributing to the recent increase of Hispanic-American members in the House is the numerical strength of Hispanic voters in many districts. The population growth of Hispanics by itself did not necessarily translate directly into increased numbers of Hispanic-American members of Congress. Since Hispanic voters have tended to vote for Hispanic candidates, increasing the number of Hispanic-majority districts has tended to produce an increase in the number of Hispanics serving in Congress. In the 1980s there were nine districts whose populations were 50 percent or more Hispanic. In 1983 Hispanic members represented five of those nine districts, and by 1990 Hispanics represented eight of the nine districts. By the 1990 census there were 19 congressional districts whose populations were 50 percent or more Hispanic. Hispanics represented 15 of these 19 districts. This increase of 111 percent in the number of Hispanic-majority districts occurred when there was a 53 percent increase of Hispanics in the general population. The growth in the number of Hispanic-majority districts helped explain why the number of Hispanics in Congress tripled between 1980 and 1998.

Many more Hispanic-majority districts were created after the 1990 round of congressional redistricting as a result of the 1982 amendments to the VOTING RIGHTS ACT OF 1965 and a Supreme Court decision upholding the constitutionality of the amendments. The 1982 amendments expanded the scope of the Voting Rights Act by requiring the Justice Department to examine the effect of voting laws, including redistricting, on minority vote dilution. Thus, the act now goes beyond assuring Hispanics access to the voting booth to seeing that Hispanics are elected to Congress. The law set the course for states to create majority-minority districts in the 1990 round of redistricting to avoid being in violation of the law.

Hispanic Americans benefited from the amendments to the 1982 Voting Rights Act in the 1992 round of redistricting. Hispanic majority districts were created as Hispanic Americans were found 1) to be sufficiently large enough as a population in compact areas to create congressional districts, 2) to share similar policy preferences and other socioeconomic characteristics, and 3) to have their preferred candidates defeated by white majorities.

Though Hispanic Americans have made recent gains in winning seats in Congress, the first Hispanic American elected to serve in Congress was in 1822. Joseph Marion Hernandez served until 1823 as the first DELEGATE from the Territory of Florida. In 1845 Hernandez ran unsuccessfully for the Senate as a Whig candidate. The first Hispanic-American senator was Octaviano Larrazolo, a Republican from New Mexico. Larrazolo was elected in 1928 to complete Senator Andieus A. Jones's term. Larrazolo served only six months before dying in office in 1930. Dennis Chavez, a Democrat from New Mexico, was the first Hispanic to serve an entire six-year Senate term. In fact, he remained in office from 1935 to 1962. In 1964 New Mexico elected another Hispanic American to complete Larrazolo's unexpired term. Joseph Manuel Montoya served until he was defeated in 1976. The first Hispanic-American woman to serve in Congress was Ileana Ros-Lehtinen, a Republican from Florida, who was elected in 1989. She was also the first Cuban American to serve in Congress and Florida's first Hispanic representative in more than 160 years. During the early 1900s until 1960, nine of the 17 Hispanic Americans to serve in Congress were resident commissioners from the annexed territory of Puerto Rico.

Hispanic Americans have been elected to Congress from Arizona, California, Florida, Illinois, Louisiana, New Jersey, New Mexico, New York, and Texas and as delegates from Guam, Puerto Rico, and the Virgin Islands. Delegates do not enjoy full voting privileges in the House, though they were permitted for a brief time (the 103rd Congress) to vote in the COMMITTEE OF THE WHOLE. Delegates since 1973 have been allowed to serve and vote on committees.

In 1976 the Congressional Hispanic Caucus was formed by five Hispanic House members. Herman Badillo, a Democrat from New York, Baltasar Corrada del Rio, a delegate from Puerto Rico, Eligio "Kika" de la Garza, a Democrat from Texas, Henry B. Gonzalez, a Democrat from Texas, and Edward R. Roybal, a Democrat from California, formed the caucus to address and work for the needs of Hispanic Americans in Congress. The caucus has worked on issues related to immigration, citizenship and naturalization, education, welfare reform, language promotion, international relations, housing and community development, health, and voting and civil rights. The caucus, which is limited to Hispanic-American legislators, has grown to 20 members.

Further reading:
Hispanic Americans in Congress. Available online. URL: http://www.loc.gov/rr/hispanic/congress. Accessed 12 December 2005.

—Charles Tien

membership: Native Americans

Though constituting less than 1 percent of the U.S. population, a dozen American Indians have served in Congress (see table). The first century of the republic saw a gradual change as the U.S. government began to treat American Indian tribes less as independent sovereign nations and more as "domestic dependent nations," to use the terminology of the time. By 1871 Congress had ended the process of signing treaties with Indian tribes and by 1913 had begun treating Indian affairs as part of the normal

AMERICAN INDIANS WHO HAVE SERVED IN CONGRESS

Member, Party, and State	Years of Service	Ethnic Background Tribal Affiliation
House		
Charles B. Curtis (R-KS)	1893–1907	Kaw
Charles D. Carter (D-OK)	1907–1927	Choctaw
W.W. Hastings (D-OK)	1915–1921, 1923–1935	Cherokee
Will Rogers (D-OK)	1933–1943	Cherokee
Will Rogers, Jr. (D-CA)	1943–1945	Cherokee
William G. Stigler (D-OK)	1945–1953	Choctaw
Ben Reifel (R-SD)	1961–1971	Rosebud Sioux
Clem Rogers McSpadden (D-OK)	1973–1975	Cherokee
Ben Nighthorse Campbell (D-CO)	1987–1993	Northern Cheyenne
Brad Carson (D-OK)	2001–	Cherokee
Tom Cole (R-OK)	2003–	Chickasaw
Senate		
Charles B. Curtis (R-KS)	1907–1913, 1915–1929	Kaw
Robert Latham Owen (D-OK)	1907–1925	Cherokee
Ben Nighthorse Campbell (R-CO)[3]	1993–	Northern Cheyenne

[3] Campbell switched party affiliation from the Democratic to Republican Party in 1995.

legislative agenda. These transitions, in part, made election to Congress an important concern for some American Indians. Though American Indians were not uniformly granted citizenship rights until 1924 and faced restrictions on voting in some states as late as 1962, the first American Indian was elected to Congress in the late 19th century.

Though some have considered Matthew Quay, a senator from Pennsylvania beginning in 1887, the first American Indian member of Congress, his Abenaki or Delaware ancestry has never been confirmed. Thus, Charles B. Curtis, representative and then senator from Kansas, is typically credited with being the first American Indian federal legislator. His successful political career culminated in his election to the vice presidency in 1928. Like some who followed him, Curtis was not generally considered pro-Indian in his political positions. Curtis's election was followed by 11 others. In fact, there was at least one Indian legislator

in Congress for 90 of the 112 years between 1893 and 2003. That being said, the table also reveals that while there have been some successes, American Indians have never attained seats in Congress in equal proportion to their population in the United States. Indeed, as of 2003 American Indians constituted 0.9 percent of the U.S. population but held only three (0.6 percent) of the 535 congressional seats.

Senator Ben Nighthorse Campbell, a Republican of Colorado, served in Congress from 1987 until 2005. As the most prominent American Indian elected official, Campbell was the recipient of both extra attention and extra pressures. His position afforded him a platform to sponsor legislation and speak out on issues that affect American Indians, but his role as the only American Indian in Congress for much of his tenure also meant that some treated him as the representative of all Indian concerns. Not only was such a burden unfair, it potentially limited the time he had to act on behalf of his non-Indian constituents. On the whole Campbell took these pressures in stride. He effectively served the citizens of Colorado, regardless of ethnicity, and helped Indian causes elsewhere as well.

The characteristics of American Indians who have served indicate that a majority have been Democrats from Oklahoma and that the Cherokee tribe has been the most typical tribal affiliation of American Indian legislators. Such demographics are not surprising, given that much of the state of Oklahoma was held as Indian Territory before being admitted to the Union in 1907. American Indians made up more than 8 percent of the state's population in the early 20th century, and the Cherokee tribe is the state's largest. Perhaps a more surprising characteristic is to be found among states that have not elected American Indian legislators. Arizona has not elected an American Indian to Congress despite having a population that was more than 20 percent Indian early in the 20th century. Likewise, Alaska, with an Indian population of more than 15 percent today, has never elected an American Indian or Alaska Native to office, though several have run.

What does the future hold for American Indian representation in Congress? If current trends persist, the American Indian presence in Congress will continue to be small, but Indian candidates can be successful when they run. Of the nine Senate races featuring an American Indian candidate through 2002, seven were successful. Moreover, a number of American Indians currently hold legislative or execute positions at the state level, important experience for a potential run for federal office.

Further reading:

Martin, Mart. *The Almanac of Women and Minorities in American Politics.* Boulder, Colo.: Westview Press, 1999; Utter, Jack. *American Indians: Answers to Today's Questions.* 2d ed. Norman: University of Oklahoma Press, 2001;

Viola, Herman J. *Ben Nighthorse Campbell: An American Warrior.* New York: Orion Books, 1993; Wilkins, David E. *American Indian Politics and the American Political System.* Lanham, Md.: Rowman & Littlefield, 2002.

—Charles C. Turner

membership: women

Between 1917 and 2003 a total of 215 women served in Congress, according to the Center for American Women and Politics (CAWP): 26 in the Senate (15 Democrats, 11 Republicans), 182 in the House (117 Democrats and 65 Republicans), and 7 (5 Democrats, 2 Republicans) in both houses. This includes a total of 30 women of color (28 Democrats, 2 Republicans), with one Democratic woman who served in the Senate and 29 women (27 Democrats, 2 Republicans) who served in the House.

In the earliest years after women won the vote, women often entered Congress by succeeding their husbands. Of the women who have served in Congress, 45 succeeded their husbands, including eight in the Senate and 37 in the House. More recently, women have built their own political careers, often first holding office at the local or state level. Of the 59 women serving in the House in 2003, for example, 44 (75 percent) held previous elective office. A total of 10 (77 percent) of the women serving in the Senate held elective office prior to entering Congress.

Few women have achieved significant leadership roles in Congress. A milestone was reached in 2002, when Representative NANCY PELOSI of California was chosen House Democratic Leader, the highest position achieved in a House minority party. Five other women (three Democrats and two Republicans) hold leadership positions in the 108th Congress, including Representative Deborah Pryce of Ohio, who chairs the House Republican Conference. Few women have chaired congressional committees. Two women chair Senate committees in the 108th Congress: Senator Susan Collins, a Republican from Maine, chairs the Committee on Governmental Affairs, and Senator Olympia Snowe, a Republican from Maine, chairs the Committee on Small Business and Entrepreneurship. Only two other women have chaired Senate committees before them. In the House no woman has chaired a committee since the 104th Congress.

Research has shown that women in Congress as a group differ from their male colleagues in two important ways: the policies they promote and the ways they work. These differences—inevitably mediated by institutional forces, partisanship, and the political climate—resemble differences found between men and women in state legislatures.

In particular, women in Congress say they have a special obligation to represent women, although each may interpret that responsibility differently. Numerous sources

Congresswoman Jeanette Rankin *(Library of Congress)*

report that many congresswomen tell varying versions of the same scenario: Whether or not they ran for Congress intending to be a voice for women, they discovered upon arriving in Washington that certain issues or perspectives were being addressed inadequately, if at all, and if the women in Congress did not speak up, women's interests would be neglected.

Also, women have changed the congressional agenda by highlighting new issues, framing policy concerns in distinctive ways, and expanding the terms of debate over legislation. Women's health concerns, including health care and research, are most frequently cited as areas in which the presence of women in Congress has resulted in noticeably different policies. Welfare policy and reproductive rights have also been noted by researchers as areas in which the distinctive impact of women lawmakers can be observed.

In 1977 15 women members formed a group known initially as the Congresswomen's Caucus, which was later reorganized and named the Congressional Caucus for Women's Issues. The bipartisan caucus, cochaired by a Democrat and a Republican in each Congress, describes

FIRSTS FOR WOMEN IN CONGRESS			
Achievement	**Name, state, party**	**Year(s)**	**Additional information**
First woman elected to House	Jeannette Rankin R-MT	1917–19, 1941–42	Only member of Congress to vote against U.S. entry into both world wars
First woman to serve in Senate	Rebecca Latimer Felton, D-GA	1922	Appointed to fill a vacancy, served only one day
First woman to chair a House committee	Mae Ella Nolan, R-CA	1923–25	Committee on Expenditures in the Post Office Department
First woman to chair a Senate committee	Hattie Wyatt Caraway, D-AR	1933–45	Committee on Enrolled Bills
First woman of color in Congress and first Asian-Pacific Islander woman in Congress	Patsy Takemoto Mink (D-HI)	1965–77, 1990–2002	
First African-American woman in Congress	Shirley Chisholm (D-NY)	1969–83	
First Hispanic woman in Congress	Ileana Ros-Lehtinen (R-FL)	1989–present	
First woman of color and first African-American woman in Senate	Carol Moseley Braun (D-IL)	1993–99	
First woman in top leadership role	Nancy Pelosi (D-CA)	2002–present	House Democratic Leader

itself as an informational clearing house on Capitol Hill and an advocate for women and families. Participation is voluntary, and not all women choose to be members. Initially the caucus included only women members; later, in order to secure sufficient funds for viability, it established itself as a LEGISLATIVE SERVICE ORGANIZATION and invited sympathetic men to join and contribute to its resources. When Congress abolished Legislative Service Organizations in 1995, the caucus reorganized as an informal group including only women that informs other members and staff of important information and develops legislation relating to women's health, economic equity, education, domestic violence, child care, child support, sexual harassment, and international women's issues.

Further reading:
Center for American Women and Politics. "Women in Congress: Leadership Roles and Committee Chairs" (fact sheet). April 2003; Center for American Women and Politics, "Women in the U.S. Congress 2003" (fact sheet). January 2003; Center for American Women and Politics. "Women in the U.S. Senate 1922–2003" (fact sheet). January 2003; Dodson, Debra L., Susan J. Carroll, Ruth B. Mandel, Katherine E. Kleeman, Ronnee Schreiber, and Debra Liebowitz. *Voices, Views, Votes: The Impact of Women in the 103rd Congress.* New Brunswick, N.J.: Center for American Women and Politics, 1995; Hawkesworth, Mary, Debra Dodson, Katherine E. Klee-

man, Kathleen J. Casey, and Krista Jenkins. *Legislating by and for Women: A Comparison of the 103rd and 104th Congresses.* New Brunswick, N.J.: Center for American Women and Politics, 2001; Rosenthal, Cindy Simon, ed. *Women Transforming Congress.* Norman: University of Oklahoma Press, 2002; *The Women's Caucus Page.* Women's Policy, Inc. Web Site. Available online. URL: http://www.womenspolicy.org/caucus/history.html. Accessed January 24, 2003.

—Kathy Kleeman

Merchant Marine and Fisheries Committee, House
The House Merchant Marine and Fisheries Committee existed as a standing committee of the U.S. House of Representatives for 107 years, 1887–1995. The committee was responsible for legislation and oversight of the maritime industries and the physical environment of oceans and the coastal zone.

The focus of the committee in its early years was exclusively on maritime shipping, culminating in the 1936 Merchant Marine Act. The development of radio was initially most important for shipping and maritime communication, and a name change to Merchant Marine, Radio, and Fisheries resulted when the committee initially oversaw this technology. A dispute over jurisdiction arose with the House Committee on Interstate and Foreign Commerce in the 1930s regarding the appropriate overseer for radio. A compromise was struck in 1965 with Commerce taking radio policy and Merchant Marine and Fisheries resuming its original name in addition to accepting an expansion of its oversight responsibilities to include, among other things, all modes of water transportation, the Coast Guard, and the Panama Canal. The committee had an integrated focus after the compromise that positioned it to expand into legislation concerning the physical environment as well as oversight of scientific exploration in oceanography.

In 1959 the National Academy of Sciences released "Oceanography 1960–1970" a 12-volume report commissioned by a consortium of the government bureaus and agencies having missions that required an understanding of oceans. This report spurred congressional action, providing an impetus for the Merchant Marine and Fisheries Committee to take a prominent role in coordinating and shaping national policy. The National Sea Grant College Act of 1966 was one component of national oceans policy. Concern for environmental protection on the land in the 1960s was quickly taken to heart by the committee, particularly as the potential consequences of off-shore petroleum exploration were experienced by the fishing industry. A Presidential Commission on Marine Science, Engineering, and Resources, chaired by Julius Stratton, produced its report in January 1969, two weeks before the off-shore oil well near the coast of Santa Barbara blew out and produced the first catastrophic oil spill for the U.S. coast. The Santa Barbara blowout sent approximately 3.3 million gallons of crude oil ashore, galvanizing public opposition to offshore drilling and bringing the committee directly into the environmental protection policy arena.

The committee was responsible for bringing the National Environmental Policy Act (NEPA) of 1969 to the floor under the leadership of Representative John Dingell of Michigan, chair of the Fisheries and Wildlife Subcommittee. The National Oceanic and Atmospheric Administration was created by executive order in 1970 with the support of the committee, which had pressured President Nixon to implement this particular recommendation of the Stratton report. The first attempt to eliminate the Merchant Marine and Fisheries Committee came in 1974. The committee emerged at that time with a larger membership to handle its expanded jurisdiction over oceanography and marine affairs, including coastal zone management and international fishing agreements.

This jurisdiction led to an activist environmental protection policy agenda in the committee throughout the 1970s. The Coastal Zone Management Act of 1972 and amendments strengthening its provisions followed in 1976, 1978, and 1980. The Endangered Species Act of 1973; protected coastal waters were extended to 200 miles offshore in 1976; the Antarctic Conservation Act in 1978; alteration in offshore oil and gas development and outer continental shelf petroleum leasing, also in 1978; and the Deep Seabed Minerals Resources Act in 1980 were just some of the environmental protection legislation reported from the committee in that decade. The changes in political climate and economic conditions of the 1980s and 1990s slowed the environmental protection work of the committee as well as constrained the national support traditionally given to the maritime industry.

The Merchant Marine and Fisheries Committee along with two other committees (District of Columbia, and Post Office and Civil Service) were eliminated at the beginning of the 104th Congress as a cost-saving measure that was part of the reforms promised by the Republican congressional candidates in the Contract with America during the 1994 elections. The final jurisdiction of the committee in the 103rd Congress included the merchant marine generally, oceanography and marine affairs including coastal zone management, the Coast Guard, fisheries and wildlife, regulation of common carriers by water, navigation, the Panama Canal, registering and licensing of vessels and small boats, rules and international agreements to prevent collisions at sea, U.S. Coast Guard and Merchant Marine Academies, international fishing agreements, and the Outer Continental Shelf Lands Act.

Further reading:
U.S. House of Representatives, Committee on Merchant Marine and Fisheries. *History of the Committee on Merchant Marine and Fisheries.* 101st Cong., 2d sess., 1990; U.S. House of Representatives. *Committee on Merchant Marine and Fisheries. Final Report on the Activities of the Committee on Merchant Marine and Fisheries in the 103rd Congress.* 103rd Cong. 2d sess. House Rept 103-887, 1995; Steinhart, Carol E., and John S. Steinhart. *Blowout: A Case Study of the Santa Barbara Oil Spill.* North Scituate, Mass.: Duxbury Press, 1972.

—Karen M. McCurdy

Michel, Robert Henry (1923–) *Representative, House Minority Leader*

Michel was born to Charles Michel, a toolmaker who had immigrated to the United States from France in 1911, and Anna, a domestic who worked for wealthy families in Peoria, Illinois. He was the oldest of three children; his twin sisters were four years his junior. Michel attended public schools in Peoria, graduating from Peoria High School in 1940. He entered Bradley University in his hometown but enlisted in the U.S. Army in 1942 following the attack on Pearl Harbor. He served as a combat infantryman in the 39th Infantry Regiment in the European theater during World War II. He was wounded by machine gun fire during the Battle of the

Bulge. He received two Bronze Stars, a Purple Heart, and four battle stars. In one encounter with the enemy, he captured 28 German prisoners without firing a shot.

Following his discharge as a disabled veteran in 1946, Michel entered Bradley University, earning a bachelor of science in business administration in 1948. He married Corinne Woodruff, who he met while they were students at Bradley. They have three sons, Scott, Bruce, and Robin and a daughter, Laurie.

In 1949 he was hired, upon the recommendation of Bradley president David Owen, as an administrative assistant to Representative Harold Velde, who had just been elected to represent Illinois's 18th District. When Velde retired in 1956, Michel was elected to succeed him, winning a four-way primary in the overwhelmingly Republican district. He campaigned on the themes of reducing government and waste, issues that he would continue to emphasize throughout his congressional career. He would go on to serve 19 terms in the HOUSE OF REPRESENTATIVES, from 1957 to 1995. His toughest reelection battle took place in 1982, when the national recession caused serious economic problems in his district (including a strike by the United Autoworkers against Caterpillar, Inc., the largest employer in the district), resulting in a strong challenge by the Democrats. He defeated G. Douglas Stephens, a labor attorney from Peoria, by 6,000 votes.

Michel holds the distinction of winning more consecutive terms in the House as a member of the minority party than anyone else in American history. In speaking of his career in the minority, in 2003 Michel said that,

> of my 38 years as a member of the minority party. Oh, those were frustrating years. But . . . I never really felt I was out of the game or that I had no part to play. Under the rules of the House, the traditions of the House . . . there is a role to play for the minority. . . . We struck a deal, we made a bargain . . . to craft good legislation for the country—that was the joy of it!

During President Ronald Reagan's administration Michel was able to achieve a number of legislative victories despite his party's minority status, notably the enactment of Reagan's budget and tax reduction plan of 1981. He would later say of the plan that "we ran up one healthy deficit for our kids out there." Many of the other victories of this period were sustaining the vetoes by Reagan of legislation passed by the majority Democrats. He was also instrumental in winning House approval of the 1991 Persian Gulf War.

In 1988 Michel found himself at the center of a controversy following a televised interview in which he spoke fondly of the old radio show *Amos 'n' Andy*, a program denounced by civil rights organizations for its stereotypical portrayals of African Americans. Michel went on to say that "it's too bad" that school children could no longer wear blackface and appear in minstrel shows. After protests from African-American leaders, Michel apologized: "My regret is more profound because I believe my public record as a Congressman is without the slightest blot of bigotry or racial insensitivity." In his later years in the House, Michel was faced with a growing number of conservative Republicans, led by NEWT GINGRICH of Georgia, who were critical of Michel's leadership style. They questioned his collegial style and suggested that his efforts to compromise with the Democrats on issues made him an ineffective Republican leader. Gingrich supporters, calling themselves the Conservative Opportunity Society (COS), won their first victory in the power struggle with Michel in 1989, when Gingrich defeated Michel protégé Edward Madigan of Illinois to become Republican WHIP (the second-ranking leadership post). The following year Gingrich led a revolt against a budget deal that President George H. W. Bush had struck with the congressional Democrats.

If Michel had not retired, he would have probably been challenged for the Republican leadership by Gingrich after the 1994 elections. Instead, Michel chose to retire, and Gingrich became Speaker of the House after the Republicans took control of the House in the 1994 election. Michel explained the conflict with Gingrich and his followers by noting that "There's a big generational gap between my style of leadership, my sense of values and my whole thinking processes . . . and I accept that." Michel was succeeded by Ray LaHood, his chief of staff, who had served on his staff for a number of years.

Michel was a delegate to every Republican National Convention between 1964 and 1996. In 1984 he chaired the Republican National Convention that nominated President Ronald Reagan for a second term. He also presided over the 1988 and 1992 conventions that nominated George Herbert Walker Bush.

Michel received high honors for his service. In 1989 Reagan awarded Michel the Presidential Citizens Medal. In 1994 President Bill Clinton gave Michel the Presidential Medal of Freedom, the highest civilian honor conferred by the U.S. government. In 2003 he was part of the first group to receive the Congressional Distinguished Service Award.

After leaving Congress in 1995, Michel joined the Washington firm of Hogan and Hartson as senior adviser for corporate and governmental affairs. He also joined the board of directors of the Public Broadcasting System and the Chicago Board of Trade and the board of trustees of Bradley University.

Further reading:
Broder, David. "Role Models, Now More Than Ever." *Washington Post*, 13 July 2003; Epstein, Shelley. "Michel's

Rebound." *Peoria Journal Star*, 28 March 1999; Locin, Mitchell, and Elaine S. Povich. "Bob Michel's Parting Warnings." *Chicago Tribune*, 25 November 1994; Mathis, Nancy. "House GOP Leader Michel Will Retire." *Houston Chronicle* 5 October 1993; Unsigned article. "American Notes; Congress: Amos 'n' Bob." *Time Magazine*, 28 November 1988.

—Jeffrey Kraus

Mills, Wilbur Daig (1909–1992) *Representative*

Wilbur Mills was born in 1909 in Kensett, Arkansas. He was the eldest of three children. His father, Ardra, was a businessman who operated a general store, cotton gin, and the Bank of Kensett. Mills attended public school in nearby Searcy and graduated from Hendrix College in 1930. In his senior yearbook it was said of Mills,

> High above the common rabble Wilbur towers, undisturbed by life's ups and downs. Something fine within him prompts his gay outlook on life. His splendid grades are indicative of much "gray matter." Wilbur walks life's straight paths and is a boon companion for anyone who is "down and out."

Mills left Arkansas to attend Harvard Law School. While many observers subsequently credited him with receiving a law degree—he was later admitted to the Arkansas bar—he returned to Kensett in 1933 without completing his law degree.

In 1934 Mills began his political career by challenging a longtime incumbent, Foster White, for White County judge. When he entered the contest, Mills's father let him know he planned to vote for White. Using the slogan "Give a young man a chance" and accusing White of corruption and nepotism, Mills eventually won the support of both his father and a majority of White County voters. He won the election 2,457 to 2,100.

Following the death of Senator JOSEPH ROBINSON, a seat opened up in the Arkansas congressional delegation, and Mills was elected to represent the Second District in 1938. He was initially placed on the Banking and Currency Committee. In 1942 he took a place on the WAYS AND MEANS COMMITTEE, a post he would hold until his retirement in 1977. The Ways and Means Committee was considered the most desirable of all committee assignments and had a great deal of influence over public policy because it had jurisdiction over Social Security, trade, taxation, and the national debt. Moreover, the Democrats on Ways and Means at that time also served as the party's Committee on Committees, determining all committee assignments for the party.

As one of "Sam Rayburn's boys," Mills received much advice from the SPEAKER OF THE HOUSE that he seemed to take to heart. Rayburn reportedly told Mills, "[d]on't ever talk until you know what you're talking about." Mills took this advice seriously and spent a great deal of time learning about the various issues that fell within his committee's jurisdiction. He explained

> I was told by everyone in those days that my job was to learn the jurisdiction of the committee, and that took a lot of work. So, I undertook to memorize the Internal Revenue Code, and almost did, I guess. I spent an awful lot of time studying it, and Social Security legislation, reciprocal trade legislation, debt legislation, welfare programs, unemployment compensation, all these matters that were within the jurisdiction of the Ways and Means Committee. I was told that if I was to have any influence in the House, it would depend upon the members feeling that I had knowledge of the subject matter that was superior to their knowledge, that my judgment was sound and so on.

Not only did Mills master the legislation, he developed an extensive network of experts upon whom he could rely for advice and information. Mills consulted lawyers, economists, civil servants, and scholars. He participated in deliberations about implementing Social Security and amendments to the Social Security Act during the 1940s. During the 1950s the Ways and Means Committee undertook a major reevaluation of the tax system. Committee members reviewed more than 17,000 proposals for tax revisions. Mills chaired three subcommittees that were crucial to this process: the Subcommittee on Fiscal Policy, the Subcommittee on Internal Revenue Taxation, and the Joint Economic Committee. He became the principal adviser to Speaker Rayburn, Ways and Means Committee chair Robert Doughton, and the Washington press corps on tax issues.

Wilbur Cohen, assistant secretary of the Department of Health, Education and Welfare, once said of Mills, "[h]e comes from a little town of 2500, which is a small, rural town, but he nevertheless is a Harvard Law School graduate who has got an incisive mind." In order to understand Mills, Cohen asserted, one must understand the tensions presented by living in both of those worlds. During the late 1950s and throughout the 1960s those worlds collided over the issue of civil rights, and Mills found himself in the unenviable position of trying to satisfy his constituents and the governor of Arkansas, Orval Faubus, while also trying to maintain his credibility in the national Democratic Party. Moreover, redistricting after the 1960 census reduced Arkansas's congressional representation from six to four. Mills was placed in the same district as arch segregationist Dale Alford. Though his personal opinion about desegregation is difficult to determine, Mills consistently voted against civil rights legislation. He also signed the Southern Manifesto, which opposed the Supreme Court's decision in *Brown v. Board of Education* (1954). Many have suggested that his position on civil rights prevented him from becoming Speaker of the House following Sam Rayburn's death in 1961.

In 1958 Wilbur Mills became the youngest man to chair the House's most distinguished committee. Mills's leadership of the Ways and Means Committee became legendary, not only because of his remarkable ability to master facts and information; he was known to quote long passages from the tax code from memory. Mills's leadership of Ways and Means was notable for his ability to coax a highly partisan group to work together in the spirit of collegiality. Ways and Means is a committee that deals with such highly technical subject matter that its bills are often considered under a closed rule governing House floor debates, which means no amendments can be offered from the floor, and all amendments required the committee's approval. Thus, the committee produced bills that were complete after thoroughly debating potential amendments. Moreover, Ways and Means dealt with subjects such as taxation that tended to divide members along party lines. Despite the divisive nature of its subject matter and the need to thoroughly evaluate all alternatives, Mills's Ways and Means Committee had a reputation as a nonpartisan committee. The committee seemed to have developed an internal process of socialization. Members were expected to interact in a nonpartisan manner, focusing on the issues rather than each other, though the final votes often broke down along party lines. Senior committee members from each party enforced these expectations by serving as mentors for their junior colleagues.

John Manley conducted several studies of Mills's Ways and Means Committee in an effort to understand committee leadership. He concluded that Mills used three types of leadership simultaneously. He kept the group focused on the task ahead of them (instrumental leadership). He dealt with the interpersonal disputes that sometimes arise in groups (affective leadership), and he knew more about the subject, whatever the subject was, than anyone else on the committee (expert leadership). Moreover, Mills modeled the type of constructive, nonpartisan interaction that was expected of other committee members in his interaction with ranking member, John Byrnes, a Republican from Wisconsin. The two enjoyed a friendly and cooperative relationship despite their philosophical differences.

Beginning in the early 1950s national health insurance for the elderly became a serious topic of conversation. Some argued that it was a natural extension of Social Security. The legislative debates were complex and divisive, and Mills and the Ways and Means Committee were at the center of the storm. Mills believed, since his days as a judge in White County, that government entities had a responsibility to assist the less fortunate. He initiated an early and limited form of Medicaid in Arkansas during the Depression by making public funds available to the needy. Still, Mills worried about Americans' willingness to absorb yet another tax increase and the long-term costs of medical care. In 1960 Mills was instrumental in passing the Kerr-Mills Act, an early version of Medicaid, which set aside federal funds for the states to use for medical care for the needy. It was never very successful since state governments were reluctant to develop legislation that would allow them to use the federal funds.

By the mid-1960s, with a Democratic president and Democrats firmly in control of Congress, the Ways and Means Committee conducted hearings on three different health care proposals. Instead of taking a position on any of the three bills, Mills proposed an alternative, the Mills bill, which combined aspects of all three proposals. It contained three sections. Part A provided hospitalization insurance for the elderly (Medicare). Part B provided optional insurance that would cover physicians' services, and Part C extended medical insurance to the poor (Medicaid). The House passed the bill 313-115; the Senate did likewise, and the Mills bill in large part created Medicare and Medicaid.

Building on Mills's reputation as a bipartisan policy expert, Representative James Burke, a Democrat from Massachusetts, organized the "Draft Mills for President" movement. At first Mills appeared to be a reluctant draftee, though he pledged to work hard if nominated by his party. In February 1972 he announced his candidacy for president of the United States. Democrats hoped Mills could capture the votes of the business community in addition to the traditional Democratic strongholds. However, Mills's candidacy never really took off. In the New Hampshire primary he received a paltry 4.8 percent of the vote. After receiving only 3.6 percent of the vote in Massachusetts, he promptly withdrew from the race.

Mills's distinguished career came to an abrupt and unfortunate end in the early 1970s, when he was besieged by personal scandal. While working on a plan for national health insurance, Mills's extramarital affair with a former striper, Annabel Battistella, became public knowledge. He was stopped by the police, and she jumped out of the car and into the Tidal Basin. Though Mills initially denied a romantic relationship, Battistella admitted the two had been involved for two years. Moreover, it gradually became clear that Mills had a serious drinking problem. In 1974 Speaker of the House Carl Albert (D-OK) asked Mills to resign as chair of the Ways and Means Committee. Mills announced in 1976 that he would not seek reelection.

In a career that spanned five decades, Wilbur Mills had an enormous impact on social and economic policy as well as the American political process. A southern fiscal conservative who ushered in the modern welfare state, Mills came to accept a large role for the federal government in both social policy and civil rights. He invited scholars, lawyers, and other experts into the policy-making process and in his darkest hour brought media attention to focus on the personal lives of politicians rather than on their work.

Further reading:
Goss, Kay C. "The Grassroots Politics of Hard Times: Wilbur D. Mills' Career as a White County Judge." *Arkansas Historical Quarterly* (2000); Manley, John. "Wilbur D. Mills: A Study in Congressional Influence." *American Political Science Review* (1969); Manley, John. *The Politics of Finance: The House Committee on Ways and Means.* Boston: Little, 1970; Morrissey, Charles T. *Oral History Interview with Wilbur D. Mills: Member of Congress from Arkansas, 1939 to 1977,* 1979; Zelizer, Julian E. *Taxing America: Wilbur D. Mills, Congress and the State, 1945–1975.* Cambridge: Cambridge University Press, 1998.

—Kimberly Maslin-Wicks

Minority Leader, House

The floor leader, chief strategist, and spokesperson of the minority party in the HOUSE OF REPRESENTATIVES has been commonly called the Minority Leader. However, since 1980 the leader of the minority party also has been called simply the Democratic or Republican leader, depending on which party is in the minority.

Historically, the Minority Leader was the candidate of the party who was not elected SPEAKER OF THE HOUSE. The power of the Minority Leader is derived from the size of the minority party in the House, the leader's personality, and his or her relationship with the Speaker, the HOUSE MAJORITY LEADER, and the president of the United States. The Minority Leader works to maintain party unity and serves as the guardian of the minority's rights in the House. The most important task of the Minority Leader is to get minority party candidates elected to the House in numbers great enough to become the majority party. If successful, the Minority Leader, now the leader of the new majority party, typically has been elected Speaker.

After being elected Minority Leader in 1980, ROBERT MICHEL, a Republican from Illinois, presented his thoughts about his leadership role, emphasizing the challenges of leading the minority party:

First of all, I look upon it as a role to be shared by those you will elect to fill out our leadership ranks. We do that for the purpose of dividing up the responsibilities around here and I like to delegate additional authority to those willing and able to lend a helping hand.

Secondly, I do not personally crave the spotlight of public attention. What I am interested in is seeing to it that the spotlight is focused on the vast array of individual talent we have assembled here in this room. My job is to orchestrate your many talents in such a way as to give us the best possible overall performance rating.

To use the symphonic analogy, I know some of you prefer speaking softly as strings, others more vocally as woodwinds, some very loudly as brass and finally those boisterous ones for percussion, but in any event, the measure of our success will be how well we harmonize and work together.

Having said that, I want to take this opportunity to remind everyone before curtain time that we are going to be performing under one serious handicap. Notwithstanding our great victories in winning the White House and control of the Senate, we Republicans are still outnumbered in this House 243 to 192. That's a 51 vote Democratic majority!

We deserve a 4 to 5 ratio on committees, but the Democratic majority still has the power and the votes to work their will, particularly on Rules, Ways and Means, and Appropriations.

Representative James Richardson, a Democrat from Tennessee, was Minority Leader at the beginning of the 20th century. He served as Minority Leader until 1903. John Sharp Williams, a Democrat from Mississippi, served as Minority Leader from 1903 until 1908. JAMES BEAUCHAMP CHAMP CLARK, a Democrat from Missouri, was Minority Leader from 1908 until he became Speaker in 1911. He also was the leader when the Democrats were in the minority during the 66th Congress (1919–21). While Clark was Speaker, James Mann, a Republican from Illinois, was the Minority Leader. North Carolina Democrat Claude Kitchin, Tennessee Democrat Finis Garrett, and Texas Democrat JOHN NANCE GARNER served as Minority Leaders during the 1920s. Garner became Speaker of the House when the Democrats gained control of the chamber in 1931.

Bertrand Snell, Republican of New York, served as Minority Leader during the long period of Republican minority status in the 1930s. Snell did not seek reelection to the 76th Congress (1939–40), and Joseph Martin, Jr., a Republican from Massachusetts, was elected Minority Leader. Martin served as Speaker during the 80th (1947–49) and 83rd (1953–55) Congresses. After the Republican Party lost 48 seats in the 1958 elections, younger members of the Republican Caucus replaced Martin with Charles Halleck of Indiana. Halleck served as Minority Leader until the caucus elected Michigan representative Gerald Ford after the 1964 Democratic landslide. Ford continued as Minority Leader until being nominated and confirmed as vice president of the United States in

1974. John Rhodes of Arizona was elected Minority Leader and served through the end of the 96th Congress in 1980.

After a spirited campaign for party leader, Robert Michel of Illinois was elected Minority Leader in 1980. One of his first actions as the new leader of the Republicans was to begin referring to himself as the "Republican Leader" because he thought "Minority Leader" suggested permanent status as the minority party. Michel continued as Minority Leader until he retired from Congress at the end of the 103rd Congress.

The Republican Party was the majority party in the 104th Congress (1995–96), and the previous Speaker of the House, THOMAS FOLEY of Washington, was defeated in 1994. The Democratic Caucus elected RICHARD GEPHARDT party leader. Following Michel's custom, he referred to the position as Democratic Leader. After he failed to produce a Democratic majority in the 2002 elections, and to focus on a possible presidential campaign in 2004, Gephardt stepped down as Democratic leader. In the leadership elections before the opening of the 108th Congress, the Democratic Caucus made history by electing Representative NANCY PELOSI of California to the post of Democratic leader. Pelosi became the highest-ranking female member of Congress in the history of the legislative branch.

Further reading:
Connelly, William F., Jr., and John J. Pitney. *Congress' Permanent Minority? Republicans in the U.S. House*, 1994. Lanham, Md.: Rowman & Littlefield; Davidson, Roger H., Susan Webb Hammond, and Raymond Smock. *Masters of the House: Congressional Leadership over Two Centuries.* Boulder, Colo.: Westview Press 1998; Hulse, Carl. "Pelosi Easily Wins Election for House Democratic Leader." *New York Times,* 15 November 2002.

—John David Rausch, Jr.

Minority Leader, Senate

The title Minority Leader is given to the head of the minority party in the SENATE. The minority leader is selected in a secret ballot vote by his or her party colleagues in a CAUCUS meeting. The formal position of Minority Leader was created in the 1920s, when it was institutionalized in Democratic and Republican Party rules and recognized in the formal precedents of the Senate. The formal powers of the Minority Leader under the Senate's standing rules are important but limited. More fundamental to a Minority Leader's power than the Senate's standing rules are Senate precedents, which date back at least to the 1930s. By custom, for example, the presiding officer gives the Minority Leader priority in obtaining recognition to speak on the floor of the Senate.

Everyday duties of the Minority Leader correspond to those of the MAJORITY LEADER, except that the Minority

Leader has little authority over scheduling legislation. Minority Leaders face roughly similar leadership tasks as do Majority Leaders, though their opportunities are somewhat more limited and their resources less extensive. When the Minority Leader has a president of his or her own party in the White House, he or she has the traditional duties of trying to carry out the administration's program and answering partisan criticisms of the president. Conversely, when the Minority Leader faces a chief executive of the opposite party, the Minority Leader needs to determine the level of opposition to the president. Besides deciding to what extent to support the president, the Minority Leader must decide whether to offer alternatives to the majority's proposals, whether to barter with the majority in return for concessions, or whether to resist what the majority desires.

Within his or her own party, the Minority Leader is as powerful as the Majority Leader. To advance whatever strategy they choose to employ, Minority Leaders can use inducements similar to those available to the opposition, such as committee assignments, information, and campaign assistance. From time to time, the Minority Leader appoints minority members to task forces and also has statutory responsibilities to fill positions on commissions.

The Minority Leader is expected to serve the personal political needs of party colleagues. Individualistic and outward-looking senators create problems for the Minority Leader. Senators have come to expect scheduling favors and party support in their political endeavors. The strategies of Minority Leaders in performing their basic responsibilities have changed over the years. Minority Leaders have been forced to expand party service functions, share leadership duties with more senators, and employ their procedural and organizational resources more creatively.

Pursuing the collective policy objectives of the party is a primary responsibility of the Minority Leader. As leader of the Minority Party in the Senate, the Minority Leader works with the party conference to set the party agenda, message, and strategy. The Minority Leader also promotes party cohesion and searches for votes on the majority side. One way of doing this is to develop policy alternatives to majority initiatives. Due to the consensual nature of the Senate, however, the ability of the Minority Leader to dictate the party's agenda is limited. The Senate Minority Leader must consult continually with the Majority Leader. For the Minority Leader to get things done requires cooperation across party lines.

The ultimate goal of the Minority Leader is to become Majority Leader after the next election by having his or her party win a majority of Senate seats. THOMAS DASCHLE (D-SD) was one Minority Leader who was successful (although only temporarily) in this quest. Daschle became Minority Leader in 1995 after the Democrats, at the time in the minority, selected him to be their leader in the Senate. When the Democrats took majority control of the Senate after Senator JAMES JEFFORDS (I-VT) left the Republican Party in June 2001, Daschle became the Majority Leader, a position he held until the Republicans won a majority of Senate seats after the 2002 elections, after which Daschle once again became Minority Leader.

The Minority Leader, therefore, has much at stake in the electoral success of his or her party colleagues in the Senate. As a result, Minority Leaders tend to do all they can to help colleagues of their own party when campaigning. The Minority Leader can help other minority party members by offering endorsements, attending receptions in Washington, and traveling to colleagues' home states as attractions to fund-raisers and other events. Minority Leaders also influence the use of the party campaign committees' resources and often contribute small sums themselves.

The Minority Leader has increasingly become an extremely important national spokesperson for his or her party. As television has become the dominant means of political communication, effectiveness as a party spokesperson has become a central ingredient of senators' expectations of the Minority Leader. Minority Leaders are expected to help create a favorable reputation for their party and seek to do so by cultivating favorable media coverage. As such, the success of the Minority Leader is due at least in part to the perception of whether the Minority Leader is helping the national party.

Further reading:
Oleszek, Walter J. *Congressional Procedures and the Policy Process.* Washington, D.C.: Congressional Quarterly Press, 2001; Rieselbach, Leroy N. *Congressional Politics: The Evolving Legislative System.* 2d ed. Boulder, Colo.: Westview Press, 1995; Smith, Steven. "Congress Reconsidered." In *Forces and Change in Senate Party Leadership and Organization,* edited by Lawrence Dodd and Bruce Oppenheimer, Washington, D.C.: Congressional Quarterly Press, 1993..

—Patrick Fisher

Mitchell, George (1933–) *Senator, Senate Majority Leader*

George J. Mitchell was born to Mary Saad, a factory worker, and George Mitchell, a laborer. He spent his youth in Waterville, Maine, attending Waterville High School. He received his bachelor's degree from Bowdoin College in 1954 and became an officer in the U.S. Army. He was stationed in West Berlin, where he was a counterintelligence officer. After leaving the military in 1956, Mitchell earned a law degree from Georgetown University in 1960 and was admitted to the bar in the District of Columbia and the state of Maine later that year.

Mitchell worked as a trial attorney in the U.S. Justice Department's antitrust division for two years (1960–62). He then joined the staff of Senator Edmund S. Muskie, a Democrat from Maine, as his executive assistant, serving from 1962 to 1965. Muskie would play a major role in Mitchell's political career.

In 1965 he returned to Maine to practice law in Portland while taking an active role in Democratic Party politics. He was state chair of the Democratic Party (1966–68) and a member of the Democratic National Committee (1969–77). Following the 1968 Democratic National Convention, Mitchell was a member of the Commission on Structure and Delegate Selection of the Democratic National Committee, which was known as the McGovern Commission after its chair, South Dakota senator George McGovern. The commission initiated major reforms in the party's delegate selection process, including the requirement that delegates to the national convention be selected through caucuses or primaries and that they be distributed among the candidates through a system of proportional representation based on the primary or caucus result. These measures opened the nomination process to party "outsiders" while diminishing the influence of national and state party leaders and organized labor. In 1972 he unsuccessfully sought election as chair of the Democratic National Committee, losing to Robert S. Strauss of Texas. He was deputy director of Muskie's vice presidential campaign (1968) and of his unsuccessful campaign for the Democratic Party's presidential nomination in 1972.

Mitchell made his first foray into electoral politics in 1974, when he was an unsuccessful candidate for governor of Maine. Winning the Democratic nomination in a primary campaign in which he promised to protect the environment and build a strong economy, Mitchell and the Republican candidate, James Erwin, were upset by James Longley, an independent.

In 1977 President Jimmy Carter appointed Mitchell the U.S. attorney for Maine. In 1979 Carter named Mitchell to a newly created U.S. district court judgeship. In May of 1980, Mitchell was appointed by Governor Joseph Brennan to the U.S. Senate to complete the unexpired term of Muskie, who became secretary of State in the Carter administration following the failed rescue on April 25, 1980, of Americans held hostage at the U.S. embassy in Iran. Cyrus Vance, Muskie's predecessor, resigned because he had opposed the rescue plan. Mitchell was recommended for all three appointments by Muskie.

Senator Mitchell was elected to the seat in his own right in 1982, with 61 percent of the vote, defeating Congressman David Emery, the Republican candidate, and reelected in 1988 with 81 percent of the vote, the highest percentage ever received by a candidate in a contested statewide election in the state's history.

In the Senate Mitchell served on the Finance Committee (1980–94), the Environment and Public Works Committee (1980–94), the Veterans Affairs Committee (1980–94), the Governmental Affairs Committee (1987–88), and the Joint Select Committee on the Iran-Contra Affair (1987) and, by virtue of his position as Majority Leader, served as a nonvoting ex-officio member of the Senate Select Intelligence Committee (1989–94).

Mitchell's work led to the enactment of nursing home standards in 1987 and the evaluation of medical care outcomes in 1989. In the environmental policy field Mitchell played a major role in the reauthorization of the CLEAN AIR ACT in 1987 and 1990, the latter including new controls on acid rain toxins. He also wrote and sponsored the North American Wetlands Conservation Act of 1989, which provided for funding for conservation projects and for the protection of additional acreage.

Mitchell rose to prominence in the Senate for his part in the Iran-contra scandal. He was appointed to the senate select committee investigating the arms-for-hostages plan engineered by members of President Ronald Reagan's National Security Council staff. Under the plan military aid for the Nicaragua contra rebels was provided between October 1984 and 1986, notwithstanding a prohibition on such aid. The aid was financed with funds obtained through the sale of U.S. arms to Iran, in violation of stated policy. Linked to these sales was the release of American hostages being held by Islamic radical groups. In response both houses of Congress appointed select committees. Mitchell's performance on the committee made him a prominent national political figure and helped him become Senate Majority Leader.

In his first full term (1983–89) in the Senate, Mitchell moved into the ranks of Democratic Party leadership. In 1984 he was appointed chair of the Democratic Senatorial Campaign Committee (DSCC). Under his leadership the Democrats gained 11 seats in the 1986 midterm elections and recaptured control of the Senate for the first time since 1980. In 1987 he became cochair of the Democratic Policy Committee. He was also elected by his colleagues to Deputy President Pro Tempore of the Senate in recognition of his work with the DSCC. Following the 1988 elections, when Robert Byrd of West Virginia resigned to become President Pro Tempore of the Senate, Mitchell was elected to replace him as Senate Majority Leader, a position he held until he retired from the Senate in 1995.

As Majority Leader, Mitchell led the Senate in passing the Americans with Disabilities Act, which extended civil rights protection to the disabled. Other significant legislation enacted under Mitchell's leadership included the Minimum Wage Act of 1989, which raised the wage for the lowest-paid working Americans; the Intermodal Surface Transportation Equity Act (ISTEA) of 1990, which pro-

vided additional federal funding for highways, railroads, and urban mass transportation systems; the North American Free Trade Agreement, which eliminated (over a period of time) trade barriers between the United States, Canada, and Mexico; and the creation of the World Trade Organization.

In 1994 Mitchell announced he would not run for reelection. Shortly thereafter, President Bill Clinton offered him the seat on the Supreme Court being vacated by Harry Blackmun. Mitchell declined, stating that he wanted to work on health care reform during his remaining time in the Senate.

After leaving the Senate Mitchell returned to practicing law, joining the firm Piper, Rudnick in Washington, D.C., as a partner. While no longer in the Senate, Mitchell became an important actor in international politics. As President Clinton's special adviser for economic initiatives in Ireland, Mitchell worked for three years (1995–98), first organizing a conference on trade and investment in Northern Ireland and later brokering an agreement among the governments of the Republic of Ireland, Great Britain, and Northern Ireland, and a number of Northern Ireland's political parties. The Belfast Agreement (also known as the Good Friday Agreement), signed April 10, 1998, was approved by public referendum on May 22, 1998. The agreement's key provisions included the establishment of a Northern Ireland legislative assembly and created a British-Irish Council and other bodies that would facilitate cooperation between the governments and a commitment that Northern Ireland's future would be decided by democratic means. For his efforts Mitchell received the Presidential Medal of Freedom, the Philadelphia Liberty Medal, the Truman Institute Peace Prize, and the UN Educational, Scientific and Cultural Organization (UNESCO) Peace Prize.

As President Clinton's second term neared its end, he again called on Mitchell, asking him to chair the Sharm el-Sheikh International Fact Finding Committee, which was charged with making recommendations to allow the state of Israel and the Palestinian Authority to resume their peace process. The report of the committee, submitted to President George W. Bush in April 2001, called on the parties to reaffirm their commitments to existing agreements, cease hostile actions, and resume peace negotiations. Despite the recommendations, the violence in the region continues.

Mitchell's post-Senate positions have included chancellor of the Queen's University of Belfast (1999 to the present), president of the Economic Club of Washington (1999 to the present), chair of the International Crisis Group (1995 to the present), a nonprofit organization dedicated to the prevention of crises in international affairs, and chair of the board of directors of the Walt Disney Company (2004 to the present).

Further reading:

Gould, Alberta. *George Mitchell, in Search of Peace.* Farmington, Maine: Heritage Publishing, 1996; Mitchell, George J. *Making Peace.* New York: Knopf, 1999; Mitchell, George. *Not for Americans Alone: The Triumph of Democracy and the Fall of Communism.* New York: Kodansha International, 1997; Mitchell, George. *World on Fire: Saving an Endangered Earth.* New York: Scribner, 1991.

—Jeffrey Kraus

morning hour

Morning hour refers to the opening period in both the HOUSE OF REPRESENTATIVES and SENATE when formalities and routine business transpire. Unfortunately, the term is something of a misnomer because these activities need not occur before the noon hour, and the time involved may exceed an hour. Tradition constrains both chambers from revising the name.

On most days the House formally convenes at or after the noon hour. However, the floor is available up to 90 minutes before the gaveling of the formal session, and members may speak for five minutes on any subject they wish. Time must be reserved in advance and is split equally between both parties. This is known as morning hour speeches. These speeches became an important vehicle in the 1980s for dissatisfied Republican conservatives, as they used the time to criticize the Democratic majority and its legislative programs. Broadcast over C-SPAN, the speakers became champions of the radical right. In response, the SPEAKER OF THE HOUSE, THOMAS P. ("TIP") O'NEILL (D-MA) ordered the C-SPAN cameras to pan the empty chamber in an attempt to discredit the speakers. The practice of highly partisan speeches continues today during the morning hour.

Once the House officially convenes, usually in the early afternoon, the daily order of business is conducted: a prayer is offered by the House CHAPLAIN, the Pledge of Allegiance is recited, the journal for the previous day's session is approved, and messages are officially accepted from the president and the Senate. One-minute speeches may also be delivered as well as corrections and insertions to the CONGRESSIONAL RECORD. This routine business is the morning hour, though it may absorb only 30 minutes or extend to more than two hours.

For approximately the first two hours after formally convening, usually in the early afternoon, the Senate's morning hour occurs. The order of the proceedings is roll call of members; prayer; the Pledge of Allegiance; a reading of the journal of the previous day's activities; petitions, memorials, and other communications; introduction of bills and resolutions of all types by senators; the filing of committee reports; and the receipt of bills and resolutions from the House and messages from the president and cabinet secretaries. Senate leaders may request unanimous consent to dispense with the morning hour or any part of it. Additionally, unanimous consent may also be sought by the leadership to have members speak for up to five minutes on any subject they wish. The time may be extended via unanimous consent. These speeches are sometimes referred to as morning business. Senate rules permit its committees to hold meetings during morning hour.

Because it is most common for the Senate to recess rather than adjourn at the end of a calendar day, a morning hour would not occur at the next meeting of the Senate. Instead, unanimous consent may be sought to conduct morning business and receive communications from the House and government officials.

Further reading:

Oleszek, Walter J. *Congressional Procedures and the Policy Process.* 5th ed. Washington, D.C.: Congressional Quarterly Press, 2001.

—Thomas J. Baldino

Morris, Robert (1734–1806) *Senator*

Robert Morris was a senator from Pennsylvania (1789–95). His six-year term in the U.S. Senate marked the culmination of a career spent in public service. Born in Liverpool, England, on January 20, 1734, Morris immigrated to the United States in 1747. Morris's father, a tobacco exporter in Maryland, died in 1750, leaving Morris an orphan. He entered into an extremely successful trading partnership with Thomas Willing in 1751. In 1769 Morris married Mary White. The couple had five sons and two daughters. He was a signer of the Declaration of Independence and had also served in the Continental Congress, the Pennsylvania assembly, and the Federal Convention and as superintendent of Finance during the Revolutionary War. Morris's biographers report that he was Washington's first choice for secretary of the Treasury, and it was only after Morris declined the position and recommended Alexander Hamilton that Washington nominated Hamilton to the post, though the accuracy of these reports has recently been challenged.

As superintendent of Finance, Morris was one of the most powerful figures in the country. Moreover, in this capacity his public responsibilities and private business interests converged, as the Continental Congress contracted with his trading company. He most likely used his personal credit to secure public loans and perhaps vice versa. Morris worked tirelessly to secure funding for the war effort and afterwards to stabilize the economy of the young nation. Under the Articles of Confederation, Morris proposed establishing a federally chartered bank, funding the debt, creating a federal mint and currency, and creating a permanent system of taxation.

During his tenure in the U.S. Senate, Morris was instrumental in securing the passage of Hamilton's economic program, arguably the most important legislative issue of the early Congress, which not coincidentally bore a striking resemblance to the plan he proposed under the Articles of Confederation. Morris enjoyed close personal and professional relationships with both George Washington and Alexander Hamilton, and it was through these relationships that he assumed the role of floor leader with respect to the economic program. Morris was possibly Washington's closest friend and political adviser during his tenure as president. The Morrises were frequent guests at Washington's dinners and levees. Both Robert and Mary Morris are said to have occupied "places of honor" immediately to the right of the host and hostess. While the federal government was housed in Philadelphia, the Washingtons lived at the home of Robert and Mary Morris (190 High Street), and the Morrises moved to another house just down the street.

Probably the most important legislative proposal and certainly the most important proposal from the executive branch in the first Senate was Hamilton's economic program. While the source of the ideas and inspiration for Hamilton's financial program is a matter of some dispute, there seems little doubt that one of the individuals he did consult was Robert Morris. Hamilton's financial program was based on the goal of consolidating all state and federal debts and indefinitely financing these debts rather than retiring them in the foreseeable future. A permanently funded debt would have the advantage of inducing stability not only in the public credit but also in land values and assuring an adequate money supply. Paying off the debt immediately was an option Hamilton never addressed in his report since the foreign debt alone was just over $10 million. Hamilton did not view it as either feasible or desirable to raise enough revenue to retire the debt since it would have a long-term negative impact on the young economy. The financial program consisted of four separate yet interdependent and interrelated bills. The first provided for the federal government to assume state debts. The second reduced the interest rate. Hamilton proposed giving foreign investors some alternatives to a straight cut in interest rates. Investors could refuse the interest rate reduction, but their payments would be given the lowest priority in annual appropriations. Hamilton proposed a 4-percent interest rate and offered creditors land in exchange for the reduction. Finally, investors had the option of retaining the 6-percent interest rate with a severe limitation imposed on principal that could be redeemed in a single year. Moreover, Hamilton proposed to increase revenue by raising taxes on coffee, tea, and liquor. Finally, Hamilton proposed the creation of a sinking fund for the purpose of financing the debt over the long term. The fund would consist of surplus revenues and a new foreign loan.

Hamilton found himself, however, in an awkward position with respect to his economic program. Congress had instructed him to prepare this report, and it was clear that both Congress and Washington expected him to lead the young republic toward financial stability. At the same time, both the House and the Senate jealously guarded their institutional turf and resisted Hamilton's efforts to turn grave concern over the economy into a precedent that compromised the legislature's independence by allowing executive department officials to appear before Congress to present their proposals. Moreover, Hamilton's financial program, which ultimately came before Congress as five separate bills, required each of those elements in order to be successful, though some modest compromises were possible without undermining the whole program. Morris sincerely supported Hamilton's proposal, no doubt in part because it was partially based on his own ideas and philosophy of public finance. In addition, Morris had the political connections, the knowledge, and the leadership skills to effectively serve as the committee chair, floor leader, and whip that Hamilton needed in the Senate.

Morris was an active participant in Senate committees. He is reported to have served on 44 committees and reported for 16 of them. He primarily served on committees that dealt with trade and commerce issues. In regard to Hamilton's financial program, he served on committees that dealt with settlement of accounts, payment of debts, settlement of accounts and funding, duties on distilled spirits, duties on teas, and the National Bank. Moreover, Morris reported for three of these committees (settlement of accounts, duties on distilled spirits, and the National Bank) that dealt with some of the most contentious issues. The assumption of state debts and the question of creating a national bank were widely regarded as among the most contentious issues of the Hamilton financial program. While the Senate did not formally designate a chair or convener, the senator listed first in the Senate Journal was responsible for reporting to the Senate the results of the committee's deliberations.

Beleaguered by charges of mismanagement of public funds and profiteering, in 1790 Morris requested a congressional investigation into his conduct as superintendent of Finance and was cleared of any wrongdoing. His woes did not end there, however. In the 1780s Morris had attempted to corner the market on tobacco trade with France. The failure of those ventures depleted his considerable fortune and left him in debt. In an effort to recoup his losses, he turned to land speculation. When those investments did not yield the expected returns, Morris found himself unable to pay his creditors. One of his creditors, probably Charles Eddy, had him arrested, and he was jailed in debtors' prison from 1798 to 1801. Two years after his imprisonment, Congress passed the bankruptcy act, which led to his release in 1801. Morris died in Philadelphia in 1806.

Further reading:
Chernow, Barbara Ann. *Robert Morris: Land Speculator, 1790–1801.* New York: Arno Press, 1978; DiGiacomantonio, William Charles. "Robert Morris." In *Documentary History of the First Federal Congress, 1789–91,* edited by Kenneth Bowling, Charlene Bangs Bickford, Helen Veit, and William Charles DiGiacomantonio, Baltimore: Johns Hopkins University Press, 1995; Nuxoll, Elizabeth. "The Financier as Senator: Robert Morris of Pennsylvania, 1789–1795." In *Neither Separate nor Equal: Congress in the 1790s,* edited by Kenneth Bowling and Donald R. Kennon. Athens: Ohio University Press, 2000; Oberholtzer, Ellis Paxson. *Robert Morris: Patriot and Financier.* New York: Macmillan, 1903; Sumner, William Graham. *The Financier and the Finances of the American Revolution.* 2 vols. New York: Augustus M. Kelley, 1968; Young, Eleanor. *Forgotten Patriot: Robert Morris.* New York: Macmillan, 1950.

—Kim Maslin-Wicks

motions, Senate

Motions are an important aspect of Congress. They are necessary to the legislative process, which, in the SENATE, operates largely by UNANIMOUS CONSENT. When senators cannot reach a unanimous consent, motions are used in order to continue the process. If it were not for motions, the voting stage could not be reached. They allow senators to consider and dispose of bills and legislation. Different motions can be used to support or oppose a bill. This is important especially for the minority party members, who can use motions to make their voices heard. Each motion has a specific function. Senators can offer motions only when the presiding officer recognizes them.

In his article on motions in the Senate in the third edition of the *Encyclopedia of the United States Congress,* Robert B. Dove noted that the most used motions in the Senate are the motion to proceed to consideration and the motion to invoke CLOTURE. The motion to proceed to consideration is used when the Majority Leader wants to proceed to bills that are on the CALENDAR. It can be used only when the bill has been on the calendar for at least one legislative day and a report has been available for 48 hours in a printed version. This motion is debatable, and a majority vote is needed to carry the motion.

The motion to invoke cloture is used to limit the amount of time spent on debate. After a cloture motion has passed, all activities cease after 30 hours, including the procedural motions and votes, which can greatly increase the amount of time spent on debate. This motion is also debatable, and it needs three-fifths of the total membership of the Senate to pass.

Some other motions used in the Senate include the MOTION TO TABLE, TO RECONSIDER, and to adjourn or recess. The motion to reconsider is used following a vote, giving senators a chance to change their votes. It can be offered only by a senator who has not voted or a senator who voted with the wining side and only on the day of the vote or during the following two days of session.

The motion to table is used to block legislation from being passed or other motions from being adopted. In order for the motion to be adopted, it requires a majority vote. If a tabling motion is approved, it is not debatable and is considered the final disposition on that issue. Senators in general prefer to block a motion rather than bills, especially when a controversial bill is in question. This way they do not go on record as voting directly on the bill. A motion to table is usually offered after a motion to reconsider.

The Senate ends its session by a motion to adjourn or to recess. The motion to recess is more commonly used since it is followed by fewer requirements than the motion to adjourn. When the Senate recesses, it picks up its activities right where it left off; if it adjourns, the legislative day ends and a new one begins at the next meeting, starting with some time-consuming activities. Adjournment is sometimes necessary since the Senate can consider a piece of legislation only after it has been on the calendar for at least one legislative day and also since the only way to begin a legislative day is by adjourning.

According to the rules of the Senate, some motions have precedence over others. For example, a motion to table has precedence over a motion to reconsider. The senators then vote on the motion to table, and if it is adopted the motion to reconsider becomes cancelled. The motion to adjourn takes precedence over the motion to table. Therefore, an offer to adjourn cannot be blocked by a motion to table the request to adjourn.

Some motions in the Senate are necessary to daily procedures, while others are clearly used to delay those procedures. It all depends on whether the senators use them for the purposes for which they were created.

Further reading:
Congressional Quarterly. *How Congress Works.* Washington, D.C.: Congressional Quarterly Books, 1998; Greenberg, Ellen. *The House and Senate Explained: The People's Guide to Congress.* New York: Norton, 1996.

—Arthur Holst

motion to reconsider (House)

One of the rules of the HOUSE OF REPRESENTATIVES is the motion to reconsider. This allows representatives to take a second look at their voting decisions on a certain piece of legislation. The motion to reconsider a vote provides the representatives with the opportunity to affirm or change their mind about a vote they have cast. If it is adopted within two days of a vote, then the vote is held again. The motion to reconsider is adopted only if it receives a majority vote.

The motion to reconsider can be made by any member of the majority in the House, and when adopted it takes precedence over all other questions except when a conference report or a motion to adjourn are being considered. Once offered, the motion to reconsider cannot be withdrawn following the first day without the consent of the House.

A representative can make a motion to reconsider at any time without discarding a motion that he or she has previously made and that is still pending. During House proceedings a delegate or resident commissioner may not make this motion. When the representatives have voted on a bill or resolution and the outcome is a tie vote or two-thirds, then only a member of the prevailing side can make a motion to reconsider. If the individual votes have not been recorded in the journal, any member of the House can propose a motion to reconsider, regardless of whether he or she voted for the prevailing side. A member of the House who is absent or does not vote cannot make a motion to reconsider. Members who cast their votes by proxy, when proxy voting is permitted, are also not allowed to make a motion to reconsider.

Even though a bill or resolution may have gone to the Senate or the president, a motion to reconsider it can still be adopted. This, however, can be achieved only by unanimous consent. If a bill, petition, memorial, or resolution has been referred to a committee or is reported from a committee for printing and recommitment, it cannot be brought back into the House through a motion to reconsider.

During House proceedings the motion to reconsider is usually followed by a motion to table (or to lay on the table), which is meant to "kill" the bill is being discussed or voted on. This motion can be countered by the motion to reconsider, and, if adopted, the representatives recast their votes on whether to adopt or reject the motion to table. A motion to reconsider can be laid on the table only before the chair of the House has put it to a vote. These tactics are usually used to either change the outcome of a very close vote or as a delaying tactic to consume floor time. The motion to reconsider can be either debatable or undebatable, depending on whether the question that is proposed to be reconsidered is debatable.

Further reading:
Johnson, Charles W. *Constitution Jefferson's Manual and Rules of the House of Representatives of the United States One Hundred Fifth Congress.* Washington, D.C.: Government Printing Office, 1997; Jefferson, Thomas. *A Manual of Parliamentary Practice for the Use of the Senate of the United States.* Washington, D.C.: Government Printing Office, Reprint edition, 1993.

—Arthur Holst

motion to reconsider (Senate)

One of the rules of the SENATE is the motion to reconsider. This allows senators to take a second look at their voting decisions on a certain piece of legislature. The motion to reconsider a vote provides senators with the opportunity to affirm or change their mind about the vote they have cast. This motion is usually followed by a MOTION TO TABLE, which prevents the motion to reconsider from being adopted. After the motion to reconsider has been tabled, the voting outcome stands unaffected.

Before a motion to reconsider can be adopted, it has to be offered by a senator. Once it has been offered, it then has to be called to reconsider. After the motion to reconsider has been called, the Senate votes on whether it will adopt it. In order for the motion to reconsider to be adopted, it needs a majority vote of the senators present on that day of the session. If it is adopted and the legislation that is being reconsidered is not debatable, then the senators recast their votes without debate. If, on the other hand, the legislation that is being reconsidered is debatable, they begin by debating and then vote on the question.

During Senate proceedings those senators satisfied with the outcome of a vote usually like to keep it from being changed. In order to make sure that this happens, two senators rise at the same time, and one moves to reconsider while the other follows by moving to table, thus locking in the vote.

The motion to reconsider is used following a vote and can be offered only once. It can be offered only by senators who have not voted or senators who voted with the wining side. The time restrictions on this motion allow the senators to offer the motion to reconsider only on the day of the vote or during the following two days of the session. Whenever the motion to reconsider a vote is adopted, the senators recast their votes.

Once a motion to reconsider a vote has been adopted, no other motion to reconsider can be adopted unless it is done so by unanimous consent. Once a bill that has been voted on has moved from the Senate to the HOUSE OF REPRESENTATIVES, a motion to reconsider can still be offered, but only if it is accompanied by a motion to request the House to adopt a motion to reconsider, which it adopts immediately. If the legislation does not pass the House, no more motions to reconsider can be offered.

When voting outcomes are close, sometimes party leaders of the losing side change their votes in order to be on the winning side only so they can get the chance to present a motion to reconsider and hopefully persuade other senators to change their votes in order to change the outcome of the vote. This, however, is unlikely and does not happen often.

Further reading:
Slack, Lana R. *Senate Manual Containing the Standing Rules, Orders, Laws, and Resolutions Affecting the Business of the United States Senate: Declaration of Independence, Articles of Confederation, Ordinance of 1787 and the Constitution of the United States.* Washington, D.C.: Government Printing Office, 1993; U.S. Senate. Reconsideration. Available online. URL: www.senate.gov/legislative/common/briefing/Standing_Rules_Senate.htm. Accessed January 17, 2006.

—Arthur Holst

motion to table

A motion to table a proposition or for a measure to be laid on the table, if adopted by a majority vote, has the effect of permanently killing a pending measure and ending any further debate on it in both the U.S. HOUSE OF REPRESENTATIVES and the SENATE. Tabling a proposition under consideration is a widely used parliamentary procedure. It is not debatable and cannot be amended.

When members of Congress assemble to transact business, they use parliamentary procedure to conduct their business with speed and efficiency while safeguarding the privileges of the individual members. Article I, Section 5, of the U.S. Constitution authorizes each chamber to determine rules governing its proceedings. Accordingly, both the House and the Senate have adopted such rules, and the rules associated with motions to table are somewhat different in each chamber, partly because the House is larger than is the Senate, and bigger groups have found it helpful to be more strict and formal in conducting their business.

Under the Standing Rules of the Senate a motion to lay on the table is in order any time a measure is pending before the Senate, except in instances in which Rule XXII provides precedence or priority to other privileged motions (e.g., to adjourn, to recess, or to proceed to consider executive business such as nominations and treaties). If the Senate is debating an amendment and the tabling motion for that amendment is successful, Rule XV indicates it will not prejudice or adversely affect the underlying bill or measure that was subject to amendment.

Consequently, the Senate has made great use of the motion to table. For example, tabling motions on amendments effectively end debate on those pending amendments and can be used to defeat amendments without having senators being recorded as voting for or against the specific amendments. While procedural votes in favor of tabling have the same effect as voting negatively on substantive amendments, they often do not carry with them recorded votes that could bring political consequences. Indeed, motions to table can often secure more votes than can votes against amendments because members can avoid direct yes-or-no votes on those measures. Moreover, because a tabling motion is not subject to debate, this motion is also useful to immediately kill the amendment that would otherwise take up more time in debate. Tabling motions can also test the strength or support for the amendment.

Great use of the motion to table is made in the Senate in connection with the MOTION TO RECONSIDER a vote taken on the same day or on either of the next two days of sessions thereafter. Motions to reconsider allow senators to change their minds about their previous votes and can be made by any senator who voted with the prevailing side or who did not vote. Rule XIII authorizes a vote to lay on the table motion that has precedence over the motion to reconsider, and if the motion to table the motion to reconsider is successful, no further motion to reconsider can be made except by unanimous consent, thus routinely bringing final disposition to the original vote approving a measure.

In the House there are more restrictions on the tabling motion. Unlike the Senate, where the tabling of proposed amendments does not affect the underlying bill or measure, the tabling of an amendment in the House does have the effect of also tabling the underlying proposition and is therefore less used. Furthermore, this motion is not in order in a number of instances, such as motions to adjourn and other propositions that are not debatable or amendable. When the tabling motion is made orally from the floor, it is subject to a timely demand that it be in writing (this is also the case in the Senate). Lastly, while in some instances it is in order in the House, it is never in order in the COMMITTEE OF THE WHOLE, where much of the work of this chamber is done, including work on bills and resolutions, Senate amendments involving taxes, raising revenue, and making appropriations.

Congressional practice in the use of the motion to lay on the table does differ noticeably from general parliamentary usage, such as under Robert's Rules of Order. Under Robert's Rules a motion to lay on the table is used to set aside the matter temporarily for more urgent business. However, as explained above, the tabling motion in both the House and the Senate is generally equivalent to a final disposition of the matter and does not merely represent a refusal to consider.

Further reading:
Schneider, Judy. *House and Senate Rules of Procedure: A Comparison.* Washington, D.C.: Congressional Research Service, 2001; U.S. House of Representatives. Constitution, *Jefferson's Manual, and Rules of the House of Representatives.* 108th Congress. Compiled by Charles W. Johnson, Parliamentarian. 107th Cong., 2d sess., 2001. H. Doc. 107-284; U.S. House of Representatives. *House Practice: A Guide to the Rules, Precedents, and Procedures of the House.* Compiled by William Holmes Brown and Charles W. Johnson. 108th Cong., 1st sess., 2003; U.S. Senate. *Riddick's Senate Procedure: Precedents and Practices.* 101st Cong. 2d Session, 1992. S. Doc. 101-28; U.S. Senate. *Senate Committee on Rules and Administration. Authority and Rules of Senate Committees, 2003–2004: A Compilation of the Authority and Rules of Senate and Joint Committees, and Related Materials.* 108th Cong., 1st sess., 2003. S. Doc. 108-6.

—Robert P. Goss

N

Narcotics Abuse and Control, House Select Committee on

A select committee in the HOUSE OF REPRESENTATIVES from 1976 until 1993, the Narcotics Abuse and Control Committee studied and reviewed the problems of narcotics abuse and control. The House created the Select Narcotics Abuse and Control Committee in July 1976. The committee's original mission was to conduct a continuing comprehensive study and review of the problems of narcotics abuse and control. It also was given the task of reviewing any recommendations made by the president or any executive agency relating to narcotic drug programs and policies. The creation of the select committee was a response to the growing concerns over drug abuse and control problems in the country. The committee's original sponsors argued that this issue was too broad for any one standing committee to supply adequate oversight.

The SPEAKER OF THE HOUSE appointed the members of the committee. At least one member had to be chosen from each of the following standing committees with jurisdiction over some aspect of the drug issue: Agriculture, Armed Services, Government Operations, Foreign Affairs, Energy and Commerce, Judiciary, Merchant Marine and Fisheries, Veterans' Affairs, and Ways and Means. The first committee consisted of 12 Democrats and six Republicans. The final committee consisted of 21 Democrats and 14 Republicans.

The select committee had only three chairs, all Democrats from New York City. In the 94th through the 96th Congresses, Lester L. Wolff was the chair. Leo C. Zefferetti was the chair during the 97th Congress. In the 98th Congress through the 102nd Congress, the chair was Charles B. Rangel.

Much of the select committee's work revolved around reviewing the efforts of executive branch agencies and presidential initiatives in the area of drug control. Despite the fact that throughout most of its existence the committee had to work with Republican administrations, it regularly supported many executive branch initiatives. Primarily, the committee advocated increases in federal resources for antidrug programs.

As a select committee, it did not have any legislative authority. It could work to enact legislation only by advising standing committees. The select committee's greatest success was in keeping drug abuse and control a priority on the national policy agenda. Some observers also credit the committee and its chairs with getting cooperation from other governments in the American antidrug effort.

Select committees are temporary bodies and have to be reconstituted at the beginning of each Congress. The Select Committee on Narcotics Abuse and Control was regularly reauthorized by wide vote margins in the House. The first real threat to the committee's existence came in December 1992, while the Democrats were reorganizing for the 103rd Congress to start in January 1993. Maryland representative Benjamin L. Cardin led an effort to phase out House select committees by limiting their reauthorization to one year instead of the traditional two years of each Congress. Cardin's plan was approved by the House Democratic leadership, but strenuous opposition by Representative Charles Rangel, the chair of the Select Narcotics Abuse and Control Committee, forced the leadership to change its mind.

On January 26, 1993, the House of Representatives voted 180-237 against a resolution that would have reauthorized the Select Committee on Narcotics Abuse and Control for the 103rd Congress. Those who voted against the resolution argued that the select committee had outlived its usefulness and was a waste of money. The ranks of the opponents included Democrats and Republicans, veteran House members and freshmen. To continue his efforts to reduce the flow of illegal drugs into the United States and to solve the nation's continuing drug abuse crisis, the last chair of the select committee, Charles Rangel, established the Congressional Narcotics Abuse and Control Caucus.

Further reading:

Alston, Chuck, and Richard Sammon. "Foley Foresees Quiet Death for Select Committees." *Congressional Quarterly Weekly Report.* 20 March 1993; Kurke, Martin L. "Congressional Review of National Problems in Drug Abuse and Its Control." *Behavioral Sciences & the Law* 3, no. 3 (1985): 241–248; Ponessa, Jeanne. "Fate of Select Panels in Doubt after House Rejects One." *Congressional Quarterly Weekly Report,* 30 January 1993, p. 207.

—John David Rausch, Jr.

National Labor Relations Board (NLRB) v. Jones & Laughlin Steel Corp. 301 U.S. 1 (1937)

In 1935 Congress passed the National Labor Relations Act (NLRA) as part of Franklin D. Roosevelt's New Deal package. The NLRA was designed to protect interstate commerce from injuries caused by industrial strife. The act provided for collective bargaining, or in other words, open contract negotiations, between employees and employers. Prior to 1935 such attempted negotiations by employees were often met with the firing of those who sought to negotiate and the hiring of new employees willing to work for whatever the employer was willing to pay. Aspects of employment other than wages, such as leave, health benefits, hours of employment, and working conditions, were similarly not open to negotiation for most companies. Congress viewed this as a hindrance to productivity during the time of economic recovery of the New Deal. The NLRA did not require that an agreement be reached, only that the employer negotiate in good faith.

Jones & Laughlin Steel Corp., as well as the other corporations involved in the case, including transportation, hauling, and clothing corporations, challenged the constitutionality of the act. They claimed that because their business was conducted within the borders of a single state, they were not engaged in interstate commerce sufficiently to allow Congress to regulate their business. The Supreme Court held that Congress did have the right to regulate these and other corporations because they were engaged in interstate commerce since most of the raw materials used in the manufacturing of the products and the final products were shipped in interstate commerce. This expansive reading of the Commerce Clause was a significant change from previous interpretations of New Deal programs. Those previous rulings had limited Congress's ability to regulate wages, hours of employment, working conditions, and even child labor. Until this case Congress was limited primarily to regulating only products that were actually shipped in interstate commerce, not the businesses themselves.

This case was important beyond its impact on regulating labor and interstate commerce. The famous "switch in time that saved nine" came about through this case. The Supreme Court's anti–New Deal stance in a series of cases led President Franklin D. Roosevelt to propose a change in the membership of the Supreme Court. While short of impeachment Congress may not remove a justice from the Supreme Court, Congress does have the power to increase the number of justices serving on the Court. The proposal considered by Congress was to increase the number of justices by adding a junior justice for each senior justice over the age of 75. The plan would have increased the Court in 1937 to 15 justices and would have given President Roosevelt the opportunity to appoint six justices who would presumably support the New Deal programs. The justices on the Court seemed to change their minds about the constitutionality of New Deal programs almost overnight in this decision.

Congress's commerce power continued to expand with the support of the Supreme Court from the 1940s through the 1980s, when the power was once again limited by the Supreme Court, but only marginally. *NLRB v. Jones & Laughlin Steel* opened the door for Congress to regulate almost all aspects of any business with even a minimal relation to interstate commerce. This included regulation of race and gender discrimination and even regulating subsistence farming even when the products of the farm were solely consumed by the residents of the farm, since such farming affects interstate commerce because the farmer was able to avoid purchasing those self-produced commodities on the open market, reducing purchase of interstate commerce goods. As a result of the Court's ruling in *NLRB v. Jones and Laughlin Steel,* the Court remained with nine members, though eight of the nine members of the Court in 1937 retired by 1941. Congress gained constitutional authority to regulate interstate commerce extensively, and President Roosevelt saved the New Deal programs.

Further reading:

Baker, Leonard. *Back to Back: The Duel between FDR and the Supreme Court.* New York: Macmillan, 1967; *Hammer v. Dagenhart,* 247 U.S. 251 1918; *Heart of Atlanta Hotel v. United States,* 379 U.S. 241 1964; Howard, John R. *The Shifting Wind: The Supreme Court and Civil Rights from Reconstruction to Brown.* Albany: State University of New York Press, 1999; McKenna, Marian C. *Franklin Roosevelt and the Great Constitutional War: The Court-Packing Crisis of 1937.* New York: Fordham University Press, 2002; *National Labor Relations Board (NLRB) v. Jones & Laughlin Steel Corp.,* 301 U.S. 1 1937; *Wickard v. Filburn,* 317 U.S. 111. 1942.

—Corey Ditslear

Natural Resources, House Committee on

The House Natural Resources Committee is concerned with legislation dealing primarily with the use of natural resources. The committee includes five subcommittees, Energy and Mineral Resources Subcommittee; Fisheries

Conservation, Wildlife and Oceans Subcommittee; Forests and Forest Health Subcommittee; National Parks Recreation and Public Land Subcommittee; and Water and Power Subcommittee, designed to address topics of the committee more specifically.

This committee is traditionally comprised of a majority of representatives from the western United States, who frequently deal with the committee's legislative outputs in their represented areas. The role of the Resources Committee in the U.S. Congress has expanded throughout its existence. Today this committee holds primary jurisdiction over most environmental issues and policy.

The committee began under the name Committee on Public Lands in 1805. The transitory jurisdiction of this committee caused largely by changes in HOUSE OF REPRESENTATIVES leadership has led to its renaming over its 200 years in existence. The 1946 committee reforms designated primary environmental issues in the scope of the Committee on Public Lands as a result of the consolidation of 44 committees into 19. A renaming of this committee occurred in 1951 to become the Committee on Interior and Insular Affairs. The 1995 committee reforms changed the name and scope of the Natural Resources Committee. Republicans changed the name from Natural Resources to its name today, Resources Committee. Merchant and Marine Fisheries, which once was its own committee, was placed under Resources, as was endangered species jurisdiction. This committee has a history with other committees, invariably claiming jurisdiction from Commerce, Military Affairs, Indian Affairs, and Agriculture over environmental and land issues. Contentious legislation and policy for this committee in the past and present include nuclear waste disposal, water projects, conservation and preservation issues, and petroleum conservation on public lands.

The role of this committee also extends to the insular issues of the nation's policy. Included in this committee is the Office of Native American and Indian Affairs. Policy concerning commonwealths, territories, and freely associated territories of the United States are discussed in this office. Currently, representatives from Guam, Puerto Rico, the Virgin Islands, and American Samoa sit on the committee as nonvoting members.

Due to the multidimensional nature of environmental issues and the way environmental policy often cross-cuts other issue areas, the House Natural Resources Committee must work together with various other committees with related jurisdictions, including but not limited to the committees that deal with energy issues, defense, and transportation (all of which impact the environment). The upside of shared jurisdictions is the possibility of working together and sharing expertise to improve policy making in a given area, such as on the natural environment. Indeed,

committees have done great things in authorizing and funding the CLEAN AIR ACT and the CLEAN WATER ACT, for example. However, when committees with similar jurisdictions do not see things in the same light (i.e., they disagree on preferences or priorities), then committee wrangling can occur. The Natural Resources Committee is one of several institutions on CAPITOL HILL that must walk this tightrope of having to interact with other committees to get things done, but also needs to guard its jurisdiction from encroachment by rival bodies.

Leadership in this committee includes members committed to environmental policy. Morris Udall, a Democrat from Arizona, who sat on the committee for 16 congressional terms, was preceded by Wayne Aspinall, Democrat of Colorado, who for 12 congressional terms sat on the committee. Representative Don Young, Republican from Alaska, is in his 16th term sitting on the committee. As leadership changes in the House and as the composition of natural resource issues evolves, this committee, as it has in the past, is likely to see jurisdictional change and thus change in its composition.

Further reading:
King, David. *Turf Wars: How Congressional Committees Claim Jurisdiction.* Chicago: University of Chicago Press, 1997; Nelson, Garrison. *Committees in the US Congress 1947–1992.* Vol. I. Washington, D.C.: Congressional Quarterly Press, 2002; United States Congress. *Rules of the House of Representatives, Organization of Committees Rule X, 1(I),* 19 January 1999.
—Glen S. Krutz and Justin LeBeau

neutrality debates
In the wake of the disillusionment that followed American participation in World War I and the bitter partisanship that doomed Woodrow Wilson's League of Nations treaty, the American public retreated into isolationism in the 1930s, even as war clouds loomed once again in Europe. Convinced that arms trading and bank loans to belligerents had dragged the country into the Great War in 1917, isolationists in Congress forced President Franklin Delano Roosevelt to acquiesce to a series of neutrality acts designed to keep the United States from involvement in future foreign conflicts. As the Great Depression raged, internationalists and isolationists both within and outside of Congress debated over the best means to promote American exports while simultaneously keeping the country out of another world war.

Concerned over the remilitarization of Germany, Italy, and Japan and fueled by congressional outrage over North Dakota senator Gerald P. Nye's investigation into World War I profiteering by munitions makers, Congress passed the Neutrality Act of 1935 prohibiting arms sales to belligerents following a presidential proclamation that a state of war existed. Despite his concern that the act did not afford him sufficient discretion in deciding when to implement an embargo, Roosevelt signed the legislation in August to avoid a confrontation with the congressional isolationists, led by Nye and Senator Bennett C. Clark of Missouri. By October the president was forced to invoke the new law limiting arms sales following Italy's invasion of Ethiopia, although U.S. exports to Italy of oil, copper, scrap iron, and other materials not covered by the treaty increased sharply. In February 1936 Congress extended the Neutrality Act for another six months and added a prohibition against loans to belligerent governments. Following the outbreak of civil war in Spain in summer 1936, Roosevelt proposed in 1937 that Congress adopt a joint resolution applying the Neutrality Act's arms embargo to civil conflicts as well.

Isolationist sentiments reached their peak early in 1937 following Hitler's remilitarization of the Rhineland, and Congress responded with yet another Neutrality Act in April of that year, prohibiting Americans from traveling on belligerent ships, maintaining restrictions on arms sales and loans to belligerents, and authorizing the president to negotiate the sale of nonprohibited items to nations at war on a cash-and-carry basis. Although Congress's intention was to prevent the country from being drawn into a European war as it had been in the 1910s, President Roosevelt was increasingly concerned that U.S. policy was inadvertently favoring the interests of aggressive powers in Europe and the Far East. Consequently, when Japan attacked China in July, Roosevelt used his discretionary authority under the 1937 act to allow arms and supplies to be sold and shipped to both sides.

By 1938, as Hitler began to make territorial demands in Europe, Roosevelt became increasingly certain that opposing aggression was preferable to keeping the United States out of war, but public opinion and Congress remained unconvinced. Although Roosevelt unsuccessfully lobbied for new legislation to replace the 1937 Neutrality Act that would allow the country to sell arms to Britain and France should war break out, Congress refused to act until after Germany's invasion of Poland on September 1, 1939, started World War II in Europe. At Roosevelt's request Congress, voting largely along party lines, authorized short-term loans and the sale of arms and other materials on a cash-and-carry basis to Britain and France, but prohibited American vessels from transporting war materiel to these countries.

In the months that followed, Roosevelt paid lip service to isolationist demands to remain neutral in the European war from Charles A. Lindbergh's America First Committee, even as he pursued policies to supply Britain and France and to forestall an Axis victory. During the summer of 1940, Roosevelt requested a congressional appropriation of $4 billion in military spending and plotted to evade the Neutrality Acts by "loaning" 50 U.S. destroyers to Britain in return for the lease of British naval bases in the Caribbean, Bermuda, and Newfoundland. As isolationist sentiment wavered in fall 1940, Congress responded to events overseas by instituting the first peacetime draft in U.S. history.

Safely reelected to an unprecedented third term, in 1941 Roosevelt pursued new policies to supply Great Britain with the vital supplies necessary to hold Nazi Germany at bay without running afoul of the Neutrality Acts. Roosevelt proposed to Congress in January 1941 $7 billion for armaments and other military supplies that the president could then transfer through sale, lease, trade, or exchange to any country whose defense was deemed vital to that of the United States. Congress passed the "lend-lease" program two months later, and the aid soon began making its way to Great Britain and, later, the Soviet Union. In the months that followed, the U.S. Navy took an increasingly active role in policing the North Atlantic against German submarines in what would become an undeclared war. By the time of the Japanese attack on Pearl Harbor on December 7, 1941, the congressional debate over neutrality was largely over.

Further reading:
Divine, Robert A. *The Reluctant Belligerent: American Entry into World War II.* New York: Wiley, 1979; Heinrichs, Waldo. *Threshold of War: Franklin D. Roosevelt and American Entry into World War II.* New York: Oxford University Press, 1990; Russett, Bruce M. *No Clear and Present Danger: A Skeptical View of the United States Entry into World War II.* Boulder, Colo.: Westview Press, 1997
—William D. Baker

New Deal

New Deal, as initially conceived, denoted an array of measures directed toward domestic issues that were implemented during the early years of President Franklin D. Roosevelt's (FDR) administration (1933 to 1939). But the term evolved and today is used to refer to FDR's overall public policy, domestic and foreign, during his entire presidency (1933 to 1945). The New Deal approach continues to be reflected in the ideology of the liberal wing of the Democratic Party. Originally, the New Deal legislation represented an active approach to relieve the national crisis precipitated by the Great Depression, when as many as one-fourth the labor force was unemployed. In retrospect, implementation of New Deal initiatives marked the beginning of the transformation of public perception of the appropriate scope of the federal government, from limited (i.e., in Thomas Jefferson's words, "the least government is the best") to positive government (governmental regulation of the economy and promotion of human rights at home and abroad).

Samuel I. Rosenman, a speech writer and close adviser to Roosevelt, drafted the portion of the president-elect's acceptance speech at the June 1932 Democratic National Convention in Chicago that coined the term *New Deal*. Roosevelt's call to action in that speech declared, "I pledge you, I pledge myself, to a new deal for the American people. Let us all here assembled constitute ourselves prophets of a new order of competence and courage." Later, in his first inaugural address, Roosevelt implied that his New Deal extended abroad. He announced a "Good Neighbor" policy toward Latin America. The characterizations were picked up and repeated in the media. Today the New Deal represents the greatest legislative program of the 20th century. The Good Neighbor policy identifies a period in which the United States became friendlier to Latin America than at any other time in history and stopped American military interventions there for several decades.

Unlike the British Labour Party's blueprint for the creation of its social welfare state, the New Deal represented a pragmatic, ad hoc approach to eradicating the Great Depression. It evolved from joint presidential and congressional actions, a fact sometimes overshadowed by FDR's legacy. For example, only two of the 15 major pieces of legislation passed during the "First Hundred Days" originated with the president himself. Ironically, these presidential initiatives, the Civilian Conservation Corps (CCC) and the Economy Act, were budgetary contradictions. The CCC increased expenditures to place youths in parks and forests for conservation work, while the Economy Act tried to balance the budget.

Scholars identify phases in the New Deal. The First New Deal occurred in 1933 and 1934, when the administration's chief concerns were with national planning among government, business, and labor to achieve relief and recovery. It featured the work of Robert Moley, Rexford Tugwell, Hugh Johnson, and Lewis Douglas. After adverse criticism from business and decisions by the U.S. Supreme Court, as well as populist challenges from Senator Huey P. Long, a Democrat from Louisiana, Father Charles Coughlin, and Dr. Francis Townsend, the administration changed gears.

The Second New Deal abandoned national planning in favor of social reform, antitrust policy, and federal spending to spur the economy. The legislation enacted during the "Second Hundred Days" of 1935 was unprecedented. Lawyers Thomas Corcoran and Benjamin Cohen and law professor Felix Frankfurter attempted to restore a competitive economy while establishing labor union rights (National Labor Relations Act, 1935) and provision for old-age pensions (Social Security Act, 1935).

Although the New Deal continued at home and abroad, it was not until the coming of World War II that the American economy recovered following the economic downturn in 1937. The G.I. Bill of Rights in 1944 helped to solidify the American version of the modern welfare state at home, and Roosevelt's efforts to end colonialism abroad and establish the United Nations represented the Third New Deal, which First Lady Eleanor Roosevelt promoted through the UN. In short, through the legislative package that collectively created the New Deal, a new and expanded role was created for the federal government at home and throughout the world.

Further reading:
Daynes, Bryon W., William D. Pederson, and Michael P. Riccards, eds. *The New Deal and Public Policy*. New York: St. Martin's Press, 1998; Howard, Thomas, and William D. Pederson, eds. *Franklin D. Roosevelt and the Formation of the Modern World*. Armonk, N.Y.: M. E. Sharpe, 2003; Kennedy, David M. *Freedom from Fear. The American People in Depression and War, 1929–1945*. New York: Oxford University Press, 1999; Leuchtenberg, William E. *Franklin D. Roosevelt and the New Deal*. New York: Harper & Row, 1963; Moley, Raymond, and Elliot A. Rosen. *The First New Deal*. New York: Harcourt, Brace & World, 1966.

—William D. Pederson

news media and Congress

The relationship between Congress and the news media is complex. It is negative, disappearing, symbiotic, critical, or reactive—depending on the context. This entry analyzes how the media coverage of Congress has changed over time, variations between national and local coverage, and variations between institutional and individual coverage.

At the dawn of the republic, Congress was the center of policy making and of primary importance. Because of its predominance, Congress dominated national news coverage and especially outdistanced presidential news coverage. Congress was in the enviable position of being about to dictate much of its relationships with reporters. Newspapers such as the *National Intelligencer* not only covered Congress, they were under contract to provide the journal of its floor proceedings. Consequently, news coverage focused on floor speeches, which members were able to edit before publication.

Reflecting the era, newspapers and their coverage were partisan. Correspondents interpreted events according to their newspapers' party preferences. However, reporters were dependent on members for more than juicy tidbits of information. Since most newspapers paid their congressional correspondents only for the months that Congress was in session, many reporters augmented their salaries by accepting congressional clerkships or LOBBYING positions. Such arrangements allowed party leaders to reward sympathetic reporters for their favorable coverage, and the reporters themselves had access to story leads they otherwise would not have.

In spite of this symbiosis, the relationship between the news media and Congress had its contentious moments. Periodically Congress would vote to expel reporters or embark on investigations of leaks. However, Congress continued to dominate news coverage until the Progressive Era, when President Theodore Roosevelt began courting reporters and cultivating media coverage.

There is little good news for Congress in analyses of congressional news coverage today. First, the news coverage of the institution, when it is not neutral in tone, is usually negative except in periods of unusual leadership or national crisis. This trend has been underway at least since the end of World War II. Second, Congress is ill-suited to the modern medium of television. Its share of television news time is small, especially in comparison to the president, and has been declining. There are several reasons for this trend. One is that television must tell a visual story as well as a verbal story. Much of the work of Congress involves "talking heads," whether on the floor or in committee; neither provides compelling television drama. Moreover, many important decisions may be made elsewhere, such as in cloakrooms, on basketball courts, or in private telephone conversations, all of which are far away from television cameras. In addition, Congress is a hydra-headed beast. Unlike the executive branch, which seeks to control the messages it presents to the media on any given day, members of Congress speak for themselves and offer a variety of opinions.

Ironically, one reason for the poor news coverage of Congress is that Congress generates so much news. The dozens of committee hearings and mark ups, floor debates and votes, briefings, investigations, and reports in any given week are simply overwhelming. While newspapers do a better job of covering Congress, deciding which stories to cover is a daunting task for any reporter. However, committee hearings, mark ups, briefings, and such are single whistle-stops on the much longer train ride known as the legislative process. Even with each passing milestone, the outcome of legislation may remain uncertain. Thus, even though public opinion polls register significant interest in so-called process stories, editors often pass over them. They prefer to wait until a floor vote takes place and will accept stories at this point.

Covering Congress this way has its price as well. For one, such stories tend to focus on the politics of the debate rather than the substance of the legislation. Legislation is complex; it is difficult to summarize the details or nuances of competing plans in a single newspaper story and impos-

sible to communicate in a 30-second television spot. Moreover, by the time legislation reaches the floor debate, it may have been on the congressional agenda for a year or more. Thus, the substance of current proposals is no longer newsworthy; alternative proposals that have been abandoned are certainly not newsworthy. The political stories have currency and simplicity. However, the public is left with an incomplete and inaccurate picture of Congress and a cloudy understanding of the legislative process.

Even at the floor vote stage, most legislation receives little or no news coverage. Many issues are not controversial and thus lack the drama of a good news story. As a result, reporters tend to focus on issues that highlight conflict: Republicans vs. Democrats, president vs. Congress, House vs. Senate. As a result, news coverage ignores the issues in which consensus emerges and thus paints a picture of Congress that is obstructionist, disagreeable, and contentious.

Congress is a bicameral institution with two chambers of equal power. This dimension further complicates media coverage. For most of the post–World War II period, the Senate received more coverage than the House. This is due in part to the Senate's role in foreign policy, which was particularly important during the cold war and the post–cold war era, and the Senate's confirmation power. The House of Representatives receives more coverage when the Senate majority is the same party as the president, such as in the early 1908s and the mid-1990s. The latter was also particularly newsworthy because of the many reforms instituted by the newly elected Republican majority.

Congress is less frequently depicted as an institution in its own right. With the dominance of the presidency, Congress is very likely to be depicted as reacting to the president's proposals. Leaders of the president's party are quoted supporting administration initiatives. However, capitalizing on conflict, the congressional leadership of the party that does not occupy the White House becomes particularly important. Former House Speaker THOMAS P. "TIP" O'NEILL (D-MA) gained national prominence because he was the leading Democratic critic of Reagan administration policies. Former House Speaker NEWT GINGRICH (R-GA) played this role opposite President Clinton, and Minority Leader TOM DASCHLE (D-SD) played this role opposite the George W. Bush administration.

Finally, news coverage of Congress is waning, especially on network television. Some network officials argue that this is part of a larger trend to de-emphasize coverage of Washington in general. However, studies have found that this shift does not include less coverage of the president, only less coverage of Congress. Part of the decline might be due to the fact that Congress is ill-suited to the medium of television. Part might be the increasing importance of the executive branch. The proliferation of cable news sources, specialized publications, and the Internet may also be partially to blame. Since audiences who desire particular information about Congress can find it in so many other places, network television executives are under less pressure to adequately cover the institution.

In the 1950s freshmen members of Congress were advised to eschew publicity in favor of working hard on their committees and getting legislation passed. The perception was that so-called show horses might have a national media presence, but the work horses were those who earned the respect of their colleagues and wielded power in the institution. The show horse–work horse dichotomy, however, appears to have waned in importance. At least by the 1980s, those who had the greatest media presence were also among those most dedicated to legislative tasks.

National news coverage of individual members varies dramatically, and these differences cannot be attributed simply to working hard in the institution. Some members never receive any mention in the national media, even if they serve for years; others are regulars on the Sunday morning talk shows. There are numerous reasons for these differences.

Some of the differences are not surprising. For example, persons in official positions of power, such as party leaders and committee chairs, are more newsworthy than back-benchers. Leaders of the majority party, including committee chairs, are newsworthy because they control the congressional agenda and are likely to dictate what laws are enacted. Leaders of the party that is not in control of the White House are newsworthy as leaders of the opposition. Similarly, reporters like members who are quotable political mavericks and are willing to be interviewed on a variety of issues. These members become minor media celebrities in their own right, and their very familiarity prompts even more exposure.

Also not surprisingly, individual senators are more newsworthy than are individual House members. There are fewer U.S. senators. Thus, they are individually more powerful, their positions of leadership are more widely distributed, and they are likely to develop expertise on a wider range of issues. Second, the Senate is considered a breeding ground for presidential aspirants in a way that the House is not.

Last, the amount and the nature of media coverage also differ by race and gender, even though women and African-American members of Congress do present themselves much like their white male counterparts. They are more likely to be quoted in articles concerning issues of importance to women or racial minorities, such as affirmative action, abortion, family leave, sexism, and racism. As such, they are depicted as narrowly focused on these topics or on topics of local interest only. Even in the 1990s coverage of women members of Congress tended to make note of personal characteristics such as a "winning smile," their families, and their dress.

In spite of the dismal state of national news coverage of Congress and its members, some individual members do expend considerable time and resources pursuing news coverage in the national media, and with some measurable success. Their motivations are myriad. They include personal aggrandizement, ambition for higher office or a leadership post, enhancement of credibility with constituents, and desire to shape the national policy agenda and public policy outcomes.

However, most members' media relations are focused, predictably, on local news media. Such efforts are important to members' reelection efforts, and they are also much more likely to yield results. As early as the 1970s, media critics discussed a symbiotic relationship between local media and members of Congress. Local reporters, especially those working for small media outlets, were hungry for news stories. Members of Congress were hungry for favorable local coverage. Thus, members and reporters enjoyed a mutually beneficial relationship whereby members' news releases might be reproduced in the media with little or no editing or alternative perspectives included.

More recent studies have debunked the idea that the relationship between members and reporters is strictly symbiotic and found that local news coverage of Congress and its members mirror broader trends of negativity and being reactionary. Nonetheless, most individual members cultivate relationships with local reporters and continue to work with them, even when displeased with some elements of their coverage. They are wise to do so, since public support of individual members of Congress appears to increase even when the voters realize that their opinions diverge from their members' voting record. Knowledge, even knowledge of disagreement, appears to forge public support among constituents.

Members, however, have widely differing experiences with the local news. There are 50 states, 435 congressional districts, and 210 media markets in the United States. The latter only imperfectly correlates with either of the former. The luckiest members are those whose districts correlate closely with a media market or whose districts' boundaries completely encompass one or more than one media market. They are likely to find that their efforts to generate local news coverage are easily rewarded. This is not so for members whose districts are in media markets in another state or whose districts are split between several different media markets. These members have a more difficult time generating local news coverage. The same can be said for members who represent a portion of a metropolitan area in which several districts and/or states are included in one media markets. They must compete with each other for whatever congressional coverage is included.

Further reading:
Cook, Timothy. *Making Laws and Making News: Media Strategies in the U.S. House of Representatives.* Washington, D.C.: Brookings Institution Press, 1989; Hess, Stephen. *The Ultimate Insiders: U.S. Senators in the National Media.* Washington, D.C.: Brookings Institution Press, 1968; Kedrowski, Karen. *Media Entrepreneurs and the Media Enterprise in the U.S. Congress.* Cresskill, N.J.: Hampton Press, 1996; Ritchie, Donald A. *Press Gallery: Congress and the Washington Correspondents.* Cambridge, Mass.: Harvard University Press, 1991; Vinson, C. Danielle. *Local Media Coverage of Congress and Its Members: Through Local Eyes.* Cresskill, N.J.: Hampton Press, 2003; Zilber, Jeremy, and David Niven. *Racialized Coverage of Congress: The News in Black and White.* Westport, Conn.: Praeger Publishers, 2000.

—Karen M. Kedrowski

nullification

Thomas Jefferson and James Madison are considered to be the architects of the doctrine of nullification, and John C. Calhoun, a Democratic member of the House and Senate from South Carolina as well as vice president in 1824 and 1828, helped to rejuvenate and redefine the doctrine. Nullification, according to its supporters, gives the states the right to interpose themselves between the federal government and the people and declare federal laws unconstitutional. Three times in American history, immediately after the formation of the American national government and the emergence of political parties, in the period prior to the Civil War, and in the 1950s, the doctrine of nullification emerged as a significant political concept. Although a significant political concept, nullification has emerged as a doctrine completely lacking in legal justification. Nullification is, in essence, a doctrine that is legally null and void.

Madison, in his 1798 Virginia Resolutions, asserted the rights of states to interpose their authority and declare unconstitutional the Federalist-sponsored Alien and Sedition Acts. The following year, in the Kentucky Resolution, Jefferson evoked the doctrine of nullification as a means to oppose the expansion of federal power at the expense of the states. The Virginia and Kentucky Resolutions became the cornerstone of the states' rights movement throughout the nation, particularly in the South.

Madison was later embarrassed when his writings were used to defend the actions of South Carolina during the 1828–33 nullification controversy. Madison argued that nullification did not give any state the right to declare any federal law unconstitutional. Nullification, according to Madison, was meant to foster cooperation among states trying to amend the Constitution or overturn federal laws.

Jefferson biographer Merrill D. Peterson writes that nullification "was the pivot upon which many states' rights Jeffersonians swung toward the policies of sectionalism, slavery and secession." John C. Calhoun, vice president under Andrew Jackson, became so concerned about the growing power of the national government that he resigned the vice presidency and became the leading champion of states' rights and sectionalism. His *South Carolina Exposition and Protest* (1828) became the philosophical Bible of the nullification movement. In the *South Carolina Exposition* Calhoun argued that the federal constitution was a compact between the sovereign states and the federal government. Under this compact the states delegated specific and limited powers to the federal government. If the federal government encroached on the sovereign rights of the states, the states could call a special convention to declare the federal law to be unconstitutional and null and void in the state. If the Constitution was amended to give the federal government authority over the state, each state had the right to accept the newly established power of the federal government, or the state could secede from the union. This was precisely the justification used by the 11 southern states when they seceded from the union and precipitated the Civil War.

Calhoun and other advocates of nullification viewed the doctrine as essential to preserving the rights of the minority in a democratic system of government. Critics of nullification, such as Presidents Andrew Jackson and Abraham Lincoln, viewed nullification as both revolutionary and treasonous. The Union could not endure if any state could secede whenever it disagreed with the actions of the federal government. From the publication of Calhoun's *South Carolina Exposition* in 1828 until the outbreak of the Civil War in 1860, nullification became increasingly associated with states' rights and the southern defense of slavery. Although nullification is usually associated with the South and the southern defense of slavery, Calhoun's writings deserve attention as one of the most significant defenses of minority rights in American democracy. Calhoun became one of the foremost critics of American democracy and a leading political thinker of the 19th century.

After the Civil War little was heard about the doctrine of nullification until the modern Civil Rights movement. The *Brown v. Board of Education* (347 U.S. 483) decision in 1954 resulted in renewed interest in the doctrine of interposition and nullification among southern states. Several states, including Virginia, South Carolina, and Florida, passed interposition and nullification laws declaring the Supreme Court's school desegregation decision to be null and void in their states. Lewis Powell, Jr., an adviser to Virginia politicians and later a member of the U.S. Supreme Court declared, "No court is known to have sustained this doctrine as a legal right, and no court is likely to do so. It is simply legal nonsense." It was apparent at this time that the doctrine of nullification lacked any legal standing and that southern legislators were invoking nullification as an exercise in symbolic politics. In other words, declaring the *Brown* decision to be null and void may have been the politically correct decision to make for southern politicians, but it was a doctrine that lacked any legal justification.

Further reading:
Ketcham, Ralph. *James Madison: A Biography.* New York: Macmillan, 1971; Peterson, Merrill D. *The Jefferson Image in the American Mind.* New York: Oxford, 1960; Wiltse, Charles M. *John C. Calhoun, Nullifier, 1829–1839.* Indianapolis: Bobbs-Merrill, 1949.

—Darryl Paulson

oath of office

All members of Congress, when taking their seat for the first time or returning from reelection at the start of a new Congress, are required to take the oath of office:

> I do solemnly swear (or affirm) that I will support and defend the Constitution of the United States against all enemies, foreign and domestic; that I will bear true faith and allegiance to the same; that I take this obligation freely, without any mental reservation or purpose of evasion; and that I will well and faithfully discharge the duties of the office on which I am about to enter: So help me God.

Article Six of the Constitution requires that all members of Congress "be bound by oath or affirmation to support this Constitution." Unlike the presidential oath of office, however, the exact form of words to be used is not stipulated. For the first 75 years of the republic, member of Congress were required only to swear that they would "support the Constitution of the United States."

The current oath has its origins in the American Civil War. As conflict divided the United States, the issue of loyalty to the Union became one of great significance. In 1862 Congress devised the "Ironclad Test Oath," by which government employees not only were required to swear their current loyalty to the Union but also to affirm that they had never previously engaged in disloyal conduct. The requirement to take this version of the oath was extended to members of Congress in 1864. In the Senate members were also required to sign their name to the oath, a practice that continues to this day.

Following the cessation of hostilities and the return of representatives and senators from Confederate states to Congress, the requirements were again changed so that former Confederates could opt out of the first part of the oath, regarding previous conduct. In 1884 the strict first section of the oath was repealed for all members, leaving just the second section that has remained the oath of office since.

Further reading:

Oleszek, W. J. *Congressional Procedures and the Policy Process.* Washington, D.C.: Congressional Quarterly Press, 2001.

—Ross M. English

objectors

Objectors are members of the HOUSE OF REPRESENTATIVES composed of three members from the majority and three members from the minority. They conduct a careful study of each and every BILL or resolution on the Private Calendar. Their role as official objectors is to object to all bills or resolutions to which they feel an objection should be made. They also are responsible for objecting to those bills or resolutions that do not conform to the requirements of the calendar, which are set by the objectors at the beginning of a new Congress.

All bills in this calendar are generally private bills, which deal with individual cases such as claims against the government, immigration and naturalization, land titles, and so on that benefit an individual or an entity. Private bills do not become public law. Instead, they become private law. The calendar is called on the first Tuesday of every month and may also be called on the third Tuesday by the Speaker of the House.

In general practice, bills are "passed over, without prejudice." By doing this the objectors give the sponsor of the bill a chance to address whatever concerns they might have before the bill is called again in the order in which it is listed in the calendar. Objectors are present and on the floor during House proceedings, and it is their responsibility to object on behalf of their party. Before the official objectors positions existed, House members served as objectors on their own free will. Proposals were made in

384

1932 to have official objectors that were later adopted by the House.

Further reading:
Congressional Quarterly Inc. *How Congress Works.* 2d ed. Washington, D.C.: Congressional Quarterly, 1991; Schneider, Judy, and Michael L. Koempel. *Congressional Deskbook 2001–2002* 107th Congress, Alexandria, Va.: TheCapitol Net, 2001.

—Arthur Holst

Office of Technology Assessment

The Office of Technology Assessment (OTA) was created as a support agency to provide independent technological assistance and expertise to members of Congress. The office existed for 23 years until closing in September 1995, eliminated in a move to cut congressional expenses.

The agency left a legacy of objective and authoritative analysis of the complex scientific and technological issues before the legislature in the late 20th century. The growth of science and technology in the mid-20th century and the expansion of public policy decisions using technical information provided the impetus for creating the agency in 1972. Executive-legislative tensions in addition to the growing economic impact of basic science research being funded by the national government, beyond the $18 billion annually in the late 1960s, when the OTA was being planned, compounded by the emerging awareness in the public of the serious long-term environmental consequences resulting from science innovation, were used successfully by proponents of creating the independent congressional support agency. Issues such as the impact of the insecticide DDT in the food chain, the consequences of low-level radiation exposure in children from mine tailings, and the health effects of various toxins produced in industrial processes required scientific expertise not typically present in elected representatives or their staff. OTA was created to fill that type of knowledge void.

The OTA was organized as an independent consulting agency to Congress. Speculation exists that the very neutrality of the agency designed into its structure was responsible for its demise. It had a governing board of 12 members called the Technology Assessment Board (TAB), divided equally between House and Senate members and Democratic and Republican Party members. Further, a nonelected scientific advisory board provided general advice to the OTA in the Technology Assessment Advisory Council, composed of eminent scientists from around the country, the comptroller general of the United States, and the director of the CONGRESSIONAL RESEARCH SERVICE. The director of the OTA, selected by the TAB, served a six-year term.

The OTA typically produced 50 reports annually on topics ranging across a broad technological field including medical research, climate change, the space program, genetic engineering, telecommunications policy, and defense against nuclear weapons. All OTA technical reports are available electronically in The OTA Legacy. The argument for elimination of the OTA centered on the ideological preferences for streamlining government and fiscal responsibility contained in the 1994 Republican CONTRACT WITH AMERICA. Further, Representative Robert S. Walker, a Republican from Pennsylvania who became chair of the House Science Committee when Republicans gained the majority, was displeased with OTA reports being published after legislation and the amount of time required for reports, typically 18 to 24 months. Others argued that the work done by the OTA was duplicative of that done in other government agencies, particularly executive agencies. The charge that OTA efforts were redundant is at the heart of the rationale behind an independent congressional technical agency, one that was leveled against the OTA during its existence.

The possible long-term consequences of the agency closing include that the legislative branch is once again reliant on the technical expertise of the executive branch. The OTA may have been doomed by the circumstances at its inception, when the president was crippled by the WATERGATE SCANDAL and Congress was intent on retaking power and influence lost to the executive. The other institutional innovations like the OTA that resulted from the reformist 1970s, the WAR POWERS RESOLUTION and the CONGRESSIONAL BUDGET OFFICE, together were bulwarks against an encroaching imperial presidency. The OTA was caught between two competing visions of what it would become, an agency for an independent early warning system, or technology monitoring mechanism function, or a support agency responding to congressional information requests. That it could not negotiate a role between those endpoints is more reflective of the tension and animosities within the House of Representatives at the end of the 20th century relating to a liberal agenda favoring environmental preservation over a conservative agenda of economic development than perhaps the administrative talents of the OTA directors or the quality of technical advice provided by the agency.

Further reading:
Kunkle, Gregory C. "New Challenge or Past Revisited? The Office of Technology Assessment in Historical Context Technology in Society," *Technology in Society* 17, no. 2 (1995): 175–196; Leary, Warren E. "Congress's Science Agency Prepares to Close Its Doors." *New York Times,* 24 September 1995, p. 14N; U.S. Congress. *Office of Technology Assessment. The OTA Legacy, 1972–1995.*

Washington, D.C.: Government Printing Office, 1996; U.S. Congress. Office of Technology Assessment. *An Experiment in Technology Policy-Making: Fifteen Years of the U.S. Office of Technology Assessment.* 100th Cong. 1st sess., 1987.

—Karen M. McCurdy

offices, Capitol Hill

Congress, like the other branches of government, has grown considerably since its inception. Originally, representatives and senators had no government-provided offices. The part-time nature of congressional service before the 20th century did not require that members of Congress have either a staff or office space. By the turn of the century, however, representatives and senators were increasingly becoming full-time legislators. Coupled with the growing size of Congress, the professionalization of legislators required more office space than was available in the CAPITOL BUILDING alone.

On March 3, 1903, Congress authorized the construction of an office building for the House. The building was completed by January 10, 1908, and later designated the Joseph G. Cannon House Office Building. An additional story was added to the structure in 1914, which is now accessible only by a separate elevator, making it the least favorable office space on CAPITOL HILL.

The growing size of member and committee staffs required the construction of a new building for the House. The Nicholas Longworth House Office Building was completed in 1933. Currently the building contains 251 member offices and 16 committee rooms, along with a cafeteria and several shops in the basement. The final House office building was completed in 1965. Named the Sam Rayburn House Office Building, it contains 169 member offices and 17 committee rooms.

The Rayburn Building is often cited as the most frustrating building on Capitol Hill. Its architecture has been described as resembling a Texas penitentiary, and it is full of purposeless space. Although the building was added to provide more room for member offices, critics quickly pointed out that member offices make up only a small fraction of the floor space. Even more disappointing is the floor plan. The Rayburn Building is the only office building on Capitol Hill that is full of dead ends, making even simple trips take far longer than necessary.

Following the lead of the House, the Senate also began construction of its own office buildings. A building the Senate was using as temporary office space was condemned and replaced with what is now called the Richard Brevard Russell Senate Office Building in 1909. The design for the Russell Building was based on the plans for the Cannon Building, hence their similar appearance. The Russell Building, however, does not have any floors that are difficult to access.

In order to provide more committee and Senate office space, the Everett McKinley Dirksen Senate Office Building was completed in 1958, and the Philip A. Hart Senate Office Building was occupied in 1982. The Hart Building was the subject of intense debate over its immense cost ($137,700,400). Considering that the Hart Building is essentially an annex to the Dirksen Building and that its cost was far higher than any of the other office buildings, it is not surprising that its construction was fraught with controversy. Along with the most expensive office building on Capitol Hill, it is also the most distinctive. It has an immense atrium that houses Alexander Calder's equally immense sculpture *Mountains and Clouds*. The Hart Building also is unique because its office suites are furnished with cubicles for staff members, a feature that is not always popular with staffers moving from one of the other buildings.

In addition to the six major office buildings, Congress maintains office space in the Capitol Building and has some offices in the Gerald R. Ford House of Representatives Office Building. Primarily used as a residence for congressional pages, the Ford Building has some committee space but does not contain any member offices. In 2002 the Thomas P. O'Neill, Jr., House of Representatives Office Building, which held mostly committee space and no member offices, was demolished and is currently a parking lot.

House member offices are typically a two or three room suite. There is a public lobby, staff office room, and the member's private office. Senate offices vary far more than House offices, but they include the same three distinct areas. Since Senate staffs are usually much larger than their House counterparts, Senate offices often have a room for each major component of the staff (i.e., the press staff and correspondence staff would have their own rooms). In general, Senate offices have far more space for staff than House offices.

The House and Senate each have different methods of selecting office assignments. The Senate assigns offices by length of service. In the case of a tie, service time as the vice president or in the House is counted. If a tie still remains, the senator representing the most populous state is given priority. Members of the House choose their offices based on their drawings in a lottery that is weighted by seniority.

Competition for choice offices can be fierce. The relative value of offices depends on many factors, including the building in which it is located, size of the member's private office, size of the staff area, and its view. Large offices with views of the Capitol dome are the most highly prized, and the most shunned are those on the top floor of the Cannon Building.

Further reading:
Congressional Quarterly. *Congressional Quarterly's Encyclopedia of American Government.* Washington, D.C.: Congressional Quarterly Press, 1993; Congressional Quarterly. *Congressional Quarterly's Guide to Congress.* 3d ed. Washington, D.C.: Congressional Quarterly Press, 1982; U.S. Congress. Joint Committee on Printing. *2003–2004, Official Congressional Directory, 108th Congress.* 108th Cong., 1st sess, 2003.

—Brian M. McGowan

offices, district

These offices are located in home districts for representatives and states for senators, from which members of Congress may serve their constituents. History does not record when members of Congress first began to maintain offices in their states and districts. Most representatives and senators did not have offices in their states and districts until about the middle of the 20th century. In *Congress: Keystone of the Washington Establishment,* political scientist Morris Fiorina indicates that the number of congressional staff more than doubled from 1960 to 1974. In 1960 14 percent of congressional staff were identified as working in a state or district office. By 1974 that number had reached 34 percent. He also points out that state and district offices are permanent operations. Nearly 30 percent of all members of Congress reported that their district offices were open only when they were present in the district in 1960. He found little evidence of "intermittent staff operations" in the districts by 1974. He also found that the number of district offices had increased as well, from only 4 percent of all members of Congress reporting more than one district office in 1960 to most members having multiple offices in 1974. A 1999 Senate Staff Employment Survey and a 2000 House Staff Employment Survey, both by the Congressional Management Foundation, found that senators have an average of four state offices with about a third of their staff, while representatives have an average of 2.3 district offices with about half of their staff.

State and district offices allow representatives and senators to maintain a presence among their constituents even when they are in Washington while Congress is in session. Constituents are able to contact the local office and have their requests passed on to the office on CAPITOL HILL. Congressional staff working in state and district offices handle most of the CASEWORK the flows into a member of Congress's office.

Federal law and the rules of the House and the Senate regulate the establishment and maintenance of state and district offices. The SERGEANT AT ARMS of the Senate secures for each senator office space for the senator's official use in cities and towns designated by the senator in the senator's home state. The space obtained by the Sergeant at Arms is in post offices or other federal buildings. If space is not available in post offices or other federal buildings, a senator may lease other office space. Leases, of course, are limited to the length of the senator's term. The Senate Sergeant at Arms maintains records of these leases.

Senators are limited in the amount of office space they may occupy. These limits are based on the population of the state represented by a senator. A senator representing a state with less than 3,000,000 people may occupy no more than 5,000 square feet. A senator representing a state with a population of 17,000,000 or more may occupy 8,200 square feet. Senators may also lease a mobile office for use in his or her home state. The size of this mobile office is included in the space limitations of all office space.

According to the *Members' Congressional Handbook* published by the Committee on House Administration, there is no limit on the number and size of district offices a representative may establish. District offices may be located in federal buildings, commercial buildings, state, county, or municipal buildings, or in mobile offices. District offices must be in the representative's district unless there is no suitable office space in a federal building in the district. Offers of free office space may not be accepted from private entities, although private office space may be leased at fair market value. Representatives may accept free office space from federal, state, or local government agencies when that office is located in the district.

Further reading:
Fiorina, Morris. *Congress: Keystone of the Washington Establishment.* 2d ed. New Haven, Conn.: Yale University Press, 1989; O'Keefe, Eric, and Aaron Steelman. *The End of Representation: How Congress Stifles Electoral Competition.* Cato Policy Analysis No. 279. Washington, D.C.: Cato Institute, 1997; United States Congress. Joint Committee on the Organization of Congress. *Organization of Congress, Final Report.* House Report 103–413. Washington, D.C.: Government Printing Office, 1993.

omnibus bills

One of the more notable trends in the character of legislation in recent decades has been the use of ever larger bills or packages of bills, which are often several inches thick when they are eventually bound. These large bills or packages are dubbed "omnibus bills," making reference to old-style omnibuses used in Europe that permitted droves of riders to board a double-decker vehicle for travel through the city. Likewise, omnibus packages provide a suitable means for bills to traverse the legislative process because their packaging allows party leaders to forge large coalitions of supporters.

Since the early 1950s there has been a juxtaposition between the rise of omnibus packages and the decline of the total number of public laws passed in a two-year Congress. One of the most robust trends in omnibus packages is that once constructed, they rarely fail; nearly all successfully traverse the legislative process. A prominent and recent use of the omnibus technique was the forging of the remainder of the FY 2005 federal budget in December 2004 as one bill.

Omnibus bills alter the traditional lawmaking process in important ways. First, omnibus bills typically are fast-tracked compared to the care that is given to individual bills. In other words, if omnibus packages were broken apart and all the smaller components were processed as individual bills, that process would take several times longer than the time taken to move the packaged version. Second, because of their size, members rarely know the particulars of the entire bill when they vote on it. In fact, omnibus packages are not typically bound until after they pass one chamber and are submitted to the other chamber. When the first chamber considers them, they are often left in a piecemeal fashion in the party cloakrooms for members and their key staff to consider. Third, omnibus bills empower party leaders to the detriment of regular members. Party leaders have a huge informational advantage in constructing the bills and can play favorites to forge partisan coalitions.

Since they have what in some cases have been called less than ideal effects, why are omnibus bills increasingly used in Washington? Several scholars have noted that omnibus packages typically contain a nucleus, often a budgetary item, that is widely supported.

Party leaders, who construct omnibus packages, then add other items to the nucleus that, it is assumed, might not make it successfully through the legislative process as stand-alone bills. Omnibus bills, then, are useful vehicles for moving controversial smaller bills through Congress and to the president. Indeed, many of the attachments to omnibus bills are bills that have some locus of opposition within Congress or are bills the president opposes. The basic idea is that the opponents favor the majority of the bill and are thus willing to support it even though smaller items they oppose are attached.

In addition to the typical political play on omnibus bills discussed above, scholars attribute the rise of packaged legislation to increasingly challenging governing circumstances in the post–World War II era. In this perspective omnibus bills are a creative means to get things done in an increasingly complex decision-making environment. Several factors relate here, including the rise of divided party government between Congress and the president, deficit politics, and increased partisanship on CAPITOL HILL. As these various constraints exhibit their effects (the president and Congress of different parties, rising deficits that make decision making all the harder, and rancorous partisanship), leaders rely on unorthodox methods of lawmaking, including omnibus use. At this level of analysis, omnibus bills are seen less as politically expedient deal-making magic tricks and more as tools of lawmaking by adaptive governing institutions.

How does one know an omnibus bill when one sees one? The definition of omnibus legislation is still somewhat vague. Many scholars assume that any piece of legislation with the word *omnibus* in the title is an omnibus bill. However, because members are responsible for naming the bills they introduce, and because there is no agreed-upon definition of an omnibus bill among members of the HOUSE OF REPRESENTATIVES or SENATE, simply using this criterion is less than satisfactory. In fact, members have an incentive to use the word *omnibus* liberally in order to make their bills sound important and worthy of chamber consideration. Moreover, several obvious omnibus packages do not have the word *omnibus* in the bill title, such as certain reconciliation packages.

Regardless of how they are defined, omnibus bills seem to now be a permanent fixture of the lawmaking landscape in Washington, although policymakers and media pundits argue over their worth. In a particularly nasty lambasting of omnibus bills, columnist George Will likened them to garbage pails, with the idea being that once enough refuse is thrown in, the bill is ready for passage. Others see omnibus use as a positive change in lawmaking that has permitted Congress to pass important policies, such as health care reauthorizations and deficit reduction legislation. In documenting omnibus use and packaging systematically from 1949 to 1994, researchers have found omnibus propensity to be highest in the budget process, health care, and crime policy. At some point or another, just about every area of American government has been included in an omnibus bill.

Further reading:
Krutz, Glen S. *Hitching a Ride: Omnibus Legislating in the U.S. Congress.* Columbus: Ohio State University Press, 2001; Sinclair, Barbara. *Unorthodox Lawmaking.* Washington, D.C.: Congressional Quarterly Press, 1997; Smith, Steven S. *Call to Order: Floor Politics in the House and Senate.* Washington, D.C.: Brookings Institution Press, 1989.

—Glen S. Krutz

O'Neill, Thomas P. ("Tip") Jr. (1912–1994)
Representative, Speaker of the House

As a member of the U.S. HOUSE OF REPRESENTATIVES from Massachusetts, Thomas P. O'Neill, Jr., eventually gained the distinction of serving the longest consecutive tenure as Speaker. A liberal Democrat, O'Neill led the

House during the presidencies of Jimmy Carter and Ronald Reagan. He was known as a gregarious politician who enjoyed public service.

Born on December 9, 1912, in Cambridge, Massachusetts, O'Neill was the youngest of three children. His grandfather emigrated to the United States from Ireland as a bricklayer, a trade his father continued. His mother died of tuberculosis when Thomas was just nine months old; he was reared with the help of a housekeeper until his father remarried. He was educated in Catholic schools. As a youth he was given the nickname "Tip," a reference to a St. Louis Browns baseball player by the same last name who was famous for walking after hitting a slew of foul balls. O'Neill gained an appreciation of public service from his father, also named Thomas, who was elected to the Cambridge city council, appointed a superintendent of sewers, served as president of the St. Matthew's Temperance Society, and led the North Cambridge Knights of Columbus.

O'Neill began participating in politics himself at the age of 15, when he campaigned for Democrat Al Smith in the 1928 presidential election. In 1935, while still a senior at Boston College, O'Neill lost a bid for a seat on the Cambridge city council. His first defeat would be his last. He began a stellar public career in 1936 with a successful campaign for the Massachusetts state house of representatives. Balancing a family with private sector positions as an insurance agent and realtor, O'Neill worked his way up the leadership ladder. He was elected minority leader in 1946 and speaker of the state House in 1948. His election to the latter post was historic: He was the first Roman Catholic so honored, the second-youngest speaker in the history of Massachusetts, and the first Democrat elected to the position in more than a century.

In 1952 O'Neill ran for the U.S. House seat vacated by John F. Kennedy. He would become a fixture in the House, winning reelection 16 times and serving a total of 34 years. He gained early influence in the House through his appointment to the RULES COMMITTEE. In 1971 he was chosen MAJORITY WHIP. Just a year later, following the sudden death of MAJORITY LEADER Hale Boggs, O'Neill was selected to fill that position. He was popular among veteran and freshman legislators alike. Long-time legislators admired his courageous opposition to the Vietnam War, while newer House members sided with him during the WATERGATE SCANDAL. With the retirement of Speaker CARL ALBERT in 1976, O'Neill was elected Speaker in early 1977.

Ironically, Speaker O'Neill had as much trouble in dealing with Democratic president Jimmy Carter as he did the ensuing chief executive, Republican Ronald Reagan. Both presidents ran as anti-Washington outsiders, and both were intent on reducing the role of government in society. In Carter's case O'Neill complained that the White House lacked a clear set of priorities and did not give him neces-

sary access to the president. Still, O'Neill helped to guide passage of several important initiatives, including the administration's energy policy and legislation pertaining to the environment, nuclear proliferation, age discrimination, airline deregulation, community reinvestment, veterans' health care, trade, and refugee resettlement. O'Neill showed political deftness by remaining neutral in the 1980 presidential nomination contest between Carter and fellow Massachusetts native Edward Kennedy.

The victory by Ronald Reagan in the 1980 presidential election was a severe blow to the Democrats, who lost control of the SENATE to the Republicans for the first time in almost 30 years. However, Democrats remained in control of the House and kept faith in O'Neill's leadership as Speaker. President Reagan, who survived an assassination attempt two months into his first term, had a very effective first year, in which defense spending increased, taxes were cut, and social spending came under attack. Though he won reelection in 1984, Reagan never matched his initial year as far as legislative success. O'Neill retired in 1986 amid the revelations over the Iran-contra affair and the recapturing of the Senate by Democrats.

Thomas P. O'Neill, Jr. *(Library of Congress)*

After his service in Congress, O'Neill gained the financial security that had previously eluded him. His memoirs, *Man of the House*, was enormously successful. Later he published another book whose title, *All Politics Is Local*, derived from the advice his father imparted after he lost the Cambridge city council race. O'Neill earned many accolades for his public service, including being named a two-time recipient of the Freedom Medal, bestowed by the Franklin D. Roosevelt Institute. Additionally, he was awarded the Presidential Medal of Freedom in 1991 by President George H. W. Bush. In 1987 the newly completed Boston federal building was named after him. Following his death on January 5, 1994, a plaque was erected in his honor in his family's ancestral town of Mallow in Ireland.

Further reading:
Clancy, Paul, and Shirley Edler. *A Biography of Thomas P. O'Neill, Speaker of the House.* New York: Macmillan, 1980; Farrell, John A. *Tip O'Neill and the Democratic Century.* Boston: Little, Brown, 2001; O'Neill, Tip, with Gary Hymel. *All Politics Is Local and Other Rules of the Game.* New York: Times Books, 1994; O'Neill, Thomas P., with William Novak. *Man of the House: The Life and Political Memoirs of Speaker Tip O'Neill.* New York: Random House, 1987; Peters, Ronald M. *The American Speakership in Historical Perspective.* Baltimore: Johns Hopkins University Press, 1990.
—Samuel B. Hoff

one-minute speeches

One-minute speeches (commonly called "one-minutes") are one of three forms of nonlegislative debate in the HOUSE OF REPRESENTATIVES (the others being SPECIAL ORDER ADDRESSES and MORNING HOUR debate). One-minutes are considered nonlegislative for two reasons. First, they occur outside the arena of legislative business. More specifically, they usually take place at the beginning of the day before the House of Representatives has commenced legislative business. Second, one-minutes provide an opportunity for members of Congress to discuss any topic they wish, policy or nonpolicy in nature. This characteristic is especially valuable considering the House's usual requirement that debate be confined to pending legislative business.

Mary Mulvihill notes that the rules of the House do not provide for one-minutes. Instead, they evolved as a UNANIMOUS CONSENT practice of the House. Thus, any member of the House can object to the practice of daily one-minutes (this rarely happens, however). But the lack of formal recognition does not excuse members from adhering to the rules of the House during the one-minute period. On the contrary, members must abide by the usual rules that govern debate, decorum, and the power of RECOGNITION of the SPEAKER OF THE HOUSE. For example, members must abide by the chamber's precedents as well as the Speaker's announced policies.

The Speaker's announced policies refer to the Speaker's policies on certain aspects of House procedure, such as decorum in debate, which are usually announced on the first day of a new Congress. One important policy with regard to one-minute speeches is the Speaker's power of recognition. Under his or her power of recognition, the Speaker decides when to entertain unanimous consent requests to address the House for one minute and how many one-minute speeches will be allowed.

The one-minute period usually takes place at the beginning of each legislative day after the daily prayer, the Pledge of Allegiance, and approval of the previous day's JOURNAL. But when pressing legislative business is before the House, the Speaker may decide to postpone one-minutes until after legislative business or to forgo them altogether. He or she also determines the number of one-minutes permitted during the period. Though the number varies from day to day, the majority and minority leadership usually receive advance notification of any limitations.

Political parties use the relatively unconstrained nature of one-minutes to their advantage. It is common practice for "theme teams" to organize one-minute speeches and special order addresses. Party leaders often coordinate party members to deliver one-minutes on the issue designated as the party's daily message. Members slated to deliver coordinated messages are usually given priority for recognition purposes. The themes range from policy, such as pending legislation or current events, to nonpolicy issues, such as tributes to national dignitaries.

In sum, when recognized by the chair, individual members have one minute to address their issue. They cannot ask unanimous consent for additional time. If members cannot finish their remarks in one minute, they have the option of completing their speech in writing in the *CONGRESSIONAL RECORD*.

Who participates in one-minutes? First, research generally has found that legislatively disadvantaged members of Congress participate in one-minutes (and nonlegislative debate in general) at disproportionate levels. Because freshmen, the ideologically extreme, and other rank-and-file representatives have traditionally faced significant challenges in conventional forms of policy making, they often have to turn to one-minute speeches to influence policy. For this reason one-minutes and other nonlegislative debate has been referred to by some as a legislative "safety valve." Second, party leaders and their designees have used one-minutes to advertise their agendas, claim credit for their policy records, and take positions on pressing issues. One-minutes have been especially valuable to individual members of the House because they often supply the media with sound bites to be played by news programs in their districts.

Third, members of the minority party have used one-minute speeches more heavily than members of the majority. One-minutes provide an opportunity for minority members to criticize the majority party and thus take advantage of the electorate's bias for negative information (known as negativity bias). For example, NEWT GINGRICH, a representative from Georgia, and other Republicans used the forums extensively in the 1980s and 1990s to attack the Democratic majority. Some have argued that Representative Gingrich's innovative use of one-minutes (and other forms of nonlegislative debate) contributed to his party's eventual rise to majority party status and his own accession to the House Speakership.

Further reading:
Fenno, Richard. *Congressmen in Committees.* Boston: Little, Brown, 1973; Mulvihill, Mary. *One-Minute Speeches: Current House Practices.* CRS Report for Congress, Order Code RL30135, 1999; Wawro, Gregory J. *Legislative Entrepreneurship in the US House of Representatives.* Ann Arbor: University of Michigan Press, 2000.

—Michael S. Rocca

Organization of Congress, Joint Committee on the

In 1992 the Joint Committee on the Organization of Congress was created with the passing of resolutions by the SENATE and the HOUSE OF REPRESENTATIVES. The Senate passed resolution S. Con. Res. 57, otherwise known as the Boren-Domenici Resolution, sponsored by Senators David L. Boren, a Democrat from Oklahoma, and Pete V. Domenici, a Republican from New Mexico, on July 30. The House passed resolution H. Con. Res. 192, sponsored by Representatives Bill Gradison, a Republican from Ohio, and Lee H. Hamilton, a Democrat from Indiana, on June 18 by a vote of 412-4. Public criticism and demand for change prompted the creation of the joint committee.

The objective of this committee was to conduct a full study of the current organization of Congress and propose changes in order to make it more efficient and its operations simpler. Another objective was to make recommendations to improve Congress's relations with other branches of government and its oversight of them. Some of the issues that the committee dealt with were the budget process, ethics rules, committee structure, and staff and scheduling. The first examination of the organization of Congress had taken place 47 years earlier.

The committee was made up of 28 members with an equal number of members from each chamber of Congress. The members from each chamber were equally divided between Democrats and Republicans. Committee members were chosen by the MAJORITY LEADERS and MINORITY LEADERS of the Senate and House. Senator

Boren and Representative Hamilton served as cochairs, while Senator Domenici and Representative David Dreier, a Republican from California, served as vice chairs. Representative Dreier had replaced Representative Gradison, who retired in January 1993.

Even though the Joint Committee on the Organization of Congress seemed like a good way to approach reorganization, it was not welcomed by everyone, especially party leaders who were afraid of losing power. House Democrats were also concerned that they would lose control of the House. This clearly showed in the lack of consensus that followed during the hearings. Committee and party leaders tried to delay proceedings.

The committee conducted an intensive study of the organization of Congress, especially during its first six months. During this time it conducted 36 hearings and interviewed 243 witnesses. Among the witnesses were 133 members of the House, including 14 former members, 15 former and current staff members, and 44 outside witnesses. The committee also conducted surveys and contracted companies to conduct studies for them. It also commissioned several CONGRESSIONAL RESEARCH SERVICE (CRS) reports and consulted with scholars and those who had opinions on how to reform.

Since few agreements could be reached during hearings and behind-the-scenes negotiations, the Senate and House had to conduct separate mark-up sessions. The Senate held a one-day mark-up session on November 10, 1993. The issues they discussed included abolition of joint committees, committee assignment limitations, limiting the time allowed for debate on a motion to proceed to two hours, committee oversight agendas, limits on postcloture delays, and streamlined legislative branch staffing. They voted to report out what they had agreed upon.

The House mark-up session took much longer than that of the Senate, convening on November 16 and adjourning on November 22. Their mark-up draft included issues that were agreed upon by the majority of House members and avoided controversial issues. Some of the issues included in the draft were the reduction in the number of subcommittees, handling of ethics complaints, changes in bill referral procedures, application of laws to Congress, oversight planning, biennial budgeting and multiyear authorizations, and committee and subcommittee assignment limits. As a result of the deliberations, the Legislative Reorganization Act of 1994 was introduced in February.

Further reading:
House of Representatives. *Joint Committee on the Organization of Congress.* Available online. URL: http://www.house.gov/rules/JointCom.html. Accessed January 19, 2006; Schneider, Judy, and Michael L. Koempel. *Congressional Deskbook 2001–2002.* 107th Congress. TheCapitol.Net, Inc.

—Arthur Holst

P

pages

Pages are high school juniors who serve as messengers for members of Congress. Pages primarily serve as messengers carrying documents between the House and the Senate,

A Senate page at work in the Senate Chamber *(Senate Historical Office)*

members' offices, committees, and the Library of Congress. They also work to prepare the House and Senate chambers by distributing the CONGRESSIONAL RECORD and other documents. When Congress is in session, a careful watcher of C-SPAN coverage will notice several pages sitting near the dais waiting to be summoned by members needing assistance.

Approximately 100 students served as pages during the 108th Congress. All pages must be high school juniors and at least 16 years of age. Applicants for page positions must be sponsored by members of Congress. Chamber leadership establishes the criteria to be a page as well as determines the members eligible to sponsor a page. During their term of service, pages participate in educational programs managed by the House and the Senate. A number of members of Congress and staffers were pages during their youth.

It is widely believed that Senator Daniel Webster appointed the first SENATE page in 1829. House records indicate that the HOUSE OF REPRESENTATIVES employed pages as early as 1842. The first female pages were employed in 1971.

Pages have been subjects of controversy. In 1983 pages were alleged to have been involved in sexual misconduct with several members of Congress. In response the House offered supervised housing near the Capitol and established a common age requirement. After more disciplinary cases emerged in 2002 and 2004, the House Page Board, the body supervising House pages, established more strict application guidelines and reduced pages' terms of service.

Further reading:
Amer, Mildred. *Pages of the United States Congress: Selection, Duties, and Program Administration.* Washington, D.C.: Library of Congress, 2003; Congressional Research Service and Bill Severn. *Democracy's Messengers: The Capitol Pages.* New York: Hawthorn Books, 1975.

—John David Rausch, Jr.

pairing

Pairing is a procedure that allows an absent member of Congress to record his or her position on a specific question by arranging with a member of the opposite side who is present at the vote to announce the pair. In the HOUSE OF REPRESENTATIVES pairing is governed by House Rule XX, Clause 3, but neither the House nor the SPEAKER OF THE HOUSE exercises jurisdiction over pairs. Interpretation of the terms of a pair rests solely with the participants. Prior to a rules change at the start of the 106th Congress in 1999, the House recognized three types of pairs. One type was the live pair, whereby one member is absent and the other present for the vote. The term *live pair* no longer appears in House rules. The two types of pairs abolished by the House in 1999 were the specific pair and the general pair. In a specific pair, also known as a special pair or a dead pair, both members were absent, but they made their positions known beforehand. The members' names were listed in the *CONGRESSIONAL RECORD* after the vote. In a general pair the members' names were listed in the *Congressional Record* without an indication of their position.

House Rule XX, Clause 3, outlines the power of the Speaker to direct the CLERK OF THE HOUSE to conduct a record vote or QUORUM CALL by call of the roll. Members appearing after the second call but before the result is announced may vote or announce a pair. The member who is present casts his or her vote, withdraws the vote, announces that he or she has a pair, identifies the absent member of the pair, and then announces the opposing position on the vote. Neither vote counts. Following the recording of the vote in the *Congressional Record,* the pair is shown. On two-thirds votes, a pair would need to consist of three members.

Pairing is used in the SENATE, although there is no provision for it in Senate rules. A senator who is part of a live pair refrains from voting and announces that he or she is paired with an absent senator. Because senators must provide an excuse for not voting on a roll call and pairing is not officially sanctioned by Senate rules, pairing does not automatically qualify as an excuse. The Senate deals with pairing by ignoring it. The clerk and the presiding officer take no notice when a pair is announced, and the pair is ignored in calculating the results of a roll call.

Further reading:

Johnson, Charles W. *Constitution, Jefferson's Manual, and Rules of the House of Representatives.* House Document No. 107-284. Washington, D.C.: Government Printing Office, 2003; Riddick, Floyd M., and Alan S. Frumin. *Riddick's Senate Procedure: Precedents and Practices.* Senate Document No. 101-28. Washington, D.C.: Government Printing Office, 1992; Sachs, Richard C. *Pairing in Congressional Voting: The House.* Washington, D.C.: Library of Congress, Congressional Research Service, 2001.

—John David Rausch, Jr.

parliamentarian

Parliamentarians are officers of the HOUSE OF REPRESENTATIVES and the SENATE whose duties include providing expert assistance and advice on the meaning and application of their chamber's legislative rules, precedents, and practices. The first parliamentarian in the House was named by the SPEAKER OF THE HOUSE in 1927. The Senate's first parliamentarian was recognized in 1935. The House parliamentarian serves with the consent of the Speaker of the House and operates in a nonpartisan role, advising House members from both parties. The Senate parliamentarian serves at the pleasure of the Senate MAJORITY LEADER and works under the direction of the Secretary of the Senate. Two deputies, three assistants, and two clerks assist the House parliamentarian, while the Senate office includes the parliamentarian, two senior assistant parliamentarians, the assistant parliamentarian, and the parliamentary assistant. Sitting parliamentarians are able to name their own assistants. The tradition is for the assistants to become parliamentarian when a vacancy occurs.

Parliamentarians in both houses are responsible for advising the member of Congress presiding during a day's session. The parliamentarian advises the chair in formulating responses to parliamentary inquiries and rulings on points of order. The House parliamentarian on duty stands to the right of the chair or sits close by the chair on the rostrum. The Senate parliamentarian sits on the lower tier of the rostrum just below the presiding officer. While the presiding member of Congress may ignore the recommendations of the parliamentarian, most follow the recommendations because few members of Congress have the vast knowledge of legislative procedure and process held by the parliamentarian. During times when the chamber is not in session, parliamentarians and their staffs are in their offices available to give advice to members upon request.

The House and Senate parliamentarians also have other duties related to their knowledge of the legislative process. They provide recommendations for referral of BILLS to STANDING COMMITTEES. Their recommendations are based on House and Senate rules and the precedents that define committee jurisdictions. Each office in both chambers is also responsible for maintaining, compiling, and publishing the rules and precedents of its chamber. The Senate office is responsible for the Standing Rules of the Senate and Riddick's Senate Procedure. The House office publishes the biennial editions of the House Rules and Manual, additional volumes of Deschler-Brown Precedents, and House Practice:

A Guide to the Rules, Precedents and Procedures of the House.

Members of the House and Senate may confer with their chamber's parliamentarian or his or her other staff before introducing a bill to learn how that bill might be referred to a standing committee. Members also may ask about procedures that may be available during House or Senate consideration of a bill, amendment, or motion. The House and Senate parliamentarians do not advise committees on their work, but they may provide insight about the interpretation of House or Senate rules that may be applicable to committee meetings.

The office of House parliamentarian evolved from earlier offices designed to assist the Speaker of the House. In 1857 Thaddeus Morrice was appointed "Messenger." Because of his ability to remember House precedents, Morrice assisted the Speaker in his role as presiding officer. After Morrice's death in 1864, the position of Messenger was continued. In 1869 the title was changed to "Clerk to the Speaker" and then to "Clerk to the Speaker's Table." The title of parliamentarian was adopted in 1927. Lehr Fess was the first person to be called House parliamentarian. Lewis Deschler replaced Fess in 1928 and served in the position until retiring in 1974. William Holmes Brown served from 1974 until he retired in 1994. Charles Johnson, Brown's deputy, was appointed House parliamentarian in 1994 and served until retirement in 2004. Johnson was replaced by his deputy, John Sullivan.

The first Senate parliamentarian was recognized in 1935. The title of the Senate Journal Clerk, Charles L. Watkins, was changed to parliamentarian and Journal Clerk. In 1937, the two positions were separated and Watkins became the first Senate parliamentarian. Watkins was succeeded by Floyd M. Riddick in 1965. Murray Zweben became Senate parliamentarian when Riddick retired in 1974. Robert B. Dove replaced Zweben in 1981. Alan Frumin replaced Dove in 1987, when the Democratic Party regained the majority in the Senate. In 1995, after the Republicans became the majority party in the Senate, Frumin was demoted to senior assistant parliamentarian, and Dove was appointed Senate parliamentarian. Senate Majority Leader TRENT LOTT, a Republican from Mississippi, fired Dove in May 2001 after Dove's rulings on amendments to the federal budget made it difficult for the Republicans to enact the party's taxing and spending goals. Dove was replaced by Frumin.

Further reading:
Campbell, Colton C., and Stanley Bach. *The Office of the Parliamentarian in the House and Senate.* Washington, D.C.: Library of Congress, 2003; Congressional Research Service and Andrew Taylor. "Senate's Agenda to Rest on Rulings of Referee Schooled by Democrats." *CQ Weekly,* 12 May 2001, p. 1053.

—John David Rausch, Jr.

party voting

Party voting refers to the propensity of the members of a political party to vote together and against the position favored by the opposition. The traditional measure of a party unity vote is one in which a majority of one party votes against a majority of the other party. Party unity scores represent the percent of the time a member of Congress votes with his or her party on party unity votes. The normative importance of party voting revolves around the concept of democratic accountability; if the parties are voting against each other, it is easier for citizens to distinguish between the competing groups and control public policy through their votes.

The extent of party voting varies for several reasons. First, the proportion of first-term members in the chamber indicates the degree of electoral change. Partisan turnover indicates a restless electorate that is distinguishing between the parties on policy questions. Similarly, new members lack socialization to the institution and hence are more likely to follow the cues of party leaders. Second, homogenous parties make for intraparty unity and interparty conflict. Legislators with clear signals from a partisan constituency base that correlates strongly across districts are more likely to vote together and easily find disagreement with the opposing party. Third, and closely related to the last variable, is a centralized leadership structure that has the ability to offer sanctions and rewards for party loyalty. The Democratic Caucus or Republican Conference is prone to grant more institutional power to its leaders when there exists a policy consensus within the group. Such empowered leaders can effectively set an agenda that meets members' goals while also reining in dissent and promoting loyalty from members at the fringes of the party who are cross-pressured by constituency concerns. Fourth, the agenda of the institution sets the groundwork for conflict. Leaders may choose to pursue a more or less confrontational agenda. Last, the partisanship of the president and divided government affects party voting. Party leaders have more leverage to convince a majority party to support the president's agenda when the president is of the same party and his electoral fate is likely to produce coattail effects for the party. Similarly, a minority party may wish to unite in opposition to an unpopular president. In periods of divided government the president and the majority party are likely to frequently come into conflict and take opposing positions in an attempt to convince voters to change either the majority party or the party in the White House.

Many political scientists bemoaned the decline in party voting and democratic accountability in the post–World War II era. Party voting, however, has risen substantially since the early 1980s, with several elections leading to great turnover and leaving close margins in both the HOUSE OF REPRESENTATIVES and the SENATE, an increase in the homogeneity in the primary constituencies of both parties and polarization between them, the centralization of power in the hands of party leaders who have pursued partisan agendas (particularly on budgetary issues), and long stretches of divided government with polarizing presidents. These factors have seen the level of intraparty cohesion and interparty conflict in Congress approach levels unseen since the 19th century.

Party voting in the United States, however, is generally lower than that found in parliamentary systems. Three variables explain this difference. First, since the Progressive era party nominations have been decided by primaries. The former system of choosing nominees by party conventions generally led to the choice of candidates who were party loyalists rather than candidates able to appeal to local sensibilities. Primaries also favor incumbents who can exploit their name recognition and accomplishments against challengers in elections that deny voters party cues to distinguish between the candidates.

Second, parties in Congress have generally been secondary to committees as a mechanism for pursuing influence. Whereas parliamentary parties are hierarchical and ascent to the top is based on party loyalty, members of Congress could prove to be party mavericks yet accumulate seniority on committees, translating that seniority into influence over policy.

Last, private campaign finance in the United States funnels money directly from the contributor to the candidate's campaign. Candidates have control over how to run their general election campaigns, allowing them to attempt to differentiate themselves from their party's positions and reputation. Parliamentary systems generally practice a much more centralized collection of campaign resources whereby the prime ministerial candidates control the national campaigns and set the tone of the election. Voters in this system judge candidates in light of the positions taken by their party leaders and the policy successes and failures of the incumbent government, rather than by any personal trait or position taken by the legislative candidates in the voters' particular districts.

In addition to the issue of accountability, debate among political scientists about the importance of party voting increasingly has come to revolve around whether parties as institutions in Congress are consequential to shaping policy outcomes. In other words, the question is whether party voting simply reflects the similarity in preferences within a party and its constituents or reflects the efforts of party leaders to shape coalitions and the content of bills. In the case of the former, bills are written with an eye to what will pass on the floor. In the case of the latter, coalitions form at the behest of leaders shaping bills that otherwise would not pass in the same form without leadership intervention. This is an ongoing debate that continues to fuel much research on party voting in Congress.

Further reading:
Cox, Gary W., and Mathew D. McCubbins. *Legislative Leviathan: Party Government in the House.* Berkeley: University of California Press, 1993; Krehbiel, Keith. "Where's the Party? *British Journal of Political Science* 23 (1993): 235–66; Mayhew, David R. *Congress: The Electoral Connection.* New Haven, Conn.: Yale University Press, 1974.
—Bill Kubik

patronage

Patronage, spoils system, political machine—regardless of what it is called, it is all the same—political figures exchanging favors. The most significant decision in regard to patronage is *Rutan v. The Republican Party of Illinois*, which the U.S. Supreme Court decided in 1990. Rutan argued that she was denied a promotion because she did not support the Republican Party. Four others who were fired, demoted, or passed up for promotion because they did not support the party accompanied her. The Republican Party claimed political hiring and firing was necessary to run an efficient government with efficient workers, and having other party members working would subvert the government. The Supreme Court ruled patronage hiring and firing unconstitutional claiming

> Patronage hiring, as much as political firing and other patronage practices related to jobs, deprives an individual of his right to freedom of speech, belief and association.

The typical understanding of patronage is what occurred in *Rutan*, but patronage in Congress is different. Congress initially fought presidential patronage as a part of the legislative-executive power struggle. In 1820 Congress passed the Four Year Law that would allow presidents to appoint people to positions for four years. Presidents during this time did not embrace the law to the full extent. Andrew Jackson was the first president to elevate rotation in office into a principle of democratic government. Jackson's motivations were not completely partisan, as he truly believed appointing party politicians who were men of power and opposition at the local level would bolster the government's legitimacy and in turn its effectiveness. However, Congress wanted to have control of patronage.

In 1883 Congress passed the Pendleton Act, creating a national merit system for civil service jobs; politics was the motivating factor for this creation. Republicans feared losing their congressional majority in the 1882 elections followed by a loss in the 1884 presidential race would cause all their appointees to be removed. Congress's control over presidential patronage grew in 1939 and 1940 when it passed the Hatch Acts. These acts made it illegal for almost all federal employees to participate in partisan activities, regardless of whether civil service laws protected them. These acts also included state and local government employees if they were even partially paid by the federal government.

Like Jackson, many presidents have recognized that they could use patronage as a way to leverage members of Congress. Presidents could give the responsibility of appointing some jobs to members of Congress in return for future support, but that also extends to all members of Congress. But what are the results of patronage? Martin and Sue Tolchin wrote *To The Victor,* which, while exploring patronage in Congress, poignantly asks:

> To what extent [was] the Vietnam War continued because members have been compromised by their patronage needs? To what extent has tax reform been evaded because of the patronage needs of the congressmen? To what extent has pollution been ignored because its foes lacked the patronage to dispense to congressmen? How much has the war on poverty suffered because the principal recipients of antipoverty patronage lacked the national clout to make themselves effective?

Patronage in Congress comes in many forms: the private sector, constituents in home districts, committee members, government agencies, and political parties. Patronage from the private sector occurs to influence votes in its favor. In return, it promises support in the form of votes and money at election time. Pressure from labor unions can also have committee chairs holding up legislation

Constituents can benefit or suffer from congressional patronage. Constituents are always pleased with their senator or representative when they can get a job as a result of his or her efforts. Tax patronage can positively impact constituents, too. The "Leo Sanders amendment" enabled its namesake to save taxes on $995,000 in government income. Likewise, a community where 40 percent of the families lived below the poverty level was going to get a $250,000 golf course to please the senator from the area because he was on the Appropriations Subcommittee of the Agriculture Committee.

Patronage to constituents and to government agencies can often be in conflict. Constituents will try to use their member of Congress to stop "bureaucratic inertia." Members of Congress on important committees or those who hold a high post on a committee can be highly involved in patronage. Any members on a committee with control of money, such as the Senate Finance, the House Ways and Means, or the Appropriations Committees of either chamber, are influential people. The committee members of Congress are placed on is determined by the influence of his or her political party leaders. These different types of

patronage are not isolated, though. An example from the Tolchins' book describes it best.

> Considered valuable patronage plums, federal buildings are valued not only for the federal jobs they bring permanently to the district but for all the contracts (architectural, engineering, and construction), employment, and business opportunities benefiting the district while the building is being constructed.

This example illustrates the importance of getting on a committee that has the authority to build new federal buildings, which is directly connected to both party and committee patronage. This results, obviously, in constituent patronage. To conclude, the Tolchins' questions are right on target. Patronage, or the lack of it, certainly influences what gets done and how in both the House and the Senate.

Further reading:
Freedman, Anne. *Patronage.* Chicago: Nelson-Hall Publishers, 1994; Tolchin, Martin, and Susan Tolchin. *To The Victor.* New York: Random House, 1971.
—Nancy S. Lind

pay and perquisites

In 1989 representatives adopted a reform prohibiting themselves from receiving honoraria for speeches given to interest groups or articles written for publication. However, they succeeded in giving themselves a pay raise to compensate for their loss of income stemming from passage of the reform proposal. Senators adopted a similar proposal two years later, but only through an unpublicized and late night vote.

Then, the Twenty-seventh Amendment to the Constitution was ratified in 1992, which directed that member pay raises could not go into effect until after the next regularly scheduled election. This amendment enabled citizens to register their reaction to the latest pay raise before it could be put into effect.

Members have enjoyed traditional personal perks established by their chamber, such as a members-only swimming pool, gymnasiums, dining rooms, elevators, hideaway offices (for selected leaders), and vehicle parking places on CAPITOL HILL and at area airports. However, most of their perks have more commonly been associated with easing their effort to do their job or, more prominently, to help them win reelection. Members are authorized a budget with which they can finance their offices on Capitol Hill and at home. Such expenditures include furnishing the office and providing telephones, computers, and other ways to transmit and receive communication. Members also use their office funds to finance their personal staff to be assigned duties and deployed (between Capitol Hill and their home state) as they see fit. Representatives and senators also have access to their chambers' special Capitol Hill television and radio studios and photographers.

Members of each chamber establish and are governed by their own set of rules. All representatives are allocated the same amount of funds for their office staff budgets, while senators are allocated a budget based on the population of the state they represent. Funds not spent each year are returned to the government treasury. Members also are allocated funds to finance trips home to interact with constituents. Allocations to representatives are based on a formula reflecting the distance from their district to Capitol Hill. Senators are allocated money based on the population of the state they represent. Members of both chambers also are authorized to do overseas travel for fact-finding missions.

Perhaps the longest-standing congressional perk is the FRANKING PRIVILEGE, the right of legislators to send mail bearing their signature rather than buying a stamp. This free mail privilege dates from the First Congress and in recent years has increasingly become the target of critics who have alleged that such mail is sent seeking political advantage with constituents. The theory behind the frank was to enable members of Congress to communicate with their constituents the events and issues on Capitol Hill. Such criticism led to a series of reforms adopted in the 1990s that ultimately have led to the reduction but not elimination of member use of the franking privilege. Observers have also speculated that the growing use of e-mail has contributed to the decline in the use of the franking privilege.

Finally, in 1991 one widely considered minor House perk was eliminated quickly amid a massive wave of negative publicity. A General Accounting Office study found that the House bank was allowing representatives to cash checks from accounts with insufficient funds without suffering any consequences. Subsequent reports revealed that numerous representatives from both major parties had either knowingly or inadvertently bounced checks. While the House responded quickly by dissolving its bank, the action came too late for several members, who subsequently were defeated for reelection.

Members of Congress enjoy a pay scale well above that of the average American plus a number of perquisites (or perks) that overall have tended to contribute to their winning reelection. The Constitution authorizes members of Congress to determine their own pay. Voting themselves pay raises traditionally has been a politically difficult task for members of both the SENATE and the HOUSE OF REPRESENTATIVES. Over the years their salaries have been the same, regardless of the chamber in which they served or their seniority or size of constituency (for senators). Although by 2003 their annual salaries had climbed to $154,700, the journey upward seldom was uneventful. For example, members commonly have been reluctant to hold roll-call votes to determine their own pay raises. In 1967 members of both chambers established a system whereby the president, after receiving a recommendation of a commission studying legislator salaries, would propose a pay raise that would go into effect unless vetoed by Congress. Exactly 20 years later senators voted 88-6 to reject a pay raise recommend by President Ronald Reagan, fearing a voter backlash because of the record deficits being accumulated at that time. Meanwhile, representatives were more creative. They rejected their pay raise but took their vote one day after their 30-day window for rejecting the proposed increase.

—James Norris

Pelosi, Nancy (1940–) *Representative, Minority Leader*

Nancy Pelosi represents California's Eighth Congressional District, which includes most of the city of San Francisco. She has served in the House since 1987, when she took office in a special election to replace Democratic representative Sala Burton, who had died in office. On November 14, 2002, House Democrats elected Representative Pelosi House Democratic Minority Leader, replacing RICHARD GEPHARDT of Missouri. Thus, Pelosi because the highest-ranking women in the history of the U.S. Congress and the first women to lead a major political party.

Congresswoman Pelosi grew up in a Catholic family in Baltimore's Little Italy. The youngest of six children and the only girl among five brothers, she received her political education early. Her father, Thomas D'Alesandro, Jr., served in the House of Representatives for five terms; during his tenure he was a member of the Appropriations Committee. He was elected mayor of Baltimore and held that office for 12 years, where he ran a traditional Democratic machine. Young Nancy was educated in the tradition of "retail politics" as she watched her father distribute patronage and call in favors. He built a coalition of Italians, Poles, Jews, blacks, and Irish and used his power to get things done for the city. Her brother went on to become mayor as well.

In the late 1950s Pelosi graduated from the all-girls Institute of Notre Dame and attended Trinity College, a women's college in Washington, D.C. While in college, she served as an intern in the office of a Maryland politician where one of her fellow interns was Steny Hoyer, the Democratic congressman from Maryland she was later to defeat in her bid to become the House Democratic Whip. In 1962 she married Georgetown University graduate and San Francisco native Paul Pelosi. Following the latter's career as an investor and businessman, the couple moved to

San Francisco. There Pelosi had five children in six years and immersed herself in being a full-time mother. One of her children remarked that she was the kind of mom who made Halloween costumes, drove her kids to school in a red wagoneer, attended all their games, and was always baking cookies.

As her children grew older Pelosi became increasingly active in Democratic politics. She chaired the Northern California Democratic Party from 1977 until 1981, when she became state chair. She was also a member of the Democratic National Committee and helped lure the 1984 Democratic National Convention to San Francisco. During this time she allied herself with then representative Phillip Burton, San Francisco's congressman for two decades. When he died in 1983, he was succeeded by his wife, Sela. The latter died of cancer before the end of her second term. Before her death, however, she urged Pelosi to seek her seat. The Burton family's support was crucial to her victory in a special election in 1987.

Before her election as Minority Leader, Congresswoman Pelosi held a number of important positions in the House. She has been ranking Democrat on the House Permanent Select Committee on Intelligence and a member of the House Appropriations Committee and Appropriations Subcommittee on Labor, Health and Human Services and Education. She was the former ranking Democrat on the Appropriation Subcommittee on Foreign Operations and Export Finance. She chaired the Congressional Working Group on China, cochaired the AIDS Task Force of the House Democratic Caucus, and cochaired the Bio-Medical Research Caucus. She also served on the House Committee on Standards of Official Conduct.

In 2001 Representative Pelosi narrowly defeated Representative Steny Hoyer (D-MD) to become House Minority Whip. A year later she won the leadership race in the House Democratic Caucus by a wide margin when centrist Martin Frost (D-TX) pulled out of the race. Ms. Pelosi received 177 of 206 votes.

Pelosi has a special talent for charming disparate wings of her party. Perhaps because she is a politician's daughter, she understands the importance of developing personal relationships. An important foundation for these relationships has been her prodigious fund-raising efforts. The latter is one of the primary reasons for her rise in congressional party politics. She helped raise almost $8 million for fellow Democrats and the Democratic Congressional Campaign Committee in the 2002 campaign, surpassing former Democratic Minority Leader Richard Gephardt and most of the House Republicans.

Congresswoman Pelosi has called herself a "liberal but also a pragmatist." In general, her positions on issues fit those of her progressive constituency of San Francisco. She has been a consistent advocate for AIDS funding for treatment and support of patients. She strongly opposed the House's prohibition of needle exchange programs, arguing that offering clean needles to drug users helps to stop the spread of AIDS. She acquired funding for a mass transit system for the San Francisco Bay area.

Her position as Chair of the Working Group on China gave visibility to her strong stance against human rights violations in that country. After the Tiananmen Square massacre in 1989, she sponsored legislation to give Chinese students the right to remain in the United States. She unsuccessfully challenged President Clinton's efforts to establish normal trade relations with China, insisting on improvements in the latter's human rights record.

Congresswomen Pelosi leads her party's opposition to most of President George W. Bush's domestic and foreign policy agenda. Indeed, in 2001 and 2002 she opposed Mr. Bush approximately 75 percent of the time. Her party cohesion score, that is, the measure that indicates whether one is voting with a majority of one's party members, consistently exceeds 95 percent. She voted against the Bush tax cut and against the resolution authorizing force against Iraq. She also opposed the president's executive order prohibiting family planning groups from receiving U.S. aid if they promote or perform abortions.

Abortion is one of several positions that puts Congresswomen Pelosi on the opposite side of the Republican Party's social and economic agenda. She voted against voucher programs, claiming they hurt public schools; she also opposed a constitutional amendment allowing prayer in public schools. She supported the ban against drilling for oil in the Alaskan Arctic National Wildlife Refuge as well as legislation raising the minimum wage. A friend to labor, she strongly supported the Clinton administration's rules on ergonomic safety in the workplace and opposed the Bush administration's successful bid to nullify them.

Congresswoman Pelosi's election as the congressional Democratic leader initiated a wide spectrum of comments. Predictably, her opponents focus on her political liabilities, while her supporters emphasize her potential for strong leadership. Republicans and their supporters point out that many of her positions seem outside the mainstream of the American electorate. They use terms such as "San Francisco liberal" to show that she represents the most liberal wing of her party and that she is out of touch with a majority of Americans. Indeed, some Republican supporters were enthusiastic about her election because they considered her an easy target for attacks.

Pelosi's supporters, however, emphasize her pragmatism and her political skills, and are confident that she can forge bridges within the party. They point to her traditional background as a wife and mother, her support for issues that appeal to swing voters such as education, health care, housing, and the environment, and, most of all, to her impressive political skills. Her pragmatism echoes her father's examples of coalition building and "retail politics." Her fund-raising skills and collegial style of leadership should help to bridge the various factions within her party. Supporters also maintain that her strong positions on many issues will help to establish a clearer Democratic plan to counter the Republicans for future control of the House.

Further reading:
Dart, Bob. "New House Leader Steeped in Politics, Church, Family." *Atlanta Journal-Constitution,* 15 November 2002; Ferrechio, Susan. "Representative Nancy Pelosi." *CQ Weekly* 60, no. 49 (2002); Feuerherd, Joe. "Roots in Faith, Family and Party Guide Pelosi's Move to Power." *National Catholic Reporter On-line,* 24 January, 2003; Jones, Mary Lynn F. "Woman on Top: Nancy Pelosi Is the Democrats' Mid-Course Correction." *American Prospect,* 16 December 2002, p. 11; "Nancy Pelosi's Record." *Washington Times,* 18 November 2002.

—Cynthia Opheim

Persian Gulf War of 1991

This was a brief war in 1990 between Iraq and a coalition of Western and Arab countries led by the United States. The coalition's actions included both defensive (Operation Desert Shield) and offensive operations to liberate Kuwait (Operation Desert Storm). A disagreement between some members of America's executive and legislative branches regarding the constitutionality of the use of force in this case precipitated a dramatic policy debate.

In the American system of checks and balances, the Constitution (Article I, Section 8) gives the power to declare war to the legislative branch. In cases of aggression or invasion, however, the president may act in self-defense on his own authority as commander in chief. The founding fathers made it clear: Decisions concerning going to war are the purview of the legislative branch, although reality has been distinctly different. In the 220-plus instances in which American armed forces have been used, only five have involved a declaration of war (in 1812, 1846, 1898, 1917, and 1941).

In the latter part of the 20th century, scholars argued that the legislative branch lost a great deal of power and influence in foreign and defense policy in relation to the executive branch. Congress has been in part responsible for that trend. For example, in 1950 Congress failed to debate seriously the issue of declaring war or even to require the president to seek its approval for combat operations in Korea. Through the 1964 Gulf of Tonkin Resolution, Congress provided President Lyndon Johnson approval to make retaliatory air raids in response to an alleged attack on a U.S. Navy destroyer without realizing the full implications of its decision. The approval effectively provided a blank check for U.S. military involvement in the Vietnam War, far beyond what Congress expected. As a result of this event, the WAR POWERS RESOLUTION OF 1973 was passed over the veto of President Richard Nixon. The law required the president in every possible instance to consult Congress before committing U.S. forces to imminent hostilities and to report to Congress within 48 hours of sending forces into combat and required that U.S. forces be withdrawn from such operations within 60 days unless Congress declared war or otherwise provided the requisite authorization.

One of the explanations given for congressional acquiescence in 1950 and 1964 was the Democratic Party's control of both branches. The Persian Gulf War, however, took place in a political environment of divided government: Republicans controlled the executive branch and Democrats dominated the legislative branch (House 267–167 and Senate 56–44). Therefore, the issues of war-making power with its tangled legal and historical legacies was further complicated by the realities of modern partisan politics.

Immediately following the Iraqi invasion of Kuwait on August 2, 1990, the UN Security Council adopted a series of resolutions condemning the act and authorizing an embargo. Between August and late October approximately 200,000 coalition soldiers were positioned in the Persian Gulf as part of Desert Shield. Because the number of troops in the theater precluded offensive actions, Congress believed they were there strictly for defensive purposes and could not be used in an offensive manner without further build-up, thus allowing time to request congressional authorization. President George H. W. Bush stated on several occasions he believed he had the authority to take military action to enforce the UN resolution and therefore did not need congressional approval. Up to this point there had been no real consultation with Congress, which recessed on October 28. Several days after the midterm election in November 1990, President Bush announced a second-stage build-up critics argued would allow for unilateral offensive action. Now the administration had the assets in place to conduct offensive operations to liberate Kuwait. With the changed tactical situation in the Persian Gulf, the administration's view that it did not need congressional authorization, together with the constitutional issues involved, made this more than an interesting academic debate.

On November 20 a fear that President Bush was going to act without congressional authorization led Ronald V. Dellums, a Democrat from California, and 45 House Democrats to file suit in U.S. district court to obtain an injunction barring Bush from using force to liberate Kuwait without congressional approval. On December 12 Judge Harold H. Greene ruled, in *Dellums et al. v. Bush,* that it was premature for the court to comment because Congress as a whole had not taken a stand but added that Congress alone possessed the power to declare war.

On November 29, 1990, Bush's hand was strengthened when, by a 12-2 vote, the UN Security Council adopted Resolution 678 authorizing the use of force to expel Iraq if it did not withdraw from Kuwait by the January 15, 1991, deadline. Congress faced a dilemma: vote for an authorization to use force, possibly providing a blank check, as with the Gulf of Tonkin Resolution, or do nothing, as with Korea, and cede more war-making authority to the executive branch. Increasingly, members of Congress and the public were calling for a formal resolution authorizing the president's use of force in Kuwait. The administration's position, however, was made clear on December 3, when Secretary of Defense Richard Cheney told a Senate hearing, "the president is within his authority at this point to carry out his responsibility" [i.e., go to war]. The political conflict continued to escalate, culminating with three days, January 10–12, of debate. In the end, competing resolutions were simultaneously introduced in both chambers, just three days before the UN deadline. In both chambers the Democratic resolutions were introduced first. The Democratic sponsored resolutions focusing on continued economic sanctions and not authorizing the use of force were defeated in both the House (183-250) and the Senate (46-53). The Republican versions, drawing on the language of section 8(a) (1) of the War Powers Resolution authorizing the use of force, pursuant to UN Security Council Resolution 678, passed both the House (250-183) and the Senate (52-47).

Although the vote in Congress provided the Bush administration a political victory, authorizing the use of force in support of Resolution 678, it was a defeat for the administration's position that it did not need congressional approval to go to war under such circumstances. In the end, by seeking a vote Bush tacitly admitted the need for congressional authorization to send troops into combat. The months of hearings and debates, in which the gravity of the decisions were constantly discussed, meant Congress could not be criticized for failing to take a stand (Korea, 1950) or adopting a resolution without a full understanding of the consequences (Vietnam, 1964).

Further reading:
Tiefer, Charles. *The Semi-Sovereign Presidency: The Bush Administration's Strategy for Governing without Congress.* Boulder, Colo.: Westview Press, 1994; Relyea, Harold C., and L. Elaine Halchin. *Informing Congress: The Role of the Executive in Time of War.* New York: Novinka Books, 2003.
—Craig T. Cobane

petitions and memorials
Requests for Congress to take action have been made by people, in the case of petitions, and state and local government, in the case of memorials. The First Amendment to the U.S. Constitution guarantees Congress shall make no law abridging the right of the people to petition the government for a redress of grievances. Individuals, groups, and organizations are allowed to petition Congress to take action or to not take action on a specific subject. Petitions are sent to individual House members and senators and do not have to be from the House members' or Senators' constituents. In the House the procedure for handling petitions and memorials is governed by Clause 3 of Rule XII: If a member, delegate, or resident commissioner has a petition, memorial, or private bill to present, he or she shall endorse his or her name and deliver it to the Clerk and may specify the reference or disposition to be made thereof. Such petition, memorial, or private bill (except when judged by the Speaker to be obscene or insulting) shall be entered on the journal with the name of the member, delegate, or resident commissioner presenting it and shall be printed in the CONGRESSIONAL RECORD. The petition is forwarded to the committee having jurisdiction over the petition's subject.

Senate Rule VII governs petitions in the Senate. Senators having petitions, memorials, bills, or resolutions to present after the morning hour may deliver them in the absence of objection to the presiding officer's desk, endorsing upon them their names, and with the approval of the presiding officer, they shall be entered on the journal with the names of the senators presenting them and in the absence of objection shall be considered as having been read twice and referred to the appropriate committees. A transcript of such entries shall be furnished to the official reporter of debates for publication in the *Congressional Record,* under the direction of the Secretary of the Senate.

Only a brief statement of the contents of petitions and memorials is printed in the *Congressional Record.* The publication of more than a brief statement requires a vote of the Senate, except when the petition or memorial is from the legislatures or conventions, lawfully called, of the respective states, territories, and insular possessions. These petitions and memorials are always published in full. Senate Rule VII, paragraph 4, outlines the rarely used procedure in which the Senate may vote without debate on a particular petition or memorial:

Petitions or memorials are referred, without debate, to the appropriate committee according to subject matter on the same basis as bills and resolutions if signed by the petitioner or memorialist. A question of receiving or reference may be raised and determined without debate. But no petition, memorial, or other paper signed by citizens or subjects of a foreign power shall be received unless the same be transmitted to the Senate by the president.

Petitions received by early Congresses dealt with such controversial issues as contested election results, the National Bank, the expulsion of Cherokees from Georgia, land distribution, the abolition of dueling, government in the territories, the Alien and Sedition Acts, and the slave trade. Since petitions were read at the start of each day's business, too many petitions could stop legislative business. The slavery debate before the Civil War created a flood of petitions from abolitionist groups as well as organizations trying to maintain the institution of slavery. In reaction to the number of petitions received, in 1840 the House of Representatives enacted a GAG RULE. No petitions or resolutions asking for the abolition of slavery were to be received by the House. Former president and member of the House of Representatives John Quincy Adams worked to end the gag rule because he believed that citizens had the right to petition their government.

Historically, memorials were sent by state legislatures seeking to instruct their senators in Washington. This practice ended with the direct election of senators in 1913. Now state legislatures send memorials as a formal means of communication asking for congressional action rather than demanding it.

The *Congressional Record* of July 21, 2004, recorded that the Senate received several petitions and memorials, including a concurrent resolution adopted by the house of representatives of Louisiana relative to income guidelines for senior citizens. The petition was referred to the COMMITTEE ON AGRICULTURE, NUTRITION, AND FORESTRY. Another petition was a resolution adopted by the senate of Michigan relative to emergency supplemental appropriations to strengthen security and increase staffing at United States–Canada border crossings. This petition was referred to the COMMITTEE ON APPROPRIATIONS. On that same day the House reported receiving three memorials from the legislature of Hawaii and two petitions from the legislature of Rockland County, New York.

Further reading:
Higginson, Stephen A. "A Short History of the Right to Petition Government for the Redress of Grievances." *Yale Law Journal* 96 (1986): 142–166; Rundquist, Paul S. *Messages, Petitions, Communications, and Memorials to Congress.* Washington, D.C.: Library of Congress, Congressional Research Service, 2003.

—John David Rausch, Jr.

point of order

A point of order is a parliamentary claim voiced from the floor by a member of the SENATE or HOUSE OF REPRESENTATIVES that a pending action violates a chamber rule or violates a chamber procedure in a specified way. If a member of the House or the Senate believes that an action violates a chamber rule or procedure, he or she is allowed to make the claim by rising and asking for a point of order.

The presiding officer must hear the point if the member is recognized. No points of order may be brought against certain decisions of the chair or after the challenged action has been completed. The presiding officer issues a ruling on the point of order. If the point of order is upheld, the pending action is prohibited. Debate on the point of order is for the purposes of informing the presiding officer, and he and she controls that debate. No debate is allowed in the Senate. All business is postponed until the chair rules on whether the point of order is valid.

In the Senate any senator may appeal the ruling of the chair. The Senate then decides the point of order, usually by majority vote, when it votes on the appeal. The chair's ruling has been overturned on occasion. The chair also has the option of submitting a point of order to the Senate for a decision without issuing a ruling. Such action is required only when constitutional questions or certain Senate rules are involved.

Appeals in the House are rare, and reversals of the chair's rulings even rarer. There are two reasons why appeals are rarely made in the House. Usually the correctness of the ruling is not in doubt because the chair consulted with the parliamentarian before making the ruling. The parliamentarian based his or her recommendation on actions taken on similar questions. The members of the House from the majority party are expected to support the ruling made by the presiding officer, who also is a member of the majority party.

Rulings on points of order set precedents. The rulings made by the full chamber are the most authoritative.

Points of order are not the same as parliamentary inquiries. Parliamentary inquiries are questions posed to the presiding officer about the current parliamentary situation. The presiding officer's responses are explanations, not rulings, and they are not subject to appeal.

Further reading:
Brown, Wm. Holmes, and Charles W. Johnson. *House Practice: A Guide to the Rules, Precedents, and Procedures of the House.* Washington, D.C.: Government Printing Office, 2003; Riddick, Floyd M., and Alan S. Frumin. *Riddick's Senate Procedure: Precedents and Practices.* Senate Document No. 101-28. Washington, D.C.: Government Printing Office, 1992.

—John David Rausch, Jr.

political action committees

Political action committees are commonly referred to by the acronym PAC. PACs are organized groups created to influence the electoral process. They serve as political mechanisms for unions, corporations, health care groups, trade associations, political leaders, and other citizen-based groups. Industries that are heavily regulated by the government are more likely to form PACs and be involved in electoral politics. PACs play a significant role in campaign financing today; in 2000 PACs spent nearly $260 million on federal candidates.

In 1943 the Smith-Connally Act restricted union campaign contributions. The Taft-Hartley Act of 1947 made the provisions of the Smith-Connally Act permanent—unions and corporations were not permitted to give monetary contributions to federal campaigns. Responding to these restrictions, the CIO (Congress of Industrial Organizations) formed the nation's first PAC in 1943. Since unions and corporations deal with other activities that exist outside the realm of the political arena, PACs were formed to solely deal with electoral politics, a completely separate entity from the union or corporation. Not all union members or corporate employees contribute to the PAC, and not all PAC contributors are union members or employees of a specific corporation. By creating PACs these groups were in full compliance with the Smith-Connally Act.

The Federal Election Campaign Act (FECA) of 1971 created individual contribution limits and explicitly permitted the establishment of separate and segregated funds (or PACs). PACs were permitted to contribute $5,000 per candidate per election. Also, corporations with government contracts began organizing PACs due to the restrictions placed on their acceptable political activity.

The FECA of 1974 lifted the ban on corporations with government contracts contributing to federal campaigns. This spurred a more rapid growth in the number of corporate PACs. In 1975 the Federal Election Commission (FEC) ruled that the parent organization of a union or corporation could cover the administrative and fund-raising costs for the PAC.

In 1976 the Supreme Court ruled in the case *Buckley v. Valeo* that PACs could spend unlimited amounts of money on issue advocacy, advertising that supports a particular issue position but does not explicitly call for the election or defeat of a candidate. During the 1990s PACs dramatically increased their spending on issue advocacy. While the ads did not directly support or oppose a candidate, many of the ads indirectly supported a particular candidate.

The regulation of PACs evolved most recently with the Bipartisan Campaign Reform Act of 2002. Senators John McCain (R-AZ) and Russell Feingold (D-WI) were the sponsors of this legislation that proposed numerous changes to the FECA of 1971. The most notable changes for PACs were significant limitations on issue advocacy. Under the new law unions and corporations could not use issue advocacy showing a candidate's photo or likeness within 60 days of a general election. In addition, any group spending more than $10,000 a year on issue advocacy was required to file a report with the Federal Elections Committee. Finally, political parties are no longer able to collect or spend soft money—money donated to political parties for noncampaign purposes. The Supreme Court ruled that this new law was constitutional in *McConnell v. FEC* (2003).

Common PAC affiliations include unions, corporations, and citizen-based groups. These PACs can be classified as connected or nonconnected. Connected PACs have a parent organization that can cover all the expenses of the PAC. As of 2000, corporations made up the largest percentage of connected PACs, with just over 1,200 PACs. There were 900 trade/membership/health PACs and 350 labor PACs.

Nonconnected (independent) PACs do not have a parent organization. There has been a dramatic increase in the number of nonconnected PACs in the past decades, with over 1,300 active independent PACs in 2000. These independent PACs may be created to focus on political leadership, political issues, or a political ideology.

Corporations and unions typically have the most active PACs, as data from the 2004 general election indicate. As of June 2004 the 20 most active PACs represent businesses, including Wal-Mart and the United Parcel Service; labor unions, such as the International Brotherhood of Electrical Workers; and trade associations, such as the Association of Trial Lawyers of America and the National Beer Wholesalers Association.

PACs have adopted a wide variety of strategies to influence elections. PACs focus their spending on majority leaders, committee chairs, and incumbents. Understanding the high reelection rates in the House and Senate, most PACs contribute to incumbent candidates; in 2000 75 percent of PAC funds went to incumbent candidates.

PACs have adopted unique ways of allocating their resources. Bundling occurs when PACs collect checks from their members and send them all to the candidate at the same time. One notable PAC that has implemented this strategy is EMILY's List, which helps elect Democratic women. PACs also have adopted the strategy of funneling money through other PACs and political parties that share a similar ideology.

PACs prefer to allocate their money to races in which they can have the greatest impact. For example, union PACs generally believe that Democratic candidates are more likely to support their goals. Therefore, they strive to maximize the number of Democratic seats in Congress. In fact, labor union PACs gave 92 percent of their contributions in 2000 to Democratic candidates. On the other hand, businesses and other conservative PACs contribute more to the Republican Party, 67 percent in the 2000 election. Many PACs are willing to contribute to either party depending on which party holds the majority. These organizations understand the importance of keeping a civil relationship with the majority party and its leaders.

It is expected that PACs will alter their political strategies in order to comply with the Bipartisan Campaign Reform Act. In previous years soft money contributions to political parties and issue advocacy played a large role in the funding of campaigns by PACs. The new regulations will require PACs to develop new strategies. PACs may choose to give funds to special interest groups rather than political parties. On the other hand, PACs may choose to give funds to 527 political organizations that are not classified as political parties but rather focus on voter education. These groups, such as the liberal organization MoveOn.org, are similar to political parties, with broad goals and issue interests. Finally, it is expected that PACs will develop new advertising techniques to comply with the Bipartisan Campaign Reform Act, such as more direct mail and print advertising.

Further reading:
Biersack, Robert, Paul S. Herrnson, and Clyde Wilcox, eds. *After the Revolution: PACs, Lobbies, and the Republican Congress.* Boston: Allyn & Bacon, 1999; Cigler, Allan, and Burdett Loomis, eds. *Interest Group Politics.* 6th ed. Washington, D.C.: Congressional Quarterly Press, 2002.
—Melinda Mueller and Michael Woods

Pollock v. Farmer's Loan and Trust Co. 157 U.S. (1895)

In this case a divided Supreme Court struck down the Income Tax Act of 1894 and in doing so interpreted the Constitution in such a way as to greatly restrict Congress's power to tax. This was done despite the fact that the Court had unanimously upheld an income tax in *Springer v. United States* in 1881.

The Constitution delegates to Congress the power to lay and collect taxes, but it recognizes different classes of taxes that place different kinds of obligations on Congress. The Constitution recognizes duties, imposts, and excises. It requires that when Congress enacts such taxes, they must be uniform throughout the United States. The Constitution also recognizes a class of taxes called direct taxes, does not define that term, but requires that they be apportioned among the states based on population.

In 1895 Chief Justice Melville Fuller, writing for the Court's majority, found the income tax unconstitutional. Fuller considered that a tax on a person's entire income, whether derived from real estate or from stocks and bonds, amounted to a direct tax. Taxes on real estate had long been considered direct taxes, and this law covered income from a person's land, which Fuller considered the equivalent of a tax on the land itself. He considered it a direct tax that Congress had not apportioned among the states based on their population. Therefore, it was unconstitutional. He held a similar view of taxes on income from stocks and

bonds. Fuller went on to argue that deductions and exemptions written into the law so deprived it of uniformity as to put it in violation of the Fifth Amendment's guarantee of due process of law.

The dissenters were highly critical of the majority's interpretation of the Constitution, as well as what they believed to be the majority's disregard for established precedent. The dissenters noted that in the early case of *Hylton v. United States* (1796) all the justices agreed in separate opinions that no tax could be a direct tax if it would make no sense to apportion it among the states according to population. It would certainly make no sense to apportion an income tax, since to do so would mean that people with identical incomes could have to pay different tax amounts depending upon the states in which they resided. Moreover, there was the precedent of *Springer v. United States* upholding an income tax in 1881. Some of the dissenters were also concerned that the *Pollock* decision would create two classes of citizens: one class that could not have its income taxed because it was derived from land or stocks and bonds, and another class that derived its income from the labor of hands or minds and whose income could be taxed, without any need for apportionment among the states. As for the argument that the income tax lacked uniformity due to deductions and exemptions permitted by the law, Justice Henry Brown stated that Congress was within its authority as long as the deductions and exemptions were based on some principle and were not purely arbitrary.

Although the dissenters' arguments failed in the Court, the position of the majority failed in the political arena. Reformers believed that American citizens should pay for the cost of government and that the wealthy should bear more of the cost. There were several unsuccessful attempts to overrule the *Pollock* decision by amending the Constitution to authorize Congress to enact an income tax. Special interest lobbying, however, was able to defeat such efforts in Congress. In 1909 Congress finally succeeded in proposing the Sixteenth Amendment, primarily because Senator Nelson W. Aldrich, a Republican from Rhode Island and chair of the Finance Committee, misread the political climate. He introduced the proposal to amend the Constitution to draw attention from a tariff bill he sponsored, believing that the states would never ratify the amendment. Senator Aldrich was wrong. By February 3, 1913, the required three-fourths of the states had ratified the Sixteenth Amendment, which empowered Congress to tax incomes, regardless of their source, without any need to apportion the tax among the states according to population. The *Pollock* decision had been overruled.

Further reading:
Bernstein, Richard B., with Jerome Agel. *Amending the Constitution: If We Love the Constitution So Much, Why*

Do We Keep Trying to Change It? Lawrence: University Press of Kansas, 1993; Kelly, Alfred H., and Winfred A Harbison. *The American Constitution: Its Origin and Development.* 4th ed. New York: Norton, 1970; Schwartz, Bernard. *A History of the Supreme Court.* New York: Oxford University Press, 1993.

—Patricia A. Behlar

Populists in Congress

From 1891 through 1903 (52nd–57th Congresses), 50 Populists served on CAPITOL HILL, seven in the SENATE and 43 in the HOUSE OF REPRESENTATIVES. At its peak in the 55th Congress (1897–99), the Populist delegation numbered six senators and 25 representatives, plus one delegate from the Oklahoma Territory. Except for two from Minnesota and one each from Michigan and Illinois, all the congressional Populists were from the South or states west of Missouri. The states with the most Populist members of Congress were Kansas (13), Nebraska (8), and North Carolina (7).

The Populist Party (officially, the People's Party) grew out of three farmers' organizations in the late 1880s—the Northern Alliance, the Southern Alliance, and the Colored Farmers' Alliance. Although state parties elected Populists to office earlier, the national party was officially established in 1892. Its presidential candidate in 1892, James B. Weaver, won 8.5 percent of the popular vote and 22 electoral votes.

The platform of the Populist Party was principally aimed at the needs of farmers in the wheat and cotton belts and western miners, but it also contained planks aimed at other economic reform. The main three Populist demands were for financial reforms, including a flexible currency and unlimited coinage of silver; transportation, including government ownership of railroads and telephone and telegraph companies; and land reform. The Populists also fought for what would today be called agricultural price supports. Some of their nonfarm demands included labor's right to organize, black political and economic rights, direct election of senators, and extensive public works projects to counter the depression of the 1890s.

In the West Populists came from both the Republican and the Democratic Parties, although more came from the Democrats. In the South Populists came almost entirely from the Democratic Party. During the 1890s free coinage of silver, always a Populist demand, grew in importance. The Populists in the West found that they needed to unite with Democrats to win elections, and "free silver" was the issue used to unite the two parties. Other demands faded as "free silver" became the movement's dominant demand.

By the late 1890s pure western Populists were replaced by "Fusionist" Populist-Democrats. By the 57th

Congress (1901–03) all three of the western Populist senators and four of the five representatives were Democratic Fusionists. Meanwhile, in the South black Populist voters were disfranchised, and white Populists were killed, intimidated, or distracted by Jim Crow. By the 57th Congress there were no southern Populists in Congress. No Populists served in Congress as Populists after 1903, although some former Populists subsequently served as Republicans and Democrats. While not especially successful in advancing its program during the 1890s, many of the Populist demands, such as a flexible currency and farm price supports, were eventually adopted and are taken for granted today.

Further reading:
Clanton, Gene. *Congressional Populism and the Crisis of the 1890s.* Lawrence: University Press of Kansas, 1998; ———. "Hayseed Socialism on the Hill: Congressional Populism, 1891–1895." *Western Historical Quarterly* 15 (April 1984) 139–162; Goodwyn, Lawrence. *The Populist Moment.* New York: Oxford University Press, 1978; Hicks, John D. *The Populist Revolt.* Minneapolis: University of Minnesota Press, 1931; Pollock, Norman. *The Populist Response to Industrial America.* New York: Norton, 1962.

—Russell G. Brooker

pork barrel

This is the traditional political practice of Congress allocating funds for projects benefiting interests in a clearly defined local area more than in the nation as a whole. The term originated during the Civil War years when food such as pork was distributed in large barrels. By the end of the 19th century the term became loaded with negative connotations. Contemporary CAPITOL HILL critics decry what they believe to be wasteful spending as "pork."

The most common allegations of pork barrel projects have been congressional expenditures for public works projects such as roads, bridges, ports, and harbors. Construction of new facilities or expansion of existing projects most often has been based on the cooperation between leaders of government agencies and members of Congress. Agency leaders traditionally have sought to distribute their facilities, such as veterans' hospitals or rivers and harbors projects to an array of states and regions as a way to broaden their support on Capitol Hill. Critics, particularly members of Congress representing regions not receiving such projects, have decried such decisions as being made on the basis of political considerations rather than on the merit of the plans.

Classic pork barrel efforts are part of a LOGROLLING effort whereby members will trade votes for other projects for support for a project favoring their constituents. This has been the classic method for passing farm sub-

In this cartoon by Robert Carter, President Woodrow Wilson is chastising a donkey, labeled "U.S. Congress," outfitted for war along with a small pork barrel. *(Library of Congress)*

sidy support legislation throughout the 20th century. Other common pork barrel logrolling efforts have included OMNIBUS BILLS setting tax, tariff, and trade policies. Such efforts have meant that each member partici-

pating in the logroll will receive something for the folks back home.

Members of the SENATE and HOUSE OF REPRESENTATIVES alike are widely expected to win their fair share of projects for constituents. David Mayhew has termed such practices as earning "particularized benefits for grateful constituents." In turn, members of Congress claim credit for winning such benefits, particularly reminding voters just before subsequent election days. Pork barrel benefits such as federal grants and construction funding are clearly targeted to specific recipients rather than scattered around the nation, such as benefits from entitlement programs.

The term *pork barrel spending* often is used to decry the allocation of federal funds for grants to finance studies to gather information critics find laughable. Critics also have maintained that what they see as wasteful pork barrel spending dominates the federal budget. Others have defended most congressional expenditure practices as going toward transfer entitlement programs and interest on the debt or to fund programs supported for their merits and their ability to produce meaningful results.

Further reading:
Mayhew, David. *Congress: The Electoral Connection.* New Haven, Conn.: Yale University Press, 1974; Evans, Diana. "The Distribution of Pork Barrel Projects and Vote Buying in Congress." In William T. Bianco, ed. *Congress on Display, Congress at Work.* Ann Arbor: University of Michigan Press, 2000; Ferejohn, John. *Pork Barrel Politics.* Stanford, Calif.: Stanford University Press, 1974; Wildavsky, Aaron, and Naomi Caiden. *The New Politics of the Budgetary Process.* 5th ed. New York: Longman, 2003.

Post Office and Civil Service Committee, House

A defunct standing committee of the U.S. HOUSE OF REPRESENTATIVES, the Post Office and Civil Service Committee functioned from 1947 to 1995. The committee was established on January 3, 1947, as part of the LEGISLATIVE REORGANIZATION ACT OF 1946. It absorbed the jurisdictions of the Committees on Post Offices and Post Roads (1808–1946), Civil Service (1924–46), and the Census (1901–46). The committee was also given jurisdiction over the National Archives, which had been under the House Committee on the Library (1806–1946). In 1995, at the beginning of the 104th Congress, the committee was abolished, and its jurisdiction was transferred to the House Committee on Government Reform. At the time of its dissolution the committee included five subcommittees: Census, Statistics and Postal Personnel; Civil Service; Compensation and Employee Benefits; Oversight and Investigations; and Postal Operations and Services.

The rules of the House of Representatives stipulated that the committee's formal jurisdiction included the census and the collection of statistics generally; federal civil service generally; National Archives; postal savings banks; postal service generally, including the railway mail service and measures relating to ocean mail and pneumatic-tube service, but excluding post roads; and the status of officers and employees of the United States, including their compensation, classification, and retirement (U.S. Congress, 1967: 350). One of the committee's functions was to publish the U.S. Government Policy and Supporting Positions, popularly known as the Plum Book, a listing of government patronage positions first issued in 1960. The committee alternated with the Senate GOVERNMENTAL AFFAIRS COMMITTEE in publishing the book after each presidential election.

The Postal Service Act abolished the cabinet-level Post Office Department and replaced it with a government-owned corporation, the U.S. Postal Service. The Postmaster General was removed from the president's cabinet and would be an appointee of the Board of Postal Governors, which would be responsible for the management of the corporation. Nine members would be appointed by the president (subject to the advice and consent of the U.S. Senate) for nine-year terms. The Postmaster General and deputy Postmaster General are also members of the board. The legislation also transferred responsibility for approving changes in postage rates from Congress to a new regulatory body, the U.S. Postal Rate Commission. The five-member body, appointed by the president with advice and consent of the Senate, recommends postal rates and classifications to the board of governors. The act also authorized a postal career service, a separate merit system for postal employees.

The Civil Service Reform Act of 1978 restructured the merit system by creating the Senior Executive Service, a cadre of senior civil servants, and reorganizing the U.S. Civil Service Commission into two separate agencies, the Office of Personnel Management and the Merit Systems Protection Board. The Office of Personnel Management administers the civil service, conducts civil service examinations, and supervises the Senior Executive Service. The Merit Systems Protection Board was given authority for discipline of civil servants and for hearing appeals from civil servants and job applicants. The statute also established the Federal Labor Relations Authority, a body analogous to the National Labor Relations Board in the private sector, codifying the rights of federal employees to join unions and engage in collective bargaining on certain subjects.

In 1983 the committee supported legislation designating civil rights leader Martin Luther King, Jr.'s, birthday a federal holiday, bringing to a conclusion a 15-year-long effort that began after King's assassination in 1968. In 1990 the committee reported out the Federal Employee Pay Comparability Act (Public Law 101-509), which restructured the compensation system for federal white-collar employees and attempted to improve employee retention by ensuring that those in government would receive pay comparable to those performing similar work in the private sector. The act replaced a nationwide general schedule for compensation with a system that made adjustments for pay based on the differences in the cost of living around the country.

Further reading:
U.S. Congress, House of Representatives, Constitution. *Jefferson's Manual, and Rules of the House of Representatives of the United States, 90th Congress.* H. Doc. 529, 89th Cong., 2d Sess., 1967; Schroeder, Patricia S. *24 Years of House Work and the Place Is Still a Mess: My Life in Politics.* Kansas City: Andrews McMeel Publishers, 1998.

—Jeffrey Kraus

Powell v. McCormack 395 U.S. 486 (1969)

The challenger in this case was Adam Clayton Powell, Jr., an African-American Democratic congressman from New York City. In 1967 he was suing JOHN MCCORMACK, then the SPEAKER OF THE HOUSE and also a Democrat. The case raised several complicated legal matters, but it also carried troublesome racial overtones.

Along with William Dawson from Chicago, Powell was for many years one of the only two African-American members of Congress. Powell was first elected by his Harlem constituency in 1944 and was reelected regularly thereafter. His seniority in the majority party brought him to the chair of the House Education and Labor Committee in 1961. Sometimes abrasive, sometimes charming, Powell embarrassed his colleagues with his extensive and highly publicized travel, ostensibly on government business, which took him to nightspots in foreign capitals as well as the Bahamas. He had tax problems with the Internal Revenue Service and was held in contempt of court in New York for avoiding payment of a libel judgment against him there. His wife was on his staff payroll but did not work in Washington, D.C., or in his constituency, as House rules required. As a committee chair, he delayed legislation reported by his own committee as a means of bargaining with other people and interests. In 1966 his committee revolted against his control, adopting new committee rules to circumvent his delays and to limit his power over the expenditure of committee funds. Despite these difficulties with his colleagues, Powell was overwhelmingly reelected by his constituency.

When Congress resumed in 1967, the House Democratic CAUCUS stripped Powell of his committee chair. The whole House voted to deny him his seat pending an investigation by a select committee. The select committee documented Powell's shortcomings, recommending several remedies, including a $40,000 fine and the loss of his seniority rights. Nevertheless, it recommended his seating. However, on March 1, 1967, the House amended the resolution of its select committee. The substitute amendment stated that Powell was excluded from membership in the 90th Congress. The House passed the substitute by a vote of 278-176.

A week later Powell filed his suit, *Powell v. McCormack,* in the District of Columbia to regain the seat and his congressional salary. Powell argued that his exclusion violated his constitutional rights because he fulfilled the constitutional requirements for the office to which he was elected. He was of age, a qualified citizen, and an inhabitant of the state in which he was elected.

On April 7, 1967, the district court dismissed the suit saying it lacked jurisdiction. Powell appealed, and the court of appeals agreed with the lower court dismissal, adding that the case raised a "political question," in which the judiciary should not violate separation of powers by intruding on Congress.

On June 16, 1969, the Supreme Court announced its decision to reverse the earlier court decisions. By an 8-1 majority the Supreme Court rejected the claim that this intruded on the prerogatives of the House. It said that the Constitution allows the House no authority to exclude any person who is duly elected and meets the constitutional requirements for office. Moreover, the Court asserted that it has responsibility as the "ultimate interpreter of the Constitution" to overrule variant determinations by other branches of government.

The Court's decision was careful to say it was not expressing any limit on the power of Congress to expel or otherwise punish its members under Article 1, Section 5, of the Constitution. The issue raised in Powell's case was exclusion rather than expulsion.

However, Powell returned to the House before the Supreme Court decided in his favor regarding his exclusion. The Harlem congressional seat was declared vacant, and a special election was held to fill it. Powell won the special election with 86 percent of the vote but made no attempt to be seated during that term. In 1968 he won reelection again with more than 80 percent of the vote. Before seating him on January 3, 1969, the House passed a resolution, milder than the one recommended in 1967, calling for a $25,000 fine and stripping his seniority. He was then sworn into office and seated. He served out his term but was defeated in the primary election of 1970 by Charles Rangel. Powell died in Miami on April 4, 1972, at the age of 63.

See also QUALIFICATIONS OF MEMBERSHIP.

Further reading:
Powell v. McCormack 395 U.S. 486 (1969); Mikula, M., and L. M. Mabunda, eds. *Great American Court Cases.* Vol. 4. Detroit: Gale Group, 1999; *Congress and the Nation.* Vol. 2. Washington, D.C.: Congressional Quarterly Service, 1969; *Congress and the Nation.* Vol. 3. Washington, D.C.: Congressional Quarterly Service, 1973.

—Jack R. Van Der Slik

POW/MIA (Prisoners of War–Missing In Action) Affairs, Senate Select Committee on

On August 2, 1991, the U.S. SENATE passed a resolution introduced by Senator Robert Smith, a Republican from New Hampshire, creating the Select Committee on POW/MIA Affairs. The resolution was introduced due to suspicions that American soldiers captured during the Vietnam War might still be alive in Southeast Asia. The 12-member committee was chaired by a veteran of the Vietnam War, Senator John Kerry, a Democrat from Massachusetts. Senator Smith served as vice chair. It was made up of six Democrats and six Republicans. The committee began its work on November 5, 1991.

Its purpose was to examine all the U.S. government's actions, intelligence, and policies relating to POWs and MIAs for the previous 20 years. The committee's goals were to ensure that the government adequately followed up on live-sighting reports, to make the accounting process more comprehensible so that the statistics used in the discussions would become easier to understand, and to add to the executive branch's efforts in obtaining cooperation from foreign countries, mainly Southeast Asian, in the search for missing soldiers. Other goals were to make it possible for the committee itself and for the public to reach their own informed conclusions by declassifying POW/MIA documents in the government's possession. Furthermore, the committee examined unresolved issues regarding POWs and MIAs from World War II, Korea, and the cold war but focused mainly on the Vietnam War. The investigation lasted 15 months, and the committee released a report on January 13, 1993, signed by all members. All the members with the exception of two concluded that no convincing evidence had been found that suggested that American soldiers were still being held in Southeast Asia.

The committee held many hearings and reviewed government documents from several governmental agencies to examine how they handled POW and MIA cases. The committee also sent delegations to Vietnam, Laos, Cambodia, and Thailand to assess the possibility of resolving the POW/MIA issue. One of the delegations included Senator Kerry, vice chair Senator Smith, Senator Chuck Grassley, a Republican from Iowa, Senator Hank Brown, a Republican from Colorado, and Senator Chuck Robb, a Democrat from Virginia. According to Kerry during a Senate floor speech on April 29, 1992, the trip was a success. He claimed that there were very good prospects that progress could be done with proper follow-up from the State Department, especially with the Vietnamese government. The Vietnamese provided the senators with access to military bases and prisons they wanted to visit. The Vietnamese government also expressed its desire to meet the demands of the U.S. government. The demands that were put forth by the delegation included access to locations where the United States might suspect that American soldiers were present or live-sightings had been reported and access to archives, prison records, hospital records, former military personnel, and people whose names had been given by returning POWs. Furthermore, the delegation also asked that the United States be provided with needed logistical support to operate within Vietnam and the return of all soldiers' remains that might still be in Vietnam's possession.

The committee's temporary authorization expired on January 3, 1993. Several of its members expressed their intentions to continue to press for more answers on the POW/MIA issue.

Further reading:
American Memory. United States Senate Select Committee on POW/MIA Affairs. Federal Research Division, 22 July 2004. Available online. URL: http://lcweb2.loc.gov/pow/senate_house/investigation_S.html. Accessed January 19, 2006; Kerry, John. Senate Floor Speech—Report of the POW-MIA Committee Trip to Southeast Asia. 29 April 1992; Government Printing Office. Authority and Rules of the Select Committee on POW/MIA Affairs, United States Senate. Washington, D.C.: Government Printing Office, 1991.

—Arthur Holst

presidential appointments

Under several provisions of the Constitution, both explicit and implied, the president has the authority to appoint individuals to serve in a variety of positions within the federal government. The mechanics of the appointment process vary depending on the position in question and depending on which part of the Constitution provides the basis for the appointment.

Appointments to major positions in the federal government are governed by provisions of Article II, which specifies that the president will appoint, "by and with the advice and consent of the Senate," individuals to serve as federal judges, ambassadors, and "other public ministers" in high-ranking federal positions. Major appointments include cabinet and subcabinet officers, the heads of independent agencies, the members of regulatory commissions, the directors of government corporations, ambassadors, and federal judges. When a president makes a major appointment, his selection must be approved by the Senate, which engages in a confirmation process in order to determine a prospective appointee's qualifications for office.

The president may also appoint individuals to serve in less significant posts within the government. These are so-called "political appointments" because they are not subject to Senate scrutiny and are therefore considered to be patronage appointments that the president can make at his own discretion. These appointments include lower-level positions in each of the cabinet departments, within agencies or offices at the subcabinet level, and in independent agencies.

The White House Presidential Personnel Office controls the process of selecting most appointees and has been the driving force behind presidential appointments since its creation in 1969. The Presidential Personnel Office was created to routinize and standardize the process of identifying potential appointees. (Prior to 1969 loose associations of presidential advisers would brainstorm informally among themselves and with interested parties to identify nominees. Not only was this inefficient, it limited presidents to appointing individuals who were acquainted—however distantly—with members of staff.) Today the process of identifying qualified prospective appointees is done in conjunction with the Presidential Personnel Office's other main purpose, which is the identification of vacancies in government and the determination of appropriate qualifications to fill the positions.

Once a vacancy has been identified and a list of required qualifications established, the Presidential Personnel Office coordinates the recruitment and application phases of the appointment process. The president's aides in this office and throughout the administration work closely with the Presidential Personnel Office to screen candidates. Candidates for presidential appointment must complete a formal job application, disclose personal information concerning their finances, agree to be investigated by the Federal Bureau of Investigation, and submit to any additional background checks required by the position for which they are being considered.

Once the Presidential Personnel Office has compiled a short list of names of prospective appointees, Congress is also likely to be consulted. In the case of appointments requiring Senate confirmation, this is more than mere courtesy; it is in the vital interest of the president to ensure that his nominee is unlikely to face substantial organized opposition in the Senate. However, the White House Office of Legislative Affairs and the congressional relations staff will also seek out professional opinions from members of the House and the Senate on a wide range of prospective appointments. Especially important are the members of congressional leadership from the president's party.

Presidents themselves are unlikely to be involved in the selection of the vast majority of their administration's appointees, even those requiring Senate confirmation. When presidents do involve themselves, they are likely to be involved only at the later stages of the process, although this varies from president to president. In rare cases presidents will "hand pick" nominees to vacant federal positions.

The contemporary appointment process has come under fire in recent years. G. Calvin Mackenzie, a political scientist and longtime observer of the process, notes that there are three major problems with the process today:

> it takes too long for a new president to staff the senior positions in the administration; . . . nominees are exposed for too long to too much investigation and criticism; . . . because the costs and risks of service are so high, it becomes increasingly difficult to recruit the highly qualified people necessary to manage the complex affairs of modern government.

Members of Congress, interest groups, and the media have begun to understand that the thousands of appointments made by the president during his tenure in office have important consequences for public policy. As a result, each of these groups has begun to scrutinize presidential appointments more closely, which has constrained the president's ability to select the candidate he believes is most suitable. At the same time, presidents themselves have contributed to problems with the appointment process because they have refused to turn their political appointments into civil service positions and because they frequently put political considerations ahead of staffing considerations when seeking to make appointments to positions in government.

Further reading:
Mackenzie, G. Calvin. *The Politics of Presidential Appointments.* New York: Twentieth Century Fund, 1981; Mackenzie, G. Calvin. *Obstacle Course: The Report of the Twentieth Century Fund on the Presidential Appointments Process.* New York: Twentieth Century Fund, 1996; Sanford, Jonathan. *Senate Disposition of Ambassadorial Nominations, 1987–1996.* Washington, D.C.: Congressional Research Service, 1997.

—Lauren Bell

previous question

The previous question is a motion used in the HOUSE OF REPRESENTATIVES to end the debate and bring the pending matter to a vote. It is the only parliamentary procedure used to both close debate and prevent further amendment. This motion cannot be offered when the House meets in the COMMITTEE OF THE WHOLE. This motion is not in order in the SENATE.

During the first hour of debate or at its conclusion, the majority floor manager moves the previous question. This motion, which is not debatable, asks the House if it is ready to vote on the pending matter. If a majority votes for the motion, no more debate on the bill is in order and no amendments may be offered. The House usually votes immediately whether to approve the pending matter. If the

House votes not to order the previous question, debate on the pending matter may continue into a second hour, during which amendments are in order. It is unusual for the House not to vote for the previous question.

If the motion for the previous question is defeated, the Speaker then recognizes the member who led the opposition to the previous question, usually the minority floor manager, to control an additional hour of debate, during which germane amendments may be offered to the pending matter. The member controlling the floor then moves the previous question on the amendments and the pending matter.

The House first adopted a rule for the previous question in 1789. It was not used as a procedure for ending debate until 1811. In 1880 the previous question rule was amended to apply to single motions or a series of motions as well as to amendments. The motion to commit pending the motion for the previous question or after the previous question is ordered to passage also was added in 1880. From 1880 until 1890 a motion for the previous question was in order only on third reading, and it was then made again for final passage. When the House recodified its rules in the 106th Congress, it combined the former Clause 1 of Rule XVII and a provision included in former Clause 2 of Rule XXVII into Rule XIX.

Further reading:
United States House of Representatives. *Constitution, Jefferson's Manual, and Rules of the House of Representatives of the United States, 108th Congress.* Compiled by Charles W. Johnson. House Document 107–284. Washington, D.C.: Government Printing Office, 2003.

—John David Rausch, Jr.

Printing, Joint Committee on

The Joint Printing Committee is the panel that oversees the Government Printing Office (GPO), the official government printer, as well as any aspect of government printing and binding. Before the GPO was established in 1860, the federal government contracted with private printing firms for its printing needs. That process soon led to corruption. A congressional investigation in 1840 showed that printers contracted by Congress during the previous seven years gained profits of almost $470,000. A similar scandal in 1846 contributed to growing embarrassment over the state of public printing in the United States.

To counter public disillusionment, Congress approved a joint resolution that directed the principal officers of the HOUSE OF REPRESENTATIVES and the SENATE to advertise and obtain sealed bids for printing, with the lowest bid in each case winning the contract. This resolution became law on August 3, 1846. To oversee this new

arrangement, Congress created the Joint Committee on Printing, which was composed of three senators and three representatives. Though the committee did not directly receive legislative proposals or directly act on them, it did receive and report on motions to print extra copies of literature for their respective chambers. The committee was given the powers to:

> use any measures it considers necessary to remedy neglect or delay on the part of the contractor . . . and to make a pro rata reduction in the compensation allowed, or to refuse the work altogether, should it be inferior to the standard.

The original joint committee then set printing and binding regulations, which it continues to do to the present. The panel's 1846 mandate also directed it to "audit and pass upon all accounts for printing." These mandates are still part of the joint committee's charge, as shown in U.S. Code, Title 44, which gives the current Joint Committee on Printing its authority.

In 1860 a joint resolution established the GPO and made the Joint Committee on Printing (JCP) its board of directors. The JCP approved physical plant and machinery purchases, as well as setting standards for the paper used in government printing. The JCP and its remedial and financial powers were reinforced in the Printing Act of 1895, which also gave the committee some additional oversight and management responsibilities.

The LEGISLATIVE REORGANIZATION ACT OF 1946 modified the membership of the committee to include the chair and two members of the SENATE COMMITTEE ON RULES AND ADMINISTRATION and the chair and two members of the COMMITTEE ON HOUSE ADMINISTRATION. In 1981 this structure was expanded to include the chair and four members of each committees from both houses. The JCP chair rotates between the chairs of the House and Senate administration committees.

Further reading:
United States Congress. Joint Committee on Printing. *Government Printing and Binding Regulations.* Washington, D.C.: Government Printing Office, 1990; United States Code, Title 44: *Public Printing and Documents and Miscellaneous Statutes Identifying the Authority of the Joint Committee on Printing.* Washington, D.C.: Government Printing Office, 1997; United States Congress. Joint Committee on Printing. *Oversight of the Government Printing Office: Hearing Before the Joint Committee on Printing, Congress of the United States, One Hundred Fifth Congress, First Session.* Washington, D.C.: Government Printing Office, 1997.

—Mary S. Rausch

private bill

Private BILLs are legislation that provides benefits to specified individuals, including corporate bodies. When enacted, these bills become private laws.

People write their senators and representatives for help with personal problems. Sometimes the assistance required is at such a level that the help must be approved by the entire Congress as a bill. Individuals request a private bill when other administrative or legal remedies have been exhausted. Congress is more likely to take this action when no other remedy is available and when the legislation will create equity.

House rules do not define what bills may qualify as private. Most private bills have official titles stating that they are to be for the benefit of named individuals. Clause 4 of House Rule XII prohibits private bills for granting pensions, building bridges, correcting military or naval records, or settling claims eligible for action under the Tort Claims Act. These prohibitions resulted from the adoption of the LEGISLATIVE REORGANIZATION ACT OF 1946. Common subjects of private bills include immigration issues, domestic claims against the government, foreign claims against the government, patents and copyrights, taxation, public lands, veterans benefits, civil service status, and armed services decorations.

Private bills travel through the legislative process in a manner similar to other measures. They are commonly introduced by the representative who represents the individual who will receive the benefits. Although it is not required, most private bills are introduced in the HOUSE OF REPRESENTATIVES as the body that represents individuals. The bills are referred to committees and subcommittees based on their subject matter. When the committee reports the bill, floor consideration is governed by Clause 5 of Rule XV. Private bills go on a special calendar called the Private Calendar. Bills on this calendar are considered on the first and, at the discretion of the SPEAKER OF THE HOUSE, third Tuesdays of each month. The House usually approves the bills by voice vote after very little debate.

If two representatives object to the consideration of a private bill, the bill is automatically sent back to the committee that reported it. Each party appoints objectors, members responsible for reviewing the bills on the Private Calendar and preparing objections to those they believe are inappropriate. If a private bill is recommitted, the committee may report the bill as a paragraph of an omnibus private bill, which has priority consideration on third Tuesdays. A motion to strike the paragraph from the omnibus bill may still defeat the bill. Once recommitted, committees seldom rereport private bills.

If passed by the House, the private bill must be passed by the SENATE and then signed by the president. The pres-

ident may veto the private bill, and the veto may be overridden in the same way as public bills.

The number of private bills in the modern Congress has declined dramatically. From 1817 through 1971, most Congresses passed hundreds of private laws. In the 96th Congress (1979–80) 123 private bills were passed. By the 104th Congress (1995–96) only four private bills were passed. Several factors explain the decline. Congress has delegated significant discretion to administrative agencies, allowing them to handle many of the situations that used to require private bills. Private provisions also have been inserted into public measures. Finally, members of Congress have become leery of private bills because they have the potential for creating trouble for the member who introduces a private bill benefiting an individual who has an imperfect record.

Further reading:
Beth, Richard S. *Private Bills: Procedure in the House.* Washington, D.C.: Library of Congress, 2004; Johnson, Charles W. *Constitution, Jefferson's Manual, and Rules of the House of Representatives.* House Document No. 107-284. Washington, D.C.: Government Printing Office, 2003; Oleszek, Walter J. *Congressional Procedures and the Policy Process.* 6th ed. Washington, D.C.: Congressional Quarterly Press, 2004.
—John David Rausch, Jr.

privilege

Privilege is a parliamentary status granting certain legislative business priority of consideration. There are two types of privilege that can be conferred on an item in Congress. Permanent privilege is granted to an item by the rules of the chamber, the chamber's precedents, the Constitution, or a statute. Temporary privilege is granted in the HOUSE OF REPRESENTATIVES by the adoption of a special rule from the HOUSE COMMITTEE ON RULES and in the SENATE by a unanimous consent agreement.

Privileged business is a matter entitled to priority and possibly immediate floor consideration. Such privileged matters include conference reports, amendments in disagreement with the other chamber, and messages from the president of the United States. Motions that are given priority over other motions are called privileged motions. These motions include the motion to adjourn, the motion to recess, and the motion to table a bill. Privileged business and privileged motions may interrupt the chamber's regular order of business.

Questions of the privileges of the House are identified in Clause 1 of Rule IX and include "those affecting the rights of the House collectively, its safety, dignity, and the integrity of its proceedings." Questions relating to the seating of members and the organization of the House at the beginning of a Congress have been held to be questions of the privileges of the House. Issues relating to the health and safety of representatives and their staffs have also been raised as questions of privilege. Such questions are presented in the form of a resolution that must be disposed of by the House. The Senate does not have similar questions of privilege.

Questions involving individual members are called questions of personal privilege. A member rising to ask a question of personal privilege is given precedence over almost all other proceedings. House rules note that the privilege rests primarily on the Constitution, which gives a member of Congress a conditional immunity from arrest and an unconditional freedom to speak in the House. Members have raised questions of personal privilege to respond to allegations about matters such as misuse of public funds, conflicts of interest, abuse of the FRANKING PRIVILEGE, corruption and bribery, criminal conspiracy or perjury, violation of the securities laws, and knowingly making a false statement with the intent to deceive. Members may rise to questions of personal privilege to respond to such public criticisms, whether made by other members or, for example, in private publications. However, a question of personal privilege "may not be based on language uttered on the floor of the House in debate," according to House practice, because the offended member may make an appropriate demand that the objectionable words be taken down.

House members are entitled to address the chamber on a question of personal privilege for up to an hour. Senate rules do not specify limits for members of that body. On October 6, 1917, Senator Robert LaFollette, a Republican from Wisconsin, rose on a question of personal privilege and spoke for three hours on the "right of the people to discuss war in all its phases and the right and duty of the people's representatives in Congress to declare the purposes and objects of the war."

Further reading:
Brown, Wm. Holmes, and Charles W. Johnson. *House Practice: A Guide to the Rules, Precedents, and Procedures of the House.* Washington, D.C.: Government Printing Office, 2003; Byrd, Robert C. *The Senate, 1789–1989: Classic Speeches.* Washington, D.C.: Government Printing Office, 1994; Riddick, Floyd M., and Alan S. Frumin. *Riddick's Senate Procedure: Precedents and Practices.* Senate Document No. 101–28. Washington, D.C.: Government Printing Office, 1992.

—John David Rausch, Jr.

Progressive Era and Congress

The Progressive Era began toward the end of the 19th century and gradually phased out after World War I. The early 1900s were a time of peace, prosperity, and progress, but American life changed dramatically between 1900 and 1915, when more than 15 million immigrants came to the United States, exceeding the total for the previous 40 years. Most of the new immigrants came from non–English speaking European countries with different cultures from America. They needed jobs, and the cities were where factories and small businesses were growing. A total of 30 percent of the nation's population moved to the cities seeking more material goods, shopping advantages, and recreation. Department stores, shopping centers, parks, sports stadiums, and amusement parks were quickly being built. Increasing use of the automobile was affecting how people spent their money and their leisure time. But the demand for public utilities and services could not keep up with the rapid growth. While the buying power of upper and middle classes made city life good, for the poor immigrants and farmers who came to work life was often worse. Factory wages provided substandard living conditions and no way out. One in three were close to starvation, living in overcrowded housing on unpaved streets with inadequate water supplies and disease. Soon it became clear that change was needed if America was to maintain stability.

The Progressive movement was characterized by a distinctive set of attitudes aimed at reforming the social and industrial life of Americans. Those attitudes were based on an optimistic belief that people could improve their condition and the environment through persistent human intervention. The optimism was fueled by evangelical Protestant religion and new developments in scientific knowledge. Religious reforms were intended to rid the world of sin, but the offer of help was often tainted by intolerance for less than the highest moral standards. Other reformers were from the new disciplines of the social sciences—economics, sociology, statistics, and psychology—developed around the turn of the century. Scientists tested their theories using factual scientific investigation, trained experts, and government authorization.

The temperance movement was typical of most Progressive reforms. Based on moral issues and supported by the middle class, its aim was to control the makers of liquor and their corrupt political allies in government. Alcohol had long been thought to be the cause of many social ills, including poverty and insanity. First successful at local and state levels, especially in the southern and western states, prohibition of alcohol became national in 1918 when Congress passed the Eighteenth Amendment to the Constitution prohibiting the manufacture, transportation, and sale of alcoholic beverages. The following year it was ratified by the states. Soon gangs of "bootleggers" made "bathtub gin," and secret "speakeasy" bars flourished. What President Herbert Hoover called the "noble experiment" was hard to enforce and finally repealed in the 1930s.

By 1910 the number of employed women had tripled, to 7.8 million. Reformers had worked for years to establish the economic and political equality of women. Through their efforts women had gained the right to control their earnings, own property, and have custody of their children after divorce. Finally, in 1919, with passage of the Nineteenth Amendment to the Constitution, the women's suffrage movement succeeded in expanding the right to vote to include women.

While some reformers focused on improving living and working conditions, others addressed environmental issues and the conservation of disappearing resources. By the late 19th century Americans had developed a "tradition of waste" with natural resources. Progressives counteracted that tradition with new legislation. The Newlands Act of 1902 funded irrigation projects by selling federal lands in the West. The Inland Waterways Commission was appointed in 1907 to study rivers, soil, forests, waterpower, and water transportation, and the National Conservation Commission of 1909 was formed to preserve resources. President Theodore Roosevelt was influenced by naturalist John Muir to begin the federal government's "conservation" movement to preserve the nation's resources, stop wasteful use of raw materials, and reclaim lands.

Roosevelt also increased public safety through the Meat Inspection Act and the Pure Food and Drug Act and enacted the Hepburn Act to regulate railroads and pipelines. President William Howard Taft enacted the Mann-Elkins Act, whereby the telephone and telegraph systems became regulated by the Interstate Commerce Commission. In 1913 the Pujo Committee of Congress led a public investigation into the concentration of power in the banking industry. During the presidency of Woodrow Wilson, Congress established the Federal Trade Commission to control monopolies and passed the Federal Reserve Act to regulate money and the banking system. The Sixteenth Amendment established the federal graduated income tax, and the Seventeenth Amendment provided for the direct election of senators by popular vote instead of by state legislature. Other election reforms included the "recall" and the "referendum." Although the Commission on Industrial Relations conducted Senate hearings on the labor-management conflict, it was left to the states to pass laws addressing fair wages and working hours, factory safety inspections, and worker compensation for injury.

Widespread business and labor disputes fostered the growth of socialism. In 1910 the first member of the Socialist Party was elected to Congress, and the following year 73 Socialist mayors and 1,200 lesser officials in 340 cities and towns were elected. The press called it "The Rising Tide of Socialism." Incorrectly portrayed as communism, socialism was not supported by the business community or the average citizen. With the congressional declaration of war in 1917, spreading democracy to the world became another Progressive goal. The Espionage Act was created to define acts of treason, and accusations of insubordination or disloyalty were used to imprison Americans who spoke or wrote against the Great War. As a result, few in Congress voiced any opposition.

Although after World War I the popularity of Progressivism began to dwindle, it remains notable as the first reform effort to draw the attention of the entire nation. While protestors and radicals were often more visible in organizing reforms, few were accomplished without the tacit approval of big business. Only wars and depressions can compare to the widespread public awareness, support, and success of the Progressive movement.

Further reading:
Fink, Leon, ed. *Major Problems in the Guilded Age and the Progressive Era*. Boston: Houghton Mifflin, 2001; Hofstadter, Richard. *The Age of Reform: From Bryan to F.D.R.* New York: Knopf, 1955; Link, Arthur. *Woodrow Wilson and the Progressive Era: 1910–1917*. New York: Harper & Brothers, 1954.

—Karen Aichinger

public approval of Congress

Public approval of Congress is the degree to which citizens have a positive evaluation of the collective job performance of the legislative branch of the national government. For the most part, scholarly attention to the topic of congressional approval dates back only as far as the mid-1970s, in the wake of highly visible congressional activity on major issues such as the Vietnam War and the Watergate scandal, coupled with significant changes in congressional procedures and norms. Prior to this period measurement of congressional approval was highly sporadic and featured question formats different from the standard items used today. Since 1980, however, a new standard question format has come to be asked with great regularity by several major survey organizations. The question "Do you approve or disapprove of the way the U.S. Congress has been handling its job?" for example, is asked every two years by the American National Election Studies (ANES) conducted by the University of Michigan. Similar questions are now regularly asked by Gallup and the CBS/New York Times poll, among others. Several distinct findings emerge from the survey data that have been collected regarding public approval of Congress. First, public approval of Congress varies considerably over time. Data from ANES, presented in Figure 1, show that approval of Congress rose from the early to mid-1980s, then fell to a low point in 1992, only to rise steadily again over the next decade.

Another finding that emerges from survey data is that even with the evident variation in the ratings, the percentage of Americans who approve of Congress generally does not compare favorably to the approval ratings of other political actors on the national stage. In particular, surveys consistently find that Americans give higher marks to the president. During the same time period depicted in Figure 1, approval of the president has been, on average, approximately 14 percentage points higher than approval of Congress. While measured less often, evidence suggests that ratings of the Supreme Court are generally higher as well.

Surprisingly, this trend also holds true when comparing public approval of Congress with other aspects of Congress itself. For example, the public's level of trust in Congress as an institution is always higher than the traditional approval rating of the job being done by the collection of representatives in Congress. Even Americans' approval for the performance of their own member of Congress outpaces their approval of the performance of Congress as a whole—generally by almost 20 percentage points. The idea that Americans love their own members of Congress but hate Congress is sometimes referred to as "Fenno's paradox"—named after the political scientist Richard Fenno, who first wrote about this seeming contradiction.

Scholars have identified several factors that appear to affect public approval ratings of Congress's job performance. First, national contextual circumstances have an impact on approval of Congress. When the public perceives that things in the nation are going well, it is more likely to approve of Congress. One of the most influential contextual factors is the state of the economy. A stronger economic picture tends to correlate with higher public approval ratings for Congress, as was the case in the mid-1980s and again in the late 1990s. There is some evidence that a citizen's personal finances may matter even more than national economic conditions in forming attitudes toward Congress, but in either case the effect is similar. Since the economy and other national conditions affect presidential popularity in much the same way that they affect Congress's popularity, it is not surprising that presidential approval and congressional approval have been found to be somewhat positively correlated.

Contextual factors that are specific to Congress also impact approval of that body. One such factor is the presence of a congressional scandal. For example, the House Bank overdrafts scandal in the early 1990s has been shown to have significantly depressed aggregate public approval of Congress during that period.

Congress's legislative actions also affect its approval ratings. Studies suggest that higher levels of legislative failure and associated legislative conflict, such as wrangling over Senate filibusters, serve to depress congressional approval. There is some evidence that even the enactment of major legislation can also lower approval of Congress.

This may be because whenever Congress wades into a policy issue, some group of citizens is bound to be disappointed regardless of whatever particular decision is ultimately made.

Factors particular to individual citizens are also related to approval of Congress. One such factor is interest in politics. Citizens who are more interested in politics tend to be less approving of Congress. This relationship could be explained by the finding by some scholars that media coverage of Congress is generally negative in tone. As a result, those who pay more attention to politics in the news may be understandably less likely to have a positive image of Congress.

Research also suggests that negative attitudes toward Congress stem in part from public attitudes toward the legislative process itself. In particular, the public has concerns about inefficiency in the legislative process and also the disproportionate influence that special interest groups have in that process. Those individuals who feel that the organization and operation of Congress are inefficient are less likely to give Congress high marks. And those who feel Congress is less responsive to ordinary citizens than to special interests are also less likely to approve of Congress.

A citizen's party identification also affects evaluation of Congress. People who align themselves politically with the congressional majority party are more likely to approve of the job Congress is doing, while members of the minority party are more likely to disapprove of Congress. This relationship has been found during both Democratic-controlled Congresses and during Republican-controlled Congresses.

Furthermore, individuals appear to care about the particular ideological direction of Congress's policy activity under the control of the majority party. The smaller the ideological difference citizens perceive between themselves and the majority party in Congress, the more likely they are to approve of the job Congress is doing. Conversely, the greater the ideological difference citizens perceive between themselves and the majority party in Congress, the less likely they are to approve of Congress. This relationship holds true above and beyond the effects of party identification alone.

The degree to which Americans approve of Congress carries important political consequences. First, despite the fact that support for Congress is generally lower than support for one's own member, there is some evidence that citizens who are less approving of Congress are marginally less likely to approve of their own member. This suggests that as much as individual incumbents may work to distance themselves from an unpopular collective Congress, they are not completely immune from these public attitudes.

Other research has focused on electoral effects of congressional approval. The basic finding is that in the voting booth the public mainly holds the majority party responsible for Congress's job performance. Those who approve of Congress are more likely to vote for the majority party can-

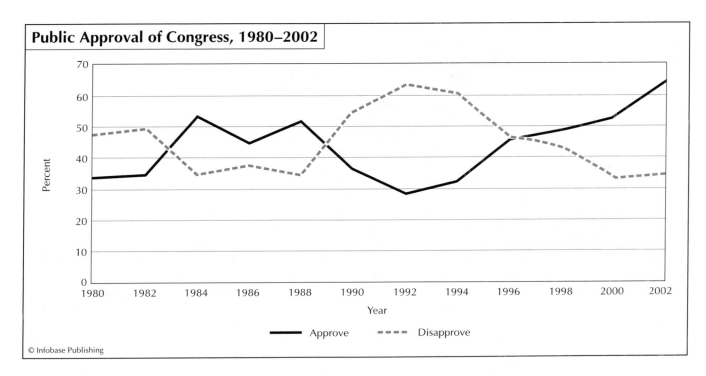

Public Approval of Congress, 1980–2002

© Infobase Publishing

didate in the election. Those who disapprove of Congress are more likely to vote for the minority party candidate in the election. Interestingly, this effect holds true regardless of incumbency. Not only does higher approval of Congress help the electoral prospects of majority party incumbents but also of majority party candidates who challenge a minority party incumbent and of majority party candidates competing for an open seat. These electoral effects have been found in both House races and Senate races.

The relative strength of these electoral effects appears to be partially conditioned by certain factors. First, the effect of congressional approval on voting is strongest among citizens who can readily name the party that holds the majority of seats in Congress. Nevertheless, even those who cannot immediately name the majority party still display similar patterns of voting behavior. Second, in keeping with the party responsibility theme, evaluations of Congress are more likely to affect an incumbent's chances for reelection when that incumbent has been a staunch party-line voter while in office than when the incumbent has been a party maverick.

Public approval of Congress is also important for reasons that go deeper than electoral politics. At its heart, congressional approval is an indicator of whether Congress has the consent of the governed. Consistently low levels of support may signal that Congress has been insufficiently responsive to the citizenry. As a result, some scholars suggest that disapproval of Congress can lessen the perceived legitimacy of Congress in the eyes of the public. In turn, the relative level of support for Congress can affect citizen

compliance with the laws it passes. Finally, congressional approval is relevant to the broader American political system. Research demonstrates that the higher the level of public approval of Congress's job performance, the greater the level of public trust in government as a whole.

Further reading:
Cooper, Joseph, ed. *Congress and the Decline of Public Trust.* Boulder, Colo.: Westview Press, 1999; Durr, Robert H., John B. Gilmour, and Christina Wolbrecht. "Explaining Congressional Approval." *American Journal of Political Science* 41 (1997): 175–208; Fenno, Richard F. "If, as Ralph Nader Says, Congress Is the 'Broken Branch,' How Come We Love Our Congressmen So Much?" In *Congress in Change: Evolution and Reform,* edited by Norman J. Ornstein, New York: Praeger, 1979; Hibbing, John R., and Elizabeth Theiss-Morse. *Congress as Public Enemy: Public Attitudes towards American Political Institutions.* New York: Cambridge University Press, 1995; Jones, David R., and Monika L. McDermott. "The Responsible Party Government Model in House and Senate Elections." *American Journal of Political Science* 48 (2004): 1–13.
—David R. Jones

public law
Public law is an important outcome of the congressional lawmaking process, the often hoped for result when members of Congress introduce legislation. Yet beyond including

the general laws passed by Congress having nationwide applicability, public law has a much broader meaning as well, for it describes a wide swath of topical content within the entire legal field. Under this latter definition, Congress has significant duties and responsibilities.

The branch of law that is concerned with the actions of government—public law—includes the fields of constitutional law, administrative law, and criminal law. Generally, laws that cover the structure, administration, and functioning of government are all within the field of public law, as are those that deal with the responsibilities of government employees. Even government-to-government relationships, such as those with foreign governments and federal-state-local government interactions, are part of this extensive field. Thus, when Congress is engaged in the process of amending the U.S. Constitution or passing laws that define and clarify the definitions of crime and specify punishments, and when the SENATE approves treaties, and when Congress delegates administrative rule making to government agencies, there is essential congressional participation in the development of or the changing of public law. Of course, actions of the executive and the judicial branches, as well as the legislative branch at all levels of government, contribute to the creation and development of public law in this broader sense, such as when presidents or governors issue executive orders, or a government agency promulgates regulations, or a court interprets the Constitution or a STATUTE or agency regulation in deciding a case.

The most frequent use and special applicability of the term *public law* to Congress occurs, however, when the process of lawmaking has been completed, and certain bills or joint resolutions have been introduced, amended where needed, and finally approved with identical wording in both the HOUSE OF REPRESENTATIVES and the Senate. When these acts of Congress are signed by the president, or passed over a presidential veto, or become law without the president's signature when Congress is in session and the president cannot exercise a pocket veto, enactment of legislation occurs. At the time of enactment, such bills and joint resolutions (except joint resolutions that propose constitutional amendments that are transmitted to the states for ratification, and which in accordance with Article V of the Constitution do not receive presidential approval) that have been characterized as public ones become public laws or statutes, and those characterized as private bills or joint resolutions become private laws or statutes.

Members of Congress have the opportunity to introduce public bills or private bills as well as joint resolutions dealing with public or private matters. Bills and joint resolutions characterized as private affect individuals, families, or small groups. Often they concern injuries to citizens from governmental activities or cases in which government agency rulings against people are being appealed (for example, when deportation is ordered because an individual has been found to have violated immigration laws). Private enactments turn into statutes that are identified by the National Archives and Records Administration as private ones, and are sequentially numbered based on the order of enactment with the identifying information of the session of Congress. "Private Law" (or the abbreviation "Pvt.L") followed by the congressional session number, and then the number of the law assigned by this agency headed by the U.S. Archivist, identify such a statute. For example, Private Law 107-1 granted permanent U.S. residence to an individual. Private statutes are far less common than public statutes. Moreover, they are excluded from the definition of public law.

Public laws include those that affect the whole of society and are of general applicability nationwide. These much more frequent public laws or statutes are numbered in a similar manner to private laws by the U.S. Archivist. To illustrate, Public Law 108-1 (alternatively Pub.L 108-1), the first act passed by the 108th Congress on January 8, 2003, provided for a five-month extension of unemployment insurance benefits for eligible individuals. Subsequent public bills or joint resolutions passed by the 108th Congress received sequentially numbered public law identifications based on the order of their enactment, continuing with Public Law 108-2, and so forth. Each public and private law enacted is first published as a "slip law" in an unbound single-sheet or a pamphletlike form so to be immediately useable; slip laws contain identifying information that includes, in addition to the public or private law number, the date of approval, the bill or joint resolution number, and a legislative history. Later a permanent bound volume of the U.S. Statutes at Large is printed, containing all the public and private laws in order of their enactment for each session of Congress. The slip laws and the bound volumes are official sources for and evidence of the laws and resolutions. They are published by the Government Printing Office, an agency of Congress. Prior to 1874, when Congress transferred the publication of the Statutes at Large to the Government Printing Office, publication had been undertaken by the private firm of Little, Brown and Company. In addition to citing a statute by its public law number as described above, citation may also be by volume and page number from the statutes (e.g., 117 Stat. 1309).

In summary, public bills and joint resolutions (but not including constitutional amendments, which are joint resolutions) that have completed the congressional lawmaking process consistent with the Constitution, including both authorization and appropriation acts, are public laws of the United States and are available in several forms—slip laws, U.S. Statutes at Large, and the U.S. Code. Public laws are distinguished from and do not include private laws, which go through a similar congressional process and are published in these same forms.

Further reading:
1 U.S. Code, chap. 2 and 3; Black, Henry Campbell. *Black's Law Dictionary.* 4th ed. St. Paul: West Publishing Co., 1968; Johnson, Charles W. III. *How Our Laws Are Made.* Washington, D.C.: U.S. House of Representatives, 2003.
—Robert P. Goss

public works

Congress authorizes and appropriates funds to construct and maintain the nation's infrastructure, more commonly known as public works projects. Congress has always funded infrastructure projects. In early Congresses the federal government supported the construction and maintenance of forts, arsenals, and armories as well as funding harbor improvements and lighthouses necessary for national defense and foreign trade. There were questions about the constitutional power of the federal government to fund internal improvements such as roads, canals, and river and inland harbor projects. While the constitutional questions continued, Congress felt pressure from western settlements to enact legislation approving the funding of internal improvements to make travel easier. In 1806 Congress enacted legislation to survey and build a national turnpike from Cumberland, Maryland, to the Ohio River. Congress avoided the constitutional question by providing that the states of Pennsylvania, Maryland, and Virginia had to give their assent to the construction of a road through their territories.

Congress also subsidized road construction projects done by the states. The legislative branch also funded projects to improve rivers and harbors. The Rivers and Harbors Act of 1826 included 22 projects spread over 10 states. Subsequent legislation authorized and appropriated funds for conducting surveys, beginning construction on new projects, and continuing construction of projects already underway. Despite the fact that the projects benefited a number of states, congressional action began to attract negative comments from the press. By 1832 the term LOGROLLING began to be attached to public works legislation by the press. Rivers and harbors bills later were called PORK BARREL legislation because legislators would dip into the federal treasury to bring projects to their districts.

One of the problems with public works legislation was that it resulted in wasteful spending. An analysis of the Rivers and Harbors Act of 1890 found that 59 percent of the appropriations were for works that provided a purely national benefit, 22 percent provided a large national benefit, 18 percent funded works of comparatively small national benefit, and as little as 0.003 percent benefited only a local area. President Chester Arthur recommended the end of omnibus public works legislation in order to control the pork barrel nature of the bills.

While Congress continued to fund internal harbors and rivers improvements, the legislature stopped funding the construction and improvement of roads. Congress returned to the practice of funding roads in 1916 by helping states build highways. In 1913 the HOUSE OF REPRESENTATIVES established a Committee on Roads to consider legislation on road building. Congress did not have to decide which individual projects to fund because the states would decide. The first federal legislation on highways in 1916 and the legislation enacted in 1921, 1956, and 1991, outlined the principles and procedures governing the federal roads program. States are responsible for planning, construction, and maintenance of highways and for determining which projects will be financed by the federal government.

The 1916 legislation did not specify any road projects, but the 1921 law required that each state designate a system of highways upon which all federal funding would be spent. Legislation enacted in 1944 specified a third category, extending the funding into urban areas. By 1956 Congress specified that funding would go to developing the Interstate highway system. The highway act of 1991 added more roadways to the program.

In 1998 Congress approved a large public works program. The legislation authorized $200 million over six years for roads, bridges, buses, subways, ferries, and even parking garages. The projects were spread across virtually every congressional DISTRICT. Because the federal budget had reached balance, members of Congress felt better about spending large amounts of money on transportation. The bill increased federal transportation spending by 44 percent from the $145 billion appropriated in the previous six-year plan. The House approved the bill by a vote of 297-86, and the SENATE approved it 88-5. President Bill Clinton signed the bill. The bill, known as the Transportation Efficiency Act for the Twenty-first Century, replaced the Intermodal Surface Transportation Efficiency Act.

In enacting public works legislation, Congress works with the executive branch to identify projects and determine funding levels. Congress can authorize and appropriate money for individual projects or authorize lump-sum appropriations for programs of public works, including formulas for allocating the money, typically in the form of grants to state and local governments. These projects are selected and built by state and local governments. A third type of public works legislation authorizes lump-sum appropriations for programs and defines the characteristics of projects that are eligible for federal funding. A department or agency in the executive branch is delegated the power to choose which programs to fund.

Further reading:
Dao, James. "$200 Billion Bill for Public Works Passed by Congress." *New York Times,* 23 May 1998, p. A1; Kelly,

Brian. *Adventures in Porkland: How Washington Wastes Your Money and Why They Won't Stop.* New York: Villard Books, 1992; Maass, Arthur. *Congress and the Common Good.* New York: Basic Books, 1983.

—John David Rausch, Jr.

purse, power of the

The power of the purse is the authority granted Congress under the U.S. Constitution to tax, borrow, and spend federal funds. Along with the power of the sword, the military power of the federal government, the power of the purse is thought to be the most powerful of governmental functions and the most formidable weapon at the legislature's exclusive disposal. In the words of Alexander Hamilton in Federalist 30,

> money is with propriety considered as the vital principle of the body politic; as that which sustains its life and motion, and enables it to perform its most essential functions.

Put another way, there is little meaningful governmental activity that can take place without funding.

As a general matter, the power of the purse is a means toward effecting governmental ends in two different ways, one indirect, the other direct. The powers to tax and borrow largely affect policy ends indirectly by providing incentives and disincentives to individuals and organizations. The power to spend, on the other hand, can directly affect policy ends by channeling federal funds toward certain goals. The exercise of all three powers has tremendous economic and social ramifications for the country. This has particularly been the case since the New Deal of the 1930s as the reach of the federal government has become a major part of everyday life in the United States.

The power to tax flows from Article I, Section 8, of the U.S. Constitution and from the Sixteenth Amendment. The former authorizes the federal government to collect revenue through tariffs, imposts, customs duties, and excise taxes, and the latter, ratified in 1913, authorizes the federal government to collect income taxes from whatever source Congress desires. In 1895 the Supreme Court invalidated a congressional attempt to collect personal income taxes, thus necessitating the amendment. Today income taxes (personal, social insurance, and corporate) make up the vast majority of federal tax revenue. For the fiscal year 2002 these taxes made up approximately three-quarters of all federal revenue (in excess of $1.7 trillion).

There is little limitation on the constitutional power of Congress to tax. Courts have generally interpreted the fiscal power of Congress to be expansive. Taxes are considered constitutionally valid even if used predominantly for regulatory and not fiscal purposes. One of the most obvious examples is the power of Congress to establish tariffs to protect American industries from overseas competition.

As with the power to tax, the power to borrow funds also stems from Article I, Section 8, of the Constitution. It provides that Congress has the authority to "pay the debts" of and "borrow money on the credit of the United States." The power to borrow is the authority Congress provides to the executive branch to sell government obligations (such as Treasury notes and bills) to raise federal revenue.

When expenditure exceeds revenue, the result is a deficit. (When the opposite is true, the government enjoys a surplus). When a deficit exists the government must borrow funds to make up the difference. The sum total of annual federal surpluses when added to the sum total of annual federal deficits equals the national debt.

While the Constitution places no restriction on Congress's authority to borrow, Congress has limited itself by statute. In 1917 Congress passed a law setting a limit on the amount of national debt that the federal government could incur. If this limit were to be breached, the country would default on its obligations to bondholders. Amendment of this statute to raise the debt ceiling has become routine, although it has never been a popular vote since it reflects the unwillingness of Congress and the president to control the federal deficit.

The power to spend, of course, is the obverse of the power to tax and borrow. Instead of raising federal revenue, the power to spend involves the expenditure of federal monies. This power stems primarily from Article I, Section 9, of the U.S. Constitution, which provides that

> no Money shall be drawn from the Treasury, but in Consequence of Appropriations made by Law.

This power has five main thrusts. These are the ability of Congress 1) to prohibit the use of funds for certain activities, 2) to establish spending ceilings that the executive branch cannot exceed, 3) to set spending floors below which the executive branch cannot descend, 4) to set conditions on the expenditure of funds, and 5) to ensure that specific sums are appropriated for specific purposes.

Currently, more than two-thirds of all federal spending goes toward mandatory spending programs (programs that automatically allocate funds according to formulas and eligibility criteria, such as Social Security and Medicare) and interest on the national debt. More than half of the remaining third of federal spending consists of defense-related expenditure. The remaining monies fund the nondefense operations of the federal government.

The power to spend is not without limit. For instance, Congress may not use its spending power to infringe unduly upon the operations of the other branches (e.g., by lowering presidential or judicial salaries). Nor may it use the spending power to restrict constitutional rights.

Congress's assertion of its spending power has waxed and waned over the years. Since the Washington administration, for example, there has been much debate over the degree of specificity Congress should prescribe in its spending bills. Congressional attempts to delegate formally some of its discretion over expenditure through the Line Item Veto Act and the Gramm-Rudman-Hollings Act have met with failure in the courts.

For nearly two centuries Congress lacked a formalized mechanism for reconciling these three distinct aspects of the power of the purse. During much of the 19th century, two committees, the House Ways and Means Committee and Senate Finance Committee, controlled both taxing and spending, but there existed no institutionalized mechanism for ensuring that a comprehensive legislative budget policy resulted. Beginning in 1921 Congress required the executive branch to submit a comprehensive budget document, but Congress did not require itself to produce one. That changed in 1974 with the enactment of the Congressional Budget and Impoundment Control Act. This statute provided a detailed budgetary process for both the executive branch and Congress to follow. It also created budget committees to scrutinize the executive branch's proposed budget and to set forth annually Congress's own fiscal policy.

Whether this effort has been a success is an open question, although most authorities would deem it somewhat of a disappointment.

More than two centuries ago James Madison in Federalist 58 wrote that the power of the purse was

> the most compleat and effectual weapon with which any constitution can arm the immediate representatives of the people, for obtaining a redress of every grievance, and for carrying into effect every just and salutary measure.

The intervening years have witnessed a dramatic expansion in the scope of federal activity, ensuring that Madison's words ring perhaps even truer now than they did then.

Further reading:
LeLoup, Lance T. *The Fiscal Congress: Legislative Control of the Budget.* Westport, Conn.: Greenwood Press, 1980; Schick, Allen. *Congress and Money: Budgeting, Spending and Taxing.* Washington, D.C.: Urban Institute, 1980; Schick, Allen. *The Federal Budget: Politics, Policy, Process.* Washington, D.C.: Brookings Institution Press, 1995; Wilmerding, Lucius, Jr. *The Spending Power: A History of the Efforts of Congress to Control Expenditures.* New Haven, Conn.: Yale University Press, 1943.

—Roy E. Brownell, II

qualifications of membership

The U.S. Constitution states the qualifications for members of Congress. Representatives must reside in the state from which they are elected, must be at least 25 years of age, and must have been citizens of the United States for at least seven years. Senators must be residents of the state before they are elected, must be at least 30 years old, and must have been American citizens for at least nine years. Article I, Section 5, of the Constitution grants each house of Congress the power to "be the Judge of Elections, Returns and Qualifications of its own members." Should a dispute about the age, residence, citizenship, or election returns arise, the matter is decided in the Senate or House. If it appears as though the legislative body went beyond the constitutional qualifications in determining membership, the Supreme Court may be asked to intervene.

In 1967 the House of Representatives denied Representative Adam Clayton Powell (D-NY) his seat because he had misused House funds. Powell sued, arguing that the House could use only age, residence, and citizenship in determining his qualifications for membership. In POWELL V. MCCORMICK (395 U.S. 486 [1969]) the Court held that Congress's power was limited to the three criteria stated in the Constitution and that Congressman Powell was entitled to his seat.

The states also are not allowed to add to the qualifications listed in the Constitution. In 1807 the House of Representatives seated a member-elect who was challenged for not being in compliance with a state law imposing a 12-month residency requirement in the district. The House determined that the additional residency requirement was not constitutional. The Supreme Court definitely answered the question of the states' abilities to add to the constitutional qualifications in U.S. TERM LIMITS V. THORNTON (514 U.S. 779 [1995]). Voters in the state of Arkansas, along with 22 other states, enacted maximum numbers of terms that members of Congress could serve. The Supreme Court held that the Constitution's qualifications clauses estab-

lished exclusive qualifications for members that may not be added to by either Congress or the states. The opinion of the court in *Thornton* presented a very detailed history of the qualifications clauses and the challenges raised under the clauses during the history of Congress.

Further reading:
Biskupic, Joan. "Congressional Term Limits Struck Down." *Washington Post*, 23 May 1995, p. A1; Maskell, Jack. *Congressional Candidacy, Incarceration, and the Constitution's Inhabitancy Qualification.* Washington, D.C.: Library of Congress, 2002; Polet, Jeff. "A Thornton in the Side: Term Limits, Representation, and the Problem of Federalism." In *The U.S. Supreme Court and the Electoral Process,* edited by David K. Ryden, Washington, D.C.: Georgetown University Press, 2000.

—John David Rausch, Jr.

quorum

A quorum is the number of members of the HOUSE OF REPRESENTATIVES or SENATE, or members of their respective committees, required to be present to do business. The U.S. Constitution, in Section 5 of Article I, specifies "a majority of each House shall constitute a quorum to do business." A smaller number of members are required to adjourn or to vote to compel absent members to attend. While the constitutional provisions seem simple, a number of questions remained open for some time. One of these questions was what is "business" for purposes of the quorum requirement. The rules of the House of Representatives and the chamber's precedents illustrate that not all parliamentary activity is considered business. The prayer, administration of the oath of office, and motion for adjournment are not forms of business and therefore are not subject to the quorum requirement.

A second important question that remained unanswered for many years was the question of what constitutes a "house" under the constitutional requirement. Is the house the full number of members or a smaller number determined by circumstance? This question arose clearly during the Civil War when the Confederate states did not elect representatives to send to Washington. In 1861 the SPEAKER OF THE HOUSE ruled that a quorum consisted of "a majority of those chosen." Speaker THOMAS REED, a Republican from Maine, clarified this definition in 1870 to mean "all Members chosen and living." In 1903 Speaker JOSEPH CANNON, a Republican from Illinois, established the modern interpretation that a quorum is "a majority of the Members chosen, sworn, and living, whose membership has not been terminated by resignation or by the action of the House." In the 108th Congress a quorum was 218 members, except when the chamber had resolved into the COMMITTEE OF THE WHOLE House on the State of the Union, when the rules specified that a quorum was 100 members.

The Senate interpretation of a quorum is similar to the one used by the House. In 1864 the Senate adopted a rule stating that a quorum consisted of "a majority of Senators duly chosen." The rule was amended in 1868 to read "a majority of the Senators duly chosen and sworn." In the 108th Congress, the number of senators required for a quorum was 51.

Both chambers operate under the assumption that a quorum is present unless proven otherwise. House rules discourage points of order questioning the presence of a quorum. In 1890 Speaker Reed ruled that it was sufficient to have simply the presence, not the votes, of a majority of House members. Previously, a House member had to cast a vote to be considered present. A group of members could be present but not vote and stop progress on a bill due to a lack of a quorum. QUORUM CALLS rarely happen in the House except when accompanied by a recorded vote.

Quorum calls are common in the Senate, since the chamber's rules permit senators to suggest the absence of a quorum at virtually any time. There are two types of quorum calls in the Senate: the "live" quorum call in response to a point of order establishing the actual absence of a quorum, and the "constructive delay," a quorum call designed to slow proceedings in order to accomplish some other task. In the absence of a quorum, no business except a quorum call or a motion to adjourn may be transacted.

Committees are allowed to establish their own quorum rules. A majority of a committee's members are required to report a piece of legislation. For other actions House and Senate rules permit committees to set quorums as low as one-third of the membership. Quorums in committees require the physical presence of the members in the committee room, but both chambers use a process of "rolling" quorums. Members record their presence on a ledger so that a quorum may not be physically present at all times.

The terrorist attacks of September 11, 2001, raised the question of what to do if a majority of the members of Congress are killed or incapacitated in an attack. Several pieces of legislation were introduced in response to the issue of a lack of quorum. Among these bills were proposals to encourage states to expedite special elections if disaster strikes. A commission on the continuity of government in the United States also reviewed the issues related to a major terrorist attack on Washington, and several committees held hearings.

Further reading:
Johnson, Charles W. *Constitution, Jefferson's Manual, and Rules of the House of Representatives.* House Document No. 107-284. Washington, D.C.: Government Printing Office, 2003; Ornstein, Norman. "Defining Quorums Down: A Bad Idea That's Ripe for Abuse." *Roll Call* (21 July 2004). Available online by subscription. URL: http://www.rollcall. com/issues/50_10/ornstein/0613-1.html. Accessed February 9, 2006; Riddick, Floyd M., and Alan S. Frumin. *Riddick's Senate Procedure: Precedents and Practices.* Senate Document No. 101-28. Washington, D.C.: Government Printing Office, 1992; U.S. House of Representatives, Committee on Rules. *Hearing on the Continuity of Congress: An Examination of the Existing Quorum Requirement and the Mass Incapacitation of Members.* Washington, D.C.: Government Printing Office, 2004.

—John David Rausch, Jr.

quorum call

The procedure used to determine the absence of a quorum in the HOUSE OF REPRESENTATIVES and the SENATE is termed a quorum call. The Constitution requires that a majority of members of each chamber be present for the House or the Senate to do business. The rules of both chambers presume that a quorum is present until the absence of a quorum is proven. A quorum call is used to determine the absence of a quorum.

In the Senate a senator who has the floor may suggest the absence of a quorum at any time, triggering a quorum call. Senate rules usually prohibit the presiding officer from counting senators to determine whether a quorum is present. When a senator suggests the absence of a quorum, the presiding officer directs the Clerk to begin a roll call of senators. When a majority of senators responds, a quorum is present and the Senate returns to business. There are two types of quorum calls in the Senate. One type is referred to as "constructive delay." This quorum call is a strategic move to delay Senate proceedings for a number of reasons, including to allow time for informal negotiations or to allow a senator to make his or her way to the floor to make a speech or propose an amendment. The second type of quorum call is the "live quorum call." The purpose of this quorum call is to bring a majority of senators to the floor.

Quorum calls in the House of Representatives are much more limited. The purpose of a quorum call in the House is to bring a majority of members to the floor to record their presence after an absence of quorum has been established. Members of the House may make a point of order that a quorum is not present, usually only when a vote is taking place. The Speaker (or the chair of the COMMITTEE OF THE WHOLE) counts to determine if a quorum is present. If a quorum is not present, the House must adjourn or take steps to get members to the floor to create a quorum.

Further reading:

Johnson, Charles W. *Constitution, Jefferson's Manual, and Rules of the House of Representatives.* House Document No. 107-284. Washington, D.C.: Government Printing Office, 2003; Riddick, Floyd M., and Alan S. Frumin. *Riddick's Senate Procedure: Precedents and Practices.* Senate Document No. 101-28. Washington, D.C.: Government Printing Office, 1992; U.S. House of Representatives, Committee on Rules. *Hearing on the Continuity of Congress: An Examination of the Existing Quorum Requirement and the Mass Incapacitation of Members.* Washington, D.C.: Government Printing Office, 2004.

—John David Rausch, Jr.

R

Randolph, John B. Cawsons (1773–1833)

Representative, Senator

A representative and senator from Virginia and U.S. minister to Russia, John B. Randolph was born in Chesterfield County, Virginia, on June 3, 1773. Known as John Randolph of Roanoke to distinguish him from the other members of his family, Randolph was the first American conservative and a proponent of the view that the federal government's powers were limited to those explicitly granted in the Constitution.

Randolph was descended from an influential and wealthy family and claimed that the Indian princess Pocahontas and her husband, John Rolfe, were his ancestors. He was the youngest of three sons (the others were named Richard, who lived from 1770 to 1796, and Theodorick, who lived from 1771 to 1792) born to John Randolph (1742–75) and Frances Bland Randolph (1752–88). A younger sister, Jane, lived only 16 days (November 10–26, 1774). The elder Randolph, who was a planter, died in 1775, and young Randolph was raised by his mother and stepfather, St. George Tucker (1752–1827), a legal scholar who was the American editor of *Blackstone's Commentaries* and the author of *A Dissertation on Slavery* (1795), a collection of lectures attacking slavery that he gave at the College of William and Mary. A half brother of Randolph's, Henry St. George Tucker (1780–1848), served as a representative from Virginia in the 14th and 15th Congresses (1815–19).

John Randolph studied with private tutors, attended Walker Maury's School in Burlington, Orange County, Virginia, and studied briefly at the College of New Jersey (now Princeton University) in 1787, Columbia College (now Columbia University) in 1788–89, and William and Mary College in 1789, although he never earned a degree. In 1790 and 1791 he studied law in Philadelphia under his cousin Edmund Randolph (who served in George Washington's cabinet as attorney general and, after Jefferson's resignation, as secretary of State), but he never practiced law. In 1792 Randolph suffered a mysterious illness that according to

Dawidoff "left him beardless, with a soprano voice and, it is generally presumed, without sexual capability."

In 1799 John Randolph was elected as a Republican to the U.S. House of Representatives and was elected to six more consecutive terms, serving from March 4, 1799, to March 3, 1813. First elected at the age of 26, when he was sworn in he was asked by the Speaker Theodore Sedgwick, if he were old enough to serve? Randolph replied "Ask my constituents."

Defeated for reelection as an anti-Madison candidate in 1813, he was returned to the House in the following election, serving from March 4, 1815, to March 3, 1817, but was not a candidate for reelection two years later. He was elected again in 1818 and served from March 4, 1819, until he resigned on December 25, 1825. Randolph was then appointed to the U.S. Senate to complete the unexpired term of James Barbour, who had resigned. Randolph served in the Senate from December 26, 1825, to March 3, 1827. He was an unsuccessful candidate for the Senate in 1827 but was again elected to the House of Representatives, serving from March 4, 1827, to March 3, 1829. He served for the last time in the House of Representatives from March 4, 1833, to his death on May 24, 1833.

From 1801 to 1807 (and again from 1827 to 1829), Congressman Randolph was chair of the House Committee on Ways and Means, making him the de facto leader of the Jeffersonians in the House of Representatives. He was one of the managers appointed by the House of Representatives in January 1804 to conduct the impeachment proceedings against John Pickering, a judge of the U.S. district court for New Hampshire. Pickering was convicted by the Senate and removed from office in March 1804. In January 1805 Randolph led the prosecution in the impeachment case against Samuel Chase, associate justice of the U.S. Supreme Court. Chase was acquitted, ending the Jeffersonians' attacks on Federalist judges.

In Congress Randolph, as the first Jeffersonian chair of the Ways and Means Committee, supported President

Thomas Jefferson's retrenchment policy by urging economy in public expenditure and reduction of taxation and the Revolutionary War debt. He rallied support for Jefferson's Louisiana Purchase in 1803. In 1805 he fell out of favor with Jefferson after opposing the president's appropriations bill and plan to buy Florida from Spain. He took the leadership of a small anti-Jefferson faction in Congress known as the Quids. The Quids believed that Jefferson and James Madison, once committed to states' rights, had become nationalists. Randolph believed that the federal government could not exercise more authority than it was explicitly granted in the Constitution. In 1808 the Quids attempted to block Madison's election as president by supporting James Monroe. They were unsuccessful, as Jefferson used his prestige to secure the Democratic-Republican Party's nomination for Madison.

Randolph was a firm believer in states' rights. He once said that "Asking one of the States to surrender part of her sovereignty is like asking a lady to surrender part of her chastity." He contended that members of Congress were delegates of the states and were responsible to their states rather than to the people of the United States. He argued that this was the intent of the framers, since had they intended for members of Congress to represent the nation, then the district lines would be drawn without regard to state boundaries. He opposed the rechartering of the Bank of the United States in 1816 because he believed it was unconstitutional and that it would lead to management of the economy by the federal government. Similarly, he opposed Henry Clay's proposals for internal improvements in 1824, arguing that the proposed surveys for roads and canals were based on his strict constructionist view of the Constitution, beyond the powers of the federal government.

The owner of a 5,000-acre plantation and hundreds of slaves in what is now Charlotte County, Virginia, Randolph believed that the federal government had no constitutional right to legislate on the institution of slavery. He vehemently opposed the Missouri Compromise of 1820, labeling the northern members of Congress who voted for it "Dough-faces." He opposed the compromise because he believed it amounted to interference by the federal government into a matter (slavery) over which it lacked constitutional authority. He became the bitter enemy of Henry Clay of Kentucky for having supported the compromise and for Clay's support of John Quincy Adams when the presidential election of 1824 was thrown into the House of Representatives. In 1826 Randolph and then-secretary of State Clay had a bloodless duel. It was not the first time Randolph had challenged one of his colleagues to a duel. He once had challenged Daniel Webster, who refused to take up the challenge.

Randolph was also a committed isolationist. He opposed the War of 1812 (which caused his sole electoral

defeat), and the "meddling" of the United States in the affairs of Europe (Greek independence in 1824) and South America (the Panama Congress of 1826). He was particularly concerned that President John Quincy Adams's acceptance of an invitation from Mexico and Colombia to attend a conference would lead to failure: "You can no more make liberty out of Spanish matter than you can make a seventy-four out of a bundle of pine saplings." The newly independent Latin American nations had emancipated their slaves, and Randolph questioned whether the United States could join in an alliance with such "revolutionaries."

In Congress Randolph was known for his eloquence and wit. Physically tall, he was described as being a mixture of aristocrat and Jacobin.

In 1829 Randolph served as a member of the Virginia constitutional convention. The following year President Andrew Jackson appointed him minister to Russia. He served from May to September of that year, when he resigned due to poor health. After returning from Russia, Randolph denounced Jackson's proclamation against nullification of the tariff by South Carolina.

In his later years Randolph became addicted to alcohol and opium. On May 24, 1833, Randolph died in Philadelphia and was buried facing west so, according to his own instructions, he could continue to keep an eye on his old enemy, Henry Clay. Randolph's will ordered that his 318 slaves be freed. He was originally buried at his residence, Roanoke, in Charlotte County, Virginia. He was later reinterred at Hollywood in Richmond, Virginia.

Further reading:
Adams, Henry. *1882 John Randolph*. Armonk, N.Y.: M. E. Sharpe, 1996; Bouldin, Powhattan. *Home Reminiscences of John Randolph of Roanoke*. Richmond, Va.: Clemmitt & Jones, 1878; Bruce, William Cabell. *John Randolph of Roanoke: 1773–1833: A Biography Based Largely on New Material*. New York: Octagon Books, 1970; Dawidoff, Robert. *The Education of John Randolph*. New York: Norton, 1979; Johnson, Gerald White. *Randolph of Roanoke: A Political Fantastic*. New York: Minton, Balch & Company, 1929; Kirk, Russell. *Randolph of Roanoke: A Study in Conservative Thought*. Chicago: University of Chicago Press, 1951; Sawyer, Lemuel. *A Biography of John Randolph, of Roanoke*. New York: Robinson, 1844.

—Jeffrey Kraus

Rankin, Jeannette (1880–1973) *Representative*

Jeannette Rankin was born in 1880 near Missoula, Montana. She was the eldest of seven children of John Rankin and Olive Pickering. John Rankin was a businessman who worked as a logger, carpenter, and rancher. Jeannette Rankin grew up on a ranch in a fairly well-to-do family, though she was not shielded from hard work. The eldest child in a large family had many responsibilities both in the home and on the ranch. She had little exposure, however, to the poverty, despair, and horrific living conditions that would make such an impression on her later in life. Rankin completed secondary school and received a B.A. in biology from the University of Montana.

She became active in politics, beginning with the suffrage movement. After women gained the right to vote in Montana, Rankin was the first woman elected to the House of Representatives in 1916. She served one term and was reelected in 1940, again serving just one term. Rankin is most often noted as a peace activist. She voted against U.S. entry into both world wars. Her stance against war, which gained her notoriety in 1917 and public contempt in 1941, made her a symbol for both the women's movement and the peace movement during the Vietnam War. In six decades of social activism, Rankin advanced a theory of representation that required the inclusion of women for the betterment of humankind.

Struggling to find a purpose for her life after graduation, Rankin traveled to San Francisco to visit her uncle. She visited a settlement house on Telegraph Hill and was captivated by the struggles of the immigrant women she met. Rankin worked at the settlement house for four months and found her life's work: social activism. She enrolled in the New York School of Philanthropy, where she was exposed to the intellectual roots of the Progressive Movement and gained hands-on experience with dire poverty and the struggles of immigrants on the Lower East Side. She wrote her mother about her heart wrenching experiences:

> I took the dearest sweetest little boy to an orphan society. He was about three years old and the mother had two younger. The father is missing. If I had been near home I'm sure I would have wanted to keep him. He was so full of joy and life. The mother didn't mind losing him. She just waved her hand and said, 'by-by.'

Rankin graduated in 1909 with a degree in social work. In 1910 a suffrage leader from the state of Washington recruited her to join their efforts. It was through the suffrage movement that Rankin learned how to organize a grassroots movement and gained confidence in her public speaking ability. She also began to formulate the ideas that would drive her life's work and bring coherence to the variety of different social causes for which she worked.

Rankin thought and argued that the lack of suffrage for and meaningful representation of women was at the heart of many of the social ills confronting the United States in the early 20th century. Women, because of their unique role in society, were more empathetic to the concerns of women and children in society. Women were also less likely to be influenced by the large corporations that, according to Rankin, lay behind the low wages, poor working conditions, and pro-war propaganda. Women were less likely to be driven by profit motives in their politics. In short, women needed to enter the political sphere because it would be unjust for them to be governed by laws that they had no voice in creating. Moreover, once women gained a voice in and confidence in the political realm, the system would become attentive to social problems, and the influence of the major corporations would be reduced or at least balanced by the perspective that women could bring to political discourse.

The state of Washington adopted female suffrage in 1910, and Rankin headed back to Montana, where a similar bill was pending before that state's legislature. In the next six years Rankin worked for the cause of women's suffrage in Montana, New York, California, Ohio, and Florida. In the summer of 1915, Montana women gained the right to vote, and shortly thereafter Rankin declared herself a candidate for the HOUSE OF REPRESENTATIVES. Her brother, Wellington, managed her campaign, and in 1916 she became the first woman elected to the U.S. House of Representatives. The first issue to come before the House in 1917 when Rankin took her seat was U.S. entry into World War I. Along with 55 of her male colleagues, Rankin voted no. The resolution was adopted, however, and as Rankin had feared, the war effort monopolized the legislative agenda, leaving little time, energy, or money for domestic and social issues.

Rankin followed through on her pledge to press Congress to improve the lives of women and children. During her single term she cosponsored two bills. The first would have allowed women who married foreigners to maintain their U.S. citizenship. The second was an attempt to educate women about venereal disease and birth control. Neither bill passed. She was more successful in her effort to improve working conditions in the Bureau of Printing and Engraving. It came to her attention that the bureau was in violation of several federal statutes, including the requirement for an eight-hour workday. She collected complaints from the employees, mostly women, and took them to the secretary of the Treasury, threatening a congressional investigation. The Treasury Department conducted its own investigation, found the bureau in violation of federal law, and restored the eight-hour workday. Though her effort endeared her to the labor movement, it could not erase the antiwar vote in the memory of her constituents. As her brother, Wellington, predicted, Rankin lost her bid for reelection.

Convinced that corporate greed was to blame for the war effort and most of the social ills facing the country, Rankin resolved to live a simple life devoted to the search for peace. Convinced that the South would be more receptive to a peace movement, Rankin bought a small house in

Georgia without indoor plumbing or electricity. She continued her political activism, creating the Georgia Peace Society and the Georgia Conference on the Cause and Cure of War. She worked for the International League for Peace and Freedom and the National Council for the Prevention of War, touring, speaking, and lobbying.

During the 1930s Congress began an investigation into charges that corporations had bribed members of Congress to support entry into World War I. Rankin spoke before a committee as a representative of the National Council for the Prevention of War. She urged the committee to find a way to remove the profit motive from war efforts. Though the committee failed to figure out a way to divorce profits from the war effort, the investigation did result in the Neutrality Act. In June 1940, spurred by concern about entry into yet another world war, Rankin again declared herself a candidate for the House of Representatives. Focusing on peace as her platform, she was again elected to represent Montana. In the months before the Japanese attack on Pearl Harbor, Rankin introduced various bills aimed at promoting peace, but to no avail. When Congress was again called on to vote on whether to enter another world war, Rankin voted no. This time she was the only member of either the House or the Senate to oppose the war. Again, as her brother had predicted, public opinion turned sharply against her and killed her chance for reelection.

As the war drew to a close, Rankin, who had become intensely interested in Gandhi's teachings, traveled to India to learn more about his work. She continued to warn of the dangers presented by an alliance between business and government and viewed participatory democracy as the only potential solution. She spent much of the next 20 years traveling extensively, frustrated with her inability to have much of an impact at home. Her frustrations abated somewhat as the Vietnam War became increasingly unpopular and interest in peace efforts increased. In the late 1960s peace activists proposed a march on Washington and asked Rankin's permission to use her name. Not only did she consent, but at age 87 she led the way; the Jeannette Rankin Brigade marched toward the U.S. Capitol in January 1968.

In her six decades of social and political activism, Jeannette Rankin not only paved the way for women's participation in the political sphere, she modeled for them what that participation ought to look like. In her voting record she responded to her own conscience, not political expediency. She worked tirelessly both in and out of office for peace and better living and working conditions for women and children.

Further reading:
Davidson, Sue. *A Heart in Politics: Jeannette Rankin and Patsy Mink.* Seattle: Seal Press, 1994; Giles, Kevin. *Flight of the Dove: The Story of Jeannette Rankin.* Beaverton,

Ore.: Lochsa Experience Publishers, 1980; Josephson, Hannah. *Jeannette Rankin, First Lady in Congress: A Biography.* Indianapolis: Bobbs-Merrill, 1974; Richey, Elinor. *Eminent Women of the West: Jeannette Rankin, Woman of Commitment.* Berkeley, Calif.: Howell-North, 1975.

—Kimberly Maslin-Wicks

Rayburn, Samuel Taliafero (1882–1961)
Representative, Speaker of the House

Sam Rayburn, or "Mr. Sam" as he was known to many, was born in Kingston, Tennessee, on January 6, 1882. He was the eighth of 11 children. The family moved to a farm just outside Bonham, Texas, when he was five years old, and Rayburn called Bonham home until he died there in 1961. He finished secondary school at the age of 18 and earned a bachelor's degree from Mayo Normal College in Commerce, Texas.

He was teaching school in Texas when he heard Texas senator Joseph Bailey deliver a speech. After that he turned his attention to a career in politics, telling a friend that he would spend three terms in the Texas state house of representatives before moving on to the U.S. House of Representatives. Rayburn followed through with his plan. He served three terms in the Texas house, including one term as Speaker, and he earned a law degree along the way. In 1912 he became the Democratic candidate for the U.S. House of Representatives from the Texas Fourth District.

He won the election in the fall and almost immediately became a protégé of JOHN NANCE GARDNER, a prominent representative from Texas who would go on to a distinguished career in the U.S. Senate and serve as Franklin Roosevelt's vice president. Gardner suggested to Rayburn that one of the most important committees in the House was the Committee on Interstate and Foreign Commerce. Rayburn was assigned to that committee and in 1930 became the chair. It was the only committee on which he ever served. Rayburn moved steadily through the ranks of the Democratic Party. He was elected Speaker of the House in 1941 and served as Democratic leader until his death in 1961. In a career that spanned five decades, Rayburn liked to say "I never served under any President . . . I served with eight."

Gardner proved to be exactly right about the importance of the Committee on Interstate and Foreign Commerce. In the early 1930s it became the clearinghouse for much of Roosevelt's NEW DEAL. By that time Rayburn had sufficient seniority to earn the chair. From that position Rayburn became Roosevelt's right-hand man and pushed through many of the key elements of the New Deal, including the Securities Act of 1933, bills creating the Federal Communication Commission and the Securities and Exchange Commission, Railroad Holding Company Act of

1933, the Public Utilities Holding Act of 1935, and the Rural Electrification Administration Act of 1936. During this time Rayburn earned the respect of his colleagues and, of course, Roosevelt.

Rayburn's mettle as Speaker was tested shortly after he assumed the Speaker's chair just months before the U.S. entered World War II. In September 1940 Congress had enacted and Roosevelt had signed the Selective Training and Service Act, requiring 12 months of military training for all men between the ages of 21 and 35. The act was about to expire, and Congress was debating an extension as the political situation in Europe grew increasingly volatile. President Roosevelt and Rayburn supported the extension. Republicans almost universally opposed it. Without an extension of the draft the U.S. military would have been reduced from 1.6 million to 400,000. Franklin Roosevelt had left for a meeting with Winston Churchill in Newfoundland, leaving Rayburn to fight this unpopular battle alone. In August 1941, just three months before the Japanese attacked Pearl Harbor, the House began deliberations on the draft extension. Rayburn called in all the personal favors he could, and the bill passed 203-202.

As Speaker, Rayburn employed a leadership style that can probably best be described as personalized. He had an open-door policy with members. They were always welcome in his office, and anyone could get in to see him as long as they were willing to wait. In comparing Sam Rayburn's style of leadership with other prominent Speakers, Booth Mooney wrote:

> Henry Clay had led the House by the force of his personal magnetism, [Thomas Brackett] Reed by vastly superior brain power, [Joe] Cannon by a combination of bulldozing and good-fellowship backed up by rigidly restrictive rules. Rayburn led the House—and for nearly as long a period as the three earlier Speakers combined—by friendly persuasiveness, a desire to be helpful to members, rock-bound integrity, and by reaping the dividends of service so extended that, at the last, almost every political figure of importance in the Democratic party owed the Speaker favors in return for favors received.

Rayburn owed much of his political education to the "Board of Education" as employed by Republican Speaker Nicholas Longworth and Democratic leader John Nance Gardner. The Board of Education was an informal meeting by invitation only at which House leaders would gather after hours to plot legislative strategy and engage in a kind of preemptive troubleshooting. Members were encouraged to speak freely, and alcohol was available. The sessions were informal, friendly, and frequently included other prominent Democrats such as, LYNDON JOHNSON and Harry Truman. Many deals were struck in these sessions, and they provided the young Rayburn with invaluable information about the inner workings of the House and its members. As Speaker, Rayburn continued to use these sessions. They allowed him to collect information about potential problems and to maintain a sense of how members were likely to react to different issues and proposals.

Rayburn enjoyed a similarly friendly relationship with journalists. He was always available and like Roosevelt often shared with them much information "off the record." In fact, many of his press conferences took place off the record. Perhaps more importantly, like his interactions with his colleagues, Rayburn took an interest in the personal lives of the people he encountered. That personal attention and kindness inspired loyalty and cooperation. Booth Mooney relayed the following story of Rayburn's extraordinary thoughtfulness:

> Rayburn's inborn kindliness was combined with a frontier instinct to aid people in times of distress. The morning after the daughter of a young Washington newsman died, the father answered the doorbell to find the Speaker of the House standing on his stoop. The reporter was surprised, for he knew Rayburn only from occasional attendance at his news conferences.
>
> I just came by to see what I could do to help, Rayburn explained. Nothing, the grieving father told him, all arrangements had been made. Well, have you and your wife had your coffee this morning? No, said the reporter. Well, I can at least make the coffee, Rayburn said, and proceeded to do so. The reporter remembered that the Speaker had been scheduled to have breakfast at the White House that morning. He mentioned this.
>
> Well, I was, but I called the President and told him I had a friend who was in trouble and I couldn't come.

One of the last battles Sam Rayburn waged in his illustrious career laid the groundwork for the eventual passage of the civil rights legislation of the 1960s, though Rayburn would not live long enough to see the final product. During the first half of the 20th century, the southern states were referred to as the "Solid South," solidly Democratic. Democratic candidates faced little competition from Republican opponents; most of the real competition came from within the Democratic Party. Once they established themselves, Democratic senators and representatives were often reelected with ease. Southern Democrats were able to focus their efforts not on reelection campaigns but on building important relationships in Washington and moved through the party ranks quickly. Thus, in the 1950s and 1960s southern Democrats held most of the important leadership posts within the party, though as a percentage of the Democratic Party their influence was declining.

One such post was the chair of the Rules Committee, occupied by Howard Smith (D-VA). The Rules Committee was established in the early 1900s as an extension of the House leadership. It is charged with setting time limits on debate and establishing the guidelines under which debate will take place. All bills must clear the Rules Committee before the House may vote on them. Under Howard Smith the Rules Committee became a venue for conservatives to block progressive legislation. The committee would simply refuse to act on any bills of which it did not approve or would require substantive revisions to bills before granting a ruling.

In the early 1960s the Kennedy administration was understandably concerned about Rayburn's ability to move its legislative program through the Rules Committee, particularly progressive bills such as civil rights, federal aid to education, and an increase in the minimum wage. Rayburn met with Smith in an attempt to persuade him that the entire House ought to determine the fate of Kennedy's proposals. Smith agreed to allow votes on five of Kennedy's proposals. Civil rights was not among them. Dissatisfied, Rayburn designed two plans for dealing with the recalcitrant Rules Committee. First, he proposed to remove William Colmer (D-MS) from the committee as a punishment of sorts for his refusal to support the Kennedy-Johnson ticket and replace him with a more moderate Democrat. This proposal drew much criticism from south-

Samuel Rayburn *(Library of Congress)*

ern Democrats. Second, he suggested enlarging the Rules Committee, which would allow him to appoint more moderate members and break Smith's stranglehold over legislation. Smith and many other southern Democrats opposed any efforts to emasculate the Rules Committee, since, in his words, it would open the door to all sorts of vicious legislation. Rayburn offered this interpretation of the showdown: "The issue is very simple. Shall the elected leadership of the House run its affairs, or shall the chairman of one committee run them?"

In January 1961 the House voted on a proposal to enlarge the Rules Committee despite the fact that Rayburn was not sure he had the votes. He offered these final words before the vote:

> Whether you vote with me today or not, I want to say that I appreciate your uniform kindness and courtesy that has been displayed toward me. This issue, in my mind, is a simple one. We have elected to the Presidency a new leader. He is going to have a program that he thinks will be in the interest of and for the benefit of the American people. I think he demonstrated yesterday that we are neither in good shape domestically or in the foreign field. He wants to do something about that to improve our situation in the United States of America and in the world. . . . Now I have here a letter that if I were easily insulted would do rather so to me. The gentleman from Virginia [Mr. Smith], chairman of the great Committee on Rules, sent out a letter, and in that letter he used the words "stack" and "pack" four times. The gentleman from Virginia, nor any other Member of this House, can accuse me of ever packing any committee for or against anything. . . . Away back in 1933 we . . . packed the Committee on Rules with the gentleman from Virginia [Mr. Smith] . . . and then in 1939, the gentleman from Mississippi [Mr. Colmer] came to me and said he very much desired to go on the Committee on Rules. I told him I thought it was a mistake . . . for various reasons. But he insisted and then we packed the committee with Mr. Colmer. . . . [T]he only way that we can be sure that this program [Kennedy's] will move when great committees report bills, the only way it can move, in my opinion, my beloved colleagues, is to adopt this resolution today.

The resolution passed 217–212, opening the door for the Civil Rights Act of 1964, the Voting Rights Act of 1965, Medicaid, Medicare, and the school lunch program. While the Kennedy-Johnson administration's legislative opportunities were just beginning, Rayburn's career was ending. He left Washington in August 1961 complaining of back pain. He was diagnosed with cancer in October and died in November 1961.

In short, Sam Rayburn developed a highly personalized and extraordinarily time-consuming leadership style that allowed him to guide the House through a phase sometimes referred to as the "era of the committee barons," an era in which committee chairs such as Howard Smith exercised nearly dictatorial control over their legislative domain and the Speaker had few tools with which to compel the barons to action. His victory on the Rules Committee enlargement vote was a signal that things were about to change.

Further reading:
Champagne, Anthony. *Congressman Sam Rayburn.* New Brunswick, N.J.: Rutgers University Press, 1984; Gould, Lewis L., and Nancy Beck Young. "The Speaker and the Presidents: Sam Rayburn, the White House, and the Legislative Process, 1941–1961." In *Masters of the House,* edited by Roger H. Davidson, Susan Webb Hammond, and Raymond W. Smock, Boulder, Colo.: Westview Press, 1998; Hardeman, D. B., and Donald C. Bacon. *Rayburn: A Biography.* Austin: Texas Monthly Press, 1987; Mooney, Booth. *Mr. Speaker: Four Men Who Shaped the United States House of Representatives.* Chicago: Follett Publishing, 1964; Steinberg, Alfred. *Sam Rayburn: A Biography.* New York: Hawthorne Books, 1975.

—Kimberly Maslin-Wicks

readings of bills

Rules of the HOUSE OF REPRESENTATIVES and SENATE alike require that each BILL be read aloud three times on the floor of the chamber. Formal chamber rules state that each bill is to be read when it is introduced, at the start of floor deliberation, and preceding a vote to consider final passage. However, the three full readings of bills, which can be more than 100 pages long, rarely occur. Most of the time legislators waive the reading of the complete bill and instead opt for a time-saving measure by having the short title of the bill read aloud.

In practice, the first reading of a bill occurs when it is introduced to a chamber and referred to one or more STANDING COMMITTEES. This normally consists of publishing the number of the bill and its title in the *CONGRESSIONAL RECORD.* The second reading occurs when the chamber meets as a COMMITTEE OF THE WHOLE. Depending on prior agreed-upon rules governing floor debate on the measure, the bill may be read one section at a time. A briefer version of this procedure might feature the reading of the title of each section prior to floor debate on that part of the measure. The final reading normally is confined to the title only and occurs just before the final floor vote. The practice of reading legislation aloud stems from an English tradition necessitated because many members of Parliament were illiterate.

Further reading:
Oleszek, Walter J. *Congressional Procedures and the Policy Process.* 6th ed. Washington, D.C.: Congressional Quarterly Press, 2004.

recess appointments

The Constitution gives the president of the United States the power of appointment, but only with the ADVICE AND CONSENT of the Senate. In the early years of the republic, the Senate was in session only for short periods and was routinely in recess from March through December. The problems of transportation also meant that senators often arrived late, leading to further delays before the Senate could reach a quorum. The founding fathers were aware that such difficulties could lead to a situation in which top posts in the executive and judiciary remained unfilled as the president awaited the return of the Senate. To counteract this eventuality, Article II of the Constitution included a provision that gave the president the "Power to fill up all Vacancies that may happen during the Recess of the Senate, by granting Commissions which shall expire at the End of their next Session." Accordingly, not only can the president make an interim appointment without the approval of the Senate, but also those appointments can continue unconfirmed until the end of the following session of Congress.

Today the problems that inspired the provision for recess appointments have all but disappeared; the Senate sits for longer sessions and the developments in transportation have meant that senators can travel between the Capitol and their states with little delay. However, the ability of the president to make such appointments has remained, despite challenges in the courts. The power is now used more for political expediency than due to practical limitations. Recess appointments are a convenient and constitutional way for presidents on occasion to avoid, at least temporarily, a potentially perilous Senate confirmation procedure. Unsurprisingly, such appointments can lead to controversy.

In recent years all presidents have taken full advantage of the recess appointment clause. President Clinton made 140 such appointments, President George H. W. Bush made 78, President Reagan made 239, and President Carter made 68. Appointments have not been limited to minor posts: Since 1791 15 Supreme Court justices have been appointed using the procedure, the latest being Justice Potter Stewart in 1958. In total, more than 300 recess appointments have involved the judiciary. The appointment of federal judges and Supreme Court justices during the Senate's recess has caused particular controversy, as they appear to conflict with Article III of the Constitution, which guarantees members of the federal judiciary "during good behaviour" security of tenure and "a Compensation, which shall not be diminished during their Continuance in Office." In contrast to these constitutional guarantees, judges appointed during a recess benefit from neither a secure tenure (if not confirmed by the Senate, they will be removed at the end of the following Senate term) nor compensation (Congress forbids any recess appointment from receiving compensation from the federal government for services).

President Eisenhower arguably made the most controversial appointment when he used the clause to appoint Earl Warren as chief justice of the Supreme Court in 1953. Warren was still serving as a recess appointment when the landmark case *Brown vs. Board of Education* was reargued before the Court. This led to accusations that Eisenhower had placed Warren in an untenable position whereby he would be aware that his decisions in such a high-profile case would have a direct impact on the outcome of the impending Senate confirmation procedure, or even that Eisenhower might choose to withdraw his nomination before the Senate had an opportunity to consider it. Despite such concerns regarding the legitimacy of judicial recess appointments, the Second and Ninth Circuits have upheld the practice in *United States v. Allocco* (1962) and *United States v. Woodley* (1985), respectively.

Since 1964, however, only two recess appointments have involved the judiciary. In 1980 President Carter appointed Walter M. Heen to the U.S. District Court for the District of Hawaii, and in December 2000 President Clinton appointed Roger Gregory to the U.S. Court of Appeals for the Fourth Circuit. Both appointments caused controversy, as they were made in the last few days before both presidents left office. An added interest surrounded the appointment of Gregory, as he would become the first African American to serve on that court, a pertinent issue considering that the Fourth Circuit serves a larger African-American population than any other. Both Heen and Gregory experienced the same fate; neither was given the opportunity to face confirmation by the Senate, as their nominations were withdrawn by the incoming presidents, Reagan and Bush. Indeed, all of Clinton's 62 last-minute executive and judicial appointments were withdrawn by his successor in the White House. Appointments to the executive made during recess have suffered from less controversy, with the presidency and Senate working together to avoid having disputes settled in the courts.

See also APPOINTMENT POWER.

Further reading:
Castellano, J. S. "A New Look at Recess Appointments to the Federal Judiciary, *United States v. Allocco*." *Catholic University Law Review*, 1963; Chanen, S. J. "Constitutional Restrictions on the President's Power to Make Recess Appointments." *Northwestern University Law Review* 79, no. 1 (1984): 191–215; Fisher, L. *Constitutional Conflicts between Congress and the President.* Lawrence: University Press of Kansas, 1997.

—Ross M. English

recognition

The presiding officers of the HOUSE OF REPRESENTATIVES and SENATE have the power to recognize members and allow them to speak from the floor of their respective chambers. The power of recognition held by the SPEAKER OF THE HOUSE is defined in Clause 2 of Rule XVII, which states "When two or more Members, Delegates, or the Resident Commissioner rise at once, the Speaker shall name the Member, Delegate, or Resident Commissioner who is first to speak."

This provision, originally adopted in 1789, was in Clause 2 of Rule XIV before the House recodified the rules in the 106th Congress. Under the 1789 rule, if two or more members rose at nearly the same time, the Speaker determined who was the first to stand. The other member was allowed to appeal to the House to overturn the Speaker's decision. In the modern House there is no right to appeal the Speaker's decision.

In the early House the small size of the body allowed a simple procedure of recognition. The Speaker recognized the first representative to rise to his feet. As the size of the House grew, a fixed order of business was developed. The Speaker's power of recognition is almost absolute based on a report from the HOUSE RULES COMMITTEE that declared that members of the House could not appeal a decision of the Speaker on the subject of recognition. In 1881 the Speaker declined to hear an appeal of his decision on a question of recognition.

The Speaker of the House plays a dual role as the leader of the majority party as well as the House presiding officer. The Speaker uses parliamentary and political power to manage House floor proceedings. He or she has the power to recognize, or not recognize, members to speak. When a member seeks recognition, the Speaker asks, "For what purpose does the Gentleman (Gentlewoman) rise?" The question is asked to allow the Speaker to determine what business the member wants to conduct. The Speaker may deny recognition if the business does not have precedence. There are established House practices of recognition, such as giving members of the committee reporting a bill priority recognition for offering amendments from the floor.

The Senate's Rule XIX governs recognition in that body. Since the Senate's presiding officer, the vice president, is not a member of the chamber, his or her powers of recognition are somewhat limited. The vice president rarely presides over the Senate. The Constitution requires that a President Pro Tempore preside over the Senate in the absence of the vice president. Most of the time the

President Pro Tempore appoints an acting President Pro Tempore to preside.

The presiding officer is required to recognize the first senator standing and seeking recognition. When several senators seek recognition at the same time, Senate precedents allow the presiding officer to recognize the MAJORITY and MINORITY LEADERS and the majority and minority floor managers, in that order. The senator seeking recognition is not required to state the purpose of his or her rising and seeking recognition.

Further reading:
Johnson, Charles W. *Constitution, Jefferson's Manual, and Rules of the House of Representatives.* House Document No. 107-284. Washington, D.C.: Government Printing Office, 2003; Riddick, Floyd M., and Alan S. Frumin. *Riddick's Senate Procedure: Precedents and Practices.* Senate Document No. 101-28. Washington, D.C.: Government Printing Office, 1992.

—John David Rausch, Jr.

recommittal

A parliamentary motion to return a BILL to a committee, with or without instructions, is termed a recommittal. If approved, such motions usually mark the death of a piece of legislation.

After the third reading of a bill in the HOUSE OF REPRESENTATIVES, but before the SPEAKER OF THE HOUSE orders the vote on final passage, a motion to recommit the bill, with or without instructions, is in order. This procedure is outlined in House Rule XIX. The minority uses this motion to amend or kill a bill.

There are two types of motions to recommit. A motion to recommit without instructions, or a simple motion to recommit, has the effect of killing a bill if adopted. Such a motion is not debatable. The second type, a motion to recommit with instructions, returns a bill to the originating STANDING COMMITTEE, and that committee is required to amend the bill as indicated in the instructions. This type of motion is debatable for 10 minutes unless the majority floor manager asks that the time be extended to one hour.

After the House has voted on a CONFERENCE COMMITTEE report, a motion to recommit the report to the committee is in order only if the SENATE has not already acted on the report. If the Senate has already voted on the report, the Senate conferees have been discharged from committee service and there is no conference to which to recommit the report.

The motion to recommit is derived from the motion to commit a piece of legislation to a committee that has existed in House rules since 1789. A rewrite of House rules in 1880 provided for a motion to recommit, with or without instructions, before or after the previous question has been ordered to bring the bill to a vote on final passage. The rules change was designed to present the House the opportunity to show that the bill was in a form most agreeable to the members of the chamber.

In 1909 a revolt against Speaker JOSEPH CANNON, a Republican from Illinois, led to the adoption of rules changes that included an addition to the recommit rule. Preference was to be given in recognition to a member opposed to the measure under consideration.

The right of the minority to offer a motion to recommit eroded by 1934. A special rule was reported out of the HOUSE RULES COMMITTEE providing for the consideration of the appropriations bill for the executive branch and various independent agencies. The rule prohibited any amendment to Title II of the bill during the consideration of the bill, effectively prohibiting a motion to recommit. Speaker Henry Rainey, a Democrat from Illinois, interpreted the rule as still permitting the minority to make a simple motion to recommit.

In the 95th Congress (1977–78), Speaker THOMAS P. O'NEILL, a Democrat from Massachusetts, further diminished the power of the minority to have a bill returned to a committee. The special rules crafted by the Rules Committee did not limit the power to recommit entirely but established prohibitions on certain types of amendments that could be included in the instructions. The minority's ability to use the motion to recommit was further eroded through the 1980s. In the 102nd Congress (1991–92) the Republican minority began to challenge the restrictive rules. When the Republicans became the majority in the House in the 104th Congress, they adopted new rules prohibiting the Rules Committee from reporting special rules that denied a motion to recommit with instructions if offered by the Minority Leader or his or her designee. This provision appears in Clause 6c of Rule XIII.

A motion to recommit is rarely adopted. When a motion comes close to being adopted, it means that the minority has formed a coalition with some faction of the majority party. This coalition almost occurred in 2001 during the consideration of a bill to establish President George W. Bush's "faith-based" social services proposal (HR 7). A group of moderate Republicans joined with the Democrats in a motion to recommit. The House leadership pulled the bill from the floor after hearing about the coalition's concerns. The moderate Republicans were concerned by language in the bill that would have allowed religious groups that receive federal funding to avoid local and state laws prohibiting discrimination.

The motion to recommit in the Senate is not typically just used by the minority. Supporters of a bill may use the motion to reconsider the legislation after it has been amended too many times. Senators also may seek to recommit a conference report. When this occurs it is a sign that the Senate does not agree with all the changes in language negotiated by the conference committee.

Further reading:
Forestel, Karen, with Lori Nitschke. "Revolt of the Moderates Tests House Leadership." *CQ Weekly,* 21 July 2001, pp. 1,744–1,747; Johnson, Charles W. *Constitution, Jefferson's Manual, and Rules of the House of Representatives.* House Document No. 107-284. Washington, D.C.: Government Printing Office, 2003; Wolfensberger, Don. "The Motion to Recommit in the House: The Rape of a Minority Right." *Congressional Record,* 4 June 1991, pp. 772–787.

—John David Rausch, Jr.

reconciliation

The reconciliation bill and process helps Congress reach its annual spending and revenue targets set out in its congressional budget resolution. The CONGRESSIONAL BUDGET AND IMPOUNDMENT CONTROL ACT OF 1974 required Congress to pass a budget resolution by April 15 for the upcoming FISCAL YEAR that starts on October 1. Under GRAMM-RUDMAN-HOLLINGS (GRH) I and II, when Congress passed its initial budget resolution it was making a decision on how it wanted to reach the deficit target for that year. Congress could decide to rely entirely on spending cuts to meet the GRH target or Congress could decide to also rely on tax increases and entitlement cuts or both. If the reconciliation bill failed to become law before October 15, then sequestration was supposed to go into effect. The BUDGET ENFORCEMENT ACT OF 1990 did away with the GRH deficit targets. Reconciliation, however, is usually still the process used to enact tax increases and entitlement cuts through the tax writing committees and the authorizing committees.

The establishment of the spending and revenue targets is the first step of the multistep reconciliation process. Reconciliation instructions in the budget resolution require virtually all major congressional STANDING COMMITTEES (except Appropriations) to make changes in existing laws regarding taxes or entitlements (such as Medicare, Medicaid, Social Security, veterans' benefits, farm subsidies, etc.). The goal of the changes is to raise revenues or cut spending. The reconciliation instructions tell committees how much to raise in revenues or how much to cut in spending, but they do not tell committees how to reach these targets. In the next step, the committees decide what specific changes to laws must be made to reach the revenue or spending targets.

When more than one committee is given reconciliation instructions, another step in the reconciliation process is required. A committee, usually the Budget Committee, must then compile the work of the different committees and offer them as a package bill to the full chamber. This bill is usually called an omnibus budget reconciliation act.

In the Senate the "Byrd Rule," named after Senator ROBERT BYRD, a Democrat from West Virginia, requires that all reconciliation acts and provisions be related to budgeting. The rule is codified in section 313 of the 1974 Congressional Budget and Impoundment Control Act, and a three-fifths vote is required to waive it. The Senate's presiding officer determines what is nongermane to the budget under the Byrd Rule, and his or her ruling can be overturned with 60 votes.

Further reading:
Schick, Allen. *The Federal Budget: Politics, Policy, Process.* Washington, D.C.: Brookings Institution Press, 1995; Shuman, Howard E. *Politics and the Budget: The Struggle between the President and the Congress.* 3d ed. Upper Saddle River, N.J.: Prentice Hall, 1992.

—Charles Tien

records of Congress

The Center for Legislative Archives maintains the official records of the U.S. House of Representatives and Senate. These records document the history of the legislative branch beginning with the First Congress in 1789. While the House and Senate retain legal ownership of the records, the Center for Legislative Archives is responsible for preserving the records and making them available to the public. The Center for Legislative Archives is part of the National Archives and Records Administration located in Washington, D.C.

The House and Senate each determine the rules of access for their records and are exempt from the Freedom of Information Act. Access to House records is governed under House Rule VII, 106th Congress, and is subject to the determination of the CLERK OF THE HOUSE. House Rule VII specifies that records not previously made available to the public by the House remain closed for 30 years. Exceptions to this rule include investigative records that contain personal information relating to a specific living person, personnel records, and records relating to hearings closed under clause 2(g)(2) of Rule XI, all of which remain closed for 50 years. Senate rules mandate that investigative files relating to individuals, personnel records, and records of executive nominations remain closed for 50 years. Most other Senate records are opened to the public after 20 years.

The Center for Legislative Archives also maintains records from joint committees of Congress, the publications of the Government Printing Office, and a series of special collections. The special collections include congressional oral histories and research interviews and 2,600 original pen-and-ink drawings by political cartoonist Clifford K. Berryman from the U.S. Senate Collection.

Researchers considering using congressional records should determine which chamber and committee dealt with the issue being researched. Researchers may find this information by consulting the indexes and text to the Annals of Congress, Register of Debates, Congressional Globe, and CONGRESSIONAL RECORD. More than any other agency of the federal government, Congress publishes an extensive record of its activities. These publications are available in the library of the National Archives and may also be available in government depository libraries located throughout the United States. Personal papers of members of Congress can be found at the Library of Congress and numerous other archival repositories throughout the United States.

Before being transferred to the National Archives, most of the records of Congress were housed in the offices, attics, basements, and storage rooms of the U.S. CAPITOL BUILDING. The records suffered from damage, neglect, and a number of abuses. Many early House records were lost when British troops burned the Capitol building during the War of 1812. Imprecise rules for preservation also contributed to the loss of records. For example, prior to 1946 Senate rules did not clearly specify which committee documents should be included in the Senate's official files.

In 1936, shortly after the creation of the National Archives as the depository for federal records, the archives staff began to look into the records storage practices of the SECRETARY OF THE SENATE and CLERK OF THE HOUSE. Their findings revealed poor storage conditions for the records—some were on the floor in damp rooms where they were subject to extensive growths of mold and fungi, insect infestation, rodents, dust, exposure to extreme heat and cold, and were accessible for pilfering. The National Archives recommended the transfer all but the most recent of congressional records to the new archives building in Washington, D.C. In April 1937 the Senate sent approximately 4,000 cubic feet of records to the National Archives.

The LEGISLATIVE REORGANIZATION ACT OF 1946 was the next step in preservation of the records of Congress. It required committees to maintain a record of their proceedings, providing for the first time a continuous record of committee votes and hearings. The act also mandated that committee staff and personal staff remain separate, thereby reducing intermingling of personal and committee papers. Finally, the act gave the secretary greater authority over all Senate committee records and required the House to transfer all of its records for the first 76 Congresses (1789–1941) to the National Archives. The passage of the Federal Records Act of 1950 completed the legal structure that currently governs the records of Congress. This act authorized the Administrator of General Services (authority has since been transferred to the Archivist of the United States) to accept for deposit within the National Archives the records of Congress that are determined to have sufficient intrinsic and historical value.

Further reading:
Baker, Richard A. "The Records of Congress: Opportunities and Obstacles in the Senate." *Public Historian,* (summer 1980): 62–72; Kepley, David R. "Congressional Records in the National Archives." *Prologue: Journal of the National Archives* 19 (Spring 1987): 23–33.

—Jessie Kratz

Reed, Thomas (1839–1902) *Representative, Speaker of the House*

Thomas Brackett Reed was born in Portland, Maine, on October 18, 1839, the son of Thomas Brackett Reed, Sr., a fisherman, and Mathilda Prince Mitchell. He was educated in Portland and attended Bowdoin College. While at Bowdoin he rowed on the crew team, edited the college newspaper, and was a member of the debate team. He taught school to help pay his college expenses. He graduated from Bowdoin in 1860.

After teaching school for a year in Maine, Reed traveled to California, where he taught school and read the law. He returned to Portland in 1863, where he enlisted in the U.S. Navy. He spent 18 months as an acting assistant paymaster on ships patrolling the Tennessee and Mississippi Rivers. After his navy service Reed returned to Portland, was admitted to the bar, and began private practice. He married Susan Merrill Jones, a widow, in 1870. They had two children.

In 1867 Reed was elected to the Maine legislature as a Republican. He served two terms in the house of representatives and a term in the senate before being elected Maine's attorney general in 1870. He was defeated in 1873 and returned to Portland to serve as the city attorney. In 1877 he was elected to the U.S. HOUSE OF REPRESENTATIVES to replace James Blaine, who had vacated the seat to move to the SENATE.

Upon arriving in the House, Reed was appointed to the special committee investigating the charges of corruption in the disputed presidential election of 1876. He was reelected to his House seat in 1878, defeating Greenback and Democratic Party candidates. He was reelected again in 1880 by defeating "Fusionist" opponents. After 1880 the district in southern Maine became much more safely Republican, and Reed was reelected 12 more times.

Reed was appointed to the HOUSE JUDICIARY COMMITTEE in the 46th Congress (1879–81). He became the chair of the committee during the 47th Congress (1881–83).

He also was appointed to the HOUSE RULES COMMITTEE. In the 48th Congress (1883–85) he gained a seat on the HOUSE WAYS AND MEANS COMMITTEE. Reed's activities on these committees gained him the respect of his Republican colleagues. While the Democrats controlled both houses of Congress and the White House in 1885, Reed was the Republican nominee to become SPEAKER OF THE HOUSE.

As a member of the House, Reed took positions similar to those of other northeastern Republicans. He supported the gold standard and worked with President Grover Cleveland, a Democrat, to repeal the Silver Purchase Act of 1890. He opposed the Democratic Party's efforts to reduce government expenditures. He also opposed the Democrats' efforts to keep African Americans from voting in the South. He voted for immigration restrictions and the introduction of the merit system into the civil service. Reed did not believe that the national government should become involved in regulating business or intervene in labor disputes. Reed supported protective tariffs as a way that governmental power could be used to promote economic development. He argued that high tariffs promoted the growth of American industry and increased workers' wages, producing higher consumption. Reed was selected to serve as the leader of the attack on Democratic efforts to reduce customs duties.

His leadership abilities and his energy in defending Republican principles attracted the attention of national Republicans. In 1889 the Republicans became the majority party in the House of Representatives. Reed was elected Speaker of the House. He initially led a chamber whose rules facilitated obstruction and delay. The primary method of frustrating majority rule was the "disappearing quorum," in which members who remained silent during roll calls were not counted toward a QUORUM. The House could not do business without a quorum. The other method was the use of DILATORY MOTIONS, such as repeated motions to adjourn. Both parties used these tactics when they were in the minority. As Speaker, Reed became frustrated with the tactics and sought a way to change the rules to get around obstruction.

As Speaker in the 51st Congress (1889–91), Reed found a way to exercise his power during a vote to take up a contested election case. He overruled a Democratic point of order that a quorum was not present. Ignoring precedent, Reed ordered the CLERK OF THE HOUSE to record as present any member who was physically in the chamber but who did not respond during the roll call vote. Reed announced the names of the silent members, all of whom were Democrats. The House erupted into chaos as the Speaker refused to hear the minority party's objections. The Democrats remained angry with "Czar Reed" for days. At first the members of the minority used the traditional methods of delay, and then they tried hiding under their desks. Finally, they boycotted the chamber.

The chaos ended when the House, on straight party votes, adopted "REED'S RULES." The new rules based quorums on the physical presence of members in the chamber, allowed the Speaker to ignore what he believed to be delay tactics, reduced the quorum necessary to do business in the COMMITTEE OF THE WHOLE, and streamlined the order of business in the House. The new rules also linked the House leadership to the majority party by allowing the Speaker to appoint members of the Rules Committee and to chair the committee. Among the members Speaker Reed appointed to the committee were two prominent Republicans, William McKinley of Ohio and JOSEPH CANNON of Illinois.

As a result of the new rules, the Republicans were able to enact much of their party's program into law. The 51st Congress enacted the McKinley Tariff and the Sherman Anti-Trust Act, liberalized military pensions, established authority for the president to protect national forests, created the federal appeals courts, provided grants to the state agricultural colleges, and prohibited interstate lotteries. A bill to protect the voting rights of African Americans in the South was passed by the House, but it died in the Senate. The 51st Congress is sometimes known as the "Billion Dollar Congress" even though it appropriated slightly less than a billion dollars. The Congress did spend more money than its predecessors.

In 1890 the Democrats regained the majority in the House of Representatives. Reed was determined that the Democrats adopt his ideas. When the Democrats restored their old rules for the 52nd Congress (1891–93), he led Republicans in filibusters until the new majority had to adopt Reed's Rules. Reed successfully used the same tactic in the 53rd Congress (1893–95). An economic depression led voters to return the Republicans to majority status in the House in 1894. Reed was elected Speaker and reinstituted his rules package with little opposition in the 54th Congress (1895–97). The Democratic Party was divided over the gold standard issue, and the Republicans sensed the possibility of winning the presidency.

Speaker Reed was encouraged by national Republican leaders to run for president. While he enjoyed national prominence as Speaker, Reed was not able to attract wide Republican support. He did not want to make political deals, and he refused to solicit the large financial contributions necessary to run a nationwide campaign. William McKinley's campaign overwhelmed Reed's effort for the White House.

In 1896 McKinley led a Republican sweep of the White House and Congress. Reed was reelected Speaker when the new Congress met. Now very powerful, he was able to enact the Dingley Tariff before committee assignments were announced. Despite his power and oratorical skills, Reed was not able to keep Congress from helping the

Cubans become free from Spanish rule. The Speaker did not support American expansionism. He opposed any war with Spain but deferred to President McKinley's request rather than publicly oppose the president. Following his 1898 reelection, Reed resigned from the House rather than attack Republican foreign policy.

Speaker Reed will be remembered for his reforms of congressional procedure. He also led the efforts to create the modern LIBRARY OF CONGRESS through increased appropriations. After retiring from politics, Reed went to work for the New York law firm of Simpson, Thatcher, and Barnum. He died in Washington, D.C., on December 7, 1902.

Further reading:
Mooney, Booth. *Mr. Speaker: Four Men Who Shaped the United States House of Representatives.* Chicago: Follett Publishing, 1964; Peters, Ronald M. *The American Speakership: The Office in Historical Perspective.* Baltimore: Johns Hopkins University Press, 1990; Robinson, William A. *Thomas B. Reed: Parliamentarian.* New York: Dodd, Mead, 1930.

—David Rausch, Jr.

"Reed's Rules"

"Reed's Rules" refer to two different but related concepts. The first is the historic actions taken by Speaker THOMAS B. REED in the House of Representatives in January 1890. The second is the book published by Reed in 1894 entitled *Reed's Rules of Parliamentary Law.* Each of these will be discussed in turn.

Historically, Reed's Rules refer to actions taken by Speaker Reed in the late 19th century that dramatically increased both the power of the Speaker of the House as well as the ability of the majority party to conduct business without obstruction. Thomas B. Reed was first elected Speaker of the House in the 51st Congress (1889), after having come to Congress in the 45th Congress (1877). During the years preceding his term as Speaker, a practice had developed in the House of Representatives that had become known as a "disappearing quorum." A vote in Congress is legitimate only if a sufficient number of representatives are present during the vote. Having the required number creates a QUORUM, and once a quorum is reached a vote can be taken and recorded, and it becomes binding. A quorum is typically half the membership of the House of Representatives.

The "disappearing quorum" was the practice of representatives refusing to cast a vote and simply sitting in their seats silent. The minority party could then frustrate the activities of the majority simply by pretending not to be present in the chamber. Although the majority party would necessarily have more than enough members to create a quorum if they all came to the chamber for every vote, this was in practice impossible to accomplish. Thus, a minority party had become able to block legislation or any decision making not by having enough votes to stop it, but by simply not voting at all.

This was exactly the situation when Reed became Speaker of the House. The Democratic minority, aware that Reed and the Republicans had only the barest majority in the House, adopted the practice of the disappearing quorum when they were in danger of losing a vote. Although previous Speakers had ruled that calling the roll was the only way to produce a quorum, Reed, anxious to get ahead with legislating, was determined to break the practice.

On January 29, 1890, a contentious party vote was taken over a disputed election in West Virginia. The Democrats refused to vote and after the vote demanded that a quorum count be taken. Only 163 Members had voted (a quorum was 166). Reed, however, did not go through with the quorum count. Instead, he directed the Clerk of the House to record the Democrats each as "present but not voting." This sent the Democrats into an uproar. Several objected to the move as contrary to parliamentary procedure. Reed held his ground and defended his action with legal and constitutional reasoning.

For three days the House floor became the stage for a debate of staggering energy and rage. The Democrats attacked Reed in speech after speech, arguing that he had violated House rules and precedents. Reed admitted to violating precedent but argued that the Constitution understood a quorum as being the presence of half of the membership of the House, not the vote of half of the membership of the House. At the end of debate Reed won a vote to sustain his ruling. Later, the Supreme Court sustained the constitutionality of the ruling.

Although the Democrats repealed the rule when they reclaimed Congress the following year, it was reinstated several years later. Since then it has remained a rule of the House and remains a strong check against minority attempts to delay business.

In 1894 Reed published a book, *Reed's Rules of Parliamentary Law.* The book outlines the basic practices that a legislature should follow during its proceedings. The book has become a popular reference, the basic rules for many legislatures in North America as well as thousands of private associations that engage in democratic debate and decision making. Many of the important ideas in the book were incorporated into the rules of the House of Representatives, most famously the change in the quorum as described above.

The book itself contains chapters that cover debate, voting, organization, rights and duties of members, committees, motions, and many other important tasks for a democratic decision-making body. Although Reed's Rules are generally used as a guide in the House of Representatives, they do not have controlling power, as Jefferson's manual is used as the principal guide to rules that are not explicitly defined by the specific rules adopted by the House at the beginning of each session.

Further reading:
Reed, Thomas B. *Reed's Rules of Parliamentary Law.* Chicago: Rand & McNally, 1894; Schickler, Eric. *Disjointed Pluralism: Institutional Innovation and Development in the U.S. Congress.* Princeton, N.J.: Princeton University Press, 2000.

—Matthew Glassman

referrals

BILLS and resolutions introduced by members in the HOUSE OF REPRESENTATIVES and SENATE are generally referred or transmitted to one or more SELECT or STANDING COMMITTEES by the presiding officer of the chamber, so that those committees can consider the proposed legislation or measure. This process of transfer, or transmittal, is called referral. The term *referral* is also used to describe the process of transferring or assigning bills reported from committees to the proper CALENDAR of a chamber, and it is similarly used in the House when bills reach the floor from committee and are assigned or referred to a committee known as the COMMITTEE OF THE WHOLE House on the State of the Union. House and Senate referral activities are governed by the rules of their respective chambers under Article I, Section 5, of the Constitution.

House members introduce bills and resolutions by depositing them in the hopper at the desk of the CLERK OF THE HOUSE while the chamber is in session. Sometimes members have a bill drafted in a particular manner to assure or possibly avoid its assignment to a given committee. Once a measure has been introduced and it becomes the property of the House, the SPEAKER OF THE HOUSE refers it to a standing or select committee with jurisdiction over the subject matter with which the measure deals. Committee jurisdictions are set forth in House Rule X and form the basis for the Speaker, with advice from the parliamentarian, deciding the appropriate committee to handle the measure. Prior referral of bills and resolutions dealing with similar or identical subject matters may serve as precedent for committee referral by the Speaker. In addition, a bill may be referred to any committee, without regard to Rule X, by action of the full House through a floor motion to refer.

Prior to 1975 a House bill could not be divided between two or among more committees, even though the measure involved matters that could properly be within the subject jurisdiction of several committees. But under House Rule XII every referral by the Speaker must be made so as to ensure to the maximum extent feasible that each committee that has jurisdiction over a subject may consider a particular provision and report back to the full House. Thus, the Speaker can refer a measure to more than one committee jointly, with each able to consider the measure concurrently or simultaneously, even though designating one committee as having "primary" jurisdiction. The Speaker may also sequentially refer a measure to one or more additional committees for consideration, either initially or after the matter has first been reported by the committee of primary jurisdiction. Last, the Speaker may make a split referral and assign only a portion of the measure (such as by title or section of the bill) to one committee, while to another committee is assigned other parts or components of the measure. In accordance with Rule XII, the Speaker may place a time limit or other appropriate conditions on referrals to committees. The multiple referrals described are usually needed only for measures that are complex, as they often have the effect of reducing the likelihood of a bill being approved by the House.

The Senate uses a similar but not an identical referral process, partly because of its smaller size. It rarely has more than one committee to which a measure is referred, although by unanimous consent under Rule XVII multiple committee referrals, either joint or sequential, are permitted involving legislation that crosses jurisdictional boundaries. In joint referral cases only one combined report can be made. The presiding officer of the Senate, with advice from the parliamentarian, otherwise makes all referrals to just one committee that has jurisdiction over the subject matter that "predominates" in such proposed legislation, a more flexible rule than the one that exists for the House. Senate Rule XXV delineates the policy fields handled by each of the standing committees, and it is that rule that governs the decision of the presiding officer, whose decision can be appealed by members. As in the lower chamber, the Senate may place time limits for consideration of a measure referred as well as discharge the committee from consideration of the measure. Referral is an important step in the legislative process, as it exemplifies a significant power of presiding officers, gives meaning to the subject matter jurisdictions of the committees and the division of labor they represent, and places constraints upon committees to report when they have not had particular bills or resolutions referred to them, absent specific authority to report or authority to originate measures in committee.

Further reading:
U.S. House of Representatives. *Constitution, Jefferson's Manual, and Rules of the House of Representatives, 108th Congress.* Compiled by Charles W. Johnson. 107th Cong., 2d sess., 2001; H. Doc. 107-284; U.S. House of Represen-

tatives. *House Practice: A Guide to the Rules, Precedents, and Procedures of the House.* Compiled by William Holmes Brown and Charles W. Johnson. 108th Cong., 1st sess., 2003; U.S. Senate, Senate Committee on Rules and Administration. *Authority and Rules of Senate Committees, 2003–2004: A Compilation of the Authority and Rules of Senate and Joint Committees, and Related Materials.* 108th Cong., 1st sess., 2003 S. Doc. 108-6.

—Robert P. Goss

reorganization of Congress

Both chambers of Congress have made periodic efforts to reorganize by changing either their structures or their procedures. Congress reorganizes itself at the start of each session. Much of the regular reorganization has been marginal and occasionally cosmetic. This reorganization often has included rules changes, alterations in committee jurisdiction, and changes in leadership powers and titles. More significant reforms have occurred at intervals in congressional history. Reacting to members' concerns about efficiency and effectiveness and public perception of a need for congressional reform, both the HOUSE OF REPRESENTATIVES and the SENATE have made changes to their operations and structures. Sometimes reorganization involves changing the rules; other times a major piece of legislation is enacted. Rules changes usually involve reorganization in one chamber, while legislation often changes the structure and operations of both chambers at the same time.

The revolt against Speaker JOSEPH CANNON, a Republican from Illinois, in 1910–11 was one of the first major reorganizations in the House. The rules adopted over Speaker Cannon's objections stripped the SPEAKER OF THE HOUSE of the ability to manage the House directly through his or her power as party leader. The rules changes led to the development of committee power in the House.

The modern congressional budget process, itself a subject of major reorganization in the 1970s, can be traced to the enactment of the BUDGET AND ACCOUNTING ACT OF 1921. The legislation gave the president the task of writing an executive budget. It created a budget process to replace the process of each part of the executive branch requesting funding through the appropriations process.

The first comprehensive review of Congress's organization and operation was the LEGISLATIVE REORGANIZATION ACT OF 1946. The bill was crafted as the result of hearings conducted in 1945 by the JOINT COMMITTEE ON THE ORGANIZATION OF CONGRESS. The committee was chaired by Senator Robert LaFollette, a Republican from Wisconsin, with Representative Mike Monroney, a Democrat from Oklahoma, as vice chair. The act reduced the number of STANDING COMMITTEES in the House and the Senate, provided for permanent professional and clerical staff for standing committees, and provided for the writing of a legislative budget. It also included the requirement that lobbyists register with the House and the Senate.

In 1965 Congress created the Joint Committee on the Organization of the Congress, cochaired by Senator Mike Monroney and Representative Ray Madden, a Democrat from Oregon. Created during a period when the public and the media were concerned about legislative effectiveness, the mission of the JOINT COMMITTEE was to review congressional organization and operations. The committee's review formed the basis of the LEGISLATIVE REORGANIZATION ACT OF 1970. The act opened Congress to greater public visibility, strengthened the legislative branch's ability to make decisions, and increased the rights of the minority party. Recorded teller votes were required in the COMMITTEE OF THE WHOLE House. Minority party committee members were allowed to call their own witnesses during one day of hearings. The 1970 law also created a SENATE VETERANS AFFAIRS COMMITTEE and improved the capabilities of the CONGRESSIONAL RESEARCH SERVICE and the GENERAL ACCOUNTING OFFICE.

Congress engaged in a number of reform efforts during the 1970s and 1980s. The House created a Select Committee on Committees in 1973. The select committee, chaired by Richard Bolling, a Democrat from Missouri, reviewed the House's committee structure. The committee's output was a realignment plan that balanced committee workloads, limited members' assignments, and consolidated committees. The committee also recommended a heightened oversight plan, granted the Speaker power to refer bills to multiple committees, and increased the number of committee staff personnel. The House rejected committee consolidation but adopted the rest of the committee's recommendations.

In 1975 the Senate adopted a proposal to establish a blue ribbon, private citizens' commission to study Senate administration, management, information sources, public communications, use of senators' time, oversight, space availability and use, and other related topics. The proposal was sponsored by Senator John Culver, a Democrat from Iowa, who had been a member of Representative Bolling's committee when Culver was in the House. Chaired by former senator Harold Hughes, a Democrat from Iowa, the commission produced its report on December 31, 1976. The commission's report did not result in any specific legislation, but the Senate has worked to implement many of its recommendations.

The House created a mixed Member–General Public Commission on Administrative Review in 1976. Established during a period of ethical controversies regarding the House's internal administration, the commission was chaired by Representative David Obey, a Democrat from Wisconsin. The commission's mission was to study ways to improve the House's administrative services, ways to more efficiently manage member's time, and ways to ensure integrity in the conduct of the House's legislative business. The House adopted the commission's recommendations on financial ethics while rejecting proposals to centralize the House's administrative functions into an Office of House Administrator and to create a Select Committee on Committees. House leadership adopted the commission's idea to streamline House scheduling and create an annual schedule of district work periods.

In March 1976 the Senate established a Select Committee to Study the Senate Committee System, chaired by Senator Adlai Stevenson, a Democrat from Illinois. The committee reviewed the chamber's committee system and proposed reforms to make the system more effective and efficient. The Senate adopted most of the committee's recommendations in 1977. The number of standing committees was reduced, with the Committees on Aeronautical and Space Sciences, District of Columbia, and Post Office merged into other committees. The jurisdictions of the remaining committees also were consolidated.

The House established a Select Committee on Committees in 1979 to work on committee reorganization. Chaired by Representative Jerry Patterson, a Democrat from California, the committee proposed a few changes that were adopted by the House. Among its suggestions was the creation of an Energy Committee, the establishment of limits on the number of subcommittee assignments held by individual members, and new scheduling arrangements to avoid conflicts.

In 1982 the Senate created the two-person Study Group on Senate Practices and Procedures to find ways to make Senate operations more efficient. Former senators Abraham Ribicoff, a Democrat from Connecticut, and James Pearson, a Republican from Kansas, composed the study group. They reported their findings and recommendations to the Senate COMMITTEE ON RULES AND ADMINISTRATION in 1983. The former senators recommended limitations on FILIBUSTERS, the election of a permanent Senate Presiding Officer, committee consolidation, and a greatly simplified budget process. The Senate failed to take any formal action on the study group's recommendations.

The Senate established the Temporary Select Committee to Study the Senate Committee System in June 1984. Chaired by Senator Dan Quayle, a Republican from Indiana, the committee was another effort to restructure the Senate's committee system. The committee issued its report in December 1984, recommending that committee assignments for senators be limited. The select committee also proposed the creation of a Joint Intelligence Committee, a procedure to restrict nongermane floor amendments, and limitations on filibusters. The Senate seriously considered the committee assignment restrictions while rejecting the other recommendations.

In 1992 Congress created the second Joint Committee on the Organization of Congress to review reform proposals and issue a report by December 31, 1993. The committee, comprised of equal number of members from each party and each chamber, was headed by Senators David Boren, a Democrat from Oklahoma, and Pete Domenici, a Republican from New Mexico, and Representatives Lee Hamilton, a Democrat from Indiana, and Bill Gradison, a Republican from Oregon. Gradison resigned from the House on January 31, 1993 and was replaced by Representative David Dreier, a Republican from California. The committee recommended a number of changes including a reduction in committee assignments, converting to a two-year budget cycle, and limiting Senate filibusters. Senate members of the committee approved their recommendations unanimously, while the House members adopted theirs by an 8-4 vote with the objection that the proposals did not go far enough. The report was issued too late in the session, so legislation incorporating the joint committee's recommendations was introduced in February 1994 in the House and the Senate. Few of the recommendations were adopted, but many were reintroduced when the Republicans became the majority in the 104th Congress.

Republicans captured control of both houses of Congress after the 1994 elections. At the start of the 104th Congress, Republicans in both chambers adopted a number of rules changes that had the effect of changing much about how Congress conducted its business. The House abolished three standing committees and merged their jurisdictions with those of other committees. The jurisdictions of the Post Office and Civil Service Committee and the District of Columbia Committee were transferred to the Government Reform and Oversight Committee. The jurisdiction of the Merchant Marine and Fisheries Committee was split between three other committees. The names of many committees were changed to reflect their new jurisdictions. The number of staff were reduced by one-third from the employment level of the 103rd Congress. The number of subcommittees allowed for each committee was limited. Proxy voting in committees was banned. All committees and subcommittees were prohibited from closing their meetings to the public except when an open meeting would endanger national security, compromise sensitive law enforcement information, or affect the reputation of a person. The Speaker of the House was no longer allowed to send a bill to more than one committee simultaneously. The Speaker was limited to no more than four consecutive two-year terms, and committee and subcommittee chairs were limited to serving no more than three consecutive terms.

Changes also affected floor procedure in the House. A three-fifths vote in the House was required to enact any increase in income tax rates. Members of the House were prohibited from deleting or changing remarks made on the floor and published in the CONGRESSIONAL RECORD. The EXTENSION OF REMARKS would appear in a different typeface. The minority leader or his or her designee was guaranteed the right to offer a motion to recommit a BILL with instructions. Commemorative legislation was abolished and would not be allowed to be introduced or considered.

The Office of Doorkeeper was abolished and its functions transferred to the office of the SERGEANT AT ARMS. The position of Chief Administrative Officer was created and would be nominated by the Speaker and elected by the full House. All Legislative Service Organizations were defunded and abolished.

The Senate did not enact significant reorganization measures when the Republicans gained control. In part, Republicans controlled the Senate from 1981 through 1987, so they did not need to change as many structures and processes as in the House. Senate Republicans created working groups to coordinate legislative strategy in the Senate, a move toward greater centralization.

In reaction to the terrorist attacks of September 11, 2001, Congress reorganized the federal government, combining several agencies into the Department of Homeland Security. This action forced Congress to evaluate its oversight of homeland security and the intelligence community and led to several proposals reviewed by both the House and the Senate during the 108th Congress (2003–04). One proposal would have created a Joint Committee on Intelligence, an idea without significant support in either chamber. The Senate convened a 22-member task force on reorganization of Senate antiterrorism oversight that issued recommendations in September 2004. Among the proposals were the creation of an intelligence oversight subcommittee in the Senate's Select Committee on Intelligence. The intelligence committee would be reduced in size, and the majority party would be prohibited from having more than a one-vote majority on the panel. A subcommittee on intelligence funding also would be created in the SENATE APPROPRIATIONS COMMITTEE. The HOUSE APPROPRIATIONS COMMITTEE already had created such a subcommittee.

Further reading:
Adler, E. Scott. *Why Congressional Reforms Fail: Reelection and the House Committee System.* Chicago: University of Chicago Press, 2002; Dewar, Helen. "Senators Offer New Oversight Structure." *Washington Post,* 5 October 2004, p. A4; Hook, Janet. "New Congress Poised to Turn Tradition on Its Head." *Congressional Quarterly Weekly Report,* 31 December 1994, pp. 3,591–3,594; Rieselbach, Leroy N. *Congressional Reform: The Changing Modern Congress.* Washington, D.C.: Congressional Quarterly Press, 1994; Towell, Pat. "GOP's Drive for a More Open House . . . Reflects Pragmatism and Resentment." *Congressional Quarterly Weekly Report,* 19 November 1994, pp. 3,320–3,321.

—John David Rausch, Jr.

representation

A crucial concept of democratic theory, members of Congress may represent their constituents in either or both a literal and substantive sense. Literal, or descriptive, representation focuses on the extent to which members of the SENATE and HOUSE OF REPRESENTATIVES resemble their constituents. The Constitution directs formal institutional representation to be two senators for each state and one representative for groups of constituents within state boundaries. The Apportionment Act of 1929 froze the size of the House at 435 members, while the size of the Senate continued to grow by two for each state subsequently admitted to the union, to its current 100 members. By the start of the 21st century members of the House were representing more than 650,000 people, while senators were representing states with populations ranging up to more than 30 million people.

Concerning literal representation, throughout the nation's history most members of Congress have tended not to be typical of the people they represent. Most members of Congress tend to be better educated, wealthier, and older than the average American. Overwhelmingly, the most popular occupations are business and law. Members of Congress are more likely than the average American to claim a religious affiliation. Episcopalians, Presbyterians, and Baptists tend to be more numerous in Congress than among the populace. Americans consistently underrepresented have been the less well educated, manual laborers, and women.

Members of Congress also can represent constituents in a substantive sense. Edmund Burke, an 18th-century member of the British Parliament, maintained that legislators could adopt a personal role of being either a delegate or a trustee. A delegate perspective features the legislator being guided solely by a perception of constituent preference. Hence, a member's floor vote on a bill would be determined by constituent feedback. Senators likely would find taking a delegate position much more difficult than representatives. Senators represent entire states, which normally are much more heterogeneous than congressional districts, which are more likely to be much less populous and hence more homogenous.

On the other hand, a legislator guided by a trustee perspective would vote based on his or her best personal assessment of the best policy choice, regardless of constituent pressure. Many members of Congress have reported taking one or more conscience votes during their careers whereby they took a position despite forceful and vocal opposition from constituents. To be sure, such votes can carry political risk—possibly significantly reduced electoral support or even defeat in the next election.

Roll-call voting studies have revealed that junior members of Congress and those feeling electorally vulnerable were the most likely to assume delegate roles. Conversely, members most likely to see themselves as trustees were senior legislators and those consistently winning reelection by comfortable margins. A study of members of the House by Roger Davidson found that an equal percentage of legislators saw themselves as delegates or trustees, while half the chamber reported being a combination of the two. Their explanation was that they would assume a trustee role unless they received a lot of pressure from constituents, at which time they would switch and become delegates. Davidson classified these representatives as a separate category he termed *politicos*. This perspective was perhaps best summed up by Senator EVERETT M. DIRKSEN, a Republican from Illinois, who concluded, "I see the light when I feel the heat."

Regardless of the role assumed, most senators and representatives alike consistently claim to possess an accurate sense of the prevailing preferences of their constituents. On the other hand, most districts and states tend to select members of Congress who naturally have viewpoints similar to the majority of voters. Prevailing viewpoints can change over time in response to the onset of new prevailing issues, redistricting, or population changes that significantly alter a member's constituency.

Further reading:
Davidson, Roger H. *The Role of the Congressman.* Indianapolis: Bobbs-Merrill, 1969; Pitkin, Hannah F. *The Concept of Representation.* Berkeley: University of California Press, 1967.

—William Culver

Republican Steering Committee, House

The House Republican Steering Committee dates back only to the 104th Congress. It is a symbol of the tremendous changes brought on by the Republican takeover of the House in 1995, becoming the majority party in the House for the first time in 40 years. In some ways the creation of the Steering Committee is more impressive than the Republican resurgence in the House, given that its creation replaced an institution—the Republican Committee on Committees—that was created in 1919.

Prior to the 104th Congress the executive committee of the Republican Committee on Committees made committee assignments for Republican House members. For the better part of 80 years the executive committee was dominated by states that sent a large number of Republicans to Congress, large states such as New York, Illinois, Michigan, and California. Even after some of the smaller states were allowed to elect representatives to the executive committee beginning in the 97th Congress, the large states maintained their power through a system of weighted voting that granted most of the votes in the executive committee to the large states. As Scott Frisch and Sean Kelly demonstrate, throughout the period there was an enduring large state–small state division in the committee assignment process, which created hard feelings within the Republican Conference. One Republican member expressed the feelings of many small state Republicans:

> On the Republican side of the aisle the business of filling vacancies simply boils down to a decision to be made by about four people. If you don't set well with any one of them, you can't get on. They come from big states and they have the votes to select whomever they want.

The Republican surge in the 1994 midterm elections returned the party to the majority for the first time in 40 years and increased the prestige of Speaker-to-be NEWT GINGRICH, who was widely credited as the architect of the historic victory. One of the important changes in the structure of the House Republican Party implemented by Gingrich was restructuring the committee selection process. Maintaining the weighted voting scheme used in the Committee on Committees in the past, Gingrich created a system in which the Speaker and party leadership were granted more than half the votes in the new Steering Committee. Similar to the DEMOCRATIC STEERING COMMITTEE, regional groupings designed for geographic compactness and relatively equal size elected one member each to the committee, each having one vote. As Frisch and Kelly demonstrate, the configuration of the Steering Committee now allows the Republican leadership to nearly dictate committee assignments.

Using the committee assignment process during the 104th Congress, Gingrich and the leadership were able to advance first-term and less-senior party loyalists into committee assignments previously reserved for more senior members of the party. Gingrich and others in the party argued that it was important to make committee assignments, especially to key committees such as Appropriations and Ways and Means, based on loyalty and to put first-term members into influential positions that would help them electorally, helping to preserve the new Republican majority. This was met with some resistance from more senior Republicans and committee chairs. One former member of the Steering Committee explained the tenor of the time in an interview with the authors:

If you were a freshman, you would never get on Ways and Means, Commerce, and Appropriations. Those were really saved for the senior people. The first time it happened was in 1994 when the Republicans took over the majority. I was on the Steering Committee . . . and a bunch of us argued for the fact that if we were going to keep the majority we needed to make sure that some of our freshman do have expertise for interests in these more powerful committees had access to senior spots. It was kind of interesting because we did go up against sort of the changing world of Congress where some of the committee chairs said "that's outrageous, we don't want this, we don't want this young person who doesn't know how committees work." But we fought for it, and that has changed, and that largely changed in 1994. . . . [It was] somewhat incumbent protection but also acknowledging that Congress has changed and the days of people being in Congress for 20 or 30 years had changed.

Equally important reforms made at the same time added to the strength of the Steering Committee. Republican standing committee chairs are chosen by the Steering Committee and limited to three terms as chair. In the 104th Congress Gingrich and the Steering Committee often ignored the seniority rule, which would dictate that the most senior Republican on a committee ascend to the committee chair, choosing significantly less senior but more loyal members of the party for those important positions. As the term limits began to have an effect in the 107th Congress, seniority again played less of a role in the chair selection process, with the Steering Committee focusing instead on party loyalty. With the resignation of Gingrich and the installation of Dennis Hastert as Speaker, the leadership became somewhat less overtly aggressive in the committee assignment process. Consistent with more consensual leadership style, Speaker Hastert was not as willing to try to impose selections on the Steering Committee, as Gingrich had done, preferring consensus within the Steering Committee instead and only exercising his power in the process sparingly.

See also CAUCUS, PARTY; AND COMMITTEE ASSIGNMENTS.

Further reading:
Brewer, Paul R., and Christopher J. Deering. "Interest Groups, Campaign Fundraising, and Committee Chair Selection: House Republicans Play 'Musical Chairs.' " In *The Interest Group Connection: Electioneering, Lobbying, and Policymaking in Washington.* Paul S. Herrnson, Ronald G. Shaiko, and Clyde Wilcox, eds. New York: Chatham House Publishers, forthcoming; Frisch, Scott A., and Sean Q. Kelly. *Committee Politics.* Norman: University of Oklahoma Press, forthcoming; Masters, Nicholas A. "Committee Assignments

in the U.S. House of Representatives." *American Political Science Review.*

—Scott A. Frisch and Sean Q. Kelley

rescission

Rescission is the withholding of federal government funds previously approved in a budget bill. Rescissions can be initiated by either the president or Congress but are normally associated with presidential impoundment and, briefly, the line-item veto. Rescissions can take place for a variety of reasons, such as making budgetary room for new spending, changing program needs, eliminating PORK BARREL projects, and assisting congressional and executive oversight of federal agencies.

It is this last objective that made rescission a necessary but controversial presidential power in the 20th century. According to Louis Fisher, in the Anti-Deficiency Act of 1905 and its amendments in 1906 and 1950 the president was given power to impound funds already appropriated to executive agencies for two main reasons: to prevent agencies from getting more money from Congress at a time when parts of the federal bureaucracy were known to spend their allocations too quickly, and to adjust appropriations if agencies performed their tasks before the full budget cycle was complete. But a long history of congressional deference to presidential discretion on impoundments ended when Republican president Richard Nixon began to use these laws in the early 1970s as a way to stop various social services spending he disagreed with that had been previously approved by the Democratic-dominated Congress.

In response to Nixon's actions and a general institutional desire to gain more budgetary power, Congress passed the CONGRESSIONAL BUDGET AND IMPOUNDMENT CONTROL ACT in 1974. In addition to creating the House and Senate Budget Committees, the CONGRESSIONAL BUDGET OFFICE, and a new annual budget process, the 1974 reform increased congressional oversight of presidential withholdings. After 1974 presidents could request temporary funding "deferrals" as well as permanent rescission, but in both cases Congress now had explicit powers to stop these actions if a majority so desired. A deferral could not occur if either chamber of Congress passed a disapproval bill, but this form of congressional oversight was dropped in light of the Supreme Court's 1983 decision in *IMMIGRATION AND NATURALIZATION SERVICE V. CHADHA* eliminating one-chamber legislative vetoes, among others. Although the 1974 act's rescission provisions were even more pro-Congress, they were not at issue in the *Chadha* case and remain in effect today. Rescission was defined as the permanent withholding of funds, which can be part of a project or its entire budget authority. To propose a rescission the president must transmit a special message to Congress detailing the reasons and impact of the action, and if Congress agrees, it must pass a bill approving all or part of the president's proposal within 45 days. If Congress ignores a presidential request entirely, the funds are released.

After 1974 presidents had varying success using the new process, and by the early 1980s critics of the current process argued it was tilted too much toward Congress's preferences. Although presidents got tens of billions of their rescission proposals approved over two decades with the new procedure, they did not always get their way, especially during times of divided government. At the same time, Congress initiated its own rescissions and ultimately withheld more dollars than presidents' requests called for. Still, presidents and their supporters in Congress, mostly Republicans, argued the president should be given greater rescission power in the form of the line-item veto.

Most governors have a line-item veto, through which they can eliminate a budget item from a bill and sign the rest into law, but this power on the federal level would require a constitutional amendment. So item veto advocates largely pushed for greater presidential rescission power and called it by the simpler name. The Line-Item Veto Act of 1996 was really an "enhanced rescission" reform that reversed the 1974 process, in that congressional inaction would now automatically allow the president's rescissions to take effect. However, if Congress wished to stop any one or all of the rescissions, it could pass a disapproval bill, which would be subject to the normal veto and override procedures. As veto overrides are very rare, the enhanced rescission alternative was as close to a real line-item veto as the president could get. Some Congress and budget watchers found this reform curious not only because it disadvantaged Congress against the executive branch but also because it was pushed by a Republican majority when Democrat Bill Clinton was president. The reform proved to be short-lived when it was struck down by the Supreme Court in a 1998 case, *Clinton v. City of New York,* as an unconstitutional alteration of the lawmaking process. The 1974 rescission process is in force again, but Congress has recently investigated other ways of enhancing presidential power after the Court's decision.

The line-item veto movement gathered steam during a time of high deficits, but the kinds of spending rescissions target are a minority of the federal government's outlays, known as discretionary spending. While rescission is an important tool for Congress and the president to manage federal programs, it will never be a magic bullet for imbalanced budgets.

Further reading:
Fisher, Louis. *Presidential Spending Power.* Princeton, N.J.: Princeton University Press, 1975. Government Accounting Office. Available online. URL: http://www.gao.gov. Accessed January 19, 2006. Congressional Budget Office. Available online. URL: http://www.cbo.gov. Accessed January 19, 2006.

—Jasmine L. Farrier

resolutions, concurrent
Concurrent resolutions are passed by both the HOUSE OF REPRESENTATIVES and the SENATE to represent the viewpoint or preferences of a majority of the members of Congress. This is the only way in which concurrent resolutions differ from simple resolutions, which affect the behavior of only one chamber of Congress. Moreover, like simple resolutions, concurrent resolutions lack the force of law and are not subject to presidential review.

Concurrent resolutions commonly are used to implement organizational rules affecting both chambers, such as setting the time and date for adjournment for more than three days and ending each session of Congress. Near the end of the 20th century members of Congress had begun using concurrent resolutions to establish guidelines for passing subsequent federal budget provisions such as appropriations levels and anticipated revenue totals. These concurrent resolutions then would establish parameters affecting congressional behavior but lack the force of law and not govern the behavior of the president. Concurrent resolutions are designated by their chamber of origin, such as H. Con. Res. for the House and S. Con. Res. for the Senate, followed by the number of the concurrent resolution.

Further reading:
Oleszek, Walter J. *Congressional Procedures and the Policy Process.* Washington, D.C.: Congressional Quarterly Press, 2004.

—James Norris

resolutions, joint
Joint resolutions are similar to bills passed by Congress. Identical forms of joint resolutions must be passed by both the HOUSE OF REPRESENTATIVES and the SENATE before being signed by the president of the United States. However, proposed amendments to the U.S. Constitution are passed by Congress in the form of joint resolutions and sent directly to the states for ratification. Presidents cannot act on that type of joint resolution.

Unlike either SIMPLE RESOLUTIONS or CONCURRENT RESOLUTIONS, joint resolutions have the force of law following either the signature of the president or the congressional overturning of a presidential veto.

Joint resolutions most commonly differ from bills by focusing on narrower topics or taking actions that are temporary. On the other hand, the most prominent joint resolution was the WAR POWERS RESOLUTION OF 1973, which sought to set parameters on presidents committing military forces abroad. Passed over the veto of President Richard Nixon, the War Powers Resolution remained a controversial policy affecting relations between subsequent presidents and congresses. Joint resolutions are designated by their chamber of origin, such as H. J. Res. for the House and S. J. Res. for the Senate, followed by the number of the joint resolution.

Further reading:
Oleszek, Walter J. *Congressional Procedures and the Policy Process.* Washington, D.C.: Congressional Quarterly Press, 2004.

—Vincent Pollard

resolutions, simple

Rules of the HOUSE OF REPRESENTATIVES and the SENATE each allow for three types of resolutions: JOINT RESOLUTIONS, CONCURRENT RESOLUTIONS, and simple resolutions. Approval of a simple resolution is confined to one chamber. Designated by a number proceeded by either H. Res (for the House) and S. Res (for the Senate), the simple resolution represents the viewpoint of a majority of the members of the chamber passing the resolution.

Simple resolutions are mechanisms by which the House or Senate can applaud, condemn, or offer public condolences, for example. In addition, resolutions have been popular tools for members to adopt rules governing their chamber. However, simple resolutions lack the force of law. They may only govern the behavior or organization of the members of the chamber passing the resolution.

When passing a simple resolution a chamber is acting alone, without approval of either the other chamber or the president of the United States. Hence, presidents are unable to veto congressional resolutions.

One of the most common uses of simple resolutions occurs at the beginning of each new Congress when each chamber passes a simple resolution to adopt rules for governing and administering that chamber over the next two years of the congressional term. For example, simple resolutions are used to assign members to committees, allocate committee jurisdictions, and set the order of business on the chamber's floor. All simple resolutions may be amended or overturned entirely by subsequent resolutions passed by the chamber in question.

Further reading:
Oleszek, Walter J. *Congressional Procedures and the Policy Process.* Washington, D.C.: Congressional Quarterly Press, 2004.

Resources Committee, House

The House Resources Committee is charged with oversight of the nation's natural resources and federally owned or managed lands. It has jurisdiction over a very wide range of legislative concerns. In the 108th Congress, for example, the committee held hearings or considered bills on proposed oil drilling in the Arctic National Wildlife Refuge, a program to assist low-income households pay for energy costs, an initiative to provide forest fire relief, and efforts to acquire historic lands to add to the National Park System.

The breadth of responsibilities in the present Resources Committee is a result of a long process of congressional evolution dating back nearly to the founding of the nation. As American territories grew in size and scope and as the nation's demands for energy resources grew, so did the size and scope of this committee. The earliest predecessors of the contemporary committee were the House Public Lands Committee, established in 1805, and the Committee on Post Offices and Post Roads, created in 1808. Numerous additional committees were added over the course of the 19th century, including Private Land Claims, Indian Affairs, and Irrigation of Arid Lands. By the mid-20th century the existing committee structure had become unwieldy, with a large number of committees possessing partial or overlapping jurisdictions in a number of areas. The LEGISLATIVE REORGANIZATION ACT OF 1946, an effort to end this confusing state of affairs, placed the jurisdiction of five additional committees (Territories, Mines and Mining, Indian Affairs, Irrigation and Reclamation, and Insular Affairs), as well as responsibility for military parks, battlefields, and some cemeteries, under one newly constituted Committee on Public Lands. Reflecting this change of mission, the body was renamed the Committee on Interior and Insular Affairs in 1951.

In the next major series of congressional committee reforms, during the 1970s, the Interior and Insular Affairs Committee lost some of the authority it had gained during the consolidation of the 1940s. Jurisdiction over areas such as environmental research and development and Indian education were transferred to other committees in 1974. In 1977 the committee gained partial jurisdiction over nuclear energy legislation, though this was removed in 1995. Also in 1995 it absorbed most of the jurisdiction of the recently abolished Merchant Marine Committee. To reflect some of these changes, Congress changed the name of the committee to Natural Resources in 1993 and to Resources in 1995. As an indication of the expansion and contraction of jurisdiction that has taken place since 1947, the size of the committee's staff has ranged from 4 to 85 over this time period, with about 57 paid staffers employed during the 107th Congress.

As of the 108th Congress there were 52 members of the Resources Committee, including the chair, Republican

Richard Pombo, representative from California. Since many of the nation's most valued natural resources and public lands are located in the western United States, it should not be surprising that the committee's membership has historically been comprised mainly of legislators from western states. In the 108th Congress, for example, only about 20 percent of committee members hailed from states east of the Mississippi River. In addition to the representatives who serve as members, there is also a long history of territorial delegates serving on this committee. Since Resources is charged with jurisdiction and oversight for American territories, the delegates from American Samoa, the Virgin Islands, and Guam and the Resident Commissioner of Puerto Rico all sit on this committee.

As the committee is charged with diverse and complex concerns, it conducts most business at the subcommittee level. The numbers and names of these subcommittees have changed to adapt to the changing legislative needs of the country. In the 108th Congress, for example, Resources had five subcommittees: National Parks, Recreation, and Public Lands; Forests and Forest Health; Energy and Mineral Resources; Water and Power; and Fisheries Conservation, Wildlife, and Oceans. In addition to these subcommittees, the Resources Committee handles legislation falling under other areas of its jurisdiction at the full committee level. For example, the committee conducts business regarding American Indian policy in full committee.

Its wide-ranging jurisdiction and the growing salience of energy and environmental concerns have meant that the Resources Committee has weighed in on a large number of bills over the past two decades. In the 107th Congress, for example, 643 bills were referred to the Resources Committee, resulting in the passage of 84 public laws. The committee has tackled bills on the expansion of National Forests, the settlement of American Indian claims against the government, the status of Puerto Rico, offshore oil drilling, logging in National Parks, and acceptable uses of lead, to name a few. The committee's heavy responsibilities will continue as the nation searches for new and more sustainable uses of its resources and more equitable treatment of its territories and trust lands.

Further reading:
Committee on Resources. *FAQ Sheet.* 20 March 2003. Available online. URL: http://resourcescommittee. house.gov/107cong/faq.htm. Accessed 12 April 2003; Congressional Research Service. *The House Committee on Resources: A Jurisdictional Sketch.* Washington, D.C.: Government Printing Office, 2002; Fenno, Richard F., Jr. *Congressmen in Committees.* Boston: Little, Brown, 1973; Library of Congress. THOMAS: *Legislative Information on the Internet.* Available online. URL: http://thomas.loc.gov/. Accessed 12 April 2003; Nelson, Garrison. *Committees in*

the U.S. Congress, 1947–1992. 2 vols. Washington, D.C.: Congressional Quarterly Press, 1993.
—Charles C. Turner

rider

A rider is an amendment to a bill that is not germane to the bill. The term *rider* comes from the image of a hitchhiker thumbing a ride. If the bill to which a rider is attached becomes law, the rider also becomes law. Riders affect both policy issues and political dynamics in both houses of Congress.

Attaching a rider to a bill is a parliamentary tactic used to address the fact that the rider is probably controversial and unlikely to succeed legislatively on its own merits. Riders can also be used to force a recorded vote on an issue. The supporter(s) of a rider seek to force other legislators or the president to accept the rider as a necessary evil to be suffered to gain more important legislation. The opponents to a rider may be legislators of the HOUSE OF REPRESENTATIVES, the SENATE, and even the president. However, presidents may at times support a rider.

While nongermane amendments are technically prohibited in the Senate, many senators believe they are just practical politics. Consequently, riders occur most frequently in the Senate. Riders are prohibited by the rules of the House; however, nongermane amendments do occur. One reason is that a "rider" to one legislator may be a germane amendment to another legislator. Additionally, sometimes a rider can be linked to funding, such as a rider to limit funding for abortions.

Riders have the best chance of success if they are attached to certain types of legislation, such as appropriations bills, OMNIBUS BILLS, continuing funding resolutions, tax bills, trade bills, budgets for the District of Columbia, urgent legislation, and emergency funding bills. Other types of bills may also be used. The decision to attach a rider to a piece of legislation is a political decision. The sponsor of the rider will seek to use a bill with a strong chance of passage. Thus, the nongermane amendment will "ride" on a bill likely to pass even with the rider attached.

Single APPROPRIATIONS BILLS and omnibus appropriations bills are frequent targets for riders because they are major pieces of business that are usually considered in the last days of a session of Congress. Frequently, both the president and the congressional leadership have settled on the particulars of the appropriation bill. The rider, an undesirable addition, will either be passed with the spending bill or mean its defeat. The political price is to accept the rider rather than endure the defeat of the bill.

Appropriations bills must begin in the House. After passage by the House the Senate can consider the appropriations the bill(s) contain. In is not unusual for senators to attach riders to this type of legislation. The Miller-Tydings Act of 1937 was a rider to the budget for the District of Columbia.

Tax bills also must arise in the House. When the Senate handles tax bills it is not unusual for this type of legislation to attract the interests of business groups. Riders of this type can turn a bill into a special interest "Christmas tree bill."

Trade bills are also targets for riders. Senators may attach a rider(s) to address economic, social, or political concerns. For example, a rider may address human rights violations by a regime that will benefit from the trade. Or the rider(s) may add to the trade bill political conditions or security restrictions important to private or governmental interest groups.

CONTINUING (funding) RESOLUTIONS are frequently used in Congress to provide funding for an agency or program until a new permanent funding package can be passed. Usually there is some urgency in the measure so that a rider has a good chance of passage along with the temporary funding. The GRAMM-RUDMAN-HOLLINGS ACT OF 1968 was a rider to a bill on the federal debt limit.

Emergency funding bills, following a natural disaster such as fires, floods, storms, or some other crisis may attract riders. Riders serving special interests can be part of the political trading that is required for passage.

Urgent legislation responding to a national crisis such as the 9/11 terrorist attack can also be a magnet for riders. Again, the pressure to pass a measure may allow riders to be successfully attached.

Riders are often allowed by the floor managers of a bill in the expectation that the rider(s) will be purged in a CONFERENCE COMMITTEE. Or they may allow one or more riders to be attached as prospective "trading material" in a conference committee.

Legislation passed by Congress must pass both houses in exactly the same wording. When the Senate and House have passed different versions of the same bill, the differences must be settled in an ad hoc committee called a conference committee. The House and Senate members of the conference committee are selected by the leadership of their respective houses. Usually the members of the conference committee are the principal supporters of the bill.

The House members, serving on only one committee, are usually legislative specialists and know the details of the bill. The senators, as generalists, are more inclined to seek a bipartisan solution or compromise. The political dealing that is part of the negotiations that are necessary to reach a consensus on the bill can include purging or retaining a rider(s).

Riders can also be used to influence the president. A bill that the president might veto can be "sugar-coated" with a rider giving the president desired legislation.

Governors in many states have the line-item veto, which can be used to veto riders. The line-item veto is not a veto power enjoyed by the president of the United States. Consequently, nongermane amendments to bills are likely to continue to "ride" to the president's desk in the Oval Office until a line-item veto is made constitutional.

Further reading:
Bach, Stanley. *House Consideration of Nongermane Senate Amendments.* Washington, D.C.: Library of Congress, Congressional Research Service, 1976; Baker, Ross K. *House and Senate.* 3d ed. New York: Norton, 2001.
—Andrew J. Waskey

rights of witnesses

During the height of the communist scare in the United States in the early 1950s, Congress established the House UN-AMERICAN ACTIVITIES COMMITTEE. In establishing this committee, Congress explained that it was its responsibility to investigate and hold hearings, either by full committee or by subcommittees, to determine the extent of subversive activities directed against the U.S. government.

In the landmark case of *Watkins v. United States* (1957), the petitioner was subpoenaed to testify before the House Un-American Activities Committee. The reason for this subpoena was that the petitioner had been heavily involved in labor union activities between 1935 and 1954. The petitioner freely and without reservation testified about his own activities and associations but refused to answer questions about whether other persons had been members of the Communist Party. He based his refusal to testify on the grounds that the committee's questions exceeded their jurisdiction. Subsequently, the petitioner was convicted of a misdemeanor due to his refusal to answer all questions put to him by the committee.

The U.S. Supreme Court ruled that while Congress clearly had the power to conduct investigations, this power was not unlimited. Furthermore, Congress did not have the authority to expose the private affairs of individuals without a legitimate justification related to the activities of Congress. Additionally, the Bill of Rights is applicable to congressional investigations, and due process requires that witnesses not be compelled to testify before a congressional investigating committee, at risk of criminal prosecution, if they do not first know "the question under inquiry."

The controversy that arose in the *Watkins* case was related to the investigative powers of Congress and the limitations on those powers. The rights of witnesses in congressional investigations were spelled out. As decided in the *Watkins* case, a congressional committee cannot abridge individual rights of free expression (First Amendment), compel a witness to testify against himself or herself (Fifth Amendment), or subject a witness to unreasonable searches and seizures (Fourth Amendment). In short, Congress can never violate the constitutional rights of its witnesses.

Further reading:
Watkins v. United States, 354 U.S. 178 (1957).
—Nancy S. Lind

Robinson, Joseph Taylor (1872–1937)
Representative, Senator

Joseph Taylor Robinson was born in 1872 near Lonoke, Arkansas, the ninth of 10 children. Although he never finished high school, Robinson earned his teaching certificate and taught for two years before enrolling at the University of Arkansas. In 1894 he was elected to the state legislature, where he served one term and then enrolled at the University of Virginia Law School. In 1896 he began practicing law in Lonoke. Robinson was elected to the House of Representatives in 1902 and served 10 relatively quiet years in the House during Joe Cannon's tenure as Speaker. In July 1911 Robinson announced his intention to run as a gubernatorial candidate. He ran a bitter race against two-term incumbent George Donaghey and won. In 1913 Senator Jeff Davis died suddenly, and the Arkansas legislature elected Joe Robinson to replace him. Robinson resigned the governorship after one month in office. Thus, in a period of only two months, Joe Robinson held three major political offices, congressman, governor, and U.S. senator. An editor from the *Memphis Commercial Appeal* warned that Robinson "had better be watched on his way to Washington in case he saw a vacant office and stopped off to pick it up for his collection."

In 1920 Senator Robinson was named permanent chair of the Democratic National Committee. Two years later he was elected Democratic leader in the Senate in a surprising victory over Furnifold Simons of North Carolina. Robinson held both posts until his unexpected death in July 1937.

It was in the U.S. Senate that Robinson distinguished himself as a loyal Democrat and an effective politician. Robinson made a name for himself as an intense and combative young man. He was nicknamed "Scrappy Joe." Those personality characteristics as well as the nickname carried over to his service in the U.S. Senate. Senator Robinson is most often noted for his powerful oratorical skills and his loyalty to Democratic presidents of that era, Woodrow Wilson and Franklin Roosevelt in particular. Robinson worked tirelessly to enact Roosevelt's NEW DEAL, compromising his own health, even when he did not personally support individual measures. While Robinson is probably remembered more for his approach to public service and Senate leadership than for any particular public laws that bear his name, during the course of his career he worked tirelessly on behalf of a couple of notable public policies, the use of

an international assembly to promote goodwill, and in defense of small businesses.

Robinson first gained national prominence in 1917, when he delivered a scathing speech on the Senate floor that was intensely critical of Senator Robert M. LaFollette of Wisconsin and his antiwar, antiadministration rhetoric.

> You had the right to question the war if your honest judgment doubted it. . . . But when Congress declared war, then . . . by God, you ought to stand here and support the flag and the President, [instead of] going about the country stirring sedition, gathering the Socialists and discontented elements, and seeking to influence them against your flag, your country, and your President. . . . If I entertained your sentiments, I would apply to the Kaiser for a seat on the Bundesrath.

As a congressman in 1909, a decade before the League of Nations, Robinson introduced House Joint Resolution 250, which attempted to create an international representative body for the purpose of promoting international cooperation and conflict resolution. The Committee on Foreign Affairs never reported the bill, but Robinson's efforts on behalf of international cooperation did not end there. He continued to reintroduce similar legislation and became one of the principal supporters of Wilson's League of Nations. Senators Robinson and Hitchcock attempted to push the measure through the Senate's Foreign Relations Committee, feeling that once on the floor of the Senate public opinion could be brought to bear on the discussion, thus pressuring senators to pass the treaty. They were, of course, unsuccessful, and in March 1920, seeing the handwriting on the wall, Senator Robinson lamented the failure and predicted dire consequences:

> If the Republicans win the issue, the United States must always be prepared for war on land and sea. She must arm and train her sons in preparation for fiercer conflicts than the world has ever seen. Already there has been too much delay. The treaty must be ratified to preserve the interests of the United States.

In the aftermath of World War I, Robinson found himself in the role of minority leader and critic of a number of policies of the federal government. Moreover, he became gravely concerned about the lack of coherent public policy. In Europe the United States took no part in the Reparations Commission since it had failed to ratify the Treaty of Versailles, but still American troops patrolled. In an attempt to call attention to this and other inconsistencies in federal policy, Senator Robinson displayed both his wit and the pragmatic approach to politics that had endeared him to Arkansas's voters:

The Senator from California (Mr. Johnson) is willing to hold an economic conference; indeed, that he is anxious to do so, provided it be stipulated in advance that no economic question shall be discussed and no action taken respecting any subject at issue. The Senator from California says that he is heartily in favor of Senators, and other representatives of the government of the United States, communicating their advice to foreign courts, provided it be understood that the advice be rejected, and that if rejected, we take no action and make no recommendations. . . . With no definite plan of action, we seem to be pursuing what is at once the most dangerous and least promising course possible. The ship of state is drifting without chart or compass, the helmsman apparently asleep at his post.

In addition, Robinson displayed his insight into foreign affairs in the early 1930s as one of the few senators who, citing *Mein Kampf,* warned that Adolf Hitler's treatment of Jews was a planned policy of extermination rather than a spontaneous outburst of patriotism.

During his 35 years in national political office, Robinson debated and orchestrated the passage of countless pieces of federal legislation, yet only one bears his name, the Robinson-Patman Act. In the late 1920s many small, independent retailers were disappearing, unable to compete with the large chains. In 1928 the Federal Trade Commission (FTC) began an investigation into the disappearance of small retailers and the business practices of the large chains. Many large retailers not only obtained discounts for purchasing in bulk, they also received "advertising allowances," despite the fact that the large chains often did not advertise and the allowances served only as a kick-back or rebate. In a survey conducted by the FTC, 25 percent of manufacturers reported that retailers used "threats and coercion" to obtain better prices on merchandise. Senator Robinson and Representative Wright Patman, a Democrat from Texas, introduced the Robinson-Patman bill. The bill 1) prohibited price distinction between different retailers purchasing goods "of like grade and quality," 2) prohibited advertising allowances, and 3) prohibited "retailers from 'induc[ing] or receiv[ing] a discrimination in price,'" making retailers as well as manufacturers liable for transgressions. While Roosevelt supported the bill and signed it, the responsibility for generating support for the controversial measure, despite considerable opposition from the business sector, fell to Robinson, who was by then the acknowledged leader of the Senate. The pro-business contingent succeeded in having some additional provisions, aimed at watering down the bill, added during the Senate debate, though Robinson had them removed in the CONFERENCE COMMITTEE.

In short, "Scrappy Joe" Robinson enjoyed a long and distinguished career in national political office, particularly the U.S. Senate. He was the unchallenged leader of the Senate for 15 years and used that post in order to advance his own belief that the "chief function of government is to protect the weak against the strong." He literally died trying. As a tireless advocate for the New Deal, Robinson pushed himself and the Senate to enact Roosevelt's New Deal quickly, despite the warnings of his doctors and colleagues that he was killing himself. He died of a massive heart attack in 1937 during the debate over Roosevelt's court-packing scheme.

Further reading:
Bacon, Donald C. "Joseph Taylor Robinson: The Good Soldier." In *First Among Equals: Outstanding Senate Leaders of the Twentieth Century,* edited by Richard A. Baker and Roger H. Davidson. Washington: Congressional Quarterly Press, 1991; Grant, Gilbert Richard. "Joseph Taylor Robinson in Foreign Affairs." *Arkansas Historical Quarterly* 1950; Towns, Stuart. "Joseph T. Robinson and Arkansas Politics: 1912–1913." *Arkansas Historical Quarterly,* 1965; Weller, Cecil E. Jr. "Joseph Taylor Robinson and the Robinson-Patman Act." *Arkansas Historical Quarterly,* 1988; Weller, Cecil E., Jr. *Joe T. Robinson: Always a Loyal Democrat.* Fayetteville: University of Arkansas Press, 1998.
—Kimberly Maslin-Wicks

Rules, House Committee on

The Committee on Rules, more commonly referred to as the Rules Committee, is a standing committee of the HOUSE OF REPRESENTATIVES with principal responsibility for regulating the flow of legislation to the floor of that chamber. Considered by many to be among the most powerful House committees, it proposes "special orders," or "special rules," that define the length of debate and the nature and extent of amendment for every major bill considered on the floor. Technically, a "rule" is a resolution that must be adopted by majority vote of the full House before debate on a bill using the terms of the rule can occur. Failure to adopt a rule causes the House to debate a measure under its standing order of business, something that is time consuming and likely to lead to the defeat of a bill.

In the contemporary House, the Rules Committee is generally regarded as an instrument of the leadership of the majority party because of its ability to influence significantly the passage of legislation. Members vie for seats on the 13-member committee based on seniority, but members do not acquire seats without the blessings of their respective party leaders.

The Rules Committee has a long tradition in the House. Beginning with its first session in 1789, the House formed an 11-member SELECT COMMITTEE called Rules to define its standing rules and general order of business, but it was a temporary committee in that it was quickly dissolved upon the completion of its responsibilities. Subsequent Congresses over the next 90 years created similar committees at the start of each Congress to recommend amendments to the rules of the prior Congress, so it was not until 1880 that the House voted to make Rules a STANDING COMMITTEE of five members, despite the fact its stature had been enhanced in 1859 when the SPEAKER OF THE HOUSE was added as the committee chair. By 1883 the modern Rules Committee emerged when it was empowered to issue the types of rules for which it is known today: setting the terms and length of debate for bills coming to the floor.

In the era of strong Speakers of the late 19th and early 20th centuries, particularly under THOMAS REED and JOSEPH CANNON, Rules became a tool through which the Speaker could extend his control over his party's rank and file as well as the entire chamber. Perceived capricious and arbitrary decisions by Cannon led to the famous "revolt" against the Speaker in 1910 that brought major changes to Rules. Led by George Norris, a Republican from Nebraska, a coalition of insurgent Republicans, a vocal, disaffected group within the majority Republican Party, and Democrats, headed by Champ Clark, a Democrat from Missouri, voted to remove the Speaker from Rules, enlarged its membership from five to 10 (six from the majority party and the remainder from the minority), allowed the House to vote members onto Rules, and established seniority as the method by which members could acquire seats on all other standing committees. In later years those elected to Rules were likely to be the senior lawmakers bidding to fill vacancies on the committee. The size of the committee fluctuated over the years from 10 to 17, depending on the will of the majority party and the magnitude of its vote margin in the chamber.

Despite the changes, Rules remained a powerful tool of the majority party leadership until the committee came under the effective control of the CONSERVATIVE COALITION from 1939 to 1967. Conservative Democrats, mostly from the South, along with Republicans held a majority of seats on Rules and voted together to block liberal social legislation. The period from 1955 to 1967 proved to be the most difficult as Howard D. Smith, a Democrat from Virginia, chaired the committee. "Judge" Smith, as he was commonly addressed, was a fiercely independent and strongly opinionated man who used Rules to impose his personal values on public policy. Rather than having his committee objectively evaluate the rules requested by the chair of the reporting committee, Smith believed he could apply his own criteria based on the contents of a bill and his personal preferences, often blocking bills he opposed and advancing those he favored, heedless of the pleas of his party's leaders. During his tenure as chair, Rules bottled up civil rights and social welfare legislation, and it was anticipated that he would obstruct much of Kennedy's New Frontier agenda. In an effort to break Smith's hold over Rules, Speaker Sam Rayburn, a Democrat from Texas, in 1961 sought to increase the number of seats on the committee from 12 to 15, with the three new members being liberal Democrats who would oppose Smith. (Though there were eight Democrats and four Republicans on Rules at this time, two Democrats were southern conservatives, giving Smith his control.) In an unprecedented move President John Kennedy publicly intervened and supported the expansion of the committee's membership, a bold stroke that succeeded in enlarging Rules.

Additional subtle but important changes came to Rules in the mid-1970s. At the instigation of liberal Democrats, their caucus voted to change its rules and required that all committee chairs stand for election rather than assuming the chair via seniority. In addition, the caucus also voted to allow the Speaker to nominate members to serve on Rules, and those named were then confirmed by a vote of the full caucus. The Republican Conference followed suit in 1989, when it permitted its leader to name all its members to Rules.

The Rules Committee currently has 13 members, 9 Republicans and four Democrats, which dates from 1983, the 98th Congress. It also has two subcommittees: Legislative and Budget Process, and Technology and the House.

The Rules Committee's principal function is to assign to each bill brought before it a "rule" that establishes the length of time the bill will be debated and how many, if any, amendments may be offered from the floor, the order in which amendments are presented, who may offer amendments, and what part or parts of the bill may be amended. While not every bill considered by the House receives a rule, most major, nonprivileged legislation does require one, and the fate of this legislation often rests with the type of rule the committee issues. The crafting of a rule may also involve the committee in settling jurisdictional disputes between and among committees that considered the same or similar bills.

A rule is a privileged, simple resolution that is taken up first before the bill associated with the rule can be debated. Each rule is debated on the floor but may not be amended, and adoption requires a simple majority vote. Once adopted, the rule gives the bill a privileged status, which means that the bill can be considered immediately, vacating the formal order of House business and allowing the House to dissolve into the COMMITTEE OF THE WHOLE to debate the bill. Failure to adopt the rule forces the House to maintain its formal procedures and established calendars, which more than likely will cause consideration of the bill to be delayed indefinitely or have the bill debated under unfavorable terms.

Bills may also find their way to the floor without a rule, but only under the following circumstances: the bill is considered on special CALENDAR days (e.g., Corrections, Private, Wednesday, and District of Columbia), the leadership seeks UNANIMOUS CONSENT or SUSPENSION OF THE RULES, or if the bill is privileged legislation (e.g., appropriations, budget resolutions, and certain special rule resolutions, motions, or questions).

Rules also exercises original (or substantive) jurisdiction over the standing rules of the House and the congressional BUDGET PROCESS. This type of jurisdiction harks back to the work of the earliest rules committees that established and reviewed the general order of House business at the start of each session. Among the most significant legislation reported by contemporary Rules Committees are the LEGISLATIVE REORGANIZATION ACT OF 1970, the BUDGET AND IMPOUNDMENT CONTROL ACT OF 1974, the resolution to create a permanent Select Intelligence Committee, the Bipartisan House Ethics Reform Recommendations of 1997, and the Comprehensive Budget Process Reform Act of 1999. Since the events of September 11, 2001, Rules has held hearings on maintaining the continuity of Congress should the CAPITOL BUILDING be attacked and a large number of representatives be killed.

In order for a bill to receive a rule, the committee chair reporting out a bill requests in writing that Rules schedule a hearing and also states his or her preferences for the details of the rule. The Rules Committee is under no obligation to act on the request, however; without a rule, the bill dies in the committee. Should the committee fail to act on a request, any member who wishes to have the blocked legislation brought to the floor may follow the procedures to obtain discharge petition.

The Rules Committee chair then schedules and holds a hearing during which the only witnesses are members of Congress, usually the reporting committee chair, the subcommittee chair that considered the bill, the bill's sponsor(s), committee members who opposed the bill, and any members who may wish to offer amendments to the bill. This opportunity to explain and defend the bill to the Rules Committee has been called a "dress rehearsal" for the floor debate that is likely to occur in the House, as each side tests its arguments. At the conclusion of the hearings, Rules Committee members debate alternative rules, consult with the majority leadership, and draft the specifics of the rule to be proposed. The influence that the majority leadership exerts over the committee cannot be overstated, because in recent history few rules have been issued that the leadership had not endorsed.

The Rules Committee chair reports and files the special rule with the Clerk of the House while simultaneously consulting with the majority leadership, including the Speaker, to determine when the bill should be brought to the floor. When a day has passed from the filing of the rule, the House may consider it any time thereafter. A two-thirds vote is required to debate a rule on the same day it is reported from Rules. On the floor, debate on the rule occurs under the so-called hour rule, though the hour rule is rarely followed. The presiding officer recognizes a majority member of Rules, who serves as floor leader, recognizing a few people to speak for and possibly against the rule. The floor leader then asks to "move the previous question," which, if the motion passes, ends all debate and amendments to the rule, and a vote on the rule is taken immediately. Thus, opponents of the rule will urge lawmakers to vote against the motion to move. If the motion is defeated, debate on the rule can drag on, leaving the prospects for the bill's passage in serious doubt.

If the motion passes, then the rule will pass as well, at which point the House dissolves to the Committee of the Whole, where it debates the bill as privileged legislation under the terms of debate described in the rule. Should the rule be defeated, the bill may be withdrawn, or it may be debated by the House under its regular order of business, without privileged status and subject to amendment.

The average rule includes the following: the length of time for deliberation, stipulations on amendments that may be offered, if any, and by whom, and what parliamentary rules and procedures may be waived, if any. Under most circumstances, the length of time granted in a rule is a function of the importance of the legislation: The more significant the bill to the leadership or president, the more time for deliberation. However, if the legislation is controversial, the majority party may shorten the floor debate as much as possible to stifle the opposition's ability to capitalize on the situation. Opponents, in this instance, would demand more time for debate.

There are four main types of rules that deal with amending bills: open, modified open, modified closed, and closed. A closed or gag rule forbids any and all amendments to a bill. A modified closed or structured rule can limit the total number of amendments offered, what sections of a bill can be amended, and who can offer amendments. For instance, a rule can specify that amendments can be offered by members of the reporting committee to Titles I and IV of a bill but not Titles II, III, V, and VI.

An open rule permits any member to offer an amendment, under the five-minute rule, to any part of a bill so long as the amendment is germane to the bill and is in compliance with all other standing rules of the House. A modified open rule may allow all or a select group of members to propose germane amendments under the five-minute rule on parts of a bill. For example, a rule can specify that Titles I, II, III, and V of a bill may be amended, while Titles IV and VI are off limits. (What distinguishes modified open and modified closed rules is the relative number of amendments permitted or restricted, i.e., if more of a bill is open to amendment, the rule is modified open, while if less of a bill is subject to amendment, the rule is modified closed.)

Typically, proponents of a bill favor closed rules for reasons as varied as the complex nature of the legislation (e.g., tax measures, appropriations bills), or they are emergency measures, or because the highly fragile coalitions created to report the bill out of committee will disintegrate should the language of the bill be disturbed through amendment. Opponents, on the other hand, challenge any limit on amendments as they attempt to defeat or significantly alter bills on the floor.

Among the relatively modern but important innovations for sequencing the consideration of floor amendments are the "King-of-the-Hill" and "Queen of-the-Hill" rules. Invented by Rules chair RICHARD BOLLING, a Democrat from Missouri, during the budget reconciliation season of 1982, the King-of-the-Hill rule allows the consideration of many amendments offered as substitutes to the main bill, any or all of which may be drastically different from the original bill. Each amendment is voted on, and many may receive a majority of the votes cast. However, the *only* amendment that counts, that is, moves forward in the legislative process, is the *last* amendment voted on to receive a majority. Republican leaders complained bitterly about the hypocrisy of this process because it allowed members to be on all sides of an issue. When they took control of the House in 1994, Speaker NEWT GINGRICH, a Republican from Georgia, created a Queen-of-the-Hill variation that he believed corrected the problem. Under this rule, a number of substitute amendments are offered, but the amendment receiving the *most* votes is the amendment that is reported out of the Committee of the Whole. Should two amendments receive the same number of votes, the *last* amendment voted on is forwarded to the Committee of the Whole.

Yet another aspect of a rule may involve the temporary waiver of specific House procedures; a waiver may be incorporated in any of the rules discussed above. Waivers may be categorized as either focused or blanket. A focused or specific waiver identifies one or more particular parliamentary procedures and sets them aside during floor action for a bill. A blanket waiver bans all points of order brought during floor action on a bill. House leadership will most often seek waivers for legislation brought to the floor near the end of a session, when the press of business and the need to move expeditiously are highest. Without such waivers the flow of legislation would slow to a trickle.

The variety of rules described above is not meant to be exhaustive of all the kinds of rules that the committee may devise. The history of the committee and its work, especially in the contemporary era, is marked by creativity and innovation, usually driven by the desire of the majority party to secure expeditious and unadulterated passage of its legislative agenda.

Further reading:
Brown, William H. *House Practice: A Guide to the Rules, Precedents, and Procedures of the House.* Washington, D.C.: Government Printing Office, 1996; Cummings, Milton C., Jr., and Robert L. Peabody. "The Decision to Enlarge the Committee on Rules: An Analysis of the 1961 Vote." In *New Perspectives on the House of Representatives.* 2d ed., edited by Robert L. Peabody and Nelson W. Polsby, Chicago: Rand McNally, 1969; Matsunaga, Spark M., and Ping Chen. *Rulemakers of the House.* Urbana: University of Illinois Press, 1976; Oleszek, Walter J. *Congressional Procedures and the Policy Process.* 6th ed. Washington, D.C.: Congressional Quarterly Press, 2004; Robinson, James A. *The House Rules Committee.* Indianapolis: Bobbs Merrill, 1963; House Rules Committee. Available online. URL: http://www.house.gov/rules.htm. Accessed 19 January 2006.
—Thomas J. Baldino

Rules and Administration, Senate Committee on

Since January 3, 1947, the Senate Committee on Rules and Administration has prepared the Senate Manual, published during the second session of each Congress as Senate Document 1, which contains the standing rules, orders, laws, and resolutions affecting the SENATE. The origin of the committee dates to April 7, 1789, when a panel was created to prepare a system of rules for conducting business. The committee consisted of Oliver Ellsworth of Connecticut, Richard Henry Lee of Virginia, Caleb Strong of Massachusetts, William Maclay of Pennsylvania, and Richard Bassett of Delaware. Their proposal was adopted by the Senate on April 18, 1789. Over the next 75 years eight additional special committees were created to review Senate rules.

In April 1867 a Select Committee on the Revision of the Rules was created and functioned until 1874, when it was designated a standing committee by the Senate and named the Committee on Rules. Major revisions of the Senate rules were proposed by the committee and approved by the Senate in 1877, 1884, and 1979. In 1917 committee members proposed an amendment to the rules providing for a CLOTURE procedure, which for the first time placed limits on debate in the Senate.

The LEGISLATIVE REORGANIZATION ACT OF 1946 merged the jurisdictions of a number of standing committees into the new Committee on Rules and Administration. The standing committees terminated included the Committee on Enrolled Bills (created in 1789 as a joint committee), which had responsibility for examining all bills, constitutional amendments, and joint resolutions (in 1947 this responsibility, by virtue of S. Res. 55, 80th Congress, was transferred to the Office of the Secretary of the Senate); the Committee to Audit and Control the Contingent Expenses of the Senate (created in 1819 as a standing committee); the Committee on Printing (created in 1841 as a standing committee); the Committee on the Library (created in 1806 as a joint committee; continued as a standing committee in 1849); the Committee on Privileges and Elections (created in 1871 as a standing committee); and the Committee on Rules (created in 1874).

In 1986 the Senate approved a Rules and Administration Committee recommendation to allow for gavel-to-gavel television coverage of the Senate's proceedings. The Senate gave committee chairs the authority to adopt rules for the telecast of their committees' meetings. The Committee on Rules and Administration has authority to promulgate rules for televising chamber proceedings.

In 1997 the committee, pursuant to its charge that it rule on the credentials and qualifications of members of the Senate, conducted an investigation into the 1996 Louisiana Senate election. The committee, after investigating charges of voter fraud, voted to uphold the election of Senator Mary Landrieu, who had defeated her Republican opponent, Woody Jenkins, by 5,788 votes out of nearly 1.7 million ballots cast.

In 2004 the committee was made up of 19 members, 10 Democrats and nine Republicans. The committee has jurisdiction, under the Standing Rules of the Senate (Rule 25.1), over the following subjects: administration of the Senate Office Buildings and the Senate wing of the Capitol; Senate rules; corrupt practices; credentials and qualifications of members of the Senate; federal elections; presidential succession; the Senate library; services to the Senate, including the Senate restaurant; the Library of Congress; the Smithsonian Institution; and the Botanic Gardens. The committee is also responsible for making recommendations on improvement of the organization and operation of Congress, including strengthening the institution, simplifying its operations, improving its relationship with the other branches of the federal government, and enabling it to better meet its constitutional responsibilities. The committee is also charged with bringing to the Senate's attention any court proceeding or action it feels is of vital interest to Congress.

The committee's most important legislative work has been on the conduct of federal elections. In 1971 the committee approved what became the Federal Elections Campaign Act (FECA) of 1971, which established more stringent reporting requirements of contributions and expenditures by candidates for federal office.

Three years later, following the revelation of campaign finance abuses during the 1972 election cycle, the commit-

tee approved the legislation that established the Federal Elections Commission (FEC) to administer FECA.

In 1993 the committee approved the National Voter Registration Act, popularly known as the Motor Voter Act. The act was intended to increase the number of eligible citizens who register to vote in elections for federal office by allowing them to register to vote when applying for a driver's license.

Following the contested presidential election of 2000, the committee supported the passage of the Help America Vote Act (Public Law 107-252). The law provided funds to the states to introduce new elections technology, created an Election Assistance Commission to assist states with the administration of elections, and mandated that states verify the identity of new voters in order to ensure the integrity of the electoral process.

In 2002 the committee supported the Bipartisan Campaign Reform Act of 2002. Popularly known as McCain-Feingold (after its two Senate sponsors, John McCain of Arizona and Russ Feingold of Wisconsin), the statute prohibited soft money, unlimited political contributions made by corporations and labor union political action committees to political party organizations.

Further reading:
U.S. Senate, Committee on Rules and Administration. *History of the Committee on Rules and Administration*, United States Senate. Senate Document 96-27. 96th Congress, 1st Session. Washington, D.C.: Government Printing Office, 1980.

—Jeffrey Kraus

rules and procedures, House

The rules and procedures of the HOUSE OF REPRESENTATIVES are significantly different from those of the SENATE. While the rules and procedures of the Senate have changed relatively little over time, those of the House have historically undergone more significant alterations.

Seats in the House of Representatives are apportioned according to population. In addition to the 435 members representing the 50 states, there is a nonvoting Resident Commissioner from Puerto Rico elected for a four-year term and nonvoting delegates from the District of Columbia, Guam, and the Virgin Islands elected to two-year terms. Over the past century most representatives in the House have been members of either the Democratic Party or the Republican Party. At any given time the smaller of the two is called the minority party, while the larger is known as the majority party and is responsible for organizing the business of the House. The majority party in the House chooses the SPEAKER OF THE HOUSE and has a majority on each committee. It also controls the appointment of the committee chairs and most committee staff members.

Beginning in the 1920s the House followed the rule of seniority for determining members' rank on standing committees and in selecting committee chairs. The member of the majority party with the longest continuous record of service on each House committee automatically became its chair. But in an effort to democratize the selection process, the seniority system was reformed in the early 1970s. Now all members of the majority party can participate by secret ballot in selecting committee chairs and each member may be elected to the chair regardless of seniority rank.

How the agenda of each new House is organized is significantly influenced by the recesses between Congresses. The House establishes the rules of its own proceedings at the start of each new Congress. The Speaker of the House, as presiding officer, is the principal arbiter of the procedural rules and is assisted in this by the House PARLIAMENTARIAN, an appointed official. But a vote by the majority of the House members can overrule the Speaker's interpretations or applications of the rules of procedure. In addition, each House committee adopts its own formal rules and procedures.

Any representative may introduce legislation, usually called a BILL. Following precedent, the Speaker refers the bill to the appropriate STANDING COMMITTEE. The committee and its SUBCOMMITTEES may hold public hearings on the bill before consideration by the full House. The HOUSE RULES COMMITTEE then recommends the length of time the bill will be debated on the House floor and determines what, if any, amendments may be considered. These recommendations must be approved by the full House before the bill is debated and amended. Finally, the full House votes on the bill, usually by a recorded roll call.

Further reading:
Sinclair, Barbara. *Legislators, Leaders, and Lawmaking: The U.S. House of Representatives in the Postreform Era.* Baltimore: Johns Hopkins University Press, 1995.
—Rossen V. Vassilev

rules and procedures, Senate

The rules and procedures of Congress are based on Thomas Jefferson's *Manual of Parliamentary Practice*, but the practices of the SENATE are significantly different from those of the HOUSE OF REPRESENTATIVES. How the agenda of each new Senate is set up is not influenced by the recesses between Congresses. Any unfinished work of the Senate is resumed in the next Congress as if no adjournment has taken place. Nor have the rules of the Senate been subject to much change. The rules adopted by the Senate during the First Congress in 1789 have remained essentially in

effect, except for small alterations made by occasional amendments to meet new circumstances and needs.

The authority to call up a measure is reserved by tradition for the MAJORITY LEADER, who decides on the legislative agenda in daily consultations with the MINORITY LEADER. Senate BILLS and resolutions are not divided into classes as a basis for their priority, nor are there calendar days set aside each month for their consideration. The Senate gives certain motions privileged status, and certain bills, such as conference reports, command first or immediate attention. That is because a bill that has reached the conference stage is considered privileged compared to bills that have only been reported. The presiding officer may place, or any senator may move to place, before the Senate any bill or other matter sent by the president or the House of Representatives, including veto messages, which constitute privileged business and which may be brought up at almost any time. Any pending question or other legislative business at that time is suspended or adjourned.

A senator may debate a bill or an issue without any restriction unless two-thirds of the senators agree to adopt a CLOTURE motion to end debate. The use of such delaying tactics is known as a FILIBUSTER. Senators may also propose as many amendments as they wish, even if such amendments are not related to the topic of the bill.

The Senate attaches special importance to maintaining decorum in its proceedings. No senator may speak ill of another senator or senators nor refer disrespectfully to any state in the union. No senator may interrupt another senator in debate without the consent of the latter as well as of the presiding officer. Nor are senators allowed to speak more than twice on any issue in debate on the same day. If a senator violates the rules of the Senate, the presiding officer or any senator may call him or her to order. If called to order, a senator must sit down and may not proceed without the consent of the Senate. If a senator persists in transgressing its rules and procedures, the Senate may pass by a two-thirds vote a motion of censure.

Further reading:
Howell, Wilbur S. *Jefferson's Parliamentary Writings: A Parliamentary Pocket-Book and a Manual of Parliamentary Practice.* Princeton, N.J.: Princeton University Press, 1988.
—Rossen V. Vassilev

rules for House and Senate debate

Parliamentary regulations govern debate on the floor of the House and Senate. The House of Representatives and the Senate have established different sets of rules for managing floor debate. The Senate does not have any regular limitations on debate, while House members always debate under some form of time limitation. The primary reason for the different rules is the difference in the number of members of the House and Senate. Since the House is made up of 435 representatives, more time management is required in order to dispense with the business of the House. With only 100 senators, the Senate can afford to have more lengthy discussions.

The House operates under two sets of debate rules. The "one-hour rule" manages debate during the times when the House is sitting as the House of Representatives. The "five-minute rule" manages debate when the House is meeting as the COMMITTEE OF THE WHOLE. The "one-hour rule" means that both sides of an issue each receive 30 minutes per matter under discussion. Most matters debated in the House, such as rules from the Rules Committee, conference reports, and amendments from the Senate rarely require more than an hour of debate. It is possible to extend the debate beyond one hour by unanimous consent or by defeating a procedural motion called the PREVIOUS QUESTION. These attempts to extend debate rarely succeed. The time is controlled by a majority and minority FLOOR MANAGER who decide how each side's 30 minutes will be allocated. A representative seeking to speak must request time from his or her manager. Each floor manager carefully allocates the time to make sure that all representatives are able to get their points made.

The five-minute rule governs debate after the House resolves itself into the Committee of the Whole. The five-minute rule allows five minutes per side for debate of any amendment or motion offered. Time can be extended by offering "pro forma" amendments, such as motions to "strike the last word," or by unanimous consent. Debate can be ended by the floor manager of a bill by moving to close debate on a specific amendment. The five-minute rule allows for a faster pace and more flexibility than is provided under the one-hour rule.

Debate is largely unlimited in the Senate. Once the presiding officer recognizes a senator to speak, he or she may speak for as long as he or she wants. The presiding officer must recognize the first senator seeking recognition without asking for a reason or an indication of the length of time the senator desires the floor. It is always possible for a senator to extend debate to a FILIBUSTER. To avoid the threat of a filibuster or to avoid any prolonged debate, the MAJORITY LEADER and MINORITY LEADER often try to negotiate a unanimous consent agreement between both sides to voluntarily limit debate on a specific bill, amendment, or motion. If all senators agree, a limit on debate will be set in advance and announced before the matter is brought up for consideration. The time allotted for debate can be an hour, several hours, or several days.

Under a unanimous consent agreement the debate time is divided between the majority and minority floor managers for the bill. The floor managers usually are the chair and ranking minority member of the committee that reported the bill to the floor. Senators must seek time to speak from their floor manager. During this period of controlled time, the presiding officer may specify the length of time the senator is allowed to speak.

Further reading:
U.S. House of Representatives. *Constitution, Jefferson's Manual, and Rules of the House of Representatives of the United States, 108th Congress.* Compiled by Charles W. Johnson. House Document 107-284. Washington, D.C.: Government Printing Office, 2000; U.S. Senate, Committee on Rules and Administration. *Senate Manual Containing the Standing Rules, Orders, Laws, and Resolutions Affecting the Business of the United States Senate.* Senate Document 107-1. Washington, D.C.: Government Printing Office, 2002.

—John David Rausch, Jr.

Russell, Richard B. (1897–1971) *Senator*

Richard Brevard Russell, Jr., was a Democratic senator from Georgia from 1933 to 1971 and for a quarter century was one of the most influential lawmakers in Congress. An authority on military affairs and agricultural policy, the "Georgia Giant," as he was known, was also one of the Senate's foremost experts on rules and procedures. He served as President Pro Tempore from 1969 to 1971, chair of the COMMITTEE ON APPROPRIATIONS from 1969 to 1971, and chair of the COMMITTEE ON ARMED SERVICES from 1951 to 1953 and 1955 to 1969. Unofficially, Russell was also the leader of the Southern bloc of senators who dominated the Senate throughout the 1940s and 1950s. However, he is perhaps best remembered today as the era's most formidable opponent of civil rights legislation.

Born to a highly regarded Georgia family, Russell was elected to the Georgia legislature at a young age, quickly rising to the rank of speaker of the house (the youngest in Georgia history). At the age of 33 he was elected governor of the state (the youngest in Georgia history), and in this position he built a reputation for streamlining the state's bureaucracy and for bringing economy to state expenditure. Following the death of the incumbent senator in 1932, Russell ran for the vacant seat and won handily (making him the youngest senator serving at that time).

A number of fortuitous events coincided with Russell's arrival in the U.S. Senate. The main factor was that a large number of sitting senators had been defeated in 1932 due to the anti-incumbent political climate of the Great Depression. Because of this large turnover Russell was able to ask for and receive a seat on the powerful Appropriations Committee. Due to a personal dispute between two senior

Richard B. Russell *(HarpWeek, LLC)*

members, Russell during his first year was also able to assume the chair of the Agriculture Appropriations Subcommittee. From this perch Russell played an influential role on agricultural policy for nearly 30 years, until his voluntary relinquishment of the post in 1962. Also during his first year in the Senate, Russell was named to the Appropriations Subcommittee on the War Department, the Committee on Naval Affairs (which would later merge with its sister committee to become the Committee on Armed Services), the Committee on Manufactures, and the Committee on Immigration. In time Russell would chair each of these committees.

Russell's power within the Senate stemmed from a combination of both formal and informal factors. From a formal standpoint Russell was well positioned as a member of several influential committees, particularly Appropriations and Armed Services. For much of his career, he was also a member of both the Democratic Policy Committee and the DEMOCRATIC STEERING COMMITTEE. (The former dictated what legislation came to the floor for debate and the latter determined Democratic committee assignments).

On an informal level Russell's personality was well suited to the rhythms of the Senate. He was a life-long bachelor and thus able to devote a great deal of time to his work. His diligence, quick mind, dedication to the Senate as an institution, courtly southern demeanor, mastery of the rules, and reputation for probity all helped Russell become an important player in the upper chamber. Presidents as well as his Senate colleagues valued his wise counsel and discretion.

Equally important to Russell's ascendancy was the conservative ethos that dominated the Senate for much of his tenure. Beginning in earnest in 1937 with the defeat of President Roosevelt's "court-packing" plan and lasting at least until the election of 1958, which brought in a host of liberal members, conservatives held sway in the Senate. Conservative Democrats from the South and conservative Republicans from the Midwest and West dominated the body and dictated the flow of legislative business. Due to his leadership of the southern caucus (well established by the early 1950s) and his good relations with conservative Republicans, Russell was at the heart of this conservative nexus. Therefore, although he never formally held the position of Democratic leader, he was the eminence grice of the Senate for almost a generation.

The Armed Services Committee proved to be one of the positions from which Russell came to play a major role in national policy. He not only served as chair or ranking member for 18 years, but he was also a member of the Appropriations Subcommittee on Defense for his entire career (chairing the subcommittee the last nine years of his life). In the 1960s one journalist commented: "In the field of national defense, Russell is recognized as pretty much the voice of the Senate."

Russell was a vigorous advocate of military strength during the cold war, recognizing the threat posed to the United States by the Soviet Union. Nonetheless, Russell did not believe in indiscriminate use of military force abroad. He was a skeptic about Vietnam, helping to persuade the Eisenhower administration not to intervene there following the collapse of the French position in 1954. A decade later his position was unchanged. Despite his misgivings about U.S. military involvement in Vietnam, Russell supported the war effort legislatively once troops had been committed. Russell's concern about U.S. involvement in the region only grew, however, and he repeatedly expressed his frustration to President Johnson, arguing that the United States should either assume a more vigorous posture with respect to the North or withdraw altogether.

Russell's effectiveness in the area of national defense was perhaps best reflected in 1951. That year a political firestorm erupted following President Truman's removal of General MacArthur from command in Korea. MacArthur's dismissal prompted a visceral reaction from the American people, most of whom revered the exalted general. In an effort to cool the mounting political tension, Russell chaired a joint committee of the Senate Armed Services Committee and Foreign Relations Committee to investigate the matter. Russell conducted these hearings with great political skill, slowly and methodically defusing the political passion by rigorously analyzing and ultimately discrediting MacArthur's foreign policy assertions and, by extension, reaffirming Truman's decision (and more subtly his authority) to remove the general. In the words of one commentator, Russell's "power and prestige . . . employed at a moment of great crisis in America" helped to bring the nation to its senses at a time "as close to a state of national hysteria as it had ever been in its history."

Russell's rural upbringing gave him a strong appreciation, if somewhat idealized view, of the small farmer. From his position on the Appropriations Subcommittee on Agriculture, Russell was able to play a major role in agricultural policy and to improve the fortunes of farmers nationwide. Russell was particularly concerned about providing small farmers with the wherewithal to purchase their own land and equipment. Russell was a firm supporter of agricultural price supports throughout his career and fought with some success against attempts by several administrations to reduce them. Russell supported most of the NEW DEAL agricultural measures and was an early backer of the food stamps program and a key sponsor of the Agricultural Research and Marketing Act of 1946, which aided agriculturally related conservation efforts. Russell's efforts to push through the National School Lunch Act enshrined what had hitherto been an ad hoc federal effort to assist farmers and feed low-income school children. Russell considered this bill one of his proudest achievements.

Russell's prestige and trustworthiness attracted others to him, particularly younger members. Among the more prominent members who gravitated to Russell was LYNDON JOHNSON. Aside from being his protégé, Johnson benefited from Russell's reluctance to become official Democratic leader. Russell feared losing his independence if he formally became the head of the Senate Democratic Caucus. Seeing promise in the young Texan, Russell pushed to have Johnson named Democratic leader.

Despite the tremendous power that Johnson wielded as Democratic leader, he relied greatly on the behind-the-scenes support of Russell. Johnson's reliance on Russell continued well into his presidency. For example, following the assassination of President Kennedy, Johnson appointed Russell to serve on the Warren Commission that investigated the tragedy. Despite their friendship, Russell ultimately opposed many, if not most, of Johnson's Great Society programs. The two men remained close until the last years of the Johnson administration.

Russell is perhaps best known today for his ardent opposition to civil rights. All his life Russell believed firmly in white supremacy and in segregation of the races.

Although he avoided the racist histrionics of some of his southern colleagues such as Theodore Bilbo, no one member of Congress did more to dilute and delay the enactment of civil rights legislation than Russell.

In the 1930s as a young senator, Russell played a prominent role in the southern caucus's defeat of proposed anti-lynching legislation. During World War II Russell worked diligently (albeit unsuccessfully) to abolish the Fair Employment Practices Committee, which had been established by President Roosevelt to prohibit defense contractors from practicing racial discrimination. In the 1950s he was the primary draftsman of the "Southern Manifesto," a document that decried the Supreme Court's decision in *Brown v. Board of Education*. This document was signed by scores of southern lawmakers in the mid-1950s and reflected their efforts to "use all lawful means" to have *Brown* overturned. Russell harshly criticized President Eisenhower for his decision to send federal troops to Little Rock, Arkansas, to integrate Central High School. He also battled to have the provisions of the 1957 and 1960 Civil Rights Acts rendered toothless. Finally, Russell vigorously but unsuccessfully opposed both the 1964 Civil Rights Act and the 1968 Civil Rights Act. (Russell did not take active part in the debate over the Voting Rights Act of 1965 due to illness. He did oppose the bill, however). Russell's mastery of procedure and Senate rules as well as his ability as a political strategist prevented scores of other civil rights measures from even reaching the Senate floor for consideration. Russell's implacable opposition to integration not only tarnished his historical reputation but hindered his national ambitions as reflected by his relatively weak showing during his 1952 campaign for the Democratic presidential nomination.

While never conceding his position on civil rights, it bears noting that following enactment of the Civil Rights Act of 1964, in a famous speech Russell did distinguish himself from many of his colleagues by counseling southerners to obey the new law and to eschew violence. In a personal note to Russell, President Johnson said of the speech, with perhaps only some exaggeration, that Russell's stature in the South ensured his words were "as significant as any I have heard made by a public official in this country."

Enactment of the 1964 Civil Rights Act signaled the end of an era in the Senate. No longer could the southern bloc defeat or emasculate civil rights legislation. It also in many ways reflected the beginning of the end of Russell's career. By the mid-1960s Russell's health had begun to fail, and his relations with President Johnson had become increasingly distant. Although he still commanded great respect in the Senate and continued to play an important role in defense and appropriations matters, the structural underpinnings for Russell's power—the conservative coalition—no longer dictated the course of Senate business. Russell remained in the Senate until his death in 1971. The following year what had been known as the Old Senate Office Building was renamed the Russell Senate Office Building in his honor. A statue of Russell was added to the building in 1996.

At the end of the day, few members of the Senate can match Russell's career as far as impact on the national scene. Russell's influence on national security and agricultural policy was immense, and he was a key player behind the scenes on scores of other legislative issues. Ultimately, however, Russell's legacy will always be greatly diminished because of his determined opposition to civil rights legislation. Russell's record in this area prevents him from taking rank with the greatest senators of American history.

Further reading:
Caro, Robert A. *The Years of Lyndon Johnson: Master of the Senate.* New York: Knopf, 2002; Fite, Gilbert C. *Richard B. Russell, Jr.: Senator From Georgia.* Durham: University of North Carolina Press, 1991; Goldsmith, John A. *Colleagues: Richard B. Russell and His Apprentice Lyndon B. Johnson.* Macon, Ga.: Mercer University Press, 1998; Mann, Robert. *The Walls of Jericho: Lyndon Johnson, Hubert Humphrey, Richard Russell, and the Struggle for Civil Rights.* New York: Harcourt Brace, 1996; McLeod, Calvin, and Dwight L. Freshley, eds. *Voice of Georgia: Speeches of Richard B. Russell, 1928–1969.* Macon, Ga.: Mercer University Press, 1997.
—Roy E. Brownell, II

S

savings-and-loan crisis

The crisis of the savings and loan institutions (S&Ls for short), the greatest financial scandal in the history of U.S. banking, first came to national attention in the mid-1980s. At that point the failure of the thrifts, as the savings-and-loan industry is also known, appeared to be an easily manageable problem. Both Reagan administration officials and representatives of the S&L industry gave public assurances that there was no crisis, all the while working behind the scenes to prevent a full-scale investigation by Congress. But this policy of denial and obfuscation did not succeed, because by the late 1980s it became obvious that the S&Ls were in deep trouble. However, confronting the crisis was postponed for political reasons until after the 1988 elections that brought to power incumbent vice president George H. W. Bush. This unwarranted delay by the White House cost taxpayers a staggering $1.4 trillion to bail out all the failed thrift institutions. If the government had stepped in and closed the ailing S&Ls in 1986 instead of delaying until after the 1988 elections, the cost might have been only $20 billion.

The S&L industry, whose main purpose had been to lend mortgage money to middle-class borrowers, had each deposit insured up to $40,000 per bank account by the Federal Savings & Loan Insurance Corporation (FSLIC). When in the mid-1970s the federal government tried to check a galloping double-digit inflation by restricting the money supply, one unintended consequence was a large increase in interest rates—that is, the cost to consumers of borrowing money. The thrifts were required by law to pay an interest rate of only 5.25 percent while commercial banks could lure depositors with money-market accounts that paid 12 percent or more. The S&L industry was confronted with a depositors' run on the thrift institutions. To help them out, the Reagan administration deregulated the thrift industry in the early 1980s. This was done under the guidance of the U.S. League for Savings Institutions, the S&L lobby in Washington, D.C., which is estimated to have given $11 million in campaign contributions to politicians from both major political parties in the 1980s. Congress soon followed suit by passing the 1982 Depository Institutions Act, legislation introduced by Democratic representative Fernand St. Germain of Rhode Island and Republican senator Jake Garn of Utah, both of whom were very close to bank and thrift lobbyists.

The act allowed the S&Ls to offer competitive interest rates, raised the federal insurance coverage on deposits from $40,000 to $100,000 (even though the average savings account was only around $6,000), and permitted the S&Ls to extend their lending into lucrative new markets such as nonresidential real estate and high-interest consumer loans. When signing it, President Ronald Reagan praised the Depository Institutions Act as "the most important legislation for financial institutions in the last fifty years." The Garn Institute of Finance (named after Senator Jake Garn), which had sponsored and lobbied for the deregulation of the thrift industry, received $2.2 millions in "donations" from grateful S&L executives.

But the lifting of government controls only stimulated a flood of "hot money" into the thrift industry, resulting in numerous fraudulent schemes and get-rich-quick investments of highly speculative natures on the part of S&L bankers, who took money from the institutions they were entrusted to protect. Deregulation eased regulatory and legislative restrictions to such an extent that S&L owners could now lend money to their closest friends and family members and even to themselves. For example, Texas S&L banker Don Dixon loaned friends and relatives more than $90 million without any guarantees that these loans were collectible. When 96 percent of his "loans" went bad, Dixon's bank collapsed. With many similarly risky "investments" going sour across the country, S&Ls went broke one after another. The government had to step in to bail them out—an extremely costly and protracted operation that took more than seven years and hundreds of billions of federal dollars to complete.

In the meantime, prosecutors found theft, fraud, embezzlement, and other criminal activities at every S&L they investigated. The American taxpayer was thus robbed twice—first when the thrifts collapsed and federal insurance money had to be paid to their depositors, and again when S&L assets were sold to investors at fire-sale prices and with huge federal subsidies. In one particularly outrageous case, the Federal Savings & Loan Insurance Corporation contributed $1.85 billion in federal subsidies to Arizona investor James M. Fail, represented by former Bush aide Robert J. Thompson, to purchase 15 failing Texas S&Ls. Fail, who had been indicted for securities fraud, put up just $1,000 of his own money in the deal, even though he had been outbid by a rival without a criminal record.

When the S&L debacle busted a federal budget that was already deeply in the red, President Bush had to renege on his famous "read my lips—no new taxes" election pledge. The Democrats, who were also up to their necks in the S&L mess, remained mostly silent, preferring to talk only about the president's son Neil Bush, the 30-year-old director of a failed Denver thrift institution named Silverado, who became the "poster boy of the S&L crisis" after Silverado had to be shut down at a cost of more than $1 billion.

The thrift fiasco seems to have been forgotten in the post–September 11 era, even though citizens are still saddled with dutifully making up for all the "missing deposits" and other financial losses brought about by the S&L high rollers. Ironically, in the few cases when S&L bankers who had stolen millions did go to jail, their sentences were typically only one-fifth that of the average bank robber.

See also "Keating Five" scandal.

Further reading:
Long, Robert Emmet, ed. *Banking Scandals: The S&Ls and BCCI.* New York: Wilson, 1993; Mayer, Martin. *The Greatest Ever Bank Robbery: The Collapse of the Savings and Loan Industry.* New York: Charles Scribner's Sons, 1990; Stephen, Mary Fricker, and Paul Muolo. *Inside Job: The Looting of America's Savings and Loans.* New York: McGraw-Hill, 1989.

—Rossen V. Vassilev

Science, House Committee on

The House Committee on Science dates to the launch of the Soviet earth-orbiting satellite *Sputnik 1,* which began the space race on October 4, 1957. The House Select Committee on Astronautics and Space Exploration was created by Speaker SAMUEL RAYBURN, a Democrat from Texas, with Majority Leader JOHN W. MCCORMACK, a Democrat from Massachusetts, as the chair and the House Minority Leader, Joseph W. Martin, Jr., a Republican from Massachusetts, as its ranking minority member. The committee gained standing status in 1959 as the Committee on Science and Astronautics. A series of name changes culminated in 1995 with the present name, the Science Committee, but began in 1975 with the House Science and Technology Committee, followed in 1987 with the Committee on Science, Space and Technology.

The importance of the committee policy matter is reflected in the growth in its size, beginning with 25 members and growing to 30 in the 1961 to 1975 period. Growth in membership continues, with the committee marking 40 members by 1977, 55 members in the 102nd Congress, and hovering slightly under 50 in the 108th Congress (2003–05). The subcommittee structure grew to as many as seven subpanels, although the current configuration includes just four subcommittees.

The present jurisdiction of the House Science Committee spans all nondefense federal scientific research and development. Agencies that fall within the authorization and oversight functions of the committee are the National Aeronautics and Space Administration (NASA), Department of Energy (DOE), Environmental Protection Agency (EPA), National Science Foundation (NSF), Federal Aviation Administration (FAA), National Oceanic and Atmospheric Administration (NOAA), National Institute of Standards and Technology (NIST), Federal Emergency Management Agency (FEMA), U.S. Fire Administration, and U.S. Geological Survey (USGS). The Science Committee's jurisdiction is divided into four subcommittee arenas: Energy; Environment, Technology, and Standards; Research; and Space.

The importance of the committee for space exploration gave way to management of government research and development programs in 1974 after jurisdiction was expanded and the name was changed to reflect the expansion beyond space exploration. Since the Committee on Science and Technology transformation, the needs of the space programs, both manned and unmanned, needed to be balanced by committee members with other national scientific research priorities. The committee was chaired by Representative George E. Miller, a Democrat from California, during the golden years of U.S. manned space programs, from President John Kennedy's call to place a man on the moon in 1961 through the successful Apollo moon landings between 1969 and 1972. The expense of manned space missions contrasted with the unmanned programs was unsupportable in the economic stress of the 1980s. Further, loss of life in the manned programs with the *Challenger* explosion in January 1986 and controversial cost overruns in NASA tarnished the luster of the manned space program. Difficulties with collaborations in building the *International Space Station* were compounded by the loss of a second shuttle orbiter when the *Columbia* disintegrated upon reentry in February 2003, further complicating the role of manned space missions in the U.S. space exploration program.

The Science Committee has been noted for its long tradition of being on the vanguard of scientific innovation and having a highly competent technical staff. This reputation allowed the committee to alert the country to the potential opportunities represented in scientific discoveries. Topics such as recombinant DNA research, supercomputer technology, and long-range renewable energy sources are at the current cutting edge of science being promoted by the committee as likely spurs to future societal and economic change. Superconductivity, intellectual property, and global warming are past innovative policy arenas that the committee has overseen. Representative Sherwood L. Boehlert, a Republican from New York, proposed three priorities for the committee when he became chair in 2001: science and math education, energy policy, and the environment. Cyberterrorism, the role of technology in homeland security, striking a balance between the needs of open research and secrecy required by security concerns, and related issues became committee priorities after September 11, 2001.

Atypical of Congress, the committee has been chaired by a number of technologically trained individuals. Three of the eight chairs had backgrounds in science before their service in Congress or on the committee. Miller, the second chair (from 1961 to 1973) was a civil engineer; Representative Robert A. Roe, a Democrat from New Jersey, another engineer, headed the committee from 1987 to 1991; and Representative George E. Brown Jr., a Democrat from California, who was trained in physics and employed as a professional civil engineer before entering Congress, chaired the committee from 1991 to 1993.

Further reading:
Hechler, Ken. *Toward the Endless Frontier: History of the Committee on Science and Technology, 1959–1979.* Washington, D.C.: Government Printing Office, 1980.

—Karen McCurdy

seating disputes/contested elections

Seating disputes in Congress have occurred when a large number of the members of one of the houses asserted that a member was not qualified to sit in that body, possibly because they strongly disapproved of the behavior or the ideology of an elected member, or when an unsuccessful candidate has attributed his or her defeat to a miscounting of votes or to fraud committed by the winning candidate or his or her supporters. Seating disputes arise more frequently as a result of contested elections than as a result of behavioral or ideological disapproval. Contesting candi-

dates seek redress from the appropriate house of Congress or in a judicial forum. Such election contests may involve a mixture of partisan politics and law. Although they may occur in either house of Congress, they have been more frequent in the House of Representatives.

The role of partisan politics in seating disputes can be seen in a late 19th-century clash between Democrats and Republicans in the House of Representatives. In December 1899 the Republicans held an eight-seat majority. There were also eight seats in dispute. The Republicans made their majority more comfortable after ruling against the Democrats on all eight disputed seats. The outraged Democrats retaliated against the Republican majority by refusing to answer when their names were called on QUORUM calls. Without a quorum business could not go forward. Speaker of the House THOMAS REED of Maine asked Congressman JOSEPH G. CANNON of Illinois, a Republican member of the House Rules Committee (and future Speaker of the House), to try to find a way to deal with the situation. On the basis of Cannon's report to him, Reed instructed the Clerk to count as present all those who answered the roll call as well as those who were present but did not answer. Speaker Reed did this even though the House had not yet adopted Cannon's report, although it did adopt it later. In time, such blatant partisanship in settling election disputes became less common.

Law plays a significant role in the resolution of seating disputes. The Constitution, the supreme law of the land, has something of relevance to say. According to Article I, Section 4: "The times, places and manner of holding elections for senators and representatives shall be prescribed in each state by the legislature thereof; but the Congress may at any time by law make or alter such regulations." Article I, Section 5, states "Each House of Congress shall be the judge of the elections, returns, and qualifications of its own members." From this it should be clear that candidates involved in contested elections may appeal to the Constitution, to federal statutes, and to state laws.

Article I, Section 5, has led each house of Congress to claim the dominant role in resolving seating disputes and contested elections of its members, although courts have also had a role. In 1969, in a case originating in the House of Representatives, the Supreme Court made it clear that Article I, Section 5, did not give unlimited power to refuse to seat a person on grounds that the House had adjudged him to lack the qualifications of a member. The person was Representative Adam Clayton Powell, Jr., a flamboyant African American from the Harlem section of New York. Among Powell's offenses was his refusal to pay a civil judgment against him in a New York court. He was also alleged to have misused public funds. After his constituents reelected him, the House refused to seat Powell, claiming the authority to do so came from Article I, Section 5. The

Supreme Court, however, in *POWELL V. MCCORMACK* (1969), held that authority under Article I, Section 5, was limited to deciding whether Powell met the requirements set forth in the Constitution concerning age, residency, and citizenship. The House of Representatives, according to the Court, lacked the authority to add anything to those requirements. The *Powell* case was a seating dispute but not a contested election case. Many seating disputes, however, do result from contested elections.

Contested elections are not unusual. Most commonly, they involve claims of election fraud and generally involve federal and state laws as well as other federal and state institutions. In an effort to create a more orderly process for resolving such contests, Congress passed the Federal Contested Elections Act of 1969. Under this legislation only the losing candidate has standing to sue. But the losing candidate is not the only person harmed by election fraud. Voters who supported the losing candidate are also harmed. Although they lack standing to sue, they may file a protest with the relevant house of Congress. The complaint is referred to a committee to investigate its merits.

The 1976 election in Louisiana to choose a representative for the First Congressional District illustrates the intersection of state and federal institutions and procedures. The leading candidates were both Democrats: New Orleans city councilman James Moreau and state representative Richard Tonry. Tonry was certified as the winner of the Democratic primary by a very close margin. He then went on to win the general election. Moreau brought suit in state court alleging fraud. Moreau was unsuccessful, and Tonry was sworn in as a member of the House of Representatives. Moreau supporters then brought their claim to the House of Representatives, and the House appointed a committee to investigate and report back to its parent body. At a new trial a state court found evidence of enough fraudulent votes that Moreau would have won but refused to take further action because the Constitution gave to each house of Congress the authority to judge the elections of its members. When the House committee received the report of its investigators, Congressman Tonry resigned. New elections were held in Louisiana. Tonry lost in the Democratic primary, and Moreau, who had changed parties, lost in the Republican primary. The winner of the special election was ROBERT L. LIVINGSTON, a Republican who held the seat until 1999.

The contested election in Louisiana's First Congressional District in 1976 was, in one major aspect, atypical. Congresspersons who have taken their oaths and are seated usually survive challenges. When losing candidates bring suit, courts are ordinarily reluctant to infringe on what they see as the constitutional authority of Congress. Moreover, challengers have a very short time frame in which to gather the evidence to support their claims. The contest in the First Congressional District of Louisiana was typical in that the challenger did not win the congressional seat.

Senate elections, too, have sometimes been contested. The one that took place in New Hampshire in 1974 was unusual in that the Senate was unable to exercise its constitutional authority successfully. The state was attempting to elect a successor to Senator Norris Cotton, a Republican who had retired after 20 years of Senate service. The candidates were Congressman Louis Wyman, a Republican who was expected to win the election, and John Durkin, a Democrat who had been the state insurance commissioner. While Wyman had greater name recognition, he also had the burden of running as a Republican in the year of the WATERGATE SCANDAL. It was a close election, and Wyman came out on top by 355 votes on the first count. A recount by the secretary of state indicated that Durkin had won by a margin of 10 votes. A recount by the Governor's Ballot Commission had Wyman the victor by two votes. It appeared that the Senate might exercise its constitutional authority to judge the election and returns to determine who had lawfully won the Senate seat. The Senate was controlled by Democrats. A Republican member threatened a FILIBUSTER. Although the Senate Rules Committee investigated the election in New Hampshire, the clash within the Senate, with each side defending its partisan interests, prevented the body from deciding the controversy. The Senate declared the seat vacant, and New Hampshire held a special election in September 1975. John Durkin won easily and became New Hampshire's second U.S. senator nearly a year after the first election.

When congressional elections have been contested and seats are in dispute, Congress has ordinarily exercised its constitutional authority. Partisan politics has not always determined the outcomes of the disputes, but it has generally been a part of the mix. Moreover, other institutions, such as federal and state courts, have had roles in the resolution of some disputes. Congress, however, has had the dominant role.

Further reading:

Barone, Michael, Grant Ujifusa, and Douglas Matthews. *The Almanac of American Politics, 1978.* New York: E. P. Dutton, 1977; Bolles, Blair. *Tyrant from Illinois: Uncle Joe Cannon's Experiment in Personal Power.* New York: Norton, 1951; *Contested Elections and Recounts,* 3 vols. Prepared by School of Public and Environmental Affairs, Indiana University. Washington, D.C.: National Clearinghouse on Election Administration, Federal Election Commission, 1978; Donsanto, Craig C., and Nancy S. Stewart. *Federal Prosecution of Election Offenses.* 6th ed. Washington, D.C.: U.S. Department of Justice, 1995.

—Patricia A. Behlar

Secretary of the Senate

The Secretary of the Senate is an elected officer of the U.S. SENATE responsible for the supervision of Senate employees who expedite the daily operations of the Senate. The first secretary was chosen in 1789. The secretary has the responsibility of keeping the minutes and records of the Senate as well as for buying supplies required by the senators. The secretary supervises preparation of the daily agenda and all histories and journals related to the Senate. The secretary must also be an expert in parliamentary procedure as he or she serves as a consultant to the Senate and its Rules Committee on matters of parliamentary interpretation.

As the powers of the Senate increased, so did the duties of the secretary. Other duties include the disbursing of payroll checks, the training and education of Senate PAGES, and maintaining the chamber's public records. This position is considered a position of great trust and responsibility. Thus, the Secretary of the Senate has administrative, financial, and legislative roles.

Some famous secretaries include Samuel Otis, the first Secretary of the Senate, who had previously served as a member of the Continental Congress; William Cox and Charles Bennett, former House members; and Charles Cutts and Walter Lowrie, former senators. The first woman to be elected to the post was JoAnn Coe in 1985.

Further reading:
"Secretary of the Senate." Available online. URL: http://www.senate.gov/reference/office/secretary_of_senate.htm. Accessed February 7, 2003.

—Nancy S. Lind

Seminole Tribe of Florida v. Florida 517 US 44
(1966)

On March 27, 1996, the Supreme Court issued a 5-4 decision in the case *Seminole Tribe of Florida v. Florida*. The case involved a conflict between the Seminole tribe and the state of Florida over the latter's alleged failure to negotiate a tribal gaming compact in good faith as required by the Indian Gaming Regulatory Act (IGRA). Chief Justice William Rehnquist, writing for the majority, held that the act, in part, violated the Eleventh Amendment to the Constitution. Though Rehnquist recognized Congress's authority to regulate Indian affairs through the Indian Commerce Clause found in Article I of the Constitution, he rejected the part of the IGRA that allowed tribes to sue states that failed to negotiate with them in the federal courts. Rehnquist found that providing tribes with this power presented a violation of the states' sovereign immunity from lawsuits in federal courts, a protection provided to them by the Eleventh Amendment.

Dissenting opinions were issued by Justices John Paul Stevens and David Souter. Stevens argued that precedents assuming that Congress had the power to create enforcement mechanisms like that employed in the IGRA dated back more than 100 years. Stevens noted that the Eleventh Amendment only prevents a state from being sued by citizens of another state or by foreign citizens and does not apply to suits brought by American Indians (or others) who are citizens of that state. His opinion expressed concern that the majority decision would hinder citizens' abilities to hold states accountable for violations of federal rights. In other words, while the Constitution expressly empowers Congress to pass laws regulating commerce, the majority's decision might make some of those laws unenforceable. In the specific case at hand, the decision meant that American Indian tribes could find themselves unable to force a state to negotiate gaming compacts with them, even though federal law now required the state to do so.

Souter's dissent echoed many of the same concerns and went on to observe that the Court's opinion produced a new and, to him, unacceptable interpretation of the Eleventh Amendment in a case in which that amendment, because the plaintiffs were citizens of the state they were suing, should not even apply. Moreover, since states do not possess any sovereignty over Indian commerce, they had no basis by which to assert sovereign immunity.

The *Seminole* case has two important federalism implications for Congress. One involves the regulation of American Indian tribes, and the other involves the application of the Eleventh Amendment. Regarding the former issue, while the 1996 *Seminole* decision remains the law of the land, the story of Indian gaming and state and federal regulation of it starts much earlier. Though gaming traditions among American Indian nations date back centuries, the gaming issue began to attract government attention in the 1980s. In the 1987 case *California v. Cabazon Band of Mission Indians* the Court held that state laws could not limit bingo operations on American Indian reservations because tribal sovereignty is subordinate to state law only when Congress explicitly gives states jurisdiction over an issue. This case symbolized both the potential for state-tribal conflict over gaming and the need for federal action. As a result in 1988, after several years of negotiation, Congress passed the IGRA. This law created a formal process for states and tribes to enter into agreements (called "compacts") regarding tribal development of casino style gaming. Though the law faced opposition from both states and tribes, many viewed its passage as a successful compromise. The law allowed tribes to pursue and develop casinos but subjected these ventures to a greater degree of state regulation and, as a result, taxation, than Indian nations, due to their sovereign status, typically face. One immediate result of the Seminole decision was that tribes lacked legal recourse when states failed to negotiate in good faith. Fortunately, lawsuits had been intended only as a last resort under the

IGRA. The law also contains provisions for a mediation process when negotiations break down. This process has helped a number of tribes and states resolve their differences, though some states have taken advantage of the lack of judicial remedies to stall or otherwise resist tribal gaming initiatives.

The second set of congressional concerns raised by *Seminole* regards enforcement of the Eleventh Amendment. The Court's finding not only prevented Congress from limiting states' sovereign immunity in Indian Commerce cases, it also overturned a precedent that had affirmed this congressional power in another arena. In the 1989 case *Pennsylvania v. Union Gas Co.* a plurality of the Court legitimated congressional limitations on sovereign immunity when created as an enforcement mechanism for legislation developed under the Interstate Commerce Clause. In overturning this precedent the *Seminole* decision made clear that state governments are protected from being sued without their consent. While this change was a victory for states, it has limited enforcement options for federal laws. In other words, if Congress passes a law that requires certain actions of the states, it cannot provide the federal courts as a forum for citizens to seek state compliance.

In sum, the *Seminole* case alters the relationship between Congress and the states and between the states and American Indian tribes by protecting the states' sovereign immunity from federal lawsuits. The immediate effect was felt by tribes seeking gaming compacts, but the future implications could extend much further.

Further reading:
California v. Cabazon Band of Mission Indians, 480 U.S. 202 1987; Indian Gaming Regulatory Act. Public Law 497, 100th Cong., 2d sess., 17 October 1988; Mason, W. Dale. *Indian Gaming: Tribal Sovereignty and American Politics.* Norman: University of Oklahoma Press, 2000; *Pennsylvania v. Union Gas Co.,* 491 U.S. 1 (1989); *Seminole Tribe of Florida v. Florida,* 517 U.S. 44 (1996).

—Charles C. Turner

Senate

The Senate is one of the two chambers of the U.S. Congress, the legislative branch of the federal government created in 1787 by Article I, Section I, of the U.S. Constitution. The other chamber of Congress is the HOUSE OF REPRESENTATIVES, upon which the Senate, with its broader and more heterogeneous electorate, was designed to provide a restraining influence.

The first meeting of the Senate—with only 20 senators—took place in 1789, when the first Congress convened in Federal Hall in New York City. The reason the Senate has been sometimes referred to, rather erroneously, as the upper chamber and the House of Representatives as the lower chamber of Congress is that when Congress first met from March 7, 1789, through August 12, 1790, the Senate was located on the floor above the House of Representatives. Otherwise, the two chambers are considered constitutionally equal, reflecting the basic principle of separation of powers, including legislative powers, that the framers of the Constitution adopted for the entire federal government.

The Senate consists of two senators from each state, currently 100, who may serve an unlimited number of elective terms. In order to provide the originally contemplated distance between the Senate and the fickle passions of public opinion, all senatorial terms are for six years, expiring in January following the election. Every two years approximately one-third of the total Senate membership is elected. Senators were elected by state legislatures until 1913, when the Seventeenth Amendment to the Constitution required that they be chosen by a direct popular vote. Also established by the Constitution, a senator must be at least 30 years of age, a U.S. citizen for at least nine years, and a resident of the state in which the senator is elected.

Under the Constitution the vice president of the United States is the presiding officer, or President of the Senate. Because the vice president normally is present only at ceremonial occasions or to cast a tie-breaking vote, in his absence the most senior senator of the majority party acts as the President Pro Tempore of the Senate. Each is addressed as "Mr. President" when presiding over Senate proceedings. Given his seniority, the President Pro Tempore is also often absent, usually due to other duties as a chair of some Senate committee. The duty of presiding over the Senate normally is then assigned to junior senators from the majority party who rotate during the Senate sessions, each spending about an hour in the chair.

The agenda of the Senate is usually set by the Senate MAJORITY LEADER and the Senate Majority Whip. The other floor leaders are the Senate MINORITY LEADER and the Senate Minority Whip. Most of the work in the Senate is transacted by STANDING COMMITTEES in which senators from both the majority and the minority parties are represented but are chaired by members of the majority party.

There are 16 standing committees in the Senate, AGRICULTURE, NUTRITION, and FORESTRY (21 members); APPROPRIATIONS (29 members); ARMED SERVICES (25 members); BANKING, HOUSING, AND URBAN AFFAIRS (21 members); BUDGET (23 members); COMMERCE, SCIENCE, AND TRANSPORTATION (23 members); ENERGY AND NATURAL RESOURCES (23 members); ENVIRONMENT AND PUBLIC WORKS (19 members); FINANCE (21 members); FOREIGN RELATIONS (19 members); GOVERNMENTAL AFFAIRS (17 members); HEALTH, EDUCATION, LABOR, AND PENSIONS (21 members); JUDICIARY (19 members);

United States Senate

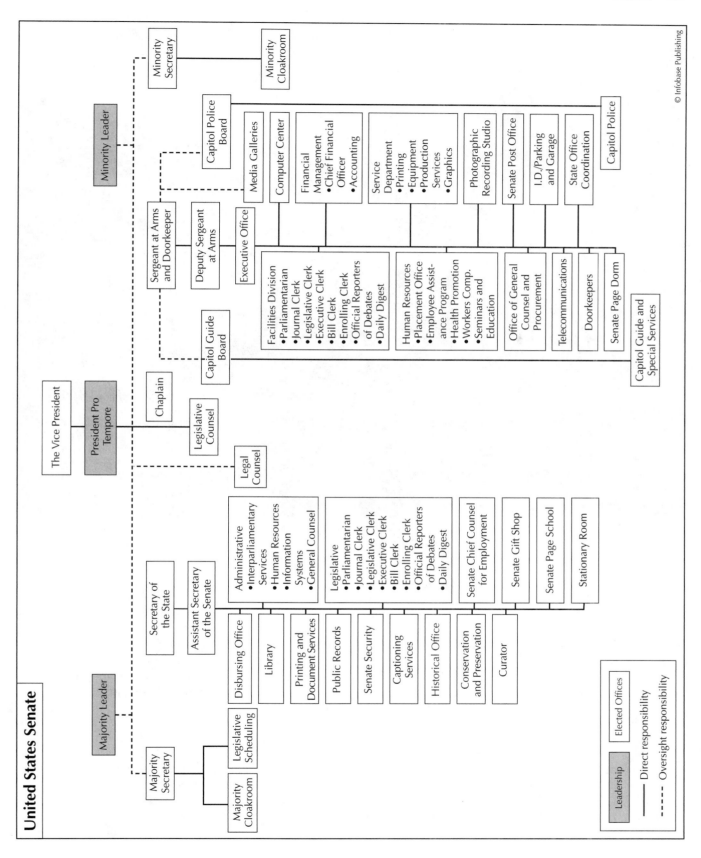

Senate Chamber in the U.S. Capitol, 1952 *(Library of Congress)*

RULES AND ADMINISTRATION (19 members); SMALL BUSINESS AND ENTREPRENEURSHIP (19 members); and VETERANS' AFFAIRS (15 members). In addition there are four special or select committees of the Senate: AGING (21 members); Ethics (6 members); INDIAN AFFAIRS (15 members); and INTELLIGENCE (17 members). There are also four JOINT COMMITTEES of the Senate and the House of Representatives: ECONOMIC (10 senators); the LIBRARY (5 senators); PRINTING (5 senators); and Taxation (5 senators).

Each chamber has an equal voice in Congress, although the Constitution directs that revenue bills must originate in the House. Both chambers must pass identical legislation for it to be signed by the president into law. Whenever an item of legislation is approved in varying forms by the Senate and the House, the bill must have its differences reconciled by a joint (or conference) committee that includes members of both chambers. A presidential veto of congressional legislation can be overridden by a two-thirds vote in each of the two chambers.

The Constitution has also given the Senate the exclusive powers of ADVICE AND CONSENT. The Senate must ratify all treaties negotiated by the president with foreign governments or international organizations by a two-thirds vote. It also confirms important presidential appointees, such as cabinet officers, ambassadors, and federal judges.

Further reading:
Hickok, Eugene W., Jr., *The Senate: Advice and Consent and the Judicial Process.* Washington, D.C.: National Legal Center for the Public Interest, 1992; Lee, Francis E., and Bruce I. Oppenheimer, eds. *Sizing Up the Senate: The Unequal Consequences of Equal Representation.* Chicago: University of Chicago Press, 1999; Oppenheimer, Bruce I.,

ed. *U.S. Senate Exceptionalism.* Columbus: Ohio State University Press, 2002.

—Rossen V. Vassilev

Senate Manual

The *Senate Manual* is a handbook of rules governing the operations of the U.S. SENATE. Officially titled the *Senate Manual Containing the Standing Rules, Orders, Laws, and Resolutions Affecting the Business of the United States Senate,* this publication is the rulebook for the Senate. It is prepared during the second session of each Congress by the Senate COMMITTEE ON RULES AND ADMINISTRATION and contains the standing rules, orders, laws, and resolutions affecting the Senate as well as copies of historic U.S. documents, such as JEFFERSON'S MANUAL, the Declaration of Independence, the Articles of Confederation, the Constitution of the United States, and selected statistical information on the Senate and other government entities. It is issued each Congress as Senate Document 1. The book is printed biennially at the beginning of a new Congress.

Since the Senate is a continuing body, it does not readopt its rules at the beginning of a Congress. Proposed changes to existing rules must be adopted subject to provisions of the existing rules.

The first list of rules governing the Senate was a manual of parliamentary procedure prepared by Vice President Thomas Jefferson in 1797. Interestingly, the House made it a formal part of its rules in 1837, but the Senate has not granted Jefferson's Manual the same status.

Besides the standing rules of the Senate, the *Senate Manual* includes a list of the Nonstatutory Standing Orders and Resolutions Affecting the Business of the Senate, the Rules for Regulation of the Senate Wing of the Capitol and Senate Office Buildings, Rules for Impeachment Trials, Cleaves' Manual of Conferences and Conference Reports, and a list of General and Permanent Laws Relating to the Senate. The book then presents a set of historic documents including the Declaration of Independence, the Articles of Confederation, the Ordinance of 1787, and the U.S. Constitution. The end of the book has historic lists of Senate officers, tables of electoral votes received by presidential and vice presidential candidates, a list of Supreme Court justices, a list of cabinet officers, and information relating to the states and territories of the United States.

The Senate has made seven general revisions of its rules since 1789. The last general revision of the rules occurred when Senate Resolution 274 was adopted on November 14, 1979. The resolution was introduced by Majority Leader ROBERT BYRD, a Democrat from West Virginia, and Minority Leader HOWARD BAKER, a Republican from Tennessee. Changes to the rules after 1979 are indicated by footnotes in each succeeding edition of the *Senate Manual.* Curiously, there is no record of a *Senate Manual* for the 105th Congress.

Further reading:
United States Senate, Committee on Rules and Administration. *Senate Manual Containing the Standing Rules, Orders, Laws, and Resolutions Affecting the Business of the United States Senate.* Senate Document 107-1. Washington, D.C.: Government Printing Office, 2002.

—John David Rausch, Jr.

senatorial courtesy

A senatorial courtesy is a custom that permits individual senators to block a presidential appointment. Senators from the home state of a presidential nominee who are also of the president's party can block a nomination to an office within the senator's state. Senatorial courtesy also can be used to block a nominee of a president from another party if the senator is of the majority party in the SENATE. Senators from the minority party have been able to block nominations on occasion. Most presidents have honored this unwritten rule that derives from the Senate's constitutional role in the appointment process.

The use of senatorial courtesy dates back to the First Congress. In 1789 President George Washington nominated Benjamin Fishbourn to be the naval officer of the port of Savannah, Georgia. Fishbourn had military experience and had served in the Georgia state government. He was qualified for the position. He did not have the support of Georgia's two senators, however. The senators wanted the job to go to another candidate. The other members of the Senate voted against Fishbourn's confirmation as a courtesy to the Georgia senators.

Senatorial courtesy is based on the idea that courtesy means one senator will honor the objection of another senator to a nomination in the first senator's home state. A senator may exercise senatorial courtesy in rejecting appointees only for positions within the state represented by the objecting senator. These positions generally are U.S. marshals, U.S. attorneys, and federal district court judges. Objections may be presented to a STANDING COMMITTEE or on the Senate floor.

The process of invoking senatorial courtesy has changed slightly since the early days of Congress. Historically, a senator has taken the floor of the Senate and indicated that the nomination was "personally obnoxious." In 1934 Louisiana senator Huey Long expanded the statement by presenting the grounds of his objection. The Senate was debating the nomination of Daniel D. Moore to be collector of internal revenue in Louisiana. Senator Long rose and began, "I first state to the Senate that this nomination is offensive to me personally." He continued by outlining his objections. Despite Long's objection to the nominee, the Senate confirmed Moore. Shortly thereafter senators reconsidered the vote and ordered the nomination recommitted to committee. The committee reported the nomination again, but Moore was not confirmed.

Senators use the "blue slip" as one method of indicating senatorial courtesy. The SENATE JUDICIARY COMMITTEE informs the home-state senators about a nomination to the U.S. courts of appeal or district courts or for a U.S. marshal or U.S. attorney by letter, usually typed on light blue paper. The senators are asked to indicate whether they approve or disapprove of the nominee. The senators mark the appropriate box on the sheet and return the paper to the Judiciary Committee. Blue slips are used only by the Senate Judiciary Committee and have been used since at least 1917.

The importance of the recommendations of the home-state senators as noted on the blue slip is determined largely by the actions of the Judiciary Committee chair. During his two decades as Judiciary Committee chair (1956–78), Senator James O. Eastland, a Democrat from Mississippi, had a policy that if he did not receive two blue slips endorsing a nominee, the nomination would not be reported out of committee. Other chairs have been more flexible, indicating that the blue slip would be considered but that a negative recommendation would not necessarily kill a nomination. In order to delay action on a nomination, some senators have refused to return a blue slip sent to them by the committee. The blue slip process developed because senators wanted a way to express their displeasure with a presidential nomination when a president did not involve them enough in the advice phase of the nomination.

With the growth of the merit system in federal appointments and the decline of PATRONAGE, some observers expected that senatorial courtesy would become less important in the appointments process. However, it is as important in the 21st century as it was in the 18th century. In a 2003 floor speech, Senator Orrin Hatch, a Republican from Utah, argued that senatorial courtesy continued to be followed. Hatch was chair of the Senate Judiciary Committee during the last six years of President Bill Clinton's administration. He explained that a number of the judges nominated by Clinton were not confirmed because they lacked the support of their senators, whom Clinton did not consult before making the nominations.

Further reading:
Binder, Sarah A., and Forrest Maltzman. "The Limits of Senatorial Courtesy." *Legislative Studies Quarterly* 24, (2004): 5–22; Denning, Brannon P. "'The Judicial Confirmation Process' and the Blue Slip." *Judicature*. (March–April 2002): 218–226; Gerhardt, Michael J. *The Federal Appointments Process: A Constitutional and Historical Analysis.* Durham,

N.C.: Duke University Press, 2000; York, Byron. "The Brawl over Judges." *National Review*, 28 May 2001.
—John David Rausch, Jr.

seniority system

The seniority system is not a rule of Congress but a custom and tradition that has been, and continues to be, the subject of modification and adjustment. The seniority system is unique to the U.S. Congress and is not used by other national legislative bodies or the 50 state legislatures. Seniority is also a relatively new custom, and it was not until the revolt against House Speaker JOSEPH CANNON in 1911 that it came to be used by that chamber.

There are actually two important forms of seniority in Congress; congressional seniority and committee seniority. Congressional seniority is used to determine office assignments and seating at social occasions. Congressional seniority is based in the SENATE on the length of uninterrupted service, either starting from the opening day of the Congress to which a member was elected or commencing with the date on which a governor certifies the appointment of a replacement senator. The HOUSE OF REPRESENTATIVES gives credit for nonconsecutive service. For example, if one served two terms and then left the House for whatever reason, if one later were elected to another House term one would receive credit for the earlier service. The Senate gives credit only from the date of one's most recent election and does not credit earlier service.

Committee seniority is what most people think of when they think of the seniority system, and it is also the system most subject to criticism. Committee seniority is used to determine the ranking minority and majority members of a committee and is still the most significant aspect of selecting committee chairpersons. To become a chair of a congressional committee, one must first be a member of the majority party. No member of the minority party is going to chair a committee of Congress. Committee chairs are determined primarily by being a member of the majority party with the longest consecutive years of service on a particular committee. This means that members who change committee assignments or lose an election and later return to Congress will have to begin their committee seniority all over again. What about members who change parties? Recently Senator JAMES JEFFORDS of Vermont announce he was leaving the Republican Party to become an independent but that he would caucus with the Democrats. In order to try to encourage such defections, both parties are likely to give credit for committee seniority. Although an independent, Jeffords was appointed to chair the Senate Environment and Public Works Committee, a position he held until the Republicans regained control of the Senate in the 2002 elections.

Criticisms of the seniority system are that it favors members of Congress from one-party states, favors members from safe districts, and provides no guarantee that the most qualified person will be chair. Supporters contend that most states now have competitive two-party systems and that most members of Congress, whether Republican or Democratic, come from safe districts, so there is no real advantage gained. Although supporters agree that the seniority system does not guarantee the selection of the most qualified chair, they argue that no system can guarantee that will happen. Supporters argue that the seniority system promotes legislative harmony by providing a neutral, nonpolitical method for selecting chairs. In other words, it keeps politics and interest groups out of the process of selecting committee chairs. By placing an emphasis on longevity, supporters also contend that it ensures chairs who will have expertise on the legislative process as well as on the subject matter. Finally, supporters contend that there is no better alternative to the seniority system.

What are the alternatives to the seniority system? One suggestion is to impose a rotation in the chair with each new term of Congress. Although this would assist in preventing the concentration of power in one person, it would also ensure that at some point the least competent person on the committee would be the chair. A second suggestion is to have the chair elected by the committee members or by the whole House or Senate. While this would result in chairs selected by majority vote, it would create numerous other problems. Coalitions might form across parties resulting in the selection of a chair from the minority party. It would certainly politicize the chair selection process. Members might promise all sorts of favors in exchange for someone's vote, and interest groups would clearly have a vested interest in which individual was elected chair. Finally, the party leadership could select chairs, as it is done in most state legislatures. This would provide for the selection of chairs loyal to their party. Critics contend that it may result only in the selection of chairs loyal to the leadership. They also point out that the House abandoned this method in 1911 because of the abuses by Speaker Joseph Cannon. As Stewart Udall, a former Democratic congressmen from Arizona said, "It is not that Congress loves seniority more, but the alternatives less."

Both parties have moved away from rigid adherence to the seniority system. House Democrats in 1975 bypassed five senior members with 179 years of combined seniority in favor of less senior Democrats to chair certain committees. The more senior Democrats who were ousted were accused of being too conservative and often siding with the Republicans. Some 20 years later newly elected Republican Speaker NEWT GINGRICH bypassed several senior Republicans to chair committees in favor of individuals that he believed would not only provide better leadership but would also be more loyal to the Speaker.

Further reading:
Goodwin, George. "The Seniority System in Congress." *American Political Science Review* (1959): 412–436; Polsby, Nelson. "The Growth of the Seniority System in the U.S. House of Representatives." *American Political Science Review* (1969): 787–807; Wolfinger, Raymond, and Joan Hollinger. "Safe Seats, Seniority, and Power in Congress." *American Political Science Review* 80 (1965): 337–349.
—Darryl Paulson

sequestration

Sequestration was added to the budget process by the 1985 Balanced Budget and Emergency Deficit Control Act (better known as the GRAMM-RUDMAN-HOLLINGS ACT [GRH I]). It was invoked if the regular process of budgeting failed to meet deficit targets as determined in GRH I and then the 1987 Emergency Deficit Control Reaffirmation Act (GRH II). Sequestration under GRH II required the Office of Management and Budget (OMB) to issue equal across-the-board cuts to defense and nondefense spending to meet the GRH target if the president and Congress failed to do so through any mix of spending cuts and tax increases. Sequestration was the part of GRH that supporters believed would force the president and Congress to meet the annual deficit targets. Social Security, Medicaid, and parts of other entitlements that make up around 70 percent of the budget, however, were exempt from sequestration cuts.

GRH required the president to submit a budget that met the GRH targets and required the congressional budget resolution (passed by April 15 as required by the 1974 act) to decide through what mix of discretionary spending and entitlements cuts and tax increases it wanted to reach the deficit target for that year. Congress could decide to rely entirely on discretionary spending cuts to meet the GRH target, or Congress could decide to also rely on tax increases or entitlement cuts or both. Therefore, the early budget resolution determined the overall spending level for discretionary spending. If Congress wanted to maintain spending levels for discretionary programs and also meet the GRH target, it had to either increase taxes or cut entitlements or do both. Tax increases and entitlements cuts are usually enacted through a RECONCILIATION bill passed by the tax writing committees and the authorizing committees. If the reconciliation bill failed to become law before October 15, then sequestration would go into effect.

The sequestration process under GRH I started with a snapshot of the deficit by the Office of Management and Budget (OMB) and the CONGRESSIONAL BUDGET OFFICE (CBO) on August 15. The snapshot included estimates for revenues and expenditures for the fiscal year ending on September 30. If the estimate was within $10 billion of the

GRH target, then no further actions were required from the GRH sequestration process. However, if the estimated deficit was not within the $10 billion cushion of the GRH deficit target, then OMB and CBO were to recommend sequestration to get the deficit within the $10 billion cushion of the deficit target. The recommendation came in the form of a joint report issued on August 20 to the comptroller general of the GAO, which was a fiscal watchdog for Congress. The comptroller general was supposed to then turn around and issue a report to the president on August 25 that estimated the deficit and the required spending reductions to get the deficit under the GRH target. The president then issued the sequestration on October 1 in accordance to the GAO's comptroller general report. On October 5, CBO and OMB issued another report that estimated any reductions in the deficit from actions taken (if any) by Congress between August 25 and October 5. The GAO then issued a revised report to the president on October 10, and on October 15 the final presidential order for sequestration was to take effect. A lawsuit brought by Representative Mike Synar (D-OK) and other members of Congress in 1986 charged that GRH was unconstitutional. The Supreme Court found that it was unconstitutional to give Congress (through it's comptroller general in the GAO) the authority to execute a constitutional responsibility of the executive.

GRH II altered the sequestration process by removing the CBO from the sequestration process. Under GRH II sequestration involved an OMB (and not a CBO) budget deficit estimate taken on August 15 for the upcoming fiscal year. If sequestration was required under GRH II, it was the OMB who would issue equal across-the-board cuts to defense and nondefense spending to meet the GRH target.

Members of Congress originally described sequestration as the "sword of Damocles," "Draconian," and a "planned train wreck." Proponents of the law believed that sequestration would be so distasteful to members of Congress that it would force members to act on their own to lower the deficit. This meant that either Congress would pass a budget resolution that reduced the deficit by only reducing spending or Congress would pass a budget resolution that also included orders for a reconciliation bill. Only once during GRH's existence was a full-year sequestration carried out, and that was in the first year of the law (FY 1986). The FY 1988 sequestration was rescinded, and the FY 1990 sequester was in effect for only five months.

Further reading:
Schick, Allen. *The Federal Budget: Politics, Policy, Process.* Washington, D.C.: Brookings Institution Press, 1995; Shuman, Howard E. *Politics and the Budget: The Struggle between the President and the Congress.* 3d ed. Upper Saddle River, N.J.: Prentice Hall, 1992.

—Charles Tien

Sergeant at Arms

The Sergeants at Arms in both the HOUSE OF REPRESENTATIVES and the SENATE are the police officers of their chambers. The Sergeants at Arms are elected at the beginning of each Congress by the membership of the chamber.

Either the Sergeant at Arms or his or her assistant attends all sessions of his or her respective chamber. They serve as the chief law enforcement officers of the chambers and as such both enforce rules of decorum and order as well as ensure the safety of all members of Congress, congressional staff, visiting foreign dignitaries, and tourists. To these ends, the Sergeant at Arms for each chamber along with the ARCHITECT OF THE CAPITOL make up the Capitol Police Board. As such, they work together supervising the Capitol police force, which provides safety and security to the Capitol buildings. The same three-member body, made up of the Senate Sergeant at Arms, the House Sergeant at Arms, and the Architect of the Capitol, also oversees the Capitol Guide Service, which provides visitors with tours of the Capitol.

Another responsibility of the Sergeants at Arms is to perform many ceremonial duties. They lead the processions for their respective chambers at presidential inaugurations. The Senate Sergeant at Arms escorts the Senate into the House chamber for both joint sessions of Congress as well as formal addresses to Congress. The Sergeants at Arms also escorts foreign dignitaries during their visits to the Capitol and also supervise all congressional funeral arrangements when a member of Congress dies in office. Other responsibilities of the Sergeants at Arms include escorting the president, other heads of state, and official guests of either chamber who are attending official functions at the Capitol.

In order to assist the Sergeants at Arms in keeping peace and order within the chambers, the Senate Sergeant at Arms has custody of the Senate gavel, while the House Sergeant at Arms is authorized to use the HOUSE MACE. In addition, the Sergeants at Arms can also be ordered to compel absent members to attend their respective chambers' sessions in order to achieve QUORUM by escorting them to the chamber. However, both of these practices, using the mace and gavel and making members attend sessions have rarely been used since the turn of the 20th century.

Further reading:
Davidson, Roger H., and Walter J. Oleszek. *Congress and Its Members.* 8th ed. Washington, D.C.: Congressional Quarterly Press, 2002; Tong, Lorraine H. "CRS Report for Congress: House Sergeant at Arms: Fact Sheet on Legislative and Administrative Duties." Available online.

URL: http://www.house.gov/rules/98-835.pdf. Accessed January 16, 2006.

—Lisa A. Solowiej

Seventeenth Amendment

Contrary to popular belief, popular elections were not popular with the framers of the U.S. Constitution. The founding fathers, after all, created a government that consisted of a president who was to be appointed by an Electoral College, a judiciary appointed by the president and confirmed by the Senate, and a Senate appointed by their respective state legislatures. Members of the House of Representatives were the only federal officials popularly elected by citizens. However, all of that changed 126 years later with the passage of the Seventeenth Amendment in 1913. The Seventeenth Amendment states: "The Senate of the United States shall be composed of two Senators from each state, elected by the people thereof, for six years; and each Senator shall have one vote. The electors in each state shall have the qualifications requisite for electors of the most numerous branch of the state legislatures." So why were senators initially appointed by state legislatures?

The founding fathers were circumspect about federal power. Accordingly, they structured the government in a manner that made it difficult for the federal government to encroach on either state or individual rights. They created a federalist system of government that divided power between the states and national government. They then established a separation of powers in the federal government by creating a legislative body to make the law, an executive body to enforce the law, and a judicial body to interpret the law. The framers then created a system of CHECKS AND BALANCES to prevent any of these branches of government from dominating another. For example, the president has a limited veto power over Congress and nominates members of the judiciary. Congress can override a presidential veto with a two-thirds vote and has the authority to impeach both the president and members of the federal judiciary. The Senate also confirms presidential appointments. The judiciary has the power of judicial review, giving it the authority to declare legislative and presidential acts unconstitutional.

The framers also created a bicameral legislature consisting of the House of Representatives and the Senate. Each was to serve a very specific function. The House of Representatives was viewed as the "people's body" and was responsible for incorporating the views of the masses into government. The Connecticut Compromise established that the number of representatives per state would be based upon population, whereas each state would be equally represented with two senators. The purpose of the House was to establish the social contract between the government and the people. This linkage was ensured by first allowing citizens to select their representatives and strengthened by requiring frequent elections every two years.

Senators were not viewed as representatives of the people by the founding fathers. Instead, senators were viewed as guardians against national power and the protectors of states' rights. Allowing state legislatures the authority to appoint senators was viewed as a compromise to the Anti-Federalists, who were fearful that the national government would come to tyrannize the states. As James Madison pointed out in Federalist 39, it was far less likely that the national government would come to dominate over a state if state legislatures were directly involved in appointing federal officials.

The framers also wanted senators to remain impervious to the whims of the electorate. Political theorists from Plato to Madison warned against the excesses of popular government. The Senate was therefore viewed as a stable counterweight to the passions emanating from the House. This upper chamber was designed to sagaciously grapple with salient state, national, and international issues free of electoral considerations. That is why the Senate has the exclusive power to ratify treaties and confirm presidential appointments.

The Seventeenth Amendment is important because it transformed the Senate selection process from an appointive to an elective one. Ratification of the Seventeenth Amendment was the result of a decades-long movement to democratize the Senate selection process. So why did this change occur? The selection process was amended for three fundamentally distinct reasons. First, the process itself was substantially flawed. Most states required senatorial candidates to win approval in both houses of the legislature. The first major problem stemmed from the fact that the chambers often disagreed and would sometimes remain deadlocked for substantial periods. Delaware, for instance, was without any Senate representation from 1901 to 1903 because of this form of legislative infighting. Second, some state legislatures were vulnerable to corrupting influences. Senators were increasingly viewed as political pawns of state party bosses and corporate tycoons. Rather than serving as the protectors of states' rights, senators were increasingly viewed as the protectors of party bosses and corporate elites. Third, the American political culture changed dramatically during the latter half of the 19th century. The "Jacksonian Democracy" era of the first half of the 19th century fueled democratic fires in the United States. The movement sparked the democratization of the Electoral College, judicial elections in many western states, and a fundamental belief that government should be accountable to the people. This movement, in conjunction with advances in mass communications and a more informed electorate, sounded the drumbeat for change.

Amending the Constitution is a two-stage process, which includes a proposal and a ratification stage. The most common method for proposing an amendment calls for a two-thirds vote in the House and Senate. The most common method for ratifying an amendment requires approval from three-fourths of state legislatures. The House approved a direct election of senators proposal in 1893, 1894, 1898, 1900, and 1902 before sending it to the Senate. These proposals never made it out of committee and thus never came to a full Senate vote during these years. A grassroots movement emerged, and the issue quickly found its way as planks in many third-party platforms. The Prohibition Party, the Populist Party, the Anti-Monopolist Party, and the Union Labor Party all began to weigh in on the issue. The Senate ultimately brought the issue to the floor and rejected it on five occasions.

Frustrated by the Senate's unwillingness to pass the proposal, the states creatively amended state law to give voters greater input in the process. Some states allowed citizens to vote in primaries, thus reducing the field for their respective state legislatures. The movement was also bolstered when the Democratic Party included it as part of its platform in 1909. The Senate ultimately passed the proposed amendment on June 12, 1911, by a vote of 64-24, and the House followed suit 11 months later by a vote of 238-39. The amendment was made official when it was ratified by the 36th of the then 48 states on May 31, 1913.

Further reading:
Hoebeke, C. H. *The Road to Democracy: Original Intent and the Seventeenth Amendment.* New Brunswick, N.J.: Transaction Publishers, 1995; Rossum, Ralph. *Federalism, the Supreme Court, and the Seventeenth Amendment.* Lanham, Md.: Lexington Books, 2001.

—Joseph N. Patten

shadow senators

Shadow senators was a term used to describe the status of individuals who had been elected to the U.S. SENATE from areas desiring admission to the union but that had not yet been granted statehood. They also were known as "Tennessee Plan" senators. Lacking official status, they were elected to lobby and monitor Congress as part of an area's efforts to achieve statehood. Since the beginning of the republic there have been 15 shadow senators from seven areas.

In 1795 the settlers of the territory south of the Ohio River held a constitutional convention that wrote a state constitution and authorized elections to be held for state offices in March 1796. The newly elected Tennessee legislature then elected territorial governor William Blount and William Cocke to the U.S. Senate. On May 23, 1796, the Senate approved a resolution stating that

Mr. Blount and Mr. Cocke, who claim to be Senators of the United States, be received as spectators, and that chairs be provided for that purpose until the final decision of the Senate shall be given on the bill proposing to admit the Southwestern Territory into the Union.

Blount and Cocke were given the privileges of the floor during the debate on the bill admitting Tennessee to the union. On June 1, 1796, Tennessee became a state, and both Blount and Cocke were sworn in as members of the Senate. Blount was expelled from the Senate in July 1797 for having instigated the Indians to assist the British in conquering the Spanish territories of Florida and Louisiana. Cocke served three separate terms in the Senate.

In November 1835 the Michigan Territory elected Lucius Lyon and John Norvell as senators. Senator THOMAS HART BENTON of Missouri presented the credentials of the two to the Senate and made a motion to assign them seats "until the decision of the question of their admission as Senators." Benton's motion was tabled in the face of opposition from southern senators who were against admitting another nonslave state to the union. Benton then made a motion to grant Lyon and Norvell the same status of spectators that had been granted to the Tennessee "senators" in 1796. A motion granting Novell this status passed the Senate on December 16, 1835. The rationale for amending Benton's motion was that since Lyon was already the Michigan territorial delegate to the House of Representatives, he already had the right to a privileged spectator's seat in the Senate. Following Michigan's admission to the union in January 1837, Lyon and Norvell were both seated as senators. Lyon served in the Senate until March 3, 1839, and Norvell until March 3, 1841.

On March 13, 1850, Senator Stephen Arnold Douglas of Illinois presented the Republic of California's petition for admission to the union to the Senate. He also presented the credentials of William M. Gwin and John C. Frémont as senators-elect from the prospective state. California's admission as a free state was opposed by a number of senators, and the territory was admitted to the union as part of the Compromise of 1850. On September 10, 1850, Frémont and Gwin were permitted to take their seats. Frémont (who would be the Republican Party's first presidential candidate in 1856) served in the Senate until March 3, 1851. Gwin, who had represented Mississippi in the House of Representatives from 1841 to 1843, served in the Senate until March 3, 1855. When the California legislature failed to elect his successor, he returned to the Senate on January 13, 1857, and remained in the Senate until March 3, 1861.

In December 1857 the Minnesota territorial legislature elected James Shields to serve in the Senate. Shields's credentials were presented to the Senate on February 25,

1858. The senator also submitted a letter arguing that he should be seated immediately since the territory had satisfied the terms of the Enabling Act for a state of Minnesota, which had been enacted by Congress in February 1857. On March 4, 1858, the Senate Judiciary Committee reported that Minnesota had, by satisfying the requirements of the Enabling Act, been admitted to the union. Shields (who had represented Illinois in the Senate from 1849 to 1855 and would later briefly represent Missouri in 1879) took his seat on May 12, 1858. He would serve until March 3, 1859.

In July 1858 the Oregon territorial legislature elected territorial delegates Joseph Lane and Delazon Smith to the Senate. They did not present their credentials to the Senate until Oregon joined the union on February 14, 1859, and they were given the oath of office the following day. Smith was an unsuccessful candidate for reelection in 1858. Lane did not seek reelection in 1860, as he was the Democratic Party candidate for vice president.

On October 6, 1956, more than two years prior to its admission as the 49th state, Ernest Gruening and William A. Egan were elected Alaska's shadow senators. Gruening, who was known as the "father of Alaska statehood," and Egan were admitted to the Senate's diplomatic gallery on January 14, 1957. They were not given floor privileges. In November 1958 Gruening was reelected as shadow senator and Alaska's territorial delegate to the House. Edward Lewis Bartlett was elected to succeed Egan, who had decided not to run for reelection. Alaska was admitted to the union on January 3, 1959, and Gruening and Bartlett took their seats as U.S. senators four days later. Gruening was reelected in 1962 but was defeated for the Democratic nomination for the Senate in 1968.

In 1990 the voters of Washington, D.C., elected civil rights leader Jesse Jackson, Sr., and Florence Howard Pendleton as the district's first shadow senators. In 1993 the House of Representatives rejected, by a vote of 277-153, the New Columbia Admission Act (H.R. 51). Jesse Jackson did not run for a second term in 1996 and was succeeded by Paul Strauss.

Further reading:
Gruening, Ernest. *The Battle for Alaska Statehood.* Seattle, Wa.: University of Alaska Press, 1967; Kefauver, Estes. *The Congressional Record.* Washington, D.C.: Government Printing Office, 1957.

—Jeffrey Kraus

Shaw v. Reno, 509 U.S. 630 (1993)

This landmark reapportionment case marked the beginning of the end for so-called RACIAL GERRYMANDERING for generations of disenfranchisement of African-American voters. For background, in *Gomillion v. Lightfoot* (1960) the U.S. Supreme Court held that deliberate use of race in redistrict-ing for the purpose of diluting minority voting power was impermissible under the Fifteenth Amendment. Subsequently, in BAKER V. CARR (1962) the Court recognized reapportionment as justiciable under the Equal Protection Clause of the Fourteenth Amendment, ushering in the so-called reapportionment revolution. In 1965 Congress enacted the VOTING RIGHTS ACT, Section 5 of which empowers the Department of Justice (DOJ) to review state reapportionment decisions. Since that time majority-minority districts have been employed, sometimes at the insistence of the DOJ, to remedy past efforts to dilute the voting power of African Americans and Hispanics in congressional elections.

In *Shaw v. Reno* the Rehnquist Court confronted for the first time a constitutional challenge to racial gerrymandering favoring minority voters, that is, the creation of majority-minority districts. In a divisive, controversial 5-4 decision, the Court held that racial gerrymandering presumptively violates the Equal Protection Clause and is subject to strict scrutiny. Thus, in order for a majority-minority district to pass constitutional muster, it must further a compelling state interest. Writing for the majority, Justice Sandra Day O'Connor stated that disregarding traditional districting principles such as compactness, contiguity, and respect for political subdivisions such that the only plausible explanation for a district's boundaries is to place distinct racial groups in a common district bears an uncomfortable resemblance to political apartheid. She also rejected (without explicitly overruling) the Burger Court's holding in *United Jewish Organization of Williamsburgh v. Carey* (1977) that compliance with Section 5 of the Voting Rights Act, particularly meeting the demands of the DOJ, satisfies strict scrutiny.

In dissent, Justices John Paul Stevens and Byron White derided the assertion that the white majority had been denied equal protection. Justice Stevens stated that the Equal Protection Clause is violated when the majority uses gerrymanders to enhance its power at the expense of minority groups, but not "when the majority acts to facilitate representation of minorities." Noting that the Court had upheld gerrymandering to benefit rural voters, union members, and political parties, he described the Court's barring gerrymandering to benefit the very group whose history in the United States gave birth to the Equal Protection Clause as perverse. Justice David Souter also dissented, arguing that the mere placement of voters in different districts denies no one a right or benefit provided to others, and therefore should not be treated the same as affirmative action in areas such as government contracts.

Subsequently, in *Miller v. Johnson* (1995) the Court expanded the *Shaw v. Reno* precedent to invoke strict scrutiny of reapportionment efforts even when the state legislature employs traditional districting principles if it appears that race was given more weight than those principles. Under *Miller* a majority-minority district need not be a bizarre shape to be subject to exacting judicial scrutiny. Accordingly, as a result of *Shaw* and *Miller*, the Court today treats racial gerrymandering as no different from other affirmative action policies, that is, presumptively unconstitutional and acceptable only to combat explicit racial discrimination. Racial gerrymandering is thus severely limited as a remedy for discrimination in congressional district apportionment.

As for the fate of North Carolina's 12th District, the Supreme Court again rejected the original boundaries in *Shaw v. Hunt* (1996). The district was redrawn by the state legislature in 1997 and 1998 and was reviewed by the Supreme Court in *Hunt v. Cromartie* (1999) and a final time in *Easley v. Cromartie* (2001). (This case is commonly referred to as *Hunt v. Cromartie*. However, the Court officially renamed the case following Easley's inauguration as governor in 2001.) In *Easley* the Court finally accepted District 12 based on the district court's factual determination that partisanship rather than race was the primary factor in determining the district's boundaries. That race closely correlated to partisanship did not, according to the majority, trigger the Equal Protection Clause, notwithstanding the history of the district.

Further reading:
Gomillion v. Lightfoot, 364 U.S. 339 (1960); *Baker v. Carr*, 369 U.S. 691 (1962); *Miller v. Johnson*, 512 U.S. 622 (1995); *Shaw v. Hunt*, 517 U.S. 899 (1996); *Hunt v. Cromartie*, 526 U.S. 541 (1999); *Easley v. Cromartie*, 532 U.S. 254 (2001).

—Daniel E. Smith

Sherman, John (1823–1900) *Representative, Senator*
John Sherman was the eighth of 11 children. He was the younger brother of William Tecumseh Sherman, a leading general in the Union army during the American Civil War. His father, Charles Robert Sherman, a lawyer, and mother, Mary Hoyt Sherman, had moved from Norwalk, Connecticut, to Ohio in 1811. The family settled in Lancaster, Ohio, and Charles Sherman practiced law in Ohio and Michigan. Charles Sherman became a member of the Ohio state supreme court (1821–29) but died of typhoid fever when the younger Sherman was six years of age.

Sherman attended private schools for eight years, two at the Homer Academy in Lancaster (from which he was expelled), four years in Mount Vernon, Ohio, and then two more years at the Homer Academy. At the age of 14 he left school to work as a junior rodman on the canals being constructed to make the Muskingum River navigable from Zanesville to Marietta, Ohio. He was later placed in charge of the construction of a lock and dam on the canal. His work on the canals ended in 1839 following the election of a Democratic governor who replaced the chief superintendent of the project and his subordinates (including Sherman) with Democratic Party loyalists. Moving to Mansfield, Ohio, in 1840, he studied law under his oldest brother and uncle and was admitted to the Ohio bar in 1844. He practiced law for 10 years before entering politics. He married Margaret Sarah Cecelia Stewart, whose father was a judge in Mansfield, in 1848. He moved to Cleveland in 1853.

Sherman entered politics as a member of the Whig Party, serving as a delegate to the 1848 and 1852 national conventions. An opponent of slavery expansion, he joined the new Republican Party in 1854 and helped organize the party in Ohio, serving as chair of the party's first state convention in 1855.

Sherman was elected to the U.S. HOUSE OF REPRESENTATIVES in 1854. He served in the House from March 4, 1855, until March 21, 1861, when he resigned to take a seat in the SENATE. In 1859 Sherman sought to become SPEAKER OF THE HOUSE of Representatives during the 36th Congress (1859–61). The House lacked a majority (there were 109 Republicans, 101 Democrats, and 27 members of a third party, the American Party). After eight weeks of failing to elect a Speaker, Sherman withdrew from the contest, and William Pennington, who had not served in the House before, was elected. Sherman became chair of the WAYS AND MEANS COMMITTEE. Under his leadership the committee experimented with delegating work on appropriations bills to individual committee members. The practice led to the committee's use of SUBCOMMITTEES during the Civil War. While he was chair the House passed the Morrill Tariff Bill, which was signed into law by President James Buchanan on March 3, 1861, two days before he was succeeded as president by Abraham Lincoln. The Morrill Tariff Bill was a protectionist measure favored by the Republican Party. The bill raised the average tariff rate from 15 percent to 37.5 percent and expanded the number of items that were subject to the tariff.

He was elected to the U.S. Senate in 1861 to fill the vacancy caused by the resignation of Salmon P. Chase, who became secretary of the Treasury in President Lincoln's cabinet. Sherman served in the Senate from March 21, 1861, until he resigned on March 8, 1877. In the Senate he was chair of the Committee on Agriculture (1863–67) and chair of the Committee on Finance (1863–65, 1867–77). In the Senate he supported the Legal Tender Act of 1862, which authorized the issuance of U.S. notes as the first national currency, and the National Banking Act of 1863, which created the first national banking system, but opposed Treasury secretary Hugh McCulloch's plan to retire the $450 million in "greenbacks" (paper money) in circulation and instead proposed resuming specie payment. A proponent of hard money, he was a leading force behind the Resumption Act of 1875, which required that the U.S. Treasury be prepared to resume the redemption of legal tender notes (greenbacks) in specie (gold) by January 1, 1879, while also reducing the number of greenbacks in circulation.

Sherman was nominated by President Rutherford B. Hayes to be the 32nd secretary of the Treasury. He served from March 10, 1877, until March 3, 1881. As secretary he oversaw the implementation of the Resumption Act. He also recommended in 1880 that major changes be made in public service in order to retain valuable employees. His recommendations ultimately led to the passage of the Civil Service Reform Act by Congress in 1883. Known as the Pendleton Act, the law classified certain government positions, removed them from patronage appointments, and established a Civil Service Commission to administer a personnel system based on merit rather than political connections.

In 1880 Sherman sought the Republican Party's presidential nomination. He hoped to emerge as a compromise candidate at a convention that was divided into two factions: the Stalwarts and the Half-Breeds. The Stalwarts, led by Senator Roscoe Conkling of New York, supported former president Ulysses S. Grant, who was being promoted for a third term after leaving office three years earlier. The Half-Breeds, who advocated political reform, supported Senator James G. Blaine of Maine. Instead, on the 34th ballot Sherman's campaign manager, U.S. Representative (and Senator-elect) James Garfield was nominated. On two additional occasions Sherman unsuccessfully sought the Republican presidential nomination (1884, and 1888).

Ironically, Sherman was again elected to the Senate in 1881 to replace Garfield, who had been elected president, Sherman was reelected in 1886 and 1892, serving until he resigned to become secretary of State in 1897 (he was replaced in the Senate by Marcus A. Hanna). During his second sojourn in the Senate, Sherman was the Republican Conference chair (1884–85, 1891–97), President Pro Tempore of the Senate (1885–87), and chair of the Committee on the Library (1881–87) and the Committee on Foreign Relations (1885–93, 1895–97). He supported the Civil Service Reform Act, arguing that "the evil of the civil service occurs in the filling of subordinate offices." He was the prime sponsor of the Sherman Anti-Trust Act in 1890. The legislation was intended to reduce the influence of monopolies, which were becoming powerful in the American economy during the later years of the 19th century. The act prohibited any business combination that restrained trade or commerce. Violations could be punished by a $5,000 fine and/or one year's imprisonment. He also authored the Sherman Silver Purchase Act. The act, which was part of a compromise whereby congressional Democrats agreed to the protectionist McKinley Tariff Bill in exchange for Republican support on silver, obligated the federal government to purchase more than 4 million ounces of silver each month at market rates and issue notes that were redeemable in gold or silver. By 1893 the law had driven down the price of silver (forcing mine owners to cut wages to miners and triggering labor violence) while nearly depleting the government's gold reserves. During the Panic of 1893 President Grover Cleveland summoned Congress into a special session to repeal the act.

In 1897 Sherman was appointed secretary of State by President William McKinley. As secretary of State, Sherman completed negotiations (begun during the last days of President Cleveland's administration) with the Republic of Hawaii for annexation of the island republic to the United States. After the treaty was rejected by the Senate, the annexation of Hawaii was accomplished by a joint resolution of Congress in July 1898. Sherman resigned as secretary of State in April 1898 due to his failing health and to his opposition to President McKinley's decision to declare war on Spain. In his 1895 *Recollections* Sherman wrote that "Our family of states is already large enough to create embarrassment in the Senate, and a republic should not hold dependent provinces or possessions. Every new acquisition will create embarrassments." After leaving office he publicly opposed the annexation of the Philippines.

On June 5, 1900, his wife of more than 50 years passed away. He died in Washington, D.C., on October 22, 1900, and was buried in Mansfield Cemetery in Mansfield, Ohio.

Further reading:
Burton, Theodore E. *John Sherman.* New York: AMS Press, 1906; Kerr, Winfield Scott. *John Sherman: His Life and Public Services.* Boston: Sherman, French, 1972; Randall, James G. "John Sherman and Reconstruction." *Mississippi Valley Historical Review* 19 (December 1932): 1908; Sherman, John. *Recollections of Forty Years in the House, Senate, and Cabinet, 1895.* New York: Greenwood Press, 1968; Thorndike, Rachel Sherman, ed. *The Sherman Letters: Correspondence between General and Senator Sherman from 1837 to 1891.* New York: AMS Press, 1971.

—Jeffrey Kraus

Shreveport Rate Case

Decided by the Supreme Court in 1914 as *Houston, East & West Texas Railway Co. v. United States* (234 U.S. 342), this case illustrates the Court's refusal to recognize two separate and distinct categories of commerce, interstate and intrastate, with the latter foreclosed to congressional regulation by the Tenth Amendment of the Constitution.

Railroads were extremely important to the commerce of the nation, but they were also important to the commerce of individual states. The early 20th century saw state governments enacting regulations that discriminated against interstate commerce while working to the benefit of their own commerce. Between 1902 and 1907 nine states set intrastate rates that railroads were not permitted to exceed.

The Shreveport Rate Case grew out of such discriminatory rate setting by the Texas Railroad Commission. Freight rates from Dallas to points in eastern Texas were lower, even though the distance was greater, than rates between points in eastern Texas and Shreveport, Louisiana, which was only a short distance across the state line. The higher rate governing shipments between Shreveport and eastern Texas was set by a federal agency, the Interstate Commerce Commission (ICC). Therefore, the Louisiana Railroad Commission filed a complaint with that agency. The ICC found merit in the complaint and ordered the railroads to charge no higher rates between eastern Texas and Shreveport than for the same distance within Texas. Alternatively, the railroads could raise their rates in eastern Texas, despite the Texas law, so that they were not lower than the interstate rate.

The railroads raised several interrelated arguments against the ICC order. They took the position that because the ICC had already upheld the interstate rates as reasonable, it could not lower them, since that would make them unreasonable. The intrastate rates were said to be beyond the reach of Congress. Therefore, the ICC could not order them raised. The argument continued that even if Congress did have power to order an adjustment in intrastate rates, it had not done so, which meant that the ICC had exceeded its authority.

The arguments were not accepted by the Supreme Court. Justice Charles Evans Hughes, writing for the majority, noted that the Constitution gave Congress the power to regulate commerce among the several states so that it could protect interstate commerce and prevent its destruction by the rivalries of state and local governments. Such rivalries had existed during the era of the Articles of Confederation to the point that they had jeopardized national unity.

Justice Hughes stated that the congressional power to regulate commerce meant that Congress was authorized to provide for government of interstate commerce. Congress could protect and promote interstate commerce, ensure that it was carried out with fairness, and ensure that it was not crippled, retarded, or destroyed. Hughes recognized that a railroad's interstate and intrastate transactions could be so closely related that the regulation of one greatly affected the other. Whenever that was the case, it was Congress and not the state that would determine the binding rule. To decide otherwise would allow the state, rather than the nation, to exercise supreme power over a national field of activity. That the Court was unwilling to do. Congress had the authority to protect interstate commerce, and it could exercise that power through a subordinate body. The Interstate Com-

merce Commission was the subordinate body through which Congress had acted.

The Supreme Court had interpreted the constitutional authority of Congress, but it had not laid the controversy to rest. State railroad commissions in some states did not interpret the Shreveport decision as striking down their power to set intrastate rates. The result was that railroads found themselves caught between state and federal regulators. The ICC reviewed its rule in the *Shreveport* case at the request of shippers who contended that the ICC had jurisdiction over rates between Texas and Shreveport but not between points within Texas. The shippers, however, did not receive satisfaction; the ICC reaffirmed its *Shreveport* decision. In its annual report for 1916, the ICC stated that it had already followed the Supreme Court's *Shreveport* decision in more than 50 cases to come before the commission.

To the extent that any doubts remained concerning whether the Interstate Commerce Commission was an instrument by which Congress exercised its commerce power, or whether it was a bureaucratic agency pursuing its own agenda, Congress spoke in 1920. It legitimized the ICC's actions when it enacted legislation to amend the Interstate Commerce Commission Act. According to the amendment, whenever the ICC found discrimination against interstate commerce, after holding a full hearing it could set the rate that it determined to be necessary to remove the discrimination, regardless of any contrary state laws. By taking this action Congress demonstrated its acceptance of its commerce power as set forth by the Supreme Court in the Shreveport Rate Case.

Further reading:
Dixon, Frank Haigh. *Railroads and Government: Their Relations in the United States, 1910–1921.* New York: Charles Scribner's Sons, 1922; Kolko, Gabriel. *Railroads and Regulations: 1887–1916.* Princeton, N.J.: Princeton University Press, 1965.

—Patricia A. Behlar

Small Business and Entrepreneurship, Senate Committee on

The Senate Committee on Small Business and Entrepreneurship considers issues that affect small businesses and conducts oversight of the Small Business Administration. Since 1940 there have been several committees in the Senate that have considered issues relating to American small businesses. The Senate established the Special Committee to Study and Survey Problems of Small Business Enterprises (also known as the Special Committee to Study Problems of American Small Business) on October 8, 1940. The committee was allowed to continue after the LEGISLA-

TIVE REORGANIZATION ACT OF 1946 did not provide for a standing committee on small business in the Senate. The Committee on Banking and Currency established a Subcommittee on Small Business in January 1947. The select committee and the subcommittee existed simultaneously until January 31, 1949, when the select committee's authorization was not renewed. Small business issues continued to be considered by the subcommittee of Banking and Currency.

Senators Kenneth Wherry of Nebraska and James Murray of Montana, the former chairs of the defunct select committee, worked to establish a full standing committee to deal with small business issues. According to Wherry, the subcommittee of the Committee on Banking and Currency could not consider all the needs of small business without taking jurisdiction from other committees. The Senate agreed and responded by limiting the subcommittee's jurisdiction. Wherry's call for a standing committee on small business threatened to reduce the jurisdiction of a number of established standing committees, such as Commerce, Banking and Currency, and Finance. In order to avoid jurisdictional conflicts but still provide a regular Senate forum where American small businesspersons could be assured a hearing, on February 20, 1950, the Senate created the Select Committee on Small Business.

The mission of the Select Committee on Small Business was to survey and study all problems of American small business. As a select committee it could not consider proposed legislation or have any legislative jurisdiction. In 1955 the select committee became the first permanent select committee, a source of controversy in the Senate. As a permanent select committee, its members did not need to be reappointed by the Senate president at the beginning of each Congress.

Senator John Sparkman of Alabama was appointed the first chair of the Select Committee on Small Business and served in that position until 1967, except for the 83rd Congress (1953–54) when the Republicans were the majority party. One of the most important activities of the select committee was casework. The National Archives reports that in the last half of 1950, the committee worked to aid 2,100 businesspersons who had been referred by individual senators and advised 6,700 more who asked for help by mail.

In 1976 the Senate gave the Select Committee on Small Business legislative authority over the Small Business Administration. It also maintained its mission to study small business–related problems. Despite the new legislative authority it continued to be called the Select Committee on Small Business.

The Senate reorganized in 1977, but differences of opinion hindered the creation of a standing committee on small business. Many senators believed that a small business committee was not necessary and proposed that the Small Business Select Committee be eliminated. During floor debate another group of senators proposed that the committee be given permanent and independent standing committee status. The result was that the Select Committee on Small Business was continued without change.

In March 1981 the Senate again considered the status of the select committee. The select committee was terminated on March 25, 1981, when it became the standing Committee on Small Business. The committee's existence was threatened again in 1993, when former senators Adlai Stevenson of Illinois and Bill Brock of Tennessee proposed to the JOINT COMMITTEE ON THE ORGANIZATION OF CONGRESS that the jurisdiction of the Small Business Committee be given to the Banking Committee. This proposal was not acted upon.

On June 29, 2001, after the Democrats became the majority party in the 107th Congress, Massachusetts senator John Kerry became the chair of the Committee on Small Business. One of his first acts as chair was to change the name of the committee to the Committee on Small Business and Entrepreneurship. The name change was to reflect more fully the spectrum of small businesses and allow the committee to focus some of its efforts on the entrepreneurial spirit that fuels the start up of fast-growing small businesses. When the Republican became the majority in the 108th Congress (2003–04) they kept the new name.

The Small Business and Entrepreneurship Committee was one of 16 standing committees in the 108th Congress. With 19 members (10 Republicans and 9 Democrats), it was a moderate-sized committee. The committee had no subcommittees. The committee's jurisdiction during the 108th Congress included oversight of the Small Business Administration. Measures reported by other committees that directly related to the Small Business Administration were to be referred to the Small Business Committee at the request of the chair prior to the measures being considered by the Senate. The committee also studied and investigated all problems of American small business enterprises.

Further reading:
Foerstel, Karen. "Sharp Cuts in Committees Ahead?" *Roll Call*, 22 April 1993, p. 1; United States Senate, Committee on Small Business & Entrepreneurship. *Summary of Legislative and Oversight Activities during the 107th Congress.* Senate Report 108-1. Washington, D.C.: Government Printing Office, 2003.

—John David Rausch, Jr.

Small Business Committee, House

The Small Business Committee is a standing committee of the HOUSE OF REPRESENTATIVES that considers issues that affect small businesses. Throughout the history of the House, a variety of committees have considered small business issues. In 1941 the House created the Select Committee on Small Business, which remained in existence until 1974. Because it was a select committee it could study small business issues, but it had no legislative authority. The legislative authority remained with the Banking and Currency Committee. The Banking and Currency Committee established a subcommittee on small business during each Congress.

In 1974 the House adopted a reorganization plan and restructured the jurisdiction of a number of committees. One of the changes was to create a standing Committee on Small Business to replace the Select Committee on Small Business. The new committee received jurisdiction of small business issues from the Banking Committee.

Observers have noted that the Small Business Committee has been closely associated with small business constituencies. The Select Committee on Small Business was created in response to the emergence of small business interest groups such as the National Small Business Union. The Small Business Committee regularly took the lead in protecting the vast small business interests in the United States. In 1985 the committee was successful in protecting the Small Business Administration (SBA) when President Ronald Reagan attempted to eliminate the agency. After the terrorist attacks on September 11, 2001, the committee struggled to find ways to help small business owners affected by the attacks.

A position on the committee has been attractive to members of the House because of its close ties to an important constituency. Membership on the committee also provides members the ability to perform direct services for their constituents, many of whom are small business owners. Despite the apparent political clout the committee should have, it has had to guard against threats of dissolution. In 1993 the Joint Committee on Congress examined a proposal to fold the Small Business Committee into the House Banking Committee. The argument was that House members served on too many committees and did not have time to adequately consider legislation. The House did not act on the joint committee's proposal. When the Republican Party became the majority in Congress after the 1994 elections, the proposal to abolish the House Small Business Committee was revisited. Republicans decided to save the committee in part because it would have a woman as chair. Kansas representative Jan Meyers was the first female head of a standing committee since the 1970s. She advocated increased committee oversight of the Small Business Administration and a reduced regulatory burden on small businesses.

The House Small Business Committee was one of 19 standing committees in the 108th Congress (2003–04). With 36 members (19 Republicans and 17 Democrats), it was a moderate-sized committee. The committee had four subcommittees: the Subcommittee on Workforce, Empowerment, and Government Programs; the Subcommittee on Regulatory Reform and Oversight; the Subcommittee on Tax, Finance, and Exports; and the Subcommittee on Rural Enterprises, Agriculture, and Technology. The committee's jurisdiction during the 108th Congress was assistance to and protection of small business in the United States, including financial aid, regulatory flexibility, and paperwork reduction and the participation of small-business enterprises in federal procurement and government contracts.

During the 108th Congress, Rule X, Clause 2(d)(1), of the Rules of the House required each standing committee to adopt an oversight plan. The Small Business Committee's plan included oversight of the Small Business Administration and other financial and management technical assistance programs. The committee planned to work with the new Office of Veterans Business Development and the National Veterans Business Development Corporation to develop ways to enhance small business services to veterans. In an effort to improve the environment for small businesses to succeed, the committee planned to examine changes in federal procurement processes as well as examine the ways that the federal government competes with small business in providing goods and services. Finally, the committee was prepared to continue its strict oversight of the federal government's regulatory activities.

Further reading:
Foerstel, Karen. "Sharp Cuts in Committees Ahead?" *Roll Call,* 22 April 1993; Jacoby, Mary, and Gabriel Kahn. "Future of 22 House Panels." *Roll Call,* 14 November 1994; United States House of Representatives, Committee on Small Business. *Summary of Activities.* Report 107-806. Washington, D.C.: Government Printing Office, 2003.

—John David Rausch, Jr.

Social Security Act

Perhaps the most notable federal program of the 20th century, the Social Security Act was established with a variety of subjects. It was signed by President Franklin D. Roosevelt on August 14, 1935. The nation was in the grips of the Great Depression, and Roosevelt intended the legislation to contribute to economic recovery and social reform. Almost 20 percent of the workforce was unemployed. Therefore, unemployment compensation was an important part of the act. The legislation also included such things as aid to dependent children, maternal and child health care provisions, and aid to the blind. Since poverty among the elderly was a national problem, the legislation created a program under which workers would receive retirement payments at age 65 if they worked in covered employment for the required time. This program was paid

A poster for Social Security, 1934   *(Library of Congress)*

the president have not ignored problems associated with Social Security because the older Americans who benefit from it have been politically active and organized.

Social Security is a pay-as-you-go system. That is, the payroll taxes of current workers and their employers are used to pay for the benefits that current retirees receive. It is due for a jolt in the second decade of the 21st century, when the "baby boom" generation, born from 1946 to 1965, begins to retire. There will be a significant decrease in the number of workers relative to retirees, barely more than two workers to each retiree, after having approximately 40 workers per retiree in the early years of the program.

The last time Congress made changes in the Social Security program was in 1983. At that time the program faced a crisis because its trust fund was nearly depleted. By 2004 Congress and the president were well aware that the future included another Social Security crisis unless they were to head it off. Should Congress and the president wait until 2015 or even later, as the trust fund runs low or runs out, solving the problem will become more expensive. Taxes will rise, and benefit cuts would be deeper. It will take a bipartisan effort to avert this.

Further reading:

Altmeyer, Arthur J. *The Formative Years of Social Security.* Madison: University of Wisconsin Press, 1966; Arnold, R. Douglas. "The Politics of Reforming Social Security." *Political Science Quarterly* 113 (1998): 213–214; Light, Paul. *Artful Work: The Politics of Social Security Reform.* New York: Random House, 1985.

—Patricia A. Behlar

South Dakota v. Dole 483 U.S. 203 (1987)

In *South Dakota v. Dole* the U.S. Supreme Court examined the breadth of Congress's taxing and spending powers. In 1984 Congress passed legislation that would reduce a state's allocation of federal highway funds if it did not raise its minimum drinking age to 21. This legislation was instigated by a growing public awareness of young people being involved in alcohol-related accidents and pressure from the administration of President Ronald Reagan. There was additional evidence that when bordering states had different drinking ages, young people crossed state lines to drink and then drove home, increasing the potential for accidents. A higher uniform national drinking age seemed to be the solution. However, setting drinking ages is arguably a power reserved to the states under the Twenty-first Amendment. Therefore, a federal law that directly set a uniform national drinking age would most likely be vulnerable to a constitutional attack. Congress had prior experience with indirectly controlling state policy through the use of highway funds. In the 1970s highway funds were linked

for by compulsory contributions of 1 percent withheld from employees' paychecks and matched by employers.

Over the years the Social Security Act has been amended many times. In 1965 Medicare was created and became a Social Security program. As a result of legislation passed in 1983, compulsory contributions to Old Age and Survivors Insurance rose to 6.2 percent from employees, matched by employers, with retirement age gradually moved back to age 67.

Although the Social Security Act includes numerous programs, in ordinary discourse *Social Security* has come to refer to Old Age and Survivors Insurance—the retirement payments. Social Security has a trust fund, as does Medicare and the Disability Program. Since it was created in 1935, Social Security has felt the impact of demographic changes in the United States. The aging of the American population has placed financial strains on the program. Congress and to states lowering their maximum speed limits to 55 m.p.h. Linking speed limits to federal highway funds never made it to the Supreme Court.

The minimum drinking age legislation made its way to the Supreme Court because South Dakota law allowed the purchase of beer with a 3.2 percent alcohol content at the age of 19. The state sued the then secretary of Transportation, Elizabeth Dole, claiming the law was unconstitutional because Congress had exceeded its spending powers and violated the Twenty-first Amendment. Chief Justice William Rehnquist, writing for a 7-2 majority, laid out four requirements for upholding the constitutionality of conditional congressional grants to the states. First, the spending must be in pursuit of the general welfare as required by Article I, Section 8. Rehnquist stated that the courts should generally defer to Congress on this requirement. Nonetheless, reducing highway accidents and fatalities would contribute to the general welfare. Second, Congress must set unambiguous conditions on the states' receipt of the funds. This requirement ensures that the states make informed choices with an understanding of the consequences. Again, in this case the second requirement was met. The choice was rather simple: Raise the drinking age and lose no highway funds, or do not raise the drinking age and forfeit a share of the state's highway funds. Third, there must be some relationship between the conditions set on the federal grant and the federal interest in the purpose of the spending. Rehnquist noted that one of the main purposes of expending highway funds was safer interstate travel. The conditions placed on the funds could reasonably be calculated to improve highway safety. The fourth requirement was that there must not be any independent constitutional bar to Congress's conditional grant. South Dakota hinged its argument on this fourth requirement. The state claimed that the Twenty-first Amendment prohibits Congress from regulating the drinking age directly. Therefore, it cannot use its spending power to regulate indirectly. Rehnquist stated that the independent constitutional bar limitation on the spending power only prohibits Congress from inducing the states to act unconstitutionally. For example, the states could not be induced to discriminate invidiously or to inflict cruel and unusual punishment. Additionally, there could be a constitutional concern if the inducement were so coercive that it could be considered compulsory. However, in this instance South Dakota would only lose 5 percent of its federal highway dollars by not raising its drinking age. Rehnquist called this a relatively mild encouragement. Consequently, the Supreme Court found the federal minimum drinking age legislation to be a valid exercise of the spending power.

Justices William Brennan and Sandra Day O'Connor dissented. Brennan felt that the Twenty-first Amendment clearly gave the power to regulate the minimum drinking age to the states. Therefore, Congress cannot encroach on this power through the use of a conditional federal grant. Justice O'Connor focused more on Rehnquist's third requirement. She did not see a sufficient relationship between spending for highway construction and establishing a drinking age of 21. The regulation is both over- and underinclusive. It is overinclusive because it stops young people from drinking even if they are not going to drive. It is underinclusive because only a small percentage of highway fatalities involve alcohol and persons under the age of 21. She agreed that Congress is permitted to impose safety considerations on highway spending, but the benefits of a uniform drinking age to highway safety are too tenuous. Unlike Brennan's dissent, O'Connor's defense of the states' right to regulate in this area was not surprising.

South Dakota v. Dole is an important case because it supports an expansive reading of Congress's taxing and spending powers. Congress is able to regulate indirectly through its taxing and spending powers what it perhaps could not regulate directly. In this case Congress was able to encourage the states to implement a federal policy by placing restrictions on federal highway dollars.

See also COURTS AND CONGRESS.

Further reading:
Ducat, Craig, R. *Constitutional Interpretation: Powers of Government.* 6th ed. Minneapolis/St. Paul: West Publishing, 1996; O'Brien, David, M. *Constitutional Law and Politics: Struggles for Power and Governmental Accountability.* 5th ed. New York: Norton, 2003; *South Dakota v. Dole*, 483 U.S. 203.

—Barry N. Sweet

southern bloc

From the earliest days of the republic, southern legislators acted as a cohesive bloc to safeguard the interests of southern states. At the 1787 constitutional convention, southern delegates were successful in adding provisions protecting the institution of slavery, counting slaves as three-fifths of a white person in allocating legislative seats and ensuring that treaties that might adversely affect southern economic and trade interests would be subject to a two-thirds ratification vote in the SENATE. In return for southern legislative acquiescence to Alexander Hamilton's industrial and economic policies in the 1790s, James Madison and Thomas Jefferson secured the placement of the new national capital in the South. Although the North's surging population growth over the course of the early 19th century brought it increasing numerical dominance in Congress, some of the nation's most prominent and skilled southern legislators—Henry Clay, John C. Calhoun, Robert Hayne, James K. Polk, Jefferson Davis, and John J. Crittendon—worked tirelessly to protect southern agricultural and slavery interests through such legislative measures and controversies as the Missouri Compromise, the Nullification Crisis, the annexation of Texas, the Compromise of 1850, and the Kansas-Nebraska Act.

Following the Civil War southern legislators actively resisted congressional Reconstruction policies and ultimately achieved their objectives when congressional Democrats conceded the disputed presidential election of 1876 to the Republican candidate, Rutherford B. Hayes, in return for the withdrawal of federal troops from the South in what became known as the Compromise of 1877. In the decades that followed, southern Democrats were successful in politically disfranchising African Americans in the South, establishing and maintaining a rigid system of racial segregation in public accommodations and public education, and resisting periodic antilynching campaigns and other federal attempts to intervene in southern affairs. The southern bloc of states most commonly has been identified as the 11 states that seceded from the Union during the Civil War, plus Oklahoma, Kentucky, and West Virginia.

The Great Depression and Franklin Roosevelt's NEW DEAL presented new challenges to the southern bloc, the members of which, due to longevity and congressional seniority, controlled many key congressional committees. In his first and second terms, Roosevelt worked diligently to avoid alienating southern bloc legislators by offering only tepid support for federal antilynching legislation. However, conservative southern legislators, fearful that a more powerful and intrusive federal government might eventually intervene in southern affairs and threaten segregation, resisted federal efforts to provide relief to African Americans in the South and by 1937 had allied with northern Republicans to resist Roosevelt's policies. The president turned against the southern bloc in a July 4, 1938, speech in which he decried Southern poverty as "the Nation's number one economic problem," and he actively supported liberal challengers against conservative southern incumbents who had opposed his policies in the 1938 congressional midterm elections. Roosevelt's strategy ultimately backfired, however, when most of the southern incumbents he had opposed were reelected, effectively bringing the New Deal to an end.

The emergence of the modern Civil Rights movement in the years following World War II presented the southern bloc with its greatest challenge yet and ultimately led to its undoing as a major political force. Once again, southern bloc legislators had allied with conservative Republicans to block President Harry Truman's administration's civil rights policies and efforts to extend the New Deal. Southern Democrats opposed to Truman's candidacy and platform marched out of their party's convention and nominated South Carolina governor STROM THURMOND as the presidential candidate of the newly formed States' Rights

Democratic Party, popularly known as the Dixiecrats. Although Truman was narrowly reelected, Thurmond and the Dixiecrats won the popular vote in four Deep South states.

When the Supreme Court handed down its landmark *Brown v. Board of Education* decision in 1954, ordering an end to racial segregation in education, leaders of the southern bloc joined white southerners in outrage. As the Civil Rights movement picked up steam in 1955 following the Montgomery bus boycott and the murder of Emmett Till in Mississippi, 101 Southern legislators, including J. W. Fulbright, RICHARD RUSSELL, Russell Long, Thurmond, Lister Hill, WILBUR MILLS, and Hale Boggs in the HOUSE OF REPRESENTATIVES and SENATE signed the Southern Manifesto, attacking the *Brown* decision as "a clear abuse of judicial power." As white southerners called for the impeachment of the Supreme Court, organized White Citizens Councils, and resisted desegregation at Little Rock's Central High School and at the University of Alabama, the southern bloc actively opposed the passage of the Civil Rights Act of 1957, the first federal civil rights bill since Reconstruction, with Thurmond holding the floor of the Senate for a record-setting 24-hour filibuster in an unsuccessful attempt at preventing the measure from coming to a vote.

Even as the movement gained momentum in the late 1950s and early 1960s, the administrations of Presidents Dwight Eisenhower and John F. Kennedy were hesitant to wholeheartedly embrace the cause of civil rights for fear of alienating southern bloc legislators in Congress. It was only after nationally televised demonstrations and the murders of four African-American girls in a Ku Klux Klan church bombing in Birmingham in 1963 that President Kennedy proposed the passage of a more far-reaching civil rights act than that of 1957. Although southern bloc legislators successfully tied the legislation up in committee and filibustered it on the Senate floor, President LYNDON JOHNSON—a Texan who as Senate MAJORITY LEADER had been one of only three southern senators not to sign the Southern Manifesto—made effective use of his legislative expertise and the public mourning following the assassination of President Kennedy to shepherd the CIVIL RIGHTS ACT OF 1964 through to passage. In signing the most sweeping civil rights legislation since Reconstruction on July 2, Johnson noted to his press secretary, "I think we've just delivered the South to the Republican Party for the rest of my life and yours." Johnson made similar use of public revulsion over voter registration violence in Mississippi and Alabama to overwhelm a demoralized southern bloc in Congress and to successfully push the VOTING RIGHTS ACT OF 1965 through to passage.

As the Civil Rights movement began to wane by the early 1970s, the cohesiveness of the southern bloc splintered. Increases in African-American voting in the South following passage of the Voting Rights Act forced a number of formerly segregationist legislators, including Thurmond, Herman Talmadge, and Russell Long, to accommodate themselves to changes in their electorates as they continued to serve in Congress. Others of the southern bloc were replaced by a new generation of southern Democrats, including Dale Bumpers, David Pryor, and Albert Gore, Jr., untainted by segregationist views and willing to openly court African-American support. Finally, President Johnson's prediction proved prophetic, as the electoral preferences of white southerners since the 1960s increasingly shifted from the Democratic to the Republican Party in national and state elections, resulting in the replacement of conservative southern Democrats with conservative Republicans such as TRENT LOTT, Richard Shelby, and Thad Cochrane in the House and Senate.

See also CONSERVATIVE COALITION.

Further reading:
Caro, Robert A. *The Years of Lyndon Johnson: Master of the Senate.* New York: Knopf, 2002; Polsby, Nelson W. *How Congress Evolves: Social Bases of Institutional Change.* New York: Oxford University Press, 2003; Sinclair, Barbara. *The Transformation of the U.S. Senate.* Baltimore: Johns Hopkins University Press, 1990; Woodward, C. Vann. *The Strange Career of Jim Crow.* New York: Oxford University Press, 2001.

—William D. Baker

Speaker of the House

One of only three legislative offices mentioned in the U.S. Constitution (Article I, Section 2), the Speaker of the House is the presiding officer of the HOUSE OF REPRESENTATIVES and the only leadership position elected by the full membership of either house of Congress. Although the Constitution does not explicitly require that the Speaker be a member of the House, all 59 men who have held the position since 1789 have been current holders of congressional seats. Unlike the nonpartisan Speakers in some parliamentary systems, the Speaker of the U.S. House of Representatives is almost always elected through a partisan vote and is therefore, in practice, the leader of the House's majority party. As such, the Speaker of the House has evolved into one of the key political positions in the American system of government, especially when the House is controlled by the political party not in control of the White House.

As both the presiding officer of the House and the de facto leader of the majority party, the Speaker may exercise a wide array of formal and informal powers. When presiding, the Speaker recognizes members who wish to speak on the floor, determines the order in which congressional business will be conducted, and interprets and applies rules of the House. The Speaker also plays a key role in distributing STANDING COMMITTEE assignments to legislators, appointing SELECT COMMITTEES, and referring BILLS to committee. As a party leader, the Speaker works closely with his party's leader in the SENATE in crafting and pursuing the party's legislative agenda. Finally, the Presidential Succession Act of 1947 identifies the Speaker as second only to the vice president in the order of presidential succession, although no Speaker has ever ascended to the presidency through this mechanism.

The political importance of the Speaker's office developed over the course of the early 19th century as a result of the evolution of the House committee system and as legislative party organizations established control of nominations for the office. HENRY CLAY of Kentucky, who was elected Speaker during his first term in office and held the position intermittently between 1811 and 1825, was the first to establish the Speaker's office as an important partisan office. Under Clay the Speaker acquired greater influence over the composition of powerful legislative committees, an authority Clay skillfully used in political bartering with other House members. Although few could match his political and legislative skills, Clay's successors in the office benefited from the cohesive party organizations that the Kentuckian had helped to establish in the House. In 1890 the powers of the Speaker were further augmented with the adoption of the "REED'S RULES," named for Speaker THOMAS REED of Maine and establishing the Speaker's authority to recognize members during floor deliberations. By the early 20th century the Speaker's control of committee assignments and procedural matters had rendered the position almost as powerful as that of the president himself, and legislators who defied the will of the Speaker often found themselves demoted or even removed from choice committees and their favored legislation directed to unfriendly committees.

Ironically, the most powerful Speaker in American history also served as the catalyst for a revolt that weakened the office's authority. JOSEPH G. CANNON, a Republican known as "Uncle Joe" and "Czar" to his colleagues, wielded almost authoritarian power over the House in opposing Progressive reforms during his 1903 to 1910 tenure. His dominance ended in 1910, when a revolt among rank-and-file House members angry over Cannon's dictatorial style removed the Speaker from office. Thereafter, the Speaker lost the authority to make committee assignments and was removed from the powerful House Rules Committee, limiting his authority to control the movement of legislation from committees to the House floor.

Over the course of the 20th century, political authority in the House was largely decentralized in the hands of powerful committee chairs. The most powerful post-Cannon Speaker was SAMUEL RAYBURN, a Texas Democrat who served as Speaker for all but four years between 1941 and 1961 and who, given the reduced powers of the office and the deep divisions among House Democrats over civil rights, labor issues, and agricultural policy, was forced to rely on more informal sources of power and his charismatic personality to wield influence.

Following Rayburn's death and the explosive political divisions over civil rights and the Vietnam War in the 1960s, House Democrats moved to strengthen the Speaker's authority once again through a series of procedural reforms, although the decentralized and fragmented nature of the House committee system was further exacerbated by a series of 1970s reforms vesting greater political autonomy in subcommittee chairs at the expense of standing committees. Following the Republican takeover of Congress in 1995, NEWT GINGRICH, a Republican from Georgia, appeared poised to strengthen the position of Speaker even further, reclaiming much of the authority Cannon had held by exercising greater control over committee assignments and the House's legislative agenda. However, ethical concerns and Republican doubts over his leadership led to Gingrich's resignation from Congress in 1998, and his successor, DENNIS HASTERT of Illinois, did not attempt to strengthen the formal or procedural powers of the Speaker after taking office.

Further reading:
Davidson, Roger H., Susan Hammond Webb, and Raymond W. Smock. *Masters of the House: Congressional Leadership over Two Centuries.* Boulder, Colo.: Perseus Books, 1998; Galloway, George B. *History of the House of Representatives.* New York: Harpercollins, 1976; Hutson, James H. *To Make All Laws: The Congress of the United States, 1789–1989.* Boston: Houghton Mifflin, 1990.
—William D. Baker

special committee   *See* COMMITTEES: SELECT OR SPECIAL.

special order addresses

Special order addresses (more commonly referred to as "special orders") are one of three forms of nonlegislative debate in the HOUSE OF REPRESENTATIVES (the others being ONE-MINUTE SPEECHES and MORNING HOUR debate). Special orders are considered nonlegislative for two reasons. First, they occur outside the arena of legislative business. More specifically, they usually take place at the end of the day after the House of Representatives has completed legislative business. Second, special orders pro-

vide an opportunity for members of Congress to discuss any topic they wish, policy or nonpolicy in nature. This characteristic is especially valuable considering the House's usual requirement that debate be confined to pending legislative business.[4] The three elements of special orders are the rules that govern the forum, who participates, and their political significance.

The rules of the House do not provide for special order addresses. Instead, they evolved as a unanimous consent practice of the House. Thus, any member of the House can object to the practice of daily special order addresses (this rarely happens, however). But the lack of formal recognition does not excuse members from adhering to the rules of the House during the special order period. On the contrary, members must abide by the usual rules that govern debate: decorum and the Speaker's power of recognition. For example, a member cannot deliver a special order address longer than 60 minutes in accordance with House Rule XVII, Clause 2, which limits individual members to "one hour in debate on any question." Further, members must abide by the chamber's precedents as well as the "Speaker's announced policies." For instance, House precedent holds that members cannot deliver more than one special order each legislative day.

The "Speaker's announced policies" refers to the Speaker's policies on certain aspects of House procedure, such as decorum in debate, which are usually announced on the first day of a new Congress. One important policy with regard to special order addresses is the Speaker's power of recognition. Although special orders routinely begin once legislative business of the day has been completed, the Speaker has the power to interrupt or reschedule the special order period. For example, the Speaker may recognize representatives for special orders earlier in the day if the House plans to consider major legislation through the evening hours.

Political parties use the flexible rules to their advantage. It is common practice for "theme teams" to organize one-minute speeches and special order addresses. Party leaders often reserve a 60-minute thematic special order to present the parties' stances on a particular bill or policy issue. It is common for each party's leadership to choose a designee to deliver a leadership special order during the party's first hour of longer special order addresses. For example, on July 9, 1997, the Republicans and Democrats organized two thematic special orders dealing with tax cuts.

---

[4] The Senate does not have special order addresses, per se. Rather, senators are given an opportunity for nonlegislative debate during their morning hour, in which morning business is conducted. A period is often set aside, by unanimous consent, for senators to speak up to five minutes on events and issues of the day.

The minority's designee, Frank Pallone, a representative from New Jersey, delivered a 60-minute special order in which he and other Democratic participants criticized the Republicans' tax plan. Then the majority's designee, Representative Mike Parker from Michigan, led a 60-minute special with Jack Kingston, a representative from Georgia, on the need for tax cuts.

In conclusion, there are generally three stages to each day's special order period: first, five-minute special orders by individual representatives; second, special orders longer than five minutes (normally 60 minutes in length) by the party's leadership or designee; and third, special orders longer than five minutes by individual members of Congress.

Who participates in special order addresses? First, research generally finds that legislatively disadvantaged members of Congress participate in special orders (and nonlegislative debate in general) at disproportionate levels. Because FRESHMAN, the ideologically extreme, and other rank-and-file representatives face significant challenges in conventional forms of policy making, they often turn to special order addresses to influence policy. For this reason, special order addresses are referred to some as a legislative "safety valve."

Second, party leaders and their designees use special orders to advertise their agendas, claim credit for their policy records, and take positions on pressing issues. One representative credited C-SPAN as having turned special order addresses from tools of the individual, when they were used primarily for tributes and eulogies, to tools of the party. Special order addresses are especially valuable to the parties because, unlike during brief one-minute speeches, the forums allow for detailed discussions of platforms, policies, and records.

Third, members of the minority party use special order addresses more heavily than members of the majority. Special orders provide an opportunity for minority members to criticize the majority party and thus take advantage of the electorate's bias for negative information (known as "negativity bias"). For example, few members of Congress in recent history have used special order addresses as effectively as NEWT GINGRICH, a representative from Georgia. Some have argued that Representative Gingrich's use of special order addresses to attack the Democratic majority in the 1980s and early 1990s contributed to his party's eventual rise to majority party status and his own accession to the House Speakership.

Representatives participate in special orders for four reasons. The first and most important reason is that the forum provides a low-cost opportunity for members to communicate with a targeted audience. They offer a direct link to constituents, interest groups, external agencies, and other members of Congress. Second, participation in special orders sends signals to party leaders that they are active participants in the legislative process. This is beneficial considering members' desire for career advancement and the finding that members who engage in legislative "entrepreneurial" activities are often rewarded with promotions. Third, special orders provide an opportunity for less-experienced members such as freshmen to hone their speech-making skills. Freshmen can use the forums to become accustomed to rules and procedures of the House and speaking from the floor. Finally, special orders give legislatively disadvantaged members the opportunity to participate in the policy-making process in a meaningful manner.

Further reading:
Fenno, Richard. *Congressmen in Committees.* Boston: Little Brown, 1973; Schneider, Judy. "Special Order Practices: Current House Practices." CRS Report for Congress, order code RL30136, 2001; Wawro, Gregory J. *Legislative Entrepreneurship in the US House of Representatives.* Ann Arbor: University of Michigan Press, 2000.

—Michael S. Rocca

special rules, House

Special rules are House resolutions that set the terms and conditions for consideration of specified legislative measures. In particular, special rules affect the procedures for debating, amending, and voting on bills as well as the time spent on final action after the COMMITTEE OF THE WHOLE is finished with consideration. Because the standing rules of the House impose various limitations on the consideration of legislation, the HOUSE RULES COMMITTEE enables the full House to debate and vote on legislation that is not privileged for floor consideration or cannot be passed by either unanimous consent or under suspension of the rules. Special rules supersede the standing rules of the House by giving bills privilege to be considered, which is why most major and controversial bills are considered under this method. However, special rules must be debated and adopted by majority vote on the House floor. Thus, the House first considers the proposed rule on a bill usually in the Committee of the Whole before beginning consideration of that bill under the terms and conditions of the rule.

When tailoring consideration of a bill, the Rules Committee variously reports one of four special rules, depending on the circumstances and content of the measure. An open rule does not restrict the number of germane floor amendments that members can propose. This rule allows members to offer an amendment, including en bloc amendments, under the five-minute rule, provided that the amendment is in compliance with House rules and the Budget Act. Conversely, a closed rule generally prohibits floor amendments, except perhaps for those recommended by the standing committee with jurisdiction over the bill. In between are restrictive rules, sometimes called modified open or modified closed rules, that limit opportunities for offering floor amendments, usually by identifying the particular amendments that are to be considered. Specifically, a modified open rule allows any member of the House to offer a germane amendment under the five-minute rule subject only to an overall time limit on the amendment process, and/or a requirement that the amendment be preprinted in the *Congressional Record*. A modified closed, or structured, rule permits only those amendments designated by the Rules Committee: one to two amendments under a modified closed rule, three or more amendments under a structured rule.

The Rules Committee can devise special rules to entangle or disentangle nearly any parliamentary situation. For example, it may report rules with "queen-of-the-hill" or "self-executing" provisions that set aside some of the regular procedures and prohibitions of the legislative process. Special rules may also waive points of order against consideration of a bill, against specified provisions, against amendments, or for matters that would otherwise be privileged for floor consideration without a rule, such as appropriations bills and conference reports. Conference reports usually receive rules only or primarily to waive points of order.

Special rules are subject to one hour of debate in the full House, controlled by the majority party manager for the Rules Committee, with half this time traditionally extended to the minority. The House may not consider special rules on the same day they are reported from the Rules Committee except by a two-thirds vote of the House. Nor may special rules be amended unless the majority manager offers an amendment or yields to another member for that purpose, or unless the previous question (the motion to end debate and proceed to a final vote) is defeated. If the previous question is defeated, its leading opponent is recognized for one hour of debate and given the right to amend the rule in a similar fashion.

The authority of the Rules Committee to report special rules is traced to the 1880s, when Speaker THOMAS REED, a Republican from Maine known as the "Great White Czar," employed such resolutions to shepherd legislation through the House. Prior to that time, measures could not be considered out of their order on the calendars of the House except by unanimous consent or under a suspension of the rules, which required a two-thirds vote. Since special rules reported from the Rules Committee necessitated only a majority vote in the House, the new practice enhanced the ability of the majority leadership to depart from the regular order of business and schedule legislation according to the majority's priorities. Recent studies record a noteworthy increase in the frequency of special rules, a trend largely attributed to the growing complexity and

unorthodoxy of the legislative process, sharpened partisanship and independence of members, and House leaders' desire for predictable results.

Further reading:
Bach, Stanley, and Steven S. Smith. *Managing Uncertainty in the House of Representatives: Adaptation and Innovation in Special Rules.* Washington, D.C.: Brookings Institution Press, 1988; Sinclair, Barbara. *Unorthodox Lawmaking: New Legislative Processes in the U.S. Congress.* 2d ed. Washington, D.C.: Congressional Quarterly Press, 2000; Smith, Steven S. *Call to Order: Floor Politics in the House and Senate.* Washington, D.C.: Brookings Institution Press, 1989; Wolfensberger, Donald R. "Special Rule." In *The Encyclopedia of the United States Congress*, edited by Donald C. Bacon, Roger H. Davidson, and Morton, Keller, New York: Simon & Schuster, 1995.

—Colton C. Campbell

Speech or Debate Clause

This clause, found in Article 1, Section 6, of the Constitution, grants members of both houses of Congress immunity from having to answer for anything they said in speech or debate in any place other than the house of Congress in which it was said. The clause was not controversial at the Constitutional Convention. It merely reworded a similar statement in the Articles of Confederation.

The lack of controversy surrounding the Speech or Debate Clause is reflected in the fact that it took almost 100 years before it received any judicial interpretation. The Supreme Court first interpreted it in *Kilbourn v. Thompson* (1881) and, in doing so, rejected a literal reading of its language. The immunity accorded to members of Congress was not limited to words spoken before either house of Congress. It extended to committee reports, resolutions, and the act of voting, even when the vote was not given verbally. The immunity extended to whatever members of Congress normally did in relation to the business before that body.

It was not until the 1960s and 1970s that the Supreme Court had opportunities to provide additional Speech or Debate Clause interpretation. The Court had to contend with the question of whether the Speech or Debate Clause protected dishonest or criminal activity by members of Congress. The case of *United States v. Johnson* (1966) involved appeal by a member of the House of Representatives from convictions on several counts of violating a conflict of interest statute. The congressman had tried to influence the Department of Justice to drop criminal charges against some savings-and-loan companies, and he had accepted money to make a speech favorable to them in the House. The Supreme Court held that because the indictment had focused on the congressman's motive in giving the speech, the Speech or Debate Clause had been violated. The Court noted, however, that making the speech was only one part of the conspiracy in which the congressman had been involved, and the government was free to retry him without introducing the speech as evidence. When a former U.S. senator was charged with soliciting and accepting bribes, the Court made clear that the Speech or Debate Clause did not shield him from prosecution. Chief Justice Warren Burger, in *United States v. Brewster* (1972), noted that not every action of a legislator is legislative activity. Taking a bribe is not a legislative act. Burger argued that the purpose of the Speech or Debate Clause was not simply to protect individual legislators, but to protect the integrity of the legislative process by ensuring the independence of its members. Its purpose was never to make members of Congress exempt from the criminal laws of the nation.

Yet the Speech or Debate Clause has protected a member of Congress from prosecution in an instance in which an ordinary citizen would have been prosecuted. *Gravel v. United States* (1972) involved Senator Mike Gravel of Alaska reading documents classified "top secret" to a Senate subcommittee and then putting them in the public record. The documents were related to decision making in the Vietnam War and are better known as *The Pentagon Papers*. Senator Gravel also arranged for private publication of the documents by Beacon Press. When a grand jury subpoenaed one of his aides, the senator sought to quash the subpoena by arguing that it violated the Speech or Debate Clause. In a 5-4 decision the Court stated that Senator Gravel did not have to answer questions and was immune from prosecution for what had taken place before the subcommittee. The senator's privilege extended to his aide as long as the activity would have been protected if done by the senator himself. But Senator Gravel was not protected in his arrangement with Beacon Press, nor was his aide protected from testifying about it before a grand jury.

Eastland v. United States Servicemen's Fund (1975) saw the Court use the Speech or Debate Clause to prevent the U.S. Servicemen's Fund from obtaining an injunction stopping the implementation of Senator James Eastland's subpoena of its banking records. Senator Eastland chaired the Subcommittee on Internal Security, which was authorized to study the way in which the Internal Security Act of 1950 was being carried out. But the organization claimed that public disclosure was the sole reason for the subcommittee going after its banking records, which violated First Amendment rights. In an 8-1 decision Chief Justice Warren Burger wrote for the majority that the absolute nature of the Speech or Debate Clause protected Senator Eastland's subpoena for the records even in the face of a First Amendment claim.

As long as legislators are pursuing legislative activity, the Speech or Debate Clause immunizes them from having to justify themselves in court. Even when a subcommittee of the House Committee on the District of Columbia did a study of public education in the district and produced a report that included the names of specific children on absentee lists and for failing tests, the Court, in *Doe v. McMillan* (1973), found that the parents were not entitled to sue for damages. But Senator William Proxmire could be sued by a recipient of one of his Golden Fleece Awards, given to people Proxmire believed were fleecing the American taxpayer. In HUTCHINSON V. PROXMIRE (1979) the Court held that he was protected for anything he said in the Senate, but not for defamatory statements made outside the Senate, such as in press releases and newsletters, even if they merely reproduced Senate speech.

Further reading:
Fisher, Louis. *Constitutional Conflicts between Congress and the President.* 4th rev. ed. Lawrence: University Press of Kansas, 1997; Peltason, J. W. *Corwin and Peltason's Understanding the Constitution.* 6th ed. Hinsdale, Ill.: Dryden Press, 1973; Warren, Charles. *The Making of the Constitution.* Cambridge, Mass.: Harvard University Press, 1935.

—Patricia A. Behlar

sponsorship/cosponsorship

Sponsorship is the first formal step in the legislative process for the U.S. Congress. Members of both the HOUSE OF REPRESENTATIVES and the SENATE may sponsor legislation, which means that they are formally introducing a proposed BILL. Each bill, amendment, or resolution in Congress has at least one sponsor and may have many cosponsors. In the 107th Congress (2001–03) more than 5,100 bills were sponsored in the House, and more than 2,200 bills were sponsored in the Senate. Even though legislators sponsor thousands of bills, few of them ever get passed into law. In the 107th Congress, for instance, only 5 percent of the bills introduced in Congress were enacted into law.

If so few bills that are introduced ever get enacted, why would a legislator sponsor a bill? One reason members of Congress sponsor bills is to set the legislative agenda. Bill sponsorship is a good indicator of the types of issues that members are trying to bring to the congressional agenda. Richard Hall argues that a roll-call vote on a bill represents a legislator's preference—whether he or she favors or opposes an issue. But a simple yes or no vote does not represent how strongly a legislator feels about an issue. On the other hand, bill sponsorship shows what issues have become priorities for representatives. Representatives may also introduce new legislation to please their constituents or interest groups or to establish a reputation in a policy area. Some representatives focus on issues that are personally important to them, problems that affect their own family and friends.

In a study of Senate bill sponsorship, Wendy Schiller found that sponsorship is a strong indicator of the issues with which a senator wants to be associated. Before sponsoring a bill senators carefully consider the costs and benefits of being associated with a bill. Every bill that is sponsored by a member can be seized on by a challenger in a reelection campaign. For example, a legislator would take a significant risk when sponsoring a bill to increase taxes, since the issue could be used against him or her in the next election. Schiller also concludes that the decision to sponsor a bill depends on the legislator's power in the Senate and the opportunities that a particular bill may provide to increase publicity or power.

Party identification is probably one of the most important factors that influences the types of bills members sponsor. Democratic representatives typically focus on bills that are more associated with a liberal ideology, while Republican representatives focus on more conservative bills. Being a member of the majority party in Congress also influences bill sponsorship, as majority party members typically sponsor more legislation.

The size of a representative's state or district and the economic interests of the state or district also influence the types of bills sponsored in Congress. Representatives from large, diverse states or districts, such as California, are likely to sponsor more legislation to represent their diverse constituents. In addition, legislators from farming states such as Illinois and Iowa are more likely to sponsor agriculture policy bills than are legislators from more metropolitan states.

The type and number of committees a member sits on also influence bill sponsorship. As committee assignments increase, bill sponsorship also increases. In addition, members usually sponsor bills that fall within the jurisdiction of their committees. For example, a senator on the FOREIGN RELATIONS COMMITTEE is more likely to sponsor bills related to foreign policy.

Bill sponsorship may also be related to the race and gender of a representative. Kenny Whitby, in his study of African-American representatives, found a relationship between race and bill sponsorship. He found that senior black members were more likely to sponsor black-interest legislation compared to the junior black members. He also found that black members serving in safe districts were more likely to sponsor black-interest legislation than were those serving in competitive districts.

Michele Swers studied similar connections between bill sponsorship and gender. She found that in the 103rd and 104th Congresses, women were more likely to sponsor women's issue bills than were the male legislators. She showed that female representatives work to incorporate the interests of women, children, and families into the congressional agenda.

In addition to sponsoring a bill, legislators may also cosponsor a bill. Cosponsorship simply indicates added support for a bill by a legislator or group of legislators. However, cosponsorship may be important in helping a bill become enacted into law. Once a bill is referred to a committee, it may be more likely to have hearings and debates if the bill has many cosponsors. Different interest groups often encourage legislators to cosponsor a controversial bill that they support so the bill will be more likely to have a chance at being enacted. When both Republican and Democratic representatives cosponsor a bill, the bipartisanship may indicate wide support for the policy. For instance, the BIPARTISAN CAMPAIGN FINANCE REFORM ACT, passed in 2002, included cosponsors from both the Republican Party, with Senator John McCain, and the Democratic Party, with Senator Russ Feingold.

Overall, bill sponsorship and cosponsorship may at first glance appear to be a mere formality in the legislative process. However, on closer examination sponsorship is an important indicator of a legislator's agenda, priorities, and interests in Congress.

Further reading:
Davidson, Roger H., and Walter J. Oleszak. *Congress and Its Members.* 9th ed. Washington, D.C.: Congressional Quarterly Press, 2004; Hall, Richard. *Participation in Congress.* New Haven, Conn.: Yale University Press, 1996; Schiller, Wendy J. "Senators as Political Entrepreneurs: Using Bill Sponsorship to Shape Legislative Agendas." *American Journal of Political Science* 39, no. 1 (1995): 186–204; Swers, Michele L. *The Difference Women Make: The Policy Impact of Women in Congress.* Chicago: University of Chicago Press, 2002; Whitby, Kenny J. "Bill Sponsorship and Intra-racial Voting among African American Representatives." *American Politics Research* 30 (January 2002): 93–109.
—Melinda A. Mueller and Carmen R. Allen

staff, committee/subcommittee

Committee staff are those men and women who are employed by the committees and subcommittees of each chamber of Congress. According to Congressional Research Service reports, the average number of individuals working on each committee staff in the HOUSE OF REPRESENTATIVES was 68 in 2001; the average number of individuals employed by each of the SENATE committees was 46 that same year.

Just like their personal staff counterparts, there are a variety of roles that committee staff play. Administrative staff members typically lack prior substantive expertise in the subject areas over which the committee has jurisdiction. These staff members are largely responsible for the administrative and clerical functions required to keep the committee operating. Such functions include staffing the committee offices, responding to telephone, mail, and electronic requests, scheduling committee hearings and meetings, setting up hearings, distributing information, and staffing the committee's library. Titles that are given to administrative and clerical staff include chief clerk, deputy clerk, documents clerk, staff assistant, and librarian.

By comparison, professional committee staff are considered the staff experts on the areas for which the committee is responsible. These individuals are primarily policy experts, many of whom have advanced degrees and, often, prior experience working in the private or public sectors on similar issues. Not only are professional committee staffers more experienced than their clerical and administrative counterparts within the committee, professional committee staff are also typically older, more experienced, and better educated than the staff members who work on members' personal office staffs. In addition to tracking pending legislation, working to draft proposals and amendments, and coordinating a legislative strategy, professional committee staff members brief the members of the committee on matters of policy that are pending before the committee and on matters of concern that may ultimately be delegated to the committee at a later date. As Kenneth Kofmehl has written,

> committee staff provide high quality analyses of matters under consideration by their committees, in which they ensure that all alternatives are considered, point up the implications of proposals, assess the validity of supporting data, and the manner in which it has been analyzed, detect gaps in presentation, and so on.

In addition to the analysis they provide, committee staff frequently draft legislative reports, prepare hearing and mark-up transcripts, provide important research capacity for the committee and its members, and meet with interest groups concerning pending legislation. These staff have much less direct contact with members' constituents than do their counterparts on members' personal office staffs.

Committee staff are in frequent contact with their colleagues on the corresponding committees in the other chamber. In addition, they often must work closely with the personal office staff members who work for the members of Congress who serve on the committee. This is especially true in the Senate, which allows the individual members on each of its committees and subcommittees to select their own staff, in contrast to House of Representatives staff members, who typically work for the committee and often remain in the same positions regardless of personnel changes of the elected membership of the committees.

Further reading:
Malbin, Michael J. *Unelected Representatives: Congressional Staff and the Future of Representative Government.* New York: Basic Books, 1980; Pontius John S. and Faye M. Bullock. "Congressional Staff: Duties and Functions." Washington, D.C.: Congressional Research Service, 2001; Rundquist, Paul S., Judy Schneider, and Frederick H. Paul. "Congressional Staff: An Analysis of Their Roles, Functions, and Impacts." Washington, D.C.: Congressional Research Service, 1992.

—Lauren Bell

staff, personal

Today staff members outnumber elected members of Congress by a ratio of roughly 57 to one. These staffers work in members' personal offices, on congressional committees, and for legislative support agencies such as the CONGRESSIONAL RESEARCH SERVICE, the LIBRARY OF CONGRESS, the CONGRESSIONAL BUDGET OFFICE, and the Office of the ARCHITECT OF THE CAPITOL. Among these, personal office staff members have the most day-to-day contact with constituents and are often the "first-responders" to questions about members' legislative proposals, voting behaviors, and constituency relations.

Each house of Congress sets its own guidelines and policies relating to the size of members' personal staffs, the ethics rules the staff members are expected to abide by, and the range of appropriate staff tasks and responsibilities. Individual members of the House are permitted to determine the specific titles their staff hold, as well as to allocate duties within the office in whatever way they determine works best for them. This includes the allocation of staff resources between their CAPITOL HILL offices and their district office or offices back in their home state. In total, House members are permitted to employ up to 18 full-time and four part-time personal office staff members. In 2000 the average Washington-based House staff member earned $46,598, with district office staff members earning less than their D.C.-based counterparts.

Unlike members of the House, senators are permitted to appoint as many staff as they wish provided they stay within the total amount allocated to them for staff expenses. The total each senator receives to cover staff costs varies depending on the size of the state the senator represents. In 1999 staff allowances ranged from $1.8 million to more than $3.1 million. Senators' staffs range in size from 31 to 43, with an average of roughly 35 staff members for each senator. Just as with the House of Representatives, senators must allocate some portion of these staffing resources to provide staff for several offices within their home states.

The functions served by members' personal staffs vary widely, depending on whether the staff members are located in the home state or district, or whether the staff members work with the member on Capitol Hill. Hill staff fulfill numerous responsibilities, ranging from clerical and administrative (for example, answering and logging incoming phone calls, opening and sorting mail, organizing the schedule, and addressing personnel issues), service (for example, responding to constituency requests for information or assistance), and legislative research, analysis, and tracking (for example, monitoring the progress of legislation the member cares about and promoting the member's legislation with other congressional offices).

In the home district staff members are much more likely to be engaged in direct contact with constituents than are their Washington counterparts. In addition to serving constituents, the district office staff members work closely with state and local elected and public officials to track matters of importance to the member and to identify areas of need so that the member can more effectively serve his or her constituents.

Personal office staff members, unlike their committee counterparts, are tied closely to the member of Congress for whom they work. While individual staffers in the office may develop substantive expertise in a particular public policy area, their foremost responsibility is to provide advice to the member of Congress and to cultivate information and activities designed to foster the member's goals in relation to specific proposals. Committee staff, in contrast, are frequently called on to place the members' individual goals behind the goals of advancing the policy interests of the entire committee or to filter members' preferences through the technical requirements of the policy area under review.

Further reading:
Dwyer Paul E. *Salaries and Allowances.* Washington, D.C.: Congressional Research Service, 1999; Pontius, John S., and Faye M. Bullock. *Congressional Staff: Duties and Functions.* Washington, D.C.: Congressional Research Service, 2001; Congressional Management Foundation. *Senate Salary, Tenure & Demographic Data: 1991–2001.* Available online. URL: http://www.cmfweb.org/public/pdfs/CMF%20Senate%20Salary%20Study.pdf. Accessed January 16, 2006.

—Lauren Bell

Standards of Official Conduct, House Committee on

Until 1967 the HOUSE OF REPRESENTATIVES had no standing ethics committee. Complaints of misconduct were referred to select committees that would conduct investigations, make determinations, and report their recommendations to the House of Representatives. There were no rules for proceedings in disciplinary matters, nor was there a written code of conduct or ethics for members of the House of Representatives.

In October 1966 a House Select Committee on Standards and Conduct was established. Three years following the Senate's creation of a Committee on Standards and Conduct, the House Committee on Standards of Official Conduct was formed by a resolution of the House of Representatives on April 13, 1967. The committee issued a report recommending changes in the House rules concerning standards of official conduct. On April 3, 1968, the House voted to make the committee a standing committee and adopted a written code of ethical conduct.

Unlike other standing committees in the House, the membership of this 10-member committee is evenly divided between majority and minority members to ensure bipartisanship in the consideration of matters that are brought before it. The basis for the committee's existence is the Constitution of the United States, which provides that each House of Congress "shall be the Judge of the Elections, Returns, and Qualifications of its own Members." Further, the Constitution states that each House may "punish its Members for disorderly behavior, with the Concurrence of two-thirds, may expel a Member."

The committee has jurisdiction over members, officers, and employees of the House of Representatives. The committee, under the Rules of the House, has the authority to recommend administrative actions to establish or enforce standards of official conduct; investigate alleged violations of the Code of Official Conduct; report the substantial violation of any law applicable to the performance of official duties to appropriate federal or state authorities; render advisory opinions regarding the propriety of any current or proposed conduct by any individual within its jurisdiction; and consider requests for written waivers of the gift rule.

Disciplinary proceedings follow procedural rules, and evidence is taken in formal hearings conducted by the committee. Since 1990 the committee's procedures have required that a subcommittee review complaints and conduct preliminary investigations. If the subcommittee believes that formal ethics charges are warranted, it issues a "Statement of Alleged Violations." The remaining members of the committee then are constituted as a subcommittee to hear the evidence and determine whether the charges are proven. Formal disciplinary actions, which may include reprimand, censure, or expulsion, are recommended by the committee to the full House of Representatives, which then votes on the recommendations. This process is intended to promote fairness to the accused by not having the same group act as a grand jury, jury, and judge. The committee has occasionally issued letters of reproval or reprimand to members, but these letters are not considered to be a formal disciplinary action. The Ethics in Government Act of 1978 (5 U.S.C. app.) designates the committee as the "supervising ethics office" for the House of Representatives and charges the committee with responsibility for financial disclosure statements for members, employees, and officers of the House as well as candidates for the House.

During the 1980s and early 1990s the committee became the venue for partisan conflict. Republicans, led by NEWT GINGRICH of Georgia, begin to bring ethics charges against Democrats. Charles Diggs of Michigan was censured by the House after being convicted of mail fraud in 1980. Diggs subsequently resigned. Between 1987 and 1989 Gingrich brought a series of charges against Speaker of the House JAMES C. WRIGHT of Texas, accusing him of financial improprieties. Wright resigned as Speaker and as a member of the House on June 30, 1989.

The Democrats reciprocated a few years later, when charges were brought against Gingrich in 1995 alleging conflict of interest and financial improprieties. In 1997 Gingrich was fined $300,000 for violating House rules barring the use of tax-exempt foundations for political purposes.

Following the Gingrich case, the leaders of both parties in the House agreed to a "truce" whereby they agreed not to bring ethics charges against members of Congress. This truce remained in place until 2004, when Representative Chris Bell of Texas charged House Majority Leader TOM DELAY with soliciting campaign contributions in return for legislative favors, laundering illegal campaign contributions through a political action committee, and improperly involving a federal agency in a partisan political matter. As of this writing (2004) the matter is pending.

The committee has expelled two members. Michael Myers of Pennsylvania was expelled in 1980 after being convicted of bribery. In 2002 James Traficant of Ohio was expelled after being convicted of 10 federal counts that included bribery, racketeering, and tax evasion.

Further reading:
Baker, Richard. "A History of Congressional Ethics." In *Representation and Responsibility, Exploring Legislative Ethics*, edited by Bruce Jennings and Daniel Callahan. New York: Kluwer Academic Publishers, 1985; Congressional Research Service. *The House Committee on Standards of Official Conduct: A Brief History of Its Evolution and Jurisdiction.* CRS Report 92-686. Washington, D.C.: Government Printing Office, 1992.

—Jeffrey Kraus

standing committee   *See* COMMITTEES: STANDING.

state delegations

A state delegation is made up of the two senators from the state serving in the SENATE and all representatives from that state serving in the HOUSE OF REPRESENTATIVES. Article I, Section 2, of the Constitution requires that the number of representatives be apportioned among the states on the basis of their populations. Every state, regardless of population, has at least one representative, including seven states with relatively small populations: Alaska, Delaware, Montana, North Dakota, South Dakota, Vermont, and Wyoming. States with large populations have many seats in the House. The most populous state, California, has 53 seats; accordingly, the California state delegation consists of 55 members of Congress. The state delegation from Alaska has three members. The size of a state delegation is equivalent to that state's vote in the Electoral College.

The concept of state delegations originated with the Articles of Confederation, adopted in 1777 by the Continental Congress and approved by all the states in 1781. The articles provided that no state would be represented in the unicameral, or one-chamber, Congress by fewer than two nor by more than seven members appointed annually by the state legislature. Each person appointed could serve as many as three years during any six-year period. But no matter how many delegates each of the 13 states appointed and no matter how many of those delegates were in the capital serving their terms, each of the 13 states represented in Congress had only one vote. The approval of the Constitution by the states brought an end to the single vote per state arrangement existing under the articles that had required the delegates from each state to work together as a state delegation to cast the state's vote and represent the state's interests. The 1787 Constitution created two chambers with two senators selected by each state legislature (until ratification of the SEVENTEENTH AMENDMENT in 1913, after which senators were selected by popular vote in each state) and one or more representatives in the House elected by the people from each congressional DISTRICT.

The principal vestige under the Constitution of this state delegation concept is contained in Article II, Section 1, of the Constitution, modified by the Twelfth Amendment, and concerns the election of the president in the event that no candidate for the presidential office receives a majority of the votes from the Electoral College. Under such an outcome, the House of Representatives selects the president from the top three vote-getters in the Electoral College. This is accomplished by each state delegation in the House casting a single vote for one of the candidates, with the winning candidate the individual who receives a majority of the 50 state delegation votes. A similar process is followed with a separate vote from among the top two vice presidential candidates in the Electoral College, but this vote is cast by members of the Senate. The victorious vice presidential candidate is the person who receives a majority vote from the 100 senators.

Another remnant of the state delegation concept in the House involves the assignment of members to committees by political parties. Following the 1910 revolt against the power of SPEAKER OF THE HOUSE JOSEPH G. CANNON, the Republicans created a Committee on Committees consisting of representatives of all state delegations in the House. The state delegation representatives on this committee were able to cast votes in the committee equal to their state delegation numbers. While this specific committee no longer exists, the committee assignments are now made by party steering committees. The support of state delegations is still one factor in making committee assignments for both parties.

State delegations involving both House and Senate members now operate on an informal basis most of the time. Because state delegation members represent common populations and contiguous districts, there are strong shared interests. These in turn are strengthened by communications with constituents, businesses, and organizations that seek for their congressional delegation to work effectively and in harmony with their elected officials at the state and local levels of government. State delegations often do so when federal programs are viewed as providing the state and communities with benefits or treating other states better than the home state. Federal formulas allocating funds among states are examples. Moreover, state legislatures, governors, and local officials sometimes petition Congress. Such memorials and petitions, and similar ones from statewide interest groups, are often sent to the state delegation members with the expectation that state delegation members will cooperate on these requests. Governors, state legislative leaders, and other elected officials occasionally meet with some or all state delegation members when visiting or conducting business in the nation's capital, often working together through offices maintained by many states and some local governments in Washington, D.C. Similarly, the district office staffs of members of Congress are often in contact with state and local officials in the home state. The decennial congressional redistricting process by the state legislature is also a time of heightened interest on the part of House state delegation members, for instance.

Although a rather hollow shell of its former self, the concept of state delegations still has applicability. While a few decades ago there were often meetings of state delegations with appointed members officers, for example, there are now fewer formal institutional arrangements. During earlier periods when congressional sessions were shorter in duration, state delegation members often stayed at the same boardinghouses, and it was natural for them to work closely together. Nowadays the nearly year-round session schedule for Congress, plus the availability and frequency of airline service back to the state or district and the increasing use of communications and other technologies have diminished the former strong comradery within state delegations and the welcome delegations provided to newly elected members. To a degree, state delegation networking has given way somewhat to a wider networking of members through coalitions and caucuses of many kinds.

Further reading:
Arieff, Irwin B. "State Delegations Strive to Protect Their Interests through Concerted Effort." *Congressional Quarterly Weekly Report*, 2 August 1980; Schneider, Judy. *House Committees: Assignment Process*. Washington, D.C.: Congressional Research Service, 1999; Schneider, Judy. *House Leadership Structure: Overview of Party Organization*. Washington, D.C.: Congressional Research Service, 2001; U.S. House of Representatives. *Organization of the Congress: Final Report of the Joint Committee on the Organization of Congress*. Washington, D.C.: Joint Committee on the Organization of Congress, 1993.

—Robert F. Goss

State of the Union message

Article II, Section 3, of the Constitution dictates the president "from time to time give to the Congress Information on the State of the Union, and recommend to their Consideration such Measures as he shall judge necessary and expedient." From this constitutional duty, the modern State of the Union message has evolved. However, it should be noted that since the Constitution is not specific as to the way a president must do this task, both the delivery practices and the content have varied over time.

The first two presidents, George Washington and John Adams, delivered to JOINT SESSIONS of Congress oral addresses that were labeled "annual messages." Thomas Jefferson halted the practice of an orally delivered address, which he likened to the monarchical opening of the British Parliament, and began the tradition of sending written messages to Congress. This tradition was followed until 1913, when Woodrow Wilson renewed the practice of an oral address given to a joint session of Congress, a practice that most presidents have followed during the modern period, even though Wilson reverted to sending written messages in 1919 and 1920 due to ill health. Wilson's reinitiation of this practice was consistent with his belief in presidential leadership of Congress. Of all the presidents since Wilson, only Herbert Hoover relied solely on sending written messages; all others have delivered at least one oral address to report on the State of the Union. Occasionally, even modern presidents transmit a written message, but this is most likely to occur when a president is a lame duck. Harry Truman in 1953, Dwight Eisenhower in 1961, and Jimmy Carter in 1981 all sent written messages to Congress in the final weeks of their administrations.

A change in terminology has also taken place. The reports to Congress from the first century and a half of the republic were labeled annual messages, but since 1945 they have been referred to as State of the Union messages or addresses. In addition, an address in the first month of a new president's term is typically not called a State of the Union address. Although delivered to joint sessions of Congress, they most often are on a specific policy area and are considered special messages rather than State of the Union messages.

Presidents are under no constitutional time requirement as to when they issue their report on the State of the Union. From Washington to Franklin Roosevelt, addresses were delivered in the months of October, November, December, and January, although December was the most common month for transmittal. After the ratification of the Twentieth Amendment in 1933 placed the opening of a new Congress in January, it became standard practice for messages to be given in that month, shortly after the new Congress had convened.

Changes in technology have also had an effect on the State of the Union message. Radio in the 1920s allowed the American public to hear the president's report for the first time. Television afforded the public the opportunity to both hear and see the president's address in the 1940s. To maximize the viewing audience, Lyndon Johnson delivered the first prime-time address in 1965. With the advent of the prime-time address, presidents and their staffs became particularly concerned with crafting a message that would have public appeal.

What presidents say in their messages has evolved as well. Initially, annual messages were simple reporting documents to Congress. They then became written summaries of cabinet reports. Today presidents use State of the Union addresses to signal to Congress and also the public what their agenda will be for the coming year. The speeches are carefully crafted, and policy items are generally placed such that the highest priority items come first. State of the Union messages afford presidents the opportunity to advertise their successes in the previous year as well. In the weeks and months following a State of the Union address, the president and his administration will begin to submit a legislative agenda to Congress formally submitted by sympathetic members.

Because the president is addressing a joint session of Congress when giving the address, the vice president will be seated on the rostrum behind the president in his or her capacity as President of the Senate. The SPEAKER OF THE HOUSE will be seated there as well. Given the impor-

tance of State of the Union addresses for official Washington, the audience will not be composed of only members of the House and the Senate. The president's cabinet will be in attendance except for one member, who will be away from the Capitol building for purposes of presidential succession. One will see the members of the Supreme Court in attendance as well as the joint chiefs of staff and diplomatic corps. Other observers will be seated in the House gallery. Ronald Reagan began the tradition of inviting to the gallery a few key individuals who would be recognized for some achievement during the course of the address. Subsequent presidents have continued this practice. These individuals are commonly seated with the First Lady.

State of the Union messages, thus, have evolved over the history of the United States. Current practice dictates that presidents fulfill this constitutional duty addressing a joint session of Congress in January to claim credit for accomplishments and indicate to members and the public what their agenda will be for the coming year.

Further reading:
Cohen, Jeffrey E. "Presidential Rhetoric and the Public Agenda." *American Journal of Political Science* 39, no. 1 (1995): 87–108; Ferth, Seymour H. *The View from the White House: A Study of the Presidential State of the Union Messages.* Washington, D.C.: Public Affairs Press, 1961; Light, Paul. *The President's Agenda.* 3d ed. Baltimore: Johns Hopkins University Press, 1999; State of the Union Messages. *The American Presidency.* Available online. URL: http://www.presidency.ucsb.edu/sou.php. Accessed January 16, 2006.

—Donna R. Hoffman

statute

A statute is a law established by an act of a legislature. Congress as the national legislature creates national statutes that apply nationwide, as compared with the 50 state legislatures that create state statutory laws that apply statewide. Local government legislative bodies, such as county commissions and city councils, also create statutory law, but their laws are termed ordinances, connoting their somewhat lesser legal status compared with statutes.

Besides statutory law created by legislatures, there also exists law created by the courts through the decisions of judges. While the legislative branch of government creates statutory law, the judicial branch of government creates judge-made case law, or common law. Common law is often based on principles rather than rules and comes from judicial precedent, or cases that have been decided previously. The executive branch also creates law, such as through executive orders, executive proclamations, and the rulings of government agencies, and this law is sometimes denoted as administrative law. Both common law and administrative law can be changed through legislative statutes.

Article I, Section 1, of the U.S. Constitution provides that all national legislative power is vested in a bicameral Congress, so that no law can be passed unless both chambers have acted by approving identical language. Section 8, Clause 1, provides expressed powers to Congress, and Clause 3 goes further to indicate that Congress may make laws not just in these areas, but may also go beyond them if necessary and proper for carrying out such specific powers and others vested in the national government. This broad grant of legislative authority is manifest in the lawmaking process of Congress, allowing statutes prescribing conduct, defining crimes, appropriating monies, providing for the common defense, and promoting the public good, among others.

Congressional and presidential actions may ultimately result in national statutes if the actions are performed in accordance with constitutional authority, adhere to the means specified under legislative rules and laws, and are handled in a form that can eventually become statutory law. For example, the actions of Congress on concurrent or simple resolutions will not result in statutes because such resolutions deal only with matters, rules, or operations of one or both chambers. But complete and necessary action by Congress on bills or joint resolutions may result in statutes. Bills and joint resolutions can fail at many steps along the way, but essential congressional actions include introduction, three readings, adherence to voting requirements in each chamber, and enrollment, for example. Necessary presidential actions include approval of an enrolled bill or permitting it to become law without signing it in order for a bill to become a statute.

Several types of statutes can result from the acts of Congress and the president. One significant distinction is the difference between public and private statutes. Public statutes are those that affect the whole society, as distinguished from private ones that concern only a specific individual, family, or small group and may affect only their private rights, such as covering those who have been injured by government programs or those appealing a government agency decision. This public-private distinction can become important, for example, in court proceedings in which judges may take judicial notice of the evidence of public statutes to all persons generally but may not take such notice without a party in the case specifically arguing the applicability of a private statute to the case being considered. Statutes are also sometimes identified either as temporary, limited in duration, or perpetual, those that will remain in force without any time limitation. Last, there are affirmative statutes and negative statutes. Affirmative ones declare what shall be done and do not overturn the common law, whereas negative statutes can prohibit actions or declare what shall not be done, sometimes negating existing common law.

Once a bill or joint resolution completes the congressional and presidential processes to become a statute, it is transmitted to the U.S. Archivist for publication in order for the public to become fully aware of the new law. Initial statutory publication is by the Office of the Federal Register in the independent National Archives and Records Administration in the form of an unbound pamphlet called a "slip law" that also contains the permanent law number and legal statutory citation as well as marginal notes and the legislative history. The assigned public law or private law numbers run in sequence, beginning anew for each session of Congress with the number of that Congress. For example, within the United States Statutes at Large, a chronological arrangement of the laws exactly as they have been enacted, Pub.L. 108-10 (identifying the 108th Congress, Public Law 10) authorizes the Federal Trade Commission to collect fees for the implementation and enforcement of a consumer "do-not-call" registry. The order of law enactment determines the sequential number of the public law assigned, with a similar sequencing occurring for private statutes (appearing as Pvt.L.). The vast majority of laws passed by Congress are public laws.

While the Statutes at Large are not arranged according to the subject matter of the law, the United States Code is put together in such a fashion to make it easier to know the current law within a particular field. The code is divided by broad subjects into 50 titles (Title 11 for bankruptcy, Title 18 for crimes, etc.), generally in alphabetical order and published by the Office of Law Revision Counsel of the House of Representatives. It is published every six years, with in-between editions published as annual cumulative supplements. This code represents the present state of the law as modified through statute after statute, for laws often amend or change previous laws. Both the Statutes at Large and the code represent different ways of viewing the results of statues that have been enacted through the often long and convoluted lawmaking process.

See also PUBLIC LAW.

Further reading:
1 U.S. Code, chap. 2 and 3; Black, Henry Campbell. *Black's Law Dictionary.* 4th ed. St. Paul, Minn.: West Publishing, 1968; Johnson, Charles W. III. *How Our Laws Are Made.* Washington, D.C.: U.S. House of Representatives, 2003.

—Robert P. Goss

Steward Machine Co. v. Davis 301 U.S. 548 (1937)

In the 1937 case *Steward Machine Co. v. Davis* and its companion, *Helvering v. Davis,* the Supreme Court upheld the SOCIAL SECURITY ACT of 1935, a part of President Franklin D. Roosevelt's NEW DEAL, by a slim majority. The Social Security Act established a payroll tax for federal old-age benefits (upheld in *Helvering*), created another payroll tax for unemployment compensation, and induced states to create certain procedures to comply with the law (upheld in *Steward*). Although such federal entitlements are very popular today, when these economic reforms were first enacted they sharply divided the Supreme Court on the constitutionality of dramatic increases in federal government power over employment issues previously regarded as private or to be regulated only by local and state authorities.

At issue in these cases was whether payroll taxes to fund both Social Security and unemployment compensation were constitutional under Congress's power to "lay and collect taxes . . . and provide for the . . . general welfare of the United States." An additional question regarding unemployment taxes was whether the federal government could push the states into establishing their own funds, which employers would contribute to. Writing for the Court in both cases, Justice Benjamin Cardozo explained Congress not only had the power to initiate these programs through its enumerated and implied powers, but the Great Depression was a sufficient cause for the expansion of federal power to ensure an economic safety net for citizens, rather than leave such programs to vary at the state level, assuming states would or could fund them at all.

Regarding the federal government's effective mandate to the states to create unemployment compensation funds under the Social Security Act during the Great Depression, Cardozo wrote in *Steward*: "the fact developed quickly that the states were unable to give the requisite relief. There was need of help from the nation if the people were not to starve."

Regarding the old-age insurance provisions of the law, in *Helvering*, Cardozo wrote:

> Congress did not improvise a judgment when it was found that the award of old age benefits would be conducive to the general welfare . . . the problem is plainly national [and] laws of separate states cannot deal with it effectively.

In these ways *Steward Machine Co. v. Davis* and *Helvering v. Davis* were part of the Supreme Court's famously abrupt 1937 break with its previous decisions striking down other aspects of the New Deal. For example, the *Steward* and *Helvering* decisions differed from the 1936 decision *U.S. v. Butler,* which struck down a New Deal agricultural program that levied a tax on certain commodities processors that would be redistributed to farmers who agreed to limit production as a way of helping raise prices. In his majority opinion in *Butler,* Justice Owen

Roberts agreed with the government that the tax could be raised under Congress's constitutional authority, but he then invoked the Tenth Amendment, saying the issue of agricultural economics fell to the states under their reserved powers. By contrast, the Tenth Amendment was explicitly rejected by the majority of the Court to stop the new federal taxes at issue in the Social Security Act. In a larger sense, these two cases also signaled, along with others decided the same year, the end of a long history of the Court's thwarting the president and Congress, and sometimes even the states, as they attempted to regulate privately owned workplaces since the late 1800s.

Although President Roosevelt was often personally at the center of these years of conflict between the elected branches and the Supreme Court, larger constitutional questions during the New Deal years surrounded Congress's abilities to pass certain kinds of taxation and spending laws, also known as fiscal policy. Although the federal government's powers to both tax and spend are found in Congress's provisions in the Constitution, it is not clear from the text what the limits to these powers are, nor is there a formula to ascertain how these policies will assist the vague goals of providing for "the general welfare" of the nation. After the Court's decisions in 1937, all subsequent Congresses and presidents hammered out a variety of taxes, spending, and other regulations on states and businesses to influence the nation's economic life, and a vast majority of these laws have passed Court muster when challenged. But states and private corporations have continued to chafe under federal regulation of their actions, even as both have also turned to the government for relief. So while *Steward* is an important precedent for federal economic power and the specific provisions it sustained have remained popular, larger political controversies have continued surrounding the proper scope of federal government influence over private corporate behavior, state governments, and the economy generally.

Further reading:
Brest, Paul, and Sanford Levinson. *Processes of Constitutional Decisionmaking: Cases and Materials.* Boston: Little, Brown, 1992; Gunther, Gerald. *Constitutional Law.* 12th ed. Westbury, N.Y.: Foundation Press, 1991.

—Jasmine Farrier

subcommittees

One of the most basic building blocks of the congressional bureaucracy, subcommittees are key working components of most committees of the SENATE and the HOUSE OF REPRESENTATIVES. Subcommittees frequently perform most of the routine tasks on Capitol Hill. They gather information, oversee the federal bureaucracy, fine tune the details of legislation, provide close links to interest groups, and often provide highly specialized knowledge and expert analysis for members of the full committees. In the legislative process subcommittees normally conduct hearings, assign research efforts to staff members, mark up (carefully review and rewrite) legislation, issue a written report, and forward the bill to the full committee. However, Senate subcommittees normally do not mark up legislation.

Subcommittee members commonly take the lead in initiating and shaping the content of legislation within the policy area of their panel. They then try to sell their preferences to the parent STANDING COMMITTEE before proceeding to the chamber floor, where subcommittee members frequently manage their side of the debate. Subcommittee members also are well represented in their chamber's delegation in conference committee deliberations with members of the other chamber.

Subcommittees did not develop in Congress until the early years of the 20th century. Throughout the century a pair of forces maintained steady pressure for creating and retaining divisions of congressional committees. Members of Congress sought to be organized to meet the increasingly specialized policy issue demands of American society and its interest groups. Subcommittees tend to be composed of members attracted either by the subject matter or constituent links associated with the panel. For example, legislators from wheat-producing regions likely would seek membership on a subcommittee with jurisdiction over wheat that was part of the House or Senate agriculture committee.

In addition, members want to increase the number of leadership opportunities presented by a proliferation of subcommittees. Each subcommittee is led by a chair chosen from the ranks of the majority party and a ranking member leading the delegation from the minority party. A significant number of representatives hold subcommittee leadership positions, while a majority of senators, including even freshmen, lead one or more subcommittees. This came about primarily in the second half of the 20th century.

A major event in the development of subcommittees was the passage of the LEGISLATIVE REORGANIZATION ACT OF 1946, which reorganized and combined standing committees, thereby igniting member interest in establishing subcommittees to address vacant policy areas. Next, amid the congressional reform movement in the early 1970s came the Subcommittee Bill of Rights of 1973, which further sparked the development of subcommittees, increasing their staff sizes and policy and program jurisdictions. The number of subcommittees and the influence of their chairs grew throughout the following decade. However, by the start of the 21st century subcommittees continued to evolve.

The Republican majority in the House has won passage of a series of chamber rules governing subcommittees. In 2003 they established a maximum of five subcommittees for most standing committees. Some committees were permitted to create a sixth committee for oversight purposes only. However, five committees were permitted to exceed the set subcommittee limit: APPROPRIATIONS, ARMED SERVICES, GOVERNMENT REFORM, INTERNATIONAL RELATIONS, and TRANSPORTATION AND INFRASTRUCTURE. In addition, representatives are limited to serving on no more than four subcommittees. Finally, committee chairs were given the power to hire and fire subcommittee chairs.

By the start of the 108th Congress the 19 standing committees of the House had been divided into 88 subcommittees, an average of 4.6 subcommittees per committee. While three committees (BUDGET, HOUSE ADMINISTRATION, and STANDARDS OF OFFICIAL CONDUCT) lacked any subcommittees, the Appropriations Committee had the most subcommittees, with 13.

Across Capitol Hill Senate rules governing subcommittees are not as restrictive as those found in the House. The 16 standing committees of the Senate were divided into 68 subcommittees, with an average of 4.25 subcommittees per committee. However, four committees lacked any subcommittees (BUDGET, RULES and ADMINISTRATION, SMALL BUSINESS AND ENTREPRENEURSHIP, and VETERANS' AFFAIRS), while APPROPRIATIONS had the most subcommittees, with 13. In addition, while senators were prohibited from chairing more than one subcommittee of each standing committee, numerous leadership opportunities remained for each senator.

Further reading:
Deering, Christopher. "The Ebb and Flow in Twentieth-Century Committee Power. In *Congress Responds to the Twentieth Century*, edited by Ahuja Sunil and Dewhirst Robert, Columbus: Ohio State University Press, 2003; Evans, Lawrence, and Richard Hall. "The Power of Subcommittees." *Journal of Politics* 52, no. 2 (1990) 335–356m; Smith, Steven, and Christopher Deering. *Committees in Congress.* 3d ed. Washington, D.C.: Congressional Quarterly Press, 1997.

—Karen McCurdy

subpoena power

Congress long has had the power to issue subpoenas, legal orders compelling witnesses to testify under oath or to produce documents or other evidence sought in connection with an investigation. This power, while never authorized by the Constitution, has rested on tradition, precedent, and statute.

The tradition in the HOUSE OF REPRESENTATIVES dates from a 1792 investigation into the causes of an American military defeat. In 1946 the LEGISLATIVE REORGANIZATION ACT authorized subpoena power to SENATE but not House standing committees because of opposition from that chamber's leaders. In 1975 the House finally received statutory authorization to issue subpoenas. In addition, subcommittees of standing committees in both chambers are authorized to issue subpoenas. However, special or select committees can issue subpoenas only if they are authorized to do so by the House or Senate resolution creating the panel.

By the end of the 20th century subpoenas had become a common tool in the hands of congressional committees to investigate and oversee the agencies and departments of the executive branch of the federal government. While presidents have successfully used executive privilege to fight off subpoena inquiries, other witnesses failing to comply with such summons can be legally cited for contempt of Congress and tried in federal court. The U.S. Supreme Court twice has upheld the power of Congress to issue subpoenas: in *McGrain v. Daugherty* (1927) and *Eastland v. U.S. Servicemen's Fund* (1975).

Further reading:
Grabow, John C. *The Law and Practice of Congressional Investigations.* Upper Saddle River, N.J.: Prentice Hall, 1991; Hamilton, James. *The Power to Probe: A Study of Congressional Investigations.* New York: Random House, 1976.

sunset laws

Laws that automatically terminate at the end of a period of time unless Congress formally renews them are said to have sunset provisions. The idea of setting a date when a law or government agency will expire is almost as old as the nation itself. The Sedition Act of 1798 included a provision requiring "That this act shall continue to be in force until March 3, 1801, and no longer." Since Thomas Jefferson defeated President John Adams in the election of 1800, the law remained in effect only during the final years of Adams's presidency. In a letter written to a friend in 1816, President Jefferson advocated a form of sunset law, arguing, "Every constitution, then, and every law, naturally expires at the end of 19 years. If it be enforced longer, it is an act of force, and not of right."

The modern conception of sunset legislation emerged out of the political reform movements of the 1970s. In his 1969 book *The End of Liberalism,* Theodore Lowi proposed a "tenure-of-statutes" act that would set a limit of from five to 10 years on the life of every law creating a federal agency. Lowi saw this limit as a way to keep government from becoming too large and inefficient.

Lowi's idea gained attention in the wake of the WATERGATE SCANDAL and calls for increased government accountability. Presidential candidate Jimmy Carter made increased accountability and reduction of the bureaucracy a key part of his 1976 campaign. The proposal also had the support of the public interest group Common Cause. The Colorado chapter of Common Cause is credited with coining the phrase *sunset legislation* in 1975 to describe laws similar to Lowi's proposed tenure-of-statute act.

In 1976 Common Cause advocated a federal sunset law to battle the entrenched interests of long-established government agencies and the inefficiency in bureaucracy. The Common Cause proposal would have required strict review and evaluation of almost all featured programs every few years. Only Social Security and a few other programs would have been exempt from sunset review. Some 70 sunset bills were introduced in the 94th Congress (1975–76), but the bills became trapped in STANDING COMMITTEES by members of Congress opposed to the automatic termination provisions. No bills were enacted.

Colorado passed the nation's first sunset law in 1976. By 1980 30 additional states adopted the innovation. With the support of prominent Senate Democrats and President Carter, a federal sunset bill passed the U.S. Senate in October 1978, but it was allowed to die in the House. Similar bills have been introduced in almost every subsequent Congress.

In April 2002 the Subcommittee on the Civil Service, Census and Agency Organization of the HOUSE COMMITTEE ON GOVERNMENT REFORM held a hearing on the Federal Sunset Act of 2001, a bill introduced by Texas representative Kevin Brady. The bill would have created a Federal Agency Sunset Commission. This commission would have reviewed every agency at least once every 12 years and submitted a recommendation for the reviewed agency's continuation, reorganization, or abolishment to Congress. There was no action on the bill after the hearing. Representative Brady reintroduced the bill in the 108th Congress in 2003. While it never enacted a comprehensive sunset law affecting federal agencies, Congress has included sunset provisions in many pieces of legislation. The law enacted in 1978 creating the independent counsel included a five-year sunset provision. The law was allowed to expire in 1998. The tax cut proposed by the Bush administration and enacted by Congress in 2001 was set to terminate in 2010. A 2003 reduction of taxes on capital gains and dividends was set to expire in 2013. Several provisions of the USA Patriot Act, enacted after the September 11, 2001, terrorist attacks were to be phased out after four years unless specifically reauthorized by Congress.

Further reading:
Benjamin, Matthew. "You Gotta Have a Gimmick." *U.S. News & World Report,* 26 May 2003, p. 39; Mooney, Chris. "Short History of Sunsets." *Legal Affairs.* Available online. URL: http://www.legalaffairs.org/issues/January-February-2004/story_mooney_janfeb04.msp 2004. Accessed January

16, 2006; Palmer, Elizabeth. "Terrorism Bill's Sparse Paper Train May Cause Legal Vulnerabilities." *CQ Weekly* 59, no. 41 (27 October 2001): 2,533–2,535; U.S. House of Representatives, Subcommittee on the Civil Service, Census and Agency Organization of the Committee on Government Reform. *Reforming Government: The Federal Sunset Act of 2001.* Report 107-188. Washington, D.C.: Government Printing Office, 2002.

—John David Rausch, Jr.

sunshine rules

The HOUSE OF REPRESENTATIVES and SENATE have "sunshine" rules that require committees to hold all meetings open to the public except when a majority of committee members vote to hold a closed session or when the matter under discussion involves national security or personnel issues. Prior to 1973 most congressional committee hearings were open to the public, but a 1972 Congressional Quarterly survey found that 80 percent of mark-up sessions were closed. In a mark-up session committee members amend and vote on legislation to be sent to the chamber floor. Organizations such as Common Cause, the League of Women Voters, the National Committee for an Effective Congress, and the United Auto Workers began a campaign to get Congress to open the mark-up sessions to the public. Group members believed citizens had a right to know how pieces of legislation were altered in committee and who advocated the changes applied to bills.

In the Senate Lawton Chiles, a Democrat from Florida, and William Roth, a Republican from Delaware, pushed for sunshine rules to be adopted by their chamber. The state of Florida was an early adopter of open meeting regulations in state government. Senator John Pastore, a Democrat from Rhode Island, told the Senate that opening mark-up sessions was an important step in regaining the public's trust in Congress. He argued that Americans held Congress in low esteem because they believed it had something to hide.

The House of Representatives adopted an open mark-up rule in 1973. The Senate rejected a similar rule that year. Senator Russell Long, a Democrat from Louisiana and an opponent of opening mark-up sessions to the public, believed that closed meetings produced better policy because they reduced the power of special interest groups to exert pressure on committees.

In the spirit of political reform that marked the immediate post-Watergate era, the Senate approved a rule that opened mark-up sessions in 1975. The vote was unanimous. The Senate's sunshine rule had limits. A mark-up session could be closed when the committee voted to do so to protect national security, internal staff information, trade secrets, identification of undercover law officers or informants, or other issues requiring confidentiality. Both chambers approved rules opening sessions of conference committees in 1975.

The sunshine rules worked as designed for a number of years after their adoption. Except when national security matters were discussed, most committee meetings were open. After only a few years a countertrend began to emerge. In 1979 Representative William Natcher, a Democrat from Kentucky, became chair of the HOUSE APPROPRIATIONS COMMITTEE's Subcommittee on Labor, Health and Human Services, and Education. Because the subcommittee dealt with the largest portion of domestic spending, Natcher thought it best to meet with closed doors. He was able to get the subcommittee members to approve closed sessions, a practice that continued until he left the subcommittee.

The HOUSE WAYS AND MEANS COMMITTEE held open sessions for a few years during the chairing of Representative Al Ullman, a Democrat from Oregon. In 1980, while marking up the reconciliation bill, it, too, changed its practices. The committee regularly held closed sessions while Representative Dan Rostenkowski, a Democrat from Illinois, was chair. A partial survey published in the *Washington Post* in 1985 found that several subcommittees of the HOUSE FOREIGN AFFAIRS COMMITTEE met in closed session. The House Appropriations Committee also regularly met in closed session, as did its subcommittees on defense, HUD and independent agencies, foreign operations, and energy and water development.

In 1985 the HOUSE ENERGY AND COMMERCE Subcommittee on Health and the Environment, a subcommittee that usually held open sessions, found an innovative method to avoid the sunshine rule. Instead of holding an open meeting or voting to close the meeting to the public, the subcommittee held a closed "caucus" to discuss health budget matters. The full committee in open session then agreed to the decisions reached by the caucus.

According to the sunshine rules, a committee or subcommittee decides by majority vote to conduct a meeting in executive, or closed, session. The vote to close the meeting also had to be taken in public. While these votes were largely along party lines, members of Congress expressed the belief that compromises were more easily reached out of the sight of lobbyists and when decisions were not formally recorded. Since the media also were kept out of closed sessions, there was less tendency on the part of committee members to perform for the television cameras.

The trend toward more closed committee sessions continued into the 1990s. In 1993 48 freshman Republican House members staged a protest to show their displeasure with the practice of the House Ways and Means Committee holding closed sessions. The committee would regularly vote along party lines to keep the public and the media out of committee meetings. Led by Representative Richard Pombo, a Republican from California, the freshman displayed a sign reading "Do not disturb!!! Democrats raising taxes!!!" on the committee door. The *Washington Post* noted that the Republican FRESHMEN decided on their course of action while caucusing behind closed doors.

The Republican Party was the majority party in the 104th Congress. In the House the Republicans reemphasized the sunshine rules on committees in the rules changes adopted on the opening day of Congress. The rule was amended to require the meetings and hearings open to the public also be open to broadcast and photographic media.

The sunshine rule governing the Senate can be found in Rule XXVI of the Standing Rules of the Senate. Committee meetings are governed by procedures found in House Rule XI, and committee hearings are governed by Rule X.

Further reading:
Cooper, Kenneth J. "GOP Freshman Knocking on Closed Doors." *Washington Post,* 13 May 1993 p. A25; Johnson, Charles W. *Constitution, Jefferson's Manual, and Rules of the House of Representatives.* House Document No. 107-284. Washington, D.C.: Government Printing Office, 2003; Rich, Spencer "Hill Panels 'Sunshine' Starts Clouding Over." *Washington Post,* 10 August 1985, p. A4; U.S. Senate. *Senate Manual.* Senate Document 107-1. Washington, D.C.: Government Printing Office, 2002.
—John David Rausch, Jr.

suspension of the rules
Suspension of the rules is a procedure primarily limited to the HOUSE OF REPRESENTATIVES for expediting legislative action by setting aside the chamber's regular rules. Measures or matters brought up "under suspension" are limited to 40 minutes of debate, are not subject to floor amendments (the member offering the suspension motion may include amendments to the measure as part of the motion), and require two-thirds approval for final passage. Suspending the rules has the practical effect of waiving all House rules under which members might otherwise make points of order against a measure and any of its provisions, which is why this legislative procedure is inevitably reserved for noncontroversial legislation. Although some studies indicate that motions to suspend the rules are occasionally made for other purposes, such as agreeing to conference reports or to concurring in a Senate amendment to a House bill. It is the most commonly used method by the House for considering legislation. Recent studies indicate that between one-third to one-half of bills and resolutions passed in recent Congresses have been considered under suspension.

Motions to suspend the rules are subject to the Speaker's discretion generally on Mondays and Tuesdays of each week and during the last six days of the annual congressional session. Members arrange in advance to be recognized for this purpose. The Speaker may defer voting on a suspension motion until a later time, inevitably at the request of the chair of the committee or subcommittee with legislative jurisdiction over the measure in question. Under the rules of the House, bills that fail to pass under suspension of the rules may be considered at a later stage.

To discourage suspension procedures for complex and controversial legislation, party rules set additional boundaries on the Speaker's discretion to consider bills under suspension. For example, the rules of the Republican Conference (and previously of the Democratic Caucus) discourage the Speaker from raising bills under suspension that exceed $100 million. Furthermore, the Republican Conference currently provides that the Speaker disregard suspension motions on measures that do not include a cost estimate, are not supported by the minority, or are opposed by more than one-third of a reporting committee's members, unless waived by a majority of the party's electoral leadership.

As some suggest, suspension of the rules is a procedural nexus between considering legislation by unanimous consent and resolutions, or special rules, reported from the HOUSE COMMITTEE ON RULES. For example, legislation void of any contention is likely to be called up and passed by unanimous consent. By contrast, complex and important measures are considered in the COMMITTEE OF THE WHOLE, debated and amended under the terms of the resolutions reported by the Rules Committee and adopted by the full House. In between is suspension of the rules, which limits opportunities for debate and amendment.

Suspending rules was originally a useful way for the House to supercede the regular order of business and take up bills leadership prioritized. Toward the end of Congress's second century, however, this practice became an enticing way for individual lawmakers to bring matters of their choice to the floor, thus disrupting the orderly consideration of legislation. As a consequence the House, in piecemeal fashion, has imposed restrictions on suspension motions, first limiting the days on which they could be offered, then requiring majority votes to consider them, and finally giving the Speaker the option to allow them through his or her discretionary power of recognition. According to several studies, by the 20th century the suspension procedure became a fairly routine method for accelerating legislative action on relatively noncontroversial measures and other matters.

Motions to suspend the rules in the SENATE are rare because they are debatable and, therefore, open to FILIBUSTERS or other dilatory tactics, and because the Senate has a tradition of operating by UNANIMOUS CONSENT. As in the House, when the Senate does vote to suspend one or more rules, a two-thirds vote is required. But different from the House, the Senate votes only on the motion to suspend and not at the same time to pass a measure.

Further reading:
Bach, Stanley. "Suspension of the Rules, the Order of Business, and the Development of Congressional Procedure." *Legislative Studies Quarterly* 15 (1990); Saturno, James V. *How Measures Are Brought to the House Floor: A Brief Introduction.* Washington, D.C.: Congressional Research Service, 2001; Oleszek, Walter J. *Congressional Procedures and the Policy Process.* 5th ed. Washington, D.C.: Congressional Quarterly Press, 2000.

—Colton C. Campbell

Swift & Co. v. United States 196 U.S. 518 (1905)

On July 2, 1890, Congress passed "An Act to Protect Trade and Commerce against Unlawful Restraints and Monopolies," more commonly known as the Sherman Antitrust Act. The Justice Department was charged with enforcing it, and in 1903 a special antitrust division was created for that purpose. Section 1 of the law states that every contract, combination in the form of trust or otherwise, or conspiracy in restraint of trade or commerce among the several states, or with foreign nations, is declared to be illegal. These offenses include price-fixing; divisions of customers, markets, and volume of production; boycotts or concerted refusals to sell; and tie-in sales. Section 2 of the law states that "every person or persons, who shall monopolize, or attempt to monopolize, or combine or conspire with any other person to monopolize any part of the trade or commerce among the several States or with foreign nations, shall be deemed guilty of a misdemeanor." The U.S. government may bring a civil suit under the law, which allows for divestiture and injunctions and may also bring a criminal suit with fines of up to $100,000 for each violation, up to three years imprisonment, or both.

The law is based on the Commerce Clause of the Constitution, found in Article I, Section 8, which gives Congress the power "to regulate Commerce with foreign Nations, and among the several States, and with the Indian Tribes." The purpose behind the law was to try to do something to curb the abuses of big business combinations that were formed in the period following the end of the Civil War and continued unabated to the end of the century. Consumers were at their mercy because, by controlling the markets, the big combinations were able to set prices on basic necessities. Small business firms were put out of business through price-cutting, and once a company was ruined a combination would raise prices. The first antitrust laws

were enacted by the states because popular discontent over abuses was first felt at the state level, but they were limited because the states can regulate only intrastate commerce. Thus, Congress passed the Sherman Act.

Once the law was enacted, the Justice Department tried to break up the sugar monopoly wherein one company had 98 percent control of American sugar refining but was dealt a severe blow by the Supreme Court in 1895 when the Court held that the refineries in question were involved with the manufacture of the product, which was not part of interstate commerce. Commerce succeeds to manufacture and is not part of it, according to an 8-1 Court, which did not find any intention to put a restraint on trade or commerce. The fact that trade or commerce might be indirectly affected was not enough (*UNITED STATES V. E. C. KNIGHT Co.*).

That was how matters stood when the Justice Department decided to try to break up another monopoly, this time involving shippers of fresh meat, by bringing a suit against them. *Swift & Co. v. United States* was decided by the Supreme Court in 1905. The government alleged that the companies would not bid against each other in the livestock markets of the different states, would bid up prices for a few days in order to induce shipments to the stock yards, would fix selling prices, and to that end would restrict shipments of meat when necessary. In addition, the government said that the companies established a uniform rule of credit to dealers, kept a black list of delinquents and would not sell meats to them, made uniform charges for the delivery of meats, and secured less than lawful freight rates to the exclusion of competitors. The defense of the companies was that the alleged activities all took place within one state, and therefore there was no involvement of interstate commerce, meaning no Sherman Act violation.

This time, however, a unanimous decision authored by Justice Oliver Wendell Holmes upheld the suit and enjoined the meat packers from their activities. He used the phrase "current of commerce" in the decision, referring to the fact that the dealers and their slaughtering establishments were largely in different states from those of the stockyards, and the sellers of the cattle were largely in different states than either. In addition, the sales were to persons in other states, and the shipments to other states were pursuant to such sales. Since some allegations were made against agents of the companies in other states, that indicated to the Court that at least some of the sales were in the original packages, which the Court in 1827 (*Brown v. Maryland*) said made it fall under the Commerce Clause.

Holmes said that the combination was directed at commerce among the states and therefore had a direct effect upon it. He found intent not merely to restrict competition among the parties, but to aid in an attempt to monopolize commerce. Separating different parts of commerce when they are part of the same process would result in decisions inconsistent with the intent of law. The current, or stream, of commerce concept has been an important development in enabling the federal government to curb abuses by big business that otherwise might have gone unpunished. Further, the broad definition of the Commerce Clause enunciated in this antitrust case has been used by the Court in other areas to justify expanded government regulations.

Further reading:
Langran, Robert, and Martin Schnitzer. *Government, Business, and the American Economy.* Upper Saddle River, N.J.: Prentice Hall, 2001; *Swift & Company v. United States,* 196 U.S. 518 (1905); White, G. Edward. *Justice Oliver Wendell Holmes. Law and the Inner Self.* New York: Oxford University Press, 1993.

—Robert W. Langran

T

tabling

Tabling is a parliamentary motion that, if adopted, kills the pending matter and ends debate. The motion to table a matter in the HOUSE OF REPRESENTATIVES is a procedural move to reject the matter without voting on its merits. Originally, the motion provided that a matter could be put aside while some other matters claimed the House's attention. In the modern House, if a motion to lay on the table is adopted, the matter being considered is killed. Hinds's *Precedents* relates that the old parliamentary usage of the motion was still in effect in 1806 and 1809 based on evidence showing that bills that were tabled were taken up later by the House. In 1841 Speaker John White, a Whig from Kentucky, ruled that a pending report laid on the table could be taken up again only by SUSPENSION OF THE RULES by a two-thirds vote. If applied to a proposed amendment to a piece of legislation, the motion to lay on the table has the same effect on the underlying legislation. This feature makes the motion a significant weapon to be used by members who would like to kill a piece of legislation.

A motion to table is not in order regarding a motion to adjourn, a motion to suspend the rules, a motion to recommit, or motions relating to the general order of business. Tabling also is not in order for motions that are not debatable or amendable. When the House has resolved itself into the COMMITTEE OF THE WHOLE, the motion to table is not in order at all. In fact, the motion to resolve into the Committee of the Whole is not subject to tabling. The motion to table is not debatable.

In the SENATE the motion to table is in order any time a question is pending before the Senate, except when the question is more privileged. The motions more privileged are the motion to adjourn, the motion to recess, and the motion to proceed to the consideration of executive business. Unlike in the House, a motion to table a proposed amendment to a bill does not affect the underlying bill. A reservation proposed to a treaty, if laid on the table, does not affect the treaty. The motion is not debatable. A motion to table requires a majority vote. A tie vote means that the motion loses. The lack of limitations in the Senate has encouraged senators to use the motion to dispose of a matter immediately, to test support for an amendment, or to avoid a direct up-or-down vote on a matter.

In 2001 Senate Republicans temporarily abandoned the use of the motion to table. The Senate was evenly divided, with 50 Democrats and 50 Republicans. A motion to table succeeds on a majority vote, requiring the presence of the vice president to break ties. The Republicans realized that amendments fail on a tie vote, so they could kill unfriendly amendments without the vice president's vote. In this way unfavorable Democratic amendments could be killed, so all the Republicans needed to do was to stop trying to table.

Further reading:
Hinds, Asher C. *Hinds' Precedents of the House of Representatives of the United States.* House Document 355. Washington, D.C.: Government Printing Office, 1907; Johnson, Charles W. *Constitution, Jefferson's Manual, and Rules of the House of Representatives.* House Document No. 107-284. Washington, D.C.: Government Printing Office, 2003; Parks, Daniel J. "Senate GOP Spares Cheney, Tables Tabling" *CQ Weekly,* 14 April 2001, 816; United States Senate. *Senate Manual.* Senate Document 107-1. Washington, D.C.: Government Printing Office, 2002.

—John David Rausch, Jr.

Taft, Robert A. (1889–1953) *Senator*

Robert Alphonso Taft was the son of William Howard Taft (1857–1930), the 27th president of the United States from 1909 to 1913 and Chief Justice of the U.S. Supreme Court (1921–30). His mother was Helen "Nellie" Herron (1861–1943), whose father, John Herron, had been a lawyer from Cincinnati and partner of President Rutherford B. Hayes. He was the nephew of Charles Phelps Taft

(1843–1923), who represented Ohio in the 54th Congress (1895–97). He had two younger siblings, a brother, Charles Phelps Taft (1897–1983), who was mayor of Cincinnati from 1955 to 1957, and a sister, Helen Herron Taft (1891–1987), who would become a professor of history and dean at Bryn Mawr College. In 1914 Taft married Martha Wheaton Bowers (1889–1958), whose father, Lloyd Wheaton Bowers, had been solicitor general of the United States in President Taft's administration from 1909 to 1910. They would have four children, William Howard Taft III (1915–91), Robert Taft. Jr. (1917–93), Lloyd Bowers Taft (1923–85), and Horace Dwight Taft (1925–1983).

Robert Taft attended public schools in Cincinnati and studied under American tutors in Manila, Philippine Islands (while his father served as commissioner and territorial governor from 1901 to 1903) and the Taft School (which had been founded by his uncle, Horace Dutton Taft) in Watertown, Connecticut, from 1903 to 1906. He graduated from Yale University in 1910 and graduated first in his class from the Harvard University Law School in 1913. Taft was offered, and rejected, a clerkship with Supreme Court justice Oliver Wendell Holmes, Jr. (1841–1935).

Taft returned to Ohio and was admitted to the Ohio bar in 1913. He entered private practice in Cincinnati with

Robert A. Taft *(Library of Congress)*

the firm of Maxwell and Ramsey, the position having been arranged by his father, who had been on the University of Cincinnati law faculty with one of the partners, Lawrence Maxwell, during the 1890s. Because of his poor eyesight, he was not eligible for military service in World War I. He joined government service during the war, serving as assistant counsel in the U.S. Food Administration from 1917 to 1918 and as counsel to the American Relief Administration in 1919, the agency (both were headed by Herbert Hoover) that provided food relief to eastern Europe following the end of the war. Returning to Ohio, Taft entered electoral politics by winning a seat in the Ohio state house of representatives in 1920. He sat in the house from 1921 to 1926, serving as the speaker and majority leader in 1926. That year he decided not to run for reelection and resumed the practice of law on a full-time basis with the firm of Taft, Stettinius, and Hollister, which he had helped found in 1924. Also in 1926 he helped found the Cincinnati Country Day School, which would be attended by three of his sons, Robert, Horace, and Lloyd.

Taft returned to the legislature, serving one term in the Ohio state senate (1931–32). He lost his seat in the Franklin Delano Roosevelt landslide of 1932. He spent the next five years rebuilding the Republican Party in Cincinnati, writing a new party constitution, expanding the party executive committee, and replacing many of the old machine leaders. While he supported federal relief programs, he believed that the National Recovery Act (NRA) and the Agricultural Adjustment Act (AAA), the centerpieces of Roosevelt's NEW DEAL, unnecessarily expanded the power of the federal government in the economy. He argued that the New Deal, if unchecked, would lead to socialism and political tyranny.

Taft was elected to the U.S. Senate as a Republican from Ohio in 1938, defeating the incumbent Democrat, Robert Bulkley (1880–1965). He was reelected in 1944 and 1950.

As a senator he was known as "Mr. Republican" for his opposition to Roosevelt's New Deal policies. He was an isolationist who attempted to keep the United States neutral during World War II. He opposed military aid to Great Britain and reinstating the military draft until the Japanese attack on Pearl Harbor in 1941. A conservative, his opposition to American involvement in the war was motivated by the same fear of overarching government control on which his opposition to the New Deal was based. In 1939 Taft said that war would lead to "an immediate demand for arbitrary power, unlimited control of wages, prices, and agriculture, and complete confiscation of private property." One British intelligence officer describer him as "a limited little man with ignoble values."

His opposition to internationalism continued after the defeat of the Axis powers. He opposed the Bretton Woods

Agreement (establishing the postwar international monetary system) and the Marshall Plan, arguing that it would not be worth the high taxes and inflation that he believed Secretary of State George C. Marshall's (1880–1959) plan to rebuild Europe would cause. He opposed the creation of the North Atlantic Treaty Organization (NATO), contending that rearming western Europe was a "waste of money, and that our economic health is essential to the battle against communism . . . arms should be sent only to a country really threatened by Russian military aggression." Taft believed that America, separated by oceans from Europe and Asia, was invulnerable: "Nothing can destroy this country, except the over-extension of our resources."

In postwar domestic policy, he was the Senate sponsor of the Taft-Hartley Act of 1947 (formally known as the Labor-Management Relations Act), which was designed to "level the playing field" in collective bargaining between labor and management. The law modified the National Labor Relations (Wagner) Act of 1935 by limiting some of the rights given to organized labor by that legislation. It was passed over the veto of President Harry S. Truman, who called it the "slave labor bill." The act outlawed the "closed shop" and permitted a "union shop" only after a majority vote by the employees. It prohibited jurisdictional strikes and secondary boycotts. Another provision prohibited contributions by labor unions to political campaigns and required labor union leaders to affirm that they were not members of the Communist Party. The act also empowered the attorney general to obtain 80-day injunctions when a strike or potential strike "imperiled the national health or safety."

Serving most of his Senate career as a member of the minority party, he was cochair of the Joint Committee on the Economic Report during the 80th Congress (1947–49); chair of the Committee on Labor and Public Welfare (80th Congress), and chair of the Republican Policy Committee from the 80th through the 82nd Congress (1947–53). In 1953 Taft became Senate MAJORITY LEADER when the Republicans took control of the Senate in Dwight Eisenhower's landslide victory in 1952. He held this post until his death.

Taft sought his party's presidential nomination four times. In 1936 he was a "favorite son" candidate from Ohio. In 1940 Taft lost the nomination in a four-way race (the other unsuccessful candidates were New York County district attorney Thomas E. Dewey, who had gained fame prosecuting organized crime figures in New York City and Michigan senator Arthur Vandenberg) to Wendell Wilkie (1892–1944), whose candidacy had been promoted by *Time Magazine* publisher Henry Luce (1898–1967). In 1948 he stepped aside for Dewey (1902–71), who had been elected governor of New York in 1942 and who had been defeated by Roosevelt in 1944, and in 1952 he finished second to General Eisenhower in the balloting for the Republican nomination.

Shortly after becoming Majority Leader, Taft was diagnosed with cancer. He died in New York City on July 31, 1953. Taft is buried in the Indian Hill Episcopal Church Cemetery in Cincinnati.

His son, Robert Taft, Jr., served in the U.S. House of Representatives from 1963 to 1965 and 1967 to 1971. He then was a U.S. senator from 1971 to 1977. His grandson, Bob Taft (1942–   ), was elected governor of Ohio in 1998 and reelected in 2002.

Further reading:
Doenecke, Justin D. *Not to the Swift: The Old Isolationists in the Cold War Era.* Lewisburg, Penn.: Bucknell University Press, Cranbury, 1979; Harnsberger, Caroline Thomas. *A Man of Courage: Robert A. Taft.* Chicago: Wilcox Follett, 1952; Kirk, Russell, and James McClellan. *The Political Principles of Robert A. Taft.* New York: Fleet Press, 1967; Moser, John. "Principles without Program: Senator Robert A. Taft and American Foreign Policy." *Ohio History* 108 (1999); Patterson, James T. *Mr. Republican: A Biography of Robert A. Taft.* Boston: Houghton Mifflin, 1972; Robbins, Jhan, and June Robbins. *Eight Weeks to Live: The Last Chapter in the Life of Robert A. Taft.* Garden City, N.Y.: Doubleday, 1954; Robbins, Phyllis. *Robert A. Taft, Boy and Man.* Cambridge, Mass.: Dresser, Chapman, Grimes, 1963; Taft, Robert Alphonso. *A Foreign Policy for Americans.* Garden City, N.Y.: Doubleday, 1951; Van Dyke, Vernon, and Edward Lane Davis. "Senator Taft and American Security." *Journal of Politics* 14, no. 2 (May 1952): 177–202.

—Jeffrey Kraus

term limitations

The question of whether senators and representatives should be restricted in the number of terms they can serve in one chamber of Congress has been a point of contention since the debate surrounding the ratification of the Constitution in 1788. Although the Constitution did not allow for enforced rotation of officeholders in Congress, many states adopted such procedures for their own governments in the early 19th century. Today 18 states restrict the number of terms their state legislators can serve, and 38 states have similar restrictions on their governors. Under the Twenty-second Amendment to the Constitution, the president of the United States is limited to serving two terms. With no constitutional limitation on the number of terms members of Congress can serve, 23 states have attempted to impose a limit on their own congressional delegations. However, in *U.S. Term Limits Inc. v. Thornton* (1995), the Supreme Court voted 5-4 to declare such state provisions unconstitutional and end the practice.

For advocates of term limits, such restrictions would prevent the problems associated with a Congress populated by long-term career politicians. Members of Congress, as incumbents, hold a number of advantages over their future electoral opponents, which has led to a situation in which regularly more than 90 percent of senators and representatives who stand for reelection are successfully returned to the next Congress. Such stability of membership, it is argued, runs the danger of Congress losing touch with the opinions and priorities of the general public and makes it difficult for challengers with fresh ideas to win election; indeed, the nature of incumbency advantage can discourage potential challengers from running at all. If new people manage to gain a seat in Congress, they face a body dominated by experienced members with knowledge, connections, and control of the process via the advantages of seniority in the committee and party structures. The tendency is for Congress to act and legislate in the way that it always has done, regardless of whether other approaches might be more successful. This situation has contributed to the long periods of single-party dominance experienced by Congress throughout the 20th century. If limits were introduced, forcing members of Congress to stand down after completing a fixed number of terms, it is argued that this would guarantee more open elections and a healthy turnover of personnel, bringing new ideas and approaches to the federal legislature. It may also help to break the close relationships between longstanding members and interest groups.

Opponents of term limits argue that they are essentially antidemocratic; denying the electorate the power to reelect a member of Congress who has been doing a good job. They contend that if senators or representatives do lose touch with their voters they will be voted out at the next election and replaced with someone with ideas more attractive to the electorate. Just because a candidate is new to Congress does not mean that he or she will automatically be better at the job than the present incumbent. Experienced legislators, rather than being something to be avoided, are an important part of successful government. Not only do they bring an understanding of how government functions, but through years spent in committees members of Congress can possess a wealth of knowledge about often complex or technical issues. James Madison in Federalist 53 advanced this argument, that, "a few of the members of Congress will possess superior talents; will by frequent re-elections, become members of long standing; will be thoroughly masters of the public business, and perhaps not unwilling to avail themselves of those advantages. The greater the proportion of new members of Congress, and the less the information of the bulk of the members, the more apt they be to fall into the snares that may be laid before them." The argument continues that even if Congress did have a regular turnover of members, this would not mean that first-term senators or representatives would avoid the problems of competing with more senior members; posts in the committees and parties will still be filled with more experienced legislators.

An attempt was made to introduce term limits for members of Congress by the Republican majority leadership of the House of Representatives in the 104th Congress. The idea had been included in the House Republicans' CONTRACT WITH AMERICA. It was perhaps not surprising that Republicans seemed to be in favor of imposing term limitations considering the dominance of Democrats in the House of Representatives over the previous four decades. Under the proposals senators would be limited to two terms and House members either three or six (two options were under discussion). In the final vote a majority of House members supported the proposal (227-224), with 38 Democrats voting for and 40 Republicans voting against. In this case, however, a simple majority was insufficient to pass the measure. The Supreme Court had ruled that the introduction of congressional term limits would require a constitutional amendment, and therefore a two-thirds majority was needed to pass the measure out of the House of Representatives. Although the proposal failed, it is of note that a majority of representatives appeared to be willing to approve a constitutional amendment that would have the effect of eventually ending their careers in Congress.

While the latest attempt to impose term limitations was unsuccessful, a handful of members have chosen to adopt self-imposed limits, pledging during their election campaigns to stand down after a specified number of terms. Once elected, however, not all keep this pledge. For instance, Representative Martin Meehan (D-MA), first elected in 1992, pledged to stand down after eight years of service, and George Nethercutt (R-WA), first elected in 1994, promised he would retire after only six years. Once ensconced in Congress, both changed their minds and were still in office at the start of the 107th Congress. Nethercutt explained that "experience . . . taught me that six years may be too short a time to do the job the people . . . elected me to do." Meehan argued that campaign finance reform was of such importance that he needed to stay in the House. In contrast to Nethercutt and Meehan, some House members did indeed stick to their own personal term limits. Elizabeth Furse (D-OR), (elected in 1992), and Jack Metcalf (R-WA), elected in 1994, both declined to run for reelection after serving three consecutive terms.

Further reading:
Carey, J. M. *Term Limits and Legislative Representation.* New York: Cambridge University Press, 1998; Carey, J. M., R. G. Niemi et. al., *Term Limits in the State Legislatures.* Ann Arbor: University of Michigan Press, 2000; Grofman, B. *Legislative Term Limits: Public Choice Perspectives.* Boston: Kluwer Academic Publishers, 1996.

—Ross English

terms and sessions of Congress

Congress has organized its meetings into terms and sessions. A term for Congress is a two-year period, corresponding to the two-year term of office for members of the HOUSE OF REPRESENTATIVES indicated in Article I, Section 2, of the Constitution. For each biennium of Congress there are two sessions, with each session representing approximately one year of the two-year term, consistent with the Article I, Section 4, requirement that Congress must assemble at least once each year.

Members of Congress are elected in November of even-numbered years. Elected members then take office at noon on January 3 of the following odd-numbered year, in accordance with the provisions of the TWENTIETH AMENDMENT. All House members and approximately one-third of SENATE members complete their terms of office two years later at noon on January 3, when those terms end. This biennium, or congressional life cycle, is labeled a Congress, and Congresses have been numbered consecutively since ratification of the Constitution, when the first Congress began its service in 1789.

The following illustration should make this clear. The 108th Congress covered the period 2003–04; it was called the 108th Congress because it was the 108th Congress to convene for a biennium following the first Congress that operated during the period 1789–91. Members of the 108th Congress were elected in November 2002; they were sworn in at the beginning of the 108th Congress in January 2003; the first session of the 108th Congress began in January 2003 and ended in January 2004; and the second session of the 108th Congress began in January 2004 and ended in January 2005.

Unlike House members, who are elected for a term of two years that corresponds to a sequentially numbered Congress, Senate members are elected for a six-year term in accordance with Article I, Section 3, of the Constitution. The six-year term for senators spans three consecutively numbered Congresses, and because their individual senatorial terms do not end after each two-year term of a numbered Congress, all senators are not sworn in at the beginning of each new Congress, as are all House members. Rather, senators are sworn in only once, at the beginning of their six-year term.

While the explanation of individual House and Senate member terms and terms of Congress may seem complicated, it was even more complex preceding 1876, when a uniform election day, "the first Tuesday after the first Monday in November," was set in all the states; prior to that time the states had different election dates. Moreover, before the ratification of the SEVENTEENTH AMENDMENT in 1913, which provided for direct popular election of senators, replacing the appointment of senators by state legislatures, legislatures appointed their senators on different dates as well. And prior to the ratification of the TWENTIETH AMENDMENT, the terms of members of Congress ended on March 4. The meaning of *term* is now more settled for both Congress and its members.

The label *session* has several applications in addition to the particular first and second annual periods that make up a two-year life cycle of a specific Congress already described. When the House and Senate assemble in regular session to conduct business, they are in session on most weekdays until adjournment, usually in the fall. Article I, Section 5, of the Constitution does not permit one chamber to adjourn for more than three days without the concurrence of the other. Once a Congress adjourns sine die, or indefinitely, it meets again if the president calls a special or extraordinary session under Article II, Section 3. Chamber annual schedules do not generally include sessions on Saturdays, Sundays, or legal holidays. When in regular session—either the first regular session during the first odd-numbered year of the biennium or the second regular session during the even-numbered year of the biennium—the chambers and their committees are in "open" session and able to conduct business publicly except when they go into "closed" or "executive" session because of the sensitive nature of their discussions and work (national security, the discussion of criminal activity, etc.). There can also be a "secret" session to receive confidential communications from the president or others when members believe such matters ought to be kept secret for a time. *Joint* session refers to a combined session of members of the House and Senate, most often convened to hear the STATE OF THE UNION MESSAGE or another significant address from the president, or particular speeches from foreign dignitaries or heads of state, or even for inaugurations and electoral vote counting purposes. Joint sessions rarely take longer than part of a day.

Another type of session has the unique name of "LAME DUCK." Congresses in earlier times assembled in regular session on the first Monday in December in accordance with Article I, Section 4, of the Constitution and sometimes met until March 4 of the following year, when their terms of office then expired. When such a session occurred, the members of Congress who assembled after the November elections were lame ducks because they had been defeated by the voters or did not stand for reelection. The Twentieth Amendment to the Constitution, termed the Lame Duck Amendment, set the terms for members of Congress to begin at noon on January 3, and it also moved the opening of Congress itself to January 3 unless by law Congress designated a different day (often Congress begins its regular session later in January).

While this change had the effect of reducing the need for lame duck sessions, it has not eliminated them. Occasionally Congress has concluded to meet after the

November election to take up unfinished business, and these lame duck sessions have been convened by congressional resolution rather then presidential proclamation. Since ratification of the Twentieth Amendment, through the year 2003 there have been 13 lame duck sessions of Congress. Generally, however, there are not lame duck sessions scheduled in even-numbered years, as the November or December period after such congressional elections is used to conduct early organization, orientation, and education meetings (not sessions of Congress) to allow members to get a leg up in addressing pressing needs that will be taken up in January, when the new Congress convenes.

Further reading:

Schneider, Judy. *Congress' Early Organization Meetings.* Washington, D.C.: Congressional Research Service, 1996; U.S. House of Representatives. *Rules of the House of Representatives: 108th Congress.* Prepared by Jeff Trandahl. Washington, D.C.: U.S. Government Printing House, 2003; U.S. House of Representatives. *Session Dates of Congress.* Available online. URL: http://clerk.house.gov/histHigh/Congressional_History/Session_Dates/index.html. Accessed 15 July 2004; U.S. Senate. *Sessions of Congress.* Available online. URL: http://www.senate.gov/reference/common/generic/Sessions.htm. Accessed 15 July 2004.

—Robert P. Goss

Thomas, Clarence, U.S. Supreme Court Nomination of

On July 1, 1991, President George H. W. Bush announced his nomination of 43-year-old Clarence Thomas, a junior judge on the U.S. Court of Appeals for the D.C. Circuit, to fill the Supreme Court vacancy created by liberal African-American jurist Thurgood Marshall's retirement four days earlier. Largely because his nomination constituted what scholars have termed a "critical nomination" in that it threatened to change the ideological balance on the closely divided Court by replacing a liberal justice with a conservative one, both the White House and its allies in the Senate anticipated that winning Thomas's confirmation in the Democratically controlled Senate would be difficult.

Though he was a sitting federal appellate judge at the time of his nomination, Thomas, an African American, had relatively little experience as a jurist. In fact, because he was appointed to the D.C. court of appeals in 1990, his tenure as a federal judge spanned just more than a year. Nonetheless, his accomplishments, legal and otherwise, were impressive. He had risen from poverty-stricken rural Georgia to graduate from Yale Law School and then served as Missouri's assistant attorney general before going on to work for Senator John C. Danforth, a Republican from Missouri, as a legislative assistant. Then, after a brief stint

at the U.S. Department of Education, Thomas went on to chair the Equal Employment Opportunity Commission (EEOC) for most of the 1980s until being tapped by President Bush for an associate judgeship on the D.C. court of appeals in 1990. Still, despite his extensive career of public service, many contemporary observers remained convinced that the president had nominated Thomas to the Supreme Court largely because he was an African American.

Between the nomination's announcement in July and the beginning of Thomas's Senate hearings in September 1991, numerous interest groups and organizations began to stake out positions on the nomination. In both the Senate and political society as a whole, much of the debate centered on speculation concerning Thomas's specific attitudes toward *Roe v. Wade* and the overall question of legalized abortion. Although he would later decline to address his position on abortion before the Senate Judiciary Committee, pro-choice groups such as the National Organization for Women, the National Abortion Rights Action League, and the Planned Parenthood Federation of America wasted no time in mounting a vigorous campaign to derail his confirmation.

More generally, Thomas's conservative political ideology and tenure at the EEOC, during which some had charged him with allowing age discrimination cases to expire without action, caused other liberal lobbies including the American Civil Liberties Union, People for the American Way, and the Alliance for Justice to strongly oppose his elevation to the Supreme Court.

On September 10, 1991, Senator Joseph R. Biden, Jr., a Democrat from Delaware, convened the Senate Judiciary Committee, which he chaired, so it could formally consider the president's nomination of Clarence Thomas to be an associate justice of the Supreme Court. The committee held hearings through September 20, 1991, during which time several Democratic senators, notably Howard Metzenbaum, peppered the nominee with questions about his views on such legal issues as abortion, civil rights, and the philosophy of natural law. The Republicans, led by Utah senator Orrin Hatch and the committee's ranking Republican, Senator STROM THURMOND of South Carolina, mounted a spirited defense of their president's nominee. After Thomas had testified for five days, the committee brought in a series of witnesses who were questioned about their interactions with and impressions of Thomas's fitness for the Supreme Court.

On September 27, 1991, the Senate Judiciary Committee voted to consider recommending Judge Thomas's nomination to the full Senate. With the lone exception of Senator Dennis DeConcini, a conservative Democrat from Arizona who favored Thomas's confirmation, the Judiciary Committee's vote split along party lines and deadlocked at a 7-7 vote. Although congressional committees must generally produce a majority in order to report any action to the floor, the Senate's treatment of nominees to the Supreme Court is unique in this regard. In the case of these judicial nominations, Senate norms dictate that nominees are generally entitled to a vote on the floor of the full Senate, regardless of the outcome of the Judiciary Committee's vote. Consequently, after the committee had failed to approve the nomination, Senator Thurmond simply moved that the nomination be sent to the floor without the recommendation of the committee, and that motion passed by a 13-1 margin.

Despite the fact that the Thomas nomination was not approved by a majority of the Senate Judiciary Committee, it was generally conceded that the nomination would likely be approved when the full Senate considered it in October. However, on October 5, 1991, the dynamics of the nomination changed dramatically. On that date reporters for National Public Radio (NPR) and *Newsday* revealed they had discovered that an allegation of sexual harassment had been communicated to the Senate Judiciary Committee earlier in summer 1991 by Anita Hill, a University of Oklahoma law professor and former Thomas aide.

In her written statement to the committee, Hill had alleged that Thomas had sexually harassed her during the time she worked under him at both the Department of Education and the Equal Employment Opportunity Commission. Hill charged that Thomas's harassment included inappropriate discussions of sexual acts and pornographic films after she snubbed his repeated attempts to date her. Despite the fact that both the allegation and an FBI report on the allegation, which included interviews with both Hill and Thomas, had been given to the Judiciary Committee weeks earlier, several members of the committee were not even aware of Hill's allegations when they voted to send Thomas's nomination to the floor on September 27, 1991.

Once the story had been leaked, the Judiciary Committee reopened hearings on the Thomas nomination, largely at the request of feminist organizations and seven female Democratic members of the House of Representatives. Both Professor Hill and Judge Thomas testified at these hearings. Supporters of Hill, already angered by what they perceived to be the Judiciary Committee's prior neglect of the information, argued that sexual harassment was a serious accusation that raised serious questions about Thomas's fitness for a lifetime appointment to the U.S. Supreme Court.

Thomas's supporters, led by his political patron, Missouri senator John C. "Jack" Danforth, testified to Thomas's high moral character and raised several questions of their own about the credibility of Hill's allegations. Why, they wondered, had her accusations failed to surface until 10 years after Thomas's inappropriate behavior had allegedly occurred? They were also skeptical because of the fact that

Hill came forward with her allegations only after other efforts to defeat Thomas's nomination had apparently failed. They wondered why Hill had chosen to come forward during this particular Senate confirmation rather than one of the previous two that Thomas had undergone. Finally, they questioned why a woman who claimed she had been harassed by her employer at the Department of Education would follow that same employer to his new post at the EEOC.

Taking place against a backdrop of media coverage frenzy, this second set of hearings was in many ways nothing short of theatrical. A number of Republican senators bluntly challenged Hill's credibility and, at times, her mental and emotional stability. On the other side, Thomas's perception of his unfair treatment at the hands of committee Democrats in general and Chair Biden in particular led him to refer to the hearings as "a national disgrace, a high-tech lynching for uppity blacks who in any way deign to think for themselves, to do for themselves."

Ultimately, Hill's accusations and Thomas's vehement denial of those accusations became little more than a classic case of "he said, she said," in which neither side could definitively prove their recollection of events. The day after the Hill-Thomas hearings concluded, the nomination was debated by the full Senate, where many senators came to the floor and delivered fiery speeches both in support of and in opposition to Thomas's elevation to the Supreme Court.

Finally, on October 16, 1991, the full Senate voted to confirm Clarence Thomas as an associate justice of the U.S. Supreme Court in a 52-48 vote—the narrowest margin by which any Supreme Court nominee won Senate confirmation since 1888. All but two of the 43 Republican senators, Oregon's Robert Packwood and Vermont's James Jeffords, voted in favor of confirmation. By contrast, 11 of the 46 Democratic senators, most of whom were conservative southerners, broke party ranks to support Thomas's elevation to the Supreme Court.

The aftermath of the Thomas confirmation brought about a number of important developments. Most immediately, Thomas's ascent to the Supreme Court gave the Court a solid conservative majority that would over the coming years effectively instill that conservatism into many of the cases it decided and, on occasion, use the majority to roll back some of the Court's more liberal decisions from years past. The Thomas confirmation also awakened Americans to the issue of sexual harassment, which soon became a societal catchphrase. Finally, some have argued that the initial reluctance of the Senate Judiciary Committee to lend credibility to Hill's claims brought about a surge in the participation of women in national politics. Subsequently, 1992 was proclaimed by many to be the "Year of the Woman" after the Senate gained four new female members and 24 more were first elected to the House of Representatives in that year's congressional elections. Some observers have suggested this increase may have been a direct result of female outrage over the male-dominated Senate's handling of the Thomas-Hill controversy.

Further reading:
Danforth, John C. *Resurrection: The Confirmation of Clarence Thomas.* New York: Viking, 1994; Greenya, John. *Silent Justice: The Clarence Thomas Story.* Fort Lee, N.J.: Barricade Books, 2001; Mayer, Jane, and Jill Abramson. *Strange Justice: The Selling of Clarence Thomas.* Boston: Houghton Mifflin, 1994; Overby, L. Marvin, Beth M. Henschen, Michael H. Walsh, and Julie Strauss. "Courting Constituents? An Analysis of the Senate Confirmation Vote on Justice Clarence Thomas." *American Political Science Review* 86 (1992): 997–1,003; Phelps, Timothy M., and Helen Winternitz. *Capitol Games: Clarence Thomas, Anita Hill, and the Story of a Supreme Court Nomination.* New York: Hyperion, 1992.

—Brett Curry

Thurmond, Strom (1902–2003) *Senator*

Strom Thurmond was a legendary senator from South Carolina and catalyst in the demise of the Democratic "solid South" in electoral politics. The oldest and longest-serving U.S. senator in history, Thurmond's personal transformation on racial issues mirrored that of white southern society during the late 20th century.

Thurmond grew up in rural South Carolina the son of a lawyer and once promising politician whose career foundered over the slaying of a man who had accosted him. At age six Strom learned to shake hands from the inflammatory U.S. senator and former governor "Pitchfork" Ben Tillman. As a teenager Thurmond, a highly motivated and ambitious young man, displayed what would be lifelong passions for athletics and pursuing women. In 1919 he began studies at Clemson College, then an all-male military institution. He continued to hone an extraordinary competitiveness through sports, the campus literary society, and establishing an influential social network. Thurmond graduated in 1923 with a horticulture degree and spent most of the next five years teaching high school while dabbling in failed financial ventures. In 1928 he won election as a county superintendent of education and proceeded to rejuvenate a woefully inadequate public school system.

Once engaged in politics, Thurmond's rise proved meteoric. He passed the bar exam in 1930 and campaigned successfully for state senator two years later. As a Democrat and F. D. Roosevelt supporter, Thurmond concentrated on issues concerning education and public works. In 1938 he became the state's youngest circuit court judge.

Although his occupation exempted him from military service, the former army reservist reported for duty after the Pearl Harbor attack. As a civil affairs officer in the First Army, he volunteered to land behind enemy lines with the 82nd Airborne during the invasion of Normandy. Thurmond participated in the Battle of the Bulge and the liberation of the Buchenwald concentration camp. He retired from active duty in 1945 as a lieutenant colonel with a Purple Heart and Bronze Star among numerous decorations. Remaining in the Army Reserve, he ultimately reached the rank of major general.

Thurmond parleyed his growing stature in South Carolina into a successful gubernatorial bid in 1946 as a progressive Democrat. While campaigning he maintained a low profile on racial matters that would not last for long. In 1947 the longtime bachelor married Jean Crouch, a woman 23 years his junior. *Life Magazine* ran a photograph of Governor Thurmond in shorts standing on his head in an attempt to demonstrate physical prowess on the eve of the wedding. The two remained devoted to each other over 12 years before Jean succumbed to an inoperable brain tumor.

For the new governor national events soon dominated his political horizons. Incensed over President Harry Truman's civil rights agenda, Thurmond accepted nomination as a third-party States' Rights Democrat (Dixiecrat) candidate for the presidency, running in the spirit of segregation. Philosophically, he perceived the president's intentions as an assault on the federalist basis of the American governmental system. Politically, he probably appreciated that South Carolina governors could not succeed themselves, and therefore he had begun to position himself for higher office. Thurmond maintained that African Americans lived well in the South and that "all the laws of Washington and the bayonets of the army cannot force the Negro into our homes, our schools, our churches, and our places of recreation and amusement." To what extent the language of states' rights served as a codeword for expressing virulent notions of racial superiority remains open to interpretation. Thurmond carried four southern states and roughly 2 percent of the popular vote in the 1948 presidential election. As he predicted, the Democratic Party could no longer take the South for granted, as his insurgency signaled a major voter realignment that would crystallize in the 1960s.

Thurmond lost a bruising Democratic primary battle for a U.S. Senate seat in 1950 with incumbent Olin Johnston. After several years of practicing law, he became the first successful write-in candidate for Congress in U.S. history when he triumphed in a 1954 special Senate election created by the death of Burnet Maybank. He kept a promise to South Carolinians by resigning the office after two years but then won the 1956 election designed to fill his seat.

In response to the *Brown v. Board of Education* desegregation decision by the U.S. Supreme Court, most white southerners in Congress initially counseled a quiet resistance based on using seniority and parliamentary procedures. But Thurmond and Senator Harry Byrd, Sr., a Democrat from Virginia, spearheaded the 1956 "Southern Manifesto" as a more bellicose stance against civil rights initiatives. When the 1957 Civil Rights Act came before the Senate, Thurmond joined a southern FILIBUSTER that extracted key concessions from the bill's supporters, including Senate Majority Leader LYNDON JOHNSON, a Democrat from Texas. The southern caucus, led by Senate impresario RICHARD RUSSELL, a Democrat from Georgia, decided to accept these compromises, but Thurmond exhorted them to continue the fight by attempting a single-handed crusade. He established a Senate record by FILIBUSTERing 24 hours and 18 minutes before relenting for a cloture vote that cut off debate. Although even some southern colleagues resented the grandstanding, they respected the dogged determination and political showmanship of the junior senator.

By the early 1960s this member of the SENATE ARMED SERVICES COMMITTEE made an aggressive prosecution of the cold war a centerpiece of his political appeal. He grew increasingly convinced that the Democratic Party had endangered national security and given in to its northern prointegration wing. Declaring that "the party of our fathers is dead," Thurmond switched to the Republicans and endorsed Barry Goldwater in the 1964 presidential campaign. He maintained his Senate seniority and rose in Republican estimations by supporting Richard Nixon in 1968 instead of southern third-party candidate George Wallace. This maneuver helped solidify the Republican "southern strategy" used so effectively in Nixon's electoral triumphs. Thurmond played a leading role in challenging the appointment of Abe Fortas as chief justice of the U.S. Supreme Court in 1968 and helped convince the liberal jurist to withdraw from consideration.

Thurmond established himself as one of the most colorful members of an institution noted for eccentric behavior. In 1964 he engaged in a wrestling match outside a committee room with Senator Ralph Yarborough, a Democrat from Texas. When Thurmond attempted to dissuade colleagues from establishing a QUORUM for a hearing, Yarborough suggested that the two 61-year-old legislators and army reservists in the same unit race for the door. Thurmond knocked Yarborough to the floor and grappled with him before decorum was restored. In 1968 Thurmond enhanced his larger-than-life reputation by marrying Nancy Moore, a Miss South Carolina from just three years earlier. The couple had four children, though their oldest daughter was killed by a drunk driver in 1993. Strom and Nancy never divorced but grew estranged as the latter battled alcoholism.

In 1970 Thurmond became the only member of the South Carolina congressional delegation to hire an African

American to his staff. Thus began a gradual reconciliation process with the black community by a former race-baiter. In 1993 Coretta Scott King invited the senator to an inaugural reception, and three years later he took more than 15 percent of the black vote in South Carolina, which exceeded all previous Republican totals in statewide campaigns during the modern era.

In 1981 Thurmond took over the chair of the JUDICIARY COMMITTEE and began serving as President Pro Tempore of the Senate. He swore in Clarence Thomas as the Reagan administration's Equal Employment Opportunity Commission chair and backed the judge firmly in his subsequent confirmation as the second African-American justice in U.S. Supreme Court history. Preparing to turn 100 in 2002, Thurmond declined to seek another Senate term. Several months after retiring, he died on June 26, 2003, in his hometown of Edgefield, South Carolina. Posthumous revelations confirmed earlier reports that Thurmond fathered an illegitimate child in 1925 with his African-American maid. He and his daughter enjoyed a warm though clandestine relationship. Thurmond never explicitly apologized for his behavior concerning race relations, which raised doubts as to the sincerity of his political metamorphosis. Even his retirement generated controversy as then Senate MAJORITY LEADER TRENT LOTT, a Republican from Mississippi, referred sympathetically (though vaguely) to the implications of a Thurmond presidential victory in 1948 and ended up forced to resign his leadership position over the ensuing firestorm. Through a long career marked by calculated political theatricality and a steady response to constituent needs, Strom Thurmond left an indelible and personal imprint on American politics.

Further reading:
Bass, Jack, and Marilyn Thompson. *Ol' Strom: An Unauthorized Biography of Strom Thurmond*. Atlanta: Longstreet Press, 1998; Cohodas, Nadine. *Strom Thurmond and the Politics of Southern Change*. New York: Simon & Schuster, 1993.

—Jeffrey D. Bass

Tonkin Gulf Resolution

Enacted by Congress in 1964 at the urging of President LYNDON JOHNSON and repealed in 1970, the Tonkin Gulf Resolution was an element in the continuing give-and-take between the president and Congress about the power to make war during the Vietnam War era. It was adopted in haste by large majorities, 414-0 in the House and 88-2 in the Senate, on August 7, 1964. Participants in its enactment later disagreed among themselves about its meaning.

On August 2, 1964, when American involvement in Vietnam was quite limited, North Vietnamese patrol boats attacked American destroyers in the Gulf of Tonkin. On the president's orders American flyers struck back at their bases on August 4. President Johnson promptly addressed the American people about the counterattack in a nationally televised speech. Then he requested Congress to enact a resolution that would convince the "aggressive Communist nations" in the world that the United States was resolute in its policy to bring peace and security to Southeast Asia.

Formally titled the Joint Resolution to Promote the Maintenance of International Peace and Security in Southeast Asia, it expressed congressional support and approval for "the determination of the President . . . to take all necessary measures to repel any armed attack against the forces of the United States," and "as the President determines, to take all necessary steps" to help defend the freedom of South Vietnam. With nearly complete unanimity, the House and Senate adopted the proposed resolution prepared for them by the White House. Politically, the move was adroit. It neutralized criticism from Barry Goldwater, the Republican candidate for president in 1964, who had called for more aggressive American action in Vietnam. The Harris Opinion Polls showed a prompt increase in Johnson's popularity with the citizenry.

Although U.S. troop levels were still small in 1964 (about 23,000), they rose rapidly to more than half a million in 1968. Concerns about the war and the president's interpretation of the resolution grew in Congress as the war intensified and public opposition to it increased. In oversight hearings held by Congress, Secretary of State Dean Rusk claimed the resolution a grant of authority to justify the widening war. In 1967 Under Secretary of State Nicholas Katzenbach asserted to the SENATE FOREIGN RELATIONS COMMITTEE that the resolution was the equivalent of a declaration of war by Congress. Debate in the committee eventually resulted in a statement from it that "the question of authority to commit the United States to war is in need of clarification."

In 1968 President Johnson withdrew from the presidential campaign, and Richard Nixon came to the presidency pledging to end the war in a solution of peace with honor. The quarrel over the president's war authority continued, and some in Congress sought to pass limits on the prosecution of the war. Those efforts received greater support in the Senate than in the House. On June 24, 1970, the Senate attached an amendment to repeal the Tonkin Gulf Resolution to what was called the Military Sales Bill. The vote in favor was 81-10. Held up in the House until the end of 1970, the bill was finally cleared and signed by President Nixon (PL 91-672).

A startling new version of the event surrounding the Tonkin Gulf incident became public in 1971 because of the publication of the *Pentagon Papers,* the Defense Department's documentary history of the Vietnam conflict. President Johnson had described the counterattack on North Vietnamese patrol boats as a defensive action. New information showed that the American commander, General William Westmoreland, provoked the attacks. In fact, an early draft of what became the Tonkin Gulf Resolution already existed in May 1964. The administration and the military planned and coordinated events in the Tonkin Gulf to obtain congressional approval to enlarge U.S. action in Vietnam, and the quick passage of the resolution accomplished that purpose with a minimum of public and congressional debate.

Despite the fact that the resolution had already been repealed in 1970, the clear evidence that President Johnson had used the Tonkin Gulf incident deceptively to rally Congress behind the president's application of military power in Vietnam was instructive to members of Congress. A variety of legislative actions were attempted to limit funding for the war effort, to force withdrawal of troops, to require pauses in bombing, to limit ground actions, and the like. Eventually in 1973 Congress was able to develop and pass the WAR POWERS RESOLUTION. It not only passed the two chambers, but after a veto by President Nixon, Congress overrode the use of armed forces and required consultation with Congress and prompt written reporting by the president to the Congress about military actions. It sets a 60-day limit on troop commitments unless Congress authorizes continuation and provides that Congress can direct the president to disengage troops from hostilities. Passage of the War Powers Resolution was in part, at least, prompted by President Johnson's misuse of the Tonkin Gulf incident.

Further reading:
Congress and the Nation. Washington, D.C.: Congressional Quarterly Service, 1973; Diamond, R. A., and P. A. O'Connor, eds. *Congressional Quarterly's Guide to Congress.* 2d ed. Washington, D.C.: Congressional Quarterly Press, 1976; Herring, G. C. *America's Longest War: The United States and Vietnam, 1950–1975.* 2d ed. New York: Knopf, 1986.

—Jack R. Van Der Slik

Transportation and Infrastructure, House Committee on

The House Committee on Transportation and Infrastructure is a standing committee of the U.S. House of Representatives. It dates to 1837, when it was created as the Public Building and Grounds Committee. The modern committee emerged from the LEGISLATIVE REORGANIZATION ACT OF 1946 as the Public Works Committee in the 80th Congress (1947–49). Whereas 89 members had been serving on four committees, 27 members remained serving on Public Works after the consolidation. The committee was named Public Works and Transportation from 1975 to 1995, when, along with several other committees, it was renamed as part of the symbolism of the 104th Congress, bringing the first Republican majority in the House in 40 years.

The shift in party control of the chamber in 1995 resulted in a dramatic revamping for the committee system, including six-year term limits for committee and subcommittee chairs, elimination of three standing committees, the majority party leadership gaining enhanced authority for chair selection, and reductions in the number of subcommittees and the number of staff allowed. The committee chair in the 107th changed because of the Republican self-imposed chair term limits. Representative Don Young of Alaska became chair of Transportation and Infrastructure in 2001 after serving six years as chair of the HOUSE RESOURCES COMMITTEE. It remains to be seen if the Republicans will continue committee term limits should they retain majority control of the House until the 109th Congress, when those serving a three-year term as chair of their second committee might be called on to step aside for newer faces.

In the 108th Congress the committee jurisdiction included responsibility for the Coast Guard; emergency management; flood control; rivers and harbor improvement; inland waterways; Merchant Marine; navigation; the Capitol building and office buildings of the House and Senate; construction and maintenance of roads; construction and maintenance of the buildings in the Botanic Garden, the Library of Congress, and the Smithsonian Institution; construction of post offices, customhouses, and courthouses; pollution of navigable waters including by oil; coastal zone management; bridges, dams and other public works to benefit navigation; and transportation, including aviation, railroads, and highways. The mandate of the Transportation and Infrastructure Committee, regardless of its name, has been to create a transportation system, whether on water, over land, or through the air. That jurisdiction has meant construction contracts to be awarded and bring jobs back home to districts.

Members of the committee traditionally have been happy to engage in classic PORK BARREL politics while serving on the panel. Scholars have characterized the panel as a clientele, or constituency, committee, meaning that members are drawn to the committee because they can bring tangible projects home to the district, which is widely thought to help members gain reelection. Members have been consistently attracted to service on the panel, measured in part by the increase in committee size that accompanied expansion in its jurisdiction and reflective of the importance of transportation to the national and local economies. The committee size increased by roughly 10 members in each decade after the 1970s (37 members in 1971, 46 members in 1981, 57 members in 1991, and became the largest House committee, with 76 members in 2001). Major policy issues handled by the committee were deregulation of the airline industry in 1978 as well as the trucking industry in 1980. Future support for highways and public transportation systems generated some controversy in the nation at the end of the 20th century, as environmental protection groups pointed to the Federal Highway Bill as the primary source of air pollution in major cities. Highways and transit appeared to be the most pressing issue facing the committee at the beginning of the 107th Congress. The committee faced a tremendous change in outlook as the reality of terrorist attacks reached the United States in September 2001. The Transportation and Infrastructure Committee was involved in creating the new Department of Homeland Security, as well as securing ports and other transportation infrastructure and seeing to the financial as well as physical security of air transportation. The new considerations for transportation and infrastructure security join some of the perennial concerns that face the committee, the future of Amtrak and location of new post offices.

Further reading:
Deering, Christopher J. and Steven S. Smith. *Committees in Congress.* 3d ed. Congressional Quarterly Press, 1997; Goodwin, George, Jr. *Little Legislatures: Committees of Congress.* Amherst: University of Massachusetts Press, 1970; Ferejohn, John A. *Pork Barrel Politics: Rivers and Harbors Legislation, 1947–1968.* Stanford, Calif.: Stanford University Press, 1974; Stewart, Charles III. "Committee Hierarchies in the Modernizing House: 1875–1947." *American Journal of Political Science* 36 (1992): 835–857.

—Karen M. McCurdy

treaties

The U.S. Constitution, in Article II, Section 2, directs the SENATE to provide ADVICE AND CONSENT to the president while negotiating treaties with other nations. Treaties, legal agreements between the United States and one or more other nations, must be ratified by a two-thirds majority of the Senate present and voting before becoming legally binding. The HOUSE OF REPRESENTATIVES plays no constitutional role in the treaty-making process.

In the early years of the nation, the Senate occasionally ratified treaties, but only after adding new stipulations or demanding the renegotiation of sections of the document. However, the "advice" step soon was largely abandoned in favor of the Senate simply ratifying agreements negotiated by the president. The system evolved into one in which new treaties are first reviewed by the SENATE FOREIGN RELATIONS COMMITTEE. After reviewing the treaty the committee may either hold the document for an unlimited time or forward the agreement on to the full chamber for final consideration. The entire Senate can either defeat the treaty or pass a resolution of ratification by the mandated two-thirds majority and forward the document to the president to sign a proclamation completing the process.

However, the Senate, either from the floor or by accepting a committee recommendation, can alter the treaty employing any of four tools. Senators can alter the text of the document through "amendments," qualify the obligations mandated by the treaty by using a "reservation," assert their preferred interpretation of the document through an "understanding," and make a statement about a policy relating to the subject, but not the exact text, of the treaty—a "declaration." These statements must subsequently be ratified by both the president and the other nations signing the treaty.

The Senate traditionally has ratified most treaties without adding any conditions. Often senators, fearing to undercut a president's international standing, have grudgingly voted to approve treaties. The Senate has rejected fewer than 20 treaties outright, preferring instead to kill treaties by simply not scheduling them for consideration, thereby letting them die a quiet death without enduring a probable acrimonious and divisive public floor debate.

Yet throughout American history presidents have occasionally suffered humiliating defeats of their treaties. The most memorable defeat of a treaty occurred in 1919 and 1920 with the Senate's rejection of President Woodrow Wilson's beloved Treaty of Versailles. The president repeatedly declined to compromise, thereby setting the stage for his bitter critic, HENRY CABOT LODGE, chair of the Senate Foreign Relations committee, to lead the fight to reject the treaty. By the end of the 20th century a bloc of conservative Republican senators were successfully defeating agreements, such as the Comprehensive Test Ban Treaty in 1999, or by forcing significant changes to the multination Chemical Weapons Agreement in 1997.

Modern presidents have sought to avoid watching their treaties be defeated in the Senate. One approach has been to consult with key senators, particularly those on the Foreign Relations Committee, during the process of negotiating with other nations. However, an increasingly popular presidential approach for avoiding Senate rejection has been to negotiate executive agreements they unilaterally sign with other nations.

Executive agreements, which are international in scope and are enforceable under international law, do not require Senate ratification. Presidents are only required to submit a copy of their executive agreement to Congress within 60 days of their taking effect. Studies have revealed that the ratio of the number of executive agreements to treaties has reversed from treaty dominance in the early 19th century to overwhelming executive agreement totals two centuries later. By the last two decades of the 20th century more than 95 percent of all American international pacts were executive agreements.

See also CASE ACT OF 1972.

"Tuesday through Thursday Club"

Members of Congress who travel to Washington, D.C., to be at the Capitol from early Tuesday morning through Thursday night and spend the remainder of the week in their districts have been said to be in the "Tuesday through Thursday Club." The origin of the Tuesday through Thursday Club (also known as the "Tuesday to Thursday Club") is difficult to determine. Political scientist Alan Fiellin described the Tuesday to Thursday Club in a 1962 *Journal of Politics* article. He predicted that while spending long weekends at home may appear to be a benefit, it could be dysfunctional for a congressional career.

Writing to his constituents in 1964, Representative Morris Udall, a Democrat from Arizona, complained that the HOUSE OF REPRESENTATIVES rarely conducted legislative business on Monday or Friday because of the tradition of the Tuesday to Thursday Club. This phrase especially describes the practices of some eastern and southern congressmembers, many of whom retain active law practices and business interests at home. These members of Congress arrive on the early plane Tuesday and are ready to depart Washington, D.C., by Thursday night. Udall's complaint was that this practice caused the session to continue on to the late fall. It also created a heavier committee workload for western, midwestern, and more distant southern members of Congress who could not afford to commute.

In the early 20th century members of Congress spent about half their time in their DISTRICTS and half in Washington. Most traveled by train between their two homes twice a year, at the beginning and at the end of a session. The absence of air conditioning kept Congress working every weekday during the cooler winter and spring months. Since there was no jet travel, members did not have the luxury of being able to fly back home for a long weekend. By about mid-century, with the growth in the size of government and the introduction of air conditioning and jet travel, more members of Congress spent more time at home in their districts.

A reform movement swept through Congress, particularly the House, in the late 1960s and early 1970s. While a number of traditions and customs were affected by these new reforms, the postreform Congress maintained the Tuesday to Thursday Club. In late 1979 a group organized by Representatives RICHARD GEPHARDT, a Democrat from

Missouri; David Stockman, a Republican from Michigan; and Tim Wirth, a Democrat from Colorado worked to end the tradition. They recommended as a first step that STANDING COMMITTEES meet on Tuesdays and Thursdays without the interruption of a floor session. Floor debate would have been scheduled on Monday, Wednesday, and Friday. While the group included some important members such as Representatives Barber Conable, a Republican from New York; Richard Bolling, a Democrat from Missouri; and Richard Cheney, a Republican from Wyoming, it had little success.

In 1993 about 60 House members signed a petition calling for a more "family friendly" work schedule in which members would work for three weeks and be off the fourth week. This proposal, considered by the JOINT COMMITTEE ON THE ORGANIZATION OF CONGRESS, would have required some votes to be scheduled for Mondays and Fridays. The proposal was not enacted.

By the final decade of the 20th century, few people referred to the Tuesday to Thursday Club because most members of Congress engaged in the practice of arriving in Washington on Tuesday morning and leaving on Thursday evening. The club was temporarily disbanded in 1995 after the new Republican majority in the House of Representatives, in particular, worked to enact the Republicans' CONTRACT WITH AMERICA in the first 100 days of the session. At the end of the first 100 days, the House schedule became less intense, with the Republican leadership promising to end the practice of the Tuesday to Thursday schedule. In the 108th Congress (2003–04), members of the House, in particular, still generally arranged their schedules so that they could devote as much time as possible to trips back to their districts.

Further reading:
Beth, Richard S. *House Schedule: Recent Practices and Proposed Options.* Washington, D.C.: Library of Congress, Congressional Research Service, 2001; Fiellin, Alan. "The Functions of Informal Groups in Legislative Institutions." *Journal of Politics* (1962); King, Anthony. "The Vulnerable American Politician." *British Journal of Political Science* 27 (1997): 1–22; Nokken, Timothy P., and Brian R. Sala. "Institutional Evolution and the Rise of the Tuesday-Thursday Club in the House of Representatives." In *Party, Process, and Political Change in Congress: New Perspectives on the History of Congress, edited by* David W. Brady and Mathew McCubbins, Stanford, Calif.: Stanford University Press, ?
—John David Rausch, Jr.

Twentieth Amendment

The Twentieth Amendment to the U.S. Constitution is popularly called the "LAME DUCK" amendment. The term *lame duck* originally signified a weak person. It later was used to describe defeated or retiring politicians. The lame ducks of Congress, defeated or retiring members, would meet in lame duck sessions of Congress called the "short" session for about four months after suffering their electoral defeats.

Lame duck sessions of Congress were prominent political events until the adoption of the Twentieth Amendment. They were the product of several factors. When the national (federal) Constitutional Convention drafted the Constitution in 1787, transportation and communications systems were more primitive than would be the case in later centuries. Improvements in transportation allowed an easier return to Washington, D.C., and made it easier to engage in what was usually viewed as political self-aggrandizement at public expense in a lame duck session between the election and the end of the session on March 3 of the following year.

Second, the Constitutional Convention had mandated that Congress meet at least once a year and that the meeting should begin on the first Monday in December unless provided by law for another date (Article I, Section 4, Clause 2). In practice this meant that a member of Congress elected in November of an even-numbered year did not take office until December of the following odd-numbered year. This was 13 months after their election. The session that began in the even-numbered year a few weeks after the election would be composed of members who had been reelected and those who were lame ducks. This was the "short" session that lasted until March 3.

Third, the Constitutional Convention instructed the First Congress to meet on the first Wednesday of March in 1789, which happened to be March 4. From this developed the practice of having the two sessions of Congress be a "long" session and a "short" session.

Congress would meet in a long session beginning in December in odd years for six months, or until June. Then in even years, after the election, it would meet in a short session from the first Monday in December until March 3. These short sessions were lame duck sessions, with many defeated or retiring members of Congress. The effect was that a member of Congress elected in an even year did not take office until 13 months later.

For the next 140 years Congress would meet in two sessions, long and short. However, they were usually not productive because major legislation would be filibustered.

The system was beneficial both to presidents and to some members of Congress. Since Congress would not meet from mid-June until December, presidents would often call Congress into special sessions. In addition, presidents would make recess appointments to fill executive branch vacancies without congressional approval. Other political moves were possible without congressional approval.

The status quo was beneficial to the leadership of the HOUSE OF REPRESENTATIVES, who were able to block or promote legislation they favored. By 1900 many people were becoming frustrated with the practice of lame duck sessions.

In 1922 a Democratic senator introduced a resolution that would have blocked lame ducks from voting unless the legislation was routine. The SENATE leadership (Republicans) referred the matter to the AGRICULTURE COMMITTEE, chaired by Senator George W. Norris, a Republican from Nebraska. Norris was a Progressive and favored reform. The Agriculture Committee proposed a joint resolution that would be presented to the states as a constitutional amendment. It passed the Senate but failed to gain a vote in the House. This happened again in 1924 and 1926. In 1928 the House voted on the joint resolution when it was presented, but the vote was against the proposed amendment. Then in 1930 the Democrats captured control of the House. The Senate passed Norris's joint resolution on January 6, 1932. The House then approved it on March 2. After both Houses of Congress approved the proposed amendment by a two-thirds vote, it was sent to the states.

The Twentieth Amendment was adopted by the necessary three-fourths of the state legislatures within six months. On January 3, 1933, the 73rd Congress began under the new system. The small portion of the amendment on eliminating lame duck session has been the most active part of the amendment. Short session filibustering was eliminated by the amendment. There have been 11 lame duck sessions since the adoption of the Twentieth Amendment.

The bulk of the Twentieth Amendment focuses on the president and vice president. The amendment moved the date for the installation of the president from March 4 to January 20. The Twentieth Amendment provides for succession in case of the death or ineligibility of the president-elect. It provides that the vice president–elect would become president if the president-elect died before installation. In addition, it provided that the vice president–elect would be acting president until a president was chosen if the president had not been chosen by January 20. Furthermore, in case neither the president–elect nor the vice president–elect could qualify, then Congress would decide who would be acting president. And finally, if the election of the president and vice president were to be decided by Congress for some reason and one of the candidates died, then Congress would decide by law what should be done. These provisions were to be implemented only in case of an election crisis.

The Twentieth Amendment improves American democracy by increasing the accuracy of representation and enabling legislators to more efficiently carry out their mandate. It was the last of five constitutional amendments produced by the Progressive movement.

Further reading:
Beth, Richard S., and Richard C Sachs. *Lame Duck Sessions of Congress: 1933–1989.* Washington, D.C.: Congressional Research Service, 1990; Norris, George W. *Fighting Liberal: The Autobiography of George W. Norris.* New York: Collier Books, 1961; Palmer, Kris E. *Constitutional Amendments, 1789 to the Present.* Detroit: Gale Group, 2000.
—Andrew J. Waskey

Twenty-seventh Amendment

The Twenty-seventh Amendment to the U.S. Constitution, addressing congressional pay limits, was ratified and proclaimed a part of the Constitution in 1992. The amendment reads, "No law, varying the compensation for the services of the Senators and Representatives, shall take effect, until an election of Representatives shall have intervened." What originally could have been the 11th or 12th amendment to the Constitution if it had been ratified shortly after being passed by Congress became the Twenty-seventh Amendment 203 years after it was originally proposed.

The congressional pay limitation amendment was originally proposed as one of 12 amendments in the Bill of Rights in 1789. Of these, 10 were ratified by the required 11 out of 14 states. The final two amendments, both concerning Congress, fell short of ratification. The first of the two failed amendments would have established a ratio of representatives to population that, if ratified, would have resulted in a HOUSE OF REPRESENTATIVES of more than 5,000 members in the year 2000. This amendment was ratified by 10 of the 11 states needed and is still technically pending today. No further action from the states has occurred. The second failed amendment addressed the impropriety of allowing the elected congressmembers to regulate their own salaries. This proposal was ratified by six states (Maryland, North Carolina, South Carolina, Delaware, Vermont, and Virginia) but rejected by five states (New Jersey, New Hampshire, New York, Pennsylvania, and Rhode Island). The amendment lay dormant until 1873, when Ohio, in response to a retroactive pay increase referred to as the 1873 Salary Grab Act, attempted to send a message of contempt toward the actions of Congress by ratifying the congressional pay limits amendment. No other states followed suit. However, in a similar political statement, Wyoming ratified the amendment in 1978 in response to another pay increase passed in 1977. In 1982 as part of a paper assignment for a government course at the University of Texas-Austin, Gregory D. Watson discovered the unratified but apparently still valid amendment and began a 10-year push to garner enough state ratifications for adoption. The states slowly jumped on board, starting with Maine in 1983 and Colorado in 1984, until in May 1992 Michigan and New Jersey

DORMANT CONSTITUTIONAL AMENDMENT PROPOSALS

Year Proposed	Topic	States Ratifying
1789	Ratio of Representatives Amendment–Establishing the ratio of representatives to population of the states.	DE, MD, NC, NH, NJ, NY, RI, SC, VA, VT
1810	Titles of Nobility Amendment–Stripping the United States citizenship of any person elevated to nobility by a foreign country.	DE, GA, KY, MA, MD, NC, NH, NJ, OH, PA, TN, VT
1861	Corwin Amendment–Prohibiting Congress from amending the Constitution to abolish slavery (in an attempt to prevent civil war).	IL, MD, OH
1926	Child Labor Amendment–Allowing Congress to regulate labor and employment of children under the age of 18.	AR, AZ, CA, CO, IA, ID, IL, IN, KS, KY, ME, MI, MN, MT, ND, NH, NJ, NM, NV, OH, OK, OR, PA, UT, WA, WI, WV, WY

attempted to become the necessary 38th ratifying state. Michigan managed to ratify on the same day but before New Jersey, sending the new amendment to Congress, where the archivist proclaimed the Twenty-seventh Amendment on May 18, 1992.

The amendment was not without controversy. Most legal scholars and many senators and representatives had assumed the amendment to be dead and doubted whether a proposed amendment was still valid after such a long time. Despite these concerns, Congress acted to officially recognize the amendment on May 20, 1992. The issues raised by the ratification of the Twenty-seventh Amendment are relevant for the future. The U.S. Supreme Court, in *Dillon v. Gloss* (256 U.S. 368 [1921]) and *Coleman v. Miller* (307 U.S. 433 [1939]), had raised doubts as to whether a proposed amendment could constitutionally survive a prolonged ratification process and whether a state could change its vote about ratification (both New Jersey and New Hampshire originally rejected the congressional pay limits amendment but finally accepted in 1992 and 1985, respectively), but ultimately left the decision whether to accept such amendments to Congress. For future amendments the issue is largely moot, as Congress has included time limits for ratification on all but one proposed amendment since the 18th Amendment (1919). The exception is the Child Labor Amendment of 1939, which along with three amendments proposed between 1789 and 1861, are the only amendments still pending (Table 1). In the end, the Twenty-seventh Amendment carries little real substantive weight. The limits on congressional pay increases it regulates were passed into law in the 1989 Ethics Reform Act. The amendment simply makes it impossible for Congress to repeal the law without amending the Constitution again.

Further reading:
Bernstein, Richard B. "The Sleeper Wakes: The History and Legacy of the Twenty-Seventh Amendment." *Fordham Law Review* 61 (1992): 497; Byrd, Robert C. *Senate 1789–1989: Addresses on the History of the US Senate.* Washington, D.C.: Government Printing Office, 1989; Miller, Robert S., and Donald O. Dewey. "The Congressional Salary Amendment: 200 Years Later." *Glendale Law Review* 10 (1991): 92.

—Corey A. Ditslear

U

Un-American Activities Committee, House

The House Un-American Activities Committee (HUAC) was a standing committee of the U.S. House of Representatives from 1945 to 1975 charged with investigating disloyalty and subversive organizations. The committee was created on May 26, 1938, as a special Committee to Investigate Un-American Activities, chaired by Representative Martin Dies, a Democrat from Texas.

Representative Dies established the pattern for anticommunist investigations, which was adopted in the Senate in 1950 by Senator JOSEPH MCCARTHY of Wisconsin. While it is McCarthy's name that is associated with the greatest notoriety in the red-baiting witch hunts of the 1950s in the Senate anticommunist hearings, Representative Dies developed the paranoid style of investigations that has been negatively associated with HUAC. The pattern that became standard operating procedure on HUAC was one of intimidation: First, to pressure witnesses to name their former associates in the Communist Party; second, to presume guilt by association, no matter how casual, with leftist organizations or individuals; and third, to make sweeping accusations against individuals.

HUAC is best known for several high-profile hearings investigating communism in the United States; the Alger Hiss case in 1948 and the Hollywood Ten found in contempt of Congress in 1947. Representative Richard Nixon of California, later president of the United States from 1969 to 1974, received his first national exposure as a young congressman as a member of the committee during the Hiss hearings. The communist leanings and associations of prominent members of the entertainment industry, screenwriters, directors, and actors, was investigated in a series of hearings in Hollywood and Washington, D.C. The hearings were documented in newsreel footage and in radio broadcasts. The prepared testimony of witnesses was frequently interrupted by the gavel of its chair, J. Parnell Thomas of New Jersey, calling the witness to answer the question "Are you now, or have you ever been a member of the Communist Party?"

Following the friendly testimony of Hollywood moguls Jack Warner and Louis B. Mayer and actors Gary Cooper, Robert Taylor, Robert Montgomery, and Ronald Reagan, 11 hostile witnesses were called in 1947. German expatriate playwright Bertolt Brecht answered questions under oath, claimed he was not a communist, and immediately after testifying before the committee, returned to East Germany. The remaining 10 hostile witnesses called (director Edward Dmytryk and screenwriters John Lawson, Dalton Trumbo, Albert Maltz, Alvah Bessie, Samuel Ornintz, Herbert Biberman, Adrian Scott, Ring Lardner, Jr., and Lester Cole) refused to answer questions, claiming Fifth Amendment rights. The committee held them in contempt of Congress, upheld in court appeals, and the 10 served 6-to-12 months terms in federal penitentiary. They were blacklisted by the Hollywood film industry, beginning a period of 10 years when 324 film workers were barred from employment; 212 of whom were fired from active employment. The intensity of the cold war in the 1950s and the fear of communist incursion dominated the actions of HUAC members. The 1948 HUAC hearings were also a product of this national fear but developed in a different manner. These hearings resulted from a charge by Whittaker Chambers, a magazine editor and former Communist Party member, that former State Department official and then president of the Carnegie Endowment for International Peace, Alger Hiss, was a member of the Communist Party. Chambers further charged that Hiss had helped transport confidential government documents to the Soviet Union. The statute of limitations having expired for espionage, Hiss was indicted on two charges of perjury in December 1948. The jury in the first trial was unable to render a decision, while a second trial resulted in a guilty verdict. His was sentenced to five years in federal prison. Hiss was released in 1954, maintaining his innocence to his death. Soviet files made public in 1995 support his guilt, but the case continues to be controversial.

The aggressive investigative style of HUAC resulted in criticism throughout its existence for its disregard for the civil liberties of witnesses. It was further criticized for failing to recommend new legislation or to fulfill its mission to investigate disloyalty and subversive organizations. By the 1960s the committee had become an expensive operation, employing more than 50 staffers and holding frequent hearings around the country. Efforts to turn critical public opinion more favorable resulted in a name change in 1969 to the House Internal Security Committee. Representative Richard H. Ichord, a Democrat from Missouri, chaired the new committee. Ultimately, though, the attempt to free the committee of its red-baiting past and controversial tactics failed. The committee was abolished in 1975.

Further reading:
Carr, Robert K. *The House Committee on Un-American Activities, 1945–1950.* Ithaca, N.Y.: Cornell University Press, 1952; Goodman, Walter. *The Committee: The Extraordinary Career of the House Committee on Un-American Activities.* New York: Farrar, Straus, & Giroux, 1968; Ogden, August Raymond. *The Dies Committee: A Study of the Special House Committee for the Investigation of Un-American Activities, 1938–1944.* Washington, D.C.: Catholic University Press, 1945. *Legacy of the Hollywood Blacklist.* Video produced and directed by Judy Chaikin. Direct cinema limited distributors, 1988.
—Karen M. McCurdy

unanimous consent

Both the House and SENATE have complex rules and procedures in place to govern activities on the floor. These rules cover everything from debates to decorous behavior, from who may enter the chamber to what constitutes a QUORUM. On the one hand, such rules help to streamline the activities of an organization made up of a large number of members (and at 435 members the HOUSE OF REPRESENTATIVES is particularly unwieldy). On the other hand, complicated rules and procedures can stymie the legislative process or even just the course of doing business on the floor. In order to streamline the process, both the House and the Senate have several ways of circumventing the rules.

One of these is the use of unanimous consent. Unanimous consent means just that: every single senator or representative (or at least every single one of those present) must agree unanimously. If even one person objects, there is no unanimous consent. While this seems rather extreme in a body that is governed by majority rule (and minority rights), unanimous consent is often used for rather innocuous requests to waive the rules. Such requests include asking to allow a staff member into the chamber, rescinding a quorum call, inserting information into the CONGRESSIONAL RECORD, and adding a senator's or representative's name as a cosponsor to a

particular bill. These are more or less polite requests and are usually granted. A member will ask for unanimous consent to waive the rules, and, if there is no objection, that request is automatically granted. If, on the other hand, one or more persons object, the request is not granted, and the rules are not waived. Perhaps a better way of understanding unanimous consent is through the phrase "no objection," which is often used in requesting and granting unanimous consent. "If there is no objection, so ordered" is often heard on both the House and Senate floors. While a "simple" unanimous consent request (such as the ones mentioned previously) is generally noncontroversial and usually granted, there is a more specific type of unanimous consent request, called a "complex unanimous consent request," that is used in the Senate to bring bills to the floor. This is discussed in the next entry.

Further reading:
Krehibiel, Keith "Unanimous Consent Agreements: Going Along in the Senate." *Journal of Politics* 48 (1986): 541–563.
—Anne Marie Cammisa

unanimous consent agreement

In the SENATE, as in the HOUSE OF REPRESENTATIVES, a bill must go through several stages before passage. It must be introduced by a senator, after which it is referred to and considered in committee and subcommittee and then reported out of committee and considered on the Senate floor. In order to schedule floor consideration, the Senate uses what is formally called a "complex unanimous consent agreement" that sets the guidelines for a particular bill. The agreement (also known as a UCA or a time-limitation agreement) specifies when the bill will be considered, how long debate will take, and any limits on amendments (usually the only limitation on amendments is that they must be germane or related to the bill at hand). As in the House, the rules governing floor debate in the Senate are quite restrictive and make considering legislation cumbersome and unwieldy. A unanimous consent agreement actually waives the rules in order that legislation may be considered in a more streamlined manner.

The unanimous consent agreement is worked out in advance with the leadership of both parties. As its name suggests, a unanimous consent request requires unanimous agreement, not just a majority vote. If one single senator objects, there is no agreement, and the legislation will not be considered. Why do senators agree to unanimous consent? First, they understand that the rules must be waived in order for legislation to be considered and that their consent is not the same as an endorsement of the bill. Second, senators also know that if unanimous consent is frequently denied, it will delay all BILLS, including their own.

The Senate as an institution has historically followed norms of behavior, and one of those norms is collegiality. Having said that, however, it is not unheard of for a senator to withhold his or her consent. If there is a bill that a senator finds objectionable in its subject matter (for example, in the 1980s and 1990s Senator Jesse Helms [R-NC]) often denied his consent to bills that involved abortion), he or she might object and thus keep the bill from being considered. Alternatively, a senator might object to another senator's bill or a bill endorsed by the president as a bargaining tool. If he or she holds that bill "hostage," then perhaps the senator can gain concessions on his or her own pet legislative proposal. Such objections are usually made behind the scenes, often anonymously.

The leadership works out the unanimous consent agreement in private and, also privately, finds out if there are any objections to it. If so, the agreement will not even come to the floor. When a senator objects to a unanimous consent agreement (or threatens to use a filibuster as a method of delaying a bill), it is called a "hold." Holds, especially anonymous holds, have been used frequently in recent Congresses and have as frequently been criticized as an erosion of the norm of collegiality.

Another indication of the erosion of collegiality and rise of individualism can be seen in the use of incremental UCAs, which cover only part of a bill as it comes to the floor. Leadership, recognizing that it would be difficult to get unanimous consent for consideration of an entire bill at once, sometimes decides that the better course of action is to get unanimous consent bit by bit, section by section, until the entire bill can be considered.

A UCA is often compared to a "rule," which schedules legislation in the House of Representatives. While there are similarities (both the rule and the UCA schedule legislation and limit debate), there are important differences as well. A rule is decided in an open committee hearing and passes with a majority vote. A UCA is negotiated privately, behind the scenes, and can be thwarted by a single senator. The consent of the minority party is essential for scheduling a bill in the Senate; the majority party, since it controls the Rules Committee, can (and frequently does) ignore the minority party wishes in the House. These differences reflect differences between the two bodies. The House, the larger institution, follows stricter rules; the Senate, the smaller body, is more inclined to allow for minority and individual rights.

Further reading:
Oleszek, Walter. *Congressional Procedures and the Policy Process.* 5th ed. Washington, D.C.: Congressional Quarterly Press, 2001.

—Anne Marie Cammisa

United States Association of Former Members of Congress

The United States Association of Former Members of Congress was created in 1970. The nonprofit and nonpartisan organization was chartered by the U.S. Congress and has approximately 600 members who represented American citizens in both the SENATE and the HOUSE OF REPRESENTATIVES.

The primary goal of the organization is to promote improved public understanding of the role of Congress as a unique institution as well as the crucial importance of representative democracy as a system of government, both domestically and internationally. Beginning in 1996, the U.S. Association of Former Members of Congress and the Stennis Center for Public Service have combined their resources to administer jointly the Congress to Campus Program. In this program bipartisan teams of former members of Congress—one Democrat and one Republican—make two-and-a-half day visits to college communities throughout the United States to share their first-hand experiences of the operations of Congress. In March 2001 the U.S. Association of Former Members of Congress published a book, *Inside the House: Former Members Reveal How Congress Really Works.*

In addition, when members of Congress leave office they often are bombarded with lucrative offers to look out for the interests of major corporations. Former members of Congress are often considered the most valuable commodity in a LOBBYING firm. Consequently, a member of Congress must wait one year after leaving office before lobbying former colleagues directly. However, former members can be hired by lobbying firms as consultants or advisers immediately upon leaving Congress, then begin lobbying once the year-long "cooling off" period is over.

Further reading:
Frey, Lou, and Michael Hayes, eds. *Inside the House: Former Members Reveal How Congress Really Works.* Lanham, Md.: University Press of America, 2001; United States Association of Former Members of Congress. Available online. URL: http://www.usafmc.org/default.asp?pagenumber'1. Acessed 19 January 2006.

—Nancy S. Lind

United States v. Darby Lumber Co. 312 U.S. 100 (1941)

United States v. Darby (1941) was one of several U.S. Supreme Court decisions overruling earlier precedents to uphold NEW DEAL legislation. The Court followed its decision in *National Labor Relations Board v. Jones & Laughlin Steel* (1937) in paying greater deference to the judgment of Congress in wielding its Commerce Clause authority.

Fred Darby was indicted for violations of the Fair Labor Standards Act, which prohibited interstate transport of goods not produced in compliance with minimum wage or 44-hour workweek requirements. The Supreme Court had ruled in *Hammer v. Dagenhart* (1918) that Congress's commerce power did not extend to regulating the workplace. In that earlier decision, involving restrictions on child labor, the Court held that while Congress could prohibit transport of "harmful" commodities such as gambling paraphernalia, prostitutes, and impure drugs, it could not restrict goods that "are of themselves harmless." To do so, the Court had said, would bring "all manufacture intended for interstate shipment . . . under federal control to the practical exclusion of the authority of the states."

The decision in *Darby* overruled *Hammer v. Dagenhart*. The Court pronounced the distinction made in the earlier case to be "a departure" from other case law that had "long since been abandoned." Congress, the Court said, could follow "its own conception of public policy concerning the restrictions which may appropriately be imposed on interstate commerce [and] is free to exclude from the commerce articles whose use in the states for which they are destined it may conceive to be injurious to the public health, morals, or welfare, even though the state has not sought to regulate their use." The Court noted that to allow interstate transport of articles from states with "substandard labor conditions" would give an unfair competitive advantage to businesses in those states.

Further reading:
Hammer v. Dagenhart 1918 247 U.S. 251; *United States v. Darby* 1992 312 U.S. 100; *National Labor Relations Board v. Jones & Laughlin Steel* 1937 301 U.S. 1.

—Jackson Williams

United States v. E. C. Knight Co. 156 U.S. 1 (1895)

The Supreme Court's decision in *U.S. v. E.C. Knight* ushered in an era of judicial obstruction of congressional efforts to regulate the national economy. The Court articulated a remarkably narrow and formalistic definition of commerce that excluded pretransaction activities, thus blocking Congress's efforts to legislate for what the justices deemed illegitimate purposes.

The case concerned the American Sugar Refining Company's acquisition of E.C. Knight and three other refining companies, which gave American Sugar control of more than 98 percent of the nation's sugar refining business. When the Department of Justice invoked the Sherman Antitrust Act of 1890 in an effort to block the transaction,

E.C. Knight asserted that manufacturing was not interstate commerce and therefore was not subject to the act.

In an 8-1 decision, the Court agreed with E.C. Knight that the production of goods is distinct from distribution, which is considered commerce, and that Congress may only regulate the latter. Wrote Chief Justice Fuller: "The fact that an article is manufactured for export to another state does not of itself make it an article of interstate commerce, and the intent of the manufacturer does not determine the time when the article or product passes from the control of the state and belongs to commerce."

In dissent, Justice Harlan hearkened back to Justice John Marshall's warning in *GIBBONS V. OGDEN* (1824) that "strict construction of the Constitution could divorce the document from its plain meaning and intent." His complaint, echoed by Justice Holmes in subsequent cases following *E.C. Knight*, was that monopolies over production clearly hinder free trade among the states; denying Congress the power to regulate them is harmful to the nation and unnecessary to protect the autonomy of the states.

For more than 40 years following *E.C. Knight* the Court relied on the production-distribution distinction as a means to restrict Congress's power to regulate the national economy. Most prominent among *E.C. Knight's* progeny were *HAMMER V. DAGENHART*, 247 U.S. 251 (1918), and *Carter v. Carter Coal, Inc.*, 298 U.S. 238 (1936). There were a few exceptions during this period, such as *Houston, East & West Texas Railway Company v. U.S.* (the SHREVEPORT RATE CASE), 234 U.S. 342 (1914), which allowed Congress to regulate intrastate railroad rates that had a "close and substantial effect on interstate commerce." The Court finally repudiated the production-distribution distinction in *NATIONAL LABOR RELATIONS BOARD V. JONES & MCLAUGHLIN STEEL CORP.* (1937), which accepted NEW DEAL legislation and invited Congress to expand its regulatory authority under the Commerce Clause.

Further reading:
Hammer v. Dagenhart, 247 U.S. 251 (1918); *Houston, East & West Texas Railway Company v. U.S.*, 234 U.S. 342 (1914); *Carter v. Carter Coal, Inc.*, 298 U.S. 238 (1936); *NLRB v. Jones & McLaughlin Steel Corp.* (1937).

—Daniel E. Smith

United States v. Eichman 496 U.S. 310 (1990)

In 1989 the U.S. Supreme Court struck down the Texas Venerated Objects Law in the celebrated flag-burning case *Texas v. Johnson*, 491 U.S. 397 (1989). In response to the *Johnson* decision, Congress passed the Flag Protection Act of 1989. The statute included the following language,

Whoever knowingly mutilates, defaces, physically defiles, burns, maintains on the floor or ground, or tramples upon any flag of the United States shall be fined under this title or imprisoned for not more than one year, or both.

The law exempted from punishment those who disposed of a "worn or soiled" flag.

The law was tested by protestors in separate flag-burning incidents in Seattle and in the nation's capital. Both the U.S. District Court for the Western District of Washington (*United States v. Haggerty*) and the U.S. District Court for the District of Columbia (*United States v. Eichman*) struck down the Flag Protection Act of 1989 as unconstitutional. The cases, both decided in 1990, were consolidated, and the U.S. Supreme Court heard oral argument in May 1990. Less than one month later the Court ruled that the Flag Protection Act of 1989 was unconstitutional. The vote was 5-4.

While the Court acknowledged that "no explicit content-based limitation on the scope of prohibited conduct" was contained in the language of the Flag Protection Act, the Court argued that the statute was not content-neutral. That is, the statute did not in reality treat various forms of speech, which might involve the flag, in an impartial manner. The Court majority also reaffirmed the position it had staked out in *Johnson* that flag burning was a form of expressive conduct protected by the First Amendment. In contrast, the dissenters on the Court argued that the government had a "legitimate interest in preserving the symbolic value of the flag." They also argued that while the Flag Protection Act prohibited certain forms of protest, those wishing to engage in protest had other avenues available to them through which they could express their views.

The Flag Protection Act of 1989 was not the first piece of legislation passed by the U.S. Congress that attempted to protect the flag. The high Court's treatment of legislation in this area has led scholars to argue, however, that those wishing to protect the flag should seek to do so by passing a constitutional amendment. Congress has attempted to pass such an amendment many times since the *Johnson* decision. It has yet to succeed in this endeavor.

Further reading:
Goldstein, Robert Justin. "The Great 1989–1990 Flag Flap: An Historical, Political, and Legal Analysis." *University of Miami Law Review* 45 (1990): 19–106; Pollitt, Daniel H. "Reflection on the Bicentennial of the Bill of Rights: The Flag Burning Controversy: A Chronology." *North Carolina Law Review* (1992); *United States v. Eichman*, 496 U.S. 310 (1990).

—Peter Watkins

United States v. Harris 106 U.S. 629 (1883)

This was a U.S. Supreme Court case concerning the issue of congressional authority. R. G. Harris and 19 other men were indicted for violating four counts of the Revised Statutes of the United States, Section 5519, which makes it illegal for two or more people to disguise themselves to deprive any other person of equal protection and due process of law.

The defendants, members of the Ku Klux Klan in Tennessee, were charged with depriving the rights of Robert Smith, William J. Overton, George W. Wells, Jr., and P. M. Wells of equal protection of the law. These four men were charged with crimes and were entitled to have their persons protected from violence during their incarceration. On August 14, 1876, the defendants had broken into the jail where the four black men were held and attacked them.

The 20 defendants, however, challenged the constitutionality of Section 5519, arguing that the creation of the law was not within the jurisdiction of Congress and claiming that the section's creation of offenses was unconstitutional and an infringement of the rights of states. They filed a demurrer on February 5, 1878. The case was heard in the circuit court, which referred the case to the Supreme Court. The demurrer questioned the power of Congress to pass the law under which the indictment was found. It was, therefore, necessary to look to the Constitution to determine if this power was granted. There are only four paragraphs in the Constitution that can have any reference to the question at hand. These are Section 2 of Article IV, of the Constitution and the Thirteenth, Fourteenth, and Fifteenth Amendments of the Constitution.

The decision in the case was delivered by Justice Joseph Story. In regard to the Fifteenth Amendment, the Court ruled that it did not apply to this case because it dealt merely with the issue of voting at that time. In reviewing its own precedents, the Court found no warrant for the application of the Fourteenth Amendment. Likewise, it was clear to the Court that the Thirteenth Amendment, besides abolishing forever slavery and involuntary servitude within the United States, gave power to Congress to protect all persons within the jurisdiction of the United States from being in any way subjected to slavery or involuntary servitude except as a punishment for crime. Congress had, by virtue of this amendment, enacted that all persons within the jurisdiction of the United States should have the same right in every state to have equal benefit of all laws and proceedings for the security of persons and property. The question with which the Court had to deal was whether the Thirteenth Amendment warranted the enactment of Section 5519 of the Revised Statutes. They believed that it did not. They argued that if Congress has constitutional authority under the Thirteenth Amendment to punish conspiracy between two persons to do an unlawful act, it can punish the act itself, whether done by one or more persons. The only way, therefore, in which one private person can deprive another of the equal protection of the laws is by the commission of some offense against the laws that protect the rights of persons, as by theft, burglary, arson, libel, assault, or murder. If Section 5519 is warranted by the Thirteenth Amendment, the Court should by virtue of that amendment accord to Congress the power to punish every crime by which the right of any person to life, property, or reputation is invaded. There is only one other clause in the Constitution of the United States that can be argued to sustain the section under consideration, namely, Section 2 of Article IV, which declares that "the citizens of each state shall be entitled to all the privileges and immunities of citizens of the several states." But this section, like the Fourteenth Amendment, is directed against state action. It was never supposed that the section under consideration conferred on Congress the power to enact a law that would punish a private citizen for an invasion of the rights of a fellow citizen, conferred by the state of which they were both residents on all its citizens alike. The Court therefore was unable to find any constitutional authority for the enactment of Section 5519 of the Revised Statutes.

Further reading:
Miller, Loren. *The Petitioner: The Story of the Supreme Court of the United States and of the Negro.* New York: Pantheon, 1966; Moreland, Louis. *White Racism and the Law.* Columbus, Ohio: Charles E. Merrill, 1970.
—Nancy S. Lind

United States v. Lopez 514 U.S. 549 (1995)

After the Supreme Court's "switch-in-time" capitulation to the New Deal's expansive view of national regulatory power in 1937, the Court adopted a remarkably deferential approach to Congress's regulatory authority under the Commerce Clause. In WICKARD V. FILBURN the Court stated that Congress need only identify a connection between interstate commerce and the activity to be regulated, however remote, for the regulation to be constitutional. In HEART OF ATLANTA MOTEL, INC. V. U.S. and *Katzenbach v. McClung* (1964), Congress sustained the CIVIL RIGHTS ACT OF 1964 under the Commerce Clause rather than the Equal Protection Clause of the Fourteenth Amendment, because the former more clearly established Congress's power over private (as opposed to state) actors. That the purposes of the act were not directly related to commerce did not offend the Commerce Clause.

More than 50 years after Wickard and 30 years after the Court upheld the Civil Rights Act, a 5-4 majority on the Supreme Court emerged in *U.S. v. Lopez* to disavow this expanded reading of the Commerce Clause and begin a

concerted effort to redraw the boundaries between the national government and the states. Together with SEMINOLE TRIBE OF FLORIDA V. FLORIDA, *Lopez* signaled an end to judicial deference to Congress in matters of federalism.

The facts of the case paint a persuasive picture for Justice William Rehnquist's opinion for the majority. The Gun-Free School Zones Act of 1990, which established federal criminal sanctions for bringing a firearm within 1,000 feet of a designated school zone, was not an attempt to regulate commerce. Nor was the law, on its face, drafted so as to use an explicit regulation of commerce to serve social or political objectives. The connection between home-grown wheat (in *Wikard*) and interstate commerce was remote, but the legislation was designed to regulate commerce; here, the statute was not about commerce. Justice Rehnquist, writing for the Court, found the relationship between guns in and around schools and commerce to be so attenuated that to accept the statute under the Commerce Clause would allow Congress unlimited regulatory power. While not rejecting decisions such as *Wickard,* the Court signaled that the "direct-indirect" test discarded during the NEW DEAL retained at least some vitality.

The *Lopez* decision thus retreated from a half century of expansive interpretation of the Commerce Clause. Equally important, it signaled an end to the deference the Court had accorded Congress in federalism cases. Not only did five justices find the guns-commerce relationship too remote to sustain under the Commerce Clause, they also declined to give weight to Congress's factual conclusions on the remoteness issue. Initially, the message to the legislature appeared to be "if you want the Court to uphold such a regulation, you must document the relationship to commerce much better."

But in *U.S. v. Morrison* (2000) the Court, following *Lopez,* again used its own judgment in striking down the Violence against Women Act of 1994, which authorized victims of gender violence to sue their attackers in federal court. Anticipating the Court's concerns, members of Congress amassed tens of thousands of pages of data over four years of hearings; these data showed a multibillion-dollar economic burden in the years leading up to passage of the act. In dissent, Justice Souter noted that far less evidence had been provided to establish the effect on interstate commerce of racial discrimination when the Court decided *Heart of Atlanta* and *Katzenbach v. McClung,* and that therefore the Court's reasoning severely undercut the authority of the Civil Rights Act of 1964 and its successors. That the Court declined to credit this evidence confirms that *Lopez* effected a major shift in the relationship between the Supreme Court and Congress as well as a sea change regarding Congress's regulatory power over the states. It also firmly established the Rehnquist Court's five-justice majority, consisting of Justices Rehnquist, Scalia,

Thomas, Kennedy, and O'Connor, that has limited Congress's powers under the Tenth and Eleventh Amendments as well as the Commerce Clause.

Further reading:
Seminole Tribe of Florida v. Florida, 517 U.S. 44 (1996); *U.S. v. Morrison,* 529 U.S. 598 (2000); *Heart of Atlanta Motel, Inc. v. U.S.,* 379 U.S. 241 (1964).
—Daniel Smith

U.S. Term Limits v. Thornton 514 U.S. 779 (1995)

This U.S. Supreme Court ruling established that neither the states nor Congress may set TERM LIMITATIONS on members of the U.S. Congress without an amendment to the Constitution. In 1992 Arkansas voters adopted Amendment 73, a citizen initiative limiting the terms of elected officials, including the Arkansas delegation to Congress. Between 1990 and 1994 23 states enacted such limits on their congressional delegations. Section 3 of Amendment 73 specifically denied access to the ballot in congressional elections to any person who had served three or more terms in the House of Representatives or two or more terms in the Senate. Incumbents who had exceeded the limits would be allowed to run only as write-in candidates. Representative Ray Thornton, a Democrat from Arkansas, and a number of groups, including the Arkansas League of Women Voters, filed suit arguing that Section 3 of Amendment 73 violated Article I of the U.S. Constitution by establishing an additional qualification for U.S. representatives and senators. The circuit court ruled in favor of Thornton, and the state appealed to the Arkansas supreme court. By a 5-2 ruling the Arkansas supreme court affirmed the lower court's decision. The state of Arkansas petitioned the U.S. Supreme Court for a writ of certiorari, which was granted.

Justice John Paul Stevens wrote the opinion of the Court joined by Justices Anthony Kennedy, David Souter, Ruth Bader Ginsburg, and Stephen Breyer. The Court held that the ballot access restriction was an additional qualification not allowed under Article I of the Constitution. Specifically, the Constitution did not allow states to add to or alter the qualifications identified in Article I. This power was not an original power of the states, and thus it could not be a reserved power under the Tenth Amendment. The fact that Amendment 73 was written as a restriction on ballot access and not a limit on additional service did not make the restriction constitutional because Arkansas was trying to accomplish indirectly what it was prohibited from doing directly.

Justice Kennedy wrote a separate concurrence stressing the nature of federalism described in the ruling. He wrote that the people have a federal right of citizenship in their relationship with the national government. The Arkansas term limit amendment interfered with this federal right.

Justice Clarence Thomas, joined by Chief Justice William Rehnquist and Justices Sandra Day O'Connor and Antonin Scalia, dissented. In his dissent Thomas argued that there was nothing in the Constitution depriving the people of each state the power to enact qualifications for their members of Congress. The Constitution's silence on this issue did not prohibit action on the part of states or the people. The dissenting opinion proposed that the reserved powers only prohibited the states from removing all qualifications for members of Congress. Thomas wrote, "The ultimate source of the Constitution's authority is the consent of the people of each individual state, not the consent of the undifferentiated people of the nation as a whole."

The *Thornton* decision marked an important point in the history of the term limitation movement. While the decision had no effect on the limits placed on state legislators, congressional term limit laws were voided in all 23 states with such laws. The ruling also forced U.S. Term Limits, the leading national term limits organization, to alter its strategy. The new strategy continued the focus on limiting congressional terms but using a more indirect process. Voters in numerous states were asked to enact "informed voter" laws, dubbed "scarlet letter" laws by their opponents. These new initiatives instructed members of Congress to support a particular constitutional amendment limiting House members to three terms and senators to two terms. The U.S. Supreme Court ruled that these new initiatives also violated the U.S. Constitution in COOK V. GRALIKE (531 U.S. 510 [2001]).

Further reading:
Polet, Jeff. "A Thornton in the Side: Term Limits, Representation, and the Problem of Federalism." In David K. Ryden, ed. *The U.S. Supreme Court and the Electoral Process.* Washington, D.C.: Georgetown University Press, 2000; Rausch, John David. "Understanding the Term Limits Movement." In Rick Farmer, John David Rausch, and John C. Green, eds. *The Test of Time: Coping with Legislative Term Limits.* Lanham, Md.: Lexington Books, 2002.
—John David Rausch, Jr.

V

vacancy

In political affairs a vacancy refers to a political office, such as a seat in the U.S. House or Senate, that has no incumbent officeholder. Because the electoral process regularly fills elective offices and because national elections occur every even-numbered year, there is a period of time in which such an office may fall vacant. The typical cause of such vacancies is death or resignation. In rare situations a vacancy results from the expulsion of an incumbent by the chamber in which that member serves.

Deaths among members of Congress are not rare. On average, the age of House members is the early 50s. The average for senators is the late 50s. However, in both chambers it is commonplace that there are senior members in their 70s, 80s, and even older. Disease and accidental death take a steady toll, removing three to five members per year.

Vacancies by resignation have a variety of explanations. Not infrequently, members of Congress, particularly those of the president's party, receive appointments to positions in the executive branch and occasionally to the courts. The president controls valued positions on his or her own staff, including positions for persons to lobby Congress for the president's legislative program. Appointees who were members of Congress sometimes fill positions at the cabinet or subcabinet levels as well as ambassadorships and the like.

The rules of the game regarding all such appointments apart from the legislative branch require that the member of Congress resign from the legislative branch in order to serve elsewhere. Article I, Section 6, of the U.S. Constitution clearly provides that members of Congress are to hold no other office concurrent with their congressional service. This, of course, is in sharp contrast with the parliamentary systems on the British Westminster model. In the United Kingdom and elsewhere the prime minister is a member of Parliament, and so are his cabinet ministers. Both Alexander Hamilton and James Madison in the FEDERALIST PAPERS (55 and 76) took note of how the American requirement would help maintain the constitutional principle of separation of powers. The founders wanted to prevent a president from putting legislators on the executive payroll while staying in Congress as the president's servants, voting his wishes into legislation. Thus, for any member of Congress to join the executive branch necessitates resignation from the legislative position. The rule applies, likewise, to anyone in the executive branch. A cabinet official may win election to Congress but would have to resign the executive position in order to be seated in the House or Senate. Sometimes, of course, members of Congress run for state or local offices, such as attorney general, governor, and mayor. While they may retain congressional office during their candidacy, upon winning election they must resign the congressional office in order to assume the state or local position.

Vacancies due to expulsion have been rare in American history. There have been only two such vacancies, both in the House, since the Civil War era. In 1980 the House expelled Representative Michael Myers, a Democrat from Pennsylvania, who accepted money from undercover agents of the Federal Bureau of Investigation. The agents were impersonating Arab businessmen engaged in bribery. In 2002 the House expelled James A. Traficant, a Democrat from Ohio, who had been convicted of 10 felonies, including the use of his congressional office for personal gain.

Vacancies in the Senate constitute a loss of representation for the home state of the previous incumbent. The Constitution provides that the state's executive authority shall name the replacement, as the Seventeenth Amendment provides, "until the people fill the vacancies by election as the Legislature may direct." With six-year terms, any vacancy is filled by appointment until the next regular election. Candidates then run for the remaining unexpired term of two or four years. In the case of a House vacancy, the state executive sets a date for a special election. As the people's house, no appointive arrangement was considered to be constitutionally appropriate, so a special election is the only means for filling such a vacancy.

Because in the last half of the 20th century turnover rates for the House of Representatives have been low and the electoral successes by incumbents have been high, special elections to fill vacancies in the House typically attract many candidates. With no incumbent in the race, a variety of hopefuls come forward, often including someone from the member's staff seeking to win the seat.

An alternate pattern, referred to in the past as "widow's succession," is for someone bearing the family name of the previous incumbent to take advantage of that name familiarity with the electorate. Such successors typically have a better-than-even likelihood of gaining election.

Since the terrorist bombing in New York on September 11, 2001, there has begun to be consideration of constitutional or statutory changes regarding the prompt filling of multiple vacancies in case of a massive attack that would eliminate many high officials, including members of Congress. At this writing, however, proposals are only in the beginning stage of discussion.

Further reading:
Hamilton, A., J. Madison, and J. Jay. *The Federalist Papers.* C. Rossiter, ed. New York: New American Library 1961; Martinez, G. "Traficant's Ouster Decided but Not Relished by his Peers." *Congressional Quarterly Weekly* 27 July 2002, pp. 2036–7.

—Jack R. Van Der Slik

Veterans' Affairs, House Committee on

The House Committee on Veterans' Affairs reviews veterans' programs; examines, evaluates, and makes recommendations regarding existing laws and reports; and, whenever appropriate, provides guidelines to strengthen existing laws concerning veterans. Specifically, the committee deals with veterans' health care including veterans hospitals, medical care and proper and adequate treatment of veterans, disability compensation, education and job training, life insurance policies, pensions of all the wars of the United States, vocational rehabilitation, readjustment of servicemen to civil life, home loan guarantees, and measures related to veterans' cemeteries.

The committee has oversight responsibility for the Department of Veterans' Affairs (VA). The committee covers hearings that examine issues such as VA compliance with various statutory provisions, VA effectiveness in providing appropriate benefits and quality health care, and implementation of sound management practices and efficient expenditure of resources.

Three subcommittees work under the House Committee on Veterans' Affairs. The Subcommittee on Benefits has eight members and a chair. It has jurisdiction over veterans' matters affecting disability compensation, pensions, memorial affairs, education, life insurance, rehabilitation, small business, employment and reemployment, and housing. The subcommittee oversees programs administered by the VA's Veterans' Benefits Administration, National Cemetery Administration, Small Business Administration, and Office of Personnel Management. This subcommittee also has oversight over Arlington National Cemetery, situated just across from the Potomac River from Washington, D.C., the site that includes graves of numerous war veterans and deceased presidents such as John F. Kennedy.

The Subcommittee on Health has 16 members and a chair. The subcommittee has legislative and oversight jurisdiction for the Department of Veterans' Affairs Health Care Program. The committee makes periodic reviews of the health care network, which includes overseeing 600 health care facilities including medical centers, nursing homes, and community outpatient clinics throughout the United States. Hearings by the subcommittee have included matters such as health care cost sharing among VA and army, navy, and air force; VA employment and reemployment; patient safety; VA research facilities; and adequacy of VA health care funding to meet specialized and personalized needs of veterans.

The Subcommittee on Oversight and Investigation has seven members and a chair. The subcommittee reviews the benefits of health care services that the federal government provides to eligible veterans of U.S. wars and their family members. It also oversees the progress and various operations of the Department of Veterans' Affairs, as well as those of other federal agencies that pertain to the issue of veterans. The subcommittee conducts regular hearings and onsite visits to different places nationwide related to veterans' welfare. The Subcommittee on Oversight and Investigation also requests reports from the General Accounting Office, the VA's Office of the Inspector General, and the CONGRESSIONAL RESEARCH SERVICE in order to streamline its oversight activities.

Although the legislative responsibilities of the House Committee on Veterans' Affairs cover a wide range of veterans' issues, the committee does not, however, have legislative jurisdiction over the following matters: military retiree issue (Committee on National Security), Survivor Benefits Program (Committee on National Security), tax status of veterans benefits (Committee on Ways and Means), veteran preference in civil service hiring (Committee on Government Reform and Oversight), and congressional charters for veterans' service organizations (Committee on Judiciary).

Further reading:
Jewell, Malcolm, and Samuel Patterson. *The Legislative Process in the United States.* New York: Random House, 1986; Ragsdale, Bruce A. *The House of Representatives.* New York:

Chelsea House, 1989; Smith, Steven, and Christopher J. Deering. *Committees in Congress.* Washington, D.C.: Congressional Quarterly Press, 1984.

—Mohammed Badrul Alam

Veterans' Affairs, Senate Committee on

One of 16 standing committees in the SENATE in the 108th Congress (2003–04), the Senate Veterans' Affairs Committee has jurisdiction over matters concerning military veterans. These issues include veterans' benefits and pensions, readjustment of service members to civilian life, military life insurance benefits, veterans' hospitals and medical facilities, vocational rehabilitation and education of veterans, and national cemeteries. The committee has no subcommittees.

The Senate Veterans' Affairs Committee was created by the LEGISLATIVE REORGANIZATION ACT OF 1970 and was organized for the first time at the start of the 92nd Congress on January 3, 1971. It was the first standing committee of the Senate to specifically consider legislation of concern to veterans. The committee maintains a low public profile and has a fairly narrow scope of policy to consider. The committee's constituency is made up mainly of veterans and veterans' organizations. Veterans' Affairs has developed close working relationships with veterans' groups and often begins each session of Congress with public hearings to receive each group's legislative agenda for the year.

Veterans' Affairs has had a precarious existence from the very beginning. When the LEGISLATIVE REORGANIZATION ACT OF 1946 created the modern congressional committee system, the HOUSE OF REPRESENTATIVES established a Veterans' Affairs Committee, but the Senate did not. Instead, in the Senate legislation pertaining to veterans was referred to several different committees, including the FINANCE COMMITTEE, the Labor and Public Welfare Committee, the Interior Committee, and the Post Office and Civil Service Committee. A number of senators sympathetic to veterans' groups who wanted a Senate standing committee for veterans' issues made several attempts to create one in the years between 1946 and 1970.

During the 1970 legislative reorganization, the Senate Veterans' Affairs Committee was finally established. Only six years later, in 1976, a legislative reorganization committee recommended that the committee be abolished. It survived because the Senate Rules Committee did not adopt the recommendation.

The need for a Senate committee dedicated to the affairs of veterans was the subject of numerous debates. Proponents of such a committee argued that there should be a parallel committee structure in the House and the Senate. They also believed that veterans' issues should be consolidated into one committee rather than distributed across several committees. Proponents also believed that a veterans' committee would relieve some of the workload of the broader policy committees. Opponents of such a committee argued that there was no clear need to have a parallel structure in the two legislative chambers. They also disapproved of the close links between the committee and its constituents and clientele. Opponents also believed that the workload of veterans' policy issues was not very heavy and that having a separate committee dedicated solely to veterans' issues would increase the workload and committee assignments of senators. It also would increase the number of staff, the amount of office space required, and other expenditures.

The committee's first chair, Vance Hartke, a Democrat from Indiana, held the position from 1971 to 1976. Hartke was an outspoken critic of the Vietnam War but proved to be an effective supporter of America's veterans. He successfully worked for the enactment of several veterans' benefits laws, including the Vietnam Era Veterans Readjustment Assistance Act and the National Cemeteries Act. Hartke's successors as chair of the Veterans' Affairs Committee tended to continue in that tradition. The committee is one of the very few congressional committees to operate free of partisanship, since the committee members prefer to work together to reap the political benefits of championing veterans' causes.

Some of the more recent legislation that has come before the Senate Veterans' Affairs Committee covers a number of issues, including responses to the September 11, 2001, terrorist attacks. Much of this legislation affected the Department of Veterans Affairs. The Homeless Veterans Comprehensive Assistance Act of 2001 (Public Law 107-95) coordinated services for homeless veterans by establishing a number of Veterans' Administration programs, including counseling, drug abuse treatment, rehabilitative services, vocational counseling and training, and transitional housing assistance for homeless veterans. The Department of Veterans' Affairs Emergency Preparedness Act of 2002 (Public Law 107-247) mandated that the Veterans' Administration establish centers for medical emergency preparedness within the Veterans' Health Administration to carry out research on detecting, diagnosing, preventing, and treating injuries and illnesses that might arise from terrorist attacks. Another provision of this law mandated that the Veterans' Administration develop strategies to provide mental health counseling and assistance not only to veterans but also to emergency response providers, active duty military personnel, and others seeking medical care at Veterans' Administration medical centers following a bioterrorist attack or other public health emergency.

Further reading:
Keller, Bill. "How a Unique Lobby Force Protects over $21 Billion in Vast Veterans' Programs." *Congressional Quarterly Weekly Report,* 14 June 1980; Sorrells, Niels C., and

Jonathan Allen. "Veterans Look for Sympathy in Senate After Bipartisan Betrayal in House." *Congressional Quarterly Weekly,* 4 October 2003, pp. 2,459–2,961; Sorrells, Niels C. "Few Changes for Veterans' Affairs." *Congressional Quarterly Weekly,* 9 November 2002, pp. 2,928–2,929; U.S. Senate, Committee on Veterans' Affairs Legislative and Oversight Activities during the 107th Congress by the Senate Committee on Veterans' Affairs. Senate Report 108-139. Washington, D.C.: Government Printing Office, 2003.

—Mary S. Rausch

veto, presidential

The U.S. Constitution empowers the president to reject, or veto, legislation passed by both houses of Congress. This power makes the president a major factor in the legislative process.

The president of the United States has four options when presented with enrolled bills, pieces of legislation passed by both houses of Congress. The bills may be signed into law within the 10-day period specified by the Constitution. The president may allow an enrolled bill to become law without signature after 10 days if Congress remains in session. If the president does not sign the bill within 10 days and Congress has adjourned, the legislation is rejected, a procedure called the pocket veto. The president may also veto the bill and return it to Congress with a message outlining the reasons for its rejection. All bills and joint resolutions, with the exception of proposed constitutional amendments, must be presented to the president before they may become law.

Congressional action on a vetoed bill begins when Congress receives the returned bill with its accompanying presidential message. The house passing the bill first also reconsiders the vetoed bill first. The process of reconsideration is not described in the Constitution, so procedure and traditions govern the process of reconsidering vetoed legislation. The chamber receiving the bill publishes the president's veto message in its journal. At this point the chamber may lay the measure on the table, essentially ending further consideration of the legislation. The vetoed bill may be referred to committee, delaying its consideration by the whole chamber. The legislation also may be reconsidered immediately upon receipt.

The House and the Senate must vote to override vetoed legislation in order for the bill to become law. A two-thirds majority vote by members present is required to override a presidential veto. If the override vote fails in one chamber, the other house does not attempt to override. Action on a veto may be taken at any time during a Congress in which the veto is received.

From 1789 through 2004, 35 of the 43 presidents have vetoed legislation on 2,550 occasions. Most of these vetoes, 1,484, or 58 percent, have been returned vetoes. The remainder have been pocket vetoes. Only 7.1 percent of the regular have been overridden by Congress, evidence that presidential vetoes are effective tools of public policy.

Early presidents vetoed few bills because they believed that they should veto only legislation they believed to be unconstitutional. President George Washington vetoed two bills. President Andrew Jackson vetoed 12 bills, primarily those dealing with either the creation of a national bank or public works projects. President John Tyler was the first president to have a veto overridden. He vetoed 10 bills, with one bill being overridden in 1845.

Veto use expanded after the Civil War. Presidents serving from 1789 through 1868 vetoed 88 bills. From 1868 until 2004, presidents vetoed 2,462 bills. President Franklin Roosevelt vetoed 635 bills in four terms in office, with nine of those vetoes overridden. President Grover Cleveland averaged 73 vetoes per year, with a total of 584 vetoes. In the late 20th century President John F. Kennedy vetoed 21 bills in his shortened term in office. President LYNDON JOHNSON vetoed 30 bills. President Richard Nixon vetoed 43 bills, with 7 overrides. In his short term in office, President Gerald Ford vetoed 66 bills, with 12 overrides. President Jimmy Carter vetoed 31 bills and experienced two overrides. President Ronald Reagan vetoed 78 bills, with nine overrides. President George H. W. Bush vetoed 44 bills with only one override. President Bill Clinton vetoed 36 bills, and two of those vetoes were overridden. President George W. Bush did not veto any bills during his first term in office.

The use of the veto usually has negative consequences for a president. Americans usually view a president as a positive and assertive force, so a president who uses the veto numerous times risks being seen as lacking leadership. President Ford used the veto to control an assertive Congress under strong Democratic leadership. The extensive use of the veto suggested to some in the American public that President Ford lacked assertive leadership. President George H. W. Bush was criticized for overusing his veto power, even though only one bill, a measure to regulate cable television, was overridden, in October 1992.

Presidents are more likely to use the veto during periods of divided party government, when the executive branch is controlled by one party and the legislative branch is controlled by the other. A president with little congressional experience also is more likely to veto legislation. Research has documented that presidents are most likely to vetoes bills during the second and fourth years of their term. Congress is most likely to override a veto during divided party government, when the president is suffering from low public approval, after a midterm election, and in times of national economic crisis.

A process has developed by which a president decides which bills to veto. The Office of Management and Budget (OMB) reviews all enrolled bills, those pieces of legislation that have passed both houses of Congress but need to be acted on by the president. The OMB contacts the departments affected by bills and compiles the views of those affected by the bills under examination. This process has been used since the 1930s and has been adjusted only to focus on the president's priorities over the independent opinions of affected agencies.

The pocket veto has been a source of controversy since the ratification of the Constitution. The Constitution provides that any bill not returned by the president "within ten Days (Sundays excepted)" shall become law, "unless the Congress by their Adjournment prevent its Return, in which Case it shall not be a Law." The pocket veto was first used in 1812 by President James Madison. Since a pocket veto is not returned to Congress, it is not subject to a veto override. The primary controversy affecting the use of the pocket veto has been determining when Congress has adjourned. Several cases during the Nixon administration appeared to specify that a pocket veto could occur only after the final adjournment of Congress at the end of the second session. Presidents Ford and Carter accepted this decision and agreed not to use the pocket veto in the middle of a session or between the first and second sessions. Presidents Reagan, Bush, and Clinton did not follow this agreement and returned bills to Congress. This action raised the issue of whether Congress could vote to override. Efforts to legislate the definition of adjournment have been unsuccessful. The scope of using pocket vetoes has been determined by tradition and political agreements between the executive and legislative branches.

Further reading:
Copeland, Gary W. "When Congress and President Collide: Why Presidents Veto Legislation." *Journal of Politics* 45, no. 3 (1983): 696–710; Glover, K. Daniel. "The Road to Presidential Veto," *National Journal*, 25 June 2005, 2,062; Sollenberger, Mitchel A. *The Presidential Veto and Congressional Procedure.* Washington, D.C.: Library of Congress, Congressional Research Service, 2004; Spitzer, Robert J. *The Presidential Veto: Touchstone of the American Presidency.* Albany: State University of New York Press, 1988.

—John David Rausch, Jr.

vice president of the United States
John Adams, the first vice president of the United States, described the post as "the most insignificant office that ever the invention of man contrived or his imagination." JOHN NANCE GARNER, Franklin Roosevelt's first vice president,

famously derided his job as "not worth a pitcher of warm spit" (the exact wording is disputed) and said that accepting the role was "the worst damn fool mistake I ever made." On declining his party's vice presidential nomination in 1848, DANIEL WEBSTER stated, "I do not propose to be buried until I am dead." Such quotes condemning the second-highest office in the United States, of which many can be found, contain certain ironies; Adams, like many of his successors, went on to hold the presidency, Garner was recognized as one of the most influential vice presidents in history, and while Webster never achieved the presidency he desired, Millard Fillmore, who accepted the nomination Webster declined, succeeded to the presidency when Zachary Taylor died in office. A total of 14 presidents have previously held the vice presidency, with nine of those assuming the office following the death or resignation of the president.

In the early years of the republic, the vice presidency was awarded to the person coming in second in the Electoral College vote for president. The process inevitably led to difficulties, with political opponents serving together in the executive. The Constitution was amended in 1804 to provide for separate votes for the two posts. This has evolved into the current situation whereby the major parties' conventions nominate a partnership for president and vice president to be elected together. The choice of running mate has frequently been decided on a desire to "balance" the ticket in terms of geography, ideology, or experience. This convention was successfully challenged in 1992, when Bill Clinton chose Senator Al Gore (D-TN) as his running mate, assuring that young moderates from southern states filled both places on the Democrat ticket. It must still be noted that a certain balance was retained in terms of experience, with Clinton's background being governor of Arkansas while Gore gained his political prominence in the U.S. Senate.

The Constitution of the United States says very little about the job of the vice president, assigning the post only two formal roles. The vice president is second in line to the presidency; Article II states that "in case of the removal of the President from office, or of his death, resignation, or inability to discharge the powers and duties of the said office, the same shall devolve on the Vice President." This in itself is vague and was the subject of much debate as to whether "the same" referred to the office of president or only to the powers, a distinction that would determine whether the vice president in such instances should be sworn in as president or merely assume the role in an acting capacity. This was a particularly pertinent question should the president be unable to "discharge the powers" but subsequently recover. A precedent was set in 1841, when John Tyler took the presidential oath, assuming the powers and office, following the death of President William Henry Harrison. When President James

Garfield was shot and incapacitated in 1881, his vice president, Chester A. Arthur, fearing a constitutional crisis should the president recover, did not attempt to take the oath of office until Garfield died later that year. Following the assassination of President John F. Kennedy in 1963, the Constitution was amended to clarify the procedures; the Twenty-fifth Amendment enshrined the precedent that the vice president assumes the office on the death, resignation, or removal from office of the president, but only acts in his or her place should the president be temporarily unable to discharge his or her duties.

The second constitutional role given to the vice president is to be the presiding officer of the U.S. Senate, a curious provision in a system founded on the separation of powers. This is largely a symbolic role, with the vice president able to cast a vote only when the Senate is deadlocked. In practice the vice president performs this function only on ceremonial occasions or when the Senate is likely to be closely divided on an important issue. There have been occasions, however, when the ability to provide the casting vote has afforded the White House a crucial influence. When the election of 2000 produced a Senate equally divided between 50 Republicans and 50 Democrats, it was the vote of Vice President Dick Cheney that placed control of the chamber in the hands of the Senate Republicans. This arrangement was short-lived, ending when Senator JAMES JEFFORDS of Vermont left the Republican Party to become an independent, giving the Democrats the thinnest of majorities and as such control of the Senate.

The degree to which the vice president can assert any influence in the administration is largely in the hands of the president. As the quotes above suggest, the vice presidency has frequently been regarded as a powerless office. However, this caricature has not always been accurate. John Nance Garner brought a new authority to the post by using his knowledge and experience of Washington politics to help President Franklin Roosevelt pass much of his New Deal program through Congress. Garner was also the first vice president to attend cabinet meetings, a practice that still continues. Among others, Walter Mondale became one of President Carter's closest advisers as well as his vice president, and Dick Cheney has become a central figure in the George W. Bush administration. Today the vice president also serves on the National Security Council and on the president's Domestic Council. As the office of vice president has grown in the modern era, the holder has frequently been used by the president to work on a wide range of issues and task forces.

Further reading:
Ingram, S. *The Vice President of the United States.* San Diego, Calif.: Blackbirch Press, 2003; Timmons, B. *Garner of Texas: A Personal History.* New York: Harper, 1948.
—Ross M. English

vote ratings by interest groups

In order to influence the political process, many interest groups publish ratings of members of Congress. To create ratings interest groups select particular votes, typically ranging from 10 to 40 in each house of Congress, that the groups feel are relevant to their cause. If a member of Congress supports a group's positions on all the selected votes, the member receives a "perfect" score of 100. Conversely, members who oppose the interest group on all its selected roll calls receive a score of 0. Generally, a legislator's rating equals the percentage of the selected votes in which the member of Congress favored the group's position, though some groups weight votes in their ratings, giving more value to votes that the group believes are more important.

Interest groups that issue vote ratings can be relatively narrow in scope, focusing on issues such as environmental policy (League of Conservation Voters) or gun rights (National Rifle Association), or can be broad in scope, focusing on a variety of public policy issues (American Conservative Union). Labor unions (United Auto Workers), business and industry associations (Chamber of Commerce), and farm organizations (National Farmers Union) also rate members of Congress according to votes that are considered important to them.

A group with a broad ideological orientation that issues vote ratings is Americans for Democratic Action (ADA). ADA is a liberal group that annually rates all representatives and senators according to a "Liberal Quotient" from 0 to 100 based on votes on 20 issues each year that ADA deems most important. The advantage of measuring the overall ideological leanings of members of Congress based on the ADA scores is that since the ADA is an overtly ideological organization dedicated to encouraging legislators to take liberal positions on issues, the ADA Liberal Quotient scores tend to give a general impression as to where a member stands on the liberal-conservative ideological spectrum. The ADA rates members of Congress in an attempt to encourage legislators to support liberal positions, but at the same time conservatives can use low ADA scores as a measure of ideological "correctness."

An example of a group with a relatively narrow public interest mission that has tried to influence members of Congress by releasing vote ratings is the Concord Coalition. The coalition's so-called Fiscal Responsibility Scorecard gives each legislator a score between 0 and 100. Votes deemed to have a significant impact on deficit reduction are assigned various weights according to their relative importance. The Concord Coalition calculates the raw scores by adding the weights of a legislator's "fiscally responsible" votes and dividing this figure by the total weighted value of the votes cast by that legislator. To the Concord Coalition, "fiscal responsibility" is voting in favor of reduced spending or increased taxes and voting against increased spending or reduced taxes. Thus, the Concord Coalition's congressional vote scores can be seen as a means of measuring individual representatives and senators willingness to support the principles of balancing the budget from both the revenue side of the budget as well as the expenditure side of the budget.

The Concord Coalition is atypical of interest groups that publish congressional vote ratings in that those who receive the organization's highest (and lowest) ratings are not consistently on one end of the political spectrum or the other. Generally, the main distinction between interest groups is where they stand on the liberal-conservative axis. Nothing distinguishes the evaluations of interest groups other than where the group stands on the ideological spectrum.

Interest group ratings also tend to be closely related to partisanship. Members of Congress tend to have a bias toward certain groups and certain interests, and these groups and interests are determined to some degree by the party he or she represents. Partisanship, however, is not an infallible predictor of interest group ratings; roll calls often split one or both of the parties. These splits are in a large part due to the fact that legislators have parochial interests.

Nonetheless, interest groups may have a polarizing effect on legislators. Political activists, including the leaders of interest groups, tend to have more ideologically extreme opinions than the mass public. Attempts by legislators to take moderate positions may invoke criticism from interest groups at both ends of the ideological spectrum. Most interest group ratings, however, are to the exterior of members of Congress, meaning that the influence of interest groups encourages legislators to move away from moderate positions.

It is important to note that by no means should a rating be viewed as an irreproachable indicator of a representative's intentions. The imperfections of interest group ratings are in part due to the fact that they are based on a relatively small number of roll calls. Interest group ratings are also influenced by the distribution of the roll calls selected, which makes legislators' views appear to be more extreme than they actually are. Yet, though imperfect, over the long run interest group vote scores can provide a good indication of a legislator's behavior in office.

Further reading:

Poole, Keith T., and Howard Rosenthal. *Congress: A Political-Economic History of Roll Call Voting*, New York: Oxford University Press, 1997; Clausen, Age. *How Congressmen Decide: A Policy Focus*. New York: St. Martin's Press, 1973; Kiewiett, D. Roderick, and Mathew McCubbins. *The Logic of Delegation: Congressional Parties and the Logic of Delegation*. Chicago: University of Chicago Press, 1991; Snyder, James M., Jr. "Artificial Extremism in Interest Group Ratings." *Legislative Studies Quarterly* 17 (1992): 319–345.

—Patrick Fisher

voting in Congress

Member voting is a centerpiece of legislative activity. A legislator's voting record is the major legacy of his or her congressional career. Each calendar year members of Congress cast thousands of votes during subcommittee, standing committee, conference committee, and floor deliberations. They constantly are called to vote on procedural issues, amendments, and final consideration of bills on their chamber floors.

Most public attention traditionally has been focused on chamber floor voting. There are three ways of voting on the floor of the HOUSE OF REPRESENTATIVES. The simplest method is by taking a voice vote whereby members simply say "aye" or "nay." However, members uncertain of the outcome of a voice vote can demand that a division vote be taken. A more accurate approach is to take a formal vote by a "division of the house" method whereby members stand near their desk to vote in favor of or opposed to the question called. The choices of individual members are not recorded in either a voice or division vote, which are most frequently taken on procedural or minor issues.

Sometimes members desire a public record of the preferences of representatives' votes. In this case the House employs a record vote, which since 1972 has been cast using an electronic system to record member preferences. Electronic voting stations are scattered around the House floor. Logging on using their personal plastic voting cards, members then press a "yes," "no," or "present" button. Members make their choices before the deadline for ending the vote. Most often they are given 15 minutes to vote. This system provides an accurate record of both the final tally and how each member voted on the question.

A fourth system, although rarely used now, is a "teller" system. This approach features representatives stating their voting preference to designated "tellers," who then record the member and his or her preference. Although this system has been used in the House, it has never been used in the Senate.

Tie votes in the House normally can be broken by the SPEAKER OF THE HOUSE, who customarily never votes except to break a tie. Tie votes in the Senate are broken by the VICE PRESIDENT OF THE UNITED STATES.

In many ways senators are similar to representatives in their voting methods. They also have voice and division of the house votes, for example. However, senators often have avoided casting potentially politically charged recorded floor votes by first considering a motion to table. Casting even a recorded vote on a tabling motion has allowed senators to explain to inquiring constituents that the vote simply was a procedural one and not on the merits of the issue. Voting to table a bill essentially defeats the proposal, but members are not on record for ever voting on the bill.

However, rules often requiring super-majority support on floor votes have been how the Senate most differs from the House. The best-known rule is the one requiring 60 senators to support a CLOTURE vote to end a FILIBUSTER. This rule has enabled a cohesive minority of 41 or more senators to successfully block controversial measures. Senate majority parties seek to capture 60 or more seats with which to govern, while House majority parties need only a simple majority to assure passage of measures.

Under certain circumstances members may opt for an alternative to voting. One is a process called "pairing" between two members unable to attend a vote. A legislator on one side of an issue finds another favoring the opposite side so their mutual absences would in a sense cancel out one another. Members are certain to announce publicly their preferences on issues on which they are paired.

A second process is proxy voting, whereby a member will assign his or her voting right to a trusted colleague attending the voting session. Although neither chamber has ever permitted proxy voting on the floor, both have allowed it in committees. However, when the Republicans gained control of the House in 1995, they immediately banned the practice in committees. Their rule has frequently inconvenienced them and led committee chairs to either reschedule votes or at times even suffer defeats when supporters were attending other panel sessions. The Senate, under strict guidelines, allows limited proxy voting in committees.

Overall, members of Congress want to participate in as many votes as possible because a high absentee rate can quickly become an issue in their next reelection campaign. Members of both chambers have tended to average about a 95-percent participation rate for recorded floor votes.

Voting processes in committees and subcommittees are similar to those governing floor votes. Depending on the rules of the panel, members typically cast voice or recorded votes. Often only the final tally, without identifying individual members, is recorded. Committee members may make numerous votes during a lengthy session marking up a major or controversial bill.

Members have been found to consider numerous factors when deciding how to cast their votes. Important factors include party affiliation, constituent pressures, member ideology, and presidential positions. Significantly, members also look to fellow members as important sources of information and advice on how to vote.

Overall, studies have documented political party affiliation to be the most important factor influencing member voting. Political party identification does not automatically predict how a member will vote, however. Unlike legislators in most nations throughout the world, members of America's Congress can and often do break ranks from their fellow party members. Yet, since the early 1980s the prevailing trend in Congress has been toward increased partisanship in voting. A prime indicator of this has been the steady increase in instances when a majority of Democrats will vote on one side of an issue against a majority of Republicans on the opposite side.

Members' ideological views most commonly mirror their party affiliation. Democratic members of Congress tend to be left of the political center, while Republican members tend to be right of the political center. Few members of Congress are in the ideological middle. These factors underscore the growing distinct voting polarization between the political parties.

Another powerful factor influencing member voting is their constituency. Member ideology and party affiliation commonly are closely linked to their constituencies. As residents of the areas they represent, legislators naturally possess views similar to their constituents. In addition, members want to reflect the views of their constituents in order to assure reelection. If a legislator's natural inclination ever needs reinforcing, he or she need look no further than his or her e-mails, telephone calls, and postal delivery to hear from constituents volunteering advice on how to vote. In sum, all members of Congress fear their voting straying too far from the views of their constituents.

Presidents have also influenced congressional voting. By taking stands on major issues and seeking to set the CAPITOL HILL legislative agenda, presidents are actively engaged with Congress. Presidents lobby to win approval of their favored programs and threaten to veto bills they oppose either in part or entirely. Most modern presidents have tended to enjoy congressional support for more than two-thirds of the bills they support publicly. While presidents obviously have been more successful in winning the support of their fellow partisans on Capitol Hill, such support is not given automatically. As noted earlier, members of Congress respond to distinctive constituent and reelection pressures. On the other hand, members from the rival party might be able to increase constituent support by voting against a president's proposal. Moreover, congressional support of a president's legislative program tends to decline throughout his or her term in the White House.

Finally, before voting many members of Congress often consult the opinions of allied legislators. These peers normally are of the same political party, ideology, and region as the member consulting them. Members often share advice on how to explain their vote to constituents and interest groups. Being able to explain an important vote can be as important politically as casting the vote itself.

See also CONSERVATIVE COALITION.

Further reading:
Cain, Bruce, John Ferejohn, and Morris Fiorina. *The Personal Vote: Constituency Service and Electoral Independence.* Cambridge, Mass.: Harvard University Press, 1989; Kingdon, John. *Congressmen's Voting Decisions.* 3d ed. Ann Arbor: University of Michigan Press, 1989; Oleszek, Walter. *Congressional Procedures and the Policy Process.* 6th ed. Washington, D.C.: Congressional Quarterly Press, 2004; Poole, Keith, and Howard Rosenthal. *Congress: A Political-Economic History of Roll Call Voting.* New York: Oxford University Press, 1997; Smith, Steven. *Call to Order: Floor Politics in the House and Senate.* Washington, D.C.: Brookings Institution Press, 1989.

Voting Rights Act of 1965

This sweeping civil rights act marked the high point of the Civil Rights movement during the 1960s. It suspended literacy tests that were long used in the southern states to prevent African Americans from voting. The U.S. attorney general was authorized to appoint federal registrars to oversee voter registration in political subdivisions where literacy tests were previously used and where fewer than half the voting age residents were registered to vote or actually voted in 1964. The focus of this enforcement was particularly on the southern states of Alabama, Georgia, Louisiana, Mississippi, North Carolina, South Carolina, and Virginia.

The Civil Rights movement gained ground slowly in the 1950s. The first civil rights act since the Civil War passed Congress in 1957. It gave power to the U.S. attorney general to protect federal voting rights, created a civil rights commission, and provided a civil rights division in the Justice Department. A 1960 act strengthened the enforcement provisions for the earlier act and added tools to enforce school desegregation orders. The 1964 CIVIL RIGHTS ACT was a major step forward. It passed Congress after the Senate broke a historic FILIBUSTER. It outlawed discrimination in public accommodations and employment. It set up the Equal Employment Opportunity Commission and strengthened enforcement of voting laws.

In 1964 Democrat LYNDON JOHNSON won a sweeping election victory over Barry Goldwater, his Republican opponent, with a 61 to 39 percentage victory. The partisan advantage favored Democrats over Republicans by 68 to 32 in the Senate and 295 to 140 in the House. Significant as the 1964 Civil Rights Act was, voting participation by blacks, particularly in states in the former Confederacy, was inhibited by literacy tests, poll taxes, and intimidation. Black civil rights leaders chose Selma, Alabama (Dallas County), for demonstrations on behalf of voting rights beginning in March 1965. According to the CONGRESSIONAL QUARTERLY, despite a clear majority of voting age blacks in the Dallas County population, of 9,877 registered

voters, 9,542 were white and 335 were black. In the previous two years only 93 of 795 black applicants were allowed to register, but 745 of 1,232 whites were accepted.

President Johnson addressed the issue with a nationally televised speech and had an administration bill introduced in the Senate with 66 cosponsors on March 18, 1965. Southern Democrats attempted to slow and pick the bill apart with amendments. They succeeded in eliminating a ban on poll taxes from the bill. The Senate closed debate with a CLOTURE vote that carried on May 25. The cloture vote was only the second one in the Senate's history to pass to bring a civil rights bill to the Senate floor for a vote. The bill passed the Senate the next day 77-19. Yes votes were by 47 Democrats and 30 Republicans. Opposing were 17 southern Democrats and two Republicans.

The House version of the bill did include the poll tax ban. It was delayed in the HOUSE RULES COMMITTEE by its southern chair, Howard W. Smith (D-VA), but passed in July by a 333-85 vote. In conference the poll tax ban was dropped, and a conference report passed 328-74 in the House and 79-18 in the Senate. President Johnson signed the bill into law (PL 89-110) on August 6, 1965.

The results of the law and the work of the federal registrars in registering new voters produced immediate and dramatic results. In the former Confederate states the number of registered black voters increased by nearly 1 million between 1964 and 1968. Registration by blacks in Alabama rose from 23.0 percent of voting age population in 1964 to 56.7 percent in 1968. In Mississippi it rose from 6.7 percent to 59.4 percent in the same period. White voter registration and especially election turnout rose dramatically as well. Comparing turnout in 1962 to 1968, the number of participants rose from 10 million to nearly 15 million voters in the old Confederacy. Moreover, in the first decade of the act the number of black elected officials in the seven targeted southern states grew from fewer than 100 to 963.

Having lost in Congress, southerners opposed to the Voting Rights Act brought to the federal courts their argument that the federal law was an unconstitutional intrusion on the right of the states to enact and administer voting and election laws. South Carolina challenged the validity of the law and sought a Court injunction to prevent Attorney General Nicolas Katzenbach from enforcing it. Five states filed briefs in support of South Carolina, and 21 filed in support of the attorney general. Chief Justice Earl Warren wrote the opinion for a nearly unanimous Court:

> The Voting Rights Act was designed by Congress to banish the blight of racial discrimination in voting, which has infected the electoral process in parts of our country for nearly a century. The Act creates stringent new remedies for voting discrimination where it persists on a pervasive scale, and in addition the statute

strengthens existing remedies for pockets of voting discrimination elsewhere in the country. Congress assumed the power to prescribe these from [paragraph] 2 of the Fifteenth Amendment, which authorizes the National Legislature to effectuate by "appropriate" measures the constitutional prohibition against racial discrimination in voting. We hold that the sections of the act which are properly before us are an appropriate means for carrying out Congress' constitutional responsibilities and are consonant with all other provisions of the Constitution. We therefore deny South Carolina's request that enforcement of these sections of the Act be enjoined.

The Voting Rights Act of 1965 was written to be effective for five years. In 1969 President Nixon proposed to extend the act for another five years but remove the focus on seven southern states. Civil rights leaders wanted the act unchanged and simply extended for five years. The president's version passed the House, but the Senate adopted a five-year extension of the 1965 law with the addition of a provision to reduce the voting age from 21 to 18 years of age. In June 1978 the House accepted the Senate version. President Nixon signed the bill, although he disapproved of changing the voting age by law instead of by a constitutional amendment. The Supreme Court upheld the lower voting age but limited its effect to federal elections. (In 1971 Congress proposed the Twenty-sixth Amendment to constitutionally empower 18-year-olds with the vote, and it was ratified by the states in record time.)

In 1975 voting rights proponents moved to extend the 1965 act for 10 years with coverage for Spanish-speaking Americans. Although there were efforts from southern Democrats to delay the bill, two successful cloture votes paved the way to passage. However, an amendment reduced the extension to seven years. The House accepted the Senate amendments, and the bill passed easily and was signed by President Gerald Ford.

By 1982 a broad coalition of civil rights groups had organized a widespread popular and lobbying effort to renew and extend the life of the Voting Rights Act. The extension of the law was never in serious political jeopardy. It extended for 25 years the enforcement provisions of the law, requiring states with a history of discrimination to get Justice Department approval for changes in their election laws or procedures.

As amended, the act allows private parties to prove a violation of the act by showing that some election procedure "results" in voting discrimination. In court cases applying the law, the court would judge the "totality of circumstances" to conclude whether there had been a violation of the law. This "results" provision was a particular response to an earlier Supreme Court decision that required proof of "intent" to discriminate. Results would be easier to demonstrate than intent.

Having chosen to enforce results rather than intent, the Senate passed the amended bill 85-8, and the House accepted the Senate's amendments without debate by UNANIMOUS CONSENT. Most of the prior opposition from the South had been extinguished by the fact that blacks were a significant part of the electorate, increasingly represented in their interests by the senators and representatives of the southern states.

While the original Voting Rights Act had enormous consequences on voting participation by both blacks and whites in the southern states, the 1982 amendments were highly consequential as well. In a landmark case arising in North Carolina, *Thornburg v. Gingles* (1986), the U.S. Supreme Court forbade the state from drawing congressional districts that would dilute minority voting strength. North Carolina summarized the rules from *Thornburg* and cases following it for its legislators after the 2000 Census:

> All 100 counties are subject to Section 2 of the Voting Rights Act, which may require drawing districts which contain a majority minority population if three threshold conditions are present: 1) a minority group is large enough and lives closely enough together so that a relatively compact district in which the group constitutes a majority can be drawn, 2) the minority group has a history of political cohesiveness or voting as a group, and 3) the white majority has a history of voting as a group sufficient to allow it to usually defeat the minority group's preferred candidate. The totality of circumstances, including a past history of discrimination that continues to affect the exercise of a minority group's right to vote, must also be taken into consideration.

While there remain unresolved questions about redistricting, it is clear that the Voting Rights Act as amended has broad application and that its provisions have enhanced opportunities for minority candidates in the electoral process. The results of the Voting Rights Act have dramatically and literally changed the complexion of public office holders. The 107th Congress included 36 African-American members in the House along with 19 Hispanics. Black elected officials after 2000 numbered 9,040, a sixfold increase since 1970. In fact, the number of black elected officials (1,628) in Mississippi and Alabama at last report exceeded the number for the entire nation in 1970. Recent trends suggest that increasingly minority elected officials win office from constituencies without a majority of minority voters. Moreover, Hispanics have become the largest minority in the United States, whose electoral prospects benefit from the Voting Rights Act.

See also MEMBERSHIP: AFRICAN AMERICANS; MEMBERSHIP: HISPANIC AMERICANS.

Further reading:
South Carolina v. Katzenbach 383 U.S. 301 (1966); *Congress and the Nation.* Washington D.C.: Congressional Quarterly Press, 1977; Bositis, D. A. *Black Elected Officials: A Statistical Summary.* Available online. URL: http://www.jointcenter.org/. Accessed 12 December 2002. and *North Carolina Redistricting.* Available online. URL: http://www.ncga.state.nc.us/GIS/Redistricting. Accessed December 12, 2002.

—Jack R. Van Der Slik

Wagner Act

The Wagner Act, also known as the National Labor Relations Act of 1935, was created by Congress to protect the rights of workers to unionize. The legislation also created a new government agency, the National Labor Relations Board (NLRB), which would be responsible for enforcing the law. The act applies to all employers involved in interstate commerce, with the exception of airlines, railroads, agriculture, and the government itself, and instructs the NLRB to assess whether employees want union representation and investigate any violations of labor practices by employers and unions.

The Wagner Act guarantees nonsupervisory employees the right to self-organize, select their own representatives, and engage in collective bargaining activities. The Wagner Act makes it illegal for employers and unions to interfere with these rights. The NLRB, in enforcing the Wagner Act, consists of five appointees each selected by the president and confirmed by a majority vote in the U.S. Senate for five-year terms. Regional offices are scattered throughout the nation to assist in the enforcement of the terms of the Wagner Act.

The rationale behind the Wagner Act is that the inequality of bargaining power between employees who do not possess freedom of association and employers who are organized into corporate structures substantially burdens the flow of commerce and tends to aggravate depression situations by keeping wage rates artificially low and reducing the purchasing power of employees. The Wagner Act states that experience has proven that protecting employee rights to organize and bargain collectively promotes the flow of commerce. The policy of the U.S. government in 1935 was to eliminate the causes of substantial obstacles to the free flow of commerce and to reduce those obstructions when they occurred by encouraging the practice of collective bargaining and by protecting the rights of workers to have freedom of association, self-organization, and selection of bargaining representatives of their own choosing.

In its enforcement of the Wagner Act, the NLRB has two primary functions. The first is to determine through secret ballot elections the choice by employees of whether they wish to have union representation, and if so, by which union. The second function is to prevent and remedy unfair labor practices by either employers or unions when they occur. The NLRB, however, is a reactive administrative agency only and cannot bring charges on its own. It processes only those charges that are filed under the Wagner Act with the NLRB. The Wagner Act was significantly amended in 1947 with the Taft-Hartley Act, which added provisions allowing unions to be prosecuted, enjoined, or sued for a variety of activities, and in 1959 with the Landrum-Griffin Act, when Congress imposed further restrictions on union activities.

The passage of the Wagner Act galvanized union organizing in the United States. It clearly limited the rights of employers to harass, interrogate, or dismiss employees for union activities. It specified that employers could not issue threats, warnings, or orders to employees to restrain from union activities, as that would constitute coercion under Section 8 of the Wagner Act. Similarly, the law declared that employers could not take disciplinary actions such as suspensions, demotions, or discharges against employees engaging in collective bargaining or union activities. Section 8 also prohibits unfair labor practices such as failure to guarantee fair representation to all members of the bargaining units. The Wagner Act sets out the general rights and responsibilities of employers and employees.

Further reading:
"The National Labor Relations Act." Available online. URL: www.http://www.nlrb.gov/facts.html. Accessed 8 February 2003.

—Nancy S. Lind

Walter L. Nixon v. U.S. 506 U.S. 224 (1993)

Article I, Section 3, Clause 6, of the U.S. Constitution states that the Senate shall have the sole power to try all impeachments. In *Walter L. Nixon v. U.S.* the Supreme Court unanimously confirmed that the power given the Senate includes flexibility in establishing procedures for and conducting impeachment proceedings. The Senate traditionally conducted impeachment proceedings on the Senate floor, with the full body hearing evidence and deliberating as a jury. In the 1980s, however, the Senate began using a new expedited procedure in which a committee of 12 conducts the evidentiary hearing and delivers a report to the full Senate, which then deliberates and votes. Nixon, a judge for the southern district of Mississippi impeached for perjury and "bringing the judiciary into disrepute" (he was impeached only after refusing to resign and continuing to receive his salary while serving in prison for perjury before a grand jury), challenged his Senate conviction, arguing that the expedited impeachment procedure was unconstitutional.

Seizing upon the constitutional language, particularly the words *sole* and *try,* Chief Justice William Rehnquist's opinion for the Court stated that Nixon's claim was nonjusticiable because the Senate's sole power to try impeachments leaves no role for the judiciary in evaluating the process. Nor, according to Rehnquist, does the word *try* in the clause constitute an "identifiable textual limit" on the Senate's authority. Concurring in the result, Justices Byron White and William Blackmun would have reached the merits of the case but concluded that the Senate's procedures were constitutionally acceptable; the impeachment clause, wrote Justice White, "was not meant to bind the hands of the Senate beyond establishing a set of minimal procedures."

—Daniel Smith

war powers

War powers are vague constitutional provisions allowing military action to protect the United States from enemies. The framers of the Constitution divided war powers between the legislative and executive branches. Article I, Section 8, of the U.S. Constitution grants Congress the power to tax and spend for the common defense, to declare war, to raise and support armies and a navy, and to make rules for the government of such military forces. Article II, Section 2, makes the president commander in chief. While Congress has the power to declare war, presidents have claimed the authority to place military in foreign countries and to wage war. There have been only five declared wars in American history: the War of 1812, the Mexican-American War, the Spanish-American War, World War I, and World War II. In the case of the War of 1812, Congress debated the merits of declaring war. In the other conflicts Congress acknowledged that the United States was already at war and readily agreed to approve the president's request for a declaration of war. U.S. military forces have been deployed in military actions abroad more than 200 times without a congressional declaration of war.

The Supreme Court has been asked to decide war power disputes between the legislative and executive branches numerous times in American history. The Court ruled in *Bas v. Tingy* (4 Dallas [4 U.S.] 37 [1800]) that Congress could authorize a war both by a formal declaration and by passing statutes that recognized a state of "limited," "partial," or "imperfect" conflict. In the *Prize* cases (67 U.S. 635 [1863]) the Supreme Court ruled that President Abraham Lincoln had the constitutional authority to order a blockade of Confederate ports. The Court argued that the president did not have the power to initiate a war, but he did have the authority to react with military force when threatened with military force without special legislative authority. The Court added to the president's power in foreign policy in its rulings in *United States v. Curtiss-Wright Export Corp.* (299 U.S. 304 [1936]) and *United States v. Belmont* (301 U.S. 324 [1937]). According to the Court, the president represented the nation in its foreign relations and affairs and, therefore, needed to be able to act without seeking legislative approval.

As the United States became a world power in the 20th century, executive power in foreign affairs grew, especially during the tensions of the cold war after World War II. The judicial branch has been less willing to involve itself in the conflict between the legislative and executive branches over war powers. The courts have called the issue a political question not appropriate for judicial action. In 1973 Congress sought to more clearly define the constitutional allocation of war powers by enacting the WAR POWERS RESOLUTION over President Richard Nixon's veto. The law established time and communications requirements on any troop deployments by the president. Rather than settle the war powers question, the act has caused additional controversy, as each president since 1973 has claimed that the act is unconstitutional while working to fulfill its requirements.

Further reading:
Fisher, Louis. *Presidential War Power.* Lawrence: University of Kansas Press, 1995; Stern, Gary M., and Morton H. Halperin. *The U.S. Constitution and the Power to Go to War: Historical and Current Perspectives.* Westport, Conn.: Greenwood Press, 1994.

—John David Rausch, Jr.

War Powers Resolution of 1973

The War Powers Resolution of 1973 is a joint resolution (PL 93-148) that attempts to limit the president's ability to engage U.S. combat forces in foreign conflicts and to reassert congressional authority in matters of war and, by extension, foreign affairs. While the proximate cause of its passage was America's involvement in the Southeast Asian conflict, the remote cause was the historic constitutional tension between presidents, who need speed and flexibility in responding to threats to national security, and lawmakers, who expect to be consulted by the president and to vote on the decision to use force.

Following an alleged attack on U.S. ships in the Gulf of Tonkin in 1964, President LYNDON B. JOHNSON requested congressional approval to send the U.S. military to Vietnam, and Congress obliged by passing the TONKIN GULF RESOLUTION. By 1972 the scope of the conflict had been expanded by President Nixon to include Cambodia and Laos without a formal declaration of war or direct authorization by Congress. Many lawmakers in both houses sought to end the U.S. military involvement, and they drafted bills to prevent any future military adventure from occurring without Congress's expressed consent. Led by Jacob K. Javits (R-NY), Thomas F. Eagleton (D-MO), and John Stennis (D-MS) in the Senate and Clement J. Zablocki (D-WI), chair of the FOREIGN AFFAIRS COMMITTEE, among many others, in the House, both chambers passed different bills that died in conference committee in December 1972. Work resumed in 1973, with the House devising a stronger version of its 1972 bill and the Senate holding firm to its earlier proposal. The major differences between the bills involved the length of time troops could be committed by the president without congressional approval (30 days and 120 days, Senate and House versions, respectively), and the circumstances under which the president could dispatch U.S. forces absent Congress's blessing (the Senate enumerated these, while the House's broad statement appeared to give the president great discretion). Senator J. William Fulbright (D-AR) offered an amendment in the Senate comparable to the House version but was opposed by Eagleton, who viewed such sweeping language as granting the president excessive authority. Conferees ultimately adopted the Fulbright amendment and compromised on the length of deployment at 90 days (60 plus a 30-day extension, if requested), and returned the joint resolution to each chamber. H J Res 542 cleared Congress but was vetoed by Nixon on October 24, explaining in his veto message that the joint resolution was "both unconstitutional and dangerous to the best interests of our nation," and "would seriously undermine this nation's ability to act decisively and convincingly in times of international crisis." As each of Nixon's prior vetoes had been sustained, it was something of a surprise that first the House (284-135) and then the Senate (75-18) voted to override the veto on November 7.

The resolution allows the president to send American troops into combat on foreign soil under the following conditions: when Congress votes to declare war; when Congress specifically authorizes the use of force by law; and when a foreign attack on the United States, its territories or possessions, or its armed forces causes a national emergency. The president must immediately inform Congress of any of the above situations, and "in every possible instance," consult with Congress before dispatching troops. If forces are deployed to the field, the president must inform the SPEAKER OF THE HOUSE and the President Pro Tempore within 48 hours. (The Speaker and the President Pro Tempore are given the power to convene Congress to receive the president's message should Congress be adjourned.) If Congress does not declare war, vote to sustain the president's decision to use force, or is unable to meet because of an attack on the country, the president must withdraw the troops within 60 days. The president may ask Congress to extend the deployment for an additional 30 days if the president certifies to Congress that the safety of the troops would be jeopardized with a quicker withdrawal. Congress can require that the president remove U.S. forces from hostilities at any time by passing a concurrent resolution—an action that cannot be vetoed by the president—so long as there was no formal declaration of war or specific congressional authorization to use force.

Legal scholars differ in their interpretations of the constitutionality of the War Powers Resolution. Some believe that Congress was correct in reasserting its authority and that the resolution remains an effective instrument, while others claim that the resolution was ill-conceived and unconstitutional or that it was effectively rendered unconstitutional with the Supreme Court's 1983 decision in *IMMIGRATION AND NATURALIZATION SERVICE V. CHADHA*, which negated the legislative veto. But since neither branch has ever directly challenged the constitutionality of the resolution in court, its political consequences remain. Since 1975 presidents have sent more than 50 reports to Congress informing it of hostilities overseas, but only President Ford detailed his use of force in response to the Mayaguez incident of 1975. In every case presidents have refused to recognize the resolution as controlling, while Congress attempted to invoke it. There have been a number of instances in which presidents negotiated compromises that loosened the restrictive language of the resolution. For example, President Reagan was able to send marines to Lebanon in 1983 for 18 months following a deal with Speaker THOMAS P. O'NEILL (D-MA). Presidents have also sought congressional approval to use any means necessary, including force, to deal with hostile actors, as both Presidents Bush did in 1991 and 2003. With the increasing number of NATO and UN security and peace-keeping actions that have involved American forces, the resolution has allowed Congress to question the president's decisions, and it will continue to do so for the foreseeable future.

Further reading:
Avella, Joseph R. "Whose Decision to Use Force?" *Presidential Studies Quarterly* 26: 485–495; Farrar-Myers, Vic-

toria A. "Transference of Authority: The Institutional Struggle over the Control of the War Power." *Congress and the Presidency* 25 (1998): 183–197; Fisher, Louis, and David Gray Adler. "The War Powers Resolution: Time to Say Goodby." *Political Science Quarterly* 113 (1998): 1–20; Rubner, Michael. "Antiterrorism and the Withering of the 1973 War Powers Resolution." *Political Science Quarterly* 102 (1997): 193–215.

—Thomas J. Baldino

Watergate Committee

This committee, also know as the Ervin Committee, was formally called the Senate Select Committee on Presidential Campaign Activities. The SENATE's purpose in creating it was to investigate the raising and spending of funds for the presidential election of 1972 as well as illegal or unethical behavior in that election. The effect of the Senate Watergate Committee's work was the energizing of the more hesitant HOUSE JUDICIARY COMMITTEE, which recommended articles of impeachment against President Richard M. Nixon. The latter committee relied heavily on witnesses, testimony, and evidence developed by the Senate Watergate Committee.

The initial impetus for the committee came from the Majority Leader, Senator Mike Mansfield, a Democrat from Montana. Mansfield had grave concerns about actions of the Committee for the Reelection of the President, headed by John N. Mitchell, who had resigned his position as attorney general in order to assume this position. Senator Mansfield was particularly concerned that the president's campaign committee had raised large cash contributions from corporate executives and stashed the money in safes and secret accounts to keep the sources of the funds secret. The spending of the funds also concerned Mansfield because he believed that they paid for the dissemination of vicious, deliberate lies about candidates for the Democratic presidential nomination, candidates who polls indicated could have run a competitive race against President Nixon. Mansfield further believed that the president's campaign committee has used its vast resources to pay for five men to break into the headquarters of the Democratic National Committee (DNC) located in the Watergate office and apartment complex. On June 17, 1972, the burglars had been arrested in the DNC offices by local police.

On February 7, 1973, the Senate unanimously approved Mansfield's recommendation and created a bipartisan select committee, with Senator Sam J. Ervin, Jr., a Democrat from North Carolina, as its chair. Prior to his election to the Senate, Ervin had had extensive legal experience as a trial lawyer and a judge. In the Senate he had earned a reputation for independence. Once the committee hearings began, they received gavel to gavel television coverage.

Senator Ervin had expected the investigation to find that overzealous members of the president's campaign committee and perhaps some overzealous White House aides were the primary culprits involved in the planning and cover-up of the break-in. In mid-May President Nixon issued a statement acknowledging that there had been a White House cover-up but that he had had no knowledge of it prior to March 21, 1973. Senator Ervin's expectations began to change, however, and the president's credibility was jeopardized by the testimony of John W. Dean III, a White House aide.

The committee gave John Dean immunity for his testimony—that is, his testimony could not be used as evidence against him in a criminal trial. However, the government could prosecute him for things about which he testified if the government had evidence against him obtained independently of his testimony. Although his title was counsel to the president, he took orders from H. R. Haldeman and John Ehrlichman, the president's closest White House advisers. Dean confessed that he had obstructed justice and committed perjury. His testimony included a lengthy written statement. It took the entire first day of his testimony to read it. In it he told of wrongdoing by high-level White House officials, including the president. Dean, in his public testimony, told of a secret meeting with the president on September 15, 1972, which convinced him that the president was aware of the Watergate cover-up. Nixon, however, had stated that he knew nothing about the cover-up prior to March 21, 1973. Dean told Sam Dash, chief counsel to the Watergate Committee, that he was convinced that his meeting with President Nixon was being recorded.

It was on Friday, July, 13, 1973, that the Watergate Committee's staff found out that there were indeed tapes of conversations in the Oval Office and certain other offices in which the president engaged in discussions. The staff learned this while interviewing Alexander Butterfield, a former aide of H. R. Haldeman. Butterfield had no role in the Watergate cover-up, but he did testify that voice-activated tape recording devices were installed in 1971.

The Watergate Committee issued a subpoena for certain tapes, but the president refused to comply, asserting executive privilege—that is, the president's right to confidentiality in his communications with his subordinates. As a compromise Nixon offered summaries of the tapes. That was unacceptable to the committee. The committee filed a civil suit against the president in federal district court but was unsuccessful both there and in the court of appeals. The committee did not appeal to the Supreme Court because its authority was due to expire on February 8, 1974.

The fight for the tapes was continued by Archibald Cox, the special prosecutor investigating the Watergate affair. In what is known as the "Saturday Night Massacre," President Nixon ordered Attorney General Elliot Richardson to fire Cox. Richardson refused and resigned from office. Richardson's deputy attorney general, William Ruckleshaus, also refused to fire Cox and was himself fired. Solicitor General Robert Bork carried out the president's order. These events forced the House Judiciary Committee seriously to consider impeachment. Leon Jaworski, the new special prosecutor, continued the quest for the tapes and ultimately succeeded before the Supreme Court in *United States v. Nixon* (1974). It was, however, the work of the Senate Watergate Committee that laid the groundwork for the special prosecutor and the House Judiciary Committee.

See also IMPEACHMENT OF PRESIDENT RICHARD NIXON.

Further reading:
Dash, Samuel. *Chief Counsel: Inside the Ervin Committee—The Untold Story of Watergate.* New York: Random House, 1976; Ervin, Sam J., Jr. *The Whole Truth: The Watergate Conspiracy.* New York: Random House, 1980; Fields, Howard. *High Crimes and Misdemeanors: The Dramatic Story of the Rodino Committee.* New York: Norton, 1978.

—Patricia A. Behlar

Watergate scandal

Popularly known under the heading Watergate, the scandal in the administration of President Richard Nixon spanning the years 1972 to 1975 was the most serious constitutional crisis of the 20th century and the gravest institutional crisis in the history of the presidency. Congress played its constitutional role by gathering information that ultimately led to the nation's only instance of forced resignation of a sitting president.

Watergate stemmed from a lengthy list of conspiracies including burglary, illegal wiretapping, extortion, money laundering, forgery, spying, fraud, playing political dirty tricks, and attempting to cover up these illegal activities. Most of the allegations involved activities supporting President Nixon's reelection campaign of 1972.

Although the scandal stemmed from the behavior of leaders of the Nixon administration, attempting to resolve the crisis required the efforts of both Congress and the federal court system. Both houses of Congress became involved in terms of investigating the Nixon administration and in initiating impeachment proceedings against the president.

The SENATE created a Select Committee on Presidential Campaign Activities, more popularly known as the WATERGATE COMMITTEE or the Ervin Committee, after its chair, Senator Sam Ervin, a Democrat from North Carolina. The fact-finding efforts of the committee were publicized in great detail each day and were frequently televised, often live. Their efforts subsequently helped provide evidence to help the HOUSE JUDICIARY COMMITTEE vote out articles of impeachment on the president.

The House Judiciary Committee, chaired by Peter Rodino, a Democrat from New Jersey, also conducted an investigation while additionally receiving evidence gathered by a federal grand jury. The committee's often dramatic hearings, deliberations, and impeachment votes were televised live and followed closely not only nationally but internationally as well. Meanwhile, the SENATE JUDICIARY COMMITTEE on May 7, 1973, voted to support the nomination of Elliot Richardson to become the new attorney general on the condition that he agree to appoint an independent special prosecutor to investigate Watergate-related allegations.

The constitutional boiling point of the crisis occurred with the struggle to compel the president to release audio tapes of conversations about Watergate activities and the cover-up he planned with the help of key aides. In late June 1973 John Dean, the White House counsel, told the Senate's Watergate Committee that the president had extensive early knowledge about the Watergate break-in and attempted cover-up. His testimony also suggested that the president's conversations with key aides had been recorded. The following month a White House staff member, Alexander Butterfield, told the senators that presidential conversations held in rooms throughout the executive office complex and even at Camp David were indeed routinely recorded.

This revelation ignited a lengthy and increasingly intense legal struggle pitting the president against the House Judiciary Committee, the Senate Watergate Committee, and the independent prosecutor's office. The president cited executive privilege and declined to release the tapes. He also directed the special prosecutor, Archibald Cox, to abandon lawsuit efforts to win release of the tapes. Cox rebuffed the president's order. Nixon, during the famous "Saturday night massacre," subsequently fired Cox, accepted the resignation of his attorney general, William Richardson, who declined to fire the special prosecutor, and fired his deputy, William Ruckelshaus, for failing to carry out the order to fire Cox.

The subsequent explosion of public, media, and congressional protest at the "massacre" greatly weakened the president's political position. On April 30, 1974, Nixon reluctantly relinquished extensively edited printed transcripts of selected White House conversations. Members of the House Judiciary Committee immediately rejected the documents as incomplete. The newly appointed special prosecutor in the case, Leon Jaworski, quickly sought a

Supreme Court ruling to compel the president to relinquish the tapes themselves.

The beginning of the end of the crisis occurred on July 24, 1974, when the president reluctantly agreed to relinquish the tapes themselves after the Supreme Court ordered him to do so by a 8-0 vote. (Justice Rehnquist declined to hear the case because he had been in Nixon's administration before recently joining the Court.) The unanimous verdict proved to be important because White House insiders leaked reports that Nixon was seriously considering not obeying such a ruling by the Court if there appeared to be deep divisions among the justices.

However, the release of the tapes intensified the pressure on the president. First, the tapes provided solid evidence that the president had played a leading role in obstructing justice, thereby supporting at least one article of impeachment. However, the tapes ignited yet another firestorm of protest when they revealed an 18-and-a-half minute gap in a critical conversation between Nixon and Haldeman on June 20, 1972. The president and his personal staff were unable to provide an explanation for the blank space on the tape, which satisfied neither congressional nor public critics.

With the final documentation in hand, congressional committees quickly began brining their efforts to a conclusion. On July 12, 1974, the Senate Watergate Committee released its final report, which included the testimony of 63 witnesses and 2,217 pages of documentation. A few weeks later the House Judiciary Committee, which had received numerous drafts of articles of impeachment dating back to the previous fall, began formally considering articles of impeachment. With his likely ouster increasingly appearing to be imminent, President Nixon formally resigned on August 9, 1974, and departed the White House for his home in San Clemente, California.

See also IMPEACHMENT OF PRESIDENT RICHARD NIXON; WATERGATE COMMITTEE.

Further reading:
Genovese, Michael. *The Watergate Crisis*. Westport, Conn.: Greenwood Press, 1999; Kutler, Stanley. *The Wars of Watergate*. New York: Norton, 1992; *United States v. Nixon*, 418 U.S. 683 (1974); *Watergate: Chronology of a Crisis*. Washington, D.C.: Congressional Quarterly Press, 1975.

—Robert E. Dewhirst

Ways and Means, House Committee on
Among the oldest, most prestigious, and influential standing committees of the HOUSE OF REPRESENTATIVES, Ways and Means bears the constitutional responsibility assigned to the House in Article I, Section 7, that "all bills for raising revenue shall originate in the House of Representatives but the Senate may propose or concur with amendments as on other bills." Thus, the committee's central purpose is to consider legislation designed to finance the operation of the federal government. It reviews bills dealing with taxation in its many forms, for example, corporate and individual income taxes; tariffs, excise, estate, and gift taxes; federal bond sales; the national debt; international trade; and beginning in the 20th century, several large programs that disburse federal funds, such as, Social Security, Medicare, and a number of social welfare and unemployment programs. The committee currently has 41 members and six permanent subcommittees: Trade, Oversight, Health, Social Security, Human Resources, and Select Revenue Matters.

As directed in the Constitution, the House has principal responsibility for money matters, particularly revenue legislation. However, in the early days of the republic, the executive branch, in the person of Alexander Hamilton, President George Washington's secretary of the Treasury, dominated fiscal policy formation. Though the House created a select Committee of Ways and Means consisting of 11 members on July 24, 1789, it never met and was disbanded in September 1789, nearly concurrently with the establishment of the Treasury Department. In so doing the House essentially relinquished responsibility for fiscal policy to Hamilton, who brought his proposals before the full chamber for discussion. Hamilton's measures generally passed, but as his proposals became increasingly controversial, they divided the members and contributed, by many accounts, to the formation of parties in Congress. In an effort to reassert some degree of oversight of Hamilton, the House appointed a select committee in March 1794 to study revenue issues. The Fourth Congress in 1795 saw the creation of a "standing" (though, in contemporary terms, select) Committee of Ways and Means, which, coupled with Hamilton's retirement, gave the committee somewhat greater latitude to operate. It demanded detailed estimates of expenditures and revenues, reviewed them, and reported bills to the House as necessary. The next two Congresses voted to reestablish the committee, though its size fluctuated between seven and 16 members.

Not until 1802, with the Jeffersonians in firm control of the government, did the House vote to establish a true standing Ways and Means Committee, when it revised its rules that year. It also revised the committee's jurisdiction to add appropriations, which gave the committee even more influence. From 1801 to 1807 the brilliant JOHN RANDOLPH, a Democrat from Virginia, chaired the committee and brought distinction to its work. During the so-called Era of Good Feelings, the Jeffersonian Republicans repealed the excise taxes, financed the Louisiana Purchase and the War of 1812, and in 1816 wrote the country's first protective tariff. Responsibility for tariffs passed from Ways and Means to the Committee on Manufactures the next year but returned to Ways and Means in 1832. With its increased responsibility the committee began to use subcommittees frequently, and this practice continued through the Civil War. Among its accomplishments during this time were the Tariffs of 1833, 1842, 1846, 1857, and 1861. It was also intimately involved in the debate over a national bank and to a lesser extent, the battle over slavery.

The Civil War brought increased work with the obvious need to fund the war and more changes to the committee. Under the leadership of Thaddeus Stevens, a Republican from Pennsylvania, the committee drafted the nation's first income tax, recommended increasing protective tariff rates several times, drafted and passed the Legal Tender Act that authorized the Treasury Department to issue paper currency, and considered numerous military appropriations bills. The demands to handle both revenue and appropriations legislation seriously overextended the committee's capacity, so in 1865 the House revised its rules to remove jurisdiction over appropriations, banking, and currency from the committee and assigned these matters to two new committees.

In the postwar years the committee focused its energy on revenue bills, particularly tariffs, though it did find time to conduct several investigations employing subcommittees into financial scandals such as those involving the Sanborn contracts and the Pacific Mall Steamship Company. During this period the committee's size increased from 13 to 17. In 1865 the House gave the committee the privilege to report its bills to the floor at any time, the committee's name changed subtly, and in 1885 the chair of the committee, who was appointed by the SPEAKER OF THE HOUSE, was made one of the three majority members of the HOUSE RULES COMMITTEE. These changes brought additional influence to the committee and made service on it a plum assignment. However, the committee had its detractors, mostly among reformers who sought changes in the tariff system. One of them, Representative James McKenzie, a Democrat from Kentucky, referred to the committee as the "gorgeous mausoleum" where bills intended to change revenue and customs duties are "buried." In fact, Republican control of Congress during much of the Gilded Age (1865 to 1890) ensured that revenue sources would favor the interests of big business and not those of the individual or small businesspeople.

The transition to the new century brought more changes to the committee than just its name, as it became known as the Committee on Ways and Means after 1880. Much of the committee's time was devoted to funding two wars, the Spanish-American and World War I, and tariff rates, either increasing or decreasing them depending on which party was in control. Among the more memorable tariffs were McKinley (1890), Payne-Aldrich (1909), Underwood (1913), and Smoot-Hawley (1930). With the ascendance of Oscar W. Underwood, a Democrat from Alabama, to the chair from 1911 to 1915, the committee significantly lowered tariff rates, eliminating protectionist provisions that favored certain industries, and passed the first corporate and personal income taxes, consistent with the Sixteenth Amendment, which was ratified in 1913. While the income tax remained, much of the tariff reforms were rolled back following the resumption of Republican control in 1920.

Beyond its role in crafting revenue bills, the committee's importance to the political life of the House was fully realized during this time. The "revolt" against "Czar" JOSEPH CANNON, a Republican from Illinois, that caused the diminution of the Speaker's powers led to increased authority for all the committee chairs. Democrats reformed their party's rules to give Ways and Means responsibility for making committee assignments. Thus, Democrats on Ways and Means became their party's committee on committees. Moreover, the party voted to make membership on Ways and Means exclusive, meaning that its members could serve on no other standing committees. Republicans followed suit in some of these areas but not others. They created a separate committee on committees in 1917, stripped the Ways and Means chair from serving as Majority Leader, and removed all standing committee chairs from serving on the Rules Committee. Interestingly, Democrats revised their rules when they returned to the minority to match those of the Republicans, with the exception of creating a distinct committee on committees.

Democrats assumed control of Congress in 1931 and dominated the legislature for most of the next six decades, and while the partisan change affected the committee, it was President Franklin Roosevelt's (FDR) response to the Great Depression with his NEW DEAL legislative agenda as well as the preparation for and conduct of World War II that brought its most serious challenges. With the passage of the Reciprocal Trade Agreements Act in 1934, which authorized the president to negotiate tariff rates directly with U.S. trading partners, the committee effectively relinquished its power to set import duties, but the committee continued to monitor trade agreements to assure favorable conditions for America's businesses. Its passage also meant tariff legislation would no longer consume as much of the committee's time. Instead, the committee would devote its attention to other forms of revenue, especially income taxes.

The committee embraced FDR's Wealth Tax of 1935 as well as a series of revenue acts from 1936 to 1951, each designed as progressive income taxes to distribute the tax burden fairly and pay for many social programs and the costs of fighting World War II and the Korean War. One of

FDR's and the committee's crowning achievements was the passage of the SOCIAL SECURITY ACT in 1935, which was amended in 1939 and again in 1954. The House gave the committee responsibility for establishing Social Security tax and benefit rates, eligibility, and other critical elements of the program, which over the years captured more and more of the committee's attention. Unfortunately for FDR, by 1940 his ambitious social programs were stalled in Congress by the CONSERVATIVE COALITION, which opposed them. A majority of the committee's members were part of the coalition, which meant that Ways and Means often took the brunt of FDR's and later Truman's anger. Interestingly, President Dwight Eisenhower experienced similar frustrations with the coalition on the committee even when the Republicans took brief control of Congress from 1953 to 1955, for Eisenhower intended to balance the budget and needed to maintain tax rates at their current levels while the coalition's members, led by the committee's chair, Daniel Reed, a Republican from New York, sought to reform the tax code and roll back tax rates. Ike prevailed, but the compromises necessary to balance the interests of liberals seeking more progressive tax rates and conservatives desiring lower overall rates increased the complexity of the income tax code beginning with the Internal Revenue Code of 1954.

The ascension of WILBUR MILLS, a Democrat from Arkansas, to chair Ways and Means in 1958 marked the beginning of a 16-year period that can arguably be labeled the "Mills Era," for he was an accomplished and effective leader, and his legislative achievements many, most noteworthy considering that he negotiated with four presidents from both parties. For approximately the first 12 years of his tenure, Mills was admired as a skilled consensus-builder and savvy politician. He knew when to act, react, and not act, or as described elsewhere, he understood when to lead as well as follow. When he assumed the chair, the committee occasionally used subcommittees, but from 1961 to 1973 Mills centralized the committee's work in the full committee under his direct control, employed a small, professional staff, and closed the committee's meetings to the press and public. He also carefully vetted all members seeking appointment to his committee, admitting only those who were willing to compromise and who shared his fiscally conservative views. He was thus able to dominate revenue policy formulation in what appeared to be secretive and authoritarian means. In fact, working behind closed doors allowed Mills to cut the types of bipartisan deals that made the committee's—and his—reputation so impressive. When coupled with the committee's right to bring bills to the floor under closed rules (meaning no amendments were allowed), Mills had an astonishingly high floor passage rate. Moreover, he was effective in bargaining with senators in conference committees, where his versions

of revenue bills were regularly adopted. Among his legislative achievements were the Revenue Act of 1962 (Kennedy's tax cut bill), the Medicare Act (1965), and amendments to the Social Security Act in 1967 and 1972, the latter of which indexed the amount of future recipient benefit increases to the consumer price index and made them automatic rather than continuing the practice of subjecting each rate increase to a congressional vote.

Times changed, but Mills failed to adapt, and by the early 1970s Mills was widely perceived as arrogant and dictatorial, particularly by the growing number of liberal Democrats entering the House. A series of House and Democratic Party rule changes brought major reforms to the committee: The size of the committee was increased from 25 to 37; the committee was required to create at least four standing subcommittees with fixed jurisdictions; committee assignment responsibility for the Democrats was shifted to a new Steering and Policy Committee; multiple referrals were permitted, which meant that a revenue bill or a bill that contained some revenue provision could be referred to more than one committee at a time, allowing leaders to work around an obstructionist chairperson; and the BUDGET AND IMPOUNDMENT CONTROL ACT OF 1974 created budget committees in each chamber that could go toe-to-toe with revenue and appropriations committees to bring about balanced budgets. Ultimately, Mills was forced to resign from Congress following a personal indiscretion, but it was obvious that his colleagues no longer valued his methods and perspective.

The new chair was Al Ullman, a Democrat from Oregon, who served from 1975 to 1981. He was nearly the antithesis of Mills in terms of style and ideology, as he ran the committee openly, democratically, and with a liberal philosophy. Few major bills were passed during his tenure, with a notable exception being the Tax Reform Act of 1976.

Dan Rostenkowski, a Democrat from Illinois, took the committee's helm in 1981 and held it until 1994, when he resigned while under criminal investigation. Under his more heavy-handed leadership, the committee grappled directly with the country's economic problems, including larger and larger annual budget deficits. Though some compared him to Mills, Rostenkowski was far more liberal but not as knowledgeable of the tax code as the legendary chair, but his leadership style and his penchant for seeking bipartisan support for the committee's legislation were similar. Rostenkowski centralized the committee's work in his office as much as possible given the earlier reforms. Despite two early defeats at the hands of President Ronald Reagan with the passage of the Economic Recovery Tax Act and the Omnibus Budget and Reconciliation Act in 1981, Rostenkowski thereafter worked intently to achieve consensus prior to sending bills to the floor, where, as in the past, bills were debated under closed rules. Subsequent legislation of note were the Tax Equity and Fiscal Responsibility Act (1982), the Deficit Reduction Act (1984), the Tax Reform Act (1986), the Family Support Act (1988), and the Omnibus Trade and Competitiveness Act (1988). His efforts to reform Social Security and Medicare were never fully realized, but his legislative legacy is substantial. Under Rostenkowski's direction the committee regained much of the prominence it enjoyed during the Mills era. With Rostenkowski's rather abrupt and shocking departure, Sam Gibbons, a Democrat from Florida, became chair in 1994 and turned it over to Bill Archer, a Republican from Texas, in 1995 following the Republican capture of the House.

Ways and Means generally has been regarded as having become more partisan since 1995. As Republicans moved to implement their 1994 legislative agenda, the CONTRACT WITH AMERICA, efforts to work in a bipartisan manner were abandoned in favor of speed. Passage of the Temporary Assistance of Needy Families Act (TANF) in 1995 required Democratic support, however, as President Bill Clinton worked with Republicans to win passage of the legislation.

Major accomplishments since 2001 included passage of President George W. Bush's large tax cut in 2001 and the Medicare Prescription Drug, Improvement, and Modernization Act of 2003, which added prescription drug coverage to Medicare. The work of the committee has also been influenced by the events of September 11, 2001, requiring the funding of the war on terrorism, the Iraq War, and establishing the Department of Homeland Security.

Further reading:
Birnbaum, Jeffrey H., and Alan S. Murray. *Showdown at Gucci Gulch: Lawmakers, Lobbyists and the Unlikely Triumph of Tax Reform*. New York: Random House, 1987; Ippolito, Dennis S. *Congressional Spending: A Twentieth Century Fund Report*. Ithaca, N.Y.: Cornell University Press, 1981; Manley, John F. *The Politics of Finance: The House Committee on Ways and Means*. Boston: Little, Brown, 1970; Schick, Allen. *Congress and Money: Budgeting, Spending and Taxing*. Washington, D.C.: Urban Institute, 1980; Strahan, Randall W. *New Ways and Means: Reform and Change in a Congressional Committee*. Chapel Hill: University of North Carolina Press, 1990; Zelizer, Julian E. *Taxing America: Wilbur Mills, Congress and the State, 1945–1973*. New York: Cambridge University Press, 1998.

—Thomas J. Baldino

Webster, Daniel (1782–1852) *Representative, Senator*
Known as "Godlike Dan" for his oration and "Black Dan" because of his political opportunism and failure to pay debts, Webster developed a reputation as the nation's greatest orator during the first half of the 19th century. Webster was the ninth of 10 children born to Ebenezer and Abigail Eastman Webster. Ebenezer was a poor farmer who tended a plot of land granted him for his service in Rogers' Rangers during the French and Indian War. He later fought as a captain in the New Hampshire militia during the American Revolution, served in the New Hampshire legislature, and was a delegate to the convention when New Hampshire ratified the federal Constitution. He eventually became a lay judge for the court of common pleas. Webster's mother was the daughter of a preacher.

Webster's parents enrolled him with a private tutor when he was four years of age and briefly sent him to Phillips Academy in Exeter, New Hampshire, in 1794 before again placing him with private tutors. It is believed that his parents withdrew him from Phillips because they could no longer afford the tuition. Webster entered Dartmouth College in 1797 and graduated in 1801. While at Dartmouth he developed his rhetorical skills as a member of a literary society known as the United Fraternity. Shortly after graduating from Dartmouth, Webster made his first public speech at an Independence Day celebration in Hanover, New Hampshire, in 1801.

After graduation from Dartmouth he began serving as a legal apprentice in Salisbury. For one year (1802–03) he was the headmaster of a school in Fryeburg, Maine, earning enough money so that his brother, Ezekiel, could attend Dartmouth. He resumed his study of law in 1803 and finished his studies in Boston under Christopher Gore, who would later be governor of Massachusetts (1809–10) and a U.S. senator (1813–16). Admitted to the bar in 1805, Webster opened a law practice in Boscawen, New Hampshire. He moved to Portsmouth, New Hampshire, in 1807. In Portsmouth Webster became well known in legal circles and the pro-British Federalist Party. In 1808 he married Grace Fletcher, a schoolteacher from Salisbury, who bore him three children: Daniel Fletcher, who was killed in the Second Battle of Bull Run; Edward, a U.S. Army major killed during the Mexican War; and Julia. Following Grace's death in 1828 he married Caroline LeRoy (1829).

In 1812 Webster was elected to the U.S. HOUSE OF REPRESENTATIVES because of his opposition to the war with Britain. The war had crippled New England's shipping and was opposed by many in the New England states. Appointed to the Committee of Foreign Relations, Webster opposed President James Madison's conduct of the war, although he did not join the Hartford Convention, which called for an end to the war. He was later removed from the Foreign Relations Committee because of his opposition to the administration. Webster also opposed a bill that would have created a government-run national bank.

Webster served two terms as a member of the House from New Hampshire before moving to Boston in 1816.

One of his last votes in Congress was to increase the salaries of members of Congress from $6 a day to $1,500 a year. The law was unpopular, and a number of House members were defeated for reelection. Webster was also challenged to a duel by JOHN RANDOLPH of Virginia, but he refused to duel Randolph "for words of a general nature" used in debate.

During the next few years Webster established himself as one of the nation's leading lawyers. He argued and won a number of major constitutional cases before the U.S. Supreme Court. These included *Dartmouth College v. Woodward* (in which he successfully argued that the state of New Hampshire could not take over Dartmouth by altering the college's royal charter, arguing that this constituted an "impairment of the contract by the State," which is prohibited by the Constitution); *GIBBONS V. OGDEN* (in which he argued that a federal law, enacted pursuant to the Commerce Clause, superseded a state-granted steam ferry monopoly under the Constitution's Supremacy Clause); and *McCULLOCH V. MARYLAND* (in which he argued that the Necessary and Proper Clause granted Congress the power to charter the Bank of the United States). It was during this time that Webster also developed his reputation as a great orator, delivering his Plymouth oration (1820), the oration at the dedication of the Bunker Hill Monument (1825), and his eulogies of John Adams and Thomas Jefferson (1826).

He entered Massachusetts politics by serving as a presidential elector in 1820. He was a delegate to the Massachusetts constitutional convention of 1820–21, where he supported giving greater independence to the state's judiciary. He was elected to the Massachusetts state house of representatives in 1822 and later that year was again elected to the U.S. House of Representatives, this time as a member from Massachusetts. He served as chair of the JUDICIARY COMMITTEE during the 18th and 19th Congresses (1823–27), overseeing the revision of the U.S. criminal code. He served in the House until May 30, 1827.

In 1827 he was chosen by the Massachusetts state legislature to join the U.S. SENATE (he was reelected in 1833 and 1839). He joined the new National Republican Party and aligned himself with HENRY CLAY of Kentucky in supporting federal aid for road building in the western states. He was chair of the Senate FINANCE COMMITTEE during the 23rd and 24th Congresses (1835–39).

Originally an advocate of free trade, having opposed tariff bills as a member of the House in 1816 and 1824, in 1828 he supported the passage of a high tariff bill that was vehemently opposed by southerners, who feared that it would harm the cotton trade. South Carolina's Robert Hayne, along with Vice President John C. Calhoun, argued that his state had the right to nullify the tariff. This was based on their belief that the Union was a compact between the states. Responding to this challenge, Webster rejected the Calhoun-Hayne compact theory of federalism, contending that the Union was an agent of the people and not the state governments: "It is, Sir, the people's Constitution, the people's government, made for the people, and answerable to the people."

These remarks cemented Webster's reputation as one of the leading advocates of American nationalism. Webster supported President Andrew Jackson during the nullification crisis of 1832–33, winning him the title "Defender of the Constitution."

While supporting Jackson on the tariff, Webster opposed the president on many other issues, including Jackson's attacks on the Bank of the United States. Webster's support of the bank was based on the relationship he had developed with Nicholas Biddle, president of the Second Bank of the United States. As Richard Current wrote,

> Webster was connected to the bank as legal counsel, director of the Boston branch, frequent borrower, and Biddle's friend. . . .
>
> When the bill to re-charter the bank passed Congress in 1832, Jackson vetoed it, condemning the bank as "unauthorized by the Constitution, subversive to the rights of the States, and dangerous to the liberties of the people."
>
> In the Senate, Webster said that the veto "manifestly seeks to inflame the poor against the rich. It wantonly attacks whole classes of the people, for the purpose of turning against them the prejudices and resentments of other classes."

Webster introduced another bill to recharter the bank, but it did not pass, the Whigs losing the bank war.

Webster joined other Jackson opponents, led by Clay, in what become the Whig Party, taking their name from the English opposition party. In 1836 Webster ran for president as one of three Whig candidates. He carried only his home state of Massachusetts.

On March 6, 1841, Webster became secretary of State in the cabinet of William Henry Harrison, the first Whig candidate elected president of the United States. Harrison died of pneumonia after one month in office and was succeeded by Vice President John Tyler, a former Democrat. Within six months of taking office Tyler and Clay split over Tyler's anti-bank and anti-tariff positions, sharply dividing the Whig Party. In September 1841 Webster was the only member of Tyler's cabinet who did not resign at Clay's behest. As Tyler's secretary of State, Webster negotiated the Webster-Ashburton Treaty of 1842, resolving a border dispute between the United States and Great Britain by establishing an agreed-upon border between the state of Maine and what would eventually become Canada. Pressure from the Whigs as well as Tyler's support for Texas annexation finally caused Webster to resign as secretary of State on May 8, 1843.

In 1845 Webster was reelected to the Senate with the support of businessmen from New York and Boston who raised money to supplement his income. House Democrats called him "the pensioned agent of the manufacturing interest." In the Senate he opposed the annexation of Texas and the resultant Mexican War because he feared the country would have to confront the issue of the expansion of slavery. While opposing expansion, Webster also feared that the Union would dissolve over the issue. In his last important speech in the Senate (March 7, 1850) he supported Clay's Compromise of 1850.

In July of 1850 President Millard Fillmore appointed Webster to serve for a second time as secretary of State, a position he would hold until his death. One of his major responsibilities was enforcement of the Fugitive Slave Act, which required the return of escaped slaves to their owners. His strict enforcement of the law divided the Whig Party and probably cost him any chance of ever becoming president, but it helped preserve the Union for another decade. As secretary of State Webster authored the "Hulsemann Letter," which was written in response to a letter from the Austrian ambassador to the United States, Johann Georg Hulsemann, which alleged that the United States had violated the law of nations and interfered with Austria's internal affairs by sending A. Dudley Mann in 1849 to see if a newly created Hungarian government would be able to maintain its independence from Austria. Hulsemann claimed Mann's presence indicated American support for Hungarian independence. Webster rejected Hulsemann's assertions, stating that the United States would continue to refrain from interfering in European affairs but would have a "lively interest in the fortunes of Nations, struggling for institutions like their own."

In 1852 Webster unsuccessfully sought the Whig presidential nomination. While at his farm, Marshfield, he was thrown from his horse, partially crushing his skull, on October 23, 1852. He died a day later, probably of a brain hemorrhage. He was buried in the Winslow Cemetery.

Further reading:
Adams, Samuel Hopkins. *The Godlike Daniel.* New York: Sears Publishing, 1930; Bartlett, Irving H. *Daniel Webster.* New York: Norton, 1978; Baxter, Maurice G. *One and Inseparable: Daniel Webster and the Union.* Cambridge, Mass.: Balknap Press, 1984; Belz, Herman. *The Webster-Hayne Debate on the Nature of the Union: Selected Documents.* Indianapolis: Liberty Fund, 2000; Benson, Allan Louis. *Daniel Webster.* New York: Cosmopolitan Book, 1929; Brown, Norman D. *Daniel Webster and the Politics of Availability.* Athens: University of Georgia Press, 1969; Carey, Robert Lincoln. *Daniel Webster as an Economist.*

New York: AMS Press, 1966; Current, Richard. *Daniel Webster and the Rise of National Conservatism.* Boston: Little, Brown, 1955; Dalzell, Robert F., Jr. *Daniel Webster and the Trial of American Nationalism, 1843–1852.* Boston: Houghton Mifflin, 1973; Fuess, Claude M. *Daniel Webster.* New York: Da Capo Press, 1968; Nathans, Sydney. *Daniel Webster and Jacksonian Democracy.* Baltimore: Johns Hopkins University Press, 1973; Remini, Robert V. *Daniel Webster: The Man and His Time.* New York: Norton, 1997; Smith, Craig R. *Defender of the Union: The Oratory of Daniel Webster.* New York: Greenwood Press, 1989.

—Jeffrey Kraus

Wesberry v. Sanders 376 U.S. 1 (1964)

The *Wesberry* case was one of a line of cases following BAKER V. CARR in which the U.S. Supreme Court spelled out the standards for establishing equitable representation of the people in the U.S. HOUSE OF REPRESENTATIVES, state legislatures, and councils of local governments. The focus of this case was representation in the U.S. House.

Wesberry was a voter in Fulton County (Atlanta), Georgia. He resided in the Fifth Congressional District, one of 10 congressional districts created by an act of the Georgia legislature in 1931. Demographic changes in Georgia during the next 30 years were substantial. The 1960 CENSUS found the Fifth District to have a population of nearly 824,000 people. The least-populated Georgia district was the Ninth, with fewer than 273,000 people. The average population for the 10 districts was 395,000 people. Wesberry claimed the right under the Constitution to have his vote for Congress be equal in weight to those of other Georgians.

The case was heard by a three-judge federal district court. While acknowledging gross population disparities in the existing districts, a majority dismissed the complaint citing Justice Felix Frankfurter's opinion in *Colegrove v. Green.* They deemed it "a strong authority for dismissal" in a "political question involving a coordinate branch" regarding "a political question posing a delicate problem."

On February 17, 1964, the Supreme Court decided in favor of Wesberry's appeal by a vote of 7-2. One of the seven, Justice Tom Clark, joined the decision but dissented on the grounds articulated for the majority by Justice Hugo Black. Black's decision cited *Baker v. Carr* to say that the conclusions developed there applied equally to this case: The Court has jurisdiction, the voters have standing to sue for relief, and the issue is a justiciable matter.

Black asserted his interpretation of the constitutional meaning of this case clearly: "as nearly as is practicable one man's vote in a congressional election is to be worth is much as another's." There was some surprise that the grounds Black asserted for the decision were in Article I, Section 2, of the Constitution.

Black reviewed the records of the Constitutional Convention and the advocacy of James Madison in the FEDERALIST PAPERS. He said that "when the delegates agreed that the House should represent 'people' they intended that in allocating Congressmen the number assigned to each state should be determined solely by the number of the State's inhabitants." Thus, the House, representing people as individuals, would embody "complete quality for each voter." He concluded by saying,

> While it may not be possible to draw congressional districts with mathematical precision, that is no excuse for ignoring our Constitution's plain objective of making equal representation for equal numbers of people the fundamental goal for the House of Representatives. That is the high standard of justice and common sense which the founders set for us.

Despite a compelling dissent against Black's reasoning about the constitutional basis for the equality principle by Justice John Harlan, the several opinions make clear that eight of the nine justices agreed that apportionment questions were clearly justiciable and that the "political question" concern given in 1946 in *Colegrove v. Green* would no longer bar consideration of any such cases. Moreover, the applicability of the Equal Protection Clause of the Fourteenth Amendment was available for further interpretation and effectuation. That came four months later in a series of state legislative cases consolidated with and cited as *Reynolds v. Sims.*

Before the end of the decade, the Supreme Court decided two more cases in 1969 that rejected a maximum of 3.1 percent variation from mathematical equality in the congressional districts of Missouri and a plan for New York that achieved equality only in "defined substates" but not in the state as a whole. The Supreme Court showed it was serious about obtaining strict compliance with the population equality standard, especially for the U.S. House.

State legislatures responded to the courts. By the end of the 1960s 39 of the 45 states that had multiple representatives in the House had redrawn their congressional district lines. In 1970 another census provided relevant population data for congressional redistricting. According to CONGRESSIONAL QUARTERLY, for 385 of the 435 districts for the 93rd Congress (elected in 1972), the variation in population from the several state averages had been reduced to less than 1 percent. By contrast, 10 years earlier only nine of the 435 districts were that close in population to their state's average. Then, in fact, for 236 districts the variation was 10 percent or more. While it remains problematic how to achieve equitable representation for protected minorities in congressional districts, the principle of one person, one vote has been both rec-

ognized and vigorously applied to the American system of representation.

Further reading:
Diamond, R. A., and P. A. O'Connor, eds. *Congressional Quarterly's Guide to Congress.* 2d ed. Washington, D.C.: Congressional Quarterly Press, 1976; Auerbach, C. A. "The Reapportionment Cases: One Person, One Vote—One Vote, One Value." In *1964 Supreme Court Review*, P. B. Kurland, ed. Chicago: University of Chicago Press, 1964; *Wesberry v. Sanders* 376 U.S. 1 (1964).

—Jack R. Van Der Slik

whips

Party leaders in the SENATE and HOUSE OF REPRESENTATIVES responsible for maintaining party discipline and cohesion are called whips. The position of whip is part of the British parliamentary heritage. The *whipper* is a British term for the person responsible for keeping foxhounds from leaving the pack while on a hunt. Edmund Burke is credited with first using the term *whip* to denote a party leader during a debate in the British House of Commons in May 1769. Neither party in the House or Senate had official whips until the late 19th century, although some members unofficially served in a similar capacity. It was not until strong parties emerged that party leaders realized a need for some official to maintain strong party discipline.

In 1897 Representative James Tawney, a Republican from Minnesota, was appointed whip by the SPEAKER OF THE HOUSE, THOMAS REED, a Republican from Maine. A Democratic whip was appointed in 1901, when the Democratic floor leader appointed Representative Oscar Underwood of Alabama. In the Senate Hamilton Lewis, a Democrat from Illinois, became the first whip in 1913. Senate Republicans elected James Wadsworth of New York as whip and conference secretary in 1915. One week later the party decided to divide the responsibilities into two positions, and Senator Charles Curtis, a Republican from Kansas, was elected whip. From 1935 until 1944, the position of Republican whip was vacant. The pace of the Senate's work was slow, and there were only 17 Republicans after 1936 and 28 Republicans after President Franklin Roosevelt's 1940 reelection. Particular Republican senators were appointed to serve as whip on specific pieces of legislation.

In the modern House the Republican whip is elected by the Republican Conference. In 1987 the Democrats began electing their whip instead of having the position filled by the floor leader in consultation with the Speaker. Both parties' Senate whips are chosen by election.

As the congressional workload increased, the majority and minority whips in both chambers became busier, working to maintain party discipline. The number of assistant whips expanded in both chambers. In the House the Democrats created a deputy whip position in 1955. A Democratic chief deputy was created in 1972. In 1981 the Democrats appointed four deputy whips. The Democratic leadership appointed four chief deputy whips in 1992. In 2002 two additional chief deputy whip positions were created. The Democratic Party in the House has an extensive whip system that includes members from different regions of the country, different classes of members, and different groups of members such as women, Hispanics, and African Americans. The Republican whip organization was not as structured or formalized until the party became the majority in the House in 1995. Because of its smaller size and collegial nature, whips in the Senate do not play as significant a role as do House whips.

Party whips have several functions. The most important is to "count heads" on a pending issue to find out how many party members support or oppose an important position. This information is given to party leaders to allow them to decide when to put an issue up for a vote. Whips also provide information on the schedule to members and work to ensure that members are present in the chamber for important votes. Whips work to promote party unity and help disseminate the party's message. As a position in the party leadership ladder, the whip also seeks to establish him- or herself as a potential party leader.

Further reading:
Eilperin, Juliet. "The Making of Madam Whip." *Washington Post Magazine,* 6 January 2002 p. w27; Oleszek, Walter J. *Majority and Minority Whips of the Senate.* Senate Document 98-45. Washington, D.C.: Government Printing Office, 1985.

—John David Rausch, Jr.

Whitewater investigation

An investigation into a failed real estate investment that President Bill Clinton and the First Lady, Hillary Rodham Clinton, made 25 years before he became president was called "Whitewater" after the name of the company involved. It eventually resulted in a number of investigations by congressional committees and a special prosecutor that led to Clinton's impeachment by the U.S. HOUSE OF REPRESENTATIVES and a trial in the SENATE, where the president was acquitted.

In 1978 Arkansas attorney general Bill Clinton and his wife, Hillary, an attorney in the Little Rock, Arkansas, based Rose Law Firm, joined with their friends James B. and Susan McDougal to borrow $203,000 to purchase 220 acres of land in the Ozark Mountains. They formed the Whitewater Development Corporation to build vacation homes on the land. Shortly after the purchase was com-

pleted, Clinton was elected governor of Arkansas. James McDougal joined Clinton's gubernatorial staff as an economic adviser.

In 1982 James McDougal bought a small savings and loan and renamed it Madison Guaranty. At Bill Clinton's behest, he hired the Rose Law Firm in 1984, where Hillary Clinton had become a partner, to do legal work for the savings and loan. In 1986 James McDougal was forced to resign from the company, and Mrs. Clinton ended the Rose Law Firm's retainer agreement with the savings and loan.

In 1989 Madison Guaranty collapsed after making a number of bad loans. The Resolution Trust Corporation (RTC) spent $60 million on the bail-out of this failed savings and loan. In 1993, following their investigation, the RTC named the Clintons as "potential beneficiaries" of illegal activities of the savings and loan.

Whitewater became an issue in the 1992 presidential campaign. A report commissioned by the Clinton campaign said the Clinton's lost about $40,000 on their investment. Shortly before taking office as president, Clinton sold his interest in the property to James McDougal for $1,000.

After Clinton took office his administration was embroiled defending against several attacks, including those surrounding the firing of employees in the White House Travel Office and the filing of three years of delinquent Whitewater corporate tax returns by Deputy White House counsel Vincent Foster. Shortly after filing the returns, Foster was found dead in a Washington park. While his death was ruled a suicide, there was speculation that Foster's suicide was related to the developing Whitewater investigation. This speculation was fueled by the disclosure that chief White House counsel Bernard Nussbaum had removed documents concerning the Whitewater Development Corporation from Foster's office.

In January 1994 U.S. attorney general, Janet Reno, named Robert B. Fiske, Jr., as special counsel to investigate the Clintons' involvement in Whitewater and the legality of the Whitewater transactions. Fiske announced that he would investigate the Foster suicide and two additional accusations: that Clinton had exerted pressure on an Arkansas businessman, David Hale, to make a loan that would benefit him and the owners of Madison Guaranty, and that an Arkansas bank had concealed transactions involving Clinton's 1990 gubernatorial campaign. Fiske determined that Foster's death was a suicide and that Clinton aides had not improperly interfered with the RTC investigation into Madison Guaranty.

In August 1994 a U.S. court of appeals panel refused to reappoint Fiske as special counsel, citing a possible conflict of interest since Fiske had been appointed to his post by Clinton's attorney general. Kenneth W. Starr, a former court of appeals judge (1983–89) and solicitor general of the United States (1989–93), was appointed to investigate matters relating to Whitewater and Madison Guaranty.

At around the same time began a series of congressional investigations into the activities that collectively became known as Whitewater. The probes could be divided into two distinct eras: those undertaken while the Democrats controlled Congress, until January 1995, and those continued or launched under Republican control beginning in 1995. Generally speaking, the Republican-led panels were more combative with Clinton and his allies than the Democratic-dominated panels had been.

During summer 1994 the House and Senate Banking Committees held hearings on Whitewater. A total of 29 members of the Clinton administration were subpoenaed or testified at the hearings. Roger Altman, deputy Treasury secretary, resigned after the Senate's hearings into contacts between the White House and the Treasury Department revealed inconsistencies in his testimony.

In January 1995 the Democratic majority on the SEN-ATE BANKING, HOUSING, and URBAN AFFAIRS COMMIT-TEE, released a report finding that no laws were broken in the Whitewater matter. Similar conclusions were reached by the House Banking and Financial Institutions Committee when it released its report during summer 1995.

When the Republicans took control of the Senate, they empanelled a Special Whitewater Committee, chaired by Alphonse D'Amato of New York. The committee held hearings for nearly a year, holding 60 sessions and taking 10,729 pages of testimony and 35,000 pages of depositions from 245 people. The Republican majority alleged that President and Mrs. Clinton had stonewalled the investigation, while the Democratic minority charged that the Clinton's had been maligned by a "fishing expedition" engineered by D'Amato and his Republican colleagues.

In August 1995 the House Banking and Financial Institutions Committee began investigating whether the Clinton administration had improperly tried to influence the RTC investigation of Madison Guaranty and Whitewater. In contrast to the elongated Senate hearings, the House committee limited its hearings to five days and turned over its records to the special prosecutor's office.

The House GOVERNMENT REFORM COMMITTEE released in September 1996 its report on the firing of the staff in the White House Travel Office. The Republican majority accused the president of abusing executive privilege and obstructing their investigation.

In 1994 Paula Jones, an Arkansas state employee, filed a sexual harassment lawsuit against Clinton, which was unrelated to Whitewater. Clinton gave a deposition in this lawsuit in 1998 in which he denied having an affair with Monica Lewinsky, a White House intern. Unknown to Clinton or Lewinsky, Linda Tripp, a former White House staff member, had tape recorded telephone conversations in which Lewinsky had described her affair with the president. Tripp turned over her tapes to Starr, who then sought and received permission to expand his inquiry to cover the president's testimony in the Paula Jones case.

Starr sent a report to the House in which he charged Clinton with perjury, obstruction of justice, witness tampering, and abuse of authority. In November 1998 the House opened impeachment hearings. Starr, in his testimony, cleared Clinton in the "Travelgate" (firing of the staff in the White House Travel Office in 1993) and the "Filegate" (the improper collection of Federal Bureau of Investigation files in 1996) controversies.

Clinton was impeached by the House in December of 1998 on charges of perjury and obstruction of justice. In the trial before the Senate, Clinton's defenders said the charges brought against him did not rise to the level of "high crimes and misdemeanors" since they had nothing to do with the president's official duties. They contended that the charges were the product of a partisan witch hunt based on the president's personal life. Clinton's accusers said that the president was the nation's chief law enforcement officer and that his repeated lies and false testimony were a sufficient basis for his removal from office.

Clinton was acquitted on both counts in January 1999 and served out his last two years in office. In April 1999 Judge Susan Webber Wright found Clinton in civil contempt for misleading testimony in the Jones case. Facing the possibility of disbarment, Clinton voluntarily surrendered his Arkansas law license. In January 2001 Robert W. Ray, who had succeeded Starr as special prosecutor in October 1999, released a report that stated while evidence does exist to indicate Governor Clinton's knowing participation, that evidence was ultimately of insufficient weight and insufficiently corroborated to obtain and sustain a criminal prosecution beyond a reasonable doubt.

Further reading:
Blumenthal, Sidney. *The Clinton Wars.* New York: Farrar, Straus, & Giroux, 2003; Ray, Robert W. *Final Report of the Independent Counsel in Re: Madison Guaranty Savings and Loan Association.* Washington, D.C.: Government Printing Office, 2001.

—Jeffrey Kraus

Wickard v. Filburn 317 U.S. 111 (1942)

Arguably the Supreme Court's most expansive reading of the Commerce Clause of the U.S. Constitution, this case set the tone for nearly 50 years of unrestrained congressional power to regulate interstate commerce. When Filburn challenged his fine under the Agricultural Adjustment Act of 1938, he was not interested in undercutting New Deal legislation, he simply wanted to harvest 23 acres of wheat without paying the statutory penalty for exceeding the 11-acre quota. He claimed that Congress lacked the authority to impose limits on the wheat crops of farmers who did not engage in interstate commerce. Far from selling or transporting his wheat across state lines, Filburn did not sell or barter any of his wheat crop; he used substantially all the grain to feed the livestock on his dairy farm, to feed his family, and to sow crops the following season.

The Court's decisions in NATIONAL LABOR RELATIONS BOARD V. JONES AND MCLAUGHLIN STEEL CORP. and UNITED STATES V. DARBY LUMBER CO. had already resolved the question of Congress's power to regulate indirect effects on commerce and whether the production of wheat is included under the definition of commerce. The question left for the Court in Wickard was the question of scope—how remote and insubstantial could a potential effect on commerce be for Congress to wield its constitutional power to regulate commerce? The Court's answer was unanimous and emphatic. If Congress has the power to regulate the wheat industry, which is unquestioned, it must also have the power to regulate wheat production and consumption that affect the wheat industry. That Filburn by himself could not damage the market, which prior to U.S. v. Darby would have been grounds to strike down the regulation, was deemed irrelevant. Instead, the justices asked whether farmers producing and consuming their own wheat can, in the aggregate, have a substantial effect on commerce. The justices viewed this type of regulation as not merely constitutionally justified, but essential. The Court's message: If Congress can reach the Filburns of the nation, there is little related to commerce that Congress cannot regulate. Following this case the Supreme Court did not seriously question Congress's authority under the Commerce Clause until 1995, in UNITED STATES V. LOPEZ.

Further reading:
Dickson, Del, ed. *The Supreme Court in Conference (1940–1985).* Oxford: Oxford University Press, 2001; *NLRB v. Jones & McLaughlin Steel Corp.,* 301 U.S. 1 (1937); *U.S. v. Darby Lumber Co.,* 312 U.S. 100 (1941).

—Daniel Smith

Wright, James Claude, Jr. (1922–) *Representative, Speaker of the House*

James C. Wright, Jr., was born in Fort Worth, Texas, on December 22, 1922. He attended Weatherford College for two years and enrolled at the University of Texas in Austin in fall 1941. Following the Japanese attack on Pearl Harbor in December 1941, Wright left the university to enlist in the Army Air Corps. He was commissioned as a second lieutenant 10 days prior to his 20th birthday and was sent to Australia to join the Fifth Air Force four months later. Wright flew bombing missions in the South Pacific in B-24 Liberators, earning the Distinguished Flying Cross.

Wright began his political career soon after returning from overseas, and it was immediately apparent that he was a man of large ambition. At the age of 23, he was elected to the Texas state legislature. Wright was not reelected in 1948 after a bizarre campaign during which one of his opponents was murdered. Allegations that radical supporters of Wright committed the murder contributed to Wright's 39-vote defeat. In January 1950 he was elected mayor of Weatherford, Texas. At age 26 he was the youngest mayor in Texas. In 1954 he defeated incumbent Wingate Lucas in the Democratic primary for the 12th Congressional District of Texas at a time when the winner of the Democratic primary was virtually assured of election. He took his seat in Congress on January 3, 1955, and was elected to 18 consecutive terms.

Although he initially desired a seat on the Foreign Affairs Committee,

> . . . Speaker Rayburn and my Texas colleagues asked me to consider Public Works instead. As a favor to them and to our state, I did. I never regretted it.

As a member of Public Works, the committee responsible for authorizing highway and water projects, Wright was often in a position to do favors for other members and to provide projects to his Fort Worth district. Wright also became known as one of the best public speakers in the House.

Wright ran unsuccessfully for the Senate seat that was vacated by LYNDON JOHNSON in 1961; he finished third and failed to qualify for a runoff. The seat was ultimately won by Republican John Tower. A subsequent attempt to run for the Senate in Texas in 1966 was abandoned when it became apparent that Wright would not be able to raise sufficient funds relying on small individual donations to make a competitive race.

Just as it appeared that Wright's burning ambition would have to be satisfied by the likelihood that he would some day assume the chair of the Public Works Committee, Wright decided to make a long-shot bid for the position of Democratic MAJORITY LEADER in 1976. In a four-way race Wright defeated John McFall (CA), Phillip Burton (CA), and RICHARD BOLLING (MO). Wright had not been considered the favorite in the race, as he had not been a reformer in the Democratic Caucus, but he ultimately defeated Burton on the final ballot 148-147. It has been alleged that Wright's victory was unintentionally aided by an effort on the part of the Burton forces to eliminate Bolling in the second round of balloting. Burton is alleged to have asked some of his supporters to vote for Wright on the second ballot, thereby assuring that there would be only one reformer available on the final ballot and that Burton would easily defeat Wright. The strategy apparently backfired, as Bolling's supporters were encouraged to vote for Wright on the final ballot, producing a narrow victory for the Texan.

Wright served as Majority Leader from the 95th through the 99th Congresses. As Majority Leader, Wright developed a close working relationship with Speaker THOMAS P. "TIP" O'NEILL, and he worked hard to ensure that he would be elevated to Speaker when the time came. Upon O'Neill's retirement Wright was elected by the Democratic Caucus to be their candidate for Speaker in the 100th Congress without opposition. He was sworn in as SPEAKER OF THE HOUSE on January 6, 1987.

As Speaker, Wright consolidated power in the Speaker's office and became the most powerful Speaker of the House since JOSEPH CANNON. Wright tightly controlled the Democratic agenda, wresting power away from the committee chairs. He pushed for passage of important bills by specific dates. He used the office of Speaker to influence U.S. foreign policy, particularly regarding the Central American peace process. He was able to use the RULES COMMITTEE as an arm of party leadership, limiting the number of open rules and guaranteeing favorable action on many key agenda items. He used committee assignments, especially assignments to the Rules Committee, in an attempt to ensure member loyalty to party leadership. According to Wright:

> . . . since the Speaker appoints the Rules Committee I was able to call the fellows in one by one and say, I hope that you will be on the Rules Committee, I just want to make sure that the Speaker's wishes will be followed. I'm asking you if you want to serve again. They were a little bit shocked. Although if they had said no I can't do it, I can't support you, then they wouldn't have been appointed. And that would have been a break. Even Rayburn appointed Howard Smith back on the Committee.

A number of major pieces of legislation were enacted during Wright's first Congress as Speaker, including Clean Water Act amendments, an omnibus highway reauthorization, a major trade bill, a welfare reform package, and catastrophic health insurance. It was one of the most productive sessions of Congress in a generation.

As Speaker, Wright used his power in a way that provoked considerable partisan opposition. One Republican House member who strongly opposed Wright's tactics was NEWT GINGRICH (R-GA), then a Republican back-bencher with a reputation as a bomb thrower. Gingrich became an outspoken critic of Wright, calling him the least ethical Speaker of the 20th century. In May 1988 Gingrich filed a complaint against Wright with the Ethics Committee (formally known as the HOUSE COMMITTEE ON STANDARDS OF OFFICIAL CONDUCT). The public interest group Common Cause joined with Gingrich in calling for an investigation of Wright's finances, lending credibility to the Georgian's allegations.

The Ethics Committee investigation, led by an aggressive counsel with strong political ambitions, Richard J. Phelan, eventually found that there was reason to believe that Wright violated three House rules (resulting in 69 separate charges). The three alleged violations involved: 1) Whether Wright's wife, Betty, performed work to earn an $18,000-a-year salary from an investment company owned by Wright supporter George Mallick; 2) Whether the use of an apartment in Fort Worth by the Wright's constituted an illegal campaign contribution; and 3) Whether Wright violated House rules through sales of a book he authored called *Reflections of a Public Man*. Wright allegedly used sales of his book to hide speaking fees from groups that were otherwise banned from providing the Speaker with honoraria.

On May 31, 1989, Wright announced his resignation as Speaker (effective with the election of a successor on June 6) when it became apparent that the Ethics Committee intended to go forward with its charges. Unlike his predecessor, O'Neill, Wright never had been extremely popular with his Democratic colleagues, and his aggressive domination of the House agenda created tensions with many House Democrats. As media accounts of the ethics charges continued to escalate, Wright found himself with few hardcore supporters. In a dramatic speech before a packed House, Wright announced his intent to resign, defended himself against the Ethics Committee's charges, and decried the partisanship and nastiness that afflicted the House. Wright stated:

> . . . it is grievously hurtful to our society when vilification becomes an accepted form of political debate and negative campaigning becomes a fulltime occupation. When members of each party become self-appointed vigilantes carrying out personal vendettas against members of the other party. In God's name, that's not what this institution is supposed to be all about. When vengeance becomes more desirable than vindication, harsh personal attacks on one another's motives and one another's character drown out the quiet logic of serious debate on important issues, things that we ought to be involved ourselves in. Surely that's unworthy of our institution, unworthy of our American political

process. All offices, both political parties must resolve to bring this period of mindless cannibalism to an end. There's been enough of it.

Wright resigned from the House of Representatives on June 30, 1989. In his retirement Wright has taught courses in political science at Texas Christian University and has written frequently for newspapers and magazines.

Further reading:
Barry, John M. *The Ambition and the Power.* New York: Viking, 1989; Rohde, David W. *Parties and Leaders in the Postreform House.* Chicago: University of Chicago Press, 1991; Wright, Jim. *Balance of Power: Presidents and Congress from the Era of McCarthy to the Age of Gingrich.* Atlanta: Turner Publishing, 1996.

—Scott A. Frisch and Sean Q. Kelly

Yellow Dog Democrats

For much of the 20th century a Yellow Dog Democrat was an individual who would vote for the Democratic candidate regardless of the candidate's voting record, personal life, or evidence of corruption. In the 21st century a Yellow Dog Democrat is a complimentary term that refers to an extreme party loyalist who remains loyal to the Democratic Party through thick or thin. It is the name for several state party publications and state and college organizations.

The earliest reference to Yellow Dog Democrats is from the 1928 presidential election. Senator Tom Heflin, a Democrat from Alabama, refused to support Democratic presidential candidate Al Smith. Alabama voters who disagreed with Heflin's decision to support Republican Herbert Hoover began to use the phrase "I'd vote for a yellow dog if he ran on the Democratic ticket." Other versions of the origin of the phrase include one in which a Yankee reporter asked an old east Texas farmer if he would vote for the Republican presidential candidate. The Texas farmer spit a little tobacco juice between the shoes of the reporter, pointed at a dog lying in the dust of the road, and said, "I'd sooner vote for that 'ole yeller [not yellow] dog than some dang fool Republican."

From the late 1920s to the 1960s, the vast majority of voters in the Old South were Yellow Dog Democrats. The presence of this breed of voter and the absence of viable Republican candidates ensured a solidly Democratic South in which southern members of the U.S. House and Senate were always members of the Democratic Party. These creatures are relics of the past and an endangered species.

Further reading:
Mickels, Ilona. "What Are 'Blue Dog' Democrats? Are They Any Relation to 'Yellow Dog' Democrats?" Available online. URL: http://www.c-span/questions/weekly55.htm. Accessed 19 January 2006;"What's a Yellow Dog?" Available online. URL: http://www.geocities.com/CapitolHill/3470/yellowdog/htm. Accessed January 19, 2006.

—John Forshee

yielding

When the HOUSE OF REPRESENTATIVES and the SENATE meet, there are several forms of motions that can be made asking for permission to speak. If a senator is speaking on a legislative bill or amendment, he or she may be asked to "yield the floor." This is when the speaker is finished with his or her remarks and another member of the chamber may be called on to speak. The Senate also tries to control the amount of time devoted to debate on a particular bill by unanimously limiting the time for debate and allowing the floor managers to recognize who will speak on the issue and for what length of time. A senator will be allowed to speak only if the floor manager yields the senator a specific amount of time for debate. The senator may then speak only for that amount of time. This is known as "yield time."

In addition, in the U.S. House of Representatives no member may be allowed to speak unless the member currently speaking on the floor yields. The permission to speak can be granted only by the legislator currently recognized on the floor. This is called "yielding" and it is most commonly recognized in legislative hearings by the following phrase: "Will the gentleman from the 7th District of Wisconsin yield to me?"

Further reading:
"Yield the Floor," "Yield Time," and "Yielding," Available online. URL: http://www.thecapitol.net/glossary/tuvwxyz.htm, Accessed 9 February 2003.

—Nancy S. Lind

Selected Bibliography

Aberbach, Joel D. *Keeping a Watchful Eye: The Politics of Congressional Oversight.* Washington, D.C.: Brookings Institution Press, 1990.

Ahuja, Sunil, and Robert E. Dewhirst, eds. *Congress Responds to the Twentieth Century.* Columbus: Ohio State University Press, 2003.

Arnold, R. Douglas. *Congress and the Bureaucracy: A Theory of Influence.* New Haven, Conn.: Yale University Press, 1979.

Arnold, R. Douglas. *The Logic of Congressional Action.* New Haven, Conn.: Yale University Press, 1980.

Baker, Richard A., and Roger H. Davidson, eds. *First among Equals: Outstanding Senate Leaders of the Twentieth Century.* Washington, D.C.: Congressional Quarterly Press, 1991.

Baker, Ross K. *Friend and Foe in the U.S. Senate.* New York: Free Press, 1980.

——. *House and Senate.* 3d ed. New York: Norton, 2001.

Bianco, William, ed. *Congress on Display, Congress at Work.* Ann Arbor: University of Michigan Press, 2000.

Binder, Sarah A. *Minority Rights, Majority Rule: Partisanship and the Development of Congress,* Cambridge: Cambridge University Press, 1997.

——. *Stalemate: Causes and Consequences of Legislative Gridlock.* Washington, D.C.: Brookings Institution Press, 2003.

——, and Steven S. Smith. *Politics or Principle? Filibustering in the United States Senate.* Washington, D.C.: Brookings Institution Press, 1997.

Binkley, Wilfred *President and Congress.* New York: Knopf, 1947.

Bond, Jon R., and Richard Fleisher, eds. *Polarized Politics: Congress and the President in a Partisan Era.* Washington, D.C.: Congressional Quarerly Press, 2000.

Cain, Bruce, John Ferejohn, and Morris Fiorina. *The Personal Vote: Constituency Service and Electoral Independence.* Cambridge, Mass.: Harvard University Press, 1987.

Cannon, David T. *Race, Redistricting, and Representation.* Chicago: University of Chicago Press, 1999.

Cox, Gary W., and Mathew D. McCubbins. *Legislative Leviathan: Party Government in the House.* Berkeley: University of California Press, 1993.

Davidson, Roger. H. *The Role of the Congressman.* Indianapolis: Bobbs-Merrill, 1969.

——, Susan Webb Hammond, and Raymond W. Smock, eds. *Masters of the House: Congressional Leaders Over Two Centuries.* Boulder, Colo.: Westview Press, 1998.

Deering, Christopher J., and Steven S. Smith. *Committees in Congress.* 3d ed. Washington, D.C.: Congressional Quarterly Press, 1997.

Edwards, George C. *At the Margins: Presidential Leadership of Congress.* New Haven, Conn.: Yale University Press, 1989.

Evans, C. Lawrence. *Leadership in Committee: A Comparative Analysis of Leadership Behavior in the U.S. Senate.* Ann Arbor: University of Michigan Press, 1991.

——, and Walter Oleszeck. *Congress Under Fire: Reform Politics and the Republican Majority.* Boston: Houghton Mifflin, 1997.

Fenno, Richard F., Jr. *Home Style: House Members in Their Districts.* New York: Addison-Wesley Longman, 2003.

——. *Congressmen in Committees.* Boston: Little, Brown, 1973.

Fisher, Louis. *Constitutional Conflicts between Congress and the President.* 4th ed. Lawrence: University Press of Kansas, 1997.

Fiorina, Morris P. *Congress: Keystone of the Washington Establishment.* 2d ed. New Haven, Conn.: Yale University Press, 1989.

Gaddie, Ronald Keith, and Charles S. Bullock III. *Elections to Open Seats in the U.S. House: Where the Action Is.* Lanham, Md.: Rowman & Littlefield, 2000.

Galloway, George B. *History of the House of Representatives.* Rev. ed. New York: Crowell, 1976.

Hall, Richard I. *Participation in Congress.* New Haven, Conn.: Yale University Press, 1996.

Herrnson, Paul S. *Congressional Elections: Campaigning at Home and in Washington.* 4th ed. Washington, D.C.: Congressional Quarterly Press, 2004.

Hibbing, John R. *Congressional Careers: Contours of Life in the U.S. House of Representatives.* Chapel Hill: University of North Carolina Press, 1991.

————, and Elizabeth Theiss-Morse. *Congress as Public Enemy.* Cambridge: Cambridge University Press, 1995.

Jacobson, Gary C. *The Politics of Congressional Elections.* 6th ed. New York: Pearson-Longman, 2004.

Jones, Charles W. *Separate but Equal Branches: Congress and the Presidency.* 2d ed. New York: Chatham House Publishers, 1999.

Josephy, Alvin M., Jr. *On The Hill: A History of the American Congress.* New York: Simon & Schuster, 1980.

Kazee, Thomas A., ed. *Who Runs for Congress? Ambition, Context, and Candidate Emergence.* Washington, D.C.: Congressional Quarterly Press, 1994.

King, David C. *Turf Wars: How Congressional Committees Claim Jurisdiction* Chicago: University of Chicago Press, 1997.

Kingdon, John W. *Congressmen's Voting Decisions.* 3d ed. Ann Arbor: University of Michigan Press, 1989.

Krasno, Jonathan S. *Challengers, Competition, and Reelection.* New Haven, Conn.: Yale University Press, 1994.

Krehbiel, Keith. *Information and Legislative Organization.* Ann Arbor: University of Michigan Press, 1991.

————. *Pivotal Politics: A Theory of U.S. Lawmaking.* Chicago: University of Chicago Press, 1998.

Krutz, Glen. *Omnibus Legislating in the U.S. Congress.* Columbus: Ohio State University Press, 2001.

Longley, Lawrence D., and Walter J. Oleszek. *Bicameral Politics: Conference Committees in Congress.* New Haven, Conn.: Yale University Press,

Loomis, Burdett. *The New American Politician.* New York: Basic Books, 1998.

————, ed. *Esteemed Colleagues: Civility and Deliberation in the U.S. Senate.* Washington, D.C.: Brookings Institution Press, 2000.

MacNeil, Neil. *Forge of Democracy: The House of Representatives.* New York: McKay, 1963.

Maltzman, Forrest. *Competing Principals: Committees, Parties, and the Organization of Congress.* Ann Arbor: University of Michigan Press, 1997.

Mayhew, David R. *Congress: The Electoral Connection.* New Haven, Conn.: Yale University Press, 1974.

Mayhew, David R. *Divided We Govern: Party Control, Lawmaking and Investigating, 1946–1990.* New Haven, Conn.: Yale Universtiy Press, 1991.

Oleszek, Walter. *Congressional Procedures and the U.S. Policy Process.* 5th ed. Washington, D.C.: Congressional Quarterly Press, 2001.

Peters, Ronald M., Jr. *The American Speakership: The Office in Historical Perspective.* 2d ed. Baltimore: Johns Hopkins University Press, 1997.

Polsby, Nelson W. *How Congress Evolves: Social Bases of Institutional Change.* New York: Oxford University Press, 2004.

Pool, Keith T., and Howard Rosenthal. *Congress: A Political-Economic History of Roll Call Voting.* New York: Oxford University Press, 1996.

Price, David E. *The Congressional Experience: A View from the Hill.* 2d ed. Boulder, Colo.: Westview Press, 2000.

Rohde, David W. *Parties and Leaders in the Postreform House.* Chicago: University of Chicago Press, 1991.

Schickler, Eric. *Disjointed Pluralism: Institutional Innovation and the Development of the U.S. Congress.* Princeton, N.J.: Princeton University Press, 2001.

Sinclair, Barbara. *Legislators, Leaders, and Lawmaking: The U.S. House of Representatives in the Postreform Era.* Baltimore: Johns Hopkins University Press, 1995.

————. *The Transformation of the U.S. Senate.* Baltimore: Johns Hopkins University Press, 1989.

————. *Unorthodox Lawmaking: New Legislative Processes in the U.S. Congress.* 2d ed. Washington, D.C.: Congressional Quarterly Press, 2000.

Smith, Steven S. *Call to Order: Floor Politics in the House and Senate.* Washington, D.C.: Brookings Institution Press, 1989.

Swift, Elaine K. *The Making of an American Senate: Reconstitutive Change in Congress, 1787–1841.* Ann Arbor: University of Michigan Press, 1996.

Thurber, James A., ed. *The Battle for Congress: Consultants, Candidates, and Voters.* Washington, D.C.: Brookings Institution Press, 2001.

Wilson, Woodrow. *Congressional Government.* Baltimore: Johns Hopkins University Press, 1981.

Index